The Dragon in Medieval East Christian and Islamic Art

Islamic History and Civilization

Studies and Texts

VOLUME 86

The Dragon in Medieval East Christian and Islamic Art

With a Foreword by Robert Hillenbrand

By

Sara Kuehn

BRILL

LEIDEN • BOSTON
2011

This book is printed on acid-free paper.

Kuehn, Sara.
The dragon in medieval East Christian and Islamic art / by Sara Kuehn ; with a foreword by Robert Hillenbrand.
p. cm. — (Islamic history and civilization ; v. 86)
Includes bibliographical references and index.
ISBN 978-90-04-18663-7 (hardback : alk. paper)
1. Dragons in art. 2. Islamic art and symbolism. 3. Christian art and symbolism—Medieval, 500-1500. I. Title. II. Series.

N7745.D73K84 2011
704.9'47—dc22

2011008359

ISSN 0929-2403
ISBN 978 90 04 18663 7

FSC www.fsc.org MIX Paper from responsible sources FSC® C004472

PRINTED BY DRUKKERIJ WILCO B.V. - AMERSFOORT, THE NETHERLANDS

For my parents

Wie sollten wir jener alten Mythen vergessen können, die am Anfange aller Völker stehen, der Mythen von den Drachen, die sich im äußersten Augenblick in Prinzessinnen verwandeln; vielleicht sind alle Drachen unseres Lebens Prinzessinnen, die nur darauf warten, uns einmal schön und mutig zu sehen.

Rainer Maria Rilke "Briefe an einen jungen Dichter"

CONTENTS

NOTES ON THE BIBLIOGRAPHY, TRANSLITERATION, DATING AND ILLUSTRATIONS

The bibliography is limited to works and articles that are cited in the study. All bibliographic references for books and periodicals are given in abbreviated form in the footnotes with complete citations appearing in the bibliography. Encyclopaedia articles and dictionary entries are cited only in the notes. Unless passages are quoted, editions of classical authors are not cited.

The system of transliteration of Arabic, Persian and Turkish words used in this work is based on that of the *Encyclopaedia of Islam*, second edition, with several modifications:

"q" replaces "ḳ"; "j" is used instead of "dj." "Th," "kh," "dg," "sh" and "gh" are not underlined.

With the exception of certain words such as Qurʾān, neither italics nor diacritical marks are used for those Arabic, Persian or Turkish names and terms that have entered into common English usage like large cities, geographical locations and dynasties.

Where specific dates pertaining to the Islamic realm are referenced, both Islamic *(hijrī)* and Christian (Gregorian) dates will be given, the Islamic date appearing first. Where a century or decade is mentioned only Christian dates are cited.

Photographs included in the illustrations were taken by the author unless otherwise noted.

FOREWORD

This book is part of a much longer and comprehensive study on which Dr Kuehn has been labouring for over a decade and whose aim is to trace the iconography of the composite mythical creature known as the serpent-dragon from the mists of antiquity to the later middle ages. Her geographical focus in the study as a whole is principally Western and Central Asia but she remains continually alert to the manifestations of her theme in neighbouring cultures to the east (including India and China) and the west. The continuity of this arresting image across vast gulfs of space and time in the most diverse cultures of the Old World from the Atlantic to the Pacific is quite startling.

That continuity in itself constitutes a major challenge to anyone seeking to tell a connected story that extends across continents, cultures and millennia. The volume of scholarship on the art of Western and Central Asia has grown exponentially in the last couple of generations. In the field of Islamic art alone, it is clearly no longer a reasonable ambition to produce a companion volume to Creswell's magisterial *Bibliography of the Architecture, Arts and Crafts of Islam to 1st Jan. 1960*; such a work would need to be several times the size and weight of that huge tome in order to cover what has been produced in the last fifty years. But as the volume of scholarship expands, so, by a seemingly ineluctable law, does its scope contract. More and more people write about less and less. The dangers of over-specialisation and tunnel vision loom large. Artificial boundaries, whether chronological, geographical, cultural or confessional, are set and then ferociously policed. Scholarship operates in watertight compartments, to the detriment of that open-mindedness, that cross-fertilisation of disciplines and, more generally, the linking of disparate bodies of information that have traditionally been regarded as the litmus text of creative thinking in academe.

Iconographical studies are especially vulnerable to this shift from the macroscopic to the microscopic mode. Images readily adapt to changes in use, in faith and context, not to mention changes in location or scale, but they do tend to guard their core meanings most tenaciously. Nevertheless, an altered context, especially if it involves a transfer from one faith to another – such as Isis suckling Harpocrates, often regarded as an immediate model for the Christian image of the Virgin and Child – can trigger unexpected accretions and adaptations of meaning. Thus there can develop over the centuries a pool of ideas associated with a given image, and it requires expert judgment and erudition to make the right choices from that pool in any particular case. The body of evidence and allusion that accumulates in this way becomes increasingly difficult to control and to understand.

Such, then, are some of the difficulties confronting an extensive iconographical study of the kind that Dr Kuehn has produced. To overcome those difficulties calls for a special kind of scholar, one that was much more commonly encountered several generations ago. Happily Dr Kuehn fits that bill, and has the sheer erudition, the wide-ranging sympathies, the creative imagination and the indefatigable intellectual curiosity to match. Methodically and passionately she follows the leads of her research wherever they take her, crossing numerous disciplinary boundaries *en route*.

The result is a many-textured study of remarkable boldness and finesse that, firmly grounded in the thought-worlds of Bronze Age Central Asia and the Hellenistic empire, explores the full flowering of the serpent-dragon motif in medieval East Christian and Islamic art, most especially in Anatolia. The range of reference is extensive – from the mythic origins of the theme to such detailed aspects as the dragon tamer, combat scenes, the significance of knotting, and the serpent-dragon as an element of personal adornment. We learn of its interaction with other animals and how it functioned as an emblem of war and of the hunt, as a guardian of treasure and as an avatar of chthonic powers; and its sinister side helps to explain its appearance in Christian contexts in association with such saints as George and Theodore. Yet it also had multiple royal and heroic associations, as shown for example by the dracontine throne with its apotropaic role. Small wonder that this fabulous creature developed an apocalyptic significance and figured largely in the Islamic sciences

– whether in star lore or toxicology, magic or cosmology. These various excurses reveal a many-layered thought world shared by Arabs, Persians and Turks as by Byzantine, Armenian, Syriac and Georgian Christians. The serpent-dragon appears on mausolea and gravestones, on mosques and *madrasas*, on monasteries and churches, on bastions and caravansarais, on city gates and palace frescoes, on pottery galore, on coins and figured silks, on mirrors and belt buckles. Usually it carries a symbolic charge, for example as an amulet or talisman, but it is also at home in narrative contexts.

Altogether this is pioneering original work, and it demonstrates an enviable capacity to move from one culture to another – classical, Christian, Zoroastrian, Islamic – in a remarkably sure-footed way. It is packed with cogent arguments and unexpected insights. Dr Kuehn is a born explorer and has a natural affinity for cross-cultural work. She disdains the quick fix and is ready to do whatever is required to prove her point. Her list of authorities is startling in its length and completeness. But those authorities are merely a means to an end – the tale's the thing, and it casts a potent spell.

Robert Hillenbrand
University of Edinburgh

ACKNOWLEDGEMENTS

The topic of dragon iconography in medieval Islamic art was suggested to me for my doctoral thesis by my Doktorvater Professor Claus-Peter Haase in 1999. I am immensely grateful to him for having given me the opportunity to work on the tremendous and awe-inspiring yet, at the same time, exceedingly challenging topic that now forms the basis for this book. I especially valued his continued support and advice while he was extremely busy as director of the Museum for Islamic Art in Berlin.

During the years in which I was engaged in this research, I regularly worked on the preparation of curatorial documentation for the al-Sabāh Collection, Kuwait National Museum, in Kuwait. This allowed me to gain an insight into one of the most outstanding collections of Islamic works of art, among whose treasures are many objects bearing revealing manifestations of the dragon. I would like to express my gratitude to His Highness Shaykh Nasser Sabāh al-Ahmed al-Sabāh and his wife Her Highness Shaykha Hussah Sabāh al-Salem al-Sabāh for generously granting me permission to publish several objects from their collection. I am much indebted to the curators of the collection, Manuel Keene and Sue Kaoukji, for their long-standing encouragement and help. My thanks also extend to my colleagues at the Dar al-Athar al-Islamiyyah.

It took ten years to complete this vast research project and put it into writing. The text has been read with keen intelligence and an extraordinary editorial eye by Jill Tilden who moreover was a valued source of intellectual support and encouragement throughout these years. I feel profoundly grateful for the privilege of her friendship.

In addition, I wish to thank Professor Eberhard König of the Free University of Berlin, second reader of my thesis, for his sympathetic reading of my interpretations and his continuous generous support.

Reverend Dr Vrej Nersessian of the British Library, London, read the sections concerning Armenian art, sharing with me some of his profound knowledge on Armenian art and offering additional valuable suggestions. For this I am extremely grateful. My thanks also go to Dr Hratschja Tamrasjan, Director of the Matenadaran in Yerevan, Armenia, as well as to the curator Dr Lilith Zakarian, for their generous help.

I am further indebted to Professor Dr Peter Zieme of the Berlin-Brandenburgische Akademie der Wissenschaften for reading the text and making valuable comments and suggestions.

I owe particular thanks to my editors, especially Ms Kathy van Vliet-Leigh and Ms Ellen Girmscheid, for inviting me to submit my text for publication in this series and for their formative guidance, patience and support throughout the publication process. For comments and criticisms on earlier versions of this work I also thank the anonymous readers for Brill. For their kind assistance in obtaining images and line drawings, grateful thanks are moreover due to Prof. James Allan, Ms Katherine Baker, Dr Wolfgang Baum, Dr Sheila Canby, Ms Maria Teresa Fortuna Canivet, Dr Stefano Carboni, Prof. Dr Falko Daim, Dr Catherine Depierraz, Mr Alfred Diwersy, Dr Joachim Gierlichs, Prof. Dr Claus-Peter Haase, Dr Navina Haider, Mr Isao Kurita, Dr Sophie Makariou, Ms Armine Melkonyan, Dr Nahla Nassar, Rev. Dr Vrej Nersessian, Mr Harvey B. Plotnick, Dr Christoph Rauch, Prof. Dr Scott Redford, Prof. Dr Mehmet Öz, Prof. Dr Yasser Tabbaa, Dr Hratschja Tamrasjan, Dr Nicole Thierry, Dr Jean Michel Thierry, Dr Lilith Zakarian. I am particularly indebted to Prof. Dr Piotrovsky, Ms Elena Obuhovich and Prof. Dr Alexander Nikitin for their tremendous help.

Above all, my deep gratitude is due to Professor Robert Hillenbrand, Professor Emeritus of the University of Edinburgh, for his inspired vision and open-hearted generosity of spirit that I will not forget. His constructive guidance was instrumental in allowing this work to be successfully delivered from the dragon's maw.

All errors and inadequacies that remain are, of course, to be attributed to me alone.

Finally, immeasurable thanks are due to my parents, Heidi and Michael Kuehn, who generously helped me emotionally and financially to complete this project. Their manifold support and tolerance have sustained me throughout. For all these reasons, the book is dedicated to them as a small token of my thanks.

PART ONE

INTRODUCTION

INTRODUCTION

The aim of this research is to contextualise and chart, as far as possible, the complex iconography of the dragon in the medieval Islamic world,[1] by interrogating the many factors, contexts and contingencies that helped to shape and transform it.[2] The study focuses on the identification of the dragon imagery in a medieval Central Asian[3] cultural context, in what may be described as Irano-Turkish territories, from where it was disseminated by people of predominantly Turkic and Iranian stock.[4] It necessarily draws on a vast corpus of imagery of long artistic and iconographic tradition which originates from an equally vast geographic area of enormous cultural and ethnic complexity, with a primary emphasis on the transmission of the dragon iconography from Central Asia to Anatolia. Importantly, the latter comprises to a large extent parts of the region that formed part of the empire of Alexander the Great at his death in 323 BC, constituting ancient Sogdia, Bactria, the Indus Valley, Parthia, Media, the Transcaucasus and Anatolia. A common feature of these regions is therefore to have been subject for three to four centuries to intermittent waves of Hellenistic influence.

Arab conquests of Central Asia began to gain momentum from 86/705 when Qutayba ibn Muslim was appointed governor of Khurasan, from where he led incursions into neighbouring regions.[5] This led to a process of Islamicisation in the city states of sedentary Central Asia and the subsequent transformation of the entire region into a centre of Islamic civilisation. It also resulted in the assimilation and subsequent Islamicisation of the steppe peoples of Turko-Mongol heritage.

Islamic-period Central Asia naturally inherited artistic traditions from preceding dynasties such as the Sasanians (*c.* 224–651) and the Sogdians (fifth–eighth centuries). A true melting pot of peoples and cultures, the region had from earliest times served as a mediator and transmitter of artistic trends as they passed from east to west Asia and vice versa. This phenomenon was taken even further in the vast spatial entity of Islam, where economic links facilitated the transmission of knowledge as well as cultural and artistic exchange among peoples of different backgrounds and thus, in spite of the multicultural setting, conveyed a feeling of unity and a sense of belonging to a common civilisation.[6] Medieval Islamic society was a mixture of several regional cultures which included Muslims and non-Muslims speaking many languages, including Arabic, Persian, Syriac, Hebrew, Armenian, Turkish, Kurdish and various local dialects. The approach in the following essays is thus necessarily broadly comparative since evidently, as Julie Scott Meisami has aptly put it, "the medieval world does not stop at, say, the border between Christian Byzantium and Islamic territories, it is also clear that valuable insights may be gained from comparing the various manifestations of what is, to a great extent, a unified tradition, which shares certain basic attitudes and assumptions despite the par-

---

1 Throughout this investigation the traditional historical era, commonly referred to as the medieval period, is defined as spanning the eighth to the thirteenth century.

2 On the history of the study of iconography in Islamic art, see the recent resumé of Ernst Grube (2005, pp. 13–33) with an extensive list of references.

3 Today "Central Asia" has acquired a narrower meaning associating it with its use in the former Soviet Union and can be said to include the territories of Uzbekistan, Turkmenistan, Tajikistan, Kyrgyzstan, Kazakhstan as well as Mongolia, the Tibet Autonomous Region and the Xinjiang Uighur Autonomous Province in northwest China. However throughout the present study the term is used in its broader sense following the cultural definition of Central Asia given by UNESCO in two meetings of experts, held in 1978 and 1979, which is anchored in the multi-volume *History of Civilization of Central Asia*. The Final Report of 12 February 1979, Paris, reads that the spatial dimensions include "territories lying at present within the boundaries of Afghanistan, the western part of China, northern India, northeastern Iran, Mongolia, Pakistan and the [former] Central Asian Republics of the USSR." See Miroshnikov, 1992, repr. 1999, pp. 259–80 (the discussion also includes a brief outline of the historical usage of the term). The problems of defining the conceptual geographies of Central Asia are revisited by Akiner, 1998, pp. 3–62.

4 The words "Turkic" as well as "Iranian" are used as general designations to denote people whose ruler or majority spoke a Turkic or an Iranian language. Tribal confederacies in Central Asia were very heterogeneous and under various cultural influences. Cf. Frye, 2005, p. 149, n. 1.

5 On the Muslim Arab campaign in Central Asia and subsequent consolidation of power, see the classical study of Gibb, 1923.

6 The accounts of medieval travellers show that there were, in fact, apart from sea frontiers, no clearly defined boundary lines within the Islamic empire. See Bauer, 1995, pp. 34–6.

ticular local colouring of the individual cultures that make up the whole." Therefore, since it pertains to more than one culture and geographical region, the study necessarily addresses the multicultural and hybrid facets of the dragon motif as it evolved in these regions and examines how the motif was accepted and incorporated into the artistic repertory.

An investigation into the visual phenomenon of the dragon, which evolved from its pre-Islamic origins to manifest itself in varied but analogous and interrelated forms across this wide spatial and temporal entity, necessitates a broad overview of the entire spectrum of images as they appear on diverse media. In doing so the study, moreover, inevitably exhibits some of the difficulties arising from the necessity of crossing academic boundaries. An interdisciplinary method of analysis has been pursued, involving not only art historical but literary, epigraphical and historical evidence. During the ten years it took to compile the vast body of data the sheer scope of the material, in cultural, confessional, geographical and chronological terms, threatened to overwhelm all attempts at containment and control. Necessarily, given the vastness of the subject, only certain aspects of the multilayered and multivalent character of the topic can be treated. This study identifies and discusses specific themes pertaining to the dragon iconography which can be observed over a long period of time.

The likeness of the dragon is commonly associated with Asia and more specifically with China, being a paramount Chinese emblem. Yet its iconographic expression was known and used in a Central Asian context during the Bronze Age period, i.e. from the late third to early second millennium BC,[7] and was again extensively employed in the so-called "animal style" which was transmitted in the wake of the migrations of the ancient nomads of the Scytho-Siberian culture.[8] The late outflows of the culture which produced this style include, for instance, the Xiongnu of Mongolia and the Yuezhi (Rouzhi), who were driven out of present-day Gansu province in China by the Xiongnu in the second century BC and migrated to the region of Bactria that lies between the mountains of the Hindu Kush and the classical Oxus river (known as Āmū Daryā). Known as the Kushāṇas, they entered the Eurasian heartlands and the Indian subcontinent in the first or second centuries AD. Under subsequent Central Asian dynasties such as the Sasanians and Sogdians (who were closely linked with the Turkic empires and played the role of active agents of cultural interaction), the dragon motif continued to be extensively employed and was to become a prominent emblem of the Great Saljuq Turks.

This so-called "Saljuq-style" dragon was a motif in common currency from Central Asia to Anatolia (Rūm, the "Roman"/Byzantine lands) long before its place was taken by a so-called "Chinese-style" dragon, introduced in the aftermath of the Mongol invasion during the rule of the Chaghatayids (624/1227–764/1363), the Batu'ids (624/1227–907/1502) and the Ilkhanids (654/1256–754/1353) when China marked one pole of the Mongol empire at its time of greatest territorial expansion. This gave rise to a Chinese and Chinese-inspired but Mongol version of the dragon that began to appear for instance on the tile revetments of the Ilkhanid summer residence at Takht-i Sulaimān, built in the 1270s in the Azerbaijan region of present-day Iran, as well as in some early fourteenth-century manuscripts. The transmission of the visual rendering of the motif was the result of an acculturation process in which it was translated into a Central Asian context. The focus of this study is precisely on the manifestations of the dragon as evinced in the cultural and artistic context of the medieval Central Asian world *before* the phenomenon of the "Chinese-style" dragon occurred in the arts of Islam during the latter half of the thirteenth and fourteenth century with the establishment of the Mongols in Central Asia. Examples dating to after the Mongol invasion are employed only in so far as they illustrate a particularly pertinent symbolic feature in the stylistic continuation of the "Saljuq-style" dragon (the term "Saljuq" being used throughout this study in an extended sense, geographically and chronologically). The issue of

[7] The dragon (together with its smaller relative, the serpent, as will be shown) is a universally attested motif, perhaps generated simultaneously by a number of cultures. An "Eastern," and more specifically "Central Asian," provenance can therefore not be inferred for one of the most ancient iconographies of mankind. However extensive material evidence of the motif, so far fairly unknown, has been discovered in the Central Asia region from at the least the late third millennium BC. This body of evidence is investigated by the present writer in a separate, forthcoming monograph which discusses the dragon iconography from 2500 BC to 650 AD. See also Kuehn, 2009, pp. 43–67.

[8] The application of this term has been questioned since it seems to exclude geographically the important branch of the same culture that inhabited Mongolia. Cf. Jacobson, 1999, p. 173.

inherent parallels in artistic expression as well as the adaptation and incorporation of seemingly "Chinese" and Chinese-inspired Mongol stylistic formulae, in particular under the Ilkhanids, and their amalgamation with the visual contexts of the Central Asian region will be addressed in the first part of the Epilogue.

Characteristics of the (serpent-)dragon

Since earliest antiquity the dragon has been a richly multivalent symbol of complex mythical and symbolic value characterised by a coalescence of maleficence and beneficence. Owing to this inherent polyvalence and ambiguity, it has been called "one of the most complex symbolisms of the history of cultures."[9] Its iconography is a recurring and popular image in the architecture and the arts of the medieval Islamic world. Yet despite its wide diffusion, the symbolism that survives from the Central Eurasian world of the medieval period is often elusive and even cryptic.

The composite mythical creatures are endowed with features or parts belonging to various animals generally recognisable across cultural-aesthetic boundaries, the reptilian, feline and raptorial motif being prevalent in the overall composition; they thus often carry chthonic, aquatic and aerial aspects. It is however the reptilian characteristics that predominate in the iconography of the medieval Central Asian dragon. This is not only displayed in visual information but also demonstrated by written sources. In a passage from the Arabian collection of tales of the *Alf layla wa-layla* ("Thousand and One Nights"),[10] the physician asks the slave girl Tawaddud to name him a serpent that lays eggs. In response she names the dragon, in other words, a grown serpent.[11] The same notion is expressed by the Ghaznawid poet Masʿūd-i Razī when he advises *sulṭān* Masʿūd ibn Maḥmūd of Ghazna (r. 421/1030–432/1040):

> Do not extend security and do not give time and opportunity [to the enemy]
> Given time the snake turns into a dragon.[12]

The tenth-century compilations of the *Ikhwān al-Ṣafā*ʾ (Brethren of Purity), a sect of the Ismāʿīlis, similarly note that the dragon, king of all crawling creatures, has the viper as *wazīr*.[13] That the dragon is in fact a large serpent is noted much earlier in the writings of the fifth-century Armenian apologist, Eznik of Koghb.[14]

Literary sources of various types, from practical writings (that is to say, pharmacopoeia, travelogues or books on magic), to theological and exegetical writings, poetry, fables and in particular epics,[15] such as the early eleventh-century Persian-language masterpiece, the *Shāh-nāma* ("Book of Kings"), prove invaluable in the effort to establish a relationship between dragon iconography and its possible iconological content, in other words the endlessly varied contemporary cultural concepts that generated these notions. Such variations result in an apparently limitless repertoire of iconographical formulae for the dragon which, according to the *Shāh-nāma*:

> lived in the water and overland now in the river and anon in the sun [i.e., on the earth], and could pull a ferocious elephant with its tail.[16]

This verse describes the dragon's ability to undergo environmental and spatial changes. In his well-known bestiary, *Ḥayāt al-ḥayawān al-kubrā* ("The Life of the Biggest Animals"), the fourteenth-century scholar Kamāl al-Dīn al-Damīrī (745/808–1344/1405) similarly observes that:

> Serpents are originally in their nature aquatic [creatures] and can live in the sea after having been land ones, and on land after having been marine ones.[17]

Allusions such as these reveal that the dragon was able to cross boundaries within its natural environment, metamorphosing from land to sea creature and vice versa. The physical changes accompanying such shape-shifting all form part of the dragon iconography in medieval Islamic art so that the creature is, for instance, portrayed variously without legs, with two forelegs or with

---

[9] Le Goff, 1980, p. 162.

[10] A collection of stories in Arabic, *Thousand and One Nights,* appears to have formed around a Persian framework and to have developed with many additions from various locations from the ninth and tenth centuries, taking final shape in the thirteenth century. Cf. Littmann, "Alf layla wa-layla," *EI*² I, 358b.

[11] Cf. *Tausendundeine Nacht* (Brandenburg, 1973, p. 70), which contains this episode.

[12] Rīzā Qulī Khān Hidāyat, *Majmaʿ al-fuṣaḥā*ʾ, ed. Muṣaffa, M., 6 vols., Tehran, 1961, vol. 2, p. 1170, as cited in Daneshvari, 1993, p. 17, n. 13.

[13] *Ikhwān al-Ṣafā*ʾ, tr. and ed. Dieterici, 1858, pp. 83–4.

[14] *Elc alandoc*ʿ, tr. and ed. Mariès and Mercier, 1959, pp. 593–4, ch. 133.

[15] For a discussion of Islamic mythology comprising the creation myths, the lives of the Prophets and eschatology, see Thackston, 1990, pp. 186–201.

[16] Tr. and ed. Mohl, 1838–1878, vol. 6, p. 41, ll. 427–9.

[17] Tr. Jayakar, 1906, vol. 1, p. 636.

four legs. It may thus have a quadruped body, a serpentine body or a quadruped protome extending into ophidian coils. Overall however the serpentine body with or without legs enjoyed greater prominence.

In its astrological manifestation, the dragon necessarily has a celestial quality which, as the sage astrologer Jāmāsp relates to Gushtāsp (Av. Wishtāspa, the Greek Hystaspes), the Kayanian king of Iranian traditional history and first Mazdaist on the throne, is all-powerful:

> No one can safely pass that fateful wheel. Who has by wisdom or by manliness escaped the knife-sharp claws of that celestial dragon? What has to be will be. There is no doubt. The shrewdest man has not escaped his fate.[18]

The avian aspect of the dragon is often expressed through its portrayal with wings. The latter are associated with the power of flight, a well-known vehicle for the transition from one realm into another.

An early Armenian translation of the third-century Christian theologian Origen's writings underlines the fiendish nature of the dragon:

> And we call *vishap* many of the largest animals; of those on land, the elephant and the serpent, and an evil and violent man, but when the names are once applied, they do not change their nature. We call *vishap* also the invisible evil power, which, asking power of the Lord, struck the righteous man with grievous blows, not in one part, but in all his parts, outer and inner.[19]

Yet it is also interesting to note the assertion that *vishaps* (Av. *vishāpa*) can fly, as stated by the thirteenth-century Armenian philosopher and historian, Wahrām Wardapet (also known as Rabuni Sevleṛntsʿi), in a letter to the Armenian king Hetʿum of Cilicia (Lesser Armenia, Armenian kingdom from 1198–1375):

> Many men have seen *vishaps* ascend from earth to heaven.[20]

However, unlike in most of Christian culture where the overall image of the serpent or dragon is predominantly associated with its portrayal in the Bible as the epitome of evil and sin,[21] the position of serpents and dragons in Islamic culture is ambiguous and can have benevolent as well as malevolent connotations. The serpent as symbol of evil does not exist in the Qurʾān where it appears only once in the story of the staff of Mūsā (Moses) metamorphosed into a serpent (*sūra*s 20, 20; and 79, 16).[22] However, both serpents and dragons figure more frequently in Persian than in Arabic tradition. This ambiguity in the nature of the dragon is also mirrored in the Persian language, the word for dragon *(azdahā)* being used to describe "a strong and brave man," or "passionate testy person" as well as "a tyrant."[23]

A positive image of serpents or dragons as powerful, friendly and helpful beings persists in Arabic as well as Persian poetry.[24] A grateful serpent is depicted in the pre-Islamic Arab writings of the sixth-century poet ʿAbid ibn al-Abraṣ who when travelling through the desert with members of his tribe, the Banū Asad, took pity on a serpent that was tormented by thirst and gave it his last drops of water to drink. During the night the camels bolted and vanished. When ʿAbid, close to despair, was searching for his mount, he heard the voice of the grateful serpent offering him a camel to ride. Because of his meritorious act ʿAbid was thus one of the surviving members of the outing to return to the clan.[25] Another story of a life-saving serpent is recorded by al-Damīrī, citing the shaykh Abu ʾl-Ḥasan ʿAlī ibn Muḥammad al-Muzayyin al-Ṣagīr al-Ṣūfī (d. 328/939–40), who fell into a well in the desert of Tabūk and was saved by a viper which, he states:

> ...wound itself round me, whilst I remained perfectly still in my heart without any emotion; it then twisted its tail round me and took me out

[18] *The Story of Rustam and Isfandiyār*, tr. and ed. Clinton, 1999, p. 33; for Gushtāsp's family tree, *idem*, pp. 24–5.

[19] Yerevan, Matenadaran MS 6036, fols. 124b-125a, cited by Petrsyan, E., and Najaryan, H., eds., *Nshkharner Oroginesi haykakan tʿargmanutʿyunnericʿ*, vol. 1, Ejmiatsin, 1979, pp. 2, 22, as referred to by Russell, 1987, p. 207.

[20] Alishan, G., *Hin hawatkʿ kam hetʿanosakan krōnkʿ Hayokʿ* ("The Ancient Faith or Pagan Religion of the Armenians"), Venice, 1910 ed., p. 187, as cited in Russell, 1987, pp. 206–7. It is of note that before the Fall the Genesis serpent is described as a winged creature with legs. Such a giant winged quadruped serpent is portrayed, for instance, in the wall paintings showing events related to the book of Genesis on the drum of the dome (far right) in the Armenian pala tine church of the Holy Cross at Aghtʿamar (915–921). See Mathews, 1982, pp. 245–57; Thierry, 1987, p. 384, fig. 266. The fact that the Genesis serpent is winged is also mentioned in the Jewish *Apocalypse of Moses*, 26; Ginzberg, 1909–38, repr. 1946 and 1955, vol. 5, pp. 123–4, n. 4.

[21] On the positive aspect of the serpent in western medieval symbolism, cf. Le Goff, 1979, pp. 53–90, repr. 1978, pp. 236–79; English tr., pp. 159–88.

[22] For the figure of the serpent in Arabic culture, cf. Ruska, "Ḥayyā," *EI*² III, 334b; Kopf, "Afʿā," *EI*² I, 214b.

[23] Steingass, 1892, repr. 1981, p. 45.

[24] Touching stories of helpful serpents were also known in antiquity; see Pliny, *Naturalis Historia* VIII 61; Aelian, *De Natura Animalium* 6.17 and 63.

[25] The story goes back to Ibn al-Kalbī and is dismissed

of the well, and then untwisting its tail from my body went away.[26]

Farīd al-Dīn ʿAṭṭār's (b. *c.* 513/1119) hagiography *Tadhkirat al-awliyā*ʾ ("Memoirs of Saints") contains another image of a benign serpent, described as fanning the mystical lovers from time to time "with a branch of narcissus held in its mouth."[27] In Abū Ṭāhir Ṭarsūsī's twelfth-century compilation of prose narratives, *Dārāb-nāma* (an Iranian recension of the *Alexander Romance*), the hero, Dārāb (Darius), is confronted with a sympathetic dragon which helps him to find his abducted mother, queen Humāy.[28] The story of Ardashīr in the same epic begins with the tale of the origin of a dragon that evolved out of a worm in an apple, perhaps representing a romanticised account of the introduction of sericulture into Iran,[29] when the sight of silkworms transforming into spinning cocoons must not have been uncommon. Among the collection of fables entitled *Marzubān-nāma* ("Tales of Marzubān") recorded by Saʿd al-Dīn Warāwīnī in 607–22/1210–25, who presented his collection to Abu 'l-Qāsim Rabīb al-Dīn, the vizier to the Ildeñizid/Eldigüzid *atābeg* of Azerbaijan (Ādharbyjān), Özbek ibn Muḥammad, there are five stories about serpents. One of these accounts deals with a pious, generous serpent who has the power to interpret dreams and who saves a weaver from punishment by helping him to remind the king of his forgotten dreams. It selflessly continues to help the weaver even though the latter deceives the serpent on two occasions.[30] The stories thus portray the serpent-dragon's compassion as a sign of innate benevolence, high merit or kindness, exemplifying human virtues.

On the other hand, the awesome and terrifying nature of the serpent-dragon forced humans into a subordinate, defensive role, thus for instance the Yasht hymn ("Songs of Praise") collection of the surviving Avestan texts, the earliest scriptures of the ancient Persian religion, Zoroastrianism, lists not only various types of legendary or mythical "first man" or "first king," but also dragon men and killers of dragons, transmitted mainly from the Indo-Iranian period.[31] The later Zoroastrian scriptures of the Vidēvdāt (Vendidād), perhaps influenced by the customs of the Median priests, the Magi,[32] contained a radically reconfigured view of the universe. The "law against the *daevas*" divided "creation into two mutually antagonistic halves—the creatures of the Holy Spirit on the one hand and the creatures of the Destructive Spirit on the other."[33] According to this understanding serpents or dragons (Av. *azhi-*, Pahl. *azh-*) were identified as creatures of the "hostile spirit" Ahriman. They were defined as evil, noxious, harmful to man and his animals and crops (Av. *khrafstra*)[34] and thus deserving of death.[35]

This inherent ambiguity is exemplified in the demon Azhi Dahāka/Azhdahāk found in the Avestan texts, the notorious dragon who tried to seize the *khᵛarənah-* (Mid. Pers. *khwarrah* "glory, God-given fortune, splendour") of Iran's Aryan rulers of traditional history, attempting, in other words, to make himself ruler of the Aryans.[36] After several great battles, he was overcome by the dragon-fighter Thraētaona/Frēdōn (the Avestic counterpart of the Vedic dragon-slayer Indra). Hence from an early time, variants of this epic seem to have attributed to usurpers some traits that seem to have been borrowed from the dragon-man.[37] Long familiar as a monstrous tyrant,[38] he becomes in New Persian or Arabic narratives the Babylonian tyrant Ẓaḥḥāk (al-Ḍaḥḥāk)/Dahāk, who belonged to the Pīshdādian, the early mythi-

---

by Abu 'l-Faraj (XXII, 85–6) as a "manifest fabrication." Cited after Kilpatrick, 2003, p. 117.

[26] *Ḥayāt al-ḥayawān al-kubrā*, tr. Jayakar, 1906, vol. 1, p. 58.

[27] Ed. Nicholson, R.A., Tehran, 1370/1991, pp. 46, 184, as cited in Gohrab, 2000, p. 86. Cf. al-Hujwīrī, *Kashf al-Maḥjūb*, p. 118; Gohrab, 2003, p. 81.

[28] Gohrab, 2000, p. 85.

[29] Yamamoto, 2003, p. 75.

[30] Tr. Levy, pp. 222–7.

[31] Christensen, 1931, tr. 1993, p. 23.

[32] According to Zaehner (1961, p. 162): "...the extraordinary zest with which the Magi are alleged to have killed 'with their own hands' flying and creeping things, can scarcely be accounted for except on the supposition that they thought such creatures to be the handiwork of an evil power. It is they, then, who would be responsible for the cut-and-dried division of creation into two mutually antagonistic halves—the creatures of the Holy Spirit on the one hand—and the creatures of the Destructive Spirit on the other. Thus they can be regarded as the true authors of that rigid dualism that was to characterize the Zoroastrianism of a later period, but which is only implicit in the Gāthās ["songs"] of Zoroaster."

[33] Zaehner, 1961, p. 162.

[34] Boyce, 1975, repr. 1996, pp. 90–1. The special stick used by the Zoroastrians to kill noxious creatures of various kinds is called a *mār-gan* ("snake-killer"); Russell, 1987, p. 461. The custom of killing of *khrafstras* is also mentioned by Plutarch (*De Iside et Osiride 46*; *De Invidia et Odio* 3.537B; *Questiones Conviviales* 4.5.2.670D).

[35] Vidēvdāt 14.5; 18.73.

[36] Cf. Christensen, 1931, tr. 1993, p. 26; Gershevitch, 1959, p. 59; Zaehner, 1961, pp. 150–3; Sarkhosh Curtis and Stewart, eds., 2005, pp. 102–3.

[37] Christensen, 1931, tr. 1993, p. 27.

[38] Yasht 5.29–30; 15.19.

cal Iranian kings who established civilisation, and, in turn, became the son of a king of the Arabs.[39] Having overthrown the Iranian king Jamshīd (Av. Yima Khshaēta "Yima the brilliant") with popular support, Dahāk is corrupted by Iblīs/Satan,[40] and from this time snakes issue from his shoulders, his demonic human-to-hominoid-dragon transformation thus representing a form of moral retribution.[41] He then imposes his tyranny on Iran for a thousand years until he in turn is overcome by the conqueror Frēdōn who imprisons him in Mount Damāwand.[42]

It is noteworthy that this paradigm of an evil king nevertheless also enjoyed a favourable reputation in Iranian history.[43] One of the astrologers of the ʿAbbasid caliph Hārūn al-Rashīd, Abū Sahl al-Faḍl ibn Nawbakht, working at the caliph's proverbial Treasure House of Wisdom *(Khizānat al-ḥikma)*, the great library, translation bureau and institute for the promotion of the philosophical sciences, describes Ẓaḥḥāk as founder of palaces of science and as living in a domain governed by the beneficent planet Jupiter.[44] Hence, by implication, ibn Nawbakht equals Ẓaḥḥāk, the founder of palaces of science, with the caliph, who was the founder of the celebrated *Khizānat al-ḥikma*.[45] Furthermore, tribal confederacies, dynasties and heroes identified with the dragon and claimed their descent from the demonic king. Rustam, the hero *par excellence* of the Iranian epic (in particular in Firdawsī's *Shāh-nāma*), traces his descent to Ẓaḥḥāk/Dahāk,[46] as did the Kushāṇas of the Yuezhi confederacy (*c.* first–third centuries) who ruled over the Central Asian regions which comprise present-day Tajikistan, Afghanistan, Pakistan and northern India[47] as well as the Islamic dynasty of Ghūr.[48] As Shapur Shahbazi has cogently argued, Dahāk is believed to have been "the eponymous father of a formidable Iranian people,"[49] the Dahae/Dahī, Sacians who formed the core of the Arsacid invaders (12–428) of Parthia, one of the five divisions of the Iranians.[50] Descent from Dahāk was moreover claimed by the Armenians of the region near Lake Sevan.[51] Finally, in the Turkish epic *Ṣaltūq-nāma* ("Book of Ṣaltuq"), the first ruler of the world, Eslem, son of Adam, becomes the father of Ẓaḥḥāk the Turk, ancestor of all Turkish sovereigns.[52]

However, at the same time the dragon Azhi Dahāka/Dahāk was in some cases regarded as "the incarnation of the demonic *par excellence*."[53] His symbolic value was drastically "historicised" and identified by various societies or groups with real or external enemies such as foreign nations or oppressive powers or rulers.[54] In his *Patmutʿiwn*

---

39 See Yarshater, 1983a, pp. 426–9.

40 In Qurʾānic tradition Iblīs is both an angel (*sūra* 20, 34) and "one among the *jinn*" (*sūra* 18, 50). An important difference between Islamic and Christian perceptions regarding Satan (from the Hebrew *śāṭān*, "adversary") hence lies, according to Arent Jan Wensinck ("Iblīs," *EI*² III, 668a), in the fact that: "Muslim thought remains undecided as to whether he was an angel or a *jinn*, and does not pronounce an opinion on the possibility of his being a "fallen angel.""

41 See a detailed description of this episode in al-Thaʿālibī, *Taʾrīkh Ghurar al-siyar*, tr. and ed. Zotenberg, 1900, pp. 19–27. Cf. *Shāh-nāma*, tr. and ed. Mohl, 1838–1878, vol. 1, pp. 63–5, ll. 178–97, pp. 69–71, ll. 14–44; vol. 2, pp. 45, 60, 75.

42 Cf. Boyce, 1975, repr. 1996, pp. 67, 91, 98, 100, 103, 283, 289, 293. *Shāh-nāma*, tr. and ed. Mohl, 1838–1878, vol. 1, p. 113, ll. 518–27.

43 Shahbazi, 1993, p. 159.

44 Ibn Nawbakht, *Kitāb al-nahmaṭān*, quoted in Ibn al-Nadīm, *Kitāb al-Fihrist*, Cairo, n.d., pp. 345–8, as cited in Pingree, 1968, p. 9 and ns. 2–4, p. 10, n. 1, pp. 11–2, 69.

45 Pingree, 1968, p. 12.

46 With the approval of his grandfather Sām, Rustam's father, Zāl, married Rūdāba, the daughter of Mahrāb, the king of Kābul, a descendant of Dahāk; al-Thaʿālibī, *Taʾrīkh Ghurar al-siyar*, tr. and ed. Zotenberg, 1900, pp. 73–97. Cf. Khāleqī-Moṭlaq, 1971, pp. 31, 35, 39–40; Monchi-Zadeh, 1975, pp. 109–10; de Bruijn, "Sām," *EI*² VIII, 1011a. For Rustam's family tree, see *The Story of Rustam and Isfandiyār*, tr. and ed. Clinton, 1999, p. 26. In the *Shāh-nāma* Mahrāb is described as idolater; Monchi-Zadeh (1975, pp. 109–11, 142–3) associates the name of the king of Kābul, Mahrāb, with the title Mahrāj (= Mahārāja), hence linking him with India. Cf. von Spiegel (1871, p. 567) who has considered him to be Buddhist.

47 This is indicated by the story of Kūsh, the nephew of Ẓaḥḥāk and founder of the Shar-i Kūshan (= Kūshānshar), noted in an epic of Īrānshāh, the son of Abu 'l-Khayr (Safa, *Ḥamāsa sarāʾī dar Iran*, pp. 296–300; cf. *The Mujmal al-Tawārīkh*, pp. 89, 187, 189), as cited in Shahbazi, 1993, p. 159.

48 Quoted by ʿUthmān ibn Muḥammad al-Jūzjānī (fl. *c.* 685/1260), the historian of the Ghurids; Bosworth, "Ghūrids," *EI*² II, 1099a. Cf. Shahbazi, 1993, p. 159.

49 Movses Khorenatsi, *Patmutʿiwn Hayocʿ* ("History of the Armenians"), p. 127: "The one they [= the Persians, in other words *some* Iranians] call Biurasp [Bīwarāsp] Azhdahak was their ancestor," cited after Shahbazi, 1993, p. 159 and n. 123.

50 Bailey, 1959, pp. 71–115.

51 Khorenatsi, *Patmutʿiwn Hayocʿ*, II.49, cited after Shahbazi, 1993, p. 159. According to a reference by Khorenatsi (*Patmutʿiwn Hayocʿ*, I.30) as well as Thomas Arcuni's *Collection des historiens Arméniens*, Petersburg, 1874, p. 47, there even existed an Armenian noble family called Azhdahāk; cited after Widengren, 1969, p. 17 and n. 35.

52 Mélikoff, 1960, vol. 1, p. 43 and n. 1; Dedes, 1996, p. 29, n. 80.

53 Russell, 1987, p. 43.

54 For a brief discussion of the Greek word *drakōn* as appellation of a historical person or a people in Hebrew, Aramaic and Greek literature, see Schlüter, 1982, pp. 44–6.

Hayoc' ("History of the Armenians"), which is ostensibly written in the fifth century but probably dated to the mid-eighth century in its present form,[55] the Armenian historian Moses of Chorene (Movsēs Khorenatsi) calls the neighbouring Medes, *mar*, which is a homonymic of the Persian word *mār* ("snake"). The *History* refers to their offspring as "progeny of the dragon" *(vishap-azun)*, or human snakes,[56] while the archetype of evil misrule, Azhi Dahāka/Azhdahāk, the dragon in man-shape (or the human in dragon-shape)[57] of the Sasanian epics, is identified with the historical Median king Astyages (Med. Rishtivaiga) against whom the Armenian king Tigran rebelled.[58] Khorenatsi also refers to the first century AD invading Alans, an Iranian people of the Caucasus, and their offspring, as descendants of Azhdahāk.[59] The name of the latter continued to be used as a symbol for historical enemies; in particular, the new world power of the Saljuq Turks, whose conquests provoked a sense of the apocalyptic in medieval Christian Transcaucasia.[60] The eleventh-century Armenian scholar and theologian, John (Yovhannes) of Tarawn, declared that the Antichrist – the dragon bound, at the time of the Crucifixion, for a thousand years – was now free once again and had returned with the help of the Saljuq Turks.[61]

In the discussion of the story of Paradise in post-Qurʾānic canonical traditions, the serpent-dragon's inherent ambivalence is also expressed. In the primordial Paradise the serpent is said to have been the most beautiful and strong of animals,[62] who was:

> ...shaped like a camel and like the camel, could stand erect. She had a multi-coloured tail, red, yellow, green, white, black, a mane of pearl, hair of topaz, eyes like the planets Venus and Jupiter, and an aroma like musk blended with ambergris.[63]

Owing to the instigation of the bird of Paradise, the peacock *(ṭāʾūs)*, which he saw at the gate of Paradise, Iblīs made use of the serpent and managed to trick her by speaking to her in a soft voice until she had confidence in him:

> she opened her mouth, ... Iblīs jumped in and sat down between her fangs (thus the fangs of snakes became poisonous until the end of the ages)[64]

and so he eluded the angels guarding Paradise who would not have admitted him. A narrative ascribed to Wahb ibn Munabbih (b. 34/654–5), a Yemenite descendant from a family of Persian origin, describes the Fall which led to the expulsion from Paradise:

> When Iblīs wanted to cause [Adam and Eve] to slip, he entered into the stomach *(jawf)* of the serpent; the serpent [then] had four legs and was like a Bactrian [camel] *(bukhtīya)*, one of the most beautiful creatures God had created. When the serpent entered the garden, Iblīs came out of its stomach *(jawf)*; he took [a fruit] from the tree [the Tree of Immortality (Qurʾān, *sūra* 20, 116–21)] that God had forbidden to Adam and Eve and brought it to Eve.[65]

As a consequence of the service rendered to Iblīs, the serpent is not only banished from Paradise, but loses her legs, which reenter her body; she will dwell in dark places and only earth will be her food;[66] she is condemned to crawl on her belly becoming "malformed and deprived of the power of speech, mute and forked-tongued."[67]

---

55 See, for instance, the "Introduction" of *Khorenatsi: History of the Armenians*, tr. and ed. Thomson, 1978, repr. 1980.

56 Ishkol-Kerovpian, "Višap," *WdM* IV, 1, pp. 155–7; Russell, 2004, p. 627.

57 Cf. Schwartz, 1980, pp. 123–4.

58 Purporting to transmit a report of the earlier historian Mar Apas Catina, Khorenatsi notes this in a passage of his *Patmut'iwn Hayoc'* (tr. Langlois, 1872, p. 39). Russell, 2004, p. 1170.

59 Alemany, 2000, p. 285.

60 Cf. White, 1991, p. 193.

61 Their invasion is described by Matthew of Edessa (Matt'ēos Uṙhayetsi), who uses visionary apocalyptic imagery: the Turks are "winged serpents" *(ojk' t'ewawork')* or "death-breathing dragons" *(vishapn mahashuntch)*. Russell, 2004, p. 883.

62 Cf. Wheeler, 2002, p. 25.

63 Al-Kisāʾī, *Qiṣaṣ al-anbiyāʾ*, tr. Thackston, 1978, p. 38.

64 *Idem*, pp. 39, 53. It is of note that of all the animals in Paradise the serpent and the peacock are singled out to become the pawns of Iblīs; both were severely punished (*idem*, pp. 46–7) but only the peacock was rehabilitated (*idem*, p. 53).

65 Al-Ṭabarī, *Mukhtaṣar taʾrīkh al-rusul wa 'l-mulūk wa 'l-khulafāʾ*, vol. 1, p. 108; see also *idem*, *Jāmiʿ al-Bayān*, I, p. 235, cited after Katz, 2002, p. 179. Jewish Midrashic literature similarly records that the serpent of the Garden of Eden originally had feet; Gray, 1906, p. 186. It is worth mentioning that in the Qurʾān it is not Eve who entices Adam to disobey God; Iblīs speaks to both and in one instance only to Adam (*sūras* 7, 20–2; 20, 120–2).

66 Al-Kisāʾī, *Qiṣaṣ al-anbiyāʾ*, tr. Thackston, 1978, p. 53; al-Ṭabarī, *Mukhtaṣar taʾrīkh al-rusul wa 'l-mulūk wa 'l-khulafāʾ*, vol. 1, pp. 525–6.

67 Al-Kisāʾī, *Qiṣaṣ al-anbiyāʾ*, tr. Thackston, 1978, p. 46. See also the second-century BC Hebrew work, *Book of Jubilees* 3.28, as well as Philo of Alexandria, *De Opificio Mundi* 55.156.

Existing contributions to the study of dragon iconography

As far as the symbolism of the dragon is concerned, the field for the greater part has been prepared through valuable studies in stylistic and iconographic development, of which those of Giovanni Curatola, Katharina Otto-Dorn, Gönül Öney and Abbas Daneshvari rank foremost.[68] Considering the prominent position accorded to the dragon motif in the arts of the medieval Islamic period, it is however surprising that so far only Giovanni Curatola has devoted a study exclusive to this iconography and its characteristics. His study, which investigates the overall relation of the dragon to Chinese and Central Asian sources as well as its appearance in manuscripts of the post-Timurid period,[69] leaves room however for the exploration and identification of the larger phenomenon, its manifestations and crosscurrents across a period of many centuries and many cultures. Some studies have concentrated on a specific medium. Otto-Dorn[70] and Öney[71] have focused in particular on the monumental sculpture of Anatolia, providing an extensive catalogue of known monumental stone reliefs. Individual reliefs were investigated by Jean-Paul Roux[72] and Özden Süslü[73] in Saljuq-period Anatolia and by Joachim Gierlichs in northern Mesopotamia (the Jazīra).[74] In a more recent work Gierlichs established an important *catalogue raisonné* of animal reliefs on monuments of the Saljuq and Artuqid periods and their successors throughout Anatolia and the Jazīra, focusing also on the depiction of the dragon.[75] The mass of data thus assembled is truly exhaustive and provides a firm foundation for further research.

The present study consists of a total of 14 chapters. Chapter 1 outlines the historical and cultural context within which the dragon iconography flourished in the medieval Islamic world from Central Asia to Anatolia. Representations of the dragon on monumental sculpture, both Islamic and Christian, of the medieval period, mainly in the form of architectural decoration, are discussed in chapter 2. The symbolic significance attributed to the dragon is closely interlinked with the perception of how the boundaries between the realm of the supernatural creature and man are negotiated. It serves as a liminal marker, constituting at the same time a powerful protective device. Chapter 3 turns to portable art, where the dragon appeared as an expression of fundamental social, moral and sociological concepts as well as a metaphor of sociopolitical authority and ideal rulership. The symbolic appropriation of the dragon and control over it figured also among the paraphernalia of heroism and rulership as well as appearing on objects of personal adornment and on vessels. It is moreover noteworthy that, while there is a large body of dragon depictions on portable items from the entire Central Asian region, of which a selection is examined here, their existence on architectural structures in the Western Central Asian (previously also "Eastern Iranian")[76] world has so far not been documented. This is due to the fact that no figural sculpture is associated with the brick architecture of the Iranian world from about 1000 to 1200. Moreover, comparatively little architecture of this period survives from the "crossroads of Asia," i.e. the region of present-day Afghanistan. Hence, only the representation of dragons on monumental settings in regions west of Iran are considered.

Many pre-Islamic thought systems and practices were assimilated into early Islamic culture. Beliefs in spirits or *jinn* and their manifestation as serpent genii have been studied for example by Joseph Henninger[77] and Ernst Zbinden,[78] and these are considered in chapter 4, which analyses the intricate connection of dragon iconography with a multiplicity of natural phenomena as the means through which the continuous correlation and interchange between human society and the natural world were mediated. Dragons are paramount symbols of the elements or forces present or active in the cosmic world. This chapter focuses on the dragons' association with the four great ele-

[68] Curatola, 1979; *idem*, 1982; and *idem*, 1989; Otto-Dorn, esp. 1978–9, pp. 25–36; Öney, 1969a, *eadem*, 1969b, and *eadem*, 1978; Daneshvari, 1993.

[69] Curatola, 1979; *idem*, 1982; and *idem*, 1989.

[70] Otto-Dorn, 1959, pp. 63–5, *eadem*, 1963, pp. 131–3, *eadem*, 1978–9, esp. pp. 25–36.

[71] Öney, 1969a, *eadem*, 1969b, and *eadem*, 1978.

[72] Roux, 1972, and *idem*, 1980.

[73] Süslü, 1987.

[74] Gierlichs, 1995.

[75] *Idem*, 1996, pp. 28–40; also *idem*, 1993, and *idem*, 1998.

[76] The term is used in a geographical sense to indicate all the regions that stretch from the Caspian Sea and the Central Iranian desert in the west to the Indus river in the east, and from the coastal strip along the Arabian Sea in the south to the banks of the Syr Daryā in the north; hence comprising part of present-day Iran, Afghanistan, Pakistan, Turkmenistan, Uzbekistan and Tajikistan.

[77] Henninger, 1963.

[78] Zbinden, 1953.

ments—earth, water, fire and wind. They express, in a mythical language, aspects of the natural setting and the positive or dangerous qualities of those aspects, such as rain, drought or flood. Their particular connection with the medium of water involves a nexus of ideas which also determines the dragon's affinity with other symbols of fertility of the vegetal world. The chthonic nature of the mythical creature may be associated with the belief in dragons guarding both treasures hidden in the earth and the sources of nature's abundance. The ability of serpents and dragons to undergo physical change underlay, moreover, their association with numinous or demonic power. The overall physical division of animals from humans and the great diversity and physical distinctiveness among animal species have made animals the preferred medium for the representation of the other, non-human, sphere, which was often characterised by the effortless passage across physical and geographical boundaries. Dragons within the "natural" animal species and the realm of the supernatural and the strange, as well as the visual fusion of two or more animals, are looked at in chapter 5.

Beyond a relation with the "natural" world, the dragon is embued, on a cosmic level, with a more complex meaning as a bringer of stability or disorder, stasis or dynamism, life or death. As mentioned earlier the mythical creature has a similar meaning on a "social" or "political" level, symbolising the enemies or, as will be shown, in some cases, the champions of a society, group or class. By using the iconography of the dragon, rulers aimed to ensure symbolic control over subject dominions. This pivotal role accorded to the dragon, which figures prominently in royal and heroic symbolism and as an indicator of political power, intellectual supremacy and socio-religious dominance, is discussed in chapter 6. Among those who have worked on these concepts is Eva Baer,[79] who has formulated the expression and thoroughly explored the iconography of "the ruler in the cosmic setting," a form of imagery closely linked to the ancient concept of the royal or heroic dragon-tamer. The dragon's overall symbolism as well as the dragon-fighting myths in Old and Middle Iranian and Persian literature have been examined in depth, respectively, by Prods Oktor Skjærvø and Djalal Khāleqī-Moṭlaq,[80] while its Armenian aspect is treated by James Russell.[81] In his book, *How to Kill a Dragon: Aspects of Indo-European Poetics*, Calvert Watkins similarly looks in detail at the structure of the ancient myths on the slaying of dragons, which recur throughout the Indo-European poetic tradition.[82] Many of these topics have most recently been reinvestigated and expanded by Michael Janda in his wonderful 2010 book, *Die Musik nach dem Chaos: Der Schöpfungsmythos der europäischen Vorzeit.*[83] The dragon combat motif played a central role mainly in the chronicles of heroic combat, in tales of romance, or in allegories of mystical initiation or religious teaching.[84] The slaying or subduing of a dragon by a hero or divinity in ancient myth, and its iconography and mode of transmission in the medieval Islamic world as well as in the Eastern Christian sphere, are explored in chapter 7. A further important aspect is the eschatological role fulfilled by some dragon fighters. The role of the equestrian warrior saints as dragon-slayers has been extensively researched by the prominent scholar of Byzantine hagiography and art, Christopher Walter.[85] More recently Oya Pancaroğlu has examined the role of the itinerant dragon-slayer in medieval Anatolia.[86]

Chapter 8 aims to uncover further layers of dragon iconology in the context of astrology, a highly esteemed science in the east, its association with light and its role as a vehicle to convey cosmological ideas. The dragon representation in medieval Islamic astrology has been addressed in a number of studies, foremost among which remains that of Willy Hartner (1938) who demonstrated over seventy years ago the influence of the conceptualisation of the two pseudo-planetary "lunar nodes" *(al-ʿuqdatāni)* on Islamic artisans.[87] Guitty Azarpay seeks to explain the theme of the

[79] Baer, 1981.

[80] Skjærvø, "Aždahā I," *EIr*; Khāleqī-Moṭlaq, "Aždahā II. In Persian Literature," *EIr*.

[81] Russell, "Aždahā IV. Armenian Aždahāk," *EIr*, and *idem*, 2004.

[82] Watkins, 1995. In the mythologies of Indo-European speaking societies (Indic, Iranian, Hittite, Greek, Roman, Germanic and Armenian) versions or traces of a type of myth have been found wherein a god or hero overcomes a mythical dragon-like creature.

[83] I am indebted to Professor Almut Hintze for pointing it out to me.

[84] Russell, 2004, pp. 1032, 1285–6.

[85] Walter, 1989a; *idem*, 1995; *idem*, 1999, and *idem*, 2003.

[86] Pancaroğlu, 2004.

[87] Hartner, 1938; *idem*, 1959, and *idem*, 1973–4, as well as *idem*, "Al-Djawzahar," *EI*^{2} II, 501b. Cf. Öney, 1969a, pp. 193–216; Otto-Dorn, 1978–9, pp. 125–36; Azarpay, 1978, pp. 363–74.

interlaced dragons in the light of its astrological significance.[88] Moreover, two more recent exhibitions on celestial imagery in Islamic art in New York and Paris also included the astrological association of the dragon.[89]

Chapter 9 surveys a theme that has previously attracted little attention: the survival within medieval Islamic tradition of the *ouroboros*, the iconography of a serpent devouring its own tail. Similarly, the motif of the drinking dragon on medieval Islamic and Christian two- and three-dimensional art represents the visual remnants that survived the mutations of an ancient belief. Likewise the knotted dragon motif in the Islamic period, related to the ancient magical practice of knot tying for apotropaic ends, discussed in chapter 10, has barely been addressed other than in connection with alchemy.[90]

The dragon figure also plays a role in the various branches of knowledge that comprise the science of alchemy as well as the more esoteric or occult sciences which include talismanic astrology. Chapter 11 introduces aspects of the dragon as prophylaxis and cure in the province of magic and divination. It discusses the dragon's association with the theriaca as illustrated in the famed *Kitāb al-diryāq*. It also looks at serpents, their venoms and other characteristics as well as the corresponding antidotes, chiefly theriaca and bezoar-type stones. The dragon's role in esoteric or magical sciences, in particular sympathetic and talismanic astrological magic, as well as in the preparation of talismans is examined in chapter 12. The supernatural power of the serpent-staff is the subject of the second section of the chapter, which has been explored in terms of Jewish influences on Islamic magic by Alexander Fodor in the context of a thirteenth-century treatise in which the motif of Moses' serpent-rod is discussed as a magical device.[91] In chapter 13 the association of the dragon with the sound-world is considered. One of these aspects is the speaking dragon; another more rare occurrence is its link with sounds transformed into music.

Chapter 14 then concludes the discussion, focusing on the dragon as pre-eminent symbol and paradigm of change and transformation, thus addressing a key aspect of its phenomenology. The most important study of the iconography of the dragon in the cult of the saints and mystics is provided by Abbas Daneshvari,[92] whose research moreover offers a significant contribution to the iconological interpretation of the multivalent symbolism of the dragon by underlining its beneficial and apotropaic aspect.[93] In medieval Ṣūfīsm *(taṣawwuf)*, the mystical dimension of Islam, the symbolism of the dragon illustrates the theme of moral transformation on the spiritual path, often mediated by the figure of a mystic.

The first part of the Epilogue shows how in the wake of the Mongol invasion dragon imagery appears in different stylistic guises. The first half of the Ilkhanid period presents a transitional period in which a new "Chinese," "Mongol" or, more broadly, "Central Asian" style appears which in the second half of their reign gradually overtakes and amalgamates with the conventional "Saljuq-style" dragon. This emergence in the Mongol period of a hitherto unknown style, termed "Islamic chinoiserie," from the relationship between Chinese and Iranian art, has been investigated by Yuka Kadoi.[94] The second part demonstrates the eminent role played by the dragon, itself the ideal image of incarnate liminality, in frontier societies in Transoxania, Khurasan and Anatolia characterised by *ghāzī*s fighting for the defence and victory of Islam. This is evident in the epic-chivalrous frontier narratives describing *jihād* against dragons, as for instance in the early Turkish Anatolian epic, the *Baṭṭāl-nāma* ("Book of Baṭṭāl"), which was more recently translated by Yorgos Dedes,[95] or the epic romance of the Türkmen Dānishmend ruler, the *Dānishmend-nāma* ("Book of Dānishmend"), also based on orally transmitted traditions and composed in the twelfth or early thirteenth century, translated by Irène Mélikoff,[96] who in the romance is identified with Sayyid Baṭṭāl.[97] This phenomenon was complemented by the cross-cultural convergence of saintly cults prominently

88 Azarpay, 1978.

89 *Following the Stars*, 1997; *L'Apparence des cieux*, 1998.

90 Rogers, 1969; Moulierac, 1987; Savage-Smith, 1997, pp. 324–33.

91 Fodor, 1978.

92 In December 2004 Abbas Daneshvari gave a series of four lectures (the Yarshater Lectures) at the School of African and Oriental Studies in London on the iconography of the dragon in Persian art. His publication on the subject is eagerly awaited.

93 Daneshvari, 1993.

94 Kadoi, 2009.

95 Dedes, 1996.

96 Mélikoff, 1960.

97 *Eadem*, 1960, vol. 1, p. 103.

involving the dragon in which Islamic, Turko-Mongol, Jewish and Christian beliefs overlapped and amalgamated.

Since there are no previous comprehensive studies of the dragon in the Islamic world,[98] the present exercise is prone to all the risks that are characteristic of such an endeavour. Depictions of dragons in the material culture of the medieval Islamic period have never been fully catalogued as a corpus, hence in what follows only a representative sampling will be considered in which the selected objects are individually discussed. Inevitably, numerous potentially relevant objects may have been overlooked or considered too briefly, and the aim of tracking down the exact symbolic significance of the serpent and its greater relative, the dragon, may not have been fully realised. Nevertheless, the approach adopted here will at least bring into focus the complexity of the semantic horizon associated with these images. This endeavour is particularly precarious since modern perception of the elements that determine different modes of interpretation will not necessarily reflect the meaning and mental associations attributed to them by the medieval populations studied. Imagery that elicited clearly identifiable connotations and allusions in the cultural milieu of the medieval Central Asian world often remains incomprehensible for modern people. Because of the refractory nature of the evidence, some iconographic elements of the period are based upon a number of deductions while some others necessarily remain elusive, even impenetrable. It is therefore the intention of the present study to locate certain iconographic details that so far have not been understood or, perhaps, even recognised. At the same time it has to be borne in mind that what may be considered a symbol in the twentieth century may well represent an authentic transfer of a reality for man in medieval Central Asia and beyond. Even so it is hoped that the following chapters will shed some light on the perception of the great dragon beast within the overall intellectual and visual universe of the medieval Irano-Turkish world.

Finally, the path that has led to the realisation of this study has been long and tortuous: the serpent is not called a dragon for nothing. Nonetheless, this study represents but a small contribution to a better comprehension of the complex multivalent symbolism of the dragon in the medieval Islamic sphere. Some propositions consequently have a provisional character that, with the help of new material, specialists will confirm or invalidate.

[98] Giovanni Curatola's thorough work on the dragon focuses on the overall relation of its iconography to Chinese and Central Asian sources as well as its appearance in manuscripts of the post-Timurid period. Curatola, 1979; *idem*, 1982; and *idem*, 1989. Other previous studies cited above have mainly focused on particular topics.

CHAPTER ONE

THE MEDIEVAL ISLAMIC WORLD FROM CENTRAL ASIA TO ANATOLIA: THE HISTORICAL AND CULTURAL CONTEXT

With its rapid expansion to the status of world power, the Islamic world became increasingly open culturally to the transmission and active appropriation of ancient learning from Graeco-Roman and Indo-Iranian sources. The westward movement of the culture of Western Central Asia, in particular that of greater Khurasan, resulted not only in an outflow of savants and artists from this region but in a general tendency to "Easternise." This coincided with the westward migration of ever-growing numbers of Turkic-speaking tribes into Western Asia which increased from the late tenth century onwards. From the end of the eleventh century until the onslaught of the Mongols in the mid-thirteenth century, the Saljuqs and their "successor states" ruled a large region from India to Egypt, perpetuating the heritage of Western Central Asian art and culture in their new homeland.

Two major currents profoundly influenced the formation of the Islamic world from its inception. One was the transmission of ancient learning from the Greek, Central Asian (in particular the Iranian) and Indian cultural realms, provoking an intense intellectual ferment in the Islamic world.[1] This was linked with and reflected by the second, which saw the culture of Western Central Asia flowing westwards, facilitated by the large-scale migrations of Turkish-speaking people into Islamic lands from the late tenth century onwards.[2]

With the establishment of the Islamic polity (*dār al-islām*, "abode of Islam") in the wake of the Arab conquests after the death of the Prophet Muḥammad in 10/632, the lifting of political and religious barriers from Morocco to India promoted greater movement of goods, people and ideas across a vast region.[3] It united areas and people that for over a millennium, since Alexander the Great (r. 356–323 BC), had been subject to varying degrees of Hellenisation.

Throughout the Umayyad period (41/661–132/750), and possibly beyond the mid-eighth century, Greek was widely current in greater Mesopotamia and Palestine as the native language of a significant portion of the population[4] and was moreover cultivated in the many Christian monasteries and cloisters. The cultivation of Hellenistic philosophy and science at centres of learning that had flourished during the first six centuries of the Christian era was well entrenched and further developed in the regions that were part of the Roman, later the Byzantine and Sasanian empires, and finally the caliphate, throughout the Fertile Crescent, from Edessa (al-Ruhā) and Qinnasrīn in the west, through Nisibis and Mosul in northern Mesopotamia to Jundaysābūr in Khūzistān, well into western Iran.[5] To these should be added at least two other major centres of Hellenistic science and learning, Ḥarrān (ancient Carrhae) in northwestern Mesopotamia just south of Edessa. In 47/667 the Muslim armies crossed the river Oxus and by 95/713 Transoxania had come within the expanding fold of Islam. The Eurasian heartlands, in particular the cities of Marw and Balkh in Khurasan (covering a wide extent of land comprising regions in present-day Afghanistan, Turkmenistan and Iran),[6] which were well-known for their libraries until their destruction by the Mongols in the early thirteenth century, constituted an important locus for integrating and transmitting knowledge.[7]

After the ʿAbbasid revolution, the transfer of the seat of the caliphate from Syria to Iraq and the building in 145/762 of a new capital, Baghdad (close to the ruins of the Sasanian capital of

[1] The most in-depth monograph on the Graeco-Arabic translation movement and the political and social factors involved in it is certainly that of Gutas, 1998.

[2] While the migratory routes of peoples were mostly from east to west, there were also significant concurrent flows in the opposite direction as well as southwards.

[3] Gutas, 1998, p. 13; Bauer, 1995, pp. 34–6.

[4] Gutas, 1998, p. 117.

[5] *Idem*, p. 14.

[6] *Idem*, p. 14.

[7] Ruska, 1926. Cf. Needham and Wang, 1965, p. 369; Gutas, 1998, p. 50 and n. 39.

Ctesiphon), placed the ʿAbbasids (132/750–656/1258) in the heartlands of the former Sasanian empire (*c.* 224–651). During Sasanian times scholarly activity was partly motivated by a Zoroastrian imperial ideology that would see all learning ultimately derive from the Avestan texts, the Zoroastrian canonical scriptures. It is perhaps in this context that the burgeoning Graeco-Persian translation activities which culminated in the reign of Khusraw I Anūshirwān (r. 531–578), generating a culture of translation that survived into early ʿAbbasid times, are best understood.[8] Political and economic support from the Western Central Asian world, in particular from greater Khurasan (in other words the wider Iranian world), was indispensable for the ʿAbbasid victory.[9] The early ʿAbbasid caliphs tried to legitimise their rule by expanding their ideology to include the concerns of the "Persian" contingent, thereby bringing about the incorporation of Sasanian culture, still dominant for large parts of the population east of Iraq, into mainstream ʿAbbasid culture.[10] Two components of the Sasanian culture, Zoroastrian imperial ideology and political astrology, proved to be of immense significance to the caliph al-Manṣūr, who was in many ways the actual founder of the ʿAbbasid caliphate, in helping him to consolidate the ʿAbbasid cause.

Between the second half of the eighth and eleventh centuries, intense scientific activity was accompanied by a prodigious effort to garner and then translate, assimilate and cultivate scientific and pseudo-scientific treatises, for instance on theology, medicine, astrology and logic, mostly via Syriac and Persian (Pahlawī) into the Arabic sphere. Especially in the field of astronomy and astrology translations were often also made from Persian or Sanskrit.[11] The translation movement was actively patronised by the ʿAbbasid rulers while at the same time representing a "social phenomenon" which was "subsidized by an enormous outlay of funds, both public and private."[12] Support for these undertakings "cut across all lines of religious, sectarian, ethnic, tribal and linguistic demarcation. Patrons were Arabs and non-Arabs, Muslims and non-Muslims, Sunnīs and Shīʿites, generals and civilians, merchants and land-owners, etc."[13] While the most widely known evidence for Muslim cultural borrowing lies in this vast corpus of Arabic translations, the simultaneous cultural appropriation was much broader, pervading all modes of life. By the twelfth and thirteenth centuries, Islamic culture had fully internalised and synthesised concepts emerging from a multitude of scientific works acquired largely from Graeco-Roman and Indo-Iranian sources.

The movement of craftsmen from eastern Islamic lands, in particular from greater Khurasan, westwards was a decisive process, which accelerated between the fall of the Iranian dynasty of the Samanids (204/819–395/1005) and the late thirteenth century, a period that might broadly be described as the Turko-Mongol era. Hemmed in by deserts both to the south and the north, the Khurasan mountain range and the plains along its slopes have always represented a significant, and often the most important communication artery between east and west. The tendency to easternise was initially an internal phenomenon within Western Central Asia which began with the Iranian Samanid dynasty that ruled in Transoxania (known during the Middle Ages as *mā warāʾ al-nahr*, "the land which lies beyond the river [Oxus]" at the eastern margin of Khurasan facing the still pagan Turks) and then in Khurasan from the ninth century onwards. For a time, the Samanids constituted the border between the Islamicised lands and the still incompletely Islamicised Turkic dynasty of the Qarakhanids. East of the regions dominated by the Qarakhanids were the lands of the Oghuz tribes from whom the Saljuqs would emerge.

Under the aegis of the Samanids and that of other petty courts of the east, Iranian literature flourished, reaching an extraordinary stage of maturity and eloquence with authors such as Rūdakī, Daqīqī and al-Kisāʾī of Marw.[14] It was at this time that the ancient Iranian epic traditions were rekindled, and in 346/957 the governor of Ṭūs in Khurasan, Abū Manṣūr Muḥammad ibn ʿAbd al-Razzāq, commissioned the translation of Pahlawī (that is, the Middle Persian of the Sasanians) texts of the national epic into New Persian. These were taken up by the great poet Abu ʾl-Qāsim Firdawsī of Ṭūs (*c.* 329–30/940–1–*c.* 411/1020 or 416/1025), author of the monumental versified epic retelling of the history of the pre-Islamic Iranian kings and heroes

---

8 *Idem*, 1998, pp. 25–6.
9 Cf. Frye, 2005, p. 4.
10 Gutas, 1998, p. 29; Spuler, 1976, pp. 342–7.
11 Pingree, 1963.
12 Gutas, 1998, p. 2.
13 *Idem*, pp. 2, 5, see also 134–5.
14 Cf. Bosworth, "Samanids," *EI*² VIII, 1025b.

from mythico-legendary times until the arrival of Islam, which in the context of the period may be seen in terms of an Iranian revival characterised by an interest in national history. Known as the *Shāh-nāma*, it was completed in 400/1010 after about thirty years of writing. Together with Asadī Ṭūsī's (d. *c.* 465/1072) slightly later heroic epic *Garshāsp-nāma* ("Epic of Garshāsp"), the oldest of the epics complementary to Firdawsī's *Shāh-nāma*, it serves as one of the main sources for various descriptions of dragons comprising the following range of features that not only incorporate characteristics of various species into a single body but had the ability to cross boundaries within the natural environment it inhabits and was found in different locations:

> [The dragon] is sometimes described as a wolf, a tiger, *shīr-e kappī*, i.e., a sort of sphinx (combined lion and ape), or simply as a *patyāra* (maleficent creature), or a black cloud. ... it has one head and mouth, exhaling fire and smoke from its hellish mouth, and inhaling with enough force to suck in a horse and rider, or a crocodile from the water, or an eagle from the sky. ... It is big as a mountain. Its head resembles a thicket of hair and its bristles stretch down to the ground like nooses. It has two horns the size of the branch of a tree, ten *gaz* or eighty cubits long. Its eyes are the size of wagon wheels or like two tanks of blood. They shine from afar as brightly as stars at night, as two glittering diamonds, as two blazing torches, or as two mirrors held beneath the sun. It has two tusks, each the length of the hero's arm or of a stag's horns. Humans and animals hang from its teeth. When it sticks its long, black tongue out of its mouth it hangs down onto the road like a black tree. Its skin has scales like a fish, each as big as a shield. It has eight feet, though most often it drags itself over the ground, and when it moves it makes the valleys and plains tremble, and a river of yellow poison as deep as a spear flows from its tail and nose. Its color is variously described, e.g., as dark yellow or gray, black, blue. ... Its lair, guarded day and night, is on a mountain (usually said to be near the sea, whence the *azhdahā* itself originated) or rock the same color as its body and is shunned by all living things, animals and plants. The sources variously locate it on the Kashaf-rūd near Ṭūs, on Mount Shekāwand in Kabul, India, "Māzandarān," on Mount Saqīlā in the land of the Romans, Mount Zahāb in the Yaman, or in Ṭabarestān.[15]

At the same time there was a florescence of local arts and crafts. With this cultural background, some of the Turkic tribes, in particular the Oghuz and Qarluq (henceforth known as Türkmen/Turkoman),[16] converted to Islam and became heirs to the local Muslim civilisations, Iranian and then Arabic. By the late tenth century Selchük (transcribed in Arabic as Saljūq), the son of Toqaq Temir Yaligh, commander of the Oghuz Yabghu, embraced Islam and became a *ghāzī* (Muslim warrior for the faith) against his still pagan fellow-tribesmen. He and his followers soon became embroiled in a power struggle with the weakening Samanids, a vacuum filled shortly after by the emerging Turkic dynasties, the Ghaznawids and Qarakhanids, thus setting the stage for the rise of the Great Saljuq Empire.

Turkic tribes had long been in contact with Western Central Asian culture. The Ghaznavid dynasty of Turkish origin was founded by Sebüktigin, a general and governor for the Samanids and with its capital in Ghazna lasted for over two hundred years, from 367/977–8 to 583/1187. The Ghaznawids were favourably disposed towards Iranian culture, and their courts became outstanding cultural centres. They thus fulfilled what was expected of royal patrons, as the polymath of the age, Abu 'l-Rayḥān Muḥammad ibn Aḥmad al-Bīrūnī, who finished his days at Ghazna, put it: "to do this [sc. to honour learning and its representatives is] ... the duty of those who rule over them, of kings and princes. For they alone can free the minds of scholars from the daily anxieties for the necessities of life, and stimulate their energies to earn more fame and favour, the yearning for which is the pith and marrow of human nature."[17] The Indian campaigns of Maḥmūd ibn Sebüktigin (r. 389/999–421/1030) brought a great influx of plundered temple treasures into the capital, Ghazna. The empire reached its zenith under Maḥmūd: no expense was spared in beautifying the capital and the *sulṭān* brought scholars, craftsmen and artisans from the lands he had conquered to Ghazna as well as to such provincial centres as Herat, Balkh and Lashkarī Bāzār, resulting in a flowering of the arts, and of architecture in particular.[18]

---

[15] Khāleqī-Moṭlaq, "Aždahā II," *EIr.*

[16] The term Türkmen appears in Islamic sources from the tenth century onwards. See Bosworth, 1968, p. 17.

[17] *Kitāb fī Taḥqīq mā li-l-Hind* ("Book of Inquiry into India"), tr. Sachau, 1887, p. 152.

[18] Bosworth, 1963, pp. 139–41. Cf. Bombaci and Scerrato, 1959.

Although Firdawsī makes the Oxus the traditional boundary between Iran and Tūrān (the Central Asian region beyond the Jayḥūn/Āmū Daryā), the land of the nomadic world of Western Central Asia, and states that there was a natural dislike between the two groups, which were like "two elements, fire and water, which rage against each other in the depths of the heart,"[19] there was never, as Bosworth has pointed out, a cut and dried distinction between the two racial groups.[20] They had a long history of interaction and the Turkish people were well-known to the Iranians, who had often been invaded by steppe peoples of diverse ethnic origins. The antithesis between Iran and Tūrān, emblematising a dualistic conception of the world and of history, thus appears by Firdawsī's time to have been more a literary and archaising preconception of the Iranian national consciousness than a reflection of the actual state of affairs.[21] The Qarakhanid Muslim philologist, Maḥmūd al-Kāshgharī, remarks in his lexicographic encyclopaedia *Dīwān lughāt al-turk*, written in 463/1071, that all of Transoxania, which was closely linked with the Eurasian steppe, was once inhabited by Turkic peoples, "but when the Iranians *(al-Furs)* became numerous, it became just like Persian territory *(bilād al-ʿAjam)*."[22] Thus the two worlds had to a large part become intermingled culturally as well as ethnically.

The westward migration of ever-growing numbers of Turkic-speaking tribes, the dominant force being the Saljuqs, into Western Asia increased from the late tenth century onwards. This accelerated following their decisive victory under Ṭoghrıl Beg over the Ghaznawids at Dandāndaqān (located between Marw and Sarakhs) in 431/1040, after which all of Iran lay open before them. In 447/1055 Ṭoghrıl Beg entered Baghdad and in 449/1058, when he entered for the second time, the ʿAbbasid caliph al-Qāʾim legitimised his rule by the bestowing of honorific titles. The victory of the second Saljuq *sulṭān* Alp Arslan against the Byzantine ruler Romanus IV Diogenes at Manzikert/Malāzgird, north of Lake Van, in Dhu ʾl-Qaʿda 463/August 1071, on a day following a moonless night,[23] effectively destroyed the ability of Byzantium (Rūm) to defend its eastern boundaries. This led to the gradual settlement of hellenised Asia Minor, or Anadolu/Anatolia as it was later to be known under the Turks, by successive waves of mostly nomadic Turkic tribes, and to the establishment of the sultanate of the Saljuqs of Rūm *(Saljūqiyān-i Rūm)*[24] in the central and eastern territories. By the end of the century the entire territory from the Armenian and Georgian marches to the Aegean sea was in Saljuq hands. In their new homeland, the Turks perpetuated the heritage of Western Central Asian art and culture with a "markedly Khurasanian flavour."[25] This was facilitated by the fact that the migratory movement of Turkic peoples swept along migrant craftsmen from the Central Asian, in particular East Iranian, world, a process much intensified by the invasion of Khurasan by the Mongol army under Genghis Khān in the 1220s.[26] The signature of master craftsmen on Anatolian tilework suggests that innovation on Anatolian Saljuq architecture owed much to craftsmen from Khurasan or Ghurid Herat[27] and points to Eastern Iran as one of the earlier and most important centres of artistic innovation. Katharina Otto-Dorn has proposed that some of the tile revetments at the now destroyed palace-citadel at Kubadabad (623/1226–634/1237), southwest of Konya, built

[19] Kowalski, 1939–49, pp. 87–9. The moon was a pre-eminent Turkish emblem and the sun a Iranian one; *idem*, pp. 98–9.

[20] Bosworth, 1963, p. 205.

[21] *Idem*, p. 206.

[22] Tr. Atalay, B., vol. 3, Ankara, 1939–1943, pp. 149–50, as cited in Bosworth, 1963, p. 206.

[23] Hillenbrand, C., "Malāzgird," *EI*² VI, 242b.

[24] The use of the ethnic/dynastic term Rūm by the Anatolian Saljuqs whose principality was based on the region of Konya and southern Cappadocia reflected their conception as heirs to the Byzantines in south-central Anatolia, territories which continued to be strongly Greek in ethnos. Bosworth, "Rūm. Relations between the Islamic powers and the Byzantines," *EI*² VIII, 601a.

[25] Melikian-Chirvani, 1974, pp. 112, 114. Note however Oleg Grabar's caveats (2006, pp. 314–5) with regard to an argumentation for a Khurasan "style" or "mode" as being hypo-thetical on visual and historical grounds and merely indicative of "an active industry or artisanship of metalwork in Khurasan."

[26] On the large-scale movement of metalworkers to western Iran, Anatolia, the Jazira, Syria and Egypt, see Ward, 1993, pp. 79, 87.

[27] The signature of the *bannāʾ* Muḥammad ibn Muḥammad ibn ʿUthmān al-Ṭūsī, who probably came from Khurasan, found on the tile-mosaic of the Sırçalı *madrasa* in Konya (640/1242–3) is discussed by Meinecke, 1976, vol. 1, pp. 35–45, and *idem*, vol. 2, no. 71. For further examples of craftsmen who, judging from their geographical epithet (*nisba*; generally pointing to someone's tribal, geographical or religious affiliation) may have come from the eastern Islamic lands to the west, see, for instance, those listed in *idem*, vol. 1, pp. 187–9, addendum II (i.e., Aḥmad ibn Abī Bakr al-Marandī, *c.* 612/1215, or *miʿmār* Badr al-Dīn Tabrīzī, post-672/1273); Pickett, 1997, pp. 37–41. See however the cautionary remarks on this subject, *idem*, n. 349.

at the apogee of Saljuq power by *sulṭān* ʿAlāʾ al-Dīn Kay Qubādh I (r. 616/1219–634/1237), may have been made by Iranian craftsmen.[28] Moreover, the extent to which the Rūm Saljuqs (just like their Iranian cousins, the Great Saljuqs) embraced the Iranian tradition of kingship was particularly marked, as also evidenced by their tendency to choose pre-Islamic Iranian royal names.[29] Furthermore, Persian was the official language of the court and administration in the sultanate of Rūm, which welcomed streams of poets and mystics (*ṣūfis*, "those who wear wool") from the Western Central Asian world, the most celebrated of whom was certainly Jalāl al-Dīn Rūmī (Rabīʿ I 604/30 September 1207–5 Jumāda II 672/1273), who had left Balkh (ancient Bactra) at the age of twelve with his family.[30] On the other hand, the sedentary population over which the Saljuqs ruled was extremely heterogeneous and included large numbers of Armenian, Georgian and Greek Christians.

The transmission of art and culture from the greater Khurasan region was also apparent in the Transcaucasian region, particularly in thriving twelfth-century Georgia[31] and Armenia, regions, valuable repositories of ancient oral and iconographical traditions that had been in the orbit of successive stages of Iranian culture since antiquity.[32] Marriage alliances between eleventh- and twelfth-century Muslim ruling families and Georgian[33] and Armenian[34] royal families resulted in a nexus of Christian-Muslim relations, while providing intermediaries between Christians and Muslims. More Islamic culture penetrated into Georgia during the reign of queen Tʿamar of Georgia (1184–1211/2), whose territory stretched from Azerbaijan to the borders of Cherkessia, and from Erzurum to Ganja, forming a pan-Caucasian Empire. The evidence of this can be seen in Georgian literature[35] and manuscript illustration[36] based on Iranian models. This influence is also discernible in metalwork from Daghistan, located east of Georgia and west of Iran.[37]

In spite of internecine strife the successive and partly overlapping major dynasties of the Ghaznawids, the Ghurids, the Qarakhanids, the Great Saljuqs, the Zangids, the Ayyubids and the Saljuqs of Rūm succeeded in spite of the ethnic diversity of their subjects in creating a comparatively unified culture from India to Egypt. In particular the artistic traditions of the Western Central Asian world, the Caucasus, Transcaucasia, northern Syria, eastern Anatolia and northern Mesopotamia certainly had to varying degrees a symbiotic development. In the twelfth and thirteenth centuries, the region underwent

---

28 Otto-Dorn and Önder, 1969, pp. 468–9. Cf. Melikian-Chirvani, 1974, p. 115 and n. 25.

29 At least from trom the time the Saljuqs entered Iran, the Turks came under the influence of Iranian culture. The impact of this influence is reflected, for instance, in al-Juwaynī's account of the last Great Saljuq *sulṭān* of Iran and Iraq, Ṭoghrıl III ibn Arslan (r. 571/1176–590/1194), reciting verses from the *Shāh-nāma* (ed. Vullers, p. 188, ll. 1060–2) while wielding his heavy mace in battle:

> "When the dust arose from the countless army,
> the cheeks of our worthies turned pale.
> As for me I raised the mace that kills with a single blow and felled that host upon the spot.
> I uttered a yell from my saddle saying, 'The earth has become a millstone upon them.'"

Cited after *Taʾrīkh-i jahān-gushāy*, tr. Boyle, 1912–37, vol. 2, p. 302.

30 Cf. Melikian-Chirvani, 1974, pp. 114–5.

31 The close relationship between cultures in the twelfth century appears to have been a result of the Christian-Islamic symbiosis at Tbilisi among the ruling families (Minorsky, 1953, p. 157; attested by king Dimitri's attendance at Friday prayers in 548/1153 (as recorded by al-Fāriqī), and p. 135 (Christian-Islamic marriages)). Cf. Melikian-Chirvani, 1974, p. 112 and n. 15.

32 Baltrušaitis, 1929, pp. 43–5; Melikian-Chirvani, 1974, pp. 113–5 and ns. 17, 18, 20.

33 After his incursions into Georgia against Bagrat IV, the Saljuq *sulṭān* Alp Arslan (455/1063–465/1073) strengthened his influence there by marrying one of the king's nieces (Allen, 1932, pp. 91–2). The ruler of Erzurum ordered his son, Mughīth al-Dīn Toghrıl, to convert to Christianity to marry Rusudan (1223–1247), the daughter of queen Tʿamar of Georgia, and heir to the throne after the sudden death of her brother, whose daughter was in turn married to the Saljuq *sulṭān* of Rūm, Giyāth al-Dīn Kay Khusraw II (634/1237–644/1246); after his death she married the Parwāna Muḥammad ibn Sulaymān Muʿīn al-Dīn (executed in 676/1277), one of the most powerful Anatolian magnates of the thirteenth century. Cf. Minorsky, 1953, p. 135; Melikian-Chirvani, 1974, p. 113, n. 17; Rogers, 1976, p. 316.

34 The eleventh-century ruler of Dwīn, Abu 'l-Aswār Shawūr, of the minor Armenian dynasty of the Shaddādids, was married to a sister of the Armenian king of Tashir, David Anholin. Akhsatān ibn Manuchihr ibn Afrīdūn, ruler of Ani, and son of this princess, also married an Armenian princess of the Bagratid house (Minorsky, 1953, p. 81). See also Melikian-Chirvani, 1974, p. 113, n. 17.

35 For instance the close similarities between the eleventh-century narrative poem, *Wīs u Ramīn*, and Shota Rustaveli's twelfth-century epic *Vepkhis-tkaosani* ("The Knight in the Panther's Skin"); see *idem*, 1974, p. 112 and n. 14.

36 See, for instance, a Georgian astrological treatise of 1188, illustrated under Islamic influence which Melikian-Chirvani (1974, pp. 112–3 and n. 15) interpretes as Persian, detecting Khurasanian influence in the Kufic inscriptions. Amiranašvili, 1966, pls. 56–66 and pp. 28–30, where the writer also connects the Iranian stylistic influence with the Persianising aspect in Georgian literature.

37 Melikian-Chirvani, 1974, p. 113 and n. 16.

sweeping socio-political, economic and artistic changes that made "northern Mesopotamia" – a geographical entity known in medieval Islam as the Jazīra ("island"), the northern part of the territory located between the Tigris and Euphrates rivers (today divided between eastern Syria, northern Iraq and southeastern Turkey) – "one of the liveliest regions."[38] Political stability, though not hegemony, brought about relative prosperity. Following the decline of the Great Saljuq dynasty from around 512/1118, the area was divided into a number of Turkish and Kurdish principalities.[39] The Saljuq "successor states" included the Artuqids of Amīda/Diyārbakr (end of the fifth/eleventh to the beginning of the ninth/fifteenth century), the Zangids of northern Syria (521–2/1127–8 until 579/1183 in Aleppo and until 631/1233 in Mosul), the Ayyubids of Syria and Egypt (564/1169–658/1260) and the Saljuqs of Rūm (Anatolia, *c.* 483/1081–*c.* 707/1307). The rapid increase of small principalities founded by *atābegs/atābaks* ("father-beys") or various members of the Saljuq dynasty resulted in the establishment of numerous courts, all competing with each other for cultural prestige, which may well have provided the impetus for the proliferation of innovative images. However, this was severely disrupted under the impact of invasions from the east, first by the Turkic Khwārazm shāhs in the 1220s and shortly after by the Mongols, which brought about a cataclysm with great social upheavals, destruction and discontinuity. After the battle of Köse Dagh in the region of Sivas (Sebasteia) in 641/1243, the Mongols occupied Anatolia and Saljuq autonomy was lost forever. For a time the Saljuq sultanate continued as a Mongol province, although some Türkmen emirs maintained small principalities of their own in distant mountainous districts, but finally the Saljuq dynasty came to its end.

---

38 Ettinghausen and Grabar, 1987, pp. 297–9.

39 For an outline of the political, religious and cultural climate of the region, see Hillenbrand, C., 1985.

CHAPTER TWO

DRAGONS ON MONUMENTAL SETTINGS IN REGIONS WEST OF IRAN

Carved friezes or high-relief sculpture on stonework of the medieval Islamic period, very often figural in nature and including a repertory of animals and fabulous beasts, were portrayed in particular on architectural monuments. These could include the gates, archivolts and doorways of secular monuments such as city walls, palaces and caravanserais, as well as religious monuments like mosques, *madrasas* and funerary structures.

Among the mythical creatures depicted on medieval Islamic monuments, the dragon occupies a significant place.[1] However, while the iconography is entirely absent from Western Central Asian monumental art until the fifteenth century,[2] it is characteristic of the area to the west of Iran. As noted earlier, this is due to the fact that no figural sculpture is associated with the brick architecture of the Iranian world from about 1000 to 1200, whereas the dragon motif is conspicuous on portable items from the greater Khurasan region, where the motif has a very ancient history. Its appearance on the architecture of eleventh- and twelfth-century northern Mesopotamia, the Jazīra, Syria and Anatolia,[3] may on the one hand be due to depictions in the so-called "minor arts" whose very nature is their potential for portability, allowing for the long-distance diffusion of motifs.[4] This may be compounded by another reason which may be sought locally. The principal building material employed for the architecture of these regions is cut-stone with brick playing a minor role. The preference for this material is due to its availability as well as the local builders' mastery of stone masonry, a skill which was naturally made use of by their new rulers, the Saljuqs. The subjugated local population was largely Christian, who only gradually converted to the faith of their rulers, and not only employed their traditions of stone-carving, woodwork, stucco and tile-mosaic but also their decorative repertoire.[5]

It is evident that dragon motifs were not limited to Islamic monuments or portable objects, but were used equally by Christian artists and the artists of other faiths. The iconography of the dragon clearly enjoyed cross-cultural popularity in the medieval era. In fact representations of the motif on stone-carved architectural reliefs in the predominantly Christian Transcaucasian realm (that is most of present-day Armenia, Georgia and Azerbaijian) precede its first known depictions in neighbouring eleventh- and twelfth-century northern Mesopotamia, Syria and Anatolia. In particular in the Armenian and Georgian regions this type of imagery can be found from about the ninth century onwards, especially the dragon combat motif (the earliest depictions of which may be datable to the seventh century), which will be examined in chapter 7.

Often depicted in mirror image, dragon themes appear above or around entrances and portals which represent the boundary between the exterior and interior. The placement reflects the sensitivity of the threshold (Lat. *limen*) as both a metaphor for the monument it protects and the

---

[1] For dragon imagery on Islamic architecture, see in particular the monograph by Öney, 1969a, as well as the research of Otto-Dorn, 1978–9, esp. pp. 25–36.

[2] Two large yellow dragons set against a blue background in mosaic faience were shown in the tympanum of the portal arch of Abu 'l-Qāsim Babur's mosque dating from 848/1444–5 situated in the shrine complex of Jamāl al-Ḥaqq wa 'l-Dīn at Anau near Ashgabat in Turkmenistan, which was destroyed when the area was struck by an earthquake in 1948. Some of the dragon mosaic has been recovered and is now housed at the Fine Arts Museum of Ashgabat. The portal was photographed by the German art historian Ernst Cohn-Wiener in the 1920s, whose collection of photographs taken in west Turkestan is kept at the British Museum and published online in the digital library of archnet.org; ArchNet Image ID ICW0120. For a discussion of the Anau dragon motif, see Pugachenkova, 1956, pp. 125–9. Dragons also appear in the spandrels of a fifteenth-century mosque at the shrine-complex of Turbat-i Sheikh Jām halfway between Mashhad and Herat in Khurasan; see Daneshvari, 1993, pl. I, fig. 1.

[3] It is also noteworthy that the dragon motif was not introduced into Egypt and the Maghrib until Mamlūk times, when this transmission probably took place through Mosuli craftsmen. Ibrāhīm, 1976, pp. 12, 15–6.

[4] Cf. Hoffman, 2001, pp. 17–22.

[5] I would like to thank Professor Robert Hillenbrand for drawing my attention to this point. Cf. Meinecke, 1976, vol. 1, pp. 5–6.

liminal or transitory realm within which the passage from the perilous exterior to the secure interior might be negotiated.[6] The doorway, gates and further openings, or other vulnerable zones, were considered to be a favourite abode of dangerous spirits, hence the particular precautions, rites of spatial passage and apotropaic sacrifices enacted in these areas on special occasions.[7] One of the primary uses of the iconography of the dragon was therefore to identify the threshold and thereby operate as liminal marker. The choice of the dragon in this capacity reflects a consistently followed principle according to which anyone entering a building is confronted by the dragon figure. While the dragon's intermediate position and hybrid character itself is marked out as incarnate liminality, characterised by ambiguity, its fierce, menacing aspect is here found in a "helpful" context in that it is directed towards the outside world, warding off all hostile attack, and turning into a symbolism of defence of those that are "inside." It is employed in its apotropaic capacity to ward off evil and afford protection by taking a defensive role against baleful creatures and dangerous influences such as natural catastrophes. Its semantic horizon is thereby extended to include the function of guardian of the threshold akin to a "tutelary spirit" imbued with prophylactic and talismanic power.[8]

The apotropaic and protective function of the dragon may further be associated with belief in the Evil Eye, the blighting glance of envy, which belongs to one of the most ancient concepts of humanity, prevalent in medieval Islamic culture and referred to in the Qurʾān (*sūra* 68, 51–3).[9] The Evil Eye was feared and apotropaic symbolism, sometimes in the form of fixed representations of the Eye attached to architectural structures, was used to ward off its malevolent gaze, to disseminate evil and to warrant protection. It may further be noted that the Evil Eye was often considered to be most harmful to those in the liminal stages of life, such as newborn children, the newly married or pregnant women. Moreover, in keeping with ideas relating to the protection of deceased individuals entering the liminal and transitional states, burials are sensitive sites. At funerary sites and mausolea, the dragons serve as markers of sacred spaces.

The depiction of dragons may be associated with the fact that some dangerous animals, in particular vipers, are held to have a poisonous glance.[10] This is illustrated by the story of the marine dragons reported by the renowned tenth-century Arab geographer and traveller, Abu 'l-Ḥasan ʿAlī ibn al-Ḥusayn ibn ʿAlī al-Masʿūdī (d. 345/956). Marine creatures are said to have so frightened the workmen who built Alexandria as to prevent Iskandar (Alexander the Great) from constructing the city. He is therefore said to have dived into the sea in a glass box inserted into a wooden box from where he drew pictures of the sea monsters. These images were used to construct metal effigies which were then set up opposite the place where building was being carried out. When the dragons emerged from the sea and saw the images they fled, enabling Iskandar to complete the building of Alexandria.[11] This ruse was hence linked to the idea that if confronted by representations of themselves, dragons would be repelled by their own noxious power.

The account has a precedent in the biblical story of the plague of poisonous snakes which so devastated the people of Israel that Moses intervened on their behalf, setting a bronze image of a serpent upon a pole (Numbers 21:6, 7 and 9):

> The Lord sent *seraph* serpents against the people. They bit the people and many of the Israelites died. The people came to Moses and said, "we sinned, by speaking against the Lord and against you. Intercede with the Lord to take away the

[6] Cf. Flood, 2006, p. 149.

[7] Kitzinger, 1970, p. 640 and n. 7; Engemann, 1975, pp. 44–8; Henninger, 2004, pp. 14 and n. 66, p. 22 and ns. 109–11, pp. 31–2; Zbinden, 1953, pp. 36, 44.

[8] Kühnel, 1950, pp. 4–18. Cf. also Otto-Dorn, 1959, p. 75 and n. 38, and *eadem,* 1978–9, p. 130; Öney, 1969a, pp. 214–25; Roux, 1972, p. 393.

[9] Schimmel, 1994, p. 91. Cf. Marçais, "ʿAyn," *EI*² I, 786a.

[10] Al-Damīrī (*Ḥayāt al-ḥayawān al-kubrā*, tr. Jayakar, 1906, vol. 1, pp. 55, 633) records that the face of a certain kind of serpent, called *al-Aṣalah*, whose looks kill by the mere sight, "is like that of a human being, that it is of an immensely large size, and that it remains in the same condition even if a thousand years pass over it." For other stories about poisonous snakes whose looks alone are enough to kill, see Ullmann, 1992, p. 111; Ruska, "Almās," *EI*¹ I, p. 313; Ruska and Plessner, "Almās," *EI*² I, 419a. The poisonous serpent or basilisk whose glance could kill a man was already known in antiquity (cf. Pliny, *Naturalis Historia* VII 1.2 and 49.70; VIII 33).

[11] Al-Masʿūdī, *Kitāb murūj al-dhahab*, tr. and ed. Barbier de Meynard and de Courteille, 1917, vol. 2, pp. 425–7. See also Pseudo-Callisthenes, *Historia Alexandri Magni*, ed. Kroll, 1926, p. 32. The story is also recorded by Ibn Khaldūn who discounts the practical aspect of it and observes "the story of the many heads they have is intended to indicate ugliness and frightfulness. It is not meant to be taken literally." *Muqaddima*, tr. Rosenthal, 1958, vol. 1, p. 73.

> serpents from us!" And Moses interceded for the people. Then the Lord said to Moses, "Make a *seraph* figure and mount it on a standard. And if anyone who is bitten looks at it, he shall recover." Moses made a copper serpent and mounted it on a standard; and when anyone was bitten by a serpent, he would look at the copper serpent and recover.[12]

The expedient relates to the magical principle of effecting a cure for snake venom by viewing the image of the serpent, thus following the principle of homeopathic (or imitative) magic, *similia similibus*, according to which things are believed to act upon each other, even at a distance, if they are alike in some relevant manner. The purpose of the bronze image was therefore therapeutic: anyone bitten by a serpent could be healed by looking at it. Since the peril was identified with the demonic power within the serpent, the bronze image upon a pole constituted a counter-equivalent power which served as effective prophylaxis. The famous copper alloy serpent column, the triple-headed serpent tripod of Delphi in the Hippodrome of the city of Constantinople, is an example of apotropaic sculpture intended to afford protection from poisonous creatures, including serpents.[13] The early tenth-century Arab captive, Hārūn ibn Yaḥyā, notes four copper serpents in Constantinople that served as talismans[14] to render noxious creatures inoffensive.[15] The sixteenth-century Ottoman historian Aḥmad ibn Yūsuf al-Qaramānī (d. 1019/1610) similarly reports:

> Serpents and snakes appeared in [Constantinople] and decimated men and cattle alike. Those who survived fled, and it remained empty for a while. Then, to drive these calamities away, one sultan [Byzantine emperor] ... fabricated a talisman, possibly the bronze one now presently shaped like three serpents.[16]

ʿIzz al-Dīn Muḥammad ibn Shaddād (613/1217–684/1285), the chronicler of the cities of Syria and the Jazīra in the thirteenth century, mentions a dragon tower *(burj al-thaʿābīn)* in Aleppo that was supposed not only to prevent the detrimental effects of snake-bites but also to protect the city's inhabitants.[17] The late Mamluk topographer Abu ʾl-Faḍl Muḥammad Ibn al-Shiḥna (active 1400–1450) more clearly specifies that the tower referred to as *burj al-thaʿābīn* serves as a talisman against serpents conferring immunity from snake bite in Aleppo.[18] Such apotropaic renditions were not unique to Islamic architecture but were also found in the Christian environment. This is evidenced by the twelfth-century ascetic Abu ʾl-Ḥāsan ʿAlī ibn Abī Bakr al-Harawī (d. 611/1215), who in his description of sacred sites of Anatolia describes a talismanic design of a double-headed serpent in the church of Mart [*sic*; perhaps a corruption of Mār] Dāris in Mayyāfāriqīn, northeast of Diyārbakr.[19]

The conception of the existence of a serpent with heads at both ends of its body appears to have been widespread in the medieval Islamic world. It is discussed in the best-known book on animals of the Arab world, the *Kitāb al-Ḥayawān* ("Book of Animals"), written by the ninth-century littérateur Abū ʿUthmān ʿAmr ibn Baḥr, known by his nickname al-Jāḥiẓ ("the google-eyed"; 159/775–6–255/868–9). He quotes the Arabic

---

[12] Tr. after Wilson, 2001, p. 75. The term *seraph* (Hebr. *saraf*) appears to be the general name for poisonous snakes whose poison, metaphorically, *soref* ("burns") the body. See also Astour, 1965, pp. 232–3; Hendel, "Neshutan," *DDD*, pp. 615–6.

[13] The Greek cities had dedicated the serpent column to the Delphic temple to commemorate victory over the Persians at Plateia in 479 BC. During the rule of Constantine I (r. 306–337) the column, which originally was eight meter high, was brought to Constantinople to decorate the *spina* (central divider) of the Hippodrome. The intertwined heads of the serpents, into which the names of the victorious cities had been engraved and which once carried a golden tripod, can be seen in sixteenth-century Ottoman miniatures and remained in place until about 1700. Only the shaft of the monument remains *in situ*; one of the serpent heads is preserved in the Istanbul Archaeological Museum. Cf. Eder, W., "Schlangensäule," *DNP* 11, 2001, p. 184; "*Picatrix*," tr. and eds. Ritter and Plessner, 1962, p. xli and n. 1.

[14] The word talisman *(ṭilsam)* is used throughout the text to denote any type of object made to protect the owner, that is to say to avert the power of the Evil Eye, and to promote well-being; it also relates to architectural sculptures that served an apotropaic function.

[15] The text is included in Ibn Rusteh's early tenth-century geographical work, *Kitāb al-aʿlāq al-nafīsa*. See El-Cheikh, 2004, p. 148.

[16] *Akhbār al-duwal wa athār al-uwal fī al-tārīkh*, 3 vols., eds. Saʿd, F., and Ḥaṭiṭ, A., Beirut, 1992, vol. 3, p. 192, cited after El-Cheikh, 2004, p. 221.

[17] *Al-Aʿlāq al-khaṭīra*, the part on Aleppo, tr. and ed. Sourdel, D., Damaskus, 1953, p. 123. Cf. Herzfeld, 1955, pp. 24–5; Meri, 2002, p. 206, n. 360.

[18] *Durr*, cited after Herzfeld, 1955, p. 25. To this may be added the tradition that Balīnūs (the Pseudo-Apollonius of Tyana), known as the great master of talismans (*ṣāḥib al-ṭilasmāt*), is reported to have left in many towns charms for protection against such adversities as serpents, scorpions or storms. Cf. the *Kitāb Ṭalāsīm Balīnās al-akbar,* Paris, Bibliothèque Nationale, Ms. 2250, fols. 84–134; see Vajda, 1953, p. 696; Sezgin, 1971, pp. 77–90.

[19] *Kitāb al-Ishārāt ilā maʿrifat al-ziyārāt*, tr. and ed. Sourdel-Thomime, 1957, p. 65. Cf. Meri, 2002, p. 206, n. 360, and *idem*, 2006, p. 162.

translation or paraphrase of the Aristotelian *Historia Animalium* and, while duly noting his personal scepticism as an educated man, records the following anecdote:

> The Master of Logic (Aristotle) states that a serpent with two heads was observed.
>
> I asked a bedouin about that, and he asserted that it be [*sic*] true. Whereupon I said to him: In the direction of which one of the two heads does it creep, and with which one does it eat and bite? He replied: As to its creeping it does not creep (at all), but proceeds towards its aim by rolling itself as do boys on the sand. As to its eating it takes its evening meal with one mouth and its breakfast with the other. As to its biting it does so with both its heads.[20]

Depictions of double-headed serpents, or amphisbaena, are a recurrent feature on architecture, most often positioned above gates, as will be shown in the following. Many city gates also carried prominent epigraphic panels commemorating a victory, invoking good fortune or deflecting evil influences.[21] Qurʾānic verses in particular are considered the most powerful of all "talismans."[22] Often these protective inscriptions were complemented or replaced by images of the dragon which served a prophylactic and talismanic (in the sense of apotropaic) function. It was thus their purpose to protect, avert the power of evil, and to promote well-being.

In 579/1183–4 Diyārbakr (Diyarbakır), the historic city of Āmid, was conquered by the Türkmen Artuqids who in the same year made significant additions to the striking black basalt city walls to commemorate the victory.[23] A large frieze graces the West Gate (the former Rūm Gate and present Urfa Gate) and eulogises the patron Abū ʿAbdallāh Muḥammad ibn Qara Arslan ibn Dāwūd ibn Suqmān (561/1166–581/1185) with extensive titles and Qurʾānic verses (*sūra*s 48, 18; and 61, 13) which were deemed to have specific powers relating to the attaining of victory: "Help comes from God and victory is near."[24] The protective power of the inscription is augmented by carved reliefs: a pair of symmetrical confronted dragons with forelegs is surmounted by the composition of a bird of prey, probably an eagle, wings outstretched, and standing atop the horns of a bull's head, the nose of which is threaded through with a large copper alloy ring carved onto the keystone of the arched gate. The dragons are rendered in formal pose with one foreleg raised (sometimes considered to be "heraldic"), their elongated twisting serpentine tail arranged first in a so-called pretzel-like (or heart-shaped) knot and then into two loops; their supernatural properties are represented by the presence of wings and by the long sinuous tongues protruding from the open mouths (fig. 1).[25] These details which represent a "heraldic" stylisation of the creature establish not only the symbolism of the Saljuq-period dragon but indicate at the same time a ceremonial and ritual of subjugation and domestication.

However in contrast to some of the later Saljuq-period dragon sculpture, discussed below, that was intended to be highly visible from far away, the Diyārbakr dragon reliefs, which represent the earliest surviving such examples of the medieval Islamic period, are rather discreetly portrayed: they are too small to be detected from a distance and thus remain curiously invisible. It may be hypothesised that the inconspicuous nature of the depictions reflects a formative level of the conceptualisation; hence, the craftsmen were still rather unfamiliar with the dragon iconography and thus perhaps did not wish to display it too ostentatiously. Yet the fluidly rendered portrayal, which is in line with later distinctive representations when the motif had become increasingly common, betrays this assumption. Indeed it may be noted that, with exceptions such as the Konya dragon sculptures discussed below, the iconic image of the dragon was generally not conspicuously displayed throughout the medieval period. This may be due to the fact that size and associated visibility were not considered to be essential criteria for the inherently propitious and apotropaic powers of the sculptures to take effect.[26]

Related but much larger, plastically carved decoration was characteristic of the early thirteenth-century city walls, gates or citadel of the Saljuq capital Konya (ancient Iconium) in central Anatolia, built by *sulṭān* ʿAlāʾ al-Dīn Kay Qubādh I (r. 616/1219–634/1237) to protect the city from

[20] Kopf, 1953, p. 400.
[21] Van Berchem and Strzygowski, 1910, p. 73.
[22] Porter, 2006, p. 794.
[23] Gabriel, 1931, vol. 1, pp. 166–8, fig. 136; van Berchem and Strzygowski, 1910, pp. 82–4; Kühnel, 1950, p. 8.
[24] Cf. Hauptmann von Gladiss, ed., 2006, pp. 31–2.
[25] Van Berchem, 1910, p. 82, fig. 30 B (drawing), pl. 17, Öney, 1969a, figs. 30 a (photograph of the entire composition) and b (line drawing); Gierlichs, 1996, pl. 48.5 (photograph of the dragon to the left).
[26] I am most grateful to Professor Robert Hillenbrand to have raised this subject for discussion.

the Mongol advance. A group of double-headed dragon reliefs from these now destroyed monuments is preserved in the İnce Minare Müzesi, Konya.[27] Iconographic and stylistic variations certainly exist between the dragon sculptures of this period, but the basic conception remains the same for all surviving examples. Akin to the Artuqid Diyārbakr dragon reliefs the Konya sculptures are thus similarly portrayed with their inner forelegs raised, the "Saljuq-style" heads with cusped pricked up ears projecting at the top, the wide-open jaws terminating in upward curled tips revealing sharp teeth and the tongues thrust out to reveal bifid tips. The upswept, curved wings with tightly curled tips project from the haunches; their serpentine tails are knotted at mid-section. In these fragments however the tails curve backwards and then taper to a small dragon head that snaps with its snout at the dragon-tail (fig. 60). Although preserved as individual panels, the dragons would probably have been represented as antithetical pairs.[28] In contrast to the shallowly rendered Diyārbakr dragon reliefs, these dragons are plastically sculpted, the monumentality of their size adding to their visually dramatic appearance. The large stone panels may have been placed on or near the city gates and would have made an impressive sight on the city wall, visible from afar. The chronicler of the history of the Rūm Saljuqids, al-Ḥusayn ibn Muḥammad ibn ʿAlī al-Jaʿfarī al-Rughadī, known as Ibn al-Bībī (d. after 684/December 1285), who was head of the chancellery of the Secretariat of State,[29] describes the elaborate royal ceremonies the Saljuqs were known to have staged at the city gates where they received visitors before conducting them into the city.[30] The placement of several dragon sculptures on the city walls and gates would have amplified the impression of power and good fortune which the sculptures were probably meant to convey.

Closely related dragon figures are known from the interior decoration of Saljuq palaces. Two small fragments have been discovered at the now destroyed palace-citadel at Kubadabad on the west bank of Lake Beyşehir, near Akşehir, of the *sulṭān* ʿAlāʾ al-Dīn Kay Qubādh I (r. 616/1219–634/1237), whose reign marked the height of Rūm Saljuq power. One of these is a fragmentary stone relief-carved with a dragon's head,[31] the other is a star tile showing paired dragons whose necks cross over and whose wide-open confronted jaws reveal rows of pointed teeth and bifid tongues.[32] A third piece was discovered while excavating the ruins of the pavilion *(köshk)* on Konya's citadel, which was probably built during the reign of the Rūm Saljuq *sulṭān* Rukn al-Dīn Qılıch Arslan IV (r. 646/1248–647/1249, 655/1257–664/1266).[33] It represents a plaster fragment moulded in low relief with a pair of related addorsed dragons separated by a braided band; their gaping snouts are turned backwards, the feathery wings raised, and the tails form a pretzel-like knot and a loop before tapering to a point.[34]

One of the most outstanding examples of the dragon iconography on city gates certainly must have been the monumental sculptures on the archivolt of the so-called Talisman Gate (Bāb al- Ṭilasm) in Baghdad (figs. 2, 139a and b) which was destroyed in 1917 during the First World War.[35] As indicated by the name of the gate, built in 618/1221–2 under the great caliph Abu l-ʿAbbās Aḥmad al-Nāṣir li-Dīn Allāh (577/1181–620/1223), this type of imagery had talismanic (as also implied by the gate's name), or at least apotropaic connotations. It showed a seated figure

---

[27] Konya, İnce Minare Müzesi, inv. no. 889 (Sarre, 1909, p. 14, fig. 16; Önder, 1961, p. 70, fig. 2; Öney, 1969a, p. 195, fig. 3; Otto-Dorn, 1959, pl. VIII, fig. 36; Gierlichs, 1996, p. 197, cat. no. 43, and pl. 38.1), inv. no. 890 (Sarre, 1909, p. 13, fig. 15; Önder, 1961, p. 70, fig. 1; Diyarbekirli, 1968, p. 370, fig. 5; Öney, 1969a, p. 194, fig. 1; Gierlichs, 1996, p. 198, cat. no. 44, and pl. 38. 2), and inv. no. 1394 (Öney, 1969a, p. 195, fig. 2; and *eadem,* 1978, p. 46, fig. 32; Gierlichs, 1996, p. 200, cat. no. 46, and pl. 39.1; Grube and Johns, 2005, p. 230, fig. 77.2).

[28] Otto-Dorn, 1978–9, p. 125. Cf. Gierlichs, 1996, p. 197.

[29] Cf. Duda, "Ibn Bībī," *EI*² III, 737b.

[30] Such as the welcome accorded to shaykh ʿUmar Suhrawardī at Konya; *al-Awāmir al-ʿAlāʾiyya fī ʾl-ūmur al-ʿAlāʾiyya* ("History of the Rūm Saljuqs"), completed in 680/181, tr. Duda, 1959, pp. 102–3.

[31] Öney, 1969a, p. 196, fig. 4; Otto-Dorn, 1978–9, p. 125.

[32] Otto-Dorn, 1978–9, p. 125; Arik and Arik, 2008, p. 313, fig. 300 (colour reproduction).

[33] Rogers, "Saldjūḳids," *EI*² VIII, 936a.

[34] Plaster fragment. Konya, Alaeddin Palace. Thirteenth century. Height 33 cm, width 19.5 cm. Konya Museum, inv. no. 1029. Öney, 1969a, p. 196, fig. 4; İnal, 1970–1, fig. 6; *The Anatolian Civilisations*, 1983, p. 36, D.39. On the dating of the *köshk*, see Sarre, 1936, pp. 36–7; Meinecke, 1976, vol. 1, pp. 71–2.

[35] Preusser, 1911, p. 16 top; Sarre and Herzfeld, 1920, vol. 2, pp. 152–6, vol. 3, pls. 10 (lower photograph) – 11; Hartner, 1938, fig. 26; Sarre, 1936, fig. 26 (detail); Kühnel, 1950, p. 11, fig. 12. Gierlichs, 1996, pl. 66.1. Meinecke, 1989, p. 58, fig. 7. Hauptmann von Gladiss, ed., 2006, p. 114, fig. 12.

that presumably represented the caliph in the act of subduing a pair of mighty confronted dragons whose expansive serpentine bodies entirely filled the rest of the archivolt. The monumental sculptures, moreover, are not only to be seen as images of power, for the added symbolism of the central figure contributes an important authoritative component as will be considered in chapter 6.

A pair of monumental intertwined double-headed dragons guards one of the monumental entrance gates to the citadel of Aleppo, which was legendary for its impregnability.[36] The large relief-carved frieze with the interlaced dragons surmounts a pointed archivolt with a raised frame at the main portal known as Serpent Gate (Bāb al-Ḥayyāt, re-built probably around 606/1209–10)[37] at the eastern tower of the citadel rebuilt under the Ayyubid ruler al-Malik al-Ẓāhir ibn Salāḥ al-Dīn (568/1173–613/1216). The two heads, one at the springing of the arch and the other at the apex, are crowned by a pair of cusped ears and punctuated with small round eyes; their pointed snouts reveal a row of prominent pointed teeth with bifid tongues thrusting out. Scaly ruff-like collars from which project what appear to be tiny, upswept, cusped wings accentuate the base of the necks and delineate the bodies. Their slender, serpentine bodies are thrice knotted on either side into evenly spaced, pretzel-like shapes. The entwined necks at the apex result in an addorsed position of the dragon heads that with wide-open jaws appear to grasp or attack their bodies; this is mirrored in the lower necks and heads of the dragons at the tail tips that are twisted around roundels enclosing eight-pointed star-rosettes (figs. 3a and b),[38] which Willy Hartner has interpreted as solar symbols.[39]

Astrological symbolism may however be but one component of the commanding composition which in its fantastic, fierce, and awe-inspiring aspect, as Yasser Tabbaa points out, exudes above all also a symbolism of power.[40] What is more, the motif serves to strengthen the belief in the impregnability and inviolability of the citadel and to function as a powerful protective device. Added to the talismanic aspect is the potent symbolism of the mysterious interlace of the dragons[41] and the knotting of their bodies, a conspicuous feature on many depictions of the dragon, as discussed below in chapter 10.

Significant relations between the Islamic world and the Caucasus region, in particular Armenia, were established in early ʿAbbasid times. Later on, with the Saljuq conquests of the eastern Anatolian region, the Armenian iconographic repertoire served as a source of inspiration, and reciprocal contacts between the Saljuqs and the cultural sphere of the Caucasus were established.[42] The close geographic proximity led furthermore to a natural sharing of iconographic emblems.

After the Saljuq raids that led to the capture of Ani, the ancient Armenian capital, near Kars, in 456/1064, the city continued to flourish under the Kurdish Shaddādid emirs who subsequently bought the city from the Saljuqs in 464/1072. During the Shaddādid period, as a result of the Byzantine and Muslim wars which led to the interruption of direct trade, Ani became an intermediary of the trade between Iraq and the Black Sea and thus developed into an important and wealthy trading centre.[43]

The long stylised bodies of a pair of dragons horizontally circumscribe two round towers (nos. 46 and 62) of the northern city wall of Ani. Their bodies are rendered in the form of a thick diagonally hatched moulding, resembling a twisted rope, and end in large heads in profile with gaping mouths revealing rows of teeth and tongues with bifid tips that flank a frontally rendered bovine head which in one case holds a ring in its mouth (fig. 130).[44] The Shaddādids of Ani (*c.* 464/1072–595/1198–9 with interruptions) ordered work on the walls, though the reliefs may equally well have been added when the Shaddādid Abū Shudjāʿ Minūchihr ibn Abi ʾl-Aswār Shāwur (d. *c.* 512/1118) was governing the city.[45] In the same vein as ʿIzz al-Dīn Ibn Shaddād's thirteenth-century elucidation of serpent imagery on a tower in Aleppo which was meant not only to prevent the detrimental effects of snake-bites but also to protect the

---

[36] Cf. Tabbaa, 1997, pp. 54, 76.

[37] Herzfeld, 1954–5, p. 85, no. 36; Tabbaa, 1997, p. 75.

[38] Cf. Roux, 1980, pp. 316–7, fig. 10; Gierlichs, 1996, pl. 65, 1–3; Tabbaa, 1997, figs. 25, 26.

[39] Hartner, 1938, p. 144.

[40] Yasser Tabbaa (1997, p. 77) mentions yet another fragmentary dragon sculpture in the form of a stone block which was reused in the late Ottoman rebuilding of the western wall of the Damascus citadel.

[41] Cf. the discussion in Herzfeld, 1954–5, pp. 236–9.

[42] Cf. Otto-Dorn, 1978–9, p. 104.

[43] Minorsky, 1953, pp. 104–5.

[44] Öney, 1969a, pp. 206–7, figs. 28, 29; Gierlichs, 1996, pl. 70.2, 3.

[45] The sculptures have been variously dated to the late tenth century (977–989), the Armenian period; to the late eleventh and twelfth century when the Shaddādids carried out work on the walls and added much of the ornamentation; and to the thirteenth century when the Zakʿarids renewed the walls. Sinclair, 1987, vol. 1, pp. 360–2; Gierlichs, 1996, pp. 96–8 with further references.

city's inhabitants,[46] the two paired dragon sculptures probably served as powerful protection for the citizens of Ani. The added potency conveyed by the symbolism of the dragons flanking a bull's head is examined in chapter 7. The dragons' sculpted representations on the Ani towers however show that their symbolism was not restricted to just one religious creed, as Muslims and Christians alike made use of the iconography.

One of the most striking features of Anatolian Saljuq architecture is the chain of caravanserais (*khāns*) that link the principal cities of the Sultanate of Rūm. Their prime function was evidently to service the north-south overland trade, in other words to provide for and protect travelling merchants. However, as Michael Rogers has pointed out, the east-west trade was much less developed and in spite of the increasingly difficult terrain, the density of distribution of caravanserais east of Sivas noticeably decreases. Nonetheless, to facilitate trade along the Araxes, the local Georgian dynasty built their own chain of caravanserais, which appears to have been modelled on the Saljuq system.[47]

The depiction of the dragons on the *khāns* afforded further protection for travellers and caravans from any evil such as raids. A pair of monumental antithetical dragons are depicted on a deeply carved relief band at the back of the entrance *īwān* at Karatay Han on the former trade road linking Kayseri with Malatya. According to the epigraphic frieze above the main door, the *khān* was built during the reign of *sulṭān* Ghiyāth al-Dīn Kay Khusraw II, son of ʿAlāʾ al-Dīn Kay Qubādh I, in 638/1240–1.[48] The expansive serpentine bodies, entirely stylised by three parallel moulded bands, are formed of a horizontal guilloche band which extends to frame the entire arch and interlaces at the apex to form a central circular motif, presumably alluding to stellar symbolism, as will be further discussed below. Tongues with bifid tips touch the edges of the central motif, projecting from the toothed jaws of the substantial dragon heads which are finely carved in profile with slightly gaping long wrinkled snouts, the tips terminating in a tight curl. The heads have small, almond-shaped eyes and the cheeks are enlivened by fine spiralling motifs. A pair of cusped ears crowns the heads; the mane is swept back and covers the uppermost section of the finely carved scaly neck (figs. 4a and b).[49]

The same *khān* includes a spring housed in a *türbe*-like building that is circumscribed by an elaborate *muqarnas* frieze, comprising a menagerie of fifteen animals among which is the atypical depiction of a single dragon.[50] Unusually, the dragon's body forms not only a pretzel-like knot just below the neck but the very long serpentine tail is knotted to form a maze of interlace (fig. 5). The dragon's hide is covered allover with a spotted pattern. Its head with wide-open mouth is turned backwards towards a bird perched in an adjacent niche that holds a round object in its beak. It may be reasonable to propose that the accumulation of knotted interlace in the dragon's tail symbolised an increase in the protection against evil influences. The resulting maze probably denoted the ability to resist disentanglement by Evil Eyes and may have been considered as added potency. At the same time the complex tangle ensured that the innate forces of the dragon itself are also securely bound in the maze of its own making. Katharina Otto-Dorn, followed by Gönül Öney, associates the reliefs with the twelve animal cycle,[51] a view which has been challenged by Jean-Paul Roux on the basis that the discrepancy between the animals depicted on the frieze and the animals associated with the twelve animal cycle is too great.[52]

At the now partly destroyed thirteenth-century caravanserai, Susuz Han (Susuz Khān), dated *c.* 644/1246,[53] located about one kilometre south of Bucak just off the Burdur-Antalya road, the ogives of a pair of recessed *muqarnas* niches that flank the portal are each surmounted by a pair of antithetically presented dragons in profile. The heads of the mythical creatures are crowned by curved horns, they have elongated wide-open snouts ending in curled-up tips, the sinuous necks are covered with scales and from the protomes project curved wings and short forelegs. At the

[46] *Al-Aʿlāq al-khaṭīra fī dhikr umarāʾ al-Shaʾm wa ʾl-Jazīra*, the part of Aleppo, tr. and ed. Sourdel, D., Beirut, 1953, p. 123, as cited in Meri, 2002, p. 206, n. 360.

[47] Rogers, 1976, pp. 322–6, and *idem*, "Saldjūḳids," *EI*² VIII, 936a.

[48] Erdmann, 1961, pp. 123–4, no. 32.

[49] Cf. Öney, 1969a, p. 198, fig. 10; Roux, 1972, p. 393, figs. 16 and 17; Gierlichs, 1996, pl. 10.1, 2; Grube and Johns, 2005, p. 234, fig. 79.2.

[50] Roux, 1972, pp. 386–9, figs. 13–5; Önder, 1987, p. 595; Gierlichs, 1996, pls. 8.3 (complete view of the frieze with fifteen animals); 9.2 (dragon); Hakkı, ed. 2007, p. 362, fig. 2 (drawing of animal frieze), p. 370 (photograph of the frieze).

[51] Otto-Dorn, 1963, p. 143. For a brief discussion of the twelve animal cycle of years, see the Epilogue.

[52] Roux, 1972, pp. 387–92.

[53] Erdmann, 1961, p. 114.

apex the confronted dragon mouths flank a small, rounded human head with clearly demarcated eyes, ears, nose and mouth (figs. 7 and 124, detail of one *muqarnas* niche).[54] The dragons' stylised festooned tail, which echoes the contemporary festoon on the arches of the "Kiosk Mosque" at Sultan Han (discussed below), frames the entire arch (without however ending in a second head at the tail tip as shown on the south-facing ogive arch at Sultan Han).[55] The composition is further distinguished by a pair of winged figures flanking a central now destroyed motif that seem to hover protectively over the composition and can be assumed to have celestial significance.[56] Their presence seems to bestow a honorific dimension upon the enigmatic iconography of the mask-like human heads tightly enclosed by the dragons' gaping jaws, a feature examined further in chapter 7. The dragon occurs once more on the caravanserai but as a single depiction (fig. 6). Set within the tight angular interlacing strapwork to the right side of the façade of Susuz Han is the small figure of a single dragon entwined in a pretzel-like knot, its re-curving tail end passing through the knot, which additionally contains, lower down, another depiction of a human face and rosettes.[57]

An interesting composition involving the dragon occurs on the façade above a window on Kesikköprü Han situated on the Kırşehir-Kayseri Road to the south of Kırşehir in central Anatolia. It shows a frontally rendered projecting bovine head from the mouth of which springs a pair of addorsed dragons, with upward arching and once looped or knotted necks, their wide-open jaws oriented to the top.[58] An inscription dates the *khān* to 667/1268–9 and names Jibrāʾīl ibn Chāchā, vizier and governor of Kırşehir under *sulṭān* Ghiyāth al-Dīn Kai Khusraw III (664/1266–680/1281), as its patron.[59]

As mentioned earlier, Ani, the ancient Armenian capital, had become an important and wealthy trading centre during the Shaddādid period.[60] In 1124, under David II, Ani was conquered by the Georgians who built their own chain of caravanserais.[61] David II laid the foundation for the power of the Georgian pan-Transcaucasian monarchy (in Peter Golden's term)[62] that reached its zenith under queen Tʿamar (1184–1211/2). The queen's victories were chiefly due to the military successes of the Christianised Kurdish generals Zakʿare and Ivane, whose family name in Georgian is Mkhargrdzeli "Longomani."[63] The brothers took Ani in 1199 or 1201 and the queen bestowed it on them as fief.[64] Under the rule of the Zakʿarids (the dynastic name of the Mkhargrdzelis), which survived for a while even after the Mongol conquest in 1239, the city experienced a renaissance and became again an important centre of international trade. The route passed through Armenia to the Black Sea ports where Trebizond had become the

[54] It is noteworthy that in addition to the contemporary carved decoration one also finds the reuse of late antique and Byzantine architectural elements at the *khān* which includes an example of a section of a lintel carved with a vegetal frieze enlivened with small human faces projecting from the recesses; documented during the author's visit in October 2008.

[55] Riefstahl, 1931, p. 67, pl. 125; Kühnel, 1950, p. 8; Gierlichs, 1996, pp. 95, 162–4, pl. 11.1–2.

[56] The motif recalls the winged figures or angels, generally referred to as Nike (Victory) or Tyche (Fortuna), depicted on the sides of the now destroyed Larenda Gate of Konya (Texier, 1862; Sarre, 1910, pl. CIX, and *idem,* 1936, pp. 8–9, figs. 3, 4; cf. the bas-relief of winged figures of *c.* 617/1220, now preserved in the İnce Minare Müzesi, Konya, inv. nos. 883, 884) and may also be compared to the *victoriae* set into the spandrels of the monumental rock-cut arch at Ṭāq-i Bustān built by Khusraw II Parwīz (590–628), or the early Christian motif derived from the Roman composition of the *imago clipeata* held by winged figures (cf. L'Orange, 1953, pp. 90–102); for instance, the flying figures holding aloft a cross within a wreath rendered on the south façade of the seventh-century church of Ptghni (Ptghavankʿ), Ararat (Thierry, 1987, p. 365, fig. 199); or on the façade of the church of Dshwari of Mzcheta, built between 586–7 and 604–5 (Baltrušaitis, 1929, pl. LXXVI, fig. 125). The motif can also be observed on portable objects such as the sixth-century Byzantine ivory bindings of the Ejmiatsin Gospels (Der Nersessian, 2001, p. 155, cat. no. 77). Cf. Redford, 1993, pp. 153–5. According to Christian church doctrine the souls of the faithful were carried to heaven by angels who guarded them from dangers on the way. The need to curb the cult of angel veneration as it appeared increasingly idolatrous is reflected in the canons of the council of Laodicea (*c.* 363–364). Protective imagery of this type occurs at entry points of Transcaucasian churches. On each side of the central window of the sixth- to eighth-century church at Ōdzun, for instance, an angel holds what appears to be the coiling tail of a serpent and the serpents' bodies intertwine to form a knot at the apex (however on account of the advanced surface deterioration the composition is unfortunately difficult to assess; cf. Redgate, 2000, p. 126); a similar serpent knot surmounts the window of the south portal at the seventh-century church of Mren (*c.* 640).

[57] Öney, 1969a, p. 199, figs. 15 a (line drawing) and b (photograph); Gierlichs, 1996, pl. 11.3–4.

[58] Öney, 1969a, pp. 184, 207–8, fig. 31; İnal, p. 160, fig. 12; Gierlichs (1996, pp. 171–2, pl. 17.6) suggests that the relief carving might be a spolia. When the author visited the *khān* in 2008, it had just been renovated and the relief with the bovine head between two dragons, which previously had been in very weathered condition, no longer existed.

[59] Erdmann, 1961, p. 77.

[60] Minorsky, 1953, pp. 104–5.

[61] Rogers, 1976, pp. 322–6, and *idem,* "Saldjūḳids," *EI*² VIII, 936a.

[62] Golden, 1983, p. 66.

[63] Minorsky, 1953, p. 102.

[64] *Idem,* p. 103. Cf. Barthold [Minorsky], "Ānī," *EI*² I, 507a.

Byzantine capital (1204) after the fall of Constantinople to the crusaders.[65]

In Ani two caravanserais were built under Zakʿarid rule. The façade of the southern caravanserai (596/1200–633/1236)[66] was richly decorated with a pair of confronted dragons with wings and what appear to be forelegs above mythical winged quadrupeds carved onto the spandrels of the ogival arch which was originally covered with a bi-coloured inlay of carved polygons (fig. 8).[67] The overall decorative scheme should however, as Rogers notes, be seen in the context of the evident taste of the Zakʿarid governors of the city for Anatolian Saljuq decoration which had resulted in the creation of a new "semi-Saljuq" Transcaucasian style that continued to flourish in Armenia and metropolitan Georgia long after the decline of the Zakʿarids.[68]

In the context of the confronted dragon representations in the spandrels of the early thirteenth-century caravanserai in Ani, it is worth mentioning that a near-identical location was reserved for the hybrid beasts in the upper section of architectural structures recorded in the two-dimensional medium of an Armenian manuscript of slightly earlier date, transcribed and illuminated in Cilician Armenia. The shift in geography of Armenian cultural centres from the Armenian plateau westwards occurred after Saljuq raids that led to the capture of Ani in 1064 and Kars the following year, at which time the king, Gagik-Abas, was driven into Cappadocian exile. This led to massive western migrations of Armenians which contributed to the re-Armenisation of ancient Armenia Minor as well as Cappadocia and Cilicia to the south. In the kingdom of Cilicia in Tarsos, miniature painting attained a high degree of excellence. Here in the monasteries of Mlich and Skevra the L'viv (Lemberg) Gospel was transcribed and lavishly illuminated from 1193 until 1198/99.[69] The ten canon tables are set within architectural frames consisting of two columns supporting arches. Interestingly in the first two tables the uppermost sections of the rectangular headpieces carry confronted winged dragons, with long raptor-like forelegs, in the spandrels that surmount the archivolts. The beasts are set against curling foliage, which is held in the dragons' snouts on the headpiece over the Letter of Eusebius to Carpianus on the second canon table (fig. 9).[70] The iconography of the dragons on these miniatures is clearly identifiable as Eastern Christian, or perhaps particularly Armenian, distinguishable from the Jazīran and Anatolian "Saljuq-style" dragon by the long raptor-like legs and the shorter snouts. The Armenian predilection for representing dragons may perhaps be associated with the fact that in Armenia the dragon *(vishap)* belongs to the pre-Christian substrate[71] and as a result is part of an ancient iconographical tradition, combined here with canonical scenes from Christian iconography. In spite of the fact that these represent two-dimensional compositions on paper, they nonetheless suggest that placing paired dragons in the spandrels of an arch was not rare in pan-Transcaucasian architecture. This is further corroborated by an analogous composition found on the arch of a thirteenth- or fourteenth-century wooden door from Godaïk in Ararat province, which is carved with confronted dragons represented without wings or legs.[72] The placement of the dragons in the arch of a door may once again support the supposition that a protective function was intended.

A stone relief, now no longer extant, of paired confronted dragons with a quadripartite knot at mid-section with further knotted interlaces above and below was found at the hospital *(darüşşifa)* of the *atābeg* Lālā Jamāl al-Dīn Farrukh during the reign of the Rūm Saljuq *sulṭān* ʿAlāʾ al-Dīn Kay Qubādh I of Konya in Çankırı (Gangra),

[65] Manandian, A., *O torgovle i gorodakh Armenii*, Erevan, 1954, p. 278, as cited in Barthold [Minorsky], "Ānī," *EI*² I, 507a. Cf. Redgate, 2000, p. 258.

[66] Rogers, 1976, p. 324.

[67] A photograph of the dragon relief in the right spandrel is reproduced in Sakisian, 1940, pl. XVIII, fig. 33.

[68] Rogers, 1976, pp. 315–26.

[69] Prinzing and Schmidt, eds., 1997, pp. 18–21.

[70] Akinian, 1930, p. 7, fig. 1; Prinzing and Schmidt, eds., 1997, pls. I, II. Comparable dragons, likewise positioned in the spandrels of the rectangular structures that surmount the archivolts, feature also in thirteenth-century Armenian manuscripts, such as in the Gospel book commissioned in 1273 by Ter Simeon, the abbot of the monastery of Skevra (Istanbul, Topkapı Sarayı Museum, Library, Ms. 122, fol. 8, Letter to Eusebius, see Der Nersessian and Agemian, 1993, vol. 2, fig. 318, page to the right).

[71] Russell, 2004, p. 453. Of note are the large carved stone steles found throughout the Transcaucasus and beyond, perhaps datable to the first two millennia BC, often referred to as *vishap* stones, that are generally erected near a spring or reservoir; hence, they probably are of some ritual or religious significance. Cf. Marr and Smirnov, 1931; Piotrovskiy, 1939. The steles are also sometimes called *vishap azhdahā* on account of their prodigious size by analogy with *azhdahā mard*, "giant man"; *azhdahā kʿar*, "megalith"; and *vishap kʿar*, "stone fish." See Tchukasizian, 1964, p. 326 and n. 21 with further references.

[72] Hovsépian, 1937, pp. 164–5, fig. 67.

outside Ankara, built according to the inscription in Muḥarram 633/1235.[73] The serpentine bodies were oriented to the left, their confronted heads with open jaws demarcated by almond-shaped eyes and topped by cusped ears, revealing sharp teeth and tongues.[74] The heads would probably have been confronted although it is no longer possible to reconstruct this on account of the deteriorated condition of the lower dragon head (fig. 175). Interesting in this regard is the record by Albert Gabriel of Süheyl Ünver's suggestion that the paired dragons, joined at mid-section by a quadripartite knot, were an ancient symbol of healing used on hospitals, transmitted through the Saljuqs,[75] an interpretation followed by Mehmet Önder who also associates the dragon iconography on the *darüşşifa* with healing.[76]

A second affiliation of the dragon with hospitals in Anatolia is found among the plaster reliefs on the façade of the Kay Kāwūs Darüşşifa in Sivas, datable to 614/1217, built during the reign of Kay Kāwūs I ibn Kay Khusraw I (r. 608/1211–616/1220). Now in very poor condition, they show traces of the body of one dragon with forelegs and spiralling tail, which can be presumed to have been complemented by a second dragon.[77]

Only three examples of the representation of dragons are known from Islamic sacred architecture from the period of the Saljuqs and their "successor states." One example is the stone relief at a mausoleum *(türbe)* known locally as that of the Emir Saltuq after whom the Türkmen Saltuqid dynasty (*c.* 465/1072–598/1202), former commanders of the Saljuq army, is named. It is the largest and most unusual of a complex of three tombs (Üç Kümbetler) just south of the walled city of Erzurum, near the Tabriz Gate.[78] The drum is circumscribed by eight fan-shaped arched niches formed by the gables of the octagon's roof, inside which are carved animal, vegetal and geometric compositions.[79] Among the reliefs is a pair of upright confronted dragons whose wide-open elongated fleshy snouts with upward-curling tips reveal a row of sharp teeth and projecting tongues and touch at the tips to form a diamond-shaped enclosure. Small, rounded eyes and small, pointed ears demarcate the heads. Their bodies entwine to form a loop at mid-section and interlace again at the bottom angle of the niche whence they curve upward to frame both diagonal sides. The two creatures thus entirely fill the architectural space into which they are fitted (fig. 10).[80]

A striking parallel to the dragons on the *türbe* of Emir Saltuq is found at the church of Saint Gregory, which belonged to a monastery, located at the edge of Ani above the cliffs of the Arpa Çay gorge. The presence of a new class of wealthy merchants that formed during the eleventh and twelfth century in Ani is attested to by the inscription of the merchant Tigran Honentsʿ on the church he erected in 1215 and dedicated to Saint Gregory the Illuminator. The Greek-Orthodox tendency favoured during Zakʿarid rule continued to predominate in the architectural design of this church.[81] However the depiction of the dragons, which appears on the fan-shaped spandrels of a blind arcade, follows the well-established Saljuq-period conventions. The recumbent confronted dragons are carved in a horizontal arrangement in the upper section. They are portrayed resting on their forelegs, their heads crowned by a pair of pointed ears. The hybrid creatures have squinting eyes and the characteristic wide-open jaws with rolled-up ends, sharp teeth and flickering tongues with bifid tips which nearly touch at the centre. The sizable upper bodies extend into tapering tails which loop twice then arch over the back (fig. 11).[82] It is interesting that the placement of the dragons in a niche is not the only feature to recall the dragons depicted on the *türbe* of Emir Saltuq, the date of construction of which is uncer-

[73] Meinecke, 1976, vol. 2, p. 103. Cf. the general references in van Berchem, 1910, pp. 82–4; Gabriel and Sauvaget, 1940, vol. 1, p. 166, fig. 137.

[74] The relief has been lost since 1940 and is only known from photographs and drawings done before this date. Cf. Gierlichs, 1996, p. 156.

[75] Cited after Gabriel and Sauvaget, 1940, p. 168, n. 1.

[76] Cf. Süslü, 1987, p. 641. By the Ottoman period, the hospital became a place of spiritual healing and snake charming. Terzioğlu, A., *Mittelalterliche islamische Krankenhäuser*, Technische Universität, Berlin, 1968, p. 126, as cited in Tabbaa, 2003, p. 112. The conspicuous knotting aspect of the dragons is discussed in chapter 10.

[77] Öney, 1969a, p. 198, fig. 9.

[78] The city withstood the Saltuqid onslaught until 473/1080, when it became the capital of the Saltuqid principality. It is during the period of their rule, which lasted for about thirty years, that Otto-Dorn (1964, p. 151) suggests that the construction of the *türbe* took place. A later dating before the city was taken by the Mongols in 639/1242 has also been put forward. Ünal, 1968, p. 160; Gierlichs, 1996, p. 146, n. 6. For a mid- or late fourteenth-century dating, see Sinclair, 1998, p. 212.

[79] Cf. Sinclair, 1998, p. 212. The compositions have been associated with the animal cycle, see Otto-Dorn, 1978–9, pp. 126, 144.

[80] Öney, 1969a, fig. 23; Otto-Dorn, 1978–9, p. 126, fig. 22; Gierlichs, 1996, pp. 145–7, pl. 1.8.

[81] Barthold [Minorsky], "Ānī," *EI*² I, 507a.

[82] Otto-Dorn, 1978–9, p. 127, fig. 23; Gierlichs, 1996, pl. 70.6.

tain. The dragons on the mausoleum are rendered upright with doubly entwined bodies and without forelegs, whereas the dragons on the church of Saint Gregory have a more horizontal orientation with individually looped tails. Nevertheless, there is a consistency in the overall iconographic programme, which is why the dragon sculptures on the so-called *türbe* of Emir Saltuq may probably be asigned a thirteenth-century date.

The second Saljuq dragon sculpture on Islamic sacred architecture is found on the small "Kiosk Mosque" situated in the arcaded rectangular courtyard of the double-section caravanserai Sultan Han, located northeast of Kayseri, on the main road that once linked Konya, Kayseri and Sivas to the east (Iraq and Iran). It is the second largest Saljuq caravanserai in Anatolia and was built between 629/1232 and 633/1236 on the orders of ʿAlāʾ al-Dīn Kay Qubādh I of Konya, as attested by an inscription on the portal. Resting on a four-bay substructure, the south- and east-facing monumental ogival arches are both symmetrically framed with a complex serpentine festoon. The latter is composed of reciprocally arranged pretzel-like shapes, culminating at the apex in confronted dragon protomes. The heads with large, almond-shaped eyes, topped by backward-projecting pointed ears, have wide-open jaws revealing sharp teeth and tongues (fig. 12).[83] Both the south- and east-facing reliefs are closely related but while the dragon protomes on the south side do not touch each other at the apex, the bodies of the dragon protomes on the east side are joined and enlivened by dots.[84] Moreover, on the south-facing arch the dragon festoons end in small, inverted dragon heads with large eyes, necks bent inwards, with the open jaws appearing to hold the tip of the outer edge of the festoon-band;[85] it is thus interesting to observe that they seem to bite (in other words "swallow" or "disgorge") their own tail tip, an aspect discussed in chapter 9 (fig. 13). While this feature is not recognisable on the east-facing arch (possibly on account of the surface deterioration), it shows, interestingly, an additional upward oriented, small dragon head, growing out of one of the bends of the dragon festoon to the left (fig. 14).[86] Also of note is the fact that both serpentine festoons are surmounted by a further band enclosing a tightly woven knotted composition distinguished by a small eight-petalled star-rosette in the interstitial area at the apex (although on the east side, on account of the surface deterioration, this is no longer identifiable). Otto-Dorn interprets the rosette as a planetary symbol suggesting an astral-mythological reading of the iconography.[87]

The third example is found in the relief sculpture of a pair of dragon protomes which spring from the base of a central vegetal composition topped by a double-headed eagle on the façade of the Çifte Minare *madrasa* at Erzurum (probably before 640/1242–3).[88] The relief featuring dragons springing from a conventionalised vegetal or tree-like composition, whose important symbolism is examined in chapter 4, is set within ogival niches at either side of the main façade, but only the relief to the right was completed (fig. 43).[89] Rogers associates the Çifte Minare *madrasa* as well as the buildings of the Great Mosque and hospital at Divriği (626/1228–9 or later) with elements of a Caucasian building tradition (in particular with the influence of western Georgia (Tao-Klargeti)).[90]

A fourth, yet less conspicuous, instance of dragons on sacred architecture of the Saljuq period may be noted in passing. The end of one of the inscriptions at the façade of the Ak Mosque (617/1220–634/1237) at Anamur near Alanya shows a single double-headed dragon, knotted at mid-section and terminating at either end in an ophidian head.[91]

In the sacred architecture of the pan-Transcaucasian realm the dragon, as mentioned above,

---

83 Cf. Riefstahl, 1932, p. 92; Kühnel, 1950, p. 8, fig. 15; Erdmann, 1961, pp. 94–5, fig. 152; Öney, 1969a, p. 197, figs. 6, 7, 7a, and *eadem*, 1978, p. 45, fig. 31; İnal, 1970–1, p. 163, fig. 23; Otto-Dorn, 1978–9, p. 127, fig. 24; Grube and Johns, 2005, p. 234, fig. 79.4. For a detailed description, see also Roux, 1980, pp. 316–7 and fig. 10.

84 Öney, 1969a, figs. 6, 7; Gierlichs, 1996, pl. 6.1, 2.

85 This detail is documented by Öney, 1969a, fig. 7a. Cf. Gierlichs, 1996, pl. 6.1, featuring the entire festoon on which however it is difficult to discern this feature.

86 See detail in Gierlichs, 1996, pl. 7.3.

87 Otto-Dorn, 1978–9, pp. 130–1, fig. 24.

88 Michael Rogers (1965, pp. 63–85 and 1974a, pp. 77–119, esp. 117–9) suggests that the fall of Erzurum to the Mongols in 1242–3 represented an architectural (as well as political) *terminus ad quem* for the dating of the Çifte Minare *madrasa*. For a comprehensive list of suggested dates of the Çifte Minare *madrasa*, see Meinecke, 1976, pp. 136–7.

89 Cf. Bachmann, 1913, pl. 66; Öney, 1969a, p. 208 and fig. 32, and *eadem*, 1969b; Otto-Dorn, 1978–9, p. 127, fig. 25; Gierlichs, 1996, pl. 12.1, 4, 5.

90 Rogers, 1974a, pp. 103–6 and ns. 76, 77. Cf. *idem*, "Saldjūḳids," *EI*² VIII, 936a.

91 Roux, 1980, p. 316; Öney, 1969a, p. 176, figs. 12 a and b.

is found already at a much earlier date. While its different manifestations will be examined in the following chapters, a noteworthy example, part of a frieze on the eastern façade of the Georgian church of the Virgin in Mart'vili in western Georgia, founded by king George II of Aphkhasia (912–957),[92] may be mentioned in this context. The frieze, which is finely carved with scrolling vines bearing clusters of grapes, also features several composite animals: a winged dragon, shown in profile with forelegs, is flanked on either side by other imaginary creatures. On its left is a centaur-like depiction with quadruped body in profile, extending into a frontally rendered human upper body with large, stylised heart-shaped head which appears to be crowned by a halo, while on its right is a composite mythical animal now commonly identified as Sasanian-style *sēnmurv*. It is rendered in profile with the protome of a canine dragon and the characteristic peacock tail.[93] The dragon's head is turned backwards towards the centaur, its long gaping snout revealing a row of teeth, the bifid tongue projecting towards its raised, unfolded wing. The creature's very long sinuous ophidian body forms a large loop, ascending behind the body to descend and taper to a point below the body of the centaur, whose forelegs rest on the attenuated tail end. Of note is the ruff-like loop around the dragon's neck, the ends of which curve sharply upwards, a feature which appears to be shared by the centaur (fig. 15). The apotropaic character of these mythical animals, which are also a salient feature on the façade of the Armenian church of the Holy Cross at Aght'amar (915–921), may be presumed.[94] Further of note is the striking difference in the depiction between this apotropaic dragon, rendered with forelegs, and the relief with a bicephalic ophidian dragon speared by two riders shown above the western entrance of the church, discussed below (fig. 107).

Another important architectural feature is found at the Armenian monastic ensemble at Sanahin, near Alaverdi in Lori province, Armenia, which was established in 966. The monastery, which also served as Bagratid necropolis, not only functioned as a religious retreat but was an intellectual academy with a scriptorium for the copying and illuminating of manuscripts as well as a library. Significantly, it is in the latter which was added in 1063 that relief-carved interlaced dragons are prominently depicted on a column capital. After the destruction by the Mongol invasion decades earlier, the library was restored by bishop Stephen Sarkis and his disciples Herapet, David, Hesou and Karapet, in the late twelfth century (fig. 16).[95]

Of particular significance is the dragon iconography in the Eastern Christian sphere of the Jazīra. Extremely interesting are its representations at the thirteenth-century monastery of Mār Behnām, also called Deir al-Khiḍr, southeast of Mosul, near the ancient Assyrian city of Nimrud situated between the river Tigris and the upper Zab.[96] The large, fort-like monastery was founded in the second half of the fourth century as a memorial to the Christian martyrs Behnām and his sister Sarah.[97]

The lintel immediately above the southern outer door in an internal corridor of the monastery carries a relief-carved depiction of a pair of addorsed recumbent dragons resting on their forelegs. Their expansive finely scaled ophidian tails form a pretzel-like knot followed by a loop and are interlaced to form a horizontally oriented figure of eight along the central axis. Small narrow wings attached to the haunches extend towards the back. The creatures are flanked by seated lions portrayed in profile with head en face. The paws of the inner legs are slightly raised and the long tails are drawn behind the flank of one of the hind legs and ascend in a slight curve terminating in dragon-headed finials behind the arched back. A weathered frontally rendered lion head

[92] The church of the Virgin in Mart'vili is variously dated between the seventh and the tenth centuries, cf. Baltrušaitis, 1929, p. 104 ("Mart'vili"). Mepisaschwili und Zinzadze (1987, p. 160, fig. 234) date it to the seventh century.

[93] For a detailed discussion of the *sēnmurv*, see Harper, 1961–62, pp. 95–101, and Schmidt, 1980, pp. 1–85.

[94] Cf. Der Nersessian, 1965, figs. 23, 28, 29, 43.

[95] Baltrušaitis, 1929, pl. LXIV, figs. 99, 100; Sakisian, 1939, fig. 30; Manoukian, Agopik and Armen, eds., 1967–9; Khal'pakh'chian, 1971, p. 145, fig. 110, right side (drawing).

[96] The dating of the reliefs is uncertain. Inscriptions in the church show that renovations of the choir were undertaken by the patriarch Mār Athanasius of Antioch in 559/1164 (Pognon, 1907, pp. 134–5, no. 75). Herzfeld (Sarre and Herzfeld, 1920, vol. 2, p. 266) dates the reliefs to the period of Badr al-Dīn Lu'lu' (618/1222–657/1259). Further extensions and renovations were undertaken between 1248 and 1295. It is further of note that a 33 line Syriac inscription engraved on the walls of the church attests that the monastery was spared from destruction by the Ilkhan Baidu in 1295. Pognon, 1907, pp. 132–42, 235, no. 76; Fiey, 1959, p. 50, and *idem*, 1965, pp. 584–5. For a detailed discussion of the dating, see *idem*, 1965, pp. 590–7.

[97] The monastery is named after Behnām, allegedly of the Assyrian family of Sennecherib II, the governor of Nineveh, who was killed together with his sister during the persecution of the Christians by Ardashīr (279–283), son of Shāpūr. Cf. *idem*, 1965, vol. 2, pp. 565–74.

projects above the centre of the relief. Below, on the actual lintel, a Christian cross, from whose base also spring *regardant* quadruped dragons, is flanked, in turn, by pairs of confronted *regardant* birds whose tail feathers end in dragon heads with gaping jaws snapping at the birds' tails (figs. 17a and b, details figs. 50 and 74).[98] The symbiosis of birds or felines with the dragon will be further examined in chapter 5.

The bilaterally symmetrical configuration of the dragons shows them with entwined tails tapering to a pointed tip and forming a vertically oriented figure of eight. Their scaly serpentine bodies are doubly intertwined in a pretzel-like knot and a simple loop. The large heads, with characteristic wide-open jaws revealing two long pointed fangs and twisted forked tongues, face stemmed cups. The almond-shaped eyes seem to squint slightly; small, cusped ears project at the top of the head. Their supernatural properties are underlined by a pair of arched narrow horns, swept towards the back, and by the slender, curved wings that spring from an ornament that winds around the dragons' haunches, terminating in an angular curl (a detail which can also be seen in the Cizre dragon-knockers, fig. 83). The inner front leg is slightly raised, a feature that is paralleled in the figures of the flanking lions.

Significant are equally the closely related carved mouldings that provide an enlarged frame for the entire portal both at the monastery of Mār Behnām and at the thirteenth-century mausoleum of Imām Bahir in Mosul,[99] which was possibly erected at the order of Badr al-Dīn Luʾluʾ (618/1222–657/1259).[100] In both cases stylistically and iconographically closely related compositions of six pairs of dragons form trilobed arch-shaped niches that accentuate a portal.

At Mār Behnām the second southern portal leading to the chapel of the baptistery is framed by a moulding in the form of a knotted interlace composed of the bodies of six dragons that enclose a total of twenty-one niches (fig. 18).[101] The horizontal section of the portal is defined by the entwined necks of the addorsed dragons, with the exception of the central arch-shaped enclosure that is topped by a projecting lion head en face. The dragon heads are crowned by arched horns and small, cusped ears folded to the back; they are rendered with the characteristic wide-open mouths revealing a long tongue, the elongated upper jaws terminating in a rolled-up tip. At the base the tails form a single loop. The vertically interlaced ogival arch-shapes each comprise eight niches: three enclose hooded standing figures holding a book in the left hand and a cross in the right hand, probably representing monks,[102] while the others contain the symbol of the cross. The horizontal interlace encloses a tall standing figure next to a small, nude figure and a rider on horseback,[103] also alternating with the cross motif. The lintel carries a central Christian cross which extends at the base into a stemmed palmette.

At the portal leading to the vestibule at the mausoleum of Imām Bahir the frame is similarly set off with a knotted interlace, here accentuated with a scaly pattern, enclosing twelve niches, which contain foliate arabesques surmounted in the arched section with a tiny *muqarnas* (fig. 19).[104] The lintel is inscribed with the words "Muḥammad, al-Malik, Allāh, ʿAlī." The outer dragon pairs form a vertical interlace that encloses

---

[98] Cf. Preusser, 1911, p. 11, pls. 5, 6.2; Fiey, 1959, p. 145, n. 1 a, fig. 12; and *idem*, 1965, vol. 2, pp. 565–9, esp. pp. 605–6; Kühnel, 1950, p. 12, fig. 14; Gierlichs, 1996, pl. 59.1 (upper section of door).

[99] Located near Bāb Sinjār. The entire portal frame was brought to Baghdad in 1939, cf. Fiey, 1965, p. 595, n. 1; Gierlichs, 1996, p. 230, n. 455. Ministry of Culture and Arts, ed., *Guide to the ʿIraq Museum*, 1979, fig. 49.

[100] Farès, 1953, p. 52. An inscription on the eastern wall gives the date 699/1300; however it is unclear whether this date refers to the construction or a renovation of the monument. Another inscription on the southern wall names the builder, ʿAbd al-Rāḥim ibn Aḥmad. See Uluçam, 1989, p. 141.

[101] Preusser, 1911, pl. 12; Fiey, 1965, pl. E; Gierlichs, 1996, pl. 59.4 (upper section of portal).

[102] Two figures are identified by inscriptions; Fiey, 1965, p. 601.

[103] The two carvings are often referred to as relating to the scene of the baptism of Sarah by Mār Matta, yet on account of the nude figure it has been suggested that they might either represent the baptism of Mār Behnām (Fiey, 1965, p. 599 and n. 2), or the baptism of Christ (Sarre and Herzfeld, 1920, vol. 2, p. 247); the other carving has been interpreted as the entry into Jerusalem (*eidem*, 1920, vol. 2, p. 247).

[104] Also published in *Mossoul au temps des Atabeks*, ed. Saʿīd al-Daywahchī, Mosul, 1958, fig. 36; ʿAṭṭa al-Hadīthī and Hanāʾ ʿAbd al-Khāliq, *al-Qibāb al-Makhrūṭiyya fī ʾl-ʿIrāq* ("Conical Domes in Iraq"), Baghdad, Ministry of Information, Directorate General of Antiquities, 1974, pl. 82; Janabi, 1982, fig. 170 B; Uluçam, 1989, pp. 141–3, figs. 314, 315. The tomb chamber of the mausoleum, which carried fragments of the *Āyat al-Kursī*, the Throne Verse (*sūra* 2, 255), on the four walls of the chamber, a *mihrab* with a hanging lamp and prayers for the holy family of Shīʿism on the *qibla* wall, is discussed by al-Suyūfī (d. 1901), *Majmūʿ al-kitābāt al-muḥarrarah fī abniyat al-Moṣulʾ*, ed. Saʿīd al-Daywahchī, Mosul, 1956, pp. 141–7; Ibn Faḍlallah al-ʿUmarī, *Manhal al-awliyāʾ wa mashrab al-aṣfiya min sādāt al-Moṣul al-hadbāʾ*, ed. Saʿīd al-Daywahchī, Mosul, 1967, pp. 225–6; both cited after Khoury, 1992, pp. 23–4, ns. 20, 28. Shrines with references to Shīʿī imams and their descendants are thought to have played a propagandistic role in Badr al-Dīn Luʾluʾ's campaign to convert *madrasas* into Shīʿī shrines. Cf. also Khoury, 1992, p. 14, n. 29, with reference to Janabi, 1982, pp. 53–4.

four niches each, knotted with a simple loop at the points of juncture. At the top the dragons terminate in the same manner as on the portal of Mār Behnām; however at the bottom of the niches the slightly tapered tails entwine to form a loop, whence they curl inward to terminate in a bird's head with curved beak which pecks at the tail (comparable to the birds on the tail tips of dragons on the Cizre door-knockers (fig. 83) and on the wing tips of the dragons at the Bāb al-Ṭilasm in Baghdad (fig. 139a)). Just like the bottom mouldings, the central niches terminate at the top in addorsed heads and at the bottom in tail ends that entwine to form a loop and thence taper to a pointed tip. Also of note are the small star-rosettes which on both portals are set into the interstices of the vertical bands.

The representation of dragons situated at the approach to the most sacred part of the building, both in the case of the monastery of Mār Behnām, where they feature on the second portal leading to the chapel of the baptistery, and at the mausoleum of Imām Bahir, where they appear on the portal leading to the vestibule, indicates that their depiction was intended to serve as monumental apotropaion and to guard the entrance to a sacred space.

CHAPTER THREE

THE DRAGON MOTIF ON PORTABLE OBJECTS

a. *Overview*

By their very nature, portable artefacts are characterised by their potential for movement across geographical, cultural and religious boundaries.[1] Most of the objects under discussion testify to an overall westward migration of the dragon iconography from the Western Central Asian regions, facilitated by the movement of ever growing numbers of Turkic-speaking tribes, the dominant force being the Saljuqs, into Western Asia. The latter took much from the artistic traditions of the Ghaznawids whose state they had destroyed.[2] During the Saljuq period, the main artistic centres were located in greater Khurasan and northern Iran, with merchants and artisans becoming the principal bearers of cultural traditions.[3] Able to move freely in the enormous empire, which reached from Khurasan to Syria and Asia Minor, the population aided the diffusion of prevailing styles and tastes which had a "markedly Khurasanian flavour."[4]

Belonging to a wider, shared visual culture across the medieval Central Asian sphere, portable objects shared emblematic themes, reflected also on monumental representations. The dragon motif is found on a great variety of artefacts, notably in the category of personal objects: specifically on accoutrements pertaining to the hunt or war and objects of personal adornment. The semantic value of the dragon motif on the former would naturally have served to enhance the efficacy of these items. When personal in nature and worn on the body, objects with this motif were popularly believed to provide the wearer with a prophylactic or apotropaic safeguard against a variety of real or imaginary dangers. The belief in the magical power of images meant that they could function as talismans intended, for instance, to promote well-being and to protect from the power of evil. This is related to the age-old belief in the agency of envy and jealousy and the Evil Eye, which certainly survived through the medieval Islamic period,[5] and the neutralisation of the harm that was intended to the person by wearing such a piece. Hence the serpent or dragon comes to be looked upon as harbinger of good luck and bestower of prosperity. In addition, such objects were often believed to endow their owners with certain abilities or powers. One of the most widespread functions of talismans was in the form of amulets (*tamāʾim*, sing. *tamīma*, or *taʿāwīdh*, sing. *taʿwīdh*) intended to gain the assistance of unseen, supernatural forces that were believed to influence the affairs of humankind to achieve certain desired outcomes. It is of course impossible to fathom how "potent" the motif was for the wearer, it may indeed be that some did not consider the dragon motif to have such explicit powers, using it as an ornament, but with prophylactic intent. In general, though, it may reasonably be conjectured that the dragon iconography carried implicit semantics imbued with passively apotropaic, that is to say protective or actively beneficial properties, in other words empowering qualities designed to be imparted to the wearer.

Other objects such as vessels with this iconography may often have functioned as portable "apotropaia." In spite of the fact that many pieces have a very varied iconography of which the dragon is only part, it may be hypothesised that dragon motifs, too, served to magnify the

[1] Cf. Hoffman, 2001, pp. 17–22.

[2] Marshak, 1986, p. 358.

[3] Melikian-Chirvani, 1974, pp. 112, 114; Marshak, 1986, p. 359.

[4] Cf. Melikian-Chirvani, 1974, pp. 112, 114. See also p. 18, n. 25.

[5] In his *Qaṣīdah Sāsānīyah*, the tenth century poet Misʿar ibn Muhalhil al-Khazrajī al-Yanbūʿī, known as Abū Dulaf, refers to beggars who wrote out talismanic charms and sold little clay tablets allegedly made from the earth of the tomb of al-Ḥuseyn in Karbalāʾ, undoubtedly alluding to the production of amulets. For this and further references, see Bosworth, 1976, vol. 1, pp. 86–8, 90, 128, vol. 2, pp. 192, 198–9, 221, 243.

intended effect of the vessels which were presumably meant to protect their maker[6] and more often their owner, so functioning as protective devices. This is emphasised by inscriptions invoking familiar expressions of wishes for blessings, luck, health, or long life for the mostly anonymous owner, which are frequently of amuletic character in themselves; these are rendered often in combination with figural decorations of a symbolic or "magical" significance such as the dragon. A clear function of the dragon's iconography was thus to reinforce the propitious, apotropaic, or even magical or supernatural powers of such portable objects.

b. *The dragon motif on accoutrements relating to the hunt or war*

Dragon imagery is attested on weapons and banners from early Zoroastrian times. It is particularly associated with the mace and with the finials of ceremonial weapons or staffs which may carry sculpted dragons with a human or animal figure in their maw. Dragon banners, an important part of military insignia from ancient times, appear in Iranian art and literature. The dragon motif similarly occurs on weapon fittings, ritually significant belt/strap fittings and equestrian accoutrements. The use of such imagery on the paraphernalia of heroism and rulership communicated mastery over the dragon and appropriation of its formidable qualities. When featured on objects of personal adornment such as jewellery or belt-ornaments, the motif endowed such items with prophylactic or apotropaic powers.

The dragon motif on weapons

Cudgels seem to have been the most widespread weapon in early Mesopotamia and Iran. "Cast in yellow bronze,"[7] they were the most powerful and the most victorious of all the weapons of the Vedic and Avestan gods.[8] Cudgels or maces were also associated with the dragon-fighting Indo-Iranian mythical heroes,[9] and hence possibly serve to characterise them as primordial warriors.[10] Significantly, the mace of the legendary dragon-fighting hero Kərəsāspa (Garshāsp in New Persian poetry), celebrated already in the Zoroastrian Yasna and Vidēvdāt, is said to have been carved in the shape of a dragon head.[11] Similarly the Mathura portrait statue of the Kushāṇa king Kanishka is shown with a giant club tapering to an open-mouthed head of a dragon-like creature.[12] The representation of the dragon on ceremonial weapons must be evidence of the intention to endow the weapon and hence its owner with the magical powers of the dragon.

The club was greatly favoured by the Parthians (250 BC–226 AD), too. The club of Herakles, the most popular of Greek heroes, even appears as architectural decoration in the early Parthian monument referred to as the "Round Hall" in Nisa, the Parthian metropolis in present-day Turkmenistan.[13] Maces and battle axes were used in the Parthian and Sasanian periods.[14] An important depiction is found on a bas-relief from a small house-temple in Parthian Hatra in northern Mesopotamia (an integral part of Iran in Parthian and Sasanian times), which shows the composite figure of Herakles-Nergal,[15] the god of the realm of death and the underworld, who can

---

[6] Cf. the twelfth-century large silver-inlaid brass ewer, now in the Georgian State Museum, Tbilisi, Georgia, which bears the inscription:

> ... seven heavenly bodies, however proud they may be, are protection for the one who works so.

Allan, 1982a, repr. 1999, p. 49.

[7] Yasht 10.96; cf. for instance, also, "cudgel of bronze" (Rigveda 1.80.12). Gershevitch, 1959, p. 121; Watkins, 1995, p. 411.

[8] Watkins, 1995, pp. 411–3.

[9] *Idem*, pp. 331–2.

[10] Wikander, 1938, pp. 60, 64–6, 99; Widengren, 1969, p. 249.

[11] Asadī Ṭūsī, *Garshāsp-nāma*, p. 269, l. 10, referred to by Khāleqī-Moṭlaq, "Aždahā II," *EIr*; De Blois, "Garshāsp-nāma (or Karshāsp-nāma)," *EIr;* Boyce, 1975, repr. 1996, p. 63; Sarkhosh Curtis, 1993, p. 26; Bivar, 2000, p. 24.

[12] Rosenfield, 1967, figs. 2, 2b (photograph on the left). The heads of the mythical creatures, the Indian composite marine creature, *makara*, and the Central Asian dragon, were sometimes portrayed in a stylistically closely related manner. Since only the head is portrayed, it is impossible to identify it with a degree of certainty as belonging to either creature, though both the *makara* and the Central Asian dragon can to a large extent be considered semantically equivalent. Clubs terminating in dragon-like heads are featured in the seventh-century wall paintings at Sogdian Afrāsīyāb; see Albaum, 1975, fig. 13. On the *makara* in Indian iconography, see Vogel, 1929–30, pp. 133–47; Coomaraswamy, 1928–31, repr. Delhi, 1971, pp. 47–56, esp. pp. 47–9; Combaz, 1945, pp. 146–55; Bosch, 1960; Rosenfield, 1967, pp. 179–83; Boardman, 1986, pp. 451–3.

[13] Colledge, 1986, p. 21 and pl. XLIa.

[14] Chegini and Nikitin, 1996, repr. 1999, p. 53.

[15] Bivar, 1975a, vol. 2, pl. 4a; Drijvers, 1978, p. 172; Winkelmann, 2004, pp. 248–51, fig. 102.

be at once life- and death-giving,[16] whose attribute is the serpent.[17] Clad in Parthian garb he is shown wielding with one hand a double-bladed battle axe, the right blade of which is replaced by a serpent, and clasping the hilt of a dagger in his other hand. The god is girded with a snake-like rope to which three quadrupeds, probably dogs, are connected, the tail of one of the quadrupeds being also in the form of a serpent. Serpents spring from the god's shoulders and rise from either side of his waist, while another serpent rests at his feet. To his right he is flanked by a large cult-standard *(semeion)*, near the foot of which another snake and a scorpion are featured.

The close association of the ophidian creature with the archaic weapon is reflected in the Persian word *gurza* which not only means "a large wooden club or mace," but also "a large headed serpent."[18] Among the Iranian and Turkish tribes the *gurz* was a weapon of special ceremonial importance.[19] Mace bearers were part of the guard of the Samanid and Ghaznawid *sulṭān*. As attested by the Ghaznawid historian Abu 'l-Faḍl Muḥammad ibn Ḥusayn Bayhaqī (d. 470/1077), the mace was the favourite weapon of *sulṭān* Masʿūd ibn Maḥmūd of Ghazna (r. 421/1030–432/1040).[20] The mace even appears on the decoration of silver-inlaid metalwork: among the planets depicted on the cover of the twelfth-century Vaso Vescovali in the British Museum, London, is an eight-armed deity, identified as the planet Mars, holding different weapons among which is a dragon-headed club.[21]

The iconography of a dragon head holding a quadruped or a human being in its open jaws is found on several finials of ceremonial weapons or staffs. Dragons are often represented as fierce, devouring creatures. However, since the animal or human being appears in the dragon's jaws it is not clear whether the act is one of ingestion or expulsion. The heads are portrayed as characteristic "Saljuq"-type dragon heads[22] which are typically represented as ophidian, the elongated lips (sometimes only the upper lip) curved upwards and rolled outwards revealing a proportionately deep cavity with large fangs.

An important example of such a ceremonial copper alloy mace terminating in a " Saljuq-type" dragon head with characteristic gaping jaw revealing teeth and tongue, perhaps made in Afghanistan and datable between the eleventh to the thirteenth centuries, is housed in the David Collection in Copenhagen (fig. 20). Finials of such dragon staffs are preserved in several collections worldwide. An example in the Furusiyya Art Collection in Vaduz which is thought to come from twelfth- or thirteenth-century Anatolia is fashioned with large almond-shaped eyes, small, rounded ears, and curved horns, and the back of the neck is embellished with elongated drop-shaped cartouches enclosing spiralling foliage. The particular feature of the mace head is that the dragon's maw holds the body of a quadruped, possibly a feline (fig. 21). The wide-open jaws of another twelfth- or thirteenth-century copper alloy dragon-headed finial with curved horns, small pointed ears and with a small loop for attachment at the back of the ophidian neck, is filled, in a corresponding manner, with the seated figure of a human being (figs. 22a and b).[23] The finial may have topped a ceremonial staff, thought to be either from Iran or the Jazīra region, and is now in the Musée du Louvre in Paris. The dragon head's very long jaws with drawn-up lips ending in curved tips have paired fangs that frame the human figure at top and bottom. The stylised figure is rendered with a rounded mask-like head. Another closely related twelfth- or thirteenth-century finial is in the David Collection in Copenhagen (fig. 23). Thought to come from Iran or Afghanistan, or perhaps Anatolia, it is cast in the form of a dragon

[16] Dhorme, 1949, pp. 40–3, 51.

[17] For further related examples of chthonic deities with the serpent as attribute, see Winkelmann, 2004, pp. 252–9, figs. 103–6.

[18] Cited after Steingass, 1892, repr. 1981, p. 1082.

[19] Herzfeld, 1927, vol. 2, pl. LXVI. Cf. *Furūsiyya*, 1996, vol. 2, p. 97.

[20] Abu 'l-Faḍl Bayhaqī, *Ta'rīkh-i Masʿūdī*, ed. Ghanī and Fayyūḍ, Tehran, 1324/1945, as cited in Bosworth, "Lashkar-i Bāzār," *EI*² V, 690b; *idem*, 1963, p. 120.

[21] Hartner, 1973–4, pp. 119–20 and fig. 17, no. 5.

[22] Cf. *L'Islam dans les collections nationales*, 1977, p. 102, cat. no. 161. In the scene of Mūsā, Aaron (Hārūn ibn ʿImrān) and the Israelites watching the Egyptians drown in the Red Sea, depicted in the illustrated copy of the *Jāmiʿ al-tawārīkh* ("Compendium of Chronicles") by Rashīd al-Dīn Ṭabīb, made in Tabriz in 714/1314, Mūsā holds an elongated staff which ends in a closely related open-jawed dragon head. Talbot-Rice, 1957, p. 61, cat. no. 11.

[23] A further eleventh- or twelfth-century silver- and copper-inlaid copper alloy dragon-headed finial, probably a sword pommel, thought to come from greater Khurasan or the Jazīra/Anatolia, shows the monster holding a stylised human being in its wide-open maw. Vaduz, Furusiyya Art Collection, inv. no. RB-94. *L'art des chevaliers*, 2007, p. 107, cat. no. 71 (only depicting the profile).

head holding in its wide-open mouth a bovid, whose protome peers out of the dragon's jaws.[24]

Interesting in this regard is the use in medieval Iranian poetry of the metaphor "caught in the dragon's maw" (akin to "held in the dragon's claws") which is conventionally used to reflect a potentially fatal calamity. In the pre-Islamic epic, *Wīs u Rāmīn* ("Wīs and Rāmīn"), translated (from Pahlawī into classical Persian) and versified by Fakhr al-Dīn Asʿad Gurgānī around 442/1050, the protagonist Rāmīn uses it, for instance, to describe his separation from his beloved Wīs, the daughter of the queen of Media who is the wife of his older brother, king Mūbad of Marw:

> ...I have left my hostage heart with you...
> It is as if, upon your soul I swear,
> I'm in a dragon's jaws when you are not there.[25]

In the *Shāh-nāma*, in which the ancient history of Iran, from its legendary origins down to the extinction of the Sasanian dynasty in 652 was recorded, this metaphor is used to describe a political misfortune, such as the defeat of the Iranians by the Türkmen:

> The world thou wouldst have said, "is in the dragon's maw, Or Heaven level with earth.[26]

Or, the hopelessness of a political situation, as expressed by one of the last Sasanian rulers, Khusraw II (Khusraw Parwīz, r. 591–628):

> But what can this avail now that my head is in the dragon's maw?[27]

In Islamic culture dreams were considered an important means of communication with the world of the unknown. Their meaning would be explained, often as a prophetic message from the world of the unseen.[28] Hence, it is interesting to consider a dream interpretation recorded in al-Damīrī's fourteenth-century para-zoological encyclopaedia which reverses the generally negative associations of the ophidian-devouring process. He states that:

> He who dreams of a serpent swallowing him, will obtain power.[29]

In the heroic epic *Garshāsp-nāma* composed by Asadī Ṭūsī in 456–8/1064–6, the eponymous hero, who is the great-great uncle of the legendary warrior Rustam, is requested by Ẓaḥḥāk at the tender age of fourteen to slay a dragon that dwells on Mount Shekāwand having emerged from the sea following a storm.[30] The hero accomplishes the feat by clubbing the beast to death with a cudgel carved in the form of a dragon head.[31] Employ-

---

[24] The iconography of the dragon devouring or disgorging a human being or an animal such as a felid or a bovid is also known in the Christian iconography of the Caucasus. A dragon with quadruped forelegs and a looped tail, portrayed in profile and depicted in the process of swallowing or delivering a proportionally small human figure, is shown above the southern entrance of the mid-tenth-century Georgian church of Beris-Sakdari, near the village of Eredwi in the Patara Liakhvi Gorge. The depiction is probably related to the story in the book of Jonah in the Old Testament of a sea-monster or *ketos* who devoured and cast up the hero under divine command. For the *ketos*, translated *vishap*, which swallowed Jonas in later Christian Armenian art, see Russell, 2004, p. 373. The imagery of the dwelling-place of sinners "in the midst of the jaws of the dragon of the outer darkness" also repeatedly appears in the Gnostic-Christian writings of the *Pistis Sophia* (*c.* fourth century) which are further discussed in the following chapters; *Pistis Sophia*, text ed. Schmidt and tr. Macdermot, 1978, bk. III, ch. 108, p. 551, ch. 119, p. 609, ch. 121, p. 617. The fact that the imagery was depicted above the entrance to the church also indicates that its iconography was associated with the warding off of evil and the affording of protection. Referring to the work of Vladimir Propp, Boris Marshak has pointed out the archaism of the theme of the hero being devoured by a monster (Propp, V.Y., *Istoricheskie korni volshebnoi skazki* ("The Morphology of a Fairy Tale"), Leningrad, 1946, pp. 200–23, as cited in Marshak, 2002, p. 49, n. 39). According to Propp (1984a, pp. 116–8, 207, 208, and *idem,* 1984b, p. 96) the imitation of devouring and expectorating of a hero by an animal such as a dragon was sometimes part of an initiation process, the successful completion of this ritual entitling the initiate to start a new phase of life or existence. An analogous relief probably representing Jonah in the maw of a mythical creature, a "whale" with quadruped forelegs (only the protome is featured) is shown above the south door (east side) of the Georgian Tao-Klardjeti monastery church of Haho (Georgian Khakhuli), modern Bağlar Başi in northeastern Turkey, datable between the tenth and eleventh centuries (Baltrušaitis, 1929, pl. LXXI, fig. 118; Winfield, 1968, pp. 62–3 (line drawing, fig. 6), pl. 30b). However, whereas on the relief of the Georgian church of Beris-Sakdari, the human figure is depicted with its head in the dragon's maw (as if being swallowed), the Haho relief shows the figure's upper body and head topped by small fish projecting from the beast's jaws (as if being spat out).

[25] Tr. and ed. Davis, 2008, p. 388; the same metaphor is employed on pp. 143, 166 and 230.

[26] Tr. and ed. Mohl, 1838–1878, vol. 6, p. 538.

[27] *Idem*, vol. 6, p. 88. For further examples cited in the *Shāh-nāma*, see, for instance, *idem*, vol. 3, p. 171, l. 377, p. 469, l. 670; vol. 4, p. 13, l. 95; vol. 5, p. 13, l. 95; vol. 6, p. 233, l. 876.

[28] Marzolph and van Leeuwen, 2004, p. 542.

[29] *Ḥayāt al-ḥayawān al-kubrā*, tr. Jayakar, 1906, vol. 1, pp. 655–6.

[30] Khāleqī-Moṭlaq, "Aždahā II," *EIr*; Yamamoto, 2003, p. 115.

[31] Asadī Ṭūsī, *Garshāsp-nāma*, p. 269, l. 10, cited after Khāleqī-Moṭlaq, "Aždahā II," *EIr*. In the *Shāh-nāma*, the hero employs serpent-like sword (tr. and ed. Mohl, 1838–1878, vol. 5, p. 341, l. 728).

ing the principle of sympathetic magic – "like affects like" – Garshāsp succeeds in killing the dragon by means of a weapon carved with its own likeness. This magical power appears to be contagious and can be transmitted from its source, in other words from the dragon onto different kinds of implements such as the mace[32] or a staff, as evidenced, for instance, by a story recorded by al-Kisāʾī. Here Mūsā similarly employes a mimetic or "homeopathic" principle by using his serpent-staff to strike a giant serpent that has devoured all the sheep of the Prophet Shuʿayb's flock that pass through an exceptionally fertile valley thereby cutting it in two.[33]

Literary accounts of the medieval Islamic period describe the bejewelled weapons that were paraded on ceremonial occasions.[34] Sabres were probably introduced into the central Islamic lands by the Turkic guard of the ʿAbbasid caliph al-Muʿtaṣim (218/833–227/842), which can be seen on a representation of a ninth-century wall painting in a building at Nīshāpūr that depicts a horseman with a belt with hanging straps designed to support a sabre.[35] Quillon blocks extending into downward-curving prongs that terminate in dragon heads are a common feature on twelfth- or thirteenth-century sabres or daggers, as for instance on a gilded copper alloy sword guard fragment, or a nielloed silver scabbard, both thought to be from Syria or Palestine and now preserved in the Furusiyya Art Collection, Vaduz (fig. 111).[36] Literary sources such as the *Shāh-nāma* similarly use the image of the (serpent-)dragon to describe swords, as for instance, those belonging to the dragon-fighting Kayanian king Gushtāsp,[37] to Iskandar[38] or to Fūr (Porus), king of India, who stopped Alexander's advance in India.[39]

The Turks attributed magical properties to jade (nephrite) and called it the "stone of victory." They used it extensively for fittings of weapons such as handles and quillon blocks, as well as for objects of adornment such as belt fittings and rings, in the belief that its presence would aid in attaining victory over their opponents.[40] Very informative in this regard is the entry under the heading *yashf* ("jade") of al-Bīrūnī's pharmacological work, the *Kitāb al-Ṣaydala fi 'l-Ṭibb* (composed in 442/1050), which states that dragon iconography was engraved on jade and used by the Turks to adorn swords:

> The *yashf* stone: this is *yashb* on which they engrave the radiate dragon [*al-shuʿāʿ* is translated as "ray of light" in Steingass]. We tested it without the engraving and it delivered [a result]. Its characteristic, they say, is to dispel stomach pains. "The stone of victory" is a variety of it and that is why the Turks adorn their swords with it.[41]

The affiliation of the dragon with arms was also made by the great twelfth-century poet Ilyās ibn Yūsuf Niẓāmī Ganjawī (535–40/1141–6–575–613/1180–217) in his romance *Haft Paykar* ("Seven Portraits"), when he compared to dragons the blades of the idealised fifth-century Sasanian king Bahrām Gūr's (Wāhram V, r. 420–38) army, and its arrows to the serpents of Ẓaḥḥāk, the tyrannical foreign ruler of Iran in the *Shāh-nāma* from whose shoulders sprouted the notorious serpents.[42] Similarly, the panegyrist and epistolographer Rashīd-i Waṭwāṭ (508–9/1114–5–573/1177–8 or 578/1182–3), who was born in Balkh, and spent most of his life as poet at the court of Khwārazm-shāh Atsïz, writes in his *dīwān*:

> Thousands of lion-hearted and elephant-bodied warriors
> Are eaten by dogs [after being slain] by your dragon-lance.[43]

A thirteenth-century silver chape is completely covered with the depiction of a pair of upright dragons that are addorsed along a central vertical ridge. The chape was found together with its long knife in Herat, in present-day Afghanistan, and is now in the al-Sabāh Collection in Kuwait

[32] Jeffers, 1996, p. 95.

[33] *Qiṣaṣ al-anbiyāʾ*, tr. Thackston, 1978, p. 223.

[34] Cf. the description of a celebration at the Ghaznawid *sulṭān* Masʿūd's court in 429/1038 by Abu 'l-Faḍl Bayhaqī, (*Taʾrīkh-i Masʿūdī*, ed. Ghanī and Fayyūḍ, Tehran, 1324/1945, pp. 539–41). Cf. Bosworth, 1963, pp. 135–7.

[35] The wall painting is now preserved in the National Museum of Iran, Tehran. Hakimov, 2000, p. 445, fig. 30.

[36] *L'art des chevaliers*, 2007, p. 154, cat. no. 147 and pp. 155–7, cat. no. 148; *Chevaux et cavaliers arabes*, 2002, pp. 118–9, cat. no. 57. An Iranian jade (nephrite) quillon block from the hilt of a sword, dated to the first half of the fourteenth century, is preserved in the Metropolitan Museum of Art, inv. no. 64.133.3. See Melikian-Chirvani, 1997a, p. 159, fig. 27.

[37] Tr. and ed. Mohl, 1838–1878, vol. 4, p. 341, l. 728.

[38] *Idem*, vol. 4, pp. 153, l. 628.

[39] *Idem*, vol. 5, pp. 151–5.

[40] Melikian-Chirvani, 1997a, pp. 131–3.

[41] Ed. ʿAbbās Zariyāb, Tehran, 1370/1991, p. 203, as cited in Melikian-Chirvani, 1997a, p. 131.

[42] Tr. Meisami, 1993, p. 91.

[43] Ed. Nafīsī, S., Tehran, 1960, p. 53, cited after Daneshvari, 1993, pp. 16–7, n. 7.

(fig. 24). The so-called "Saljuq-style" heads of the fabulous beasts are turned towards the back thus confronting each other with their wide-open jaws terminating in upward curled tips and revealing the tongues, the long cusped ears projecting at the top. The quadruped protomes with snugly-fitted feet are oriented towards the edge of the chape, their serpentine bodies with slender, curved wings forming five loops attenuating towards its tip. It is interesting to note a closely related depiction found on a twelfth- or thirteenth-century silk fragment from Samangan province in present-day Afghanistan, also housed in the al-Sabāh Collection in Kuwait, which is woven with an upright pair of dragons with gaping jaws, here in confronted position and wearing beaded collars, their winding serpent-like bodies having clusters of three dots in the bends and set against a background of foliate scrolls (fig. 25).

The dragon motif on banners

In the Middle Iranian period, a dragon *(azhdahā)* was often depicted on standards carried in battle as a symbol of martial valour, intended to frighten the enemy by its ferocious aspect and to show the ruler's power.[44] These banners are referred to several times in the *Shāh-nāma*, in which the ancient history of Iran, from its legendary origins down to the dissolution of the Sasanian dynasty was recorded, as *azhdahā-paykar* ("having a dragon's body").[45] In his *De historia conscribenda sit* (XXIX) the second-century Greek writer Lucian describes the war against the Parthian king Vologesus III who defeated the Romans at Elegia in 162, destroying the Roman legion and killing the commander Severianus. Lucian notes that the Parthians used banners with different emblems to differentiate the divisions of their army, a dragon ensign *(dracōn)* preceding a thousand-man division. He refers to another historian's vivid report of these dragon ensigns, which were made of light material, attached to open-jawed heads and mounted on poles, so that they would move in the breeze like enormous serpent-dragons, so much so that they appeared to the Romans to be:

> ...alive and of enormous size; that they were born in Persia a little way beyond Iberia; that they are bound to long poles, and raised on high, create terror while the Parthians are coming from a distance; that in the encounter itself at close quarters they are freed and sent against the enemy; that in fact they had swallowed many of our men in this way and coiled themselves around others and suffocated and crushed them.[46]

Later on the emblem was introduced into the Roman army where the standard-bearer bore the title *draconarius*. Such a banner with a dragon ensign belonging to the Dacians and their Sarmatian allies is portrayed on the narrative reliefs of Trajan's column which commemorates the Dacian wars of the early second century AD. The fluttering dragon ensigns were described by the contemporary Greek historian Flavius Arrian in his *Tactica* (XXXV 2–5) as being of "Scythian" origin:

> Scythian ensigns are serpents of good length, tied to staffs. They are made out of pieces of dyed material. The heads and the bodies through to the tail are made in order to appear as terrifying as possible ... They swell in the wind of a ride so that they look like those serpents and even begin to whistle when the breath of air is strong enough.[47]

The dragon banner in the Roman army appears to have been instituted in the wake of the deployment of new tactical divisions as part of the Roman emperor Diocletian's (r. 284–305) reorganisation of the military machinery.[48] Such dragon banners are again described by the fourth-century Roman historian Ammianus Marcellinus, who served in the army of Constantine II (337–361) in Persia, in his *Rerum gestarum libri* (XVI 10.7 and 12.39). In his record of Constantine's entry into Rome in 357 (XVI 10.7) Marcellinus writes that the emporer:

> ...was surrounded by dragons, woven out of purple thread and bound to the golden and jewelled tips of spears, with wide mouths open to the breeze and hence hissing as if roused by anger, and leaving their tails winding in the wind.[49]

---

[44] It is of note that the Indian *makara*, discussed above (p. 36, n. 12), also formed the head of the battle standard *(makaradhvaja)* of Rudra or Shiva, and was later also carried by Siddhārtha's son, Rāhula. It served as battle standard for the hosts of Mara, who attacked the Buddha. The *makara* also served as designation for specific battle formation of troops that take the form of a *makara* during battle manoeuvres. Cited after Beer, 2004, p. 68.

[45] Skjærvø, "Aždahā I," *EIr*.

[46] Lucian, *Quomodo historia conscribenda sit*, tr. Kilburn, K., London, 1959, vol. VI, pp. 42–3. Cf. Widengren, 1969, pp. 17–8 and n. 38; Shahbazi, "Derafš," *EIr*.

[47] Arrian, *Tactica* (XXXV), cited after Lebedynsky, 1995, pp. 93–4.

[48] Haussig, 1992, p. 29.

[49] Cf. Widengren, 1969, p. 18, n. 39 (with further references).

According to Moses of Chorene, in commemoration of the Armenian king Tigran's resettlement of the defeated Medes to the area of Goghtʿn and around the foot of Mount Ararat, the windsock-like silk dragon *(vishap)* banner, adopted from the Parthians, became the Armenian king's heraldic sign.[50] In his account of the battle of Jiraw the sight of the banners (III.37) is similarly vividly conveyed:

> the sinuous rippling of the dragon [banners], puffed up by the blast of air, their jaws yawning frightfully.[51]

An account of the anonymous fifth-century Armenian *Epic History* or *Buzandaran Patmutʿiwnkʿ* (IV.2) also describes the battle standard of the Arsacid Armenians (54–428) as a silk dragon banner.[52] A description of the advance of the Iranian army is given in the grand heroic epic, Firdawsī's *Shāh-nāma*, which states that:

> behind each banner, there followed another banner – some with dragons, others with the image of eagles

showing that different royal emblems could be used concurrently.[53]

A dragon banner may be depicted on a bone plaque which is incised with a battle scene and probably served as a belt element.[54] It was found in a necropolis near the village of Orlat in the district of Koshrabad, west of Samarqand, and, according to Boris Marshak, does not reflect a local but a Central Asian nomadic tradition.[55] The mail-clad combatants are wielding lances, bows, swords and battle axes.[56] Strapped to the lancer on the lower left is a military emblem, which may have served as badge of rank, a long, flowing banner on a pole akin to the dragon banners represented on wall paintings in Chinese Turkestan (present-day Xinjiang), discussed below. Marcus Mode tentatively ascribes the plaque to the reign of the Xiongnu king of Sogdiana (Su-te) in the 30s of the fifth century attested by *The History of the Wei (Wei-shu)*.[57] The Xiongnu were known to have fought under the dragon banner, a traditional ensign of the military forces of the steppes.[58]

Similar banners, some rendered in serpent or dragon-like form, are depicted on wall paintings in Chinese Turkestan, a region whose pivotal position at the crossroads between China and Central Asia resulted in a broad cultural synthesis which embraced the western Turks or Kök Türks (*T'u-chueh* or *Tujue*). In the Cave of the Painter at Kizil (Kezier), a sixth- to seventh-century wall painting illustrates an army with a dragon banner.[59] During the German Turfan expeditions at the beginning of the twentieth century, Albert von le Coq recorded several such banners. At Kizil, in the "Cave of the Dove," a seventh- or eighth-century wall painting features a *senāpatiratna*, a deity who symbolises the wrathful power to overcome enemies, carrying a banner in the form of a serpentine body terminating in a swallow-tailed pennant with projecting dragon head with gaping jaws,[60] and in the "Caves with Fireplace," a warrior riding a war elephant also holds such a dragon banner.[61] A wall painting discovered in the eighth-century "Cave of the Doves" at Kirish, the ruins of Simsim, portrays a dragon-king *(nāgarāja)* above whom floats a large banner with lupine head and what appears to be a serpentine body.[62] The wolf was one of the prevalent emblems on the military standards of Turkish tribes; other such emblems seem to have been the moon or the dragon.[63]

---

[50] Russell, 2004, pp. 621–40, esp. 624 and 622–23 (for a discussion of the historical Tigrans that could have inspired the orally transmitted legend); also pp. 1047–8 (with a translation of the late twelfth-century Armenian Catholicos Nersēs Šnorhali's text *Interpretive Explanation, Mingled with Supplication, of the Standards of the Kings of Armenia* which recalls the king and his banner).

[51] *Idem*, p. 627.

[52] *Idem*, pp. 624–5 and n. 9. It is interesting to observe that such dragon standards are still represented in thirteenth-century Armenian miniatures (Washington, DC, Freer Gallery of Art, Ms. 32.18, p. 513; "Judas leading the Multitude," see Der Nersessian and Agemian, 1993, vol. 2, fig. 251).

[53] Tr. and ed. Mohl, 1838–1878, vol. 3, p. 589, ll. 2107–2108.

[54] Mode, 2006, p. 420 and n. 4.

[55] Marshak, B.I., "Iskusstvo Sogda," *Tsentral'naya Aziya. Novye pamyatniki pis'mennosti I iskusstva. Sbornik statey*, eds., Piotrovskiy, B.B. and Bongard-Levin, G.M., Moscow, 1987, p. 235, as cited in Mode, 2006, pp. 421–2. Cf. Brentjes, 1989, p. 41.

[56] Bone plaque with battle scene. Orlat, Koshrabad district, west of Samarqand, present-day Uzbekistan. Ilyasov and Rusanov, 1997–8, pl. IV:1; Mode, 2006, p. 444, fig. 1. Cf. Brentjes, 1989, p. 40, fig. 3.

[57] Mode, 2006, p. 433. For a comprehensive list of suggested dates of the plaques, cf. esp. pp. 421–2, 433.

[58] *Idem*, p. 433.

[59] G. 356; von Le Coq, 1925, p. 54, fig. 50.

[60] G. 274; *idem*, p. 72, fig. 117.

[61] G. 50; *idem*, p. 55, fig. 53.

[62] G. 432; *idem*, p. 68, fig. 101. The lupine figures recall the fact that the Tʿu-chüeh tribe, which was part of the Xiongnu confederacy, is said to have depicted a wolf on their banners; Eberhard, 1979, pp. 52–3.

[63] Roux, 1979, p. 170. The seventh-century Chinese dynastic annals, the *Pei shih*, as well as the *Chou shu* (50, 4a), explicitly state that the Turks put wolf heads on their standards; Sinor, 1982, p. 233 and 1996, repr. 1999, p. 329; Liu, 1958, p. 9. It is interesting to observe that wolf-standards were sometimes referred to as dragon-standards; see Schmidt, 1980, p. 63. The dragon, the wolf and the moon were also emblems on the respective flags of Rustam, Gurgīn and Farīburz (*Shāh-nāma*; tr. and ed. Mohl, 1838–1878, vol. 3, p. 66).

In Asadī Ṭūsī's *Garshāsp-nāma* the eponymous hero's victory over the dragon was commemorated by a flag *(dirafsh)* embellished with the representation of a black dragon *(azhdahāy-i siyāh)* and a pole surmounted by a golden lion, in turn topped by a moon.[64] The banner was passed on to Garshāsp's descendants and became his family's coat of arms.[65] Likewise, the standard of the paladin Rustam, whose ancestors are thought to have been Saka people who came to Sakastān/Sīstān and Zābulistān in the late second century BC,[66] was "blazoned with the dragon's form and from its tip a golden lion roars."[67] His grandfather, Sām, also had a dragon banner,[68] as did Rustam's son, Farāmarz.[69] The *Shāh-nāma* account records that when Bahrām Chōbīn received the supreme command, the Sasanian king Hurmuz IV (578–590) handed him the purple dragon banner with the words: "You are indeed a second Rustam."[70] Not only did Bahrām Chōbīn receive the distinguishing emblem which likened him to the great hero, but, in addition, he claimed Arsacid Parthian descent and was thus heir to the traditional Arsacid dragon banner.[71] Dragon banners bearing the effigy of a gold-coloured dragon without legs or wings, the open mouth revealing the tongue, set against red and black grounds alternately, are featured on a page from a dispersed *Shāh-nāma*. Painted in Shiraz in 742/1341, the miniature, which was formerly in the collection of the prince and the princess Sadruddin Aga Khan, now in the Aga Khan Foundation, portrays the victory of the dragon-slayer Bīzhan, grandson of the Iranian commander, Gūdarz, over Hūmān, brother of the Tūrānian commander, Pīrān;[72] the banners being displayed in commemoration of the celebrated feat carried out by Farāmarz, son of Shahrbānū Irem and Rustam, in slaying a dragon called hissing serpent *(mār-i juwshā)*.[73] An extended list of heroes thus seems to have claimed the right to own a dragon banner as emblem. The visual appropriation of the dragon's likeness on individual and dynastic banners not only communicated mastery over the mythical creature but also implied that through victory the vanquisher had been able to appropriate the formidable qualities of the dragon.

The dragon motif on belt/strap fittings and equestrian accoutrements

Girding with a belt was a rite of passage in all Central Asian, in particular Iranian, societies from ancient times.[74] Adorned parade belts played an important role in the investiture of warriors in the Indo-Iranian world and were insignia of cultic or ritual significance as well as symbols of social distinction.[75] In the Armeno-Parthian dynasty the belt was presented to the *dihqāns* ("members of the lesser feudal nobility") along with a ring and a banner as tokens of royal service.[76] The origin of the custom has been attributed to the sacred rope-girdle (*kustī*) of the Zoroastrians, for whom, however, such girding was an act of consecration, as in the rite of initiation. In Turkish and Islamic society the belt was of great importance; it was an integral part of male costume, often presented by the ruler, and hence regarded as an insignia of rank.[77]

The nomadic warrior seems to have been girt with a pair of belts[78] adorned in accordance with

64 Widengren, 1969, p. 17, n. 35; Asadī Ṭūsī, *Garshāsp-nāma*, pp. 49–63 (63.35–6), as cited in Khāleqī-Moṭlaq, "Aždahā II," *EIr*. A dragon-shaped long narrow flag floating from the mast of a boat is featured on a ninth-century lusterware plate from Nīshāpūr. Papadopoulo, 1979, fig. 420.

65 *Op. cit.*

66 De Bruijn, "Rustam," *EI*² VIII, 636b. Cf. the discussion in Shahbazi, 1993, pp. 157–8.

67 *Shāh-nāma*, tr. and ed. Mohl, 1838–1878, vol. 3, p. 107, ll. 1224–1255, p. 113, ll. 1292–1293; vol. 5, pp. 85, 89; *The Tragedy of Sohráb and Rostám*, tr. and ed. Clinton, 1987, pp. 95, 549–50. Cf. Shahbazi, 1993, p. 159; Melikian-Chirvani, 1998, p. 179.

68 Widengren, 1969, p. 17, n. 35, with reference to the *Garshāsp-nāma*, as also cited by Shahbazi, 1993, p. 159.

69 Khāleqī-Moṭlaq, "Aždahā II," *EIr*.

70 *Shāh-nāma*, tr. and ed. Mohl, 1838–1878, vol. 6, pp. 587–9, ll. 525–31. It is of note that like the dragon banners surrounding Constantine when he entered Rome, as described by Ammianus Marcellinus (see above), the *Shāh-nāma* account specifies that the colour of Bahrām Chōbīn's dragon banner was – just like that of Rustam – purple; tr. and ed. Mohl, 1838–1878, vol. 6, pp. 587–9, ll. 525–31.

71 Shahbazi, "Derafš," *EIr*.

72 "Victory of Bīzhan over Human." Page of a dispersed *Shāh-nāma*. Iran, Shiraz. 1341. Height 36.9 cm, width 30.7 cm. Collection of the Prince and the Princess Sadruddin Aga Khan, Ms. 006/E. *Chevaux et cavaliers arabes*, 2002, p. 161, cat. no. 119. A further example of a dragon banner is illustrated in an Ilkhanid-period *Shāh-nāma* manuscript; Pope and Ackerman, eds., 1938–9, repr. 1964–81, vol. 10, pl. 834.

73 *Farāmarz-nāma*, London, British Museum, Ms. Or. 2946, fols. 24, 25, as cited in Khāleqī-Moṭlaq, "Aždahā II," *EIr*.

74 It is of note that the belt did not play an important role in Greek tradition. Cf. Brentjes, 1989, p. 42.

75 Cf. Widengren, 1969, pp. 21–32.

76 Brentjes, 1989, p. 43. The Parthian king Uthal is depicted with a belt whose central belt plaques are rendered with winged and apparently bearded dragons with coiled serpentine tails resting on their forelegs. See Winkelmann, 2004, pp. 10–3, fig. 5b.

77 Cf. the discussion of Katharina Otto-Dorn, 1961–2, pp. 9–13.

78 As evidenced for instance by the first-century AD finds in the Sarmatian *kurgan* near Porogi, nomadic warriors customarily wore two belts. Simonenko, 1991, p. 215, fig. 1.

rank and ancestry.[79] Hence on one belt a diagonally suspended bow in a long narrow bow-case and a quiver filled with arrows could be carried, while a sword or sabre and a dagger might be suspended from the second.[80] Paired belts, a ceremonial main belt and another with straps from which the sword and other weapons were suspended, were, according to the *Tarikh-i Bukhārā*, worn by the young attendants *(bandagān)* at the court of the queen of Bukhara.[81] Reports on the Turks in their homeland emphasise the importance of belts, which in addition to their utilitarian function served as status symbols. The Turks are described as rich in cattle, horses and sheep and possessing "many vessels of gold and silver. They have many weapons. They have silver belts..."[82]

The Avars, an Ibero-Caucasian people who were subjects of the Turks, followed in the wake of the great migrations of nomadic peoples from the Eurasian steppes, fleeing to the north Caucasus region in 558 and from thence migrating westwards.[83] Late Avar period iconography is preserved almost exclusively on items of personal adornment, in particular compartmentalised belt sets with multiple plaques figuring more naturalistic *tamgas* in the form of fabulous creatures reflecting "ancestral, totemic ideas."[84] Often these are shown in combat with ungulates or human beings perhaps symbolising "the cycle of death and rebirth." Among the animals another hybrid creature with a long history in the Near East, the griffin, appears to have been particularly prevalent, however the dragon also made an appearance as did natural animals such as horses, eagles and wild boars.[85] An elongated silver tongue-strap fitting ("Hauptriemenzunge") with one arched end featuring a quadruped dragon was unearthed from grave 292 of an Avar necropolis in Abony, Hungary, attributed to the second half of the seventh century (fig. 26).[86] The beast is rendered in profile with elongated open snout, the upper lip curving upwards revealing a pointed tongue, crowned by horns or ears, with a beard projecting from the chin; the elongated, undulant, serpentine body covered with a spotted pattern is demarcated by crest-like, spiky protrusions, and rests on three curved legs with pointed protrusions at the feet, probably representing unsheathed claws. Depicted at mid-section of the body is what appears to be a small version of the dragon. An association of this representation with the Chinese dragon through Byzantine mediation has been proposed by Falko Daim on the grounds that the depiction of the dragon is comparatively rare in Avar iconography.[87] Samuel Szádeczky-Kardoss however relates this iconography to Hellenistic (that is Seleucid and Parthian) and Sasanian influence, while underlining that "the subject matter [of the Avars] is taken from the body of beliefs proper to the peoples of the steppe."[88]

Belts also had an important ceremonial significance and were a symbol of authority for the Samanids, Ghaznawids and Saljuqs.[89] Tenth- or eleventh-century Western Central Asian belt hooks were commonly *S*-shaped with a central cuboctahedral or spherical knob, terminated at either end by a horned dragon head, one end bent to a closed position and with a heavy rectangular strap-slot.[90] The dragon heads are shown with the wide-open snouts characteristic of the "Saljuq" type, the upper lip curving upwards and revealing a deep cavity with stumpy fangs. A roughly contemporary horned dragon with open snout and sinuous body also occurs on narrow essentially rectangular copper alloy belt strap fittings from present-day Afghanistan, some of which are gilded.[91]

79 Szádeczky-Kardoss, 1990, p. 126.

80 Cf. the belts of the sandstone statue of the Śaka satrap Caṣṭana (first half of the first century). Czuma, 1985, pp. 112–3, cat. no. 43; Azarpay, 1981, pp. 122–5.

81 Schefer, 1892, pp. 7–12.

82 Gardīzī, *Zayn al-akhbār*, in V.V. Bartol'd (W. Barthold), *Otč o poezdke v Srednyuyu Aziyu s naučnoy tsel'yu 1893–1894 gg.*, in *Zapiski Imperatorskoy Akademii Nauk*, ser. VII, t. i, 74–175. Pers. text and Russ. tr. repr. in *Sočineniya*, Moscow 1963–73, vol. 8, p. 35, cited after Golden, "Pečenengs," *EI*² VIII, 289a.

83 Pohl, 1988, pp. 28–9; Barthold and Golden, "Khazar," *EI*² IV, 1172a.

84 Szádeczky-Kardoss, 1990, pp. 126–8.

85 Pohl, 1988, p. 289.

86 Cf. *Xi'an*, 2006, p. 356, cat. no. 271.

87 Daim, 2000, pp. 134–6, fig. 60; *Xi'an*, 2006, p. 356, cat. no. 271 (catalogue entry by Falko Daim).

88 Szádeczky-Kardoss, 1990, p. 128. It is interesting to observe that a plaque in the form of a reptilian mythical creature with large gaping snout bearing the images of fish on its belly, datable between the sixth and the eighth century, can be detected among the animal copper alloys from the governorate of Perm, north of the Caspian; see Oborin and Tshagin, 1988, p. 93, cat. no. 69.

89 Bosworth, 1963, p. 38.

90 Several of these examples are preserved in Kuwait, al-Sabāh Collection, Kuwait National Museum, such as inv. nos. LNS 617 J, LNS 1122 J, LNS 1123 J, LNS 1125 J b, LNS 2762 J.

91 See an example in Kuwait, al-Sabāh Collection, Kuwait National Museum, inv. no. LNS 3103 J; putative origin: Herat, Afghanistan.

An unusual depiction of a standing quadruped dragon appears on a richly gilded copper alloy fitting, probably for the strap of a parade belt, now in a private collection (fig. 27). The head, turned backwards, has gaping jaws with fleshy folds, the upper lip terminating in a tight curl revealing rows of teeth, conspicuous projecting fangs and a long flickering tongue. Small, circular eyes punctuate the head, which is crowned by small, cusped ears and extends into the long sinuous neck surmounted by a crest defined by deep hatching. A split palmette projects from the haunches at the front and another extends from the tip of the long sinuous tail which curves under the flank to ascend vertically above the back. The legs with delineated four-clawed feet are firmly planted on two platforms that project to form the base of the fitting, adding to the imposing plastic effect of the creature. In spite of the uncommon appearance, its powerful and expressive monumentality must be the result of a long-established tradition. Remarkably, distant cousins of the enigmatic beast, albeit no dragons, appear to survive on the low-relief carvings that cover a large part of the exterior of a cathedral of Saint Dmitry (1193–1197) in Vladimir in the northeastern principality Vladimir-Suzdal of Rus' situated around the river Volga. Named after the warrior saint Demetrius of Salonika, the cathedral was commissioned by prince Vsevolod III (1176–1212) for his own use. Contacts with the east on the part of this principality, by way of the Volga, were much closer than with western Europe and it is generally thought that most of the characteristic local artistic features are due to Caucasian influences.[92] Vladimir-Suzdal had close contacts with Armenia and Georgia, exemplified by the fact that prince Yuri Bogolyubsky, Vsevolod's nephew, was chosen as husband for the famed Georgian queen Tʿamar (1184–1211/2) in 1184. On all three middle pediments of the cathedral the biblical king David is portrayed as surrounded by the animals, several of which are rendered with stylistic aspects reminiscent of the dragon on the fitting, such as the elongated necks, the long legs ending in forceful delineated feet and, in particular, the elongated tails that curve under the haunches to project vertically above the back, ending in a split-palmette.[93] The stylistic and iconographic stimuli for these relief sculptures are to be sought in post-Sasanian, Islamic and Transcaucasian art which may well have been well-known through textiles and other portable items.[94] As a reflection of these eastern stimuli the late twelfth-century date of creation of the Vladimir relief sculptures thus provides an approximate *terminus ante quem* for dating the fitting with its forceful relief featuring a standing quadruped dragon which, in contrast to the more tame appearance of the beasts in the Vladimir reliefs, is characterised by an immediacy and innate animal nature, imbued with the vigour, physical power and lively spirit of wild beasts.

The dragon motif also extends to horsemanship. Niẓām al-Mulk, the celebrated vizier of the Saljuqid *sulṭān* Alp Arslan and former Ghaznawid functionary, used the figurative expression "Exalted Stirrup" *(riqāb-i ʿālī)* in his *Siyāsat Nāma* when referring to the *sulṭān*.[95] The metonym was used at Turkish as well as Iranian courts to denote "the sovereign himself or his presence, the foot of the throne."[96] It is thus fitting that a pair of standing quadruped dragons are depicted on the shoulders of a cast copper alloy horse stirrup which is probably from the Ghaznawid world, datable to the eleventh or twelfth century, now in the Nasser D. Khalili Collection of Islamic Art, London (fig. 28).

c. *The dragon motif on objects of personal adornment*

In the Western Central Asian world the dragon also features prominently on objects pertaining to personal adornment. Quadruped dragons appear on an eleventh- or twelfth-century soft stone mould of rectangular outline used for tooling leather, reportedly from Herat in northern Afghanistan and housed in the al-Sabāh Collection in Kuwait (figs. 29a and b). Next to the patterning for two faces of a pouch featuring astrological and hunting scenes (as well as two small flaps), the mould is intaglio-carved with a pair of large, confronted quadruped dragons portrayed

[92] Buxton, 1934, pp. 24–5.

[93] Allenow et al., 1992, figs. 205 and 228.

[94] *Eidem*, p. 35. The style has also been compared with Transcaucasian relief sculptures on the seventh-century church of Ptghni (Ptghnavankʿ) in Ararat province and the church of the Holy Cross of Aghtʿamar on Lake Van built between 915 and 921. See Buxton, 1934, pp. 25–6.

[95] *Siyāsat Nāma*, p. 133, pp. 98–9; cf. Silverstein, 2007, p. 131.

[96] Deny, "Riqāb," *EI*² VIII, p. 528b. The use of the term is also attested in Ibn Bībī, *al-Awāmir al-ʿalāʾiyya*, tr. Duda, 1959, pp. 95–6.

with elongated slender bodies standing on tall, splayed legs, with one leg raised in a formal stance. Their snarling heads with long wide-open snouts reveal protruding sinuous tongues, while the top of the head has pricked ears and prominent elegantly curved horns. The creatures are characterised by very long, narrow wings that surmount the back, and thin, elongated *S*-shaped tails.

The dragon also makes an appearance on a range of jewellery. A roughly trapezoidal twelfth-century grey steatite jewellery mould from Maimana province (Faryab) in Afghanistan, now in the al-Sabāh Collection in Kuwait, is deeply carved for a simple loop ear wire, terminating at one end with a dragon head and a vent.[97] An eleventh- or twelfth-century copper alloy ring from northern Afghanistan, preserved in the same collection, has tapering shanks that terminate on either side at the apex in double-collared, bulging-eyed dragon heads, their lower jaws joining at the tips.[98]

Intertwined dragon protomes, joined by a single loop, appear as appliqués on the shoulders of a twelfth-century niello-inlaid gold finger ring, also in the al-Sabāh Collection in Kuwait. The creatures are defined by confronted wide-open snouts with upward-curling tips that hold up a rectangular bevelled-edged agate seal stone which is inscribed in reverse Kufic script: "my sufficiency is in God and [it] suffices" (fig. 30). These pious words were probably a supplication for help to overcome difficulties.[99] The efficacy of the prayer was buttressed by the entwined dragons which in turn would have helped to enhance the ring's protective properties.

The motif of the entwined dragons is further shown on an unglazed earthenware press mould of tapering rectangular form from Balkh in northern Afghanistan also in the al-Sabāh Collection in Kuwait. The twelfth-century mould has a remarkable pictorial programme. It shows a pair of addorsed *regardant* quadruped dragons in rampant posture with geometrically patterned elongated bodies. Importantly, the winged creatures entwine at mid-section. Their heads are crowned by long, curved horns and the open jaws revealing long tongues touch the scrolling foliage bearing round buds or fruit, possibly pomegranates, against which the entire composition is set and which itself again terminates in gaping dragon heads. A small feline *couchant*, probably a lion, is framed between the legs of the dragons, which are surmounted in their turn by addorsed upright quadrupeds alternating with a pair of confronted human figures seated, legs folded back, on a horizontal platform. Three stacked round objects that closely resemble the produce of the flowering branches (which are perhaps pomegranates, the fruit associated with the concept of fertility) appear between these figures (figs. 31a and b).

To this may be added a very important and more complex composition of paired entwined dragons in mirror image, joined at the centre by a quadripartite knot. This composition, considered below in chapter 10, is featured on a matrix for belt ornaments which can be connected to the Ghurid *sulṭān* Ghiyāth al-Dīn Muḥammad ibn Sām (r. 569/1173–599/1202–3), the builder of the minaret of Jām, or his younger brother, Mu'izz al-Dīn Muḥammad ibn Sām (r. 569/1173–602/1206), with whom he ruled in partnership and also shared the *ism* (name) Muḥammad and the *nasab* (a person's relation to his forefather) ibn Sām (fig. 169).[100]

In this context it is interesting to note that the motif of the interlaced dragons was minted as an added emblem on the coinage of Fakhr al-Dīn Qara Arslan ibn Dāwūd (539/1144–562/1167), the Artuqid ruler of Ḥiṣn Kayfā and Khartpert, which otherwise follows late Byzantine conventions (figs. 32a and b). The dragon protomes are represented addorsed but with necks twisted backwards so that the open-mouthed heads are confronted. Their raised wings touch at the centre in a circular tip while the forelegs extend down and forward to the medallion edge. The lower ophidian body entwines once and forms a quadripartite loop which then extends to frame the lobed medallion. The addition of the dragon motif countermark, superimposed on the lower left quadrant of a reproduction of a late Byzantine coin type featuring an enthroned nimbate Christ holding a book,[101] may be seen not only as an example of Türkmen efforts to create a multi-cultural

[97] Length 8.53 cm, width 2.94 cm. Kuwait, al-Sabāh Collection, Dar al-Athar al-Islamiyyah, Kuwait National Museum, inv. no. LNS 2619 J.

[98] Height 2.59 cm, width 2.4 cm. Kuwait, al-Sabāh Collection, Dar al-Athar al-Islamiyyah, Kuwait National Museum, inv. no. LNS 1596.

[99] The formula is a well-known supplication in modern times.

[100] From a set of 77 copper alloy matrices for belt/strap fittings, Kuwait, al-Sabāh Collection, Dar al-Athar al-Islamiyyah, Kuwait National Museum, LNS 2558 J a-x2.

[101] This type of motif is seen on coins of Manuel I Komnenos (1143–1180). See Lane Poole, p. 123, no. 329.

paradigm, embracing as it does both Byzantine Greek and Türkmen visual traditions, but also as a step towards asserting the identity of this Artuqid ruler. The choice of this particular motif as emblem by a Türkmen leader is particularly important since it gives weight to the hypothesis that the interlaced dragon figure was introduced into Islamic art from Central Asia via the Turkish dynasties.[102] The use of a symbol which must have carried Iranian cultural associations may thereby represent a conscious effort to revive a visual heritage from the past which at the same time served as a means of self-identification.

Dragon imagery on Central Asian objects of personal adornment was also found at the frontier town of Ūtrār, located at the confluence of the Aryss and the Syr Daryā rivers. Excavations yielded a signet ring featuring a rider on horseback killing a dragon, an iconography that will be discussed in greater depth in chapter 7, together with bracelets terminating in dragon heads.[103] The incident at Ūtrār where a Mongolian caravan was massacred by Khwārazmian officials led to the invasion of Transoxania by Genghis Khān's troops in the autumn of 616/1219 and the city's destruction shortly thereafter. It signalled the beginning of the Mongol conquest of Western Asia.

Whereas the Central Asian world yields a wide range of objects of adornment decorated with the likeness of the dragon, comparable finds from Anatolia and the Jazīra from the eleventh to the thirteenth century are generally extremely rare. However, on the back of an early- to mid-thirteenth-century Saljuq gold-inlaid steel mirror, which would have been a prime accoutrement, now in the Topkapı Sarayı Müzesi, the dragon occurs three times with different connotations. The central field is decorated with a mounted falconer on a richly caparisoned horse with a hunting dog attached by a leash to the saddle. A small, looped dragon with raised, gaping head appears just in front of the horse's hooves, a quadruped, probably a fox, seeks cover at the back, and a game bird flies above. The benedictory inscription in minute letters on the horse's harness underlines the rider's elevated position. The scene is circumscribed by a band enclosing a procession of symmetrically arranged real quadrupeds as well as mythical creatures, the latter including a centaur-archer whose tail terminates in a dragon head. The band is crowned at the top by a pair of expressive dragons with small wings and forelegs whose upper bodies cross (but do not loop) so that the gaping mouth of each appears to snap at the other dragon's looped tail end (fig. 33).[104] Their position at the apex, as Priscilla Soucek notes, brings to mind the use of architectural dragons as guardians at gates.[105]

Such a mirror would have belonged to the requisites of the nobility and may well, as Oya Pancaroğlu proposes, have been used as instrument "of allegorical reflection and divination." This mirror thus "embodies a vision of kingship that extends beyond the horizons of temporal human dominion while affirming the universality of its royal centre."[106] Mirrors have a long history of association with apotropaic properties in antiquity and the medieval period, for they have the power of turning evil back upon itself.[107] They are often linked with magic and the Latin version of the magical manual *Ghāyat al-ḥakīm* ("The Philosopher's Goal"), attributed to Abū Maslama Muḥammad al-Majrītī (who wrote between 443/1052 and 448/1056),[108] includes instructions on how to make a magic mirror, ascribed to Jābir ibn Ḥayyān, the semi-legendary eighth- or ninth-century author of a large body of Hermetic alchemical literature. The owner of this mirror was said to have power over the winds, humankind and demons.[109] The amplified depiction of the dragon on such a multi-layered object, as pair at the apex, below the horse's hooves and as the centaur's tail, shows that it was considered an extremely valued and compelling iconography that was deemed necessary to further increase the potency of the mirror's inherent properties.

[102] Azarpay, 1978, p. 366, n. 20.

[103] Baipakov, 1992, p. 110; the date of the pieces is not mentioned. They could also date to the period after the destruction by the Mongols in 617/1220, since the city regained some of its commercial prominence by the middle of the thirteenth century, as attested by the travelling Armenian king Het'um II of Cilicia (Lesser Armenia, Armenian kingdom from 1198–1375) who in his *Account of the Eastern Kingdoms* (p. 128, as cited in Bretschneider, 1888, repr. 1967, p. 57) called Utrār (Otrar) "the greatest city of Turkestan."

[104] Cf. Öney, 1969a, p. 171, fig. 21; Erginsoy, 1978, pp. 456–7, figs. 225 a and b; *Glory of Byzantium*, 1997, p. 424, cat. no. 282; *Turks*, 2005, cat. no. 72.

[105] *Glory of Byzantium*, 1997, p. 424 (catalogue entry no. 282 by Priscilla Soucek).

[106] *Turks*, 2005, p. 395, cat. no. 72. Cf. also Pellat, "Mirʾāt," *EI*² VII, 105b.

[107] Ullmann, 1992, pp. 55–61; Maguire, 1994, p. 267.

[108] On Abū Maslama Muḥammad al-Majrītī, see Sezgin, 1971, pp. 294–8.

[109] Cf. Strohmaier, 1989, p. 267.

d. *The dragon motif on vessels*

The depiction of the dragon is frequently found sculpted as part of vessels, for instance on the arched handles of two celebrated buckets both of which are now preserved in the State Hermitage, St. Petersburg. One of these is the richly silver- and copper-inlaid copper alloy bucket, named after its collector, Count Alexei Bobrinsky, the famous "Bobrinski bucket," which was purchased in Bukhara in 1885 by N.N. Shavrov, the adjuntant of General Chernyayev, governor general of Turkestan (fig. 34). It was probably made in Herat, one of the main cultural centres of the province of Khurasan which flourished especially under the Ghurid dynasty, during whose rule the vessel was produced as indicated by the date *muḥarram* 559/December 1163 inscribed in Kufic at the top band of the handle of the bucket.[110] The loops of the handle are in the form of a leaping lion and on the inside a dragon protome, from whose gaping mouth issues the four-sided arched section inscribed on two sides in *naskhī* with benedictory inscriptions (fig. 56).

The second bucket, which in the mid-nineteenth century was in the Parisian collection of Louis Fould before coming into the possession of the St. Petersburg jeweller, A.K. Fabergé, is signed by its maker, Muḥammad ibn Nāṣir ibn Muḥammad al-Harawī. The toponymic *(nisba)* al-Harawī ("from Herat") perhaps indicates the origin of the maker, and indeed the bucket is thought to have been made in late twelfth- or early thirteenth-century Khurasan, probably in Herat.[111] Yet nothing is known of the maker who could also have migrated from Khurasan westwards; moreover, on the basis of its faceted body and gilt ground as well as several decorative elements, it has recently been attributed to the early thirteenth-century Jazīra, northern Syria, or possibly Anatolia.[112] Its handle is closely related to that of the Bobrinski bucket and is similarly held in place by loops in the form of curved dragons topped here by projecting lion-headed knobs (fig. 57).[113]

The dragon's close connection with water has been manifested since ancient times and its ensuing depiction on vessels containing liquid is known at least from the early medieval period. Often this is expressed in dragon-headed spouts. This feature appears on an automaton depicted in the treatise written by the court engineer Abu 'l-ʿIzz Ismāʿīl ibn al-Razzāẓ al-Jazarī (fl. second half of sixth/twelfth century) which details the various automata commissioned by the Artuqid ruler Nāṣir al-Dīn Maḥmūd ibn Muḥammad al-Malik al-Ṣāliḥ (r. 597/1201–619/1222) for the court's amusement. The resulting work, *Kitāb fī maʿrifat al-ḥiyāl al-handasiyya* ("Book of Knowledge of Ingenious Mechanical Devices"), dates to *c.* 1200.[114] Al-Jazarī's "Hand-washing machine," which was designed for ritual ablutions, is depicted with a dragon-spouted ewer on a leaf from the earliest extant manuscript of this work dated to the end of Shaʿbān 602/about 10 April 1206, copied by Muḥammad ibn Yūsuf ibn ʿUthmān al-Ḥaṣkafī ("of Ḥiṣn Kayfā") at Diyārbakr, and now preserved in the Topkapı Sarayı Library, Istanbul. When the machine was turned on, water flowed from the cistern in the servant's chest into the ewer, the bird on the lid of the vessel whistled and the liquid poured out of the gaping mouth of the dragon-headed spout (fig. 35).[115] Such a spout is also portrayed on a Jazīra-type copper alloy ewer (with recently replaced silver inlay), the so-called "Homberg Ewer," now preserved in the Keir Collection in London, which has an overall decagonal outline. The lower part of the neck is inscribed with the signature of the artist, Aḥmad al-Dhakī, the engraver, al-Mawṣilī and the date 640/1242.[116]

The dragon motif in manifold variations is frequently found as part of the decorative programme of vessels, as for instance on a rectangular brass tray inlaid with silver and with a central cruciform depression in which four pairs of dragons

---

[110] Cf. Loukonine and Ivanov, eds., 2003, pp. 114–5, cat. no. 116. Cf. Pope and Ackerman, eds., 1938–9, repr. 1964–81, vol. 13, pl. 1308; Rice, 1955, pls. XIX–XX; Mayer, 1959, p. 61; Ettinghausen, 1943, pp. 193–208; Hartner, 1973–4, p. 122, fig. 18.

[111] See however Eva Baer's (1983, pp. 301–2) caveat with regard to the assumption that the *nisba* carried a geographic association that indicates the place of the artist's workshop. Not only could the artist have left his native town but it could also have indicated a special product or specialised technique.

[112] Ivanov, 2004, p. 174; see also *idem*, n. 19 with reference to Oktay Aslapana (1971, p. 284), who came to the same conclusion many years ago.

[113] Another thirteenth-century bucket of Anatolian provenance with handles terminating in dragon heads was sold at Sotheby's, London, 1990; cf. Ivanov, 2004, p. 175, fig. 2.

[114] For al-Jazarī's sources, see *Kitāb fī maʿrifat al-ḥiyāl al-handasiyya*, tr. Hill, 1974, p. 74.

[115] Cf. Rogers, tr., exp. and ed., 1986, p. 30, cat. no. 10.

[116] Fehérvári, 1976, p. 105, cat. no. 131, pl. I.

are portrayed with their heads turned back and their tails intertwined. The well-wishing Arabic inscriptions are typical of Western Central Asian metalwork. In the medieval Islamic world inscriptions bestowing blessings on the owner were often combined with figural decorations of a symbolic or magical intention,[117] in order to magnify the overall apotropaic function intended to benefit the maker and owner of the objects. Not least because of the epigraphic bands which are typical of Khurasani metalwork, the tray has been attributed to the first half of thirteenth-century northeastern Iran; however on the basis of the creatures' entwined tails an Anatolian or Jazīran provenance has recently been suggested.[118]

A related composition also fills the inner band of three zigzag bands that circumscribe the conical base of a thirteenth-century copper alloy candlestick base, inlaid with silver, which is preserved in the Metropolitan Museum of Art, New York. It comprises bilateral compositions of confronted pairs of quadruped dragons in profile. The tail tips of the creatures are entwined with the contiguous addorsed dragons' tails (fig. 36). They are portrayed with their inner forelegs raised, their wide-open jaws revealing the tongues and the upswept, curved wings with tightly curled tip projecting from the haunches. The dragons' hide is covered with scales, the tails knotted at mid-section to form a figure of eight. Importantly, the tapering tail tips transform into small dragon heads which appear to grasp or snap at the serpentine coils.[119] An epigraphic frieze around the shoulder invokes blessings such as glory, prosperity, perfect health, good fortune, felicity, etc., upon the owner. It is notable that the paired dragons have close analogies to the dragon figures carved in low relief on three relief-carved stone panels from the now destroyed city walls, gates or citadel of Konya (618/1221) (fig. 60). Like their monumental cousins, the miniature versions of the dragons on the candlestick base may well have conveyed an impression of might and good fortune, thus augmenting the impact of the epigraphic blessings.

[117] Cf. Kerner, 2004, pp. 218–9 and ns. 79, 80.

[118] Ivanov, 2004, p. 174. The tray is published in the exhibition catalogue *Islam and the Medieval West*, 1975, cat. no. 58. Dimensions 8 inch square. At the time of publication the piece was in the collection of N. Anavian.

[119] Cf. d'Avennes, 1877, pl. 161–5, fig. 3; Dimand, 1926, p. 197, fig. 5.

PART TWO

THE DRAGON AND THE NATURAL WORLD

CHAPTER FOUR

DRAGONS AND THE POWERS OF THE EARTH

a. *The dragon and the elements*

Equally at home on land and sea, the dragon is associated with remote places and phenomena of the natural world. Its aquatic nature is profoundly ambivalent: as water dweller it can be both benevolent guardian and malevolent destroyer. In its threatening manifestation the creature is linked to adverse climatological phenomena such as thunder, rain, lightning or earthquakes.

The symbolic complexity of the dragon is thus expressed through its ability to cross boundaries within the natural environment it inhabits. The distinction between land- and sea-beast is often blurred. That the dragon or the large serpent can be both aquatic and terrestrial was noted in the fifth-century Armenian theological writings of Eznik of Koghb.[1] According to the texts of the *Ikhwān al-Ṣafā'* (Brethren of Purity, established *c.* 373/983), the likeness, character and manner of the dragon is like the sea serpent.[2] Both aquatic and terrestrial, the dragon, like its close cousin the amphibian serpent, is thus characterised by a wet-dry dichotomy as noted by the fourteenth-century scholar Kamāl al-Dīn al-Damīrī in his *Ḥayāt al-ḥayawān al-kubrā*.[3] They dwell not only in springs, wells, rivers, lakes or sea water, but also in mountains, forests, caverns, caves, crevices and other subterranean enclosures, hence lending themselves to association with the underworld and chthonic forces. In tunnelling into the earth and resurfacing again above ground, they are associated with the fertilisation of the earth. Their absence and re-emergence according to the cycle of the seasons (during the dormant season it hibernated in the ground)[4] may also be seen as a metamorphosis.

In the Rigvedic pantheon a primordial "serpent of the deep," *Ahi Budhnyà*, is known;[5] the Vedic *áhi-* meaning "serpent, snake," while *budhnyà-* is an adjectival derivative of *budhnàs* "bottom, base." The origin and abode of the "dragon of the deep" is the dark bottom of heavenly waters, he is "sitting in the depth of rivers" *(budhne nadīnāṃ rajaḥsu sīdan)*.[6] In the Rigveda (dating from 1500–1000 BC) *budhnàs* is used of the root (in heaven) of the cosmological Nyagrodha tree (1.24.7),[7] hence associating the serpent with a tree.[8] In later Indian literature water is known as the abode of serpent demons.[9] Apart from the aquatic monster Gandarəβa who lives in Lake Vārukasha (originally perhaps denoting a specific location such as Lake Aral or the Caspian Sea), the Iranian Zoroastrian dragons were terrestrial creatures, "inhabitants of this world," and the connection with water is less evident in Zoroastrian literature, with the exception of some references to river-dwelling dragons.[10] Yet in almost all of the stories in Iranian literature, the dragon's lair is close to either a source of water or the sea,[11] for instance, the dragon-fighter Garshāsp in the *Garshāsp-nāma* kills a dragon which had emerged from the sea and made its abode on Mount Shekāwand, while Sām in the *Shāh-nāma*[12] slays

[1] *Elc alandoc'*, tr. and ed. Mariès and Mercier, 1959, pp. 593–4, ch. 133.

[2] Tr. and ed. Dieterici, 1858, pp. 114–6.

[3] Tr. Jayakar, 1906, vol. 1, p. 636. See p. 5.

[4] This observation is recorded by al-Bīrūnī in his *Kitāb al-Āthār al-Bāqiya* ("The Chronology of Ancient Nations") (tr. and ed. Sachau, 1876–8, p. 248) in which he states that during the cold season he himself found that:

> ...in Khwārizm, they gather in the interior of the earth and roll themselves up one round the other so that the greatest part of them is visible, and they look like a ball. In this condition they remain during the winter until this time.

[5] Oldenberg, 1894, repr. 1977, pp. 71–2; Watkins, 1995, pp. 460–2.

[6] Grassmann, 1873, repr. 1976, cols. 909–10. Cf. Watkins, 1995, pp. 460–2.

[7] Watkins, 1995, p. 460.

[8] After he was killed by Indra, the Rigvedic hymns (1.32.5) state the following about the dragon Vṛtra: "As trunks of trees, what time the axe hath felled them, low on the earth so lies the prostrate dragon" (tr. Hotchkin Griffith, 1889, p. 20).

[9] Oldenberg, 1894, repr. 1977, p. 71; Vogel, 1926, pp. 32–33, 115–6, 209, 244; Bosch, 1960, pp. 33–4, 51–3, 136–7.

[10] Boyce, 1975, repr. 1996, pp. 90–1.

[11] Cf. Khāleqī-Moṭlaq, "Aždahā II," *EIr*.

[12] Tr. and ed. Mohl, 1838–1878, vol. 1, p. 309,

a dragon from the river Kashafrūd in Khurasan.[13] The dragon's aquatic nature is clearly perceptible in the Armenian *vishap* (Georgian *veshapi*, also a fabulous serpent; Syriac *wshp*; a loanword from the Avestan *vishāpa-*, "whose saliva is poison") was used as an epithet to *azhi*, "serpent,"[14] which was said to dwell in the waters of a lake.[15]

In the ancient Semitic world the predominant belief was that both wood and water are potent generating forces,[16] a notion which continued to exist in the medieval Islamic period.[17] Holy trees are known either by direct assertion or by implication to be associated with spring shrines.[18] Often the sacred spring or well spirit or numen was an accompaniment of a sacred tree[19] or sacred place.[20] Sources of life such as wood and water are also considered to be channels of a greater power; the power that is contained in them is thought to be "contagious."[21]

In the Islamic period trees and twigs as part of trees were widely used for religio-magical purposes, and by extension, any magic rods or wands used in such practices were related to the idea of woody plants.[22] The association of vegetation and the dragon is reflected in the description by the universal historian Abū Jaʿfar Muḥammad ibn Jarīr ibn Yazīd al-Ṭabarī (*c.* 224–5/839–310/923) of the rod of Mūsā (Moses) as a:

> ...two-pronged fork with a crook under the meeting point of the twigs and when it was turned into a serpent, the two twigs formed the mouth of the serpent with its forked tongue, while the crook took the shape of the crest.[23]

The numinous power inherent in the serpent, discussed further below, is also reflected in the Qurʾānic story of Mūsā's rod turning into a serpent, which is an example of the living power of the rod.[24]

The ancient association of the dragon with water is revealed in the names of streams, lakes, pools or springs that are also often compared with each other in poetic simile. The serpent as guardian and custodian of a water source is referred to by the ancient Greek term *drakōn* in the second-century AD compilations of Pseudo-Apollodorus.[25] According to the Byzantine historian Procopius of Caesarea, a river in Bithynia was called Drakōn because its shape resembled that of the fabulous monster.[26] The sacred fountain of Ephca at Palmyra, which is a sulphurous spring, is associated with a demon in serpent form.[27] As William Robertson Smith has pointed out, there are indications that in certain instances the original sanctuary was at a well beneath the town as was the case of the original sanctuaries of Jerusalem, such as the fountain of En-Rogel (1 Kings I, 9, 38) where Adonijah held his sacrificial feast, located near the "serpent's stone" which may possibly be identified with the "dragon well" (Nehemiah II, 13).[28] Sacrifices offered at the well of Abraham at Mamre were said to be eaten by the serpent denizen of the water.[29] In Syria sacred springs were thought to be guarded by spirits in the form of giant pythons.[30] The chronicler of the early Byzantine period, Ioannes Malalas (d. *c.* 570/580), mentions that the partly subterranean river Orontes in Asia Minor was called Drakon,[31]

ll. 1175–176. In the Pahlawī Riwāyat of Garshāsp, the hero fights in the sea with the dragon Gandarw for nine days and nights; after his victory he slaughters fifteen horses and eats them. See Monchi-Zadeh, 1975, p. 138.

[13] The early thirteenth-century historian Ibn Isfandīyār (I, p. 89), probably a native from Āmul, has similarly recorded a tale from Māzandarān in which Sām had vanquished a dragon at an otherwise unknown location called Kāva Kalāda in the same province near the sea; see Khāleqī-Moṭlaq, "Aždahā II," *EIr*.

[14] *Nirangastān* 48, cited after Ananikian, "Armenia (Zoroastrian)," *ERE*, vol. 5, part 2, 1914, p. 800; Skjærvø, "Aždahā I," *EIr*; Boyce, 1975, repr. 1996, p. 91, n. 42.

[15] Russell, 2004, p. 373.

[16] Robertson Smith, 1889, repr. 1927, pp. 132–3, 135–6, 166–7; Jeffers, 1996, p. 145.

[17] Cf. Whitehouse, "Holiness (Semitic)," *ERE* 6, 1913, p. 754.

[18] Cf. Wood, 1916, p. 19.

[19] Robertson Smith, 1889, repr. 1927, p. 136; Jeffers, 1996, p. 163 and n. 107.

[20] *Eadem*, pp. 169–70; Whitehouse, "Holiness (Semitic)," *ERE* 6, 1913, p. 754.

[21] Jeffers, 1996, p. 145.

[22] Cf. Schimmel, 1994, pp. 29–30.

[23] Al-Ṭabarī, *Mukhtaṣar taʾrīkh al-rusul wa ʾl-mulūk wa ʾl-khulafāʾ*, I, Cairo, n.d., p. 401; al-Thaʿlabī, *ʿArāʾis al-majālis fī qiṣaṣ al-anbiyāʾ*, Cairo, n.d., p. 90, cited after Fodor, 1978, p. 4.

[24] Schimmel, 1994, p. 30. It is also of note that Ezekiel (17.3-10) likens the king to a vine and (19:11) calls the vine "fit to be carved into a royal scepter."

[25] Apollodorus, *Bibliotheca* III 4.1. The central episode of the myth of Kadmos is his victory over the spring-guarding *drakōn*, Ares' son, whose teeth he sowed in the earth and out of which grew armed warriors (the *Spartoi*). On the Kadmos myth, see Fontenrose, 1959, repr. 1980, pp. 306–20; Astour, 1965, pp. 156–61.

[26] Procopius VII, *Buildings* V 2.3-10.

[27] Robertson Smith, 1889, repr. 1927, pp. 168–9.

[28] *Idem*, p. 172, n. 3.

[29] *Idem*, p. 177.

[30] Whitehouse, "Holiness (Semitic)," *ERE* 6, 1913, pp. 751–3; Chelhod, 1955, p. 105 and n. 6. For other examples in Syria and Palestine, cf. Robertson Smith, 1889, repr. 1927, pp. 168, 176–7.

[31] *Chronographia*, tr. and ed. Dindorf, 1831, p. 38,1. Cf. Robertson Smith, 1889, repr. 1927, pp. 171–2;

and was, according to Strabo, also known as Typhon and Ophites.[32] The continued association of the Orontes with the mythical dragon is shown in a Turkish legend from Hatay which states that the river was created when the dragon took flight from the mysterious immortal Islamic Prophet Khiḍr by digging underground channels.[33] In Persian the close affiliation between the serpent and the stream of water is reflected in the word *liwāʾ* which comes to mean "the winding of the river" as well as "the twisting or coiling of a serpent."[34] A serpent spring also makes an appearance in the *Kitāb-i Samak ʿAyyār* ("Book of Samak the Adventurer"), collected by Farāmarz ibn Khudādādh al-Arrajānī and written down by Ṣadaqa ibn Abu 'l-Qāsim Shīrāzī,[35] which is thought to be rooted in the Parthian period.[36] The association of the dragon with water is similarly evident in the Transcaucasian tradition. The appellation of the Armenian river Awji near Awjaberd in Geghark'unik' province contains just like the toponym the word *awj* (serpent).[37] One of the most ancient Armenian cults, that of tree worship, is often connected with water sources and serpents. In his collection of Armenian folklore entitled *Krots-Prots* (ch. 9), the eighteenth-century clergyman Garegin Servantsian records the ancient belief that aged serpents come to a certain source to shed their skins, eat a flower which only they know, bathe in the spring and are then rejuvenated. Anyone who finds the same flower and eats it and then drinks three times from the water in which the serpent bathed will similarly become immortal.[38] In pre-Islamic Central Asia, in particular in the regions of present-day Afghanistan, the connection of dragons with water was expressed by the pan-Indic serpent deities *(nāgas)*, the serpent genii, who dwell in terrestrial water sources, and to whom were attributed tempests and floods.[39] In Kashmir, the word *nāg* occurs in a variety of names of springs, rivers, or reservoirs, for instance, Lake Nīla Nāg in the region of Nāgām (ancient Nāgrāma).[40]

This close association of the dragon with the element of water also led to its depiction on waterspouts. This is evidenced in the Islamic period in the example of Karatay Han situated between Kayseri and Malatya. Two of the conduits used for drainage from the gutters of the roof (gargoyles) of the mid-thirteenth-century caravanserai have the appearance of winged dragonite protomes that hold in their wide-open mouths what appears to be the stylised upper body of a human being whose hands clutch the monsters' forelegs (fig. 37).[41]

The dichotomy of the dragons is evident in their activities either as guardians of natural sources or as ravagers in the form of destructive natural phenomena. In the popular mind dragons lent themselves naturally to functioning as symbols for the mysterious and destructive forces of the earth. The notion of dragons as guardians of water

Fontenrose, 1959, repr. 1980, pp. 277–8.

[32] Reportedly this is because the wounded *drakōn* Typhon had crawled into the underground channels of the source of this river to seek shelter from the thunderbolts of Zeus (Strabo, *Geography* XVI, 750). The name of the Greek she-dragon Pythōn (*phuth-* from Vedic *bhudh-*) who is slain by Apollo with his arrow (Fontenrose, 1959, repr. 1980, pp. 13–45) also demonstrates the inherent designation of a serpent creature of the watery deep (Watkins, 1995, p. 461). The Pythōn myth, as Joseph Fontenrose (1959, repr. 1980, pp. 77–93, 193) shows, largely corresponds with that of Typhon. In the Greek tradition the outer ring of the world's water, the ocean (Ogenos-Okeanos), is also the lair of Ophioneus (Ophiūchus), the serpent-man who tried to overcome Zeus (Janda, 2010, pp. 71–89; Russell, 2004, p. 718). In *Phaedo* Plato's literary figure, Socrates, compares the rivers to the serpent: "There are some, then, that after having encircled the earth with one or more coils, like snakes, descend so deeply that they come out at the lowest point of Tartarus," as cited in Mastrocinque, 2005, p. 29. Cf. Robertson Smith, 1889, repr. 1927, p. 176 and n. 4.

[33] Franke, 2000, pp. 100, 547–9.

[34] Cited after Steingass, 1892, repr. 1981, p. 1130.

[35] See the preface of the Oxford *Kitāb-i Samak ʿAyyār* (Bodleian Library Ms. Ouseley 379–81); Sachau and Ethé, 1889, pp. 422–3; Gaillard, 1987, pp. 10–1.

[36] Gaillard, 1987, pp. 64, 155.

[37] Alishan, G., *Hin hawatk' kam het' anosakan krōnk' Hayok'* ("The Ancient Faith or Pagan Religion of the Armenians"), Venice, 1910 ed., pp. 165–6, as cited in Russell, 2004, p. 461.

[38] Ishkol-Kerovpian, "Baum- und Pflanzenkult," *WdM* IV, 1, pp. 105–6.

[39] The *nāgas* are genii of lakes and springs, and are worshipped for their beneficent as well as destructive aspects as powers of the waters. They are considered also as guardians of treasure and givers of vital forces stored up in springs and wells. The accounts of the seventh-century Chinese pilgrim Xuanzang (Hsüan-tsang) show that the *nāga* cult was still flourishing in parts of Western Central Asia and northern India in the seventh century. Cf. *Si-yu-ki*, vol. 1, tr. Beal, 1884, repr. 2000, pp. 121–3. For an in-depth study of the *nāgas* in Indian iconography, see Vogel, 1926.

[40] *Idem*, pp. 227–31, with further examples.

[41] See Erdmann, 1962, pl. IX. Roux (1972, pp. 373–5, figs. 1 and 2), however, recognises these spouts to be sculpted in the form of a fantastic leonine animal. Gargoyles in the form of dragon heads are also found at the fourteenth-century Araboğlu Mosque in Karaman, south of Konya. See *idem*, p. 373, n. 2.

sources, which was well-known in ancient Greek sources,[42] is recorded in the medieval period by the twelfth-century Byzantine scholar Ioannes Tzetzes, a commentator on Lycophron.[43] By contrast, destructive natural phenomena attributed to dragon monsters, also well-established themes in ancient Greek sources,[44] were mentioned by the tenth-century Arab encyclopaedist al-Masʿūdī who associates meteorological phenomena with the mythical creatures. He reports that the Caspian and the Mediterranean (near Tripoli and Latakia) were "prolific in sea monsters" *(kathīr al-tanānīn)*, adding that according to tradition the sea monster *(al-tannīn)* was a "black wind nurtured in the depth of the sea, which ascends to the zephyrs." He adds the account that the *al-tannīn* were:

> ...black serpents existing in the plains and mountains, in which places there are floods and rainstorms, carrying them down into the sea, where they feed upon the sea-creatures so that their bodies attain great size, and their age is extended, and in the end some of them achieve the age of 500 years, and become the lords of the sea. These stories are by no means denied by the Persians, who assert that the monsters have seven heads, and are called *Ajdahā* [*Azhidahāka*].[45]

The celebrated thirteenth-century cosmographer and geographer Zakariyyāʾ ibn Muḥammad ibn Maḥmūd al-Qazwīnī (*c.* 600/1203–4–682/1283), who originated from an Arab family that had been Iranised after settling at Qazwīn, similarly relates that the Iranians believed "the sea-dragon to be either a hurricane or a black serpent dwelling on the sea bottom."[46]

The *Ikhwān al-Ṣafāʾ*, whose *Rasāʾil* (Epistles) appeared in the tenth century, states that, on account of the formidable fire created by the venom which sits between his jaws and moves freely in flames within his body, the dragon endeavours to obtain relief in freezing temperatures. The text describes that as a result of the intensity of the fiery heat of his venom, the dragon-king seeks as abode the peaks of high hills and mountains, above the regions of mild air, in a region where the cold is so intense that there can be neither clouds nor rain, and where neither plants nor animals can survive.[47] Citing Ibn ʿAbbās, al-Masʿūdī, moreover, reports the medieval Islamic idea that "when the tail of a dragon strikes a large edifice, (like) a tree or mountain, it destroys it. Furthermore, at times when the dragon breathes it sets fire to large trees,"[48] apparently describing natural manifestations such as earthquakes. This association between dragons and fire is similarly mentioned in the *Kitāb-i Samak ʿAyyār*.[49] The fiery breath of the notoriously pelagic biblical Leviathan is also described in Job (41:11–3):

> Out of his mouth go burning torches, and sparks of fire leap forth. Out of his nostrils goes smoke, as out of a burning pot or cauldron. His breath kindles coals and a flame goes out of his mouth.

Moses of Chorene's writings also preserve pre-Christian Armenian religious poetry which describes the birth of Vahagn, god of strength and victory. Sudden storms or winds on Lake Van are a sign that dragons *(vishap)* live in the lake, growing there until they are large enough to destroy the world, at which point Vahagn (probably conflated in this story with the Hurrian weather god Teshub, the Urartean Teisheba)[50] drags the dragons up from the depths to take them into the sky to burn up in the sun.[51] The twelfth-

[42] A giant dragon *(drakōn)* guarded the local spring, sacred to the god Ares, at the future site of the Boeotian city Thebes (Apollonius, *Argonautica* 3.1178–87; cf. also Euripides, *Phoenician Women* 930–5 and *Bacchae* 1274, 1314–5).

[43] *Ioannis Tzetzae Historiae*, ed. Leone, P.A.M., Naples, 1968, p. 404, 399, as cited in Bouras, p. 67 and n. 41.

[44] The contumacious Greek primeval monster Typhon was defeated by Zeus but as punishment lived on under the earth (under volcanoes or in Tartaros); he personified volcanism, being thus associated with volcanic eruptions. The classical Greek lyric poet Pindar, for instance, ascribes the volcanic action of Etna in Sicily to the *drakōn* Typhon who was imprisoned under the mountain (*Pythian Odes* 1.15–28; see also Aeschylus, *Prometheus Bound*, 351–72). Typhon also appeared as demon of storms and whirlwinds (Hesiod, *Theogony* 846, 869–80).

[45] *Kitāb marūj al-dhahab*, tr. and ed. Barbier de Meynard and de Courteille, 1917, vol. vol. 1, pp. 266–7.

[46] *Kitāb ʿajāʾib al-makhlūqāt*, ed. Wüstenfeld, 1849, repr. 1967, p. 129. See also Badiee, 1978, pp. 120–1.

[47] Tr. and ed. Dieterici, 1858, pp. 115.

[48] *Kitāb marūj al-dhahab*, tr. and ed. Barbier de Meynard and de Courteille, 1917, vol. 1, p. 267. For a translation of the passage into German, see Monchi-Zadeh, 1975, p. 159, n. 33.

[49] Gaillard, 1987, p. 63.

[50] Geo Widengren (1966, p. 444) suggests an amalgamation of Iranian beliefs held by Armenians with the older Anatolian substratum of the Hurrian song of the monster Ullikummi, whom the weather god Teshub (Urartean Teisheba) smites. Cf. Ishkol-Kerovpian, "Vahagn," *WdM* IV, 1, pp. 149–52; Schwartz, 1975, p. 416; Russell, 1987, p. 29, and *idem*, 2004, pp. 357–61, 373; Mahé, 1994. However, according to Mary Boyce (1975, repr. 1996, p. 64, n. 279), the tale of Vahagn killing a monster may be a late development.

[51] *Patmutʿiwn Hayocʿ*, tr. Langlois, 1872, p. 41 and n. 1. See also Russell, 2004, pp. 357, 361, 617–8 and n. 23, 631 and n. 38, 1132, 1287, n. 39; van Lint, 2009, pp. 257–8.

century Armenian historian Matthew of Edessa (Matt'ēos Uṛhayetsi) relates the eruption of volcanoes to the fiendish nature of dragons, referring to this phenomenon metaphorically as the dragons of Mount Ararat fighting those of Mount Aragac.[52]

An echo of the ancient association of dragons with water seems distantly to reverberate in the ancient Iranian festival of Sada, the celebration of which, according to the historian of the Ghaznawid dynasty, Abu 'l-Faḍl Bayhaqī, resumed during Ghaznawid times. For the celebration of Sada, a festival held fifty days before Nawrūz (the celebration of the return of spring), large fires are lit in commemoration of the Pīshdādian king Hūshang (Haoshyaṅha), the first lawful king who reigned over the seven climes of the world, over the demons and the sorcerers, and according to al-Bīrūnī, and later Firdawsī, was the inventor of fire. As stated by the latter, Hūshang also originated the idea of using irrigation canals. Firdawsī, moreover, records the king's feat of valour in vanquishing a monstrous dragon that infested the country and which the king himself attacked with stones, "when one of them falling with prodigious force upon another, struck fire and set herbage and surrounding trees in a blaze, and consumed the dragon in the flames."[53] The writer adds that the legendary pre-Islamic monarch "gave orders that prayers should be said facing a fire, saying: It is the spark given by God (Īzād); worship it if you are wise."[54]

Sada was held in winter "to strengthen the sun and to help bring back warmth and light to the world."[55] As was customary, *sulṭān* Mas'ūd of Ghazna (the son and successor of Maḥmūd) chose to celebrate it beside a stream, where a fire was lit[56] to aid symbolically the stream of water "in his subterranean task of protecting plants and springs from frost."[57]

The affiliation between dragon, water and earth also becomes apparent in the *Alexander Romance* by the Pseudo-Callisthenes, thought to have originated at some time prior to the third century AD as a collection of oral legends and other material. A good portion of the material was progressively gathered in written form, probably assembled in Alexandria, and entered the Iranian tradition no later than the Sasanian period. In this romance Iskandar (Alexander) is flying through the air on the back of the eagles when, at the highest point of the sky, he sees an enormous serpent whose coils enclose a disc representing the world surrounded by the ocean.[58]

In medieval Iranian poetry, the transformative power of the dragon is sometimes evoked as a portent to signal changes in the course of human events or impending alterations in the cosmic cycle. This type of metaphor is employed in the verse romance, *Wīs u Rāmīn*, composed by Fakhr al-Dīn Gurgānī for the governor of Iṣfahān on behalf of the Saljuqids. The story relates how Rāmīn has become unfaithful to Wīs who remonstrates with him in a long elaborate letter reminding him of her love. Rāmīn sets off to Marw in the hope of a reconciliation with his beloved, but when he arrives on horseback, a snowstorm is in progress. The meteorological phenomenon is figuratively associated with the dragon to evoke human emotions:

> ... the skies became like some vast dragon breathing tongues of flame; the snow was like a poison, since within it men's hearts would freeze and stiffen in a minute, black clouds were massing, blocking out the light, choking back breath, depriving eyes of sight; the snow blew with such force that elephants could not have stood its vehemence.[59]

The natural phenomenon thus described correlates with the human event by functioning as a form of inauspicious portent. A dragon in the form of a black cloud appears also in the epic poem *Bahman-nāma* ("Book of Bahman"), in which Ādar Barzīn, the son of the dragon-slayer Farāmarz, recognises that the cloud is a transformed dragon which came out of a mountain every spring to violate the daughter of the local ruler, Bīwarāsp/Dahāk. He kills the dragon with

[52] Abeghyan, M., *Erkeri Zhoghovadsu* ("Collected Works"), Erevan, 1966–75, vol. 7, p. 65, and *Avandapatum*, no. 11, as cited in Russell, 1987, p. 206.

[53] Cited after Steingass, 1892, repr. 1981, p. 663.

[54] Massé, "Hūshang," *EI*² III, 637b.

[55] Boyce, 1983, p. 800.

[56] Bayhaqī, *Ta'rīkh-i Mas'ūdī*, ed. Ghanī and Fayyūḍ, Tehran, 1324/1945, p. 278, as cited in Lambton, "Marasīm: 3. In Iran," *EI*² VI, 518a.

[57] Boyce, 1983, p. 801.

[58] Pseudo-Callisthenes II, ch. 41, tr. and ed. Stoneman, 1991, p. 123. Cf. the imagery described in Reitzenstein, 1904, p. 31; Millet, 1923, p. 94; Grabar, 1951, pp. 47–8; see also the discussion on the astral ascension of the Sasanian king in L'Orange, 1953, pp. 64–79, which argues for a primeval oriental origin of the motif of Iskandar's heavenly ascent (p. 69).

[59] Tr. and ed. Davis, 2008, p. 448.

arrows and then washes at a spring.[60] In this story the killing of the dragon is followed by contact with water. In the *Shāh-nāma* a similar reference is made. Both heroes, Rustam, after he had killed the dragon Babr-i bayān which came out of the sea once a week, and Borzū, after he had vanquished the dragon on Mount Zahāb, lose consciousness, and on reviving also wash themselves in a spring.[61] Likewise in another episode of the *Shāh-nāma*, after accomplishing the third of his seven trials *(haft khʷān)*, that of slaying the dragon, Isfandiyār, one of the prince-heroes of the epic and eldest son of *shāh* Gushtāsp, loses consciousness. On reviving, "he called for a new garment, and then immersed himself in a nearby stream, washed the dirt from his body. Thus cleansed, he came before the Lord. Down on the ground again, contorting and writhing like a serpent, he cried out:

> Must it not be that the dragon-slayer is constantly sustained by the One who grips the world?

The troops invoked blessings upon their leader, and all of the company bowed low before the Just Provider."[62] Frequent reference is thus made in the legends to a loss of consciousness of the hero in the aftermath of the dragon-slaying and his subsequent contact with water that is known to have a "magical" cleansing effect and to be a transformative agent. The purification thus constitutes a rite of separation from the act that has been accomplished.

That water is an agent of transformation is further evidenced in an account of the slaying of a dragon *(shīr-i kappī)* in Turkestan by Bahrām Chōbīn, Sasanian commander of Hurmuz IV (r. 578–590), rival to the throne of his son Khusraw II Parwīz. However, in this case it is the dragon that would become invulnerable if it went to a certain spring and wetted its hair.[63]

b. *The serpent(-dragon)* jinn

Sources of water such as wells or streams, manifestations of life around which vegetation spread, were thought to be endowed with properties of generation, cleansing and in some cases with medicinal or healing virtues.[64] These were sometimes also regarded by the Arabs and other Semites as inhabited by the serpent genie *(jinn)*, and hence had a sacred significance.[65] Serpents as well as the *jinn* (pl. *ajnān*, "genii"),[66] the supernatural spirits invisible to the human eye, whose existence is recognised in the Qurʾān (*sūra*s 72, 130; 37, 158; 51, 56; and 55, 15), were considered from the oldest times as the general earthly genius loci of trees, in particular roots of trees, as well as caves, springs and wells.[67] According to a tradition of the Prophet Muḥammad cited by al-Damīrī in his para-zoological encyclopaedia, chthonic creatures such as serpents represent one of three categories of *jinn*.[68] While usually invisible, the *jinn* liked to manifest, according to Muslim popular belief, as creeping creatures, reptiles and amphibians, in particular serpents.[69] In pre-Islamic Arabia, the *jinn* were regarded as semi-divinities.[70] The serpents' close association with metamorphosis was motivated by their mutant nature, manifested by behaviour such as the periodical sloughing off their skin, living in water or tunnels beneath the earth and alternating between land and water. This aptitude to metamorphose was often seen

---

[60] *Bahman-nāma*, BM Or. 2780, fols. 180, 181, as cited in Khāleqī-Moṭlaq, "Aždahā II," *EIr*. Cf. Hanaway, "Bahman-nāma," *EIr*.

[61] Cf. Khāleqī-Moṭlaq, "Aždahā II," *EIr*.

[62] Tr. and ed. Mohl, 1838–1878, vol. 4, p. 503, ll. 1702–1714. English tr. as cited in Dickson and Welch, 1981, vol. II, p. 201. See also al-Thaʿālibī, *Taʾrīkh Ghurar al-siyar*, tr. and ed. Zotenberg, 1900, pp. 309–12.

[63] Khāleqī-Moṭlaq, "Aždahā II. In Persian Literature," *EIr*.

[64] Robertson Smith, 1889, repr. 1927, p. 168.

[65] Whitehouse, "Holiness (Semitic)," *ERE* 6, 1913, p. 754; Robertson Smith, 1889, repr. 1927, pp. 119, 168, 171–2, 176.

[66] Closely related to the nature of the *jinn* seem to be the Armenian *shahapet*s, serpent genii of places, and as such "supernatural protectors" of tombs, homesteads or rural sites, often also residing in vegetation, especially trees. Aghatangelos, pp. 56–7, as cited in "461.šahap," "462.šahapet," Hübschmann, 1895, pp. 208–9. On the *shahapet*s, see Ananikian, 1925, pp. 74–6; Ishkol-Kerovpian, "Šahapet," *WdM* IV, 1, p. 136; Russell, 1987, pp. 329–34. The fifth-century Armenian apologist, Eznik of Koghb (fl. *c.* 430–*c.* 450), Bishop of Bagrewand, notes that they:

> ...appeared sometimes as a man, sometimes as a serpent, because of which it was made possible for serpent-worship to be introduced into the world.

*Elc alandoc*ʿ, tr. and ed. Mariès and Mercier, 1959, p. 594, ch. 138; see also pp. 574–5, ch. 64. The theme of the serpent as *genius loci* occurs also in the *Alexander Romance*; Pseudo-Callisthenes I, ch. 32, tr. and ed. Stoneman, 1991, p. 65.

[67] Wellhausen, 1897, pp. 106, 212, 214. Robertson Smith, 1889, repr. 1927, p. 120, n. 1. Macdonald [Massé], "Djinn," *EI*² II, 546b. Zbinden, 1953, p. 49.

[68] Tr. Jayakar, 1906, vol. 1, p. 449.

[69] Nöldeke, 1860, pp. 412–4, and *idem*, 1913, p. 669; Robertson Smith, 1889, repr. 1927, pp. 120, 129; Ruska, "Ḥayyā," *EI*² III, 334b; Gohrab, 2000, p. 87.

[70] Robertson Smith, 1889, repr. 1927, pp. 121–3, 138. Cf. Macdonald [Massé], "Djinn," *EI*² II, 546b.

as a source of numinous or demonic power. As primarily chthonic creatures, yet able to undergo so portentous a transformation, the *jinn* embody "the undefined and innominate divine,"[71] having a very close and necessary link with the serpent.[72]

The close association of some *jinn* with trees through their characterisation as the spirit that resides in vegetation,[73] is exemplified in the story of Ḥarb ibn Omayya and Mirdās ibn Abī ʿĀmir, historical persons who lived a generation before Muḥammad. When the two men set fire to an inaccessible, knotty thicket, the *jinn,* taking the form of white serpents, flew out of the burning grove of al-Qurayya with doleful cries and the intruders died soon afterwards.[74] It is believed that the *jinn* slew them "because they had set fire to their dwelling place" and thus violated their haunt.[75]

In the Islamic period the pagan gods of the so-called Jāhiliyya period, considered to be the time of ignorance and false beliefs, were broken, their sanctuaries destroyed and their guardians dispersed.[76] The gods and demigods were subsequently downgraded into *jinn.*[77] The serpent was one of the most ancient sacred symbols of the pre-Islamic cults,[78] however since Islam broke with these pre-Islamic practices, Muḥammad gave orders to kill the serpent *(amara bi-qatli-l-aym)* even in the midst of prayer,[79] even if the believer is in a state of sacralisation *(iḥrām)*, or in the sacred enclosure of the Meccan sanctuary.[80] Yet these pre-Islamic cults were only gradually and hesitantly abandoned.[81] The ninth-century historian of Mecca and its sanctuary, al-Azraqī (d. 222/837), reports on the authority of Ṭalq ibn Ḥabīb that in the first century of Islam a male serpent circumambulated the Kaʿba, the most sacred building of Islam, called the House of God *(bayt Allāh)*, located in the centre of the Great Mosque of Mecca, and when warned by the Muslims that were present, suddenly took to the skies and disappeared:

> We were seated with ʿAbd Allāh b. ʿAmr b. al-ʿĀṣ in the Ḥijr; the sun having come there (the shade having contracted) the assembly rose up, when we beheld the glistening of a serpent which had come out of the gate of the Beni-Shaibah [Banū Shayba]. The eyes of the men were raised to look at it; it went the circuit of the House seven times and prayed with two bendings of the body behind the place of Abraham, when we went and said to it, 'O thou visitor, God has ordained thy blood to be shed, and there are in our land slaves and fools of whose mischief to thee we are afraid?' It then went away in the direction of the sky and we did not see any more of it.[82]

Theodor Nöldeke has associated the behaviour of these Muslims with the belief in *jinn*,[83] probably in order to give an explanation for such vestiges of the ancient cults.[84] Even so the Prophet Muḥammad insisted on regarding the serpent as

[71] Wellhausen, 1897, repr. 2007, p. 106.

[72] Nöldeke, 1860, p. 413.

[73] The ancient conception of trees as animated beings (in ancient Greece, for instance, Aristotle, *De plantis*, I, p. 815; Plutarch, *De placitis philosophorum*, V, 26; for Hebrew lore, see Judges, 9–10; 2 Kings, 9), also explains the particularly close association of *jinn* with trees; cf. Robertson Smith, 1889, repr. 1927, pp. 132–3.

[74] Abu 'l-Faraj, *Aghānī* VI, p. 92 and XX, pp. 135–7; Yāqūt, *Muʿjam al-buldān* III, p. 85, as cited in Wellhausen, 1897, repr. 2007, pp. 152–3; Robertson Smith, 1889, repr. 1927, p. 133; Zbinden, 1953, p. 76. Moreover, killing a serpent is said to make enemies of the spirits; see Henninger, 2004, pp. 15–6.

[75] Abu 'l-Faraj, *Aghānī* VI, p. 92 and XX, 135–7, cited after Robertson Smith, 1889, repr. 1927, p. 133.

[76] Atallah, 1975, p. 166.

[77] Robertson Smith, 1889, repr. 1927, p. 120.

[78] Atallah, 1975, p. 166. There was a custom to take sacred oaths "by the serpent between the two *ḥarra* [basaltic lava fields]," recorded in Ibn Hishām's edition of the Ibn Isḥāq's *Sīra*, ed. Wüstenfeld, 1857, p. 16; Ibn al-Athīr, *Nihāya*, I, p. 450; *The History of al-Ṭabarī*, vol. 5, tr. and ed. Bosworth, 1999, p. 179 and n. 460. Cf. Robertson Smith, 1889, repr. 1927, p. 130, n. 1; Atallah, 1975, p. 167. Wahib Atallah (pp. 162–9) moreover conclusively deduces that the translations for the sacred phrases, *Aymu-l-Lāh* and *Aymu-l-Kaʿba* were "by the serpent of God" and "by the serpent of the Kaʿba," respectively, and hence meant that, just like the oath discussed above, these formulas were made "by the sacred serpent."

[79] For this as well as further traditions, see Ḥamd Allāh al-Mustawfī al-Qazwīnī, *The Zoological Section of the Nuzhatu-l-qulūb*, tr. and ed. Stephenson, J., London, 1928, Persian text, pp. 55–6, tr. p. 38, as cited in Ettinghausen, 1955, p. 277.

[80] Al-Azraqī, *Kitāb Akhbār Makka*, I, pp. 377–9, as cited in Atallah, 1975, p. 166.

[81] *Idem*, p. 166.

[82] Cited in al-Damīrī, *Ḥayāt al-ḥayawān al-kubrā*, tr. Jayakar, 1906, vol. 1, p. 221. The French translation of the text more precisely states: "…"Être pieux, *muʿtamir*, Dieu a agrée ta prière et ta visite du lieu saint. Mais, notre pays ne manque pas d'esclaves ni d'hommes incapables d'apprécier le bien, *sufahāʾ*. Nous craignons qu'il t'arrive malheure." Alors, le serpent gonfla sa tête en forme de boule, *baṭḥāʾ*, il enroula sa queue autour de cette boule, il s'énleva dans les airs et disparu dans le ciel." Al-Azraqī, *Kitāb Akhbār Makka*, I, p. 263, as cited in Atallah, 1975, p. 166.

[83] Nöldeke, 1860, p. 415.

[84] In his commentary on Ibn Hishām (ed. Wüstenfeld, vol. 2, pp. 41–2) ʿAbd al-Raḥmān al-Suhaylī notes that in several cases an orthodox Muslim is said to have wrapped a dead serpent in a piece of his cloak and to have buried it.

an enemy of Islam,[85] as shown in several canonical traditions (the so-called *ḥadīth*)[86] such as: "We have not made peace with serpents since the time we became their enemies;"[87] "whoever leaves them [the serpents] (alone) is not one of us;"[88] "whoever leaves a serpent alone from fear of its revenging itself on him, has on him the curse of God, the angels and men, – all of them;"[89] "whoever kills a serpent will have as it were killed a man believing in the plurality of gods, and whoever leaves a serpent (alone) fearing retaliation from it, is not one of us."[90]

Yet these dictates had to be eased with regard to domestic serpents[91] and it is known that Muḥammad saw in each serpent not only a maleficent but also a benign spirit,[92] thus continuing to ascribe to them a certain positive power. According to tradition, it is forbidden to kill serpents that dwell in human habitation because these are beneficial *jinn*.[93] Before killing a domestic serpent it has to be forewarned three times, or during three days,[94] of the danger it faces and of the obligation of the faithful to pursue it.[95] The persistent adherence to the belief that every house has its serpent guardian that is the real owner of the place – probably linked to the belief in ancestral spirits – may in some way be connected with this tradition.[96] Al-Damīrī also records the interpretation of a dream in his *Ḥayāt al-ḥayawān al-kubrā* which underlines the continued importance accorded to domestic serpents:

> If one dreams as if the serpents out of a place have disappeared, there will be an epidemic (of plague), and the mortality in that place will increase, for serpents indicate life.[97]

Post-Qur'ānic traditions thus portray the (serpent-)dragon as no more than the genius loci, fulfilling solely the function of guardian.[98] Yet it appears that in spite of official strictures, the cult of the serpent was abandoned only slowly under Islam, while domestic serpents, considered as beneficial *jinn* in their role as genius loci, continued to be tolerated.

The traditions also maintain that the Ka'ba, the most famous sanctuary of Islam, was built upon a serpent. When Abraham (Ibrāhīm) wished to build the Ka'ba, the Sakīna (the Hebrew *shekhīnā*, "dwelling," or "presence," is usually considered the source for the Arabic *sakīna*)[99] unfolded itself like a snake on the first foundations which had already been laid by Adam or the angels, saying, "Build upon me,"[100] "and so he built; hence every Bedouin in flight and every powerful person inevitably circumambulates the sanctuary under the Sakīna's protection."[101] Al-Ṭabarī expounds on this tradition and describes the serpent as

In order to justify these vestiges of the ancient cults the serpent was said to represent "a believing *jinn*"; cf. al-Damīrī, I, p. 233, cited after Robertson Smith, 1889, repr. 1927, p. 444, n. 1.

[85] Al-Damīrī, *Ḥayāt al-ḥayawān al-kubrā*, tr. Jayakar, 1906, vol. 1, p. 649. Cf. Atallah, 1975, p. 166.

[86] The term *ḥadīth*, or "communication," denotes codified reports that convey the normative sayings and deeds of the Prophet Muḥammad, based, according to Muslim belief, on first-hand accounts of reliable witnesses to those utterances and events; after the Qur'ān, the *ḥadīth* constitute the second most important basis of Islamic law.

[87] Al-Damīrī, *Ḥayāt al-ḥayawān al-kubrā*, tr. Jayakar, 1906, vol. 1, pp. 649–50. Cf. Atallah, 1975, pp. 166–7.

[88] *Op. cit.*

[89] *Op. cit.*

[90] *Op. cit.*

[91] Atallah, 1975, p. 167. Cf. Massé, 1938, vol. 1, pp. 201–2.

[92] Nöldeke, 1860, p. 415; Wellhausen, 1897, repr. 2007, p. 153.

[93] Nöldeke, 1860, pp. 415–6; Wellhausen, 1897, repr. 2007, pp. 151, 164; Zbinden, 1953, p. 76; Henninger, 2004, p. 31.

[94] Al-Damīrī, *Ḥayāt al-ḥayawān al-kubrā*, tr. Jayakar, 1906, vol. 1, pp. 650–1; cf. Atallah, 1975, p. 167.

[95] Ibn al-Athīr, *Nihāya*, ed. Zāwī, Cairo, 1963, "ḥarağ," I, p. 362, cited after Atallah, 1975, p. 167.

[96] Donaldson, 1938, repr. 1973, p. 168; Atallah, 1975, p. 167. These house snakes are revered also throughout the Persian-speaking world; see Russell, 1987, p. 461. The fifth-century Armenian author Eznik of Koghb writes for instance that "now if there be a heathen who may think a being evil by nature, let him be opposed by the co-practitioners of his own art, the worshippers of serpents, for they now tame serpents to such a degree that they can call them into houses of talismans *(yuṙt 'iwk')* and offer them food, as did the Babylonians with the dragon they worshipped, but the beloved of God killed it with the same accustomed food." *Elc alandoc'*, tr. and ed. Mariès and Mercier, 1959, p. 575, ch. 65. The dragon-killing mentioned by Eznik refers to the apocryphal book of the Old Testament Bel and the Dragon in the book of Daniel LXX in which there was giant serpent *(drakōn)* worshipped at Babylon which was killed by feeding lumps of a concoction of pitch, fat and hair to the dragon, causing it to burst. Cf. Gunkel, 1895, pp. 320–3. There is a distinct possibility that ophiolatry and ophiomancy (cf. al-Bīrūnī, *Kitāb al-Āthār*, tr. and ed. Sachau, 1876–8, pp. 217–9, see *Jadwal al-ikhtiyārāt* ("Table of Selections"); Panaino, 2005, p. 73–89) was practised in the Persian-speaking world. In this connection it is of interest to note that the Yezidis venerate a serpent carved at the height of a man and painted black on the wall to one side of the entrance to their holiest shrine, Shaykh 'Adī, near Mosul in Mesopotamia. See Russell, 1987, p. 461; Bachmann, 1913, pls. 14–6.

[97] Tr. Jayakar, 1906, vol. 1, p. 656.

[98] Wensinck, 1916, repr. 1978, p. 60.

[99] Fahd, "Sākīna," EI^2 VIII, 888b.

[100] Al-Azraqī, *Kitāb Akhbār Makkah*, ed. Wüstenfeld, 1858–61, p. 30, as cited in Wensinck, 1916, repr. 1978, p. 60. Fahd, "Sākīna," EI^2 VIII, 888b.

[101] *Op. cit.*

"a stormy wind with two heads. One of them followed the other till it reached Mecca; there it wound itself like a serpent on the spot of the sacred house."[102] The foundation of the Kaʿba is further described as "a wind called the wind Al-Khadjūdj which had two wings and a head like a serpent's."[103] A similar description is given by Ḥusayn ibn Muḥammad al-Diyārbakrī in his *Taʾrīkh al-khamīs* in which it is said to possess "two serpents' heads, one behind the other."[104] Such traditions endow the great serpent with a sacred as well as a mythological character.

In Islamic tradition, the (serpent-)dragon is thus closely associated with the foundation of the Kaʿba. It evidently has not only a mythological or apotropaic function but a sacred character, following the ancient Semitic and Iranian traditions.[105] Its supernatural qualities are manifest in the winged and double-headed appearance. It is further significant, as Arent Jan Wensinck points out, that in most of the traditions the Meccan serpent is either the Sakīna or a being sent by God, hence "not a demoniac but a divine being."[106]

Finally, a madman was said to be supernaturally possessed by *jinn (majnūn)*.[107] At the same time, *jinn* sometimes endowed men with special knowledge as seems to be implied by the word for the mantic figure of a poet *(shaʿīr)*, who was thought to be endowed with demonic or supernatural inspiration. The close association of the *jinn* with serpents is also emblematised in Iranian literature. In his romantic epic of the popular legend *Laylā wa Majnūn*, Niẓāmī of Ganja in Azerbaijan uses ophidian imagery to depict the lovers.[108] In particular Majnūn's serpent-like appearance and his dwelling in a cave or ruin underline the fact that he is possessed by *jinn*:

> There, in that particular ruined place,
> He is creeping like a serpent over a stone.
> He is insane, in pain and distressed,
> and like a demon, he is far from the eye of man.
> Due to his wounds, his soul is pierced;
> the marrow of his bones can be seen.[109]

c. *The treasure-guarding dragon*

Just as the dragon keeps the wealth of the waters concealed, it also keeps, by implication, guard over the wealth which is concealed in the earth. The belief concerning dragons guarding treasures hidden in the earth and the sources of nature's abundance may be linked with their chthonic nature.[110]

Within the sanctuary of the Kaʿba in Mecca a deep pit or well was situated, called *khizāna* ("treasury"), on account of the offerings of jewellery and precious objects that were thrown

---

102 Al-Ṭabarī, *Mukhtaṣar taʾrīkh al-rusul wa ʾl-mulūk wa ʾl-khulafāʾ*, vol. 1, tr. and ed. de Goeje, 1879–1901, p. 275, 8–10, cited after Wensinck, 1916, repr. 1978, p. 61 and n. 2. The pre-Islamic origins of the belief in serpents as guardians of graves and foundations in general (see Wensinck, 1916, repr. 1978, p. 60) are supported by Gustaf Dalman's research in Petra, where he photographed a large conical stone carved in relief with a coiled serpent (1908, vol. 1, pp. 218–20, figs. 141–3). It was placed upon a gigantic stone block under which is a large room with niches for the reception of the deceased.

103 Al-Ṭabarī, *Mukhtaṣar taʾrīkh al-rusul wa ʾl-mulūk wa ʾl-khulafāʾ*, vol. 1, ed. de Goeje, 1879–1901, p. 276, 16–7, as cited in Wensinck, 1916, repr. 1978, p. 61.

104 Vol. 1, Cairo, 1283, p. 98, as cited in Wensinck, 1916, repr. 1978, p. 61.

105 Cf. Wensinck, 1916, repr. 1978, p. 60.

106 *Idem*, p. 65.

107 Robertson Smith, 1889, repr. 1927, p. 128.

108 Cf. Gohrab, 2000, pp. 83–95, esp. 87–93.

109 Ed. Asgharzada, A.A., and Babayev, F., Baku, 1965, ch. 20, 51–3, cited after Gohrab, 2000, p. 87. Closely related imagery is abundantly used in the romance *Wīs u Rāmīn*, tr. and ed. Davis, 2008, pp. 29, 89, 195, 209, 236, 473.

110 In an Ugaritic poem of Baal V AB:D 35–44, the goddess ʿAnat declares that:

> Did I not crush El's Darling, Sea?
> Nor destroy River, the great god?
> Nor muzzle Tannin full well?
> I crushed the writhing serpent,
> The powerful one of seven heads,
> ...
> I fought and I inherited gold.

Hence by fighting one or more dragons, which apparently guarded the gold, ʿAnat obtained the precious metal. Cited after Astour, 1965, pp. 291–2. In ancient Greek lore the great dragon *(drakōn)* who guards some treasure or holy site was an important theme, and either protects its holdings as its own possession or was placed there by the owner of the site as its guardian. The subterranean golden apples located in the uttermost parts of the earth in the garden of the Hesperides were guarded by the Nymphs, daughters of Atlas, and the *drakōn* (Hesiod, *Theogony* 333–5); the oracle at Delphi was protected by the female dragon (*drakaina*) Pythōn that was killed by Apollo; the spring at Thebes was watched over by a *drakōn* killed by Kadmos, and the golden fleece was guarded by a *drakōn* killed by Medea or Jason. Euripides (*Herakles* 397, tr. after Buschor, Munich, 1952) calls the treasure-guarding serpent the "reddish *drakōn*, the formidable coiled gurdian." Plato notes that owing to his sharp sight, the dragon guards hidden treasures as well as temples and oracles (*Phaedrus*, 4.20.3–4); cf. Merkelbach, "Drache," *RAC* IV, 1959, pp. 226–7. For post-biblical Jewish sources describing the Genesis serpent as possessing "silver, gold, gems, and pearls," before the Fall, see Ginzberg, 1909–38, repr. 1946 and 1955, vol. 1, p. 71. The treasure-guarding serpent is also known in Indian lore, such as the fable in the into it and preserved there.[111] This was probably done with the intention, as Wensinck suggests, of appeasing the god of the netherworld.[112] Islamic tradition relates how in the period shortly before the rise of Islam, at a time when the ancient Arab tribes of the Jurhum controlled the Kaʿba, these treasures were stolen from the sanctuary.[113] Thereupon, according to the *Kitāb Akhbār Makkah* ("Book of Information on Mecca") assembled by al-Azraqī, the ninth-century historian of Mecca and its sanctuary,[114] God sent "a serpent which had a black back and a white belly and a head like the head of a he-goat; this serpent guarded the sacred House [and its treasure] during five hundred years."[115] The serpent is called a "large serpent" and has its dwelling place in the pit of the Kaʿba, where it guards the treasures.[116] It is fed by daily food offerings thrown into the sacred pit by the faithful and basks in the sun on the stones of the Kaʿba.[117] This is further elaborated in the biography of the Prophet Muḥammad by the Arab author ʿAlī ibn Burhān al-Dīn al-Ḥalabī who writes that "Allāh sent a white serpent with a black head and a black tail and its head was like the head of a he-goat. It had to dwell in this pit in order to guard the objects there."[118] Al-Azraqī notes that as a result the treasure of the Kaʿba held all the votive offerings, including arrows used for divination, jewellery for adorning idols, and gold,[119] and also that Muḥammad uncovered a large amount of gold in the well.[120] During the pre-Islamic period, sacred serpents were also known to have guarded the sanctuaries at Nakhla where the cult of the goddess al-ʿUzzā prospered as well as at Dawmat al-Jandal where the god Wadd was served.[121] These sacred serpents were also fed at the sanctuaries, often with milk.[122]

According to the tenth-century Arabic geographer Abū Muḥammad al-Ḥasan ibn Aḥmad al-Hamdānī (d. 334/945–6), a treasure lay hidden near the high mountains Ḥufāsh and Milḥān (Rayshān) in south Arabia. Many Arabs sought this treasure but they were always prevented from reaching it by a serpent in the shape of a high mountain which barred their approach.[123]

The indirect association of the serpent with wealth in the interpretation of a dream is recorded by al-Damīrī in his *Ḥayāt al-ḥayawān al-kubrā* according to which:

> He who dreams of being bitten by a serpent, in consequence of which the bitten part is swollen, will obtain great wealth, for the poison indicates wealth and the swelling indicates an increase in it.[124]

Panchatantra of the hooded serpent in the anthill who daily bestows a gold piece on the poor Brahmin Haridatta (Vogel, 1926, pp. 173–4) or the legend of the gold-guarding black serpent of Rājagṛiha who was subdued by the Buddha (*Avadāna Śalākā* IV, 1, ed. Spencer, vol. 2, pp. 289–91, as cited by Vogel, 1926, p. 21). Al-Bīrūnī records an episode from the *Saṁhitā* in which Varuṇa's son, Agastya, devoured the water of the ocean so that it disappeared, revealing the lower parts of Mount Vindhya:

> ...whilst the *makara* and the water animals were clinging to it. They scratched the mountain till they pierced it and dug mines in it, in which there remained gems and pearls.

Kitāb fī Taḥqīq mā li-l-Hind, tr. Sachau, 1887, p. 93. The simile of the pearl-guarding monster similarly appears in *Wīs u Rāmīn*, tr. and ed. Davis, 2008, p. 473.

[111] Al-Azraqī, *Kitāb Akhbār Makkah*, ed. Wüstenfeld, 1858–61, pp. 41, 14–6; 49, 1; 106, 14–6; 111, 11; 169; 171, 4; as cited in Wensinck, 1916, repr. 1978, pp. 29–30. Atallah, 1975, p. 164.

[112] Wensinck, 1916, repr. 1978, p. 30; see also Wellhausen, 1897, repr. 2007, p. 103; Atallah, 1975, p. 164.

[113] Al-Azraqī, *Kitāb Akhbār Makkah*, ed. Wüstenfeld, 1858–61, p. 48, 8–10, cited after Wensinck, 1916, repr. 1978, p. 63.

[114] The book was put together before 251/865, although it also includes references from as late as 310/922–3; cf. Grabar, 1985, p. 2 and n. 12.

[115] Ed. Wüstenfeld, 1858–61, p. 48, 8–10, German tr. vol. 4, pp. 12–3, 85, as cited in Wensinck, 1916, repr. 1978, p. 63. Cf. Atallah, 1975, p. 164.

[116] Ed. Wüstenfeld, 1858–61, p. 170, 10, cited after Wensinck, 1916, repr. 1978, p. 63. On the account of the serpent in the well of the Kaʿba, sent by God to guard its treasury in the time before the Kaʿba was secured with doors and a lock, see Canova, 1994, pp. 421–5.

[117] Atallah, 1975, p. 164. The role of the paternal grandfather of the Prophet, ʿAbd al-Muṭṭalib, in providing security for the treasury of the Kaʿba is also of relevance with regard to the possible existence of a serpent cult at the site in pre-Islamic times. Cf. Nöldeke, 1869, p. 416; Fahd, 1968, esp. pp. 40–1; Atallah, 1975, p. 166.

[118] *Al-Sīra al-Ḥalabiyya*, Cairo, 1292, vol. 1, p. 189, 3–5, as cited in Wensinck, 1916, repr. 1978, pp. 63–4 and n. 1.

[119] *Kitāb Akhbār Makkah*, pp. 119–24.

[120] *Idem*, p. 124; al-Qāḍī al-Rashīd ibn al-Zubayr, *Kitāb al-Hādāya wa 'l-Tuḥaf* ("Book of Gifts and Rarities"), tr. Ghādah al-Ḥijjāwī al-Qaddūmī, no. 175.

[121] Atallah, 1975, p. 165.

[122] *Idem*, pp. 164–6. The notion that serpents are drawn to milk appears also in the tale of the "Queen of the Serpents" included in *Alf layla wa-layla* where the Serpent-Queen is enticed into a cage by bowls of milk and wine (*The Book of the Thousand Nights and a Night*, tr. Burton, 1885, vol. 2, pp. 594–6).

[123] *Ṣifat Jazīrat al-ʿArab*, ("Description of the Arab Peninsula"), ed. Müller, Leiden, 1884, p. 68, as cited in Schleifer, "Ḥufāsh," *EI*² III, 548b.

[124] Tr. Jayakar, 1906, vol. 1, p. 655.

In another interpretation, the dreamer is not bitten by a serpent but merely dreams of a smooth serpent that he can take wherever he likes, which is interpreted as a sign that the dreamer will become wealthy:

> If one dreams of possessing a sleek (smooth) serpent which he has taken wherever he likes, [he] will obtain riches and become prosperous.[125]

Moreover a dream of a black serpent (instead of a smooth serpent) is said to indicate the acquisition of power and governance:

> He who dreams of possessing a black serpent will acquire a kingdom and government.[126]

The motif of a black snake as positive augury also appears in the *Shāh-nāma* when the young Buzurjmihr, the later minister of Khusraw Anūshirwān, was breathed on by a black snake which was interpreted by his companion who witnessed the scene as a sign that Buzurjmihr would attain a position of great power.[127]

The association of the colour black with the concept of royalty is interesting and may perhaps be related to the black banner of the ʿAbbasids (black being supposedly the colour of the Prophet's banner) but could also be a vestige of conceptualisations that were introduced by the Turko-Mongol dynasties for whom the colour carried exalted associations.[128]

In his romance *Haft Paykar*, which was completed in 593/1197, the poet Niẓāmī Ganjawī refers to "dragon-like locks on treasures rested."[129] Surviving examples of such dragon locks are rare.[130] However dragon knockers that have a part attached to a door, and another part linked to it by a hinge that may be lifted and used to strike a plate fitted to a door are used to gain entrance to a monument. Well-known examples are, for instance, the copper alloy knockers discussed below that adorned the doors of the Great Mosque (Ulu Cami) of Cizre (the former Jazīrat ibn ʿUmar), now in the Türk ve İslam Eserleri Müzesi in Istanbul (figs. 82 and 83).

The motif of the treasure-guarding dragon appears also in the first part of Niẓāmī's prose romance *Iskandar-nāma* ("Alexander Romance"), called *Sharaf-nāma* ("Book of Honour"). He describes how a certain Balīnūs, whose name is the Arabic version of Apollonius (of Tyana), a renowned sage and magician of the first century AD and author of several handbooks on magic, accompanied Iskandar, represented as an Islamicised Graeco-Iranian hero,[131] on his conquest of

---

[125] *Idem*, p. 656. It is interesting to compare this with the Zoroastrian practice of taking snake omens as recorded in the New Persian text, the *Mār-nāma* ("Book of Snakes") included in the Persian Riwāyats of Dastūr Dārāb Hormazdyār that date from 1679; one of the verse-lines stating, for instance, "If you see a snake on the day of Hormazd, your honour, property and income will increase." See Panaino, 2005, p. 79.

[126] *Idem*, p. 656.

[127] Tr. and ed. Mohl, 1838–1878, vol. 6, pp. 247–9, ll. 1037–1045.

[128] The adjective *qara*, literally "black," designates the prime compass point of the north, the place of origin of the Altaic tribes, hence acquiring the meaning "principal," "chief" (in contrast to other compass points which are also described in terms of colour such as *ak* ("white") indicating the south). Cf. Pritsak, 1950–5, pp. 244–5, 255. *Qara* was used in the onomastic of the Turkish tribes (for instance, the eighth-century seasonal camp of the eastern Turks, Qara Qum; the Uighur capital from 744 to 840, Qarabalghasun; the southern Uighur capital after 840, Qara Xocho; and the first Yuan capital, Qaraqorum) and as an epithet to the names of Xiongnu and Turkic rulers. There are also the Qara-Qitai ("Black Qitan") who after the fall of the Liao empire ruled over nearly the whole of Central Asia from the Oxus to the Altai mountains until 1175 and the Qarakhanids that ruled in the lands of Central Asia straddling the T'ien-shan mountains from the tenth to the early thirteenth centuries. It also carries the meaning "strong, powerful" (Kramers, "Ḳarā," *EI*² IV, 572b) as evidenced by its use in personal names of the Islamic period, such as the name of the Artuqid ruler Abū ʿAbdallāh Muḥammad ibn Qara Arslan ("black lion") ibn Dāwūd ibn Suqmān (561/1166–581/1185).

[129] Tr. Meisami, 1993, p. 221.

[130] Such a lock is featured on a gilded and nielloed silver casket, now in the Treasury of St. Mark's, Venice. Thought to have been either in crusader possession (Marshak, 1986, pp. 119–20 and n. 89, figs. 163–7) or the product of a southern Italian or Spanish workshop (*Nobilis Officinae*, 2005, pp. 171–2, cat. no. 13; *Venise et l'Orient*, p. 123, cat. no. 93), the casket has been variously dated from the twelfth to the fourteenth century: Anna Schwinger dates it to the twelfth century, or alternatively, proposes it as a thirteenth- or fourteenth-century reproduction (*Nobilis Officinae*, 2005, p. 171, cat. no. 13), while Boris Marshak (1986, p. 435) has suggested to date it to the second half of the thirteenth century. Most recently Francesca Leoni has proposed that the casket originates from southern Italy, or possibly Spain, and should be dated to the end of the thirteenth or the early fourteenth century (*Venise et l'Orient*, p. 123, cat. no. 93; catalogue entry by Leoni). The flat lid is framed at the sides by epigraphic bands in Kufic, flanking two seated musicians whose depiction conforms to the usual Islamic courtly iconography. The decoration on the front of the casket includes two large interlaced ornaments each enclosing a central cross-shape, suggesting that it may have been made for the Western market. One of the sides depicts a human-headed harpy with a tail terminating in a large dragon head with gaping mouth. Of particular note are the three extremely finely worked yet prominent hinges that terminate in two confronted dragon heads, their wide-open mouths touching at the tips. The lock, which ends in closely related dragon heads, fastens just above a pair of lion heads.

[131] In spite of mythologising features that go back to the Pseudo-Callisthenes, it is noteworthy that medieval Islamic authors differentiated between the legendary and

Iran. Through his talismanic powers Balīnūs helped the king to defeat Āẓar Humā, the powerful priestess of a fire temple, who in the form of a dragon guarded the holy fire, in other words, the treasure of the temple.[132] The same motif is extensively used in Niẓāmī's *Haft Paykar*, considered in chapter 14, and also in his *Laylā wa Majnūn*. When the news of Laylā's death reaches Majnūn, he hastens madly to her grave and:

> ...rolls in the same way as a serpent,
> Or a worm coiling beneath the earth,
> With a thousand toils, he coiled himself around
> The grave-stone like a serpent on a treasure.[133]

Even in her death Majnūn continues to keep watch over the grave of his beloved, Laylā, like a serpent guarding a treasure:

> The cavern is always the home of a snake;
> O Moon, why has the cavern become your residence?
> I will lament in your cave for you are my beloved;
> you are the companion of the cave *(yār-i ghār)*, how can I not weep?
> You turned out to be a treasure in the earth;
> If you are not a treasure, why are you then thus [in the earth]?
> Every treasure, which is in a cave,
> has a serpent upon its skirt.
> I am a serpent which is the sentinel of your grave
> watching the treasure on your grave.[134]

Serpents as guardians of treasures are a widely known topos in folk tales, as recorded in the *Alf layla wa-layla*, for instance the giant fire-spitting serpent guarding Solomon's magic ring in the story of the adventures of Bulūqiyā inserted into the story of the *Queen of the Serpents*.[135] The story of the Valley of the Diamonds, which recurs in many eastern sources, associates serpents with diamonds. It is found in the legend of the Hellenistic Orient represented by *De XII gemmis*, the tale of the fourth-century bishop of Constantia (Cyprus), Epiphanius,[136] as well as by Pseudo-Aristotle.[137] It is retold in the *Alexander Romance*[138] and also recorded by al-Bīrūnī in his *Kitāb al-Jamāhir fī maʿrifat al-jawāhir* ("Comprehensive Book on the Knowledge of Precious Minerals"),[139] by Niẓāmī in his *Iskandar-nāma*,[140] by the Arabian mineralogist Aḥmad al-Tifāshī (580/1184–651/1253),[141] in the collection of travel narratives of Sindbād in the *Alf layla wa-layla*[142] as well as later in the travelogue of the merchant explorer Marco Polo (*c.* 1254–*c.* 1324).[143] It recounts that in the east on the extreme frontier of Khurasan there is a deep valley in which diamonds lie, guarded by poisonous snakes upon which no man can gaze without dying; however this power endures only so long as the serpents live. On his way to India Iskandar, the Dhu 'l-Qarnayn ("two-horned") of the Qurʾān (*sūra* 18, 82–98), is said to have ventured into such a diamond pit. He outwitted the serpents by holding up mirrors as shields in which the serpents saw their own reflection and died.[144] The association of diamonds with serpents may also explain the belief in the toxicity of diamonds first advocated in the Pseudo-Aristotle, which cautions its readers "against taking the diamonds into their mouths, because the saliva of the snakes adheres to it so that it deals out death."[145]

The association of dragons with gems is also recorded in Armenian epic lore, as related by the eleventh-century Armenian scholar Grigor Magistros (990–1058) in a letter addressed to prince Tʿornik Mamikonean:

> A fish called Azhdahāk (i.e., Azhi Dahāka) ... gave a concubine a huge pearl... she took it to the king, who had it set into a crown ... The king then ordered that the gods be honoured with rich offerings, and that this fish be carven, together

---

the real figure of the Macedonian conqueror, as evidenced by al-Bīrūnī's *Kitāb al-Āthār* (tr. and ed. Sachau, 1876–8, p. 127) in which he comments upon the catastrophic consequences of the historical Alexander's invasion in 330 BC which led to the extinction of the Achaemenid empire.

132 *Dīwān*, pp. 974–5, cited in *Pseudo-Apollonius of Tyana*, tr. and ed. Weisser, 1990, p. 27. The theme of Alexander as dragon-slayer appears in the Syriac version of the Pseudo-Callisthenes, ch. 7, tr. and ed. Budge, 1889, repr. 2003, pp. lxxiv, 107–9, as well as in the Ethiopic version, *idem*, p. ciii.

133 Ed. Asgharzada, A.A., and Babayev, F., Baku, 1965, ch. 62, 42–3, cited after Gohrab, 2000, p. 90.

134 *Idem*. Cf. *idem*, 2003, p. 83.

135 Marzolph and van Leeuwen, 2004, p. 130.

136 Laufer, 1915, p. 20.

137 *Das Steinbuch*, tr. and ed. Ruska, 1912, pp. 14–6.

138 Stoneman, 1991, p. 2.

139 P. 99, 11–102, 5, as cited in Ullmann, 1994, p. 107. Cf. Ruska, "Almās," EI^1 I, p. 313; Ruska [and Plessner], "Almās," EI^2 I, 419a.

140 See Laufer, 1915, pp. 10–1.

141 Raineri Biscia, A., *Fior di pensieri sulle pietre preziose di Ahmed Teifascite*, Bologna, 2nd ed., 1906, pp. 21, 54. In this version the serpents are "able to swallow an entire man ("inghiottiscono un uomo intero")," cited after Laufer, 1915, p. 13 and n. 1.

142 Marzolph and van Leeuwen, 2004, p. 385.

143 Laufer, 1915, pp. 10–21, esp. pp. 11, n. 2, 14, and 18, n. 1.

144 *Idem*, pp. 10–21. Ullmann, 1992, p. 111. Cf. Ruska, "Almās," EI^1 I, p. 313; Ruska [and Plessner], "Almās," EI^2 I, 419a.

145 Laufer, 1915, pp. 40–1.

with the effigies of the other divinities, and that sacrifices be made on the banks of the river Phison, where it had appeared to the concubine.[146]

d. *The dragon and vegetal compositions*

An instance of the association of the serpent with a tree has already been noted in the figure of the Rigvedic primordial "serpent of the deep," *Ahi Budhnyà*, which resides at the roots of the tree. This may be related to the notion of the giant serpent as custodian of a tree, often represented as stylised vegetation, which became an important iconographical motif, reflected in particular on the decoration of portable objects found throughout the Central Asian regions. The prevalence of this theme in these regions is corroborated in the depiction of a fork-shaped harness ornament, datable between the sixth and the eighth centuries, which was excavated from a tomb at Kebinai in southern Siberia (fig. 38). The pendant is cast in openwork with paired antithetical dragons emerging from a stylised vegetal composition that springs from a horned mask-like head at the bottom.

Long-necked *regardant* dragon protomes with deep-set eyes, lupine or canine snouts and feathery wings, springing from a central foliate stalk and emitting or biting the leaves are shown on a belt fitting serving as hinge joint, cast in openwork. The fitting was unearthed in Novocherkassk in the lower Don region and is attributed to the second half of the eighth century (fig. 39).[147] A Byzantine attribution has been suggested on the basis that Byzantine workshops are thought to have existed in the proximity.[148]

In the Central Asian world the iconography is further recorded on a small early medieval ancestral fire altar *(chirāgh khāna)* from Samarqand.[149] The niche, which formed the nucleus of a house, is decorated on both end panels with a stylised tree-like vegetal composition flanked by a pair of perching birds with long florid tails, probably representing peacocks. Springing from the trunk of the tree are arched *regardant* dragons that flank a large central crescent-shaped bracket, above which flutters a pair of small birds (figs. 40 a and b). After the destruction of the fire temples following the advent of Islam, these *chirāgh khāna*, miniature imitations of fire temples, were placed as small altars in private houses for the luminaries that manifest the presence of the eternal fire. A small fire was lit in the niche, the denomination *chirāgh khāna* translating as house of the lamp, in other words a domestic "fire temple." Together with the dragons that spring from the central tree this altar contains images of roosters. The rooster motif is a well-known visual element harking back to Sasanian and early Islamic iconographies. The idea of the rooster (Av. *parō. dərəs-*, "he who foresees [dawn]") as a sacred bird or a bird endowed with special powers was characteristic of Iranian beliefs. In the Avesta it is considered as the bird of Sraosha, the angel who defends mankind from demons.[150] Generally in Zoroastrianism it is regarded as an ally of the powers of light and goodness, as an enemy to evil and demonic beings, and as a symbol of royalty and true religion; thus in the Vidēvdāt Ahura Mazdā says of the rooster:

> That bird lifteth up his voice at the mighty dawn (saying), 'Arise, O men, laud Best Righteousness, contemn the demons'.[151]

---

[146] Tchukasizian, 1964, p. 325.

[147] Cf. Daim, 2000, p. 128, fig. 51.

[148] *Idem*, p. 130. The paucity of early medieval records of this important visual element from the wider Central Asian world warrants a brief geographical digression. It is interesting to point out that the motif also exists on eighth-century Lombard and Frankish art such as the sarcophagus of Abbess Theodota [*sic*], Pavia, I. 720–30 (Atroshenko and Collins, 1985, p. 139, fig. 88; Daim, 2000, drawing on p. 319, fig. 13.3), on the Baptistry of Callisto (so-called Sigualdus), dated 762 to 776, in the Museo Archeologico Nazionale, Cividale del Friuli (Daim, 2000, p. 128, fig. 52, drawing on p. 319, fig. 13.2), and on the eighth-century silk-embroidered white linen tunic of the Frankish queen, Saint Bathilde of Chelles, which is thought to have been made at the Merovingian court under Byzantine influence (Vida, 2000, p. 312, fig 6.2; cf. Vierck, 1978, pp. 521–64). The iconographic expression was probably transmitted to Europe in the wake of the great migrations of nomadic peoples from the Eurasian steppes such as the Avars, subjects of the Turks, who fled to the north Caucasus region in 558 and then migrated westwards into the province of Pannonia (which lay to the east of northern Italy), where later waves of Avar migrants continued to join them (cf. Pohl, 1988, pp. 28–9; Barthold and Golden, "Khazar," *EI*² IV, 1172a). The motif of dragon protomes projecting from vegetal compositions that is found on eighth-century Lombard and Frankish art may thus have been inspired by Central Asian prototypes.

[149] Rempel', 1983, p. 127, fig. 49.5; *idem*, 1987a, p. 103, fig. 42a; and *idem*, 1987b, pl. LI, fig. 11, altar to the left side.

[150] Vidēvdāt 18.14–5; Gershevitch, 1959, p. 62. In Jewish post-biblical scriptures (*Yoma* 21a) the crowing of the cock is likewise known to drive demons away, see Ginzberg, 1909–38, repr. 1946, and *idem*, 1955, vol. 5, p. 173, n. 16.

[151] Vidēvdāt, *Fargard* 18.2.14 (*The Zend-Avesta*, tr. Darmesteter, 1880); *Bundahishn* 19.33 (*Sacred Books of the East*,

In antiquity, the religious significance of the cock as sacred bird of the sun whose rising he announces is described by the second-century Greek geographer Pausanias.[152] In medieval Islam it was similarly associated with light and Paradise, as well as with royalty, but also with the magician-king Sulaymān ibn Dāwūd who was acquainted with the speech of birds and animals (Qur'ān 27, 16–9).[153] In his *Kitāb 'ajā'ib al-makhlūqāt* al-Qazwīnī notes a prophetic *ḥadīth* according to which God placed under the divine throne a rooster whose wingspan extended from east to west. At the approach of dawn the rooster would beat his wings and cry out loud: "Glory to God, the Almighty!" At this all the roosters in the world would respond in similar fashion, praising God by beating their wings and crowing.[154]

A similar type of imagery as the one on the *chirāgh khāna* can also be found in a Buddhist context in Chinese Turkestan (present-day Xinjiang). When the near one-hundred-year steppe empire of the Uighurs in Mongolia (744–840), which had essentially been a continuation of the Turkic qaghanate, was destroyed in 840, one group fled westward into the region of Chinese Turkestan, where they ultimately founded two kingdoms. Here the Uighurs became the culture bearers of Central Asia.[155] On a wall painting from Cave 19 in Uighur Bezeklik in Qocho (present-day Turfan), datable between the ninth and the eleventh centuries, a pair of dragons in "Central Asian Chinese-style" springing from a water pool are closely associated with abundant vegetation. The confronted snarling dragons ascend in upright position, their tail ends entwined. Dramatically presented with their raptor-like legs raised and extended talons unsheathed, they guard between them a treasure, shown springing from the lotus throne and floating over a flaming pearl, the Buddhist *ruyi baozhu* (Skr. *cintāmaṇi*),[156] from which sprout the formidable, profusely reticulated branches of a tree. Its luxuriant growth is nourished by the fructifying waters of the pool in which small dragons cavort (fig. 41).[157] A pair of knotted dragons features in a related depiction of the same period from a now destroyed wall painting, also from the cave monastery of Bezeklik, recorded only by a drawing made by the German archaeologist Albert Grünwedel during the third German expedition to Chinese Turkestan in 1906 to 1907 (fig. 168).[158]

A similar conceptualisation of the dragon and the tree is emblematically portrayed in an Islamic context as part of a large water-clock automaton. It is described in an illustrated horological treatise attributed to Archimedes of which several medieval Arabic versions survive.[159] The second section of this treatise gives an account of a tree with silver birds set between two mountains behind which serpents hide:

> We will now describe how a tree is made, upon whose branches are birds. This tree is to be fixed vertically between two mountains, with a finger-length between each mountain and the stem of the tree. When an hour elapses then a snake emerges from a hole in the mountain's foot. The hole is inside the floor of the tree or opposite the birds that are on the branches of the tree. When the two snakes emerge the birds shriek and whistle as long as the snakes are visible. Then the snakes go back inside their holes and the shrieking and whistling of the birds ceases.[160]

While parts of the Pseudo-Archimedes treatise are first mentioned in Islamic sources of the tenth century, this type of clock seems to belong to a much earlier tradition and was known to have been built in Sasanian and Byzantine times.[161] During the medieval Islamic period, automata in the form of silver gilded trees with artificial singing birds were known as expressions of imperial

tr. West, E.W., Oxford, 1897); see also *The Zohar*, vol. 4, p. 369 (*Wayikra* 22 b) (tr. Simon, M., New York, 1949) in which the cock calls upon men to praise God and study law; cited after Bonner, 1950, p. 125 and n. 11. Cf. Harper, 1978, p. 65; Schwartz, 1985, p. 661.

152 *Graeciae Descriptio* V 25, 9. Cf. Bonner, 1950, p. 127.

153 Viré and Baer, "Ṭāwūs, Ṭā'ūs," *EI*² X, 396a.

154 Tr. and ed. Giese, 1986, p. 219.

155 Golden, 2004, p. 22.

156 The pearl (Skr. *maṇi*) was a symbol of the Buddha and of law. In Sino-Indian traditions it was "a wishing jewel, granting the desires of its possessors." Moreover it was associated with the moon. The "dragon-pearl" symbolises the full moon, the Buddhist *ruyi baozhu* (Skr. *cintāmaṇi*), the wish-fullfilling jewel of the Indian *nāgas*, which symbolises transcendent wisdom. See Schafer, 1963, pp. 181, 243. For the reception of the motif consisting of three points surmounting two wavy lines, called *çintamani* in Persian and Islamic art, see Soucek, "Cintāmani," *EIr*, and Kadoi, 2006–7, pp. 33–49.

157 This mural painting, which was taken to Berlin by the German expedition, is presumed to have been destroyed during the bombing of World War II.

158 Grünwedel, 1912, fig. 590.

159 Hill, 1976; cf. *idem*, 1984, p. 230.

160 *Idem*, 1976, pp. 30–1, figs. 14, 15. See also *idem*, 1984, pp. 229–30, fig. 12.2 for the design of the water machinery from Archimedes.

161 *Idem*, 1984, p. 230.

might, particularly in ʿAbbasid times;[162] slightly later they are also recorded as having surrounded the throne of the Byzantine emperor.[163]

The motif of the tree with serpents is rendered on a two-dimensional medium, a polychrome-enamel overglaze-painted ceramic bowl (so-called *mīnāʾī* ware) from Rayy, datable to the second half of the twelfth century. Here a central tree springs from a small mound at the base of the bowl. At mid-section the tree trunk is separated by a mound-like conical motif around which a dragon appears to be coiling and from the tip of which emerges the giant upward oriented gaping jaws of a dragon with bifid tongue. The trunk grows out of this creature's maw into a treetop with lush foliage topped by a pair of perched birds. The scene is flanked on either side by a rider and in turn by a figure seated cross-legged (fig. 42).[164]

An analogous motif is represented by the well-known relief sculptures that decorate the stone minaret buttresses of the Çifte Minare *madrasa* at Erzurum, probably built just before the fall of the city to the Mongols in 640/1242–3.[165] Set within an ogival arch-shaped niche surrounded by a triple torus frame, the composition was intended to appear at either side of the main entrance of the *madrasa*, but only the relief to the right was completed.[166] The sculptures are carved to form a pair of dragon protomes that spring from the stem of a central palm tree with a double-headed eagle at its summit (fig. 43).[167] The scaly upward-curving serpentine necks extend into large, upward oriented heads with large, almond-shaped eyes and small, pointed ears, their open jaws with outward curled tips replete with rows of teeth and tongues with bifid tips. Just behind the heads, the slender necks are embellished with guilloche chains, a feature they share with the dragons that flank a central bovine head on the city walls of Ani (fig. 130) and the dragons that frame the large, composite star-rosette from Konya (fig. 154). The dragons' curving ophidian bodies are once looped, then join to grow upwards into the stemmed vegetation above, while an inverted stemmed palmette springs from the interstice created below the point of juncture of the bodies. Out of the large, crescent-shaped bracket which encloses the stem grow eight large "palmate" leaves that fan out symmetrically and bear what appears to be fruit, probably pomegranates; on the tips of the side fronds (second leaves from the bottom) perch small birds. The pomegranates, anomalous in the context of a palm tree, link the tree with the idea of fertility and immortality – both in itself and as a dwelling place for birds.

Öney interprets the dragons as chthonic symbols (in contrast to the solar/light symbol of the double-headed bird) which guard the tree.[168] Similarly, Otto-Dorn reads this form of imagery in the light of astrological lore, according to which the dragons threaten the luminaries represented by the crescent-shaped bracket and the double-headed eagle.[169] The serpent at the foot of the tree seems to have been a well-known conceptualisation in medieval Islam, as is evidenced by a saying recorded by the fourteenth-century encyclopaedist al-Damīrī and attributed to ʿAbd Allāh ibn ʿAmr ibn al-ʿĀṣ, a contemporary of the Prophet Muḥammad, in which he compares himself to the serpent at the foot of the tree:

> I support [equally well] good and evil, and am inexorable,
> Like the serpent at the foot of the trees. [170]

[162] The wonders contained in the newly built caliphal palace, such as an automaton in the form of trees, are reported in al-Khātib's account in the *History of Baghdad* of the arrival of Byzantine ambassadors to the ʿAbbasid capital in 305/917–18. They described seeing a silver tree in a large pond with silver or gilded whistling birds perched on its branches. *Idem*, p. 205 and n. 17.

[163] In the Byzantine treatise of "The Throne of Solomon" in Constantinople, the throne of the emperor is depicted as surrounded by automata which included a jewel-encrusted tree with artificial singing birds, roaring lions and moving beasts, a description which is corroborated by Liutprand, Bishop of Cremona, who visited Byzantium as envoy in 336/948 and again in 355/966. Cf. *idem*, p. 205. The tree stood in the chrysotriclinium before the emperor's throne; outside there was a fountain with a silver eagle that covered the conduits by holding a serpent in its talons. Ebersolt, 1923, pp. 55–7. See also Soucek, 1997, p. 405 and ns. 13–8 with further references.

[164] İnal, 1970–1, fig. 17. The bowl does not seem to have been published elsewhere; its overall condition and the extent of possible overpainting which could have a bearing on the imagery are not known to the author. However, in spite of these uncertainties, the bowl was nonetheless included as it represents a rare example of this iconography.

[165] See p. 31, n. 87.

[166] Above the tree in the right hand panel is a double-headed eagle, the equivalent part in the left hand panel is left unfinished. On the side faces of the portal are similar compositions but without dragons. See also Gierlichs, 1996, pl. 12.1, 4, 5.

[167] Cf. *idem*, pl. 12.1; Öney, 1969a, p. 208 and fig. 32, and *eadem*, 1969b.

[168] Öney, 1969a, p. 208.

[169] Otto-Dorn, 1978–9, pp. 133–4.

[170] *Ḥayāt al-ḥayawān al-kubrā*, tr. Jayakar, 1906, vol. 1, p. 634.

The close assocition of the tree and the serpent is also evident in the *Risālat* of Ibn Faḍlān, secretary of the caliphal mission to Volga Bulgaria from 309/921 to 310/922, that relates the story of a tree being cut to size which then begins to move and crawl away in the form of a giant dragon.[171]

Given the historical relations of Armenians with the principality of Erzurum (Karin), which at various times belonged to Armenia and under Islamic rulership also had a Christian Armenian population, it is interesting to relate the Çifte Minare *madrasa* motif to earlier as well as contemporary Armenian references preserved in manuscript illumination. A significant variant on the imagery is presented in a collection of sermons of 1216 illustrated by Barsegh K'ahanay (the priest) in Skevra monastery, Cilician Armenia (fig. 44). It portrays a tall multi-branched tree bearing large foliage, buds and fruit that are pecked at by different types of birds that perch on the branches. Yet instead of growing out of the base of the tree and rearing up from there, the interlaced slender trunks of the tree are here shown to be enclosed by an entwined pair of giant scaly serpents forming a double loop. The motif represents an example of the standard depiction of the tree or pole together with the serpent forming the figure of eight (both open and closed) as also repesented in the symbol of the caduceus *(kerykeion)* discussed below. The reptiles gnaw, with heads upreared, at the uppermost leaves. A small bird is perched on the summit of the tree while a pair of confronting human-headed birds, probably harpies, flanks the base of the trunk. The latter bears an intricate interlace terminating in pendant palmette-shaped buds. The tree-with-serpents motif certainly alludes here to a complex of ideas, not least the serpent and the fruit-bearing tree in the Garden of Eden.[172] Painted about three decades before the construction of the Çifte Minare *madrasa*, the miniature thus documents a variation of the motif in a Christian context.[173]

A large marginal ornament from an Armenian Gospel of Luke illuminated in 1323 shows open-mouthed dragons with projecting tongues that touch the base of a more stylised, tree-like vegetal motif. The latter contains the symbols of the four Evangelists set amidst foliage that tapers to an arched apex. It is surmounted by an ornate cross flanked by clusters of grapes instead of the birds that top the tree-like compositions on the collection of sermons of 1216 and the mid-thirteenth-century Çifte Minare *madrasa*. The ornament was illustrated by the miniaturist T'oros Taronatsi in the important scriptorium of the monastery of Gladzor in southern Armenia (fig. 45).[174]

In view of the close analogies between the dragon compositions on the façade of the Çifte Minare *madrasa* and contemporary Armenian stone carvings, Rogers has referred to the reliefs as "barely islamicised versions of Armenian *khatchk'ars* (commemorative cross-stones)."[175] This is particular evident on *vishap*-type Armenian Christian sepulchral steles or commemorative cross-stones *(khatchk'ar)*, such as a twelfth- or thirteenth-century example from Makravank' in Ararat province, on which a closely related form of imagery can be deduced. On this *khatchk'ar* a pair of stylised dragons springs from the base of a cross, whence their serpentine bodies bifurcate, form a loop and then curve upwards to terminate in stylised heads with wide-open jaws. Just below the heads, ornamental bands enclose collars in the form of a figure of eight which accent the ophidian necks and delineate the bodies, the latter being enlivened by parallel decorative stripes. The bases of the small crosses are shown to rest on the tips of short tongues projecting from the dragons' mouths whose lips end in inward-curling tips (fig. 46).[176]

---

[171] Ed. Dahhān, S., Damascus, 1959, pp. 127–8 (fol. 4 206 *wāw*), as cited in Montgomery, 2006, p. 72.

[172] A reference to the tree is also found for instance in the Proverbs of Solomon: "A Tree of Life is wisdom for those who acquire it" (3.18). On the meaning of the Tree of Knowledge and the Tree of Life, see Agathangelos, *Teaching of St. Gregory*, tr. and ed. Thomson, 1970, ch. 277; *The Armenian Commentary on Genesis Attributed to Ephrem the Syrian*, tr. Mathews, 1998, pp. 21–2, 27–8, 32–3, 37 and n. 116, 39; see also Wallace, 1985, pp. 101–32.

[173] I am grateful to Professor Robert Hillenbrand for pointing this out to me.

[174] For a closely related example, see British Library Ms. Add. 15,411, fol. 92a, dated 1321, which is also illustrated at the monastery of Gladzor in southern Armenia by T'oros Taronatsi; see *The Christian Orient*, 1978, pl. 13 (caption 119). The same conceptualisation can be observed in an eleventh- or twelfth-century Georgian illustration of the Gospel book from Ghelati near Kutaisi in northwestern Georgia which shows a tree-like composition from the base of which projects a root-like vertical extension that carries a single curved serpent with gaping mouth revealing a bifid tongue. Georgia, Tbilisi, Institute of the Academy of Sciences of Georgia, Ms. A 908, fol. 16; see Amiranašvili, 1966, fig. 35.

[175] Rogers, "Saldjūḳids," *EI*² VIII, 936a.

[176] For another closely related *vishap*-type *khatchk'ar* with small crosses issuing from the gaping dragon heads, see *Armenië*, 2001, p. 52, photograph, lower left side, third *khatchk'ar* from the left.

It is notable that *khatchk'ar* decorated with the cross, the "Sign" of God or "Wood of Life," as the main decorative motif, symbolise primarily the salvation of the souls of the departed in whose memory they were erected.[177] In the case of *vishap*-type *khatchk'ar* it appears therefore less likely that the dragons are shown ingesting the crosses and it may be presumed that, conversely, the mythical creatures are represented as deliverers and as givers of fecundity and prosperity.

The visual conflation of dragon bodies with knotted ornaments is perhaps indebted to the canon-tables of Armenian Gospel books.[178] An important marginal ornament features a cross resting on an inverted heart-shaped interlace of split-palmettes which evolves into two confronted dragon heads, the necks enclosed in narrow ornamental collars. Just as on the *vishap*-type *khatchk'ar* discussed above, the creatures are distinctly portrayed with their tongues darting from the wide-open mouths to touch the base of the cross (fig. 47). The ophidian heads are capped by pointed ears, the most characteristic aspect being however the wide open, curved snouts, the upper lip ending in a rolled-up tip. The ornament is portrayed on Mark's first page, copied by the priest Hohannes [*sic*], son of the priest Manuk, in 1171 in Edessa (now known as Urfa) in southeast Anatolia.[179]

The rendering of the dragons on the *vishap*-type *khatchk'ar* as well as the Edessan marginal ornament reveals analogies with the arch-shaped double-headed knotted dragons with wide-open jaws, pointed ears and horn-like protuberances, the bodies covered with an interlaced palmette scroll, that are featured on some of the funerary steles at the vast cemetery of Akhlāṭ. The latter is situated at the northwest corner of Lake Van between Eski Akhlāṭ and the Ottoman *qal'a* and was principally erected between 1250 and 1350 (figs. 48 and 49).[180] The points of resemblance are noted by Rogers who hypothesises that the overall decoration of the richly carved tombstones, some of which become highly stylised,[181] "was a reaction to the traditional decoration of Armenian *khatchk'ar*."[182]

Representations that associate the dragons yet again with the Christian cross are moreover found at the monastery of Deir Mār Behnām in Mosul. On the lintel of the southern outer door, just below the relief-carved representation of a pair of entwined dragons (figs. 17a and b), examined above, is a central Greek cross. From its base extends an arched cartouche which encloses a pair of stylised *regardant* quadruped dragons viewed from behind, whose arched bodies are crossing (fig. 50).[183] The dragons' gaping mouths and their projecting tongues touch the tip of the cusped lower end of the cross. An interesting parallel occurs on the portal leading to the chapel of the baptistery at Mār Behnām, where the frame is carved with a knotted serpentine moulding forming ogee arch-shaped niches which also enclose crosses whose lower ends extend into stemmed palmettes.

An important *khatchk'ar* in the church of Surb Astvatsatsin (Holy Mother of God) in Sevanavank', located on the northwestern shore of Lake Sevan in the eastern Armenian province of Geghark'unik', depicts the scene of God expelling Adam and Eve from Paradise flanked by a pair of dragons with knotted tails and open mouths revealing the tongues (fig. 51). It is interesting to note the early rabbinic assessment of the association of Adam and Eve with the serpent: "the serpent is your [sc. Eve] serpent and you are Adam's serpent."[184] Yet for its role in the fall of Adam and Eve, God condemned the serpent forever to eat "earth" (Genesis 3.14). However rather than being portrayed as evil, it is once again shown to touch the bottom tip of the long cross held by God in his right hand with its projecting tongue.[185] This ambiguity inherent in the figure of the serpent(-dragon) is elucidated in a passage from the *Epistle of Barnabas* in which Moses says:

[177] Der Nersessian, 2001, p. 110. In the Armenian Hymnal the rod is referred to as Holy Cross and Tree of Life, a staff that gives life *(kensatu)*, a staff of power *(zawrut'ean)*. Russell, 2004, p. 1148.

[178] Cf. Rogers, "Saldjūḳids," *EI*^{2} VIII, 936a.

[179] Izmailova, T.A., "Edesskaia rukopis 1171 goda (M. 313)," *Kultura i iskusstvo nardo vostoka* 8, *Trudi gosudarstvennogo Orgena Lenina Ermitazha*, 19, Leningrad, 1978, pp. 84–101 (English summary, pp. 117–8), as cited in Der Nersessian and Agemian, 1993, p. 30.

[180] Rogers, 1988, p. 109.

[181] Four steles carved with dragons are said to be extant; Süslü, 1987, p. 640. Cf. Karamağaralı, 1972, p. 187, nos. 734–234a (no. 72, epitaph dated 23 Ṣafar 700/7 November 1300). Öney, 1969a, fig. 11.

[182] Rogers, 1988, p. 120.

[183] Researched by Preusser, 1911, n. 11, pp. 5–6, pls. 5, 6.2. Cf. Fiey, 1965, vol. 1, pp. 565–09, esp. pp. 605–6; Kühnel, 1950 (church of Khiḍr Ilyās).

[184] Genesis *Rabbah* 20; Wallace, 1985, p. 148.

[185] Tr. Lake, 1914, vol. 1, p. 385.

> Whenever one of you, he said, be bitten, let him come to the serpent that is placed upon the tree, and let him hope, in faith that it though dead is able to give life, and he shall straightway be saved.

In the Armenian apocryphal tradition a promise was made to Adam at the expulsion that he will be restored as ruler of Paradise after the Second Coming, an event which may be implied in the carving with the giant serpents appearing to guard the gates of Paradise.

At least from the beginning of the fifth century, the cross was regarded as a powerful amulet,[186] hence in the early Christian period crosses placed on or near entrances served primarily protective and apotropaic functions.[187] The Christian cross together with the dragons thus undeniably has a special function as an apotropaion guarding a threshold.

The association of the dragon with the cross may be related to the symbol of the serpent as it appears in the Gospel of John (3:14):

> And as Moses lifted up the serpent in the wilderness, even so must the Son of Man be lifted up.

In his homily on the Gospel of John, the fourth-century archbishop of Constantinople, John Chrysostom (*c.* 347–407), similarly compares the "lifting up" of the serpent with the manner of Jesus' death and parallels the Christ himself with the likeness of the serpent:

> In the former, the uplifted serpent healed the bites of the serpents; in the latter, the crucified Jesus healed the wounds inflicted by the spiritual dragon. In the former, there was the uplifted brass fashioned in the likeness of a serpent; in the latter, the Lord's body formed by the spirit.[188]

The tenth-century polymath al-Bīrūnī, one of the most eminent literary and scientific figures of the medieval Islamic period, records a Christian source which also relates the brazen serpent to the cross:

> God ordered the Israelites to make a serpent of brass and to hang it on a beam, which was to be erected, for the purpose of keeping off the injury done by the serpents when they had become very numerous in the desert. Now from this fact they infer and maintain that it was a prophecy and a hint indicative of the Cross (of Christ).[189]

Correspondingly, as Hans Leisegang asserts in his discussion of the *Epistle of Barnabas*,[190] the serpent lifted up by Moses is characterised as a representation of Jesus, an identification that became an established motif in Christian symbolism, and the counterpart of the satanic serpent in Paradise.[191]

At the same time, the multivalent aspect of the symbol of the cross, employed as metaphor for both the crucifixion and the resurrection[192] of Christ, has to be taken into account. In Armenian exegetical works the *khatchkʿar* is often elaborated as "Wood of Life" *(pʿayt kenats)*.[193] The equation of the "living" cross with vegetation[194] provides an

[186] Canaan, 1938, p. 175, n. 249.

[187] Kitzinger, 1970, p. 640.

[188] Tr. Sr. Thomas Aquinas Goggin, 1957–60, 1:262–3.

[189] Although he derides this reference as indulgence in "tricks and hallucinations"; *Kitāb al-Āthār*, tr. and ed. Sachau, 1876–8, pp. 292–3.

[190] XII 5–6, tr. Kirsopp, L., *The Apostolic Fathers*, London and New York, 1914, vol. 1, p. 385, cited after Leisegang, 1955, repr. 1979, p. 229. Cf. Daniélou, 1964, pp. 92, 271; Thomson, 1970, ch. 473, n. 1.

[191] *Apocalypse of Moses* 16–9; Justin, *Dialogue* 124; Origen, *De principiis* 3.2.1. In this connection it is interesting to consider an eighth-century Armenian text in which the church is said to be "a paradise planted by God which evil cannot enter; for from that first one we were expelled through the wiles of the serpent, but we enter this one through Christ ... In that other paradise was planted a tree of life, forbidden to the firstborn; while here we have the cross of life, planted by the same planter, and which has taken root and has blossomed through His life-giving blood." Aucher, J.B., *Domini Johannis Ozniensis Philosophi Armenorum Catholici Opera*, Venice, 1834, pp. 290–2, as cited in Der Nersessian, 1965, p. 42 and n. 96.

[192] With regard to the Christian Feast of the Apparition of the Flaming Cross in Heaven, al-Bīrūnī records that, according to Christian scholars, Constantine's mother, Helena, went to Jerusalem to find the cross of Christ which when placed upon a dead body could resurrect the dead. He further notes that the wood used for the cross is referred to as "the wood of Paeonia," which is frequently "attached to a man who suffers from epilepsy, being considered as a symbol of the resurrection of the dead" (*Kitāb al-Āthār*, tr. and ed. Sachau, 1876–8, pp. 293–3). For related narratives on the association of the Cross and the Tree of Life, see Wünsche, 1905, pp. 15–7.

[193] See the Homily by David Anyaghtʿ, cited in Russell, 2004, pp. 630 and 1194. In Agathangelos' fifth-century theological teachings, *Teaching of St. Gregory*, the cross is praised as a "Tree of Life rooted in the earth" (tr. and ed. Thomson, 1970, pp. 7–9, 21–3, and chs. 577–86, 618–31). On the cult of the Tree of Life in Armenia, see Russell, 1987, p. 33. The Tree of Life as prefiguration of the Cross of Christ is mentioned in the Christian Syriac *Meʿārath gazzē (Cave of Treasures*, tr. and ed. Budge, 1927, p. 34).

[194] Cf. *Teaching of St. Gregory*, tr. and ed. Thomson, 1970, pp. 159–62, and chs. 641–54.

analogy to the dragon's inherently close relation with vegetation and the associated beneficial qualities of fertility/fecundity. This in addition to the shared special apotropaic functions naturally accords the dragon the preeminent position of a vehicle that issues, thus perhaps wittingly emits or, by extension, one may hypothesise, delivers, and henceforth protects the "living" cross.

***

Yet another manifestation of symmetrical dragon heads is found in an embroidery on cotton ground from the greater Khurasan region, now in a private collection. Here the motif is takes the form of addorsed symmetrically arranged monster heads with tall floppy ears springing from a central vegetal composition, probably representing a conventionalised tree motif visualised as stylised plant. The necks of the creatures extend into the "branches of the tree" in such as way that the bodies are fused with the scrolls. The textile has been radiocarbon dated to the thirteenth or fourteenth century (fig. 52). In his ground-breaking article on "pseudo-planetary nodes" in Islamic art, written in 1938, Hartner has identified these monster heads with long ears growing from scrolling tendrils as "the dragon progeny threatening the luminaries or, vicariously, their *domicilia* and *exaltations*."[195] However, he qualifies the astrological interpretation by suggesting that "in all probability, various elements – astronomical, astrological and mythological – were here fused in one."[196] The iconography of the "inhabited scroll" which includes not only dragon heads, but other animal as well as human heads is ubiquitously applied specifically on late eleventh- to early thirteenth-century works of art, in particular metalwork, from Western Central Asia, especially the greater Khurasan region.[197]

The long-eared dragon heads are also a common feature on contemporaneously dated press-moulds, most of which have a Khurasani provenance. Ralph Pinder-Wilson hence identifies these scrolls as having their origin in Khurasan, first occurring on marble reliefs, attributed to one of the Ghaznawid palaces (perhaps of Masʿūd III (r. 492/1099–508/1115) or Bahrām Shāh (r. 511/1117–552/1153) or of a later date) excavated at Ghazna by the Italian Archaeological Mission to Afghanistan.[198] Spiralling tendrils transforming into dragon- and other mythical heads are figured on a mould which bears a dedicatory inscription to a Ghurid general and governor of Herat, ʿIzz al-Dīn Ḥusayn ibn Kharmil (d. 607/1210–1).[199] Openwork gilded silver plaques found in the valley of Kotchkar in the Semirechye, now in the State Hermitage in St. Petersburg, are further examples of vegetal scrolls inhabited with the monster and animal heads, among which the dragon is prominently represented.[200] *Rinceaux* with such heads also form the all-over decoration on the doublures of a Qurʾān from Anatolia or the Jazīra, datable to the mid-thirteenth or fourteenth century.[201] This ornamenting of the doublures of the sacred book of Islam with vegetal scrolls from which spring mythical and naturalistically rendered zoomorphic heads offers an interesting parallel to the practice, evidenced in Ilkhanid Anatolia, of decorating the façades of sacred architecture, such as mosques and *madrasas*, with such "inhabited scrolls." A more detailed discussion of this can be found below in the Epilogue.

The wide distribution of the motif is, moreover, attested by its representation throughout the Caucasus region, such as on an archivolt fragment from Daghistan in the eastern Caucasus. It is carved with a vivid depiction of a mighty winged dragon pursuing a slender cervid, the

[195] Hartner, 1959, pp. 237–9, and *idem,* 1973–4, p. 112, 118. An anachronical but perhaps not completely irrelevant depiction exists on a late Parthian-period stucco capital (the imagery is 24 cm square) from Qalʿa-i Yazdigird. On the capital a pair of interlaced dragons with slender snouts and long floppy ears, for which there appear to be no prototypes, is shown. Keall, 1967, p. 115, fig. 6.

[196] Hartner, 1973–4, pp. 112–3.

[197] Cf. Melikian-Chirvani, 1982, p. 145, fig. 51; Pinder-Wilson, 1997, p. 343.

[198] Bombaci and Scerrato, 1959, pp. 13–5 and figs. 11, 12; Baer, 1965, pp. 15, 66, pl. XLVII, figs. 82, 83. Although on the two surviving marble panels no creatures that can be identified as dragons inhabit the scrolls, it is noteworthy that the hexagonal interlace enclosed within the border of one of the panels includes a winged and horned quadruped with a long gaping snout which may be recognised as a quadruped dragon (Bombaci and Scerrato, 1959, fig. 12; Baer, 1965, fig. 83). The fabulous creature is rendered just below a similar such quadruped which however is distinguished by a bird's beak and small pointed ears and thus clearly typifies as a griffin.

[199] Pinder-Wilson, 1997, pp. 346–7, cat. no. 215.

[200] See Strzygowski, 1916, p. 214, fig. 180 (outer vertically-oriented plaques).

[201] Doublures of two sections of a 30-part Qurʾān from Anatolia or the Jazīra, dated to the mid-thirteenth or fourteenth century. The Nasser D. Khalili Collection of Islamic Art, London, inv. nos. QUR433 and QUR132. Pinder-Wilson, 1997, p. 342, fig. 11.

inner edge being framed by a *rinceau* terminating in gaping dragon heads with projecting tongues (figs. 63 and 53, detail).[202] The dragon's vegetal affiliation, conveyed through its repetitive projection from the foliate bends, was presumably not merely decorative, intending rather to underline the associated, apparently positive and beneficial, semantic meaning of the visual expression.

During the twelfth and thirteenth centuries, *rinceaux* that evolve into gaping dragon heads and protomes also figure in Armenian miniature painting, the earliest dated examples of the motif appearing in marginal ornaments of the famous so-called Homiliary of Mush executed on parchment leaves at the monastery of Avagvankʿ near Erēz/Erznga(n) (present-day Erzincan)[203] in northeastern Anatolia between 1200 to 1202 (figs. 126–129, 131–133). The fusion of a winged dragon's body with the leafy branches is also shown in a headpiece in the same manuscript, which is further discussed below. The hind parts of the mythical creatures are transformed here into vegetal scrolls, thereby highlighting the emergence of two confronted dragon protomes with forelegs, the necks are again enlivened by ornamental collars (fig. 61). A more detailed *rinceau* appears in a headpiece of a later manuscript, copied in the scriptoria of Sis, the capital of the Armenian Kingdom of Cilicia, in 1274, which had a princely sponsor, Marshal Oshin, son of Kostandin of Lambron and queen Keran's uncle. It features on the first page of the Gospel of Luke and is filled with an animated all-over foliate interlace "inhabited" by animal and human heads among which the dragon is prominently represented. For the most part the stems are issuing from animal and dragon necks, the tips of the wide-open dragon jaws, and the pointed tips of the tight-fitting headdress worn by the human heads. The headpiece is crowned at the apex by a foliate interlace in the form of an inverted heart-shape from which project two large, confronted dragon heads whose gaping jaws reveal the tongues that touch the upper edge of the headpiece and whose lower jaws extend into split-palmettes that curve along the same edge (fig. 54).

In another version of the dragon's association with vegetation, rather than vegetation sprouting dragon heads or dragon bodies growing into or out of vegetal stems, the mythical creature itself issues vegetation. This is represented on a Samanid-period bowl excavated near Tashkent, Uzbekistan, featuring a sketchy composition of a stylised rider with large, round head and raised hands mounted on a recumbent dragon, from whose elongated open snout and hindquarters sprout two twigs of undulant foliage (fig. 55).[204]

The iconography of the dragon as producer of vegetation is further exemplified by two analogous depictions on the arched handles of the two celebrated silver- and copper-inlaid copper alloy buckets, cited above, both preserved in the State Hermitage, St. Petersburg. The loops of the handle of the so-called Bobrinski bucket (inscribed with the date *muḥarram* 559/December 1163) are fashioned out of dragon protomes enlived by a spotted pattern. From the open mouths springs (a devouring interpretation may be presumed to be incongruous) the four-sided arched section inscribed on two sides in *naskhī* with benedictory inscriptions and on the top band of the handle in Kufic with the date *muḥarram* 559/December 1163. On the outside the mythical creatures are flanked by leaping lions (fig. 56). The so-called Fould bucket (signed by its maker, Muḥammad ibn Nāṣir ibn Muḥammad al-Harawī, and recently attributed to early thirteenth-century Jazīra, northern Syria, or possibly Anatolia) has a handle that is similarly held in place by loops in the form of arched dragons topped at the outside by projecting lion-headed knobs. From the dragons' open mouths emerges the six-sided arched handle, decorated on all facets with scrolling foliage in place of the benedictory inscriptions of the Bobrinsky handle. On either side of the handle the foliage gives way to lion heads that frame a square link inlaid with a composite quadripartite interlaced knot at the apex (originally topped by a now lost finial) (fig. 57).[205]

Yet another aspect of the dragon's relation with vegetation is shown in the Eastern Christian world in the eleventh-century Georgian church

[202] Cf. Bashkirov, 1931, p. 95 and pl. 72.

[203] When Ibn Baṭṭūṭa visited the city in 731/1331, he described the inhabitants of the town as predominantly Armenian. See *Tuḥfat al-nuẓẓār fī gharāʾib al-amṣār wa-ʿajāʾib al-asfār*, tr. Gibb, vol. 2, p. 437.

[204] This as yet unpublished bowl has been handled and photographed by the author. It was excavated together with other Samanid-period earthenware bowls; in spite of the fact that the piece has not been tested, its body and glazing are characteristic of this period, hence in spite of the rather crude and perhaps unusual depiction displayed on it, it has been deemed sufficiently interesting to be included as a reference, albeit one of a more folkloristic character.

[205] Cf. Mayer, 1959, pl. X; Loukonine and Ivanov, eds., 2003, pp. 123–4, cat. no. 126.

of Çengelli, located near Kağizman in the steep mountains that soar above the Aras valley, south-west of Kars, curiously placed within a formerly Armenian community. Inside the church the northern capital is carved in relief with a recumbent looped serpent portrayed with upstretched head which reaches towards a cluster of grapes suspended just above its gaping mouth (fig. 58). The head is capped by a pair of small, cusped ears and the upper lip of the elongated snout terminates in the curled-up tip characteristic of the "Saljuq-type" dragon. The other face of the capital features the relief sculpture of a composite tree bearing pomegranates and bunches of grapes, both kinds of fruit generally carrying paradisical associations.[206]

[206] Composite vine scroll friezes bearing grapes and sometimes also pomegranates frequently appear on the façades of tenth-century Armenian and Georgian churches, the most prominent example being the Bagratid church of the Holy Cross of Aghtʿamar (915–921) at Lake Van where in addition to bands of pomegranate framing the exterior window arches, two continuous vine friezes circumscribe the exterior of the church. Cf. Der Nersessian, 1965, pp. 11, 25, pl. 31. The pomegranate is one of the symbols of the Iranian fertility goddess Ardvī Sūrā Anāhitā (Mid. Pers. Anāhīd, Grk. Anaïtis) who was venerated by the Armenians that shared the religion of the Persians and the Medes. See Soudavar, 2003, pp. 58, 74, pl. 165, fig. 71. For an example of comparable decoration on Georgian churches, see the tenth-century church of the Virgin in Martʿvili; Mepisaschwili und Zinzadze, 1987, p. 160, fig. 234. Of note is further the description of the holy garment decorated with pomegranates and bells which was ordered by Moses in Exodus 39. Much earlier examples of these motifs are portrayed in the carved decoration of the church of Saint Polyeuktos (*c.* 524–527) in Constantinople (Istanbul) featuring, for instance, the combination of pomegranates and split palmettes on a modillion or a vine growing out of a vase on a column capital. Cf. McKenzie, 2006, pls. 559, 567. According to Genesis (9:20), the Tree of Life was probably the stem of a vine.

CHAPTER FIVE

DRAGONS AND ANIMALS OF THE NATURAL AND THE MYTHICAL REALMS

a. *The dragon in animal combat scenes*

Ancient Near Eastern animal motifs such as the theme of combatant animals figure prominently in the decorative repertoire of the medieval Islamic period. Animal combat scenes also appear to reflect the visual language of so-called Steppe Empire Eurasian "animal style" art.[1] Dragons locked in combat with each other or with other real or imaginary creatures played a particularly significant part in the artistic vocabulary of many Eurasian pastoral peoples.

This ancient iconographical theme of animal combat, in which the dragon is pitted against another animal, continues to appear in both Islamic and Christian contexts. A fluidly rendered representation, evoking the immediacy and innate animal nature intrinsic in wild beasts, is found in a twelfth- or thirteenth-century openwork decoration of a brazier from the Iranian world or Anatolia. The scene depicts the combat of two exceedingly fierce and powerful creatures, a feline quadruped with a quadruped dragon.[2] The latter has an elongated ophidian body tapering to the tip of a long tail and is twisted around the entire body of its striding adversary, beginning at the right hind leg, circling the body once, and then the neck, re-emerging behind the feline's head, biting with an elongated snout into the feline's neck, who in turn mauls the mythical creature's shoulders. The densely patterned fur of the felid and scaly hide of the fabulous beast are finely contrasted (fig. 59).[3] This type of imagery has been interpreted as a classical metaphor of the dragon as eclipse symbol swallowing the lion, symbol of the Sun (the zodiacal sign of Leo is known as the house of the Sun).[4] It is moreover generally assumed that the creature emerging victorious from the combat would assimilate some of the essential qualities of the vanquished party; in this case the dragon perhaps absorbing qualities attributed to the lion such as bravery, courage and magnanimity as well as ferocity, voraciousness and wildness.

A comparable spirit seems to pervade the dragon reliefs preserved from the now destroyed city walls of the Saljuq capital Konya (618/1221), now in the İnce Minare Müzesi in Konya. The dragons' expansive knotted tails curve upwards and terminate in small dragon heads with open mouths that appear to grasp or attack the tails, hence visually conflating two dragons (fig. 60).[5] The influence of the bestiaries that populated the imaginary world of the medieval period perhaps stimulated the visual fusion of two or more animals, often of a different type, a common feature

---

[1] In his study on the theme of animal combat, Jean-Paul Roux (1981, pp. 5–11) came to the conclusion that the cultivation of shamanism among the Eurasian peoples perhaps played a role in the development of the motif.

[2] An engraved copper alloy plaque in the form of a haloed sphinx *passant* shown in combat with a winged dragon whose body is circling the body once and then the neck, re-emerging behind the sphinx's head and aiming to bite the back was sold at Sotheby's, London, 13 April, 1988, lot 252.

[3] Cf. *L'Etrange et le Merveilleux en terres d'Islam*, 2001, p. 97, cat. no. 64 (dated here to the twelfth or thirteenth century); Hauptmann von Gladiss and Kröger, 1985, p. 54, cat. no. 264 (dated here to the fourteenth century). Sections probably belonging to the same artefact are found in several collections, such as Copenhagen, the David Collection, inv. no. 31a/1975; von Folsach, 1990, p. 197, cat. no. 327, and *idem*, 1991, p. 53, cat. no. 91 (catalogued with an Iranian provenance and dated to the thirteenth or fourteenth century). For a complete side of the brazier with such openwork decoration, formerly in the Harari Collection, Cairo, see Erginsoy, 1978, p. 331, fig. 175, and further fragments of side panels, fig. 176 A (in the Grenoble Museum) and fig. 177 B (in Baltimore, Walters Art Gallery). Cf. Grube and Johns, 2005, p. 221, fig. 72.7.

[4] Cf. *L'Etrange et le Merveilleux en terres d'Islam*, 2001, p. 97, cat. no. 64. As has been demonstrated by Hartner and Ettinghausen, the lion combat motif dates back to ancient Mesopotamia and Iran having been interpreted as an astronomical symbol for the constellations Leo and Taurus that developed into a royal and finally a religious symbol. Hartner and Ettinghausen, 1964, pp. 161–71. See also Kuz'mina, 1987, pp. 729–45.

[5] Sarre, 1909, p. 13, fig. 15; Önder, 1961, p. 70, fig. 1; Diyarbekirli, 1968, p. 370, fig. 5; Öney, 1969a, p. 194, fig. 1; Gierlichs, 1996, p. 198, cat. no. 44, pl. 38. 2.

in the arts of Western Central Asia, particularly from the eleventh to the thirteenth century. Often however compositions represent a physically strong animal attacking a weaker one. The interesting depiction of an apparent contest between two dragons, hence two fabulous creatures of equal strength, perhaps symbolises the perpetual act of predation.

An animal combat also appears as part of a bilaterally symmetrical foliate interlace which fills a headpiece in the Mush Homiliary illuminated at the monastery of Avagvankʿ near Erznga(n) between 1200 and 1202. It terminates at one end in the protomes of two confronted winged dragons with forelegs and at the other in two goat heads topped by long curved horns, the latter snapping at the dragon wings while the dragon snouts clinch the goat necks (fig. 61).[6]

The façades of Armenian churches are similarly adorned with combatant animals, also featuring the likeness of the dragon or giant serpent. The bas-relief of a bird in combat with an ophidian dragon is shown over the window on the southern façade of the small twelfth- or thirteenth-century chapel behind the main church of Surb Astvatsatsin, which forms part of the monastic complex Makaravankʿ in Tavush province, Armenia.[7] Here the long serpentine body of the dragon is slung around the neck of the bird that in turn hacks with its large beak at the dragon's neck (fig. 62).[8]

A certain archaism of representation displayed in the vividly expressed animal nature of the creatures is preserved in the north Caucasus region – clearly featuring the dragon as antagonistic force in animal combat. The depiction echoes the theme of a lion killing a weaker animal which had been current in the Near Eastern and Central Asian world for millennia.[9] The portrayal certainly reflects the immediacy of mythic animal combat. Used as architectural ornament, the dragon is portrayed as a predatory and voracious creature, mauling another quadruped, presumably a cervid, shown with backward turned head, on an archivolt fragment from Daghistan in the eastern Caucasus (fig. 63).[10] The dragon's head is crowned with slanted cusped ears that are folded to the back, the flame-like mane is composed of four large, contiguous, cusped teardrop shapes that project from the sinuous necks; the slender wing that springs from the haunches is stiffly raised over the back ending in a small curl at the tip. The mythical creature is rendered with a pair of muscular forelegs, the inner leg raised as if to attack its prey, while the other balances the weight of the body; its elongated undulating serpentine tail forms a central loop and terminates in a curl.

b. *The dragon and mythical creatures*

The visually conflated dragons of the Konya reliefs (fig. 60) show that the body of the dragon was itself seen to be subject to mutations. Similarly, hybrids resulted from the dragon incorporating parts of other animals and mythical creatures and vice versa other animals and mythical creatures merging with parts of the dragon. Most commonly it was the head that was assimilated. The multiplex creatures thus juxtapose two principles into a unified being creating a duality, an ambiguity which simultaneously contrasts and fuses two metaphorical principles, as, for instance, the well-known example of the bird and the serpent or dragon representing two eternal antagonists which are discussed in the following. The nature of such hybrid beings is frequently associated with transitory or liminal states exemplified in such

[6] This depiction may be an allusion to *vishap-a-kagh*, a term employed in Armenian legend (from *vishap* and *kagh*, the latter meaning "male goat," *hircus*). It may be associated with the god Vahagn of the ancient Armeno-Parthian pantheon who bears the epithet *vishapakʿagh*, "dragon-slayer." I am grateful to Rev. Dr Vrej Nersessian (personal communication) for elucidating this point. Cf. Ishkol-Kerovpian, "Vahagn," *WdM* IV, 1, pp. 149–52, esp. p. 150.

[7] See *Makaravankʿ, Documents of Armenian Architecture/Documenti Di Architettura Armena*, vol. 22, Venice, 1993.

[8] The same motif is found frequently in marginal ornamentation of Armenian manuscripts. For instance, in a Gospel book, vellum, 318 fols., dated 1290, copied in Drazark, Cilician Armenia, by the scribe Tʿoros and illuminated by Tʿoros Roslin, Ms. 5736, fol. 10b. Mnatsakanyan, 1955, p. 532, fig. 1040.

[9] Cf. Ettinghausen, 1972, pp. 44–5.

[10] Bashkirov, 1931, pl. 72; Baltrušaitis, 1929, pl. LXVI, fig. 107. Anatoli Ivanov (1976) has revised Bashkirov's twelfth- to fourteenth-century dating of most Daghistan sculpture preserved in the walls of the mosques of Kubachi, on the basis of tombstones from Kubachi and a neighbouring village as well as an inscribed archivolt (fig. 133 in the publication) datable to the fourteenth or early fifteenth century. However, the archivolt fragment with the dragon and cervid was not part of the group of pieces discussed and published by Ivanov, nor do the carvings of the published tombstones (figs. 123, 126, 127, 130, 135, 136) bear any stylistic resemblance to the carving on the fragment (on the basis of the photographs), which is why a twelfth- or thirteenth-century dating still seems justified. The contention that most of the reliefs were not made in Kubachi but elsewhere in Daghistan (p. 203), is certainly worthy of notice.

tales as the *Alexander Romance* which recount Alexander's journey to the outer reaches of the earth, the land of darkness, without Sun, Moon or stars, where he meets such mythical creatures. Antecedents for dragon head motifs issuing from different zoomorphic junctures, for instance, from the tips of the wings or the tail ends,[11] may ultimately be found in the ancient "animal style."[12]

The synthesis with the dragon is portrayed on animals from the real and the imaginary realm. Among the theriomorphic examples, the dragon-tailed lion was one of the most common, as will be shown in the following. Predominant among the dragon-tailed fabulous creatures from the mythical realm are those usually defined as griffins and unicorns.[13] A thirteenth-century relief from the now destroyed fortress in Konya portrays a winged unicorn with prominent dragon tail in pursuit of a bovid (fig. 64).[14]

Often however the creatures fusing with parts of the dragon were therianthropomorphic beings combining the form of a human with those of an animal. Human-headed mythical creatures, generally identified as harpies, sphinxes[15] or centaurs, were portrayed with limbs transforming into dragon heads on diverse objects of the Eastern Islamic world. A harpy (a human-headed bird) whose florid tail terminates in a large upward-curving dragon protome with forelegs and gaping mouth serves as finial of an eleventh-century copper alloy incense burner typical of artistic production from the greater Khurasan region.[16] A sphinx (a human-headed quadruped, often represented with a female head and the body of a feline, frequently a lion(ess)) and a griffin (a hybrid of a bird and a quadruped), both with their upwardly curving tails terminating in dragon heads with open mouths that are oriented towards the heads of the fantastic animals, are prominently rendered on a frieze which runs around the body of a twelfth-century gilded and nielloed silver jug from Iran.[17]

Anatolian examples include architectural manifestations such as the carved reliefs of two winged quadrupeds with dragon-tails, possibly representing a sphinx and a griffin, on the bastion *(burç)* in the southwest of the city wall of Diyārbakr (Ulu Bandan tower no. 31) which according to the inscription was built in 604/1208–09 by the builder *(bannāʾ)* Ibrāhīm ibn Jaʿfar under the patronage of the Artuqid ruler Nāṣir al-Dīn Maḥmūd ibn Muḥammad al-Malik al-Ṣāliḥ (597/1201–619/1222).[18] A star tile unearthed during the 1992 excavations of the the now destroyed small palace at Kubadabad (623/1226–634/1237) built by *sulṭān* ʿAlāʾ al-Dīn Kay Qubādh I shows a gracefully rendered sphinx *marchant*, the haloed head in profile turned backwards and the tail ending in a dragon head capped by pointed ears, a wisp of flowing hair at the back of the neck and open jaws revealing the tongue (fig. 65). A pair of confronted perched harpies whose upstretched wing tips terminate in dragon heads are found on the *türbe* of Hüdavend Hatun/Khudāwand Khātūn (712/1312) in Niğde, examined in more detail below (fig. 66). An example of a portable object, representing perhaps a fountain head, is the small twelfth- or thirteenth-century pierced copper alloy figure of a recumbent lion-bodied sphinx with a tall crown whose raised curving wings as well as the upward-curling tail end in gaping dragon heads.[19]

To this dragon-tailed menagerie may be added a dragon-tailed sphinx portrayed to the left of the portal of a caravanserai in the Selim moun-

[11] Body parts of natural and mythical animals could also transform into body parts, mostly the heads, of other animals of the natural world. For instance, an eleventh- or twelfth-century copper alloy incense burner in openwork from present-day Afghanistan in the form of a standing lion has a tail that terminates in a bird head (David Collection, Copenhagen, inv. no. 48/1981; see von Folsach, 1991, p. 44, cat. no. 30, ill. on p. 15). Birds whose heads transform into those of hares are found on the cavetto of a twelfth- or thirteenth-century silver-inlaid dish with polylobed cavity from the Khurasan region, in the Musée du Louvre in Paris, inv. no. OA 6479 (Paris, Musée du Louvre, Département des Antiquités orientales, Section Islamique; Pope and Ackerman, eds., 1938–9, repr. 1964–81, p. 1315; *L'Etrange et le Merveilleux en terres d'Islam*, 2001, pp. 50–2, cat. no. 32, (see detail of cat. no. 32)).

[12] Cf. Otto-Dorn, 1978–9, pp. 130, 136.

[13] For a discussion of the unicorn-elephant fight, see Ettinghausen's monograph on the unicorn, 1950, pp. 84–91 (with a further dragon-tailed example, pl. 31, left).

[14] Cf. Gierlichs, 1996, pl. 37.2–3.

[15] For an in-depth study on sphinxes and harpies in medieval Islamic art, see Baer, 1965. For a more general study which includes modern interpretations of the sphinx, see Regier, 2004.

[16] Berlin, Museum für Islamische Kunst; Pope and Ackerman, eds., 1938–9, repr. 1964–81, vol. 13, p. 1278 B; Erginsoy, 1978, p. 158, fig. 70.

[17] Berlin, Museum für Islamische Kunst, inv. no. I.2210; Gierlichs, 1993, p. 53, cat. no. 50.

[18] Cf. Gabriel and Sauvaget, 1940, p. 98, fig. 72, pp. 120, 171, fig. 14, pls. LVIII. 2, LXVIII. 1; Gierlichs, 1996, pl. 51.5 and 6.

[19] Previously Diyārbakr Müzesi, Erginsoy, 1978, pp. 447–8, figs. 222 a and b; Baer, 1965, fig. 29. Now in Copenhagen, the David Collection, inv. no. 5/1978; von Folsach, 1990, p. 197, cat. no. 326.

tains in southern Armenia. The mythical creature has a powerful, perhaps bovine, quadruped body structure, topped by a slender neck which supports the frontally depicted human head whose features are no longer identifiable on account of the weathered condition with a prominent three-pronged crown-like headdress. The creature's tail curves upward to form a pretzel-like knot terminating above the slender wings with curled tip in a dragon head whose open jaws reveal the protruding tongue. According to the Persian inscription on the outside lintel the caravanserai was built in 727/1326–7 whereas the Armenian inscription on the right inside the portal states that it was constructed six or seven years later by Chesar Ōrbēlian and his brothers (fig. 67); just like the *türbe* of Hüdavend Hatun, the caravanserai was erected during the reign of the last Ilkhanid ruler Abū Saʿīd Baḥādur Khān (r. 717/1316–736/1335).

Hence in contrast to the animal combat in which the victorious antagonist would assimilate some of the essential attributes of the defeated animal, the hybrid examples referred to above amalgamated not only the form but presumably also the nature of the disparate elements, in other words their innate characteristics and attributes. This fusion was a conspicuous feature perhaps intended not only to reinforce the visual impact but also to augment the intended effect of a potent symbol. It has been shown that one of the most commonly depicted themes is that of dragon heads issuing from the tails or wing tips of real or imaginary creatures some of which may sometimes be identified as one of the constellations visualised as one of the twelve signs of the zodiac, as discussed below. It may be surmised that these depictions, other than those in an astronomical or astrological context, do not have a special astrological connection,[20] but reflect a general eastern spirit of *ʿajāʾib*, akin to that of the western *merveille*, at the mythical creatures of God's Creation *(al-makhlūqāt)* that are thought to exist beyond the limits of the known world. This is expressed in visual hybridisations that were particularly pervasive during the twelfth and thirteenth century in the medieval Central Asian world and beyond.

c. *The dragon and the bird*

From ancient times the bird and the serpent represented two of the mightiest cosmic entities. Their interaction harks back to well-known mythic themes recorded from ancient Mesopotamia,[21] Greece[22] and India.[23] In these archaic accounts a bird is identified with the theft of the elixir of eternal life, whose custodian the serpent would once have been.

Early Islamic histories, such as Balʿamī's *Tarjumat-i tārīkh-i Ṭabarī*, record several stories in which the rooster is considered apotropaic. In a passage of the chapter on Gayūmart (Av. *gaya marətan* "mortal life"), the mythical First Man of the Mazdean myth of creation, Balʿamī describes him witnessing the scene of a white rooster victoriously attacking a serpent in the middle of the day and then crowing gleefully. Gayūmart thence pronounces the rooster to be an auspicious portent. The same chapter notes that contrarily a rooster's

---

[20] Cf. Rogers, 1969, pp. 154–5 and ns. 15 and 16; Badiee, 1978, pp. 255–6.

[21] The Babylonian myth of Etana (surviving in Old Babylonian, Middle Assyrian and Neo-Assyrian recensions) that contains the fable of the serpent and the Zu bird relates how both lived in peaceful coexistence, "in the shade of the styrax tree begets the serpent; on its crown begets the eagle" until one day the eagle treacherously devoured the young of the serpent and the serpent, in revenge, broke the eagle's wings and threw him into a deep pit where he was doomed to perish. Etana found and healed the eagle who to show his gratitude took him to heaven to bring from there the "plant of birth" without which Etana could have no offspring. See Knipe, 1967, pp. 340–5; also Küster, 1913, pp. 52–3, 127–31, Astour, 1965, p. 235, and Reiner, 1991, repr. 2003, p. 301. It is of note that the Zu bird represents the evil protagonist against the the serpent as victim.

[22] Homer (*Iliad* XII 202–9; see also verse 220) describes the battle between eagle and serpent with the words:

> ...and a bird came ... a high-flying eagle ... holding a huge scarlet snake *(drakōn)* in its talons, alive still, twitching. Nor did it give up the fight. It struck the one who held it between chest and neck, twisting backward. And he dropped it to the ground, hurting with pain, and it fell in the midst of the army while he gave a cry and flew off down the wind. The Trojans shivered to see the shining snake *(ophis)* which lay among them, a portent from Zeus of the aegis.

Tr. after Redfield, 1975, repr. 1994, p. 144. The motif similarly appears in Aristophanes' *Equites* 218–22 and in Plutarch's *Vita Themistocles* 26.

[23] In the Vedic myth recorded in the Rigveda (4.26–7) it is Indra mounted on an eagle or falcon who steals the elixir (Av. *haoma*, Ved. *sóma*) from the atmospheric *gandharvas*. The antagonism between the mythical bird or bird-like creature (often an eagle-like predatory bird), *garuḍa*, and the *nāgas* is a favourite theme in Indian literature which finds its origin in the ancient fable of the rival sisters, Kadrū, the mother of the *nāgas*, and Vinatā, the mother of *garuḍa*, recorded in the *Mahābhārata* (*Ādi-parvan* 25–34); Vogel, 1926, pp. 51–3. Cf. Denis, E., *La Lokapaññati et les idées cosmologiques du Bouddhisme ancien*, Paris, 1977, vol. 1, 170–1, as cited by Strong, 1992, pp. 200–1, with further examples on pp. 29, 188–9, 200–8.

crowing at night was considered an inauspicious sign. Its crowing at such an unusual hour served as a warning that saved Siyāmak, Gayūmart's grandson (according to the *Bundahishn*), from being attacked by a serpent.[24]

Cosmological concepts associating the bird with the serpent are recorded in the Meccan tradition, according to which Allāh sent:

> ...from the cupola of heaven a bird in the form of an *ʿuqāb*, a bird with a black back, a white breast and yellow claws. While the serpent on the wall of the Kaʿba opened its mouth in order to repel the bird, the latter came, caught it by its head and took it to the mountain Ajjād.[25]

Wensinck interprets this tradition as a reference to the three cosmological powers, "the sun [symbolised] by the bird, the ocean by the serpent, and the earth by its navel, the sanctuary [the Kaʿba]."[26] He further notes that the age-old symbolism of:

> ...the eagle with the serpent in its mouth or between its talons is a striking illustration of the idea of cosmic victory. ... Eagle and serpent are the representatives of two of the mightiest cosmic entities, the sun and the ocean.[27]

Yet although birds and (serpent-)dragons are depicted as opposing symbols, the sky and water/earth, above and below, they are often conjoined into a composite generated from the same stock of concepts and images.[28] This visual conflation of the bird with the dragon can be seen in particular on textiles, which due to their portability and high status, were a prime luxury medium for the transmission of a visual vocabulary. The motif is exemplified, for instance, on a twelfth- or thirteenth-century silk samite fragment from Samangan province in Afghanistan, of elongated rectangular form, featuring pairs of large and stately confronting birds, probably roosters, with prominent combs and florid tails terminating in dragon heads, which flank elaborately rendered palmette trees (fig. 68).[29]

Islamic textiles largely survive in relatively good condition because they were included in medieval church treasuries.[30] The bird and dragon motif can be found on one such fragment which was preserved in the shrine of Saint Apollinaris at the church of Saint Servatius in Siegburg. Dragon heads project from spiralling volutes that emerge from the outer wing tips of a double-headed bird (probably an eagle) with "ears" set within shield-shaped medallions. The expressive crested dragon heads are rendered with large, circular eyes and particularly wide-open snouts tapering to pointed tips and revealing the tongue (figs. 69a and b).[31] The silk has been attributed by Friedrich Sarre to an Anatolian manufactory, where it might have served as a Saljuq coronation robe,[32] and has been dated to the first quarter of the thirteenth century.[33]

Comparable imagery of the double-headed bird of prey is preserved in architectural ornamentation at the confines of the same cultural sphere. The same bird with "dragon-wings" can also be found on either side of the western gateway of the thirteenth-century Great Mosque of Divriği (Diwrīgī), situated on the borders of Armenia and Cappadocia. The dragon heads are rendered with elongated wide-open mouths emitting curving, tongue-like foliage, which in turn extends to the outspread wing tips of the double-headed birds (figs. 70a and b).[34] The mosque was built in 626/1228–9 (or later) by native craftsmen of Akhlāt (northwest of Lake Van) for the Türkmen Mengüjükid ruler Aḥmad Shāh and his wife, Tūrān Malik, who were under Saljuq suzerainty.[35] The epigraphic band above the main portal of the mosque mentions the name and title of ʿAlāʾ al-Dīn Kay Qubādh, presumably in recognition of his overlordship.[36]

---

[24] Recorded in Balʿamī's Persian translation of Ṭabarī's *History*; tr. and ed. Lazard, 1956, pp. 206–7, 211.

[25] Ibn Hishām's edition of the Ibn Isḥāq's *Sīra*, ed. Wüstenfeld, 1857, p. 125; al-Diyārbakrī, Ḥusayn ibn Muḥammad, *Taʾrīkh al-khamīs*, vol. 1, Cairo, 1283, p. 112, cited after Wensinck, 1921, repr. 1978, p. 47. Cf. Atallah, 1975, p. 164.

[26] Wensinck, 1921, repr. 1978, p. 47.

[27] *Idem*, p. 46.

[28] The theme of the transformation of a serpent into an eagle occurs for instance in the *Alexander Romance*; Pseudo-Callisthenes I, ch. 10, tr. and ed. Stoneman, 1991, p. 42.

[29] Related imagery occurs on a mid-thirteenth-century *lampas* weave which carries addorsed felines and double-headed eagles in the interstices grasping curled outer tail feathers that end in dragon heads; preserved in the Cleveland Museum of Art, inv. no. 1990.2. Watts and Wardwell, 1997, cat. no. 43.

[30] Cf. Shalem, 2004, pp. 125–30.

[31] Cf. Jacques and Wencker, 1967, pp. 472–527 and 487–90. A smaller fragment (length 22.5 cm, width 21 cm) is preserved in Staatliche Museen Preussischer Kulturbesitz, Kunstgewerbemuseum, Berlin, inv. no. 81.745. *The Arts of Islam*, 1976, p. 79, cat. no. 14; von Wilckens, 1992, p. 43, fig. 66, colour pl. on p. 48; Gierlichs, 1993, p. 30, pl. 10, cat. no. 84.

[32] Otto-Dorn, 1978–9, p. 119.

[33] von Wilckens, 1992, p. 43, cat. no. 66.

[34] Otto-Dorn, 1978–9, p. 120, fig. 18; Enderlein, 1990, p. 88; Firat, 1996, no pagination. Gierlichs, 1996, pl. 3, 1–4.

[35] Sourdel-Thomine, "Diwrīgī," *EI*² II, 320a.

[36] Van Berchem, 1910, pp. 97–8; Otto-Dorn, 1978–9, p. 121.

The mutation of the bird into a dragon also occurs in the illuminations of Armenian manuscripts. In a marginal ornament in a ninth- or tenth-century missal from Ejmiatsin ("the Only-begotten descended") in Armavir province confronted mythical creatures have the bodies of birds, their long necks interlacing to terminate in dragon heads that turn backwards and appear to bite into the upright foliate tail tips (fig. 71). Not the heads of the birds but more frequently their tails end in dragon heads as shown in the L'viv Gospel transcribed and illustrated in Cilician Armenia in 1198/1199.[37] The eighth of the ten canon tables is framed by birds that are perched on vertically interlaced vines, their tails extending into a spiral from which grow dragon heads crowned by long rabbit-like ears,[38] their open mouths revealing tongues with bifid tips that touch the tips of the birds' beaks (fig. 72).[39] In the same manuscript on the opening page of the Gospel of Luke, a pair of long-legged birds flanking the central cross and surmounting the frame of a headpiece are shown in the same posture, their heads turned backwards, the beaks inserted into the open mouths of yet another type of dragon with a scaly body and long pointed ears. Importantly this depiction portrays the symbiosis of the entire dragon body with that of the bird, the dragon's tail tapering towards the bird's head and extending towards the beak which, held in the dragon's jaws, closes the loop (fig. 73). Similes associating the serpent and the dove are recorded in Agathangelos' fifth-century literary composition entitled *Teaching of St. Gregory*, one of the earliest Armenian theological texts, which states that man will learn the wisdom of the serpent, strip off all ephemeral impurities as a serpent sloughs off its skin, and receive the pure simplicity of the dove.[40]

A comparable feature portraying a fusion of the bodies of the bird and the dragon can be observed on the stone relief above the southern outer door at the monastery of Mār Behnām/Deir al-Khiḍr. Here the upward-curling tips of the tail feathers of the confronted, *regardant* birds transform into characteristic dragon heads that peck at the tail tips (fig. 74).

The inverse mutation of the tail or wing ends of dragons transforming into raptorial bird heads is exhibited, for instance, on a copper alloy dragon knocker that was fastened to the wooden door of the Great Mosque (Ulu Cami) of Cizre (fig. 83) or the dragon reliefs carved on the now destroyed Talisman Gate (Bāb al-Ṭilasm) in Baghdad (fig. 139b), both discussed in the following.

d. *The dragon and the feline*

The symbiosis of the dragon with a feline predator, two creatures carrying associations not only of great danger, but of royalty (discussed below in chapter 7), is alluded to in Iranian literature. The phenomenon is illustrated in a *Shāh-nāma* account which describes how Rustam, the chief epic hero of Iran, when fourteen years old, vanquishes in India the sea- and land-dwelling dragon known as Babr-i Bayān. Rustam has the slain beast flayed and then makes out of the skin or hide a coat for himself, the *babr-i bayān*.[41] In nature when an animal dies its flesh decays while the skin and hair remain. This fact may have given rise to the association of animal hides with special powers. The dragon's skin may be considered to represent the essence of the living beast. Being covered with its skin was believed to symbolise the acquisition of this fundamental nature and to induce a transformation of the wearer. The *babr-i bayān* was invulnerable, proof against fire and water and impregnable to any weapon. The hero thus wore it before going into battle, placing it above his chainmail tunic which was reinforced by iron-plated armour.[42] The *babr-i bayān* was visualised as either the pelt of a tiger *(babr)* or that of a leopard *(palangīna)*.[43] The dragon Babr-i

[37] Prinzing and Schmidt, eds., 1997, pp. 18–21.

[38] The extensive range of the repertoire of zoomorphic visual fusions resulting in fantastic beasts on artefacts from the Irano-Turkish region is exemplified, for instance, by birds with the heads of hares, depicted on the cavetto of a twelfth- or thirteenth-century silver-inlaid dish with polylobed cavity. See p. 75, n. 11.

[39] Cf. Akinian, 1930, p. 16, fig. 7; Prinzing and Schmidt, eds., 1997, p. 50, pl. VIII.

[40] Tr. and ed. Thomson, 1970, p. 29, and chs. 602–10.

[41] The legend is known among the Mandeans of Iraq in which Rustam kills the Babr-i bayān in China when he is twelve years old. Petermann, 1860–1, vol. 2, pp. 107–9. See Khāleqī-Moṭlaq, "Aždahā II" and *idem*, "Babr-e bayān," *EIr*.

[42] *Shāh-nāma*, tr. and ed. Mohl, 1838–1878, vol. 3, p. 129, ll. 1470–6. Melikian-Chirvani, 1998, p. 173.

[43] *Idem*, vol. 3, p. 129, l. 1474; 227, l. 1035; this identification is confirmed by its reference in a Sogdian text

bayān thus seems to have acquired features of a feline predator endowed with dragon-like characteristics.[44] By clothing himself in the *babr-i bayān* Rustam implicitly signalled his symbolic appropriation of the dragon's qualities as well as his mastery over the hybrid creature. It is of note that such composite animal imagery associating the feline, in particular the lion, with the dragon is also apparent in ancient Near Eastern myth.[45]

The visual conflation of dragon and feline is expressed in Central Asian art from at least the eleventh century onwards. It appears on a matrix from the set of 77 late twelfth-century copper alloy matrices for belt/strap fittings, considered earlier in chapter 3, one of which bears an inscription in the name of the Ghurid *sulṭān* Ghiyāth al-Dīn Muḥammad ibn Sām. The matrix is symmetrically cast in relief with a pair of small, addorsed lions *couchant*. These are surmounted by ascending, exaggeratedly long, imbricated tails that interlace in a lozenge-shape before overlapping again at the tip and terminating in disproportionately large, confronted dragon heads. The creatures' open snouts touch at the tips, thus forming another small lozenge, and are crowned by prominent curving horns with curling tips (fig. 75). Another small matrix from the same set, with lozenge-shaped outline topped by a trefoil finial, features a single seated lion in high relief whose upward-arching tail also ends in a large, horned, snarling dragon's head with gaping mouth revealing the tongue (fig. 76).[46] The conflation of the king of animals, the personification of kingly power *par excellence* (lion hunting being the prerogative of Islamic rulers), with the dragon presented an apt symbolism for the strap fittings of a royal belt.

The iconography of a dragon-tailed lion is also shown on the portal of several thirteenth-century Islamic and Christian monuments located in particular in southeast Anatolia and northern Mesopotamia. It appears on the so-called royal door of the monastery of Mār Ḥūdéni/Mār Aḥūdēmmeh in Mosul,[47] the monastery of Mār Behnām/Deir al-Khiḍr at the southeast of Mosul (fig. 77),[48] on the men's entrance of the Chaldean church[49] and on the main portal of the Jacobite church (fig. 78),[50] both located in Cizre. The seated lion is portrayed in profile, the head rendered frontally or in three-quarter view, his long tail winding around the hind legs, under the belly and extending over the back transforming into a dragon's neck and head. The mythical creature is portrayed with a curved horn and gaping jaws, revealing a long tongue with bifid tip entwined at mid-section, snapping at the lion's back. At Mār Ḥūdéni the lion's tail again forms a pretzel-like knot, and at the Jacobite church the dragons' bifid tongues entwine at mid-section (the same feature can be observed on the addorsed entwined dragons at Mār Behnām, figs. 17a and b, 160). Of note is moreover the conspicuous placement and orientation of the dragon-tailed lions towards the opening of the doorways drawing attention to the threshold.

Similar depictions appear also in the two-dimensional medium of manuscript illumination such as in a Gospel book painted by Bartholemew (Bardagh) in the Armenian province of Siunikʿ, in which two confronted lions are seated on the tips of the Armenian initial "U" of the first word of Mark's Gospel (Սկիզբն, the beginning). The two lions represent here the symbol of Saint Mark,[51] their heads being rendered in frontal view

(Benveniste, E., *Textes Sogdiens*, Mission Pelliot III, Paris, 1940, pp. 134–6), as cited in Khāleqī-Moṭlaq, "Babr-e bayān," *EIr*. Cf. Melikian-Chirvani, 1998, p. 173.

[44] It is worth mentioning the analogy to the Greek legend of the pre-eminent hero Herakles, whose exploits included strangling a lion, which could not be slain in any other way because its pelt was invulnerable, and wearing its skin as a coat over his shoulders as though becoming part lion himself.

[45] The story of "The Slaying of the Labbu" (Cuneiform texts from Babylonian tablets in the British Museum 13.33–54; Heidel, repr. 1951, pp. 141–3) recounts the victory of the god Tishpak over the dragon referred to variously as *labbu* (Akkadian for "lion"), *bašmu* and *mušḫuššu*. The latter two are listed as separate members of Tiamat, the personified primordial water-chaos, and her battalions in the Akkadian epic of creation, *Enūma Elish* (I.121; II.27; III.31,89), of Babylon. See Wilson, 2001, pp. 30–2.

[46] Kuwait, al-Sabāh Collection, Dar al-Athar al-Islamiyyah, Kuwait National Museum, LNS 2558 J 'a-x2' 's2' and 't2'; 't2' being entirely covered with reddish corrosion products; 's2' height 2.69 cm, width 1.53 cm, 't2' height 2.92 cm, width 1.87 cm.

[47] Height 22,5 cm, width 27 cm. Sarre and Herzfeld, 1920, vol. 2, p. 294 (drawing), fig. 281, and, *eidem*, 1911, vol. 3, pl. 106, fig. 3. Fiey, 1959, pp. 144–6, fig. 11.

[48] Preusser, 1911, pl. x; Hartner, 1938, fig. 27; Fiey, 1959, fig. 12; Gierlichs, 1996, pl. 59.1.

[49] The church no longer exists; recorded *in situ* by Preusser, 1911, p. 25, pl. 35.2 (Preusser refers to it as Jacobite church); reproduced by Hartner, 1938, pp. 143–4, fig. 24; Willy Hartner also notes the fact that as "manly animal" *par excellence*, the lion reliefs were absent from the women's entrance of the Chaldean church, fig. 25.

[50] Height 45 cm, width 56 cm. The church does not exist any more; recorded *in situ* by Preusser, 1911, p. 25, pl. 34.2 (reproduced by Hartner, 1938, pp. 143–4, fig. 23); the reliefs are preserved in the Archaeological Museum, Diyārbakr, inv. nos. 64, 65. Öney, 1969, p. 209, and n. 50, fig. 34; Gierlichs, 1996, pl. 60.5, 6.

[51] I would like to thank Rev. Dr Vrej Nersessian for this information.

at an angle, each with one raised foreleg meeting at the central axis and their ascending tails ending in dragon heads with open snouts revealing long tongues (fig. 79).

Artistic cross-fertilisation in plastic and pictorial art between Islamic Anatolia and Christian Armenian and Georgian regions is reflected in the depiction on a thirteenth-century relief on the hall portal of Kesikköprü Han (667/1268–9) in central Anatolia. It shows a lion in profile with frontally oriented head whose tail curves under its belly and then upwards to terminate in a dragon head just above the back. The head with small, pointed ears is oriented backwards to face a long-tailed bird which perches on the lion's hindquarters and pecks at the dragon's open mouth (fig. 80).[52] This type of imagery with a bird pecking with its beak at the open mouth of a dragon is a recurrent feature in Armenian miniatures (see figs. 72 and 73).

It is probable that the dragon motif that was seen on the royal silks (*parang* or *parniyān*) or their representation on wall paintings in Central Asia, in particular Sogdiana, the later Māwarā al-Nahr of the early Islamic period, and Turkestan became a favoured emblem of royalty, next to the lion and the eagle, on medieval Islamic silks. Al-Ḥusayn ibn Muḥammad ibn ʿAlī al-Jaʿfarī al-Rughadī, known as Ibn al-Bībī al-Munajjima ("the son of the "lady," the astrologer"), who was head of the chancellery of the Secretariat of State at the court of the Rūm Saljuqids,[53] relates in his memoirs, *al-Awāmir al-ʿAlāʾiyya fī ʾl-ūmur al-ʿAlāʾiyya*, that after his ascension to the throne, the Rūm Saljuq *sulṭān* ʿAlāʾ al-Dīn Kay Qubādh I of Konya followed the ancient custom[54] of bestowing lavish gifts upon his emirs amongst which the receiving of robes of honour (*khilʿa* or *tashrīf*) constituted the greatest honour.[55] A conflation of dragon and lion can be seen on a royal textile, a silk woven in gold, set against a pink ground, which bears the name of *sulṭān* ʿAlāʾ al-Dīn Kay Qubādh, probably referring to Kay Qubādh I. The textile is decorated with circular medallions enclosing a pair of addorsed *regardant* lions in rampant posture with frontally presented heads from whose open mouths spring volutes that form a central vegetal composition. The lions' curling tail ends transform into dragon heads with wide-open jaws (figs. 81a and b).[56]

The conjunction of dragon and lion was also used on door handles, which seem to have had a special place in the tradition of southeast Anatolia. An example intended for the palace door at Diyārbakr is illustrated in a copy of the celebrated treatise on automata written by the master craftsman al-Jazarī (the *nisba* pointing to an affiliation with Cizre, also known as Jazīrat ibn ʿUmar), begun when in the service at the court of the Artuqid ruler Nūr al-Dīn Muḥammad ibn Qara Arslan (562/1167–581/1185) in the principality of Ḥiṣn Kayfā (Hasankeyf)[57] (fig. 134).[58]

In 577/1181 Nūr al-Dīn was awarded Diyārbakr as fief and transferred his court to the city. There al-Jazarī created a monumental door with cast brass plates inlaid with copper and silver for the ruler's palace,[59] now only surviving in draw-

[52] To the left of the portal there is another lion relief, probably a spolium, which on account of its poor state of preservation (only the protome is extant) is difficult to assess; Gierlichs, 1996, pp. 171–2, pl. 17.3. When the author visited Kesikköprü Han in 2008, the building had just been renovated and the relief with the dragon-tailed lion with bird did not exist anymore.

[53] Duda, "Ibn Bībī," *EI*² III, 737b.

[54] The Patriarch Jacob is recorded as having chosen his favourite son Joseph from amongst his brothers to honour him with a ceremonial or royal robe, *ketōnet passīm* (Genesis 37,3). This custom was first recorded in Islam with the Prophet Muḥammad bestowing the *burda* he was wearing on the poet Kaʿb ibn Zuhayr; cf. Ibn al-Athīr, *Kāmil*, Cairo, 1301, vol. 2, pp. 133–4, cited after Stillmann, "Khilʿa," *EI*² V, 6a.

[55] *Al-Awāmir al-ʿAlāʾiyya*, tr. Duda, 1959, p. 95. Allsen (1997, pp. 85, 87–9) remarks upon the "impressive continuity" of the ancient practice of the bestowing of garments. Gordon (2001, pp. 5–6) hypothesises that the practice of investiture with "luxurious robes" began with the early nomads, "first perhaps as a semi-diplomatic relation with the sedentary culture but soon as a prerogative of a nomadic leader," which set a prototype for later investiture ceremonies.

[56] Cf. Diez and Arslanapa, 1956, pp. 259–60; *The Arts of Islam*, 1976, p. 79, cat. no. 13; Arrizoli-Clémentel, 1990, p. 55.

[57] *Al-Jāmiʿ bayn al-ʿilm wa ʾl-ʿamal an-nāfiʿ fī ṣināʿat al-hiyal*, ed. Aḥmad Yūsuf al-Hassan, Institute for the History of Arabic Science, Aleppo, 1979; facsimile ed. of Ms. Ahmet III no. 3472, Istanbul, Topkapı Sarayı Museum, Library, Kültür Bakan-lığı, ed. *Olağanüstü mekanik araçların bilgisi hakkında kitap*, Ankara, 1990. Cf. Meinecke, 1996, p. 62, n. 18. The treatise, which al-Jazarī compiled and illustrated, was completed at the beginning of the thirteenth century for the Artuqid ruler of Diyārbakr. The original manuscript does not survive, but a copy was made shortly after its completion by another artist from Hisn Kayfā, a certain Muḥammad ibn Yūsuf ibn ʿUthmān al-Hiskafī, now preserved in Istanbul, Topkapı Sarayı Museum, Library. Meinecke, 1996, p. 63 and n. 26.

[58] Cf. *idem*, 1996, p. 139, pl. 21a. This type of imagery is also used as marginal ornament in Armenian manuscript illumination, see the collection of sermons, copied on vellum, 607 fols., dated 1205, transcribed and illuminated in the monastery of Ghazarvankʿ by the scribe Vardan; Ms. 7729, fol. 237a. Mnatsakanyan, 1955, p. 517, fig. 1024.

[59] Since Muḥammad ibn Qara Arslan had started only two years before his death in 581/1185 to furnish his residence, the doors may well have been made during this period, cf. Meinecke, 1989, p. 57, and *idem*, 1996, p. 62.

ings.[60] It consisted of two hinged leaves, each framed with a broad epigraphic band in Kufic containing eulogies of the ruler and fitted with cast copper alloy knockers,[61] which are fashioned, according to al-Jazarī's description:

> Then I made for each leaf [of the door] ring [i.e. a knocker] from cast brass in the shape of two connected serpents, the head of each facing the head of the other. Their mouths are open as if they wished to devour the head and neck of a lion. This lion's head and neck are the extension of an iron staple which is nailed to the door. The fangs of the serpents are in two holes in the lion's neck...[62]

Only a copy of al-Jazarī's drawing of the door knocker and not the actual device survives. However the knockers were much imitated. Copper alloy examples of this type as well as brass plaques adorned the wooden doors of the Ulu Cami of Cizre, now in the Türk ve İslam Eserleri Müzesi (fig. 82). According to the inscription on the upper panel of the door, it was endowed by the local Zangid *atābeg* Maḥmūd ibn Sānjar Shāh who resided in Cizre from 604/1208 to 638/1241.[63] Hence the Cizre knockers were probably made about two decades after al-Jazarī's creations.[64] In contrast to the drawing of the knocker in the copy of al-Jazarī's compendium of 602/1206 in which the heads of the dragons that flank the central lion-headed knob (serving as hinge and attachment to the door) are facing each other, the dragon heads of the Cizre copper alloy knockers are portrayed addorsed, thus with heads turned away from the lion head. The dragon heads, rendered with small cusped ears and almond-shaped eyes outlined by curving lines, have characteristic wide-open jaws and a curled tip of the snout. They are shown to grasp or attack the small, curved wings which spring from an ornament that curls around their haunches. The dragons' paired forelegs touch at the tips, their scaly ophidian bodies forming a loop at the centre, and tapering to the entwined tail ends from the tips of which spring small raptorial bird heads (fig. 83).[65] Several other dispersed examples of near-identical dragon-knockers dating from the late twelfth to the early thirteenth century exist in slightly varying sizes.[66]

The imagery of the dragon guarding a treasure is a central theme in Niẓāmī's romance *Haft Paykar*, completed in 593/1197.[67] In the same work the poet, who spent most of his life in Ganja in present-day Azerbaijan, talks about "dragon-like locks on treasures rested"[68] which may indicate that the dragon knockers designed by al-Jazarī and their counterparts at the Ulu Cami of Cizre and other mosques were part of a well-established iconographic genre which extended far beyond southeastern Anatolia and was well-known in the medieval world.[69] As doorknockers the interlaced dragons were fastened to the doors at the entrance

[60] Cf. al-Jazarī, *Kitāb fī maʿrifat al-ḥiyāl al-handasiyya*, tr. Hill, 1974, pp. 192–3, 267. The earliest extant copy (Istanbul, Topkapı Sarayı Müzesi, Ms. Ahmet III, A.3472, fol. 165b) contains a colophon with the date "end of Shaʿbān 602" (about 10 April 1206) but as noted by David King in his review of *The Book of Knowledge of Ingenious Mechanical Devices: Kitāb fī maʿrifat al-ḥiyāl al-handasiyya* by *Ibn al-Razzāz al-Jazarī* (*History of Science* XIII, 1975, pp. 284–9, esp. n. 4) this refers not to the date of Ms. Ahmet III, A.3472, but to the date of the manuscript from which the Istanbul manuscript was copied.

[61] Height 450 cm, width 300 cm; Meinecke, 1996, pp. 62 and 136, pl. 18 a. Cf. al-Jazarī, *Kitāb fī maʿrifat al-ḥiyāl al-handasiyya*, tr. Hill, 1974, pp. 191–5; Hauptmann von Gladiss, p. 32, fig. 10. For a modern reconstruction of the Artuqid palace door at Diyārbakr, see Meinecke, 1989, p. 57, fig. 6.

[62] *Kitāb fī maʿrifat al-ḥiyāl al-handasiyya*, tr. Hill, 1974, p. 194.

[63] Cf. Hauptmann von Gladiss, ed. 2006, p. 69.

[64] Meinecke, 1989, p. 57.

[65] One of a pair of door knockers from the Ulu Cami of Cizre, now in Istanbul, Türk ve İslam Eserleri Müzesi, inv. no. 3749; see *The Anatolian Civilisations*, vol. 3, 1983, pp. 60–1, nos. D. 95–7; Ölçer, 1993, and *idem*, 2002, pp. 98–9; Roxburgh, 2005, pp. 130–1, 399–400, cat. no. 87. The other pair is preserved in Copenhagen, the David Collection, inv. no. 38/1973; see *The Arts of Islam*, 1976, no. 194; Erginsoy, 1988, p. 170, fig. 141; von Folsach, 1990, p. 196, cat. no. 323, *idem*, 1991, p. 44, cat. no. 32, and idem, 1996, fig. 110, cat. no. 362; Hauptmann von Gladiss, ed., 2006, p. 68, fig. 25. The lion-headed pin of the Copenhagen knocker is in Istanbul, Türk ve İslam Eserleri Müzesi, inv. no. 3750. The knockers were documented *in situ* by Preusser, 1911, pp. 25–6, pl. 36. Cf. Öney, 1969a, fig. 17; Meinecke, 1989, p. 56, fig. 5, and *idem*, 1996, p. 136, pl. 18b.

[66] Door knocker, preserved in Berlin, Museum für Islamische Kunst, inv. no. I.2242; see Kühnel, 1925, p. 136, fig. 100 and *idem*, 1950, p. 13, fig. 16; Meinecke, 1989, p. 56, fig. 4 and *idem*, 1996, p. 139, pl. 21b; Gierlichs, 1993, p. 41, cat. no. 7; Grube and Johns, 2005, p. 230, fig. 77.6. Two examples are in the Nasser D. Khalili Collection of Islamic Art, London, inv. nos. MTW1407&1428; height 40 cm, width 40 cm; see Piotrovsky, ed., 2000, p. 98, cat. no. 3; Bilici, 2006, figs. 9, 10.

[67] Tr. Meisami, 1995.

[68] *Idem*, p. 221.

[69] Another type of copper alloy knocker, now preserved in Paris, Musée du Louvre, features a circular openwork ring composed of five confronted pairs of dragon protomes with wide-open jaws held by a central lion-headed knob and in earlier publications has been attributed to Iran or Syria and the twelfth century (*L'Islam dans les collections nationales*, 1977, p. 99, cat. no. 153) but has now been assigned a Jazīran

to a sacred building where they served to protect the building. In their function as "guardians" of entrances to sacred places or to "treasures" they were endowed with an apotropaic function.

e. *The dragon and the elephant*

The ingenuity of al-Jazarī was further proven when later in his career he entered the service of Qutb al-Dīn Suqmān (581/1185–597/1201) and began inventing mechanical devices, such as the so-called "elephant water-clock." This water-clock was amongst the devices originally compiled and illustrated by al-Jazarī, and is shown on a leaf from the *Kitāb fī maʿrifat al-ḥiyāl al-handasiyya* which was copied by Muḥammad ibn Yūsuf ibn ʿUthmān al-Ḥaṣkafī at Diyārbakr, and dated to the end of Shaʿbān 602/about 10 April 1206, now preserved in the Topkapı Sarayı Library in Istanbul (fig. 84). "The passage of constant hours,"[70] the concept of the ebb and flow of time and the seasons, is indicated by a scale adjusted by a small person seated atop an elephant *passant* within a tall tower that supports the device. Perched on top of the tall domed tower, a bird spins around every half an hour, whereupon the elephant driver strikes his elephant and another figure causes the falcon to release a pebble. In his description of the central mechanism al-Jazarī states:

> ...transversely between the centres of the pillars is an axle on which are two serpents, the claws of each one grasping the axle, its tail around the axle like a ring, its head tilted backwards, the mouth open as if to swallow the falcon,[71] the edge of the lower lip is touching the front of the castle [the tower], and the upper lip is spread, with the two fangs bared.[72]

It is interesting to note that the representation of the serpent body coiled around the central pole also has an analogy in ancient Hindu mythology, in which the body of the great cosmic dragon Vāsuki ("Possessor of Treasures") serves as giant churning rope to rotate Mount Mandara in the well-known myth of the "Churning of the Ocean" *(Samudramanthana)* which produces the nectar *(amṛta)* of divine immortality.[73] In the course of the story, the demons Rāhu and Ketu become involved, an episode which is discussed below in chapter 8.

The motif of the serpent that appears to threaten the birds is based on a related design by an earlier craftsman, acknowledged by al-Jazarī,[74] the late eighth-century Pseudo-Archimedes,[75] whose work included frequent representations of the dragon on clocks, knockers or as spouts of ewers. From this it appears that motifs ultimately derived from Hellenistic sources enjoyed widespread popularity in the medieval Islamic world. And although he has suggested no symbolic meaning for his creations, al-Jazarī may well have taken for granted that his audience was well aware of the overall symbolism, in which case the omission is inconclusive. The depictions may therefore have well been part of an apotropaic and, perhaps, talismanic tradition.

On textiles of the early medieval period the imagery of the elephant, the giant among animals, was fairly frequent. It has been preserved on several Umayyad[76] and Byzantine textiles[77] made in imitation of late Sasanian examples.[78] In the medieval Islamic period elephants had great value and regal status and as such were often richly caparisoned.[79] Such noble pachyderms are shown together with disproportionately diminutive quadruped dragons on a saddle cloth,

provenance and a late twelfth- or early thirteenth-century date (*L'Etrange et le Merveilleux en terres d'Islam*, 2001, p. 232, cat. no. 160). Paris, Musée du Louvre, Département des Antiquités orientales, Section Islamique, inv. no. MOA 97. Rouault and Masetti-Rouault, eds., 1993, cat. no. 471 (colour photograph).

[70] Tr. Hill, 1974, p. 48.

[71] *Idem*, p. 59 and 1984, p. 238.

[72] *Idem*, p. 68.

[73] Cf. Long, 1976, pp. 177–81.

[74] *Kitāb fī maʿrifat al-ḥiyāl al-handasiyya*, tr. Hill, 1974, pp. 272, 279 and *idem*, 1998, ch. XII, "The Banū Mūsà and their "Book of Ingenious Devices," p. 73; Meinecke, 1996, p. 63 and n. 27.

[75] Possibly the work of a late eighth-century Muslim inventor who based his work on several earlier sources including probably Philon and Heron. Cf. *Kitāb fī maʿrifat al-ḥiyāl al-handasiyya*, tr. Hill, 1974, p. 10.

[76] Jerusalimskaja, 2000, p. 114 and n. 13.

[77] Grabar, 1951, p. 35. Cf. the "Elephant Silk" from the tomb of Charlemagne, Treasury of Aachen Cathedral (Grabar, 1951, p. 35, fig. 3); or, an eleventh-century Armenian painting showing king Gagik-Abas of Kars (1029–1064), sitting in state with his wife and daughter on a low throne covered with a textile decorated with pearl roundels containing elephants (illustration from the Gospel book of Gagik-Abas of Kars, perhaps painted in Kars, *c.* 1050. Jerusalem, Armenian cathedral of Saint James, Ms. 2556, fol. 135bis. Der Nersessian, 1945, p. 119, pl. XXIII.2; *Glory of Byzantium*, 1997, p. 353, photograph to the left); king Gagik himself is shown to wear a garment with a comparable pattern and a *tiraz* with Kufic letters at the upper arms, indicating an Islamic origin. This led André Grabar to suggest that the garment may have been a gift by a Muslim sovereign. It moreover shows that this pattern was evidently linked to both Armenian and Islamic contexts.

[78] Grabar, 1951, pp. 40–2.

[79] Bosworth, 1963, p. 117.

known as the celebrated Khurasanian "Elephant Silk," which was preserved as the shroud of Saint Jodokus (Saint Josse) (fig. 85a).[80] The silk samite survives as a group of fragments which show two superimposed pairs of large, confronted elephants in the central field. The great beasts are lavishly caparisoned with saddle blankets, their heavy feet with articulated toes being singled out for emphasis. These potent symbols of power are each paired with a disproportionately tiny quadruped dragon with a very long sinuous neck almost disappearing between its legs. The four-legged dragons rest on feet with separated toes and long, needle-pointed talons, their stiffly raised wings terminating in a small curled tip following post-Sasanian conventions, and their raised undulant tails terminating in a pointed tuft of hair (fig. 85b).[81] The depiction is framed above and below by a Kufic inscription in mirror image which includes glory and good wishes to the owner, Qāʾid Abu ʾl-Manṣūr Bākh-tigīn, the Turkish *āmir* of Khurasan, whose execution in 349/960–1 by order of his Samanid sovereign ʿAbd al-Malik ibn Nūh presents a *terminus ante quem* for dating the textile.[82] The silk is framed in the style of a carpet by a procession of camels with flying scarves and roosters with beaded neckbands in each of the corners. It thus provides a combination of Sasanian style elements with Central Asian aspects such as the dragons and the camels. Belenitskii and Bentowitsch note analogies in the motifs to Sogdian art, in particular with the eighth-century wall painting frieze of the Red Hall at the Sogdian palace at Varakhsha, northwest of Bukhara, featuring elephants being attacked by long-necked mythical creatures.[83] The authors suggest that the dynamic representation of dragons and elephants on the Varakhsha wall paintings may be a translation of the same theme onto a textile in a more static manner and without any apparent connection to the combat theme portrayed at the Varakhsha wall paintings.[84]

The name of the pachyderm certainly appears as title and opening verse of the early Meccan *sūra* 105 of the Qurʾān alluding to the failed expedition of the Yemenite king Abraha against Mecca. His troops had been accompanied by an elephant which on arriving at the frontier of Meccan territory, knelt down and refused to advance further towards the city. The episode is related to the tradition according to which the birth of the Prophet is said to have taken place at this time, in the "year of the Elephant."[85]

These majestic quadrupeds had a special status and were covetously guarded by the *sulṭāns*. Rulers bestowed elephants only as a great favour or when a commander was appointed to a particularly responsible post.[86] Among the Būyids, ʿAḍud al-Dawla had war elephants *(fuyūl muqātila)* which he used against his cousin Bakhtiar ibn Muʿizz al-Dawla in 366/977.[87] It was also the Ghaznawid *sulṭān* Masʿūd's favourite mount for hunting.[88] On formal occasions involving solemn processions *(mawākeb)* the *sulṭān* rode on an elephant, as in September 422/1031, when Masʿūd proceeded to the plain of Shābahār outside Ghazna to preside over a session of the *maẓālim* court held for the redress of wrongs.[89] The representation of lavishly caparisoned elephants must therefore have served as a proclamation of power and authority for the Turkish *āmir* Qāʾid Abu ʾl-Manṣūr Bākh-tigīn. The unusual depiction of elephants together

[80] The saint whose seventh-century tomb is in Runiacum, present-day Saint-Josse-sur-Mer, near Pas-de-Calais, Musée de Louvre, Paris, inv. no. 7502; Pope and Ackerman, eds., 1938–9, repr. 1964–81, vol. 6, pl. 981; text, vol. 3, pp. 1928–39 and 2002; Ettinghausen, Grabar and Jenkins-Medina, 1987, repr. 2001, p. 244, fig. 260; von Wilckens, 1991, p. 48, fig. 43, and p. 347, n. 47; technical analysis in *Bulletin de liaison du CIETA* 33, 1971, pp. 22–57. A silk fragment of uncertain date featuring a related elephant pattern is found at Siegburg; cf. Meredith-Owens, "Fīl," *EI*² V, 690b. Étienne de Blois, count of Bologne and commander of the first Crusade, is said to have procured the precious textile together with his two brothers Godefroy de Blois and Baudoin, and to have offered it to the Abbaye Saint-Josse of which the counts were benefactors. Cf. *La France romane*, 2005, p. 177, cat. no. 124.

[81] It is interesting to note that closely related depictions of these unusual, extremely long-necked quadruped dragons with their uplifted feathery wings and vertically raised tails are prominently portrayed flanking a tree-like composition in a headpiece of the Armenian Gospel book of Mughni, datable to the second half of the eleventh century and probably executed somewhere in the Ani region (Yerevan, Matenadaran Ms. 7736, fol. 9r); see Gevorkian and Abgarian, eds., 1996, pl. 54.

[82] Combe, Sauvaget and Wiet, eds., 1933, vol. 4, no. 1507, with bibliographical data. Cf. Ettinghausen, Grabar and Jenkins-Medina, 1987, repr. 2001, p. 401, n. 66.

[83] Belenitskii, 1980, p. 228; Belenitskii and Bentowitsch, 2000, pp. 44–5.

[84] *Eidem*, 2000, p. 45.

[85] See al-Azraqī, *Kitāb Akhbār Makkah*, ed. Wüstenfeld, 1861, vol. 4, German tr., pp. 48–9.

[86] Bosworth, 1963, p. 117.

[87] See Christensen, 1944, p. 208. Anon., *Taʾrīkh-i Sīstān*, ed. Bahār, M.S., Tehran, 1314/1935, p. 206; Miskawayh, *Tajārib al-umam*, tr. and ed. Margoliouth, 1921, vol. 5, p. 402.

[88] Bosworth, 1963, p. 118.

[89] Bayhaqī, *Taʾrīkh-i Masʿūdī*, ed. Ghani and Fayyāz, Tehran, 1324/1945, pp. 372–3, as cited in Bosworth, "Court and courtiers: In the Islamic Period to the Mongol Conquest," *EIr*.

with dragons appears thus to combine the royal symbolism accorded to the elephant with that of the dragon.

The expression Zanda-pīl, "the furious elephant" is, moreover, a common metaphor used in Persian epic poetry for a *pahlavān* (hero),[90] such as the well-known epithet of Rustam being *pīltan*, "elephant-bodied."[91] In *Wīs u Rāmīn* Fakhr al-Dīn Gurgānī praises Wīs' brothers, the trusted champions of Rāmīn, as "two elephants, two lions like no others," thereby putting both creatures on a par with each other.[92] A proverb from an Afghan manuscript which states that "only Zāl can manage the elephant" (Zāl most likely representing the nephew of Ẓaḥḥāk, the historicised hominoid dragon, in the late eleventh-century epic *Kūsh-nāma*), might furthermore point to the possibility that the elephant was, as Gianroberto Scarcia has shown, a significant component of the ancient legends of the eastern frontier province of Zābulistan.[93]

***

Aspects of the dragon's association with other animals are encapsulated in a figural scheme portrayed on a gilded copper alloy lantern with a pyramidal cover in openwork which has been dated to the second half of the thirteenth century, and was used in the Mevlevī Dergāhı in the Rūm Saljuq capital of Konya.[94] The front face features double doors with a lobed arch that allow for the insertion of a candle into the cuboid body of the lantern. This small lamp, which could serve as a miniature architectural model, shows two upright addorsed "Saljuq-style" dragons crowned with pointed ears with gaping mouths and looped bodies that flank a large, six-petalled star-rosette. The dragons face towards open-mouthed lions, each with a raised foreleg and tail that arches over the back ending in a dragon head with closed jaws. The composition is set just above the double doors, which are flanked by double-headed birds of prey with looped necks, outspread wings and legs whose tail feathers terminate in the form of a large, inverted palmette bud. A cursive inscription at the lower edge of the front face reveals the name of the maker, Ḥasan ibn ʿAlī al-Mawlawī. The sides, back and cover of the lamp are covered with floral and stellar ornaments. The composition of the rosette flanked by dragons and in turn by dragon-tailed lions surmounting double-headed eagles can be assumed to epitomise the power of the *sulṭān*.[95] The fact that the scheme is portrayed on a lamp connects it, moreover, with the theme of light and hence also with the symbolism of the luminaries.

---

[90] Cf. Scarcia, 1967, p. 42.

[91] Steingass, 1892, repr. 1981, p. 269. See also *Shāh-nāma*, vol. 3, tr. and ed. Mohl, 1838–1878, p. 157, l. 202; Kowalski, 1939–49, p. 94.

[92] Tr. and ed. Davis, 2008, p. 388. In a eulogy the twelfth-century poet Rashīd-i Waṭwāṭ similarly associates the strength of both animals when he speaks of "lion-hearted and elephant-bodied warriors"; see p. 39.

[93] Scarcia, 1967, pp. 44–5.

[94] Erginsoy, 1978, pp. 413–4, figs. 196 a and b (dragon-tailed lion); *The Anatolian Civilisations*, vol. 3, 1983, p. 75, cat. no. D. 138.

[95] Konya Müze Müdürlüğü, inv. no. 400. Erginsoy, 1978, pp. 412–9, figs. 196 a–e; Kalter and Schönberger, 2003, p. 74; Turks, 2005, p. 394, cat. no. 70.

PART THREE

THE DRAGON AND ITS ROYAL AND HEROIC ASSOCIATIONS

CHAPTER SIX

THE DRAGON IN SCENES OF COMBAT

a. *The dragon combat in ancient myth*

Combat with the water-controlling dragon

Myths of dragon-like creatures and the vanquishing of these dragons were well-known, if not universal, in the traditions both of the Indo-Europeans and of the Near Eastern civilisations with whom the Persian speaking peoples came into contact from at least the first half of the first millennium BC.[1] In these contexts the mythical creatures are suited ideally to play the role of adversaries as they represent forces or elements that interfere with the correct order or functioning of the world, and they are defeated by deities, kings or heroes who shape and organise the cosmos. Through their victory the latter acquire authority and power over the newly ordered world. The iconography of the dragon combat or encounter, part of the Indo-Iranian literary theme of heroic mythological exploits, draws on the immemorially ancient epic theme of this quest, an ever-recurring motif even in cultures that are culturally and geographically far removed from one another.

The cosmogonic quality of the dragon-slaying myths evidently lay in the fact that in order to construct or defend world order, the god or hero had to destroy the primeval or chaotic dragon. During the remote period of Indo-Iranian unity, an age that long played a key role in the later cultures of the Near East and India, the Indo-Iranians may well have imagined dragons harbouring and restraining the heavenly waters, so causing drought, and not releasing them until overcome by a god or hero.[2] The oldest texts of the Indo-Iranians, the Vedic texts (1500–1000 BC), are composed in Sanskrit and usually refer to the dragon by the most common word *áhi-*, while in the old Iranian Avestan texts the term used is *azhi*, which originally meant only "snake, serpent."[3] Intoxicated and strengthened by the ritual potion of Soma, the divine hero Indra fulfils a cosmogonic act by dismembering the primary denizen of the forces of chaos, the cosmic serpent-monster Vṛtra ("the enveloper") whom the Rigveda calls "the first-born of dragons" (*prathama-jā́m áhīnām*, 1.32.4).[4] Indra, who carries the Indo-Iranian epithet "smashing resistance, obstacles" (*u̯rtra-ǰhan)*,[5] is eulogised in the Sanskrit text of the Rigvedic hymn (1.32) with the words:

> I tell now the manly deeds of Indra,
> The foremost which he did armed with the cudgel.
> He slew the serpent, drilled through to the waters,
> He split the belly of the mountains.[6]

Importantly, the stone dragon is split into two halves, the upper half forming *Dyáv-* "the sky" and the lower *kṣám-* "the earth."[7] The defeated Vṛtra is referred to in the Rigvedic texts as *áhi-*, "serpent,"[8] and *dāsá*, "the pent-up waters with the *dāsá* as husband, the Serpent as guardian"

---

[1] Cf. Watkins, 1995, p. 299. The most ancient known traditions about vanquishing dragons go back to the Sumerian, Akkadian and Egyptian mythologies of the first three millennia BC. The god Enlil defeats a monstrous dragon, the Labbu, in a Sumerian text. The god Marduk vanquishes Tiamat and her conscripts in the Akkadian epic of creation, *Enūma Elish*, of Babylon. In the mythology of the ancient Syrian city of Ugarit the god Baal overcomes the monsters Yamm and Mot. The dragon Apopis is dispatched by the god Seth in Egyptian mythology. In the Hittite texts of Bogazköy, the dragon Illuyanka fights the weather god.

[2] Skjærvø, "Aždahā I," *EIr*. In Greek mythology, Zeus slays the monster Typhaon/Typhon that has a hundred snake heads (Hesiod, *Theogony* 825–626).

[3] Watkins, 1995, p. 299.

[4] Indra similarly defeats the monster Vala (*valá-*, meaning "enclosure") who may have been conceptionally identical with Vṛtra at an earlier stage of the myth being derived from the same root, *val-/var-* "to cover, to enclose"; Vala thereupon frees the goddess of dawn, Ushas, whom he had imprisoned. Janda, 2010, pp. 27, 65, 247, 266, 270.

[5] Watkins, 1995, p. 299.

[6] Cited after *idem*, p. 304. It is interesting to note the ambiguity surrounding the killing of the primordial dragon conveyed in the Purāṇic accounts in which, paradoxically, Vṛtra is said to be a *brāhmaṇa* and Indra is decried for committing brahmanicide, the most heinous of all sins. Cf. Long, 1976, p. 172, n. 3, and p. 192, n. 29.

[7] Janda, 2010, pp. 45–70, esp. 27, 63, 79, 266, 270.

[8] Rigveda 1.32.5, 1.32.8, 1.8.10, 1.61.8, 1.103.7.

(Rigveda 1.32.11). The word *dāsá* is translated by Calvert Watkins as "hostile demon," "enemy," but also "non-āryan, barbarian," as well as "slave."[9] Indra released the waters "surrounded by the serpent" *(páriṣṭhitā áhinā)* and struck down the *dāsá* (Rigveda 2.11.2).[10] The serpent and the sobriquet in Indo-Iranian may be linked as *aǰhi- dāsá-*, from which originate the Vedic *áhi- ... dāsá-* as well as the Iranian name of the dragon Azhi Dahāka.[11]

Significantly, one of the principal functions of the divinity was not necessarily to kill the huge dragon, but rather to destroy an obstacle, *vərəthra-*, which tried to withhold the flow of the generative waters, thus to fulfil a cosmogonic task.[12] The water-controlling aspect of the dragon has analogies in the figure of Vṛtra as well as Azhi Dahāka who becomes the hominoid Azhdahāk.[13] As has been suggested, the mythological character of Azhdahāk may well be older than the Zoroastrian texts which first record his name, since figures of anthropomorphised dragons already appear in Bronze Age Central Asia.[14]

In the Avestan sources the mortal hero-king Thraētaona (Pahl. Frēdōn, N. Pers. Farīdūn, Arm. Hruden), whose abode was presumably the Central Asian steppes,[15] is associated with the feat of conquering the dragon Azhi Dahāka with his mighty club and thus restoring order and justice.[16] In the Avesta the dragon is described as three-headed and six-eyed (Yasht 14.38.40; 9.8).[17] Another great Avestan dragon-fighter is Kərəsāspa who slays Azhi Sruuara (or Azhi Zairita), "the horned Azhi, the horse-swallowing, man-swallowing, venomous, yellow-green ..." (Yasna 9.11; cf. Yasht 19.40).[18] In Zoroastrian Pahlawī literature the hero also defeats the sea monster Gandarəβa (Skr. *gandharvá-*) in Lake Vārukasha after having offered a sacrifice to the goddess Ardvī Sūrā Anāhitā.[19] As has been recognised long ago, the hymns in both Indic and Iranian traditions relate to a traditional mythology which must be shared Indo-Iranian patrimony.[20]

The heroic feats associated with the two ancient Iranian festivals of Nawrūz and Mihragān, respectively, at the spring and autumn equinoxes of the solar year are of note. The vernal New Year festival, Nawrūz, the official beginning of the year in Sasanian times, was instituted according to legend by the primordial king Jamshīd (Jim), the legendary Kayānid emperor of Iran.[21] Al-Bīrūnī records the Iranian tale of a demon called Iblīs[22] who had caused a terrible drought and famine by his evil spells and threatened to destroy all life on earth. Jamshīd marched to the demon's abode and conquered him, releasing the spell and causing new fertility to burst forth.[23] On his victorious return

---

[9] Watkins, 1995, p. 311.

[10] *Idem*, pp. 311–2.

[11] The material on Azhi Dahāka has been comprehensively discussed by Skjærvø, "Aždahā I," *EIr*.

[12] Boyce, 1975, repr. 1996, p. 64; Gnoli, "Bahrām," *EIr*.

[13] Watkins, 1995, p. 312.

[14] Cf. Francfort, 1994, figs. 3–5; Kuehn, 2009, pp. 43–67.

[15] Boyce, 1975, repr. 1996, p. 101. The association of the dragon-fighter with that of a solitary figure fighting in a foreign country is interesting. In the Avesta the dragon-fighters, Thraētaona and Kərəsāspa, are associated with "frontier heroes" of the Central Asian steppes, in particular the grazing lands of southeast Afghanistan, Thraētaona being born in Varena and Kərəsāspa coming from the Pishin plain to the south Lōra river (lower Urvadhā). Sarkhosh Curtis and Stewart, eds., 2005, pp. 43–4. Cf. Boyce, 1975, repr. 1996, p. 101 and n. 58; Monchi-Zadeh, 1975, p. 114. The great dragon-fighter of the national Iranian epic, Rustam, is similarly presented in Firdawsī's *Shāh-nāma* as a non-Iranian, coming from outside Iran (Melikian-Chirvani, 1998, p. 183), and was known as a Central Asian Saka/Scythian, Skythes, that is, Sagzī (*idem*, 1998, p. 193; P'yankov, 2006, p. 505. The term *Sagzī* was also used of a native of the province of Sīstān, originally called Sakastān/Sagistān, arabicised to Sijistān. Cf. the discussion of the term in Shahbazi, 1993, pp. 157–8; also Bailey, 1958, pp. 131–54, esp. 132).

[16] Monchi-Zadeh, 1975, pp. 103–5; Boyce, 1975, repr. 1996, p. 63.

[17] Watkins, 1995, p. 313.

[18] *Idem*, p. 319; Nyberg, 1933, pp. 336–52, repr. 1975, pp. 379–95.

[19] Cf. Monchi-Zadeh, 1975, p. 114.

[20] Watkins, 1995, p. 314 and n. 3.

[21] See al-Thaʿālibī, *Taʾrīkh Ghurar al-siyar*, tr. and ed. Zotenberg, 1900, pp. 13–4. Christensen, 1934, pp. 146–8; Zaehner, 1961, p. 138.

[22] The name Iblīs is a Qurʾānic designation for the devil, although he is referred to as a *jinn* (*sūras* 18, 50; and 55, 15) and occurs less frequently than *al-shayṭān* which is used to designate the devil in the context of his maleficent intentions towards man. In the *Shāh-nāma* Iblīs is termed a demon *(dīw)*, capable of transforming himself into another being including taking on the form of a dragon; *dīws* having a strong pre-Islamic (Zoroastrian) background (going back to the Old Iranian word *daiva* and the Avestan *daēuua*). Interestingly, among the few *ḥadīth* in which the name appears, there is one in which the Prophet speaks of Iblīs as having a throne "on the Waters" thus underlining the connection of Iblīs with the element of water (*Ṣaḥiḥ Muslim* IV, p. 1472; cited after Algar, "Eblīs," *EIr*). Azhi Dahāka/Ẓaḥḥāk is seen as leader of the demons *(dīws)* that corrupted Jamshīd who thereupon taught men, who were then vegetarians, to eat animal meat (whereas the Avesta forbids blood sacrifices), he thence became too proud, lost his purity, giving himself up to profane pleasures, and thus was forsaken by his glory *(khᵛarənah)*. Cf. Huart [Massé], "Djamshīd," *EI²* II, 438b.

[23] On the problematic hypothesis that the ancient Indo-Iranian New Year festival contained, among other things, a ritual combat between a deity, or a ruler as his representative, and a dragon that has captured creative parts of nature such as rain, cattle or women and thus threatens procreation and life as such, see Widengren, 1965, pp. 41–9. Cf. most recently Janda, 2010, pp. 69–70, 102; also Nylander, 1974, pp. 144–6.

Jamshīd appeared before his people radiating like a second sun.[24] Thereafter, al-Bīrūnī relates, Jamshīd's rule was just and prosperous "until the time when Bīwarāsp [Ẓaḥḥāk/Dahāk][25] appeared who killed [him] and subdued his realm."[26]

In turn, as al-Bīrūnī reports, the dragon Bīwarāsp/Dahāk is vanquished by the dragon-fighter Farīdūn (the Avestan Thraētaona) during the festival of Mihragān, which he then instituted to celebrate his victory over the usurping tyrant, whom he bound in fetters and imprisoned in Mount Damāwand,[27] an extinct volcano in northern Iran as well as the highest peak in the country. Significantly, according to various traditions, the sun appeared for the first time on the day of Mihragān.[28] Al-Bīrūnī further states that the Persian theologians conceived the prestigious ancient festival of Mihragān:

> ...as a sign of resurrection and the end of the world, because at Mihragān that which grows reaches its perfection.[29]

The festival was also "a time for rallying the forces of good to oppose the demons of coming winter and darkness."[30] It is also interesting to note that the celebration of Mihragān was accorded great importance at the courts of most rulers in the Turko-Iranian environment until the Mongol invasion.[31] A typology of such festivals shows the constant need of society to struggle against marginal situations such as a savage exterior or awesome chaos in order to recreate social reality as Peter Berger and Thomas Luckmann have aptly pointed out:[32]

> *All* societies are constructions in the face of chaos. The constant possibility of anomic terror is actualized whenever the legitimations that obscure the precariousness are threatened or collapse. And in such situations, or more regularly in ceremonially created periods of crisis – literally: separation between two eras, situations, periods – a 'deep legitimacy' is required, referring to a mythical reality outside ours, 'the other reality', lying beyond the borders of history and space, an eternal truth that existed before time but still exists behind it and behind our reality, and occasionally mingles with ours in 'periods of exception'.

Zoroastrian myth also influenced Armenian legends. The early dragon-slaying myth of the Avestan victory god Vərəthraghna (O. Iran. Vṛtraghan, N. Pers. Bahrām), "the best-armed of the heavenly gods, the strongest in strength, ... the most victorious in victory, ... the most glorious in glory," may have been conserved in the Armenian national hero Vahagn (who carries the epithet *vishapakʿagh*, "who handles dragons").[33] According to the Armenian historian Moses of Chorene, Vahagn fought with and vanquished dragons, his deeds equalling those of Heracles.[34] The golden aspect of the god is reflected in the song of the birth of Vahagn, the oldest testimony of Armenian literature,[35] which also survived in

[24] *Kitāb al-Āthār*, tr. and ed. Sachau, 1876–8, p. 202. Cf. Carter, 1974, pp. 185–6 and n. 64. Al-Bīrūnī (*idem*, pp. 199–201) furthermore mentions presents being brought at the New Year festival, Nawrūz, which is evidenced by further sources; see Ehrlich, 1930, pp. 95–101.

[25] See al-Thaʿālibī, *Taʾrīkh Ghurar al-siyar,* tr. and ed. Zotenberg, 1900, pp. 16–8. In the *Bundahishn* Dahāk is referred to as the one "whom they call Biwarāsp" (lit. "possessor of ten thousand horses"); cf. Yasht 5.28–31, in which Azhi Dahāka sacrifices "a hundred stallions, a thousand oxen, and ten thousand sheep" to to the fertility goddess Ardvī Sūrā Anāhitā, the Yazata ("venerable one") of all waters and fertility, to obtain a wish. See al-Ṭabarī, *Taʾrīkh al-rusul wa 'l-mulūk*, tr. and ed. Brinner, 1991, p. 18, n. 107.

[26] *Kitāb 'l-Āthār*, tr. and ed. Sachau, 1876–8, p. 202.

[27] *Idem*, pp. 207–10, 213–4. Also al-Thaʿālibī, *Taʾrīkh Ghurar al-siyar*, tr. and ed. Zotenberg, 1900, pp. 35–6. See Widengren, 1966, pp. 435, 439. Cf. *Shāh-nāma*, tr. and ed. Mohl, 1838–1878, vol. 1, pp. 111–3, ll. 19–528, p. 115, l. 10. Zaehner, 1961, p. 139; Calmard, "Mihragān," *EI*² VII, 15a.

[28] Calmard, "Mihragān," *EI*² VII, 15a.

[29] *Kitāb al-Āthār*, tr. and ed. Sachau, 1876–8, p. 208. Cf. Boyce, 1983, p. 802.

[30] Boyce, 1983, p. 802.

[31] Calmard, "Mihragān," *EI*² VII, 15a. According to the Ghaznawid historian Bayhaqī's narrative, the Ghaznawid *sulṭān* Bahrām Shāh ibn Masʿūd regularly celebrated at court the two ancient Iranian seasonal festivals of Nawrūz and Mihragān. Fallāḥ Rastgār, pp. 431–3, as cited in Bosworth, "Court and courtiers," *EIr*. Stripped of their original Zoroastrian religious significance, these traditional festival patterns had also survived under the ʿAbbasid caliphs, as attested by the verses of various contemporary Arabic poets; for instance, the Nawrūz poem by Ḥusain ibn Ẓaḥḥāk Khalīʿ and the Mihragān poem attributed to the caliph al-Maʾmūn (see Masʿūdī, *Kitāb murūj al-dhahab*, tr. and ed. Barbier de Meynard and de Courteille, 1917, vol. 8, pp. 277–8, 340–2). In the sulṭānate of his predecessor, Masʿūd ibn Maḥmūd of Ghazna, the exchange of customary gifts and tribute for this festival was accompanied by much drinking of wine *(rasm)* which was associated with the celebration of Mihragān since Achaemenid times (Fallāḥ Rastgār, pp. 431–3; Browne, 1920, vol. 1, pp. 475–6; Clinton, 1972, p. 136; for the verses of Manūchihrī, see also Hanaway, 1988, pp. 69–80, as well as Bayhaqī's *Taʾrīkh-i Bayhaqī*).

[32] Berger and Luckmann, 1971, p. 121.

[33] *Patmutʿiwn Hayocʿ*, tr. Langlois, 1872, p. 40 and n. 1. The dragon-slaying characteristic of Vahagn has also been interpreted as secondary or due to local elements (Benveniste and Renou, 1934, p. 80). While Iran conserved the ancient deity, India may have fused the deity with the hero and thus Indra was associated with the characteristics and functions of Vṛtraghan; see Gnoli, "Bahrām," *EIr*.

[34] *Patmutʿiwn Hayocʿ*, tr. Langlois, 1872, p. 41 and n. 1.

[35] Cf. Russell, 2004, p. 357.

the records of Moses of Chorene.[36] The Armenian Vahagn was identified with the Sun, as also reported by the classical Armenian commentator on Genesis, "some worshipped the Sun and called it Vahagn."[37] This Armenian hymn from the Zoroastrian tradition finds, as Watkins notes, a parallel in the Vedas, in particular the hymning of Apām Napāṭ, literally the "Son of the Waters" (Rigveda 2.35), as deity and as sacrificial fire, which is probably of Indo-Iranian date.[38] After an inconclusive contest for the gleaming *khᵛarənah* between the dragon Azhi Dahāka and Fire, the *khᵛarənah* escapes to Lake Vārukasha and at the bottom of the deep lake Apām Napāṭ grabs it (Yast 19.45–54).[39] In another early Armenian epic from Sasun, southwest of Lake Van,[40] the hero Samsar (Sanasar), who was conceived after his mother drank from a magical spring,[41] slays a dragon *(vishap)* that controls the spring of water which feeds the city and must receive a girl in sacrifice each year.[42]

Parts of Central Asia, in particular in the Kushāṇa empire, were of course Buddhist from the first centuries of the millennium. It is interesting to note that in the northwest of the empire – which seems to have been the only geographical region where he fulfilled such a role – the Buddha appears in the role of a dragon-fighter.[43] He overcomes the great dragon-king *(nāgarāja)* Apalāla, the dragon who lived in the mountain spring that was the source of the Śubhavāstu (Swāt) river and who terrorised the region in northwest Pakistan on the border with Afghanistan by causing periodic destruction to the harvest though violent storms and floods.[44] There are parallels to the great Indo-Iranian dragon-fighter Indra vanquishing Vṛtra, for Apalāla like Vṛtra has aquatic features. The Buddha appears to be taking over the role of Indra when he strikes the mountain, within which the dragon resides, with Vajrapāṇi's thunderbolt.[45]

The Buddha is also said to have tamed and converted another *nāgarāja*, named Gopāla, in "Chen-t'o-lo" (Gandhāra (?)).[46] This feat is recorded in Indian texts that were translated into Chinese, such as the early fifth-century translation of the *Buddhānusmṛtisamādhi Sūtra* ("Sūtra of the Ocean-like Samādhis of Buddha Visualisation"),[47] and is described as taking place at a cave located in a mountain at Nagarahāra near present-day Haḍḍa/Jalalābad in eastern Afghanistan.[48] A pond near the cave is believed to have been the lair of a dragon-king (referred to as Gopāla in early Indian texts), his five ogress-consorts, who had been transformed into female dragons, and various small dragons that terrorised the region with adverse weather conditions. The Buddha was summoned to the area where he and his attendants tamed the dragon king. Once converted, the latter implored the Buddha to stay on for 1500 years whereupon the "World-Honoured One" left his "luminous mystical form" or "projection" (shadow) image in the cave.[49] A related

[36] *Patmut'iwn Hayoc'*, tr. Langlois, 1872, pp. 40–1; Watkins, 1995, pp. 253–4. Cf. Russell, 2004, pp. 357–70.

[37] Alishan, G., *Hin hawatk' kam het' anosakan krōnk' Hayok'* ("The Ancient Faith or Pagan Religion of the Armenians"), Venice, 1910 ed., p. 187, as cited in Russell, 1987, p. 270.

[38] Watkins, 1995, p. 254. Also Janda, 2010, p. 255. On Apām Napāṭ, see Oldenberg, 1894, repr. 1977, pp. 118–20 and n. 1; Boyce, 1975, repr. 1996, pp. 41, 44–50. Cf. Yasht 19; Boyce, 1984, pp. 29–30.

[39] Gershevitch, 1959, p. 59.

[40] Russell, 2004, p. 879 and n. 8.

[41] Azarpay, 1981, p. 99. On the motif of the supernatural conception and birth of heros, see Schirmunski, 1961, pp. 27–8.

[42] Russell, 2004, p. 1123. The Hebrew Bible similarly contains many traces of ancient mythology, wherein Yahveh, in primeval times, overcomes monsters that are extremely similar to the dragon-like beings defeated by the various Near Eastern gods. Added to names already present in the more ancient Ugaritic texts, such as Yamm, Mavet or Mot, were names such as Peten, Nahash, Rahab, Leviathan, Tannin, Behemot.

[43] Strong, 1992, p. 27. Dragon-slaying or -taming myths are not unknown in East Asian cultures. In the Chinese context the Buddha is also known in the role of "Huan Long Shi, the dragon-tamer" which may however be informed by the Central Asian prototypes. Cf. Wu Hung, 1986, p. 270.

[44] *Si-yu-ki*, vol. 1, tr. Beal, 1884, repr. 2000, pp. 121–3. A list of ancient Indian sources that were subsequently translated into Chinese recording the story of the Buddha's subduing of Apalāla and Gopāla in the Kushāṇa kingdom is provided by Rhie, 1999–2002, pp. 116–7. Cf. Strong, 1992, pp. 26–7. The theme of the Buddha converting Apalāla was a very popular subject in Gandhāran art; see, for instance, *Gandhara*, 2009, cat.nos. 173 (from the Dharmarājikā *stūpa* complex in Taxila, Taxila Museum, inv. no. C.4ID.46) and 174 (Peshawar Museum, inv. no. PM-3133). The taming of the serpent king can perhaps also be seen in the light of the successful cultivation of the Swāt valley.

[45] *Si-yu-ki*, vol. 1, tr. Beal, 1884, repr. 2000, p. 122 and n. 14. Cf. Carter, 1992, p. 70.

[46] *Aśokarājāvadāna*, I. See Rhie, 1999–2002, p. 116.

[47] Rhie, 1999–2002, p. 118–27.

[48] Caspani, 1945, pp. 49–52; Soper, 1949, p. 279; Rhie, 1999–2002, pp. 113, 136–7, and ns. 227, 242; image section 2.b and figs. 1.7a–c.

[49] Rhie, 1999–2002, pp. 117–27, and n. 242 (with reference to Soper (1949, pp. 314–30, and 13, nos. 1–2, 1950, pp. 63–75) who relates the legend to Zoroastrian and even Manichean beliefs). On the discussion of the inappropriate common translation of the Chinese character "ying" as "mirror image of the Buddha's body" (a fully-fledged Buddha image), his "projection" in other words rather than the com-

version of this story is also given by the seventh-century Chinese pilgrim Xuanzang who visited and described the dragon cave which at that time was well-known for the belief that the Buddha had once been there on a supernatural visit and had left his "luminous reflected image."[50]

It is noteworthy that whereas Indra kills the dragon, the Buddha chooses to subdue, tame and convert Apalāla and Gopāla, by opening their eyes to the destruction they had caused and by "graphically showing [them] the world as it truly is – an intolerable place of pain."[51] Rather than physical dominance or even the destruction of the dragon, he advocates introspective paths and moral transformation.

Another Buddhist story recorded by Xuanzang concerns a *nāgarāja* who lives in a lake on a mountain two hundred miles northwest of Kapisa. After many years of stirring up natural forces to destroy the monasteries and *stūpa*s founded by the Kushāṇa king Kanishka, the creature is eventually overcome by the king. The story relates how the thunderous voice of the dragon "shook the earth, and the fierce winds tore up the trees, whilst stones and sand pelted down like rain," whereupon the king summons all the accumulated merit of his past lives and "from both his shoulders there arose a great flame and smoke."[52] This form of imagery shows a solar ruler who tames the monstrous dragon-*nāgarāja* by making a pact with him: as soon as some unfavourable weather phenomenon appears, the *ghantā* (cymbal or drum) will sound to remind the dragon of his promise whereupon he will cause the danger to subside.[53]

The eschatological role of the hero

Middle Persian/Pahlawī texts describe an eschatological myth which shows the dragon as the being responsible for the lapse into chaos and death that is to take place at the end of time. As a consequence of this metamorphosis the latter has to be fought by valorous characters symbolising the *status quo*. The dragon-fighter Frēdōn (the Avestan Thraētaona) is first mentioned as fulfilling an eschatological role: he defeats but does not kill the giant dragon, binding and imprisoning him "in the most grievous punishment of confinement" at Mount Damāwand.[54] The conquering hero thereby also frees the royal women, Sauuaŋhauuāci and Arənauuāci, "the two most beautiful women in the world," the two wives of Azhi Dahāka/Ẓaḥḥāk.[55] Hence in later myths female figures appear to have replaced water and rain as symbols of fertility and life.[56] The theme of the rescue of a princess or maiden by the dragon vanquisher, which became a regular topos in most Iranian dragon-slaying stories, was introduced when the dragon became identified with a historical person, such as the foreign tyrant Ẓaḥḥāk, who imprisoned the maiden.[57] The dragon remains bound at Mount Damāwand until the end of the world approaches when the other great dragon-fighter, Kərəsāspa (who figures as Kirsāsp in Mid. Pers. and Garshāsp in N. Pers.) will be awakened (resurrected) by the divine beings Srōsh and Nēryōsang.[58] It is for him that the final victorious battle against the dragon is reserved, the final war between Good and Evil Spirits.[59] His eschatological work takes place and Kərəsāspa defeats the dragon when he emerges near the end of time from his captivity, breaks free of his fetters, wreaks havoc and causes much devastation in the world.[60]

monly used "shadow," see Rhie, 1999–2002, p. 113 and n. 227. Cf. Wang, 2005, pp. 245–6.

50 *Si-yu-ki*, vol. 1, tr. Beal, 1884, repr. 2000, pp. 93–7. Cf. Strong, 1992, pp. 28–30; Rhie, 1999–2002, pp. 132–3.

51 Strong, 1992, p. 27.

52 *Si-yu-ki*, vol. 1, tr. Beal, 1884, repr. 2000, pp. 62–6, esp. p. 65. Cf. Carter, 1974, p. 186, n. 67. For a discussion of the Kushāṇa royal solar cult, see also Rosenfield, 1967, pp. 189–91.

53 *Si-yu-ki*, vol. 1, tr. Beal, 1884, repr. 2000, p. 66.

54 Dēnkard 9.12.19, tr. West, W.E., *Sacred Books of the East*, Oxford, 1880–7, repr. Delhi 1965, p. 40.

55 Yasht 5.34; 17.34. Watkins, 2005, p. 464. In later traditions the female figures became Jamshīd's (Yima) sisters or daughters; Zaehner, 1955, repr. 1972, p. 413. The theme is also attested in Greek mythology, for instance, the hero Perseus saves Andromeda from an aquatic dragon.

56 Cf. Gershevitch, 1959, p. 45; Remmer, 2006, pp. 212–25.

57 Khāleqī-Moṭlaq, "Aždahā II," *EIr*.

58 Yasht 3.60–2. Christensen, 1931, tr. 1993, p. 95.

59 Cf. *idem*, pp. 55, 95.

60 *Bundahishn* 29.9 and in greater detail in Dēnkard 9.21.8–10. Cf. Hintze, 1999, p. 82. Like Garshāsp, Sām plays a part in eschatological events: on Mount Sagāwand he lies on his back in the cold covered by snow and guarded by ten thousand *frawashi*s (Pahl. *frawahr*) of the righteous until the dragon breaks loose and the final battle commences. *Bundahishn* 197.14–98.6; Monchi-Zadeh, 1975, pp. 108–9, 142–3. In the Avesta Sāma is the name of a clan, to which Thrita as well as his sons Kərəsāspa and Urvākhshaya belonged (Yasna 9.10); Monchi-Zadeh, 1975, p. 109. From Sasanian times onwards, however, Sām and Garshāsp began to be taken as the names of separate persons.

Zoroastrianism which is a prophetic religion with a revealed scripture offers salvation to the souls of its adherents and humanity can be redeemed. The dualistic worldview inherent in its belief system[61] dictates that "Evil must be annihilated by Good, if God is to save his creation."[62] Hence in the Younger Avestan hymns the myth of the dragon-fighter inherited from Indo-European times acquired an additional semantic component, that of the coming world saviour or Saoshiiaṇt (Pahl. Sōshyans). This Saoshiiaṇt is characterised by the epithet "victorious" (Av. *vərəthrajan-*)[63] who, in the last days, "is conceived of as not only utterly defeating Evil but also as ushering in a new age."[64] "He is the one who brings about the Renovation of the world (Av. *frashō.kərəti*) in which Ahura Mazdā's good and perfect Creation is restored and freed from all Evil."[65] Significantly, his victory over the monstrous dragon became the "pre-condition for the resurrection of the dead and the beginning of a new era."[66]

The Zoroastrian eschatological myth recounts the coming of the final cosmic saviour, who is believed to come from the region of the Helmand river (Haētumaṇt, "with dams" in the Avesta) in Sakastān/Sīstān in southeastern Iran and southwest Afghanistan.[67] He is the son of Vīspa. tauruuairī, who became pregnant by the Prophet Zarathushtra's own seed while bathing in Lake Kasaoiia, his seed being miraculously preserved in the depth of the lake guarded by "guardian spirits."[68] She will bear a son called Astuuaṭ.ərəta, the last and greatest of the ancient Avestan valiant warriors, who will brandish the victorious weapon borne by other heroes before him, especially Thraētaona when he slew the dragon Dahāka.[69] With this weapon (which belongs to the terminology of the Indo-European myth of the hero killing a dragon, Av. *azhi-* "snake, serpent, dragon," *jan-* "to kill") he will drive out Falsehood from the world of Truth (Zamyād Yasht 19.93).[70] The corresponding Vedic adjective *vṛtrahán-* ("slayer of Vṛtra," lit. "breaking the defence")[71] is used especially by the Vedic god, Indra, who slays the dragon whose name became Vṛtra in the Indian tradition.[72] The ancient myth of the dragon-fighter was thus reinterpreted in a religious way in the popular image of the Saoshiiaṇt overcoming Evil.[73]

b. *Iconography of the medieval dragon-fighter*

The visual representation of a fighter, whether mounted or on foot, doing battle with a dragon employs a traditional and enduring iconographical formula of some antiquity and wide diffusion throughout Central Asia and the Near Eastern world, part of a stock of popular imagery that survived into medieval times. The fighter takes aim at the dragon using a variety of weapons, including bow and arrow, sword, spear or long lance, while the dragon is shown either as a lively upright creature imbued with fighting spirit, or in the guise of a vanquished dragon lying on its back beneath the horse's feet with gaping upturned jaws. The representation of the single equestrian dragon-fighter may be divided into two basic groups: the rider distinguished by royal or divine attributes, as graphically depicted in the investiture relief of Ardashīr I at Naqsh-i Rustam, discussed below, or the figure of the hunter or warrior, prevalent in the medieval Islamic period, without such insignia.

In Sasanian royal imagery Ahura Mazdā/ Ohrmazd is shown on horseback crushing the head of the Zoroastrian evil principle of the universe, Angra Mainyu, known in later times as Ahriman who is likened to the serpent in the *Great Bundahishn* ("Book of Primal Creation"), Pahlawī translations based on lost Avestan scriptures of the third century AD and before and their commentaries written after the Arab conquest.[74] It describes him as having sprung:

[61] Cf. the definition of the term "dualism" by Hintze (1999, p. 75 and n. 19) referring to two separate cosmic powers.

[62] *Eadem*, p. 76.

[63] Hintze (1995, p. 94) suggests that this epithet was added because of "the connection of the concept of the Saoshiiaṇt with the myth of the hero slaying a dragon."

[64] Hintze, 1999, p. 76.

[65] *Eadem*, p. 76; cf. *eadem*, 1995, p. 96.

[66] *Eadem*, 1999, p. 86.

[67] *Eadem*, 1995, p. 96.

[68] Boyce, 1975, repr. 1996, p. 282; Hintze, 1999, p. 77. On Vīspa.tauruuairī, see Remmer, 2006, pp. 57–8, 144–8, 200–5, 253.

[69] Boyce, 1975, repr. 1996, p. 283; Hintze, 1995, p. 93 and 1999, pp. 77–8.

[70] Hintze, 1995, p. 93 and *eadem*, 1999, p. 77.

[71] *Eadem*, 1995, p. 94.

[72] *Eadem*, 1999, p. 77.

[73] *Eadem*, p. 78.

[74] See Watkins, 1995, p. 58. On the *Iranian* or *Great Bundahishn*, see also Klíma, 1968, pp. 41–3.

> ...like a snake, out of the sky down to the earth, ... thereby the sky was as shattered and frightened by him, as a sheep by a wolf.[75]

The association of the serpent with Ahriman is perhaps best portrayed in the monumental third-century investiture relief sculptures of the Sasanian king Ardashīr I (r. 224–241) at Naqsh-i Rustam. It shows a bilateral equestrian scene. The conquering king Ardashīr appears on the left, facing an anthropomorphic Ahura Mazdā with turreted crown on the right, shown in the act of bestowing on Ardashīr the gift of *khᵛarənah*, in the form of a ring to be hung over and secured around the royal crown. Ardashīr's steed is shown trampling on the head of the last Parthian leader Ardavān (Artabanus) V, while Ahura Mazdā's horse treads underfoot a creature held in the coils of serpents. The plastically sculpted reliefs draw on the age-old universally understood motif of the ruler placing his foot on a prostrate enemy as a symbolic gesture of physical as well as ideological supremacy, the horse serving in this instance as a visual extension of the ruler, his rider.[76] This visual realisation of victory is of particular significance: the vanquished enemy, his head wreathed with serpents, one of which uprears its head at the front, presumably represents the anthropomorphic Ahriman, and thus the first dated example of a symbolic synthesis of the serpent and Ahriman (figs. 86a and b).[77] The defeat of the Parthian leader is thus equated with triumphing over the powers of evil. Inscriptions in three languages, Middle Persian, Parthian and Greek, on the horses' flanks identify the god and the conqueror.[78] The representation of the paired mounted horsemen, imperial and divine, surmounting prostrate enemies, human and satanic, thus underscores the triumph by metaphorically alluding to a complex of eschatological beliefs.

A mounted dragon-fighter distinguished by a flaming halo appears on seal stones from the Iranian world[79] such as a sixth-century brown-red jasper, preserved in the State Hermitage, St. Petersburg (fig. 87). The rayed halo that surrounds the rider's head and shoulders probably symbolises the *khurrak-i Kayan* (the *khᵛarənah* of the Avestan texts and Firdawsī's *farr-i kayani*), the Royal Splendour of the Kayanids (the protagonists of a millenary struggle against Tūrān), the radiance that descends upon the heroic warrior and, above all, the ruler and renders him sacred.[80] The rider thus probably represents one of the ancient Indo-Iranian epic heroes that fulfil a mythical quest. He is seen holding a spear and battling with what appears to be a seven-headed dragon whose body coils along the edge of the seal from below the horse's hooves, rising upwards with one dragon head surmounting the other. He is flanked by the figure of a small scorpion and a star. The depiction visualises here the popular imagery of the hero as a "beneficial force" attacking a monstrous dragon representing a "malevolent force."

In the historical story in the Pahlawī text *Kārnāmak-i Ardakhshīr-i Pāpakān* ("Book of the Deeds of Ardashīr, Son of Pāpak"), written around 600, the founder of the Sasanian dynasty Ardashīr Pāpakān (224–241) himself is related to the valiant ritual of killing a dragon called Haftān-bōkht (the Haftwād of Firdawsī's *Shāh-nāma*) who lived in the village of Alār in the *rustāq* of Kojārān.[81]

Prominent depictions of the equestrian dragon-fighter are encountered on wall paintings discovered by Russian archaeologists in the city of Panjikent in Sogdiana (Zarafashān, north of the Hiṣār range), now at the State Hermitage, St. Petersburg. The depictions show pictorial epics from a variety of literatures, among them the Greek fables of Aesop and the Indian epic

---

[75] *Bundahishn* 6.10–11 (*Sacred Books of the East*, tr. West, E.W., vol. 5, Oxford, 1897). Cf. Zaehner, 1961, p. 262; Boyce, 1984, p. 50.

[76] The motif appears in the *Shāh-nāma*, tr. and ed. Mohl, 1838–1878, vol. 4, p. 81, l. 237. See also the related ancient Oriental motif of "eating/licking dust" as simile for death and the humiliation of the vanquished enemy, which is exemplified in Genesis 3.14. Cf. p. 23; also Martinek, 1996, p. 65 with further examples.

[77] Ghirshman, 1962, p. 132, fig. 168. Cf. Boyce, 1979, repr. 2001, p. 107.

[78] Boyce, 1979, repr. 2001, p. 107.

[79] For additional examples of Sasanian-period glyptics with this motif, cf. Gyselen, 2007, pls. 14.2 and 14.3; Gignoux and Gyselen, 1982, p. 58, nos. 14.1–14.3; Gignoux, 1978, p. 54, no. 6.6; Bivar, 1969, nos. BL 3, BL 4; Ghirshman, 1962, p. 243, fig. 300 (collection of H. Seyrig).

[80] The iconography of *farr(ah)*, *khᵛarənah* has been associated with figures connected with light and fire, in other words, by having flames emanating from the human body or partially surrounding it. Cf. Christensen, 1944, p. 146. For the "flaming shoulders" of divine beings or kings on Kushāṇa coins, see Rosenfield, 1967, pp. 17, 23–4, 29, 157, 197–201. Cf. Gnoli, "Farr(ah), Xᵛarənah," *EIr*; Carter, 1974, pp. 176–7 and ns. 18–20. On Firdawsī's concern with the distinctive hereditary mark of Iranian splendour, *farr-i kayani*, see Rypka, 1968, pp. 155, 159. See most recently, Soudavar, 2003.

[81] Nöldeke (1879, ch. 6) associated the story of Haftwād with the ancient myth of Apollo and Hydra; Minorsky, "Lār," *EI*[1] III, pp. 15–7.

Mahābhārata, as well as episodes from the heroic cycle, the dragon-fighter being identified by Aleksandr Belenitskii as the hero-champion Rustam.[82] The hero's ancestors were Saka people who are part of the Scytho-Siberian cultural grouping and belong to the Indo-Iranian group that came to Sakastān/Sīstān and Zābulistān in the late second century BC,[83] lands far from Sogdia. Saka heroic tales were nevertheless very popular with the Sogdians,[84] although only a fragmentary Sogdian text survives[85] and only in the tenth century was the tale taken up by Firdawsī in his *magnum opus*. The heroic cycle of Rustam's Herculean seven feats *(haft khʷān)* attains almost spiritual importance.[86] Before reaching his ultimate goal the hero has to undergo these trials,[87] which represent a kind of rite of passage.[88] During his third feat, which is reminiscent of Herakles defeating the Hydra of Lerna,[89] Rustam slays a magical dragon that is guarding a watering place which the ram has shown[90] and comes out of the forest at night and approaches the sleeping hero.[91] Twice he is woken by his formidable mount Rakhsh,[92] but each time the dragon vanishes. On the third occasion the monster fails to conceal itself in time and with the help of the faithful Rakhsh the hero succeeds in killing the dragon. Interestingly, the *Shāh-nāma* portrays the dragon with human traits such as the power of reflection[93] and speech: during the battle he declares himself master of the whole desert.[94] Correspondingly, Rustam is shown confronting the dragon as if it were a human adversary.[95]

Igor P'yankov notes the archaic style of Firdawsī's records of the Rustam cycle and has demonstrated its close parallels with ancient Greek records, particularly Herodotus' accounts of one of the genealogical myths of the Scythians (*Histories* IV 8–9).[96] According to the father of Greek historiography the hero, known by the Greeks as Herakles, comes to an arid region at the Pontus Shore (Black Sea) later inhabited by the Scythians where he loses his horses and in the search for them meets in a cave in the forest a mythical creature described as a woman with the lower body of a serpent.[97] With this anguipede woman he engenders three sons, the youngest and worthiest of whom, named Scythes, becomes the first king of the Scythians. In Firdawsī's account Rustam's first feat is his victory over a lion whose pelt he wears just like the Grecian Herakles after the latter's vanquishing of the Nemean lion.[98] The second exploit is the discovery of a spring in the desert country.[99] The third is the victory over the dragon. While there is no love theme in the third trial, the fourth episode recorded in the *Shāh-nāma* mentions a sorceress in the form of a beautiful girl who tries to seduce Rustam near a small river in the shade of some trees.[100]

Parts of the story are shown on a continuous frieze of the Sogdian wall paintings in Panjik-

---

[82] Belenitskii, 1980, pp. 103–5, 199. Cf. Azarpay, 1981, p. 195. Guitty Azarpay (1981, pp. 96–7) also points out that the "dramatis personae" were subject to change and not necessarily connected to any specific hero.

[83] Boyce, 1975, repr. 1996, p. 101 and n. 104; de Bruijn, "Rustam," *EI*² VIII, 636b; P'yankov, 2006, p. 505.

[84] P'yankov, 2006, pp. 505–6.

[85] The Sogdian fragment from Dunhuang which records part of the Rustam legend is fully quoted in Klíma, 1968, p. 53; Azarpay, 1981, pp. 6–7. Cf. Marshak, 2002, p. 51.

[86] Cf. Russell, 2004, p. 543 and n. 30. For a discussion of the close parallels of the *haft khʷān* (dragon slaying being one of the exploits) of Rustam and Isfandiyār, see Yarshater, 1983a, pp. 469–70 and n. 5.

[87] The number seven was specifically important to the "Avestan people," and plays a significant role in the rites and customs of the Zoroastrians, for whom seven is the number of the creations and of the Amahraspands (Aməsha Spəntas), the positive creatures or "Bounteous Immortals," who guard them. The number seven gained even greater prominence in the Islamic period, when it acquired additional symbolism. Cf. Hartmann-Schmitz, 1989, pp. 12–20; Schimmel, 1994, p. 27. Moreover, seven often conveys ideas of perfection and periodicity (for a list of examples, see Shahbazi, "Haft (seven)," *EIr*). It is a favourite number in eastern Semitic civilisations with magico-religious features; among the Israelites it was used in ritual incantations (2 Kings 13 and Joshua 6); and in the Old Testament seven is the number of completeness. Cf. Jeffers, 1996, p. 87, n. 286.

[88] Cf. Omidsalar, 2001, pp. 262, 265–6.

[89] For a discussion of the points of resemblance between Hercules and Rustam, see Melikian-Chirvani, 1998, p. 178. See also p. 79, n. 44.

[90] *Shāh-nāma*, tr. and ed. Mohl, 1838–1878, vol. 1, p. 515, ll. 336–41.

[91] A view of the entire scene is reproduced in Azarpay, 1981, p. 96, fig. 42. *Shāh-nāma*, tr. and ed. Mohl, 1838–1878, vol. 1, pp. 517–21.

[92] On the motif of the horse as helper of the hero, see Schirmunski, 1961, pp. 25–6.

[93] *Shāh-nāma*, tr. and ed. Mohl, 1838–1878, vol. 1, p. 517, ll. 565–70.

[94] *Idem*, vol. 1, pp. 519–21, ll. 396–400. This exploit is also recorded by the eleventh-century Armenian scholar Grigor Magistros who moreover notes that the battle took place near Mount Damāwand; see Tchukasizian, 1964, pp. 321–2. Cf. P'yankov, 2006, p. 507.

[95] Tr. and ed. Mohl, 1838–1878, vol. 1, pp. 519–21, ll. 393–5, 400–2.

[96] P'yankov, 2006, pp. 505–11, esp. pp. 506–7.

[97] Cf. Sulimirski, 1985, p. 168.

[98] It is notable that the Nemean lion was one of the offspring of the *drakōn* Typhon and Echidna, who had the face and torso of a woman and the body of a serpent (Hesiod, *Theogony* 306–8). See West, 1962, p. 161.

[99] Tr. and ed. Mohl, 1838–1878, vol. 1, pp. 513–7.

[100] *Idem*, vol. 1, pp. 521–3.

ent. The monster is depicted as a terrifying she-dragon who has coiled her elongated serpentine tail around all four legs of the horse (probably to be understood as Rakhsh),[101] her female upper body rises up, naked to the waist. With her long arms she is dragging the mounted Rustam-like hero's head towards her. The hero has succeeded in wounding the dragon twice with his axe (fig. 88).[102] In the next scene the dragon, its wounds gushing blood, is in its death-throes. In contrast to the preceding images, it now lies prostrate on the ground (fig. 89).[103] Boris Marshak explains the depiction of the serpentine she-dragon with human arms and lion's mane as a conflation of three trials mentioned in the *Shāh-nāma*, namely the fight with the dragon, the lion and the sorceress.[104] While the genealogical aspect of the myth was apparently forgotten, some analogies with the original theme of the mythical anguipede progenitrix appear to have been retained.[105]

An equestrian dragon-fighter is also portrayed on a tympanum from the medieval city of Bunjikat (20 kilometres south of the modern town of Shahristan in northern Tajikistan) in the Sogdian principality of Ustrushana, probably dating from the seventh to the ninth century. A row of pearl roundels frame the rim of the monumental wooden arch-shaped tympanum (partly destroyed by fire) that adorned the top of the portal leading to the throne hall of the Qalʿa-i Qahqaha, now preserved in the National Museum in Dushanbe in Tajikistan.[106] In one of the roundels a mounted horseman is seen taking aim at a twice-knotted dragon.[107]

While there appear to be no surviving representations of the dragon-slayer around the turn of the millennium in the Islamic realm of Western Asia, the equestrian dragon-fighter can nonetheless be seen as a leitmotif which links the pre-Islamic Sasanian and the Sogdian times with the Islamic period. After an apparent lacuna in the tenth and perhaps the early part of the eleventh century (a period during which the motif occurs in the Christian art of the Caucasus, particularly in Armenia and Georgia, as examined below), it is depicted with great regularity on Islamic works of art from Central Asia to Anatolia and the Jazīra.

The *Abū Muslim-nāma*,[108] which records the life of the charismatic Abū Muslim Khurāsānī (d. *c.* 137/754–5) who led a popular movement for the ʿAbbasid cause and became a legendary figure after his assassination, recounts the heroic exploits of the fourth caliph ʿAlī ibn Abī Ṭālib (d. 40/660), Muḥammad's cousin who married the Prophet's daughter Fāṭima. ʿAlī is portrayed as accomplishing the feat of vanquishing the dragon at a very early age and is eulogised as infant dragon-slayer with the words:

> Bare-handed in the cradle with his mighty arms
> he tore apart the dragon's jaws.[109]

---

[101] Comparable imagery is represented on a Sasanian seal in the British Museum, London, which shows a double-headed serpent coiled around each of the four legs of a bovine and rearing up above its head and inscribed with the name of the owner in Pahlawī. Mordtmann, 1864, pl. I, no. 4, republished in Ettinghausen, 1955, p. 282, pl. XXXIX, no. 8. Cf. Bivar, 1969, p. 8, pl. 15.1; Marshak, 2002, p. 43.

[102] Azarpay, 1981, pl. 6; Marshak, 2002, p. 40, figs. 17–20, colour pl. 3; Grube and Johns, 2005, p. 233, cat. no. 78.5.

[103] Azarpay, 1981, pl. 7; Marshak, 2002, p. 43, fig. 20.

[104] *Idem*, 2002, p. 51. An anachronical but perhaps not entirely irrelevant parallel exists in Kushāṇa-period chthonic creatures, sometimes referred to as *vyāla*, which were represented as half-females, half-serpents, with a female upper body whose lower limbs transform into a long spiralling serpentine tail terminating in a fan-shaped caudal fin. Cf. Czuma, 1985, p. 53, cat. no. 3.

[105] Igor P'yankov (2006, pp. 508–10) notes that traces of the ancient genealogical tales are still preserved in today's folklore of southern Tajikistan where the Scythian people once lived and where he heard oral traditions from local people about a dangerous serpentine woman who lives in the river.

[106] Unfortunately, the panel remains unpublished; it was not permitted to photograph it in the museum nor was it possible to obtain a photograph from the museum. For a description of the site, see Negmatov, 1996, repr. 1999, pp. 259–74, and fig. 41.

[107] The first fire is associated with the time of the ʿAbbasid conquest of the town in 206/822, the second with the annexation to the Samanid state by Ismāʿīl ibn Aḥmad I (279/892–295/907) providing a *terminus ante quem* for the dating of the wooden panel.

[108] The *Abū Muslim-nāma* was written by Abū Ṭāhir Ṭarsūsī (Ṭūsī), who was part of the retinue of the Turkic Ghaznawid *sulṭān* Maḥmūd (r. 389/999–421/1030). The legends of Abū Muslim are surveyed in Mélikoff, 1962. See also *eadem*, 1960, vol. 1, p. 43.

[109] The translation is based on the manuscript in Paris, Bibliothèque Nationale, Ms. Pers. 843, dated 1145–6/1732–4; Mahdjoub, 1988, p. 63. The motif of the infant dragon-slayer is repeatedly found in classical literature, for instance, in the depiction of the infant hero Herakles struggling with two serpents described by the classical Greek poet Pindar (*c.* 518–438 BC) in the *Nemean Ode* 1, 42–7. Another early classical example is given by the infant Apollo who when only a few days old shot arrows from the arms of his mother Leto at a multi-headed snake, the story being depicted on a fifth-century BC lekythos (predating Euripides' *Iphigeneia in Tauris*, 1239–1251); see Fontenrose, 1959, repr. 1980, pp. 16–7 and fig. 1. For a discussion of the epic motif of the supernatural power and acquisition of "wisdom" and certain magical abilities of infant heros from dragons, see Schirmunski, 1961, pp. 58–9.

It is interesting to compare this imagery with that of the infant Rustam whose arms are associated with courageous dragons in the *Shāh-nāma* account.[110]

The theme of the dragon-slayer appears in a mid-twelfth-century book on cosmography written in Persian and dedicated to the last Great Saljuq *sulṭān* of Iran and Iraq, Ṭoghrıl III ibn Arslan (r. 571/1176–590/1194). The story in Muḥammad ibn Maḥmūd ibn Aḥmad-i Ṭūsī's "Book of Marvels," entitled *ʿAjāʾib al-makhlūqāt* ("Wonders of Creation"),[111] illustrates the power of talismanic images hidden in the pre-conquest Byzantine capital Constantinople (al-Qusṭantīniyya).[112] Three bronze statues representing Muḥammad and two of his closest followers, ʿAlī and Bilāl (the first muezzin), were zealously guarded by the local people; they knew from past experience that damage to the statues would set off a devastating earthquake.[113] Significantly, of the three statues only the one which shows ʿAlī on horseback striking a dragon with a spear is illustrated in the manuscript.[114] While on the one hand this story is buttressed by apocalyptic traditions, such as the prophetic *ḥadīth* foretelling the city's capture by an Islamic ruler who bore the name of a prophet,[115] it is also noteworthy that it was the Byzantine capital which was associated with the figure of the equestrian dragon-slayer. However, the story also shows that the dragon-fighter represented a well-established iconographical theme in medieval Islam. It was indeed so firmly entrenched as to be deemed the most appropriate imagery for the representation of the Companion of the Prophet who for the Sunnī Muslims represents the fourth caliph and for the Shīʿites the divinely appointed successor *(khalīfa)* and heir *(waṣī)* of Muḥammad.

By the twelfth century, dragon-fighter iconography was a prevalent part of a set narrative genre often inspired by textual sources such as the early eleventh-century Iranian national epic, the *Shāh-nāma*, and was a motif of choice depicted on many portable objects produced in medieval Western Central Asia. The theme was often chosen as part of a visual narrative on metalwork, for instance on the two copper alloy buckets discussed above, the 559/1163 Bobrinski bucket probably from Herat, and the late twelfth- to early thirteenth-century richly gilded bucket made by Muḥammad ibn Nāṣir ibn Muḥammad al-Harawī, also perhaps from Herat. The third figural relief that circumscribes the body of the Bobrinski bucket also comprises a procession of riders. Behind one of the mounted warriors, a "Saljuq-style" twice looped dragon with enormous gaping mouth rears up threateningly (fig. 90), its tongue with bifid tip oriented towards the back of the horseman, the scaly body echoing the body of the dragon protome on the handle (fig. 56). A second rider charges from behind to assist the beleaguered warrior, wielding what appear to be a shield and a club. The body of the Fould bucket is divided into twelve barely perceptible vertical facets, alternately enclosing a cartouche forming an angular figure of eight framed by a benedictory epigraphic band in Kufic and enclosing riders mounted on camels, horses and mules or donkeys. One of the horsemen, a curved sabre raised above his head, turns backwards to defend himself against an upright dragon of a type closely related to the one featured on the Bobrinski bucket, who threatens him with open jaws from behind (fig. 91).[116] The prevalence of the motif on Western Central Asian metalwork is further suggested by a related depiction in which the dragon is shown with a curved horn on an early twelfth-century Herati-type copper alloy ewer inlaid with silver from a private collection (fig. 92).

A variant of the motif is found on the base of a well-known copper alloy penbox *(qalamdān)* inlaid in silver, gold and niello from Iran, which bears the name Maḥmūd ibn Sunqur and the date 680/1281–2 inscribed on the hasp. Here not the single equestrian fighter but a second genus, that of the paired horsemen, is reproduced. Two scenes of confronted fighting horsemen, separated by three large roundels filled with a geometric pattern, are shown: on the scene to the left one horseman attacks an upright double-headed dragon

[110] Tr. and ed. Mohl, 1838–1878, vol. 5, p. 353, ll. 1707–9.

[111] Ed. Sotūde, M., Tehran, 1345/1966, as cited in Pancaroğlu (2003, p. 31 and n. 4) who dates the book to the years between 562/1167 and 573/1194. Cf. Radtke, 1987, pp. 278–88.

[112] First section of chapter six which includes descriptions on talismanic portraits, statues and tombs of prophets and kings (ed. Sotūde, M., Tehran, 1345/1966, pp. 333–4); Pancaroğlu, 2003, pp. 33, 37 and appendix.

[113] *Eadem*, pp. 34, 37.

[114] First section of chapter six (Aḥmad-i Ṭūsī, *ʿAjāʾib al-makhlūqāt*, ed. Sotūde, M., Tehran, 1345/1966, pp. 333–4); *eadem*, pp. 34, 37 and appendix.

[115] See, for instance, Eisener, 1987, pp. 129–37. Cf. Pancaroğlu, 2004, p. 155.

[116] Cf. Mayer, 1959, pl. X.

with a sword while the other turns backwards to shoot a lion with bow and arrow (fig. 93).[117] The vertically oriented body of the dragon is characterised by bilateral symmetry, the addorsed heads with open jaws revealing projecting tongues and the scaly body bifurcating to form two loops before uniting and thinning to a short pointed tip. On the right, two horsemen charge at each other with long lances. The depictions are set against a background filled with a dense interlace of foliate scrolls bearing long-eared animal heads that have been identified as "dragon progeny."[118]

Another example with the motif survives in the form of a twelfth- or thirteenth-century richly gilt copper alloy polylobed openwork roundel, probably a fitting from a belt or horse-harness for attachment, now in the al-Sabāh Collection, Kuwait National Museum. The roundel depicts an elaborately dressed archer on the back of a prancing horse which has a knotted tail and carefully rendered trappings, studded with circular *phalerae* and suspended crescents. A feline, probably a cheetah, crouches behind the warrior, who draws his bow and takes aim at a dragon as it writhes below the feet of his mount (fig. 94). The serpentine body is enlivened by a dense dotted pattern and arranged in two loops.

Of the same period and from the same wider geographical region stem related depictions on polychrome painted ceramic tiles or vessels (so-called *mīnā'ī* ware) featuring a richly clad dragon-fighting rider, his mount decorated with magnificent trappings. On a star tile, now in the Freer Gallery of Art, Washington, DC, the sinuous speckled dragon is shown in a downward diagonal (fig. 95),[119] whereas on a bowl from the Vollmoeller Collection in Zurich it is rendered in the more conventional supine posture, jaws agape, tongue projecting and the serpentine body arranged in two loops (fig. 96).[120] The ophidian bodies are both demarcated with a dense pattern. On the tile the horseman seems to take aim with a bow, while on the bowl the cavalier probably brandishes a sword. Another example of the depiction of a horseman fighting an upright dragon is part of the main narrative frieze circumscribing the shoulders of a contemporary moulded flask in the Aga Khan Collection.[121]

The belief in the invulnerability of a dragon's hide, which is impervious to water, fire, or any weapon, explains why the hero usually aims at the head, eyes or mouth of the dragon or has to attack him from within.[122] This is particularly evident in one of the celebrated feats of Rustam in the legend of the battle with the Babr-i bayān.[123] As a young man Rustam was fighting the beast in a distant land and managed to kill the dragon by making it swallow oxhides filled with quicklime and stones[124] which he carried to the place where once a week the dragon came out of the

[117] Cf. *Furūsiyya*, 1996, vol. 1, p. 173, fig. IVa detail to left, and IV view of entire lid, vol. 2, p. 232, cat. no. 194.

[118] Hartner, 1959, pp. 237–9, and *idem*, 1973–4, pp. 112, 118.

[119] In its unrestored condition the tile has been published in Atil, 1973, cat. no. 49, and Grube and Johns, 2005, p. 233, cat. no. 78.7.

[120] Another example of a *mīnā'ī* bowl with the same iconography featuring the dragon head rising above the horse's head is preserved in the Calouste Gulbenkian Foundation, Lisbon. Curatola, 1989, fig. 63.

[121] *Splendori a corte*, 2007, p. 149, cat. no. 117 (the dragon-fighting theme is not featured on the side of the flask that has been reproduced in the catalogue).

[122] In the Avesta (Yasht 9.10–1) a similar story of the invulnerability of the dragon's hide is recorded, according to which Kərəsāspa/Garshāsp cooked his midday meal on the vast green flank of the sleeping Azhi Sruuara (Azhi Zairita):

> He was a young man famous for his strength, had curly hair and swung his club; he smote the horny dragon, the horse-swallowing and man-swallowing, full of poison, yellow of colour, over whom yellow poison flowed as high as a spear. On his back Kərəsāspa cooked his meal in an iron cauldron at the time of noon. And the monster felt warm and began to sweat. Then he rushed from under the iron cauldron and upset the boiling water. Affrighted rushed headlong the valiant Kərəsāspa.

As cited by Klíma, 1968, p. 12, after the German translation of Wolff, F., *Avesta: Die Heiligen Bücher der Parsen*, Straßburg, first ed. 1910, repr. 1924; see also Boyce, 1975, repr. 1996, pp. 102–3. The long time lapse before the heat began to permeate the dragon's hide to finally wake him up (Skjærvø, "Aždahā I," *EIr*) suggests, according to Khāleqī-Moṭlaq ("Aždahā II," *EIr*), "that the belief in the invulnerability of the dragon-hide was a very old component of the story." Having finally defeated the dragon, the hero, like Rustam, also made a coat out of its hide. It is noteworthy that similarly many early epic heroes were distinguished with a magical invulnerability apart from one vulnerable spot, for instance Isfandiyār in the *Shāh-nāma* who is invulnerable apart from his eyes, and so a double-pointed arrow has to be discharged into them in order to wound or kill him. Cf. Schirmunski, 1961, pp. 36–7.

[123] Two versions of the legend are found in a *Shāh-nāma* manuscript in the British Museum, London (Ms. Or. 2926, fols. 112b-115a and 118b-122b); it is also current in surviving Iranian oral folklore (Enjavī, A., *Mardom o Shāh-nāma*, Tehran, 1355/1976, pp. 217–8, cited after Khāleqī-Moṭlaq, "Aždahā II," *EIr*); a variant of the story is known among the Mandeans of Iraq (Petermann, 1860–1, vol. 2, pp. 107–9).

[124] In the *Shāh-nāma* this method of killing the dragon is similarly employed by Iskandar (tr. and ed. Mohl, 1838–1878, vol. 4, pp. 203–5, ll. 1230–1249). Analogies may be found in other mythological traditions such as the story of Bel and the Dragon in the book of Daniel LXX in which there was a giant serpent *(drakōn)* that was venerated by the Baby-

sea. When the dragon swallowed these, his stomach burst. Significantly, in stories where the dragon was presented as a historical person, the invulnerability of the hide was metaphorically transformed into the impregnability of the enemy's castle.[125]

The depiction of a fighter on foot in direct combat with a dragon whom he attacks with his sword – a motif which appears to be absent from Christian iconography – is found on the outer walls of a celebrated plate whose interior is decorated with a large battle scene featuring the siege of a citadel and inscribed with the names of the warriors. These names incorporate Turkish elements, suggesting that they may have been Saljuq fighters.[126] Datable to the early thirteenth century, the plate is housed in the Freer Gallery of Art, Washington, DC (fig. 97).[127] The outer walls show a richly clad warrior carrying bow and arrow, shown in three-quarter view and facing a writhing ophidian dragon in rampant posture. The dragon combat is one of five heroic feats portrayed on the plate, the vignettes being separated by trees. Other feats include the shooting of a wolf with bow and arrow, clubbing a feline, probably a panther, with a mace, and shooting a mythical creature with bow and arrow. A further element shows two confronted figures, one of whom is holding a feline, probably a cheetah, on a leash. An upper register contains an epigraphic band with good wishes in Kufic script.

Following the Saljuq victory at the battle of Manzikert in 463/1071 and subsequent lárge-scale Turkish penetration into Anatolia, the Saljuq *sulṭāns* of Rūm, being closely affiliated with Iranian cultural and artistic traditions, also perpetuated these semantic horizons. The image of a mounted figure fighting a dragon was applied widely to objects and architectural decoration in Anatolia and the neighbouring Jazīra.

The motif occurs on an important frieze fragment from the now destroyed pavilion (once part of the palace) of Qılıch Arslan II (r. 551/1156–588/1192), one of the greatest Rūm Saljuq *sulṭāns*, noted both for his military achievements and his patronage of the arts. It shows two haloed horsemen charging each other and attacking respectively a dragon and a lion (fig. 98). The rider on the left thrusts his long spear into the gaping jaws of the dragon. The beast is shown with curling goatee beard projecting below the chin, and a pronounced bristling crest running down the spine to the tapering tail. The second horseman turns around to grasp the lion's mane with one hand while dealing him a blow with the sword held in the other. The Rūm Saljuq depiction thus provides a parallel to the version emblematised on the Iranian penbox made by Maḥmūd ibn Sunqur (fig. 93) almost a century after the making of the frieze. This composition, moreover, again features the fight of confronted horsemen against the most dangerous and deadliest of adversaries, the dragon and the lion. The fragment must have been part of a large frieze and is a valuable example of the type of decoration that presumably once adorned not only Saljuq-period pavilions but related secular buildings throughout the entire region as far as Central Asia.[128]

One of the earliest depictions of the motif of the single equestrian dragon-fighter west of Iran is found on the coinage of Turko-Islamic Anatolia. An equestrian warrior spearing a prostrate scaly dragon appears on the reverse of a copper coin of a type minted by the last Türkmen Dānishmendid

lonians; the Jewish Prophet Daniel killed it without sword or staff by brewing a concoction of pitch, fat, and hair and then feeding cakes made of it to the dragon (Gunkel, 1895, pp. 320–3, cogently argues that this story is an adaptation of a passage of the Babylonian creation epic *Enūma Elish*, an Akkadian text; cf. *idem*, 1895, pp. 412–3, tablet IV, ll. 93–104; Pritchard, ed., 1955, repr. 1968, p. 67). The execution of enemies seems sometimes to have been inspired by the manner in which the dragon was killed in these traditions (Merkelbach, "Drache," *RAC* IV, 1959, pp. 234–5). Mithridates VI (120–163 BC), king of Pontus, for instance, gave orders to execute Manius Aquilius by pouring liquid gold down his throat (Appianos, *Mithridates*, XII 21; Pliny, *Naturalis Historia*, XXXIII 48; cf. *idem*, pp. 234–5). This method of killing the dragon is described by al-Qazwīnī in his *Kitāb ʿajāʾib al-makhlūqāt* (ed. Wüstenfeld, 1849, repr. 1967, p. 112). For the illustration of this story in the so-called Sarre Qazwīnī, now in the Freer Gallery of Art, Washington, DC, see Badiee, 1978, pl. 32. The theme is also visualised in a fourteenth-century miniature showing Ardashīr pouring molten lead down the dragon's throat, illustrated in the St. Petersburg *Shāh-nāma* (Dorn 329, f. 243r), copied in Shiraz, 30 Jumādā I 733/16 February 1333. These references not only demonstrate that this method of killing was known but perhaps also testify to its ongoing popularity in the medieval period. See also p. 58, n. 96.

[125] Khāleqī-Moṭlaq, "Aždahā II," *EIr*.

[126] Atil, 1973, cat. no. 50.

[127] In 1983 the conservation department of the Freer Gallery of Art discovered that the original plate had some overpainting and subsequently restored it back to its original state. As a consequence part of the upper body and head of the warrior and a section of the snake's protome are no longer visible after the restoration. A photograph of the plate that pre-dates the conservation was used in order to make the imagery more easily recognisable.

[128] Cf. *The Anatolian Civilisations*, vol. 3, 1983, pp. 34–5, cat. no. D.38; *Turks*, 2005, p. 392, cat. no. 58.

ruler of Malatya/Malaṭiyya (Melitene), Nāṣir al-Dīn Muḥammad ibn Ismāʿīl (r. 557/1162–565/1170 and 570/1175–573/1178), whose name appears on the obverse, minted in the 1170s.[129] Mounted on a galloping horse the rider's right foot is placed on the body of a dragon and with his right hand he grasps the end of a lance which is thrust in the small uncoiled dragon's open jaws; the left hand holds the reins. Importantly the armoured rider, clad in a short skirt and a long-sleeved coat, is here portrayed nearly in profile. The coinage was produced after the Dānishmendids' capture of Malatya, situated not far from the upper Euphrates on an important stretch of the Arab-Byzantine frontier, in 494/1101 following a three-year siege. For much of its existence the dynasty of the Dānishmendids (463/1071–573/1178), one of the earliest Türkmen principalities established in Anatolia that reigned in northern Cappadocia, maintained a frontier ethos in which the dragon-fighting *ghāzī* was a pre-eminent symbol, as will be shown in the Epilogue.

Qılıch Arslan II's conquest of Malatya in 573/1178 brought about the end of the Dānishmendid dynasty. Not long after the Saljuq conquest of Malatya, the city of the frontier hero *par excellence*,[130] a new copper coin with a horseman slaying a dragon was minted by the ruler of Malatya, Muʿizz al-Dīn Qayṣar Shāh (r. 582/1186–597/1201 with an interruption in 587/1191), a son of Qılıch Arslan II (r. 551/1156–588/1192).[131] As Nicholas Lowick tentatively suggests, the Turkish *ghāzī* rulers were perhaps "consciously or not, seeking to establish contact with an imaginary heroic world of the past, possibly under the stimulus of historical or quasi-historical works of literature."[132] The dragon-slayer iconography on Dānishmendid and Saljuq coins is thought to have been inspired by the Byzantine copper coins struck by the crusader prince Roger (d. 513/1119), who usurped the throne of Antioch in the guise of regent for Bohemond II between 1112 and 1119,[133] and can ultimately be traced back to early Byzantine coinage.[134] On Roger's coin the equestrian rider is similarly portrayed nearly in profile and leaning forward on a galloping horse to stab the mouth of a serpent with his lance. The inscription identifies the figure as Saint George. In spite of the differences in the iconographic representation of this mounted dragon-fighting warrior, in particular the depiction of the figure in profile, there is an overall consistency with the image of contemporaneous dragon-fighters throughout medieval Western Asia.

The cosmopolitan milieu and the generous patronage of Badr al-Dīn Luʾluʾ (618/1222–657/1259) in Mosul permitted the city to become a haven for master craftsmen from Central Asia who were fleeing the Mongol invasion.[135] Among them were specialist inlay workers from the greater Khurasan region (where the technique was developed).[136] Their skill is prominently displayed on a copper alloy candlestick base, probably made in the Jazīra in *c.* 1230, and inscribed with the names of the masters, Ḥājji Ismāʿīl and Muḥammad ibn Futtūḥ al-Mawṣilī.[137] The dragon-fighting theme is shown in a large polylobed cartouche depicting a rampant knotted creature that rises above the horse's rump, his large open maw with projecting tongue oriented towards the rider who turns towards it with raised sword in hand (fig. 99).[138]

The same iconography of a horseman fighting a dragon reappears in a mid-thirteenth-century glazed fritware sculpture, now preserved in the National Museum of Damascus. Possibly a fountain element, it was discovered in Raqqa, a major city in the western part of the Jazīra.[139] The warrior wears his hair in long braids under a small cap

129 Whelan, 1980, pp. 143–8, pl. 16, 5b.

130 Wittek, 1936, p. 295.

131 Istanbul, Archaeological Museum, inv. no. 1068. Süslü, 1987, p. 640, pl. 118, ill. 5 (line drawing). Cf. Pancaroğlu, 2004, p. 157, fig. 7. Another copper coin with a horseman drawing a bow against a dragon, of uncertain date, is inscribed with the name of Muḥammad ibn Salduq (*c.* 570/1174–597/1200); Lane Poole, 1877, repr. 1967, p. 114, cat. no. 310.

132 Lowick, 1985, p. 170; cf. Pancaroğlu, 2004, p. 156.

133 Schlumberger, 1878, repr. 1954, pp. 46–9, pl. 2, no. 12; Whelan, 1980, pp. 147–8.

134 Related imagery appears already on the fourth-century gold medal of the Roman Emperor Constantine II (337–361), struck after the victory over Magnentius in 353. The emperor is shown on horseback with right hand raised over a coiled dragon with the legend *debellator hostium*. Paris, Bibliothèque Nationale, Cabinet des Médailles, inv. no. 462, Vitr. XVIII; cf. Merkelbach, "Drache," *RAC* IV, 1959, p. 255, fig. 2; Lewis, 1973, fig. 31 (pls. unnumbered); Grube and Johns, 2005, p. 232, cat. no. 78.3.

135 Ettinghausen, 1962, p. 92; Hillenbrand, R., 2006, p. 20.

136 Pinder-Wilson, 1997, p. 344.

137 *The Arts of Islam*, 1976, p. 182, cat. no. 200.

138 The same motif is found on other thirteenth-century inlaid copper alloy candlesticks, cf. for example, one from Anatolia (?) in the Victoria and Albert Museum, London, inv. no. M. 711–910, and another from Siirt, Anatolia, in the Nuhad Es-Said Collection of Islamic metalwork (Allan, 1982a, repr. 1999, pp. 59–61, cat. no. 7).

139 Glazed fritware in the form of a horseman fighting a dragon, datable to the mid-thirteenth century. Discovered by Eustace de Lorey in Raqqa, Syria. Height 46.5 cm. Damascus, al-Mathaf al-Waṭanī, inv. no. A.5819. *A Concise*

and with his sword and round decorated shield defends himself against the dragon as it rears up to strike.

Images of paired dragons are prominently depicted in the Mosul area, the heart of the Jazīra, on the gateway to the only remaining caravanserai located between Mosul and Sinjār, known as Khariyyāt al-Khān or Khān al-Harārāt, which is now partly destroyed.[140] The reliefs on each half of the archivolts of the monumental archway show two horned dragons with backward-facing heads, fighting off warriors on foot distinguished by haloes and shown in three-quarter view. The dragons are closely related to those on the Bāb al-Ṭilasm in Baghdad. Curved horns project from the crown of the head. The strong forelegs end in feet with individual pointed talons and the slender arched wings have finely delineated plumes. The heads are also rendered in three-quarter view with wide-open jaws revealing sharp teeth; high vertically hatched ruff-like projections demarcate the necks. The scaly serpentine tails form a pretzel-shaped knot and a single loop before gradually tapering to terminate in another small dragon head projecting from the inward-curling tail tip. The fabulous creatures are being attacked by the lances of the long-haired bearded figures who grip the tips of the dragons' noses with one hand while holding the lance in the other. Importantly, as will be further discussed below, the dragon-fighting reliefs surmount an imposing arch charged with nine equidistantly placed cusped medallions enclosing eight-petalled star-rosettes (figs. 100a and b).

The epigraphic frieze on the portal of the *khān* identifies the Zangīd successor Badr al-Dīn Lu'lu' Abu 'l-Faḍā'il al-Malik al-Raḥīm (618/1222–657/1259) as patron, through which the *khān* can be dated between 631/1233–4, when Badr al-Dīn Lu'lu' became official ruler *(atābeg)* of Mosul, and the Mongol invasion in 656–7/1257–8, when his rule was terminated although he succeeded in keeping Mosul as vassal of Hūlāgū.[141] The inscription also gives the *atābeg*'s honorary titles and relates him in a eulogy to the Saka hero Rustam, "the Rustam-i Zāl of our time," thus showing him in a long line of kings and underlining his legitimacy as ruler.[142] It was fitting for Badr al-Dīn Lu'lu' who governed Mosul for the longest time, and who was a freedman probably of Armenian servile origin, to carry Arab names, Persian titles and to be depicted as Turkic leader.[143] The accompanying inscription also grants sanctuary to all comers[144] which underlines the protective function of the motif.

The depiction of the hand-to-hand combat of the dragon-fighter on foot on the gateway at al-Khān has a counterpart in the representation on the Mosul gate which secures the entrance to the small mountain town of ʿAmādiya, or al-ʿImādiyya, northeast of Mosul.[145] Its monumental display echoes that on al-Khān, in particular the portrayal of the fighters who attack the dragon with a sword (although not with a lance as at al-Khān). One way in which the representations differ is that at ʿAmādiya the horned dragons are shown addorsed: the protomes project in rampant posture at the apex of the arched entrance from the top of a large knot, reminiscent of the "Syrian knot," that ties their ophidian bodies. The gaping mouths reveal the bifid tongues that entwine at mid-section (the same feature can be observed on figs. 78 and 160), and again the fighters grip with one hand the tips of the dragons' noses while with the other hand aiming their swords at the dragons' necks. Significantly, the quadripartite knot encloses a composite hemispherical rosette formed of fine pointed petals arranged radially

Guide to the National Museum of Damascus, 1969, fig. 2 (35); *Furūsiyya*, 1996, p. 222, ill. 31, pp. 236–7, cat. no. 198. ii. Two further faience fountain sculptures in this series, representing a sphinx with tail and wings ending in dragon heads and a rooster with tail ending in a bird head; dated here to the late twelfth century, are preserved in Copenhagen, the David Collection, inv. nos. Isl. 56 and Isl. 57, respectively. See von Folsach, 1990, p. 104, figs. 129 and 128.

140 Van Berchem, 1906, 2v, v1, pp. 197–210, 203–4; Preusser, 1911, pl. 17 bottom, captions on this plate mistakenly reversed; Sarre and Herzfeld, 1920, vol. 1, pp. 11, 13–5; Reitlinger, 1938, pp. 149–50; Kühnel, 1950, p. 8; Ettinghausen and Grabar, 1987, p. 302, fig. 325; Gierlichs, 1998, pp. 35, 199, fig. 1; drawing of the right spandrel of the caravanserai with parts of the inscription by Ernst Herzfeld, 19 December 1907, reproduced by Hauptmann von Gladiss, ed., 2006, fig. 19.

141 Van Berchem (in Sarre and Herzfeld, 1911) vol. 1, p. 15.

142 *Idem*, pp. 14–5 and fig. 8; Hauptmann von Gladiss, ed., 2006, p. 123 and fig. 19.

143 See for instance Badr al-Dīn Lu'lu', identified by the inscription of his name on the *tiraz*, is depicted as mounted falconer on the frontispiece of the *Kitāb al-Aghānī* ("Book of Songs"), dated 616/1219, Muḥammad ibn ʿAlī Ṭālib ibn al-Badrī, now in Copenhagen, Royal Library, Ms. Cod. Arab. 169. Hauptmann von Gladiss, ed., 2006, p. 8, fig. 1; Hillenbrand, R., 2006, p. 19. Cf. Cahen, "Lu'lu'," *EI*² V, 820b.

144 Ibrāhīm, 1976, p. 13.

145 The gate was destroyed during bombing in the 1980s and then reconstructed. Gierlichs, 1995, pls. 2–3 (watercolour of 1955), and *idem*, 1998, pp. 35, 199, fig. 2; Hauptmann von Gladiss, ed., 2006, p. 122, fig. 16.

in superimposed layers. The rayed outline of the rosette adds to the overall starburst effect, underlining the identification of the rosette as a solar symbol. The base extends to form an interlaced festoon that frames the arched aperture which includes a small eight-petalled rosette at the apex (fig. 101).[146]

The solar iconography of the large central rosette adds weight to the identification of the small rosette, just like the closely related rosettes emblazoned on the gateway to al-Khān, as stellar symbol. As also shown in the above-discussed reliefs on the Bāb al-Ḥayyāt in Aleppo (fig. 3a), on Karatay Han (figs. 4a and b) and on the small "Kiosk Mosque" situated in Sultan Han (fig. 12), the latter two examples being located near Kayseri, this once again associates dragons with stellar constellations. As noted, in contrast to the depiction on al-Khān, on which the mirror image of the dragon fight is rendered in a confronted manner, the dragons are shown as addorsed. Their bodies issue from the knotted configuration that encloses the solar symbol and then extends to frame the arch. The creatures may thus be seen to hold or bind the sun by means of the knotted enclosure. Yet at the same time, they appear to emerge from the solar symbol. The relief is thus an important example of the dual symbolism inherent in the dragon's connection with the sun which has often been associated with the occurrence of the eclipse as will be seen below. Only fragments remain of the architectural inscription[147] which again names Badr al-Dīn Lu'lu' as benefactor and thus dates the relief, like the façade sculptures at al-Khān, to the period of his rule. At that time the treasury was kept at ʿAmādiya,[148] which might have provided all the more reason for Badr al-Dīn Lu'lu' to emblematise himself as a dragon-fighter set within the complex of stellar allusions on the town gate.

At the same time it is interesting to consider the identification of the standing haloed fighters with the syncretistic figure of the Islamic Prophet Khiḍr,[149] guide of wayfarers and patron saint of travellers and, moreover, identified with the Christian dragon-slayer Saint George.[150] This is especially pertinent in view of the widespread popular cult of Khiḍr at the regional monastery of Mār Behnām/Deir al-Khiḍr, located southeast of Mosul, an important place of pilgrimage for Jews, Christians and Muslims. The iconography of the dragon-slayer, regarded as Saint George as well as al-Khiḍr, played a pertinent role at the monastery. In the age of syncretism this however does not exclude the possibility that Badr al-Dīn Lu'lu' wished to benefit from these different layers of identification of the dragon-fighter motif and to build his historical charisma upon a rhetorical association of his personality with religious figures – his conscious association with al-Khiḍr – as well as "mythical" figures associated with Iranian legendary history and national epic – he is called "the Rustam-i Zāl of our time." Being an astute diplomat he thereby clearly relied on the potency and cultural resonance that these figures possessed at the time, arguably to enhance his position as powerful ruler and defender of his realm as well as to appropriate symbolically the religio-cultural space of his realm. It also demonstrates his ambition to create a cultural paradigm by embracing a multilayered symbolism which includes syncretic religious aspects as well as ancient Iranian traditions. This was visually anchored in the figure of the dragon-fighter as well as the symbol of the interlaced dragons at ʿAmādiya. It may be hypothesised that akin to the motif of the interlaced dragons, added around a century earlier to the otherwise late Byzantine style coinage of the Artuqid ruler Fakhr al-Dīn Qara Arslan (figs. 32a and b), these symbols were chosen in the spirit of a conscious revival of imagery carrying an association with the glorious Iranian past. The royal messages conveyed by the sculptures on the gateways of al-Khān and ʿAmādiya demonstrate visual expressions of both power and ideologies that are remarkably fluid, traversing geographical, religious and cultural boundaries.

Yet another manifestation of the mounted dragon-fighter is found in a mid- to late thirteenth-century Anatolian manuscript, known as *Daqā'iq al-Ḥaqā'iq*, dedicated to the Saljuq *sulṭān* Ghiyāth al-Dīn Kay Khusraw III, which is variously dated Ramaḍān 670/April 1272 and

[146] Cf. Gierlichs, 1995, pp. 195–7.

[147] On the right side, "ʿIzz li Mawlānā al-Sulṭān al-Mālik al-Malik ar-Raḥīm al-ʿĀlim al-ʿĀsil al-Mu'ayyad al-Muẓaffar al-Manṣūr al-Mujāhid al-Murābiṭ al-Mutaghir al-Ghāzī Badr al-Dunyā wa 'l-Dīn," and on the left side, "Atābak al-Aʿẓam Abu 'l-Faḍā'il Lu'lu' …," after Gierlichs, 1995, p. 202.

[148] *Idem*, p. 203.

[149] Sarre and Herzfeld, 1911, vol. 1, pp. 13, 37–8; Coomaraswamy, 1934, p. 181; Tabbaa, 1997, p. 76.

[150] Friedlaender, "Khiḍr," *ERE*, vol. 14, 1915, p. 695; Fiey, 1965, vol. 2, pp. 575–6; Franke, 2000, pp. 155, n. 512, and pp. 159–60; Baumer, 2005, p. 110. See also the discussion in the Epilogue, part 2.

mid-Shawwāl 671/early May 1273,[151] although the illustrations may be of a later date.[152] It shows the warrior as a mounted angel with long beard, wearing a three-pointed Iranian crown and shawl that streams in the wind. The figure is identified as Shamhūrash (an angel known as judge and ruler of the *jinn*), who is about to pierce a dragon with a sword.[153] The weapon of choice, a sword, recalls the stucco relief from the Saljuq palace in Konya. The dragon's head was partly cut off when the margin was trimmed, leaving only the open snout with curled tip; the long tail forms a large pretzel-like knot and a simple loop (fig. 102). The manuscript comprises a compilation of five different Persian texts on various topics related to astrology and magic, influenced to a certain extent by Byzantine prototypes. The painting is part of a treatise on geomancy and talismans which is further illustrated by the depiction of magic writing on the page, composed of rows of numbers and letters.

It may be postulated that the representations of the single fighter, mounted or on foot, and of the paired horsemen of the medieval Islamic period did not solely fulfil a decorative purpose. Illustrating the belief of the magical power of images, they very likely served as prophylactic and apotropaic representations with a talismanic function, precisely because as André Grabar has observed, "in this domain the possibility of a 'consubstantiality' of the representation and the thing represented is implicitly acknowledged."[154]

It is also worth noting that in the pictorial representations the dragon and the hero are generally shown in ongoing combat; the monster is sometimes depicted in a rampant posture engaging the hero in furious battle as if to test his valour, hence it is clearly not yet defeated. By contrast in Islamic literature of the medieval period, as also seen in the examples cited above, the dragon is generally overcome by the hero. A notable exception to this rule is the story of Isfandiyār's son, the heroic king Bahman who features in the early twelfth-century eponymous epic *Bahman-nāma* which was probably written by Īrānshāh ibn Abi 'l-Khayr between 485/1092–93 and 501/1107–8. In this account the king abdicates in favour of Humāy, the daughter of the king of Egypt, and then during a hunting expedition "in Dayr-i Gachīn between Isfahan and Ray"[155] he is killed by a dragon.[156] This may however, just like the metaphor of being "caught in the dragon's maw," be a euphemism simply intended to indicate the fact that he perished. As such it would be indicative of man's relation with the dragon as being interdependent and transformative.

c. *The Eastern Christian holy rider as dragon-fighter*

The idea of connecting the cult and iconography of the Eastern Christian warrior saints with the dragon can be traced to at least the early seventh century.[157] The dragon motif in the Christian church developed in the eastern confines of Byzantium,[158] where the so-called holy rider vanquishing a dragon was a well-established literary topos and was represented in early wall paintings.[159] Depictions are found on portable items, ranging from magical amulets to luxury objects, as well as on sacred architecture, in particular churches and funerary settings. The motif fell on particularly fertile ground in the Transcaucasus region which was part of the pan-Iranian religio-cultural realm and was steeped in its artistic conventions.

The antecedents of the victorious equestrian figure fighting a dragon have been sought further west where they have been linked to votive reliefs with Thracian horsemen, confronted or single, and a serpent sinuously rising towards the rider's

[151] Blochet, 1926, pl. XIX; Hartner, 1938, p. 143, fig. 22; Barrucand, 1990–91, pp. 113–4, pl. 3c.

[152] Rogers, "Saldjūḳids," *EI*² VIII, 936a.

[153] Winkler, 1930, p. 102.

[154] Grabar, 1957, p. 140.

[155] This detail is recorded by Mehrdad Shokoohy from the anonymous *Mujmal al-tawārīkh wa 'l-qiṣaṣ*, as noted by Bivar, 2000, p. 22. On the basis of the geographic location of Bahman's battle with the dragon, Bivar relates it to the campaign (much of which took place in Media and Susiana) between Eumenes of Cardia, whose name coincides etymologically with Bahman, and Antigonus the One-Eyed, both successors of Alexander the Great, as recorded by the Greek historian Diodorus Siculus (19.44) who wrote in the first century BC. Antigonus completely vanquishes Eumenes in 316 BC and since the latter had been more popular with the Ira-nians, Antigonus was allegorically equated with the dragon *(azhdahā)*. See Shokoohy, 1983, pp. 448 and 451; Bivar, 2000, p. 22.

[156] See Hanaway, "Bahman-nāma," *EIr*. The dragon is named Abr-i Sīyāh ("Black cloud"); Khāleqī-Moṭlaq, "Aždahā II," *EIr*.

[157] Walter, 2003, p. 140.

[158] Although the horseman was one of the most distinctive figures in the pictorial repertory of the Coptic arts of Byzantine Egypt, it is notable that he does not battle with a dragon; an example of a rider piercing a dragon on a Coptic tapestry band of the early Islamic period forming a rare exception. Cf. Lewis, 1973, p. 54, fig. 28 (pls. unnumbered).

[159] Cf. Walter, 2003, p. 37.

feet, or coiled around his staff or around a tree.[160] Similarly the god Mithras is depicted on horseback accompanied by a serpent.[161] However, there is no evidence that would establish a direct connection,[162] since, as Christopher Walter also notes, in none of the cases does the serpent seem to be a noxious beast nor does the rider seem to battle with the serpent.[163] On the contrary, in Mithraism, which became a widespread religion in the Mediterranean basin, Europe and the Near East, the serpent appears to have been "a symbol of beneficial, life-giving force."[164] It has further been suggested that the dragon-slaying iconography grew out of the tradition of associating the saints with ancient Greek mythologies,[165] in particular the legend of Perseus and Andromeda.[166] However, this theory is based on the assumption that the story of a Christian saint rescuing a princess or maiden from a dragon was ancient, whereas it dates back no earlier than the eleventh century, as will be shown below.[167]

Conversely, the iconography of a triumphant rider trampling on or slaying a fallen enemy occurs frequently in antiquity and has been widely used in different contexts.[168] The concept of killing a serpentine adversary was introduced on Roman imperial imagery for the first time to represent the victory of Constantine I (r. 306–337) over his enemy, one hundred years after the above-discussed investiture relief of Ardashīr I (r. 224–241). According to Eusebius' *Vita Constantini* (III, 3), a painting in the vestibule of Constantine's palace at Constantinople showed the emperor and his sons with a dragon writhing under their feet, identified by Grabar[169] as representing Constantine's vanquished enemy, Licinius, his former co-emperor, who was defeated and killed in 324, portrayed as being pierced and cast down into the deep.[170] The lost Constantinian composition was disseminated throughout the late empire by a widespread coin type represented by the mid-fourth-century gold medallion struck by Constantine II (317–361) after the victory over the usurper Magnentius in 353. It shows the emperor with raised right hand, mounted on a horse that rears up over a dragon framed by the legend *debellator hostium*.[171] The horse is represented with hind legs parallel, hooves touching the ground, while the forelegs are raised high over the coiled reptile. However, as Grabar has suggested, even though this newly introduced iconography of the triumphant emperor striking down or trampling a dragon

---

[160] Thierry, 1972, p. 259, fig. 22; Mazarov, I., "Opit za rekonstrukcija na hipomita v devna Trakija," *Izkustvo* 35 III, 1985, pp. 20–30, as cited in Walter, 1989a, p. 664 and fig. 2; 2003, fig. 11; *Furūsiyya*, 1996, vol. 2, pp. 221–2.

[161] Rostovtzeff, ed., 1939, pp. 112–6, pls. XIV, XV; Cumont, 1937, pp. 63–71. Cf. *idem*, 1939, p. 74. On the relationship between the Iranian Mithra and the Roman Mithra, see Zaehner, 1961, pp. 99–104.

[162] Hinnells, 1974, pp. 244–5. Khāleqī-Moṭlaq ("Aždahā II," *EIr*) tentatively suggests that the feast of Mihragān (mentioned in the *Shāh-nāma*) held after the victory of Farīdūn (Thraētaona) over Ẓaḥḥāk may possibly be connected to the story of the dragon-slaying by the god Mihr (Mithra), although no direct association between the ritual and worship of the festival and the dragon-slayer has been found. A simulated dragon-slaying by the Emperor Commodus during the mysteries of Mithras is recorded in a passage from Lampridius (*Commodus* 9); see Loisy, 1930, repr. 1983, p. 182. However, Jean Calmard ("Mihragān," *EI²* VII, 15a) calls this attempt "another attractive but faulty interpretation," based on the ancient noun *mithrakāna*, associating the suffix *kāna* (no longer *akāna*) with a variant of *ghna* (Ved. *han*, Old Pers. *jan*) meaning to strike or kill; *mithrakāna* thus refers to the killing (or sacrifice) for Mithra, analogous with the expression designating the Indo-Iranian god Verethragna. Nevertheless, it is of note that with Christianisation, the festival of *mithrakān* was consecrated to Saint George. Cf. Boyce, 1981, p. 67.

[163] Walter, 1989b, p. 664.

[164] Hinnells, 1974, pp. 244–5, 247, and *idem*, 1975, p. 295; Skjærvø, "Aždahā I," *EIr*.

[165] The representation of a horseman surmounting a coiled snake features on Greek bronze coins struck at Isinda in Pisidia during the first century BC. However the rider is generally depicted holding his lance as if to thrust it forward, rather than straight down, that is, he is rarely shown to aim at the serpent's jaws, see Hill, 1897, pp. 223–4, pl. XXXVI, 3, 4. Cf. Der Nersessian, 1965, p. 24; Whelan, 1980, pp. 146–7.

[166] Cf. Sakisian, 1937, p. 228; Fontenrose, 1959, repr. 1980, pp. 515–20; Sharon, "Ludd," *EI²*, V, 798b.

[167] In spite of the analogies of the stories of Perseus rescuing Andromeda from a sea monster at Joppa located close to Lydda, and that of the eleventh-century story of Saint George rescuing the princess from the dragon, the enormous gap of time does not allow for the establishment of a connection. Cf. Walter, 2003, pp. 121–2 and n. 82, p. 140 and n. 195.

[168] It is interesting to note, though, that in Coptic Egypt there appears to be only one rare example of a horseman vanquishing an enemy, in which case a prostrate human figure lies under the horse's hooves (fragmentary tapestry panel, late sixth or early seventh century, Washington, DC, The Textile Museum, inv. no. 71.6). See Lewis, 1973, fig. 7 (pls. unnumbered).

[169] Grabar, 1936, pp. 43–4 and 130.

[170] The earliest representation of the symbol of the serpent(-dragon) being slain by a *labarum* as metaphorical victory over evil, a special imperial standard modelled on the cross after Constantine's conversion to Christianity, appears on bronze coins minted in Constantinople in 326–7. *Eusebius*, tr. and ed. Cameron and Hall, 1999, p. 209, fig. 2. Cf. Demougeot, 1986, pp. 94–118, esp. 94–6.

[171] Paris, Bibliothèque Nationale, Cabinet des Médailles, inv. no. 462, Vitr. XVIII. Cohen, 1892, vol. 7, p. 443; Merkelbach, "Drache," *RAC* IV, 1959, p. 255, fig. 2; Lewis, 1973, fig. 31 (unnumbered pls.); Grube and Johns, 2005, p. 232, cat. no. 78.3.

under his horse's hooves remained essentially a symbol of victory, it also introduced a moral and spiritual meaning.[172]

It is this very motif which provides a link with the hagiographical iconography of the holy rider vanquishing an enemy which appears on Jewish[173] or Christian magical "amulets" that circulated in the Byzantine world. These frequently show on the obverse an anonymous rider saint spearing a prostrate figure, generally represented as female with long hair, who raises her hands in a vain attempt at supplication or defence. More rarely the figure appears to be portrayed with a bare female torso and what may perhaps be a serpentine lower body.[174] The choice of a female figure as the vanquished enemy reflects perhaps the ancient belief in dangerous female demons which may go back to the Lilith of Jewish legend.[175] Of note is that the term Druj,[176] the demoness of deceit and treachery, is applied in later Avestan texts to a whole class of female demons.[177] It has also been shown convincingly that the prostrate figure on these amulets represents a female demon who harms children and pregnant women as attested by late antique magical sources and that the amulets served as prophylactic charms against a variety of illnesses.[178] However, the systematic study of this iconography is complicated by difficulties in dating the amulets and by the frequent absence of legends which would make it possible to identify the equestrian figure. The rare accompanying legends invoke Solomon the horseman, the formidable enemy of demons, and/or Saint Sisinnios[179] (who is thought to have been a Parthian),[180] permitting identification with either or both of these figures.

Through the use of his "magical" seal and other ritual techniques attributed to him, the Jewish king Solomon was considered to be the archetypal controller of spirits and demons,[181] the quintessential warrior-magician, a figure that reflected a conflation of parallel Jewish, Christian, Greek

[172] Grabar, 1936, pp. 44, 47.

[173] While monotheism and the prohibition of images restrained Jews from developing divine or demonic figural images, the Second Commandment was not strictly observed by all Jewish communities. Special highlights of Jewish figural art are, for instance, the wall paintings of the third-century synagogue at Dura Europos (see Rostovtzeff, 1939, p. 102) and the mosaics of the sixth-century synagogue of Beth Alpha (Sukenik, 1932).

[174] For a detailed analysis of this type, see Bonner, 1950, pp. 99, 208–21, pls. XIV–XVII, nos. 294–301, 306, 309, 311, 314, 315, 318, 319, 323–7. Cf. Perdrizet, 1903, and *idem*, 1922; Peterson, 1926, p. 103, 107 (lower illustration); Engemann, 1975, p. 25 and fig. 1, p. 37 and fig. 6, n. 111 with references on the so-called seals with Solomon on horseback; Thierry, 1999, pp. 238–9 and ns. 20, drawings 2 a-c; Alexander, 1999, pp. 1076–1077, fig. 32.2. Cf. also Bank, A.V., *Gemma s izobrazeniem Solomona*, Vizantijskij Vremennik 8, Moscow, 1956, pp. 331–8; as cited in Walter, 1989a, pp. 665–6, n. 57; *idem*, 2003, fig. 14. The reverse of the amulets depict various scenes, the most common being the representation of the "all-suffering eye." The ancient symbol is usually depicted as an eye whose pupil is pierced by various sharp weapons and attacked by several fierce or noxious animals; as portrayed, for instance, at the Dura synagogue (Engemann, 1975, pp. 22–48 and p. 27, fig. 5; Doro, 1941, pp. 220–1). Cf. Walter, 1989b; Thierry, 1999, p. 240. For a recent study dedicated to Sasanian-period glyptics with this motif which however sees the subjects represented on the seals as having originated in the Mediterranean and the Near Eastern civilisations, see Magistro, 2000, pp. 167–94. For a discussion of Byzantine amulets with a rider saint spearing a prostrate she-demon, see Spier, 1993, pp. 25–62, esp. pp. 60–2, and pl. 2, nos. a, 15, and b, 21, pl. 3, no. a, 33 and pl. 6, no. d.

[175] Cf. Hutter, "Lilith," *DDD*, pp. 520–1; Bonner, 1950, p. 210.

[176] See, for instance, *Bundahishn* 2.3.3.23–4; Boyce, 1984, p. 50.

[177] Cf. Langton, 1949, p. 70; Bonner, 1950, p. 210.

[178] Bonner, 1950, pp. 210–8; Spier, 1993, pp. 25–62, esp. pp. 33–44. For the transmission from early Near Eastern to Jewish and classical Greek mythology of the belief in a female demon, bringer of harm to children and pregnant women, see Barb, 1966, pp. 1–23. The aid of Saint Sisinnios is also invoked in Armenian talismanic scrolls against the female demon Āl, known throughout the Persian-speaking world, who is believed to be the personification of puerperal fever which strikes women in childbed. Cf. Russell, 2004, pp. 447–8. On the Āl, see also Goldziher, 1896, vol. 1, p. 16; Winkler, 1931, pp. 104–7; and, in particular, the monograph of Eilers, 1979.

[179] The most elaborate visual representation of the mounted Saint Sisinnios appears on the seventh- or eighth-century fresco found on the west wall of chapel XVII in the Apa Apollon monastery at Bawīṭ in Upper Egypt where he spears a prostrate female figure identified as the demoness "Alabasdria." Excavated in 1901–2 by Clédat, 1904–6, xii.2, pp. 79–81; Perdrizet, 1922, pp. 13–5; Lewis, 1973, fig. 30 (pls. unnumbered).

[180] Perdrizet, 1922, p. 13; Maguire, 1995, p. 57. Peterson (1926, p. 118) considers the Sisinnios legend to have an Iranian origin. Rika Gyselen (1995, pp. 89–90), moreover, remarks upon the resemblance of the name (and apparent function) of Saint Sisinnios and that of the Iranian "mage" Sāsān found on many Sasanian magical seals while excluding the possibility of an inverse influence (on the figure of Sāsān, pp. 55–6).

[181] Solomon evolved as legendary magician, endowed with exceptional wisdom and believed to be skilled in the art of exorcising spirits and demons. A detailed description of an exorcism is related by the first-century historian Josephus (*Antiquitates Iudaicae* 8.45–9) as well as by the late antique *Testamentum Salomonis*, an uncanonical religious text which appears to be a Christian adaptation of a contemporary demonological Jewish text entirely devoted to Solomon's power over demons (ed. from manuscripts at Mount Athos, Bologna, Holkham Hall, Jerusalem, London, Milan, Paris and Vienna by McCown, 1922, esp. chs. 3–18). Cf. Bonner, 1950, p. 209.

and Iranian traditions when moreover interest in extraneous doctrines and cults was very active.[182]

These visual images of triumph over the enemy or over the powers of evil were naturally adopted for the presentation of warrior saints,[183] the actual systematisation of their cult probably having taken place in Constantinople.[184] The image of the dragon being trampled by a potent rider's horse, traceable to at least the early seventh century, thus mirrors the symbolic meaning of spiritual triumph over the persecutions of tyrannical pagan rulers, representing the crushing of evil and Satan through conversion and the destruction of pagan temples.[185]

The close parallels in iconography between the Iranian and the Judaeo-Christian traditions expressing the fundamental juxtaposition between victor and vanquished, however, may in large part be due to the influence of Iranian dualist notions on the religions of the Near East from the Achaemenid period to the early centuries of the present era.[186] The strong dualistic character of Jewish eschatology, including the belief in the coming of a saviour (messiah),[187] a final struggle between Good and Evil, and the resurrection of the dead, seems also to suggest the strong possibility of a borrowing from Zoroastrian doctrine,[188] where according to Yasna 30.3–5 the good and bad spirits were "twins" (separate, independent individuals as stated by orthodox Zoroastrianism),[189] as is evidenced by the Qumran texts, early Christianity and all Gnostic religions (Hermeticism, Gnosticism, Manichaeism).[190] Christianity, in turn, inherited most of its eschatological perspective from the Iranian-inspired apocrypha of the Old Testament and the Jewish writings of the period just before its emergence.[191]

The eschatological concept in the struggle against a dragon in Judaeo-Christian tradition has close analogies in ancient Iranian texts, cited above. In the Old Testament the resurrection is connected with the myth of Leviathan (Hebrew *liwyātān*; Ugaritic *ltn*) who is slain by Yahweh and thus plays a role in the eschatological struggle.[192] In the Syriac *Apocalypse of Baruch* (29.4; perhaps early second century AD) Leviathan together with another mythical monster, Behemoth, rises out of the sea at the coming of the Messiah.[193] In the Apocalypse of John (20.1–3) the "old dragon" is identified with Satan, evil incarnate. An angel descends from heaven with a key to the abyss, the underworld, and a chain to fetter the dragon there for one thousand years.[194] Once this term has expired, the dragon is freed to take part in the great final struggle in which it will be decisively defeated, resulting in the resurrection of the dead and the coming of a new age in which death and evil are no more.[195] Almut Hintze concludes:

---

182 Bonner, 1950, p. 18; Alexander, 1999, p. 1077; Walter, 2003, p. 35; Pancaroğlu, 2004, pp. 152–3.

183 Der Nersessian, 1965, p. 24.

184 Walter, 1989a, p. 663.

185 Especially during and after the exile of the Jews in Babylon, Iranian influence may have been instrumental in bringing about the change in the conception of Satan from a servant of God (for instance, in Zechariah, 3.1–3.3) to his adversary (Duchèsne-Guillemin, "Ahriman," *EIr*). At least in part a Jewish apocalyptic movement, the early Christian faith inherited a worldview in which Satan played a vital role as the ultimate adversary or opponent of God and his agents. In the visions of John, Satan is portrayed as composite beast, which emerges from the sea (Daniel 7), drawn from the myth of a cosmic struggle between a god and a sea monster or dragon informed by a Mesopotamian mythic pattern (cf. also the general discussion in Gunkel, "Die Drachentraditionen," 1895, pp. 29–90, and "die Traditionen vom Urmeer," 1895, pp. 81–111) to which Satan "gave his power and his throne and great authority" (Revelation 13.2). This imagery was used in polemical discourses and played an important role in the "demonisation" of either external enemies or internal adversaries of which the Roman imperial power was a designated agent.

186 Boyce and Grenet, 1991, pp. 361–490; Gnoli, "Dualism," *EIr*; Hintze, 1999, pp. 72–9, esp. pp. 75–6.

187 In connection with the concept of messianism in Judaism it is of interest to note the identification of the saviour and the serpent, which is supported by the numerical equivalence of the Hebrew letters of the words *naḥash* ("serpent") and *mashiaḥ* ("messiah"), both being equivalent to 358, therefore by the rules of gematria these words are considered to have a close affinity. The idea that the serpent-messiah would destroy the evil serpent is expressed in the thirteenth-century writings of Isaac Cohen of Soria in Spain, published by Scholem, 1926, p. 273.

188 The main locus of contacts between Jews and Mazdāyasnians was most likely to be Persia and Babylonia where Jews lived among the predominantly Persian population; Hintze, 1999, p. 78. Cf. Shaked, "Eschatology," *EIr*.

189 Boyce, 1975, repr. 1996, p. 193.

190 Shaked, "Eschatology," *EIr*; Gnoli, "Dualism," *EIr*. Cf. Zaehner, "Zoroastrianism," *CELF*, p. 159.

191 Shaked, "Eschatology," *EIr*.

192 Isaiah 27.1. Heidel, 1942, repr. 1951, p. 103; Hintze, 1999, pp. 89–90.

193 Hintze, 1999, pp. 80–1 and n. 38. Cf. 1 Enoch 60.7. Related beliefs are found in Gnostic traditions. It is interesting to consider a later fourteenth-century Samaritan chronicle which reverts to earlier Jewish, Christian and Samaritan traditions and relates of the first-century Dositheans: "These people believed that the Serpent will govern the lives of creatures until the day of resurrection." See Isser, 1976, p. 80.

194 Cf. Hintze, 1999, p. 81, n. 39 with further examples.

195 *Eadem*, p. 81, and n. 41. Cf. parallels in the book of Revelation (20.1–6) where there appears the story of the leader of the powers of darkness, also referred to as "the dragon, the primeval serpent, which is the devil and Satan," being overpowered and cast into the abyss by an angel who "sealed it over him, to make sure that he would not deceive

> It is very likely that the Jewish/Christian tradition took over the image [of the struggle against a dragon] from the Zoroastrian one in order to formulate its own eschatological myth.[196]

The metaphysical struggle between fighter and dragon of course represents in a basic sense an "antagonism of the light, celestial (sun), and the dark, terrestrial, principles."[197] By extension traditional combat depictions convey the triumph of good over evil and light over darkness. As Kiti Mačabeli observes, the older eastern model of the iconography of the light-bearing horseman lent itself naturally to Transcaucasian Christian imagery, resulting in an identification between the mounted saint as the embodiment of light and the positive principle, seen in the act of crushing the dragon, the quintessential symbol of evil and darkness.[198] One illustration of this concept in a Sasanian context is the third-century depiction of the god Ahura Mazdā/Ohrmazd on horseback crushing the head of the Zoroastrian spirit of evil, Angra Mainyu/Ahriman (figs. 86a and b).

The earliest surviving representations of the dragon-slaying model in Eastern Christian art are found, as mentioned above, on the eastern confines of the Byzantine empire in Transcaucasia. This region, and in particular Armenia, was profoundly influenced by Parthian Iranianism, hence it is safe to assume that the artistic traditions had to a certain extent developed in symbiosis with the Iranised world.[199] The model underwent a comparable process of development in neighbouring Cappadocia which was located at the crossroads of the Byzantine, Arab and Transcaucasian worlds.

Among the earliest known instances of bas reliefs with the motif is a seventh-century Georgian stone stele from Ekikilise, village of Agʿegui in Kartli region (fig. 103)[200] preserved in the Museum of Fine Arts in Tibilisi. The iconography of a single unnamed dragon-fighting equestrian figure spearing a large dragon, whose spotted body is rendered as twice coiled, succumbing at his horse's feet, can be clearly made out.[201] Just as in the later examples from the Islamic world considered above, the rider is often portrayed with his head encircled by a halo and his upper body turned so as to appear nearly frontally; the horse usually has its hooves firmly planted on the ground and the serpent is knotted or coiled beneath it. Yet significantly, the battle with the dragon is now almost exclusively reduced to the moment of triumph visualised by the weapon of choice being invariably plunged into the animal's throat, thus killing it.

An important, possibly seventh-century, wall painting with confronted warrior saints fighting two dragons is found in Cappadocia, now in a very poor state of preservation, in the rock-cut church known as Mistikan kilise in the village of Güzelöz (Mavrucan), region of Çavuşin.[202] It is one of the earliest surviving examples of the conceptual doubling, in other words the paired

---

the nations again" for a thousand years. Cf. Boyce and Grenet, 1991, pp. 421, 446.

196 Hintze, 1999, pp. 86–7.

197 Hartner, 1938, p. 143, n. 45.

198 Cf. Mačabeli, K., *Pozdneantičnaja torevtika Gruzii: Pomaterialam torevtiki pervych vekov nashej ery*, Tbilisi, 1976, p. 85, translated into German by Scholz, 1982, p. 245.

199 Sasanian-style iconography is found in reliefs with scenes of the hunt on the seventh-century church of Ptghni (Ptghnavankʿ) in Ararat province. On the right side, below the archivolt on a window of the south façade, is a galloping rider armed with bow and arrow taking aim at the protome of an excessively long-necked monster with large gaping mouth. The accompanying inscription identifies the rider as Manuel Amatuni (d. 389), who has been portrayed in the same manner as was customary for the Sasanian kings who were overlords of this part of Armenia (Der Nersessian, 1945, p. 89). The weathered condition of the carving makes it difficult to determine the long-necked mythical creature with long agape snout and forelegs. It was identified by Der Nersessian (1945, p. 88) as a griffin; the description mistakenly confuses the attribution of the lion and the standing man with the griffin and the rider; however on account of its very long sinuous neck and the excessively long wide open mouth with what appears to be a projecting tongue, it might represent a dragon. *Eadem*, 1945, pl. X.1 (photograph represented mirror-inverted); Thierry, 1987, p. 365, fig. 199.

200 The stele bears the inscription of which one can only decipher the word "...assomtavrouli..." ("...serpent..."). I would like to acknowledge my debt to Nicole Thierry who provided me with this information (the inscription was read by Mrs. Kétino Abachidzé); she identifies the rider as an early representation of Theodore. Another contemporary, yet unpublished fragmentary relief with the same motif from Berdadzor is also preserved in the Museum of Fine Arts in Tibilisi. Thierry, 1999, p. 236. An early example appears on one side of a fragmentary capital, dated to the sixth century, found at Dwīn, the ancient Armenian capital, now preserved in the Historical Museum, Yerevan, inv. no. 2604, featuring a serpent protome beneath the hooves of a horse. The rider's hand is shown holding the horse's reins but he is not shown holding a weapon, hence it is unclear whether he is intended to represent a mounted warrior. Khalʿpakhʿchian, 1980, p. 92, pl. 9.

201 Thierry, 1999, pp. 236, 240, fig. 4. The stone relief is also reproduced in Süslü, 1987, p. 644, pl. 119, ill. 27 (wrongly identified as coming from Ani and as preserved in the Historical Museum, Yerevan).

202 It is noteworthy that while the wall paintings are very faint, the overall composition could still be clearly discerned when the present writer visited the church in October 2008 (which is probably due to the fact that this particular church is hardly ever visited). Thierry (1972, pp. 258–63; *eadem*, 1984–5, pp. 293–302, esp. pp. 300–2, fig. 88, pl. 156a;

portrayal, of the equestrian warrior saints, a significant characteristic, as will be seen in what follows, introduced to augment and reinforce the intended effect, making the paired dragon-fighters a doubly potent emblem. Here a unique feature is added to the symmetrical composition of the two horsemen in that they direct their spears at two horned dragons which are entwined around the "trunk" of a central tree-like composition (fig. 104).[203] Portrayed with frontally rendered curved horns, globulous eyes and long open muzzles whose slightly bulging tops are demarcated by small wrinkles and which exhibit the lupine characteristic of the steppe dragons, the dragons' heads come to face the horses' heads. The equines do not prance or rear up on their hind legs, but pose heraldically with one foreleg raised. Nicole Thierry sought to explain the composite aspect of the iconography by the fact that Cappadocia served as a large military encampment from where Byzantine troops, among whom were large mercenary contingents, in part of different nomadic origins,[204] went to wage war against the Persians and later against the Arabs. The influence of the mercenary troops was also felt in the progressive adaptation of military techniques and equipment of a "Turanian cultural community," which sometimes occurred directly or through Parthian or Sasanian mediation.[205]

The depiction is in the tradition of widely employed symmetrical Sasanian imagery exemplified in the third-century investiture relief of Ardashīr I at Naqsh-i Rustam with the equestrian scene of Ardashīr facing Ahura Mazdā whose horses' hooves are shown to trample, respectively, the head of a dead enemy and the serpent-wreathed head of Ahriman (fig. 86b).[206] This conceptual pairing aspect is also found on different media, notably on Sasanian and Sogdian textiles.[207] Here, too, the pairing of the iconography was presumably not purely intended to create the effect of pictorial symmetry but rather aimed at reinforcing its potent benefit. Hence the visual symmetry of the dragon-fighters was also intended to bring into play the belief in a double protection through the agency of its essential meaning, the triumph of good over evil.[208] Yet while the influence of the Iranian symbolic repertoire is certainly felt in the symmetrical composition of horsemen and the tree-with-serpents, it is represented here in a Christian context. The motif therefore may allude, just like the much later above-discussed miniature from the *Yachakhapatum*, or a book of homilies, of 1216 illustrated at Skevra monastery in Cilician Armenia (fig. 44), to the subject of the serpent and the fruit-bearing tree in Paradise. Hence, the representation may be seen as a compound motif linking the dragon-fighting horsemen and the tree-with-serpents.

Comparable symmetrical imagery of two confronted equestrian warriors also flanking a large stylised tree with curling foliage is found on a now lost stone relief plaque (extant only as a drawing) from a church in Ani. Mounted on caparisoned horses with large saddle blankets, the horsemen again mirror each other's actions. Yet instead of directing their weapons at serpents entwined around a tree as in the early, possibly seventh-century, Cappadocian wall paintings at Mistikan kilise, the warriors plunge their long lances down the upturned throats of the dragons whose prostrate bodies are arranged in three loops under the horses' hooves (fig. 105).[209] The depiction in the Ani relief thus follows more common visual conventions current both in Christian and Muslim contexts.

In another Cappadocian wall painting, found above the vestibule door of the late ninth- or tenth-century funerary chapel known as Yılanlı kilise ("serpent church") in the Ihlara valley, paired warrior saints thrust their lances into the gaping

eadem, 2002, no. 13) dates this painting as early as the seventh century, a date that Walter (2003, p. 125 and n. 99) cautions as perhaps being too early. It is of note however that in a late sixth-century church, dedicated to Saint George, at Zindanönü, near Çavuşin, traces remain of a fighting warrior saint, identified by an inscription as Saint George (only the upper section featuring the upper body of the saint holding a long lance and the frontally represented head of his horse remain, so it is unknown what he is spearing below).

[203] Cf. Thierry, 1999, p. 242, drawing 4, and *eadem*, 2002, p. 124; Walter, 2003, p. 56, fig. 27.

[204] Cf. Darkó, 1948, pp. 85–97, esp. pp. 90–1.

[205] Cf. *idem*, 1935, pp. 443–69, esp. pp. 463–9. See Thierry, 1972, pp. 263 and n. 67 with further references.

[206] Ghirshman, 1962, p. 132, fig. 168.

[207] See for instance Otavsky, 1998, figs. 65, 68, 83–8, 97–9, 103, 104, 106, 108–111; also, the *zandaniji* silk with the scene of Abraham's sacrifice of Isaac from Moshchevaya Balka. Belenitskii, 1980, p. 228, line drawing at the upper right; Jerusalimskaja, 2000, p. 98, fig. 11.

[208] Pancaroğlu, 2004, pp. 153–4. See also Henry Maguire's discussion (1994) on the significance of regular repetition of geometric designs in early Christian floor mosaics and textiles as protective devices.

[209] Strzygowski, 1918, pp. 287–90, fig. 329, drawing after Brosset, 1860, p. 33, text, pl. XXXVII. The church is dated 622 and Josef Strzygowski suggests a contemporary dating for the relief; however Marie-Félicité Brosset, who recorded the relief in his *Ruines d'Ani* published in 1860 (after a drawing by M. Kästner), believed that it could not have been carved earlier than the Islamic conquest in 1072.

mouths of a powerful bicephalous dragon, elaborately speckled, who rears up diagonally across the space between the two horses; the larger of the two dragon heads is horned (fig. 106).[210] Just above the two dragon heads is a cross with an inscription running on either side that establishes a semantic relation between the idea of Christ's triumph over evil on the cross and the victory of the saints over the dragon.[211] The pictorial and textual elements in the composition of this painting above an entrance have been interpreted as apotropaic in intention.

A related composition is found on a relief frieze on the western entrance to the Georgian church of the Virgin in Mart'vili, founded by king George II of Aphkhasia (912–957). Here two confronted unidentified holy riders with fluttering cloaks are shown to spear the raised gaping heads of a massive twice looped bicephalous scaled dragon (fig. 107).[212] As in the wall painting at Yılanlı kilise, one of the dragon heads is larger, has a more pronouncedly curved upper snout and is crowned by what appear to be long pointed ears. A pair of winged figures, probably angels, hover on either side of the riders, extending to them crowns from the arc of heaven that were won by the martyrs for their courage in the struggle with demons and invisible enemies.[213]

Among the military saints Theodore and George were predominantly associated with the miracle of dragon-slaying and often appear together.[214] In the hagiographical tradition, Saint Theodore clearly preceded Saint George in the role of dragon-slayer.[215] Prior to the eleventh century Saint George is almost invariably depicted in combat with a man. Then during the eleventh century the visual expression alters and the saint is increasingly represented slaying a dragon.[216] The earliest dated and visually identifiable representation of Saint George, killing a man and not yet a dragon, seems to be a relief depiction on the façade of the Armenian church dedicated to the Holy Cross which stands on the small island of Aght'amar situated southeast of Lake Van (now in eastern Turkey), erected by king Gagik Artsruni, ruler of the southern Armenian kingdom of Vaspurakan between the years 915 to 921.[217] In addition to Saint George, two further mounted warrior saints, Theodore and Sergios, are portrayed. The rendition of three equestrian saints, an example of the serialisation of the images, again illustrates the intent to amplify their role visually and thereby intensify their beneficial effect as apotropaic devices. The Armenian martyr Saint Sergios, traditionally considered the defender *par excellence* against all kinds of evil and dangers, was here added to the commonly paired military saints Theodore and George. He is depicted killing a feline, probably a panther, while Saint George tramples a supine fettered human figure that in eleventh-century legends is sometimes identified as his persecutor, the emperor Diocletian (fig. 108).[218] Saint Theodore is shown thrusting a lance into the upraised open mouth of a dragon, portrayed without wings or legs, its

[210] This visual differentiation between the two dragon-heads might also indicate two different identities. Cf. Thierry, 1999, p. 234. See also *eadem*, 2002, p. 155. A visit to the church in October 2008 showed that the imagery was effaced to the point of being barely recognisable.

[211] An inscription above the cross states the words that are uttered by the pierced serpent heads: "Cross, who made you shine? The Christ, he who is struck in me!" Thierry (1999, p. 234) interprets these words as the serpent, the personification of evil and death, recognising the defeat inflicted upon it by Christ through his death.

[212] Cf. Aladaşvili, 1977, pp. 48–56, 150–1, pls. 149, 150; Thierry, 1999, p. 240 and n. 40, fig. 5.

[213] Walter, 1995, p. 301; Thierry, 1999, p. 243 and n. 64.

[214] Walter, 1995, and *idem*, 1999. See also, *idem*, 2003, pp. 44–66 and 109–44. For a discussion of the cult of saints, in particular the cult of Saint George, in Georgia, see Schrade, 2001, pp. 169–98.

[215] There are two saints called Theodore in the Orthodox tradition: Theodore Tyron ("the recruit") and Theodore Stratelates ("the general"). On the confusion between the two Theodores, see Oikonomidès, 1981, pp. 327–35. The legend of the Theodore Tyron mentions that he was "born in an eastern land" and died in Amaseia (Amasya), in present-day Turkey (from where his remains were taken to Euchaita, present-day Avkat). His exploit of vanquishing a dragon with a spear only appeared in the second state of his *Passio Prima* (dated 890); *Bibliographica hagiographica graeca*, 1762d in Paris *graec.* 1470. Walter, 1995, p. 309 and n. 87, and *idem*, 2003, p. 50 and n. 38. Cf. Hengstenberg, 1912, pp. 78–106, 241–80; "Theodore Teron," *ODB*, vol. 3, pp. 2048–9. Some antecedents of Theodore's dragon-slaying feat may be found in the seventh-century *Passion* of Marina of Antioch. Cf. Merkelbach, "Drache," *RAC* IV, 1959, pp. 246–7; Boulhoul, 1994, pp. 255–304, esp. p. 263; Thierry, 1999, p. 242, n. 52.

[216] Thierry, 1999, p. 241. The earliest dated example of Saint George piercing a dragon is depicted in Cappadocia at the church of Saint Barbara at Soğanli (1006 or 1021). See De Jerphanion, 1925–1942, vol. 2, pl. 189. 2; Thierry, 1999, p. 241. It is noteworthy, however, that in Cappadocia George was never represented as killing a man; cf. Walter, 2003, p. 128. The fullest repertory of Georgian representations of Saint George piercing a human figure with his lance is given by Tschubinashvili, G.N., *Georgian Repoussé Work*, Tbilissi, 1957, cited after Walter, 1989a, p. 665.

[217] Cf. Der Nersessian, 1965, p. 19, figs. 49, 50.

[218] Scholz, 1982, p. 242 and n. 1; Walter, 1989a, p. 665, and *idem*, 2003, p. 56 and n. 64, and p. 129 and ns. 125 and 126.

body patterned with spots and tied into a heart-shaped knot (fig. 109).[219] The warrior saints hold long cross-ended lances and are portrayed in full military attire according to iconographic types derived mainly from elements borrowed from antiquity, such as the chlamys tied on the right shoulder, the cuirass, short tunic and buskins.[220]

An early eleventh-century depiction of paired confronted horsemen, identified here as the two saints George and Theodore, spearing respectively an anthropomorphic figure and a twice-looped dragon and surmounted by a stern image of Christ, appears twice on the church of Nik'orc'minda built during the last years of Bagrat III's reign (1010–1014) in the mountainous region of western Georgia, in the province of Racha (fig. 110).[221] The scene is once shown on the large tympanum over the western portal and again on the eastern façade.

The belief in the saints' power to vanquish evil probably inspired the representation of the motif on the interior and the exterior of churches and funerary structures. Its recurrent depiction in the Transcaucasian region, notably on Georgian churches, attests to the great importance accorded to the motif. Dragon-slaying riders were progressively identified as warrior saints and can conclusively be interpreted as exercising an apotropaic or protective function.[222]

The legend of Eastern Christendom's best known and most venerated dragon-slayer, who also enjoyed considerable popularity in the Latin West, partly as a result of the Crusades,[223] is first attested in the eleventh century when miracles were introduced into the Saint George cycle which includes the feat of rescuing a princess from a dragon.[224] One such typical story is recorded in an eleventh-century Georgian manuscript preserved in the Patriarchal Library, Jerusalem.[225] It describes how Saint George stopped at a lake where he saw a weeping girl about to be sacrificed to the dragon and there performed the miracle of vanquishing the dragon; thereafter the saint accompanies the princess who leads the dragon on a leash towards the city of Lasnia while her father, king Selenios, and the citizens look on. The miraculously subdued beast is tamed and symbolically tied to a leash and led about, a crucial detail that establishes the ceremonial and ritual of the subjection of the dragon. The earliest dated manuscript in which this story is illustrated is also found in Georgia at Pavnisi (*c.* 1170–1180).[226] However there are other Georgian examples that can be dated earlier on stylistic grounds: Adish (late eleventh century),[227] Boč'orma (*c.* 1100),[228] and possibly Ik'vi (twelfth century).[229] Thereafter the dragon miracle was incorporated as a regular feature in the iconographical repertoire of Saint George. Yet in Greek the miracle of the dragon is first attested in a late twelfth-century manuscript as an appendix to an account of the Passion of Saint George, and in a roughly contemporary illustration from Anargyroi in Kastoria (*c.* 1180).[230] It is therefore very possible that the story of Saint George and the dragon miracle originated in the Transcaucasian region, probably in Georgia, from where it spread.[231]

The depiction of the saintly dragon-slayer on a funerary stele from Maraş in southeast Anatolia, now in the Archaeological Museum of Adana,[232] attests to the continued importance of the motif. A beardless rider distinguished by a circular nimbus and with fluttering scarf is shown to hold a lance in both hands and thrust it into the large gaping jaws of a dragon, depicted with backward thrown head and short forelegs, that succumbs at his feet. The dragon's body is rendered according to the

219 The cross-ends of his lance are broken off. Cf. Der Nersessian, 1965, p. 19.

220 Walter, 2003, p. 22.

221 Baltrušaitis, 1929, pl. LXVII, fig. 108; Neubauer, 1976, fig. 57; Aladaşvili, 1977, pp. 147, 158–9, pl. 156; Thierry, 1999, pp. 244, fig. 6. The bas-relief on the eastern façade is reproduced in Scholz, 1982, fig. 2.

222 Cf. Walter, 1989a, p. 665.

223 The town Ludd (Lydda) in Palestine to the southeast of Jaffa is traditionally believed to be the birthplace of Saint George. Cf. Sharon, "Ludd," *EI*² V, 798b.

224 Walter, 1995, pp. 320–2, and *idem*, 2003, pp. 128–9; Schrade, 2001, p. 177, n. 56.

225 Georgian manuscript, datable to the eleventh century, Greek Patriarchal Library, Jerusalem, cod. 2. The Georgian text has been translated into English by Walter (1995, pp. 321–2 and *idem*, 2003, p. 141) on the basis of the translation into Russian (Privalova, 1977, p. 73 and n. 57).

226 A thrice-looped dragon; Privalova, 1977, pp. 16–7, 19, fig. 5 (line drawing). Cf. Thierry, 1999, p. 241, n. 50.

227 Undulant dragon; Privalova, 1977, p. 77, fig. 18 (line drawing), pl. XVIII, figs. 1, 2.

228 On account of the weathered surface, the drawing is too indistinct to identify whether the body was looped or knotted; *eadem*, p. 83, fig. 20 (line drawing).

229 Horned undulant dragon with long, flaring snout and goatee beard; *eadem*, p. 80, fig. 19 (line drawing), pl. XIX, figs. 1, 2. Reproduced in Walter, 1989b, p. 357, fig. 3.

230 Aufhauser, 1911, pp. 31–3; Walter, 1989b, pp. 350–1.

231 Walter, 1989b, p. 351, and *idem*, 1995, p. 322.

232 Height 56 cm, width 30 cm, thickness 4 cm. Adana, Archaeological Museum, inv. no. 76B. Süslü, 1987, p. 638, pl. 118, ill. 1.

standard iconography with a pretzel-like knot at mid-section followed by a further loop. A pair of flying figures hovers over the canopy of the rider in a sign of glorification. A three-line inscription in Syriac as well as in Arabic associates the stele with the Christian minority and gives the date, 701/1301–2, as well as the name of the master, Ibn Bahri.[233] Given that it is utilised as a symbol of victory in a funerary context, the presence of the dragon-slaying motif on this stele appears to echo the popular eschatological notions of the wall painting above the entrance of Yılanlı kilise in the Ihlara valley.[234]

The iconographic semantics of the equestrian dragon-fighter – from the greater Khurasan region to Asia Minor – in its heroic as well as saintly incarnation, thus owe much to ancient prototypes that germinated in the syncretistic melting pot of the great Near Eastern religions. These were probably inspired to a large extent by ancient Iranian dualist notions, and specifically eschatological thought systems, which resulted in close parallels between Iranian and Jewish concepts, inherited, in turn, by Christianity.[235] As can be seen in both material culture and written sources, there is overwhelming evidence that the figure of the Iranian holy rider battling the dragon (more rarely also visualised as fighting on foot) largely served to articulate the many strands of this complex image. The latter thus informed a visual vocabulary that proved to be meaningful as an internationally recognisable symbol for adherents of different religions in the medieval Central Asian sphere. As a consequence it allowed for effortless re-contextualisation and seems to have served as connecting symbol between different cultural and religious spheres on a popular level, in some ways coming to symbolise a cultural syncretism.

These strong syncretistic aspects are evident on a twelfth- or thirteenth-century nielloed silver scabbard, which sets the dragon-slaying iconography alongside the dragon's inherently prophylactic aspect. It moreover represents an example of a pastiche expressing in visual form the coexistence of themes from different religio-cultural repertoires. The scabbard is inscribed around the rim with customary good wishes in Arabic rendered in cursive script. Whereas the epigraphic frieze is worked in relief, an unusual, shallowly incised depiction is shown below. It differs not only in subject matter but also in style and execution from motifs shown on metal objects fabricated in the medieval Islamic world:[236] a warrior saint in crusader attire is shown to aim at a prostrate dragon, its slender serpentine body forming a pretzel-like knot at mid-section, and the "Hand of God" projecting from the right to point at the warrior (fig. 111). The dragon-slayer motif surmounts a register containing an ancient iconographic theme of almost worldwide currency, again executed in relief, showing a bird of prey attacking a quadruped, probably a deer. Below this a similarly time-honoured theme, a procession of animals of the hunt, is set against foliate scrolls, typical for the decorative repertoire of a local workshop which conceivably employed craftsmen belonging to one of the monotheistic religions of the Near East, where this sheath is thought to have been made for a Christian, probably crusader, client.[237] In contradistinction however to the dragon-slaying motif on the scabbard decoration, the quillon block of the accompanying dagger, both preserved in the Furusiyya Art Collection, Vaduz, extends into downward-curving prongs that terminate in dragon heads, a feature frequently employed on quillon blocks and imbued with an inherent apotropaic function.[238] However, the rendering of the dragon heads is already highly stylised, perhaps suggesting that the heads had lost some of their original protective quality to become a more decorative feature.

[233] Erdmann, 1957, p. 372, n. 32.
[234] Cf. Pancaroğlu, 2004, p. 161.
[235] Cf. Shaked, "Eschatology," *EIr*; Hintze, 1999, pp. 86–7.
[236] I would like to thank Professor Robert Hillenbrand for drawing my attention to this point.
[237] Cf. *Chevaux et cavaliers arabes*, 2002, pp. 118–9, cat. no. 57; *L'art des chevaliers*, 2007, pp. 155–7, cat. no. 148. For a discussion of Islamic metalwork objects with Christian themes made for Muslim and Christian patrons, cf. Baer, 1989, pp. 41–9.
[238] See chapter 3. Also *L'art des chevaliers*, 2007, p. 154, cat. no. 147.

CHAPTER SEVEN

THE DRAGON IN RELATION TO ROYAL OR HEROIC FIGURES

a. *Royal and heroic associations of the dragon in literary accounts*

In Iranian legends the dragon combat was one of the wonders and heroic feats required as proof of the king's or hero's legitimacy, so becoming by extension an important device of royal or heroic ideology.[1] A royal victory over the dragon was intended to manifest virtuous conduct and to endow the royal persona with heroic qualities. The visual enactment of this victory communicated mastery over the mighty mythical creature as well as implying metaphorically that through this deed of prowess the vanquisher was able to take on the formidable qualities of the dragon, that is to say, assume part of the dragon's nature, as will be shown below.

Just as in the visual arts the dragon's powerful likeness was evoked, so it served also in literature as a simile in the formulation of praise and panegyric for rulers and their entourage. Drawing on the dragon's qualities of instilling fear and dread as well as awe and reverence, the creature was evoked metaphorically as a lively expression of the heroic qualities of the *mamdūḥ* ("the praised one"). Repetitive reference to the dragon was thus a rhetorical device used by poets and historians, among them Firdawsī, the celebrated poet from a village near Ṭūs, near present-day Mashhad in Khurasan, who began writing the *Shāh-nāma* during the last decade of Samanid sovereignty and completed it during the rule of the Ghaznawids. The latter were ethnically Turkish but were deeply imbued with the Persian and Islamic courtly traditions. In the opening verses, Firdawsī eulogises the royal patron, *sulṭān* Maḥmūd of Ghazna (r. 389/999–421/1030), with the words:

> At his banquets *(bazm)*, he is a heaven of fidelity
> In combat *(razm)*, he is a dragon with sharp claws.[2]

By thus creating a visual image like a frieze or bas-relief, the court poet uses his skill to publicly display and celebrate the virtues and accomplishments of the patron.[3] Firdawsī's flattering rhetoric is echoed by that of the foremost panegyric poets at the Ghaznawid court, Abu 'l-Ḥasan Farrukhī Sīstānī (d. 429/1037–8), who called his royal patron an "illuminating sun" at banquets and a "roaring dragon" in combat.[4] The imagery of the dragon seems to have represented a heroic ideal and was frequently used in panegyrics in the *Qābūs-nāma* ("Book of Qābūs"), written in 475/1082–3 by the Ziyārid prince ʿUnṣur al-Maʿālī Kay Kāwūs ibn Iskandar ibn Qābūs, for the edification of his son. In this well-known "Mirror for Princes" the 63-year-old prince remarks upon the fashion for court poets to liken the "mighty" to a "dragon" or a "lion;" urging his son to weigh carefully such eulogies.[5]

Dragon symbolism was not only reserved for the *sulṭān*; Manūchihrī Dāmghānī, poet at the court of Maḥmūd's successor, *sulṭān* Masʿūd of Ghazna (r. 421/1030–432/1040), also performed services for the *sulṭān*'s chief vizier, Aḥmad ibn ʿAbd al-Ṣamad, by extravagantly praising his virtues in an ode *(qaṣīda)* in which he too calls upon the symbolic meaning of the dragon:

> With such petty enemies why should the Khwājah do battle?
> The dragon is shamed who fights with a chameleon.[6]

That this metaphorical or allegorical use of the dragon image was in widespread currency is further attested by its use in a *qaṣīda* by Ẓahīr al-Dīn al-Fāryābī (550/1156–598/1201–2; as indicated by his *nisba* he was perhaps born at Fāryāb near Balkh). In his *dīwān* the poet glorifies the courage of the last Great Saljuq ruler in the west, *sulṭān* Ṭoghrıl III ibn Arslan with the words:

---

[1] Khāleqī-Moṭlaq, "Aždahā II," *EIr.*

[2] Tr. and ed. Mohl, 1838–1878, vol. 1, p. 25, ll. 221–2.

[3] Cf. Clinton, 1972, p. 130.

[4] *Dīwān-i Hakīm-i Farrukhī-i Sīstānī*, p. 363, l. 7354, as cited in Melikian-Chirvani, 1997a, pp. 143–4.

[5] Tr. Levy, 1951, p. 133. Cf. Klíma, 1968, p. 95.

[6] *Dīwān*, p. 25, cited after Clinton, 1972, p. 45.

> When his enemies saw his dragon countenance
> They raised their hands above their heads like scorpions.[7]

In a dramatic double simile in the *Iskandar-nāma,* Niẓāmī brings together the heroic qualities of the dragon with those of the lion to describe:

> ...an Alan knight, similar to a fierce lion, [who] came forth like a black dragon, with a mace in his hand, hard to bear for less than seventy men and able to split Mt. Alborz.[8]

The mythical creatures are thus invoked in order to endow the subject of eulogies, by association, with praiseworthy superhuman qualities.

In the *Haft Paykar* Niẓāmī again jointly invokes the lion and the dragon in the allegorical description of king Bahrām seizing the crown from between two lions:

> The golden crown in two black lions' jaws as in two dragons' jaws a (lustrous) moon-
> A moon escaping with a basin's noise the cloud, but the basin eke a sword,
> The two vindictive lions lashed their tails upon the ground like dragons twain (in wrath);
> To say, Who'll seize from us this golden crown? Who'll dare a lion or a dragon rob?
> They knew not of that man of iron heart, who captured lions, dragons hunted too.[9]

Firdawsī evokes related heroic imagery in the *Shāh-nāma* in the story of the demon Akwān who at royal command was slain by Rustam who himself is repeated likened to a dragon.[10] The hero assures the king that "whether demon, lion or male dragon, it will not escape my sharp sword," and is himself described as arriving at the battle scene "like a male lion riding a dragon."[11]

The court poet Masʿūd-i Rāzī was exiled to India by the Ghaznawid *sulṭān* Masʿūd ibn Maḥmūd for daring to admonish the *sulṭān* during the festival of Mihragān in Dhu 'l-Ḥijjah 430/September 1039 with the lines:

> Your enemies were ants, but now they have become vipers; hasten to destroy these ants turned vipers.
> Give them no more time, and do not tarry, for if given time a viper will become a dragon.[12]

Similar allegorical language is also used in the *History of the Saljuqs* by Ibn Bībī (d. after 684/December 1285) who referred to rebellious youths as "young serpents that grow into dragons"[13] and likened the victorious Saljuqs to "threatening dragons."[14]

Rustam, the legendary prince of Sistān, is conspicuous for his role in the battles with his archenemy Afrāsīyāb, the legendary king of Tūrān in the Iranian epic. In the "Book of Qay Qubād" of Firdawsī's *Shāh-nāma*, his father Zāl however warns him about going to war with the Tūrānian who is identified as a Turk and as a powerful "male dragon":

> Zāl told him, "Listen my son
> Today, for once, think hard:
> In war, this Turk is a male dragon
> In skirmish and in combat he is a cloud of calamity. [15]

In literary tradition the dragon is hence used to emphasise the heroes' and rulers' superhuman qualities by allegorically transforming them into dragons whose likeness was often singled out as apt symbol of royalty and superiority.[16] This is also noticeable in the visual language, for instance on a large marble slab relief-carved with addorsed *regardant* "Saljuq-style" dragons in rampant posture with forelegs and unfolded wings. Significant are their long interlaced tails. Their open mouths reveal enormous fangs with long bifid tongues thrust out, their forelegs with separated talon-toed paws rest on their long upward-curving sinuous tails. The plaque carries an epigraphic band inscribed with the formula *al-sulṭān al-muʿaẓẓam* ("the exalted sultan"), a title held by the Saljuqs (fig. 112). It comes from the cenotaph of the Mamlūk ruler al-Muʾayyad Sayf al-Dīn Shaykh (d. 1421/824) in Cairo, which Max van Berchem has identified as (much earlier) spoils from the *sulṭān*'s Mesopotamian campaigns[17] and for which Rogers suggests an Anatolian Saljuq provenance.[18] The inscription

[7] Ed. Bīnish, T., Tehran, 1958, p. 43, as cited in Daneshvari, 1993, p. 16, n. 7.

[8] Muḥammad Ilyās ibn Yūsuf Niẓāmī, ed. and French tr. of the Russian episode by Spitznagel, L., *Expédition d'Alexandre le Grand contre les russes, extrait de l'Alexandréide ou Iskèndèr-Namé de Nizâmy*, St. Petersburg, 1828, cited after Alemany, 2000, pp. 264–6 and n. 57.

[9] Tr. Wilson, p. 73.

[10] Tr. and ed. Mohl, 1838–1878, vol. 3, p. 187, l. 566.

[11] *Idem*, vol. 3, p. 275, ll. 63–5.

[12] Meisami, 1990, p. 41.

[13] *Al-Awāmir al-ʿalāʾiyya*, tr. Duda, 1959, p. 309.

[14] *Idem*, p. 212.

[15] Tr. and ed. Mohl, 1838–1878, vol. 1, p. 467, ll. 34–9.

[16] Cf. Melikian-Chiravani, 1984, p. 323.

[17] Van Berchem, 1910, p. 81, fig. 34.

[18] Rogers, J.M., *Islamic Art in Egypt 969–1517*, exhibition catalogue, Cairo, 1969, pp. 203–4, no. 194, as cited in Ibrāhīm, 1976, p. 11. Cf. Rogers, 1969, p. 154, n. 14.

explicitly identifies the iconography of the paired dragons as a royal ensign of a now anonymous *sulṭān*. It is interesting to note the analogy of this type of imagery to the stone reliefs at the *türbe* of Emir Saltuq at Erzurum (fig. 10) and at the church of Saint Gregory in Ani (fig. 11). Closely related interlaced dragons are depicted on portable items such as the twelfth-century gold finger ring from the greater Khurasan region (fig. 30) where they served to strengthen the protective function of the objects, and were chosen as emblematic motifs west of Iran for the coinage of twelfth- or thirteenth-century rulers in the Jazīra (figs. 32a and b). This spolium is evidence that not only did the motif of the interlaced dragons prove to be meaningful beyond the Central Asian realm but that the iconography could be re-contextualised in a fifteenth-century Mamlūk setting where it was distinguished as an emblem that was deemed suitable for inclusion in a royal funerary setting.

b. *Paired dragons with a central anthropomorphic figure*

Dragon symbolism and cosmic rulership

Artistic representations developed during the ʿAbbasid period projected an idealised vision of rulership which included the creation of physical manifestations of their imperial pursuits, in particular with respect to court ritual. Iranian influence on court ceremonial *(marasīm)* became noticable reflecting "the profound iranisation of customs and society."[19] Considerable importance was attached to the throne *(sarīr, kursī)*. The caliph sat on a throne placed on a dais *(ṣuffa)* when he presided over court ceremonies. Iranian features in these ceremonies sometimes included the caliph's elevation on a raised platform or throne (Pers. *takht*), rather than just a dais.[20] These influences were noticeable beyond the caliphal court. According to the tenth-century philosopher Miskawayh, the ambitious Ziyārid ruler Mardāwīj ibn Ziyār (d. 323/935) was imitating Sasanian custom when he sat on a golden throne and wore a crown.[21] The historian Abu 'l-Faḍl Bayhaqī (d. 470/1077), recorded in his *Taʾrīkh-i Masʿūdī* ("History of Masʿūd") that the Ghaznawid *sulṭān* Masʿūd ibn Maḥmūd held court sitting on a dais and in 429/1038 had his throne, originally made of wood, replaced by a golden, jewel-studded throne, three years in the making, that he placed on a dais in his new palace.[22] In the manner of the Sasanian kings he had a seventy-*man* crown suspended from golden chains.[23] The grandeur of the house of the Ghaznawids was, in the words of Bayhaqī, "resplendent as the sun."[24] The twelfth-century Khurasani poet Awḥad al-Dīn Muḥammad Anwarī (*c*. 520/1126–583/1187–8 or 585/1189–90), who was born near Abīward, had served *sulṭān* Sanjar ibn Malik Shāh and survived the collapse of the Great Saljuqs, expresses similar metaphorical notions for the enthroned sovereign:

> May the world be your servant and destiny your page
> The sky your throne and the sun your crown.[25]

His words aptly express the celestial and solar associations of royal ideology, areas in which the dragon theme played an important role. The conventional medieval Islamic depiction of rulership shows a frontally rendered human figure, the head in three-quarter view, seated cross-legged on a raised platform between two poles, which serve as the arms of the "chair," and which are topped by dragon heads, their wide-open jaws revealing tongues commonly oriented towards the head of the human figure. The figure is often shown with arms extended at either side, grasping the staffs just below the dragon heads. At times he holds a staff in one hand and what looks like a cup in the other, imagery suggestive of cosmic kingship.[26]

---

[19] Sourdel, 1960, pp. 121–48; cf. Spuler, 1976, p. 346.

[20] Sourdel, 1960, p. 131.

[21] *Tajārib al-umam*, tr. and ed. Margoliouth, 1921, vol. 5, p. 489. Firdawsī similarly speaks, for example, of the golden throne of Ẓaḥḥāk (*Shāh-nāma*, tr. and ed. Mohl, 1838–1878, vol. 1, p. 109, ll. 449, 590), the golden throne given by Farīdūn to his successor Manūchihr (*idem*, vol. 1, p. 167, l. 627) or the golden throne of Kay Kāwūs (*idem*, vol. 2, p. 49, l. 526).

[22] Ed. Ghanī and Fayyūḍ, Tehran, 1324/1945, p. 438, as cited in Lambton, "Marasīm," *EI*² VI, 518a.

[23] *Op. cit.* Cf. Meisami, 1999, p. 77. For the "hanging crown" in the throne hall of the Sasanian kings at Ctesiphon which perhaps was used by the Umayyad owner of the desert residence Khirbat al-Mafjar (in this case in the form of a *qalansuwa*) and later also entered Byzantine court ceremonial; cf. Ettinghausen, 1972, pp. 28–30. See also the crown suspended above the throne of Manuchehr; *Shāh-nāma*, tr. and ed. Mohl, 1838–1878, vol. 1, pp. 211, ll. 1142–143.

[24] Meisami, 1999, p. 296.

[25] *Dīwān*, vol. 1, p. 200. Cf. Melikian-Chirvani, 1984, p. 327.

[26] Cf. Baer, 1983, pp. 258–66.

The visual expression is particularly prevalent on mid-eleventh to thirteenth-century silver-inlaid metalwork and seems to have first appeared on objects produced in the greater Khurasan region.

Dragon-headed staffs flanking this traditional medieval Islamic portrayal of rulership are portrayed in one of eight roundels on the lid of the covered copper alloy bowl, inlaid with silver, known as the Vaso Vescovali, made in the Khurasan region around 1200.[27] The "ruler on a dragon-throne" is in turn symmetrically flanked by attendants while the dais is supported by a pair of addorsed feline protomes (fig. 113).[28] Since the other roundels enclose representations of the seven conventional planets, the depiction in the eighth roundel has been associated with the pseudo-planet *jawzahar*, illustrating here the eighth "planet."[29]

The earliest dated instance of the "dragon-throne" is found on the 559/1163 Bobrinski bucket, where it is repeated four times in the main register separated by an epigraphic frieze of anthropomorphic and zoomorphic *naskhī*, the lower parts of the *hastae* often terminating in dragon and other animal heads, expressing good wishes for the owner (fig. 114).[30] These roundels are encircled by 28 radiating "rays," alternately inlaid in silver and copper. The frieze is the uppermost of a series of three figurative registers that circumscribe the richly inlaid copper alloy bucket. It is interesting to investigate these dense pictographic friezes since they provide the wider context for the "ruler on a dragon-throne" iconography.

The second register encloses figures engaged in various popular pastimes ranging from backgammon and banqueting to making music and fighting with staves. The third features a hunting party with several bow-bending, sword- or lance-wielding figures on horseback and on foot involved in fighting and hunting, depicted amidst animals in flight or in pursuit and mythical creatures such as a sphinx and a dragon, which will be further discussed below. The second and third registers thus contain pictorial cycles visualising the outward declarations of very ancient Iranian royal pursuits: feasting or celebration *(bazm)* and hunting or fighting *(razm)*. Such motifs, representing royal pleasures and pastimes, were evidently transmitted directly from Sasanian art.[31] Within the Islamic cultural sphere hunting, feasting and fighting, considered the best preparation for war, are again important themes.[32] These activities were associated with heroic figures, as is the case with Rustam in the *Shāh-nāma*:

> Thus did Rustam ordain a banquet
> For he was one that ordains banquets *(bazm)*
> And that makes war *(razm)*.[33]

The rim of the bucket is circumscribed by a silver-inlaid inscription in Persian, which reads:

> Ordered by ʿAbd al-Raḥmān ibn ʿAbdullāh al-Rashīdī, made by Muḥammad ibn ʿAbd al-Wāḥid, worked by *ḥājib* Masʿūd ibn Aḥmad the decorator of Herāt, for the exalted *khwāja* Rukn al-Dīn, the pride of the merchants, the most trustworthy of the faithful, grace of the pilgrimage and of [its] two shrines, Rāshīd al-Dīn ʿAzīzī, ibn Abu 'l-Ḥusayn al-Zanjānī, may his glory be lasting.[34]

On account of the kind of eulogies offered to the dedicatee and the date recorded on the object, the month of Muḥarram, during which the pilgrimage is performed, Assadullah Souren Melikian-Chirvani suggests that "the gift consecrated a collective *ḥajj* led by the dignitary. The gift of a bucket used to contain water, perhaps for ritual ablutions, would have been appropriate."[35] Evidently, the choice of the "ruler on a dragon-throne" motif on the bucket was part of an iconographic repertoire deemed suitable for an official gift perhaps to be offered by a religious community to a dignitary, whose *nisba* indicates that he may have been from Zanjān in northwestern Persia.[36] However, since the other blessings inscribed on the bucket are directed at an anony-

[27] Otto-Dorn, 1978–9, fig. 32; Baer, 1983, p. 255, fig. 207. A colour reproduction of the lid is given in Ward, 1993, p. 79, fig. 57.

[28] Hartner, 1973–4, pp. 117–23, esp. pp. 121.

[29] *Idem*, pp. 117–23, esp. pp. 121 and fig. 17.6 (drawing of the planets on the cover of the Vaso Vescovali), followed by Baer, 1981, p. 14, and Carboni, 1997, pp. 22–3.

[30] Cf. Pope and Ackerman, eds., 1938–9, repr. 1964–81, vol. 6, pl. 1308; Ettinghausen, 1943, pp. 193–208; Rice, 1955, pls. XIX–XX; Mayer, 1959, p. 61; Hartner, 1973–4, p. 122, fig. 18; *The Arts of Islam*, 1976, pp. 170–2, cat. no. 180; Loukonine and Ivanov, eds., 2003, pp. 114–5, cat. no. 116.

[31] Cf. the discussion of Dorothy Shepherd (1978, p. 119) in which she traces these twin themes to "a very early date when ... they symbolized heroisation and apotheosis... [and by analogy] were seen as symbols of paradise that Islam promised to all true believers."

[32] This association was already pointed out by Xenophon in his *Kynegetikos* (XII.1); see Davidson, "Haft k̲ᵛān," *EIr*.

[33] Tr. and ed. Mohl, 1838–1878, vol. 3, p. 358, ll. 782–3.

[34] Reading after Ettinghausen, 1943, p. 196. Cf. Melikian-Chirvani, 1982, pp. 71, 82–3, n. 61; Ward, 1993, p. 74, fig. 54.

[35] Melikian-Chirvani, 1982, p. 83, n. 62.

[36] Cf. *idem*, p. 71 and p. 83, n. 62.

mous owner, it may be surmised that such luxury objects were designed for the market, with special inscriptions only being added to the rim or handle after purchase.[37] Hence, one may presume that the "ruler on a dragon-throne" roundels which were so prominently displayed on the bucket were an iconographic theme which was meaningful and would have been understood by most potential clients.

The motif also occurs on eleventh- or twelfth-century objects of adornment, for example on a small, circular copper alloy pendant inlaid with silver reportedly from Herat in present-day Afghanistan. The pendant shows a human figure, the features of his moon-shaped face and the folds of his voluminous pantaloons finely incised, seated cross-legged on a "throne" flanked on either side by upright rods terminating in snarling dragon heads, and in turn by tall vessels. Here the "throne" is decorated at the centre with a pendant palmette, flanked on either side by horizontally-oriented half-palmettes. The reverse is decorated with a long-legged bird of prey attacking a hare that turns its head towards the bird. A zigzag border, giving the impression of solar rays, frames the scene.[38]

Analogous iconography of the seated figure flanked symmetrically by dragon-headed staffs is employed on several other pieces of metalwork, such as a late twelfth- or early thirteenth-century copper alloy inkwell inlaid with silver also from northern Afghanistan, formerly in the Minassian Collection, New York (fig. 115). The figure, in a flat headdress from which seem to descend long fluttering ends, appears on the base of the inkwell in the same iconographical setting, his raised arms grasping dragon-headed staffs. The latter, in turn, are symmetrically flanked here by a pair of birds, instead of by palmettes as shown in the previous example or by attendants as on the Vaso Vescovali. The roundel is again set into a radiant frame, presumably conveying solar significance.[39] This equating of the ruler with the Sun goes back to the pre-Islamic concept of the divine glory conferred upon the king. The solar aspect of ancient Iranian kingship was associated with the Zoroastrian belief in the Iranian royal and divine attribute of *farr*, often rendered as *farr-i kayānī*, "the glory of the Kays (the ancient dynasty of Iran)," the distinctive hereditary mark of Iranian legitimacy.[40] This may also be reflected in the Turkic convention of *altun khān (qaghan)*, the "golden ruler."[41] The tenth-century Khwārazmian scholar al-Bīrūnī records that on the festival of Mihragān, the Sasanian king wore a radiant crown to resemble the Zoroastrian god Mihr, lord of the sun.[42]

The same scene is rendered on another inlaid copper-alloy inkwell of the same period, which features a cross-legged figure crowned by a pointed headdress and flanked by dragon-headed staffs whose gaping mouths have particularly long tongues oriented towards the figure's head. Importantly, in this example the dragons' undulant bodies descend diagonally from the staffs and thus directly associate the depiction with the entire body of the dragon, rather than – as shown above – with the staff mutating at the tip into a dragon head.[43] If the imagery should be seen as bearing some astrological meaning, the latter could also be interpreted as an abbreviated reference to the astrological "head" *(ra's)* and the "tail" *(dhanab)* of the dragon (fig. 116).[44]

A point of resemblance with the motifs discussed above (figs. 113–116) occurs on seventh-century stamp seals which depict a crudely rendered standing ithyphallic figure with arms and legs outstretched; the arms holding two upright staffs around which serpents are wound and which are topped by stellar motifs or birds.[45] Phyllis Ackerman has associated this imagery both with the astronomical sign Serpentarius and with Gayūmart (Av. *gaya marətan* "mortal life"), the mythical first man of the Mazdean creation myth. The latter was considered a semi-divine giant who stood between gods and men.[46] A different reading is offered by Marian Wenzel who attempts to link the motif of a seated or standing figure hold-

[37] Ward, 1993, p. 74, fig. 54.

[38] Height 2.61 cm incl. loop, thickness 0.17 cm. Kuwait, al-Sabāh Collection, Dar al-Athar al-Islamiyyah, Kuwait National Museum, inv. no. LNS 2535 J.

[39] Baer, 1981, p. 14.

[40] Melikian-Chirvani, 1994, p. 149 and n. 39. See also p. 93, n. 80.

[41] Bailey, 1967, pp. 95–6, 99.

[42] Boyce, 1983, p. 803.

[43] A sizable representation of a crowned seated person holding on to dragon staffs which are rendered with a finely imbricated ophidian pattern, the scales enlivened by central dots, is incised on a thirteenth- or fourteenth-century steel saddle plate from Afghanistan or Eastern Iran, housed the David Collection Copenhagen, inv. no. 30/1999; *Chevaux et cavaliers arabes*, 2002, p. 113, cat. no. 48.

[44] Cf. Pugachenkova and Rempel', fig. 196 (and fig. 197, line drawing); Hartner, 1973–4, pp. 110–1, 114, 121; Baer, 1983, pp. 256–7.

[45] Ackerman, 1936, p. 127; Bivar, 1969, pls. 5–6; Wenzel, 2005, ills. 10–1.

[46] Ackerman, 1936, p. 127.

ing up serpent staffs with the process of firemaking.[47] Yet the figure grasping staffs entwined with serpents and topped by birds or stellar symbols could indeed represent a mythical giant holding what might perhaps represent abbreviated visual formulae of a vegetal motif characterised as the "Tree of Life" with serpent motif.[48]

This interpretation gains weight through a depiction on a floor mosaic discovered in the nave of a church at Huarte, located fifteen kilometres north of Apamea in present-day Syria, and dated by inscription to the years 472 or 487.[49] On the central axis of the pavement close to the sanctuary is the large frontally rendered figure of Adam, identified by an inscription above his head. He is portrayed as fully clothed and enthroned on a backless raised platform, leaning against a cushion, and holding an open book in his left hand, while extending the fingers of his right hand in a gesture of speech. Importantly, he is framed by two slender cypress trees around each of which is coiled a serpent, its head oriented towards Adam's head, the open jaws revealing bifid tongues. Adam is surrounded by a variety of tame beasts and birds set amidst flowering vegetation indicating that the setting is the primordial Paradise before the Fall (fig. 117).[50] Since the image does not accord with the book of Genesis – Adam being represented not naked but clothed, enthroned and reading a book – Henry Maguire has proposed reading this paradisical scene not in a literal but a spiritual sense as allegory.[51] Precedent for such an interpretation is found in the notion of the Robe of Glory, which is commonly found in the writings of the early Syriac fathers and ultimately derives from early Jewish sources.[52] The imagery is repeatedly used in the hymns of the fourth-century Syriac writer Ephrem, deacon in Edessa and Nisibis, who equates the white robes of those baptised with the Robes of Glory (which he also reads as Robes of Light) lost by Adam and Eve at the Fall but regained through baptism which is understood eschatologically as re-entry into Paradise.[53] Hence the scene may be understood as depicting the robed Adam not only as ruler over the world[54] but as an image of one who through Christ has discovered the state of divine wisdom and glory.[55]

In sum, it may be noted that Adam, the first of men of the biblical creation myth, is represented just like Gayūmart, the mythical first man of the Mazdean creation myth, between two slender elongated plants around which coil serpents whose heads are oriented towards the central figure. On the late fifth-century Huarte mosaic the association of the cedars in the paradisical setting with the Tree of Life is apparent, whereas on the seventh-century stamp seals the staff-like motifs may presumably represent abbreviated visual formulae; the addition of the birds or stellar symbols at the apex of these verticals give further substance to this interpretation.[56] It may thus be postulated that both depictions portray a central figure flanked on either side by a serpent-entwined Tree of Life motif. Ackerman has moreover noted an astronomical association for the imagery on the stamp seals.[57]

The conventional medieval Islamic representation of rulership features enthroned figures flanked by dragon-headed or dragon-entwined staffs; the iconography occurring predominantly on mid-eleventh to thirteenth-century silver-inlaid metalwork produced in the greater Khurasan region (figs. 113–116). Since these are often framed by a disc with pointed rays, Eva Baer has interpreted them as artistic formulae of princely or royal images transposed in a sense to a cosmic setting, and as emblematised luminaries, or panegyrical visual expressions of the "heavenly ruler," which sometimes have an astrological

[47] Wenzel, 2005, pp. 140–58.

[48] For the imagery of the "Tree of Life," see also the discussion in chapter 9, part a. It may be notable to repeat here James L. Sauvé's view (1970, p. 181) on this time-honored symbol: "Indo-European mythology is a pan-cultural Eurasian phenomenon, and those studies that overlook the 'tree of life,' or dismiss it as marginal or incidental in importance, must fail to evaluate properly, or even approximately, many aspects of some Indo-European religions and mythologies."

[49] Canivet, M.T. and P., 1975, pp. 49–70; Maguire, 1987, p. 367.

[50] Canivet, M.T. and P., 1975, p. 61 and fig. 3; Maguire, 1987, p. 367. For similar motifs of a tree and serpent with an enthroned ruler or king, see Fodor, 1976, pp. 159–60.

[51] Maguire, 1987, p. 368.

[52] Ephraem, *Hymni de Paradiso and Section 2 of Commnetarium in Genesium*, tr. and ed. Brook, 1990, pp. 31, 67, 226–7.

[53] *Idem*, pp. 31, 66–74, 94, 112, 226–7.

[54] "God said…have dominion…over every living thing that moveth upon the earth…" (Genesis 1:28). In the Christian Syriac *Meʿārath gazzē* 2.11–25 *(Cave of Treasures*, tr. and ed. Budge, 1927, p. 34) God gave Adam power over all beings.

[55] Maguire, 1987, p. 368, n. 23, and p. 372, ns. 34, 38. In post-exilic Judaism, Midrash and Judeaeo-Christian tradition the figure of the enthroned Adam is seen as the source of supernatural wisdom, see Fodor, 1976, pp. 166–7.

[56] Of note may be the parallel given by the Greek poet Pindar of the *drakōn* Typhon who supports the column of the Etna on which perches the eagle of Zeus (*Pythian Odes* 1).

[57] Ackerman, 1936, p. 127.

character.[58] An anecdote attesting to the astral qualities of the ruler in the face of the dragon is noted by Ibn Bībī, the Rūm Saljuq chronicler, in which he metaphorically likens the meeting of the armies of the Khwārazm-shāh and the Rūm Saljuqs to the day on which:

> ... in accordance to servile custom the King of the Planets kissed the earth at the door of the King of the World and the encounter of the troops of the War-Dragon unfurled the crimson and yellow banner at the arena of the horizons.[59]

Luminary imagery is similarly used to describe the birth of Khurshīd *shāh* in one of the earliest Persian popular romances, the *Kitāb-i Samak ʿAyyār*, who throughout the story is portrayed in terms of solar metaphors and is even named "king Sun."[60]

In sum, it may be stated that the visual tradition of the medieval Islamic representation of rulership involves the imagery of a central figure flanked by serpent-dragons that top or twine around verticals which might carry a vegetal association that could distantly associate them with the Tree of Life motif as ultimate prototype. Frequently the vertical is shown only with a projecting dragon head. This may thus present yet another example of the visual conflation that was so pervasive in the medieval Central Asian world and beyond. It would be an example of a visual development that merges the figure of the dragon with that of the staff in a unified whole. The Tree of Life motif exhibited a remarkable persistence and popularity in Near Eastern and Indo-European[61] iconography which, as has been discussed above, could still be gauged in visual and textual sources of the eleventh to thirteenth century, the period when this imagery was employed with great regularity.[62] This supports the hypothesis that the prototype of the vertical may be sought in a vegetal composition. It is moreover notable that the central figure often grasps with one or two hands the verticals just below the point from which the dragon heads project. To this may be added the luminary association which transposes the motif to a cosmic setting – sometimes with an astrological character.

The pivotal role the dragon plays in these images will be further elucidated in the following, concluding in a discussion of the time-honoured symbolism of the dragon-tamer.

Issuing and devouring

The iconography of a human figure, sometimes reduced to the image of a mask-like face, flanked on either side by dragons, was one of "great symbolic potency" in the Central Asian world and beyond and existed in manifold variations.[63] The monsters not only frame the central motif but on account of their gaping jaws at first sight appear to threaten or perhaps even attempt to devour what they flank. The possibility of the latter interpretation will be discussed in the light of surviving examples of this enigmatic imagery.

The motif is prominently recorded in the visual arts of the Caucasus region, for instance on the Armenian cathedral of the Holy Apostles in present-day Kars erected by king Abas I between 930 and 943 in the adjacent secondary Bagratid kingdom of Vanand, near the border with eastern Anatolia. On the exterior of the drum above the blind arcades twelve full-length figures are carved in low relief that in folk tradition are associated with the twelve apostles. The figures have mask-like faces and are clad in long robes. In what is perhaps a unique occurrence, some are shown to raise their bent arms upwards, others place their hands on their chests, in what may have represented ritually significant gestures and may have conveyed a canonical koiné.[64] It is conceivable that the sequence of the movements played a role and even alluded to a visual narrative.[65] One of the figures is flanked by a tree-like vegetal composition.[66] Next to it is a figure with a looped serpent rising up at either side of his upper body, the heads oriented towards his ears. Significantly, the figure does not extend his arms towards the serpents but

---

[58] Baer, 1981, p. 14, and *eadem,* 1983, pp. 259–68, 274. See also the discussion on the astral transformation of the Sasanian throne in L'Orange, 1953, pp. 37–47.

[59] *Al-Awāmir al-ʿalāʾiyya*, tr. Duda, 1959, p. 170.

[60] Gaillard, 1987, pp. 124–5.

[61] Cf. Janda, 2010, pp. 320–2.

[62] See also the close association of the tree with the Iranian king in the *Shāh-nāma* account, for instance, the simile of the drying leaves of the tree of the Kayānids employed to describe the death of Farīdūn (tr. and ed. Mohl, 1838–1878, vol. 1, p. 209, ll. 1128–129) or of the noble tree that stretches far into the shadow used to depict the death of Iskandar (*idem*, vol. 4, p. 255, l. 1849).

[63] Cf. Russell, 2004, p. 1169.

[64] The folding of the arms was a deferential gesture known in the Iranised world since Zoroastrianism and was used by Christians in prayer towards God; see Russell, 2004, p. 310. Cf. Colledge, 1986, p. 16.

[65] For a line drawing of all twelve figures, see Thierry, 1978, p. 47, fig. 26.

[66] *Idem*, pl. V.3.

has the hands placed, one above the other, on his chest (fig. 118).[67] The repetition of the motif above the northwestern port-hole window ("oculus") of the church underlines the importance accorded to this iconography. Here, instead of a full-length figure a frontally presented human bust flanked by giant looped serpents is portrayed (fig. 119).[68]

Several interpretations have been proposed for the enigmatic reliefs. The portrayals are particularly puzzling since as decoration on a church façade they can be assumed to represent overall propitious and apotropaic motifs. Yet the readings of the figure flanked by serpents, in particular, have only multiplied the mystery. One explanation identifies the figure as Saint Gregory the Illuminator during his imprisonment in the snake-infested Khor Virap ("deep dungeon").[69] Another tentative suggestion is that the representation preserves an echo of the ancient myth of the Armenian dragon-fighter Hruden (the Avestan Thraētaona) who chained Azhi Dahāka.[70]

On the cathedral of the Holy Apostles in Kars, the figure is shown flanked by two serpents. An iconographical schema involving two serpents that grow out of the shoulders of a human figure was perhaps still known in medieval Armenia, where even after Christianisation vestiges of the Zoroastrian faith – in which this was a well-known form of imagery – continued to survive. In later Zoroastrian Pahlawī/Middle Persian sources (which were written down in the ninth century but incorporated material from third century AD writings and before), the formidable Avestan dragon Azhi Dahāka is transformed into an early Iranian historicised foreign king, Azhdahāk, or, as he is named in New Persian or Arabic narratives, Ẓaḥḥāk (al-Ḍaḥḥāk/Dahāk). According to an account in the *Shāh-nāma*, the dragon-king Ẓaḥḥāk was not originally evil but when Ahriman (Av. Angra Mainyu), the demonic half of ancient Zoroastrian dualist myth, tempted him, kissing his shoulders, a pair of serpents sprang from the place the Spirit of Evil had touched. These serpents, a reminiscence of Ẓaḥḥāk's original reptilian nature, had to be fed the brains of young men every day, binding him to the perpetual sacrifice of humans, who eventually rebelled and overthrew him.[71] An early example of the motif of a human figure with snakes growing out of each shoulder may be sought in greater Mesopotamia, where it is expressed in the figure of the chthonian god Nergal[72] whose iconography may per-

[67] *Idem*, pl. V.1 and 1987, p. 154, pl. 62; Russell, 2004, pp. 1167–168, and p. 1180, pl. 2. See also the depiction of a stylised figure with hands similarly placed, one above the other, on the body and flanked by a pair of crosses on a relief from Samtavro (probably twelfth century), recorded by Baltrušaitis, 1929, pl. LXXXV, fig. 144.

[68] Jean Michel Thierry (1978, p. 54, fig. 30 (line drawing), pl. VIII, 2) identifies also the bust as that of Saint Gregory. See also Gierlichs, 1996, p. 96.

[69] Russell, 2004, pp. 1168–9 and ns. 3 and 4, pp. 1178, 1288. Russell (2004, p. 631) tentatively perceives the figure to be Judas Iscariot fused with Azhdahāk and suggests that these figures are apotropaic symbols of evil. Another interpretation is given by Thierry (1978, p. 49 and *idem*, 1987, pp. 154, 544) who sees the figure as part of an ascension theme common in Byzantine art representing the Virgin; the paired serpents are explained as an artistic mishap which occurred when the artist copied the Byzantine model and mistakenly interpreted the wavy edges of the Virgin's maphorion as serpents.

[70] Russell, 2004, p. 560 and n. 21.

[71] Ṭabarī describes these as excrescences that resembled the heads of serpents which to Ẓaḥḥāk seemed like dragon heads each time he was taking off his clothes. The monstrous outgrowths were extremely painful but the application of brains appears to have assuaged the pain. See Balʿamī's Persian translation of Ṭabarī's *History*; *Tarjumat-i tārīkh-i* Ṭabarī, tr. Zotenberg, vol. 1, pp. 115–7; the story is recorded in greater detail in al-Thaʿālibī, *Taʾrīkh Ghurar al-siyar*, tr. and ed. Zotenberg, 1900, pp. 19–27. In a manuscript of the *Shāh-nāma* (fol. 8r) featuring the enthronement scene of Ẓaḥḥāk, the tyrant is depicted with a pair of "Saljuq-style" serpent protomes springing from his shoulders in bilaterally symmetrical fashion whose gaping mouths with long curving snouts are turned towards his head. Copied in Shiraz, dated 752/1352. Present location unknown. Ferrier, ed., 1990, p. 202, fig. 7. An earlier known occurrence of the same scene in a miniature from the Great Mongol *Shāh-nāma* ("Demotte"; Washington, DC, Freer Gallery of Art, Ms. 23, 5), probably copied in Tabriz and often dated to around 735/1335, shows Ẓaḥḥāk with undulant serpents in asymmetrical arrangement featured with elongated, wrinkled and fleshy snouts, slightly agape, which exhibit more East and Central Asian characteristics. Grabar and Blair, 1980, p. 59.

[72] It is possible that the motif with the serpents was inspired by sculptural images of the Semitic Underworld God, Heracles-Nergal-Ahriman, as depicted on the bas-relief from a small house-temple in Parthian Hatra in northern Mesopotamia (which was an integral part of Iran in Parthian and Sasanian times). The composite figure shows the god of the realm of death and the underworld, who can be at once life- and death-giving (see Dhorme, 1949, pp. 40–3, 51), clad in Parthian garb. The god's attribute is the serpent, a pair of which springs from his shoulders and rise from either side of his waist, while another serpent rests at his feet. Ghirshman, 1962, p. 87, fig. 98; Bivar, 1975a, vol. 2, pl. 4a. See also pp. 36–7. Cf. Drijvers, 1978, p. 172. Comparable characteristics are likewise shared by the Palmyrene healing warrior god Shadrafa, distinguished by serpents and scorpions springing from his shoulders. On a beam from the *peristylium* of Bēl's temple at Palmyra (dated *c.* 32 AD) Shadrafa is portrayed as one of the gods on foot, horseback and chariot who fight a snake-tailed female monster; significantly the combat scene is surmounted by a pair of winged creatures with human torso and serpentine coils as legs that probably represent beneficial beings. Seyrig, 1934, pp. 165–8, pl. 20. See also Drijvers, 1978, pp. 176–7; Bonner, 1950, pp. 124–5.

haps have been appropriated for the depiction of Yima, the Indo-Iranian "first man,"[73] who in the Iranian tradition becomes the ruler of the underworld after his death,[74] as well as in much earlier Mesopotamian[75] and Bronze Age Central Asian deities.[76] It also appears in archaic Greek literature as shown by Hesiod's anthropomorphic *drakōn* Typhaon/Typhon who is described as having a hundred snake heads growing from his shoulders (*Theogony* 825–626). Material evidence of this visual expression is found mainly in Western Central Asia and the Caucasus.[77] A large terracotta figure, probably made in seventh- or eighth-century Sogdia, thus before Islam had become firmly entrenched as the principal faith in the region, shows an enthroned crowned man, large-headed and with grinning mouth, from the base of whose neck a pair of serpents grow, curving upwards and around his ears before descending down to his cheeks. The man's left hand is clasped to his chest while his raised right hand clenches a now lost object, perhaps a staff.[78] As James Russell notes, it is unlikely that the figure represented an epic monster. Rather is it a supernatural figure that probably fulfilled an apotropaic function.[79] The symbolism of an anthropomorphic figure with serpents springing from the shoulders is thus characterised by an element of ambiguity that allows for a multilayered interpretation.[80] Russell remarks upon this ambiguity when he discusses the role of Yima about whom "Zoroastrian tradition preserves two separate narratives ...; in one he dies and goes down to live in a happy underground abode, while in the other version, he commits sin, wanders unhappy and dies [*Shāh-nāma*]."[81] He therefore proposes that the motif of "Azhi Dahāka in the epic is contaminated by an image of Yima [the Jamshīd of the much later *Shāh-nāma*] appropriated from Nergal ([related by inference to] Ẓaḥḥāk [who] succeeds Jamshīd in the *Shāh-nāma*)."[82]

It is interesting that a closely related motif was chosen in the anonymous fifth-century Armenian *Buzandaran Patmutʿiwnkʿ* which portrays the unfortunate Armenian king Pap (369–374) as having serpents that sprang from his breasts (though not from his shoulders) and wove themselves around his shoulders (IV.44).[83] According to the historian this was because the king was possessed by demons. The choice of symbolism may also be associated with the fact that the king, who was later assassinated by the Romans, had antagonised the Christian clergy and, in addition, had been accused of homosexuality.[84] The description of king Pap with serpents may perhaps reflect the reformulation of the beneficial aspect of the dragon when it acquired an overall symbolic meaning as a satanic force in Christian imagery.[85] The inversion of the beneficial association is graphically articulated in the later so-called "revenge miniatures" of the eleventh- or early twelfth-century Byzantine Metaphrastian Menologion volumes, in which persecuting pagan

[73] Yasht 13.130; Christensen, 1931, tr. 1993, p. 15; Zaehner, 1961, p. 134.

[74] Russell, 1987, p. 44.

[75] Nergal's iconographic characteristics link him with the ancient Sumerian Mesopotamian chthonic vegetation and healing god, Ningizzida, whose attribute is the horned dragon; when represented in anthropomorphic form two serpent heads grow from the god's shoulders. Cf. Edzard, "Ningizzida," *WdM* I, pp. 112–3; Drijvers, 1978, pp. 151–86, esp. pp. 171–80.

[76] See Aruz, 1998, figs. 3c and 3e; Francfort, 2002, p. 132, fig. 28; Kuehn, 2009, pp. 43–67.

[77] It is interesting to observe further that the symbolic concept of serpents growing from Dahāk's shoulders have a point of resemblance with the motif of the serpent crest that generally issues from the point of juncture between the neck and the shoulders of the anthropomorphic representation of the Indian *nāgas* that were frequently found in the Buddhist material culture of Central Asia; cf. Vogel, 1926, p. 40.

[78] Height 61.5 cm. The State Hermitage Museum, inv. no. GA 3053. D'yakonova, 1940, pp. 195–200, fig. 1. See also Russell, 1987, p. 441. *Grand Exhibition of Silkroad Buddhist Art*, 1996, p. 37, cat. no. 22. The bust of a man with snakes growing from his shoulders is also featured on the wall paintings of Sogdian Panjikent; Belenitskii, 1980, p. 203.

[79] Russell, 1987, p. 44.

[80] In this context it is interesting to consider a note by al-Qazwīnī in *Āthār al-bilād wa-akhbār al-ʿibād* ("Monuments of the Countries and History of their Inhabitants"), 437, 9–10, which states that serpents grew from the shoulders of the *ṣūfī* Sheikh al-Kammūnī (from whom al-Qazwīnī traces direct descent through five generations) in order to overturn the power of an unjust ruler. See von Hees, 2002, pp. 36–7, 45.

[81] Russell, 1987, p. 44. See Zaehner, 1961, pp. 134–7, esp. p. 140; Boyce, 1975, repr. 1996, pp. 92–5 and n. 69.

[82] Russell, 1987, p. 44.

[83] *Buzandaran Patmutʿiwnkʿ*, tr. Garsoïan, 1989, p. 202; Russell, 2004, p. 62, n. 36, and p. 130.

[84] According to the *Buzandaran*, once when the king was young his mother entered his room [whilst he was engaged in sodomy] and saw that white snakes had twisted themselves around him (V.22); tr. Garsoïan, 1989, p. 165. Cf. Russell, 2004, pp. 341–2.

[85] In the Christian apocalypse, Satan as the Devil is called the "great dragon" and "ancient serpent" (Revelation 12.9 and 20.2). The use of the serpent as a symbol of Evil is exemplified, for instance, by a homily on the Armenian martyr Saint Sergios by Severus of Antioch, delivered at Chalcis on 1 October 514: "We must be watchful against Satan, the snake who with sleepless eye fixed on our heels lies waiting to push us into the pit of sin by our love for pleasure, such as stuffing one's belly," as cited in Fowden, 1999, p. 23.

tyrant rulers who had martyred Christian saints were depicted with a serpent as a symbol of evil.[86]

What appears to be an abbreviated formula or contracted version of the motif of the full-length human figure or bust flanked by two serpents as shown on the tenth-century cathedral of the Holy Apostles in Kars (figs. 118 and 119), is found three times on the façade of the central monument of the fortified monastic complex of Tatʿev, located in Siunikʿ province in southeastern Armenia. The church, dedicated to the Saints Paul and Peter (Surb Poghos Petros), was constructed by the order of prince Ashotʿ of Siunikʿ under the supervision of bishop Ter Hohannes between 895 and 906.[87] Erected nearly half a century earlier than the imagery on the cathedral of the Holy Apostles in Kars, three frontally rendered mask-like heads are framed on either side by horizontally oriented dragons whose bodies form a single loop.

On the eastern façade of the Paul and Peter church the human heads with prominent ears[88] are flanked by long slender pairs of dragons, while on the northern façade a crowned moustachioed head is framed by two shorter and more voluminous dragons. All of the creatures are portrayed with mouths ajar, revealing a row of sharp teeth as well as projecting tongues, which touch the ears of the heads.[89]

The Armenian historian Stepʿanos Ōrbēlian has interpreted the heads as belonging to the donors of the church; the mustachioed head on the north façade, Grigor Supan, the ruler of Gegharkʿunikʿ (fig. 120), as well as the two heads on the east façade, prince Ashotʿ (fig. 121) and his wife Shushan (fig. 122).[90] The head identified as that of princess Shushan is framed by shoulder-length tresses. Her head is surmounted by a large composite star-rosette that has an elaborate centre, from which radiates one row of cusped petals, which may have conveyed a special significance, possibly with astral or royal connotations.[91] Khalʿpakhʿchian has suggested a protective function of the motif of the human head between dragons, since the latter are regarded by Armenians as protectors of homes *(shahapets)*, serpent genii of places.[92]

The widespread use of the symbol of open-mouthed dragons flanking a human head is also attested by its use in twelfth-century Armenian manuscripts. It is shown as an element attached to ornate initials, such as in the loop of the initial in the Cilician Gospels of Luke and of Matthew (Baltimore, Walters Art Gallery Ms. 538), written in 1193 for the Bishop Ter Karapet, at the monastery of Paughoskan near the fortress of Katen in the region of Mlich (fig. 123).[93] Here the mask-like human head is bracketed by dragon heads, which, like those flanking the heads at Tatʿev, are similarly portrayed with open jaws ending in prominently curled-up tips.

The theme of symmetrically doubled dragons flanking a human head appears on other three-dimensional constructions recorded in the Islamic world, such as at the thirteenth-century caravanserai Susuz Han, dated *c.* 644/1246, situated near Bucak, examined above. At the *khān* the symbolism is shown twice, mirrored above two *muqarnas* niches flanking the main portal, effectively once again doubling the visual impact of the potent motif (fig. 124, detail of one *muqarnas* niche). Just like the above-discussed Armenian dragon heads, those at Susuz Han are portrayed in the so-called "Saljuq-style."

[86] When a first word of a *Passion* was the name of an emperor who had martyred a saint, the evil ruler might be depicted in the initial letter as being strangled by a serpent (Patterson Ševčenko, 1990, p. 193), emperors or crowned figures may be encircled by a serpent (*eadem*, p. 90), or, as in the case of the Roman emperor Trajan, portrayed as holding a serpent in his hand (*eadem*, p. 155).

[87] Cf. Garsoïan, 1994, p. 11.

[88] It is interesting to note that comparable mask-like heads, similarly cut off immediately above the neck, appear on several Armenian sacred buildings dating from the tenth to the thirteenth century. They appear for instance among the vine branches at the Armenian church of the Holy Cross at Aghtʿamar, a few are included among the animal friezes, and two continuous rows of mask-like human female and male heads appear under the eaves on the north and south walls of the west exedra of the church (Der Nersessian, 1965, p. 26, figs. 16, 40). Sirarpie Der Nersessian has identified these schematic heads as following the tradition of Iranian motifs seen to decorate the Parthian palace of Hatra in the Mesopotamian desert (cf. Ghirshman, 1962, p. 36, fig. 49), which were also discovered at Hamadan (ancient Ecbatana) and at Qum south of Tehran (cf. *idem*, p. 38, fig. 52), which originally had an apotropaic character but became an ornamental motif in the classical period (Der Nersessian, 1965, p. 26).

[89] Khalʿpakhʿchian, 1980, pp. 173–4, fig. 6 (line drawing of three reliefs), fig. 8 (forth relief). Russell, 2004, p. 560 and n. 21, p. 631, pp. 1168, 1181, pl. 3.

[90] As cited in Khalʿpakhʿchian, 1980, p. 164.

[91] For a discussion of the significance of the rosette motif in the early Persian, Sasanian and Umayyad period, see Ettinghausen, 1972, pp. 36–41.

[92] Khalʿpakhʿchian, 1980, p. 164. On the Armenian *shahapet*s, see p. 56, n. 66

[93] Der Nersessian, 1973, pp. 6–9, 85–6, pl. C and figs. 13–29; for the ornate initial of the Gospel of Matthew, see fig. 34.

Paired dragons flanking a central motif are also featured on other architectural elements such as a thirteenth-century carved wooden door, discussed below, probably from the Tigris region, now preserved in the Museum für Islamische Kunst in Berlin. The gaping "Saljuq-style" dragons' mouths similarly flank a small central medallion that contains a heavily abraded motif, perhaps once representing a human bust (fig. 153).

Instead of a human head as central element held by open-mouthed dragons, the mythical creatures similarly flank an inscription, a vegetal composition or an animal head, for instance that of a bull or a lion. The close link between the blessings expressed in an inscription and images of fructifying vegetation is evidenced in parallel depictions on the handles of the previously mentioned Bobrinski and Fould inlaid copper alloy buckets. The handle loops of the former are made in the form of dragon protomes from whose gaping mouths spring the central four-sided arched section. Benedictory inscriptions appear in *naskhī* on two sides and in Kufic on the top band of the handle with the date *muḥarram* 559/December 1163. On the outside the loops are flanked by leaping lions (fig. 56). The handle loops on the Fould bucket are made of arched dragons topped at the outside by projecting lion-headed knobs. From the dragons' open mouths emerges the six-sided arched handle, decorated on all facets with scrolling foliage in place of the benedictory inscriptions shown on the Bobrinsky handle (fig. 57).

In a similar manner an inverted pendant palmette is flanked by open-mouthed dragon heads inserted in the loop of the initial letter on the first page of a twelfth-century Armenian Gospel of Matthew (fig. 125). Further related imagery is shown in a marginal ornament portrayed in the important Mush Homiliary, discussed earlier, transcribed and illuminated at the monastery of Avagvankʿ near Erznga(n) in northeastern Anatolia in 1200 to 1202.[94] In this illumination the excessively long looped ophidian bodies of two dragons form a pretzel-like knot at mid-section (fig. 126).[95] Their wide-open mouths revealing sharp teeth are oriented upwards, and in place of the tongues, the creatures emit vegetal scrolls bearing split palmettes and buds. The dragons' mouths thus seem to emit the foliage. This forms an interlaced composition surmounting the pretzel-knot which in turn intertwines with the ophidian bodies. The same manuscript yields further initial letters and marginal ornaments with variations of the same theme. An example of the former are two dragons in mirror image springing from vegetation and touching the foliage with the tips of their outstretched tongues (fig. 127) and of the latter, a closely-related imagery showing the beasts touching each other's tongue tips (fig. 128); correspondingly, a scrolling vegetal stalk bearing palmettes and split-palmettes is shown with a single dragon head growing out of the foliage and biting into the stalk at mid-section (fig. 129).

Yet another analogous motif is represented by the previously discussed relief sculptures on the stone minaret buttresses of the mid-thirteenth-century Çifte Minare *madrasa* at Erzurum. However here a pair of dragon protomes issues from the stem of a palm tree in such a way that they come to flank the central vegetation with its small birds and the double-headed eagle at its apex (fig. 43).

As has been shown above, in lieu of an inscription or vegetation dragons with gaping mouths flank Christian crosses on architectural representations such as on the *vishap*-type *khatchkʿar* (fig. 46) or on the lintel of a door at the Monastery of Deir Mār Behnām in Mosul (figs. 17 a and b, 50) as well as on ornaments in Cilician Armenian Gospel books (figs. 45 and 47). Hence it appears less likely that the dragons framing the Christian emblems are intended to be read as threatening or even less as ingesting the crosses. It may rather be presumed that, conversely, as in the case of vegetation or benedictory inscriptions, the mythical creatures are depicted with crosses issuing from their mouths, perhaps suggesting the active association of the dragons with this symbol of spiritual deliverance. This would suggest a role for them not only as guardians but one may cautiously hypothesise perhaps even as rescuers or deliverers, drawing on associations with the idea of Christ the Saviour and Deliverer.

---

[94] Cf. Izmailova, T.A., "Edesskaia rukopis 1171 goda (M. 313)," *Kultura i iskusstvo nardo vostoka* 8, Trudi gosudarstvennogo Orgena Lenina Ermitazha, 19, Leningrad, 1978, pp. 98–9, fig. 14, as cited in Der Nersessian and Agemian, 1993, p. 31. The interlace has close analogies to a *vishap*-type *khatchkʿar* from Yovhannavankʿ, Ararat, dated 1171, on which the pair of stylised dragons form a central interlace and their open snouts with curled tips emit what appears to be curving foliage. See Thierry, 1987, p. 408, fig. 362.

[95] For a closely related marginal ornament, see the Gospel book, copied on paper, 275 fols., dated 1331, transcribed and illuminated in the village of Agheth (Bzhnunikʿ) by the scribe Hovhannes Kʿahanay (the priest). Mnatsakanyan, 1955, p. 516, fig. 1021.

By analogy, should the imagery of dragons flanking and apparently emitting crosses carry a positive symbolism, then this would have implications for other motifs in the same position. The closely related theme of symmetrically doubled dragons flanking a central animal head survives on architectural compositions. It appears on two of the round towers of the northern city wall of the medieval Armenian city of Ani, probably added under Shaddādid rule in the early twelfth century. Here the creatures' heads with gaping jaws, revealing rows of teeth and tongues with bifid tips, frame a bovine head that in one instance holds a ring in its mouth (fig. 130). The dragons' necks carry ornamental bands as collars. The prominent depiction of the motif on the towers of the city walls certainly underlines its apotropaic intent. It may be surmised that the bovine head flanked by dragon mouths is therefore not threatened by the devouring aspect of the dragons, but, contrarily, is presumably guarded and protected.

The Mush Homiliary yields further variations of the lion's mask with paired dragon heads growing from or issuing vegetation. The mythical creatures are shown joined to the mask with the help of a knotted vegetal interlace bearing split-palmettes and buds (fig. 131). This is also modified to include paired human heads. A marginal ornament shows the central lion mask to emit two leaves from its mouth which rise along either side reaching the mask's crown and issue two human heads in profile (fig. 132).[96] It is notable that the human profiles, drawn in clear outline with large almond-shaped eyes, bulbous nose and receding chin, are closely comparable to the head of a sphinx *marchant* on a star tile from the now destroyed small palace at Kubadabad (built three decades after the inception of the paintings in the Homiliary), which is rendered with a similar tight-fitting headdress with pointed tip (fig. 65). From the apex of the leonine mask spring further vegetal stalks bearing palmettes and foliage which terminate at the top in two confronted open-mouthed dragon heads whose projecting tongues touch the central stalk.

In the same manuscript the theme of paired dragons cum lion's mask can be observed. Significantly, this imagery takes the characteristic form of a pomegranate, a fruit which for its abundant seeds symbolises fertility and immortality both in Armenia and throughout the Iranian world, thus underlining, once again, the auspicious character of the motif (fig. 133).[97]

A closely comparable visual formulation is found in the drawing of the brass door handles of al-Jazarī, intended for the palace door at Diyārbakr in southern Anatolia, which survives only in a copy of the original illustration and a description in the treatise on automata written by the master craftsman. In the illustration the knockers are shown in the form of two confronted dragons with gaping mouths and outstretched tongues that frame the lion-headed knob (fig. 134).

The popularity and wide distribution of the theme of the lion's mask with paired dragon heads is further underlined by its representation on architectural monuments such as the fine relief embellishing the upper corners just below the roof of the thirteenth-century church of Surb Karapet (John the Baptist) (1221–1227) on the east side of the monastic complex of Noravankʿ in Vayots Dzor in southern Armenia (fig. 135).

The complexity of the theme of confronted dragon heads is reflected in a zoomorphic composition at the monastic complex of Geghard, also known as Ayrivankʿ, in the mountainous region of Kotaykʿ, Armenia, that perhaps represents the coat of arms of the Proshian family.[98] The large high relief covers most of the northern wall above the archways leading to the rock carved family sepulcher of the Proshians. The funerary chamber to the northeast of the *gavit* (narthex) was constructed in 1283 and houses the remains of Khaghbakian Prosh, a vassal of the Zakʿarid dynasty who had sold the monastery to the Prosh family. A stairway west of the *gavit* leads up to a burial chamber of his son Papak and his wife Ruzukan which according to an inscription on one of the central columns was hewn out in 1288. The plastically rendered relief sculptures show a monumental bovine head at the apex holding a large ring in its mouth which is fastened to chains that are attached to the collars of symmetrically doubled confronted lions *marchant*. The long curving tails of the imposing felines evolve at the tips into large upward-looking dragon heads. Rendered with gaping snouts terminating in tightly curled tips and revealing large fangs and projecting tongues as well as ornamental bands form-

[96] Cf. Durnovo, Sargsian, and Mnatsakanyan, 1978, pl. 31 (lower right corner).

[97] See also pp. 65, 71, n. 208. On the pomegranate motif in Greek mythology, see Elderkin, 1924, pp. 1–3, 18, 25–7, 44–5, 118.

[98] Khalʿpakhʿchian, 1980, p. 325 and figs. 18 and 20.

ing collars around the necks, the dragon heads diagonally flank the bovine head from below in a triangular fashion. The composition thus offers a parallel to the two relief sculptures with paired dragons framing a bovine head (which in one instance also holds a ring in its mouth) that circumscribe two of the towers of the northern city wall at Ani (fig. 130). At Geghard the sculptures are augmented further just below the lions' frontally oriented heads by the sculpture of a commanding eagle with outspread wings whose claws grasp an ungulate – most probably a symbol of the princes' power (fig. 136).

An elaboration of the motif of dragon heads flanking a central mask-like human face is featured on the *türbe* of Hüdavend Hatun in Niğde. The monument, with a sixteen-sided pyramidal roof on an octagonal body, is of cut stone and was built in 712/1312, during the lifetime of the princess who was buried there twenty years later, and during the rule of the Ilkhanid governor Sunqur Ağa. The motif is amalgamated with the relief of a frontally presented double-headed bird of prey, almost certainly symbolising an eagle, which fills one of the carved blind niches that decorate the façade of the octagonal building. The tips of the outspread wings of the eagle extend into upward-curving dragon heads with long, upward-curved snouts and projecting tongues. A mask-like frontally rendered human head springs from between the elongated interlaced birds' necks that form a loop at the base, while the addorsed eagle heads peck at their own outspread wings (fig. 137).

As was shown earlier in chapter 5, animals can sometimes be seen merging visually with one another, thus fusing not only bodily but presumably also in terms of their innate characteristics. The motif here shows a fusion of the eagle with the dragon, both of which are rendered symmetrically with doubled heads and necks, to which the human aspect is added in the form of the central frontally represented face, resulting in a therianthropomorphic hybrid. The eagle heads are thus shown hacking with their sharp beaks at their own wings since these are at the same time an extension of the "bodies" of the dragons that spring from the wing tips. Moreover, this composite imagery offers an interesting parallel to that of the mask-like face flanked by dragon heads with wide-open mouths that appears on the above-mentioned thirteenth-century caravanserai Susuz Han near Bucak (figs. 7 and 124). However, at the *türbe* of Hüdavend Hatun the dragons appear visually merged with a double-headed eagle, the bifid tongues thrust upwards from their gaping jaws towards the eagle's heads and then towards the human head at the apex. It may be presumed that just as in the case of the conceptual doubling of representations mentioned earlier, a device prominent throughout the medieval period and seen here in the double-headed eagle and dragon, the composite hybrid portrayed here on the *türbe* is similarly an example of an intention to reinforce and augment the visual impact and intended effect of the potent symbol. The motif shown on the *türbe* may thus be seen as a visually amplified version of that on the caravanserai Susuz Han.

It is further noteworthy that the pictorial amalgamation of the dragon and the bird, as shown in the present example, is also illustrated for instance on the presumably royal Saljuq silk fragment, now preserved in the shrine of Saint Apollinaris in Siegburg (fig. 69). The representation of a closely related motif on the *türbe* of Hüdavend Hatun, the daughter of the Rūm Saljuq *sulṭān* Rukn al-Dīn Qılıch Arslan IV, underlines its royal connotations. The examples above moreover show that even during Ilkhanid rule the iconography of the dragon, stylistically and presumably also iconologically, continued to follow "Saljuq-style" conventions.

A similar conceptualisation governs a later illustration in a copy of Zakariyyāʾ ibn Muḥammad al-Qazwīnī's cosmography *ʿAjāʾib al-makhlūqāt wa gharāʾib al-mawjūdāt* ("Wonders of Creation and Oddities of Existence"), written around 668/1270. It is represented in the Sarre Qazwīnī, now in the Freer Gallery of Art, Washington, DC, the suggested dates for which have varied from 1350 to the early fifteenth century.[99] It is considered "a last living example of the long tradition of manuscript painting associated with the local iconographical tradition of Diyarbakir."[100] In the light of this attribution it may be interesting to take a closer look at what is a comparatively late representation of the motif. It shows a gigantic polycephalic scaly dragon *(al-tannīn)* with a large pretzel-like knot incorporating a small, mask-like human head. Two of the six projecting dragon heads, their confronted gaping jaws revealing pro-

[99] Cf. Badiee, 1984, p. 97.

[100] *Eadem*, 1978, p. 406, pl. 42, and *eadem*, 1984, p. 103.

jecting tongues, encircle and surmount the human head. The small head thus appears almost to grow out of the dragon's body, while being flanked at the same time by four other dragon heads that project from just below (fig. 138). It is thus literally engulfed by the dragon heads and seems almost to fuse with the body of the giant polycephalic dragon. The text to the illustration states that the dragon was so large that it snapped off the top third of the minaret of Anṭākiya (Antioch).[101]

With regard to the paired reliefs at Susuz Han, Öney has identified the human heads as sun rosettes threatened by the "underground forces and the dark moon symbol" of the dragon,[102] hence associating it with astrological functions, according to which the dragon is the cause of solar and lunar eclipses. It is important to note however, as Abbas Daneshvari has demonstrated, that the concept of the dragon solely in its role as eclipse monster threatening the light of the luminaries and, by extension, the rulers as their worldly embodiments, presents only one aspect of the multivalent symbolism of the dragon.[103] As has been shown above there exists at the same time another possibility: that of perceiving the symbolism of the gaping dragons' jaws flanking a central motif as beneficial and apotropaic. At Susuz Han this reading is supported by paired winged figures whose presence seems to bestow a honorific dimension upon the iconography of the gaping dragons' jaws flanking the mask-like human faces (figs. 7 and 124). It thus appears reasonable to assume that the iconographic theme of dragons' jaws flanking other central motifs, such as inscriptions, vegetation or animal heads may be similarly associated with a beneficial, apotropaic function.

The dragon-tamer

The representation, examined above, of the ruler transposed to a cosmic plane flanked on either side by dragons, survived mainly on portable objects (figs. 113–116), in particular on silver-inlaid metalwork from the greater Khurasan region, from where this visual expression spread westward. It is significant in this respect that the central figure is portrayed with one or both of his arms extended to hold the staffs just below the dragon heads, in other words as if grasping the necks of the dragons. The fact that sometimes the figure does not hold the creatures' necks with both hands may suggest that the actual holding of the necks is not a prerequisite. For the imagery to convey its iconological content to the contemporary beholder – namely the ruler as victor over mythical creatures which symbolise any and all hostile forces – it apparently sufficed to represent the key elements of a central figure flanked by two dragons.

In its most detailed and perhaps most complete execution, this important iconographic expression is emblematised on an architectural structure. In a powerful parallel to the widely spread iconography of the ruler flanked by dragons the extraordinary representation of a frontally portrayed figure seated cross-legged is shown grasping the tongues of a pair of mighty confronted dragons. The reliefs are carved on a now destroyed section of the Talisman Gate, the Bāb al-Ṭilasm (formerly Bāb al-Ḥalaba), one of the four gates at the east of Baghdad (figs. 139a and b).[104] The gate was part of the city wall of Baghdad, the capital of the ʿAbbasid caliphate, and according to the inscription was completed in 618/1221–2 under the caliph Abu 'l-ʿAbbās Aḥmad al-Nāṣir li-Dīn Allāh (577/1181–620/1223). In order to restore moral and political unity and to bring about a revival of the old grandeur of the ʿAbbasid empire,[105] the caliph sought to develop and incorporate in the principal Sunnī states fraternities dedicated to the classical Islamic *futuwwa* (which may be translated as "youthful manliness"), whose aim was to promote a chivalric code of behaviour.[106]

Portrayed in high relief on the upper part of the spandrels of the arched gateway were two majestic confronted horned dragons whose wide-open snouts with turned-up tips, marked by rows of sharp teeth and fangs, reveal excessively long tongues with bifid ends that are grasped with both outstretched hands by the central frontally-portrayed figure. The latter has a "moon-shaped" face flanked by long tresses, which is distinguished by a halo and a three-pronged crown, and sits cross-

[101] *Kitāb ʿajāʾib al-makhlūqāt*, ed. Wüstenfeld, 1849, repr. 1967, p. 133. See Badiee, 1978, p. 124.

[102] Öney, 1969–70, p. 200. Cf. Otto-Dorn, 1978–9, p. 131.

[103] Daneshavri, 1993, pp. 15–25, esp. pp. 20–1.

[104] Preusser, 1911, p. 16 top; Sarre and Herzfeld, 1920, vol. 2, pp. 153–6, vol. 3, pls. 10–1; Hartner, 1938, fig. 26; Sarre, 1936, fig. 26 (detail); Kühnel, 1950, p. 11, fig. 12; Gierlichs, 1996, pl. 66.1; Meinecke, 1989, p. 58, fig. 7; Hauptmann von Gladiss, ed., 2006, p. 114, fig. 12.

[105] For a translation of the inscription, see Sarre and Herzfeld, 1911, vol. 1, pp. 35–6.

[106] Cahen and Taeschner, "Futuwwa," *EI*² II, 961a.

legged just above the apex of the arch. He is clad in an ornately patterned loose long coat, belted just below the slightly protruding belly over trousers, with short boots projecting from below the hem.

The dragons have muscular forelegs depicted with toes and talonesque claws, the inner forelegs being raised. Their heads are crowned by a pair of curved horns that project from the top of the head and are flanked by small, cusped ears, folded to the back; the faces are rendered with small, almond-shaped eyes and trefoil-shaped motifs on the face and upper part of the neck, which is demarcated below the jaw line by small, contiguous curls, while larger curls accentuate the back of the neck. The enormous dragons' scaly serpentine tails twine along the arch forming two impressive knots, the first combining a pretzel-shape with an additional loop, the second a straightforward pretzel-like knot, then extend into three more loops and taper to the tip (lacunae attest to the possible existence formerly of small heads whose identity, bird or dragon heads, can no longer be verified). The dragons' feathery elegantly upswept wings project from the haunches and end in curls, the long uppermost tip curling inward and terminating in small, crested birds' heads with wattles projecting from the chin and long feathers sweeping down the back of the necks. With their small, curved beaks the birds peck at the dragons' wings.

The monumental depiction of the cross-legged central haloed and crowned figure (apparently small in size but in fact reaching about 60 cm in height)[107] subduing the giant dragons by holding their tongues seems to reflect the ancient concept of the dragon-tamer. The fact that the royal figure, who is comparatively small in proportion to the dragons, manages to subjugate the great beasts only adds to the impression of dominance and prestige the presentation intends to convey. The gesture of tightly grasping the dragons' tongues is probably the crucial aspect of the image, representing not only the control of speech but also the ritual of public subjugation of the dragons and thereby the harnessing of their forces. This time-honoured motif of victory doubtless symbolises the caliph's heroic feat of overcoming adverse forces, embodied by the dragons whose likeness was moreover sometimes used to emblematise personified historical foes.[108] The pairing of dragons observed specifically on monumental depictions was presumably intended as much to reinforce and replicate the symbolic meaning as to create an effect of pictorial symmetry. This tendency to double single units is a well-known phenomenon among Near Eastern cultures.[109] It may thus be presumed that the iconographic elements of this composition have been selected in order to convey a certain meaning or to evoke a certain response in the beholder. It is in the consciousness of the latter that the full cultural meaning of the artwork unfolds. As Ernst Gombrich has pointed out: "The form of a representation cannot be divorced from its purpose and the requirements of the society in which the given visual language gains currency."[110]

In order to provide an insight into the symbolic mindset and linguistic expression of the period during which the imagery of the dragon was commonly used as metaphor and allegory, Ernst Herzfeld refers to the report of the contemporary scholar Yāqūt, who compares the conquest of the fort of Ṭabaraq near Rayy by the Great Saljuq *sulṭān* Ṭoghrıl III in 588/1192 (previously occupied by the Khwārazm-shāh Takash) to a serpent with two heads, one in Iraq, the other in Khurasan, who opens its mouth because it wants to swallow both.[111] This double-headed giant serpent or paired dragon whose bifid tongues are immobilised and are effectively bound by the restraining hands of the central seated figure is imbued with more effective talismanic power than anything else. As suggested many years ago by Herzfeld[112] and more recently by Meinecke,[113] the

---

[107] Meinecke, 1989, p. 58.

[108] Friedrich Sarre interprets one of the dragons as symbolising the Khwārazm-shāh ʿAlāʾ al-Dīn Muḥammad ibn Takash, who had been overcome by the Mongols in the year before the erection of the monument, and the other as a personification of the Mongols themselves (Sarre and Herzfeld, 1911, vol. 1, p. 40). Max van Berchem however conceives the second dragon as representing the Ismāʿīlī Grand Master of Alamūt, Jalāl al-Dīn Ḥasan III ibn Muḥammad II who was subordinate to the caliphate since 608/1211–2. Al-Juwaynī, *Taʾrīkh-i jahān-gushāy*, tr. Boyle, 1912–37, vol. 2, pp. 364, 391, 699–701; van Berchem, "Das Baghdad Talismantor," ed. Sarre and Herzfeld, 1911, vol. 1, and *idem*, 1897, pp. 474–7. This second interpretation may be more likely since al-Nāṣir had succeeded in securing the return of the Syrian and Iranian Ismāʿīlīs to the fold of Sunnī orthodoxy in 608/1211–2. See however Marshall Hodgson (1955, pp. 215–25, esp. pp. 222–3, n. 31) who rejects van Berchem's reading of Ḥasan symbolising the second dragon. Cf. Hartmann, 1975, pp. 164–6; ul-Huda, 2003, pp. 13–40, esp. p. 35.

[109] See Kuntzmann, 1983, esp. 51–116; Anthony, 2007, pp. 134–5; Kristiansen and Larsson, 2005, pp. 264, 297.

[110] Gombrich, 1960, pp. 87–90.

[111] *Muʿjam al-buldān*, III, p. 507, cited after Sarre and Herzfeld, 1920, vol. 2, p. 153.

[112] Sarre and Herzfeld, 1911, vol. 1, pp. 38–40.

[113] The significance of the gate as potent victory

monumental sculptures almost certainly represented a victory commemoration on a triumphal gateway, which also served as entrance to the caliphal palace. Significantly, by employing the time-honoured symbolism of the dragon-tamer this victory commemoration aimed at invoking supernatural talismanic defences as a psychological safeguard against dangerous forces or catastrophic events.

The associated royal charisma may moreover be rooted in the celestial,[114] and possibly astrological, realms. Hartner sees in the central figure "the new-born child - symbol of the new moon."[115] However on account of the confronted seated lions in profile, which are carved in relief onto the imposts below the arch, the central figure could also be interpreted as a personification of the Sun whose house is in Leo.[116] However, irrespective of the visual conflation of the figure with either the Sun or the Moon, its striking imagery probably represented the triumph of the "heavenly ruler" over his enemies by employing a highly potent symbolism of great antiquity.[117] On yet another level, as has been pointed out by Herzfeld, the popularly used appellation "Talisman Gate" (Bāb al-Ṭilasm) is certainly no mere coincidence but, as noted above, may be associated with the overall propitious and apotropaic content of the iconographic visualisation.[118] This is further corroborated by the inscription, which refers to the caliph as "the *imām*, to whom the whole of humanity has to submit," as well as "the caliph who is initiated by the master of the world and who is a proof for Allāh of the entirety of beings," representing a further talismanic aspect alluding to defeated or yet to be defeated rivals of the caliph.[119]

It has been shown that the emblematic representation of the cosmic ruler flanked by and often grasping dragon-headed staffs, so ubiquitously employed on works of art, in particular on metalwork, from the mid-eleventh to the early thirteenth century, was associated with the ancient concept of the "Master of the Animals," represented here as the "Master of the Dragons." The motif gives visual form to the idea of the cosmic ruler wrestling with and subduing threatening forces, represented by the dragons. What is more, the iconographic expression portrays the ruler as dragon-tamer whose supernatural powers enabled him to subdue, contain, tame and transform the dragons rather than annihilate them. Since this iconographical theme was used as decoration on a wide range of artefacts accessible to a larger part of society (the Bobrinski bucket, for instance, was perhaps given to a religious dignitary), it seems probable that its semantic meaning was not seen as exclusively confined to the art of the court and the upper classes but rather that it was a multivalent symbol, transcending any specific level of society.[120] This was made possible by the fact that the ethos of cosmic rulership was understood to comprise the idea of victory over adverse forces as a synthesis of the fundamental royal virtues and hence itself served as a visual metaphor imbued with a more generalised auspicious and apotropaic significance.[121]

It is moreover tempting to propose that a bust or a head flanked by two dragons represented an abbreviated reference, which has close analogies to the semantic meaning of the dragon-tamer, and whose allegorical content was clear to a medieval audience. The emblematic significance of the allegorical imagery that omitted the visual manifestation of the bodies would have conveyed the same meaning as the examples of the dragon-tamer motif on Khurasani metalwork or the Bāb al-Ṭilasm in Baghdad. Yet another possibility may be considered, namely that a twofold approach was possible in reading this imagery, and that a literal as well as an allegorical conception was attached to the "abbreviated" form.

What is more, as already noted above, the representation alludes to a mythical vision of the ruler and refers to the age-old portrayal of the archetypal royal hero overcoming dangerous creatures in a mythical-heroic manner. It may be suggested with a degree of certainty that to the

monument was still relevant in not too distant memory which is reflected in the symbolic act of the Ottoman *sulṭān* Murād IV ibn Aḥmad I (1032/1623–1049/1640) who, after his occupation of Baghdad in 1638, walled up the gateway in order to prophylactically curtail the potency of the gate as victory monument, in other words, to preclude any future conquests. Meinecke, 1989, p. 58. Cf. also Sarre and Herzfeld, 1911, vol. 1, pp. 34–6.

[114] Cf. Hauptmann von Gladiss, ed., 2006, p. 115.

[115] Hartner, 1938, p. 144.

[116] Pancaroğlu, 2001, pp. 171–2, n. 29. The lion's association with the sun, which can be traced back to remote antiquity, as far as the fourth millennium BC (Hartner, 1938, pp. 115, 119), apparently originated in a purely mythological or metaphysical conception (*idem*, p. 138). The personification of the planets is discussed in chapter 8, part b.

[117] Cf. Hauptmann von Gladiss, ed., 2006, p. 115.

[118] Sarre and Herzfeld, 1911, vol. 1, pp. 38–9.

[119] *Eidem*, pp. 39–40.

[120] Cf. Pancaroğlu, 2000, p. 246.

[121] *Eadem*, pp. 246–7.

medieval mind the animal combat or the mastery of beasts was associated with the timeless image of a heroic and royal ideal associated with the ruler. Representations of the ruler between two dragons, as emblematised in the Bāb al-Ṭilasm relief, show him constraining the great powers of the dragons within the control of his realm, thereby demonstrating his mythical powers. It is conceivable that when commissioning the visual metaphor and sculptural vision of the mythical dragon-tamer for the monumental victory commemoration, the caliph al-Nāṣir's aim was to evoke the supernatural forces associated with the time-honoured Indo-Iranian concept as well as to appropriate the associated royal charisma of ancient kingship.

c. *Symbolism of the dragon's tongue*

It is inherent in the dragon's very nature that, owing to its multivalent qualities, it escapes definition. One of its many preeminent features is the conspicuous emphasis on the tongue, used to denote the supernatural quality of the creature. In most of the examples discussed earlier, the deep gaping throats of the fabulous creatures reveal tongues, which are invariably oriented towards the central motif. In the Armenian examples at the late ninth-century monastic complex of Saint Peter and Saint Paul in Siunikʿ (figs. 120–122) and the mid-tenth-century cathedral of the Holy Apostles in Kars (figs. 118 and 119), the outstretched ophidian tongues are clearly directed at the ears of the human heads. The serpent-headed staffs that flank the seated frontally portrayed figures depicted on twelfth- or thirteenth-century Islamic metalwork are also shown with the tongues projecting from the mouths towards the human heads (figs. 113–116). This may be related to the fact that a snake's tongue is known to dart out before it strikes at a foe. At the Bāb al-Ṭilasm in Baghdad of 618/1221–2 the central figure is hence portrayed as holding tightly on to the dragons' tongues (figs. 139a and b). As has been shown, this gesture is associated with the symbolism of subjugation by bridling the creatures and thereby rendering them defenceless. Reference to taming and mastering the (serpent-)dragon by means of holding its tongue is also made in al-Kisāʾī's story of Moses (Mūsa) and the pharaoh *(firʿawn)*. To save the life of the latter from the attack of the Prophet's rod turned giant serpent, Moses "cried to the serpent, which came to him as a tame dog comes to his master. Moses put his hand in its mouth and caught its tongue, whereupon it was again a staff.[122]

The vital organ of the tongue thus seems to epitomise the seat or the extension of power of the mythical creature. This underscores the inference that the use of control over this potent emblem permits the powerful creature to be overmastered. Establishing control over the dragon implies of course not only the domination of its dark and evil nature, but also of its inherent beneficial qualities. An attempt will be made in the next and subsequent chapters to describe the nature of these qualities.

Tongues are generally associated with the power of speech, a quality of the dragon that will be addressed in chapter 13. According to the Qurʾān, the magician-king Sulaymān ibn Dāwūd, the biblical Solomon, was acquainted with the speech of birds and animals (*sūra* 27, 16–9), a tradition based on I Kings 4.33.[123] In Judaism as well as in Islamic scriptural tradition the understanding of the language of animals was initially associated with the story of Paradise.[124] The early Haggada speaks of Adam understanding the language of birds and beasts[125] and of Eve[126] speaking with the serpent[127] who was considered to be the wisest, the cleverest and the most astute of all animals.[128] In the late Haggada non-Jewish folklore was censored before it was assimilated; the

[122] *Qiṣaṣ al-anbiyāʾ*, tr. Thackston, 1978, p. 228.

[123] Walker [Fenton], "Sulaymān b. Dāwūd," *EI*² IX, p. 882b.

[124] Al-Kisāʾī, *Qiṣaṣ al-anbiyāʾ*, tr. Thackston, 1978, pp. 36–46. Cf. Schwemer, 1994, p. 137.

[125] Adam lost this ability with the Fall of men but in the Messianic period this condition will be re-established. Ginzberg, 1909–38, repr. 1946 and 1955, vol. 5, pp. 94, n. 54, 119–20, n. 113.

[126] *Idem*, p. 91, n. 48.

[127] In Paradise all animals could speak, but as punishment for allowing Iblīs to seduce Eve (Ḥawwāʾ) the serpent lost not only its legs but also the ability to speak (a skill similarly denied to all the other animals). Al-Kisāʾī, *Qiṣaṣ al-anbiyāʾ*, tr. Thackston, 1978, p. 46. Cf. *Book of Jubilees* 3.28; Philo of Alexandria, *De Opificio Mundi* 55.156. Older rabbinic sources do not know of the original language spoken by man and the animals, but a passage in the Lekah on Genesis, 3.1, maintains that before the Fall only the serpent spoke the original language of man, Hebrew, whereas the rest of the animals spoke their own language which was only understood by Adam. See Ginzberg, 1909–38, repr. 1946 and 1955, vol. 1, p. 181, n. 91, and vol. 5, pp. 91, n. 48, 94, n. 58, and 100–1, n. 83.

[128] The wisdom of the serpents is also noted in the New Testament (Genesis 3.1; Matthew 10.16). Cf. Schwemer, 1994, p. 137.

biblical king Solomon took the place of the great serpent(s) and could understand and speak the language of animals as well as teach their language to others.[129] However, in spite of this assimilation the connection of the serpent with the language of animals remained widespread in folktales throughout Asia and the Near East.[130] One of the oldest recorded versions is a third-century Buddhist tale, in which a king rescues the daughter of a dragon-king who thereupon grants him a wish. The king says that he has already many precious objects but that he wishes to understand the language of the animals. The dragon-king grants him this request on condition that he will keep his ability a secret.[131]

In Armenian folktales serpents can speak and the touching of a serpent's tongue serves as a source of knowledge.[132] Vestiges of such myths may be discerned in Armenian popular traditions, which similarly record that a grateful serpent king gave the knowledge to cure all diseases to a boy who had saved his son. He transmitted this knowledge by touching the boy's tongue with his own; the boy then became the physician known also in the Turkish-speaking world as Luqmān *al-ḥakīm*.[133] In another Armenian story, the grateful serpent-prince licks a dead person back to life.[134]

According to a further tradition the grateful serpent passes on the ability to understand the language of all animals through the power of its breath.[135] Similarly in antiquity the ability to confer supernatural knowledge of the language of animals, that is to say, the art of divination, on human beings was most commonly attributed to the serpent.[136] These scattered references to human mastery of the language of the animals functioned as metaphors for the extraordinary lucidity of prophets, saints and sages.

Other widespread views held that the eating of serpent's flesh transmitted supernatural wisdom to the consumer,[137] and that knowledge of the language of animals was given to Arabs.[138] This mantic art they are supposed to have acquired by

[129] In interpretation of 1 Kings 5.13. See Ginzberg, 1909–38, repr. 1946 and 1955, vol. 4, pp. 138–40, 287–8, n. 34. In later Jewish folk tales, Leviathan replaces the great serpent (Noy, 1971, p. 177), for instance, in the Jewish variant of the "Story of the Dutiful Son" (*idem*, p. 196): "He (Leviathan) said to him: "Open your mouth!" He opened his mouth and Leviathan spat into it three times. At once, the spirit of wisdom and cleverness rested upon him, and he knew and understood the language of animals and birds, and he spoke seventy languages."

[130] For a comprehensive bibliography, see Noy, 1971, pp. 171–208.

[131] Chavannes, 1910, vol. 1, pp. 382–3. A comparable *Jātaka* story speaks of a king saving the life of a dragon-king who thereupon rewards him with a charm "giving knowledge of all sounds"; Cowell, ed., 1897, repr. 2000, vol. 3, pp. 174–7; see also Vogel, 1926, p. 22.

[132] Hoogasian-Villa, 1966, p. 67.

[133] *Eadem*, pp. 426–9 and 531–2.

[134] Surmelian, 1968, p. 232. Cf. the parallel to the Armenian mythical dogs, called *Arlez* (Arm. *aralez* or *yaralez*), one of which is black, the other white, who live with invisible powers, and who are said to have licked the bodies of wounded war heroes back to life. See Eznik, *Elc alandocʿ*, tr. and ed. Mariès and Mercier, 1959, ch. 122; cf. Karamanlian, P.A., *Die Aralezen bei Eznik* (German Resumé, pp. 705–7), as cited in Schlerath, 1954/58, p. 39.

[135] Hoogasian-Villa, 1966, pp. 401 and 528. The motif occurs in the *Shāh-nāma* recounting how Buzurjmihr, the later minister of Khusraw Anūshirwān, was breathed on by a black snake which was interpreted by his companion who witnessed the scene as indicating that Buzurjmihr would attain a position of great power (tr. and ed. Mohl, 1838–1878, vol. 6, pp. 247–9, ll. 1037–1045). See also p. 61. At the same time the Iranian national epic repeatedly invokes the metaphor of the dragon's breath to allude to an impending and potentially fatal calamity (tr. and ed. Mohl, 1838–1878, vol. 1, p. 153, ll. 450–3; vol. 3, p. 183, l. 510; vol. 5, p. 519, l. 1897). In like manner the potentially fatal power of the "slavering dragon" and of his breath is mentioned in the romance *Wīs u Rāmīn* (tr. and ed. Davis, 2008, p. 364 and 83, respectively). See also the related metaphorical imagery used by Matthew of Edessa, p. 9, n. 61.

[136] References to such phenomena are preserved in Greek tradition. The Hellenistic/Roman author Apollodorus relates that Melampus acquired the gift of prophecy after he had performed funeral rites for some serpents which had been killed by his servants and thence reared the young serpents (*Bibliotheca* I. 9. 11–2, p. 87; Scholiast on Apollonius Rhodius, *Argonautica* I.118. Cf. Eustathius on Homer, *Odyssey* XI 292, p. 1685; Pliny, *Naturalis Historia*, X 137. See also Frazer, 1888, p. 166). When these were fully grown, they crept onto each of his shoulders as he slept and cleansed his ears with their tongues. When he woke up he understood the voices of the birds and other animals, and thus acquired the gift of foretelling the future. Cassandra and her brother Helenus are said to have acquired their prophetic gift in the same manner. When young they were placed one night in the temple of Apollo and in the morning were found with serpents wreathed around their bodies, licking their ears (cf. Scholiast on Homer, *Iliad*, VII 44; Tzetzes, *Scholiast in Lycophron, Introd.* I, pp. 266–8, ed. Müller, C.G.; Scholiast on Euripides, *Hecuba*, V 86). Likewise Porphyrios is recorded as saying that perhaps all men might understand the language of all the animals if a serpent had washed their ears (*De Abstinentia*, III 4).

[137] "The reason why the serpent has the capacity to understand the language of the birds and the animals is according to Pliny (after a saying of Democritus) that they are generated from the mixed blood of diverse birds, hence anyone who eats a serpent will understand the bird language" (*Naturalis Historia*, X 70; see also XXIX 22), as cited in Frazer, 1888, p. 180.

[138] Cicero, *De divinatione* 1.92 and 94. Cf. Appian's account of his successful escape from the Jewish revolt in Egypt (*c.* 116 AD) near Pelusium thanks to an Arab guide who correctly interpreted the three screeches of a crow. Appian, *Roman History* 24,19.

eating the heart or the liver of large serpents.[139] The lasting popularity of this type of account is evidenced in its appearance in the frame tale of the *Alf layla wa-layla* in the story of the *Queen of the Serpents*. Here the queen consents to be slain and sacrifices her flesh, which when boiled and eaten has healing properties.[140] Moreover, the drinking of the elixir is said to give access to the fountains of knowledge, in other words knowledge of all sciences. Another story, the *Keys of Destiny*, tells of a place that harbours the secret of transforming base metal into gold and ultimately of gaining immortality. Access to it can only be gained by killing a serpent in a black valley and preparing an ointment from the reptile's heart mixed with other ingredients.[141] In folk tales the imbibing, ingesting or application by any means of elixirs prepared from the heart or the flesh of a serpent initiates into hidden secrets.[142]

[139] See Flavius Philostratus, who at the beginning of the third century AD, wrote a biography of the wandering philosopher Apollonius of Tyana in Cappadocia (*Vita Apollonii* 1.20, 2 vols., tr. Conybeare, F.C., London, 1980, p. 57; also 3.9, p. 249), who became master of the beasts by acquiring an understanding of the language and ideas of animals from the Arab tribes "by feeding either on the heart or the liver of the dragon." The mantic significance attributed in antiquity to (serpent-)dragons in revelations and oracles can still be gleaned from the writings of the fifth-century Greek poet Nonnos (*Dionysiaca* XLI 340–1) when he reports that *ophion* has recorded the sayings of the gods about the world *(thesphata kosmou)*. The second-century Greek traveller and geographer Pausanias (*Graeciae Descriptio* IV 10.5–6) even called a seer outright Ophioneus. It may not be irrelevant to note that in the Scandinavian version of the epic of Siegfried, the hero roasted the dragon's heart, whereby some dragon blood dropped onto his tongue, which led to his acquisition of an understanding of the bird language; see Schirmunski, 1961, p. 55.

[140] 535th Night [1830 Calcutta ed. count]. *The Book of the Thousand Nights and a Night*, tr. Burton, 1885, vol. 5, pp. 407–9. Cf. Marzolph and van Leeuwen, 2004, pp. 349–50. In a Syrian tale a dervish is said to have drunk serpent water, following which the serpents cannot bite him and he is able to talk with serpents and birds in their respective languages; *Syrische Sagen und Märchen*, tr. Prym and Socin, 1881, pp. 150–1.

[141] Marzolph and van Leeuwen, 2004, p. 251.

[142] This has certain parallels to passages in the Old Testament. Whereas Isaiah (6.6–8) and Jeremiah (1–9) are touched by God or an angel, Ezekiel (3.1–3) is ordered to eat a scroll with writing on it that tastes as sweet as honey. This intake is reminiscent of ancient initiation rituals that similarly involve the touching of the mouth, that is to say, the tongue, with a liquid substance which is then swallowed. Van Lint, 2005, p. 374. In the early Turkish Anatolian epic, the *Baṭṭāl-nāma* ("Book of Baṭṭāl"), the angel Gabriel/Jibrāʾīl instructs the Prophet Muḥammad to place a drop of saliva in the mouth of the early Muslim frontier warrior ʿAbd al-Wahhāb. The warrior swallows it but it rests in his throat "to be held in trust." He then passes the drop on to Jaʿfar, later named Sayyid Baṭṭāl Ghāzī, who on swallowing it "acquired perfect knowledge of seventy two different languages and of twelve sciences." Dedes, 1996, pp. 100, 117–8.

PART FOUR

THE DRAGON IN ASTROLOGY, ALCHEMY, MEDICINE AND MAGIC

CHAPTER EIGHT

THE DRAGON AND ASTROLOGY

a. *Astrology in medieval Central Asia*

The ancient practice of astrology,[1] the interpretation of the movement of celestial bodies as reflecting divine powers and enabling prognostication of the future, had a deep and pervasive influence on early and medieval Islamic thought and culture.[2] The history of astrology, which had been introduced into the Iranised world of Central Asia through Graeco-Babylonian influence, goes back to ancient times. Moreover, with the spread of Buddhism into Central Asia, Iran and China, Indian *nakṣatra* (lunar asterism) astrology was introduced.[3]

Interest in the science of astronomy, closely and in practice inextricably linked with astrology, is further corroborated in Central Asia by findings during excavations at the religious and funerary complex of Qoy-Qrylgan-Qalʿa (fourth/third century BC to the third/fourth century AD) in the region of Toʿrtkoʿl in Khwārazm, which might indicate that the site could have been used for astronomical observations. The findings include clay fragments and rings that could be reconstructed to form an astrolabe with a circular alidade.[4] The great tenth-century Khwārazmian scholar Abu 'l-Rayḥān Muḥammad ibn Aḥmad al-Bīrūnī, known as "the Master" *(al-ustādh)*, who devoted more than half of his extensive writings to astronomy and astrology, writes in relation to ancient Khwārazmian astronomy and astrology that the Khwārazmians "knew them [the constellations] better than the [pre-Islamic] Arabs."[5]

Later Parthian (250 BC–224 AD) and Sasanian (224–652 AD) kings are recorded as having maintained a "chief of the star-gazers" *(axtarmārānsālār)* at court where a regnal horoscope would be drawn up for each king. However, only during the reign of the Sasanian king Shāpūr I (r. 241–271) was the study of Iranian astronomy and astrology known to have been encouraged. According to the *Dēnkard* (Book IV), the ninth-century compendium of the Zoroastrian religion, the king is said to have gathered the astrological writings, "which were dispersed throughout India, the Byzantine empire and other lands."[6] Another Sasanian ruler who, according to al-Bīrūnī, encouraged Greek or Graeco-Syrian and Indian scholars in Iran was Khusraw I Anūshirwān (r. 531–579).[7] According to a tradition reported by Firdawsī, the colossal throne *(taq-i taqdis)* of his grandson, the last Sasanian king Khusraw II Parwīz (r. 591–628), was embellished with images of the seven regions as well as the seven planets and the twelve signs of the zodiac.[8] As the centre of the astrological throne the ruler represented the one who held the power to influence the stars.[9] Political crises were regarded as inevitable at acute aspects of the constellations.[10]

---

[1] Astrology seems to have been widespread and practised at a very early time by all nations in the ancient East. Cf. Jeffers, 1996, p. 147.

[2] The ʿAbbasid caliphs, in particular al-Manṣūr, accorded particular prominence to the study and practical application of astrology. Gutas, 1998, p. 16 and n. 7, and p. 33.

[3] Pingree, 1963, pp. 230–1, 240–1. The *Śārdūlakarṇāvadāna*, which contains an exposition of this system, was widely diffused (*idem*, pp. 240–1) and summarised in Chinese by the Parthian prince An Shih-kao in the second century AD (*Śārdūlakarṇāvadāna of the Divyāvadāna*, tr. Mukhopadhyaya, S., Santiniketan, 1954, pp. 213–7; and on An Shih-kao, see Zürcher, 1959, vol. 1, pp. 32–4; cited after Pingree, 1963, pp. 240–1) and fully translated twice in the third century AD (*Śārdūlakarṇāvadāna*, tr. Mukhopadhyaya, 1954, pp. xii–xiii, cited after Pingree, 1963, pp. 240–1).

[4] Schirmer, 1926–7, pp. 43–6, 63–79. According to Boyce and Grenet (1991, pp. 184, n. 133, 193, n. 173) the primary purpose of the upper storey of the tower at the complex was not, as supposed by the excavators of the site, to function as an observatory; the use of the primitive astrolabes found at the site was only secondary.

[5] *Kitāb al-Āthār*, tr. and ed. Sachau, 1876–8, p. 226.

[6] Zaehner, 1955, repr. 1972, p. 8; Pingree, 1963, p. 241; Gutas, 1998, p. 36, see also p. 41.

[7] Kennedy, 1956, p. 50.

[8] Tr. and ed. Mohl, 1838–1878, vol. 6, p. 253. Comparable imagery is reported secondhand from Theophanes through Kedrenos that in Ganzaca (Ganjak) when Heraclius captured Khusraw's palace in 624, he saw Khusraw's image in the domed roof of the palace, as though enthroned in heaven and surrounded by the sun, moon and stars. Texts cited in full in Herzfeld, 1920a, pp. 1–3; L'Orange, 1953, pp. 18–27, esp. pp. 19–21. Cf. also Carter, 1974, p. 177 and n. 25.

[9] Herzfeld, 1920, pp. 1–24 and 103–47.

[10] On court astrologers, cf. Christensen, 1944, p. 396; on

Sanskrit astrological texts were translated into Pahlawī in the Central Asian world, according to David Pingree, in particular in Sind and Afghanistan.[11] During the last centuries of Sasanian rule the influence of the sciences of astronomy and astrology, which were often a synthesis of Hellenistic and Indian theories, was particularly prevalent. The works of many early Islamic astrologers, many of whom were Iranians or Central Asians, in turn incorporated numerous Indian astronomical and astrological theories. This is reflected in the works of the ninth-century astrologer Abū Maʿshar Jaʿfar ibn Muḥammad ibn ʿUmar (d. 272/886) from Balkh who combines in his *Zīj al-hazārāt* ("The Zij of the Thousands") Hindu, Sasanian and Hellenistic astronomical and astrological traditions, claiming to have used an ancient Persian text from antediluvian times written during the reign of Ṭahmūrath (Av. Takhma Urupi), the second king of the Pīshdādian dynasty of legendary epic Iranian history.[12] Ibn al-Nadīm quotes passages from Abū Maʿshar's *Kitāb ikhtilāf al-zījāt* ("The Book on the Variations among *zījs*"), which contain calculations determining the movement of the planets:

> The people of the time of Ṭahmūrath and the more ancient Persians called these the "cycles of the thousands"; and the wise men of India and their kings, the ancient kings of Persia, and the ancient Chaldeans who lived in Babylon determined the mean longitudes of the seven planets by means of them, preferring them over others because of their accuracy and brevity.[13]

The translation movement of the early ʿAbbasid period saw an unprecedented level of activity in the sciences of astronomy and astrology. This had a profound effect on social attitudes.[14] Indeed astronomy was viewed by scholars as the "mistress of all sciences."[15] The strong astrological tradition in the Sasanian period helps to explain why the field of Arabic astrological literature in the early Islamic period was dominated by Iranian scholars,[16] who in turn maintained contact with their Indian counterparts.[17]

In fact both sciences, astronomy (*ʿilm al-hayʾa*, the "science of the figure (of the heavens)" or *ʿilm al-falak*, "science of the spheres") and astrology (*ʿilm al-nujūm*, the "science of the stars"), were for a long time so close that the word *munajjim* was used to designate both astrologer and astronomer.[18] This is based on the fact that, according to Jābir ibn Ḥayyān (known to the Latins as Geber),[19] one of the main representatives of earlier Arabic alchemy, "the astrologer must be a mathematician; he must have mastery of astronomy, this is a part of *ʿilm al-nujūm* (the "science of the stars" or astrology). For *ʿilm al-hayʾa* (astronomy) is the description of the situation of the state of the sky and what it contains *(ṣūrat waḍʿ al-falak wa-mā fīhi)*, whereas astrology is the gift of the stars *(ʿaṭāʾ al-kawākib)*.[20] Astrology, which involves calculating the position of the planets and the mathematical production of horoscopes, is often referred to as judicial (or catarchic) astrology (*ʿilm aḥkām al-hayʾa*, the "science of the judgment of the stars").[21]

Astrological predictions consisted not only of determining the fate of an individual (*mawālīd*, "genethlialogy," or horoscopic astrology) and of the auspicious and inauspicious timing of events and actions (*ikhtiyārāt*, "choices"), but also of the application of continuous horoscopes for determining the course of events for a country or dynasty or to answer specific questions (*masāʾil*, "interrogations").[22]

In spite of the fact that astrology stood in fundamental opposition to the tenets of the Islamic religion,[23] it gradually established a role in the public life of Islamic rulers.[24] Well-known astrologers included, for instance, Māshāʾallāh ibn Atharī, an Iranian Jew from Basra, and Abū Sahl al-Faḍl ibn Nawbakht, an Iranian, who converted from Zoroastrianism to Islam at the court of the second ʿAbbasid caliph Abū Jaʿfar al-Manṣūr (r. 136/754–158/775). Both

horoscopes, see Kennedy and Pingree, 1971, p. vi; see also Russell, 2004, p. 85 and n. 11.

[11] Pingree, 1963, pp. 242–3.

[12] The legendary history of king Ṭahmūrath is recorded, for instance, by al-Thaʿālibī in his *Taʾrīkh Ghurar al-siyar* (tr. and ed. Zotenberg, 1900, pp. 7–10) in which he also describes the kings's subjugation of Iblīs demonstrated by his using Iblīs as mount to perambulate the world. Cf. Pingree, 1963, pp. 243–4 and *idem*, 1968, pp. 3–4 and n. 3. The culture hero Takhma Urupi riding Angra Mainyu as his horse from one end of the earth to the other is mentioned twice in the Avesta (Yasht 15.11–2, 19.28–9).

[13] *Kitāb al-Fihrist*, Cairo, n.d., pp. 348–50, cited after Pingree, 1968, pp. 3–4.

[14] Cf. Gutas, 1998, pp. 108–10.

[15] Ullmann, 1972, p. 277, n. 5.

[16] *Idem*, pp. 296–7 and n. 6.

[17] Gutas, 1998, p. 15.

[18] Fahd, "Munadjdjim," *EI*[2] VII, 557b.

[19] On Jābir ibn Ḥayyān, see Sezgin, 1971, pp. 132–269.

[20] *Idem*.

[21] Savage-Smith, 2004, p. xxxvii.

[22] Fahd, "Nudjūm, Aḥkām al-," *EI*[2] VIII, 105b; Savage-Smith, 2004, p. xxxvii; Saliba, 1992, pp. 56–63.

[23] Saliba, 1992, pp. 45–67; Michot, 2004, pp. 277–340.

[24] Gutas, 1998, pp. 33–4.

astrologers were leading astrological advisors to this caliph and instrumental in drawing up a horoscope for him determining the day (4 Rabīʿ al-Thānī 145/30 July 762) on which the construction of the city of Baghdad should begin. The Iranophile ʿAbdallāh al-Maʾmūn (r. 198/813–218/833) was the son of Hārūn al-Rashīd by an Iranian slave girl and after his father's death in 193/809 ruled over the eastern half of the caliphate residing in Khurasan. After overthrowing his brother al-Amīn, who ruled over the western half, in a civil war, al-Maʾmūn became caliph in Marw in 198/813 and ruled the caliphate from that city for another five years, during which time he gathered around him astronomers from Ferghana, Chach, Khwārazm and greater Khurasan.[25] In his celebrated historical work al-Masʿūdī reports that under the influence of his Iranian vizier al-Faḍl ibn Sahl Zadhānfarūkh (d. 202/818), al-Maʾmūn:

> used to spend time investigating astrological rulings and prognostications, following what the stars prescribed, and modeling his conduct on that of the past Sāsānian emperors like Ardashīr ibn Bābak [Ardashīr Pāpakān I, r. 224–41] and others.[26]

When he moved to Baghdad in 204/819, he was followed by a host of astronomers and astrologers.[27] The pervasive role that astrology played may be seen in the example of the vizier Ibn Muqla (d. 328/940) who, upon the advice of the astrologers, arranged his meeting with the caliph al-Rāḍī (322/934–329/940) when the Moon was in the zodiac sign Leo governed by the Sun, considered the most auspicious time to meet for secretive affairs.

The science of the celestial bodies was thus of such significance for Islamic rulers that most of their decisions were governed by astrological considerations.[28] This predisposition was equally prevalent among rulers of Turkic stock and is also attested for the Sogdians (who were closely associated with the Turkic empires and played the role of active agents of cultural interaction) in the period immediately preceding Islam. The major assemblies of the Sogdians *(anvāzak)*, whose responsibilities included proclaiming the new king, were composed not only of local rulers and ecclesiastical dignitaries but also of astrologers and soothsayers.[29] During their campaigns, the Turkic Ghaznawid *sulṭāns*, Maḥmūd and Masʿūd were accompanied by their astrologers.[30] At the battle of Dandānaqān in 431/1040, the victorious Saljuqs had an astrologer *(munajjim)* with them, who was rewarded, presumably on account of his correct prognostications, when Ṭoghrıl proclaimed himself ruler of Khurasan.[31] Soothsaying qualities are also attested for members of the ruling house, for according to Ibn al-Athīr, even Ṭoghrıl's cousin, Qutulmish ibn Arslan Isrāʾīl, had astrological skills.[32]

Astrologers from greater Khurasan are known to have moved to the courts of the Rūm Saljuqs of Anatolia. Among them was the mother of the thirteenth-century chronicler Ibn Bībī, known as al-Bībī al-Munajjima ("the lady, the astrologer"), who was from Nīshāpūr and working as astrologer at the court of the Khwārazm-shāh Jalāl al-Dīn. There she met an ambassador of the Rūm Saljuq *sulṭān* ʿAlāʾ al-Dīn Kay Qubādh I of Konya. The meeting made such an impression on the ambassador that he informed the Saljuq *sulṭān* and in due course the family was invited to the court in Konya where she successfully predicted a military victory.[33] The services of the astrologer would frequently be requested before the undertaking of any important action. The astrologer Shams al-Dīn, for instance, is said to have determined the time of the military offensive under the Ayyubid al-Kāmil Nāṣir al-Dīn (r. 615/1218–635/1238).[34] Like their eastern cousins, the Great Saljuqs, some Rūm Saljuq rulers, such as Malik ʿAlāʾ al-Dīn Dāwud Shāh, also practised the science of astrology themselves.[35] Hence throughout medieval Islamic history the science remained popular, astrological practices being patronised not only by members of princely circles but by most segments of Islamic society.[36]

[25] Al-Najaf, *al-Maṭbaʿa al-Haydariyya*, 1368/1949, p. 133, cited after Saliba, 1992, pp. 58 and n. 78.

[26] *Kitāb murūj al-dhahab* ("Meadows of Gold"), tr. and ed. Barbier de Meynard and Pavet de Courteille, 1861–77, vol. 8, pp. 300–1.

[27] Akhmedov, 2000, p. 195.

[28] Cf. *idem*, p. 199.

[29] *Vessantara Jātaka* 64, 1a–4a, cited after Widengren, 1969, p. 117 and n. 61.

[30] Bosworth, 1963, p. 118.

[31] *Idem*, p. 217 and n. 40.

[32] *Idem*, p. 217.

[33] Ibn Bībī, *al-Awāmir al-ʿalāʾiyya*, tr. Duda, 1959, pp. 2–4, 187–8.

[34] Ibn Shaddād, *al-Aʿlāq al-khaṭīra*, vol. 3, 2, pp. 552–3, cited after Saliba, 1992, p. 58, n. 81.

[35] Ibn Bībī, *al-Awāmir al-ʿalāʾiyya*, tr. Duda, 1959, p. 150.

[36] Saliba, 1992, pp. 45–67.

b. *The dragon in medieval Islamic astrology*

The idea that eclipses of the Sun and the Moon were caused by the interference of an eclipse monster was widely held throughout the Eurasian continent and can be traced back to remote antiquity.[37] The fearful monster, which quenched the light of the supreme luminaries by seizing them in its jaws, was generally conceived as a giant serpent or dragon, an iconography thought to be of oriental origin.[38] Its function was thus seen to be that of threatening and "devouring," as well as "delivering" and protecting the great luminaries at certain irregular intervals.[39]

A number of theories arose to explain the dragon's role in the phenomena of solar and lunar eclipses and lunar waxing and waning. Khāleqī-Moṭlaq offers the following summary:

> ...a dragon comes up from hell every month on the eastern side of the sky and swallows a piece of the moon's disc every night until the night comes when no part of the moon can be seen. Then the moon-god kills the dragon from inside its belly and triumphantly re-emerges. In later times, however, the sun took over the moon's role in the celestial combats, and it was the sun which slew the dragon and rescued the moon from the dragon's belly twelve times every year.[40]

Vestiges of these and related beliefs survive in Persian poetry and will be cited below.

The idea that these phenomena were caused by a body whose head and tail intercept the Sun's and the Moon's light was probably related to the emergence of definite ideas as to the nature of the orbits of the Sun and the Moon and their opposite points of intersection between the Moon's orbit and the ecliptic.[41] The classical theory of the dragon myth seems to have been modified in accordance with developments in astrological doctrine at least from late Arsacid and Sasanian times onwards.[42] Sasanian astrologers received from India the notion of Rāhu, a celestial serpent whose head *(siras)* and tail *(ketu)* cause solar and lunar eclipses.[43] In Pahlawī Rāhu was referred to as Gōchihr, his head *sar*, and his tail *dumb*; in Arabic, the latter were respectively called *ra's* and *dhanab*.[44] The great treatise on horoscopic astrology of the first-century Hellenistic astrologer Dorotheus of Sidon, which was first translated into Persian in the third century and into Arabic in the eighth century, contains a chapter (V, 43) entitled "on clarifying the phases of the moon and the head of the dragon and its tail ..." It states that "the head is called the "ascending" and its tail the "descending" and the signs which those learned in the stars call "obscured" are from Leo to Capricorn ..."[45]

Astrology also offered support for Zoroastrian apocalyptic ideas, according to which the planetary bodies were regarded as evil; the

---

[37] Hartner, "Al-Djawzahar," *EI*² II, 501b. Cf. Massé, 1938, vol. 1, p. 172.

[38] In ancient Babylon "the 28th of the month was a day of lamentations when prayers of penitence were offered, because the moon had disappeared from view and was to remain hidden for a few days in the power of the dragon." Green, 1992, p. 29; Hartner, 1938, p. 132, n. 24. The "Chaldeans" considered the dragon to have been created even before the constellations and the planets, and guarding over the universe with its head towards the sunrise and its tail to the sunset. Mackenzie, 1964, p. 525, and *idem*, "Gozihr," *EIr*.

[39] Hartner, 1938, p. 131. Cf. Daneshvari, 1993, p. 20. See also the Babylonian Talmudic tract *Avodah Zarah* ("Mishna on Idolatry," VIII a) in which the dragon is portrayed as devouring the sun. See also Epstein, 1997, p. 76.

[40] Khāleqī-Moṭlaq, "Aždahā II," *EIr*.

[41] Khareghat, 1914, p. 129.

[42] See Panaino, 2005, pp. 73–89, esp. 74–5, who discusses the Zoroastrian practice of deducing omens through ophiomancy (that is to say, divination by serpents) which was linked with astral elements. In this connection it is interesting to consider the reference of the fifth-century Armenian theologian, Eznik of Koghb (*Elc alandoc'*, tr. and ed. Mariès and Mercier, 1959, p. 641, ch. 291) to the pre-Christian belief which saw the heavenly bodies as deities when they worshipped venomous creatures, whereby he implicitly appears to associate astrolatry with ophiolatry.

[43] For an analysis of the origin of the concept of Rāhu, see Mallmann, 1962, p. 81; Markel, 1995, pp. 55–64; Pingree, 2006, p. 240. In the Rigveda (5.40.5–9) Rāhu is known as a demonic being, *Svàr-bhānu-*, which is said to have pierced the Sun with darkness. In post-Vedic mythology *Svàr-bhānu-* is replaced by *Rāhu-*, his name sometimes being conferred upon the latter; *Svàr-bhānu-* perhaps meaning "who has the effulgence of the sun" or "who is affected by the effulgence of the sun." Advanced knowledge of periodical eclipses of the sun and the moon led to the belief in two demonic beings, the red *Rāhu-* and the black *Ketu-*. See Scherer, 1953, pp. 100–1. Representations of Rāhu in a narrative context begin to appear in Indian art slightly earlier than his iconic portrayal as a member of the planetary deities. One of the earliest known portrayals of Rāhu being in a relief of the "Churning of the Ocean" carved over the façade of the doorway of cave temple number nineteen at Udayagiri in the Vidisha district of Madhya Pradesh, which probably dates from *c.* 430 to 450. The planet is shown as a large horrific head with bulging eyes with a fierce, demonic expression turned to the right, his hands probably cupped together with palms facing upward in the gesture of scooping the elixir of immortality (on the legend, see the discussion below). Williams, 1982, p. 87 and pl. 117.

[44] Pingree, 2006, p. 240.

[45] *Dorothei Sidonii Carmen Astrologicum*, tr. and ed. Pingree, D., Leipzig, 1976, p. 322, cited by Beck, 2004, p. 172. Jews writing in Hebrew utilised the terms *ro'sh* or rather *zanav hat-teli* or *hat-tannin* for *ra's* and *dhanab*, whereas it was known in the Byzantine tradition as *hē kephalē* or *hē oura tou drakontos*. See Schlüter, 1982, p. 138.

"good" luminaries, the Sun and the Moon, were removed from the category of the seven planets whose intrusion brought injustice into the world.[46] Consequently the Sun and the Moon were substituted by two "demonic" opponents, the head and tail of the dragon (Pahl. *gōchihr* which stems from the Avestan *gao chithra*, "holding the seed of cattle," formerly the stock epithet of the Moon[47]).[48] According to the *Bundahishn*, Gōchihr is portrayed as "similar to a snake with the head in Gemini *(dō-pahikar)* and the tail in Centaurus *(nēmasp)*, so that at all times there are six constellations between its head and tail."[49]

In contradistinction to the original meaning of *gao chithra*, the light and fecundity attribute of the Moon, the dragon's head *(gōchihr sar)* and tail *(gōchihr dumb)* came to represent the demon of eclipses that intercepts the light of the luminaries, the personified dark principle and direct antagonist of the luminaries.[50] This led to the concept of a polarity of good and evil throughout the cosmos, the eclipse demon being referred to as Dark Sun and Dark Moon, "dark" meaning "obscured," and "eclipsed."[51] Thus, according to the *Bundahishn*, the serpent-like *(mār homānāg)* Gōchihr and Mūsh Parīg, with tail *(dumbōmand)* and wings *(parrwar)*, are said to be the evil opponents of the stellar constellations and are therefore bound to the Sun's path to restrain their capacity to cause harm.[52] The expulsion of evil from the sky is manifested by the plunging to earth of Gōchihr,[53] who sets the earth on fire and whose permanent body will only be destroyed by resurrection.[54] The eclipse dragon also played a part in Manichaeism as Anabibazon and Katabibazon, the head and tail of the dragon.[55] According to Manichaean cosmogony the two dragons were hung up and fettered in the lowest heaven and two angels, male and female, were placed there to cause them to revolve continuously.[56]

In the history of ancient Indian astronomy throughout the pre-Siddhāntic period, only Rāhu (the *grahaṇa*, "seizer") was held "responsible" for causing eclipses by devouring the Sun and Moon. Ketu (the tail of the dragon), understood as a planet[57] that generates comets with its fiery tail, is first mentioned in the *Atharvaveda* (19.9.8-10).[58] Both Rāhu and Ketu appear in the great epic *Mahābhārata* (1.5.15–7), in which the demon Rāhu allied himself with the celestial gods in the struggle against the world serpent, Ananta. After the victorious event, he assumed a disguise and thus succeeded in drinking from the most beneficial of substances, the *amṛta* (lit. "non-dying"; Av. *haoma*, Vedic Skt. *sóma*)[59] drink containing the miraculous herb of immortality. But the Sun and the Moon having detected his deception denounced him to the gods, whereupon Vishnu swiftly threw his discus *(sudarśanacakra)* and severed Rāhu's head. However, the drink had already produced its effect so that his head and tail both survive, immortalised, as invisible planets and intransigent enemies of the luminaries. As a consequence, the Sun and the Moon are periodically – in symbolic terms – "swallowed" or "disappear in" the vengeful monster that thus causes solar and lunar eclipses.[60]

In the later, "scientific" phase, when Indian notions were transmitted to Western Asia and the wider Iranian world, the two parts of the

---

[46] Khareghat, 1914, p. 129; Brunner, "Astronomy and Astrology in the Sasanian Period, s.v. Astrology and Astronomy in Iran," *EIr*, pp. 862–8.

[47] Zaehner, 1955, repr. 1972, p. 164, n. E; MacKenzie, 1964, p. 515, n. 26.

[48] *Bundahishn* ch. 5, A. 5, pp. 52.12–53.1, cited after Brunner, "Astronomy and Astrology in the Sasanian Period," *EIr*, pp. 862–8. Cf. Hartner, "Al-Djawzahar," *EI*² II, 501b.

[49] *Bundahishn* ch. 5 A. 5. Skjærvø, "Aždahā I," *EIr*. Cf. Zaehner, 1955, repr. 1972, p. 164, n. E. Also MacKenzie, 1964, pp. 515, 525.

[50] Hartner, 1938, p. 153. Cf. Duchèsne-Guillemin, 1990, pp. 17–9.

[51] *Bundahishn* (ch. 5.4, p. 49.13–5) and the late ninth-century catechism *Shkand-gumānīg wizār* ("Doubt Dispelling Exposition") 4.46, cited after Brunner, "Astronomy and Astrology in the Sasanian Period," *EIr*.

[52] "[The sun's opponent, the "tailed Mūsh Parīg"] is tied to the sun's chariot but occasionally becomes loose and does great harm"; *Bundahishn* ch. 5.4.5 A. 6–7, pp. 50.6–7, 53.1–5, and *Shkand-gumānīg wizār* 4.46, cited after Brunner, "Astronomy and Astrology in the Sasanian Period," *EIr*. Cf. Zaehner, 1955, repr. 1972, p. 164, n. E. MacKenzie, 1964, pp. 513, 516; Hartner, 1938, p. 151.

[53] *Bundahishn* 34.17, p. 225.1–3, cited after Brunner, "Astronomy and Astrology in the Sasanian Period," *EIr*.

[54] *Bundahishn* 30.31, cited after Khareghat, 1914, p. 128.

[55] For instance in the Coptic *Kephalaia* (ch. 69), cited after Beck, 2004, pp. 177–8.

[56] Boyce, 1975, p. 60 text y 1 with note; Skjærvø, "Aždahā I," *EIr*.

[57] For the evolution of the meanings of "ketu," see Hartner, 1938, pp. 152–3.

[58] Scherer, 1953, pp. 101–3, for further names of Rāhu and Ketu, see esp. pp. 102–5. Cf. Markel, 1995, pp. 56, 65; Santoro, 2006, p. 547.

[59] For a brief resumé on the discussion of the etymology of the term *amṛta*, see Long, 1976, pp. 181–2, n. 22. See also Janda, 2010, pp. 29, 55.

[60] Hartner, 1938, p. 131, and *idem*, "Al-Djawzahar," *EI*² II, 501b.

eclipse monster were identified with the lunar nodes, which play a crucial role in the eclipses.[61] At the beginning of celestial motion the head or forepart, Rāhu, that is to say the ascending node of the Moon's orbit upon the ecliptic, was in Gemini and Ketu, the tail or hindpart of the bisected serpent-monster, in other words the descending node, was in Sagittarius (*al-qaws*, lit. "bow"), often represented as an armed centaur.[62] The 180° extent of the dragon reflects the fact that the nodes occupy diametrically opposite points of the ecliptic. Hence the dragon's body is conceived as arched across the sky.[63]

The demon of the eclipses Rāhu is well-known not only in the Brahmanic tradition, but also in Buddhism.[64] In the Buddhist *Jātaka* stories of the previous births of Gautama Buddha, which were familiar throughout the Central Asian region, repeated reference is made to the Moon gripped between Rāhu's jaws, or being liberated from the latter.[65] Thus, in the *Gandhāra Jātaka*, the king of Gandhāra chose to become an ascetic after observing a lunar eclipse, explaining that:

> Taking the moon's orb seized by Rāhu as my theme I forsook my great kingdom and took the religious life.

because:

> There is the moon's pure orb become dark by trouble from outside; now this kingdom is a trouble to me: I will take the religious life so that the kingdom does not make me dark as Rāhu does the moon's orb.[66]

In the *Buddhacarita* Siddhārtha's son is called Rāhula "with the face of Rāhu's adversary."[67] It is of note that in some Pali texts the demon Rāhu is said not to devour the Sun and the Moon, "but merely to caress them with his hand."[68] In the well-known story of the *Candrasūtra* (Pali *Candimā-sutta*, "Discourse on the Moon") the Buddha reprimands Rāhu and directs him to release the Moon at once which Rāhu does, knowing that otherwise his head will be split into seven pieces.[69] The Buddha thus delivers the Moon (the god dwelling in the Moon), who had appealed to him for refuge, from Rāhu's clutches.[70] The contextual and conceptual metamorphoses of the motif thus attest to a mechanism of continuity of these essential thought systems which governed the Central Asian world and beyond.

Yet even when the scientific causes were clear, the mythological interpretation of the phenomenon survives. This fact and the ensuing syncretism is expounded by Hartner:

> We might suppose that clear insight into the physical causes of eclipses could have thrown mythological tradition into the background. But this has not been the case. What we observe is that mythological and astronomical elements contract an intimate fusion. The nodes of the moon's orbit are simply identified with the eclipse monster itself: with the Hindus, Rāhu becomes the ascending, Ketu the descending node; with Persians and Arabs, the head and tail of the Djawzahr play the same role.[71]

In Islamic astronomy the Persian *gōchihr,* called *al-jawzahar* or *al-tinnīn* (also *azhdahā*, "the giant dragon"), was sometimes represented as a bipartite or double-headed dragon. It is the circumpolar constellation Draco, "represented as a very long serpent with many convolutions; it is coiled around the north pole of the ecliptic,"[72] which is sometimes metaphorically applied to the Milky Way.[73] The *Viṣṇudharmottara Purāṅa* (III.67) describes how the first sacred waist band or girdle (*ayyaṅga* which is closely related to the Iranian *aiwiyaonghen* that is worn by every devout Zoroastrian) was presented to the sun god

[61] Cf. Hartner, 1938, p. 131, and *idem,* "Al-Djawzahar," *EI*² II, 501b.

[62] Brunner, "Astronomy and Astrology in the Sasanian Period," *EIr*, II, p. 867. The dragon head projecting from the centaur's tail represents the descending node's exaltation in Sagittarius; however, although the latter is the dragon's "tail" *(dhanab)* and not its "head" *(ra's)*, and hence the representation of the "head" is an iconographic inconsistency, it has come to symbolise the astrological association. Hartner, 1973–4, p. 110.

[63] *Bundahishn* 5.4, p. 49.13–5, cited after Brunner, "Astronomy and Astrology in the Sasanian Period," *EIr*, p. 867.

[64] Cf. Santoro, 2006, p. 547.

[65] Cf. *eadem*, p. 547.

[66] Cowell, 1897, repr. 2000, vol. 3, pp. 222–3.

[67] Johnston, 1936, repr. 2004, p. 29. Cf. Santoro, 2006, p. 547. The concept is evoked in yet another line: "Deliver Rāhula from grief for his parent as the full moon from eclipse by Rāhu." See Johnston, 1936, repr. 2004, p. 129.

[68] Malalasekera, G.P., *Dictionary of Pāli Proper Names*, 2 vols., 1938, repr. 1974, vol. 2, pp. 735–7, cited after Strong, 1992, p. 156.

[69] *Idem*, p. 156. The *Candrasūtra* was also translated into ancient Uighur, see Zieme, 2000, pp. 65–80.

[70] Waldschmidt, 1970.

[71] Hartner, 1938, p. 131.

[72] Al-Bīrūnī, *Kitāb al-Tafhīm*, tr. and ed. Wright, 1934, p. 71.

[73] MacKenzie, 1964, pp. 521–2, n. 53, 525. *The Mystical and Visionary Treatises of Suhrawardi*, tr. Thackston, 1982, p. 113, n. 42.

by the king of serpents, Vāsuki, and represented the starry band of the Milky Way.[74] In a verse of the late eleventh-century Iranian poet Labībī the seven heads of the dragon represent the heavenly spheres and the universe.[75]

Together with the acculturation of astronomical knowledge, astrological iconography emerged in the form of visual conceptualisations that were regularly featured in medieval imagery. These were emblematically transferred onto architectural sculpture as well as portable objects, in particular metalwork and ceramics. Astrological considerations also had a profound bearing on the artistic conventions of the iconography of the dragon. Its representation in medieval Islamic astrology has been addressed in a number of studies, foremost among which remains Hartner's, in which he demonstrates the influence of the conceptualisation of the two "lunar nodes" *(al-ʿuqdatāni)* on Islamic artisans.[76]

As seen in sources that pre-date the Islamic period, the crucial aspect of *al-jawzahar* is that it consists of two nodes of the Moon's orbit or "points at which (the) two [great] circles of the sphere intersect,"[77] in other words the two points where the course of the Moon crosses the plane of the ecliptic from south to north: the "head of the dragon" *(raʾs al-tinnīn)* is formed by the ascending node of the Moon's orbit, and, correspondingly, the "tail of the dragon" *(dhanab al-tinnīn)* by the descending node.[78] This associates it with both solar and lunar eclipses; the latter were attributed to the occurrence of a conjunction, or opposition, of the Sun and Moon (New Moon or Full Moon, respectively) in or near the lunar nodes.

In medieval Islam especially, the astrological influence of the eclipse of the Sun is considered one of the foremost signs of the impending destruction of the world.[79] In the Qurʾān the latter is repeatedly described among the signs of perturbations of heavenly bodies (*sūra* 75, 8–9; and 81, 1). Early Islamic tradition frequently describes the occurrence of an eclipse of the Sun during the period of the Prophet Muḥammad's residence in Medina.[80] On this occasion the Prophet is reported to have said "that he had never been so greatly filled with fear," and the commentaries add to this, "that he thought that the Hour had come, and to illustrate it he is reported to have said that he saw Paradise and Hell so close to him that he could have gathered a bunch of grapes from the land of the blessed, had he stretched out his hand."[81] According to Abū Saʿīd al-Sijzī's comprehensive tenth-century astrological compilation on the "Conjunctions and Revolutions of the Years of the World" which was based on earlier sources, a solar eclipse indeed indicated the death of Muḥammad as well as the accession of the first caliph Abū Bakr.[82]

The significance accorded to the eclipse is reflected in the bi-partite "dragon" that was seen as temporarily "devouring" the Sun and the Moon at certain irregular intervals, and then disgorging or "delivering," them – since the two planets always appear to emerge unscathed from their temporary eclipse by the "dragon." This non-Ptolemaic concept played a prominent role in astrological associations whereby the two nodes were treated as though they were real celestial bodies, in other words extra, albeit invisible, "planets," or fictitious nodes.[83] They were conceived as an eighth and a ninth planet, the only difference between them and the original seven planets being that contrary to the others their movement was westwards or "retrograde," rather than eastwards.[84]

Ghaznawid and Ghurid military campaigns in India brought not only extensive booty, but resulted at the same time in an influx of scholars, craftsmen and a variety of artisans, all of whom came with their own indigenous iconographies, contributing perhaps to the diffusion of the iconography of *al-jawzahar*. The great scholar Abū Rayḥān Muḥammad ibn Aḥmad al-Bīrūnī had accompanied *sulṭān* Maḥmūd, possibly as official astrologer, on several of his military expedi-

[74] Carter, 1981, p. 80 and n. 27.

[75] M. Dabīrsīāqī, *Ganj-i bāz yāfta*, Tehran, 2535/1355 Sh., 1976, cited after Khāleqī-Moṭlaq, "Aždahā II," *EIr.*

[76] Hartner, 1938, and *idem*, "Al-Djawzahar," *EI*² II, 501b. Cf. Öney, 1969a, pp. 193–216; Otto-Dorn, 1978–9, pp. 125–36; Azarpay, 1978, pp. 363–74.

[77] See the definition of *al-jawzahar* in Abū ʿAbd Allāh Muḥammand al-Khwārizmī's *Mafātīḥ al-ʿUlūm*, cited after Hartner, 1938, p. 120.

[78] Cf. Kharegat, 1914, pp. 126–8; MacKenzie, 1964, p. 515.

[79] Wensinck, 1923, p. 193.

[80] Al-Bukhārī, *Mawāqīt al-Ṣalāt*, b. 51, cited by Wensinck, 1923, p. 193 and n. 6.

[81] Al-Bukhārī, *Kitāb al-ʿItq*, b. 3, cited by Wensinck, 1923, p. 193 and n. 7.

[82] Al-Sijzī, *Kitāb al-qirānāt wa taḥāwīl sinī al-ʿālam*, as cited in Pingree, 1968, pp. 70–127, 118–9 (the table of the horoscope of the solar eclipse foreboding the death of the Prophet).

[83] Beck, 2004, p. 161 and n. 29.

[84] *Idem*, p. 161.

tions to northwest India.[85] In his *Kitāb al-Tafhīm li-awā'il ṣinā'at al-tanjīm* ("Book of Instruction in the Elements of the Art of Astrology"), written upon his return to Ghazna in 422/1031, he refers to the two fictitious nodes, the eighth and a ninth planet, as knot *('uqda)* and point of crossing *(majāz)*.[86] In spite of his statement that "they are not real planets," the same author does however record the position of the *ra's al-tinnīn* and the *dhanab al-tinnīn* in the various astrological tables included in his texts.[87] Much earlier, in the work *On The Great Conjunctions*, or the *Aḥkām Taḥāwīl Sinī al-Mawālid*, the astrologer Abū Ma'shar (d. 272/886) had already referred to the points of exaltation for the nodes of the Moon which for the dragon's head is in Gemini 3°, and for the tail in Sagittarius 3°.[88]

The "node of the Moon's orbit" however is an integral part of the iconography of the eclipse monster, portrayed as loop or twisted knot, sometimes visualised as a pretzel- or heart-shaped knot. This is reflected in the symbolism of the personification of comets, Ketu, visualised on the *navagraha* reliefs that represent the nine Indian planetary deities, which are similarly illustrated with a human torso and a serpentine tail terminating in a knot.[89] The earliest surviving representation of Rāhu and Ketu in India is carved on a *navagraha* lintel from Uttar Pradesh, dating from *c.* 600 or slightly later, in which Ketu is represented as a half-ophidian figure sitting on his coiled serpentine tail beside the cephalic Rāhu (fig. 140).[90]

Individual depictions of *jawzahar* – Draco as eighth planet next to the seven traditional planets, comprising the Sun, the Moon, Saturn, Jupiter, Mars, Venus and Mercury,[91] often portray a cross-legged figure holding a dragon in each hand. The figure is shown to hold either a pair of upright dragons, their bodies forming a loop,[92] or vertical staffs (figs. 113–116); both the coiling bodies and the allegorical staffs end in confronted dragon heads with gaping snouts. It is significant that representations of the planet *jawzahar* thereby make use of the emblematic portrayal of the cosmic ruler mentioned earlier, framed by dragon-headed staffs, ubiquitously employed on visual art from the mid-eleventh to early thirteenth century and associated with the ancient concept of the "Master of the Dragons." The choice of this cosmic symbolism underlines the prominence accorded to *jawzahar* which gives an indication of the magnitude of the potential effects the planet could have on the course of human events. The conception of the central figure as dragon-tamer thereby perhaps reflects the apparent necessity to harness the forces of this planet.

The planetary character of the two nodes of *al-jawzahar* indicates that they are traversing the plane of the ecliptic. With respect to the signs, the planets have a "domicilium" as well as a place of exaltation *(sharaf)* and dejection *(hubūṭ)*. These astronomical terms respectively define the points most distant from and closest to the earth, especially in reference to the elliptical orbit of the Moon. In astrology they relate to the point of maximum and minimum influence of one of the seven traditional planets and of the two nodes of *al-jawzahar* when they find themselves in association with one of the constellations visualised as one of the twelve signs of the zodiac.

In the Irano-Turkish territories, the eclipse pseudo-planet *(al-jawzahar)* is often shown at the point of exaltation of its head or tail in Gemini, as for instance on a silver- and copper-inlaid brass ewer from Herat, formerly in the Nuhad

---

[85] Boilot, "al-Bīrūnī (Bērūnī), Abu 'l Rayḥān Muḥammad b. Aḥmad," *EI*² I, 1136a.

[86] Tr. and ed. Wright, 1934, pp. 91–2.

[87] *Idem*, pp. 255, 258.

[88] Hartner (1938, p. 133 and n. 30) refers to *De magnis coniunctionibus*, the Latin version translated by Johannes Hispalensis, printed at Augsburg in 1489 (repr. Venice, 1515), which contains a chapter dealing with the planetary influence of the nodes as a figure of the "dragon" with its head and tail twisted around two nodes (reproduced in *idem*, fig. 10). Cf. al-Bīrūnī's references in his *Kitāb al-Tafhīm*, tr. and ed. Wright, 1934, p. 358.

[89] Ketu's serpent tail is alluded to in the *Agnipurāṇa*; see De Mallmann, 1962, p. 86.

[90] The earliest western Indian representation is found on a fragmentary lintel from Alwar district in Rajasthan, which probably dates from *c.* 600 to 650 (Markel, 1995, fig. 29; Government Museum, Alwar). For later depictions, see also Hartner, 1938, pp. 134, 138, figs. 6–8. For a discussion of the *navagraha* reliefs, see Pingree, 1964–5, pp. 249–67; Markel, 1995, pp. 19–68 and 129–76.

[91] Hartner, 1938, pp. 114–38. In later medieval Indian literature both nodes, Rāhu *(ra's al-tinnīn)*, and Ketu *(dhanab al-tinnīn)*, were attributed the same importance as the other seven planets, hence there were a total of nine planets; *idem*, p. 133, cf. also p. 151.

[92] For instance, on a late twelfth- or early thirteenth-century copper alloy inkwell inlaid with silver from Western Central Asia (Pugachenkova and Rempel', fig. 196, and fig. 197, line drawing), or on a thirteenth-century silver-inlaid copper alloy candlestick from Mesopotamia (Baer, 1983, p. 256, fig. 208).

Es-Said Collection, now in the National Museum of Qatar in Doha (fig. 141).[93] In Islamic tradition, the planetary eclipse in Sagittarius is generally rendered as a centaur taking aim with a bow at its long dragon-headed tail and shooting an arrow into the dragon's mouth. On the Qatar ewer the sign is accordingly portrayed as the protome of a winged quadruped dragon with tongue protruding from the gaping mouth rising from the looped tail (fig. 142). A sculptural example of the planetary eclipse in Sagittarius is depicted among eight astrological reliefs carved onto the pillars of the Tigris bridge, near the city of Jazīrat ibn ʿUmar (present-day Cizre), Anatolia. Among the reliefs is the upright knotted protome of a dragon with gaping mouth and curled-up snout tip, oriented towards the figure of a centaur shooting with a bow and arrow into its mouth. The bridge was commissioned by the *wazīr* of Mosul, Jamāl al-Dīn Muḥammad al-Iṣfahānī. The *wazīr*'s imprisonment in 558/1163 provides a *terminus ante quem* for the construction of the bridge and its astrological relief sculptures.[94] As pointed out by Hartner, the reliefs are one of the earliest-known sculptural examples "in which the Islamic artist obviously grants the same rights to one or both of these pseudo-planets as to the seven real ones, while in India this had been the rule centuries before."[95]

Similarly, depictions of *al-jawzahar* threatening the Sun and the Moon, or their respective zodiacal animals, the lion and the crab, became prevalent in the decorative programmes of objects, as evidenced in the depictions on the same ewer (figs. 143 and 144). The importance of the eclipse pseudo-planet is such that most of the roundels on this ewer show the signs of the zodiac and planets inhabited with monster heads with long floppy ears growing from scrolling tendrils (as shown for example in the depiction of "Moon in Cancer") that Hartner identifies with "the dragon progeny threatening the luminaries or, vicariously, their *domicilia* and *exaltations*."[96] However, he has qualified the astrological interpretation suggesting that "in all probability, various elements – astronomical, astrological and mythological – were here fused in one."[97] This shows that the astrological veracity of such details was less important than their exemplary significance. It is moreover noteworthy that the monster heads with long floppy ears issue from vegetation, which for its association with fertility generally has positive connotations. It may therefore be hypothesised that the depiction of "dragon progeny" together with the signs of the zodiac and the planets was intended to have a beneficial influence on the paths of the luminaries.

A related large silver-inlaid brass ewer, housed in the Georgian State Museum, Tbilisi, Georgia, which is decorated on the shoulder with the signs of the zodiac and the planets, bears inscriptions that not only give the name of the maker, one Maḥmūd ibn Muḥammad al-Harawī and the date, the month of Shaʿban 577/19 December 1181–17 January 1182, but also state that the "seven heavenly bodies, however proud they may be, are protection for the one who works so."[98] As James Allan states, "from this poem it is evident that the inlayer saw those images as protection for himself against evil."[99] It further underlines the overall magical and prophylactic quality that was ascribed to the iconography of the signs of the zodiac and the planets. The frequency of their

---

[93] *Jawzahar* at the points of exaltation of its head or tail in Gemini is also depicted at the top of the lid of the penbox from Iran (signed by Maḥmūd ibn Sunqur on the hasp and dated 680/1281–2; on this penbox see also pp. 96, 98 and fig. 93), which bears roundels in three groups of four containing symbols of the zodiac with their ruling planets. Cf. Hartner, 1938, p. 138 (misprint of dates), figs. 14 and 15 (roundel representing "Gemini"); *idem*, 1973–4, pp. 115 and fig. 9 (left); Pope and Ackerman, eds., 1938–39, repr. 1964–81, vol. 13, p. 1336.B; Barrett, 1949, pl. 33 top; *Legacy*, 2002, cat. no. 158, fig. 46. The same motif is shown on an early thirteenth-century copper alloy inkwell, inlaid with silver, attributed to Iran or Syria, now in the Metropolitan Museum of Art, New York; cf. Baer, 1983, p. 257, fig. 209 (detail of p. 79, fig. 59).

[94] Meinecke, 1996, p. 60. On the reliefs of Jazīrat ibn ʿUmar, see Preusser, 1911, pl. 40; Hartner, 1938, p. 134 and fig. 2 (photograph at bottom left), and *idem*, 1973–4, pp. 108, 110; Gierlichs, 1996, pl. 47.4. A Sagittarius rendered as a centaur shooting an arrow towards his own tail which terminates in a dragon head is depicted in a Georgian astrological treatise, probably illustrated under Islamic influence in 1188; Amiranašvili, 1966, pl. 56. See also p. 19, n. 36. A comparable figure is represented as centaur-archer shooting an arrow backwards at the dragon head emerging from its tail on the coinage of the Artuqid ruler of Mardin, Nāṣir al-Dīn Artuq Arslan ibn Il Ghāzī (599/1203–637/1239); Roxburgh, ed. 2004, p. 398, cat. no. 86; *What the Coins Tell Us*, 2009, p. 102; Hauptmann von Gladiss, ed., 2006, pp. 107–8, figs. 15, 16. The same emblem also figures on the coinage of the ʿAbbasid caliph al-Nāṣir (577/1181–620/1223); *eadem*, 2006, p. 107, cat. no. 15.

[95] Hartner, 1938, p. 132.

[96] *Idem*, 1959, pp. 237–9, and *idem*, 1973–4, p. 112, 118.

[97] *Idem*, 1973–4, pp. 112–3.

[98] Loukonine and Ivanov, 2003, pp. 116–7, cat. no. 117 (with the inscription in Arabic and English). Cf. Allan, 1982a, repr. 1999, p. 49; Atil, Chase, and Jett, 1985, p. 17, fig. 6. The translation given is based on the rendering by Allan. See also p. 36, n. 6.

[99] Allan, 1982a, repr. 1999, p. 49.

depiction, in particular on portable items, moreover emphasises the prodigious cultural significance of the signs of the zodiac and the planets in the medieval Islamic world. The prominent depiction of *al-jawzahar* on objects such as these Herati ewers "evidently originates," as Hartner has underlined, "not in a doctrinal astrological conception, but in a purely metaphysical, one," being associated with "the antagonism between the celestial luminaries and the terrestrial light-devouring dragon."[100]

As mentioned, a solar or lunar eclipse *(al-kusūf)* can occur only when the Moon is at one of the points of crossing *(majāz)*, or nodes. In his *Kitāb al-Tafhīm* al-Bīrūnī, moreover, notes that the latter are perceived as having separate natures, the head being hot, auspicious, and indicating increase of wealth etc. and the tail being cold, bringing misfortune, and indicating diminution of wealth, etc.[101] In addition he records the information that "some people say that the dragon's head is male and diurnal and the tail female and nocturnal."[102]

From about the twelfth-century symbolic personifications of Sol and Luna, often shown together with the dragon motif, were widely applied to portable objects, especially on metalwork, from greater Khurasan to the Anatolian region. By virtue of its very characteristic as an eclipse dragon *al-jawzahar* was directly linked to the Sun and the Moon. The two luminaries are among the representations of the eight planets (the pseudo-planet *jawzahar* is here represented as eighth "planet") on the lid of a covered copper alloy bowl, known as Vaso Vescovali, made in the Khurasan region in about 1200.[103] A three-faced Sun, akin to the one featured on the Qatar ewer (fig. 143), surmounts a winged figure who, seated on a pointed support and holding up the luminary's "dais," is symmetrically flanked by two confronted attendants behind whom long-eared *jawzahar*-like heads grow out of stems which curl behind their waists (fig. 145). The Moon consists of a human figure holding up with its four arms (an image probably informed by Indian prototypes) a large crescent which frames the entire upper body, while squatting on a "dais" supported by quadruped protomes, probably horses. The addorsed attendants are related to those of the Sun but are clad in more angular attire with the *jawzahar*-like heads growing from their waists (fig. 146). Significantly, as Hartner has observed, "the scene has no menacing character."[104] A remarkable depiction of a personified Moon in Cancer is shown on the so-called "Wade Cup," dated 596/1200–622/1225, now in the Cleveland Museum of Art, featuring a winged figure holding up a crescent moon and with splayed legs surmounting the crab; the legs of the moon figure are held in the claws of the crab and both are flanked on either side by long-eared dragon progeny that springs from the base (fig. 147).[105]

The personifications of the Sun and the Moon are also featured above a pair of addorsed knotted dragons, serving here as support for the luminaries, as part of a decorative programme on a large copper alloy basin inlaid with silver of the thirteenth-century *atābeg* Badr al-Dīn Lu'lu' (618/1222–657/1259) of Mosul (fig. 148).[106] The depictions reveal an interest in the translating of entities beyond the domain of humankind, such as the two luminaries, into human guise.[107] In this context it is interesting to recall that this also corresponds to the Turkish tradition of conceiving the two great luminaries as living beings.[108] The selective visualisation of the Sun and the Moon and the menace posed to them in the form of solar and lunar eclipses, ascribed to *al-jawzahar*, is related to the daily relevance afforded to the two luminaries in human affairs and existence.[109]

While the dragon is mainly associated with the eclipses and, hence, the "devouring of light," its positive aspect as giver of light and, consequently, as protector of light is often more difficult to gauge although references are found in Iranian poetry.[110] The polymath Asadī Ṭūsī accordingly writes in his epic *Garshāsp-nāma:*

> the dragon that gives the sun also takes it back by its poison.[111]

---

[100] Hartner, 1938, p. 138.
[101] Tr. and ed. Wright, 1934, p. 233.
[102] Al-Bīrūnī introduced these concepts into Muslim literature, though not without misgivings as to their veracity, qualifying this information as "quite illogical" (*idem*, p. 234).
[103] Cf. Hartner, 1973–4, p. 119; Ward, 1993, p. 79.
[104] Hartner, 1973–4, p. 119.
[105] Rice, 1955, pl. VII b; Hartner, 1959, p. 235, fig. 4.
[106] Cf. Saxl, 1912, p. 164 and fig. 10; Sarre and van Berchem, 1907, pp. 22, 27, figs. 1 and 13.
[107] Pancaroğlu, 2000, p. 197.
[108] Roux, 1979, p. 179.
[109] Pancaroğlu, 2000, p. 204.
[110] Cf. Daneshvari, 1993, p. 20.
[111] Asadī Ṭūsī, *Garshāsp-nāma*, pp. 475–6, cited after Daneshvari, 1993, p. 21.

The simile "the sun is delivered from the dragon" in the romantic epic, *Wīs u Rāmīn*,[112] almost certainly of Arsacid Parthian origin, expresses a related stance. It was translated and versified by Fakhr al-Dīn Gurgānī around 1050 for the first Saljuq *sulṭān* Ṭoghrıl I, his minister Abū Naṣr ibn Manṣūr, and his governor Abu 'l-Fatḥ ibn Muḥammad of Iṣfahān.

The eleventh-century Iranian poet Masʿūd-i Saʿd-i Salmān (*c.* 440/1046–7–*c.* 515/1121–2) whose family came from Hamadān, enjoyed status and fame at the Ghaznawid courts of Lahore and Ghazna in his youth and again in his later years. But he also suffered the misery of some eighteen years of incarceration, resulting in the prison-poetry *(ḥabsiyya)* for which he is renowned and in which he metaphorically employs both fire and dragon imagery:

> My heart has become like a fire temple,
> fearing it I don't breath even for a moment,
> until from the heat of my dragon-like heart
> my mouth fills with fire.

However he emerges from the dragon's clutches "like a cool cypress in a garden"[113] thereby employing the conventional metaphor which implies that he comes forth unscathed from an eclipse or other impending calamity.

Comparable imagery governs Niẓāmī Ganjawī's description in the first part of his *Iskandar-nāma*, the *Sharaf-nāma*, of Iskandar's destruction of the fire temples of the Iranian Zoroastrians during his conquest of Iran (an action for which the historical Alexander is not responsible but that perhaps reflects Niẓāmī's vague memory of an Iranian religious resistance to Hellenism).[114] Iskandar arrives at a fire temple dominated by a powerful priestess, Āẓar Humā, who transforms herself into a fire-breathing black dragon to guard the holy fire of the temple, hence implying that the dark dragon protects the fire and therefore the light and, by association, the luminaries.[115] Through his talismanic powers Balīnūs (Apollonius) helps to break the resistance of the priestess and when she is brought in front of Iskandar, Balīnūs declares "this black dragon is the moon [a moon-faced beauty]" a pun that implicitly also refers to the dragon's association with light and, by inference, perhaps his implicit role as the deliverer and protector of light.[116]

The esoteric conceptualisation of the dragon is illuminated in the allegory of a hero's spiritual journey in *A Tale of Occidental Exile* written by the mystic Shihāb al-Dīn Yaḥyā Suhravardī (d. 587/1191):

> If you desire to be delivered along with your brother [i.e., speculative reason, the guide (*ʿāṣim*)], do not put off traveling. Cling to your rope, which is the dragon's tail *(jawzahr)* of the holy sphere that dominates the regions of the lunar eclipse [the realms of the eclipse denoting the world of ascetic practice].[117]

The hero passes beyond the material world and reaches a light, the active intellect, which is the governor of this world. He places the light in the mouth of the dragon, the world of the elements, that "dwelt in the tower of the water-wheel [i.e., the sky which turns like a wheel], beneath which was the Sea of Clysma [i.e., the water below the sky] and above which are the stars the origin of whose rays was known only to the Creator and those "who are well-grounded in knowledge."" [118]

The metaphysical aspect of the bi-partite dragon is further evoked in a passage of the fables and anecdotes of the early thirteenth-century *Marzubān-nāma* with the allegorical allusion, "at dawn, when the black snake of night cast the sun's disc out of the mouth of the east,"[119] hence once again implying a double-headed dragon delivering the luminary and the creation of light.

The luminary aspect of the dragon is also reflected, as Abbas Daneshvari has pointed out, by its flanking the mount of finger rings (fig. 30).[120] In Farīd al-Dīn Aṭṭār's *Ilāhī-nāma* ("Book of God"), the magic signet ring of Solomon, an

[112] Tr. cited after Daneshvari, 1993, p. 21.

[113] *Dīwān-i ashʿār-i Masʿūd-i Saʿd, qaṣīda* 205, tr. Sharma, 2000, pp. 94–5. On Masʿūd-i Saʿd-i Salmān, see also Rypka, 1968, p. 196. Cf. the early Indian conception as expressed in the Vedic myth in which, after his defeat by Indra, the dragon Vala (*valá-*, meaning "enclosure") frees the goddess of dawn, Ushas, whom he had imprisoned. See p. 87, n. 4. Janda, 2010, pp. 45–70, esp. 27, 63, 79, 266, 270.

[114] Cf. Stoneman, 1991, p. 2.

[115] Niẓāmī, *Sharaf-nāma*, ed. Dastgardī, V., Tehran, 1936, p. 244, cited by Daneshvari, 1993, p. 21; Niẓāmī, *Dīwān*, pp. 974–5, cited in *Pseudo-Apollonius of Tyana*, tr. and ed. Weisser, 1990, p. 27.

[116] Ed. Dastgardī, V., Tehran, 1936, p. 244, cited by Daneshvari, 1993, p. 21.

[117] *The Mystical and Visionary Treatises of Suhrawardi*, tr. Thackston, 1982, p. 102 and ns. r and s.

[118] *Idem*, p. 105 and ns. uu, vv, ww.

[119] Tr. Levy, 1959, p. 51. Cf. Saʿīd al-Dīn Warāwīnī, *Marzubān-nāma*, ed. Rūshan, M., 2 vols., Tehran, 1978, pp. 96–7, cited by Daneshvari, 1993, pp. 20–1.

[120] Daneshvari, 1993, p. 21.

allusion to the sun, is guarded by a dragon.[121] By analogy, dragons flanking the cosmic ruler (figs. 113–116), further increase the luminary symbolism of the ruler.[122] Even more explicitly, Abu 'l-Ḥasan Farrukhī, the celebrated court poet of Sīstān (Seistan), links the luminous sun with the roaring dragon when he praises the character of his patron:

> In your banquets, you are an illuminating sun
> In combat, you are a roaring dragon.[123]

Reminiscences of ancient cosmogonical notions may be gauged from Armenian lore recorded by Khorenatsi relating to the Median king Astyages, the Armenian arch-enemy referred to as Azhi Dahāka, the archetype of evil misrule, whose first wife, Anoysh, was called the "mother of the dragons."[124] Her name, Anoysh, however literally signifies "immortal, luminous, perfumed."[125] Moreover, her association with the monstrous dragon, to whom she gives numerous offspring, recalls certain cosmogonies in which one of the two primordial entities is "infinite light, serene and joyous" and the other "a frightening and dark obscurity, coiled up in twisting spirals akin to those of a serpent."[126]

It is also interesting to note that the original meaning of the Sanskrit word *ketu* is "light," "clarity" (synonymous with the etymologically related adjective *citra* of the Pahl. *gōchihr*), which is in apparent contradistinction to the light-devouring function of Ketu as eclipse demon.[127] In Gnostic writings, as will be discussed shortly, the serpent is also associated with both darkness and light.[128]

---

[121] *Ilāhī-nāma*, pp. 264–5, referred to by *idem*, p. 21.
[122] *Idem*.
[123] *Dīwān-i Hakīm-i Farrukhī-i Sīstānī*, p. 363, l. 7354, cited by Melikian-Chirvani, 1997a, pp. 143–4.
[124] Mahé, 1995, p. 183.
[125] Acaryan, H., *Hayeren armatakan bararan* ("Dictionnaire étymologique arménien"), vol. 1, p. 206 b (in Armenian), cited by Mahé, 1995, p. 183.
[126] *Poimandres*, tr. and ed. Nock and Festugière, 1946, p. 7 and 12, n. 9.
[127] Hartner, 1938, pp. 152–3.
[128] Cf. Sheppard, 1962, p. 89.

CHAPTER NINE

VESTIGES OF ANCIENT DRAGON ICONOGRAPHIES

a. *The encircling dragon*

The iconography of the circular dragon biting its own tail, traditionally known by its Greek name as *ouroboros*, was also known in the Islamic tradition. This type of imagery is vividly described in surviving textual sources. The early medieval writer Muḥammad ibn ʿAbdullāh al-Kisāʾī who probably wrote not long before 1200 refers to the authority of Kaʿb al-Aḥbār, a Yemenite convert to Islam (probably in 17/638), when portraying the creation of the Canopy and the Throne of God:

> Then God created a great serpent to surround the Canopy. Its head is of white pearl and its body is of gold. Its eyes are two sapphires, and no one can comprehend the magnitude of the serpent except God. It has forty thousand wings made of different kinds of jewels, and on each feather there stands an angel holding a jeweled lance, praising God and blessing His name. When this serpent extols God, its exaltation overwhelms that of all angels...[1]

A related description of the girdling dragon is given by Abū ʿAbd Allāh al-Qurṭubī, the thirteenth-century expert in *ḥadīth*, or sacred tradition, in a commentary on *sūra* 40 of the Qurʾān:

> When God created the Throne, it said, 'God has not created anything greater than myself,' and exulted with joy out of pride. God therefore caused it to be surrounded by a serpent having 70,000 wings, each wing having 70,000 feathers in it, each feather having in it 70,000 faces each face having in it 70,000 mouths, and each mouth having in it 70,000 tongues, with its mouths ejaculating every day the praises of God ..., the number of drops of rain, the number of leaves of trees, the number of stones and earth, the number of days of this world, and the number of angels, – all these a number of times. The serpent then twisted itself round the Throne which was taken up by only half the serpent while it remained twisted around it. The Throne thereupon became humble.[2]

In the Jewish tradition a great silver serpent likewise encircles the machinery of the throne of king Solomon and by operating the wheelwork, activates the mechanism.[3] It is of note that Solomon's mechanical throne, which can be likened to a miniature universe, can only be put into motion by the serpent.[4]

In his *Qiṣaṣ al-anbiyāʾ* ("Tales on the Prophets"), Abū Isḥāq Aḥmad ibn Muḥammad ibn Ibrāhīm al-Thaʿlabī al-Nīsābūrī al-Shāfʿī (d. 427/1035), describes the Kaʿba in Mecca, the central sanctuary of the Islamic world, as a divine throne that is circumscribed by a dragon:

> Then Allāh surrounded it by a serpent. ... this serpent wound itself around the throne and the latter reaches to half the height of the serpent which is winding itself around it.[5]

In the biography of the Prophet Muḥammad, al-Ḥalabī similarly relates how the serpent that dwells in the pit of the Kaʿba to guard the treasures there, would:

> ...leave its dwelling place and appear glittering, viz. it exposed itself in the sun upon the wall of the Kaʿba while its colour assumed a glittering appearance; and often it wound itself on the wall so that *its tail approached its head* [emphasis added].[6]

---

[1] *Qiṣaṣ al-anbiyāʾ*, tr. Thackston, 1978, p. 7.

[2] Al-Damīrī, *Ḥayāt al-ḥayawān al-kubrā*, tr. Jayakar, 1906, vol. 1, p. 638; see also *ʿArāʾis al-majālis fī qiṣaṣ al-anbiyāʾ*, tr. and ed. Brinner, 2002, p. 25.

[3] *Bet ha-Midrasch,* 1853–73, vol. 5, p. 35. Cf. Ginzberg, 1909–38, repr. 1946 and 1955, vol. 4, pp. 157–9; Wensinck, 1916, repr. 1978, p. 63.

[4] *Bet ha-Midrasch,* 1853–73, vol. 2, pp. 83–5.

[5] Al-Thaʿlabī, *Qiṣaṣ al-anbiyāʾ. Musammā bi ʾl-ʿarāʾis al-majālis*, Cairo, 1290, p. 13, as cited in Wensinck, 1916, repr. 1978, p. 62 and n. 3; see also *ʿArāʾis al-majālis fī qiṣaṣ al-anbiyāʾ*, tr. and ed. Brinner, 2002, p. 151. Wensinck (1916, repr. 1978, p. 62 and n. 3) notes that there are also Greek images in which the serpent is wound around and ascends above the *omphalos*, which often has a sepulchral character (Elderkin, 1924, pp. 109–16); for a discussion of the *omphalos* in literature, see Roscher, 1913, pl. IX, no. 6; and *idem*, 1914, pl. I, no. 1, pl. II, nos. 3, 4, 14. See also p. 59 and n. 102.

[6] *Al-Sīra al-Ḥalabiyya*, Cairo, 1292, vol. 1, p. 189, 3–5, as cited in Wensinck, 1916, repr. 1978, p. 64 and n. 1.

In the Islamic tradition *(ḥadīth)*, as Wensinck points out, the description of the serpent is a metaphor for the ocean:

> ...as the Ocean, the Mekkan [*sic*] serpent is glittering in the sun and as the Ocean it is black and white.[7]

The motif of the "serpent whose tail approached its head" is well-known in Semitic cosmography. A key passage in the book of Job (26:12) states:

> He has inscribed a circle on the face of the waters at the boundary between light and darkness.

The inscribed circle refers to the line of the horizon, which separates the inhabited world from the waters that surround it.[8] These waters are symbolised by Leviathan, "the encircler," who is primarily a sea monster.[9] The name of the biblical monster Leviathan (Hebr. *liwyātān*) has been derived from *lwh* suggested by the Arabic *lwy* "turn," "twist" and the Assyrian *lamû* "surround," "encircle,"[10] underscoring the probablility of an original serpent-like nature of Leviathan.

The same motif is used by the great Andalusian Arab mystic Muḥyi 'l-Dīn Ibn al-ʿArabī (560/1165–638/1240) whose works draw on many sources, including Gnostic, Hermetic and Neoplatonic works. In his discussion of the Pole (*quṭb*; an elevated rank of sainthood in *ṣūfī* mysticism) that represents the living Messenger *(rasūl)* in the *Kitab al-manzil al-quṭb* ("Book of the Spiritual Dwelling of the Pole"), he describes an enormous serpent whose head and tail touch and that encircles Mount Qāf:

> The Pole is both the centre of the circle of the universe, and its circumference. He is the mirror of God, and the pivot of the world. ... God is perpetually epiphanized to him. ... He is located in Mecca, whatever place he happens to be in bodily. When a Pole is enthroned at the level of the *quṭbiyya*, all beings, animal or vegetable, make covenant with him ... This explains the story about the man who saw the huge snake that God had placed around Mount Qāf, which encircles the world. The head and the tail of this snake meet. The man greeted the snake, who returned his greeting and then asked him about Shaykh Abū Madyan, who lived at Bijāya in the Maghrib. The man said to it, "How do you come to know Abū Madyan?" The snake answered, "Is there anyone on earth who does not know him?[11]

According to a saying of the Prophet Muḥammad, Mount Qāf is separated from the world "by a region which men cannot cross, a dark area which would stretch for four months walking."[12] It was thus a distant, marginal area at the boundaries of the "civilised" world.[13] Such liminal regions were often inhabited by demons. Descriptions of dragons and other mythical creatures abound in such regions in the descriptions of medieval Islamic geographical and travel works.[14] Their topical proliferation serves as a "cultural marker" (in James Montgomery's words) indicating to the traveller that he is in a distant land.[15] Together with other imaginary hybrid creatures, such as sphinxes and harpies, the presence of the dragon may have signified the outer reaches of the known earth. This vision of the fabulous distant lands at the remote ends of the world is also found in the *Alexander Romance* of Pseudo-Callisthenes. In this legend many wondrous feats are ascribed to Iskandar who made his way to the furthest west and furthest east, the end of the world, entering the "regions not illuminated by the Sun, the Moon and the stars and light as day" where he encounters creatures such as human-headed birds.[16]

However, Mount Qāf does not only encircle the earth: it also encloses the ocean which "forms a girdle around the earth."[17] The symbolism also occurs in the story of Solomon of the *Alf layla wa-layla* which recounts how Solomon on his fly-

---

[7] *Idem*, p. 64.

[8] Wakeman, 1973, pp. 134–5.

[9] Gunkel, 1895, p. 47 and n. 1; Wakeman, 1973, p. 135 and n. 1.

[10] *Eadem*, 1973, p. 64. Cf. Grünbaum, 1877, p. 275.

[11] The same story, in expanded form, of a man speaking to a serpent appears in the *Risālat ruḥ al-quds*. See Chodkiewicz, 1993, p. 55 and n. 32.

[12] Cf. Streck [Miquel], "Ḳāf," *EI*² IV, 400a.

[13] In ancient Greek lore the ends of the earth were inhabited by primeval and/or mythical creatures (for instance in Hesiod's *Theogony* 270–6). Inaccessible by land, they could only be reached by the crossing of waters, often described as world-encircling.

[14] Cf. Montgomery, 2006, p. 72.

[15] The fourth marvel of Ibn Faḍlān's *Risālat* constitutes the story of a tree being cut to size which then begins to move and crawl away in the form of a giant dragon. *Risālat Ibn Faḍlān*, ed. Dahhān, S., Damascus, 1959, pp. 127–8 (fol. 4 206 *wāw*), as cited in Montgomery, 2006, p. 72. Cf. the dangerous and monstrous creatures of Greek lore that dwell at the edges of the earth, the *eschatiai*, or "most distant lands," and are very often guardians of treasure, for instance, the golden apples of the Hesperides in the far west and the golden fleece of Kolchis in the far east which are protected by giant serpents; see Romm, 1987, pp. 45–54.

[16] Pseudo-Callisthenes II, ch. 40, tr. and ed. Stoneman, 1991, p. 121. Related conceptualisations of sphinxes and man-birds appear in the *Kitāb-i Samak ʿAyyār*; see Gaillard, 1987, p. 120.

[17] Streck [Miquel], "Ḳāf," *EI*² IV, 400a.

ing carpet travels through the world and reaches the dragon that encompasses the world.[18] According to a popular belief recorded by al-Qazwīnī, the earth is supported by the biblical monsters Leviathan and Behemoth.[19] Later Jewish tradition similarly states that:

> ...the Ocean surrounds the whole world as a vault surrounds a large pillar. And the world is placed in circular form on the fins of Leviathan.[20]

Similarly a large serpent is said to encircle the bier of a righteous person, a tradition which provides a microcosmic allegory of the whole world surrounded and supported by a giant serpent.[21] It also shows that the Islamic conceptions are in some way connected with ancient biblical notions, which in turn have precedents in the Babylonian tradition of chaos.[22]

In his short tractate, the *Sod ha-Nachasch u-Mischpato* ("Mystery of the Serpent"), the thirteenth-century kabbalist, Joseph Gikatilla ben Abraham, a disciple of the Spanish mystic Abraham ben Samuel Abulafia (1240–*c.* 1292), sheds some light on the mystery of the mythical creature as a liminal symbol, situated upon the ambiguous dividing line between the divine and the demonic:

> Know that from the outset of its creation the serpent represented something important and necessary for harmony so long as it stood in its place. It was the Great Servant who had been created to carry the yoke of both sovereignty and service. Its head surmounted the heights of the earth and its tail reached into the depths of hell. Yet in all worlds it had a befitting place and represented something extraordinarily significant for the harmony of all stages, each one in its place. And this is the secret of the serpent of heaven that is known from the *Sefer Yezira*, and that sets in motion the spheres and their cycle from east to west and from north to south. And without it no creature in the sublunar world had life, and there would be no sowing and no growth and no motivation for the reproduction of all creatures. This serpent now stood originally outside the walls of the sacred precincts and was connected from the outside with the outer wall, since its tail was linked with the wall whereas its countenance was oriented inwards. It did not befit it to enter the inside, but its place and law was to affect the creation of growth and reproduction from the outside, and this is the secret of the tree and the knowledge of good and evil.[23]

This world serpent, which likewise serves as liminal motif between order and chaos by encircling the cosmos, in other words the realm of order, was a symbol of great antiquity in the Mesopotamian world and beyond.[24]

The writings of mystics such as Ibn al-ʿArabī were also influenced by the esoteric science of alchemy *(al-kīmiyāʾ)*, considered a form of revealed knowledge that had both its spiritual goals and practical applications. A special alchemical symbol is that of the tail-eating serpent, known as *ouroboros* (the etymology is from *oura*, "tail," and the root of *bora*, "food," *boros*, "voracious").[25]

Among the large pseudo-epigraphic literature of alchemical books composed in the medieval period, an Arabic alchemical treatise titled *Muṣḥaf al-ḥakīm Usṭānis fī-l-ṣināʿat al-ilāhiyya* ("Book of the Wise Ostanes on Divine Art") is attributed to Ostanes (Uṣṭānis), the renowned Median author of books on magic and gnosis of the Achaemenid period.[26] It describes how in a dream a creature with serpent's tail, eagle's wings and elephant's head devouring its own tail (like a serpent) guides Ostanes up to the seven gates of wisdom for which it gives him the keys.[27]

An important corpus of alchemical writings, compiled at the end of the ninth and beginning of the tenth century, is attributed to the celebrated alchemist Jābir ibn Ḥayyān (d. *c.* 196/812), allegedly from Ṭūs in Khurasan,[28] who according to tradition was a personal friend of the sixth Shīʿite

[18] Marzolph and van Leeuwen, 2004, p. 356.

[19] Cf. Streck [Miquel], "Ḳāf," *EI*² IV 400a. It is noteworthy that Behemot is known as Lawatyā (Leviathan, see Job 41:1), the patronymic part of the name *(kunya)* is Balhūt and Bahamūt (Behemot, see Job 40:15). Cf. al-Thaʿlabī, *Qiṣaṣ al-anbiyāʾ*, p. 4, cited after Thackston (tr. al-Kisāʾī's *Qiṣaṣ al-anbiyāʾ*), 1978, p. 338, n. 9.

[20] *Bet ha-Midrasch*, 1853–77, vol. 2, p. 63, 17–8.

[21] Babylonian Talmud *Bava Metsiah* 84b-85a, as cited in Epstein, 1997, p. 74. This is supported by the Hasidic verse *zaddik yesod olam*: "a righteous person is the foundation of the world" (Proverbs 10:25), cited after *idem*, p. 74.

[22] Streck [Miquel], "Ḳāf," *EI*² IV, 400a.

[23] Scholem, 1957, repr. 1988, p. 437.

[24] Schütt, 2002, p. 106.

[25] Needham and Wang, 1965, p. 374; Anawati, "Arabic Alchemy," *EHAS*, 1996, vol. 3, p. 863.

[26] Sezgin, 1971, pp. 51–4; Ullmann, 1972, pp. 184–5; Anawati, "Arabic Alchemy," *EHAS*, 1996, vol. 3, p. 862; Needham and Wang, 1965, pp. 333–5. In Zoroastrian pseudo-epigrapha which include those of Ostanes, the magus is said to have accompanied Khshayārshā (Xerxes) during the great Persian invasion of Greece. Cf. Boyce and Grenet, 1991, pp. 494–6.

[27] Reitzenstein, 1916, pp. 3335; Ullmann, 1972, pp. 184–5 and ns. 1 and 2; Anawati, "Arabic Alchemy," *EHAS*, 1996, vol. 3, p. 862.

[28] Ullmann, "Al-Kīmiyāʾ," *EI*² V, 110a.

imām Jaʿfar al-Ṣādiq (81/700–147/765) who initiated him into alchemy and secret teachings.[29] In his *Kitāb al-aḥjār* ("Book of Stones") Jābir ibn Ḥayyān includes several recipes for creating beasts such as serpents.[30] The earliest texts of the corpus are thought to have originated in the scientific culture of the great cultural oases the Oxus (Āmū Daryā) and Jaxartes (Syr Daryā) rivers: Marw, Balkh, Khiva, Samarqand and Bukhara, the traditional roads of exchange between east and west, from where it was transmitted to the rest of the Islamic world.[31]

Another work was the *Tabula Smaragdina* ("Emerald Tablet") attributed by Islamic sources to Hermes, which purported to reveal the key to the ultimate secret of alchemy, and which was included in the *Kitāb Sirr al-Khaliqā wa Ṣanʿat al-Ṭabīʿa* ("Book of the Secret of Creation and the Art (of Reproducing) Nature"), written in the mid-seventh century or later in about 205/820 under the caliph Maʾmun.[32] Julius Ruska, who translated the text, was the first to suggest that its origin lay further east.[33] He similarly proposes that its genesis should be sought in "the great culture-oases in the region of the Oxus and the Jaxartes rivers, of Merv and Balkh, or Khiva, Bokhara and Samarqand, those great cities which since ancient times have seen the exchange of material and intellectual goods between west and east, and where Greek traditions endured for such a surprisingly long time."[34] Ruska visualises these cities at the crossroads of Asia north and east of the Sasanian empire as filled with a mixed population of Iranians, Tūrānians, Syrians, Indians, and Chinese,[35] places where Buddhism, Manichaeism, Nestorian Christianity and Chinese cults coexisted. Here the sciences of astrology, alchemy and macrobiotics were very much alive.[36] The close analogies especially in the account of cosmic Creation with Chinese alchemy have been pointed out by Joseph Needham and Ling Wang.[37] The text expresses the alchemical concept of heat acting as male, cold as female, and their union producing humidity and dryness, which has close parallels to the Chinese theories of Yin and Yang.[38] However, these correlations could only happen due to a "trans-Asian continuity" from ancient times that was greatly enhanced after the conquests of Alexander (r. 336–323 BC), son of Philip II, king of Macedonia, and later through the traveller and explorer Chang Chhien's diplomatic and commercial expeditions (fl. *c.* 138–126 BC).[39]

In a text known as the "Congress of Philosophers" (surviving only in a twelfth-century Latin translation and hence lacking its original Arabic title), tentatively dated to *c.* 900 and attributed to a certain Abū Bakr Aḥmad ibn ʿAlī al-Kasdānī, better known as Ibn Waḥshiyya al-Nabaṭī and the *Muṣḥaf al-jamāʿa* of the *Turba philosophorum*, a symposium of philosophers and alchemists voice their divergent opinions.[40] In the speech of "Socrates" chemical reaction is compared with generation, lead is male and orpiment female. According to "Diamedes" both male and female substances are needed, mercury relating to the former and sulphur to the latter. "Ostanes" makes copper female and mercury male, while "Theophilus" offers allegories of nights between husband and wife, etc.[41]

The great emphasis on sexuality in chemical substances and reactions that are detailed in the *Turba philosophorum* is one of the main characteristics of alchemy. This is based on the belief in a universal sympathy that ultimately unites all parts of the universe, metals and stones (which are alive), males and females.[42] Further, the uniting of the opposite principles female/male, passive/active, cold/hot, humidity/dryness finds expression in the coupling of the Sun and the Moon, a cosmological motif of central importance since it symbolises the generation of all things.[43] It is believed that all metals are a result of their union

[29] Anawati, "Arabic Alchemy," *EHAS*, 1996, vol. 3, p. 866 and n. 40. Although the traditions about Jaʿfar al-Ṣādiq are persistent even in many books of the Jābirian Corpus itself, the claim that he himself is the instructor appears to be untenable. Cf. Needham and Wang, 1965, p. 390, and ns. h-k.

[30] Haq, 1994, pp. 14–21.

[31] Cf. Corbin, 1998a, pp. 45–6.

[32] Ruska, 1926. Cf. Needham and Wang, 1965, p. 369.

[33] Needham and Wang, 1965, p. 370.

[34] Ruska, 1926, p. 167, as cited in Needham and Wang, 1965, p. 370.

[35] *Eidem*, p. 370.

[36] *Eidem*.

[37] *Eidem*, p. 373.

[38] *Eidem*.

[39] Chang Chhien's expeditions are recorded by Ssuma Chhien in the *Shih Chi* (ch. 123) and the *Chhien Han Shu* (chs. 61, 96A, 96B). *Eidem*, pp. 332, 387.

[40] Sezgin, 1971, pp. 60–3; Needham and Wang, 1965, pp. 397–9.

[41] Ruska, 1931, pp. 200, 215–6, 229, 247, see also the summaries, sects. 54–5, 57, 59; Plessner, 1954, pp. 331–8. Cf. Needham and Wang, 1965, p. 401, n. A; Ullmann, "Al-Kīmiyāʾ," *EI*² V, 110a.

[42] Anawati, "Arabic Alchemy," *EHAS*, 1996, vol. 3, p. 863 and n. 35. Cf. Needham and Wang, 1965, pp. 469–70 and n. h with references.

[43] Cf. *eidem*, 1965, p. 373.

in different proportions and according to different modalities. Under the influences of the planets, these are formed in the heart of the earth by the union of the correlative hypothetical substances of sulphur, male, in which fire and air are present and which has hot and dry "natures," and mercury, female, which contains water and earth, which is cold and wet.[44] This relates also to the circular nature of the alchemical process and the agency of transformation that both devours and restores.

The *ouroboros* symbol is depicted in Arabic alchemical texts, such as the writings of Muḥammad ibn Umayl al-Ṣādiq al-Tamīmī (*c.* 287/900–287/960, known in the west as "Senior Zadith").[45] His most renowned work was the *Kitāb al-Māʾ al-Waraqī wa ʾl-Arḍ al-Najmīya* ("Book of the Silvery Water and Starry Earth"), known in Latin as the *Tabula Chemica*,[46] in which the schematic depiction of a pair of winged creatures biting each other's tails is shown (fig. 149).[47] The *ouroboros* motif is also illustrated in the work on alchemy, *Kitāb al-Aqālīm al-sabʿa [dhāt al-ṣuwar wa ʾl-tashābīh]* ("The Seven Climes") of the mid-thirteenth-century writer Abu ʾl-Qāsim Aḥmad ibn Muḥammad al-ʿIrāqī.[48] Similarly, in Abū Maslama Muḥammad al-Majrīṭī's treatise *Ghāyat al-ḥakīm* the opposing principles of positive and negative bodily temperaments are associated with the two celestial nodes (knots), the head and the tail of the "hidden essence."[49]

It is significant then that in medieval Islamic iconography the *ouroboros* dragon was doubled and is often pictured as two entwined dragons eating one another (or, in other words, threatening one another), in an act both self-destructive and at the same time parturient, the cycle that is recreated in the self-devouring.[50] In the symbolism of medieval Islamic alchemy, the paired interlaced dragons represented a fundamental polarity, on which the cosmic rhythm is based, the *solve et coagula* of the alchemical process: the sulphur and mercury of alchemy.[51]

This double aspect is echoed in the popular belief, mentioned earlier, that the earth is supported by the biblical monsters Leviathan and Behemoth.[52] It is also found in rabbinic tradition where it is stated that:

> Behemoth and Leviathan are serpents (monsters) on the edge of the ocean who encircle the earth like a ring.[53]

Concerning *nāḥāsh ʿāqallāṭōn* in Isaiah 27:1 the Talmudic commentator Rashi (*c.* 1040–1105) similarly remarks that "this *entwined* Leviathan surrounds the whole earth" [emphasis added].[54]

The *ouroboros* symbol was especially important for the Ophite (from *ophis*, the Greek for "serpent") Gnostics.[55] In the ancient Orphic mystery the great dragon was the sphere of the Sun, the supreme cosmic force, the good spirit of light, stretched like a radiant ribbon around the rim of the heaven of fixed stars; closely related to the four winds, the four quarters of the cosmos and the four seasons.[56] Writing in *c.* 400, Macrobius, moreover, describes the iconography of the dragon, which encompasses the world tail in its mouth, as like the forward and backward looking god Janus, a visible image of the universe which feeds on itself and returns to itself again.[57]

However in some Gnostic-Christian writings such as the *Pistis Sophia* (*c.* fourth century),[58] in which belief in heavenly bodies and demonology are closely connected, the serpent became the

[44] Anawati, "Arabic Alchemy," *EHAS*, 1996, vol. 3, p. 866. Cf. Needham and Wang, 1965, p. 373; Moulierac, 1987, p. 88; Kraus [Plessner], "Djābir b. Ḥayyān," *EI*² II, 357b.

[45] Cf. Sezgin, 1971, pp. 283–8; Needham and Wang, 1965, p. 378; Ronca, 1998, pp. 95–116, esp. pp. 102–9.

[46] Stapleton and Ḥusain, 1933, 12, no. 1, pp. 117–213.

[47] The highly stylised illustration is accompanied by an Arabic inscription in the Lucknow manuscript as:

> ...two Birds [with an indication of the position of the respective heads and the tails]; the Male and the Female; Two in One.

eidem, 1933, pl. I, A. A closely related, yet even more stylised, version of the motif is depicted in the Paris Ms. no. 2610, Bibliothèque Nationale, Paris, see *eidem*, pl. 2 B.

[48] Ullmann, 1972, p. 237 and n. 1.

[49] "*Picatrix*," tr. and eds. Ritter and Plessner, 1962, p. 45.16–9.

[50] Joseph Needham and Ling Wang (1965, pp. 378–9) consider this development to have been due to "Chinese influence" on the Hellenistic single tail-eating serpent motif. Cf. Schütt, 2002, pp. 106–7.

[51] Moulierac, 1987, p. 88.

[52] Cf. Streck [Miquel], "Ḳāf," *EI*² IV 400a.

[53] Goldschmidt, 1892, p. 83.

[54] Grünbaum, 1877, p. 275.

[55] Leisegang, 1924, repr. Stuttgart, 1955, pp. 111–3, 160, and *idem*, 1955, repr. Princeton, 1979, pp. 218–20. On the pivotal function of the serpent for the Ophite sects, see Schlüter, 1982, pp. 56–9.

[56] Leisegang, 1955, repr. 1979, pp. 218–20.

[57] *Saturnalia* 1.9.12. Merkelbach, "Drache," *RAC* IV, 1959, p. 227.

[58] Known as the Askew Codex, British Library, Ms. Add. 5114. See *Sacred*, ed. Reeve, 2007, cat. no. 72.

Antichrist and Satan, the Leviathan of the Old Testament.[59] The *Pistis Sophia*, which claims to record the teachings of Jesus during the eleven years following his resurrection, states:

> The outer darkness is a great dragon whose tail is in its mouth, and it is outside the world, and it surrounds the whole world.[60]

Significantly, in the apocalypse of the heavens the Sun appears as a great dragon accompanied by the seven planets and with the four horses[61] that in Greek mythology drew the chariot of the sun god Helios *(sol invictus)*, while the Moon is depicted as steered by a male and a female dragon and drawn by two white bulls.[62]

Nevertheless, the ancient conceptions of the serpent resurface in the Gospel of John in the New Testament (3:14). As noted earlier, the serpent lifted up by Moses is presented in the *Epistle of Barnabas* as a symbol of Jesus and of Christianity.[63] The formula, "I am the alpha and the omega," meaning "in my beginning is my end and in my end is my beginning," also leads to the imagery of the *ouroboros* serpent, symbol of the unity and eternal renewal of life.[64]

The *ouroboros* motif reached its apogee during the Gnostic period, which lasted from the second century BC to the third century AD, when the Greek and West Asian cultures were subsumed by a form of pan-Hellenism.[65] It is of significance, however, that the symbol had not been known in Classical Greek, Etruscan or early Roman culture.[66] Thus the *ouroboros* symbol came to serve as an image for a complex of ideas that was known by a Greek name.

An *ouroboros* serpent that encircles a lion, surmounted by a crescent and star, engraved on a fifth-century Sasanian seal (fig. 150),[67] suggests that the Sasanian representations of the serpent biting its own tail may perhaps be based on conventional renderings of the dragon in contemporaneous star-maps inspired by astrological works of the Hellenistic east.[68] In Hellenic astrology, the great celestial serpent *(draco coelestis)* dominated the heavens, encompassing all the spheres of the cosmos, coiling around the heavens and biting its tail.[69] Yet it is important also to consider the reverse of the seal, which depicts a palm tree above a pair of outspread wings with small streamers surrounded either by a decorative border or a more stylised *ouroboros*.[70] Since this represents a rare iconographic variant, Rika Gyselen tentatively suggests a magical interpretation of the seal.[71]

The motif of the paired encircling dragons also makes an appearance in the well-known legend of the Ascent of Iskandar. Certain editions of the romance of Pseudo-Callisthenes (*c.* fourth century) describe how, as Iskandar is carried to heaven by eagles, he sees a field encircled by a serpent which is explained as the world surrounded by the ocean.[72] The depiction of this scene also reflects the force and ongoing cultural resonance which the *Alexander Romance* possessed at the time; in particular, the meaning associated with this imagery. It is portrayed on a small Byzantine enamelled medallion of the eleventh century from the Pala d'Oro on the high altar of St. Mark's, now preserved in the Treasury of San Marco, Venice, representing the schematised composition of Iskandar's view of the world as seen from on high (fig. 151).[73] The plaque is decorated with a large central tree inhabited by birds and flanked by a pair of addorsed peacocks with their heads turned backwards. The composition is encircled

[59] Leisegang, 1955, repr. 1979, p. 218.

[60] *Pistis Sophia*, text ed. Schmidt and tr. Macdermot, 1978, bk. III, ch. 126, p. 635; cf. *Pistis Sophia*, tr. Mead, 1896, p. 320, sec. 319. See also Leisegang, 1955, repr. 1979, p. 218; Reitzenstein, 1916, esp. p. 41; Merkelbach, "Drache," *RAC* IV, 1959, p. 228; Sheppard, 1962, p. 88; Beck, 2004, p. 225.

[61] *Pistis Sophia*, text ed. Schmidt and tr. Macdermot, 1978, bk. IV, ch. 136, pp. 709–10; cf. *Pistis Sophia*, tr. Mead, 1896, p. 296, sec. 359; Leisegang, 1955, repr. 1979, p. 218 and n. 11; Sheppard, 1962, p. 89; Beck, 2004, pp. 225–6, n. 72. The motif of the flying chariot driven by dragons apppears also in the myth of Medea (Pseudo-Apollodorus, *Bibliotheca* I. 146; Diodorus Siculus, *Library of History* IV. 50. 6; Ovid, *Metamorphoses* VII 217, 350 and 391–3).

[62] *Pistis Sophia*, text ed. Schmidt and tr. Macdermot, 1978, bk. IV, ch. 136, pp. 709–10; cf. *Pistis Sophia*, tr. Mead, 1896, p. 296, sec. 359; Beck, 2004, pp. 225–6, n. 72.

[63] Tr. Lake, 1914, vol. 1, p. 385.

[64] Leisegang, 1955, repr. 1979, p. 229.

[65] Needham and Wang, 1965, p. 376.

[66] *Eidem*, p. 376, n. g.

[67] Cf. Gyselen, 1995, pp. 52–3, fig. 60 (photograph of seal recto, verso).

[68] Bivar (1969, p. 26) connects the *ouroboros* serpent with the Egyptian serpent deity Āpep that is regarded as the cosmic antagonist of the Sun and the Moon. According to Azarpay (1978, p. 369 and fig. 6) "representations of the *ouroboros* serpent on Sasanian seals of the fifth century suggest the currency of astrological notions about the ecliptic Dragon at an earlier period in Sasanian Persia."

[69] Leisegang, 1955, repr. 1979, p. 217.

[70] Bivar, 1969, p. 26, pl. 11, DL2; Gyselen, 1995, p. 53, fig. 60.

[71] *Eadem*, 1995, pp. 52, 76–7.

[72] Pseudo-Callisthenes II, ch. 41, tr. and ed. Stoneman, 1991, p. 123. Cf. Millet, 1923, p. 94, ch. 102. See also p. 55.

[73] Grabar, 1951, p. 48, fig. 10c (photograph).

by a pair of giant serpents with looped bodies and interlaced tails.

The significance of this imagery is underlined by Grabar who identifies it as highly characteristic of the Iranian repertoire of motifs, stating that "this image of the Universe, a distinctly Iranian iconography, deserved to be introduced into the family of medieval representations of the Cosmos."[74] Similarly the tree and the birds represented on the plaque, as Grabar has observed, represent "Iranian symbols of the garden of the Earth; in the text of the legend they are documented with the words: "fruits of the Earth.""[75] The Latin version of the text states: "orbis terrarum sicut area, in qua conduntur fruges."[76] This form of imagery thus provides a bird's eye view of the terrestrial universe current in the medieval Iranised Central Asian sphere. The motif was here adapted to a Christian context and, as Grabar notes, it is possible that the stylised cruciform motif on the apex of the tree represents a Christian cross which served to "convert" this oriental representation of the universe into a Christian one.[77] Evidently the motif had wide currency in the medieval world, both Muslim and Byzantine.

The origin of this iconography may plausibly be seen to lie in the Zoroastrian cosmological motif of the Saēna Tree, the perch of the great mythical Saēna bird (Av. *saēna-mərəya-*, Mid. Pers. *sēn murw*, Pers. *sīmorğ*).[78] The tree on which the Saēna nests grows in the middle of Lake Vārukasha (Yasht 12.17) and is called Vīspō.bish (the Gaokərəna-Tree, Mid. Pers. Gōkirn), Tree of All Remedies, because it bears the seed of all healing herbs.[79] According to the *Bundahishn* the revered Vāsī Panchā.sadvarā lives in the lake (Yasht 42.4). It appears to be a kind of sea dragon and is "so huge that if it were to rush swiftly along from sunrise to sunset it still would not have covered as much ground as the length of its own body; it rules over all denizens of the waters."[80] Islamic cosmological notions speak of the "Lote Tree on the Boundary" *(sidrat al-muntahā)*, also known as *ṭubā* ("blessed").[81] The Qur'ān describes how when the Prophet was carried on his night journey *(mi'rāj)* up to the seventh heaven, he went on as far as the *sidrat al-muntahā* beyond which no angel or any other being can pass. This tree is located to the right of the divine throne *('arsh)* and near the garden of the eternal abode (*sūra* 53, 14–5).[82]

An emblematic illustration of the city of Babylon in the manuscripts of Beatus' Commentary on the Apocalypse shows the theme of two giant serpents enclosing a city. Discussing this coincidence of imagery John Williams comments that "Christian culture shared iconographic traditions associated with the Muslim world..."[83] Babylon, which must have been notorious for its dragons, was also known in Iranian tradition as the location of the giant dragon Dahāka.[84]

The illustration of the city of Babylon serves as frontispiece for the Daniel Commentary (1.1 and 14.23) in two tenth-century manuscripts, the Morgan Beatus, dated between *c.* 940 and 945 (fig. 152), and the Girona Beatus, dated 6 July 975,[85] as well as in one mid-eleventh-century manuscript, the Saint-Sever Beatus from the monastery of Saint-Sever-sur-l'Adour (on which the city is shown to be enclosed by two dragons whose heads and tails entwine at top and bottom).[86]

In the Morgan Beatus Babylon is shown as a towering city with a large horseshoe arch-shaped main city gate framed by an inverted pair of small dragons, who touch at the tail tips, in such a manner that their undulant bodies seem to form an ogee arch-shaped enclosure around the gate. The entire composition is encircled by a sequence of two giant dragons demarcated by a fine spotted pattern in anti-clockwise arrangement, the gaping

---

74 *Idem*, p. 48. Similar cosmological concepts referring to the gigantic tree and the mythical bird sent by God to aid the hero are described in the *Kitāb-i Samak 'Ayyār*; see Gaillard, 1987, p. 113.

75 Grabar, 1951, p. 48.

76 Cited after *idem*, p. 48. Cf. Millet, 1923, p. 102.

77 Grabar, 1951, p. 48, n. 17.

78 See Boyce, 1975, repr. 1996, pp. 88–91, 137–8, 143.

79 Cf. Janda, 2010, pp. 320–1.

80 *Eadem*, p. 89.

81 On the Tree of Life in Islamic tradition, see Lechler, 1939, pp. 369–419; Wensinck, 1921, repr. 1978, p. 33; Widengren, 1955, pp. 103–4, 208–9, 212–3.

82 The Qur'ān mentions also the Tree of Eternity *(shajarat al-khuld)* (*sūra* 20, 120–1) and another tree which appears in Islamic eschatology as growing in Hell (*sūras* 37, 60–2; 44, 43; and 56, 52).

83 Williams, 1994, vol. 1, p. 139.

84 Skjærvø, "Aždahā I," *EIr*. Cf. Yarshater, 1983a, p. 426; Hintze, 1999, p. 86, n. 62.

85 City of Babylon enclosed by two dragons, frontispiece, Daniel Commentary. The Girona Beatus. Kingdom of Léon, probably Tábara. Dated 6 July 975. Museu de la Catedral de Girona, Num. Inv. 7 (11). Williams, 1994, vol. 2, ill. 376.

86 City of Babylon enclosed by two dragons, frontispiece, Daniel Commentary. The Saint-Sever Beatus. Monastery of Saint-Sever-sur-l'Adour. Mid-eleventh century. Paris, Bibliothèque Nationale, Ms. Lat. 8878, fol. 217. Williams, 1994, vol. 2, ill. 466.

dragons' snouts revealing a long tongue which nearly touches the tail of the preceding dragon.

Williams refers to an ancient Slavic version of a Byzantine epic of the city of Babylon[87] which may further elucidate the imagery of the dragons encircling the city. According to this story, thought to be of Indo-Iranian origin,[88] Nebuchadnezzar rebuilt a new city on top of "seven rocks and seven stations," the entire city being surrounded by the body of a giant dragon whose mouth and tail unite to form the gate.[89] Nebuchadnezzar also had a large sword made for himself in the form of a dragon which had magical powers and could act autonomously.[90] The image of the dragon was, in addition, chosen by the king as coat of arms of the city, and as such was applied to garments, weapons, military standards, horse harnesses and saddles, roof beams, doors and windows, vessels, plates, bowls and spoons.[91] In case of war all the "heraldic" dragons would come to life and devour the army of the enemy.[92] In the same account of Babylon it is said that following the king's death, failure to observe his commandments led to an inversion of the protective powers of the dragon. The narrative later reveals that the singing of a hymn in praise of God made the initially hostile dragons recoil as if to form a knot.[93]

This version of the epic thus makes it clear that the dragon was seen not only as a creature that struck fear in people's hearts, but as guardian of the city with inherent apotropaic powers.[94] It suggests that the encircling dragons performed a protective function as well. It is interesting to consider, moreover, that the conspicuous knotting characteristic of many dragon representations, a topic examined in the following chapter, may be an indication that the fierce aspect of the dragon is contained once its body forms a knot.

The encircling dragon iconography is also found on architectural elements such as a carved wooden door, once possibly part of a mausoleum.[95] The door, dated to the first half of the thirteenth-century, is thought to come from the Tigris region, and is now preserved in the Museum für Islamische Kunst in Berlin (fig. 153).[96] It is carved with a pair of large dragons surrounding a central medallion set within an arch-shaped frame. The latter contains an interlaced infinite star pattern, in turn outlined by an interlaced pearled band which extends at its apex into a small medallion. It is touched on either side by the sinuous tongues projecting from the gaping mouths of the dragons whose scaly serpentine bodies with raised slender wings wind tightly around the medallion. Their bodies form a pretzel-like knot and then two loops, the tail tips tapering to a point to form a tight curl at the base. On account of the surface wear of the door only the frame of the small medallion is extant, one can therefore only speculate what it was that the dragons were protecting or threatening.

A similar conceptualisation governs the depiction on a large bas-relief stone fragment carved with a pair of antithetically arranged dragons that frame a large mutlilayered composite rayed orb which carries clear solar associations, discovered near Alaeddin Tepe in Konya, now in the İnce Minare Müzesi in Konya (fig. 154). It was probably part of a thirteenth-century Saljuqid monument, which no longer exists. Only the dragon head to the left is complete, portrayed with a long, curved wide-open snout revealing sharp teeth and fangs along with a prominent sinuous tongue the tip of which touches the edge of the star rosette. The head is punctuated with almond-shaped eyes framed by long, curved lashes and crowned by a small, rounded ear. At the back of the head the dragon's neck is clasped by paired "collars," the upper part braided, the lower marked with vertical hatching. The long scaly ophidian bodies form a loop and then a pretzel-like knot. The bottom section of the stone is broken off so the tail tips are lost. Likewise, only part of the pretzel-like knot of the dragon to the right has survived.

A more complex form which may be related to the encircling motif graces the small "Kiosk Mosque" situated in the courtyard of the double-section caravanserai Sultan Han, near Kayseri (between 629/1232 and 633/1236) discussed in detail in chapter 2. Here the confronted serpent festoons end in small dragon heads, the necks bent inwards and the open jaws holding the tips

---

[87] *Idem*, vol. 1, p. 60, n. 64. The epic is known from six slightly varying text fragments of ancient Russian histories. Wesselofsky, 1876, pp. 129–43, esp. 133.

[88] *Idem*, 1876, p. 308.

[89] *Idem*, p. 133 and n. 11. It may further be noted that in another ancient Russian epic a dragon, his head touching the tip of his tail, is described as surrounding the city of Antioch. *Idem*, pp. 325–6, n. 51.

[90] *Idem*, pp. 133, 135.

[91] *Idem*, p. 133.

[92] *Idem*, pp. 133–4.

[93] *Idem*, p. 141, n. 28.

[94] *Idem*, p. 142.

[95] Cf. Hauptmann von Gladiss, ed., p. 95.

[96] Cf. Meinecke, 1989, pp. 54, 58, detail.

of the outer festoon-band. They thus appear to "swallow" or "deliver" their own tails (fig. 13). An analogy may further be drawn to the interlaced dragons that enclose the ogival arches carved with figural compositions on the portals of the Imām Bahir Mausoleum in Mosul (fig. 19) and the Mār Behnām Monastery southeast of Mosul (fig. 18).

The *ouroboros* aspect is further evident in the double frontispiece of the *Kitāb al-diryāq* ("Book of the Theriac," often referred to as "Book of Antidotes"), dated 595/1199, in the collection of the Bibliothèque Nationale, Paris, on which the encircling dragons are juxtaposed with the personification of the Moon (fig. 176), examined below in chapter 11. Although of course realised in an entirely different medium, the representations in stone and on paper probably share a relatively close geographic provenance and period of production. The astral personification on the Pseudo-Galen double frontispiece, moreover, might provide a link between what appear to be composite stellar symbols on the Berlin door (fig. 153) and the Konya architectural stone fragment (fig. 154).

The motif also features conspicuously on several Kashan-style ceramic vessels that are overglaze painted with lustre; here the encircling imagery is rendered in the form of interlacing bands comprising multiple pairs of "Saljuq-style" dragons with small pointed ears and gaping snouts with thin projecting tongues circumscribing a central composition.[97] On one bowl, now preserved in Chicago, in the Harvey B. Plotnick Collection, the ophidian bodies of the mythical creatures encircle a well-known motif, often portrayed on early thirteenth-century Kashan-style ceramic bowls, of two seated human figures conversing. Portrayed with three-quarter facing large "moon-shaped" faces with long almond-shaped eyes, arched eyebrows and gently smiling lips, flanked by long tresses embellished with diadems and flowing over the shoulders, the figures conform to the standards of ideal beauty that prevailed in Islamic lands ruled by Western Asian dynasties from the tenth century onwards.[98] The composition is encircled by an interlaced band formed of six pairs of dragons terminating in paired confronting heads with gaping mouths and projecting tongues (composed of very fine flame-like lines). Their alternately spotted and finely scaled bodies form evenly spaced circular enclosures containing vegetal motifs. The serpentine interlace is in turn framed by epigraphic bands in Kufic and cursive script in Arabic and Persian (fig. 155). The main theme of the inscriptions is love, the longing for the beloved and the anguish and suffering occasioned by love.[99] These sentiments are reflected by the two human figures whose thoughtful interaction is underlined by a distinctive right-handed gesture with delicate finger movement by one of the figures, while the other has folded hands.[100] The introspective experience of personal love was perceived as a crucial element in following the path to virtue and attaining moral perfectibility.[101] This microcosmic ideal is aptly framed by the interlaced dragons. The tall cylindrical body of a Kashan-style ewer of the same period and in a closely related style, now preserved in Paris, Musée du Louvre, is similarly encircled by eight pairs of intertwining dragons whose heads with wide-open mouths and projecting tongues confront each other on the rounded shoulder. The bodies of the fabulous beasts define five horizontal registers filled with cursive epigraphic bands in Persian written in reserve on a lustre-painted ground.[102] It may be inferred that, although generally perceived to be a mere decorative device on Saljuq-period objects, the iconography of encircling dragons may well have conveyed some cosmological and, possibly, mythological significance.

The encircling dragon motif is also found on textiles, which were a key luxury item for circulation. Their eminent portability and high status within the medieval Islamic and Eastern Christian cultures assured their important role in establishing an international visual vocabulary.[103] This led to shared decorative themes in Islamic and Byzantine textiles, and consequently to frequent

[97] Grube, 1965, pl. 28 (dated 607 H/1210, New York, Metropolitan Museum of Art). Enderlein et al., 2001, p. 51 (Berlin, Museum für Islamische Kunst, inv. no. I. 1996.2). Pope, 1945, p. 121, pl. 84 (Kelekian Collection).

[98] Cf. Holter, 1937, pp. 11–2.

[99] Pancaroğlu, 2007, p. 133, cat. no. 86.

[100] Cf. *eadem*, p. 133, cat. no. 86.

[101] Cf. Meisami, 1987, pp. 237–98.

[102] *L'Islam dans les collections nationales*, 1977, p. 148, cat. no. 293. Watson, 1985, pp. 104–6 and fig. 76. *L'Etrange et le Merveilleux en terres d'Islam*, 2001, p. 110, cat. no. 75. Paris, Musée du Louvre, Département des Antiquités orientales, Section Islamique, inv. no. MOA 444.

[103] Cf. Hoffman, 2001, p. 26.

difficulties in distinguishing between centres of production.[104]

The iconographic scheme of encircling serpents is clearly rendered on an eleventh- or early twelfth-century wine-red and gold samite, the so-called relic cover of Saint Amandus, one part of which is preserved in the Abegg-Stiftung in Riggisberg, the other in the Cleveland Museum of Art.[105] The textile fragments, which are thought to have a Western Asian provenance, possibly from the Saljuq realm, figure staggered beaded escutcheon-shaped medallions enclosing gigantic double-headed eagles with their wings outspread. The eagles surmount pairs of addorsed feline quadrupeds whose tails also terminate in dragon heads with gaping jaws. A pair of giant double-headed dragons encloses the entire composition (fig. 156).

An extended form of the encircling dragon motif is also found on the lining fabrics of the coronation mantle of Roger II (r. 1130–1154), the Norman ruler of Sicily and southern Italy. The outer face of the red silk cloak, which was woven in the royal workshop *(dār al-ṭirāz)* in Palermo and carries an inscription in Kufic dating it to the year 528/1133–4, is embroidered with gold thread and pearls with a central palm tree separating addorsed tigers attacking camels.[106] This iconography not only represents the cosmological and emblematic motifs that symbolised Roger's claim to power, but also creates a link beyond the western Norman domain to the Islamic sphere, which is underlined by the fact that the embroidered inscription along the lower hem of the garment is written in Arabic, a language used at Roger's court and in which he was fluent.[107] In view of the king's controversial status the imagery on the mantle would have been expected to convey the legitimacy of his position. The lining, however, would remain largely unseen, revealing only glimpses of the imagery which was therefore mainly reserved for the person of the king.

The lining fabrics comprise five successive sections from three different textiles that are, according to the motifs, commonly referred to as the "Dragon," the "Tree of Life," and the "Bird" cloth (figs. 157a and b).[108] All three types show a grid-like lattice composed of paired interlaced dragons with projecting tongues that define the overall surface and enclose groups of human figures, trees, birds and foliate motifs. A beaded *rinceau* runs along the body of one of the serpents while the body of the other is marked by evenly spaced stripes.[109] Since this imagery was chosen for the lining of the coronation mantle, a highly official and ceremonial vestment, its symbolic content must have been imbued with a special significance. While the outer face was intended as a visual statement of the king's claim to power and authority, the inner one may be seen as having an implicit talismanic intent. This may be compared to the use of talismanic shirts covered with Qur'ānic verses often in conjunction with astrological and magical practices and devices that were often worn under the outer garments (or armour) and of which a considerable number of Turko-Iranian examples are recorded.[110] These shirts were destined to protect the owner, avert injury or illness, and thereby bestow invulnerability. The encircling dragon motif which decorates the lining fabric that covers the inside of the coronation mantle may therefore be presumed to

[104] Soucek, 1997, pp. 405–7; *Glory of Byzantium*, 1997, p. 416 (catalogue entry no. 271 by Daniel Walker); Hoffman, 2001, pp. 18, 26.

[105] On the Cleveland fragment of the relic cover of Saint Amandus only the feathery tail and claws of the eagle survive. A further fragment is preserved in the collection of Rina and Norman Indictor, New York.

[106] The mantle was subsequently used for the coronation of the German emperors of the Roman Holy Empire and entered the treasury of the Vienna Kunsthistorisches Museum in 1801, inv. no. XIII 14; height 146 cm, length 345 cm. *Nobilis Officinae*, 2005, pp. 259–64, cat. no. 66; Tronzo, 2001, pp. 241–53.

[107] For a translation of the inscription, see *Nobilis Officinae*, 2005, pp. 259–64, cat. no. 66 (in German); Hoffman, 2001, p. 32 (in English).

[108] *Nobilis Officinae*, 2005, pp. 256–9, esp. p. 257, cat. no. 65. A textile from the tomb of Roger I, Norman Count of Sicily from 1071 to 1101, in Palermo belongs to this group, of which today only a drawing of 1784 survives. *Idem*, cat. no. 65, fig. 1 (after Daniele, F., *I regali sepolcri del Duomo di Palermo riconosciuti e illustrati*, Naples, 1784). It may further be compared to an eleventh- or twelfth-century drawing from Egypt with continuous scroll patterns, the lower band of which is composed of paired dragons with raised confronted heads, gaping mouths and projecting tongues touching at the centre, now in Berlin, Museum für Islamische Kunst, inv. no. I.6608; von Wilckens, 1997, p. 169, fig. 96. Cf. Gierlichs, 1993, p. 40, cat. no. 5; Grube and Johns, 2005, p. 260, fig. 94.5.

[109] It may not be irrelevant to note that the motif of the serpent also appears in the pavement of the main apse, the *Sancta Sanctorum*, in the Cappella Palatina, inlaid on either side with a large twice looped serpent, which, according to William Tronzo (1997, pp. 33–4, fig. 26; see *idem*, p. 34 and n. 20, for comparable examples), may have apotropaic meaning. Its association with an "Oriental" repertoire of motifs is strengthened by the existence of a panel with addorsed lions symmetrically flanking a stylised tree at the nave entrance to the choir; *idem*, p. 34, fig. 27.

[110] See *Turks*, 2005, 442, 458–9, cat. nos. 257, 322; and Tezcan, 2006.

have been intended not only to protect the king but also to endow him with certain abilities or powers.

Research into the silk and gold thread textiles underlines on the one hand the characteristics of Byzantine court production, the *panni imperiali*, while on the other pointing to stylistic features pertaining to Central Asia and the Ancient Orient. The closely related iconographies indicate the use of pattern books that seem to have circulated among different workshops involved in making the "golden textiles." In view of the complexity of cultural identification, Eva Hoffmann proposes the existence of a "shared textile vocabulary of the international courts between the tenth and the twelfth centuries from Islamic, Byzantine and Norman centres."[111]

The possibility of an eastern, and perhaps Central Asian, provenance for the overall iconography is strengthened by the discovery of a silk fragment from Samangan province in Afghanistan, now preserved in the al-Sabāh Collection in Kuwait (figs. 158a and b). In the same manner as on the "Bird Cloth," the Samangan fragment also shows a large, inverted pretzel-like interlace, formed by the ophidian bodies of four serpent-dragons. All the details of the iconographic expression, including palmette-like trees flanked by perched birds in the lobes of the interlace and the beaded or striped demarcation of the ophidian bodies as well as their projecting red tongues, are near-identical to those of the "Bird Cloth" (fig. 157a and b).

It would certainly be wrong to attempt to assign the motif to a single artistic tradition. However, it is worthy of note that the motifs enclosed by the confronted giant dragons that divide up the entire surface include the ancient Iranian cosmological motif of the tree with birds. This motif is closely related to the representation on the Byzantine enamelled medallion from the Pala d'Oro (fig. 151) which, although it was made in Constantinople, was clearly inspired by Iranian and Central Asian visual expressions. This artistic tradition permeates also the more complex iconography on the "Bird Cloth" lining fabric found in the coronation mantle of Roger II. Even though it would at first sight seem likely that the lining fabrics were inserted at the time the coronation mantle of Roger II was made (dated 528/1133–4), Anne Wardwell has tentatively dated another silk and gold textile decorated with parallel curving vines which also forms part of the lining of the mantle to the period between the third decade and the last quarter of the thirteenth century,[112] hence suggesting that a section of the lining was added at a later date. The al-Sabāh textile has been radiocarbon dated to between 1154 and 1282. Regrettably, the test results are not specific enough to be able to determine in which of the two centuries the textile was fashioned. The Samangan fragment with three-partite heart-shaped knots fashioned of serpent-dragons certainly underlines the wide circulation of this significant iconographic representation. The continued use of a motif associated with ancient Iranian ideas is not surprising given that, despite the triumph of Islam, the people of the eastern Islamic lands hung on to their pre-Islamic roots and associated iconographic notions more assiduously than those in most other areas of the Islamic world.

b. *The drinking dragon*

It is interesting to consider the exceptional motif of the drinking dragon which is depicted on the so-called "Dragon Cloth" section of the lining of the coronation mantle of Roger II. The open-mouthed dragon heads are shown with projecting tongues, apparently lapping from the contents of the stemmed cups (fig. 159).[113] The same motif is found above the lintel of the southern outer door of the monastery of Mār Behnām/Deir al-Khiḍr, an important place of pilgrimage associated with miraculous healing by both Christians and Muslims. The two addorsed intertwined dragons are portrayed with wide-open mouths and long tongues with entwined bifid tips that also appear to drink from a stemmed cup (fig. 160).

The same visual formulation can be observed in an illustration in the Vani Gospels, a Georgian manuscript transcribed and illuminated in Constantinople at Romani Monastery by the Georgian monk Ioane for the celebrated Georgian queen Tʿamar (1184–1211/2) in *c.* 1200. A canon table set within an architectural frame of columns supporting arches is surmounted at the apex by paired serpents that lap with bifid tongues at the liquid

[111] Hoffman, 2001, p. 34.

[112] Wardwell, 1988–9, p. 110, with references, and fig. 48.

[113] Cf. *Nobilis Officinae*, 2005, pp. 124, 126, figs. 1 and 2, pp. 256–9, cat. no. 65 ("Dragon Cloth"). Pairs of drinking griffins and lions antithetically placed on either side of a bowl-shaped vase are featured on the relief ornamentation of the Mshattā façade in present-day Jordan built during the early Islamic period. See Creswell, 1932, pls. 66–74.

contained within a chalice (fig. 161). The foot of the chalice is held in place by the interlaced reptilian bodies, patterned with scales, which spring from the base of a four-columned structure that holds up a fountain, probably representing the "Fountain of Life," underlining the paradisiac symbolism associated with the illumination of canon tables.[114] The composition is flanked by winged mythical creatures, a griffin to the left and a sphinx-like being playing a stringed instrument on the right.

The symbolism of a dragon with its head placed close to the vessel as if eager to reach the contents while its body serves as handle attached to jugs and ewers had been known since ancient times.[115] The motif became formalised in the post-Sasanian period with the body of the dragon becoming more stylised.[116] This type of imagery in which the gaping snout of a dragon head holds the rim of a vessel above a handle or, alternatively, releases the liquid when it serves as spout (fig. 35), is associated with the reading of the dragon as beneficent custodian, safeguarding the precious contents of the vessel.

The dragon's role as a beneficent creature, guardian of the liquid of vessels, evoked in the figure of a winged and horned dragon with elongated snout and open jaws, reaching towards the folded lip of a vessel while the frontlegs hold onto the side wall just below the rim, is featured on a late seventh- or early eighth-century pear-shaped gold jug of unknown provenance, preserved in the Moscow Historical Museum (fig. 162).[117] The proximity of the dragon protome to the vessel's rim, which is rendered as if eager to reach for the contents, was perhaps seen as token of the liquid's protection.

The motif of a serpent lapping from a vessel was a well-known theme in depictions of Greek mythology.[118] It appears on a sixth-century Byzantine gilded silver dish, preserved in the State Hermitage Museum, St. Petersburg, an example of the reception of Dionysiac motifs in sixth-century Byzantine art.[119] It shows a young woman with one knee bent at a right angle, opening with one hand the lid of a cylindrical container from which a serpent is emerging, while with the other holding a calyx-like vessel, from whose contents the serpent is lapping. The container has been identified as *cista mystica*, the iconographic emblem of the Eleusinian and Bacchic mysteries to which in late Hellenistic times a serpent issuing from the sacred *cista* was added.[120] The female figure is probably associated with a mystery cult, perhaps representing a maenad, one of the female followers of the god Dionysos (fig. 163).[121] A similar motif is associated with Hygieia, goddess of medicine, whose cult spread with that of her mythical father Asklepios and who like her father is invariably associated with a serpent, sometimes shown as drinking from a bowl held in her hand.[122] The motif of the lapping dragon, which seems to be rooted in Dionysiac lore, was also known in early Kushan-period Gandhāra (present-day Afghanistan and Pakistan). It is exemplified on a schist relief (fig. 164) with a nude boy (*eros* or *putto*)

[114] For a discussion of the overall iconography of Armenian canon tables (which however does not consider the role of the dragons), see Mathews and Sanjian, 1991, pp. 169–73, esp. p. 171. On the symbolism of the *fons vitae*, see Underwood, 1950, pp. 43–138.

[115] See chapter 3, "The dragon motif on vessels." Melikian-Chirvani identifies the representation of a feline or mythical head griping the rim of a vessel as visual metaphor of "the king drinking wine as a substitute for sacrificial blood" which goes as far back as Achaemenid times. See *idem*, 1992, pp. 101–34, *idem*, 1995, pp. 47–97, esp. pp. 54–7 for literary images of wine as substitute for blood libations, and *idem*, 1996, pp. 85–139.

[116] Cf. the parallel development of the feline, most often symbolising a panther, in post-Sasanian art, Ettinghausen, 1972, pp. 3–10.

[117] Marshak, 1971, T8, and 1986, pp. 58–9, fig. 68 (line drawing); Rempel', 1987a, 63, fig. 24b.

[118] See the discussion in Elderkin, 1924, pp. 11, 15–9, 37–8, 41–3, 137. The iconographic scheme of a serpent drinking from a vessel appears, for instance, on a marble relief from Tomis (Constanta), dated to the second century AD, preserved in Bucharest, Archaeological Institute, a serpent coiled around a tree moves to drink from a phiale held out by a rider next to an enthroned goddess. See also another marble relief, again perhaps from Tomis, dating to the second or third century AD, now in a private collection, London, where the reptile drinks from a phiale offered by a standing goddess flanked by an approaching rider. See Lane, ed., 1996, p. 142, fig. K12, p. 143, fig. K14. The motif of a goddess offering liquid from a vial to a serpent is also shown on a Roman relief in the National Museum, Palermo, inv. no. 1551 (*ibid*, p. 157) as well as on a late Roman votive relief, now in the Musée du Louvre, Paris, inv. no. MA 3316 (*ibid*, p. 148). A distant echo of the motif is found on fifth-century BC stone reliefs and terracotta plaques from Lakonia, attesting to its great antiquity. Cf. Salapata, 2006, pp. 541–60. It also appears on an archaic Laconian relief from Gerakion featuring the descent of the dead to Hades. Elderkin, 1924, pl. II, fig. 2, and p. 11 with further references.

[119] For a discussion of the reception of Dionysiac motifs in Sasanian art, cf. Ettinghausen, 1972, pp. 3–10.

[120] Burkert, 1995, p. 84. See also Kelhoffer, 2000, pp. 364–5.

[121] Cf. *Iskusstvo Vizantii v sobraniiakh SSSR*, 1977, vol. 1, p. 98, fig. 133.

[122] Cf. Thrämer, "Health and Gods of Healing (Greek)," *ERE*, vol. 6, part 2, 1914, p. 552.

attempting to quench the thirst of a dragon who seems to lap from the contents of a bowl that is offered while a second boy, also holding a cup, rides sideways on its back.[123]

In Christian iconography the Dionysiac symbol of the cup or the *kantharos* took on a new significance by becoming the Eucharistic chalice.[124] The motif of the drinking serpent appears as the serpent-topped chalice of John the Evangelist.[125] While it is likely that this form of imagery was initially imbued with ideas of healing and salvation, associated with the beneficial aspect of the serpent, the same motif later increasingly came to be reinterpreted and reformulated in a negative sense when the meaning of the myth associated with the serpent was inverted. As a result of this process the (serpent-)dragon assumed an overall meaning as symbol and instrument of a fiendish force in Christian imagery, thus frequently bearing the traces of the mental and cultural shift imposed by the new religious system.[126] In the new Christian context, numerous hagiographic and other traditions created a restructured version of ancient mythical themes pertaining to the dragon. In consequence, there was a shift in mythological paradigm, the force of the earlier myth died, was changed or suppressed and only vestiges of it remain. This inversion of meaning is attested in the eleventh- or early twelfth-century Byzantine encyclopaedia of the Metaphrastian Menologion volumes featuring so-called "revenge miniatures."[127] These show the crowned figures of Roman tyrants responsible for the deaths of martyred saints, associated with a serpent or dragon seen as an embodiment or emissary of Satan. One of these depictions portrays a crowned figure, probably representing the emperor Maximian, holding a vessel from which a serpent is drinking.[128]

Hence it is a reasonable conjecture that the drinking dragons on the "Dragon Cloth" section of the lining of the coronation mantle of Roger II, those over the door at the monastery of Mār Behnām and those in the Vani Gospels all belong to the same symbolic group, representing the visual remnants that survived the mutations of ancient beliefs. The basic association between the vessel as container of liquid and the dragon was so strong that it survived in different forms even though the original iconographic association had perhaps long been forgotten.[129] Vestiges of the importance of its former cultic associations can however still be gauged from the "revenge miniatures" in which the original intent of the iconography of the drinking serpent was inverted and survives in corrupted form.

---

[123] Kurita, 1988, repr. 2003, vol. 2, fig. 737 (erroneously catalogued as lion). Cf. Ingholt, 1957, pp. 156–7, no. 296; Boardman, 2003, pp. 139–40, fig. 10 (line drawing).

[124] See Elderkin, 1924, pp. 41–7.

[125] The motif refers to the challenge given to Saint John by the High Priest of Diana at Ephesus to drink from a poisoned cup; in order to warn him, two criminals had been given the same poison to drink and they both died immediately. However the apostle made the sign of the cross, the poison departed from the cup in the form of a serpent and John did not suffer any ill effects. Recorded in Book V of the Acts of the Apostles of the Apocrypha Abdias, reportedly from the Bishop of Babylon; Fabricius, J.A., *Codex apocryphus Novi Testamenti*, ed. secunda, Hamburg, 1719, vol. 1, p. 577, see Barb, 1953, p. 9; also Kelhoffer, 2000, pp. 449–52. While it is not specified what kind of harmful substance was contained in the potion offered to Saint John, it is of note that this deed may not be as miraculous at it appears had it contained snake venom. Already in classical antiquity it was quite well-known that a viper's venom is harmful only if it enters directly into a person's blood stream (that is, through an open wound) but not if it is imbibed. See *idem*, pp. 433–452, with further examples of "miracles" involving the drinking of snake venom.

[126] See p. 119, n. 85.

[127] Cf. the example of an eleventh- or early twelfth-century Byzantine encyclopaedia of the Metaphrastian Menologion, n. 986. Cf. Walter, 2003, pp. 52–3.

[128] Sinai, Monastery of Saint Catherine, gr. 508, fol. 234v: Inde and Domna (6F7). See Patterson Ševčenko, 1990, p. 156.

[129] Cf. the parallel transmission of the Dionysiac animal, the panther or lynx, into Sasanian and post-Sasanian art and the concluding remarks of Ettinghausen, 1972, p. 10. Note also the use of both serpent and feline (in this case interpreted as lion) on the handle of the Bobrinsky bucket (*idem*, fig. 125).

CHAPTER TEN

THE KNOTTED DRAGON MOTIF

a. *The ancient practice of knot tying*

From ancient times the tying of magical knots was a way of binding magical/supernatural powers.[1] The ritual practice of tying knots in a cord and blowing on them was one of the most common forms of harmful or therapeutic magic in pre-Islamic times.[2] The practice is connected with the concept of binding spells whose knots cannot be unloosed, thus drawing on the principles of sympathetic magic with the purpose of rendering the victim generally impotent.[3] Serpent charming may be interpreted in a similar manner since the serpents are "bound" by the charmer.[4] The knotted representations are used as symbols to conjure up the cosmic powers that are appropriate to effectively protect or, conversely, harm individuals as well as human communities.[5] Such "binding spells" are frequently employed on Aramaic and Mandaic incantation bowls. In these the magician threatens to employ a spell such as he has used to bind the sea and the dragon Leviathan, and to bind the victim with the same bonds as those constraining the sky, the earth and the seven planets.[6]

The Qurʾān warns of "the evil (arising) from those who blow (or spit) upon the knots" (*sūra* 113, 4), a practice analogous to that known as "tying the aglet," designed to keep husbands and wives apart.[7] It is notable that *sūra*s 113 and 114 are called *al-muʿawwidhatān* ("the two who preserve") and their verses are considered of special talismanic power if recited in tandem with the original signification of blowing upon the knots.[8] Interestingly, *sūra* 113 refers to the evil women "who blow upon knots," and for this reason it is believed to be "particularly efficacious against the ills of the flesh."[9]

In his commentary on *sūra* 113, the thirteenth-century Qurʾānic exegete al-Bayḍāwī refers to a related account according to which a Jew cast a magic spell on the Prophet Muḥammad by putting a cord with eleven knots into a well, whereupon he fell ill.[10] After the revelation of *sūra*s 113 and 114, the archangel Jibrāʾīl disclosed the cause of

---

[1] In Mesopotamian magic texts the verb "to bind" (Akkadian *kasâru*) was used to express the concept of "bewitchment" (Astour, 1968, p. 18). Inversely, in lengthy litanies the help of the gods was invoked to undo or dissolve the knot of a magic spell or charm which was believed to have supernatural powers (Dhorme, 1949, p. 261). In like manner the texts describe the role of the conjurer as the "knotter" (Akkadian *kashu*) or the "untangler" (Akkadian *pâtaru*) of nefarious or beneficial charms, respectively, both of which are symbolised by knots (Amiet, 1961, rev. and repr. 1980, p. 116). The apotropaic function of the knot is a recurrent phenomenon in many countries and periods. Cf. Kitzinger, 1970, p. 642 and n. 21.

[2] Cf. Wellhausen, 1897, p. 161. A scholium on a sermon of the fourth-century archbishop of Constantinople, Gregory of Nazianze, defines incantations *(epasmata)* with the words:

> The chants sung over young children by [...] old women, muttering to avert evil, and at the same time licking the babes' foreheads with their tongues and spitting, blowing to each side.

Migne, J.P., *Patrologia Graeca* 36, 907 B-C, cited after Bonner, 1950, p. 4.

[3] Jeffers, 1996, p. 32.

[4] *Eadem*, p. 32.

[5] This is corroborated by Porphyrios who in his letter to Anebon considered the tying and untying of sacred knots as means by which the theurgists induced the gods to certain actions. Cf. Chwolsohn, 1856, vol. 2, p. 138, n. 144.

[6] "Wenn ihr irgend etwas gegen ... unternehmt, dann werde ich euch bezaubern mit der großen Bezauberung des Meeres und mit der Bezauberung des Ungeheuers Leviathan ... biege ich den Bogen gegen euch und spanne die Sehne gegen euch ... bringe ich herab auf euch den Beschluß des Himmels und den Bann, den ich auf den Berg [Hermon] und auf das Ungeheuer Leviathan gelegt habe ... [binde ich euch mit der Bindung], durch die Himmel und Erde gebunden wurden ... binde ich euch mit der Bindung, durch welche die sieben Planeten gebunden wurden." Niggemeyer, 1975, pp. 70, 146.

[7] Fahd, "Siḥr," *EI*² IX, 567b.

[8] It is however remarkable that the idiom "blowing on magical knots" was still metaphorically used during the tenth-century as attested by al-Thaʿālibī's account of the literary life at the Samanid court where:

> ...men of letters ... [were] each offering to the other fragrant flowers of dialectic, and pursuing the perfumes of Culture, and letting fall in succession necklaces of pearls, and *blowing on magical knots* [emphasis added].

Yatīmat al-dahr, part IV, ch. 2, Cairo, 1377, tr. Browne, 1920, vol. 1, pp. 365–6, cited after Clinton, 1972, p. 4.

[9] Ruska and Carra de Vaux, "Tilsam," *EI*² X, 500a.

[10] Cf. Canaan, 1938, p. 75 and n. 42.

the illness and the Prophet sent ʿAlī to read the two *sūras*. At each verse *(āyaʿalāʾiyya)* a knot was untied and the Prophet was cured.[11] His third and favourite wife ʿĀʾisha is recorded as saying:

> As soon as he recited the Qurʾân over one of these knots into which a spell against him had been placed, that particular knot became untied.[12]

The Basran Muslim mystic, Abū ʿAbd Allāh al-Ḥārith al-Muḥāsibī (d. 243/857), said that God helps the man who persists in his wrongdoing and is in need of something "which unties in his heart the knots of persistence in evil, in such a way that he may return to his Lord in repentance of his offence."[13] In Muslim religious science the act of loosing or untying a knot is considered the resolving of a difficulty *(ḥulūl)* which in Hellenistic philosophy denotes the inherent accident in an object as well as the substantial union of soul and body.[14] This is also noticeable in the custom that the garments of pilgrims conducting the *ḥajj* must be knotless, which is in accordance with the widespread belief that those who officiate at either religious or magical ceremonies should have no knots on their person.[15]

Describing a magical act directed against an enemy, the historian and jurist Abū Zayd ʿAbd al-Raḥmān Walī al-Dīn al-Ḥaḍramī, known as Ibn Khaldūn (732/1332–784/1382), recounts how the magician created an image of the intended victim and then began to pronounce the spell:

> ...during the repeated pronunciation of the evil words he collected spittle in his mouth and spat upon (the picture). Then he tied a knot over the symbol in an object that he had prepared for this purpose since he considered tying knots and (making things) stick together to be auspicious (and effective in magical operations). In this manner the magician can inflict upon his victim what he had intended.[16]

Contrarily, knots were also designed to protect from harm, and served to safeguard health and love relations.[17] Release from binding spells, *ḥall al-maʿqūd* ("unbinding the tied"), is one of the stated uses of early magic-medicinal bowls. The word *maʿqūd* means one who is bound with knots, a commonly used term for a person on whom a spell has been cast. The knot is allegorically referred to in the Qurʾān, when Mūsā implores God to loosen a knot from his tongue (*sūra* 20, 27). The nightly recitations of the Qurʾān *(tahajjud)* are said to be justified on the basis that it loosens one of the knots which Satan ties in the hair of a sleeper (*sūra* 17, 81).[18]

It is notable that the same concept existed in the Turkic culture where the concept "magic" is also expressed in "bond, fetters" *(bag)*.[19] A magical association with knotting is also made in one of the earliest prose romances in Persian, the *Kitāb-i Samak ʿAyyār*, in which the magicians who are captured may be bound by a rope only if the binder knows the special types of knots and the appropriate manner of fastening them.[20]

More mundane are the allegorical associations made by the Rūm Saljuq chronicler Ibn Bībī in his *al-Awāmir al-ʿAlāʾiyya fī ʾl-ūmur al-ʿAlāʾiyya*, who writes that in spite of the waning fortunes of the empire:

> ...it occurred to no one that the knot of this empire could dissolve and that the sun of this fortune could set.[21]

For the successful conclusion of the Rūm Saljuq *sulṭān* ʿIzz al-Dīn Kay Kāwūs's marriage preparations he elaborates upon the commonly used metaphor "to tie the marriage knot" *(ʿaqdi zanāshūʾī bastan)*[22] in the following manner:

> ...when the knot of the agreement was tightened and the rope of the bond gained firmness.[23]

---

[11] Johnstone, 1976, pp. 79–80. Cf. Muslim, *Īmān*, vol. 2, p. 275, cited after Fahd, "Sihr," *EI*² IX, p. 567b.

[12] *Muqaddima*, tr. Rosenthal, 1958, vol. 3, pp. 160, 168.

[13] In his *Kitāb al-Riʿāya li-ḥuqūq Allāh* ("Book of Observance of the Rights of God"), al-Muḥāsibī includes the study of the "repentant ones," *al-tawwābūn*. Arnaldez, "al-Muḥāsibī, Abū ʿAbd Allāh al-Ḥārith," *EI*² VII, 466b.

[14] Massignon [Anawati], "Ḥulūl," *EI*² III, 570b.

[15] Frazer, 1913, repr. 1980.

[16] *Muqaddima*, tr. Rosenthal, 1958, vol. 3, p. 161. Cf. Scheftelowitz, 1912–913, pp. 15–6 and n. 1.

[17] Cf. Chwolsohn, 1856, vol. 2, pp. 138–9, n. 144. In the Talmud the third-century rabbi Abaji says that when three, five or seven knots are tied to the left arm, they have power, respectively, to protect from ill-health, to heal and to protect from magic.

[18] Abū Dāwūd, *Tatawwuʿ*, *bāb* 18. Wensinck, "Tahadjdjud," *EI*² X, 87a.

[19] The word *bag* is derived from the verb *ba-* "to bind," hence a magic spell can be bound. I would like to thank Professor Dr Zieme for elucidating this point.

[20] *Samak-i ʿAyyār* II, p. 354; V, p. 532, as cited in Omidsalar, "Magic in literature and folklore in the Islamic period," *EIr*. Cf. Gaillard, 1987, pp. 19–21.

[21] "... es niemandem ... in den Sinn [kam], daß der Knoten jenes Reiches sich auflösen und die Sonne jenes Glückes untergehen könne." Ibn Bībī, *al-Awāmir al-ʿalāʾiyya*, tr. Duda, 1959, p. 47.

[22] Steingass, 1892, repr. 1981, pp. 623, 857.

[23] "... als der Knoten des Vertrages zusammengezogen war und das Seil der Verbindung Festigkeit erhalten hatte." Ibn Bībī, *al-Awāmir al-ʿalāʾiyya*, tr. Duda, 1959, p. 79.

The allegory of the knotted dragon tail is used by the early thirteenth-century secretary in the administration of Jamāl al-Dīn Ay Ana Ulugh Bārbak,[24] Abu 'l-Sharaf Nāṣiḥ Jarbādhqānī, who records that:

> Abu 'l-Ḥasan was commanded to Sistan and with cunning, boldness and skill to bring success to this travail, which had become knotted as the Dragon's tail ... to free the troops from the straits of exile, the locks and bolts of affliction[25]

hence alluding to these military difficulties as "knots" in the dragon's tail.

It should be remarked in this connection that the use of knots as apotropaic devices perpetuates earlier practice seen in the architecture of the early Islamic period.[26] It is significant that these were also placed in or near thresholds. The desert residence of Khirbat al-Mafjar, possibly built by the eighth-century Umayyad prince and later caliph al-Walīd ibn Yazīd,[27] for instance, had specially designed mosaics with magic knot designs placed on the thresholds to ensure the magical entrapment of any evil force trying to enter the throne hall *(dīwān)*.[28] Similar knot designs were employed in contemporary churches of Syria and Palestine suggesting that the apotropaic associations of ancient times were incorporated into Christian concepts as well.[29]

The knotting aspect can also be observed in Islamic epigraphy on portable objects, for instance on the Bobrinski bucket, dated 559/1163. Circumscribing the body at mid-section is an epigraphic frieze with a benedictory content which has constantly repeated knotted hastae (fig. 34). In addition to their decorative function, the reduplication of potent signs such as complex knotted forms, in this case mainly of a quadripartite configuration, together with the reiteration of letters (an important part of magical practice), was presumably intended to intensify their beneficial effect by invoking the concept of a continuous, endless protection.[30] To this may be added the definition given by the fourteenth-century Ottoman theologian and biographer, ʿIṣām al-Dīn Ṭashköprüzāde, of the Arabic word *ṭilasm*, or talisman, as "indissoluble knot."[31]

b. *The knotted dragon*

It has been suggested that the motif of entwined dragons with necks or bodies interlaced to form a single loop, occasionally a knot, consistently employed in medieval Islamic architecture on gates and portals, is subject to different interpretations.[32] Guitty Azarpay more clearly specifies that:

> the theme of the entwined dragons finds Central Asian forerunners that doubtless contributed to the widespread use of the motif in Islamic art patronized by Turkish dynasties.[33]

This is illustrated on memorial steles, a celebrated example being the early eighth-century entwined dragons that crown the stele of the Turkic commander-in-chief Köl Tigin, inscribed with a bilingual text in Chinese and Turkic, in Chöshöö Cajdam in Mongolia (fig. 165).[34] Together with the memorial complex the stele was built in 731 with the help of Chinese palace artists sent by the Chinese emperor Xuanzong (r. 712–756). The Chinese artists worked under Turkic instructions overseen by Köl Tigin's older brother Bilgä Qaghan (d. 734), hence one may surmise that the iconographies figured in the memorial stele were intended, in accordance with Turkic cosmogonic and cosmological beliefs, to smooth the way of the deceased into the afterlife.[35] The stele was

---

[24] Jamāl al-Dīn Ay Aba Ulugh Bārbak played an important role in the politics that followed after the death of last Great Saljuq ruler in the west, Ṭoghrıl III ibn Arslan.

[25] Meisami, 1999, p. 260.

[26] For an example of the use of knots of Solomon as an apotropaic device, see the eight Solomon knots that appear as isolated motifs in the mosaic pavement that covers the threshold block of the synagogue at Sardis, rebuilt in the fourth century. Cf. Dinkler, 1978, p. 78, pl. XVII, 13.

[27] Ettinghausen, 1972, p. 42.

[28] Cf. *idem*, pp. 17–65, esp. pp. 47, 63, pls. 17–27; Farès, 1959, p. 33.

[29] Ettinghausen, 1972, p. 47; Farès, 1959, p. 52.

[30] Cf. p. 107, n. 209.

[31] In his encyclopaedia *Miftāḥ al-saʿāda wa-miṣbāh al-siyāda* I, 277, 3 to 278, 3. Ullmann, 1972, p. 362 and n. 3.

[32] Azarpay, 1978, p. 366, n. 20; Tabbaa, 1997, p. 77; Santoro, 2006, p. 550.

[33] Azarpay, 1978, p. 366, n. 20.

[34] The interlaced dragon motif has a very long history in the Central Asian region, as is exemplified by a pair of inlaid and pierced gold belt plaques with a pair of entwined lupine dragons in combat with birds, probably griffins, found at *kurgan* 3, datable to the second or first century BC, in Tchaltyr, Miasnikovski district, a region bordering Kuban in Rostov province, near the Sea of Azov in south Russia, which are part of the stylistic repertoire of Scytho-Siberian art. Museum of Azov, inv. no. KP-24444/1 and 2. Schiltz, 2001, pp. 178–9, cat. no. 198.

[35] Scharlipp, 1992, p. 51. Excavations of the Köl Tigin memorial complex revealed that its gates were oriented towards the east, the direction held sacred in Turkic belief

originally erected on the back of a pedestal in the form of a turtle, which was found nearby. The front of the stele oriented towards sunrise bears an inscription in runic Turkic script, whereas the back of the monument is inscribed in Chinese characters with the condolences sent by the Tang emperor. Another example is offered by a fragmentary monumental stone memorial stele carved with the arched body of a quadruped dragon (which formed the left side of an entwined pair of dragons) of the eighth Uighur *qaghan* (r. 808–821) at the Uighur capital Qarabalghasun (Ordu Balïq), to the south of the palace remains, in the Ötükän region of Mongolia (fig. 166). The dragon head is rendered with foreshortened snout ending in a tightly curled tip, holding a round object, perhaps a pearl, in its open jaws and with a thick curly beard at the lower jaw, extending into a prominently protruding forehead with bulging eyes and large, cusped ears swept to the back. The latter touch upon an *X*-shaped motif enlivened with small roundels in the interstitial areas that embellish the dragon's neck, while the scaled muscular body is slightly awkwardly arranged with large projecting extremities terminating in unsheathed claws. The fragment almost certainly formed one side of an interlaced pair of dragons that once crowned a colossal memorial stele inscribed, as surviving fragments reveal, with a trilingual text in Chinese, Uighur and Sogdian. The doubling aspect of the interlaced dragons has already been touched upon in preceding chapters. The pairing of the dragons, aimed at buttressing and doubling the visual impact, was a noticeable feature that may have served to augment the intended effect of the potent symbol. This may moreover be associated with the inherently ambivalent aspect of the dragon in ancient Turkish cosmology which saw the creature living underground in winter then re-appearing in the spring and soaring into the sky in the summer where it reigned at the zenith as a divine creature.[36]

The association of the Turks with the dragon is further corroborated by ethnogonic myths of different Turkic tribes which are characteristic of Central Asian founder myths and legends of origin (for instance, the mythic formulae of the origins of the ancient Scythian-Saka),[37] such as the tale of the origin of the Kimeks, recorded in the eleventh-century account of the Ghaznawid historian Abū Saʿīd ʿAbd al-Ḥayy Gardīzī.[38] The legend recounts how Shad, the ruler and "founder" of the Kimeks:

> ...one day heard a voice coming from the water as he stood on the banks of the Irtysh; the voice said, Shad, give me your hand in the water. Shad, seeing only some hair floating on the surface of the water, tethered his horse and entered the water; he grasped the hair, which turned out to belong to his wife-to-be, Khatun, and upon enquiring, he learned that she had been seized from the riverbank by a water dragon.[39]

The Kimek founder myth not only affirms the sacredness of the river Irtysh in Siberia to the Turkic tribe but also involves the motif of an ancestress that had been snatched by an aquatic dragon.

Also noteworthy is the account given by the Armenian historian Mattʿēos Uṙhayetsi (d. 1142) of the Qun migration in the mid-eleventh century, in which he mentions the "People of the Serpents" that attack the Pale Ones (*khartēshkʿ* = Cumans).[40] To this may be added the story of a Qıpchaq chieftain, Tugorkan, recounted in Rus'

as source of the sun; a concept which is not adhered to in Chinese architecture. Cf. Hersek, 2002, pp. 152, 156. The cosmic meaning of the dragon in the art of the pre-Islamic Türks of Central Asia was discussed by Emel Esin (1968–70 and 1973) and Gönül Öney (1969a).

[36] Boratav, "Drache," *WdM* VII, 1, p. 207. See also Esin, 1970–1, pp. 161–82, and a review by Rogers (1970–1, pp. 267–9), in which he disputes the cosmological significance of the dragon in Turkish art. In her reply (1973–4, pp. 151–2) Esin quotes, *inter alia*, from Yusūf Khāṣṣ Ḥājib's *Qutadghu-bilig* ("Wisdom of Royal Glory") completed in 462/1069–70, couplet 126: *Yarattı, kör, evren, tuçi evrilür Anıng birle tezginç yime texginür* ("See, He created *evren* [the dragon] which revolves continually, Together with it revolves the Ecliptic"). For a further dicussion, see Esin, 1981, p. 834.

[37] Cf. DeWeese, 1994, p. 496, n. 8. See too the Hunnic legend of origin which is rendered, albeit imperfectly, in Iordanes' sixth-century *Getica* ("Gothic History") which comprises an account by the Byzantine historian Priscus who travelled among the Huns. According to "old traditions," the Huns are descended from "witches" *(haliurunnae)*, or "magician women" *(magas mulieres)*, who consorted with "unclean spirits" of the steppes and whose offspring dwelled first in "swamps." See *Getica*, tr. and ed. Mierow, 1915, repr. 2006, pp. 85–6; Maenchen-Helfen, 1944–5, pp. 244–51; Pohl, "Hunnen," *RgA*, vol. 15, 2000, p. 248; DeWeese, 1994, p. 496.

[38] Bartol'd, V.V., "Izvlechenie iz Zain al-Akhbar," *Sochineniia*, VIII, p. 27 (text), 44 (tr.); Marquart, 1914, pp. 89–91; Martinez, 1982, pp. 109–75, esp. pp. 120–1 on the Kimek. All references as cited in DeWeese, 1994, p. 494 and n. 3.

[39] DeWeese, 1994, p. 494. See also Monchi-Zadeh, 1975, p. 234.

[40] Marquart, 1914, pp. 54–5. *Sharaf al-Zamān Ṭāhir Marwazī*, tr. and ed. Minorsky, 1942, p. 18 (Arabic), pp. 29–30 (English). Minorsky (p. 103) suggests that the "People of the Snake/Serpent" were the Qun, whereas Marquart (p. 55) leans towards identifying them with either the Qitan or Qay. All references cited after Golden, 1997, p. 89 and n. 13. On the eleventh-century migrations of nomadic peoples in the Eurasian steppe zone, cf. Vásáry, 2005, esp. pp. 4–12.

literary tradition *(byliny)*, who carries the patronymic "Tugarin Zmeevich" ("the son of the serpent-dragon").[41]

While it may not be possible to trace the chain of transmission of the interlaced dragons, they are considered to be variations in the context of a possible *sensus communis*. However, not only are the dragons portrayed as pairs with necks or bodies entwined to form a single central loop, but occasionally their own bodies incorporate a knot at mid-section. The shape of the knot varies, though it is often quadripartite in form.

Yet before discussing the motif in the Western Central Asian region it is interesting to note that the iconography of dragons joined by means of a quadripartite knot also makes an appearance in a Buddhist context in the art of eastern Turkestan. Depictions appear in the wall paintings of cave monasteries in Shorchuk, dated between the sixth and the eighth century, and Bezeklik in Qocho (Chinese Gaochang, the former capital of the western Uighur kingdom, Dakianusšhahri, located *c.* 30 km east of present-day Turfan), which has been dated to the late tenth century.[42] The Shorchuk wall painting shows donors facing confronted dragons knotted at mid-section in a similar manner (fig. 167). An analogous composition of knotted dragons is portrayed on a now destroyed wall painting from Bezeklik which survives only in a drawing by the German archaeologist Albert Grünwedel made during the third German expedition to Chinese Turkestan in 1906 to 1907. The drawing shows a pair of superimposed vegetal stems each terminating in a blossom growing out of a water pool. At the point of juncture, a pair of addorsed Chinese-derived dragons project horizontally, their hind limbs entwined to form a central quadripartite knot, while the upper blossom forms the seat of Padmapāṇi, the Bodhisattva of Compassion (fig. 168). The painting displays a fusion of Buddhist and Manichaean elements which evolved under Uighur patronage in the late tenth century. The fact that it was executed under Uighur patronage adds further weight to the possibility that the interlaced dragon figure was introduced into Islamic art from Central Asia via the Turkic dynasties.[43]

It is significant in this regard that some of the earliest extant examples of the quadripartite knot in Islamic art seem to appear in the wider Khurasan region. A key document, the starting point for the discussion that follows, is a large, elongated copper alloy matrix with cusped arch terminals, distinguished by a pair of confronted dragons in mirror image whose scaly bodies form a central quadripartite interlacing knot (fig. 169).[44] Both arch-shaped ends are filled with the protomes of the paired confronted dragons. The latter have rounded heads with wide-open snouts showing finely demarcated flews and inward-curled tips and revealing projecting tongues that touch at the centre. Their elongated twisted horns with upward-curling tips curve towards the back above the slender cusped ears. The heads are separated from the curving bodies by a finely moulded "collar." Their angled ribbed front legs with rounded feet nearly touch at the tips. The serpentine bodies of the four dragons form a large, central quadripartite knot that is enlivened at the centre by a small quatrefoil with elongated lozenge-shaped petals which may represent a stellar emblem.

This matrix, now in the al-Sabāh Collection, Kuwait National Museum, is part of a set of 77 copper alloy matrices for belt/strap fittings, one of which bears an inscription in the name of Muḥammad ibn Sām above the figure of a lion.[45] As discussed earlier, the inscription connects the set directly with the Ghurid *sulṭān* Ghiyāth al-Dīn Muḥammad ibn Sām or his younger brother, Muʿizz al-Dīn Muḥammad ibn Sām. This set of matrices could thus have appertained to either one, or both, of the brothers, although Ghiyāth al-Dīn clearly remained the elder statesman.[46] The set was, moreover, reportedly found near the

[41] Rybakov, B.A., *Drevnjaja Rus'. Skazanija, byliny, letopisi*, Moscow, 1963, pp. 102–4. In a *bylina* verse Tugorkan is depicted as riding forth with two grey wolves preceding him; Rybakov, B.A., *Kievskaja Rus' i russikie knjazhestva XII–XIII vv.*, Moscow, 1982, p. 156 (in which this verse is cited); both sources as cited in Golden, 1997, p. 89. Cf. the discussion in Schirmunski, 1961, pp. 23–4.

[42] Cf. Russell-Smith, 2005, pp. 230–2.

[43] Azarpay, 1978, p. 366, n. 20.

[44] Three further matrices feature seated lions with upward-arching tails terminating in large horned dragon-heads; Kuwait, al-Sabāh Collection, Dar al-Athar al-Islamiyyah, Kuwait National Museum, inv. nos. LNS 2558 J a-x2 'x2,' 's2' and 't2.'

[45] Kuwait, al-Sabāh Collection, Dar al-Athar al-Islamiyyah, Kuwait National Museum, inv. no. LNS 2558 J a-x2 'g'; length 4.42 cm, width 2.81 cm.

[46] Cf. Flood, 2005, p. 266.

minaret of Jām.[47] The name and elaborate titles of *sulṭān* Ghiyāth al-Dīn Muḥammad ibn Sām are given on the three lower epigraphic bands of the minaret of Jām.[48] Another important Ghurid document for assessing the evolving titulature of the *sulṭān* is a four-volume leather-bound lavishly illuminated Qurʾān dated 584/1188–9, now preserved in the Iran Bastan Museum in Tehran. The *sulṭān*'s extensive range of official and celebratory titles is recorded in the colophon,[49] combining epithets used earlier by both the Saljuqs and the Ghaznawids.[50] Even by the inflated standards of the time they are ostentatious, providing an insight into this *sulṭān*'s self-representation and imperial aspirations a decade before the Ghurid conquest of India.[51]

The choice of the dragon and the lion, both emblems of might and royalty, as symbols to represent Ghiyāth al-Dīn's rulership, under which the Ghurid empire reached its apogee, is significant. Even though he was greatly concerned with orthodoxy[52] a metrical version of the genealogy of the family, composed by Fakhr al-Dīn Mubarākshāh Marwarrūdhi, which was completed during the reign of Ghiyāth al-Dīn, traces the family back to the hominoid serpent of the ancient Iranian epic past, Azhi Dahāka. As is well-known, a pair of serpents are said to have sprouted from the latter's shoulders. After Farīdūn (arabicised from Afrīdūn) overthrew the thousand-year reign of Ẓaḥḥāk/Dahāk, his descendants were presumed to have settled in Ghūr.[53] The Ghurid descent from Dahāk seems to have enjoyed a favourable reputation. This descent was shared by Rustam, one of the greatest warriors of Iranian legends,[54] by the Kushāṇas of the Yuezhi confederacy (*c.* first–third centuries) who ruled over the region which comprises what is now Tajikistan, Afghanistan, Pakistan and northern India,[55] as well as by the Armenians of a province near Lake Sevan.[56] According to the genealogy of the Sām dynasty of Ghūr, the fourth caliph ʿAlī brought about the conversion of the family to Islam in the first century of the Islamic era, granting them the rulership of Ghūr.[57]

The knot that joins the two dragons is the so-called "knot of Solomon," which was known in the Central Asian region from at least the first centuries AD through to the Islamic period. This knot succeeded the ancient so-called Herakles/Hercules knot, the most famous knot used in ancient times, considered to have apotropaic and magical qualities, which was often depicted in the form of both ophidian and quadruped dragons,[58] and is a compelling example of continuity of meaning in spite of formal change. The symbolism of the Herakles knot still had currency in late seventh- or early eighth-century Sogdia. Moulded in the form of a pair of upright dragons that are linked by means of a large Herakles knot, the motif appears in a non-Buddhist context in the monumental sculptural decoration on the plastered mud-brick architecture of the portico of Temple II in the ancient city of Panjikent in Sogdiana (Zarafashān, north of the Ḥiṣār range) (fig. 170).

Like the Hercules knot, the knot of Solomon is a well-known apotropaic sign.[59] It is commonly associated with the magical seal of Solomon *(khātam Sulaymān)*[60] and attributed to the magician-king Solomon of post-biblical Jewish tradition[61] who controls the winds, animals, and spirits. The biblical King Sulaymān is named

[47] A pair of nielloed gold pendants, now in the al-Sabāh Collection, also inscribed with the name of the Ghurid *sulṭān*, "Muḥammad ibn Sām" was found in the same village. Kuwait, al-Sabāh Collection, Dar al-Athar al-Islamiyyah, Kuwait National Museum, inv. no. LNS 1890 J.

[48] The name and titles of the *sulṭān* Ghiyāth al-Dunya wa 'l-Dīn Abu 'l-Fatḥ Muḥammad ibn Sām are given by Maricq and Wiet, 1959, p. 27, no. 3; Pinder-Wilson, 2001, p. 168 and n. 47.

[49] Iran Bastan Museum, Tehran, Ms. 3507, fol. 198a. Cf. Flood, 2005, pp. 267–9, fig. 1.

[50] *Idem*, p. 268.

[51] Cf. *idem*, pp. 267–9.

[52] Ghiyāth al-Dīn was closely affiliated with the Karrāmiyya sect that was dominant among the population of Ghūr and instrumental in persecuting the Ismāʿīlis, but later he shifted allegiance to the Shāfiʿī school of law, while his brother, Muʿizz al-Dīn, became a Ḥanafī; *idem*, pp. 270, 281 and n. 66, p. 287.

[53] Quoted by Abū ʿAmr al-Jūzjānī, the historian of the Ghurids; Bosworth, "Ghūrids," *EI*² II, 1099a. Cf. Shahbazi, 1993, p. 159.

[54] See p. 8, n. 46.

[55] See p. 8, n. 47.

[56] See p. 8, n. 51.

[57] See p. 8, n. 48.

[58] See Belenizkii, 1980, fig. 92.

[59] The importance accorded to such plaited knots is underlined by their ubiquitous use in monumental epigraphic friezes on architecture, an early example being the tomb tower Rādkān West in the Alburz Mountains in Māzandarān finished in 411/1021. See Blair, 1992, pp. 85–7, figs. 48–52.

[60] Melikian-Chirvani, 1977, pp. 367–406. The "Seal of Solomon" was portrayed as a five-pointed star or pentagram, interchangeably used with a six-pointed star or hexagram. Cf. Doutté, 1909, p. 154; Dawkins, 1944, pp. 145–50; Ittig, 1982, p. 86; Moulierac, 1987, p. 88; Shani, 1999, p. 254 and n. 11.

[61] Cf. Henninger, 2004, pp. 20, 25. Evidence of Solomon's influence on the magical traditions of the Graeco-Roman

seventeen times in the Qurʾān (especially *sūra* 38, 30–9).[62] The *khātam Sulaymān* is thought to have been the symbol inscribed on the seal ring of Sulaymān, "which endowed his owner with power over both terrestrial and supernatural beings."[63] Melikian-Chirvani, moreover, has drawn attention to the possibility that the presence of the motif, which is "typical of the Eastern Iranian repertoire [on metalwork] seldom used in the West,"[64] indicates an esoteric intention.[65]

The motif of the knotted dragons, rendered in virtually the same manner as on the Ghurid matrix, is pictured on a "sphero-conical" unglazed earthenware vessel found in the region of the Golden Horde (Juchi Ulus), datable to the late twelfth or early thirteenth century, now preserved in the State Historical Museum in Moscow (fig. 171). The dragons are more stylised, however, and have lost their horns and forelegs, so that only their necks are shown to cross over. A great quantity of these "sphero-conical" vessels have been found throughout the Islamic world, and while the vessels probably served numerous different purposes,[66] the prevalent view is that they contained liquids such as beverages,[67] mercury or perfume,[68] while some may have been used for chemical or alchemical operations.[69] Several "sphero-conical" vessels with the same motif have been found, such as a bottle fragment from Dwīn in Ararat province, the former Armenian capital until the Arab conquest when it became the seat of the governor,[70] an example from Iran, now in the collection of Michael Rogers, London,[71] with stamped decoration and a large six-pointed star (a motif also associated with the magical *khātam Sulaymān*) as well as another unprovenanced example from a private collection.[72]

A moulded band with eight almond-shaped medallions enclosing pairs of knotted dragons circumscribes a pyriform flask of unglazed earthenware, thought to come from Iran or Mesopotamia, which is datable to the same period, now in the Musée national de la céramique, Sèvres.[73] Here the winged dragons are pictured addorsed. The heads, jaws agape, are twisted back so that their outstretched tongues meet at the centre while their forelegs are turned outwards and the bodies are linked by means of a quadripartite knot.

Like most of the "sphero-conical" vessels, the body of the flask is made of dense almost stoneware-like high-temperature fired earthenware, which makes the vessel watertight. The specificity of the paste and the esoteric connotation of the motifs evoke alchemical procedures which were practised by great physicians such as Abū Bakr Muḥammad ibn Zakariyyāʾ al-Rāzī (the Rhazes of the Latin Middle Ages) from Rayy in Iran (*c.* 250/854–313/925 or 323/935), whose interest lay particularly in practical chemistry,[74] and suggest the use of the flask in a laboratory context.[75]

In the symbolism of medieval Islamic alchemy, it seems the paired dragons connected with the use of a quadripartite knot represented a fundamental polarity on which the cosmic rhythm is based, the *solve et coagula* of the alchemical process: the sulphur and mercury of alchemy.[76] This complex theory was developed in the writings of the Jābirian Corpus, Muḥammad ibn Umayl

period, revealing the extensive influence of Jewish magic, is found in the use of his name in several incantations in magical papyri and the specific reference to the use of his seal in the following appeal: "I adjure you by the seal which Solomon placed on the tongue of Jeremiah, and he spoke." Preisendanz, 1973, p. 102 (Pap. IV, 3039–041). Cf. Perdrizet, 1903, p. 58; Aune, "Exorcism," *ISBE*, vol. 2, 1939, repr. 1994, p. 243.

[62] Sulaymān is acquainted with the speech of birds and animals (*sūra* 27, 16–9), he can control the wind as well as the demons and *jinns* who taught magic to humans (*sūras* 21, 81–2; 34, 12; 34, 12–3; and 38, 36–40).

[63] Ittig, 1992, p. 86; Shani, 1999, p. 254 and n. 10.

[64] Melikian-Chirvani, 1982, p. 178.

[65] *Idem*, 1977, pp. 367–406.

[66] On the possible usage of these vessels, see Ettinghausen, 1965, pp. 218–29; Rogers, 1969, pp. 147–58. A comprehensive list of functions based on the vessels' forms is given by Savage-Smith, 1997, pp. 324–33. The contents of "sphero-conical" vessels excavated at Nīshāpūr were tested and were thought to "hold volatile liquids, water and oil without seepage." See Hauser and Wilkinson, 1942, p. 89; Wilkinson, 1973, pp. XXXII–XXXIII.

[67] On the use of the vessels as beer gourds, containing *fuqāʿ* or *fuqqāʿ*, see Ghouchani and Adle, 1992, pp. 72–92.

[68] Ettinghausen, 1965, pp. 218–29.

[69] Rogers, 1969, pp. 147–58; Moulierac, 1987, pp. 86, 88.

[70] The History Museum of Armenia, inv. no. 1682–8, height 12 cm, diameter 9 cm. Dzhanpoladyan, 1958, p. 206, fig. 5. Cf. Ettinghausen, 1965, p. 228, fig. 15 (drawing); Rogers, 1969, p. 153, n. 12 (drawing p. 154, fig. 3); Moulierac, 1987, p. 87 and n. 28.

[71] Rogers, 1969, p. 152, pls. 1 and 2; Moulierac, 1987, p. 87; Savage-Smith, 1997, pp. 324–5, type 6, drawing below ("private collection, London").

[72] Ettinghausen, 1965, p. 224, pl. L A (photograph).

[73] Sèvres, Musée national de la céramique, inv. no. MNC 19589; see *À l'ombre d'Avicenne*, 1996, p. 143, cat. no. 56 (detail).

[74] Anawati, "Arabic Alchemy," *EHAS*, 1996, vol. 3, p. 868.

[75] Moulierac, 1987, p. 86. Flasks of comparable shape are featured on fol. 15 and fol. 17 of the Pseudo-Galen treatise *Kitāb al-diryāq* ("Book of Antidotes"), dated 595/1198–9, now in the Bibliothèque Nationale, Ms. Arabe 2964. Cf. *eadem*, p. 84.

[76] *Eadem*, p. 88.

al-Ṣādiq al-Tamīmī, and also the *Turba Philosophorum*.

In the *Kitāb al-Fihrist*, a work composed in Baghdad at the end of the tenth century, Abu 'l-Faraj Muḥammad ibn Isḥāq ibn al-Nadīm (d. 385/995 or 388/998) credits the Umayyad prince Khālid ibn Yazīd (d. *c.* 704/85) as the first Arab to have been interested in alchemy and to have ordered translations of some alchemical works.[77] By the middle of the tenth century various philosophical currents circulated in Baghdad, which also included the magical and alchemical thought-world of the writings of the Jabirian cycle.[78] In the writings of the Jabirian corpus of alchemy, the idea of a transmutational elixir *(al-iksir)* used as medicine or life-giving force, which was probably transmitted from China,[79] occurs for the first time. It could be prepared from animal, vegetal or mineral substances and could be used to prolong life or given as medicine to sick people. As already mentioned in the preceding chapter, Jābir ibn Ḥayyān (d. *c.* 196/812), purportedly an alchemist at the court of Hārūn al-Rashīd, believed all metals to be a result of their union in different proportions and according to different modalities. Under the influences of the planets, these are formed in the heart of the earth by the union of the hypothetical substances of sulphur, male, in which fire and air are present and which has hot and dry "natures," and mercury, female, which contains water and earth, and is cold and wet.[80]

Astrological components may also inform the iconographic rendering. In Abū Maslama Muḥammad al-Majrītī's magical treatise *Ghāyat al-ḥakīm* the opposing principles of positive and negative bodily temperaments are associated with the two celestial nodes (knots), the head and the tail of the "hidden essence ["verborgenem Wesen"]."[81] As mentioned earlier, al-Bīrūnī reports that the nodes have separate natures, the head of the dragon being hot, auspicious and indicating increase of wealth and the tail being cold, bringing misfortune and signifying diminution of wealth.[82] He also notes that:

> ...some people say that the dragon's head is male and diurnal and the tail female and nocturnal.[83]

It is further of note, as recorded by al-Damīrī in his bestiary, that in medieval Islam it was a popular belief that "serpents do not copulate in the usually known manner of copulation, but they twist themselves round each other (for that purpose)."[84] A sexual character of the knotted dragon motif is further supported by the universal sympathy, discussed earlier, that ultimately unites all natural opposing forces, including those of the female and the male principle, which also finds expression in the coupling of the Sun and the Moon. The use of the twisted serpents' motif as a simile for sexual intercourse appears in Gurgānī's poem *Wīs u Rāmīn* which in its essence is a celebration of an erotic relationship.[85] However, whereas the theme of the twisted serpents was frequently associated with sexual symbolism in pre-Islamic written sources,[86] it is a relatively rare occurrence in medieval Islam.

Exactly the same motif as shown on the Sèvres pyriform flask is recorded on a contemporary unglazed clay jug with filter from northern Syria, in the National Museum in Damascus. The vessel carries around the body a similar moulded band with contiguous almond-shaped medallions enclosing the same knotted dragons (fig. 172). A similar depiction, but with the dragon heads in addorsed position, is found on a shallow ceramic bowl from Raqqa of the same period, now preserved in the Metropolitan Museum of Art in New York (fig. 173).[87]

---

[77] Anawati, "Arabic Alchemy," *EHAS*, 1996, vol. 3, p. 864.

[78] Gutas, 1998, p. 104.

[79] Hill, 1990, p. 335. Cf. Needham and Ling, 1954, pp. 323–4; Needham et al., 1980, pp. 330–425, esp. pp. 339–55.

[80] Anawati, "Arabic Alchemy," *EHAS*, 1996, vol. 3, p. 866. Cf. Moulierac, 1987, p. 88; Kraus [Plessner], "Djābir b. Ḥayyān," *EI*² II, 357b.

[81] *"Picatrix,"* tr. and eds. Ritter and Plessner, 1962, p. 45.16–9.

[82] *Kitāb al-Tafhīm*, tr. and ed. Wright, 1934, p. 233.

[83] *Idem*, p. 234. Of note is also the association of Leviathan and Behemoth in the book of Job 40–1 where they appear as representatives of different orders, the one of liquids and the other of solids. In the book of Enoch 6:7–9 the sex of the monsters is differentiated: the female Leviathan dwells in the depths of the sea and the male Behemoth occupies a dry wilderness on the east of Paradise. The *Apocalypse of Abraham* 10 speaks of male and female Leviathans. Cf. also the apocryphal book of Esther (1:4–11) in which Mordecai dreams of two combatting dragons.

[84] Tr. Jayakar, 1906, vol. 1, p. 634. Cf. Ruska, "Ḥayyā," *EI*² III, 334b.

[85] Tr. and ed. Davis, 2008, p. 192.

[86] See the forthcoming publication by the present writer which discusses the dragon iconography from 2500 BC to 650 AD; also Kuehn, 2009, pp. 43–67.

[87] Lane, 1947, pl. 81 B; Dimand, 1947, p. 191, fig. 124; Grube, 1963, p. 59, fig. 15; Grube and Johns, 2005, p. 230,

An esoteric character of this dragon knot is suggested by its appearance on a hemispherical copper alloy magico-medicinal bowl, preserved in the Royal Ontario Museum in Toronto, which has been dated between the twelfth and fourteenth century.[88] The interior of the bowl features a pair of knotted confronted dragons with paired slender sinuous tails, an undulating serpent, an eight-legged scorpion and a quadruped, probably a lion.[89] The dragons are characterised by "Saljuq-type" fanged jaws with the conspicuous feature that their tongues are darting out to meet at the centre (fig. 174). The interesting serpent-lion-scorpion combination is mentioned in Aḥmad ibn ʿAlī al-Būnī's (d. *c.* 622/1225) widely circulated thirteenth-century writings on magic.[90] It also occurs on Islamic talismans such as the "Lion Seal" described by Ibn Khaldūn.[91] The bowl is circumscribed on the exterior in cursive script with a therapeutic inscription which reads:

> This holy bowl is useful for the sting of a scorpion and of a snake and the bite of a mad dog, for difficulty in childbirth, nosebleed, stomach ache and colic. The afflicted person is to drink from it three times. By the grace of god he will recover. For difficult labour drink saffron water. For stopping nosebleed and abdominal pain, snuff water from it. For colic, gulp down hot water. This has been proven by experience. The work of Muhammad ibn Yūnus – may God have mercy on him.[92]

In addition it is inscribed with Qurʾānic verses (comprising *sūras* 84, 1–4; 71, 18; and 94, 5–6), further invocations asking relief from labour pains and colic (requesting the help of four genii) as well as a series of nine letters that form the initial part of a different *sūra* (hence are endowed with a special "sympathetic quality," or *khawāṣṣ*). It is significant that although the decorative programme and the inscription suggest that talismanic power was invested in this bowl, the inscription does not attribute this power directly to a planetary representation, but instead emphasises the curative properties of the bowl. The therapeutic efficacy for an ailing person to drink from a bowl that is inscribed with Qurʾānic verses and formulae of blessing is well-known. It may be presumed that just as the medicinal effect derives its power from the contact of water with a vessel inscribed with pious inscriptions and magical invocations, the symbolism of the three animals, the quadruped, the snake and the scorpion, as well as the knotted dragons on this magico-medicinal bowl[93] serve a similar function through the agency of water. The charging of water with magico-medicinal healing through material contact with a magical object or talisman[94] is also illustrated, for instance, in the magical manual of the Pseudo-Majrīṭī, *Kitāb*

---

fig. 77.9. For a line drawing of the knotted dragons, see Rogers, 1969, p. 151, fig. 2.

[88] See a related bowl dated 565/1169–70 from Syria in the Nasser D. Khalili Collection of Islamic Art, London; Savage-Smith, 1997, p. 82, cat. no. 25.

[89] Knotted dragons also occur on another type of early Islamic magic-medicinal bowl, the so-called "poison cups," which are also of hemispherical form. In addition to the knotted dragons, they also consistently represent a serpent, a scorpion and a quadruped, in appearance something between a dog and a lion (the former would be more appropriate since the bowl serves to protect against the bite of a mad dog). These were used to provide an antidote for poison and to serve as protection against animal bites and stings. Rehatsek, 1873–4, pp. 150–4; Canaan, 1936, p. 105, 1938, p. 146; Ittig, 1982, p. 82; Savage-Smith, 1997, pp. 73–4.

[90] Canaan, 1936, pp. 101–5; Ittig, 1982, pp. 91–2; Savage-Smith, 1997, pp. 138–9; Porter, 2004, p. 185.

[91] Ibn Khaldūn states in the *Muqaddima*:

> Then there is the 'Lion Seal' which is also called the pebble seal. On a steel thimble, the sorcerer engraves the picture of a lion dragging its tail and biting on pebbles which is thus divided into two parts. A snake is represented in front of the lion. It is coiled at the feline's mouth. Upon the lion's back, a crawling scorpion is represented. In order to make the engraving, (the sorcerer) waits for a time when the sun enters the first or third decan of Leo, provided (further) that the two luminaries (the sun and the moon) are well and out of their misfortune ... People assume that the person who holds onto it (the charm) has an indescribable power over rulers and is able to have close contact with them, to serve them, and to use them for his own ends...

Tr. Rosenthal, 1958, vol. 3, p. 163. The same motif is mentioned in the *Ghāyat al-ḥakīm* ("The Philosopher's Goal"), attributed to Abū Maslama Muḥammad al-Majrīṭī. The serpent-lion-scorpion motif was current in the Islamic east in the early Islamic period. A depiction of just the lion and scorpion, without the serpent, appears on the obverse of two circular pendants from the Nīshāpūr excavation of the Iranian expedition of the Metropolitan Museum of Art (1936 to 1947). Cf. Jenkins and Keene, 1982, cat. no. 7a and b; Allan, 1982b, pp. 68–9, cat. nos. 60, 61.

[92] Ittig, 1982, p. 81.

[93] The same "decorative programme" is given also on five other "magic bowls" that were examined by Annette Ittig (1982), but the knotted dragon figures on only one of these bowls. While Ittig suggests that the inscriptions may therefore not necessarily be directly related to the motif of the knotted dragons, the depiction certainly cannot be antithetical to the content of the inscriptions and may belong to a body of magico-talismanic symbols used for related purposes that do not necessarily have to concur.

[94] The use of talismans in the region of Mosul that are written in ink and washed off with water which is then given as a potion to a person who has been bitten by a serpent, scorpion or mad dog, is described by Thompson, 1907, p. 327.

ghāyat al-ḥakīm wa aḥaqq al-natījatain (the so-called *Picatrix*), which relates that the owner of a finger ring engraved on the bezel with a serpent surmounted by a scorpion will be protected from snake bite; or again that he will be healed from any such bite when the ringstone is placed into a liquid which is then imbibed.[95]

A comparable conceptualisation connecting the knotted dragons with the subject of medicine and healing governs the depiction on a marble relief plaque of a pair of confronted dragons linked by a quadripartite knot at mid-section with further knotted interlaces above and below. The plaque was found at the *darüşşifa* of the *atābeg* Lālā Jamāl al-Dīn Farrukh in Çankırı, outside Ankara, dated by the inscription to Muḥarram 633/1235,[96] but is no longer extant (fig. 175). The serpentine bodies are oriented to the left; their confronted heads, with gaping jaws, almond-shaped eyes and cusped ears, reveal sharp teeth and tongues (the lower head is less legible on account of the deteriorated condition but may be presumed to mirror the upper head).[97]

In his discussion of the Çankırı *darüşşifa* knotted double dragon motif Gabriel drew attention some time ago to the reminiscence of the ancient Asklepian symbol (consisting of a single serpent coiled around a staff).[98] It is also of note that in some thirteenth-century star pictures the constellation Ophiūchus (Serpentarius), the "serpent-holder,"[99] is rendered knotted in such a way as to appear almost double.[100] This is of special importance for the interpretation of the iconography of the knotted dragons, taking into account that in classical antiquity Ophiūchus was also referred to as Asklepios, the god of medicine *par excellence*, whose attribute is a pair of intertwined serpents, and as Hygieia, his mythical daughter.[101] The constellation Ophiūchus governed physicians and pharmacologists as well as huntsmen and athletes.

---

[95] The German translation of the Arabic version of the *Ghāyat al-ḥakīm*, ed. Ritter, 1933, 2. Abh., 10. Absch., f115, states:

> Man graviert auf einen Ringstein das Bild einer Schlange und darüber einen Skorpion ... wer diesen Ringstein trägt, den beißt keine Schlange und er wird geheilt von ihrem Biß, wenn er ihn in eine Flüssigkeit legt und sie trinkt.

Cited after Barb, 1953, pp. 17–8, n. 119.

[96] Meinecke, 1976, vol. 2, p. 103. Cf. general references in Gabriel and Sauvaget, p. 168, n. 1, fig. 137; Kühnel, 1950, p. 8.

[97] The relief has been lost since 1940 and is only known from photographs and a drawing done before this date. Cf. Gierlichs, 1996, p. 156. Marginal ornaments in the form of two closely related dragons, knotted in a similar manner, but with a large tripartite knot, are found in an Armenian Gospel book of 1304 by the miniaturist Vardan in Astapat, Nakhichevan, Ms. 3722, fols. 290b, 319a, 171a, 280a, 232a. Mnatsakanyan, 1955, p. 517, fig. 1023; *Armenian Miniatures*, eds. Gevorkian and Abgarian, 1996, pl. 24 (upper left corner).

[98] Gabriel, 1940, p. 168, n. 1, and fig. 137. Cf. Süslü, 1987, p. 641. As noted earlier, the *darüşşifa* became a place of spiritual healing and snake charming by the Ottoman period. See p. 31, n. 75.

[99] On Ophiūchus, see Scherer, 1953, p. 184.

[100] Saxl, 1932, vol. 1, p. 293, fig. 344; "Ophis, Ophiuchus," *RE*; "Sanitas et duo dracones perplexi" in Gundel, 1936, pp. 174–6. See Rogers, 1969, p. 156, n. 17.

[101] Cf. *idem*, 1969, pp. 156–7.

CHAPTER ELEVEN

THE DRAGON AND THE MAGICO-MEDICAL SPHERE

a. *The dragon as prophylaxis and cure*

In Iranian mythology Thrita/Trita was the first of the healers. He "drove back sickness to sickness, drove back death to death; he asked for an antidote (and) obtained it from Khshthra-Vairya to withstand sickness ... and to counter-act snake-bite" (Vidēvdāt 20.2–3).[1] Thrita, "the third man who pressed the Haoma" (Yasna 9.10), appears originally to have been closely associated (if not identical) with Thraētaona,[2] for the invention of the miraculous gift of healing, in other words the granting of health, strength, fertility and fecundity, was also attributed to the latter.[3] In the Farvardīn Yasht Thraētaona had the ability to cure certain illnesses and could:

> ...counteract pain, hot fever, humours, cold fever and incontinence, and [...] the pain caused by the serpent.[4]

Knowledge of the secret causes of illness and the no less secret measures necessary to obtain a cure belonged to the duties of the healer. Accordingly, Thraētaona was also regarded as the inventor of magic.[5] In living Zoroastrian observance it is Thraētaona who is invoked, as king Frēdōn/Farīdūn, in prayers and on amulets to keep away or cure sickness.[6] The tenth-century philologist Ḥamza al-Iṣfahānī also records that Farīdūn "constructed amulets, and introduced the antidote (made) from the body of vipers, and founded medicine, and pointed out those extracts of herbs which keep away pestilence from the bodies of animate beings..."[7] Manichaean Middle Persian prayer and incantation texts reciting "names of power" frequently mention the "First Physician" *prydwn* (Frēdūn) in connection with other powerful names known in a magical context, such as Gabriel and "Sabaoth."[8]

The parallels in the magical healing abilities of both Thrita and Thraētaona are mirrored by their heroic feats. Both are known to have overcome serpent-bodied, three-headed and six-eyed dragons, respectively known as Viśvarūpa and Azhi Dahāka, the difference being that the former is a celestial and the latter a terrestrial dragon.[9] It is interesting to observe that the magical healers who are called upon to cure injuries caused by snake bites and to invent an antidote for snake venom are at the same time dragon fighters *par*

[1] Dubash, 1906, p. 173.

[2] *The Zend-Avesta*, tr. Darmesteter, vol. 2, 1880, p. 549, n. 275; Boyce, 1975, repr. 1996, pp. 98, 100. On the close etymological relation between Thrita/Trita and Thraētaona, see Watkins, 1995, pp. 314–6; Remmel, 2006, pp. 126–7.

[3] Yasht 13.131. See Boyce, 1975, repr. 1996, pp. 98, 100.

[4] Yasht 13.131 (cited after Dubash, 1906, p. 173). *The Zend-Avesta*, tr. Darmesteter, vol. 4, 1880, p. 219. Cf. Sarkhosh Curtis, 1993, p. 26.

[5]
> When Thraētaona, on his march to Bawri, the capital of Aži [...], arrived at the Tigris (the Rangha); an angel then came and taught him magic to enable him to baffle the sortileges of Aži *(Shāh-nāma)*. We have in this passage an instance of his talents as a wizard, and one which helps us to understand why Thraētaona is considered as the inventor of magic, and his name is invoked in spells and incantations.

The Zend-Avesta, tr. Darmesteter, vol. 2, p. 549, n. 275. Cf. Boyce, 1975, repr. 1996, pp. 68–9 and n. 3; Bivar, 1967, pp. 522–3. The association of Bawri (Bāvīr), the fortress of Dahāk, with Babylon seems to be a later tradition, cf. Monchi-Zadeh, 1975, p. 238 and n. 2. Two further fortresses of Dahāk were said to be located in Simbrān and in Hindūkān (*Bundahishn* 209.11–2; *idem*, p. 238).

[6] Boyce, 1975, repr. 1996, p. 98. Cf. Modi, 1894, pp. 1–24. On the basis of Farīdūn's attribute of a bull-headed mace with which he breaks the stronghold of the demon-king Ẓaḥḥāk, Bivar (1967, pp. 522–4, pl. 1, F) identifies the scene of a hero grasping a demon by the hair engraved on a Sasanian-period chalcedony seal-stone, probably an amulet, in the British Museum, inv. no. 1905-5-30, 1, with the legend of Farīdūn battling with Ẓaḥḥāk. The latter is portrayed in the process of devouring (or expectorating) a human being whose upper body, head and arms protrude from the demon's mouth. Bivar surmises that the scene represents Farīdūn in his medical role, possibly combating a fatal illness, since the demon is shown as not merely wounding but devouring a human being.

[7] Ḥamza al-Isfahani, ed. Gottwaldt, J.M.P., p. 23 and ٢٣, as cited in Bivar, 1967, p. 522, n. 25. Cf. Ḥamza al-Isfahani, *Ta'rīkh sinī mulūk al-arḍ wa 'l-anbiyā'*, Beirut, 1961, p. 34; Ṭabarī, I, p. 226; Bal'amī, *Tarjumat-i tārīkh-i Ṭabarī*, ed. Bahār, p. 148; Ibn al-Balkhī, I, p. 36; and *Tārikh-i guzīda*, ed. Navā'ī, p. 84; cited after Tafaẓẓolī, "Ferēdūn," *EIr*.

[8] Henning, 1947, pp. 39–40.

[9] Yasna 9.7; Boyce, 1975, repr. 1996, pp. 98–9.

excellence.[10] Another analogy between the two healer-heroes is provided in the Avesta which relates that the second mortal to press liquid *haoma* (Ved. *sóma*) was Āthwya, for which he received the boon of fathering Thraētaona, and the third *haoma*-presser was Thrita.[11] The sacred *haoma* plant was regarded as chief of medicinal herbs.[12] The drink, made of the *haoma* seed, intoxicated, gave heightened divine powers and mantic wisdom,[13] and was used to counter the dragon "who tosses poison around."[14]

Further manifestations of the dragon in the realm of prophylaxis and cure are found in epic narratives.[15] In Asadī Ṭūsī's heroic *Garshāsp-nāma*,[16] Ẓaḥḥāk (the historicised mythological foreign usurper and avatar of the Avestan demon Azhi Dahāka) requests the legendary hero Garshāsp to vanquish a dragon that comes out of the sea and lives on Mount Shekāwand in Kābul.[17] Before setting out to fight the dragon, Garshāsp took an antidote/theriac *(diryāq)*, a kind of universal drug which often contained the flesh of serpents (see the discussion in the following section). He finally succeeded in killing the beast with a club carved in the form of a dragon head.[18]

By slaying the dragon with a weapon carved with his own likeness, the hero thus once again applied the homeopathic (or imitative) principle of *similia similibus curantur*. After the victory Garshāsp is said to have shed his skin and lost consciousness. Hence as a result of his triumph over his mighty foe he assimilated some of his adversary's positive ophidian characteristics, such as the shedding of the skin, an act that is symbolic of long or eternal life. Thus when the hero regained consciousness, he gave thanks to an angel. The dragon's carcass was transported to the city where Garshāsp's feat was celebrated and he was honoured as *jahān-pahlavān* (chief hero), a term closely associated with the Iranian heroic tradition. The event was commemorated in a flag embellished with the representation of a black dragon and a pole surmounted by a golden lion in turn topped by a moon.[19] This was passed on to Garshāsp's descendants and became his family's coat of arms,[20] another allegorical example which suggests that the formidable qualities of the dragon were appropriated by the vanquisher. Doses of *diryāq* against the dragon's poison were also taken by Rustam's son, Farāmarz, and his helper, Bīzhan, before they slew the hissing dragon that lived on the summit of a mountain in India.[21] Similarly, the legendary hero Borzū, the son of Sohrāb, resorted to drinking *diryāq* and milk as an antidote to the dragon's venom before entering his lair on Mount Zahāb to slay him.[22]

The ancient association of the serpent with the art of healing[23] appears also in the popular tale of the serpent that introduced the healing herb,

[10] *The Zend-Avesta*, tr. Darmesteter, vol. 4, 1880, p. 219.

[11] Boyce, 1975, repr. 1996, pp. 98–9.

[12] *Eadem*, p. 161.

[13] *Eadem*, pp. 158–9.

[14] Yasna 9.30; cf. Schwarz, 2006, p. 216.

[15] The serpent is an age-old emblem of chthonic gods of fertility, healing and divination in the ancient Near East. The association of the (serpent-)dragon with medicine and elixirs is also found in the ancient Jewish tradition. According to the Jewish Midrash the angel of healing, Raphael (*Rᵉphâ'el*, who acted as a physician as well as a binder of demons), was originally called Labbi'el, who was ordered by God to provide healing for humanity (*Midrashim Konen* 26–7; *Yerahme'el* 14–5). In addition to his attribute as healer, Raphael also has a chthonic aspect being known as "Prince of Hades" (1 Enoch 20:2; 22:106). Significantly, the Babylonians reported of the constellation ᵐᵘˡ*Muš*, "serpent" (i.e., Hydra, the sea-serpent), that it was the image of the ancient Mesopotamian dragon *labbu* (see Heidel, 1942, repr. 1951, pp. 141–2). Astour, 1965, pp. 236–7; Kuntzmann, 1983, p. 97; cf. Wilson, 2001, pp. 30–1. In the Ugaritic texts the Rephaim *(Rᵉphâ'îm)*, the ghosts of the dead in the netherworld, are known for their healing abilities, Baal being known to drive out serpent demons (*KTU* 1.82:6), and another deity, Horon, to neutralise the effects of snake venom (*KTU* 1.100:61–9). See also Becking, "El Rophe," *DDD*, 1995, pp. 292–3; Kuntzmann, 1983, p. 216.

[16] Ed. Yaghmā'ī, Tehran, 1354/1975; De Blois, "Garšāsp-nāma (or Karšāsp-nāma)," *EIr*.

[17] Khāleqī-Moṭlaq, "Aždahā II," *EIr*. See also chapter 3.

[18] Asadī Ṭūsī, *Garshāsp-nāma*, p. 269, l. 10, as cited in Khāleqī-Moṭlaq, "Aždahā II," *EIr*. Cf. the related story of Mūsā killing a giant serpent with his serpent-staff; al-Kisā'ī, *Qiṣaṣ al-anbiyā'*, tr. Thackston, 1978, p. 223. See also the discussion on pp. 38–9.

[19] Widengren, 1969, p. 17, n. 35. Asadī Ṭūsī, *Garshāsp-nāma*, pp. 49–63, cited after Khāleqī-Moṭlaq, "Aždahā II," *EIr*.

[20] Asadī Ṭūsī, *Garshāsp-nāma*, pp. 49–63, as cited in *idem*.

[21] *Farāmarz-nāma*, London, British Museum, Ms. Or. 2946, fols. 24, 25; Khāleqī-Moṭlaq, 1982, pp. 22–45; *idem* "Aždahā II," *EIr*.

[22] *Borzū-nāma*, Paris, Bibliothèque Nationale, Ms. Supp. Pers. 1023, fols. 242, 243; *idem*.

[23] Pliny (*Naturalis Historia*, XXIX 4) notes the widely held belief that the snake is full of "many remedies" (*inesse ei remedia multa creduntur*). This view was shared by the early Christian theologian Cyril of Jerusalem (*c.* 315–386 AD) in his Catechesis (9.14):

> Can you know the efficacy of all herbs, or the benefit coming from every animal? Already even from poisonous vipers have come antidotes for the safety of humans. But you will say, "The snake is terrible." Fear the Lord and he [that is to say, the snake] will not be able to harm you.

Cited after Kelhoffer, 2000, p. 440.

called Persian basil, to the Sasanian king Khusraw I (r. 531–579), known as Khusraw Anūshirwān, recorded by al-Qazwīnī in his encyclopaedic treatise *Kitāb ʿajāʾib al-makhlūqāt wa gharāʾib al-mawjūdāt*. The king had saved a large serpent that crept under his throne and had sent one of his horsemen to protect it from the bite of a scorpion. The following year, the thankful serpent came again before the throne of the king and cast out of its mouth a black seed. This seed the king ordered to be sown and a basil plant grew out of it which the king used to cure his "cold in the head and pains in the brain."[24]

More all-encompassing is the popular Armenian tradition which records that a serpent king endowed the archetypal physician Luqmān *al-ḥakīm* (after whom *sūra* 31 is named) with the knowledge to cure all diseases. But seeing that the knowledge would enable men to achieve immortality, God became jealous and ordered an angel to empty out Luqmān's elixir and cast his books into the sea.[25]

b. *The dragon and the theriaca as illustrated in the* Kitāb al-diryāq

From earliest times the serpent-dragon was associated with poisons as well as antidotes. In different forms snake flesh and other ophidian elements were used as remedies for various kinds of ailment. Among the earliest extant illustrated Islamic manuscripts are two copies of an Arabic text on antidotes derived from snakes and used as a remedy for snake venom.[26] As mentioned in its title, the *Kitāb al-diryāq* ("Book of the Theriac") concerns the preparation of the theriac (a derivative of the Greek *thēriakos*), a medicinal remedy celebrated in antiquity that was considered efficacious against the poison of snakebites or the bites of other wild beasts (from *ther*, "wild animal")[27] dealing with the effects of snakebites.

The earlier of the two copies, dated 595/1199, in the collection of the Bibliothèque Nationale, Paris, since 1853,[28] has a double frontispiece.[29] The doubling of the near-identical pages, once again, serves to increase and underpin the intended effect, underlining the double potency of the symbolism of the paired images. The pages depict two seated figures each holding up large crescents with two diminutive attendants in princely dress on either side, each enclosed by two confronted dragons and four framing figures that are equally splendidly clad (fig. 176).[30] Flanking the central section of both miniatures horizontally at top and bottom are epigraphic bands in Kufic which read: "Its owner and scribe is the meekest of God's servants, be He praised, Muḥammad, son of the fortunate Abu 'l-Fatḥ, son of the rightly guided *imām*, Abu 'l-Ḥasan, son of the beneficent *imām*."[31] A second double page composition carrying an inscription on the right side states that the book was made for the library of a certain *imām* Abu 'l-Fatḥ Maḥmūd,[32] possibly a nephew of the owner/scribe named on the frontispiece, and apparently a member of the Shīʿī religious class.[33] Unfortunately the place of production is not stated. The paintings of the manuscript have been attributed to Iran, but most scholars concur that they originate in the north Mesopotamian (Jazīran) school of Mosul.[34]

The haloed and crowned female figure on the two miniatures, richly clad and bejewelled, her plaited hair falling over her shoulders, is seated with folded legs and crossed feet. One of the soles faces upwards showing the tips of the henna-tinted toes, while the uplifted hands with henna-

[24] Al-Damīrī, *Ḥayāt al-ḥayawān al-kubrā*, tr. Jayakar, 1906, vol. 1, pp. 639–40.

[25] Hoogasian-Villa, 1966, pp. 426–9 and 531–2. On Luqmān's title of *ḥakīm* in Turklish folklore, cf. Eberhard and Boratav, 1953, p. 346.

[26] Ms. Arabe 2964 in the Bibliothèque Nationale, Paris, and Ms. A.F. 10 in the Österreichische Nationalbibliothek, Vienna. For a monograph on the Paris manuscript, see Farès, 1953; for a discussion on the Vienna manuscript, see Holter, 1937, pp. 1–48, and Duda, 1992, pp. 46–69.

[27] A recipe for theriac is recorded in Moulierac, 1996, pp. 102–3. Its production is visualised in Ms. Arabe 2964, p. 5, Bibliothèque Nationale, Paris.

[28] The date given in the colophon is Rabīʿ al-awwal of the year 595/31 December 1198–29 January 1199, copied by Muḥammad Abu 'l-Fatḥ ʿAbd al-Waḥīd. Paris, Bibliothèque Nationale, Ms. Arabe 2964. Farès, 1953, pls. III–IV.

[29] In the course of reassembling the manuscript with missing folios, the double frontispiece has been repaginated to pp. 36 and 37, see Duda, 1992, pp. 48–9.

[30] Cf. Grube, 1967, pl. 27 (colour illustration); Grube and Johns, 2005, p. 230, fig. 77.1.

[31] Pancaroğlu, 2001, p. 155 and n. 6, with the transcriptions of the Arabic text. In spite of the prestigious titles the name of the scribe is unknown to chroniclers and historians; Moulierac, 1987, p. 84.

[32] Farès, 1953, pp. 8–9, pl. V; Pancaroğlu, 2001, p. 155 and n. 7, with transcr. of the Arabic text and English tr.

[33] See Pancaroğlu, 2001, p. 157 and n. 14.

[34] An Iranian origin has been suggested by Melikian-Chirvani (1967) who however does not exclude the possibility of an Artuqid (Jazīran) provenance. Farès (1953) attributes the paintings to the "school of Baghdad." Ettinghausen supports a Jazīran provenance (1962, pp. 86, 92), which was strengthened by Nassar (1985) and Ward (1985).

tinted fingertips hold a large crescent-shaped moon. The centrally facing figure is flanked on either side by two small attendants.[35] The composition is encircled by two confronted dragons whose bodies are knotted at the four cardinal points; at the top the heads, with curved horns, wrinkled snouts and wide-open jaws revealing tongues with bifid tips, extend beyond the circumference, while the slender coiling tails form an additional loop before tapering to a point at the base. The corners of the composition are filled with four winged figures, of presumably honorific and celestial significance,[36] that hold up the medallion. The central figures and the four framing figures are distinguished by a halo.

The central frontally rendered figure, possibly a symbolic personification of the planet Moon *(al-qamar)*, was a popular motif at this time[37] and one that was "generally invested with astrological and semi-magical significance."[38] The now destroyed thirteenth-century Sinjār Gate of Mosul was decorated with a relief portraying a figure holding up a crescent moon.[39] The emblem appears to have been of some importance since it is shown on the coinage of Badr al-Dīn Lu'lu' as well as on coins of other rulers of Mosul and Sinjār (between 585 and 657/1189 and 1258) and of Saladin (Mayyāfāriqīn, 587/1191).[40]

In his monograph on the manuscript, Bishr Farès perceives the lunar emblem as Nin-gal, the "Great Lady" and divine consort of the moon-god Sīn, whose attribute was the crescent, and proposes that the iconographic expression was transmitted through the Ṣābian cult of the moon-god at Ḥarrān[41] whose cult flourished well into the Islamic period. Farès associates the lunar figure with the content of the text, which he construed to be a prophylactic or talismanic device reinforced by healing powers associated with serpents against the evil powers of disease in ancient Mesopotamian and Graeco-Roman beliefs.[42]

The iconography of the Pseudo-Galen double miniature has been studied by Guitty Azarpay, who identified the depiction of the dragons juxtaposed with the anthropomorphic lunar emblem as eclipse dragons, the head and the tail of *al-jawzahar*.[43] This argument is strengthened by the fact that a partial solar eclipse did occur in the Near East on 29 Rabīʿ al-awwal 595/28 January 1199, a date which corresponds with that of the completion of the manuscript, indicating that the representations on the double miniature were intended as apotropaic devices against the potential astrological threats imminent at the very time of its production.[44] Yet rather than associating the imagery of *al-jawzahar*, portrayed with the personified moon emblem, with the actual occurrence of a solar or lunar eclipse, Pancaroğlu suggests, as proposed earlier by Farès, that the depiction has in fact a wider meaning and, more precisely, may also be semantically linked with the contents of the manuscript.[45]

Although probably being a pseudo-epigraphical original Arabic work by an anonymous author, the text of the *Kitāb al-diryāq* is falsely attributed

[35] Azarpay (1978, pp. 364–5) relates the lunar personification to Graeco-Roman and Byzantine traditions in which the Moon is female, which, she suggests, is generally perpetuated in depictions of the symbol in Islamic art. On the female nature of the Moon in Roman astrological imagery, see also Markel, 1995, p. 83, in contrast to it generally being thought of as male in Indian mythology, *idem*, pp. 32–8 and n. 33 (for an exception see, *idem*, p. 152); Pingree, 1964–5, p. 250. The henna-tinted fingernails and tips of the fingers and toes of the figure clearly identify her as female. See also the depiction of female moons on a late twelfth-century Tell Minis-style bowl, now preserved in the Paris, Musée du Louvre, Département des Antiquités orientales, Section Islamique, inv. no. OA 7872. *L'Etrange et le Merveilleux en terres d'Islam*, 2001, p. 232, cat. no. 159.

[36] Azarpay, 1978, p. 366, n. 19; Pancaroğlu, 2001, p. 163.

[37] See, for instance, on twelfth- and thirteenth-century metalwork (Saxl, 1912, p. 164, fig. 10; Pope and Ackerman, eds., 1938–9, repr. 1964–81, vol. 6, pls. 1327, 1331) and miniature painting (e.g. al-Qazwīnī, *ʿAjāʾib al-makhlūqāt*, Munich, Bayerische Staatsbibliothek, Cod. Arab. 464, realised during the author's lifetime in Wāsiṭ in 678/1279–80; Saxl, 1912, fig. 8).

[38] Azarpay, 1978, p. 364.

[39] Sarre and Herzfeld, 1920, vol. 2, pp. 213–5; Azarpay, 1978, p. 365, fig. 3; Hauptmann von Gladiss, ed., 2006, fig. 22. The lunar figure was interpreted by scholars as the emblem of the city of Mosul as well as the coat of arms of Badr al-Dīn Lu'lu' (whose sobriquet was "new moon" or "full moon of religion"). Rice (1957, pp. 321–2) however has disputed this association on the basis that the motif was not restricted to Mosul; cf. Ettinghausen, "Hilāl. ii. – In Islamic art," *EI*² III, 379a.

[40] Such as the copper coinage of the Zangid rulers of Mosul, ʿIzz al-Dīn Masʿūd I ibn Mawdūd (576/1180–589/1193) (cf. *What the Coins Tell Us*, 2009, p. 32, 15722 and 15719) or Nāṣir al-Dīn Maḥmūd ibn Masʿūd (616/1219–631/1234) (dated 627/1229; American Numismatic Society; cf. Ettinghausen, "Hilāl," *EI*² III, 379a, fig. 4). See also Lane Poole, 1877, nos. 529–33, 567–9, 589–92. The lunar emblem is also shown on the coinage of the ʿAbbasid caliph al-Nāṣir (577/1181–620/1223); Hauptmann von Gladiss, ed., 2006, p. 106, cat. no. 12.

[41] Farès, 1953, pp. 22–4, 26–7, 33.

[42] *Idem*, pp. 29–33.

[43] Azarpay, 1978, pp. 363–74, and *eadem*, 1991, pp. 1–10.

[44] *Eadem*, 1978, pp. 363–74. On the apparent discrepancy of the choice of representing a lunar eclipse when in fact it was a solar eclipse that had occured, see Pancaroğlu, 2001, p. 164.

[45] Pancaroğlu, 2001, p. 164.

to the second-century physician Galen with the commentary of Yaḥyā al-Naḥwī (John the Grammarian/Johannes Grammatikos or Johannes Philoponus) of Alexandria (*c.* 490–565),[46] and credited to the most renowned scholar of the translation movement, the Nestorian Christian Ḥunayn ibn Isḥāq al-ʿIbādī (*c.* 192/808–264/877).[47] It is a literary "hybrid"[48] comprising the biographical sketches of nine classical physicians – among whom are the physicians Galen (Jālīnūs), Andromachus the Younger (Andrūmakhus al-Qarīb al-ʿAhd), who together with his father was active at the court of the Roman emperor Nero, and the early fourth-century Philagrios (Aflaghuras) – their theriac recipes as well as their vitae, followed by a section on snakes and their classifications and further medicinal recipes.[49]

In the third painting of the Paris *Kitāb al-diryāq*, Philagrios is shown in the process of preparing an antidote in a large vessel placed on a stand over a fire which is fanned by his assistant.[50] The onlookers comprise men and women of different age groups. Seated at the lower right corner of the scene, an emaciated figure clad only in a loincloth, probably the patient, gestures to a dragon depicted just below the physician. The creature has large, wide-open jaws and its body is composed of two intertwining serpent coils. It may thus represent an ingredient in the preparation of the antidote, as indicated in the account of Andromachus the Younger that is given in the text, discussed below. Alternatively, the entwined coils may represent the caduceus-like staff, a symbol that was known in the medieval Islamic world. Writing in the thirteenth century, the physician Ibn Abī Uṣaybiʿa (599/1203–669/1270) records in his dictionary of over 380 biographies of physicians, *ʿUyūn al-anbāʾ fī ṭabaqāt al-aṭibbāʾ* ("Sources of Information on the Generations of Physicians"), that according to Galen's account:

> Asklepios is represented holding in his hand a carved staff with branches, made from the marsh mallow tree. ... Upon it, there is represented a long-lived animal, wound [i.e., coiled] around it – a snake.[51]

He explains that the association of Asklepios with the serpent is due, firstly, to:

> ...the fact that the snake is a sharp-sighted animal which is much awake and never sleeps. Thus the student of the craft of medicine must not be detracted by sleep, and he must possess the keenest possible mind in order to be able to warn (his patients) in advance of present (conditions) and (those) likely to arise in the future.[52]

He offers a further explanation, namely that the serpent has a long lifespan, perhaps possessing eternal life and hence that:

> those who employ the craft of medicine are able to live long. ... This animal – the snake – sloughs off its skin, called by the Greeks "old age." Likewise people by employing the craft of medicine, are able to slough off old age, the result of disease and regain health.[53]

Other medieval Arabic sources record that Asklepios' staff was wreathed with entwined serpents and, moreover, that Agathodaimon (Aghāthūdhīmūn), who was considered a great authority in the occult sciences, was Asklepios' teacher.[54]

In spite of their dangerous or even life-threatening qualities, serpents have long been considered to have medicinal benefits against a variety of afflictions and, as stated in the account of Andromachus the Younger included in the text of the *Kitāb al-diryāq*, were an essential ingredient in the theriac, into which he "added many drugs ... and made a single theriac ... [he also]

[46] Meyerhofer, 1932, pp. 1–21.

[47] Cf. Ullmann, 1970, p. 49; Johnstone, "Summ," *EI*² IX, 872a; Pancaroğlu, 2001, p. 156 and n. 9; Kerner, 2004, p. 167.

[48] Kerner, 2007, p. 25.

[49] In addition to the two frontispiece miniatures there are nine text miniatures and a set of illustrations of serpents and plants that have a direct bearing upon the content of the text. Farès, 1953, pls. VII–IX: portraits of physicians of antiquity, XI–XVI: themes and anecdotes treated in the text, XIX: a table of serpents, XVII–XVIII: specimens of plants. See also Moulierac, 1996, p. 101; Kerner, 2004, pp. 3–4 and n. 3.

[50] Paris, Bibliothèque Nationale, Ms. Arabe 2964, p. 15. Colour reproductions in *À l'ombre d'Avicenne*, 1996, p. 156, cat. no. 87, bottom, and Pancaroğlu, 2007, p. 26, fig. 12.

[51] Rosenthal, 1956, pp. 67–71.

[52] *Idem*, p. 70 and n. 72. The denomination *drakōn* is thought to be derived from the Greek word *derkomai*, "to see" (see also Porphyrios, *De Abstinentia*, III. 3,8); the sacred serpent is said to be the guardian of the temple of Asklepios because it is the most watchful of animals; according to Cornutus, Lucius Annaeus, "snakes are symbols of Athene, because they look frightening and are vigilant and sleep little" (*Theologiae Graecae Compendium*, 20); similarly, it is associated with Asklepios because of its ability to self-rejuvenate, to discard age, as well as its vigilance; because patients require attentive care (*Theologiae Graecae Compendium*, 33).

[53] The Greek *gerās* ("old age") is also used to denote the cast-off skin of snakes. Rosenthal, 1956, pp. 70–1 and n. 76.

[54] Ullmann, 1972, p. 176 and n. 6; Plessner, "Aghāthūdhīmūn," *EI*² I, p. 247a.

mixed into the theriac the flesh of snakes ..."[55] Three anecdotes attributed to Andromachus the Younger serve to substantiate the therapeutic properties of snake flesh. These comprise the use of snakes dissolved in wine, a mixture reported to have cured a man suffering from leprosy (known as elephantitis),[56] the homeopathic effect of snakes dissolved in water upon a snakebite, and similarly a snakebite serving as an antidote against an opium overdose.[57]

The fourteenth-century scholar al-Damīrī records in his well-known bestiary that "it is unlawful to eat serpents on account of their injurious property, and an antidote prepared out of their flesh is also unlawful." He based this on the tenth-century traditionist and Shāfʿī specialist Abū Bakr al-Bayhaqī, remarking that it is forbidden by the Shāfʿī school, "excepting in circumstances of great necessity."[58] In spite of these cautionary remarks snakes apparently continued to be a choice ingredient in the theriac or other concoctions, as evidenced also by the same scholar who cites that according to ʿĪsā ibn ʿAlī:

> The flesh [of snakes] preserves the senses, and soup (gravy) made of its flesh strengthens the sense of sight. The flesh of serpents from a part of their bodies in which there is much of it warms, dries, and clears the body, and removes diseases from it. [...] if it is burnt and kneaded with good olive oil, and a painful carious cavity in a tooth is stuffed with it, it will cure it; if it is pounded fine together with its head and applied over parts affected with alopecia, it will cause hair to grow again.[59]

Al-Damīrī notes further recipes from other authorities:

> If the fried slough of a serpent is taken and the bark of the root of capers, long birth-wort (aristolochy), and anacardium in equal parts are mixed with it, and then a person suffering from both external and internal hanging piles is fumigated (with the mixture), they will fall off. [...] if the slough of a serpent mixed with the reddish tinged bdellium both external and internal piles are fumigated, they will be cured. If an egg of a serpent is pounded with nitre and vinegar, and then applied over fresh patches of white leprosy, it will remove them. [...] [The serpent's] heart if it is hung on the body, will cure quartan ague.[60]

There was a profitable trade in the importation of vipers and other snakes *(afʿā)* chiefly from Sijistān (Sīstān), a region known for its great

---

[55] Kerner, 2004, pp. 232–3. The practice of consuming snake meat to cure a variety of illnesses has a very long history. The first-century medical writer Cornelius Celsus (d. *c.* 50 AD) reports the experience of farmers who cured abscesses in the lymphatic glands by eating snake flesh (*De medicina* 5.28.7b); cf. Hanson, 2006, p. 497. The ingredient was formalised when the Roman emperor Nero (r. 54–68 AD) developed an interest in an antidote formulated by Mithridates VI (120–163 BC), king of Pontus, for which a Persian physician had probably supplied the recipe and which the king used daily as a preventive measure against poisoning. He asked his "Leibarzt," Andromachus the Elder, to investigate and improve the compound, which subsequently was modified by the addition of snake flesh as a further ingredient, thus creating what is generally regarded as the first true theriac, the Theriaca Andromachi, being an early example of the homeopathic principle of *similia similibus curantur* (Bierman, 1994, p. 5). Thereafter, the use of snake flesh as a cure is recorded by numerous physicians, such as Aretaios and Galen (Oberhelman, 1994, p. 943 and n. 9). It is also reported in the writings of Eznik of Koghb (*Elc alandocʿ*, tr. and ed. Mariès and Mercier, 1959, pp. 574–5, ch. 64). Moreover, it is known that the ingredient was used by Jewish physicians of the medieval period when they produced the universal drug:

> ...*ṭariyāqā* in which is mixed the flesh of the viper and the eggs of that animal that is called. ...(?) mix it with dry ground leavened bread, roll it into oven loaves and dry them with the other ingredients in the *ṭariyāqā*. ...then knead it with honey.

Gil, 2004, pp. 605–6.

[56] Manuscript of the *Kitāb al-sumūm* ("Book of Poisons")/ *Kitāb al-diryāq* (a combination of the *Kitāb al-diryāq* with another toxicological treatise, the *Kitāb al-sumūm),* sold at Sotheby's *Arts of the Islamic World*, London on 25 April 2002, lot 30; the unillustrated manuscript of the *Kitāb al-diryāq is* dated 8 Jumādā al-ūlā, 622/19 May, 1225, with a tentative provenance of Mesopotamia or western Iran, fol. 44b. Kerner, 2004, pp. 17–8, 86, and *eadem,* 2007, p. 32. The anecdote is also recorded by the eleventh-century Christian physician Ibn Buṭlān, see Browne, 1921, pp. 72–3. A related account of a serpent "vomiting" into a bowl of *maḍīra* (a kind of broth made with sour milk) which is drunk by an epileptic boy who was subsequently cured is attributed to al-Rāzī; al-Faraj, vol. 2, pp. 103–4, and Ibn Abī Uṣaybiʿa, vol. 1, p. 312, cited after Browne, 1921, pp. 75–6. Yet another anecdote is related by a man called Abū ʿAlī ʿUmar ibn Yaḥyā al-ʿAlawī, which recounts that a man was cured from leprosy by eating roasted snake meat after having cut off the heads and tails; al-Faraj, vol. 2, p. 100, cited after, *idem,* 1921, p. 76. Cf. Massé, 1938, vol. 1, p. 207.

[57] *Kitāb al-sumūm/Kitāb al-diryāq*, *op. cit.*, fol. 45b, 46a. Kerner, 2004, pp. 17–8, 88–9. Cf. Pancaroğlu, 2001, pp. 160–1, figs. 6–8. Andromachus the Younger is shown together with a man who is bitten by a serpent in Ms. Arabe 2964, p. 19, Bibliothèque Nationale, Paris.

[58] Tr. Jayakar, 1906, vol. 1, p. 649. In this connection it is worthy of note that in the *Shāh-nāma* account of Iskandar's adventures the consumption of *tinnīn*, which in spring fall down from Heaven, is associated with Yājūj and Mājūj (Gog and Magog), the apocalyptic peoples known from biblical (Ezekiel 38.39, Apocalypse 20.7–10) and Qurʾānic eschatology (*sūras* 18, 93–8; and 21, 96); tr. and ed. Mohl, 1838–1878, vol. 5, p. 223, ll. 1467–1468.

[59] Tr. Jayakar, 1906, vol. 1, p. 654.

[60] *Idem*, p. 654.

number of vipers,[61] since theriac was prepared from their flesh.[62] Moreover, the city of Arīhā (Jericho) is named "the home of the theriacal serpents, and the excellence of the theriac of Jerusalem owing to the use therein of the flesh of those serpents" in an addition to a thirteenth-century manuscript copy of al-Muqaddasī's geography, *Aḥsan al-taqāsīm fī maʿrifat al-aqālīm* ("The Best Divisions for Knowledge of the Regions"), preserved in the Süleymaniye Kütüphanesi, Istanbul.[63] In the second extant copy of the *Kitāb al-diryāq*, in the Österreichische Nationalbibliothek in Vienna, a miniature in the herpetological tract illustrates the procedure of serpent hunting for the flesh of snakes used in the remedy.[64] The serpents were made to bite into leather-"dolls" with glass eyes for them to discharge their venom, making them easier to handle.[65]

The medicinal properties of serpent flesh were also known in Buddhist Central Asia where in the Swāt region Lord Śakra (Indra), an incarnation of the Buddha, sacrificed himself for the good of the people by transforming himself into a great serpent whose dead body filled the entire valley of Swāt. Since his flesh was a remedy for every kind of disease, the sick were thus delivered from their afflictions.[66] This legend has certain affinities with an assortment of tales related to the *Queen of the Serpents* which is included in *Alf layla wa-layla* collection of fairy-tales and other stories.[67] In the tale the Serpent-Queen consents to be slain and to sacrifice her flesh in order to heal the king. However just as in Andromachus the Younger's theriac recipe recorded in the *Kitāb al-diryāq* text, the consumption of snake flesh is seen here specifically as a cure for leprosy with which the king is afflicted.[68] In the tale the flesh of the reptile is to be boiled and then served to the leper. Moreover drinking the elixir, in other words the broth in which the flesh was cooked (after skimming off the "first scum" or foam which appears in the process of boiling), is said to give access to the fountains of knowledge, as well as various sciences.[69]

The consumption of snake flesh as an antidote to snake venom is recommended by ʿAlī ibn Waḥshiyya al-Nabaṭī in his ninth-century text on poisons. He notes an antidote attributed to a certain Ḥajujā which involves consuming the flesh of a viper (two ounces) cooked together with bread *(samīd)* and sipping the meat broth.[70] The benefits of serpents, in particular the healing properties of snake flesh as general antidote to its venom, is also stated in the tenth-century texts of the *Ikhwān al-Ṣafāʾ*.[71]

The symbolism of the knots formed by the two dragons on the frontispiece may be related to the number symbolism of four which, as Meisami writes, "is the number by which the categories of nature are subdivided: the four elements, the four humours, and the four seasons."[72] Medieval Islamic medicine, based largely on Greek medicine and natural history, in particular the Galenic

---

[61] Cf. *idem*, p. 56; Monchi-Zadeh, 1975, pp. 117–8, see also n. 5.

[62] Kopf, "Afʿā," *EI*² I, 214b.

[63] Copied in 658/1259. Istanbul, Süleymaniye Kütüphanesi, Ayasofya 2971. Al-Muqaddasī, *Aḥsan al-taqāsīm fī maʿrifat al-aqālīm*, tr. and ed. Collins, 1994, p. 158.

[64] Vienna, Österreichische Nationalbibliothek, Cod, A.F. 10, fol. 22b. Duda, 1992, vol. 2, fig. 39; *À l'ombre d'Avicenne*, 1996, p. 100. Interestingly, as Jaclynne Kerner (2007, p. 35, n. 92) has pointed out, the illustration sheds light on the common misperception that snake venom (which forms the basis for modern antidotes to snakebite/antivenins) was an ingredient in the theriac. However, snake venom was known to be beneficial and to act as an antidote in pre-Islamic times (see p. 157, n. 125). It was also administered in ancient India. In the chapter on the use of poison as drug recorded in the famous sixth- to seventh-century treatise *Aṣṭāṅga Saṃgraha* by Vāgbhaṭṭa the Elder, probably composed in Ujjain, in western Madhya Pradesh, it states that the person who has consumed vegetable/mineral poison should be treated with snake venom (48.3.5). The same is noted in ch. 36 of the *Aṣṭāṅga Hṛdaya* by Vāgbhaṭṭa the Younger. I am indebted to Dr Jouhar Kanjhirala Adam for this information. The use of snake venom as antidote may furthermore be gauged from Indian lore, such as the episode of the boyhood of Bhīmasena and the tale of king Nala who, being possessed by an evil spirit, was healed by the bite of the Nāga Karkoṭaka; see Vogel, 1926, pp. 71–4, and 80–1, respectively.

[65] *Kitāb al-sumūm/Kitāb al-diryāq*, *op. cit.*, fol. 49a. Kerner, 2004, pp. 17–8, 98.

[66] *Si-yu-ki*, vol. 1, tr. Beal, 1884, repr. 2000, pp. 125–6. Cf. Carter, 1992, p. 70, n. 24.

[67] 483rd to 536th Night [1830 Calcutta ed. count]. *The Book of the Thousand Nights and a Night*, tr. Burton, 1885, vol. 5, pp. 324–411. See also Marzolph and van Leeuwen, 2004, pp. 348–50.

[68] 534th to 535th Night; *The Book of the Thousand Nights and a Night*, tr. Burton, 1885, vol. 5, pp. 404–10. Cf. Brandenburg, 1973, p. 49.

[69] 535th Night. *The Book of the Thousand Nights and a Night*, tr. Burton, 1885, vol. 5, pp. 407–10. Cf. Marzolph and van Leeuwen, 2004, pp. 349–50.

[70] Levey, 1966, p. 69. Another form of consumption is recorded in the *Aṣṭāṅga Saṃgraha*. It states that a hooded serpent, which has been enraged and found emitting fumes from its mouth, should be made to bite many times on a piece of meat fastened to the tip of a stick. After carefully deciding the strength of the poison, the physician should administer the powder of this meat to the patient who has not been cured by any other anti-poison medicines (48.19.20).

[71] Tr. and ed. Dieterici, 1858, pp. 89–91.

[72] Cf. Meisami, 1993, p. 166.

humoral physiology and pathology, was informed by a structure of sympathies. The four elementary qualities or natures *(ṭabāʾiʿ)* (hot, cold, moist and dry) were regarded as the crucial constituents of all things, whether metals, minerals, plants, or animals; these qualities traditionally correspond to other quaternary groupings such as the four Aristotelian elements of earth, fire, air, and water, and to the Hippocratic-Galenic cardinal humours *(al-akhlāt)* which consisted of phlegm, yellow bile (choler), black bile (melancholy) and blood.[73]

The eleventh-century historian of the Ghaznawids, Bayhaqī, stresses the importance for man to "understand that he is composed of four elements, which must be maintained in equilibrium."[74] The actions of the poisons in the body were explained as an imbalance *(iʿtidāl)* of the four humours, or the entire constitution.[75] Moreover, as Meisami states, "the four elements and humours (i.e., the bases of all creation), when maintained in equilibrium, are symbolised by the image of a square within a circle."[76] Since this text is largely associated with medicinal preparations, Oya Pancaroğlu argues that the four winged figures which surround the central figure may have been intended to symbolise the four elements and their four humoral counterparts which, by extension, may also be reflected in the four knots formed by the two dragons that may be read as a reinforcement of this number symbolism.[77]

However, since the pillars of Galenic humoral physiology and pathology are linked to worldly existence and its material manifestations, they may also be more closely associated with the motif of the dragons with fourfold knot. This motif would lend itself as a more likely association since the representation of the dragon often served to embody the world and its material expressions.[78] The poet al-Fāryābī accordingly defines the four senses that bind humans to the world as four dragons:

> This human who is the highest of creations
> Is constantly in the throes of the four dragons
> [that make up his senses]. [79]

In a similar vein, in Niẓāmī's *Haft Paykar*:

> ...the dragon represents the "sky," that is, the material world; its four feet the four elements, its seven heads the seven planets.[80]

It is, moreover, recorded that above the throne of the Ghaznawid *sulṭān* Masʿūd, who although being ethnically Turkish was deeply imbued with Persian and Islamic courtly traditions:

> ...a gold-plated chain [was] hung from the ceiling of the chamber containing the dais, and came down over the dais where the crown and the throne were. The crown was attached to this chain, and there were four bronze figures fashioned in the shape of human beings and mounted on columns which were secured to the throne itself, so that their hands were outstretched and thus held the crown safely.[81]

Hence, the number of four figures holding up the crown above the throne may be indicative of standard patterns for enthronement scenes that were current in the Central Asian world. It may thus be possible to view the four winged figures framing the personification of the Moon that is enclosed within interlaced dragons of the *Kitāb al-diryāq* as representing the heavenly sphere, while by contrast the serpent-dragon, with its symbolism evoking potent therapeutic talismanic devices directed against the "demons" of illness, is related to the medical sphere.

c. *Studies on the properties of serpent(-dragons) and the effects of their venom*

Based largely on late antique forms of Greek medical knowledge with their magical practices and beliefs, medieval Islamic medical science, pharmacology and toxicology likewise maintained a close link between science and supernatural medical paradigms,[82] as reflected in the *Kitāb al-diryāq*.[83] Hence supernatural and magical explanations of diseases were often sought. However, while magic spells as remedies were usually prohibited they could exceptionally be resorted to in special cases such as snake or scorpion stings.[84] The use of both natural *(ʿilm sīmiyā)* and

[73] Cf. Browne, 1921, pp. 120–1; Needham and Ling, 1954, p. 459; Dols, 1984, pp. 10–24, esp. 10–1.
[74] Meisami, 1999, p. 82.
[75] Johnstone, "Summ," EI^2 IX, 872a.
[76] Meisami, 1993, p. 166.
[77] Pancaroğlu, 2001, p. 164 and n. 30.
[78] Daneshvari, 1993, p. 19.
[79] Al-Faryābī, *Dīwān*, ed., Bīnish, T., Tehran, 1958, p. 43, as cited in Daneshvari, 1993, p. 16, n. 7.
[80] Tr. Wilson, 1924, vol. 2, 1645, n. 1616, and Dastgirdī, V., *Haft Paykar*, Tehran, 1313, p. 244, n. 1; as cited in Meisami, 1987, p. 228, n. 56.
[81] Bosworth, 1963, pp. 135–6.
[82] Moulierac, 1987, p. 88.i.
[83] Cf. Bürgel, 1988, pp. 33–7. For the lands of the Fertile Crescent, see also Farès, 1953, p. 26, and *idem*, 1959, p. 162.
[84] Cf. Ullmann, 1978, pp. 2–5.

supernatural *(siḥr)* magic which was thereby involved may largely be seen as a reflection of the beliefs and practices current in contemporary society.[85]

The relationship between pharmacology, toxicology and other occult sciences is evidenced by the attribution of one of the earliest and most complete known works in Arabic on the scientific study of poisons, their detection and actions, and the treatment of the conditions they cause, the *Kitāb al-sumūm wa daf' maḍārrihā* ("Book on Poisons and the Prevention of Their Harm"), to the renowned alchemist Jābir ibn Ḥayyān which was probably written about 900 or earlier.[86] Another important text on poisons in Arabic ascribed to 'Alī ibn Waḥshiyya al-Nabaṭī who lived in the second half of the ninth century similarly exhibits a mixture of science and magic.[87]

Texts on pharmacology and toxicology, in particular, contained ideas infused with late antique concepts of magic based on the Hermetic notion of a unified cosmos of independent forces.[88] The subject of toxicology intersected above all with the Hermetic tradition of late antiquity, formulated in writings attributed to Hermes Trismegistos (including a number of astrological treatises) which had great influence on magical, divinatory and alchemical discourse in the medieval era.[89] This body of discourse emphasises the close relationship or cosmic "sympathy" between the divine and the physical world, spirit and matter, between the hidden and the seen, and was aimed at gaining intellectual and spiritual mastery of the cosmos by tapping into supernatural forces.[90]

An Arabic text ascribed to Hermes Trismegistos on the venom of serpents and other poisonous creatures, translated and compiled from the Greek most probably in the ninth century and in circulation throughout the medieval period, reveals the association between toxicology and the Hermetic notions of sympathies.[91] The belief in a link between the terrestrial and the celestial informed in particular the description of the serpents, their venom and the theriac antidotes, which were systematised in the text according to their correspondence to the twelve constellations of the zodiac and the planets. Among the serpents corresponding to the description of the planets is a dark green or black and saffron-coloured serpent which represents the head and tail of the planet of the dragon *(al-jawzahr)*.[92] A list of fantastic serpents follows, among them a deathly red serpent with black wings living in the air[93] and a large marine serpent with branching horns like those of a stag and a mane like that of a seahorse. We learn further that this marine serpent has a black neck, a white head, a red belly and a multicoloured back; that it can be caught with the help of music; that a stool made with its vertebra can both cure the sitter of podagra and serve to protect the house in which it stands from vermin, and that this serpent's head yields stones that are used for talismans.[94] Another deathly dark-green serpent from the Egyptian desert is human-headed with a curly beard.[95] A serpent from the mountains of Inner Armenia has a fishtail, a bird's head and is adorned with many colours, while another from the same region has two breasts and, if not deathly, is able to inflict harm.[96] The most vicious of all serpents is the pale yellow "Basiliskos" ("the queen"), whose head is crowned by tufts of hair. Whoever so much as sees it dies

---

[85] Levey, 1966, pp. 10–1.

[86] Tr. Siggel, 1958, p. 3; Levey, 1966, p. 16.

[87] Poison is clearly defined as "overpowering in its nature," arising "from the mixing of the soul in its makeup with its uniting substances according to the influence of the stars," destroying "that which is called the life-force," affecting the bodily organs, prohibiting breathing, and ending ultimately in death. Levey, 1966, pp. 11, 15, 25–6; see also Sezgin, 1971, pp. 318–29.

[88] O'Connor, 1994, pp. 21, 52–5, esp. 53.

[89] Cf. Peters, 2004, pp. 189–90.

[90] A large body of this literature probably originated in the city of Ḥarrān (ancient Carrhae) in northwestern Mesopotamia, a major centre of ancient scholarship, in particular in astrology and astronomy (Ullmann, 1972, pp. 289–93; Massignon, 1950, repr. 1981, pp. 384–400). During the 'Abbasid period Ḥarrānian scholars were present in large numbers in Baghdad. Many citizens of Ḥarrān, claiming to be Ṣābians, resisted conversion to Islam and the city remained largely pagan until the early eleventh century. The Ṣābians, whose liturgical language was Syriac (Chwolsohn, 1856, vol. 1, p. 159), provided some of the greatest translators and scientists of Islam. In his classic study on the Ṣābians, Daniil Chwolsohn enumerates some thirty Ṣābian scholars comprising astronomers, philosophers, doctors and mathematicians (1856, vol. 1, ch. 12); al-Battānī al-Ḥarrānī al-Ṣābi', one of the most renowned Arab astronomers, was born before 244/858, probably at Ḥarrān, into a family that formerly professed the Ṣābian religion. The theology of the Ḥarrānians, who came to be known as the Ṣābians after a visit by the caliph al-Ma'mun, is Babylonian in origin, and is a complex blend of polytheism, Gnosticism, Mithraism, Hellenistic Neopythagoreanism and perhaps even Indian cultural components in a synthesis catalysed by Hermeticism. Cf. Marquet, "Ikhwān al-Ṣafā'," *EI*[2] III, 1071a.

[91] Ullmann, 1994; for the dating of the manuscript, see *idem*, p. 159.

[92] *Idem*, p. 18.24, p. 54.187–90.

[93] *Idem*, p. 28.79.

[94] *Idem*, pp. 28–30.80–3.

[95] *Idem*, p. 30.84.

[96] *Idem*, p. 30.85–6.

on the same day,[97] and the sound of its hiss is equally deadly to the hearer. Any animal moreover that tastes the flesh of a person killed in such a way will immediately die in its turn.[98] The physicians Abū ʿAlī Aḥmad ibn ʿAbd al-Raḥmān ibn Mandawayh (d. 410/1019) from Iṣfahān and Abū ʿAlī al-Ḥusayn ibn ʿAbd Allāh ibn Sīnā who came from a village near Bukhara (whose name was latinised as Avicenna; d. 428/1037) both mention that the "Basiliskos" serpent exists in the land of the Turks.[99] In his text on poisons Ibn Waḥshiyya also mentions serpents which exist in the valley of the Khazluj in the land of the Turks noting that "if a man sees these snakes, he dies; also if the snake looks at him, he dies immediately."[100]

Al-Damīrī similarly records in his *Ḥayāt al-Ḥayawān* that the gaze of some serpents exerts a baleful influence and can indeed be mortal.[101] The same phenomenon is also described in the traditional tale of Alexander. There is said to have been a deep pit *(biʾr)* at a cemetery near Hamadān. Everybody who looked into it died at once. When Iskandar could not find a solution, he wrote to Aristotle who recommended him to place an iron mirror at the mouth of the pit and only to look into the pit when the mirror was blank. Iskandar followed this advice and for seven days the mirror was obscure, only appearing blank on the eighth day. He then ordered that someone should descend into the cavity, but his people refused. Eventually an animal was sent down and when it was clear that no harm had come to it, a slave descended in turn. At the bottom he saw a large coiled serpent with one central eye lying dead. Iskandar had it dragged from the pit. When he learned of all this, Aristotle explained to Iskandar that the serpent's eye was the source of its venom, which was why all those who looked at it died immediately. When the giant serpent saw its own reflection in the mirror it was bound to perish as well.[102] These references show that in particular the eyes of the creature are considered to be the seat of a specific fear-inspiring power which is believed to be potentially fatal.

Further evidence of the persistence in Islamic times of a tradition relating to the legendary power of the serpent's sharp-sightedness and penetrating gaze can be found in the saying that vipers and related snakes *(afʿā)* live to an age of a thousand years, and that when they become blind, regain their sight by rubbing their eyes against the fennel plant *(rāziyānaj)*.[103] The tradition is probably distantly associated with the Greek *drakōn*, synonymous with *ophis*, *serpens* and other words for serpents[104] which were used for living (real) as well as mythical serpents, said to derive its name from the root *derk*, meaning "to see."[105] Macrobius clearly derives the name *draco* from this root "for they say that this serpent has the keenest vision and counterfeits the nature of the star that is ever watchful; for this reason, furthermore, the protection of shrines, holy places, oracles, and treasures is entrusted to serpents."[106]

In this context it is interesting to note the belief in the special property of the *dhubābī* type of

---

[97] The fatal look of the basilisk is also noted by Eznik of Koghb (*Elc alandocʿ*, tr. and ed. Mariès and Mercier, 1959, p. 594, ch. 140).

[98] Ullmann, 1994, pp. 30.87–8, pp. 101–15.87–8. When discussing the basilisk's noxious influence, Pliny records that when struck with a spear the force of its poison was such that it could run up the spear and would kill not only the rider but also the horse (*Naturalis Historia* VIII 33). A reflection of this ancient belief may be found in Ibn Waḥshiyya's text on poisons which states that:

> There is a kind of snake called *mādhyānā* at the boundary of the countries of the Bājarmā [in the Arabian peninsula], between it and Media toward the side of Armenia. ... Its temper is that it bites the stone thrown at it. If this happens, then the man who threw the stone dies on the spot. This is when the thrower does not shoot at it; if he does, then he dies more quickly than the one who does not shoot.

Tr. Levey, 1966, p. 27.

[99] Ullmann, 1994, pp. 105–6, p. 141.169. On Ibn Mandawayh, see Sezgin, 1970, p. 328.

[100] Tr. Levey, 1966, p. 27.

[101] Tr. Jayakar, 1906, vol. 1, p. 633. Cf. Ruska, "Al-ḥaiya," *EI*[1].

[102] Al-Zuhrī, *Kitāb al-Jaʿrāfiyya*, pp. 598–600, as cited in Ullmann, 1994, pp. 56–7.

[103] Al-Damīrī, *Ḥayāt al-ḥayawān al-kubrā*, tr. Jayakar, 1906, vol. 1, p. 57. According to the Egyptian encyclopaedist and historian al-Nuwayrī (*Nihāya*, XI, p. 82), this happens when the reptiles leave their holes in spring. The same is noted repeatedly in al-Qazwīnī (ed. Wüstenfeld, 1849, repr. 1967, pp. 284 and 428; Wiedemann, 1970, vol. 2, pp. 336, 386). The sympathy between the serpent and the fennel plant is also mentioned by the early medieval alchemical author Jābir ibn Ḥayyān (Kraus, 1942, p. 67). A decoction of the fennel flower stalk mixed with wine was used as remedy against snake bites (Dietrich, "Basbās," *EI*[2] supplement. Cf. Kopf, "Afʿā," *EI*[2] I, 214b; Ruska, "Ḥayyā," *EI*[2] III, 334b). The assertion that snakes use fennel for skin and sight is already mentioned in antiquity (cf. Pliny, *Naturalis Historia* XX 23.95).

[104] Merkelbach, "Drache," *RAC* IV, 1959, p. 226.

[105] See p. 173, n. 52.

[106] *Saturnalia* 1.XX.1–4. Cf. Schlüter, 1982, pp. 14–5; Van Henten, "Dragon," *DDD*, p. 265.

emerald *(zumurrud)*. It was said that when this stone was brought close to the serpent's eyes they would bulge from their sockets and burst.[107] According to Ibn Waḥshiyya's ninth-century text on poisons, it is the acorn-headed viper who responds in such a manner to the sight of the green emerald.[108] The phenomenon was tested by the thirteenth-century Arabian mineralogist Aḥmad al-Tifāshī (580/1184–651/1253) and still found to be true.[109] That the belief was widespread in the medieval Islamic world is shown by its figurative use in philosophical arguments, for instance by the ninth-century Muʿtazilite theologian Ibn al-Rāwandī in his book against prophecy, which he entitled *Kitāb al-Zumurrud* ("Book of the Emerald") because as he informs the reader:

> One of the properties of the emerald is that the eyes of snakes dissolve and melt away if they look at it, and similarly, if an adversary peruses this book, he melts away [i.e., his arguments are silenced].[110]

The notion of the potency of the image, exemplified in the biblical story of the invasion of poisonous snakes which so devastated the people of Israel that Moses intervened on their behalf, setting a miraculous bronze image of a serpent on a pole (Numbers 21:4–9),[111] is related to the magical principal of effecting a cure for snake venom by looking at the image of the serpent. In other words, it is a case of correspondence magic predicated on the principle that *similia similibus curantur* where a representation of the danger or of the disease helps in some way to exorcise it.[112]

In medieval Islamic toxicological treatises the section on the preparation of poisons was as prominent as that devoted to their prophylaxis and treatments. In Ibn Waḥshiyya's text the preparation of poisons and their antidotes often also involves a mixture of magical rites, incantations and astrology.[113] The description of the preparation of a poison with a snake as main ingredient and its symptoms reads as follows:

> There is a snake found in the desert called the black snake. It is one of the strong snakes called "the black which strips" because all snakes shed their skins once a year except the black which sheds four times every season of the year. It is so called because of the frequency of its shedding. This snake is taken and put into a wide, glass or clay vessel. It is cut into four pieces so that all its blood flows in the vessel. Its head is cut as one piece, and four fingers [width] below its head for every piece. This is carried out until the four or five pieces are finished and the blood comes together in the vessel. Set the pieces aside in something else so that the blood only will be in its vessel. Pay attention to the amount of its weight for the same amount of yellow sulfur is taken. This must be pure and good; it is pulverized finely and then sprinkled on the blood as long as the blood is fluid and mixes well with it. The head and tail [of the snake] are set aside but the pieces of its body are cremated with wood of mezereon until all becomes ash. This is then added to the blood and sulfur and mixed well by pulverization in the vessel until it needs moisture for its excessive dryness. It is moistened either with the blood of an animal or with the urine of a little boy until it is wet. Then the head and tail are thrown on it, side by side, and pulverized with it until all are mixed. It is gathered into a black lead vessel and covered with a well-fitting lid [i.e., of black lead], then buried in ass manure for twenty-one days. At the time of the hunting of the black [snake], its cutting, pulverizing, and mixing and at the time of its bleeding, the Moon must be adjoined to Mars or associated with it. When it is taken out after twenty-one days, it is found that it has become deeply black and has a very bad odor with a strong sharpness. Whoever carries out this work must fortify the atmosphere with two pieces of cotton soaked in violet oil which is so pure that there is nothing dearer than it or oil of nenuphar together with oil of pumpkin. He also smells sandalwood upon which

[107] Al-Masʿūdī, *Kitāb murūj al-dhahab*, tr. and ed. Barbier de Meynard and de Courteille, 1917, vol. 3, p. 46.

[108] Levey, 1966, p. 27.

[109] *Kitāb Azhār al-afkār fī jawāhir al-aḥjār*, tr. and ed. Abul Huda, 1998, p. 84. Cf. Kunz, 1913, p. 158.

[110] Al-ʿAbbāsī, *Maʿāhid al-Tanṣīṣ*, vol. 1, p. 156, cited after McKinney, 2004, p. 270.

[111] See also the the well-known copper alloy serpent column, the triple-headed serpent tripod of Delphi, in the Hippodrome of Constantinople, as an example of apotropaic sculpture against poisonous creatures including serpents. Cf. p. 23, n. 13.

[112] Jeffers, 1996, p. 234. Cf. Wakeman, 1973, p. 86.

[113] For instance, while treatment for a viper bite is administered an incantation of Dābāth, a charm master, is to be recited while a hand-held rod is made to pass over the entire body of the victim. Levey, 1966, p. 14, see also *idem*, p. 69, for an unintelligible charm attributed to the same charm master. Ibn Waḥshiyya's exposition of poisons (see p. 177, n. 87) gives an important insight into the medieval perception that harmful properties can be combatted by antidotes. See Levey, 1966, p. 24.

> rosewater has been poured. When the cover of the black lead vessel is opened, air must be allowed to pass through for an hour to decrease the odor. If you wish that it have the power of killing within six hours, leave it so; if you wish that it be fatal immediately, without delay and tarrying, pulverize the penetrating things which are eaten and drunk. This reaches the core of the body. While one of the two is dry and the other moist, gather both together and add them to the poison you have macerated. Mix them all well. Certainly it can be lethal on the spot without delay. I recite the praise of the old one [God], the generous, the kind, the beneficent for those who know him and worship him and for those who do not know him and do not worship him!
>
> When you want to use this to kill, weigh out one carat and mix it with any food, drink, gruel, or any odoriferous substance. It works when it reaches the belly or touches a spot on the body, wounds it and then, after a while, kills him. It is penetrating and sharp.
>
> Whoever drinks this poison which is extracted from the black snake and sulfur, then his symptoms are that he becomes very restless, his eyes become red, his tongue swells, and he is so thirsty that a drink of water does not quench it [i.e., the thirst]; his tongue lolls and his voice is remote, his eyes pop out, all the veins of his body are gorged with blood, he becomes very anxious, and often he cries until he dies.[114]

Ibn Waḥshiyya, moreover, records an interesting operation which can be lethal by sound. It involves a compound agent, one of the central ingredients being three large vipers, used to anoint two hides and the wood of a drum, which when struck "kills by the sound when it is heard." Once the agent has been applied three times and has dried, the drum has to be struck with a stick made of the branch of an olive tree. Drum and stick have to be set apart and when the Sun sets on a Tuesday evening, the drum and stick have to be placed facing Mars, preferably when the Moon is adjoining Mars or when Mars is rising. This is followed by a long incantation which repeatedly focuses on the drum and stick along with fumigations. Thereafter if one wishes to kill someone, one should strike the drum when the Moon is associated with Saturn. While striking the drum one should sing in praise of Mars and "whoever hears this voice dies either on the same day or after three hours following the darkness of the night have passed."[115]

d. *The serpent(-dragon) stone*

Belief in the healing properties of a magic serpent stone (Pers. *shāh-muhra*) is ancient and widespread and refers to a precious stone located either in the head of the dragon[116] or in its mouth, that is, one that would be expectorated by the ophidian creature.[117] The idea that serpents have precious stones in their heads is recorded in the Indian *Panchatantra*, a collection of stories and fables, originally written in Sanskrit in the third century BC.[118] It is propounded in the *Koiraniden* of Hermes Trismegistos and related texts in which the occult medical effects of the organs of animals are described.[119] Examples include a large mythical serpent in the western sea with cervid-type dendritical antlers and a mane like that of the seahorse, a creature said to have stones in its head that are used for talismans.[120] Such a serpent stone is also mentioned in Ibn Waḥshiyya's ninth-century text on poisons and their antidotes. He specifies that:

> There is a bead *(kharaza)* in the neck of the viper between its head and body. It is not found and is not clear except in large vipers which have aged for hundreds of years. This bead is found on its neck. When you take this bead at the time of the rising of the sign of Aries, whatever climate it may be, with the left hand and fasten it tightly with parchment of the fawn by means of a white silk thread, and after he fastens it, if he wishes, he sews it in a tanned hide and hangs it fastened

[114] Tr. Levey, 1966, pp. 58–9, also n. 297 for further references on this species. For other preparations of poisons with snakes as central ingredient, see *idem*, pp. 52–5. Ibn Waḥshiyya also records the preparation of a compound poison which requires snake eggs, see *idem*, p. 62, and specifies an antidote for someone who drinks gall of the viper (see *idem*, p. 81). Snake gall also serves as ingredient for the preparation of a lethal agent (see *idem*, p. 107).

[115] Tr. Levey, 1966, pp. 37–8.

[116] The stone is the *dracontias* or dragon stone described by Pliny (*Naturalis Historia*, XXXVII 10.57) and Solinus (*Collectanea Rerum Memorabilium*, 30.16). According to Pliny (*Naturalis Historia*, XXXVII 158) it is to be obtained by severing the head of a sleeping dragon. Cf. Merkelbach, "Drache," *RAC* IV, 1959, p. 228. See also Hasluck, 1929, vol. 2, p. 653 and n. 1; Massé, 1938, vol. 2, p. 326.

[117] Steingass, 1892, repr. 1981, p. 728, cf. also *muhra*, p. 1354. Cf. Hoffmann-Krayer, "Schlange," *HdA*, vol. 7, 1936, p. 1122, and *idem*, pp. 1199–201.

[118] Frazer, 1888, p. 179; also Laufer and Walravens, 1987, p. 138.

[119] Ullmann, 1972, p. 404, and *idem*, 1994, p. 100, 83.

[120] *Idem*, 1994, pp. 28–30, 80–3, 100, 83.

> on his left upper arm, then it serves to keep away from him the evils of the vipers and that of all snakes ... When the vipers and any snakes touch his body, then they become soft; their hatred goes out. ...
>
> As to what Shūshā ordered, he said that the bead of the snake is taken during the rising of the sign of Aries and is tied in the slough of the snake, then sewed in a tanned hide. The man fastens it on his middle where he binds the trouser band. If snakes sting him, then it is not harmful to him. He requires only a mild remedy to avoid death, becoming black or blue in colour, and lessening in power.[121]

A "snake-stone," often linked with a bezoar (*bāzahr*, a corruption of the Pers. *pād-zahr*, lit. "protecting (against) poison"),[122] that is, a concretion or "stone," found in a snake or another animal, can be used in an amulet against the Evil Eye and illness.[123] That it is also supposed to work as an antidote against snake venom is indicated by the twelfth-century poet Niẓāmī Ganjawī when he states that:

> from the thorny rose there comes rose water; life from the snake-stone.[124]

And about two hundred years later al-Damīrī (d. 808/1405) records that there is one type of serpent, for whose bite "the bezoarstone *(al-diryâq)* is useful."[125]

Talismanic virtue is also ascribed to the *guhar-muhra*:

> a pearl said to be found in a serpent's head and to secure the owner's continual good luck.[126]

Pearls and their association with serpents also appear in a legend in the seventh-century Sanskrit text *Harshacharita* ("The Deeds of Harṣa"). According to the story a pearl necklace, "which shone ... like a cluster of stars," born of the tears of the Moon god, became an antidote to poison and came into the possession of Vāsuki, the king of serpents. The latter always carried it with himself to soothe the burning heat of poison and eventually presented it to Nāgārjuna during his stay in the Netherworld.[127]

The belief in a rain stone (Turk. *yai*, Mong. *yada*),[128] often a bezoar placed in water, which was widespread among the Altaic people of Inner Asia in the medieval period seems to have spread from the early Turks to the Mongols. The rain stone could be used in weather magic and by its means the holder could magically cause rain or snow to fall or to cease.[129] In his treatise on mineralogy, *Azhār al-afkār fī jawāhir al-aḥjār* ("Best Thoughts on the Best of Stones"), written around 637/1240, Aḥmad al-Tifāshī describes the use of such a stone in a rain-making ritual conducted by an old Turkish weather-magician in the camp of the Khwārazm-shāh Muḥammad Khān, which took place under the personal supervision of the *sulṭān*:

> ...Then [the old Turk] took a live snake of the same colour as the [rain] stone, and fixed it [by

[121] Tr. Levey, 1966, pp. 69–70.

[122] Real bezoar stones, that is to say, hard round concretions, are also said to be obtained from the body of wild goats (the concretions are believed to have formed, for instance, in the head, the heart or the intestines, especially the stomach) indigenous to Iran and the lands on the borders of China that live chiefly on poisonous serpents; the bezoar is said to form when the animal has eaten too much snake flesh. Cf. Ruska, "Bezoar," *EI*[1] I, p. 710; for a detailed description, see al-Damīrī, *Ḥayāt al-ḥayawān al-kubrā*, tr. Jayakar, 1906, vol. 1, pp. 222–5 and n. 1; Ettinghausen, 1955, pp. 280–1 and n. 29, pp. 283–5, and n. 52. The twelfth-century Jewish theologian Ibn Maymūn/Maimonides notes with regard to the bezoar:

> Of the bezoar there is no mention in Galen's writings. The bezoar stone, called animal bezoar, is an acorn-like object of green to blue-green hue. It is formed layer upon layer, like some shell heaped one upon another. People say its origin is in the medial eye-corner of the Oriental ram; others believe it is formed in the gallbladder, which is indeed the case.

Treatise on Poisons and Their Antidotes, tr. and ed. Muntner, 1966, pp. 17–8. According to other accounts, bezoar stones are also believed to be found in different animals as well as human beings; cf. Molnár with an appendix by Zieme, 1984, pp. 128–9. On the bezoar, see also Pseudo-Aristoteles, *Das Steinbuch*, tr. and ed. Ruska, 1912, pp. 147–9. A thirteenth- or fourteenth-century gold bowl with a mounted bezoar stone attached by a gold chain, perhaps produced in the Caucasus, is now housed in the Kunsthistorisches Museum, Vienna, inv. no. 1140, published by Ettinghausen, 1955, p. 282, pl. XXXIX, no. 6.

[123] Massé, 1938, vol. 1, p. 210.

[124] Meisami, 1995, pp. 25, 280, 7:54.

[125] *Ḥayāt al-ḥayawān al-kubrā*, tr. Jayakar, 1906, vol. 1, p. 636.

[126] Steingass, 1892, repr. 1981, p. 1107. For the association of dragons with pearls, see also the Iranian legend of Azhdahāk (that is, Azhi Dahāka) giving a huge pearl to a concubine. Tchukasizian, 1964, p. 325. See pp. 62–3.

[127] Bāṇa, *Harshacharita*, tr. Cowell and Thomas, 1897, pp. 250–2.

[128] See the linguistic discussion in Molnár with an appendix by Zieme, 1984, pp. 104–16.

[129] Bosworth, "Yada Tash," *EI*[2] XI, 226a. For further discussion, see Rashīd al-Dīn, tr. and ed. Quatremère, 1836, pp. 428–35. An in-depth study of the phenomenon is found in Molnár with an appendix by Zieme, 1984. Cf. DeWeese, 1994, pp. 175–6, n. 24.

its tail to the tip of a stand of three reeds that surmount the bowl], hanging head down to the reed above the bowl [filled with water], so that there was a distance of two ells between the head of the snake hanging down and the surface of the water. After that he got two pieces of stone from the keeper of the stones, and put them into the water. ... He murmured some words, raised his head towards the sky, and prayed for rain. ... Then suddenly, clouds appeared at the edges of the sky, and it began to rain heavily, the air cooled down, and the men and the animals were eased.[130]

In his *Ta'rīkh-i jahān-gushāy* ("The History of the World-Conqueror") ʿAlā al-Dīn ʿAṭa-Malik al-Juwaynī (623/1226–681/1283) reports how Genghis Khān's son Toluy resorts to using the magical stone to produce snow as a means of concealment when hard pressed by the Tungusic Jurchen army during his invasion of northern China (Chīn) in 1232. Among his army was a Qanqlī Turk, a *yaichi/yadachi* (master of the art of *yai/yada*) who was well versed in the science of this stone and whom he ordered to make use of the weather magic in warfare:

Ulugh Noyan commanded him to begin practising his art and ordered the whole army to put on raincoats over their winter clothes and not to dismount from their horses for three days and nights. The Qanqli busied himself with his *yai* so that it began to rain behind the Mongols, and on the last day, the rain was changed to snow, to which was added a cold wind. From this excessive summer chill, which was such as they had not experienced in winter, the Khitayan army were disheartened and dismayed and the Mongol army emboldened and exhilarated.[131]

The account thus details the military use of weather magic as a meteorological weapon employed to enhance nomadic martial tactics.

On yet another level, the "philosopher's stone," the universal remedy endowed with the power of transmutation, is allegorically compared to the serpent stone in the *Kitāb Mānī rasūl Allāh*, a short treatise attributed to Mani (216–*c.* 277), son of Pattēg, the founder of the dualist religion of Manichaeism, proclaiming the great secret:

Blessed be he who knoweth the Tree of Beatitude. The distinguishing mark of this noble tree is the following: it only grows where goodness and blessing is to be found. Its fruit has a sweet, bitter, sour, bilious taste, from it emanates a tomb-like stench. Only few eat from it for it is deadly poison. However if you eat knowingly from it, you will not die, since it contains both poison and theriac [or theriac as well as poison], as is the case with the serpent. Our stone resembles the serpent, one can find it in the treasuries of kings and in the houses of sages, but one can also find it on the rubbish heaps, because fools spurn it and sages and scholars err with regard to its value. When you wish to pick from the fruits of the tree, it will cry and shed tears. Do not let yourself be frightened by this, rather pick them boldly and do not be frightened by it and its tears, because its tears banish suffering and illnesses, which it can generate, into the earth.[132]

---

[130] Molnár with an appendix by Zieme, 1984, pp. 63–4. See also *idem*, pp. 120–4.

[131] Tr. Boyle, 1912–37, vol. 1, p. 193. This feat is also recorded by Ghiyāth al-Dīn Khwāndamīr (d. 942/1535) in his chronicle *Ḥabīb al-Siyār* ("Friend of Travels"); see Ross, 1895, p. 33. The historian Muḥammad Ḥaidar Mīrzā Dughlāt (905/1499–1500–958/1551), a cousin of the first Mughal ruler, Bābur, notes the continued use of the magical rain stone in his *Ta'rīkh-i Rashīdī*. In the account of the Chagatayid Tughluq Tīmūr's (d. 764/1363) invasion of *Mā warā' al-nahr*, the Khān's two forces were on the right bank of the Jayḥun (Āmū Daryā) but since they were faced with an army that:
"exceeded them in number, [they] had recourse to magic, and sought aid from the Jadah stone, which possessed supernatural properties.

The army of Jatah had not strength for the fight,
So they sought help from the magic stone.
With the stone of Jadah, who was a magician,
They filled the world with wind and rain,
The clouds roared with thunder and the winds howled.
A thunderbolt fell upon the earth.

Although the sun was in Orion, a host of dark clouds suddenly filled the sky. The thunder resounded and the lightning flashed. The elements rushed out from the ambush of destiny into the open plain of the ether, and the thunderclaps re-echoed round the azure vault of heaven. The arrows of lightning were shot out, in all directions, from the bow of the thunder-clouds, and the rain shot down its whistling darts. It seemed as if the Fates had again become prey to the love of rebellion and confusion. Such a quantity of water descended from the eyes of the stars, that the Deluge seemed to occur a second time."

Tr. Ross, 1895, pp. 32–3. The use of weather magic in warfare appears also in the *Shāh-nāma* account, tr. and ed. Mohl, 1838–1878, vol. 3, pp. 35–9.

[132] Ullmann, 1970, p. 186, and *idem,* 1972, p. 186 and ns. 1 and 2.

CHAPTER TWELVE

THE DRAGON AND THE PROVINCE OF MAGIC AND DIVINATION

a. *The dragon and talismans*

As has been seen in preceding chapters, the range of symbolic meanings associated with the figure of the dragon extends to include an important role in those branches of knowledge that encompass the more esoteric or magical sciences, in particular sympathetic and talismanic astrological magic and the preparation of verbal and material talismans. The dragon's ability to eclipse the great luminaries is allegorically treated in the quest for "mastery" of magic and the concomitant mystical illumination of life.

This is apparent in medieval Islamic literature such as Niẓāmī's *Iskandar-nāma*. The story recounts how the well-known sage and magician of the first century AD, Apollonius/Balīnūs, who in the Islamic Middle Ages became known as the great master of talismans *(ṣāḥib al-ṭilasmāt)*,[1] overcomes a powerful priestess, Āẓar Humā, who had transformed herself into a black dragon to guard the holy fire of the temple.[2] However the wise Balīnūs not only breaks the resistance of the dragon-priestess but, interestingly, also marries her and manages in so doing to acquire knowledge of many of her magical practices. Niẓāmī's account makes clear that it was only his association with Āẓar Humā that enabled Balīnūs to become a famous magician.[3] It is notable that solely through union with a priestess who has the power to transform herself into a dragon can the great talisman-maker Balīnūs acquire knowledge of the magical sciences. In one of the oldest popular Persian prose narratives, the *Kitāb-i Samak ʿAyyār*, the magnanimous hero Samak is said to be taught two charms, one for dispelling serpents and another for calling them forth.[4] Similarly, the pre-Islamic romance, *Wīs u Rāmīn*, translated and versified in the mid-eleventh century, mentions snake charming by means of sorcery.[5]

The magical aspect of the dragon is allegorically alluded to by ʿAsjadī Marwazī (as indicated by his *nisba* he was presumably a native of Marw), a court poet of *sulṭān* Maḥmūd of Ghazna, who writes:

> Don't expect the world to be good to you
> The snake is only [made] kind by the power of magic.[6]

An important magical science was talismanic astrology. On the premise that stars can predetermine the course of future events, and that those well-versed in the motions of the heavens can accordingly foretell the future, the position of Islamic religious doctrine was, as already mentioned, fundamentally antithetical to astrological science. However, while astrology contented itself with mere prediction, magic on the other hand concerned itself with harnessing the forces of the cosmos to achieve predetermined ends. Between these two categories, there was also the magic of theurgy *(ṭilsam)*, the adjuration of divine powers, which concerned itself among other things with the making and the use of talismans, a process dictated by the observance of specific conditions in the making of objects designed to protect the bearer.[7] Islam ultimately accepted the use of "magic" and theurgy under certain strict conditions. Hence binding supernatural beings to human purposes was allowed as long as the aim was not to bring harm (so-called "white" or "natural" magic, *ʿilm al-sīmiyā*), which to a certain extent validated the use of amulets and talismans. The astrological iconography of the twelve zodi-

[1] On Apollonius of Tyana, see Sezgin, 1971, pp. 77–90.

[2] Niẓāmī, *Dīwān*, pp. 974–5, cited in *Pseudo-Apollonius of Tyana*, tr. and ed. Weisser, 1990, p. 27.

[3] Dastgirdī, V., vol. 1, Tehran 1334/1956, pp. 242–4, as cited in Bürgel, 2000, p. 135.

[4] *Samak-i ʿAyyār* III, pp. 56–7, as cited in Omidsalar, "Magic in literature and folklore in the Islamic period," *EIr*. Cf. Gaillard, 1987, pp. 19–21.

[5] Tr. and ed. Davis, 2008, p. 88.

[6] *Dīwān*, ed. Shabāb, T., Tehran, 1955, p. 31, as cited in Daneshvari, 1993, pp. 21–2.

[7] Ruska and Carra de Vaux, "Tilsam," *EI*[2] X, 500a.

acal signs and the seven planets fulfils a central function in talismanic design. The visual conceptualisation of the dragon thereby also plays a role, rendered as part of particular conjunctions which form the basis for astrological prediction.

The Qurʾānic exhortation not to worship the Sun and Moon, two signs created by God, occurs once (*sūra* 41, 37).[8] The codification of Rabbinic laws, *Mishna*, also specifically refers to images of the Sun, the Moon and, in addition, of the dragon, all of which must have been commonly represented in or before at least the fifth century AD (certainly the latest possible date of the composition of the *Mishna*), resulting in the Talmudic tract *ʿAvodah Zarah* ("Mishna on Idolatry" 3, 3) which contains the following prescription:

> Whenever a vessel is found on which the picture of the sun, or of the moon, or of a dragon *(draqōn)* is shown, it must be thrown into the salt sea.[9]

Rabbi Judah explains with regard to the imagery of the dragon *(deraqon)* that it is "anything that has fringes between the joints ... of the neck."[10] Commenting on this prohibition of the use of idolatrous images of the luminaries and the dragon in *Moreh Nebukhim* ("The Guide for the Perplexed") the great twelfth-century Jewish theologian Abū ʿImrān Mūsā ibn ʿUbaid Allāh ibn Maymūn/Maimonides (1135–1204) says:

> When the picture of the sun or the moon is mentioned, this does not mean that the picture of the sun is represented by a round disk, or that of the moon by a bow, but it refers to those figures which are called *telesmata*, and which are ascribed to the stars by the men who made them. Thus, for instance, they used to represent Saturn like a black old man, Venus like a gold-adorned fair young girl, the sun as a crowned king sitting on a chariot, and likewise they ascribe many figures to all of the constellations and stars though there is no agreement on it among them ... But the picture of the dragon [*deraqon*] which is mentioned in this *Mishna* is a scaled and finned figure like that of a fish. This figure was highly renowned with them because they attribute it to a certain part of the celestial sphere. And one of them who used to make such pictures told me that this one picture represents the dragon in the sphere of the moon [*teli*] – called in Arabic "al-Djawzahar" – and that it is made after a certain model and in a certain hour. As I have never seen such a picture I asked him in what book I might find it mentioned. Whereupon he answered me that his teacher himself had devised that picture and confided it to him as a secret, together with many other things.[11]

It is interesting that Maimonides thereby equates the *deraqon* with the dragon in the sphere of the Moon *(teli)*, the meaning of the latter however remaining unclear. The commentary thus shows, as Hartner put it:

> ...that still in the twelfth century the astrological doctrines of the Djawzahar had by no means become a generally known matter but used to be treated as a secret by the initiated, in such a way that even a highly erudite scholar like Maimonides could make only a rather vague statement about it.[12]

It reveals, moreover, the extent to which the fabrication of *telesmata*, or talismans, was shrouded in secrecy. It is also associated with the fact that, like astrology, the practice of magic *(siḥr)* was frowned upon by the religious establishment.[13]

As objects which were made to protect their owner and to ward off evil, the action of talismans is based on the concept of sympathetic magic,[14] which operates through the connectedness and interdependence of all phenomena through their qualities and attributes.[15] Magic was defined by the Khurasanian theologian and religious reformer, Abū Ḥāmid al-Ghazālī (450/1058–05/1111), as "based on a combined knowledge of the properties of certain terrestrial elements and of propitious astral risings."[16]

---

[8] Fahd, "Shams," *EI*² IX, 291a.

[9] Hartner, 1938, pp. 149–50. It is of note that the serpent-dragon image is to be cast into the salt sea, that is the Dead Sea, presumably meant as symbol of death. A *baraita* (extra-canonical Mishna) similarly maintains that "all planets except the sun and moon are "permissible" as are all faces except the human face and all figures except the dragon," as cited in Epstein, 1997, p. 142, n. 38. For a detailed discussion of rabbinic texts on the theme of the dragon and idolatry, see Schlüter, 1982, pp. 62–129.

[10] Wilson, 2001, pp. 124–5.

[11] Cited after the English translation by Hartner, 1938, p. 150. For a German translation, see Chwolsohn, 1856, vol. 2, pp. 484–5; Schlüter, 1982, p. 130.

[12] Hartner, 1938, p. 150. See however Schlüter's (1982, pp. 141–1) suggestion that Maimonides, who in spite of being well-versed in astrology was, as is generally known, ill-disposed towards the science, may thus intentionally have equated the Moon *teli* with the *deraqon* (which the Mishna so expressly proscribed) partly in order to take distance from his contemporaries who placed such great importance on the Moon *teli*.

[13] Fahd, "Siḥr," *EI*² IX, 567b.

[14] *Idem*. Cf. Porter, 2006, p. 794.

[15] O'Connor, 1994, p. 67.

[16] *Iḥyāʾ*, vol. 1, pp. 49–50, as cited in Fahd, "Ruḳya," *EI*² VIII, 600a.

The influential magical manual *Ghāyat al-ḥakīm* ("The Philosopher's Goal"), attributed to Abū Maslama Muḥammad al-Majrītī, who wrote between 443/1052 and 448/1056, provides a synthesis of magic with astrology and stresses the importance of using talismans, whether material or verbal (spells).[17] The compilation was inspired by Ṣābian sources,[18] which played an important role in the transmission of esotericism from late antiquity into early Islam, and by "'Indianised' hermeticist astrology."[19]

Taking inspiration from the tenth-century compilations of the *Ikhwān al-Ṣafā'*, al-Majrītī wrote:

> ...magic essentially comprises two parts, one theoretical and one practical. The first consists in knowledge of the positions of the immobile heavenly bodies (which is where, in fact, the forms are located), the modalities of their radiation on the planets and, finally, aspects of conjunctions of the celestial spheres at the precise moment that the successful outcome of a project is desired. Under this heading the ancients placed everything having to do with discernment of the beneficial and of the baleful and with theurgy. As for practical magic, it consists in the knowledge of three domains of the created being and of the qualities of the planets which would be disseminated there.[20]

Ibn Khaldūn, who knew the *Ghāyat al-ḥakīm*, goes further in his prolegomena on the history of the world, *al-Muqaddima*, stating that:

> ... the souls of magicians possess the ability to exert influences in the universe and to tap into the spirituality of the planets, in order to use it in the exercise of their influence, by means of a psychic or satanic force.[21]

Among the images of the planetary gods described by al-Majrītī in the *Ghāyat al-ḥakīm*, one combines the Sun, the Moon and Jupiter with the imagery of the dragon.[22] In one source cited by al-Majrītī the Sun is portrayed in the form of a standing male figure holding a shield in his left hand and having under his feet the image of a dragon;[23] in another he appears as a crowned king, enthroned with a dragon under his feet and a raven in front of him.[24] The Moon resembles a woman with a beautiful countenance, girded by a dragon. A pair of serpents crown her horned head, another pair encircle her wrists while above and below her head are seven-headed dragons.[25] Again, in the first cited source the Moon is portrayed as a woman who sits on a pair of dragons, each biting the tail of the other.[26] Jupiter is a male figure with lion head and raptor's feet, with a polycephalic (or seven-headed) dragon under his feet.[27]

The significance of a talisman lies in its conjunction with the celestial bodies;[28] hence talismanic astrology plays a central role in its preparation.[29] The magician is warned of the eclipses of the Moon and the Sun and instructed to delay making the talisman until the Moon is free of the knot (node).[30] He is further warned of worse calamity when the Moon "foregoes ... the head or the tail *(taqaddama)*; because then he will be 'burnt' through the conjunction *(bi-mulāqāt)* of his body with that of the Sun,"[31] the reason being that when "passing from northern

[17] It was translated into Spanish in 1256 by order of Alfonso the Wise, king of Castile and Leon, and later became known in Latin under the title of *Picatrix*; Anawati, "Arabic Alchemy," *EHAS*, 1996, vol. 3, p. 872. Cf. Ritter, 1933; *"Picatrix,"* tr. and eds. Ritter and Plessner, 1962; also Ritter, 1921–2.

[18] The so-called Ṣābian inhabitants of Ḥarrān in northwestern Mesopotamia were particularly well-known for the practice of astronomy and astrology. Cf. p. 177, n. 90.

[19] Cf. Fahd, "Ṣābi'a," *EI*² VIII, 675a.

[20] *"Picatrix,"* tr. and eds. Ritter and Plessner, 1962, p. 9; tr. after Fahd, "Siḥr," *EI*² IX, p. 567b.

[21] *Idem* (tr. after *Muqaddima*, tr. Rosenthal, 1958, vol. 3, pp. 156–8).

[22] Citing three sources, specified as a lapidary by 'Uṭārid, a book without a title by Balīnūs (Apollonius) and a work by a certain Qrīṭūn (Kriton) on pneumatic talismans translated by Bu(i)qrāṭīs (the name Bu(i)qrāṭīs is identified by Ritter and Plessner as "Picatrix," while Ullmann, 1972, p. 420, and Strohmaier, 1989, p. 267, relate it to that of Hippocrates). Varying descriptions of the planets are given in the text which is a result of different manifestations and a syncretist evolution of the iconography of the celestial bodies; *"Picatrix,"* tr. and eds. Ritter and Plessner, 1962, pp. xliv, lxv.

[23] Citing a lapidary by 'Uṭārid as source; *eidem*, p. 115.10–3.

[24] Citing a work by a certain Qrīṭūn on pneumatic talismans translated by Bu(i)qrāṭīs; *eidem*, p. 115.14–7 and n. 1.

[25] Citing a lapidary by 'Uṭārid as source; *eidem*, pp. 116.30–117.1–5.

[26] Citing a book without a title by Apollonius as source; *eidem*, p. 117.6–8 and n. e.

[27] Citing a work by a certain Qrīṭūn on pneumatic talismans translated by Bu(i)qrāṭīs; *eidem*, p. 118.6–9.

[28] *Eidem*, p. 35.21.

[29] *Eidem*, p. 35.21.

[30] *Eidem*, p. 23.30.

[31]
> "...dem Kopf oder Schwanz ... vorhergeht *(taqaddama)*; denn dann ist er 'verbrannt' durch das Zusammentreffen *(bi-mulāqāt)* seines Körpers mit dem Körper der Sonne."

"Picatrix," tr. and eds. Ritter and Plessner, 1962, p. 24.5, cf. pp. 69.27–70.1; with emendation by Hartner, 1965, p. 445.

to southern latitudes, the Moon develops maleficent qualities."[32]

Instructions are given for the manufacture of an amuletic seal ring stone which has the extraordinary power of bringing about the disappearance of the wearer's enemies, and of instilling fear and terror into enemies. The making of it requires great precision and should be done at the hour of the zodiacal sign of Jupiter and the first decan of the *domicilium* of his exaltation, which is Cancer.[33] At this time green corundum should be engraved with the male figure of Jupiter rendered with a lion head and raptor's feet, holding a lance *(mizrāq)* with which he stabs a dragon that lies under his feet.[34]

Another interesting association with the head of the dragon *(ra's al-tinnīn)* is made in the *Ghāyat al-ḥakīm* describing in gruesome detail the severance of a man's head, carried out on a living subject, for divinatory purposes.[35] The soothsaying head is then posted in front of the *ra's al-tinnīn*, denoting probably a *navagraha* relief.[36]

Basing himself on the idea that the Intellect and the Soul have intermediary roles in the Creation of the natural world, which again echoes the well-known *Rasā'il* (Epistles) of the *Ikhwān al-Ṣafā'*, al-Majrītī allegorically states in the *Ghāyat al-ḥakīm* that if inclined towards the intellect, the soul will be illuminated by it, but if it moves away from the intellect the knot of the dragon's tail will eclipse the Sun and the Moon.[37]

Associated notions are also known in Jewish mysticism, discussed by the thirteenth-century mystic Abraham Abulafia in a passage from the *Otzar Eden HaGanuz,* where he goes so far as to refer to the knots of the *jawzahr (tᵉli)* as knots of love and mystical union:

> And the cosmic axis *(tᵉli)* is none other than the knot of the spheres, and there is no doubt that this is the subject of their existence, like the likeness of the connection of the limbs within man, and the connection of the limbs in man which are suspended in the bones at the beginning are also called the axis in man as well. And its secret is that a magician bring this knot of desire and renew it in order to preserve the existence of this compound for a certain amount of time. And when the knot is undone, the matter of the testimony of the knot will be revealed, and one who cleaves to these knots *(qešarim)* cleaves to falsehoods *(šeqarim)*, for as they are going in the future to be undone, the knots of his cleaving will also be undone, and nothing will remain with him any more, and therefore, before he loosens these, he must tie and cleave to the ropes of love those who have not loosened the knots of his love and the cleaving of his desire; and that is God, may He be exalted; and no other in any sense.[38]

b. *The dragon staff*

The supernatural and magic power of the rod has been renowned since the dawn of classical antiquity. The shape of the caduceus *(kerykeion)* appears at least as early as the middle of the sixth century BC in the form of the figure eight or in that of twisted serpents.[39] First and foremost in Greek mythology it was the attribute of the messenger of the gods, Hermes, whose chthonic character is related to his magic might.[40] The symbol's appearance in the Central Asian region is

[32] Hartner, 1965, p. 446.

[33] The *domicilium* represents the position of a planet standing in a certain zodiacal sign, while the exaltation *(sharaf)* signifies the point of the maximum power of a planet when standing in a certain zodiacal sign. Cf. Nasr, 1964a, repr. 1993, pp. 160–1, and table IV.

[34] "*Picatrix,*" tr. and eds. Ritter and Plessner, 1962, p. 129.7–13.

[35] The implied human sacrifice is also recorded by Ibn Khaldūn, *Muqaddima*, tr. Rosenthal, 1958, vol. 1, p. 221. A comparable magical practice is ascribed to the Ṣābians. Cf. Ibn al-Nadīm, *Kitāb al-Fihrist*, ed. Chwolsohn, 1856, vol. 2, pp. 15, 19–21, and n. 121; and ed. Flügel, G., Leipzig, 1871–2, p. 321; Chwolsohn, 1856, vol. 1, p. 142, and *idem,* vol. 2, pp. 19–21, 130–2, 142–4. See also Dozy and de Goeje, 1884, pp. 365–6; Green, 1992, pp. 178–80. The soothsaying head of the Ḥarrānians is mentioned in several other sources, for instance, by the fourteenth-century author al-Dimishqī, *Nukhbat al-dahr fī 'ajā'ib al-barr wa 'l-baḥr*, book 1, ch. 10, ed. Chwolsohn, 1856, vol. 2, pp. 388–9, in the chronicle of the Syrian Jacobite patriarch Dionysius Telmaharensis (d. 848) and the Nestorian church chronicle by the fourteenth-century historian 'Amr ibn Mattai, as cited in *idem*, p. VII and ns. 25, 26.

[36] "Picatrix," tr. and eds. Ritter and Plessner, 1962, pp. 146.6–147.22; with emendation by Hartner, 1965, p. 448. Green, 1992, p. 179.

[37] "*Picatrix,*" tr. and eds. Ritter and Plessner, 1962, pp. 45.19–24–46.1; cf. introduction, p. lxi.

[38] 55a Bodleian Ms. Or 606. This process of loosening and tying is conceived as the path towards enlightenment, see Idel, 1988, p. 136.

[39] Levi, 1941, p. 227. On the origin and the history of the caduceus, see also Wilson, 2001, pp. 183–94.

[40] To this may be added the Greek myth which tells of the blind soothsayer Teiresias who once came across two serpents in the act of copulation and killed the female one with his staff. He was immediately transformed into a woman and remained so for seven years. After seven years he met again two copulating serpents and this time killed the male one whereafter he became a man again. See Astour, 1965, p. 163.

testified by its representation as early as the late fourth century BC on gold coinage struck by Sophytes, who ruled over the Oxus region in northern Afghanistan.[41]

In the Semitic world the shepherd's rod, stick, or staff *(ʿaṣā)* could function as a symbol of sovereign rule. If used as such it was believed to be a repository of the power of royalty, and when bestowed upon someone it both signified and helped to effect the transfer of this royal force.[42] Following the example of the Prophet Muḥammad, the early caliphs carried a spear or staff on ceremonial occasions *(ʿanaza)*.[43]

The word serpent or snake *(ḥayya)* appears in the Qurʾān only in allusion to the staff or rod that Mūsa carried as sceptre of his authority and miraculously transformed into a serpent.[44] Of the nine miracles of which the Qurʾān speaks, Mūsā's turning of his staff into a serpent is the first (*sūra*s 20, 17–24; 27, 10; and 28, 31); he accomplishes this by throwing down the staff which takes the form of a crawling serpent. The transformation of Mūsa's symbol of sovereign rule, into a dragon, is a magical act that proves the Prophet's authenticity. In Mūsā's duel with the magicians of the pharaoh *(firʿawn)* the rods and ropes of the magicians were devoured by Mūsā's serpent-rod (*sūra*s 7, 107 and 117; 26, 32 and 45). He thereby performed a miracle by which God provided evidence of his authenticity as a Prophet. In post-Qurʾānic tradition as well as in magical writings this miracle and the miraculous character of the serpent-rod play an important part. The rod was directly associated with the shape of a serpent[45] and could also take the form of "a writhing serpent the size of a camel."[46] Mūsā is portrayed with such a rod ending in a dragon's head in one of the surviving folios of Rashīd al-Dīn's *Jāmiʿ al-tawārīkh* ("Compendium of Chronicles") transcribed and illuminated in 714/1314–5 at the Ilkhanid capital, Tabriz, which is further discussed below.[47] The complete transformation of the rod into a five-clawed quadruped dragon of Chinese derivation is portrayed in the scene of Mūsā frightening the *firʿawn* illustrated in a copy of Balʿamī's *Tarjumat-i tārīkh-i Ṭabarī*, probably made in the Jazīra and dated to *c.* 1300, now preserved in the Freer Gallery of Art, Washington, DC.[48]

Trees, and twigs as part of trees, were widely used for religio-magical purposes which relate the rod or wand to an artificial twig.[49] This is reflected in the description in Arabic sources of Mūsā's rod as a "two-pronged fork with a crook under the meeting point of the twigs and when it was turned into a serpent, the two twigs formed the mouth of the serpent with its forked tongue, while the crook took the shape of the crest."[50] The Qurʾānic story of Mūsā's rod turning into a serpent is, moreover, an example of the living power of the rod.[51]

Al-Tirmidhī records the popular eschatological belief according to which Mūsā's rod is one of the things that will reappear in the Last Days. When the Beast *(al-dābbat al-arḍ)* which is spoken of in the Qurʾān (*sūra* 27, 82)[52] becomes manifest as one of the significant signs of the approaching Hour, it will bring with it Mūsā's

[41] The dating is suggested relative to Seleucid coinage which dates from circa 305 BC. Reverse caduceus, obverse Sophytes in profile with helmet. See Bopearachchi, 1996, p. 26.

[42] Glaznov, 2001, p. 92.

[43] Miles, "ʿAnaza," *EI*² I, 482b.

[44] Ruska, "Ḥayyā," *EI*² III, 334b.

[45] Cf. al-Thaʿlabī, *Qiṣaṣ al-anbiyāʾ*, Cairo, n.d., p. 189, cited after Fodor, 1978, p. 13; see also *idem*, p. 12 and n. 73.

[46] Al-Kisāʾī, *Qiṣaṣ al-anbiyāʾ*, tr. Thackston, 1978, p. 227. Cf. Ibn Iyās, *Badāʾiʿ al-zuhūr*, Cairo, n.d., pp. 125–6, as cited in Fodor, 1978, p. 15 and n. 89. In the Old Testament, this rod belonged to Aaron, before it was turned into a serpent-rod which swallows the rods of the Egyptian magicians, then it bursts into bloom and bears almonds. See Fodor, 1978, p. 2.

[47] Martin, 1912, repr. 1968, vol. 1, p. 24, fig. 12; Talbot-Rice, 1957, p. 61, cat. no. 11. The dragon finial of the staff held by Mūsā closely resembles a twelfth- or thirteenth-century copper alloy finial from Iran or Jazīra, now preserved in Paris, Musée du Louvre, which may have topped a ceremonial staff (*L'Islam dans les collections nationales*, 1977, p. 102, cat. no. 161; *L'Etrange et le Merveilleux en terres d'Islam*, 2001, p. 110, cat. no. 74. Paris, Musée du Louvre, département des Antiquités orientales, section Islamique, inv. no. OA 6697). Another closely related finial is preserved in Copenhagen, the David Collection, inv. no. 47/1966 (von Folsach, 1990, p. 197, cat. no. 325, and *idem*, 1991, p. 44, cat. no. 33, ill. on p. 17). For related imagery in Armenian manuscripts, see the figure of a priest holding an upright undulant serpent with gaping mouth as staff portrayed in an Armenian lectionary from Erznga(n), dated 1362 (Yerevan, Matenadaran MS 4519); *Armenian Miniature*, eds. Gevorkian and Abgarian, 1996, pl. 54. Such a dragon-rod would also have been carried by a Buddhist monk, see Whitfield, R., Whitfield, S., and Agnew, 2000, p. 25.

[48] Kadoi, 2008, p. 147, fig. 4.23.

[49] Cf. Schimmel, 1994, pp. 29–30.

[50] Al-Ṭabarī, *Mukhtaṣar taʾrīkh al-rusul wa ʾl-mulūk wa ʾl-khulafāʾ*, I, Cairo, n.d., p. 401; al-Thaʿlabī, *Qiṣaṣ al-anbiyāʾ*, Cairo, n.d., p. 90, cited after Fodor, 1978, p. 4.

[51] Schimmel, 1994, p. 30.

[52] See also the the commentary on this verse of the twelfth-century Khwārazmian scholar Abu ʾl-Qāsim Maḥmūd ibn ʿUmar al-Zamakhsharī, known as Jār Allāh, verse in which he said that the beast will come forth from Ajyād without stating what or where this is; see Lane, 2005, p. xiii and n. 1. Cf. Abel, "Dābba," *EI*² II, 71a.

rod as well as the seal of Solomon *(khātam Sulaymān)*.[53]

The importance of the serpent-rod lies in its capacity to serve as an instrument for the performing of "magical" actions[54] which may be linked to the widespread association of snakes with magic.[55] In post-Qur'ānic histories of the Prophet Muḥammad, Mūsā's miracles play an important part.[56] According to al-Kisā'ī, the rod is said to come from Paradise and a long succession of pre-Islamic prophets had previously used it.[57] When discussing the contest between Mūsā and the Pharaoh's magicians, the same author states that the staff metamorphoses, as noted above, into "a writhing serpent the size of a camel."[58] According to al-Ṭabarī, an angel brought the rod.[59] Al-Tha'labī speaks of it as a miraculous rod which performed wonders such as providing water in a drought, producing milk, honey and fragrant odours, and becoming a fruit-bearing tree when placed by Mūsā in the ground. The *Qiṣaṣ al-anbiyā'* further list the following endowments: that a double dragon would appear on the two twigs, in other words, that the rod transforms itself into a double dragon, to combat enemies; that the rod was able to divide mountains and rocks and to lead its owner over rivers and seas; that it warns of danger and protects Mūsā and his herd from beasts of prey and assassins; finally that it was able to transport Mūsā at his will.[60]

In the eleventh-century magical treatise *Ghāyat al-ḥakīm* Abū Maslama Muḥammad al-Majrītī cites Plato's *Great Book of the Laws* as a source for the performance of the magical transformation of rods or ropes into serpents that can devour anyone who is thrown in front of them.[61] The magic power of Mūsā's serpent-rod was attributed primarily to the words inscribed upon it,[62] which consisted of names that were linked to the mystical divine name that was endowed with special power[63] and in Arabic magic literature is generally referred to as *ism Allāh al-a'ẓam* ("the greatest name of God").[64] The same rod was associated with the symbol of a circle considered to have the power to ward off evil.[65] In accordance with ancient Jewish and general Middle Eastern tradition, circles are a symbol of light and hence express the luminous character of the rod.[66] In his writings, which draw on pre-Islamic (comprising Hellenistic and Jewish) magical practices, the "master of the art of magic," Aḥmad ibn 'Alī al-Būnī enumerates the mystical names on Mūsā's rod with which "darkness disappeared" and "several strange things are accomplished."[67] Al-Tha'labī also records that the rod performed the miracle of shining in the darkness,[68] a feature generally considered characteristic of objects of revelation.[69]

---

53 Al-Tirmidhī, *Bāb al-Tafsīr* on *sūra* 27; *Musnad Aḥmad*, vol. 2, 295, as cited in Jeffery, "'Aṣā," *EI*² I, 680b.

54 Cf. Fodor, 1978, p. 2 and n. 6.

55 Wakeman, 1973, p. 77, n. 2.

56 See, for instance, the miracle recorded in al-Kisā'ī, *Qiṣaṣ al-anbiyā'*, tr. Thackston, 1978, p. 228. To a large extent these "miracles" are derived from rabbinic sources such as *Yalqūṭ Shim'onī*, *Midrash Wayyosha*, *Peṣiqta de-Rab Kahana*, and *Midrash Rabba*, as cited in Jeffery, "'Aṣā," *EI*² I, 680b.

57 Ādam, Hābil, Shīth, Idrīs, Nūḥ, Hūd, Ṣāliḥ, Ibrahīm, Ismā'īl, Isḥāq and Ya'qūb; *Qiṣaṣ al-anbiyā'*, tr. Thackston, 1978, p. 222.

58 *Qiṣaṣ al-anbiyā'*, tr. Thackston, 1978, p. 227.

59 Al-Ṭabarī, *Mukhtaṣar ta'rīkh al-rusul wa 'l-mulūk wa 'l-khulafā'*, vol. 1, 460–1, as cited in Heller, "Mūsā," *EI*² VII, 640a.

60 Al-Tha'labī, *'Arā'is al-majālis fī qiṣaṣ al-anbiyā'*, tr. and ed. Brinner, 2002, pp. 294–5. See also Heller, "Mūsā," *EI*² VII, 640a; Fodor, 1978, pp. 5–6.

61 "*Picatrix*," tr. and eds. Ritter and Plessner, 1962, p. 154.13–5.

62 Fodor, 1978, p. 9.

63 *Idem*, p. 10.

64 *Idem*, p. 11. According to legend, Solomon's ring was also inscribed with the divine names which gave it the miraculous power that Moses' rod had possessed; Salzberger, G., *Die Salomonsage in der semitischen Literatur* I, Diss., Berlin, 1907, pp. 117–9, as cited in Fodor, 1978, p. 13, n. 77. For an analysis of the Islamic divine names, see Anawati, 1967, pp. 7–58.

65 Canaan, 1937, p. 109; Fodor, 1978, pp. 13–5 and n. 87; Schimmel, 1994, p. 91. The association of the serpent and the circle is evidenced on an Aramaic magic bowl from the collection of V. Klagsbald, Jerusalem, which is decorated at the centre with a figure standing in a circle that is drawn around the feet. Two serpents flank the figure at either side while a serpent encircles the entire composition. Naveh and Shaked, 1985, repr. 1998, p. 198–214, drawing on p. 200, pls. 30, 31.

66 Fodor, 1978, p. 15 and n. 86.

67 *Manba' uṣūl al-ḥikma*, pp. 154–6, as cited in Fodor, 1978, p. 6.

68 Al-Tha'labī, *Qiṣaṣ al-anbiyā'*, Cairo, 1325, pp. 111–6, cited after Heller, "Mūsā," *EI*² VII, 640a. Cf. Fodor, 1978, p. 5.

69 *Idem*, 1978, p. 14 and n. 82.

PART FIVE

THE DRAGON AS MYSTICAL METAPHOR

CHAPTER THIRTEEN

THE DRAGON AND SOUND

In his biography of the Prophet Muḥammad, al-Ḥalabī describes how one day the serpent was on top of the wall of the Kaʿba when a large bird snatched it and cast it on the hill of al-Ḥajūn (where the cemetery of Mecca is located):

> [...] where it was swallowed by the earth. Some people say that this is the creature, which will speak to mankind on the day of Resurrection. It is also said that the monster will come forth from the ravine of the mountain Adjyād.[1]

He thus implicitly seems to associate the serpent with the Beast of the Earth *(al-dābbat al-arḍ)* mentioned in the Qurʾān (*sūra* 27, 82).[2] Here the serpent will raise its voice on the day of Resurrection.

Citing the seventh-century Jewish convert Kaʿb al-Aḥbār, the early medieval writer al-Kisāʾī describes the voice of the great serpent:

> When the serpent extols God, its exaltation overwhelms that of all the angels. When it opens its mouth, the heavens and the earth are lit by the lightning that flashes. Were not this serpent tempered by extolling God, it would strike down all created things with the might of its voice.[3]

In this tradition its voice is likened to the terrifying sound of thunder, thereby metaphorically associating the dragon with climatological phenomena.

The voice of a beneficial serpent saves the life of a mystic in a story recorded in Abū Ibrāhīm Mustamlī al-Bukhārī's (d. 434/1042–3) Persian commentary on the celebrated manual on Ṣūfism, *Taʿarruf li-madhhab ahl al-taṣawwuf*, by Abū Bakr al-Kalābādhī (d. 380/990):

> I heard Abu 'l-Ḥasan al-Fārsī saying: "I became so extremely thirsty in a desert that I could not move any more. I had heard that the eyes of thirsty people burst before they die. I was waiting for the bursting of my eyes when I suddenly heard a voice. I turned my face and saw a white serpent, as bright as pure silver, approaching me. I ran fearfully because fear had engendered power in me. Then due to weakness I walked slowly while the serpent was still after me. In this way I walked, till I reached water. The voice grew silent and I could not see the serpent.[4]

The powerful voice of the dragon is also referred to in an account of the dragon fight of Sām/Garshāsp, the legendary ruler of Sīstān and grandfather of the hero Rustam. When the dragon, who was fifty thousand cubits *(gaz)* in length, saw Sām, he jumped at him. Sām struck him with his mace so that the dragon fell to pieces and "uttered so fearful a cry that all of Sām's companions fell to the ground in terror."[5]

Al-Damīrī also reports that there is one species of serpent, found in abundance in the country of the Turks, whose hiss is deadly even at the distance of a bow-shot and yet another type of serpent, "the voice of which if a man hears, he dies."[6] On the other hand, he cites the interpretation of a dream according to which:

> He, who dreams as if a serpent has spoken to him, will obtain happiness.[7]

A speaking dragon appears in the epic *Shāhnāma*, during Rustam's third trial. This creature lives underground on the road to Māzandarān[8] and the hero inadvertently strays into its terrain. The dragon is endowed with the magical power of invisibility, and is portrayed as using his faculty

---

[1] *Al-Sīra al-Ḥalabiyya*, Cairo, 1292, vol. 1, p. 192, 2–4, cited after Wensinck, 1916, repr. 1978, p. 64.
[2] See also pp. 187–8.
[3] *Qiṣaṣ al-anbiyāʾ*, tr. Thackston, 1978, p. 7.
[4] *Sharḥ-i al-taʿarruf*, vol. 4, ed. Raushan, M., Tehran, 1366/1987, pp. 1792–93, as cited in Gohrab, 2000, p. 86.
[5] *Tārīkh-i Ṭabaristān*, compiled c. 613/1216 by Muḥammad ibn al-Ḥasan ibn Isfandiyār (tr. Browne, 1905, pp. 41–2).
[6] Tr. Jayakar, 1906, vol. 1, p. 633. Cf. Ruska, "Al-ḥaiya," *EI*[1].
[7] Tr. Jayakar, 1906, vol. 1, p. 656.
[8] For a discussion on the location of Māzandarān, see Monchi-Zadeh, 1975, pp. 48–79.

of thinking, expressing surprise that the hero dares to sleep in the face of the impending danger of his advance.[9] The mythical creature then approaches the sleeping hero, who is twice woken by his loyal steed Rakhsh, but the dragon vanishes. On the third approach it is unable to cloak itself and is seen by the hero. The exchange of words that ensues between the hero and the dragon serves to anthropomorphise the creature to some extent. Nevertheless, with the help of his horse, the hero manages to slay the dragon.

The speaking anthropomorphised serpent is also known in the most famous Arabian collection of fairy-tales and other stories of the *Alf layla wa-layla* in the *Journeys of Bulūqiyā*.[10] Mythical serpents endowed with the power of speech appear similarly in Indian lore, such as in the great collection of fables known as the *Panchatantra*.[11] Armenian popular tradition also preserves several tales that contain the motif of the speaking serpent such as the story of the Magic Ring.[12]

To this may be added the speaking serpents of antiquity in Ptolemy I's account of the Siwah expedition of Alexander the Great. Arrian (II.3.2) records the interesting story that Alexander was guided to and from the oracle by two giant dragons uttering speech. This aspect appears already in Hesiod's account of the hundred serpent heads that issue from the shoulders of the dragon Typhon which spoke in many voices *(phonai)*, at times those of different animals and, at times, sounds only the gods could understand (*Theogony* 825–52).

The belief in the serpent-dragon's receptivity to sounds that create a pattern such as tone, rhythm and melody, that is to say, sounds transformed into music, seems to have roots that lie in deep antiquity and which appear to have survived into the Islamic period.[13] According to a ninth-century Arabic text on the poisons of serpents, attributed to Hermes Trismegistos, music attracts mythological serpents such as the large serpent in the western sea, referred to earlier, with cervid-type dendritical antlers and a mane like the mane of a seahorse, which can be hunted with the help of music made with cymbals and shawms.[14] A comparable phenomenon is recorded by Ibn Waḥshiyya in his late ninth-century text on poisons in which he states that people from Kasadān invented a particular type of bell which brings out serpents and vipers from their holes when they hear the sound.[15] That the sound of music can lure serpents out of their caves is similarly reported by the late ninth-century author Abū Hilāl al-ʿAskarī.[16] The serpent as well as its larger relative the dragon may thus have been considered susceptible to the transformative influence of the medium of sound and music.[17]

This aspect of the dragon is given expression by its depiction on musical instruments, which appear in a number of early Ilkhanid paintings portraying a court scene with the enthroned ruler and his consort, housed in the Staatsbibliothek zu Berlin and in the Topkapı Sarayı Library, Istanbul.[18] The court ceremony shows the enthroned couple surrounded by princely relatives and courtiers, both male and female, accompanied by musicians playing a stringed instrument, which again resembles a harp, the arched string arm of which is fashioned in the form of a dragon's neck terminating in its projecting head (fig. 177). Like

[9] Cf. Omidsalar, 2001, pp. 259–93, esp. p. 269 and n. 14.

[10] Littmann, "Alf layla wa-layla," *EI*[2] I, 358b.

[11] Cf. Vogel, 1926, pp. 20–1, 28, 173–4.

[12] Hoogasian-Villa, 1966, pp. 193–7, for other tales with this motif, see pp. 224–9, 401 and 426–9.

[13] The Old Indic name *gandharva* represents a beneficent mythical being who is said to be surrounded by the heavenly waters, "which flow down at his look," and who is sometimes, mainly in later literature, portrayed as heavenly musician (Skjærvø, "Aždahā I," *EIr;* Panaino, "Gaṇdarəßa-," *EIr*). In the Rigveda these celestial beings are compared to the luminosity of the Sun and the stars of the Moon's orbit; Rigveda 8.1.2 (with the Sun), *Vājasaneyi-Saṃhitā* 9.7 (the stars of the Moon's orbit; cf. Oldenberg, 1894, repr. 1977, p. 245). Etymologically the name equals the sea monster Gandarəβa (Gandarw, Gandarb, spelled *gndlp*) which is defeated by the hero Kərəsāspa/Garshāsp. According to Prods Oktor Skjærvø, "it is through "Iranian polarisation" of the inherited Aryan mythological concepts [...] that *gandarəβa* has been turned into a sea monster" ("Aždahā I," *EIr*. Cf. Oldenberg, 1894, repr. 1977, pp. 245–50; Grassmann, 1873, repr. 1976, cols. 376–7). This associates it with the Manichean demoniacal beings called *mazans* which dwell in the ocean as sea dragons or dragon-like sea monsters. It is further notable that the *gandarəβa* survives in Sogdian as *γntrw* (Skjærvø, "Aždahā I," *EIr*).

[14] Ullmann, 1994, p. 28.81.

[15] Levey, 1966, p. 36.

[16] Ullmann, 1994, p. 100.81.

[17] See also the pact made with the tamed *nāgarāja* who lives to the northwest of Kapisa. As soon as some unfavourable weather phenomenon occurs, the sound of the *ghantā* (cymbal or drum) will remind the dragon of his pact with king Kanishka, whereupon he will cause the danger to subside. See p. 91.

[18] The dragon-headed string instrument is depicted on other fols. featuring an Ilkhanid court scene, one of which is also preserved in the Staatsbibliothek zu Berlin (*Dschingis Khan und seine Erben*, 2005, p. 258, cat. no. 286) and another in an album compiled in the late 1400s in Istanbul, Topkapı Sarayı Museum, Library, Ms. H. 2153, fol. 166a (the painting is attributed to the same period).

the overall pictorial scheme of the painting, the dragon head is rendered in an east Asian manner, the closed jaws characterised by fleshy folds on the bridge of the snout which is terminating in a prominent curl and with flowing mane and beard springing from the chin. It is interesting to consider the possibility of music as a civilising force which in turn would have had a subsuming and, hence, taming effect on the nature of the dragon, a change suggested by its appearance at the tip of a musical instrument.

The closest example to the Ilkhanid dragon harp can perhaps be found in seventh- or eighth-century Panjikent in Sogdiana. In spite of the tremendous chronological hiatus this may be of some relevance. Among the epic cycles portrayed on the Panjikent wall paintings there are at least two that depict original Sogdian legends.[19] One of these includes the well-known figure of a musician that serves as a caryatid supporting an arch. The tip of her large harp-like stringed instrument terminates in a dragon head with open mouth and elongated, curved upper proboscis-like snout whose head is turned towards the harpist (figs. 178a and b).

Another indirect association of the dragon with music is shown on one of the earliest wall paintings at Panjikent, which has been dated to the late fifth century, on the eastern wall of the northern chapel of Temple II. Here the dragon serves as zoomorphic throne for a goddess identified as deity of the river Zerafshan[20] to whose right is a rectangular musical instrument with attached bells. The affiliation of the goddess with the instrument has led Martha Carter to point out an analogy with the ancient Hindu Saraswatī (who is also known in Buddhism), goddess of music and learning, who is also a river goddess.[21]

Vestiges pertaining to elements of both the musical and the aquatic qualities of the dragon can still be found in the more recent history of Central Asia. They recur in the songs of Kazakh shamans who also use a stringed musical instrument *(kobyz)* of which they say:

> I took in my hands a *kobyz* made of a pine-tree
> And wind like a water serpent.[22]

---

[19] Marshak, 2002, p. 145. For a drawing of the entire mural, see Belenitskii and Marshak, 1981, p. 24, fig. 3.

[20] Belenitskii and Marshak, 1971, pp. 42–5, and *eidem*, 1981, p. 70; Azarpay, 1981, p. 140 and n. 61.

[21] Carter, 1992, p. 75. Revealed wisdom, which in Brahmanism is personified in Vāch, the female Logos, and later appears as Saraswatī/Prajñā, is essentially an aquatic element and had extensive influence on the formation of the character of the *nāgas*. This association explains why the *nāgas* are said to exhibit great musical skill and possess magic musical instruments (as well as excel in other arts). Cf. Bosch, 1960, pp. 137, 174–5. See also the connection of tritons (serpent-legged mermen associated with Tritōn, the son of Poseidon) with music as visualised in Gandhāran art, for instance in a schist frieze from Andan Dheri near Chakdara with tritons playing musical instruments. Chakdara, Dir Museum, inv. no. 505 (AND 533); *Gandhara*, 2009, cat. no. 75.

[22] Basilov, 1991, p. 278.

CHAPTER FOURTEEN

THE DRAGON AS SYMBOL OF TRANSFORMATION

The dragon can be said to symbolise the liminal or transitional phase in rites of passage. As such it evokes a dual response, perceived both as beneficent and an object of fear. This results also in its twin functions as deliverer and destroyer, roles that link it to the elemental cycle of birth and death. Interestingly, the Targum Onkelos, an Aramaic translation of the Pentateuch, renders the west Semitic root *nḥš* ("serpent") as Aramaic *ḥiwyaʾ* ("serpent") whose Arabic cognate is *ḥayya* ("serpent").[1] There may be, moreover, an etymological association of *nḥš* and the Akkadian *nêsu (naāšu)* meaning "to live, to stay alive, to recover." The temptation to see this cognate as an indication of a semantic relation between the terms "serpent" and "life" has repeatedly been succumbed to.[2] The hypothesis appears to be substantiated by the fact that the root *ḥyw* apparent in the word *ḥay[w]āt*, as described by Ibn Manẓūr (d. 711/1312) in his *Lisān al-ʿArab* (completed in 689/1290), entails the concept of life as opposed to death.[3] He further states that "the plural of all that is alive is *ḥay[w]āt* ("life") ... and that *ḥayawān* ("the animal kingdom") implies a notion of life *(ḥayāt)*."[4] The word *ḥay[w]āt* is once mentioned in the Qurʾān (*sūra* 29, 64) where it means "the true life" and is used of the afterlife. Ibn Manẓūr adds that "...the derivation of *ḥayya* ("serpent") from *ḥayāt* is well-known..."[5] The same author more clearly specifies that "...when the life of a man or a woman is prolonged, he or she is called *ḥayya*; this is due to the long life of the *ḥayya* and that is why the man or the woman is described as *ḥayya* for his or her prolonged life..."[6]

That childbirth was associated with the dragon in its beneficent aspect seems to have been a view widely held in antiquity.[7] Remnants of such notions seem perhaps to resonate in texts such as the *Kitāb Tadbīr al-ḥabālā wa ʾl-aṭfāl* ("Book of Children and Pregnant Women"), written by Aḥmad ibn Muḥammad al-Baladī (d. *c.* 380/990) who served as physician to the Egyptian vizier Abu ʾl-Faraj Yaʿqūb ibn Yūsuf ibn Killīs in the tenth century. There he gives the following instruction to ease birth:

> ...a snake skin wound around the hip of a woman accelerates birth.[8]

According to another tradition, a snake's scale placed on a pregnant woman, presumably when she is in labour, will ensure an easy delivery.[9] In the epic romance *Wīs u Rāmīn* these notions are reflected in Fakhr al-Dīn Gurgānī's allegorical imagery:

> ...the sun is delivered from the dragon.[10]

Serpents or dragons also play a symbolic role in the miraculous birth and apotheosis of numer-

---

[1] Wilson, 2001, p. 97.

[2] *Idem*, p. 50. See also Astour, 1965, p. 194.

[3] Beirut, n.d., vol. 14, p. 211. I am grateful to Layla al-Musāwī for elucidating this point.

[4] *Idem*, p. 214.

[5] *Idem*, p. 240.

[6] *Idem*, p. 221. Cf. Wallace, 1985, pp. 143–72, esp. pp. 144, 148, 151 and 160; also p. 108. For further etymological associations, see Lecerf, "Ḥayy," *EI*² III, 330a.

[7] In ancient Greece women would go to the sanctuary of Asklepios where a serpent would appear in their dreams and they would then get pregnant (Plutarch, *Life of Alexander* 2.2–3.4). Cf. Ferwerda, 1973, p. 107. Plutarch reports that:

> ... women ... were addicted to Orphic rites and the orgies of Dionysus from very ancient times being called Klodones and Mimallones, and imitated in many ways the practices of the Edonian women and the Thracian women about Mount Haemus, from whom, it would seem, the word *thrêskeuein* came to be applied to the celebration of extravagant and superstitious ceremonies.

Cited after Asirvatham, 2001, pp. 96–7.

[8] Ullmann, 1978, p. 109. The notion that if attached to the loins of a woman in childbirth the sloughed off skin of a snake facilitates delivery is also recorded by Pliny (*Naturalis Historia* XXX 44) who adds that care must be taken to remove it immediately after the birth.

[9] Donaldson, 1938, repr. New York, 1973, p. 169.

[10] Tr. cited after Daneshvari, 1993, p. 21. The parable of a dragon helping a doe deliver its young is recorded in a Talmudic passage of the *Bava Batra* ("The Last Gate"):

ous heroes and kings of antiquity.[11] Many traditions name them among the ancestors of heroes and as mythical ancestors of tribal confederacies and kingly dynasties.[12] The classical author Herodotus reports that the ancient Scythians who lived north of the Black Sea regarded themselves as descendants of the greatest of the Greek heroes, Herakles/Hercules, and a woman with a serpent's lower body (*Histories* IV 8–9).[13] With this anguipede woman he engenders three sons, the youngest of whom, named Scythes ("the Scythian"), was the worthiest and became the first king of the Scythians.[14] The story of the miraculous birth of the superhuman hero who issues from the encounter of a princess with a serpent appears also in one of the oldest recorded epic tales *(bylina)* compiled in the eighteenth century in west Siberia.[15] Among the tribal confederacies, dynasties and heroes claiming their descent from Dahāk, the hominoid serpent of the ancient Iranian epic past are, as mentioned earlier, the Kushāṇas of the Yuezhi confederacy, the Armenians living in the region near Lake Sevan, the Islamic Sām dynasty of Ghūr as well as the hero Rustam and his descendants. These claims are surpassed in the Turkish epic *Ṣaltūq-nāma* ("Book of Ṣaltuq"), in which the first ruler of the world, Eslem, son of Adam, becomes the father of Ẓaḥḥāk the Turk, ancestor of all Turkish sovereigns.[16]

The association of serpents with birth symbolism occurs also, albeit in a different manner, in the story of Prince Sayf al-Mulūk in the *Alf layla wa-layla*. The tale recounts how an aged childless ruler is advised by Solomon the Wise that, in order to bring about the birth of a prince, he must cook the flesh of two serpents that appear by a certain tree at noon and serve the dish to his wife.[17]

More often though, the dragon is known in its other function as the awful dragon of death. On the way to his execution the mystic and theologian Manṣūr ibn Ḥusayn al-Ḥallāj ("the wool-carder," 244/857–309/922) from Ṭūr in Fars, is said to have faced his impeding martyrdom by reciting the following verses:

> My friend doth unrelated stand to aught of ruth or clemency:
> From His own cup He bade me sup, for such is hospitality!
> But when the Wine had circled round, for sword and [executioner's] carpet called He
> Who with the Dragon drinketh Wine in [the heat of] Summer, such his fate shall be.[18]

The use of the dragon as metaphor for the inevitable fate of death occurs in a passage of the

> The doe has too narrow a womb [to permit it to give birth; therefore] when it crouches to give birth, I prepare for her a dragon that bites her belly so it grows slack and she gives birth.

Bava Batra 16b, cited after Morgenstern and Linsider, 2006, p. 85. Cf. Ginzberg, 1909–38, repr. 1946 and 1955, vol. 2, p. 168.

[11] Scipio Africanus (Livy IIVI 19.7), Alexander the Great (Plutarch, *Life of Alexander* II 4), the Messian hero Aristomenes (Pausanias, *Graeciae Descriptio* IV 14.7–8) and the future emperor Augustus after his adoption by Julius Caesar (Suetonius, *Augustus* 94.4), are said to have been born from the union of their mothers with a giant serpent or dragon. Cf. Ferwerda, 1973, p. 107; also Küster, 1913, p. 112.

[12] The Greek god Zagreus was born of the union of Persephone and Zeus who had taken the form of a dragon (Nonnos, *Dionysiaca* V 562.564; VI 155–7). Pentheus, king of Thebes, was the son of Echion, "the serpent-man" (the name Echion being the male form of Echidna, the serpent-monster; Euripides, *Bacchae* 537–44). The Greek hero Kadmos kills the *drakōn* that barred the way to the site of the future city and then sowed its teeth in the earth, hence giving rise to the *Spartoi* ("sown men") who became the first Thebans. It is moreover interesting to note that towards the end of his life both Kadmos and his wife Harmonia were changed into serpents and lived among Encheleians (Ovid, *Metamorphoses* IV 576–600). On the Kadmos myth, see Fontenrose, 1959, repr. 1980, pp. 306–20; Astour, 1965, pp. 156–61. Similarly, the Indian kings of Chhota Nāgpur claim origin from a *nāga* called Puṇḍarīka. Vogel, 1929, p. 35.

[13] Cf. P'yankov, 2006, pp. 505–11, esp. pp. 506–7.

[14] This myth was modified by Valerius Flaccus to the extent that the Scythians were said to be descendants of Colaxes (the youngest son of Targitaos who reigned in Scythia was named Colaxais; Herodotus, *Histories* IV 5) and the anguipede earth-born maiden, and in the account of Diodorus Siculus (II 43) according to which the same woman was impregnated by Zeus.

[15] Jakobson and Szeftel, 1949, pp. 13–87, esp. 21, 64; Schirmunski, 1961, pp. 58–9. It is interesting that comparable notions occur in early Christian gnostic writings, such as a text entitled *Baruch* written by the second-century Christian gnostic Justin, which survives in summarised form in the early third-century antiheretical work, *Refutatio omnium haeresium* ("Refutation of All the Sects") of Hippolytus of Rome. According to his recapitulation of the text, in the beginning creation results of the marriage of a male divine principle, Elohim, the God of creation and Lord of heaven, and a female principle, named Eden or Israel, the mother earth, who is described as looking like a woman as far as the groin and a serpent below (*Refutatio omnium haeresium* 5.24.2-3). Williams, 1996, pp. 18–9, 37–9.

[16] Mélikoff, 1960, vol. 1, p. 43 and n. 1; Dedes, 1996, p. 29, n. 80. For further examples in South Slavic epics, see Schirmunski, 1961, pp. 28–30.

[17] Marzolph and van Leeuwen, 2004, pp. 362–3. The story goes back to the age-old belief that pregnancy could be caused by ingesting magic food. See Astour, 1965, pp. 171–2.

[18] Browne, 1920, vol. 1, p. 435; see also p. 363.

Mathnawī, in which the mystic poet Jalāl al-Dīn Rūmī (604/1207–672/1273) allegorically states:

> When Destiny comes, the wide spaces are narrowed. A hundred ways and asylums may lie to left and right; yet they are all barred by Destiny, the invincible dragon.[19]

A related conceptualisation of the "invincible dragon" appears not only in Arabic and Iranian literature, but in a saying of the military commander ʿAbd Allāh ibn ʿAmr ibn al-ʿĀṣ, a contemporary of the Prophet Muḥammad, in which he likens himself to the "inexorable serpent":

> When others looked askance, I blinked not;
> Then I partially closed my eyes, but not in winking [at the sight of danger].
> You saw me return [to the charge] and continue to dash forward.
> I support [equally well] good and evil, and am inexorable,
> Like the serpent at the foot of the trees.[20]

Although the Qurʾān makes no allusion to Hell being populated by huge serpents, such a belief is preserved in later traditions. It is attested in a *ḥadīth* by the tenth-century Ḥanafī jurist Abu ʾl-Qāsim Isḥāq al-Samarqandī (d. 342/953–4), also known as al-Ḥakīm ("the Wise One"), according to which:

> ... the Prophet, blessings and peace be upon him, said that in Hell are snakes each as large as a camel and the pain of their bite will last for forty years.[21]

In his grave a sinner may be tortured by a serpent of fire which bites him until the day of judgement.[22] Another *ḥadīth* records a more explicit saying of the Prophet on the torments in Hell inflicted by dragons:

> Concerning the chastisement of the truth-concealer in his grave: ninety-nine *tinnīns* will be given mastery over him. Do you know what a *tinnīn* is? It is a serpent. There will be ninety-nine serpents, each of which has nine heads: They will gnaw at him, eat at him and blow into his body until the day he is raised up.[23]

Yet another tradition speaks of the punishment for insolence against God:

> ...as a black snake [that] winds itself around the impudent man's neck and kills him after forty days.[24]

This belief in the dragon as "inexorable death" is still echoed in the popular culture of Iran, according to which there is a serpent in every grave that will torment the dead in proportion to the number of sins committed in life.[25] Similarly, in popular belief in present-day Afghanistan it is said that following burial the mythical angel ʿIzrāʾīl/ʿAzrāʾīl, who has authority and power over death, appears and grips the tongue of the deceased for questioning.[26] This idea may reflect the Qurʾānic tradition according to which the angel of death ʿIzrāʾīl creeps into the dying man's throat to draw out his spirit (*sūra* 79).[27] In the same way, the fourteenth-century encyclopedian al-Damīrī relates the interpretation of a dream according to which:

> He who dreams of a serpent coming out of his mouth while he is ill, will die, for that indicates his life which will have come out of his mouth.[28]

The early fourteenth-century Syrian traditionist Ibn Kathīr (d. 774/1373) reports a *ḥadīth* on

---

[19] Tr. and ed. Arberry, 1961, p. 271.

[20] Cited after al-Damīrī, *Ḥayāt al-ḥayawān al-kubrā*, tr. Jayakar, 1906, vol. 1, p. 634.

[21] Tr. into Pers., ed. Ḥabībī, A., Tehran, 1969, p. 83, cited after Daneshvari, 1993, p. 18.

[22] Wensinck and Tritton, "ʿAdhāb al-ḳabr," *EI*² I, 168b.

[23] Chittick, 1992, p. 90, 9–15.

[24] Al-Qalyūbī, Aḥmad ibn Salāma, *Nawādir*, no. 29, as cited in Ritter, 2003, p. 183.

[25] Bess Donaldson (1938, repr. 1973, p. 168) remarks that this belief is mainly current "among the uneducated women."

[26] Private communication. A tradition connecting the serpent with the moment of the death of a human being was also well-known in antiquity. When a serpent passed through a hole in a wall, the ancients would say that the soul was definitely separated from the body and had started its descent into the underworld. Cf. Porphyrios, *Vita Plotini* (II, 27). According to Pliny (*Naturalis Historia* XVI 85.234), a *draco* lived in a cave near the grave of Scipio Africanus the Elder to watch over his soul. On the role of serpents as guardians of graves, see also Küster, 1913, pp. 67–71. In the *Testament of Abraham* (recension A ch. XVII) which is generally considered to be a Jewish work, datable to the first century AD (cf. Delcor, 1973, pp. 63–5, 72, 76–8), when death comes to fetch Abraham's soul, he shows him seven flaming *drakōn* heads as well as the faces of various poisonous serpents. In ch. XIX, death explains the function of the faces as the different manners of death, while the seven *drakōn* heads stand for death raging seven aeons long. Similar associations of the Greek words *drakōn* and *ophis* with death and the underworld appear in the Greek *Apocalypse of Baruch*. See Schlüter, 1982, pp. 46–8. For traditions in which Rahav and Leviathan are identified with the angel of death, see Ginzberg, 1909–38, repr. 1946 and 1955, vol. 1, p. 40 and n. 187.

[27] Cf. Wensinck, "ʿIzrāʾīl," *EI*² IV, 216b.

[28] Tr. Jayakar, 1906, vol. 1, p. 655. See also the troublesome dream of Kanaʿān ibn Kūsh, the father of Namrūd (the Nimrod of the Bible), in which his son is born and a snake enters his nose, an ominous sign which is interpreted to mean that his son will kill him. Heller, "Namrūd, also Namrūdh, Nīmrūd," *EI*² VII, 952b.

authority of Abū Hurayrah according to which the Prophet Muḥammad said:

> Anyone who does not remit the obligatory alms of the wealth which God has bestowed upon him, his wealth will appear to him on the Day of Resurrection as an ancient male serpent, bald from age and the accumulation of poison in its head, and with two projections dangling from its forehead. It shall coil itself around his neck and, grabbing him on both sides of the face, shall cry out, 'I am your wealth, I am your treasure!'[29]

In the Jewish tradition it is also the serpent that has power over life and death.[30] In the Talmudic tractate *Bava Batra* a serpent is said to be the keeper of a miraculous stone that has power of life or death.[31] In the same text the angel of death himself is called Leviathan.[32] In ancient Near Eastern[33] and Greek[34] lore the serpent is in the possession of a plant which can restore life.

The Armenian commentary on the book of Genesis, attributed to the Syriac writer Ephrem, gives further insight into contemporary Christian understanding of the relation of the serpent with death:

> ... Indeed, why did Justice, which interrogated Adam and Eve, not interrogate the serpent? And if the nature [of the serpent] was bound, why was it also condemned with those [Adam and Eve] who had free will? And if it had free will, why did [Justice] not interrogate it? [Justice] did not interrogate [the serpent] for the reason that It knew who It was with whom It was speaking. And that one who hears knows what he hears. And that the serpent was the first to receive punishment was so that [Adam and Eve] might repent, show compunction and make supplication to [God]. But when they were unwilling to turn [to Him] in contrition, [God] set upon them the decree of death, and they became dust, fodder for the serpent. '*From dust you are*,' [God] said, '*and to dust you shall return*.'[35] And to [the serpent He said, '*Dust shall become your food*.'[36,37]

The close association of the mythical creature with the departure from life is underlined by its representation in the thirteenth-century barrel-vaulted funerary chapel of Surb Grigor. Part of the monastic complex of Noravankʿ in Vayots Dzor in southern Armenia, it was added in 1275 by prince Tarsayich Ōrbēlian, governor of Siunikʿ province, at the north side of the church of Surb Karapet as mausoleum of the Ōrbēlian princes. The point of juncture of the wall arch and vaulted ceiling, above the semi-circular altar, is entirely horizontally circumscribed by two pairs of confronted dragons in low relief and highlighted with white and red pigment. The elongated serpentine bodies, which are enlivened with a spotted pattern, are arranged in evenly spaced loops (fig. 179).

In Iranian poetry death is sometimes metaphorically likened to the maleficent influence of the dragon, alluding to the belief that the moon, in eclipse, is swallowed by the eclipse dragon *(al-jawzahar)*. In Niẓāmī's *Haft Paykar* the officer who brings the false report of the execution of the "bright-faced" luminous harp girl Fitnah to king Bahrām tells him that he has "given the Moon to the Dragon," that is to say, eclipsed her life.[38]

The extent of the geographical and chronological dissemination of the dragon's allegorical role in death is attested by the life stages of a parable called the "Man in the Well" in which it figures prominently. It is of great interest since the parable's sequence of transmission can be documented. It was translated into Middle Persian (Pahlawī) from an early Sanskrit text, perhaps from the eleventh book of the great Indian epic *Mahābhārata* (chapters 5–6),[39] together with other texts from the *Mahābhārata* and the *Panchatantra*, by Burzōe of Nīshāpūr, the personal

[29] *Tafsīr al-Qurʾān al-ʿAẓīm*, vol. II, pp. 165–7, cited after Ayoub, 1992, p. 390.

[30] Cf. Epstein, 1997, p. 74.

[31] Babylonian Talmud, *Bava Batra* 74b, as cited in *idem*, p. 74.

[32] *Idem*.

[33] The serpent appears as giver of life and possessor of the magic herb of life in Babylonian literature. Searching for the secret of immortality Gilgamesh succeeds in harvesting the magic plant from the bottom of the sea (*Epic of Gilgamesh* XI 287–9), only to have it stolen from him by the serpent.

[34] For the story of Glaucos, a son of king Minos of Crete, who was restored to life by a herb placed by a serpent onto a dead serpent which thereupon was brought back to life, see Ovid, *Fasti*, VI. 749–54, and Apollodorus, *Bibliotheca* III. 3.1–4. A similar story of a young dragon being raised from the dead through the agency of a plant and the same plant being used to resurrect the Lydian hero Tylon, who had been killed by a dragon, is recorded by Pliny (*Naturalis Historia* XXV 5).

[35] Genesis 3,19.

[36] Genesis 3,14.

[37] Tr. and comm., Mathews, 1998, pp. 34–5.

[38] Tr. Meisami, 1995, 25:71. Cf. *eadem*, 1987, p. 218.

[39] De Blois (1990, pp. 34–5) shows that since the parable was recorded in several Indian texts, if it was not taken from the *Mahābhārata*, it would have come from another contemporary Indian source available to Burzōe.

physician of the sixth-century Sasanian king Khusraw I (Khusraw Anūshirwān, r. 531–579). About two centuries later Burzōe's Pahlawī version[40] of the Indo-Iranian political fable was translated into Arabic prose by ʿAbd Allāh ibn al-Muqaffaʿ (*c.* 102/720 – executed *c.* 139/756–7) as the celebrated *Kalīla wa Dimna*. In the tenth century the fables were translated into Persian under the Samanid Naṣr ibn Aḥmad (302/914–331/943), but only sections of Rūdakī's version survive in quotations.[41] The text thus evolved to include stories that originated from different cultures. Less than two centuries later they were again translated into a Persian text (which survived) by Abu 'l-Maʿālī Naṣr Allāh ibn Muḥammad for his patron, the Ghaznawid Bahrām Shāh (r. *c.* 511/1117–552/ 1157), attesting to their continued popularity.[42] A chapter in the *Kalīla wa Dimna*, entitled "The Perils of Life," relates the following story (fig. 180):

> A man fled from an enraged camel and out of necessity suspended himself in a well; his hands fell on two branches which were growing above the well and his feet obtained a foothold. Soon he could see better that his two feet were on the heads of two snakes who had emerged from their holes. His glance fell to the bottom where he saw a terrible dragon with its mouth open in expectation. At the top of the well he noticed a white and a black rat incessantly gnawing away at the roots of the branches. Meanwhile he considered how to find a way out of his misfortune. In front of him was a beehive where he found a little honey and tasted some. He became preoccupied with its sweetness, neglecting his (proper) work so that he did not think of his feet resting on the heads of the four snakes which might withdraw at any moment, or of the rats furiously nibbling the branches with no sign of slackening, until the branches broke and he fell into the maw of the dragon.[43]

Naṣr Allāh Munshī offers his own interpretation of the parable which confirms the continuous contextual and conceptual validity of the dragon's maw as metaphor for "inexorable death" in twelfth-century Central Asia:

> Thus I have compared the world to that well full of misfortune and dread, and the incessantly gnawing white and black rats to night and day whose succession works to curtail the living. The four snakes are the humours that are the basis of man's nature which when disturbed become deadly poison. The tasting of the honey and its sweetness corresponds to the pleasures of this world whose worth is little and brings grief and toil; the dragon is our inexorable death.[44]

Closely related to the ancient Indian parable of the "Man in the Well,"[45] this story was also included in the famous legend of *Bilawhar wa Būdhāsaf*,[46] the Near Eastern version of the Buddhist *Jātaka* stories of Gautama Buddha.[47] The

---

[40] Burzōe's Pahlawī translation is lost but survives in a Syriac version of about 570 by the Periodeut Būd. The transmission of the *Kalīla wa Dimna* from India is also described in the *Shāh-nāma* (tr. and ed. Mohl, 1838–1878, vol. 6, pp. 445–57); cf. Brockelmann, "Kalila wa-Dīmna," *EI*² IV, 503a.

[41] Cf. Brockelmann, "Kalila wa-Dīmna," *EI*² IV, 503a.

[42] *Idem.*

[43] Mīnuvī's 1343/1964 compilation of Naṣr Allāh's Persian version of the Kalīla wa Dimna, p. 56 l. 17 to 57 l. 13, as cited in O'Kane, 2003.

[44] *Idem.* The description of the greedy jaws of Hell occurs in Mazdaist religious texts, such as the *Ardā Wīrāz-nāmag* ("Book of Ardā Wīrāz") (see Klíma, 1968, p. 37); monstrous wide-open jaws representing death and the netherworld appear in several passages of the Old Testament (Isaiah 5.14; Proverbs 1.12).

[45] Cf. de Blois, 1990, pp. 34–5; Ch'en, 1968, pp. 220–1. There are only minor discrepancies in the Indian version according to which:

> ...a man out hunting was pursued by a unicorn and in trying to flee, fell into a well. As he was falling, he stretched out his arm and caught hold of a small tree growing on the side of the well. He thought that he was now safe, but upon closer scrutiny, he found that two mice, one white and one black, were gnawing at the roots of the slender tree to which he was clinging. He now looked down into the well and what did he see but a monstrous dragon with mouth open waiting for him to fall. He then examined the place where his feet were resting, and saw four serpents surrounding him. Now he looked up at the tree he was holding, and saw some honey dripping down from one of the branches. Immediately, the unicorn, mice, dragon, and serpents were forgotten, and his mind became intent only on securing the honey.

The Indian interpretation of this parable is closely related:

> ...the unicorn is death, the deep well is the world, the small tree is man's life, gnawed at its roots by day and night (the white and black mice), the dragon is the jaws of hell, the four serpents are the four great elements that compose the body. Surrounded by all these horrors and dangers, man forgets all and thinks only of the pleasures of life.

Cited after Ch'en, 1968, p. 221.

[46] The versions of the parable in the *Kalīla wa Dimna* and the book of *Bilawhar wa Būdhāsaf* are closely comparable; de Blois, 1990, p. 35. The name Būdhāsaf is a corruption of the Sanskrit Bodhisattva, a title acquired by meritorious beings who aspire for Enlightenment *(bodhi)*.

[47] Cf. Lang, "Bilawhar wa Būdhāsaf," *EI*² I, 1215b. The Indian transmission has been complemented with folkloristic parallels and put into an Indogermanic context by Vasil'kov, 1995.

latter provided the prototype for the popular Christian tale of *Barlaam and Joasaph,* recorded by the Georgian monk Euthymius (955–1028).[48] The parable with the dragon imagery, the snakes in the story most likely being a reflection of the likeness of the great dragon, thus proved to be meaningful in the long term both within and far beyond the Western Asian world. This is further attested by yet another version of the parable recorded by the court poet Manuel Philes (*c.* 1275–*c.* 1345) of the Byzantine emperor Andronikos II, in which however the well was represented as a tree while the dragon's role at the bottom remained a constant:

> On a picture of Life which represents a tree, in which is a man gaping upwards and quaffing honey from above, while below, the roots [of the tree] are being devoured by mice: On seeing this symbol of the shadow of [earthly] things, bear in mind, O man, the end that is hidden from you. Standing upright, you are enjoying the honey of pleasure, while a dragon with gaping mouth awaits your fall to destroy you.[49]

The parable of the "Man in the Well" thus exemplifies the potency of the visual allegory in which the dragon's maw stands for death, imagery that transcended geographic, cultural and religious boundaries and was long shared not only by the peoples of the medieval Western Asian environment but also by those of adjacent cultures.[50]

The dragon is hence credited with the possession of great transformative powers. The ability to metamorphose, to transcend a situation and respond to changing circumstances, were exactly the qualities associated with the mystic. A metaphor of change and transformation on the mystic path, the great mythical beast thus functions as an allegory of his guardianship of heavenly treasure and hidden mysteries, a hermeneutic tool[51] of particular significance for the mystic. Its affiliation with the notion of the ultimate transformative power of death converts it in the eyes of the mystic into "the dragon of freedom and detachment."[52]

This is exemplified by the story of the Iranian mystic Abū Ḥamza al-Khurāsānī told by the mystic al-Hujwīrī (d. 469/1076) in his *Kashf al-Maḥjūb*, a treatise on Ṣūfism, which again uses the well (or pit) symbolism:

> It is well-known that one day he fell into a pit. After three days had passed a party of travellers approached. Abū Ḥamza said to himself: "I will call out to them." Then he said: "No; it is not good that I seek aid from anyone except God, and I shall be complaining of God if I tell them that my God has cast me into a pit and implore them to rescue me." When they came up and saw an open pit in the middle of the road, they said: "For the sake of obtaining divine recompense *(thawāb)* we must cover this pit lest anyone should fall into it." Abū Ḥamza said: "I became deeply agitated and abandoned hope of life. After they blocked the mouth of the pit and departed, I prayed to God and resigned myself to die, and hoped no more of mankind. When night fell I heard a movement at the top of the pit. I looked attentively. The mouth of the pit was open, and I saw a huge animal like a dragon, which let down its tail. I knew that God had sent it and that I should be saved this way. I took hold of its tail and it dragged me out. A heavenly voice cried to me, 'this is an excellent escape of thine O Abū Ḥamza! We have saved thee from death by means of death.'[53]

The pit is a metaphor for life and the dragon a means of achieving liberation from it.[54]

Hagiographical literature also yields examples of saints receiving help from serpent *jinn*s as is illustrated by the story of shaykh Muḥammad al-Udfūwī who once performed the pilgrimage to Mecca with a group of *ṣūfī*s who had no provisions:

> ...so the shaykh held out a bowl and took up a collection from among them saying, "whoever has something and hopes for a divine reward in recompense should put it in this bowl." A large snake suddenly came forward with a dirham in its mouth and dropped it into the bowl saying, 'We are *jinn* who have come to make the pilgrimage with you this year.'[55]

In the mystical tradition the entire spectrum of the dragon's multivalent forces is called into play. In the hagiography of the great Khurasani mystic

---

[48] De Blois, 1990, p. 34. Cf. Der Nersessian, 1937, pp. 63–5; Ch'en, 1968, pp. 219–21.

[49] Cod. Escur., Poem no. 248. Cf. Mango, 1972, p. 247.

[50] Cf. Janda, 2010, ch. *Die Parabel vom Mann im Brunnen*, pp. 174–81.

[51] Cf. Taylor, 1999, p. 139.

[52] The phrase is borrowed from Daneshvari, 1993, p. 22.

[53] Tr. and ed. Nicholson, 1976, p. 96.

[54] Daneshvari, 1993, p. 23.

[55] Ibn al-Zāyyat, *Kitāb al-Kawākib al-Zayyāra*, pp. 157–8; also Ibn ʿUthmān, *Murshid al-zuwwār*, pp. 271–2; al-Sakhāwī, *Tuḥfat al-aḥbāb*, pp. 276–7; and Ibn al-Nāsikh, *Miṣbāḥ al-dayājī*, fols. 33v-34v; cited after Taylor, 1999, p. 156.

Abū Saʿīd ibn Abi ʾl-Khayr Mayhanī (357/967–440/1049),[56] entitled *Asrār al-tawḥīd* (compiled around 575/1180),[57] the shaykh is said to have kept company with dragons during his retreats. One day he asked one of his particularly unruly disciples to perform his ablutions at a stream and his prayers on a rock, and then wait for a "friend" of his who had been with him for seven years, and in whose companionship he had found much comfort and relaxation, to convey him his greetings:

> Then suddenly there was a dreadful clap and the mountain quaked. [The disciple] looked and saw an awful black dragon, the largest he had ever seen: its body filled the whole space between two mountains. At the sight of it his spirit fled; he was unable to move and fell senseless to the earth. The dragon advanced towards the rock, on which it laid its head reverently. After a little while the dervish recovered himself somewhat, and observing that the dragon had come to a halt and was motionless, he said, though in his terror he scarcely knew what he said, "The Shaykh greets thee." The dragon with many signs of reverence began to rub its face in the dust, whilst tears rolled from its eyes. This, and the fact that it attempted nothing against him, persuaded the dervish that he had been sent to meet the dragon; he therefore delivered the Shaykh's message, which it received with great humility, rubbing its face in the dust and weeping so much that the rock where its head lay became wet. Having heard all it went away.[58]

The same work contains a collection of sayings attributed to Abū Saʿīd ibn Abi ʾl-Khayr, in which there is a passage stating that the celebrated Islamic mystic Abū Yazīd (Bāyazīd) al-Biṣṭāmī (d. 261/874 or 264/877–8) is said to have mounted a lion brandishing a venomous serpent as a whip.[59] A depiction of the angel Abi ʾl-Ḥanaf as crowned rider on a lion holding a second crown in his right hand and an upright dragon staff in his left hand is found in a mid- to late thirteenth-century Anatolian manuscript, known as *Daqāʾiq al-Ḥaqāʾiq*, although the paintings may be of a later date (fig. 181).[60] Marianne Barrucand identifies the horned dragon with open mouth and once looped body as a sceptre.[61] In the sixth volume of the *Mathnawī*, Jalāl al-Dīn Rūmī describes the eleventh-century mystic Abu ʾl-Ḥasan ʿAlī ibn Aḥmad Kharraqānī (d. 425/1033) in the same manner, portraying him as "the model of a saint who has perfectly mastered his base soul and is therefore master over the lower animals in the world, who are bound to serve him just as his *nafs* has learned to serve him."[62] The depiction of the mystic riding a dangerous animal such as a lion or a dragon thus symbolises his

[56] For a monograph on the mystic, see Meier, 1976.

[57] Barthold, 1958, p. 311; Ritter, "Abū Saʿīd Faḍl Allāh b. Abī ʾl-Khair," *EI*² I, p. 145b.

[58] Nicholson, 1967, pp. 70–1. Cf. Gohrab, 2000, p. 85.

[59] Muḥammad ibn al-Munawwar ibn Abī Saʿīd, *Asrār al-Tawḥīd fī Maqāmāt al-Shaykh Abī Saʿīd*, Tehran 1313, repr. 1366–7, tr. O'Kane, J., *The Secrets of God's Mystical Oneness*, New York, 1992; Gohrab, 2000, pp. 85–6.

[60] Rogers, "Saldjūḳids," *EI*² VIII, 936a. See also Süslü, 1984, p. 173, and pl. LXXX, fig. 8. A related depiction in a late fourteenth-century Persian drawing, probably from Shiraz, Muẓaffarid period, shows a man riding a lioness with a snake around his waist, another in his left hand and holding on to a further snake wound around the lioness's neck. Preserved in Istanbul, Topkapı Sarayı Museum, Library, Album H. 2152, fol. 2r; Raby, 1981, p. 160 and fig. 479, where a relationship between this drawing and the motif of the snake-wielding demon Tarish (Grube and Johns, 2005, p. 216, fig. 70.8) is suggested. The miracle of the snake-wielding and lion-riding mystic appears also in the cult of the *siddhas* (mythical originators of a popular religio-magical movement popular among the Hindus in northern India in the eleventh and twelfth centuries), as recorded in the legends of the 84 *siddhas* of the Hindu Buddhist tradition. In one of the legends Guru Ḍombipa, a king who was forced to abdicate because he chose a low-caste woman as his consort in Tantric exercises, retires to the wilderness. After twelve years of practice the king in union with his consort emerges on a young pregnant tigress, holding a poisonous snake as a whip. Grünwedel, 1916, pp. 137–228, esp. p. 148; and *Buddha's Lions*, tr. Robinson, 1979, p. 35. The motif of the dragon-rider appears on Artuqid coins (for instance, on the obverse of a copper coin of 585/1189 struck by ʿImād al-Dīn Abū Bakr ibn Qara Arslan (581/1185–600/1203–4) of Khartpert, see Spengler and Sayles, 1992, p. 61; *What the Coins Tell Us*, 2009, p. 101) and on the above-discussed Samanid-period bowl (fig. 55). In the *Shāh-nāma* the hero Rustam is also describes as riding on a dragon (see p. 112). This may be compared to king Ṭahmūrath using Iblīs as mount; see p. 134, n. 12.

[61] Barrucand, 1990–1, p. 141.

[62] *Mathnawī* VI 2120–1, as cited in Schimmel, 1980, repr. 1993, p. 313. The motif is also used on talismans as exemplified by the representation of a woman clad in red knee-length pantaloons riding a lion and holding a serpent in the left hand, a seal of the planet Mars, illustrated in the *Dahīra al-iskandarīya*, 24a, -3 to 24a, -3; cf. Ruska, 1926, pp. 98–9, with the title, *Ṣanʿat al-haraz al-ṭilasmiyya al-nāfiʿa min al-amrāḍ al-ʿasīrat al-bur*ʾ, as cited in Ullmann, 1972, p. 419 and n. 4. It is noteworthy that this imagery was known in the Jewish tradition; the Talmud mentions that king Nebuchadnezzar rode a lion and held in his hands, as a bridle, a serpent (*Sabbath* 150a). The same animals, the very deadliest creatures, lions and poisonous serpents, are mentioned in biblical references, for instance "Thou shalt tread upon the lion and adder [a venomous snake]; the young lion and the dragon shalt thou trample under feet" (Psalm 91, 13), symbolising Christ's triumph over evil. Van Henten (1995, repr. 1998, p. 266) interprets this combination of the dragon and the lion as a result of Iranian influence. It may, therefore, not be irrelevant to note that in Zoroastrianism, both lion and serpent figure prominently in Pahlawī literature as creatures of Ahriman, the first as main representative of the "wolf species," the second most deadly of the *khrafstras*

subjugation of his somatic self and mastery over his *nafs*.

Following ancient popular beliefs the *nafs* ("soul" or "self") mentioned in the Qurʾān is said to take the form of a beast, often symbolised as a snake.[63] It has to be tamed to eventually overcome the stages of *nafs lawwāma* ("blaming soul"; *sūra* 75, 2) and *nafs ammāra* ("commanding soul"; *sūra* 12, 53) which correspond essentially to man's conscience,[64] to reach the state of *nafs muṭmaʾinna* ("the soul at peace"; *sūra* 89, 27).[65] In Islamic mysticism this serpent can be turned into a "useful rod" just as Mūsā's rod turned "on God's command" into a serpent.[66] The goal of disciplining the *nafs* is to train it in such a way that all negative activities associated with it become extinct;[67] this may be compared with the manner in which a good snake-charmer who receives a snake, to use a metaphor coined by al-Ghazālī, "distinguishes between the antidote and the poison, and extracts the antidote while destroying the poison."[68] This path is ultimately experienced by the mystic as being drawn upwards, as *fanāʾ* ("passing away," "effacement") in God.

The mystical path of self-recognition *(gnosis)*, in other words, the return of the self to the Self, is described by al-Biṣṭāmī by means of the analogy of the sloughing of the outward skin of the serpent.[69] By virtue of this unsheathing, the serpent gains new skin and thereby new life which is likened to the mystic's final shedding of his "I" in *fanāʾ*. Hence in the same manner as the serpent sloughs its old skin and appears newly robed, the mystic annihilates his *nafs* (lower soul) and lives eternally by undergoing a metamorphosis.[70]

A similar sentiment is expressed in a couplet of the poet Muḥammad Shīrīn Maghribī born about 750/1350 near Iṣfahān in Central Iran:

> Unless you slay the serpent of existence, you cannot find the way to the treasure;
> Because your existence is a snake upon His treasure.[71]

In his prose writings *Maqālāt*, Shams-i Tabrīzī, the spiritual master of Jalāl al-Dīn Rūmī, illustrates the breadth of the polyvalence of the dragon in the form of a two-headed serpent that has a head at either end:

> The world is a treasure and the world is a serpent. Some people play with the serpent and some with the treasure. He who plays with the serpent, must bare his heart to its bite. It bites with its tail and it bites with its head. When it bites with its tail, you will not awake, and then it starts to bite with its head. People who have turned their back on the serpent, and have not become proud of its precious stone, *mār muhra*, and its love, *mihr*, have taken elderly reason as their guide – because reason regards the glance of the serpent as an emerald. As the dragon-like serpent noticed that elderly reason conducted the leadership of the caravan, it became dejected, despised, and discouraged. In that ocean (of the world) the serpent

(noxious creatures) that infest the earth. Zaehner, 1955, repr. 1972, p. ix, and *idem*, 1961, pp. 129–30. Moreover, among the *Ahl-i Ḥaqq* ("People of the Truth"), a secret sect prevalent mainly in western Iran and parts of northeastern Iraq, both the lion and the dragon guard the first and fifth heavens through which the soul has to pass in order to reach the heaven above. *Idem*, 1961, p. 130.

[63] Cf. *Dīwān* 458/4856, as cited by Schimmel, 1980, repr. 1993, p. 112.

[64] *Eadem*, p. 270.

[65] The association of the human soul's concupiscent parts (following Plato's division into rational, irascible and concupiscent souls which correspond with the Qurʾānic souls) with the serpent is a common topos in medieval Islamic literature. Cf. Calverley and Netton, "Nafs," *EI*² VII, 880a.

[66] Schimmel (1975, p. 113) adds that "more frequent, however, is the idea that the power of the spiritual master can blind the snake; according to folk belief, the snake is blinded by the sight of the emerald (the connection of the pir's spiritual power with the green colour of the emerald is significant). Thus, his influence renders the *nafs*-snake harmless."

[67] The twelfth-century mystic ʿAmmār al-Bidlīsī (d. between 590 and 604/1194 and 1207) analyses the greater *jihād* declaring that man's lower soul *(nafs)* is the greatest enemy to be fought (*Bahjat al-ṭāʾifa*, tr. and ed. Badeen, 1999, p. 110. Cf. Hillenbrand, C., 1997, p. 161). This is related to the saying of the Prophet: "We are returning from the lesser *jihād* to the greater *jihād*" (see *Bahjat al-ṭāʾifa*, tr. and ed. Badeen, 1999, p. 110, n. 118; also Ibn ʿArabī, *al-Durra al-Fakhira, al-Rūḥ al-Quds fī Muḥāsabat al-Nafs*, tr. and ed. Austin, 1971, p. 53).

[68] Al-Ghazālī has employed this imagery when expressing his social concern about the vulnerability of the general Muslim public when reading the works of philosophers; *al-Munqid min al-ḍalāl* ("Deliverance from Error"), tr. Montgomery Watt, 1953, p. 44. The ongoing relevance in our time of the idea of an internal battle to synthesise these forces, emblematised in the figure of the dragon, is reflected in the autobiographical records of the twentieth-century shaykh Aḥmad al-ʿAlawī. He reports that in his youth he charmed a serpent for his spiritual teacher, the shaykh Sidi Muḥammad al-Būzīdī, whereupon the shaykh made him realise that his own soul was far more venomous and more difficult to subdue (Lings, 1961, p. 52). In the face of worldly temptations presented by the *nafs* "the ego is weak and pliant, but when challenged with the truth of its relativity it resists with tenacity and cunning" (Ibn ʿArabī, *al-Durra al-Fakhira, al-Rūḥ al-Quds fī Muḥāsabat al-Nafs*, tr. and ed. Austin, 1971, p. 53, n. 2).

[69] Rahman, "Abū Yazīd al-Biṣṭāmī," *EI*² I, 162a.

[70] Gohrab, 2000, p. 86.

[71] Nurbakhsh, J., *Sūfī Symbolism*, vol. 4, Tehran, 1369/1990, p. 140; the couplet belongs to *ghazal* no. 186. 1. 14, in Lewisohn, L., ed., *A Critical Edition of the Divan of Muhammad Shirin Maghribi*, Tehran and London, 1993. Cited after Gohrab, 2000, p. 89.

> was like the crocodile forming a bridge under the feet of reason. Its poison turned into sugar, its thorn into a rose. It was a highway robber, but it grew to be a guide. It was a cause of fear, but it grew to be the cause of security.[72]

As mentioned earlier, it is frequently a serpent that has the power to confer supernatural knowledge of the *manṭiq al-ṭair*, the language of birds, upon a human being. The mystics see this as the language of the soul, an interpretation of the Qur'ānic verse (*sūra* 27, 16–9) which mentions that Sulaymān understood the speech of the birds, so becoming, in mystical terms "the shaykh who converses in the secret language of the soul with his disciples."[73]

The medieval Jewish philosopher Yehuda HaLevi of Toledo (*c.* 1080–1140) explains in the *Kuzari* (4, 25; with reference to the anonymous *Sefer Yezirah* ("Book of Creation," 4, 2) that while the dragon *(tᵉli)* also has an astrological/astronomical significance; it serves above all as an allegory for veiled metaphysical aspects of the universe and hidden mysteries which cannot be grasped:

> The *Teli* in the world is like a king in his province, the heart in the soul is like a king at war. *Teli* is the name of the *juzhar* [*jawzahr*]; by this word one understands the world of the intellect because through the *juzhar* one denotes hidden things which are not comprehended by the senses.[74]

The dragon thus serves as mystical vehicle and symbol in the path to spirituality, mystical revelation and finally an enlightened state of being.[75] In consequence, the dragon that was seen to guard a worldly treasure can readily be transformed by the mystic into the dragon that guards divine and heavenly treasures.[76]

An interesting literary allegory attesting to the validity of this notion over a long period of time is found in the so-called *Hymn of the Pearl*,[77] composed before the end of the Parthian-Arsacid period in 224 AD[78] in or not far from Edessa (now known as Urfa).[79] The hymn, which recounts the story of the quest for a unique pearl guarded by a dragon, might reveal further aspects of the treasure-guarding dragon which are still relevant conceptualisations in Central Asia and the Near East in early medieval times. The protagonist, who identifies himself as the son of the "King of Kings, the great king of the East," recounts how he was sent as a young prince by his parents from their Eastern kingdom to Egypt (representing here the dark demonised world),[80] to recover a precious pearl that lay on the sea bed, encircled by a giant hissing dragon.[81] The latter appears here as ruler of the sea and guardian of a treasure. In spite of the prince's efforts to disguise himself from the Egyptians lest they recognise him as a stranger and arouse the dragon against him, he is recognised in Egypt, savours the food and falls asleep in the "dragon's inn." Only when he receives a letter from his parents, which flies to him in the form of an eagle, is he reminded of his mission. He instantly puts the dragon to sleep by a charm, snatches the pearl and makes a triumphant return to the kingdom in the east. There he dons the glittering royal robe he used to wear as a child and, like a mirror, it permits him to recognise his royal self and be reunited with it.[82] The pearl in the *Hymn of the Pearl* can be seen as a symbol of the soul itself. The story thus presents in allegorical form the Gnostic doctrine of the soul's heavenly origin and salvation through *gnosis*.[83] The prince is represented not only in the traditional guise of a hero on a quest, but also as a seeker on a spiritual journey.[84] The metaphorical use of the pearl as "soul, spiritual power, substance" is attested in the Iranian tradition.[85] The dragon that guards this soul-pearl has to be

[72] *Maqālāt-i Shams-i Tabrīzī*, ed. Muwaḥḥid, M.A., Tehran, 1369/1990, p. 313, as cited in *idem*, pp. 86–7.

[73] Schimmel, 1987, p. 89.

[74] Tr. Touati, 2006, p. 179.

[75] Cf. Daneshvari, 1993, p. 24.

[76] *Idem*, p. 23.

[77] The *Hymn of the Pearl* exists in two versions, Syriac and Greek, each represented by a single manuscript dating from the tenth and eleventh century respectively. Adam, 1959, pp. 1–28, 84–9. Cf. Parpola, 2001, p. 182. Although it appears in one of the apocryphal writings of the *Acts of Thomas the Apostle* (chs. 108–13), it has a non- and pre-Christian character. Adam, 1959, p. 61.

[78] It probably stems from a heroic cycle from Parthian Iranian culture (247 BC–224 AD) since the kingdom of the Great King is identified as Parthia in verse 40; *idem*, 1959, p. 58.

[79] Cf. Reitzenstein, 1916, pp. 44–5 and n. 2 (on p. 44); Adam, 1959, p. 75; Drijvers, 1991, pp. 380–4; Russell, 2004, pp. 1261–81; Mastrocinque, 2005, pp. 12–4 and n. 41.

[80] Adam, 1959, pp. 56–7 and n. 54; Colpe, 1983, p. 840.

[81] Cf. Russell, 2004, p. 1278.

[82] Adam, 1959, pp. 66–7. Cf. references in early Greek and Indo-Iranian literature to a colourful robe which is often likened to the sky; Janda, 2010, p. 83 and n. 126.

[83] Cf. Parpola, 2001, p. 181.

[84] Russell, 2004, p. 1284.

[85] Reitzenstein, 1916, p. 46 and n. 1; Widengren, 1960, p. 27. Colpe, 1983, p. 840.

charmed before gnosis can be attained. The importance of the *Hymn of the Pearl* in the Iranian sphere is, moreover, documented by the fact that it is later appropriated by the Manichaeans.[86] As Simo Parpola demonstrates, the story has no apparent Greek, Christian or Jewish parallels, but it is closely paralleled by several Mesopotamian myths that were popular in the Neo-Assyrian, Neo-Babylonian and Persian periods.[87]

It is interesting to consider the Parthian allegorical epic in the light of the mystical traditions of the medieval Islamic period. Analogous ideas are expressed in Niẓāmī's *Haft Paykar* in which the motif of the treasure-guarding dragon plays an important part in the biographical journey of the fifth-century Sasanian ruler Bahrām Gūr (the sobriquet Gūr, or onager (a wild ass) referring to his prowess at hunting; 420–438) from birth to death.[88] The pattern of Bahrām's life likewise recalls that of a mythic hero who must pass successive tests to prove his worth. In the first of four linked exploits an onager *(gūr)* of extraordinary beauty, described as a spiritual form *(paykar-i rūḥānī)*, leads the prince to the mouth of a remote cave before which lies a terrible dragon that guards a treasure.[89] The dragon, which has devoured the onager's foal, is slain by the mighty hunter and its belly slit open, whereupon the foal emerges unharmed and leads Bahrām to the discovery of the treasure, a necessary step on his path to kingship.[90] The story thus follows the convention of the heroic epic in which a quest must be undertaken to recover a stolen treasure from a dragon. The first and last episodes repeat the same motif, the undertaking of the spiritual quest that anticipates Bahrām's fourth trial, the final hunt, which represents the end of his symbolic journey. Again he is guided by an onager to a remote cave in which lies a deep water-filled chasm, into which the king plunges on horseback, "consigning the kingly treasure to the cave." He vanishes to become one with the "Companion of the Cave" *(yār-i ghār)*, an allusion to the historical journey of the Prophet Muḥammad from Mecca to Medina during which he found refuge in a cave with the first caliph, Abū Bakr, thus completing the cycle.[91] The king so transcends the material limits of life on earth, and the treasure is transformed into ultimate spiritual perfection.[92]

The mystical poet and thinker Farīd al-Dīn ʿAṭṭār (*c.* 537/1142–3–617/1220), who was born in Nīshāpūr, also alludes to the dragon's implicit association with spirituality:

> You are a treasure of spirituality and where your treasure is, there is the dragon.[93]

The dragon is thus experienced as a stage or threshold which functions not as an end but as a healing, transforming way station not only for a more harmonious inner and social life but also as a symbol that could lead to a distinct and higher vision of the absolutely transcendent Divine. In a passage of the *Mathnawī*, Jalāl al-Dīn Rūmī similarly describes the dragon as guarding the treasure, the hidden essence:

> Wherever men put a big lock, that is a sign that there is to be found something precious and valuable. So you see the greater the veil the better the element. Just as a snake is over the treasure, so do you not regard our ugliness, but regard the precious things of the treasure.[94]

This "hidden treasure" guarded by the dragon is the heart of man, the centre of his spiritual physiognomy.[95] The pivotal role accorded to the dragon in the journey of transformation is allegorically expressed by the poet and mystic Mawlānā Nūr al-Dīn ʿAbd al-Raḥmān Jāmī (817/1414–898/1492), born in Khardjird near Herat, in his *dīwān*:

> The teeth of the key [which open the treasure chest]
> Are the teeth of the dragon.[96]

---

[86] Russell, 2004, pp. 1261, 1264 and n. 8. For parallels in Mandean literature, see *idem*, p. 1296 and n. 51.
[87] Parpola, 2001, pp. 181–93.
[88] Meisami, 1987, pp. 211–3, and *eadem*, 1993, p. 155.
[89] *Eadem*, 1993, p. 160.
[90] Cf. Krotkoff, 1984, p. 102, n. 33.
[91] Cf. *idem*, pp. 113–4, ns. 21, 33; Meisami, 1987, p. 223, and *eadem*, 1993, p. 163 and n. 5.
[92] *Haft Paykar*, tr. *eadem*, 1995, p. 259, ch. 52, l. 27. "The traveller learns from the Guide ... what the structure of the cosmic crypt is and what dangers he must face if he undertakes the journey through and beyond it. Then he accepts the challenge and makes the sojourn through the cosmic mountains and valleys until he finally comes out of the world of formal manifestation and meets at the end with death, which symbolizes birth into a new spiritual life and also conveys the irreversibility of the process of spiritual realisation. He who has left the cosmos does not become imprisoned in it again." Nasr, 1964b, p. 44.
[93] *Dīwān*, ed. Nafīsī, S., Tehran, 1960, p. 23, cited after Daneshvari, 1993, pp. 23–4.
[94] Tr. and ed. Arberry, 1947, repr. 2004, p. 241.
[95] Cf., for instance, Farīd al-Dīn ʿAṭṭār's account of the soul's journey during its mystical meditation in a period of retreat expounded in his *Muṣībat-nāma* ("Book of Affliction"); see the exposition given in Corbin, 1993, pp. 287–8.
[96] Ed. Rāzī, H., Tehran, 1957, p. 24, as cited in Daneshvari, 1993, p. 19.

CONCLUDING REMARKS

The immense cultural significance of the serpent-dragon is best demonstrated by the fact that its iconography was known and exploited throughout Western Asia in the medieval period. Moreover, it was not restricted to just one religious creed. Jews, Christians, Moslems, Buddhists, Hindus and others were equally ready to employ its likeness in textual and visual sources while contributing, each in their own way, to the broad repository of dragon and serpent iconography.

A wide semantic range of serpent-dragon iconography and iconology evolved during its immemorial history in Western Asia. Textual and visual sources reflect the quintessential ambiguity of such imagery. Animated by the endless interplay of dichotomous forces the creature revealed itself as deliverer or destroyer, regenerator or annihilator, protector or adversary. The dragon thus served to embody the eternal opposition of two distinct forces, one seeking to preserve life, the other to destroy it, a polarity giving rise to a kaleidoscopic diversity of function and symbolism.

The serpent-dragon accrued a range of negative aspects following changes brought about by the rise of Zoroastrian cosmological dualism. A more robust symbolism was needed and the inherently powerful and combative serpent-dragon aptly came to represent the Zoroastrian evil spirit who declares to God: "I shall destroy you and your creatures forever and ever. And I shall persuade all your creatures to hate you and to love me."[1] In its new guise the dragon thus assumed the mantle of eschatological opponent, the evil principle who would be destroyed, following a millennium of conflict, in a final battle that would usher in a new age and a new creation.

Serpents and dragons thus came to be classed as noxious beings *(khrafstras)*, creatures of the "hostile spirit" Ahriman and as such evil and deserving of death. In spite of this the Greek writer Philo of Byblos (*c.* 64–141) records a saying of the magus Zoroaster/Zarathushtra according to which the serpent is not only immortal but "the director of everything beautiful ... the best of the good, the wisest of the wise ... the father of order and justice, self-taught ... and perfect and wise ..."[2] The link between these statements and historical Iranian Zoroastrianism seems tenuous. Nevertheless, as well as reflecting the Hellenistic reception of Zoroastrian ideas they may suggest that the Iranian definition of the serpent-dragon as unequivocally maleficent was perhaps not always as cut and dried as appears from surviving scriptures.[3]

The serpent-dragon's association with the mysteries of birth and death is echoed in Philo's monograph *Ethothion* (now lost but preserved in excerpts by Eusebius) in which he claims that "it is immortal and ... dissolves into itself ...; for this sort of animal does not die an ordinary death unless it is violently struck."[4] The serpent is known to be the animal most filled with the breath of life (*pneuma*).[5] Its connection with life is further suggested by the possible association of various terms for "serpent" with those of "life," traceable especially in Aramaic and Arabic. The case for tracing such serpent names (*ḥiwyaʾ* and *ḥayya* respectively) back to the root *ḥyw*, apparent in the word *ḥay[w]āt* ("life"),[6] as described by Ibn Manẓūr in the *Lisān al-ʿArab*,[7] was explored above in chapter 14. Such an etymology would elucidate the drag-

---

[1] Boyce, 1984, p. 46. This may be compared with the antagonism between Jahweh and the serpent in the Genesis narrative (2–4); see the interpretation by Rhodokanakis with addendum by Ehrenzweig, 1921, pp. 76–83.

[2] Philo of Byblos' *The Phoenician History* (as quoted by Eusebius, *Praeparatio Evangelica* 1.10.52), tr. and ed. Attridge and Oden, 1981, p. 67. Cf. *eidem*, p. 95, n. 161 for reference on Zoroaster in this text.

[3] This supposition is further corroborated by the ongoing Zoroastrian practice of ophiomancy which is in striking contradiction to the classification of serpents as *khrafstras*. See p. 58, n. 96, p. 61, n. 125 and p. 136, n. 42.

[4] Philo of Byblos' *The Phoenician History* (as quoted by Eusebius, *Praeparatio Evangelica* 1.10.48), tr. and ed. Attridge and Oden, 1981, p. 65.

[5] *Idem*, p. 63.

[6] See Wilson, 2001, pp. 50, 97, 214, 221, 240. Also Astour, 1965, p. 194; Wallace, 1985, pp. 143–72, esp. pp. 144, 148, 151 and 160; also p. 108.

[7] Beirut, n.d., vol. 14, p. 211.

on's affinity with symbols of fertility and fecundity in the vegetal world, which often spring from its mouth (hence are associated with his breath, saliva and tongue), as well as, by extension, its guardianship of treasures hidden in the earth and the sources of nature's abundance.

At the same time the serpent-dragon is known as the awful dragon of death. In medieval writings reference to its gaping mouth (as well as its breath or saliva) frequently alludes metaphorically to impending calamity. It manifests particular power in times of great danger, whether natural phenomena such as storm, flood or drought, or aspects of the heavens such as an eclipse, which may usher in calamity or disease. The dragon's association with the heavens was further underlined through its identification with astronomical and astrological manifestations.

Its manifestly dual nature confers on the serpent-dragon an intermediate status. The world-encircling *ouroboros* marks the boundary between the ordered world and the chaos around it and thereby appears itself as exponent of liminality situated upon the ambiguous dividing line between the divine and the demonic. Thus intrinsically linked with the idea of the threshold, dragon imagery appears around entrances and portals of secular and religious architectural monuments, where it serves as liminal marker and apotropaic device in the role of a guardian imbued with prophylactic and talismanic power, warding off the dangers inherent in such places.

It has also been shown that a visual hybridisation resulted from a conflation of the dragon with other animals, mythical creatures or vegetation. This fusion draws two juxtaposed principles together into a unified being, so creating a duality which simultaneously contrasts and fuses two opposites. These composites reflect an amalgamation not only of external, that is physical, but also of internal, that is innate, characteristics. This hybridisation finds an interesting parallel in the motif of the human face, animal head, vegetal ornament or benedictory inscription flanked by two dragon heads. The visual pairing of the monstrous heads is an example of the conceptual doubling aspect of representations so prominent throughout the medieval period, a device intended to reinforce and augment the visual impact and potency of the symbol. This symbolism of gaping dragons' jaws flanking a central motif, which also entails an astrological aspect, similarly affords a glimpse into the process of conflating two principles. This arresting visual trope serves as a shorthand, alluding to the act whereby the dragon has issued or will devour the central element. The processes of issuing and devouring are thereby intrinsically linked. In both the dragon nature is merged with that of the central motif. The outcome of this synthesis is probably to be seen as empowering. The imagery of the dragon heads flanking a central motif thus may be presumed to represent a beneficial iconography, serving as powerful apotropaic device.

The association of the serpent with healing powers and in turn with magic is well-known as evidenced, for example, in the classical and Punic world by its symbolic relationship with Asklepios or in the magical abilities of Thrita and Thraētaona, the earliest healers of Iranian mythology, whose invention of an antidote for snake poison is paralleled by their heroic dragon-fighting feats. The same symbolism could be associated with Moses raising the bronze serpent in the wilderness to heal the victims of a plague of serpents. Mounted on a pole, the serpent serves as antidote to death. This homeopathic principle was a frequently employed tool, also serving Iskandar according to al-Masʿūdī, when marine dragons obstructed the building of the city of Alexandria. The principle of *similia similibus curantur* involving the dragon is complemented by that of transforming alchemy. In the symbolism of medieval Islamic alchemy paired interlaced dragons illustrate the fundamental polarity on which the cosmic rhythm is based, the *solve et coagula* of the alchemical process. The dragon here serves to embody the circular nature of the alchemical process and the agency of transformation that both devours and restores. On yet another level Abū Maslama Muḥammad al-Majrīṭī represents this in his treatise *Ghāyat al-ḥakīm* as the opposing principles of positive and negative bodily temperaments which are associated with the two celestial nodes (knots), the head and the tail of the "hidden essence."

The dragon can also be said to function as a representative of the unknown, often conceived of as hostile and threatening. Resistant to rationalising and civilising influences, it came to represent wicked foreign tyrants, a paramount example being the hominoid dragon Ẓaḥḥāk of Iranian mythology who was turned into a historicised political entity, presumably blending spheres of history and mythology.

Yet the frequent use of the dragon simile in panegyrics addressed to heroes and rulers reflects at the same time both the numinous fear and the reverential awe that the creature evoked. The potency of the dragon, emblematised on paraphernalia of heroism and rulership such as banners or articles of personal adornment, relies on the same combination of fear and awe, while drawing particularly on the implicit semantics of the dragon iconography as protective and beneficial.

The significance accorded to the dragon figure is underscored by the fact that, as repeatedly noted above, it was singled out as monstrous paradigmatic adversary. This fundamental juxtaposition between victor and vanquished dragon adversary may in large part result from the influence of Iranian dualist notions on the religions of the Near East. In many ways the treatment of the great opponent also reveals a polemical trend. The Hebrew Bible represented pagan kings such as Nebuchadnezzar (Jeremiah 51.34) with the likeness of the *tannin*,[8] while in Christian imagery the dragon assumed an overall meaning as symbol and instrument of a diabolical force[9] as visually attested, for instance, in the eleventh- or early twelfth-century Byzantine encyclopaedia of the Metaphrastian Menologion volumes, featuring "revenge miniatures" employed for purposes of politico-religious propaganda. Dragon imagery thus became a significant tool in the ongoing polemic against earlier cults. Nonetheless, as has been shown, numerous examples of such imagery survived the repressions and official mutations of ancient beliefs. These survivals testify to the strength of a complex immemorially ancient heritage of traditions, rituals, beliefs and legends that circulated in the medieval Western Asian world and beyond. They illuminate the deep-rooted potency as well as fluidity and eminent adaptability of the dragon iconography, which lent itself to constant renewal and to the revival of ancient associations. More than this, the survival of this imagery also reflects popular belief in contrast to official religious and political ideology, revealing fundamental differences between two mentalities, sensibilities and needs. On the one hand there is the ruling religious and political elite, claiming the triumph of good over evil and imposing an ideology which dictates clearly delineated boundaries. On the other there is the traditional culture of popular folkloric belief shared by the general populace. Faced with the terrifying ambiguity of the dragon nature, natural prudence suggests that pacification is the wisest course. Ancient thought-patterns, equivocal, artful and at times even magical, offer the possibility of rendering the dragon inoffensive and possibly even releasing its beneficial aspect.

The enemy symbolised by a dragon is presented as formidable but generally vanquished. Yet the nature of the eminent monster is such that it can only be subdued by a warrior, frequently represented as horseman, endowed with supernatural powers and by miraculous means. This imagery was used in Sasanian political propaganda at the investiture relief of Ardashīr I (r. 224–241) at Naqsh-i Rustam and likewise employed and adapted in Jewish, Christian or Islamic contexts.

Often however the fight with the dragon was not a duel to the death, as frequently shown particularly in political or eschatological contexts, but a taming of the creature. The intent was to neutralise and contain the terrifying and equivocal forces inherent in the dragon rather than to annihilate them.

At this juncture it is important to emphasise that the intrinsic as well as extrinsic ambiguity of the serpent-dragon also entails an element of transcendence, necessarily so since the creature's mystery can only be explained as flowing from the juxtaposition of two or more levels of reality. In essence, then, it defies understanding. The cosmic aspect of the dragon, which sometimes surfaces, involves also a sacred dimension; it is interesting to note that the Latin term *sacer* means both sacred and wretched or cursed. Its inherent duality makes of the dragon image an embodiment of change and transformation, and consequently at times a cipher of upheaval.

Such associations extend the dragon's semantic territory as agent of fertility and fecundity into the realm of spiritual fertilisation. Often however the great beast serves as metaphor for spiritual realities whose meanings are obscured or veiled. Another aspect of the hero's combat with the dragon can thence be observed in the transforma-

[8] See the discussion of the serpent as a symbol of Israel's political neighbours and enemies (this probably being closely related to the fact that for instance in Canaan the serpent was worshipped) in the exegesis of the Old Testament in Martinek, 1996, pp. 53–5; also 61–2.

[9] In the apocrypha of the New Testament this is particularly evident with regard to the demonisation of female sexuality, cf. *eadem*, pp. 122–34. See also the representations of prostrate female figures as the demonised enemy who is vanquished by the victorious horseman on Jewish or Christian magical "amulets" that circulated in the Byzantine world, discussed on p. 104.

tion of the mythical warrior into a new kind of spiritual warrior *(fātā)*. The combat which takes place on an external mythical ground – symbolised by the fight with the dragon – could on another level be considered a personal spiritual struggle *(jihād)* against one's lower self, a process which was deemed to be more meritorious than physical struggle.[10] The Bāb al-Ṭilasm dragon relief in Baghdad was built under the supervision of the ʿAbbasid caliph al-Nāṣir li-Dīn Allāh who distinguished himself by trying to develop the organisation of the classical Islamic *futuwwa* brotherhoods (which were closely associated with and gradually assimilated *ṣūfi* traditions)[11] and who was dedicated to becoming a "caliph of unity."[12] The representations of the ruler between two dragons, as emblematised in the Bāb al-Ṭilasm relief, show him taming the awesome forces of the dragons. The resonance and complexity of the imagery offered al-Nāṣir the possibility of enhancing his reputation on multiple levels. The caliph acquired by association the mythical power, strength and authority of the dragons he had subdued. At the same time, the scene suggested a spiritual interpretation: portrayed as *fātā* the caliph's harnessing of the dragons' might can be seen to stand as a symbol of his personal spiritual *jihād*. The Bāb al-Ṭilasm relief thus exemplifies the way in which the users of such imagery were able to draw on many potential levels of meaning, evoking complex and subtle ideas and responses.

Finally, it is important to recall the significance accorded to the great serpent in the legendary Islamicised prophetic tales, based on the authority of learned men from the early years of Islam but recorded only from the eleventh century onwards. Related by the *quṣṣāṣ al-ʿāmm* ("narrators for the common folk") who enjoyed great success with popular audiences, the tales reveal the extraordinary aura that surrounded the fabulous beast. Not only was the great serpent said to encircle the divine Canopy, but it was singled out to:

> ...greet [the] Prophet Muḥammad on the night of his ascent into heaven and give him glad tidings concerning himself and the community.[13]

Even if the present study necessarily represents no more than a brief episode in the immemorial history of "one of the most complex symbolisms of the history of cultures,"[14] it is hoped that some of the deep layers of the dragon iconography, hinted at in narratives such as this, have been uncovered in these pages. The investigation of a wide variety of visual and textual dragon references across different cultural, confessional, geographical and chronological spheres may also illuminate and reflect the way in which medieval man perceived himself, in his interaction with such a potent and enigmatic symbol.

---

[10] Cf. Hillenbrand, C., 1997, p. 97.

[11] For an analysis of the caliph's close relation with his Minister of Religious Affairs, the mystic Shihāb al-Dīn ʿUmar al-Suhrawardī (539/1145–632/1234), see ul-Huda, 2003, pp. 13–40. His influential position allowed the *ṣūfi* shaykh to create the conditions necessary for both supporting the caliphate through Islamic mysticism *(taṣawwuf)* in conjunction with the *futuwwa* and thereby to endorse Islamic mystics by means of the caliphate.

[12] *Idem*, p. 35.

[13] Al-Kisāʾī (citing the authority of Kaʿb al-Aḥbār) in *Qiṣaṣ al-anbiyāʾ*, tr. Thackston, 1978, p. 7.

[14] Le Goff, 1980, p. 162.

EPILOGUE

a. *East-west exchange and the metamorphosis of dragon imagery*

The first part of the Epilogue explores the dragon imagery as potent symbol of cross-cultural connection and artistic exchange during the Mongol era in general and the Ilkhanid period in particular. In the Mongol visual arts, including coinage, sculptural and architectural elements, as well as in manuscript illustrations, the dragon appears in different stylistic guises as elements of Chinese and Western Asian derivation combine, testifying to the meeting and merging of cultural elements from east and west and providing evidence of early acculturation in the development of an Ilkhanid idiom. The breadth of the emerging dragon iconography is illustrated in the text and illustrations of Ilkhanid manuscripts.

More than any other creature, the dragon is identified with China,[1] also known as the land of Chīn (al-Sīn in the Arabised form), Khitay or Cathay.[2] One consequence of the Mongol invasions and subsequent Mongol hegemony was a westward movement of the arts that led to the introduction of stylistic aspects of East Asian (mostly Chinese and Chinese-inspired Mongol) derivation,[3] which include the motif of the dragon. Surviving portable and monumental art from the Ilkhanid realm, in particular the tile decoration of the royal residence at Takht-i Sulaimān and the grand illustrated copy of the most important single historical source for the Mongol empire, Rashīd al-Dīn Ṭabīb's *Jāmiʿ al-tawārīkh* ("Compendium of Chronicles") produced in 714/1314–5, bear eloquent witness to this phenomenon.

Temüjin, the leader of a small Mongol tribe, became a conqueror of the eastern part of Mongolia by defeating the Kereit ruler Ong Khān in 1203. Having been proclaimed Supreme Chief of all Mongols in 1206, Genghis Khān and his armies swiftly vanquished a vast area of the Asian continent which included most of Eurasia from the China Sea to the banks of the Dnieper. Central Asia, in the widest geographic interpretation of the term, was thus for the first time united under a single ruler and Genghis Khān was said to have carried out God's will as decreed by divine revelation in becoming master of the world.[4] When Genghis died in 1227, the Great Mongol Empire (Mong. *yeke mongghul ulus*) was divided into various khānates (appanages) ruled over by his descendants. The Great Khāns *(qaghans)*, Möngke (r. 1251–1260) and Qubilay (r. 1260–1294), both descendants of Genghis Khān's youngest son Toluy, ruled Mongolia and northern China as the Yuan dynasty (1271–1368) from their capitals, first at Qaraqorum in Mongolia and later at Khānbāliq (lit. "City of the Khāns," Chin. Dadu, now known as Beijing) in China. They were supported by three collateral principalities: the Golden Horde, descended from Genghis Khān's eldest son Juchi in most of Russia; the Chaghatayids, descended from Genghis's second son Chagatay, in the region from the Aral Sea to the Altai mountains; and the Ilkhans descended from Hülegü/Hūlāgū, in Western Asia.

---

[1] The definition of what "China" entails has been a subject of scholarly debate in the field of history of Chinese art, see Thorp and Vinograd, 2001; Hay, 1999, pp. 120–62.

[2] For a discussion of the geographical boundaries of the various names related to China and the East, see Thackston in his translation of Rashīd al-Dīn Ṭabīb, *Jamiʿu't-tawarikh*, vol. 1, 1998–9, p. 24, n. 2. As Melikian-Chirvani (1997a, pp. 127 and 164, n. 33) has shown, the descriptions of the land of Chīn in the *Shāh-nāma* refer to eastern Turkestan, the area of Khotan and Kāshghar (sometimes going as far west as the Samarqand area), the land of the Turk Afrāsīyāb (tr. and ed. Mohl, 1838–1878, vol. 3, p. 390, l. 1155), whose son Pīrān is referred to as "Constable of Chīn" *(Sepahdār-i Chīn)* (*idem*, p. 44, l. 491) as well as "Constable of the Turks" *(Sepahdār-i Torkān)* (*idem*, p. 142, l. 1630).

[3] For a discussion of the influence of so-called "conquest dynasties" on the social and cultural history of China and the often repeated associated concept of a one way "sinicisation" which necessarily leads to a one-sided interpretation of this socio-cultural phenomena, see Wittfogel and Fêng, 1949, pp. 14–5; Bol, 1987, pp. 461–538; and Crossley, 1990, pp. 1–34.

[4] This premise is evident throughout Mongol rule and exemplified, for instance, in Hülegü's letter addressed to the French king Louis IX which expresses the Mongolian worldview, namely that Mongol commands represent God's will on earth. Meyvaert, 1980, p. 249.

The control of most of Asia by the Mongols, the so-called Pax Mongolica, marked an increase in trade and cultural transmission between the Mongol empire in China and Central Asia and also led to the introduction of accoutrements associated with the nomadic culture of the Mongols. Among these are a group of twelfth- and thirteenth-century dragon-handled cups, or belt-bowls, both in silver and gold, mostly found among grave goods distributed over a wide geographical region.[5] A well-known example is the thirteenth-century gold dragon-handled cup, or dipper, which is part of the Siberian Collection of Peter the Great (fig. 182).[6]

The cup's relief-cast handle is rendered in the form of a horizontally-projecting scaly serpentine 'neck' rearing up and terminating in an outward-oriented dragon head with flowing mane and curled up snout which attaches to the rim. The head has a short snout, a ribbed upper lip and shorter, curved, lower lip; a gold ring is held in the clenched jaws. The small eyes may have been set with stones that are now missing. The beard hair projecting from the rounded flews terminates in curls. An angular gold wire extends from the dragon's forehead to the lip of the bowl. An inscription on the bottom of the cup in the "Turkic" literary language in cursive script connects it to the Ulus Juchi (Golden Horde, descended from Genghis Khān's eldest son Juchi whose centre was located in the Volga Basin in the Qıpchaq steppe). The inscription reads: "In the year since the Prophet Muḥammad went from Mecca to Medina six hundred seventeen [years of the lunar calendar] have passed." The date corresponds to 1220–1. It is however probable that the inscription was added at a later date. This type of cup was developed in the northern regions of China and Mongolia as exemplified by vessels made in the states ruled by non-Han (i.e. non-Central Plain) Chinese tribes such as the Liao (916–1125) and Jin dynasties (1115–1234).[7] The shallow drinking vessel seems to have been designed as a portable container which could be carried by travellers suspended from a belt or saddle by the loop formed by the dragon's protome.[8]

Belts set with depictions of the dragon are known to have been produced in the steppe regions of northern China from at least the Western Jin period (265–316).[9] The large number of excavated Qitan-Liao-period belt/strap fittings and harness ornaments with dragon motifs[10] moreover indicate that the dragon motif was well

[5] For a list of extant belt-bowls with dragon-headed handles found in Siberia, the Transcaucasus, the Dnieper region, the Middle Ob region, and in Bulgaria, see Kramarovsky, 2000, p. 204. To this may be added an example discovered in a tree burial in Kurgan 7 of the excavations in Olen'-Kolodez' on the left bank of the Don river (Kashirski district, Woronesch region) which can be dated to the first half of the twelfth-century (Efimov, K.J., "Zolotoordynskie pogrebenija iz mogil'nika Olen'-Kolodez," *Donskaja archeologija*, no. 3/4, 1999, pp. 93–102, referred to by Kramarovsky, 2005, p. 224).

[6] Cf. Basilov, 1989, p. 72 (upper photograph); *Golden Horde*, 2000, pp. 212–3, cat. no. 12; *Legacy*, 2002, fig. 197, cat. no. 155. Herodotus (*History*, IV 8–10) mentions the successful girding of a belt with a golden goblet attached to the clasp as a qualifying trial imposed on the forefather and first king of the Scythians. In steppe culture belts emblazoned with large, rectangular cast metal plaques were not only a predominant component of pastoral paraphernalia, but are thought to have been status indicators and royal regalia of some significance. Bunker, 1992, pp. 216–7. *Balbals*, the ancient Turkic memorial stone sculptures symbolising a man or a woman, are also often depicted with a round vessel suspended from the belt. Bayar, 2005, p. 71.

[7] For instance, a silver example was unearthed from Aohan Banner, Chifeng City, Inner Mongolia (Inner Mongolia Autonomous Region Museum, height 5.2 cm, diameter 7.7 cm. *Ao Han Wen Wu Jing Hua* ("Aohan China"), 2004, p. 203 (photograph at the bottom).

[8] Nephrite versions of dragon-handled vessels of different shapes and with different dragon heads from Central Asia and the Iranian world survive, such as a late fourteenth- or early fifteenth-century example of a wine boat in Tehran, National Museum of Iran, inv. no. 8841 (*Shah ʿAbbas*, 2009, p. 161, cat. no. 76) or fifteenth-century examples, such as a cup in the same museum, inv. no. 8842 (*Shah ʿAbbas*, 2009, p. 160, cat. no. 75), an example in London, British Museum, inv. no. 1961 2–13.I (*The Arts of Islam*, 1976, p. 129, no. 113; *Timur and the Princely Vision*, 1987, p. 143, 340, cat. no. 52; Grube, 1988–9, p. 189, fig. 10A), or another from the art market (Sotheby's, 27 April, 1981, lot 122; Grube, 1988–9, p. 189, fig. 10B), a ewer in Washington, DC, National Collection of Fine Arts, inv. no. 1928.8.292 (Grube, 1988–9, p. 190, fig. 11) or yet another cup in San Francisco, Asian Art Museum, The Avery Brundage Collection, inv. no. B60 J160 (*Timur and the Princely Vision*, 1987, pp. 222, 353, cat. no. 120). The dating of some of these nephrite vessels has been challenged by Melikian-Chirvani (1997, pp. 134–62, figs. 5–7) who dates the Avery Brundage cup much earlier, between the tenth and the eleventh century (1997, pp. 139–41, 145).

[9] White and Bunker, 1994, cat. no. 50, and *eidem*, 1999, p. 71, fig. 9.

[10] In 1005 the Qitan-Liao emperor Shengzong (Yelü Longxu) dispatched birthday gifts to the Song emperor. Among these were belts, saddles and other imperial accoutrements adorned with gold or silver fittings depicting dragons. The conscious choice of such products as diplomatic gifts, reflecting the priorities of a pastoral people, as well as their decoration with dragons, underline their importance to the Qitan-Liao. Cf. Wittfogel and Fêng, 1949, pp. 147–8. For examples of Qitan-Liao horse harness or belt accoutrements with dragon motifs, see White and Bunker, 1994, 1999, p. 71, fig. 9; So, 2004, pp. 284–5, cat. no. VI:6.

established on the accoutrements of the steppe culture that extended far beyond Mongolia. After the demise of the Qitan state of Liao in China, part of the Qitan nobility, who were most probably distant descendants of the eastern branch of the Xianbei tribal confederacies, moved westwards to Chinese Turkestan. With the help of the Uighurs, to whom they were related, they created between 1128 and 1133 the Qara-Qitai ("Black Qitan") state in the Ili Valley, which after their victory over the Saljuq Turks in 1141 near Samarqand stretched over a vast area of Central Asia as far as the northern bank of the Āmū Daryā (known to the Arabs as the Jayḥūn, "flood"). With the expansion of the Qitan, some of their iconographic expressions also moved westwards into Central Asia.

In 1206 Genghis Khān marched westwards with the main body of his army, progressively taking over the Tangut kingdom, and the empire of the Qara-Qitai, who submitted to the authority of the Great Khān and were with time assimilated by the local population. Qara-Qitai, Jurchen, Uighurs, Qarluqs, Qıpchaqs and Chinese were already fighting on the side of the Great Khān in the victorious war against the Khwārazm-shāh ʿAlāʾ al-Dīn Muḥammad ibn Takash (596/1200–617/1220).

According to Mark Kramarovsky, it follows from the description of the military gear of Jalair Mukhali (d. 1223) that the saddle and horse trappings of Genghis Khān and his elite night guard *(kebteuls)*, the most privileged military unit of the Mongol army, were decorated with dragons.[11] The workmanship and, perhaps, the choice of the motif are thought to have been influenced by the Qitan and Jurchen to the northeast of China.[12] Kramarovsky suggests that the conscious choice of the dragon as unifying heraldic symbol, reserved for the "emperor" and his elite guards, was formed in the period between 1204 to 1206 and 1217 to satisfy the needs of a rapidly growing new elite.[13] In 1221 the widespread occurrence of the dragon symbol was observed by the Chinese traveller Chang Chun during his visit to Bianjing (now Kaifeng), the former capital of the Tungusic Jurchen of the Jin dynasty.[14] Early Mongol battle and parade belts and belt buckles with depictions of dragons are known from archaeological finds brought by the first generation of Jurchids as early as the 1220s to 1240s to the European steppe zone, pertaining to finds in the Dnieper region, the Middle Don region, the steppes of the Caucasus foreland and the Middle and Lower Volga regions.[15] According to Kramarovsky, the first stratum of gilded and nielloed silver belts with heraldic dragons may be assigned to the second half of the twelfth century and the first half of the thirteenth century. Of a complete belt found at Krasnoyarskoye archaeological site in the vicinity of Astrakhān, which would have consisted of 65 to 70 elements, 29 parts survive, many carrying the emblem of a dragon (fig. 183).[16] The type and style of this belt, which is Central Asian in origin, dates from the time of the formation and the flourishing of the single Mongol state.[17] The elite night guard belonged to the elder generation of the officer corps of the Jurchids who arrived in the European part of the steppes around the middle of the thirteenth century and had disappeared by the late fourteenth century.[18]

Among these finds is a so far unrecognised composition. It appears on a belt head and expresses the ancient Central Asian conceptualisation of the "Master of the Dragons" as the dragon-tamer. The almost universal currency of the motif throughout the Central Asian world is underscored by its use on this accoutrement of rectangular outline with arched ends. It shows a frontally rendered figure with mask-like face, punctuated by small, almond-shaped eyes, angular nose, large open mouth and with large protruding ears, grasps with extended arms the necks of two imposing rampant dragons, holding them at bay (fig. 184).[19] Although the remarkably fluid rendering of the dragons with their long pointed horns owes much to the Chinese canon of these fabulous beasts, it is used here in a typically Central Asian configuration that was not prevalent in the Chinese empire. Given its evident corre-

[11] Kramarovsky, 2000, p. 203, and, *idem*, 2005, p. 225.
[12] *Idem*, 2000, p. 205, and, *idem*, 2005, p. 225.
[13] *Idem*, 2000, pp. 203–4, and, *idem*, 2005, p. 226.
[14] *Men-da bei-pu* [*sic*; *Mengda beilu* ("Thorough Account of the Mongol Tatars")], 1975, p. 76, as cited by *idem*, 2000, p. 203.
[15] *Idem*, 2005, p. 226.
[16] Cf. *Golden Horde*, 2000, p. 69, p. 151, fig. 7.2 (line drawing), pp. 216–7, cat. no. 19.
[17] Kramarovsky, 2005, p. 226.
[18] *Idem*.
[19] Cf. *Golden Horde*, 2000, p. 69, p. 151, fig. 7.1 (line drawing), pp. 216–7, cat. no. 19; *Legacy*, 2002, fig. 198, cat. no. 142; *Dschingis Khan und seine Erben*, 2005, p. 230, cat. no. 253 (bottom left, depicted in inverted position).

spondence with imagery relating to the overmastering of the dragon, this iconography can be assumed to have been implicitly imbued with favourable properties, possibly of an empowering quality, which would in turn be passed on to the owner of the buckle. At the same time it is a sign of supremacy and of victory over untamed forces. The frequent application of the dragon motif on accoutrements pertaining to a traditional nomadic lifestyle, moreover, suggests that it was not only well-known but firmly enshrined in Mongol mythological concepts and formed an integral part of their artistic repertoire even before the onset of the period of Mongol imperial rule. The fact that belief in a dragon played a significant part in the indigenous beliefs of the Mongols (see below), lends added weight to this possibility.[20]

Two years after Genghis Khān's death in 1227, his third son and designated successor, Ögödei, was confirmed as the second Great Khān (r. 1229–1241). From 641/1243–4 until 653/1255–6 his territories in greater Khurasan were overseen by governor Arghūn Āqā, who was part of the Oirat Mongol clan.[21] It was under him that in 642/1244–5 the Mongols minted their first silver coins in Arrān (the district in Transcaucasia between the Kur and Aras rivers). Not least because of the turbulent political situation in Khurasan, Arghūn chose to retain the area of Azerbaijan as one of the centres of Mongol monetary production.[22] It is significant that for the iconography of these first coins, the Mongols chose that of the dragon-fighting horseman. The latter is portrayed as a galloping archer in Mongol attire turning to aim over his shoulder at a "Saljuq-style" ophidian dragon. The arched inscription above, written in the Turkic language but in Arabic script, states: "Ūlūgh Mūnqūl ulūsh nyk/One great Mongol nation." Coins of this type were chosen for different principalities such as Ganja, the capital of Arrān, and Nakhchavān.[23] In their quest for legitimacy, the Mongols may well have given serious consideration to their choice of the motif of the mounted archer and dragon as a symbol of "inherited" sovereignty, using it as a means of propagating their ideological formula. The image here represents a victorious mounted archer in Mongol dress, combined with the traditional imagery of the dragon-fighting horseman that was easily recognisable throughout Western Asia.

Another important form of dragon symbolism, that of the tree with dragons, had made an appearance in thirteenth-century Mongolia in the form of an automaton. During Ögödei's time the designated capital of the empire at Qaraqorum in the Orkhon valley in central Mongolia, chosen by his father as early as 1220, was walled and, according to the *Yüan-shih* ("History of the Yuan dynasty"), the official history of the Yuan dynasty composed in the early Ming dynasty, Ögödei constructed a palace there in 1235.[24] In the imperial precinct his son Möngke erected a serpent-tree, which became a monument of central significance. At his orders it was built in the form of a large, gilded silver tree-fountain by the French silversmith Guillaume Bouchier, a prisoner-of-war, together with fifty local workmen.[25] The serpent-tree-fountain was of considerable size and was situated in the southern section of the main reception hall of the Khān's palace called *Tumen Amgalant* ("Myriad Tranquillities") opposite the Khān's throne.[26]

During Möngke's reign the Franciscan friar, William of Rubruck (Willem van Ruysbroeck, *c.* 1210–1270) from French Flanders visited the Mongol capital of Qaraqorum in 1254 and in his *Itinerarium* addressed to king Louis IX of France gives a detailed account of this silver tree-fountain:

[20] Spuler, 1939, repr. 1955, p. 140, with reference to Banzarov, D., *Černaja věra ili šamanstvo u Mongolov i drugija stat'i* ("Der schwarze Glaube oder der Schamanismus bei den Mongolen und andere Aufsätze"), ed. Potanin, G.N., St. Peterburg, 1891, pp. 15–6. Cf. Liu, 1958, p. 10; Roux, 1978, p. 128, also p. 143.

[21] Cf. Kolbas, 2006, pp. 100, 114.

[22] *Eadem*, pp. 114–5.

[23] *Eadem*, pp. 125–7 and n. 20; Ganja: pl. 5.1 (reverse) and cover; Nakhchavān, preserved in the Bibliothèque Nationale, Paris: the dragon's head rears up behind the horse, an arrow piercing its mouth.

[24] *Dschingis Khan und seine Erben*, 2005, p. 152.

[25] For a monograph on William Bouchier, see Olschki, 1946.

[26] Cf. a contemporary oil on paperboard painting representing the silver serpent-tree-fountain by B. Pürevsüch, Mongolia, 1980 (Mongolian Cultural Foundation, Ulan Batar, inv. no. 21); *Dschingis Khan und seine Erben*, 2005, p. 153, cat. no. 109. See also an eighteenth-century engraving of the fountain in Bergeron, 1735, p. 96, preserved in the Staatsbibliothek zu Berlin – Preußischer Kulturbesitz, Orientabteilung, Ms. 4'Uk 2408; reproduced in Olschki, 1946, pl. 3, and *Dschingis Khan und seine Erben*, 2005, p. 154, cat. no. 110.

> In the entry of this great palace, it being unseemly to bring in there skins of milk and other drinks, master William the Parisian had made for him a great silver tree, and at its roots are four lions of silver, each with a conduit through it, and all belching forth white milk of mares. And four conduits are led inside the tree to its tops, which are bent downward, and on each of these is also a gilded serpent, whose tail twines round the tree. And from one of these pipes flows wine, from another *cara cosmos*, or clarified mare's milk, from another *bal*, a drink made with honey, and from another rice mead, which is called *terracina*; and for each liquor there is a special silver bowl at the foot of the tree to receive it. Between these four conduits in the top, he made an angel holding a trumpet, and underneath the tree he made a vault in which a man can be hid. And pipes go up through the heart of the tree to the angel. [...] And there are branches of silver on the tree, and leaves and fruit.[27]

Significantly, the portrayal of the tree with serpents has certain analogies with that of the previously discussed large water-clock automaton described in a medieval Islamic illustrated horological treatise.[28] During the medieval Islamic period, automata in the form of silver gilded trees with artificial singing birds were known as expressions of imperial might, particularly in ʿAbbasid times.[29] However, the affixing of the four gilded serpent ducts from which flow four different types of liquid appears to be a unique feature which must have been meaningful to Möngke Khān and his entourage, according to whose orders the prestigious serpent-tree was designed and placed at the most central location in the palace facing the Khān's throne.

Related imagery may be sought in popular tradition and folklore. However since any diffusion of narratives took place largely through oral transmission before finding crystallisation in the literary world, it is interesting to regard oral epics popular in Central Asian folklore (which were recorded as late as the nineteenth century) as possible carriers that transmitted and thereby preserved remnants of the age-old visual concept of a tree with roots reaching the underworld guarded by a serpent or dragon. Such symbolism appears, for instance, in the Qirghiz cycle of *Er Töshtük*, in which the hero must make a mystical journey into the underworld. There he finds an elm tree whose trunk reaches through the centre of the earth, the tree's crown reaching to the sky with a dragon coiled around its base. He rescues the young of an eagle by cutting the monstrous creature in half. To show her gratitude the mother eagle swallows Er Töshtük and then disgorges him, transformed and rendered invulnerable, and after that carries him up again to the land of the living.[30]

It is of note that under Möngke's reign the building of an important Buddhist temple with central *stūpa* was completed in Qaraqorum.[31] During excavations at the site a thirteenth- or fourteenth-century copper alloy matrix for a double *vajra* ("thunderbolt") was found.[32] A concept similar to that seen on the above examples also governs the depictions on the matrix: from each of the arms of the cross grow a pair of dragon protomes that support the pyramidal jewels, representing the sacred Mount Meru as the centre. The symbolism on the matrix attests to the universality of the various manifestations of the serpent-tree-cross iconography revealing, to a great extent, a unified tradition throughout the Central Asian world, which shares certain basic beliefs.[33]

William of Rubruck's journey to Mongolia coincided with the fresh wave of extensive military campaigns launched by Hülegü (r. 654/1256–663/1265), Möngke's younger brother and expeditionary commander, across Central and Western Asia. The future founder of the Ilkhanate led the main body of the Mongol army across the Oxus river and onto the Iranian plateau. His eldest son, Abāqā, the future second Ilkhan, who was born in Mongolia in 1234, accompanied him. In 654/1256 the grandson of Ghengis Khān overcame the Shīʿa Muslim state of the Ismāʿīlīs (the Assassins) ensconced in northwestern Iran and in 652/1258 brought the ʿAbbasid caliphate in Baghdad to a violent end. Thus establishing their hegemony over most of West Asia, the Ilkhanid dynasty ruled over Mesopotamia, Iran, Western

[27] *The Mission of Friar William of Rubruck*, tr. and ed. Jackson and Morgan, 1990, ch. 16.

[28] Hill, 1976; cf. 1984, p. 230.

[29] See p. 65, n. 162.

[30] Recorded by the great Turkic philologist and archaeologist V. Radlov (1885, pp. 535–8); see also DeWeese, 1994, pp. 237–8. Closely related tales are known in Armenia and among the Kurds. Cf. Schmidt, 1980, pp. 19–20; Abełyan, M., *Erkeri zhłovacu* ("Collected Works"), Erevan, 1966–75, vol. 1, pp. 383–8, as cited in Russell, 1987, p. 311.

[31] Hüttel, 2005, p. 146.

[32] *Dschingis Khan und seine Erben*, 2005, p. 176, cat. no. 176.

[33] Cf. DeWeese, 1994, pp. 39–50.

Central Asia, Transcaucasia, and parts of Asia Minor, from 654/1256 to 754/1353.

Hülegü took the title Ilkhan and continued his allegiance to the throne of the Great Khān in China, his brother Möngke.[34] The ensuing close relationship of symbolic and commercial ties between the Mongol court in China and the Ilkhanid court created an environment of extraordinary cultural exchange in the form of gifts,[35] tribute[36] and merchandise,[37] moving in both directions between China and Western Asia. Life at the Yuan court became an "absolute model to the Ilkhans, who tried to emulate the Great Khāns in their courtly life, conducting many of their private and official affairs in the Mongolian fashion of their ancestral homeland."[38] Yuan China's art thus affected and informed the visual expressions of the Ilkhanate which was characterised by the transmission of Chinese and Chinese-inspired Mongol motifs. The blurring of the boundaries between what constitutes a "Chinese," a "Mongol" or, more broadly, a "Central Asian" style is of course the outcome of a fluidity of cultural modes (expressed in material culture), representing a long-lasting and more or less continuous state of acculturation and appropriation between different ethnic and cultural groups.

Some of the Mongols who had invaded Western Asia had been Nestorian Christians (in particular their wives),[39] but the majority followed the indigenous beliefs of the Mongols which were essentially ancestral animistic and syncretic. The cult of Heaven (Tengri) was central to the Turko-Mongol system of belief, its beginnings going back to remotest times. This concept played a fundamental role in the notion of legitimacy and sovereignty.[40] It comprised the veneration of the Sun, in particular the rising Sun, the Moon and the natural phenomena of the heavens in which, as mentioned above, the belief in a dragon played an important role.[41] As such, it provided a bridge to Chinese concepts of cosmology and sovereignty, both being linked by a similar notion of Heaven.[42]

However in the royal house and among the ruling class there was a tendency towards Buddhism, perhaps as a result of the fairly close relations with China. The rulers, Hülegü (r. 654/1256–663/1265), Abāqā (r. 663/1265–680/1282) and his sons Arghūn (r. 683/1284–690/1291) and Gaykhātū (r. 690/1291–694/1295) were probably Buddhists, hence Buddhism took a central place during the first half of Ilkhanid rule for about forty years (654/1256–694/1295). Consequently elements of Buddhist art and iconography were pervasive, visualised in the many richly endowed Buddhist temples built by the rulers.[43] One of the Ilkhanid Buddhist sites is situated in the village of Dashkasan of the district of Viār, probably named after the Sanskrit term *vihāra* for a Buddhist monastery. It is located just outside the Mongol summer quarter Qongqur Öleng (Turk. "Brown Meadow"), which later became the imperial city Sulṭāniyya (*c.* 684/1285) near Qazwīn in northwestern Iran founded by Ghāzān's younger brother and successor Öljeitü (Ūljāytū, r. 703/1304–716/1316). At the west wall of the rock-cut complex two monumental, fluidly rendered, quadruped dragons *passant* with their tails curling between the hind legs and set against undulating foliage are preserved. Carved into stone in high relief and flanked by *mihrāb*-like *muqarnas* niches, the creatures are an early testimony for the depiction of a Chinese-inspired Mongol dragon (fig. 185).[44]

The Ilkhanids maintained the nomadic practice of seasonal migrations, moving rythmically according to the time of year from summer *(yaylāq)* to winter *(qishlāq)* quarters. One of their summer encampments was at Sughūrlūq (Turk. "Marmot Meadows"),[45] in the Azerbaijan region of present-day Iran. It was chosen for its climate,

[34] Spuler, 1939, repr. 1955, pp. 224–6.

[35] *Idem*, pp. 305–6.

[36] *Idem*, p. 223; Masuya, 1997, pp. 12–3 and n. 10.

[37] Spuler, 1939, repr. 1955, pp. 220–4, 359. During the Yuan period, Chinese maritime trade exported lacquers, ceramics, combs, silk, umbrellas and bronze coins to West Asia, and imported ivory, rhinoceros horn, coral, cotton cloth, hide, wax, kingfisher and peacock feathers, dyes, raw medicine, shark skin, hawksbill turtle shell and parrots. Deng, 1997, p. 114, table 5.2.

[38] Masuya, 2002, p. 75. Cf. Allsen, 2001, p. 197.

[39] Spuler, 1939, repr. 1955, pp. 151–2.

[40] *Idem*, pp. 168–9. Cf. for instance the Mongol formula, *möngke tngri-yin küčün-dür* ("In the Might of the Everlasting Heaven"), found at the beginning of some Mongol letters; Meyvaert, 1980, pp. 253, n. 39 and 258, n. 79.

[41] See p. 212.

[42] The cult of Heaven in Chinese state rituals may have had a common origin with the veneration of Heaven as it is known among Altaic peoples. Di Cosmo, 1999, pp. 369, 380.

[43] Spuler, 1939, repr. 1955, pp. 10, 74, 149–51, 308. With the exception of a short period when there was a Muslim ruler, Aḥmad Tegüder (r. 680/1282–683/1284).

[44] See Curatola, 1982, pp. 71–88; *Legacy*, 2002, p. 110, fig. 127; Kouymjian, 2006, fig. 63; Akbarnia, 2007, fig. 29; Kadoi, 2008, p. 107–8, fig. 3.19.

[45] Rashīd al-Dīn Ṭabīb, *Ta'rīkh-i Mubārak-i Gāzānī;* partial ed. Jahn, 1957, pp. 66, 73; Masuya, 1997, pp. 72–9.

excellent pasture grounds and, as the Turkic name "place abounding in marmots" suggests, the abundant game, which enabled the Mongols to pursue their favourite pastime of hunting. As part of their sedentarisation, the second Ilkhanid ruler, Hülegü's eldest son and successor, Abāqā (r. 663/1265–680/1282) began the construction of a summer residence at Sughūrlūq in the 1270s,[46] less than fifteen years after the arrival of the Ilkhanids.

The project was completed under his son Arghūn, who also used the residence to house his imperial treasury.[47] The site, later also known as Takht-i Sulaimān ("Solomon's Throne"), remains the only surviving palatial architectural complex of the Ilkhans for which provenance and date are certain. It was built over and incorporated the remains of a pre-existing sanctuary, the important Zoroastrian fire temple of Ādur Gushnasp, the "City of the Warriors' Fire," active during the late Sasanian period, indicating that the site was perhaps not only selected for its excellent location but for its associations with ancient Iranian kingship, and was intended to appropriate the early charisma that attached to the site.[48] The fire temple is said to have been erected by Kay Khusraw, the third mythical ruler of the Iranian dynasty of the Kayānids. According to the philologist Ḥamza al-Iṣfahānī (*c.* 280/893–*c.* 350/961) he killed a dragon called Kūshīd and gave its name to the fire temple he built in the place of Ādur Gushnasp, calling it Kūshīd for Gushnasp (lit. "possessing stallions" – thought to be the name of the unknown founder).[49]

This apparently conscious selection had a precedent in the Mongols' choice of capital. Thomas Allsen convincingly argues that they "went to great lengths to properly site their capital, Qaraqorum, in the same region as the imperial city of the Türk qaghanate and Uighur empire because they believed that there inhered in that particular locale a special good fortune, a charisma (Turk. *qut*) that would favor their own political enterprise."[50] The site may therefore have been carefully selected in an effort to activate its ancient "spiritual resource" (in Allsen's words) and thereby generate *qut* which is also one of the characteristics that identifies a nomadic Inner Asian sovereign as chosen by heaven.[51] The strategic positioning of the Ilkhanids was particularly crucial: the Mongolian takeover marked a profound rupture resulting from the destruction of the five hundred year-old ʿAbbasid empire (132/750–656/1258) centred on Baghdad and the demise of the two hundred year-old Saljuq dynasty which ruled over a wide area of Western Asia during the eleventh and twelfth centuries (although it survived in Anatolia until the beginning of the fourteenth century). The radical political change necessarily also brought with it new forms of visual expression.

It was however in the introduction of mythical creatures of Chinese stylistic derivation, in particular the dragon *(long)* and the phoenix *(fenghuang)*,[52] that Takht-i Sulaimān would have the greatest impact on Iranian art. These creatures appear on star-shaped, rectangular and other polygonal glazed revetment tiles on the interior walls of the palatial buildings.[53] Excavations show

---

[46] This date is corroborated by production dates inscribed on at least 163 lustre-painted tiles excavated at the site: 670 and 671 H and 674 H, that is, 9 August, 1271 to 17 July 1273 and 27 June, 1275 to 14 February, 1276 AD; Masuya, 1997, pp. 72, 368–77. See *Legacy*, 2002, figs. 59, 79, 95, 97, 100, 101 and 205, cat. nos. 84, 99, 100, 101, 103.

[47] Masuya, 1997, pp. 200–1.

[48] See Boyce and Grenet with a contrib. by Beck, 1991, pp. 74–81.

[49] Huart, "Kay Khusraw," *EI*² IV, 815b.

[50] Allsen, 2001, p. 208, and *idem,* 1996, pp. 125–6. Cf. al-Juwaynī, *Taʾrīkh-i jahān-gushāy*, tr. Boyle, 1912–37, vol. 1, pp. 54–5, 236.

[51] Allsen, 1996, pp. 116, 131. According to a Yuan-period Uighur inscription, the word *qut* was also used in the title of their sovereign, *altun iduq qut* (lit. "golden sacred good fortune"). Geng and Hamilton, 1981, pp. 17 and 19, Uighur text, 26 and 28, French tr.

[52] See, for instance, *Legacy*, 2002, figs. 83, 92, 93, 96, cat. nos. 88–91, 105, 204; also, the reconstruction drawing of *lajvardina* star and cross tiles from the northern Octagon at Takht-i Sulaimān, fig. 205. The dragon and *sīmurgh*, both of Chinese inspiration, appear also on a large-size brass basin inlaid with gold and silver of scalloped outline, which has been dated to the early fourteenth century, now in the Victoria and Albert Museum in London, inv. no. 546–1905, one of the most striking examples of Ilkhanid metalwork. Melikian-Chirvani, 1982, pp. 202–7, no. 93; *Legacy*, 2002, fig. 211, cat. no. 169. The points of resemblance between the dragons and the *sīmurgh*s depicted on the basin with those rendered on the eleventh-century Liao imperial mausoleum at Qingling in Liaoning province have been noted by Jessica Rawson (1994, pp. 148–9). Hence by the end of the thirteenth century the influence of a Chinese-derived phoenix is noticeable in the visual imagery of the *sīmurgh*; cf. Baer, 1965, p. 41.

[53] Masuya, 1997; tile types displaying the dragon: 4-b, 4-c, 4-i, 4-s, 4-u, 6-1-f, and 6-2-2a. See also *Legacy*, 2002, figs. 59, 93, 102, 106, 275, cat. nos. 86, 91, 93, 101, 102.

that the most lavishly decorated areas of Takht-i Sulaimān were situated in the *īwān* palace hall and the complex of octagonal towers joined to the *īwān*. Various techniques were used for decorating the tiles at Takht-i Sulaimān[54] which range from underglaze painting and monochrome glazing to overglaze lustre-painting and *lājvardina* (Pers. *lājvard* meaning "lapis lazuli"), over- and underglaze (an unusual technique believed to have first been documented at Takht-i Sulaimān).[55]

The dragons portrayed on the tile revetments (figs. 186a and b) closely resemble the carved Viār dragon, datable probably to the second half of the thirteenth century. The creatures' vitality is vividly conveyed. The heads, crowned by fine antlers, show an elongated wide-open snout with curled-up proboscis revealing the deep parallel grooves on the roof of the mouth as well as the sharp fangs and the protruding sinuous tongue. Tufts of hair are growing from the nape of the neck. The quadruped bodies are densely covered with scales and the muscular raptor-like legs have formidable feet with four unsheathed talons. When shown as single entities, the dragons are either rendered *regardant* with tails raised or coiled, the head facing the expansive tail which is tucked around one of the hind legs. Similarly vigorous dragons *passant* were also carved in relief on the torus moulding of the round capitals that crowned the red sandstone columns, pairs of which stood in each of the eight corners of the south octagon (figs. 187a and b).[56] Yet although the quadrupeds bear some resemblance to Chinese or Chinese-inspired Mongol renditions of these mythical creatures, the bodies are heavier and the twists are more angular, characteristic of a Central Asian inspiration of the dragon; yet the mode of transmission of the style and conventions of the motif cannot be established with certainty.[57]

Images of dragons enjoyed wide currency in the Turkic world (figs. 165 and 166) and must have been well-known to the Mongols whose cultural interrelationship with the Türk has a long history.[58] The legendary beasts are known to have been used as architectural decoration in Mongol cities. They make a prominent appearance on the automaton tree mentioned earlier from Möngke's palace at the first Yuan capital in Qaraqorum in Mongolia. Thirteenth- and fourteenth-century literary sources also include detailed descriptions of architectural elements carved with images of dragons at the palatial buildings as well as bridges at the second Yuan capital Khānbāliq (Dadu) in China prior to its destruction in the 1360s.[59] In the summer of 1275 the Venetian merchant traveller Marco Polo (*c.* 1254–*c.* 1324) arrived at the court of Shangdu (in present-day Inner Mongolia), the summer capital of the Yuan dynasty, and left an account of the so-called "Cane Palace" which presumably relates to Qubilai's "Sira Ordu." He describes it as a temporary structure in the form of a huge tent decorated with sculpted dragons supporting the architraves:

> It is stayed on gilt and lackered [*sic*] columns, on each of which is a dragon all gilt, the tail of which is attached to the column whilst the head supports the architrave, and the claws likewise are stretched out right and left to support the architrave.[60]

The Italian explorer subsequently also visited the winter court in Khānbāliq and noted that the walls of the Khān's palace were "adorned with representations of dragons sculptured and gilt."[61] Several palatial cities were erected throughout Mongolia in the thirteenth- or fourteenth-century. Sculpted granite dragon protomes were a prominent feature at one of these palatial struc-

[54] *Eadem*, 1997. For the excavation report, see Naumann, E. and R., 1976.

[55] Masuya, 1997, p. 239.

[56] Two capitals were reportedly taken from Takht-i Sulaimān in the early twentieth century but given to the German excavators during their 1960 campaign. Kleiss, 1961, columns 58–60, fig. 14. Naumann, 1977, pp. 89–90, figs. 69 and 70. Cf. Masuya, 1997, pp. 228–9 and pl. 8.

[57] See, for example, the discussion of transmission of representations between Yuan China and Central Asia by Shatzman Steinhardt, 1987, pp. 59–71. For a study about the reception of Chinese painting and the types of material evidence found in the Timurid context, see Sugimura, 1986.

[58] Some Mongol tribes had been subjects of the Turk and Uighur empires. With the collapse of the steppe empire of the Uighurs in Mongolia in 840, which led to a westward movement of the Turks, the Mongolisation of Mongolia, previously a Turkish homeland, began.

[59] Tao Zongyi (1346–1415), *Zhuogeng Lu* ("Record of Rest from the Plow"), 1368, repr. Shanghai, 1959 ed., *juan* 21, p. 2 and Xiao Xun, *Gugong Yi Lu* ("Record of the Remains of an Imperial Palace"), repr. Taipei, 1963 ed., p. 251, cited after Shatzman Steinhardt, 1988, pp. 62–3, 71 and fig. 14. The late fourteenth-century official Xiao Xun (*Gugong Yi Lu*, 1) gives an account of Qubilai's audience hall as surrounded by a "marble balustrade carved with figures of dragons and phoenixes." During excavations at Dadu a marble panel was discovered with a dragon in relief framed above by a border enclosing two smaller dragons. *Kaogu*, 6, 1972, pl. 11, as cited in Shatzman Steinhardt, 1988, pp. 62–3 and fig. 14.

[60] *The Travels of Marco Polo*, tr. and comm. Yule and rev. Cordier, 1929, pp. 299–300.

[61] *Op. cit.*, p. 364.

tures, Kondui Palace in the Transbaikal region, which seems to have developed upon the architectural and spatial arrangement of Ögödei's palace complex *Tumen Amgalant* at Qaraqorum. The palace was built on a platform, surrounded by double-tiered terraces, the dragon sculpture being set on the upper terrace at intervals of two metres facing outwards. Of the 150 dragon sculptures that decorated the terrace, 102 were found during Sergei Kiselev's archaeological excavations in the 1940s (figs. 188 and 189).[62] The excavations revealed traces of conflagration, and it is thought that Kondui Palace was burned to the ground during raids by the Chinese army approximately at the same time as Qaraqorum was destroyed in 1380. It is worthy of note that in contrast to many of the previously discussed examples from Islamic architecture, these dragon sculptures were overall not only highly visible but were in fact integrated into the structural aspects of the palatial architecture often with a supportive function.[63]

Dragon imagery was therefore well established and had wide currency in Mongol culture. In addition, glazed roof tiles, tile terminals (the circular *goutou* and the triangular-shaped *dishui*) in particular, with moulded decoration of dragons have been found in many Mongol cities.[64] The overall depiction of the dragons on the roof tiles is closely related stylistically to that on the tiles from Takht-i Sulaimān.

In Chinese culture the dragon *(long)*[65] is one of the oldest, most significant and most pervasive symbols, recognised, according to a twelfth-century reading of the early Han-period account *Huainanzi*, as an all-encompassing creature, the antecedent of all species:

> As for the myriad creatures be they feathered, hairy, scaly or armored, they all find their ancestry in the dragon.[66]

According to ancient ritual beliefs, particularly favoured in Buddhist and Daoist traditions, dragons are a symbolic expression of fertility and fecundity, able to control rain and, if invoked, to procure rain in agricultural life.[67] Far from being a mere symbol of the natural elements, the *long* also carried imperial affiliations from ancient times.[68] This is symbolised not least by the mythologising of the miraculous conception of Gaozu, founder and first emperor of the Han dynasty, who was born as the result of his mother's union with a scaly dragon, a sure sign of a heavenly mandate.[69] Already in the *Shang shu*, one of the major historical works of early Chinese history, the dragon is thought to have been depicted together with "the sun and the moon, the stars and the constellations, the mountains, ... and the flowery animals ... on the upper sacrificial robes of the emperor."[70] In spite of this association, dragons were used outside the court context in China before and after the advent of the Mongols. Early thirteenth-century Mongols of any rank appear to have worn garments decorated with dragons and phoenixes as witnessed by the Song envoy Peng Daya who recorded his visit to Ögödei's court in the *Heida Shilue* ("Summary of the Records of the Tatars") written in 1237.[71] However, beginning with the Chinese Song dynasty (960–1279) the symbol of the dragon became an imperial prerogative and paramount imperial symbol, customarily referring to the "emperor's person: his body was the dragon body, his hands the claws, his capital the dragon's pool."[72] The Song and Jurchen Jin dynasties, fol-

[62] Kiselev, 1965, pp. 325–69; for further examples of dragon sculptures from Kondui, see *idem*, p. 340, fig. 180, and p. 343, fig. 181. At least one of the dragon sculptures remained *in situ*, cf. Artemiev, 2003, p. 306, fig. 3. For comparable architectural marble sculptures of dragon protomes from Shangdu, see *Legacy*, 2002, fig. 21, cat. no. 204. Similar sculptures were found in western Siberia in the territory of the Golden Horde, see *Golden Horde*, 2000, pp. 208–9, nos. 2, 3.

[63] I must thank Professor Robert Hillenbrand for pointing this out to me.

[64] See Kiselev, 1965, p. 319, fig. 166, p. 321, fig. 168, pl. XXXI, fig. 1 and 2; Masuya, 1997, pp. 723–4, chart XVIII; *Legacy*, 2002, figs. 22, 83, 105, cat. nos. 188–90.

[65] As a "species" the mythological *long* encompasses different subspecies. For a discussion of the dragon in ancient Chinese myth, see Allan, 1991, pp. 64–7. For the dragon in Chinese art in general, see *eadem*, pp. 157–64, 174; Rawson, 1984, pp. 93–9.

[66] *Erya yi* ("Ramifications of the Literary Expositor"), compiled by Luo Yuan (1136–1184), 28.297, cited after Sterckx, 2002, pp. 84–6. See also the study of Suetoshi Ikeda (1981, pp. 290–5) who proposes an etymological relationship between the Chinese characters *long* (dragon) and the much debated, obscure *gui* (perhaps "ancestral spirits") and considers the dragon to be an ancestral deity transformed into a mythical animal.

[67] For detailed discussions of these rituals, see Loewe, 1987, pp. 195–214; and Jing, 2002, pp. 70–3.

[68] Masuya, 2002, p. 96.

[69] Cf. Sterckx, 2002, pp. 194, 202.

[70] *Shangshu zhengyi*, 5.4b, annotated by Kong Yingda et al., in *Shisanjing zhushu*, vol. 1, cited after Sterckx, 2002, p. 53.

[71] Ed. and comm., Wang Guowei, *Menggu shiliao sizhong* ("Four Historical Sources on the Mongols"), Taipei, 1962, p. 479, cited after Masuya, 1997, p. 570.

[72] Rawski, 1998, p. 42.

lowed in 1314 by the Mongol Yuan, similarly adopted this proclamatory use of the theme and made the five-clawed *long* an exclusively imperial symbol.[73]

These multicultural symbols were presumably understood by most members of the Ilkhanid court where, according to Allsen, a large group of "Easterners" were also present such as Ongguts, Qitans, Uighurs, Tibetans, Tanguts, Mongols and Chinese.[74] The tile revetments were without doubt impressive, expressing the wealth and taste of the Ilkhanids which in turn must have conveyed an awesome message of imperial power.

Some of the lustre-painted star tiles and lustered and molded frieze tiles of Takht-i Sulaimān include inscriptions with quotations from religious texts, including Qurʾānic verses and *ḥadīth*, as well as Iranian secular poems and quotations from the epic *Shāh-nāma*, which by the Ilkhanid period was a recognised cornerstone of Iranian literature.[75] In addition to the representation of dragons and phoenixes, the subject matter of the visual decoration comprises depictions of princely or heroic activities. The verses taken from scenes of the *Shāh-nāma* located on the borders of eight-pointed lustre-painted tiles and on some of the lustre-painted frieze tiles, are especially noteworthy. Melikian-Chirvani has proposed that these inscriptions present an intentional selection of the verses in order to connect Abāqā and his successor Aḥmad Tegüder (r. 680/1282–683/1284) with the ancient kings of Iran.[76] The text has been modified in at least three cases so that it addresses the second person rather than the third as in the original context, hence directly addressing and thereby integrating the Ilkhanid rulers into the history of Iranian kings.[77] The cyclical character of the *Shāh-nāma*, where heroes and rulers in one cycle parallel the adventures of heroes and rulers in another, facilitated the inclusion of the Ilkhanid rulers within Iranian legendary history and national epic, arguably symbolising the legitimisation of their presence in the Iranian and more broadly the Western Asian world.[78] The cyclical nature of its "historical" destiny has, according to Melikian-Chirvani, made the *Shāh-nāma* a "mirror of destiny" and of the world.[79]

The eulogies contained in these inscriptions are echoed by those recorded by the minister and historian for the Mongols, ʿAlā al-Dīn ʿAṭa-Malik al-Juwaynī (623/1226–681/1283), in the extensive dynastic history *Taʾrīkh-i jahān-gushāy* ("History of the World-Conqueror"), sponsored by Hülegü, which begins with the campaigns of Genghis Khān and ends with Hülegü's own victories in Iran and Mesopotamia in 1256 to 1258. In one of these accounts the future Turkic Khwārazm-shāh Jalāl al-Dīn (617/1220–628/1231) has to flee to Shadayk during the struggle for succession. En route he engages with a Tatar army, demonstrating a courage that even Rustam, the son of Zāl, could not have mustered. To highlight the drama of the moment, Juwaynī quotes from the *Shāh-nāma*:

> The captain gave his dragon rein and dust removed
> Light from the world-[80]

In his battles with the Mongols, the decisive courage of the *sulṭān* is further compared to the very deadliest creatures, the lion and the dragon:

> ...a lion of the meadow or a Leviathan of the raging sea.[81]

The praiseworthy qualities attributed to each beast are here again brought together.

However once the die was cast and the Mongol army had prevailed, Juwaynī was the first to par-

[73] According to the *Yüan-shih*, the dynastic record of the Yuan period, the court prohibits the use of the sun, the moon, dragon and tiger on the decoration of silk and satin fabrics as soon as the Yuan dynasty was estabished; a code for the robes and colours of officers issued in 1314 further specified restrictions on "the use of designs using the *long* with five claws and two horns as well as the *feng* [phoenix] on robes, vessels, and plates, tents and carts of officers." Allsen, 1997, p. 108; Masuya, 1997, p. 570; see also *eadem*, 2002, p. 96; Kadoi, 2008, p. 22, see also the discussion on p. 25. As suggested by Masuya (2002, p. 97), "the presence of only four claws on the dragons at Takht-i Sulayman may have expressed the Ilkhan's respect for the suzerainty of the Great Khans, who claimed for themselves the exclusive use of the five-clawed dragon."

[74] Allsen, 2001, p. 6. However, very little is known about the presence of Chinese artists and craftsmen in the Ilkhanid realm. It is not clear whether Chinese artists were actually transferred to the Ilkhanid courts and trained local artists or if it was mostly a matter of wide circulation of Chinese textiles, works on paper and other works of art in Western Asia that influenced local artists. Masuya, 1997, pp. 31–5; Rossabi, 2002, p. 35.

[75] The verses taken from the *Shāh-nāma* are discussed by Melikian-Chirvani, 1991 and 1997b; and Ghouchani, 1992. Cf. Masuya, 1997, pp. 377–405.

[76] Melikian-Chirvani, 1984 and *idem*, 1991. Cf. Kadoi, 2008, p. 51.

[77] Melikian-Chirvani, 1997b, p. 155.

[78] Cf. *idem*, 1991, pp. 33–148, and *idem*, 1997b, p. 136.

[79] *Idem*, 1997b, p. 136.

[80] Tr. Boyle, 1912–37, vol. 2, p. 402.

[81] *Idem*, p. 407.

allel Mongol exploits with those of the formidable hero Afrāsīyāb, a well-known figure in Iranian epic from the Avestan texts to the *Shāh-nāma*, the mythical king of Tūrān (the Central Asian region beyond the Jayḥūn/Āmū Daryā), which after the appearance of the Turks in the sixth century was mostly used in the sense of Turkestan, or the land of the Turks,[82] the legendary nemesis of Iran. In the *Taʾrīkh-i jahān-gushāy*, Juwaynī identifies Genghis Khān as the new Afrāsīyāb:

> For that king is a male dragon panting for vengeance,
> A cloud of calamity.
> A mountain of hard rock becomes like a sea of water if
> It hears the name of Afrāsīyāb.[83]

Drawing on dragon symbolism to evoke the conqueror Genghis Khān was also part of a rhetoric that indicated a shift in political power and sought to explain the change in political fortune indicated by the metaphor of the portentous transformation of the "male dragon panting for vengeance" into a "cloud of calamity."

Pictorial and textual citations from the history of ancient Iranian kingship were long considered an appropriate subject for the decoration of palatial buildings. The inclusion of verses from the epic probably belonged to an established decorative programme, also used, according to the chronicler Ibn Bībī, in 618/1221 to decorate the walls of the palaces of the Rūm Saljuq *sulṭān* ʿAlāʾ al-Dīn Kay Qubādh I (r. 616/1219–634/1237) at Konya and Sivas.[84]

One of the episodes from the *Shāh-nāma* depicted on several tiles shows the story of the hero Farīdūn in his fight against the tyrant Ẓaḥḥāk (al-Ḍaḥḥāk)/Dahāk.[85] Another tile type shows Farīdūn with his bull-headed mace riding on a cow going into battle against Ẓaḥḥāk.[86] Yet another, which exists only in several fragments, shows a similar procession with the chained Ẓaḥḥāk on foot.[87] It is interesting that on one of the fragments the excavators of Takht-i Sulaimān recognised two snakes wound around the head of Ẓaḥḥāk[88] who, otherwise, is characteristically portrayed with snakes growing out of each shoulder.[89]

Other scenes show horsemen fighting with dragons. This is when the "Saljuq-style" dragon makes an appearance on the lustre-painted frieze tiles featuring riders with drawn swords attacking the mythical creatures.[90] Thus, notably in depictions of heroic deeds from the ancient past, artists do not draw on the newly introduced Chinese-inspired Mongol iconography to portray the dragon, preferring the well-known representation that was current throughout medieval Western Asia. Hence while the Ilkhanid period brought new iconographic themes of "Chinese" derivation, such as the dragon and phoenix, these did not immediately override earlier visual traditions. However, the combination of subject matter and styles of both Chinese and Western Asian deriva-

---

[82] Barthold, 1932–5, repr. 1962, pp. 86–7.

[83] Tr. Boyle, 1912–37, vol. 2, pp. 408–9. Cf. Melikian-Chirvani, 1984, pp. 301, 323–4. Significantly, the metaphorical association of Afrāsīyāb with the dragon is reflected in his role in the ancient scriptures of Zoroastrianism. According to the Yasht hymn, Afrāsīyāb's powers included the suppression of waters, draining of rivers, causing of drought, famine and destruction. The scriptures stress Afrāsīyāb's repeated but largely unsuccessful attempts to attain the *farr* (divine fortune, glory), which he desired by, for example, sacrificing one hundred horses, one thousand cattle, and ten thousand sheep to the fertility goddess Ardvī Sūrā Anāhitā (Yasht 5.41–53). However, as Iran's arch-enemy, only his defeat by the Iranian kings such as Zav and Kay Khusrow caused the rivers to flow and the land to prosper. The Afrāsīyāb-myths were combined with a number of legends that mirrored the recurrent attacks on Iranian settlements by the nomads of the Central Asian steppes during the migration period of the various nomadic tribes such as the Saka (the Scythians), the Yuezhi, the Kushans, the Huns, the Hephtalites, the Kidarites and the Turks. See Yarshater, "Afrāsīyāb," *EIr*; Zaehner, 1961, p. 151. The association of the king of the Tūrānians in the Iranian national epic with a Turkic ruler has a precedent in Turkic Qarakhanid culture, to whom contemporary Islamic sources often refer as *Āl-i Afrāsīyāb* ("House of Afrāsīyāb"). This is related to the epic cycle of the Qarakhanids which celebrates the exploits of Afrāsīyāb who was adopted as ancestor by the founder of the dynasty and was identified with the Turkish hero Alp Er Tonga. Maḥmūd al-Kāshgharī, *Dīwān Lughāt al-turk*, tr. Atalay, B., Ankara, 1939–1943, vol. 1, pp. 41, 159–60, 343, 381, 396, 410, 413–4, 466, 486; vol. 3, 149–51, 157, 368, as cited in Mélikoff, 1960, vol. 1, p. 43.

[84] Bombaci, 1966, p. 39, n. 5.

[85] Simpson, 1985, pp. 139–40; *Legacy*, 2002, cat. no. 95.

[86] Naumann, E. and R., 1969, p. 52, fig. 10; Simpson, 1985, fig. 15; Masuya, 1997, pp. 530–4, fig. 6-2-4, pl. 215. For a discussion of the representation of Farīdūn on medieval Islamic ceramics and metalwork, see Simpson, 1985, pp. 131–49.

[87] Masuya, 1997, p. 539, fig. 6-2-6, pl. 220.

[88] Naumann, E. and R., 1969, p. 51.

[89] See pp. 8, 39, 118, n. 71, 119, n. 77, 164, 219.

[90] Masuya (1997, pp. 536–7) identifies two tiles made from the same mould: *Okayama Shiritsu Oriento Bijutsu-kan* ("Okayama Municipal Museum of Near Eastern Art"), catalogue of the collection of the museum, Okayama, 1979, cat. no. 336; Sotheby's, *Catalogue of Islamic Ceramics, Metalwork, Arms and Armour, Glass and Other Islamic Works of Art*, London, April 12, 1976, lot no. 103.

tion on the Takht-i Sulaimān tiles might be considered an important testimony to the meeting and merging of cultural elements from Eastern and Western Asia as well as evidence of early acculturation in the development of an Ilkhanid idiom.

Both the choice of site for the palace, in its implicit appropriation of a past dynasty's legacy of power and ancient affiliations with Iranian spiritual strength, and the themes of the tile decoration with Chinese and Iranian symbols of royalty, indicate that the Ilkhanid rulers were trying to enhance their strategic representation. Their aim was to communicate the legitimacy and charisma of Ilkhanid rule as well as to accumulate "spiritual," in other words political, power since for the Mongols "the fashioning of a capital was a statement of material and spiritual riches."[91]

Until the adoption of Islam as state religion, the early Ilkhanid calendar was based on the astronomically determined twelve animal cycle of years, the so-called "Chinese-Uighur" calendar, in which the year was perceived as starting in spring and the main unit of time was the alternation between winter and summer encampments.[92] According to this system which was well-established in Central Asia, each year is associated with an animal; the cycle comprising rat, buffalo, leopard, rabbit, dragon, serpent, horse, sheep, monkey, rooster, dog and pig.[93] In ancient Turkish mythology the two animals of the twelve animal calendar, the serpent *(yılan)* and the dragon *(luu)*, are related.[94] The origin of the animal cycle has been much debated, and it remains uncertain whether it can be associated with a Chinese or Central Asian origin.[95] It was used in Khotanese, Sogdian, Buddhist Sanskrit, Tocharian, Gandhāran, and Turkic accounts as well as Chinese where the cycle had taken root during the Tang period.[96]

Some Ilkhanid-period works of art have been associated with this calendar, such as the identical animal scroll reliefs that adorn either side of the portal façade flanking the top corners of the door of the Gök *madrasa* in Sivas, where a prominent dragon head projects from amidst the cluster of animal heads (fig. 190). The construction of the *madrasa* was funded by the powerful vizier of the last period of the Saljuqs of Konya, Fakhr al-Dīn ʿAlī Ṣāḥib Aṭaʾ (d. 687/1288–9), in 670/1271–2 when the Saljuqs were vassals of the Ilkhanids. In the same year two further *madrasa*s were erected in Sivas, the Çifte Minare *madrasa* commissioned by the Ilkhanid vizier Shams al-Dīn Juwaynī and another *madrasa* ordered by al-Muẓaffar ibn Hibat-Allāh al-Barujirdī, a private individual of whom only the name is known. These were the first Ilkhanid-sponsored buildings in the city, which was the place of residence of the Mongol governors, and reflect the change from Saljuq to Ilkhanid hegemony. It is against this background that Fakhr al-Dīn ʿAlī appears to have sought to consolidate his own power base by training a group of Muslim bureaucrats at the Gök *madrasa* who would support his personal ambitions.[97] While the other two Ilkhanid sponsored *madrasa*s are devoid of zoomorphic depictions, it is noteworthy that only on the façade of the *madrasa* patronised by Fakhr al-Dīn ʿAlī are animal sculptures represented. The manner of their articulation however, in tightly grouped clusters projecting from interlaced stems, was not confined to this one site nor to architectural decoration. A closely related type of imagery with an assemblage of four interlaced dragon heads appears on a two-dimensional medium, an illumination in a thirteenth-century Armenian collection of sermons illustrated in the monastery of Surb Karapet near Baghesh (Bitlis) (fig. 191).

The dragon motif similarly makes an appearance on the Sunqur Beg Mosque in Niğde in south-central Anatolia, built in the Saljuq period but restored in 736/1335 by the Ilkhanid governor Sayf al-Dīn Sunqur Ağa during the reign of the last major Ilkhanid sovereign Abū Saʿīd Baḥādur Khān. The rectangular side panels that flank the portal are framed by *rinceaux* of vegetal scrolls which bear animal heads, including dragon heads with "Saljuq-style" snouts (fig. 192). Hence, more than fifty years after the construction of the Gök *madrasa* the iconography of the dragon remained remarkably consistent. It is, moreover, noteworthy that zoomorphic creatures, fantastic and nat-

[91] Allsen, 1996, p. 130.

[92] See Melville, 1994; van Dalen, 2002, pp. 327–56, esp. pp. 333–5.

[93] Alternatively these could be replaced by the following animals: rat/mouse, buffalo (bull/cow), feline (leopard or tiger, rarely replaced by a lion or fox), hare (rabbit), dragon (rarely replaced by a lizard, giraffe, bird or fish), serpent, horse, sheep/goat, monkey (rarely replaced by a human), rooster (cock/hen), dog (rarely replaced by a crane), and pig/boar (rarely replaced by a goat). *Rashiduddin Fazlullah's Jamiʿu't-tawarikh,* tr. Thackston, vol. 1, 1998–9, p. xxix.

[94] Boratav, "Schlange," *WdM* VII, 1, p. 248.

[95] Cf. Needham and Wang, 1954, pp. 405–6.

[96] Cf. Whitfield, 2004, London, p. 233; Panaino, "Calendar," *EIr*.

[97] Wolper, 1995, p. 44.

uralistic, are depicted in the portals of sacred monuments, such as a *madrasa* and a mosque. As discussed earlier, the placement of the dragon theme relates to its role in protecting the vulnerable zone at the threshold of the monuments representing the liminal or transitory passage, in other words the interface of the exterior with the interior. Such use invokes dragon imagery in its apotropaic capacity. As guardian of the threshold the dragon is a powerful force to ward off evil and afford protection against any dangerous influences. The dragons on the Sunqur Beg Mosque represent rare Ilkhanid-period examples[98] which continue a tradition that appears to have begun during the rule of the Saljuqs of Rūm, as evidenced by examples of sacred architecture such as the Ak Mosque (617/1220–634/1237) at Anamur, the Great Mosque (626/1228–9 or later) at Divriği, the "Kiosk Mosque" at Sultan Han (between 629/1232 and 633/1236) near Kayseri, and the Çifte Minare *madrasa* (before 640/1242–3) at Erzurum.

The association of the reliefs on the Gök *madrasa* with the duodecimal animal cycle that was introduced through the Ilkhanids was first proposed by Ernst Diez.[99] This hypothesis was elaborated by Otto-Dorn and is followed by several Turkish authors,[100] but has been challenged by Roux who does not believe that this calendar was represented in Islamic art.[101] Controversy also surrounds closely related depictions on a tile type found at Takht-i Sulaimān, of which several fragments and complete examples survive.[102] The spandrels between upper and lower bands of the lustre-painted square tiles show relief scrolls bearing animal heads among which long-eared dragon heads can perhaps be made out. The excavators of Takht-i Sulaimān, Elisabeth and Rudolf Naumann, as well as Johanna Zick-Nissen similarly associate the depiction with the duodecimal animal cycle.[103] Baer explains the motif as a reflection of the legendary talking or *wāqwāq* tree of the *Alexander Romance*[104] associated also with the Iskandar cycle of the *Shāh-nāma*,[105] which Iskandar is said to have encountered during his travels to the ends of the earth.[106] Said to grow in some of the Indian islands, this fabulous tree bears fruits resembling human heads which utter the sound *wāqwāq* when named. The theme recurs frequently in manuscripts of the "Wonders of the World" genre (for instance in the works of the thirteenth-century cosmographer al-Qazwīnī) and is perhaps related to that of the Zaqqūm tree mentioned in the Qur'ān on which demons' heads grow instead of fruit (*sūra* 37, 62–8). The iconographic rendering of the Gök *madrasa* reliefs is closely related to the "inhabited scroll" motif referred to earlier, which may have its origin in Khurasan, where the first datable instance occurs on marble slabs, possibly from a palace of a Ghaznawid sovereign at Ghazna.[107] It is therefore conceivable that the animal heads fixed to *rinceaux* do not illustrate any particular story but reflect, rather, an overall spirit of wonder at the mythical hybrids thought to exist beyond the outer reaches of the known earth and as such imbued with prophylactic and talismanic qualities.[108]

Until the death of the Great Khān Qubilai (Qūbīlāy) in 694/1295, the Ilkhanids were subordinate to the larger empire of the Great Khān in China. This became different when Ghāzān Maḥmūd Khān (r. 694/1295–703/1304), the seventh and possibly the greatest Ilkhanid ruler, marked the outset of his reign by officially professing the Muslim faith, when he declared himself *pādishāh-i Īrān va Islām* ("emperor of Iran and Islam").[109] The conversion to Islam signalled

[98] A further example is the mausoleum of Hüdavend Hatun (712/1312) in Niğde, discussed on pp. 75–6, 123.

[99] Diez, 1949, pp. 99–104.

[100] Otto-Dorn, 1963, pp. 131–3, 143, and *eadem*, 1978–9, pp. 142–5.

[101] Roux, 1978, pp. 239–41. See also Di Cosmo, 2002, p. 280.

[102] Melikian-Chirvani, 1984, figs. 3–14; Masuya, 1997, pp. 484–92, fig. 6-1-g.

[103] Naumann, E. and R., 1976, p. 48; *Museum für Islamische Kunst*, catalogue of the collection of the museum, Berlin, 1979, p. 122.

[104] Baer, 1965, pp. 66–8. On the theme of the talking tree, see the Ethiopic version of the Pseudo-Callisthenes, tr. and ed. Budge, 1889, repr. 2003, p. cii, and the Syriac versian, *idem*, pp. 104–6. The Hellenistic poet Callimachus (310/305–240 BC) even describes a contest of talking trees (*Iambus* IV).

[105] Tr. and ed. Mohl, 1838–1878, vol. 5, pp. 229–33.

[106] The *wāqwāq* tree thereby transforms into the oracular Tree of the Sun and Moon which through its heads is said to have informed Iskandar of his approaching death. Cf. Ackerman, 1935, pp. 67–72. For illustrations of the *wāqwāq* tree, see for instance Martin, 1908, repr. 1968, vol. 1, p. 21, fig. 10.

[107] See pp. 69–70.

[108] See also Baer (1965, p. 68) who suggests that in the popular imagination these *rinceaux* were imbued with a specific meaning related to magical transformation and were not merely traditional ornaments.

[109] Fragner, 2006, p. 73. The official profession of the Islamic faith is emblematised in the Arabic inscription of the *shahāda* ("There is no god but God and Muḥammad is the Messenger of God") which Ghāzān Khān had inscribed on a gold coin that was struck at Shiraz in 700/1300–1, yet at the same time he remained culturally close to his Mongol identity by inscribing the reverse in Uighur, stating "struck by Ghāzān by the Power of Heaven" and adding his Muslim

the transformation of the Ilkhanids into an Islamic dynasty, perhaps in an effort to secure their power in relation to the Mamlūks in Egypt and to relate themselves historically, ethnically and linguistically to their Muslim subjects. Ghāzān underlined the independent status he intended to take by using the title Khān.[110] Yet in spite of having thus become more independent from the Mongol empire, the Ilkhans seem to have continued to pledge their loyalty at least nominally to the Mongol institution of the *yasa*, the tribal laws of the Mongols as codified by Genghis Khān, a system that was of singular historical significance to the Mongols even though with the introduction of Islamic law it had *de facto* lost its validity.[111]

The conversion of the Ilkhans to Islam dealt, however, a heavy blow to the hitherto friendly relations of the Mongols with Cilician Armenia. In the year of Ghāzān Khān's ascension to the throne, the Cilician king Het'um II travelled for nearly two months to the Ilkhanid capital Marāgha, an important centre of Christianity during the Mongol period, in the Azerbaijan region of present-day Iran, to meet the Ilkhan ruler at his *ordu* (imperial encampment)[112] in order to receive investiture and, in turn, to present "great gifts." He was warmly welcomed and received a gift of royal apparel, which "advertised [his] right to act on behalf of the sovereign,"[113] an example of gift exchange or reciprocity as tribute which was central to Mongol imperial society.[114] He also successfully petitioned for the rescinding of an order to demolish all Christian churches.[115] The kingdom of Cilicia had friendly relations and maintained regular contact with the Mongol court in Qaraqorum and later in Khānbāliq from the mid-thirteenth century. Diplomatic relations included several journeys of Armenian princes and kings to the Mongol and Ilkhanid courts and lasted until Ghāzān Khān's death in 703/1304.[116]

Even before Het'um's travel to the Ilkhanids in 1295, depictions of dragons in Armenian manuscripts had acquired stylistic aspects that are characteristic of Chinese and Chinese-inspired Mongol art, reflecting the influence of representations on Chinese silks and other works of art that were imported to Cilicia.[117] Visual evidence of the relations between the Mongol court and their Armenian vassals can already be clearly detected at least a decade earlier in the example of the illuminated lectionary ordered by Het'um II and copied and illustrated in Cilicia in 1286.[118] The spandrels of the trilobed arch of the headpiece of folio 334 are filled with a dragon-and-phoenix motif (fig. 193). The dragon is here shown incorporating some Chinese-derived conventions such as the formidable paws with four unsheathed claws and the undulating tail tucked under one of the hind legs. The soaring phoenix is rendered with outspread wings with delineated plumage and slender fanned tail, its head portrayed with the distinctive curved beak turned upwards to face the dragon's head. Paired together the mythical creatures became symbols of imperial sovereignty in Yuan China and were as such probably deemed appropriate symbols for members of the Armenian imperial family, perhaps Het'um's parents, Levon and Keran.[119] The depiction also reflects the fascination with imaginary animals of Far Eastern derivation. An example of the direct appropriation of the image of the Chinese dragon can be seen in the donor portrait of Archbishop John (Yovhannes), the half-brother of the Cilician king Het'um I, in the Gospel he commissioned in 1289. The lower hem of his tunic carries an appliquéd piece of cloth embellished in gold with a standing Chinese dragon, the head with gaping mouth in profile, all outlined in red on a white background.[120] Sirarpie Der Nersessian surmises that the textile represents a Chinese silk which may have been brought by one of John's brothers who had visited the Mongol court or an

name, Ghāzān Maḥmūd, written in Arabic between the lines. See Phillips, 1969, p. 121, fig. 32 (drawing) and pl. 38g (British Museum).

[110] Spuler, 1939, repr. 1955, pp. 225–6.

[111] *Idem*, pp. 220–3, 312. Cf. Allsen, 2001, p. 22.

[112] Het'um II had set out to meet the Ilkhanid ruler Baidu, but when Ghāzān Khān wrested power from the latter and ascended to the throne, he paid his respects to the new sovereign.

[113] Allsen, 1997, pp. 93–4.

[114] *Idem*, pp. 27–70 and 99–106, and *idem*, 2001, pp. 31–50.

[115] *The Chronography of Gregory Abû 'l-Faraj*, tr. and ed. Budge, vol. 1, 1932, pp. 505–6.

[116] Early Armenian missions include the visit of Smbat, constable of Armenia, in 1247 to 1250, to the Mongol court of Qaraqorum, followed three years later by that of his brother, king Het'um I, in 1253 to 1255. Het'um I and his son Levon II paid several visits to the Ilkhanid rulers Hülegü, Abāqā and Arghūn from the 1250s to 1280s. See Kouymjian, 2006, pp. 305–8.

[117] Der Nersessian and Agemian, 1993, vol. 1, pp. 124–5.

[118] Yerevan, Matenadaran Ms. 979, fol. 334. See *eidem*, vol. 1, p. 124 and vol. 2, fig. 517.

[119] Cf. Kouymjian, 2006, p. 321.

[120] Yerevan, Matenadaran Ms. 197, fol. 141v, Archbishop John ordaining a priest; see Der Nersessian and Agemian, 1993, vol. 2, fig. 645.

otherwise imported silk which the archbishop may have used for his vestment.[121]

Surviving examples of textiles which were made in Central Asia at about the same time similarly present the dragon in different postures. A famous fragment of a silk tapestry *(kesi)*, which has been dated between 1200 and 1300, shows dragons in rampant posture chasing pearls.[122] Closely related stylistically to the dragons featured on the tile revetments of Takht-i Sulaimān, these are similarly shown with elongated wide-open proboscis-like snouts and their tails hooked under one of the hind legs.

Another textile, a silk and gold thread *lampas* weave, dated to *c.* 1300, which was found in Gdańsk (also known by its German name Danzig), now in the Kunstgewerbemuseum in Berlin, features paired confronted parrots with Arabic inscriptions on their wings and tails with ascending four-clawed dragons of East Asian inspiration rendered in a twisted fashion in the interstices.[123] As noted in the inscription the silk was probably made for the Mamlūk *sulṭān* al-Nāṣir al-Dīn Muḥammad I ibn Qalāwūn (r. from 693/1293 to 694/1294 and from 698/1299 to 741/1341) and offered as a gift by the last Ilkhanid ruler Abū Saʿīd following a truce.[124] A further example, also preserved in the Kunstgewerbemuseum in Berlin, which has been dated between 1275 and 1350, shows coiled dragon motifs set in lobed medallions surmounted by a band of pseudo-inscription composed of interlaced Kufic shafts. At first sight the dragons appear to be distinctly Chinese in style, closely related to the dragons portrayed on Jin brocades[125] or on Yuan textiles.[126] Yet the motif has been adapted to more Iranian interpretations with the pearl being absent and, more importantly, the dragons' tails ending in dragon heads.[127] The depiction on the *lampas* weave also reflects the imperial Mongol policy of large scale movement and resettling of specialist craftsmen drawn from diverse conquered countries to staff their workshops, transforming them into fertile ground for the creation of a range of syncretic expressions.[128]

It moreover shows that luxury items such as textiles served as primary transmitters of visual ideas, techniques, forms and fashions from the East Asian (primarily Chinese) visual culture to the West and played a prominent role in the formulation of new aesthetic idioms in Western Asia.[129] It is noteworthy that together with the monumental dragons carved at the neighbouring site of Viār (fig. 185) and the dragons that emerge in Armenian manuscripts (fig. 193), the dragons depicted in the royal residence at Takht-i Sulaimān (figs. 186a and b, 187a and b), in particular on the tile decoration, seem to be among the earliest instances of the appearance of Chinese-inspired Mongol dragons created in a Western Asian context. It is most likely that the dragon motifs portrayed on Chinese or Central Asian textiles provided a model for the dragons rendered on other media.[130]

The dragon motif continued to be an important symbol in Ilkhanid manuscript illustration, of which one of the very greatest examples, the *Jāmiʿ al-tawārīkh*, was undertaken under Ghāzān Khān. It was at his instigation that the great task of committing the Ilkhanids' universal history to writing was assigned to the eminent grand vizier and patron of learning, Rashīd al-Dīn Faḍlallāh Hamadānī Ṭabīb (*c.* 645/1247), a convert from Judaism. Intended to promote Mongol identity and transmit a written record of its distinctive history and achievements,[131] the *Jāmiʿ al-tawārīkh* centres on Mongol history. This ideological operation was made to fit into the literary mould of the subject population, aiming to place the Mongol Ilkhanids as rightful successors of the previous "legitimate" kings in Iran, thereby justifying ideologically the political process of amalgamating pre-conquest Iranian and Mongol Ilkhanid identity into one unified structure.[132] Completed only after Ghāzān's death during the

[121] *Eidem*, vol. 1, p. 158.

[122] The Cleveland Museum of Art, inv. no. 1988.33; Watts and Wardwell, 1997, cat. no. 17, for related examples see p. 55, fig. 12, p. 68, fig. 22, p. 75, figs. 26 and 27, and cat. nos. 13, 14, 18. Cf. Kadoi, 2008, p. 20, fig. 1.1.

[123] Inv. no. 1875-258. Wardwell, 1988–9, fig. 19; von Wilckens, 1992, pp. 47–8, no. 75; *Legacy*, 2002, fig. 75, cat. no. 71; Kadoi, 2008, p. 26, fig. 1.6.

[124] The inscriptions read, "Glory to our lord the *sulṭān*, the king, the just, the wise Nāṣir," at the centre is the name "Muḥammad." *Arts of Islam*, 1976, p. 80; Wardwell, 1988–9, p. 101.

[125] Watts and Wardwell, 1997, cat. no. 30; *Legacy*, 2002, fig. 2002, cat. no. 181; Kadoi, 2008, p. 27, fig. 1.8.

[126] For instance, Watts and Wardwell, 1997, cat. no. 42.

[127] Inv. no. 00.53. Watts and Wardwell, 1997, p. 139, fig. 68; Kadoi, 2008, p. 27, fig. 1.7.

[128] See Dode, 2007, pp. 100–13.

[129] The agency of the Mongols as "prime movers" in the long-distance east-west exchange and patrons of cultural transmission has been demonstrated by Allsen, 2001, pp. 3–16, 193–211. See also *Legacy*, 2002, p. 183.

[130] Cf. Kadoi, 2008, p. 107.

[131] Tr. Thackston, vol. 1, 1998–9, p. 18.

[132] *Idem*, pp. 27–8.

reign of Muḥammad Khudābandah Öljeitü in 706/1307–8, the compendium was probably transcribed and illustrated under the supervision of its author.[133] By securing the preservation of his writings and their transmission, Rashīd al-Dīn ensured that both he and the *pādishāh-i Īrān va Islām* (as both Ghāzān and Öljeitü were called) would be remembered by posterity.[134]

Rashīd al-Dīn, who served the Ilkhanids Ghāzān and Öljeitü, had entered service in the Ilkhanid court as a physician (hence his appellation Ṭabīb, the physician). Not least through realising the *Jāmiʿ al-tawārīkh*, he became one of the key figures in the relationship between Yuan China and the Iranian world during the Ilkhanid period. His first volume, devoted to an official history of the Mongols and their conquests, is particularly informative since the vizier relied very largely on oral information, partly provided by Ghāzān Khān himself, and partly by the personal representative of the Great Khān, Bolād Zhengxiang (Pers. Pūlād Chīngsāng, d. 712/1313), who repeated to him passages from the now lost so-called *Altin Defter* ("Golden Book"), the official Mongol chronicle.[135]

According to Rashīd al-Dīn's deed of endowment *(waqfnāma)* dated 709/1309, he created and sponsored a foundation, the Rab-ʿi Rashīdī ("Rashid's quarter"), in an outlying quarter of Tabriz, which served as a centre of intellectual activity with numerous buildings including a mosque, *madrasa*, *khānaqāh* (dervish lodge), a hospital as well as a vast library and a scriptorium. In the latter the *Jāmiʿ al-tawārīkh* and other texts authored by Rashīd al-Dīn (which were to be bilingual, that is to say copied in both Arabic and Persian, the two main literary languages of the Ilkhanid empire and the neighbouring states), were illustrated and illuminated, and then disseminated throughout the empire.[136]

The second volume of the *Jāmiʿ al-tawārīkh* deals with the histories of the "ancient kings," the pre-Islamic rulers, then addresses Islamic history from the time of the Prophet Muḥammad to the arrival of the Mongols. Again this relied very largely on oral reports of native informants concerning the other peoples of the world with whom the Mongols came into contact.[137]

The dragon makes an appearance in the text as well as in the paintings. In the section on the history of the Saljuqs an account is given of the Great Saljuq *sulṭān* Muḥammad ibn Malik Shāh, which details how at the beginning of his reign in 501/1108 he overthrew and killed the Mazyadid Sayf al-Dawla Ṣadaqa and the amīr Ayāz.[138] Around the contenders a large army had gathered "in such a fashion that drawing up ranks for battle, their splendour and equipment outshone the Sultans." In spite of this:

> The Sultan had the aid of heaven and the assistance of the Lord.
> They have written that, on that day of battle, black clouds, fire, thunder and lightning had appeared above the enemy, as well as the form of a dragon out of whose mouth fire was coming, so that the whole group threw away their weapons. They recognized death, and beheld the fear and terror of the Resurrection.[139]

Rashīd al-Dīn's description draws on visual signs of nature which include black clouds, fire, thunder and lightning. He appears to allude to imagery used in the Qurʾān (*sūra* 2, 55–6):

> And when you said, "O Moses, we shall not believe in you, until we see Allah manifestly," the thunderbolt struck you, while you were looking on. Then we made you alive after your death, so that you might give thanks.

The natural phenomenon of the thunderbolt thus serves the purposes of heaven, miraculously hindering human vision. At the same time Rashīd al-Dīn touches upon a Mongol belief according to which:

> ...lightning storms come from an animal like a dragon, and in that region they witness it coming down out of the air onto the ground, striking its tail against the earth, coiling around itself, and pouring fire from its mouth.[140]

---

133 Blair, 1995, p. 14.

134 Hoffmann, 2000, p. 73.

135 Spuler, 1939, repr. 1955, pp. 221–2; Allsen, 2001, pp. 73–5.

136 "Articles of Endowment of the Rab-ʿi Rashidi," tr. Thackston, 1995, pp. 114–5.

137 Two substantial groups of folios written in Arabic survive from a grand illustrated copy of the *Jāmiʿ al-tawārīkh* produced in 714/1314–5, now housed in the Edinburgh University Library, and the Nasser D. Khalili Collection of Islamic Art (formerly the Royal Asiatic Society), London.

138 For the section on the history of the Saljūqs, Rashīd al-Dīn and his compilers probably relied heavily on the *Saljūq-nāma* of Ẓāhir al-Dīn Nīshāpūrī, written in *c.* 584/1188 for the last Great Saljūq *sulṭān* Ṭoghrıl III ibn Arslan (r. 571/1176–590/1194).

139 *The History of the Seljuk Turks*, tr. Luther and ed. Bosworth, 2001, p. 73.

140 Tr. Thackston, vol. 1, 1998–9, p. 82. Cf. Roux, 1978, p. 122.

In literary sources such as the *Shāh-nāma* throne imagery is associated with the dragon. The throne of Qaidāfa, queen of Andalusia, is described for example as having dragon-like feet.[141] At the same time dragon iconography was often visually connected with scenes of enthronement. Among the earliest surviving folios that were illustrated under the supervision of Rashīd al-Dīn are four that portray rulers seated on pedestal thrones with high columnar legs and raised footstools. The edges of the segmented backrests of the thrones are decorated with horizontally projecting dragon-headed finials.[142] In the compilation of histories of the "ancient kings," the throne of Jamshīd/Yima, the legendary Kayānid emperor of Iran, who encouraged the invention of weapons and the development of the crafts, is guarded by confronted dragon heads with curved, cervid-type antlers, long, floating manes and "beards," their prominent snouts tapering to an upward curl.[143] The representation of the dragon heads thus follow a Chinese-style koiné, one of the prime characteristics of which is its stag-like horns,[144] a feature also present on the dragons depicted on the tiles of the royal residence at Takht-i Sulaimān.

The accession scene of *sulṭān* Lohrāsp in Balkh shows the back of the throne surmounted by dragon heads with closed snouts turned away from the ruler.[145] Likewise, the finials of the throne of his son, the dragon-fighter Gushtāsp (who slew a wolf with the features of a dragon and went on to slay a dragon)[146] terminate in dragon heads facing away from the ruler, which are closely comparable to those on his father's throne but with two curved horns.[147] It is notable that while Jamshīd is flanked by confronted dragon heads that appear to be attentive and hence more likely to bestow their protective qualities upon him, Lohrāsp and Gushtāsp are, on the contrary, flanked by outward-facing dragon heads.

In Rashīd al-Dīn's section on the history of India, the Kashmiri Buddhist Kamāla Shrī, who served in the Mongol court, seems to have been a source of information for the history of the later sultans of Delhi as well as of Kashmir and for Sanskrit sources of the life and the teachings of the Buddha.[148] In the illustrations for this section the king of Kashmir, Yashaskara (r. 939–948), is seated on the dragon-throne. His enthronement scene portrays nobles and Brahmans choosing the *faqīr* as new ruler, recognising that in spite of his poverty he has the power of persuasion (fig. 194). The continued use of the motif of the enthroned ruler flanked by two upright elements topped by dragon heads shows that the convention to some extent persisted in the Mongol period, with the difference that stylistically the "Saljuq-style" dragons gave way to dragon representations with a Chinese-style veneer.[149]

The dragon-throne motif appears on another Ilkhanid-period miniature in the Topkapı Sarayı Library, Istanbul, attributed to *c.* 700/1300, which illustrates a court scene.[150] It portrays an unidentified nimbate ruler in the conventional pose of rulership, seated cross-legged on the cushioned throne raising his right hand to chest level and framed by courtiers. The ruler is shown in frontal view and is larger than his attendants, whose densely drawn courtly pastimes emphasise the centrality of the sovereign's throne. The portrayal follows the iconographical canon of the frontally

[141] Tr. and ed. Mohl, 1838–1878, vol. 5, p. 187, ll. 1032–1033.

[142] Cf. Donovan's discussion (1998–9, pp. 34–41) of this type of pedestal thrones in the *Jāmiʿ al-tawārīkh*.

[143] Talbot-Rice, 1957, p. 49, ill. 5.

[144] In China the hybrid composition of the dragon came to be known as the "nine resemblances" *(jiu si)*, a definition ascribed to the ancient Chinese philosopher, Wang Fu, who writing in the time of the Han dynasty (206 BC–220 AD) claimed that the dragon incorporated the bodily parts of nine other animals (the horns of a deer, the head of a camel, the eyes of a demon, the neck of a serpent, the belly of a sea monster, the scales of a carp, the claws of an eagle, the foot-pads of a tiger and the ears of an ox). *Erya yi* ("Ramifications of the Literary Expositor"), compiled by Luo Yuan (1136–1184), 28.297, as cited in Sterckx, 2002, p. 180.

[145] Talbot-Rice, 1957, p. 71, ill. 16.

[146] *Shāh-nāma*, tr. and ed. Mohl, 1838–1878, vol. 5, p. 333, ll. 643–4; also pp. 305, l. 306; 309, l. 362; 315, l. 437; 317, l. 455.

[147] Pope and Ackerman, eds., 1938–9, repr. 1964–81, vol. 4, pl. 827 A; Edinburgh University Library. Talbot-Rice, 1957, p. 75, ill. 18.

[148] *Die Indiengeschichte des Rašīd ud-Dīn*, tr. and ed. Jahn, 1980, pp. 8–9, 19.

[149] Melikian-Chirvani (1997b, p. 160) points out that in the illustrations of the surviving folios of Rashīd al-Dīn's *Jāmiʿ al-tawārīkh*, none of the thrones of the rulers of the Islamicised world show dragon-headed finials fitted to their arched backs. However, since only part of the manuscript survives and the dragon-throne motif appears on other Ilkhanid-period miniatures, apparently for rulers of the Islamic period (see for instance the example (fig. 195) cited below), there may be no grounds for a distinction between the depiction of the thrones of rulers of the pre-Islamic and those of the Islamic world.

[150] For another example of a throne lavishly decorated with dragons, see an illustration from a *Jāmiʿ al-tawārīkh*, dated *c.* 715/1315, showing the enthroned Ilkhanid ruler Ögödei and his wife while receiving ambassadors. Martin, 1912, repr. 1968, vol. 2, pl. 43 reproduction to the left.

rendered cross-legged ruler which became ingrained in the Near and Central Asian regions at the beginning of the Christian era. The conventional depiction of the two winged flying geniis hovering over the sovereign while holding a shawl at either end was probably intended to bring heavenly fortune. On the back of the imposing throne, oriented towards the ruler, are inward-curving golden dragon-headed finials. Crowned by a pair of bifurcated antlers, the long upturned snouts revealing sharp teeth and elongated tongue, a tangled mass of mane fluttering at the back and beard projecting from the chin, they are closely related to the dragon heads in the *Jāmiʿ al-tawārīkh* produced in 714/1314–5. The figures are rendered as ethnically East Asian, presumably Mongol, identifiable not only by their physiognomies with slant eyes, small mouths and round jaws but also their attire, while the scalloped upper edge of the ceremonial chair recalls Chinese-style models and is decorated all over with floral representations that also follow sinicised conventions, gold palmette-like blossoms set against a black background (fig. 195). From the tip of the cusped apex of the throne back projects a tall, stemmed foliage bracketed at the stem from which issue stemmed blossoms held by smaller such brackets. The vegetal composition is flanked by the dragon heads. It is interesting to compare the representation to the similarly lavish descriptions known of Qubilai's throne at Khānbāliq:

> ...ornamented with dragons among clouds, and with a white awning and cushions embroidered in gold.[151]

Other emblems of power such as the dragon rod of Mūsā are also illustrated in the surviving folios of the *Jāmiʿ al-tawārīkh* of Rashīd al-Dīn, transcribed and illuminated in Tabriz under the supervision of the vizier.[152] In one of the miniatures Mūsā, Hārūn ibn ʿImrān (Aaron) and the Israelites stand watching the Egyptians drown in the Red Sea (Qurʾān, *sūra* 28, 76–82), while Mūsā is shown supporting himself on an elongated staff that ends in a typically "Saljuq-style" dragon head with small pointed ears and prominent outward-curling snout tip, the wide-open mouth revealing the teeth and the tongue.

In the same vein, the stirrup was associated with royalty in Mongol society. Juwaynī whose family from Khurasan had been accustomed to serve in the Mongol administration, records in his *Taʾrīkh-i jahān-gushāy* that "the sign of a great emir [among the Mongols] was that his stirrups were of iron."[153] The use of dragon protomes on a thirteenth-century Mongol iron stirrup fragment, excavated in Qaraqorum, may therefore reflect the exalted status accorded to the stirrup in Mongol society. The inward-facing heads, which Hans-Georg Hüttel identifies as lupine dragon heads,[154] top the crossbar of the stirrup and are pictured with gaping jaws flanking the slot for the stirrup strap (fig. 196).[155]

The affiliation of the dragon symbolism with royalty[156] took many forms. In the Avestan texts the Iranian mythic hero-king Farīdūn brilliantly defeated the three-headed, six-eyed dragon Dahāka and fettered and imprisoned the beast on Mount Damāwand,[157] achieving this feat not least on account of the magical powers attributed to him.[158] Imbued with these powers, Farīdūn was even able to assume the shape of the beast he had vanquished, which he did to test the worthiness of his three sons, Salm, Tūr and Iraj; whereupon:

> ...he roared, belched anger, sowed terror, and flames came out of his mouth. When his three sons drew near, he saw the mountains had darkened around; he arose, with the clouds of dust about his feet, bearing rage and filled the world with roar and howl.[159]

After judging his sons' reactions to these events, he divided his kingdom between them, Salm receiving the Near East, Tūr the Central Asian region beyond the Jayḥūn/Āmū Daryā (Tūrān), and Iraj the centre, Iran.[160] The scene is portrayed in a miniature from the so-called small (that is, small-format) *Shāh-nāma* group of manuscripts,

---

[151] Itō Chūta, *Shinakenchiku sōshoku* ("Chinese Architecture and Decoration"), 5 vols., Tokyo, 1943, vol. 1, p. 89, cited after Shatzman Steinhardt, 1988, p. 72.

[152] Martin, 1912, repr. 1968, vol. 1, p. 24, fig. 12; Talbot-Rice, 1957, p. 61, cat. no. 11.

[153] Tr. Boyle, 1912–37, vol. 1, p. 22.

[154] *Dschingis Khan und seine Erben*, 2005, pp. 166–7, cat. no. 151 (catalogue entry by Hans-Georg Hüttel).

[155] Cf. also a pair of stirrups in gold, silver and iron from Tibet or Mongolia, tentatively dated between the twelfth and the fourteenth century with outward-facing dragon-heads, now in The Metropolitan Museum, New York, inv. no. 1999.119a, b. See LaRocca, 2006, p. 243, cat. no. 127.

[156] See chapter 7.

[157] Yasht 5.33–5, 15.23–4; Yasna 9.7–8; Vīdēvdāt 1.18.

[158] Yasht 5.61–5. Cf. Tafaẓẓolī, "Ferēdūn," *EIr.*

[159] Dulęba, 1995, p. 58.

[160] *Shāh-nāma*, tr. and ed. Mohl, 1838–1878, vol. 1, p. 135.

datable to *c.* 1300. Even though it portrays a scene from Iran's epic past, the riders are depicted as ethnically Mongolian and/or Turkic, identifiable by their countenance and their apparel. The depiction may once again illustrate the conscious effort of the Mongols to use ancient Iranian legends "to create a visual connection between past and present, equating, and thus legitimizing, Mongol rule and rulers with that of Iran's legendary and historical dynasties."[161] The horsemen are shown with a giant horned dragon with a powerfully sinuous once looped body (fig. 197).[162] In stylistic terms the representation of this dragon essentially continues Saljuq traditions. The giant ophidian body is still rendered in looped form without legs and dorsal or pectoral fins. Yet the head of the mythical creature is now crowned by cervid-type antlers that project horizontally from the top of the head, a feature that emerged as part of the Chinese-style koiné of the dragon in the period after the Mongol invasion. In spite of the introduction of this new aspect of the head, the giant serpentine knotted body dominates the image. It is thus reasonable to assume that, in particular in the case of the representation of a scene from the *Shāh-nāma*, this stylistic modification did not have a bearing on the dragon's iconological content. Overall it may be noted that the imagery of the "Saljuq-style" dragon, at least the main characteristics such as the long gaping snout with upturned tip and long knotted ophidian body, exhibited a remarkable longevity, especially in the Anatolian region.

However, just as Salm, Tūr, and Iraj are depicted with Mongolian physiognomies and matching attire, so too the dragon, one of the key sinicising motifs introduced into Islamic art, slowly acquired certain Chinese or Chinese-inspired Mongol aspects mirroring the process of a gradual penetration of East Asian art and culture through the agency of the Mongols. The syncretism reflected in the miniature referred to above may be regarded as another example giving visual form to the transitory period of a "melding of Mongol and Persian cultural identities and traditions."[163] Hence it appears that during the second half of their reign the Ilkhanids had integrated Chinese and Central Asian elements into a visual language of their own, gradually forging a syncretic Ilkhanid dynastic ideology which merged with local visual traditions.

Over the following decades the "Saljuq-style" dragon gradually gave way to a "Chinese-style" dragon which is also exemplified, for instance, in the depictions of the dragons portrayed in a manuscript of al-Qazwīnī's *ʿAjāʾib al-makhlūqāt* preserved in the British Library, London (Ms. Or. 14140). Probably executed in the years between 694/1295 and 701/1302 – and perhaps in Mosul under the patronage of the governor Fakhr al-Dīn ʿĪsā (d. 701/1302)[164] – the London Qazwīnī distinguishes between an acquatic (*al-tinnīn*; fol. 48r) and a terrestrial (the giant serpent, *al-thaʿbān*; fol. 127r) dragon.[165] The antlered head of the sea-dragon is closely related to the heads of the dragons of the Viār sculptures or the Takht-i Sulaimān tiles, whereas its body still follows intrinsically the "Saljuq-style." Its marine quality is underlined by undulant serpents springing from from the nape of the neck in lieu of the customary tufts of hair. The Chinese-style head is accentuated by the depiction of small floating Chinese-inspired clouds, sometimes read as fungus-shaped or magical fungus *lingzhi*.[166] The so-called giant serpent is portrayed with a closely related head and, at first sight, appears to have a similar scaly serpentine body. Yet instead of the conventional knot, the fluidly rendered sinuous body, now accentuated with a crest along the spine, has acquired two muscular striding forelegs with two or three

---

[161] Simpson, 2007, p. 385. Cf. Melikian-Chirvani, 1997b.

[162] In the same manuscript a closely related huge knotted dragon is portrayed in the illustration of Isfandiyār's third labour: he fights the dragon (Ms. F1930.4b, f. 085v), whereas the dragons in the scenes of Gushtāsp killing a dragon in Rūm (Ms. F1929.46, f. 074v) and Bahrām Gūr killing a dragon in India (Ms. F1930.10b, f. 121v) are rendered in much more sinicised fashion, characterised by bulging bead-like eyes, straight, slightly gaping, jaws with fleshy flews arranged in folds and long flowing beards springing from the chin and the back of the head.

[163] Simpson, 2007, p. 385.

[164] On the provenance and patronage of the manuscript, see the discussion in Carboni, 1992, pp. 523–38.

[165] Kadoi, 2008, p. 146, figs. 4.20 and 4.21; also the serpent-like fish (*al-tinnīn*; fol. 38r) living in the Persian sea and the big dragon (*al-tinnīn al-ʿaẓīm*; fol. 47r) living in the Caspian sea; cf. Carboni, 1988–9, pp. 20–1, 26. For al-Qazwīnī's description, see *Kitāb ʿajāʾib al-makhlūqāt*, ed. Wüstenfeld, 1849, repr. 1967, pp. 109 and 128–9; also Badiee, 1978, pp. 112 and 120–1. For a discussion of the dragons in the London Qazwīnī, see Carboni, 1992, pp. 495–7. The London Qazwīnī dragons shown on fols. 33 and 47 are more clearly identifiable as giant serpents. Yet it is worthy of note that they are rendered with the typical elongated snouts ending in a rolled-up upper lip and the massive bodies knotted with a large single loop, features that are more characteristic of the "Saljuq-type."

[166] On the *lingzhi* motif, see Rawson, 1984, p. 139.

unsheathed claws. Another newly acquired feature is the band of flames that flickers along the dragon's right leg and above its back, a characteristic already known from Central Asian textiles such as the above-mentioned fragment of a silk tapestry *(kesi)*, dated between 1200 and 1300, featuring dragons chasing pearls.[167] In spite of the fact that the dragon is shown with two rather than four legs, its depiction deserves particular attention because it is one of the earliest adoptions of a complete figure of a Chinese-derived dragon in Iranian painting.[168]

This debt to China is also evident in a miniature from the Great Ilkhanid *Shāh-nāma* of 1330–1335, portraying Bahrām Gūr, one of the most celebrated rulers of the Sasanian dynasty in the *Shāh-nāma*, killing a giant dragon, now in the Cleveland Museum of Art,[169] or in a folio from the so-called "Small *Shāh-nāma*" group of manuscripts, dated 735/1335, featuring Isfandiyār's third course, the dragon-slaying, preserved in the Metropolitan Museum of Art.[170]

The new Chinese-derived elements were thus gradually assimilated into a well-established Western Asian dragon iconography. As has been shown, the iconography of the Chinese-style dragon was meaningful for the Ilkhanids and their entourage but when transmitted to a Western Asian context it gradually disintegrated, to be appropriated only in fragmentary form by the receiving cultural milieu. In the process of diffusion certain stylistic aspects of the Chinese-inspired dragon motif were combined in hybrid fashion with prevailing Islamic artistic features and gradually integrated into existing traditions.[171] The iconographic expression was thus received through a Central Asian filter, resulting in a new creation which came to be *de rigueur* after the Ilkhanid period. This assimilation through osmosis of the dragon imagery also provides eloquent testimony of the crucial role played by the pastoral nomads in the process of east-west exchange.[172] Their creative energy and determined agency underlay the forging of a distinct aesthetic combining Western Asian and East Asian motifs in the post-Mongol period.

b. *Syncretism and the dragon*

The personal interest taken by the Muslim Ilkhans in Islamic mysticism extended to the teachings of wandering dervishes known for their antinomian and heterodox outlook. These dervishes arose from a frontier milieu in Transoxania, Khurasan and Anatolia that was characterised by heroic figures, warrior adventurers and warrior saints that ensued from the age-old pastoral culture of predation but who in later Ottoman chronicles were portrayed as *ghāzīs* fighting for the defence and victory of Islam.[173] It will be shown that in these liminal societies epic-chivalrous frontier narratives were characterised by the heroic valour associated with the dragon as well as the *jihād* against the dragon. The dragon was used as a link to narrative intersections of otherwise unconnected heroic and saintly figures whose identities became connected and often amalgamated. This was complemented by the cross-cultural convergence of saintly cults prominently involving the dragon in which Islamic, Turko-Mongol,

---

[167] On the flame as chinoiserie element, see Kadoi, 2008, pp. 204–5, who also associates the motif of the "flaming dragon" with Chinese dragon paintings; *eadem*, p. 147, fig. 4.22.

[168] Another early depiction of a Chinese-derived dragon appears in a copy of al-Qazwīnī's *ʿAjāʾib al-makhlūqāt*, written and illustrated during the author's lifetime in Wāsiṭ in 678/1279–80 (Munich, Bayerische Staatsbibliothek, Cod. Arab. 464, fol. 73v; see Badiee, 1978, pl. 72). The quadruped dragon is somewhat awkwardly rendered with its hindlegs *marchant* whereas the foreshortened forelegs are slightly raised. While the head overall echoes Chinese-derived models, in spite of the fact that it is not crowned by antlers, the protome thus still follows conventional prototypes. Added features are however the flaming bands rising from the neck and an exaggerated spiky crest projecting from the dragon's back and belly.

[169] Ms. 1943.658; Grabar and Blair, 1980, cat. no. 49; *Legacy*, 2002, fig. 187, cat. no. 56. *Shāh-nāma*, tr. and ed. Mohl, 1838–1878, vol. 6, pp. 41–5, ll. 427–71.

[170] Ms. 1974.290.26; Swietochowski and Carboni, 1994, cat. no. 32. For a description of the feat, see *Shāh-nāma*, tr. and ed. Mohl, 1838–1878, vol. 4, pp. 499–503. The dragon slaying theme is also represented in the illustrations of the *Shāh-nāma* cycles of Hūshang, Farīdūn and Gushtāsp. Cf. Arberry et al., 1959, pl. 4d; Simpson, 1979, figs. 42, 58, 91 and 92; Fitzherbert, 2001, fig. 81. *Shāh-nāma*, tr. and ed. Mohl, 1838–1878, vol. 4, pp. 499–503, ll. 427–71.

[171] As Bertold Spuler (1939, repr. 1955, p. 363) succinctly observes:

> The rising tide of East Asian forms that swept in [with the Mongol onslaught] did not represent a danger to Iranian artists but rather served as inspiration for new work in almost a creative sense. With sovereign mastery they knew how to assimilate foreign elements without being untrue to themselves.

[172] Allsen, 2001, p. 211.

[173] Lindner, 1983, pp. 21–5.

Jewish and Christian beliefs overlapped and merged.

At least from the period of Ghāzān Khān's rule there was a growth in Shīʿite sects as well as a popularisation of *ṣūfī* orders together with an influx of Turkish converts.[174] The Ilkhan took a personal interest in Islamic mysticism, an interest which was shared by his successors and subordinates. While he was governor of Khurasan, even before his conversion, Ghāzān Khān visited the most important places of pilgrimage *(turbat)* of the region such as the graves of the celebrated mystics Abū Yazīd (Bāyazīd) al-Bisṭāmī (d. 261/874 or 264/877–8), Abu 'l-Ḥasan ʿAlī ibn Aḥmad Kharaqānī (d. 425/1033) and Abū Saʿīd ibn Abi 'l-Khayr Mayhanī (d. 440/1049). At that time he also went to see the shrine of the eighth Imam in Mashhad and the imposing mausoleum of *sulṭān* Sanjar near Marw. Later as ruler he paid his respects to the great Shīʿa sanctuaries in Mesopotamia, Najaf and Karbalāʾ which he richly endowed by building irrigation channels as well as accommodation for pilgrims and *sayyid*s.[175]

It is unfortunately not known which shaykh presided over Rashīd al-Dīn's *khānaqāh* and whether he represented a mystic order *(ṭarīqa)*. It is however known that numerous shaykhs visited the *ṣūfī khānaqāh*, for instance, the famed shaykh Ṣafī of Ardabīl (d. 735/1334). Among the mystics that came to visit were also some wandering dervishes *(qalandar*s*)*, often characterised by their bizarre appearance and the fact that they "deliberately embraced a variety of unconventional and socially liminal practices."[176] One prominent representative was shaykh Barāq, a crypto-shamanic Türkmen dervish from Tokat in central Anatolia who scandalised onlookers by his strange appearance. His chin was shaved but he had an oversize moustache and his upper incisor had intentionally been broken off.[177] He would go almost naked but for a loincloth and a kind of felt turban to which bovine horns were attached. Around his neck he had a rope hung with henna-dyed bovine teeth and bells, to the accompaniment of which he would dance in imitation of the movements of apes and bears.[178] When the shaykh came first into the presence of Ghāzān Khān in Tabrīz, a tiger (or, according to some accounts, a lion) was unleashed on him to test his supernatural powers, but Barāq like many mystics could communicate with animals and a shout from him was enough to subdue the wild beast.[179] Thereafter he enjoyed close links with the Ilkhanid court and is said to have exercised some influence over Ghāzān and Öljeitü. In 707/1307–8, on his way to see Öljeitü, Barāq went on an expedition to Gīlān. Near Lāhījān he and some of his followers were intercepted by a group of people, upbraided for being "friends of the Tatars" and killed. Those of his followers who survived the attack took the shaykh's bones back for burial at Sulṭāniyya where a hospice was built for his followers by the Ilkhanid ruler.[180]

The likes of Barāq Bābā arose from a frontier milieu in Transoxania, Khurasan[181] and Anatolia.[182] The boundary regions in which such elements subsisted constituted a refuge for political or religious dissidents as well as wandering bands of soldiers of fortune that provided the core population of this war-like frontier society where many divergent cultural elements came into contact with each other. The groups in which the Turkish ethnic element predominated also served as a source for mercenary recruits. Maḥmūd of Ghazna (r. 389/999–421/1030) for instance is known to have drawn heavily upon this resource of *ghāzī*s for his Indian campaigns.[183]

The Central Asian frontier of Islam became a zone of conversion by the tenth century. For the most part the *ghāzī*s adopted an Iranian version of Islam and maintained some of their own pre-Islamic traditions. Dervish preachers, often characterised by their heterodox outlook, were instrumental in the process,[184] among them Barāq,

---

[174] Spuler, 1939, repr. 1955, pp. 243–4.

[175] *Jāmiʿ al-tawārīkh*, ed. ʿAlīzāda, vol. 3, pp. 415–6 (visit of Mashhad, the graves of the mystics, and the mausoleum of Sanjar), p. 330 (Najaf and Karbalāʾ), pp. 411–2 (endowment of irrigation channels for Najaf and Karbalāʾ), as cited in Hoffmann, 2002, pp. 205–6.

[176] Karamustafa, 2006, p. 17. Cf. Meier, 1976, pp. 494–516.

[177] Meier, 1976, p. 511.

[178] Roux, 1984, p. 70; Mélikoff, 1962, p. 40; and *eadem*, 1998, pp. 11–3; ʿAsqalanī, 1385/1966, vol. 1, p. 6, cited after Algar, "Barāq Bābā," *EIr*; Karamustafa, 2006, pp. 62–3.

[179] Algar, "Barāq Bābā," *EIr*. For similar examples in the *Baṭṭāl-nāma*, see Dedes, 1996, pp. 156, 164.

[180] Dorn, 1858, pp. 148–51. Cf. Karamustafa, 2006, p. 62.

[181] Bonner, 2006, pp. 112–4.

[182] For a dicussion of the frontier setting in early Ottoman Anatolia, see Lindner, 1983, pp. 1–10, esp. pp. 24–5. The concept of the frontier and frontier societies has been the subject of Burns, 1989, pp. 307–30.

[183] Bosworth, 1963, repr. 1992, pp. 98–105, 109–10; Mélikoff, "Ghāzī," *EI*² II, 1043b.

[184] Mélikoff, 1960, vol. 1, p. 51.

who is said to have been a disciple of the dervish Ṣarī Ṣaltūq Dede, the thirteenth-century semi-legendary Turkish warrior saint,[185] and to have received from him both supernatural powers and his name (Barāq: Qıpchaq Turkish "hairless dog"). The mixed, composite cultural and ethnic elements of frontier life were a melting-pot of contradictions that in spite of its ambiguous dimensions brought about the awareness of a special identity. This was at times characterised by the common ideology of *jihād*, in its guise as holy war[186] inspired by esoteric mystic beliefs with a military following as well as guilds dominated by *akhīs*,[187] a kind of fraternal congregation comparable to the classical Islamic *futuwwa* institution,[188] and sects of heterodox dervishes.[189] The *ghāzīs* were inspired to fight the infidels and expand the frontiers of Islam but at the same time were driven by the economic motivation of having to obtain their livelihood from plunder. These regions thus witnessed a whole spectrum of countercultural occurrences, "interstitial events" or liminal phenomena, thus offering an appropriate abode for the liminal symbol *par excellence*, the dragon. A chivalric-heroic code developed in these frontier societies, propagated principally through prose epic tales in which the dragon played a key role.[190]

One of the main characteristics of these epic-chivalrous frontier narratives is the *jihād* against the dragon. In Abū Ṭāhir of Ṭūs's popular epic *Abū Muslim-nāma* ("Book of Abū Muslim"),[191] the legendary Abū Muslim Khurāsānī (d. *c.* 137/754–5), champion of the *jihād*, fights against the heretics who transformed themselves into dragons.[192] At the same time, the dragon is considered a heroic ideal and the *ghāzīs* are called upon to be as valiant as dragons in the fight,[193] a notion that can also be found in the epic *Wīs u Rāmīn*, in which the warriors are similarly urged to be as heroic as a dragon *(azhdahā-kirdār)*.[194] Muslim epic heroes such as the Iranian Abū Muslim or the Arabic Baṭṭāl Ghāzī, the latter immortalised in the Turkish romance *Baṭṭāl-nāma* ("Book of Baṭṭāl"),[195] possess pronounced supernatural skills. They represent a dervish-shaman type celebrated for their religious leadership among the wandering dervishes, and conduct *jihād* against fire-spitting underground dragons, sometimes polycephalic, in order to liberate young men and women.[196] The tales of Abū Muslim and Baṭṭāl Ghāzī provided the models for other epic works on Malik Dānishmend (Pers. "wise, learned man") and Ṣarī Ṣaltūq Dede that celebrate the exploits of the conquerors of Anatolia.[197]

In the campaign of conquest in Asia Minor, or Anadolu as it was later called by the Turks, which continued for more than three centuries, advancing Saljuq troops were harried by raids on the part of irregular, unruly and often tribal nomad elements, generally referred to as Türkmen (Turkoman). The belligerent activities inherent in their *modus vivendi* led to ravaged lands that characterised a major frontier zone called *uj* (extremity, border or border fighter), often interchangeably used with the Turkish term *aqīnjī* (raider) alongside that of *ghāzī*.[198] The ever-increasing numbers of these nomads on the Armenian and Byzantine frontiers in eastern Anatolia swelled the ranks of the Arab, Kurdish and Dailamī *ghāzīs* who had long fought their Byzantine counterparts, the *akritai*. The location of this frontier warfare stretched from Tarsus along the Taurus mountains through Cilicia up to Malatya (Melitene) and the mountains of Armenia in eastern Anatolia. The disputed land was known as *ḍawāʾiḥ al-Rūm* (the exterior lands facing the "Roman"/Byzantine lands), in other words, it was situated at the periphery of one cultural complex and adjacent to another. As the invasions into Asia Minor progressed, a gradual displacement of old boundaries towards the west took place. In Anatolia the Muslim *ghāzīs* were

[185] *Eadem*, p. 43 and n. 1.

[186] *Jihād* literally means "striving" for faith, and has been interpreted as both a spiritual struggle for religious perfection *(jihād al-nafs)* and holy war against enemies of Islam *(jihād al-akbar)*. See pp. 202, n. 67, 208. Also Bonner, 1996; *idem*, 2006; and Tyan, "Djihād," *EI*² II, 538a.

[187] Taeschner, "Akhī," *EI*² I, 321b.

[188] Cahen and Taeschner, "Futuwwa," *EI*² II, 961a.

[189] Mélikoff, 1960, vol. 1, p. 48.

[190] *Eadem*.

[191] On Abū Ṭāhir Ṭūsī who is said to have been active at the court of *sulṭān* Maḥmūd of Ghazna, see Mélikoff, 1962, pp. 31–6.

[192] *Eadem*, p. 134.

[193] *Eadem*.

[194] Cf. Widengren, 1969, p. 17 and n. 35.

[195] The epic was translated into German in 1871 on the basis of a post-sixteenth-century manuscript preserved in Dresden; Ethé, 1871. For a recent translation, see Dedes, 1996, 2 vols.

[196] Mélikoff, 1960, vol. 1, pp. 50–1, 162; *eadem*, 1962, p. 37; Dedes, 1996, p. 41.

[197] Mélikoff, 1960, vol. 1, p. 47.

[198] Cahen, 1948, pp. 5–7, and *idem*, 1968, p. 58. Cf. Bauer, 1995, pp. 45–53; Dedes, 1996, p. 14, n. 36.

fighting against the infidel Christian *akritai*, who were however themselves often recruited from among Turkish mercenaries.[199] Thus the borderlands were to a certain extent also a zone of interaction with overlapping socio-cultural spheres. As a result of the Mongol invasions the impact of the *ghāzīs* in eastern Asia Minor was again augmented through renewed waves of Central Asian Turkish tribes which also contained large numbers of wandering dervishes, fleeing from the invaded Central Asian and western Iranian provinces.

This frontier life on both sides of the border was profoundly different from that of the more stable and peaceable hinterlands. The epic prose literature that developed on both sides of the centuries-old frontier zone, both Byzantine and Arabo-Turkish, gives an insight into this phenomenon. Epics include the Turkish romance of Sayyid Baṭṭāl and the Byzantine Greek chivalric epic of *Digenis Akritas* of the eastern frontier. Owing much to the Arabic folk prose epic *Sīrāt al-amīra Dhāt al-Himma* (also known as *Dhu 'l-himma* or *Delhemma*),[200] the latter relates the fabulous exploits of the early Muslim frontier warrior al-Baṭṭāl and his companion, ʿAbd al-Wahhāb, during the early wars against Byzantium in the Umayyad period. The acts of heroism carried out on the Byzantine frontier by the Arab-Christian warrior Digenis include the feat of vanquishing a dragon.[201]

Heroic deeds of this type provided the key element for such Turkish Anatolian wondrous epics as the *Baṭṭāl-nāma*. Resembling the Byzantine hero, who is mentioned in the *Baṭṭāl-nāma*, the pseudo-historical al-Baṭṭāl becomes a prototype of popular Turkish literature as ancestor of the Türkmen *ghāzī* state of the Dānishmendids (463/1071–573/1178) in the wake of the conquest of Asia Minor. The story of the exploits of Sayyid Baṭṭāl Ghāzī, whose oral roots may be sought as early as the arrival of the Dānishmendids in Anatolia,[202] became incorporated into the religious-heroic epic cycle of the important frontier city of Malatya,[203] and is set within the historical context of the Arab-Byzantine frontier battles before they gradually turned into Turko-Byzantine wars.[204]

In the tale Baṭṭāl, who carries the sword of the hominoid dragon Ẓaḥḥāk,[205] and other heroic figures, friends as well as foes, are referred to as dragons.[206] The inherent ambiguity of the mythical creature is graphically depicted in several scenes. Baṭṭāl enters an underworld populated by fire-spitting dragons which he holds at bay by drawing a magic circle.[207] However the emerald-headed serpent king, who possesses knowledge of the healing properties of plants, comes to greet the warrior, who eight days later is pulled up to the surface of the earth by holding on to the tail of a giant dragon.[208] The dragon also appears as a defender of the faith in dreams threatening to swallow those who do not convert to Islam,[209] while at the same time its open mouth is evoked to symbolise a grave calamity.[210]

Close parallels are found in the Türkmen epic romance *Dānishmend-nāma* ("Book of Dānishmend"), also based on orally transmitted traditions and composed in the twelfth or early thirteenth century. The hero, Malik Aḥmad Dānishmend Ghāzī,[211] founder of the eponymous Dānishmendids who in the early twelfth century were as powerful as the Saljuqs, appears as a *ghāzī* in Anatolia fighting the Christian warriors of the First Crusade in Cappadocia.[212] In the romance he is identified with Sayyid Baṭṭāl.[213] Both the *ghāzīs*[214] and Malik Dānishmend,[215] whose heroic

[199] Mélikoff, 1960, vol. 1, p. 49, and *eadem*, "Ghāzī," *EI*² II, 1043b; Bauer, 1995, pp. 57–8. For a discussion of the atmosphere of religious heterodoxy and socio-cultural syncreticsm which developed in the wake of the early Ottoman conquest, cf. Lindner, 1983, pp. 1–50.

[200] For a monograph on the epic, see Steinbach, 1972. Cf. Canard, "Dhu 'l-himma, or dhāt al-himma," *EI*² II, 233b.

[201] Jeffreys, 1998, pp. 155–6. For illustrations of Akritas-like warriors slaying a dragon, see Frantz, 1940–1, pp. 87–91; *idem*, 1941, pp. 9–13.

[202] The earliest surviving manuscript of the *Baṭṭāl-nāma*, however, dates to 1436–7. Dedes, 1996, p. 13.

[203] Canard, "Dhu 'l-himma, or dhāt al-himma," *EI*² II, 233b; Dedes, 1996, pp. 9–14.

[204] Dedes, 1996, pp. 1–2.

[205] *Idem*, pp. 113, 114, 151, 196, 202, 204, 214, 270, 282, 284, 306 and 308.

[206] *Idem*, pp. 124, 144, 233, 269.

[207] *Idem*, pp. 255–6.

[208] *Idem*, pp. 256–8.

[209] *Idem*, p. 175.

[210] *Idem*, p. 295.

[211] The title *malik* ("king") was granted to one of Dānishmend's successors, Amīr Ghāzī Gümüshtigin, by the ʿAbbasid caliph al-Mustarshid for his victories against the Christians, the Armenians of Cilicia and the Franks of the County of Edessa. Cf. Bosworth, 1996, p. 215; Mélikoff, 1960, vol. 1, pp. 104–6.

[212] *Eadem*, 1960, pp. 162, 260–2, vol. 2, pp. 75–7; Franke, 2000, pp. 133–4.

[213] Mélikoff, 1960, vol. 1, p. 103.

[214] *Eadem*, pp. 333, 347, 381, 408.

[215] *Eadem*, p. 387 and pp. 346–7, see also p. 448.

achievements are also related to Rustam-i Zāl, are likewise vividly described as having fought like dragons against the infidels. Moreover, the combined actions of two of the Turkish armies are referred to with the simile:

> The Greeks found themselves caught between these two dragons.

The impact of the dragon symbolism on these frontier societies is furthermore documented by the fact, mentioned earlier, that after the Dānishmendid conquest of Malatya, the last Dānishmenid ruler of Malatya, Nāṣir al-Dīn Muḥammad ibn Ismāʿīl minted a copper coin in the 1170s featuring a dragon-slaying equestrian warrior.[216]

Similar feats are described in the mid-fifteenth-century hagiography, the epic *Ṣaltūq-nāma* ("Book of Ṣaltūq"), of the eponymous warrior saint, a religious leader among the circles of wandering dervishes. The narrative describes how Ṣarī Ṣaltūq was transported to the summit of Mount Qāf, doing battle there with a dragon that threatened the nest of a *sīmurgh*, a mythical bird from Iranian mythology.[217] At another time Ṣaltūq battles *jāżūs* (sorcerers, wizards)[218] who ride on lions and dogs brandishing serpents in their hands.[219]

Ṣarī Ṣaltūq is also known to have propagated Islam in the Crimea and the Dobruja.[220] He had joined the fleeing Rūm Saljuq *sulṭān* ʿIzz al-Dīn Kay Kāwūs II to whom the Byzantine emperor Michael VIII Palaeologus had allocated Dobruja, south of the Danube delta in Rūmeli, as a base to settle with his men.[221] The legendary frontier saint saved the kingdom and at the fortress of Kaliakra (Qilghra) killed a seven-headed dragon which had captured the daughters of a king.[222] Afterwards, the people converted to Islam and Ṣaltūq built a *tekke* (dervish lodge).[223]

According to the *Ṣaltūq-nāma*, Ṣarī Ṣaltūq is said to have had close relations with Ḥājjī Bektāsh (possibly d. 669/1270–1), the patron of the heterodox Bektāshiyya order of dervishes in Anatolia.[224] Ḥājjī Bektāsh's spiritual affiliations are linked to the great mystic Aḥmad Yasawī (d. 562/1166–7) from western Turkestan and, according to legend, he is regarded as a *khalīfa* or representative of shaykh Yasawī,[225] the eponym of the Yasawiyya that had a wide following among Turkic nomads in Central Asia. Allegedly the mystic sent him to Anatolia to propagate his order there.[226] However, before coming to Rūm (Anatolia) Ḥājjī Bektāsh accomplishes several heroic feats. According to the principal hagiographical work concerning the saint, the *Wilāyat-nāma*, written in Turkish prose between 886/1481 and 907/1501,[227] Ḥājjī Bektāsh conjures up natural disasters such as flood, drought, famine and an eclipse and as yet another manifestation of a dervish dragon-slayer he overcomes a dragon, thereby converting the people of Badakhshān (the mountainous region situated on the left bank of the upper reaches of the Āmū Daryā) to Islam.[228]

It is likely that Ḥājjī Bektāsh was part of the westward migration caused by the Mongol invasion of Khurasan.[229] According to legend the dervishes from Rūm tried to prevent him from coming to their lands from greater Khurasan. Ḥājjī Bektāsh overcomes this struggle by a well-known miracle, namely by going to Anatolia transformed as a dove.[230] Later, after changing

---

[216] Cf. *Turks*, 2005, p. 397, cat. no. 80; Pancaroğlu, 2004, p. 157, fig. 6.

[217] Mélikoff, 1962, vol. 1, p. 39.

[218] The term *jāżū* is frequently employed in Turkish epic literature. In Mazdean religion the term *jādū* (Av. *yātav*, Pahl. *yātūk*) served as the synonym of "zindīq," or heretic, unbeliever. *Eadem*, p. 199 and n. 2.

[219] *Ṣaltūq-nāma*, ff. 178–80, as cited in Mélikoff, 1962, p. 39.

[220] DeWeese, 1994, p. 253.

[221] Leiser, "Ṣarī Ṣaltūḳ Dede," *EI*² IX, 61a.

[222] Hasluck, 1929, vol. 2, pp. 430–1; Leiser, "Ṣarī Ṣaltūḳ Dede," *EI*² IX, 61a; DeWeese, 1994, p. 253.

[223] Köprülü, tr. and ed. Leiser, 1992, pp. 54–5; see also Leiser, "Ṣarī Ṣaltūḳ Dede," *EI*² IX, 61a.

[224] Leiser, "Ṣarī Ṣaltūḳ Dede," *EI*² IX, 61a. Legendary frontier heroes like Abū Muslim, Sayyid Baṭṭāl and Ṣarī Ṣaltūq were venerated by the Bektāshi. Birge, 1939, pp. 27, 51, 70, 71, 217; Mélikoff, 1960, vol. 1, p. 51.

[225] Later hagiographical tradition links Aḥmad Yasawī to another dragon-slaying saint, Osman Bābā, relating that some merchants from China came to Aḥmad Yasawī imploring him for help "to get rid of a dragon that had appeared in their country. The shaikh girded the waist of Osman, who was still a child, with a wooden sword and sent him off. He went (to China) and killed the dragon. Subsequently, Osman was given the by-name *amīr* Chīn ("Commander of China"). And he was sent to Rūm by his shaikh. There he guided a great many people to Islam." While serving the warden of the *sancak* of Bozok in 1005/1596–7, the Ottoman official and historian Muṣṭafa ibn Aḥmad ʿAlī, heard the story from the shaykh of the *tekke* (dervish lodge) of Osman Bābā, ʿUmdat al-Māchīn; ʿAlī (Muṣṭafa ibn Aḥmad), *Kunh al-akhbār* ("The Essence of Events"), 5 vols., Istanbul, 1861–9, vol. 5, pp. 58–61, cited after Köprülü, tr. and eds. Leiser and Dankoff, 2006, p. 50.

[226] Algar, "Bektāš," *EIr*.

[227] *Idem*. On the hagiographical literature of Ḥājjī Bektāsh, see Mélikoff, 1998, pp. 58–60.

[228] *Eadem*, p. 70.

[229] Algar, "Bektāš," *EIr*.

[230] Saints with a shamanic origin often seem to have had the power to metamorphose into a bird, a lion (for instance, Ḥājjī Bektāsh and his disciples) or a dragon (for instance,

into a human being again, he was met by a mystic, Sayyid Maḥmūd Hayranī from Akshehir accompanied by three hundred Mawlawī (Turk. Mevlevī) dervishes who rode lions and used serpents as whips.[231] As seen earlier, the imagery of mystics exerting power through handling snakes was prominent in the medieval Islamic world. The mystic thus demonstrated his ability to control, manipulate and effectively master the very deadliest of creatures that are also invested with great powers. As noted above, the feat of riding on animals and wielding snakes as whips is also ascribed to the *jāżūs* (sorcerers) who frequently appear in Abū Ṭāhir of Ṭūs's popular epic tales.[232] When seeing the opposing mystic on a lion and holding a serpent, Ḥājjī Bektāsh is said to have mounted a rock (or according to later traditions a wall) and ordered it to move. Forthwith it changed itself into a bird and set off. Ḥājjī Bektāsh thereby demonstrated superiority over an adversary who could only exercise control over animate beings whereas he was able to rule the inanimate as well. In this context the semi-legendary saint and patron of the Anatolian tanners' guilds, Akhī Evrān (Evran or Evren, "snake, dragon"), should also be mentioned. Not only did he free the inhabitants of Kırşehir in central Anatolia from a dragon but he was able to metamorphose into a serpent and appeared in the form of this animal in his tomb *(türbe)*.[233]

These tales demonstrate not only the pivotal importance of the potent symbolism of the dragon or its kin, the serpent, but its use as a link to narrative intersections of otherwise unconnected heroic and saintly figures whose identities became connected and often amalgamated. In this process of blending, the function of malleable stories was complemented by the role of cult sites where Islamic, Turko-Mongol and Christian beliefs overlapped and amalgamated.

The origins of the Bektāshiyya date from the aftermath of the thirteenth-century heterodox Bābāʾī insurrections during the reign of the Rūm Saljuq *sulṭān* Ghiyāth al-Dīn Kay Khusraw II. Ḥājjī Bektāsh was to some degree associated with these uprisings, not least because he became a leading disciple of a certain Bābā Rasūl-Allāh, also known as Bābā Ilyās Khurāsānī, the Bābāʾī leader who was executed at Amasya in 639/1240, the year of the revolt.[234]

Bābā Ilyās, the great-grandfather of the fourteenth-century *ṣūfī* master Elvān Çelebi, was also seen as a manifestation of the immortal Islamic Prophet Khiḍr Ilyās/Hızır-Ilyās.[235] Elvān Çelebi's hagiographic work *al-Manāqib al-qudsiyye* (760/1358–9) written in Turkish prose, which records the legend of Bābā Ilyās and the Türkmen revolt, is one of many deeds of saints and founding figures written at least a generation after the subject's death, hence often linking a recent past with a historical present.[236]

The dervish lodge of Elvān Çelebi in the village of Tekkeköy near Çorum provides an example of a multilayered composite foundation which reflects the cross-cultural encounters between Muslim and Christian societies and documents a religio-cultural symbiosis. The site has been identified with the pilgrimage site Euchaita to which the remains of the Byzantine dragon-slaying warrior saint Theodore Tyron were brought. According to Elvān Çelebi, Bābā Ilyās was a companion of Khiḍr *(Hıżır yoldašı)*.[237]

In the mid-sixteenth century, German travellers visited Elvān Çelebi's *zāwiya* and noted that the dervishes were dedicated to the cult of Khiḍr Ilyās. One of the visitors, Hans Dernschwamm, notes in his travel journal:

> the Turks esteem nor know of no other saint but Saint George whom they call Khiḍr Ilyās, … that he has not died and still lives.

He also recounts that the dervishes pointed out traces of Khiḍr's visit to the site. Among these were the remains of a dragon he had slain, a hoof

Akhī Evrān); cf. Mélikoff, 1998, pp. 11, 78, 89, 136, 157, 199.

[231] Mélikoff, 1962, p. 40; and *eadem*, 1998, p. 76.

[232] *Eadem*, 1962, p. 37; Dedes, 1996, pp. 41, 265.

[233] Akhī Evrān is moreover said to have been protected by a dragon, see Roux, "Drachen," *WdM* VII, 1, p. 314. His name has also given rise to the hypothesis of a survival of a snake cult. See Gordlevskiy, V., *Dervishi Akhi Evrana i tsekhi v Turtsii* ("The Dervishes of Akhi Evran and the Craftsmen Guilds in Turkey"), Izvestiya Akademii Nauk SSSR, 1927, pp. 1171–94 (French résumé by Vajda, 1934, pp. 79–88). Cf. Taeschner, "Akhī Ewrān," *EI*² IX, 61a; also Boratov, 1957, pp. 382–5.

[234] For a discussion of the Bābāʾī revolt and the leading figures Bābā Ilyās Khurāsānī and his disciple, Bābā Isḥāq, see Mélikoff, 1998, pp. 32–40; Ocak, 1989. Cf. Algar, "Bektāš," *EIr*. Cf. also Lindner, 1983, pp. 14–5. Cahen ("Bābāʾī," *EI*² I, 843b) and Tschudi ("Bektāshiyya," *EI*² I, 1161b) still identify Bābā Isḥāq as leader of the rebellions.

[235] Pancaroğlu, 2004, p. 158.

[236] The manuscript is preserved in the Library of the Mevlevī Dergāhı in Konya, Ms. 4937. Mélikoff, 1998, pp. 32–40; Wolper, 2000, p. 311f.

[237] Franke, 2000, p. 242.

mark made by his horse, a spring and even the tomb of his groom and sister who had accompanied him on his dragon-slaying expedition.[238] Moreover, "cures were performed at the site by the use of earth and scrapings of the wall which surrounded the place of the dragon."[239] The *zāwiya* of Elvān Çelebi thus (in Sara Wolper's words) "functioned as a place where a matrix of associations between Bābā Ilyās, local Christians and Khiḍr were linked."[240]

This cross-cultural convergence between Muslim and Christian societies throughout the Turko-Iranian region thus allowed at a popular level for an intensification of interchange, specifically with regard to saintly cults. It resulted in a double veneration at many cult sites, with the frequent equation of the saint of one faith with a saint of the other faith. This also manifested in the visual culture. The phenomenon of local transference and subsequent joint cult, which once again is manifestly exemplified in the figure of the dragon fighter, found its way into many local legends and sanctuaries.

An example of such fusion is shown in the monastery of Mār Behnām, which became an important place of pilgrimage for miraculous cures for both Christians and Muslims, known by the latter as Deir al-Khiḍr.[241] The figure of al-Khiḍr/al-Khaḍir is a very important one in the spiritual hierarchy of Islam. He is the eternal omnipresent Prophet, "the Verdant One," who appears to believers to help and advise them in need and console them in grief.[242] Khiḍr is invested with an eschatological significance in both primordial and apocalyptic times, appearing sometimes as the light of Muḥammad (*nūr Muḥammadī*; the Prophet's pre-existing entity) but more generally as his helper, as well as that of the entire Muslim community.[243] He is closely associated with the element of water and is still revered today in Mesopotamia as patron saint of water.[244] The place of pilgrimage gained in importance when the figure of the martyr Mār Behnām was conflated with Saint George, and then in turn equated with the conspicuous Islamic mythical Saint Khiḍr.[245]

Significantly, it is because of the syncretism of Mār Behnām (Saint George) and Khiḍr that in 694/1295 the Ilkhan Baidu, grandson of Hülegü/Hūlāgū (r. Jumādā I to Dhu 'l-qaʿda 694/March-October 1295), is said to have spared the monastery of Mār Behnām from destruction while other monasteries were ravaged.[246] The Ilkhan's presence at the monastery is documented by an inscription in Old Turkish (Uighur) in the crypt, invoking the blessing of Khiḍr Ilyās on behalf of the Khān and his entourage.[247] In the inscription Khiḍr is addressed as "Khiḍr Ilyās." The Islamic

[238] *Hans Dernschwamms Tagebuch*, ed. Babinger, 1923, pp. 201–6; Hasluck, 1929, vol. 1, pp. 48–9.

[239] The earth was used to cure fever, see Hasluck, 1929, vol. 1, pp. 48, 263, vol. 2, p. 571.

[240] Wolper, 2000, p. 315.

[241] The official designation of the monastery of Mār Behnām is "monastery of Khiḍr." Muslim and Yezidi pilgrims still come today to visit the tomb of Khiḍr, "the father of Muḥammad." Fiey, 1965, p. 575.

[242] Wensinck, "al-Khaḍir, al-Khiḍr," *EI*² IV, 902b; Friedlaender, "Khiḍr," *ERE*, vol. 14, 1915, pp. 694–5. For a comprehensive recent investigation of al-Khiḍr, see Franke, 2000.

[243] Franke, 2000, pp. 121–31; van Lint, 2005, p. 364. Henry Corbin (1998b, p. 55) relates how Khiḍr Ilyās, identified in Muslim tradition as unnamed guide of Mūsa (Qurʾān, *sūra* 18, 59–81), initiates the biblical Prophet "into the science of predestination." Khiḍr thus reveals himself as "the repository of an inspired divine science, superior to the [religious] law *(sharīʿa)*." Whereas Moses was invested with the prophetic mission of revealing a *sharīʿa*, Khiḍr has thus, says Corbin, shown himself to be "superior to Moses in so far as He reveals to Moses precisely the secret, mystic truth *(ḥaqīqa)* that transcends the *sharīʿa*, and this explains why the spirituality inaugurated by Khiḍr is free from the servitude of literal religion." Khiḍr, identified with Elijah, Saint George and other figures who in a number of traditions have a close affinity and whose identities have at times merged to become effectively interchangeable, is seen as an initiator of a mystic truth which emancipates the seeker from literal religion. This transcendence of exoteric religion fostered the symbiotic coexistence of Jewish, Christian and Muslim beliefs. On the Qurʾānic account of Mūsa and Khiḍr, see also Franke, 2000, pp. 60–80.

[244] Al-Khaḍir is said to live upon a green carpet *(ṭinfisa)* in the heart of the sea (al-Bukhārī, *Tafsīr*, *surā* 18, 4) and at the spring of life (al-Ṭabarī, *Mukhtaṣar taʾrīkh al-rusul wa 'l-mulūk wa 'l-khulafāʾ*, vol. 1, p. 417); Wensinck, "al-Khaḍir, al-Khiḍr," *EI*² IV, 902b; Franke, 2000, pp. 88–101. Khiḍr is considered as guardian of the Fountain of Eternal Life which symbolises the Water of Sacred Knowledge. Cf. Mélikoff, 1960, vol. 1, pp. 163–4 and n. 1; Franke, 2000, pp. 45–52.

[245] Fiey, 1965, vol. 2, pp. 575–6; Baumer, 2005, p. 110. On the frequent conflation of Khiḍr and Saint George, see Clermont-Ganneau, 1876; Friedländer, 1910, pp. 92–110 and 161–246, as well as *idem*, "Khiḍr," p. 695; Franke, 2000, p. 155, n. 512, and pp. 159–60. In his apologia the Byzantine emperor John VI Kantakouzenos (d. 1383) explains that Saint George is also venerated by Muslims who however call him Χετήρ 'Ηλίας ("Khiḍr Ilyās"). Hasluck, 1929, vol. 1, p. 322.

[246] Baidu not only returned the treasures that were looted from the monastery but added a personal donation. Pognon, 1907, pp. 132–42, 235, no. 76; Braun, 1900, pp. 50–2; Fiey, 1965, pp. 584–5.

[247] *M(a)r kıdır ilyaznıŋ kutı alkıšı elhanka bäglär hatunlarka konzun ornašzun* "May the happiness and praise of Khiḍr Elias befall and settle on the Il-khan and the nobles and the noblewomen!" The English tr. is cited after Harrak and Niu, 2004, pp. 66–70, tr. on p. 68. See also Pognon, 1907, pp. 132–42, no. 79; Fiey, 1959, p. 50. As pointed out by Professor Dr Peter Zieme (personal communication)

Prophet al-Khiḍr/al-Khaḍir and the biblical Prophet Ilyās (Elias/Elijah)[248] also known in the Qurʾān (*sūra* 37, 123–32) are thus associated as a pair and sometimes identified with one another.[249] This gives rise to a multi-layered composite character adopted also in popular Turkish tradition as Hızır-Ilyās (often contracted to "Hızırellez/Hıdrellez").[250]

At the monastery of Mār Behnām the iconographic programme of the dragon-slayer is represented as two confronted dragon-slaying horsemen who spear, respectively, a prostrate dragon with a heart-shaped knot at its mid-section, and an anthropomorphic figure, representing Satan, beneath their horses; the rider slaying Satan is identified as Saint Behnām (fig. 198).[251] The relief, which flanks a very weathered centrally projecting lion head, is shown on the lintel above the so-called "royal door" that leads to the burial chamber of Saint Behnām. In this position it not only helped to demarcate the sacred threshold, but as an auspicious and apotropaic motif served to protect the tomb. The funerary association of the imagery perhaps once again echoes popular eschatological notions similar to those expressed in the Cappadocian wall paintings above the vestibule door of the previously mentioned Yılanlı kilise in the Ihlara valley (fig. 106). To the left of the royal door is a depiction of Saint Behnām alias Saint George on horseback, here in the role of dragon-slayer, represented on a large plaster relief.[252] The depictions reflect a multifaceted notion which was deeply rooted in popular spirituality.

The connection of Khiḍr with the dragon-slaying motif appears also in the *Dānishmend-nāma*, in which Malik Dānishmend battles with a fire-spewing dragon responsible for swallowing hundreds of *ghāzīs* at a monastery called Deryānōs. After several futile attempts Malik Dānishmend finally overcomes the mythical creature which was created by the magical skills of the monks in the monastery. He accomplishes this feat through guidance received in a dream from the legendary early Arab warrior ʿAbd al-Wahhāb, who instructs him to countermand the beast's magical powers by reciting Khiḍr's prayer and then blowing in the direction of the dragon.[253]

Yet another convergence of role can be seen between Khiḍr and John the Baptist (the Armenian Surb Karapet, the Holy Precursor)[254] who assumed the qualities of the long-haired *(gisavor)* Zoroastrian dragon-fighting hero Vahagn.[255] The apostle thus became the christianised version of the important Zoroastrian figure, some of whose qualities were passed on to the "Forerunner of Christ."[256] In this way Surb Karapet, like Khiḍr, also became associated with dragon-fighting.

The attribution of such miracles as dragon-slaying to figures of legendary or saintly status, sometimes through the agency of the pivotal Khiḍr Ilyās, may be seen as part of a process of cultural adaptation in which the idea of a relative contextual and conceptual continuity becomes a cross-cultural point of contact.[257] The iconography of the dragon-fighter thus proved ideally suited to transcend a variety of religious and secular contexts while epitomising, in the words of Pancaroğlu, "the fundamental themes of rescue, relief, triumph, and resurrection."[258]

---

the inscription is notable because it represents the most western testimony of ancient Uighur during the Ilkhanid period. I am grateful to Professor Dr Zieme for the reading of the Uighur inscription which adds the word *m(a)r* to the reading of Harrak, A. and Niu Ruji, *op. cit.*

[248] Franke, 2000, pp. 159–61. It is interesting to note that Elijah's gentilic is *hat-Tišbî* (I Kings 17.1) which is thought to be located somewhere in Gilead. Since miraculous powers of provoking drought and granting rain were ascribed to the Prophet, he must have been assimilated to some extent with the storm god Teshub of the Hurranians who lived together with the Semites in northern Syria. Elijah was moreover known as the greatest healer in Hebrew legend, his miracles including even the resurrection of the dead (I Kings 17:17–24). See Astour, 1965, pp. 215, 297.

[249] This fusion also pertains to the whole complex of myths and legends associated with both Khiḍr and Ilyās. Massignon, 1956, pp. 269–90. Cf. van Lint, 2005, pp. 365–8.

[250] Cf. Hasluck, 1929, vol. 2, p. 498; Roux, "Hızır," *WdM* VII, 1, pp. 327–8; Franke, 2000, pp. 167–73; Pancaroğlu, 2004, pp. 151, 157–8. At the Turkish Hızırellez festival the meeting of Khiḍr and Ilyās coincides with the return of spring and the regeneration of nature. See Franke, 2000, p. 148.

[251] Preusser, 1911, pl. 10, top; Fiey, 1965, pl. F (drawing of Mār Behnām slaying the devil represented as a horned prostrate figure with long tail).

[252] The dating of this relief is disputed and ranges from the thirteenth to the fifteenth century (Fiey, 1965, pp. 605–7). The cult of Mār Behnām in his quality of Khiḍr was until recently the object of a divination cult whereby mainly female pilgrims would throw a handkerchief or other light cloth at the large plaster relief; if it stuck to the croup of the horse, it was taken as a sign that their prayers were answered. It is not too long ago that the "magic nails" were removed. Cuinet, vol. 2, 1890–5, repr. 2001, p. 832.

[253] Mélikoff, 1960, vol. 1, pp. 162, 260–2, vol. 2, pp. 75–7; Franke, 2000, pp. 133–4.

[254] Van Lint, 2005, pp. 349–57.

[255] Russell, 1987, pp. 202–4, 217; van Lint, 2005, pp. 364–5. For instances of the identification of Khiḍr with the Armenian Saint Sergios (Sarkis) in eastern Anatolia, see Hasluck, 1929, vol. 2, pp. 570–1; Fowden, 1999, p. 190.

[256] Cf. Redgate, 2000, pp. 123, 125.

[257] Pancaroğlu, 2004, p. 158.

[258] *Eadem*, pp. 158, 161.

LIST OF ABBREVIATIONS

CELF	*The Concise Encyclopaedia of Living Faiths*, ed. Zaehner, R.C., New York, 1959, repr. London, 1979.
DDD	*Dictionary of Deities and Demons in the Bible*, eds. van der Toorn, K., Becking, B., van der Horst, P.W., 1995, Leiden, Boston and Cologne, repr. 1998.
DNP	*Der Neue Pauly: Enzyklopädie der Antike*, eds. Cancik, H., and Schneider, H., Stuttgart and Weimar, 1996–2003.
EHAS	*Encyclopedia of the History of Arabic Science*, ed. Rashed, R., 3 vols., London and New York, 1996.
EI[1]	*The Encyclopaedia of Islam*, 1st ed., 4 vols. and suppl., Leiden and London, 1913–38.
EI[2]	*The Encyclopaedia of Islam*, 2nd ed., 11 vols., Leiden, 1960–2005, *Extract from The Encyclopaedia of Islam CD-ROM v.-1.0.*
EIr	*Encyclopaedia Iranica Online.* Available: www.iranica.com. Accessed April 2009.
ERE	*Encyclopedia of Religion and Ethics*, eds. Hastings, J., et al., 12 vols., Edinburgh and New York, 1908–21.
HdA	*Handwörterbuch des deutschen Aberglaubens*, eds. Bächtold-Stäubli, H., et al., 10 vols., Berlin and Leipzig, 1927–42, repr. 1987.
ISBE	*The International Standard Bible Encyclopedia*, eds. Orr, J., et al., 4 vols., Grand Rapids, MI, 1939, repr. 1994.
KTU	*Cuneiform Alphabetic Texts from Ugarit, Ras Ibn Hani and Other Places*, eds. Dietrich, M., Loretz, O., and Sanmartín, J., 2nd enlarged ed., Münster, 1995.
ODB	*The Oxford Dictionary of Byzantium*, ed. Kazhdan, A., 3 vols., Oxford, 1991.
RAC	*Reallexikon für Antike und Christentum*, ed. Klauser, T., 13 vols., Stuttgart, 1941–78.
RE	*Paulys Real-Encyclopädie der classischen Altertumswissenschaft*, eds. Wissowa, G., et al., Stuttgart and Munich, 1893–1980.
RgA	*Reallexikon der germanischen Altertumskunde*, 4 vols., eds. Hoops, J., Berlin and New York, 1911–9, 2nd ed. Jankuhn, H., et al., 1968–98.
Steingass	Steingass, F.J., *A Comprehensive Persian-English Dictionary*, 1892, repr. Delhi 1981.
WdM	*Wörterbuch der Mythologie*, ed. Haussig, H.W., 7 vols., Stuttgart, 1965–86.

BIBLIOGRAPHY

Primary Sources

Agathangelos
1970 *The Teaching of Saint Gregory: An Early Armenian Catechism*, tr. and ed. Thomson, R.W., Harvard Armenian Texts and Studies 3, Cambridge, MA.

al-Azraqī, Abu 'l-Walīd Muḥammad ibn ʿAbd Allāh
1858–61 *Kitāb Akhbār Makkah*, ed. Wüstenfeld, F., *Die Chroniken der Stadt Mekka*, vol. 1, *Geschichte und Beschreibung der Stadt Mekka von Abul-Walîd Muhammed ben Abdallah el-Azraki*, Leipzig.

Balʿamī
1867–74 *Tarjumat-i tārīkh-i Ṭabarī*, tr. Zotenberg, H., *Chronique de Abou-Djafar-Mohammed-ben-Djarir-ben-Yezid Ṭabarī traduite sur la version persane d'Abou-ʿAli Moʿhammed Belʿami*, 4 vols., Paris, repr. 1958.

Bar Hebraeus
1932 *Chronicon Syriacum*, tr. and ed. Budge, E.A.W., *The Chronography of Gregory Abû 'l Faraj, the Son of Aaron, the Hebrew Physician Commonly Known as Bar Hebraeus, Being the First Part of His Political History of the World*, London, 2 vols.

Barnabas, *Epistle of*
1914 tr. Lake, K., *The Apostolic Fathers*, XII, 5, London and New York.

Bet ha-Midrasch
1853–73 *Sammlung kleiner Midraschim und vermischter Abhandlungen aus der älteren jüdischen Literatur*, 6 vols., ed. Jellinek, A., Leipzig and Vienna, repr. 1967.

al-Bidlīsī, ʿAmmār ibn Muḥammad
1999 *Bahjat al-ṭāʾifa wa Ṣaum al-qalb*, tr. and ed. Badeen, E., *Zwei mystische Schriften des ʿAmmār al-Bidlīsī*, Beirut.

al-Bīrūnī, Abu 'l-Rayḥān Muḥammad ibn Aḥmad
1876–8 *Kitāb al-Āthār al-Bāqiya ʿan al-qurūn al-khāliya*, tr. and ed. Sachau, E.C., *Chronologie orientalischer Völker von Albêrûnî*, Leipzig and London.
1887 *Kitāb fī Taḥqīq mā li-l-Hind min maqūla maqbūla fi-l-ʿaql aw mardhūla*, tr. and ed. Sachau, E.C., *Alberuni's India: An Account of the Religion, Philosophy, Literature, Chronology, Astronomy, Customs, Laws and Astrology of India about A.D. 1030*, London.
1934 *Kitāb al-Tafhīm li-Awaʾīl Ṣināʿat al-Tanjīm*, tr. and ed. Wright, R.R., *The Book of Instruction in the Elements of the Art of Astrology*, repr. from British Museum Ms. Or. 8349, London.

The Book of the Thousand Nights and a Night
1885 tr. Burton, R.F., privately printed.

Buzandaran Patmutʿiwnkʿ
1989 *The Epic Histories Attributed to Pʿawstos Buzand: Buzandaran Patmutʿiwnkʿ*, tr. Garsoïan, N.G., Cambridge, MA.

Caturaśīti siddha pravṛtti
1979 *Buddha's Lions: The Lives of Eighty-Four Siddhas*, tr. Robinson, J.B., Berkeley, CA.

Chrysostom, John
1957–60 *Saint John Chrysostom: Commentary on Saint John the Apostle and Evangelist*, tr. Sr. Thomas Aquinas Goggin, The Fathers of the Church 33 and 41, Washington, DC.

al-Damīrī, Kamāl al-Dīn Muḥammad ibn Mūsā
1906 *Ḥayāt al-ḥayawān al-kubrā*, tr. Jayakar, A.S.G., *Ad-Damîrî's Ḥayât al-Ḥayawân* ("A Zoological Lexicon"), vol. 1, London and Bombay.

Dernschwamm, Hans
1923 *Hans Dernschwamms Tagebuch einer Reise nach Konstantinopel und Kleinasien (1553–5)*, ed. Babinger, F., Munich and Leipzig.

Ephraem, Syrus (Ephrem the Syrian)
1990 *Hymni de Paradiso and Section 2 of Commnetarium in Genesium*, tr. and ed. Brook, S., *Hymns on Paradise*, Chrestwood, NY.
1998 *The Armenian Commentary on Genesis Attributed to Ephrem the Syrian*, tr. and ed. Mathews, E.G., vol. 2, Corpus Scriptorum Christianorum Orientalium, vol. 573, Louvain.

Eusebius
1999 *Eusebius: Life of Constantine*, tr. and ed. Cameron, A., and Hall, S.G., Oxford.

Eznik of Koghb (Kołb)
1959 *Elc alandocʿ* ("A Treatise on God"), tr. and ed. Mariès, L., and Mercier, C., *Eznik de Kołb: De Deo*, Patrologia Orientalis, vol. 28, Armenian text, fasc. 3, French tr., fasc. 4, Paris.

al-Firdawsī, Abu 'l-Qāsim
1838–78 *Shāh-nāma*, tr. and ed. Mohl, J., *Le livre des rois*, 7 vols., Paris.
1987 *The Tragedy of Sohráb and Rostám: From the Persian National Epic, the Shahname of Abdol-Qasem Ferdowsi*, tr. and ed. Clinton, J.W., Seattle and London.
1999 *In the Dragon's Claws: The Story of Rostam & Esfandiyar from the Persian Book of Kings*, tr. and ed. Clinton, J.W., Washington, DC.

al-Ghazālī, Abū Ḥāmid Muḥammad ibn Muḥammad al-Ṭūsī
1953 *The Faith and Practice of Al-Ghazali*, tr. Montgomery Watt, W., London.

Gurgānī, Fakhr al-Dīn Asʿad
2008 *Wīs u Rāmīn*, tr. and ed. Davis, D., *Vis and Ramin*, New York.

Ḥaidar Mīrzā Dughlāt, Muḥammad
1895 *Taʾrīkh-i Rashīdī*, tr. Ross, E.D., with notes by Elias, N., *The Taʾrīkh-i Rashīdī, a History of the Moguls of Central Asia*, London.

al-Harawī, Abu 'l-Ḥāsan ʿAlī ibn Abī Bakr
1957 *Kitāb al-Ishārāt ilā maʿrifat al-ziyārāt*, tr. and ed. Sourdel-Thomime, J., *Guide des lieux de pèlerinage*, Damascus.

HaLevi, Yehuda [Hallévi, Juda]
2006 *Le Kuzari: Apologie de la religion méprisée*, tr. and ed. Touati, C., LaGrasse.

Harshacharita
1897 *Harshacharita of Bāṇabhatta*, tr. Cowell, E.B., and Thomas, F.W., *The Harsa Carita of Bana*, Bombay.

Hermes Trismegistus
1946 *Poimandres, Traites 1–12*, tr. and ed. Nock, A.D., and Festugière, A.J., *Corpus hermeticum* vol. 1, 4, Paris.
1994 *Das Schlangenbuch des Hermes Trismegistos*, ed. and tr. Ullmann, M., Wiesbaden.

Ḥudūd al-ʿālam
n.d. *The Regions of the World from East to West: A Persian Geography, c. 372 A.H.–982 A.D.*, tr. and ed. Minorsky, V., preface Barthold, W. (Bartol'd, V.; tr. from Russian), London.

al-Hujwīrī, Abu 'l-Ḥāsan ʿAlī ibn ʿUthmān ibn ʿAlī al-Ghaznawī
1976 *Kashf al-Maḥjūb*, tr. and ed. Nicholson, *The Kashf al-Maḥjūb: The Oldest Persian Treatise on Sufism, Tr. from the Text of the Lahore Ed., Compared with Mss. in the Indian Office and British Museum*, R.A., London.

Ibn al-ʿArabī, Muḥyi 'l-Dīn Muḥammad ibn ʿAlī
1971 *Al-Durra al-Fakhira, al-Rūḥ al-Quds fī Muḥāsabat al-Nafs*, tr. and ed. Austin, R.W.J., *Sufis of Andalusia: the Rūḥ al-quds and al-Durrah al-fākhirah of Ibn ʿArabī*, London.

Ibn Baṭṭūṭa, Abū ʿAbd Allāh Muḥammad
1929 *Riḥlat Ibn Baṭṭūṭa al-musammāt tuḥfat al-nuẓẓār fī gharāʾib al-amṣār wa-ʿajāʾib al-asfār*, tr. and ed. Gibb, H.A.R., *Travels in Asia and Africa 1325–1354*, 3 vols., London, repr. Cambridge, 1956–1971.

Ibn Bībī, al-Ḥusayn ibn Muḥammad ibn ʿAlī al-Jaʿfarī al-Rughadī
1959 *Al-Awāmir al-ʿAlāʾiyya fī 'l-ūmur al-ʿAlāʾiyya*, tr. and ed. Duda, H.W., *Die Seltschukengeschichte des Ibn Bībī*, Copenhagen.

Ibn Faḍlān, Aḥmad ibn al-ʿAbbās ibn Rashīd ibn Ḥammād
2005 *Ibn Fadlan's Journey to Russia: A Tenth-Century Traveler from Baghdad to the Volga River*, tr. and ed. Frye, R.N., Princeton, NJ.

Ibn Hishām
1857 *Sīrat sayyidnā Muḥammad rasūl Allāh*, tr. and ed. Wüstenfeld, F., *Das Leben Muhammeds nach Muhammed Ibn Ishâk ueberliefert von Abd el-Malik Ibn Hischâm: Aus den Handschriften zu Berlin, Leipzig, Gotha und Leyden*, Göttingen.

Ibn Isfandīyār, Muḥammad ibn al-Ḥasan
1905 *Tārīkh-i Ṭabaristān*, tr. and ed. Browne, E.G., *An Abridged Translation of the History of Ṭabaristān Compiled About A.H. 613 (A.D. 1216) by Muḥammad b. al-Ḥasan b. Isfandiyār: Based on the India Office Ms. Compared with 2 Mss. in the British Museum*, E.J.W. Gibb Memorial Series II, Leiden.

Ibn al-Kalbī, Hishām ibn Muḥammad ibn al-Sāʾib al-Kalbī Abu 'l-Mundhir
1952 *Kitāb al-Asnām*, tr. Faris, N.A.,*The Book of Idols*, Princeton, NJ.

Ibn Khaldūn, Abū Zayd ʿAbd al-Raḥmān Walī al-Dīn al-Ḥaḍramī
1958 *Muqaddima*, tr. and ed. Rosenthal, F., *The Muqaddimah*, 3 vols., Princeton and New York.

Ibn Manẓūr, Muḥammad ibn Mukarram
n.d. *Lisān al-ʿArab*, Beirut.

Ibn Maymūn, Abū ʿImrān Mūsā ibn ʿUbaid Allāh/ Maimonides, Moses
1966 *The Medical Writings of Moses Maimonides*, vol. 2, *Treatise on Poisons and Their Antidotes*, tr. and ed. Muntner, S., Philadelphia, PA.

Ibn Shaddād, ʿIzz al-Dīn Abū ʿAbd Allāh Muḥammad ibn ʿAlī al-Ḥalabī
1953 *Al-Aʿlāq al-khaṭīra fī dhikr umarāʾ al-Shaʾm wa 'l-Jazīra*, tr. and ed. Sourdel, D., *La description d'Alep d'Ibn Shaddād*, Beirut.

Ikhwān al-Ṣafāʾ
1858 *Der Streit zwischen Mensch und Thier: Ein arabisches Mährchen aus den Schriften der lauteren Brüder*, tr. and ed. Dieterici, F., Berlin.

Iordanes
1915 *Getica*, tr. and ed. Mierow, C.C., *The Gothic History of Jordanes*, Princeton, NJ, repr. 2006.

Jābir ibn Ḥaiyān, Abū Mūsā
1942–3 *Jābir ibn Ḥayyān: Contribution à l'histoire des idées scientifiques dans l'Islam*, Mémoires présentés à l'Institut d'Égypte, 44 and 45, 2 vols., tr. and ed. Kraus, P., Cairo.
1958 *Sumūm wa dafʿ madārrihā*, tr. Siggel, A., *Das Buch der Gifte des Jabir ibn Ḥayyān*, Akadademie der Wissenschaften und der Literatur, Veröffentlichungen der orientalischen Kommission 12, Wiesbaden.

Jalāl al-Dīn Rūmī
1961 *Tales from the Masnavi*, tr. and ed. Arberry, A.J., London.
1947 *Discourses of Rumi*, tr. and ed. Arberry, A.J., London, repr. 2004.

al-Jazarī, Abu 'l-ʿIzz Ismāʿīl ibn al-Razzāẓ
1974 *Kitāb fī maʿrifat al-ḥiyāl al-handasiyya*, tr. and ed. Hill, D.R., *The Book of Knowledge of Ingenious Mechanical Devices*, Dordrecht and Boston, repr. by the National Hijra Council of Pakistan, Islamabad, 1989.

al-Juwaynī, ʿAlāʾ al-Dīn ʿAṭa-Malik ibn Muḥammad
1912–37 *Taʾrīkh-i jahān-gushāy*, ed. Mirza Muhammad Qazwini, tr. Boyle, J.A., *The History of the World-Conqueror*, Cambridge, MA, 2 vols.

Kay Kāwūs ibn Iskandar ibn Qābūs, ʿUnṣur al-Maʿālī
1951 *A Mirror for Princes*, tr. Levy, R., London.

Khorenatsi, Movsēs (Moses of Chorene)
1872 *Patmutʿiwn Hayocʿ*, tr. Langlois, V., "Mar Apas Catina – *Histoire ancienne de l'Arménie*," *Fragmenta Historicorum Graecorum*, ed. Müller, K., vol. V, pp. 1–54.
1978 *Khorenatsi: History of the Armenians*, tr. and ed. Thomson, R., Cambridge, MA, repr. 1980.

al-Kisāʾī, Muḥammad ibn ʿAbdullāh
1978 *Qiṣaṣ al-anbiyāʾ*, tr. Thackston, W.M., *The Tales of the Prophets of al-Kisāʾī*, Boston.

Maimonides, see Ibn Maymūn

Malalas, Ioannes
1831 *Chronographia*, tr. and ed. Dindorf, L., *Ioannis Malalae Chronographia*, ex recensione Ludovici Dindorfii accedunt chilmeadi hodiique annotationes et ric. bentleii epistola ad Io. Millium, Corpus scriptorum historiae Byzantinae 9, Bonn.

Manūchihrī Dāmghānī
1972 *The Divan of Manūchihrī Dāmghānī: A Critical Study*, tr. Clinton, J.W., Minneapolis, MN.

Marco Polo
1929 *The Travels of Marco Polo: The Complete Yule-Cordier Edition*, 2 vols, tr. and comm. Yule, H., and rev. Cordier, H., London.

al-Masʿūdī, Abu ʾl-Ḥasan ʿAlī ibn al-Ḥusayn ibn ʿAlī
1917 *Kitab murūj al-dhahab wa-maʿādin al-jawhar*, tr. and ed. Barbier de Meynard, C., and de Courteille, P., *Les Prairies d'Or*, 9 vols., Paris.

al-Masʿūd-i Saʿd-i Salmān
1364/1985 *Dīwān-i ashʿār-i Masʿūd-i Saʿd*, ed. Nūrīyān, Mahdī, Isfahan, tr. Sharma, S., *Persian Poetry at the Indian Frontier: Masʿûd Saʿd Salmân of Lahore*, Delhi, 2000.

Meʿārath gazzē
1927 *The Book of the Cave of Treasures*, tr. and ed. Budge, E.A., London.

Miskawayh
1921–2 *Tajārib al-umam wa taʿāqib al-humam*, tr. and ed. Margoliouth, D.S., *The Eclipse of the ʿAbbasid Caliphate: Original Chronicles of the Fourth Islamic Century*, Oxford, vol. 5, *The Concluding Portion of the Experience of the Nations*, vol. 2, *Reigns of Muttaqi, Mustakfi, Mutiʿ and Taʾi.*

Mihr Yasht
1959 *The Avestan Hymn to Mithra*, tr. and ed. Gershevitch, I., Cambridge.

al-Muqaddasi, Shams al-Dīn Abū ʿAbd Allāh Muḥammad ibn Aḥmad ibn Abī Bakr
1994 *Aḥsan al-taqāsīm fī maʿrifat al-aqālīm*, tr. Collins, B.A., *The Best Divisions for Knowledge of the Regions*, Reading.

Niẓāmī Ganjawī, Ilyās ibn Yūsuf
1924 *The Haft Paikar*, vol. 1, tr. and ed. Wilson, C.E., London.
1995 *The Haft Paykar: A Medieval Persian Romance*, tr. and ed. Meisami, J. Scott, Oxford and New York.

Philo of Byblos
1981 *The Phoenician History: Introduction, Critical Text, Translation, Notes*, tr. and ed. Attridge, H.W., and Oden, R.A., Jr., The Catholic Biblical Quarterly Monograph Series 9, Washington, DC.

Picatrix, see Pseudo-Majrīṭī

Pistis Sophia
1896 *Pistis Sophia: A Gnostic Gospel (with Extracts from the Books of the Saviour Appended)*, tr. Mead, G.R. Stow, London.
1978 *Pistis Sophia*, text ed. Schmidt, C., tr. and notes Macdermot, V., Nag Hammadi Studies, IX, Leiden.

Plano Carpini, John of
1955 *The Mongol Mission: Narratives and Letters of the Franciscan Missionaries in Mongolia and China in the Thirteenth and Fourteenth Century*, tr. and ed. Dawson, C., New York, pp. 3–76.

Pseudo-Apollonius of Tyana
1980 *Das "Buch über das Geheimnis der Schöpfung" von Pseudo-Apollonios von Tyana*, tr. and ed. Weisser, U., Berlin, New York.

Pseudo-Aristoteles
1912 *Das Steinbuch des Aristoteles mit literargeschichtlichen Untersuchungen nach der arabischen Handschrift der Bibliothèque Nationale*, tr. and ed. Ruska, J., Heidelberg.

Pseudo-Callisthenes
1889 *The History of Alexander the Great Being the Syriac Version of Pseudo Callisthenes*, tr. and ed. Budge, E.A.W., Cambridge, repr. 2003.
1926 *Historia Alexandri Magni. Recensio vetusta editit*, ed. Kroll, W., Berlin.
1991 *The Greek Alexander Romance*, tr. and ed. Stoneman, R., London.

Pseudo-Majrīṭī (Abu ʾl-Qāsim Maslama ibn Aḥmad al-Majrīṭī)
1933 *Pseudo-Maǧriṭi: Das Ziel der Weisen, 1. Arabischer Text*, ed. Ritter, H., Studien der Bibliothek Warburg, vol. 12, Leipzig and Berlin.
1962 *"Picatrix." Das Ziel der Weisen von Pseudo-Maǧriṭi*, tr. and eds. Ritter, H., and Plessner, M., Studies of the Warburg Institute, vol. 27, London.

al-Qazwīnī, Zakariyyāʾ ibn Muḥammad ibn Maḥmūd
1849 *Kitāb ʿajāʾib al-makhlūqāt wa gharāʾib al-mawjūdāt* ("Wonders of Creation and Oddities of Existence"), ed. Wüstenfeld, F., *Zakarija Ben Muhammed Ben Mahmud el-Cazwini's Kosmographie, Erster Theil: Die Wunder der Schöpfung. Aus den Handschriften der Bibliotheken zu Berlin, Gotha, Dresden and Hamburg*, vol. 1, Leipzig, repr. Wiesbaden 1967.
1986 tr. and ed. Giese, A., *Die Wunder des Himmels und der Erde*, Darmstadt.
2002 tr. and ed. von Hees, S., *Enzyklopädie als Spiegel des Weltbildes: Qazwīnīs Wunder der Schöpfung – eine Naturkunde des 13. Jahrhunderts*, Wiesbaden.

Rashīd al-Dīn Faḍlallāh Hamadānī Ṭabīb
1836 *Histoire de Mongols de Perse écrite en persan par Rashid-eldin*, tr. and ed. Quatremère, É.M., Paris.
1957 *Taʾrīkh-i Mubārak-i Ġāzānī des Rašīd al-Dīn Faḍl Allāh Abī-l-Hair: Geschichte der Ilhāne Abāǧā bis Gaihātū (1265–1295)*, partial ed. Jahn, K., 's-Gravenhage.
1971 *Successors of Genghis Khan*, tr. Boyle, J.A., New York.
1980 *Die Indiengeschichte des Rašīd ud-Dīn*, tr. and ed. Jahn, K., Vienna.
1998–9 *Rashiduddin Fazlullah's Jamiʿu't-tawarikh, Compendium of Chronicles: a History of the Mongols*, 3 vols., tr. Thackston, Wheeler M.,

eds. Tekin, S., and Tekin, G.A., Sources of Oriental Languages and Literatures 45, vol. 1, Cambridge, MA.

2001 *The History of the Seljuk Turks: from the* Jāmiʿ al-Tawārīkh. *An Ilkhanid Adaptation of the* Saljūq-nāma *of Ẓāhir al-Dīn Nīshāpūrī*, tr. Luther, K.A. and ed. Bosworth, C.E., Richmond.

1995 "Articles of Endowment of the Rab-ʿi Rashidi," tr. Thackston, W.M., Appendix 1 in Blair, S.S., *A Compendium of Chronicles: Rashid al-Din's Illustrated History of the World*, The Nasser D. Khalili Collection of Islamic Art, vol. 27, London, pp. 114–5.

Rigveda

1889 *The Hymns of the Rigveda*, tr. Hotchkin Griffith, R.T., Benares.

Rubruck, William of

1990 *The Mission of Friar William of Rubruck: His Journey to the Court of the Great Khan Möngke*, 1253–1255, tr. and ed. Jackson, P., and Morgan, D., London.

Si-yu-ki

1884 *Buddhist Records of the Western World. Translated from the Chinese of Hiuen Tsiang (A.D. 629)*, 2 vols., tr. Beal, S., London, repr. 2000 (vol. 1) and 2001 (vol. 2).

al-Suhrawardī, Shihābuddīn Yaḥyā

1982 *The Mystical and Visionary Treatises of Suhrawardi*, tr. and ed. Thackston, W.M., London.

1976 *Shihâboddîn Yaḥyâ Sohravardî Shaykh al-Ishrâq: L'ange empourpré. Quinze traits et récits mystiques traduits du persan et de l'arabe*, tr. and ed. Corbin, H., Documents spirituels 14, Paris.

al-Ṭabarī, Abū Jaʿfar Muḥammad ibn Jarīr ibn Yazīd

1879–1901 *Mukhtaṣar taʾrīkh al-rusul (al-umam) wa 'l-mulūk wa 'l-khulafāʾ*, tr. and ed. de Goeje, M.J., *Annales quos scripsit Abu Djafar Mohammed ibn Djarir at-Tabarī*, Leiden.

1999 *The History of al-Ṭabarī: The Sāsānids, the Byzantines, the Lakmids, and Yemen*, vol. 5, tr. and ed. Bosworth, C.E., New York.

1991 *The History of al-Ṭabarī: The Children of Israel*, vol. 3, tr. Brinner, W.M., Albany, NY.

al-Thaʿālibī, Abū Manṣūr

1900 *Taʾrīkh Ghurar al-siyar* or *al-Ghurar fī siyar al-mulūk wa 'l-akhbārihim*, tr. and ed. Zotenberg, H., *Histoire des rois des Perses par Aboû Manṣoûr ʿAbd al-Malik ibn Muḥammad ibn Ismâʿîl al-Thaʿâlibî*, Paris.

al-Thaʿlabī, Abū Isḥāq Aḥmad ibn Muḥammad ibn Ibrāhīm

2002 *ʿArāʾis al-majālis fī qiṣaṣ al-anbiyāʾ*, tr. Brinner, W.M., *Lives of the Prophets*, vol. 24, Leiden.

al-Tīfāshī, Aḥmad ibn Yūsuf

1998 *Kitāb Azhār al-afkār fī jawāhir al-aḥjār*, tr. and ed. Abul Huda, S.N., *Arab Roots of Gemology – Ahmad ibn Yusuf al Tifaschi's Best Thoughts on the Best of Stones*, Lanham, MD, and London.

al-Warāwīnī, Saʿd al-Dīn

1959 *Marzubān-nāma*, tr. Levy, R., *The Tales of Marzuban*, London.

Zend-Avesta

1880 *The Zend-Avesta*, vol. 2, tr. Darmesteter, J., ed. Müller, M.F., Oxford, repr. 2004.

Secondary Sources

Adam, A.

1959 *Die Psalmen des Thomas und das Perlenlied als Zeugnisse vorchristlicher Gnosis*, Berlin.

Ackerman, P.

1935 "The Talking Tree," *Bulletin of the American Institute for Persian Art and Archaeology* IV, 2, pp. 67–72.

1936 "The Iranian Serpentarius and Gemini," *Bulletin of the American Institute for Persian Art and Archaeology* IV, 3, pp. 126–9.

Akbarnia, L.

2007 *Khitaʾi: Cultural Memory and the Creation of a Mongol Visual Idiom in Iran and Central Asia*, Ph.D. dissertation, Harvard University.

Akhmedov, A.

2000 "Astronomy, Astrology, Observatories and Calendars," *History of Civilizations of Central Asia*, vol. 4, *The Age of Achievement: A.D. 750 to the End of the Fifteenth Century, part 2, The Achievements*, Paris, pp. 195–204.

Akiner, S.

1998 "Conceptual Geographies of Central Asia," *Sustainable Development in Central Asia*, eds. Akiner, S., Hay, J., and Tideman, S., New York, pp. 3–62.

Akinian, N.

1930 *Das Skevra-Evangeliar vom Jahre 1197, aufbewahrt im Archive des armenischen Erzbistums Lemberg*, Materialien zur Geschichte der armenischen Kunst, Paläographie und Miniaturmalerei 2, Vienna.

Aladaşvili, N.A.

1977 *Monumental'naja skul'ptura Gruzii: figurnye rel'efy V–XI vekov* ("Monumental Georgian Sculpture: Fifth to Eleventh Century Bas-Reliefs"), Moscow.

Albaum, L.

1975 *Zhivopis' Afrasiaba*, Tashkent.

Alemany, A.

2000 *Sources on the Alans: A Critical Compilation*, Handbook of Oriental Studies, section eight, Central Asia, eds. Sinor, D., and Di Cosmo, N., vol. 5, Leiden, Boston and Cologne.

Alexander, D.

1992 *The Art of War: Arms and Armour of the 7th to 19th Century*, The Nasser D. Khalili Collection of Islamic Art, vol. 21, London.

Alexander, P.S.

1999 "Jewish Elements in Gnosticism and Magic," *The Cambridge History of Judaism*, vol. 3, *The Early Roman Period*, Cambridge, pp. 1052–1079.

Allan, J.W.

1982a *Islamic Metalwork: The Nuhad Es-Said Collection*, London, repr. 1999.

1982b *Nishapur: Metalwork of the Early Islamic Period*, New York.

Allan, S.
1991 *The Shape of the Turtle: Myth, Art, and Cosmos in Early China*, New York.

Allen, T.
2003 *Ayyubid Architecture*, published by Solipsist Press, Occidental, California, electronic publication.

Allen, W.E.D.
1932 *A History of the Georgian People*, London.

Allenow, M., Dmitrijewa, N., and Medwedkowa, O.
1992 *Russische Kunst*, Freiburg, Basel and Vienna.

Allsen, T.T.
2001 *Culture and Conquest in Mongol Eurasia*, Cambridge Studies in Islamic Civilization, Cambridge.
1997 *Commodity and Exchange in the Mongol Empire: A Cultural History of Islamic Textiles*, Cambridge Studies in Islamic Civilization, Cambridge.
1996 "Spiritual Geography and Political Legitimacy in the Eastern Steppe," *Ideology and the Formation of Early States*, eds. Claessen, Henri J.M., and Oosten, Jarich G., Leiden, pp. 116–35.

Amiet, P.
1961 *La glyptique mésopotamienne archaïque*, Paris, rev. and enlarged repr., 1980.

Amiranašvili, Š.
1966 *Gruzinskaya Miniatyura* ("Georgian Miniatures"), Moscow.

Ananikian, M.H.
1925 *Armenian, The Mythology of All Races*, vol. 7, Boston.

Anawati, G.C.
1967 "Le nom suprême de Dieu," *Estratto degli Atti del III Congresso di Studi Arabi e Islamici, Ravello, 1-6 settembre 1966*, Naples, pp. 7–58.

Anthony, D.W.
2007 *The Horse, the Wheel, and Language: How Bronze-Age Riders from the Eurasian World Shaped the Modern World*, Columbia and Princeton.

Arberry, A.J., Minovi, M., and Blochet, E.
1959 *The Chester Beatty Library: A Catalogue of Persian Manuscripts and Miniatures*, ed. Wilkinson, J.V.S., Dublin, vol. 1.

Arik, R., and Arik, O.
2008 *Tiles: Treasures of Anatolian Soil: Tiles of the Seljuk and Beylik Periods*, Istanbul.

Arrizoli-Clémentel, P.
1990 *Le Musée des Tissus de Lyon*, Lyon.

Artemiev, A.R.
2003 "Srednevekovye Mongol'skie Poseleniya XIII–XIV vv. v Zabaikal'e," *Problemy arkheologii i Paleoekologii Severnoi, Vostochnoi i Tsentral'noi Azii :* Materialy Mezhdunarodnoi Konferentsii «Iz Veka v Vek» ("Issues of Archeology and Paleoecology of Northern, Eastern, and Central Asia"), ed. Derevianko, A.P., Izdatel'stvo Instituta arkheologii i etnografii SO RAN, Novosibirsk.

Aruz, J.
1998 "Images in the Supernatural World: Bactria-Margiana Seals and Relations with the Near East and the Indus," *Ancient Civilizations From Scythia to Siberia* 5, no. 1, Leiden, pp. 12–30.

Asirvatham, S.R.
2001 "Olympias' Snake and Callistenes' Stand," *Between Magic and Religion: Interdisciplinary Studies in Ancient Mediterranean Religion and Society*, eds. Asirvatham, S.R., Pache, C.O., Watrous, J., Lanham, MD, pp. 93–126.

Aslapana, O.
1971 *Turkish Art and Architecture*, New York and Washington, DC.

Astour, M.C.
1968 "Two Ugaritic Serpent Charms," *Journal of Near Eastern Studies* 27, pp. 13–36.

Atallah, W.
1975 "Aymu-l-Lāh: Vestige d'un culte chthonien," *Arabica* 22, 2, pp. 162–9.

Atil, E.
1973 *Freer Gallery of Art Fiftieth Anniversary Exhibition, III. Ceramics from the World of Islam*, Washington, DC.

Atil, E., Chase, W.T., and Jett, P.
1985 *Metalwork in the Freer Gallery of Art*, Washington, DC.

Atroshenko, V.I., and Collins, J.
1985 *The Origins of the Romanesque: Near Eastern Influences on European Art, 4th-12th Centuries*, London.

Aufhauser, J.B.
1911 *Das Drachenwunder des heiligen Georg in der griechischen und lateinischen Überlieferung*, Leipzig.

d'Avennes, P.
1877 *L'art arabe* III, Paris, repr. London, 1983 as *Arab Art as Seen Through the Monuments of Cairo from the 7th Century to the 18th.*

Ayoub, M.
1992 *The Qur'an and Its Interpreters: The House of ʿImrān*, New York.

Azarpay, G.
1978 "The Eclipse Dragon on an Arabic Frontispiece Miniature," *Journal of American Oriental Society*, vol. 98, no. 4, October–December, pp. 363–74.
1981 with contrib. by Belenitskii, A.M., Marshak, B.I., and Dresden, M.J., *Sogdian Painting: The Pictorial Epic in Oriental Art*, Berkeley, Los Angeles and London.

Bachmann, W.
1913 *Kirchen und Moscheen in Armenien und Kurdistan*, Wissenschaftliche Veröffentlichungen der Deutschen Orient-Gesellschaft 25, Leipzig.

Badiee, J.
1978 *An Islamic Cosmography: The Illustrations of the Sarre Qazwīnī*, Ph.D. dissertation, The University of Michigan.
1984 "The Sarre Qazwīnī: An early Aq Aoyunlu Manuscript?" *Ars Orientalis* 14, pp. 97–113.

Baer, E.
1965 *Sphinxes and Harpies in Medieval Islamic Art: An Iconographical Study*, Oriental Notes and Studies 9, The Israel Oriental Society, Jerusalem.
1981 "The Ruler in the Cosmic Setting: A Note on Medieval Islamic Iconography," *Essays in Islamic Art and Architecture. In Honor of Katharina Otto-Dorn*, ed. Daneshvari, A., Malibu, CA, pp. 13–9.
1983 *Metalwork in Medieval Islamic Art*, Albany, NY.
1989 *Ayyubid Metalwork with Christian Images*, Studies in Islamic Art and Architecture, 4, Leiden and New York.

Bailey, H.W.
1958 "Languages of the Saka," *Handbuch der Orientalistik* I.IV.1, ed. Spuler, B., Leiden and Cologne, pp. 131–54.
1959 "Iranian *Arya-* and *Daha-*," *Transactions of the Philological Society*, pp. 71–115.
1967 "Altun Khan," *Bulletin of the School of Oriental and African Studies* XXX, pp. 95–104.

Baipakov, K.
1992 "Les fouilles de la ville d'Ortrar," *Archéologie islamique* 3, pp. 87–110.

Bálint, C.
1989 *Die Archäologie der Steppe: Steppenvölker zwischen Volga und Donau vom 6. bis zum 10. Jahrhundert*, ed. Daim, F., Vienna and Cologne.

Baltrušaitis, J.
1929 *Etudes sur l'art médiéval en Géorgie et en Arménie*, Paris.

Bank, A.V.
1966 *Vizantijskoe iskusstvo v sobranijach Sovetskogo Sojuza* ("Byzantine Art in the Collections of the USSR"), Leningrad and Moscow.

Barb, A.A.
1953 "Der Heilige und die Schlangen: 1. Ein Amulett gegen Gift und Kopfschmerzen," *Mitteilungen der Anthropologischen Gesellschaft in Wien* 82, 1, pp. 1–21.
1966 "Antaura, the Mermaid, and the Devil's Grandmother," *The Journal of the Warburg and Courtauld Institutes*, vol. 29, pp. 1–23.

Barrett, D.
1949 *Islamic Metalwork in the British Museum*, London.

Barrucand, M.
1990–1 "The Miniatures of the *Daqā'iq al-ḥaqā'iq* (Bibliothèque Nationale, MS Pers. 174): A Testimony to the Cultural Diversity of Medieval Anatolia," *Islamic Art* IV, pp. 113–51, and colour pls. II and III.

Barthold, W. (Bartol'd, V.V.)
1932–5 "Zwölf Vorlesungen über die Geschichte der Türken Mittelasiens," *Die Welt des Islam*, vols. 14–7, repr. Hildesheim, 1962.
1958 *Turkestan Down to the Mongol Invasion*, 2nd ed. E.J.W. Gibb Memorial Series, n.s. 5, London.

Basilov, V.N.
1989 ed., *Nomads of Eurasia*, Seattle and London.
1991 "Texts of Shamanic Invocations from Central Asia and Kazakhstan," *Shamanism in Central Asia and the Americas*, eds. Seaman, G., and Jane S. Day, Los Angeles, pp. 273–92.

Bashkirov, A.S.
1931 *Iskusstvo Dagestana* ("The Art of Daghestan: Carved Stones"), Moscow.

Baumer, C.
2005 *Frühes Christentum zwischen Euphrat und Jangtse: Eine Zeitreise entlang der Seidenstraße zur Kirche des Ostens*, Stuttgart.

Bayar, D.
2005 "Gedenkstätten und Steinskulpturen der Alttürkischen Zeit," *Dschingis Khan und seine Erben: Das Weltreich der Mongolen*, Munich, pp. 69–73.

Bauer, R.W.
1995 *Boundaries and Frontiers in Medieval Muslim Geography*, Transactions of the American Philosophical Society, Philadelphia, PA.

Bazin, L.
1974 *Les calendriers turcs anciens et médiévaux*, Paris, Université de Paris, Diss., 1972, Service de reproduction des thèses de l'Université de Lille III, Lille.
1991 *Les systèmes chronologiques dans le monde turc ancien*, Budapest and Paris.

Beck, R.
1988 *Planetary Gods and Planetary Orders in the Mysteries of Mithras*, Études préliminaires aux religions orientales dans l'Empire romain 109, Leiden, Boston and Cologne.
2004 *Beck on Mithraism: Collected Works with New Essays*, Ashgate Contemporary Thinkers on Religion, Ashgate.

Beer, R.
2004 *The Encyclopedia of Tibetan Symbols and Motifs*, Chicago.

Belenitskii (Belenizkii), A.M.
1980 *Mittelasien: Kunst der Sogden*, Leipzig.

Belenitskii, A.M., and Bentowitsch, I.B.
2000 "Aus der Geschichte der mittelalterlichen Seidenweberei (Zur Identifikation der Gewebe *zandaniji*)," *Textilien Mittelasiens: Beiträge zur sasanidischen und frühislamischen Kunst Entwicklung – Ornamente – Symbolik*, vol. 1, Mittelasiatische Studien, vol. 2, ed. Reinhold Schletzer, pp. 38–46 (repr. from *Sowjetische Archäologie*, no. 2, 1961).

Belenitskii, A.M., and Marshak, B.I.
1971 "L'art de Piandjikent à la lumière des dernières fouilles (1958–68)," *Arts Asiatiques*, vol. 23, pp. 3–40.
1981 "The Paintings of Sogdiana," *Sogdian Painting: The Pictorial Epic in Oriental Art*, Azarpay, G., with contrib. by Belenitskii, A.M., Marshak, B.I., and Dresden, M.J., Berkeley, Los Angeles and London, pp. 11–78.

Benveniste, D.
1927 "L'origine du *višap* arménien," *Revue des études arméniennes* 7.1, pp. 7–91.

Benveniste, É., and Renou, L.
1934 *Vṛtra et Vṛθragna*, Paris.

van Berchem, M.
1897 "Epigraphie des Assassins des Syrie," *Journal asiatique* sér. 9, vol. 9, pp. 474–7.

1906 “Monuments et inscriptions de l’atābek Lu’lu’ de Mossoul,” *Orientalische Studien Theodor Nöldecke zum siebzigsten Geburtstag gewidmet*, Gieszen, pp. 197–210.

van Berchem, M., and Strzygowski, J.
1910 *Amida: Materiaux pour l’epigraphie et l’histoire musulmanes du Diyar-Bekr, Beiträge zur Kunstgeschichte von Nordmesopotamien, Hellas und dem Abendlande*, Heidelberg.

Berger, P.L., and Luckmann, T.
1971 *The Social Construction of Reality: a Treatise in the Sociology of Knowledge*, Harmondsworth.

Bergeron, P.
1735 *Voyages faites principalement en Asie dans le douzième, treizième, quatorzième et quinzième siècles*, The Hague.

Bierman, A.I.
1994 “Medical Fiction and Pharmaceutical Facts about Theriac,” *Pharmaceutical Historian: Newsletter of the British Society for the History of Pharmacy* 24, 3, pp. 5–8.

Bilici, K.Z.
2006 “Bronze Door-Knockers of Cizre - Great Mosque: a New Example,” *Ērān ud Anērān: Studies Presented to Boris Il’ič Maršak on the Occasion of His 70th Birthday*, eds. Compareti, M., Raffetta, P., and Scarcia, G., Venice, pp. 111–22.

Birge, J. Kingsley
1939 *The Bektashi Order of Dervishes*, London.

Bivar, A.D.H.
1967 “A Parthian Amulet,” *Bulletin of the School of Oriental and African Studies* XXX, pp. 512–25.
1969 *Catalogue of the Western Asiatic Seals in the British Museum, Stamp Seals II: The Sassanian Dynasty*, London.
1975a “Religious Subjects on Achaemenid Seals,” *Mithraic Studies: Proceedings of the First International Congress of Mithraic Studies*, ed. Hinnells, J.R., vol. 1, Manchester, pp. 90–105, and vol. 2, pl. 4.
1975b “Mithra and Mesopotamia,” *Mithraic Studies: Proceedings of the First International Congress of Mithraic Studies*, ed. Hinnells, J.R., vol. 2, Manchester, pp. 275–89.
2000 “The Role of Allegory in the Persian Epic,” *Bulletin of the Asia Institute* 14, pp. 19–26.

Blair, S.S.
1992 *The Monumental Inscriptions from Early Islamic Iran and Transoxiana*, Leiden.
1995 *A Compendium of Chronicles: Rashid al-Din’s Illustrated History of the World*, The Nasser D. Khalili Collection of Islamic Art, vol. 27, London.

Blochet, E.
1926 *Les enluminures des manuscrits orientaux - turcs, arabes, persans - de la Bibliothèque Nationale*, Paris.

de Blois, F.
1990 *Burzōy’s Voyage to India and the Origin of the Book of Kalīlah wa Dimnah*, London.

Boardman, J.
1986 “The Ketos in India,” *Iconographie classique et identité régionale*, eds. Kahil, L., et al., Bulletin de Correspondance Hellénique, Supplément XIV, Paris and Athens, pp. 447–53.
2003 “Three Monsters at Tillya Tepe,” *Ancient Civilizations From Scythia to Siberia*, vol. 9, no. 1–2, Leiden, pp. 133–46.

Bol, P.
1987 “Seeking Common Ground: Han Literati under Jurchen Rule,” *Harvard Journal of Asiatic Studies* 47, 2, pp. 461–538.

Bombaci, A., and Scerrato, U.
1959 “Summary Report on the Italian Archaeological Mission to Afghanistan: Introduction to the Excavations at Ghazni,” *East and West*, NS 10, 1–2, March - June, pp. 3–22.

Bombaci, A.
1966 *The Kufic Inscription in Persian Verses in the Court of the Royal Palace of Masʿūd III at Ghazni*, Rome.

Bonner, C.
1950 *Studies in Magical Amulets Chiefly Graeco-Egyptian*, Ann Arbor and London.

Bonner, M.D.
1996 *Aristocratic Violence and Holy War: Studies in the Jihad and the Arab-Byzantine Frontier*, American Oriental Series, 81, New Haven, CN.
2006 *Jihad in Islamic History: Doctrines and Practice*, Princeton, NJ.

Boratov, P.N.
1957 “Vestiges oğuz dans la tradition bektaşi,” *Akten des vierundzwanzigsten Internationalen Orientalisten-Kongresses in München*, Wiesbaden, pp. 382–5.

Bosch, F.D.K.
1960 *The Golden Germ (De gounden kiem, engl.): An Introduction to Indian Symbolism*, Indo-lranian Monographs, ‘s-Gravenhage, Mouton.

Bosworth, C.E.
1963 *The Ghaznavids: Their Empire in Afghanistan and Eastern Iran 994–1040*, Edinburgh, repr. New Delhi, 1992.
1968 “The Political and Dynastic History of the Iranian World (A.D. 1000–1217),” *The Cambridge History of Iran*, vol. 5, *The Saljuq and Mongol Periods*, ed. Boyle, J.A., Cambridge.
1976 *The Mediaeval Islamic Underworld: the Banū Sāsān in Arabic Society and Literature*, 2 vols., Leiden.
1996 *The New Islamic Dynasties: A Chronological and Genealogical Manual*, Edinburgh.

Boulhoul, P.
1994 “Hagiographie antique et démonologie: Des notes sur quelques passions grecques,” *Analecta Bollandiana* 112, pp. 262–3.

Bouras, L.
1977 “Dragon Representations on Byzantine Phialae and Their Conduits,” *Gesta* 16/2, pp. 65–8.

Bousset-Gressmann, W.
1926 *Die Religion des Judentums in späthellenistischen Zeitalter*, 3rd ed., Tübingen.

Boyce, M.
1975 *A History of Zoroastrianism: The Early Period*, vol. 1, Leiden, repr. 1996.

1979 *Zoroastrians: Their Religious Beliefs and Practices*, London, repr. 2001.
1981 "Varuna the Baga," *Monumentum George Morgenstierne I*, ed. Duchèsne-Guillemin, J., Acta Iranica, xxi, Leiden, pp. 59–73.
1982 *A History of Zoroastrianism: Under the Achaemenians*, vol. 2, Leiden.
1983 "Iranian Festivals," *The Cambridge History of Iran*, vol. 3, *The Seleucid, Parthian and Sasanid Periods*, eds. Fischer, W.B., Gershevitch, I., and Yarshater, E., Cambridge, pp. 792–819.
1984 *Textual Sources for the Study of Zoroastrianism*, Manchester.

Boyce, M., and Grenet, F. with a contrib. by Beck, R.
1991 *A History of Zoroastrianism: Zoroastrianism under Macedonian and Roman Rule*, vol. 3, Leiden.

Brandenburg, D.
1973 *Medizinisches in Tausendundeiner Nacht: Ein literaturgeschichtlicher Beitrag zur islamischen Heilkunde*, Stuttgart.

Braun, O.
1900 tr. and ed., *Das Buch der Synhados oder Synodicon Orientale nach einer Handschrift des Museo Borgiano*, Stuttgart, repr. Amsterdam, 1975.

Brentjes, B.
1989 "Incised Bones and a Ceremonial Belt: Finds from Kurgan-Tepe and Tillian-Tepe," *Bulletin of the Asia Institute* 3, pp. 39–44.

Bretschneider, E.V.
1888 *Medieval Researches from Eastern Asiatic Sources: Fragments Towards the Knowledge of the Geography and History of Central and Western Asia from the 13th to the 17th Century*, repr. London, 1967.

Brosset, M.-F.
1860 *Ruines d'Ani capitale de l'Arménie sous les rois Bagratides, aux Xe et XIe siècle: histoire et description*, St. Petersburg.

Browne, E.G.
1920 *A Literary History of Persia: From the Earliest Times Until Firdawsi (to 1000 A.D.)*, vol. 1, London.
1921 *Arabian Medicine*, Cambridge.

Buddruss, G.
1975 "Zur Benennung der Schlange in einigen nordwestindischen Sprachen," *Münchner Studien zur Sprachwissenschaft*, *33*, pp. 7–14.

Buiskikh, A.
2007 "On the Question of the Stylistic Influences Reflected in the Architecture and Art of Chersonesos: 'Snake-legged Goddess' or Rankenfrau," *Ancient Civilizations from Scythia to Siberia*, Vol. 13, Nos. 3–4, pp. 157–81.

Bunker, C.E.
1992 "Gold Belt Plaques in the Siberian Treasure of Peter the Great: Dates, Origins and Iconography," *Foundations of an Empire: Archaeology and Art of the Eurasian Steppes (Nomads: Masters of the Eurasian Steppe)*, ed. Seaman, G., vol. 3, Los Angeles, pp. 201–22.

Bunker, C.E., and White, J.M., with So, J.F.
1999 *Adornment for the Body and Soul: Ancient Chinese Ornaments from the Mengdiexuan Collection*, Hong Kong.

Bürgel, J.C.
1988 *The Feather of Simurgh: the "Licit Magic" of the Arts in Medieval Islam*, New York.
1995 "Die Geheimwissenschaften im Iskandername Nizamis," *Proceedings of the Second European Conference of Iranian Studies*, Bamberg, 30 September to 4 October 1991, Societas Iranologica Europaea, eds. Fragner, B.G., et al., Rome, pp. 103–12.
2000 "Occult Sciences in the *Iskandernameh* of Nizami," *The Poetry of Nizami Ganjavi: Knowledge, Love and Rhetoric*, eds. Talattof, K., and Clinton, J.W., New York, pp. 129–40.

Burkert, W.
1995 "Der geheime Reiz des Verborgenen: Antike Mysterienkulte," *Secrecy and Concealment: Studies in the History of Mediterranean and Near Eastern Religions*, Proceedings of a Meeting held 1–4 June, 1993, Werner Reimers-Stiftung, Bad Homburg, eds. Kippenberg, H.G., and Stroumsa, G.G., Leiden, New York and Cologne, pp. 79–100.

Burns, R.I.
1989 "The Significance of the Frontier in the Middle Ages," *Medieval Frontier Societies*, eds. Bartlett, R., and McKay, A., London, pp. 307–30.

Bussagli, M.
1963 *La peinture de l'Asie Centrale*, Geneva.

Buxton, D.R.
1934 *Russian Mediaeval Architecture: With an Account of the Transcaucasian Styles and Their Influence in the West*, Cambridge.

Çağman, F., and Tanindi, Z.
1986 *The Topkapi Saray Museum: The Albums and Illustrated Manuscripts*, tr. and ed. Rogers, J.M., Boston.

Cahen, C.
1948 "La première pénétration turque en Asie-Mineure (seconde moitié du XIe siècle)," *Byzantion* XVIII, pp. 5–7, repr. London 1974.
1968 *Pre-Ottoman Turkey: a General Survey of the Material and Spiritual Culture and History c. 1071–1330*, tr. Jones-Williams, J., London.

Canaan, T.
1936 "Arabic Magic Bowls," *Journal of the Palestine Oriental Society* 16, pp. 79–127.
1937 "The Decipherment of Arabic Talismans," *Berytus Archaeological Studies*, vol. 4, pp. 69–110.
1938 "The Decipherment of Arabic Talismans," *Berytus Archaeological Studies*, vol. 5, pp. 141–51.

Canivet, M.T. and P.
1975 "La mosaïque d'Adam dans l'église syrienne de Hūarte (Ve s.)," *Cahiers Archéologiques* 24, pp. 49–70.

Canova, G.
1994 "Il serpente della Kaʿba: Una nota sulla Mecca preislamica," *Annali di Ca' Foscari: Rivista della Racolta di lingue e letterature straniere dell'Università di Venezia* 25, pp. 421–5.

Caratsch, C.
2005 "Der Futterstoff des Mantels König Rogers II. von Sizilien," *Nobilis Officinae: Die königlichen Hofwerkstätten zu Palermo zur Zeit der Normannen und Staufer im 12. und 13. Jahrhundert*, ed. Seipel, W., Vienna and Palermo, pp. 125–35.

Carboni, S.
1988–9 "The London Qazwīnī: An Early 14th-Century Copy of the *ʿAjāʾib al-Makhlūqāt*," *Islamic Art* III, pp. 15–29, pls. IV–VII, figs. 1–5.
1992 *The Wonders of Creation and the Singularities of Ilkhanid Painting: A Study of the London Qazwīnī British Library MS. Or. 14140*, unpublished Ph.D. dissertation, School of Oriental and African Studies, University of London.

Carpenter, T.H.
1991 *Art and Myth in Ancient Greece*, London.

Carter, M.L.
1974 "Royal Festal Themes in Sasanian Silverwork and their Central Asian Parallels," *Acta Iranica*, Commémoration Cyrus, vol. 1, Hommage Universel, Tehran, Liège and Leiden, pp. 171–202, pls. III–XIV.
1981 "Mithra on the Lotus: a Study of the Imagery of the Sun God in Kushano-Sasanian Era," *Momentum Georg Morgenstierne* I, Acta Iranica 21, Hommages et Opera Minora, vol. 7, Leiden, pp. 74–98 and pls. XIII–XXIII.
1992 "A Scythian Legend from Ancient Uḍḍiyāna," *Bulletin of the Asia Institute* 6, pp. 71–8.

Caspani, E.
1945 "The Cave of the Shadow of the Buddha at Nagarahara," *Journal of the Royal Asiatic Society of Bengal (Letters)*, vol. 11.

Chavannes, É.
1910 *Cinq Cent Contes et Apologues: Extraits du Tripitaka Chinois*, Paris.

Chegini, N.N., and Nikitin, A.V.
1996 "Sasanian Iran – Economy, Society, Arts and Crafts," *History of Civilizations of Central Asia*, vol. 3, *The Crossroads of Civilizations: A.D. 250 to 750*, ed. Litvinsky, B.A., Paris, repr. Delhi, 1999, pp. 35–78.

Chelhod, J.
1955 *Le sacrifice chez les arabes: Recherches sur l'évolution, la nature et la fonction des rites sacrificiels en Arabie occidentale*, Bibliothèque de sociologie contemporaine, Paris.

Ch'en, K.K.S.
1968 *Buddhism: The Light of Asia*, New York.

Chittick, W.C.
1992 *Faith and Practice of Islam: Three Thirteenth Century Sufi Texts*, Albany, NY.

Chodkiewicz, M.
1993 *Seal of the Saints: Prophethood and Sainthood in the Doctrine of Ibn al-ʿArabī*, Cambridge.

Christensen, A.
1934 *Les types du premier homme et du premier roi dans l'histoire légendaire des iraniens*, vol. 2, Archive d'Études Orientales 14, Leiden.
1944 *L' Iran sous les Sassanides*, 2nd ed., Copenhagen.
1993 *The Kayanians [Les Kayanides*, 1931], tr. Tumboowalla, F.N., Mumbai.

Chwolsohn (Chvol'son), D.A.
1856 *Die Ssabier und des Ssabismus*, vol. 1, *Die Entwicklung der Begriffe Ssabier und Ssabismus und die Geschichte der harranischen Ssabier oder der syro-hellenistischen Heiden im nördlichen Mesopotamien und in Bagdad zur Zeit des Chalifats*, vol. 2, *Orientalische Quellen zur Geschichte der Ssabier und des Ssabismus*, St. Petersburg.

Clédat, J.
1904–6 *Le monastère de la nécropole de Baouît*, Mémoires publiés par les membres de l'Institut français d'archéologie orientale du Caire, Cairo.

Clermont-Ganneau, C.
1876 "Horus et Saint Georges d'après un bas-relief inédit du Louvre," *Revue archéologique* II, pp. 196–204 and 372–99.

Cohen, H.
1892 *Description historique des monnaies frappées sous l'Empire romaine*, Paris, vol. 7.

Colpe, C.
1983 "Development of Religious Thought," *The Cambridge History of Iran*, vol. 3, *The Seleucid, Parthian and Sasanid Periods*, eds. Fischer, W.B., Gershevitch, I., and Yarshater, E., Cambridge, pp. 819–65.

Combaz, G.
1945 *Masques et Dragons en Asie*, Mélanges Chinois et Bouddhiques, vol. 7, Brussels.

Combe, E., Sauvaget, J., and Wiet, G.
1933 eds., *Répertoire chronologique d'épigraphie arabe*, Cairo.

Coomaraswamy, A.K.
1934 "Khwāja Khaḍir and the Fountain of Life, in the Tradition of Persian and Mughal Art," *Ars Islamica* I, pp. 173–82.

Corbin, H.
1993 *History of Islamic Philosophy*, vol. II, London.
1998a *The Voyage and the Messenger: Iran and Philosophy*, Berkeley, CA.
1998b *Alone with the Alone: Creative Imagination in the Ṣūfism of Ibn ʿArabī*, Bollingen Series XCI, Princeton, NJ.

Cowell, E.B.
1895–1913 ed., *The Jataka or Stories of the Buddha's Former Births*, 7 vols., Cambridge, repr. Delhi, 2000.

Creswell, K.A.C.
1932 *Early Muslim Architecture*, vol. 1, Oxford.

Crossley, P.K.
1990 "Thinking about Ethnicity in Early Modern China," *Late Imperial China* 11, 1, pp. 1–34.

Cuinet, V.
1890–5 *Turquie d'Asie: Les Provinces arabes Alep, Mossoul, Bagdad, Bassorah*, vol. 2, Paris, repr. 2001, Istanbul.

Cumont, M.F.
1937 "St. George and Mithra the Cattle-Thief," *Journal of Roman Studies* 27, pp. 63–71.

1939 "Mithra en Asie Mineur," *Anatolian Studies presented to William Hepburn Buckler*, ed. Calder, W.M., and Keil, J., Manchester, pp. 67–76.

Curatola, G.
1979 "Serpenti e 'draghi' anatolici: un'antica questione," *Studi su Harran*, Venice Quaderni, no. 6, Venice, pp. 123–46.
1982 "The Viar Dragon," *Solṭāniye III, Quaderni del Seminario di Iranistica, Uralo-Altaistica e Caucasologia dell'Università di Venezia*, 19, pp. 71–88.
1989 *Draghi*, Eurasiatica, Quaderni del Dipartimento di Studi Eurasiatici, Università degli Studi di Venezia, vol. 15, Venice.

Czuma, S.J.
1985 *Kushan Sculpture: Images from Early India*, Cleveland.

Daim, F.
2000 ed., *Die Awaren am Rand der byzantinischen Welt: Studien zu Diplomatie, Handel und Technologietransfer im Frühmittelalter*, Monographien aus Frühgeschichte und Mittelalterarchäologie, Innsbruck.

Dalman, G.
1908 *Petra und seine Felsheiligtümer*, Leipzig.

Daneshvari, A.
1993 "The Iconography of the Dragon in the Cult of the Saints in Islam," *Manifestations of Sainthood in Islam*, ed. Smith, G., Istanbul, pp. 15–25.

Daniélou, J.
1964 *The Theology of Jewish Christianity*, London and Chicago.

Dankoff, R.
1975 "Kāšgarī on the Beliefs and Superstitions of the Turks," *Journal of the American Oriental Society*, vol. 95, pp. 68–80.

Darkó, E.
1935 "Influences touraniennes sur l'évolution de l'art militaire des Grecs, des Romains et des Byzantins," *Byzantion* X, pp. 443–69.
1948 "Le rôle des peuples nomades cavaliers dans la transformation de l'empire romain aux premiers siècles du moyen-âge," *Byzantion* XVIII, pp. 85–97.

Dawkins, J.Mc.G.
1944 "The Seal of Solomon," *Journal of the Royal Asiatic Society*, pp. 145–50.

Day, J.
1985 *God's Conflict with the Dragon and the Sea: Echoes of a Canaanite Myth in the Old Testament*, Cambridge.

Dedes, Y.
1996 *Battalname*, 2 vols., Cambridge, MA.

Delcor, M.
1973 *Le Testament d'Abraham: Introduction, traduction du texte grec et commentaire de la recension grecque longue. Suivi de la traduction des Testaments d'Abraham, d'Isaac et de Jacob d'après les versions orientales*, Studia in V.T. Pseudepigrapha, Vol. II, Leiden.

De Mallmann, M.-T.
1962 *Les enseignements iconographiques de l'Agnipurāna*, Annales du Musée Guimet, Bibliothèque d'études 67, Paris.

Demougeot, E.
1986 "La symbolique du lion et du serpent sur les *solidi* des empereurs d'Occident de la première moitié du Ve siècle," *Revue numismatique*, 6th series, 28, pp. 94–118.

Deng, G.
1997 *Chinese Maritime Activities and Socioeconomic Development, c. 2100 B.C.–1900 A.D.*, Westport, CT.

DeWeese, D.A.
1994 *Islamization and Native Religion in the Golden Horde: Baba Tükles and Conversion to Islam in Historical and Epic Tradition*, University Park, PA.

Dhorme, E.
1949 *Les religions de Babylonie et d'Assyrie*, Les anciennes religions orientales, Paris.

Diakonoff, I.M.
1981 "The Cimmerians," *Monumentum George Morgenstierne I*, ed. Duchèsne-Guillemin, J., Acta Iranica, xxi, Leiden, pp. 103–40.

Dickson, M.B., and Welch, C.S.
1981 *The Houghton Shahnameh*, 2 vols., Cambridge, MA, and London.

Di Cosmo, N.
2002 *Ancient China and Its Enemies: The Rise of Nomadic Power in East Asian History*, Cambridge.
1999 "Manchu Shamanic Ceremonies at the Qing court," *State and Court Ritual in China*, ed. McDermott, J.P., Cambridge, pp. 352–98.

Diez, E.
1949 "The Zodiac Reliefs of the Portal of the Gök Medrese in Siwas," *Artibus Asiae* vol. 12, 1–2, pp. 99–104.

Diez, E., and Arslanapa, O.
1956 *Türk sanatı*, Istanbul.

Dimand, M.S.
1926 "Near Eastern Metalwork," *The Bulletin of the Metropolitan Museum of Art New York* vol. 20, pp. 193–9.
1947 *A Handbook of Muhammadan Art*, New York.

Dinkler, E.
1978 "Der salomonische Knoten in der nubischen Kunst und die Geschichte des Motivs," *Études Nubiennes*, Cairo, pp. 73–86.

Diwersy, A., and Wand, G.
2001 *Irak – Land zwischen Euphrat und Tigris*, Blieskastel.

Diyarbekirli, N.
1971 "Vestiges de croyances altaïques dans l'art seldjoukide," *Turcica, Revue d'Études Turques*, III, pp. 60–70.

Dode, Z.V.
2007 "Bestiary on Mongolian Silks: Style and Semantics of Design," *Archaeology, Ethnology and Anthropology of Eurasia*, vol. 30, no. 2, July, pp. 100–13.

Dols, M.W.
1984 tr. and with an introd., *Medieval Islamic Medicine: Ibn Riḍwān's Treatise "On the Prevention of Bodily Ills in Egypt,"* Berkeley, CA.

Donaldson, B.A.
1938 *The Wild Rue: A Study of Muhammedan Magic and Folklore in Iran*, London, repr. New York, 1973.

Donovan, D.
1988–9 "The Evolution of the Throne in Early Persian Painting: The Evidence of the Edinburgh *Jāmiʿ al-Tawārīkh*," *Persica* vol. 13, pp. 1–76.

Dorn, B.
1858 ed. and tr., *Muhammedanische Quellen zur Geschichte der südlichen Küste des Kaspischen Meeres*, vol. IV, *Auszüge aus Muhammedanischen Schriftstellern nebst einer kurzen Geschichte der Chane von Scheki*, St. Petersburg.

Doro, L.
1941 *Antioch-on-the-Orontes: The Excavations of 1937–1939*, vol. 3, Princeton, NJ.

Doutté, E.
1909 *La société musulmane du Maghrib: Magie et religions dans l'Afrique du Nord*, Alger.

Dozy, M., and de Goeje, M.J.
1885 "Mémoire posthume de M. Dozy contenant des nouveaux documents pour l'étude de la religion des Harraniens," *Actes du sixième congrès international des Orientalistes tenu au 1883 à Leide*, vol. 2, *Section: sémitique*, Leiden, pp. 282–366.

Drijvers, H.J.W.
1978 "Mithra at Hatra? Some Remarks on the Problem of Irano-Mesopotamian Syncretism," *Études mithriaques*, ed. Duchèsne-Guillemin, J., Tehran and Liège, pp. 151–86.
1991 "The Acts of Thomas," *New Testament Apocrypha*, ed. Schneemelcher, W., Louisville, KY, pp. 322–411.

Driver, S.R., and Gray, G.B.
1921 *A Critical and Exegetical Commentary on the Book of Job*, I, New York, pp. 359–71.

Dubash, S.E.
1906 *The Zoroastrian Sanitary Code, with Critical and Explanatory Notes*, Bombay.

Duchèsne-Guillemin, J.
1990 "The Dragon and the Lunar Nodes," *Bulletin of the Asia Institute* 4, pp. 17–9.

Duda, D.
1992 *Die illuminierten Handschriften und Inkunabeln der Österreichischen Nationalbibliothek*, 5, *Islamische Handschriften*, 2, Veröffentlichungen der Kommission für Schrift- und Buchwesen des Mittelalters, 1, Österreichische Akademie der Wissenschaften, phil.-hist. Kl., Wien.

Dulęba, W.
1995 *The Cyrus Legend in the Šāhnāme*, Polska Akademia Nauk Oddział w Krakowie, Prace Komisji Orientalistycznej Nr. 22, Krakow.

Dundes, A.
2003 *Fables of the Ancients? Folklore in the Qurʾan*, Lanham and Oxford.

Durnovo, L.A., Sargsian, M.S., and Mnatsakanyan, A.Š.
1978 *Ornamenty Armianskikh rukopisei* ("Ornaments of Armenian Manuscripts"), Erevan.

Du Ry, C.J.
1970 *Die Welt des Islam*, Baden-Baden.

D'yakonova, N.V.
1940 "Terrakotovaya figurka Zakhaka," *Trudy otdela Vostoka Gosudarstvennogo Ermitazha* 3, pp. 195–205.

Dzhanpoladyan, R.M.
1958 "Sferokonicheskiye Sosudi iz Dvina i Ani," *Sovetskaya Arkheologiya*, no. 1, pp. 201–13.

Eberhard, W., and Boratav, P.N.
1953 *Typen türkischer Volksmärchen*, Veröffentlichungen der Orientalischen Kommission, Wiesbaden.

Ebersolt, J.
1923 *Les arts somptuaires de Byzance: étude sur l'art imperial de Costantinople*, Paris.

Ehrlich, R.
1930 "The Celebration and Gifts of the Persian New Year (Nawrūz) According to an Arabic Source," *Dr. J.J. Modi Memorial Volume*, Bombay, pp. 95–101.

Eilers, W.
1976 *Sinn und Herkunft der Planetennamen*, Sitzungsberichte der Bayerischen Akademie der Wissenschaften, phil.-hist. Kl., Heft 5, Munich.
1979 *Die Āl, ein persisches Kindbettgespenst*, Bayerische Akademie der Wissenschaften, phil.-hist. Kl., Heft 7, Munich.

El-Cheikh, N.M.
2004 *Byzantium Viewed by the Arabs*, Harvard Middle Eastern Monographs 36, Cambridge, MA.

Eisener, R.
1987 *Zwischen Faktum und Fiktion: Eine Studie zum Umayyadenkalifen Sulaimān b. ʿAbdalmalik und seinem Bild in den Quellen*, Wiesbaden.

Elderkin, G.W.
1924 *Kantharos: Studies in Dionysiac and Kindred Cult*, Princeton Monographs in Art and Archaeology XII, Princeton, NJ.

Ellis Davidson, H.R.
1976 "Mithras and Wodan," *The King and Kingship in Achaemenid Art*, eds. Cool Root, M., and Henning, W.B., Leiden, pp. 99–110.

Enderlein, V.
1973 "Das Bilderprogramm des Berliner Mosul-Beckens," *Staatliche Museen, Forschungen und Berichte* 15, pp. 7–40.
1990 *Islamische Kunst*, Dresden.

Enderlein, V., Hauptmann von Gladiss, A., Helmecke, G., Kröger, J., and Tunsch, T.
2001 *Museum für Islamische Kunst. Staatliche Museen zu Berlin – Preußischer Kulturbesitz*, Berlin.

Engemann, J.
1975 "Zur Verbreitung magischer Übelabwehr in der nichtchristlichen und christlichen Spätantike," *Jahrbuch für Antike und Christentum* 18, pp. 22–48.

Epstein, M.M.
1997 *Dreams of Subversion in Medieval Jewish Art and Literature*, University Park, PA.

Erdmann, K.

1957 "Weitere Nachträge zu den "Beobachtungen auf einer Reise in Zentralanatolien,"" *Archäologischer Anzeiger* 71, pp. 361–72.

1961 *Das anatolische Karavansaray des 13. Jahrhunderts* I, *Istanbuler Forschungen* 21, Berlin.

1962 *Ibn Bibi als kunsthistorische Quelle*, Istanbul.

Erdmann, K., and H.

1976 *Das anatolische Karavansaray des 13. Jahrhunderts*, Bände II–III, *Baubeschreibung: Die Ornamente*, Istanbuler Forschungen Band 31, Berlin.

Erginsoy, Ü.

1978 *İslam Maden Sanatının Gelişmesi*, Istanbul.

Esin, E.

1968–70 "Büke, The Cosmic Significance of the Dragon in Early Turkish Iconography," *Cultura Turcica* VI–VII, pp. 76–108.

1970–1 "Evren, Selçuklu san'atı evren tasvirinin Türk ikonografisinde menşe'leri ("The Origins of Saljuq Cosmological Symbols in Turkish Iconography")," *Selçuklu Araştırmaları Dergisi* I, 1969, Ankara, pp. 161–82, and 19 unnumbered pls.

1973 "The Cosmic Symbolism of the Draconite Arch and Apotropaic Mask in Turkish Symbolism," *Art and Archaeology Research Papers* IV, pp. 32–51.

1981 "The Religious Terminology of *Qutadghu Bilig* (462/1070)," *Sprache und Erkenntnis im Mittelalter: Akten des VI. Internationalen Kongresses für Mittelalterliche Philosophie der Société Internationale pour l'Étude de la Philosophie Médiévale 29. August - 3. September 1977 in Bonn*, ed. Beckmann, J.P., and Kluxen, W., Berlin, IV.3, pp. 831–7.

Ethé, H.

1871 *Die Fahrten des Sejjid Batthâl: ein alttürkischer Volks- und Sittenroman*, 2 vols., Leipzig.

Ettinghausen, R.

1943 "The Bobrinski "Kettle," Patron and Style of an Islamic Bronze," *Gazette des Beaux-Arts*, series 6, vol. 24, ed. Wildenstein, G., New York, pp. 193–208.

1950 *Studies in Muslim Iconography: I. The Unicorn*, Freer Gallery of Art Occasional Papers, vol. 1, no. 3, Washington, DC.

1955 "The "Snake-Eating Stag" in the East," *Late Classical and Medieval Studies in Honor of Albert Mathias Friend*, ed. Weitzmann, K., Princeton, NJ, pp. 272–86.

1962 *Arab Painting*, Geneva.

1965 "The Uses of Sphero-Conical Vessels in the Muslim East," *Journal of Near Eastern Studies* 24, pp. 218–29.

1972 *From Byzantium to Sasanian Iran and the Islamic World: Three Modes of Artistic Influence*, The L.A. Mayer Memorial Studies in Islamic Art and Archaeology 3, Leiden.

1984 "The 'Wade Cup' in the Cleveland Museum of Art, Its Origin and Decorations," *Islamic Art and Archaeology. Collected Papers*, ed. Rosen-Ayalon, M.; intr. Grabar, O., Berlin, pp. 331–90.

Ettinghausen, R., and Grabar, O.

1987 *Islamic Art and Architecture 650–1250*, Harmondsworth, UK, and New York, repr. 2001, Hong Kong.

Ettinghausen, R., and Grabar, O., and Jenkins-Medina, M.

1987 *Islamic Art and Architecture 650–1250*, New Haven, CN, repr. 2001.

Exhibition catalogue

1975 *Islam and the Medieval West*, ed. Ferber, S., University Art Gallery, April to March 1975, Binghampton, NY.

Exhibition catalogue

1976 *The Arts of Islam*, Hayward Gallery, eds. Jones, D., and Mitchell, G., London.

Exhibition catalogue

1977 *L'Islam dans les collections nationales*, 2 May to 22 August 1977, Musée du Louvre, Paris.

Exhibition catalogue

1977 *Iskusstvo Vizantii v sobraniiakh SSSR, Katalog vystavki*, eds. Bank, A.V., Bessonova, M.A., 3 vols., The State Hermitage Museum, Leningrad and Pushkin Museum, Moscow.

Exhibition catalogue

1978 *The Christian Orient*, British Library, London.

Exhibition catalogue

1983 *The Anatolian Civilisations* III, Seljuk/Ottoman, Topkapı Palace Museum, 22 May to 30 October 1983, Istanbul.

Exhibition catalogue

1989 *Timur and the Princely Vision: Persian Art and Culture in the Fifteenth Century*, Lentz, T.W., and Lowry, G.D., Arthur M. Sackler Gallery, Smithsonian Institution, Washington, DC, 16 April to 6 July 1989, Los Angeles County Museum of Art, 13 August to 5 November 1989, Los Angeles.

Exhibition catalogue

1992 *The Royal City of Susa: Ancient Near Eastern Treasures in the Louvre*, eds. Harper, P.O., Aruz, J., and Tallon, F., Paris.

Exhibition catalogue

1993 *L'Eufrate e il tempo - Le civiltà del Medio Eufrate e della Gezira siriana*, eds. Rouault, O., and Masetti-Rouault, M.G., Milan.

Exhibition catalogue

1996 *À l'ombre d'Avicenne: La medicine au temps des califes*, 18 November 1996 to 2 March 1997, Institut du Monde Arabe, Paris.

Exhibition catalogue

1996 *Furūsiyya*, vol. 1, *The Horse in the Art of the Near East*, vol. 2, *Catalogue*, ed. Alexander, D., King Abdulaziz Public Library, Riyadh.

Exhibition catalogue

1996 *Grand Exhibition of Silkroad Buddhist Art*, Tokyo National Museum, Tokyo.

Exhibition catalogue

1997 *The Glory of Byzantium: Arts and Culture of the Middle Byzantine Era A.D. 843–1261*, eds. Evans, H.C., and Wixom, W.D., 11 March to 6 July 1997, Metropolitan Museum of Art, New York.

Exhibition catalogue

1997 *Following the Stars: Images of the Zodiac in Islamic Art*, ed. Carboni, S., 4 February to 31 August 1997, The Metropolitan Museum of Art, New York.

Exhibition catalogue
1998 *L'Apparence des cieux: Astronomie et Astrologie en terre d'Islam*, ed. Makariou, S., 18 June to 21 September 1998, Musée du Louvre, Paris.

Exhibition catalogue
2000 *Altyn Urda khezinelere/Sokrovishcha Zolotoi Ordy (The Treasures of the Golden Horde)*, The State Hermitage Museum, St. Petersburg.

Exhibition catalogue
2001 *L'Etrange et le Merveilleux en terres d'Islam*, 23 April to 23 July 2001, Musée du Louvre, Paris.

Exhibition catalogue
2001 *Armenië: middeleeuwse miniaturen uit het christelijke Oosten*, Museum Catharijneconvent, Utrecht, 3 November 2001 to 3 March 2002, Zwolle.

Exhibition catalogue
2002 *Chevaux et cavaliers arabes dans les arts d'Orient et d'Occident*, 25 November 2002 to 3 March 2003, Institut du Monde Arabe, Paris.

Exhibition catalogue
2002 *L'orient de Saladin: l'art des Ayyoubides*, 22 October 2001 to 10 March 2002, Institut du Monde Arabe, Paris.

Exhibition catalogue
2002 *The Legacy of Genghis Khan: Courtly Art and Culture in Western Asia, 1256–1353*, eds. Komaroff, L., and Carboni, S., 5 November 2002 to 16 February 2003, The Metropolitan Museum, New York, New Haven and London.

Exhibition catalogue
2003 *De l'Indus à l'Oxus: Archéologie de l'Asie Centrale*, 15 April to 31 August 2003, Musée de Lattes.

Exhibition catalogue
2004 *Ao Han Wen Wu Jing Hua* ("Aohan China"), Hohhot.

Exhibition catalogue
2004 *The Silk Road: Trade, Travel, War and Faith*, ed. Whitfield, S., 7 May to 12 September 2004, British Library, London.

Exhibition catalogue
2005 *Nobilis Officinae: Die königlichen Hofwerkstätten zu Palermo zur Zeit der Normannen und Staufer im 12. und 13. Jahrhundert*, ed. Seipel, W.,Vienna and Palermo.

Exhibition catalogue
2005 *Dschingis Khan und seine Erben: Das Weltreich der Mongolen*, 16 June to 25 September 2005, Kunst- und Ausstellungshalle der Bundesrepublik Deutschland, Bonn, 25 October 2005 to 29 January 2006, Staatliches Museum für Völkerkunde, München, Munich.

Exhibition catalogue
2005 *La France romane au temps des premiers Capétiens (987–1152)*, 10 March – 6 June 2005, Musée du Louvre, Paris.

Exhibition catalogue
2005 *Turks: A Journey of a Thousand Years, 600–1600*, ed. Roxburgh, D., 22 January to 12 April 2005, Royal Academy of Arts, London.

Exhibition catalogue
2006 "Frühe Begegnungen mit dem Westen auf den Routen der Seidenstraße," *Xi'an. Kaiserliche Macht im Jenseits: Grabfunde und Tempelschätze aus Chinas alter Hauptstadt*, 21 April to 23 July 2006, Kunst- und Ausstellungshalle der Bundesrepublik Deutschland, Bonn, pp. 354–7.

Exhibition catalogue
2006 *Venise et l'Orient: 828–1797*, ed. Carboni, S., 2 October 2006 to 18 February 2007, Institut du Monde Arabe, Paris.

Exhibition catalogue
2007 *Splendori a corte: Arti del Mondo Islamico nelle Collezioni del Museo Aga Khan*, 31 March to 3 June 2007, Palazzo della Pilotta, Parma, Milan.

Exhibition catalogue
2007 *Attila und die Hunnen*, Historisches Museum der Pfalz, Speyer, Stuttgart.

Exhibition catalogue
2007 *Sacred: Books of the Three Faiths: Judaism, Christianity, Islam*, ed. Reeve, J., 27 April to 23 September 2007, The British Library, London.

Exhibition catalogue
2007 *L'art des chevaliers en pays d'Islam: Collection de la Furusiyya Art Foundation*, ed. Mohamed, B., 26 June to 21 October 2007, Institut du Monde Arabe, Paris.

Exhibition catalogue
2009 *What the Coins Tell Us: Symbols and Multicultural Aspects in Medieval Anatolian Coins*, 30 September to 31 December 2009, Yapı Kredi Vedat Nedim Tör Museum, Istanbul.
2009 *Shah ʿAbbas: The Remaking of Iran*, ed. Canby, S., 19 February to 14 June 2009, British Museum, London.

Fahd, T.
1968 *Le panthéon de l'Arabie centrale à la veille de l'Hégire*, Paris.
1971 "Anges, démons et *djinns* en Islam," *Génies, anges et démons*, ed. Fahd, T., *Sources orientales* 8, Paris, pp. 155–214.

Farès, B.
1953 "Le livre de la thériaque. Manuscrit arabe à peintures de la fin du XIIe siècle conservé à la bibliothèque nationale de Paris," *Art Islamique* II, Cairo, pp. 1–56, pls. 1–21.
1959 "Figures magiques," *Aus der Welt der islamischen Kunst: Festschrift für Ernst Kühnel zum 75. Geburtstag am 26. 10. 1957*, Berlin, pp. 154–62.

Farmer, H.G.
1916 *The Influence of Music: From Arabic Sources. A Lecture Delivered Before the Musical Association*, London.

Fehérvári, G.
1976 *Islamic Metalwork of the Eighth to the Fifteenth Century in the Keir Collection*, London.

Ferrier, R.W.
1990 ed., *The Arts of Persia*, New Haven and London.

Ferwerda, R.
1973 "Le Serpent, le noeud d'Hercule et le caducée d'Hermès. Sur un passage orphique chez Athénagore," *Numen* 20, 1, pp. 104–15.

Fiey, J.M.
1959 *Mossoul chrétienne: Essai sur l'histoire, l'archéologie et l'état actuel des monuments chrétiens de la ville de Mossoul*, Beirut.
1965 *Assyrie chrétienne: Contribution à l'étude de l'histoire et de la géographie ecclésiastiques et monastiques du nord de l'Iraq*, Beirut, 2 vols.

Fırat, S.
1996 *Selçuklu sanatı* ("The Art of the Seljuks"), Ankara.

Fitzherbert, T.
2001 *"Balʿami's Tabari": An Illustrated Manuscript of Balʿami's Tarjuma-yi Tarikh-i Tabari in the Freer Gallery of Art, Washington (F57.16, 47.19 and 30.21)*, unpublished Ph.D. dissertation, University of Edinburgh.

Flood, F.B.
2005 "Ghurid Monuments and Muslim Identities: Epigraphy and Exegesis in Twelfth-Century Afghanistan," *The Indian Economic and Social History Review* 42, 3, pp. 263–94.
2006 "Image against Nature. Spolia as Apotropaia in Byzantium and the Dar al-Islam," *The Medieval History Journal* 9, 1, Delhi, pp. 143–66.

Fodor, A.
1976 "The Metamorphosis of Imhotep – A Study in Islamic Syncretism," *Akten des VII. Kongresses für Arabistik und Islamwissenschaft, Göttingen, 15. bis 22. August 1974*, ed. Dietrich, A., Göttingen, pp. 155–81.
1978 "The Rod of Moses in Arabic Magic," *Acta Orientalia Academiae Scientiarum Hungaricae* vol. 32, 1, Budapest, pp. 1–21.

von Folsach, K.
1990 *Islamic Art: The David Collection*, Davids Samling Kobenhavn, Copenhagen.
1991 *Fabelvaesener dra Islams Verden*, Davids Samling Kobenhavn, Copenhagen.
1996 *Sultan, Shah, and Great Mughal: The History and Culture of the Islamic World*, Davids Samling Kobenhavn, Copenhagen.

Fontenrose, J.
1959 *Python: A Study of Delphic Myth and Its Origin*, Berkeley and Los Angeles, repr. 1980.

Fowden, E.K.
1999 *The Barbarian Plain: Saint Sergius between Rome and Iran*, Berkeley, Los Angeles and London.

Fragner, B.G.
2006 "Ilkhanid Rule and Its Contributions to Iranian Political Culture," *Beyond the Legacy of Genghis Khan*, ed. Komaroff, L., Leiden, Boston and Cologne, pp. 68–80.

Franke, P.
2000 *Begegnung mit Khiḍr: Quellenstudien zum Imaginären im traditionellen Islam*, Beiruter Texte und Studien 82, Beirut and Stuttgart.

Francfort, H.-P.
2002 "Images du combat contre le sanglier en Asie centrale (3ème au 1er millénaire av. J.-C.)," *Bulletin of the Asia Institute*, n.s., Vol. 16.

Frantz, M.A.
1940–1 "Digenis Akritas: A Byzantine Epic and Its Illustrations," *Byzantion* 15, pp. 87–91.
1941 "Excavations in the Athenian Agora: Akritas and the Dragons," *Hesperia* 10, 1, pp. 9–13.

Frazer, J.G.
1888 "The Language of Animals," *The Archaeological Review* vol. 1, 3, May, pp. 161–81.
1913 *Golden Bough: A Study in Magic and Religion*, part II, *Taboo and the Perils of the Soul*, 3rd ed., London, 1980.

Friedlaender, I.
1910 "Zur Geschichte der Chadhirlegende," *Archiv für Religionswissenschaft* 13, pp. 92–110
1910 "Alexanders Zug nach dem Lebensquell und der Chadirlegende," *Archiv für Religionswissenschaft* 13, pp. 161–246.

Gabriel, A.
1931 *Monuments turcs d'Anatolie*, vol. 1, *Kayseri – Niğde*, Paris.
1934 *Monuments turcs d'Anatolie*, vol. 2, *Amasya, Tokat, Sivas*, Paris.
1940 *Voyages archéologiques dans la Turquie Orientale (Mardin, Diyarbakir, provinces au-delà du Tigre, Kharput, Malatya, Urfa)*, 2 vols., avec un recueil d'inscriptions arabes par Sauvaget, J., Institut français d'archéologie de Stamboul, Paris.

Gaillard, M.
1987 *Le livre de Samak-e ʿAyyâr: Structure et idéologie du roman persan médiéval*, Paris.

Garsoïan, N.G.
1994 "The History of Armenia," *Treasures in Heaven: Armenian Illuminated Manuscripts*, eds. Mathews, T.F., and Wieck, R.S., Princeton, NJ, pp. 2–23.

Gaulier, S., Jera-Bezard, R., and Maillard, M.
1976 *Buddhism in Afghanistan and Central Asia*, Iconography of Religions XIII, 14, part 1, Leiden.

Geng, S., and Hamilton, J.
1981 "L'inscription ouigoure de la stèle commémorative des Iduq Qut de Qočo," *Turcica* 13, pp. 10–54.

Gevorkian, A., and Abgarian, G.
1996 eds., *Armenian Miniature: Zoomorphic Ornamentation*, Yerevan.

Ghouchani, A.
1992 *Persian Poetry on the Tiles of Takht-i Sulaiman (13th century)*, Tehran.

Ghouchani, A., and Adle, C.
1992 "A Sphero-Conical Vessel as *fuqqāʿa*, or a Gourd for "Beer,"" *Muqarnas* IX, pp. 72–92.

Gibb, H.A.R.
1923 *The Arab Conquests in Central Asia*, Royal Asiatic Society, London.

Gierlichs, J.
1993 *Drache, Phönix, Doppeladler: Fabelwesen in der islamischen Kunst*, Berlin.
1995 "Das Mosul-Tor von ʿAmādiya im Nordirak.

Ein unbekanntes islamisches Figurenrelief und seine Bedeutung," *Baghdader Mitteilungen* 26, pp. 195–206, pls. 17–22.
1996 *Mittelalterliche Tierreliefs in Anatolien und Mesopotamien: Untersuchungen zur figürlichen Baudekoration der Seldschuken, Artuqiden und ihrer Nachfolger bis ins 15. Jahrhundert*, Istanbuler Forschungen 42, Tübingen.
1998 "Drache, Sphinx und Doppeladler: Bemerkungen zur figürlichen Steindekoration der Seldschuken und Artuqiden," *Eothen*, Jahreshefte der Gesellschaft der Freunde Islamischer Kunst und Kultur, 4–7, 1993–6, pp. 33–7.

Gignoux, P.
1978 *Catalogue des sceaux, camées et bulles sasanides de la Bibliothèque Nationale et du Musée du Louvre II: Les sceaux et bulles inscrits*, Paris.

Gignoux, P., and Gyselen, R.
1982 *Sceaux sassanides de diverses collections privées*, Leuven.

Gil, M.
2004 *Jews in Islamic Countries in the Middle Ages*, Leiden.

Ginzberg, L.
1909–38 *The Legends of the Jews*, 7 vols., New York, repr. Philadelphia, 1946 and 1955.

Ghirshman, R.
1962 *Iran: Parther und Sasaniden*, Munich.
1964 *Iran: Protoiraner, Meder, Achämeniden*, Munich.

Glaznov, G.Y.
2001 *The Bridling of the Tongue and the Opening of the Mouth in Biblical Prophecy*, Sheffield.

Golden, P.B.
1982 "The Twelve Year Animal Cycle Calendar in Georgian Sources," *Acta Orientalia Academiae Scientiarum Hungaricae* XXXVI, pp. 197–206.
1983 "The Turkic Peoples and Caucasia," *Transcaucasia: Nationalism and Social Change*, ed. Suny, R.G., Ann Arbor, MI, pp. 45–67.
1997 "Wolves, Dogs and Qıpčaq Religion," *Acta Orientalia Academiae Scientiarum Hungaricae*, vol. 5, pp. 87–97.
1998 "Religion among the Qıpčaq of Medieval Eurasia," *Central Asiatic Journal: International Periodical for the Languages, History and Archaeology of Central Asia*, vol. 42, 2, pp. 180–237.

Goldschmidt, E.
1892 *Das Buch Henoch aus dem Aethiopischen in die ursprünglich hebräische Abfassungssprache zurückübersetzt*, Berlin.

Goldziher, I.
1896 *Abhandlungen zur Arabischen Philologie*, Leiden, vol. 1.

Gohrab, A.A.
2000 "Majnun's Image as a Serpent," *The Poetry of Nizami Ganjavi: Knowledge, Love and Rhetoric*, eds. Talattof, K., and Clinton, J.W., New York, pp. 83–96.
2003 *Laylī and Majnūn: Love, Madness, and Mystic Longing in Niẓāmī's Epic Romance*, Leiden, Boston.

Gombrich, E.H.
1960 *Art and Illusion: A Study in the Psychology of Pictorial Representation*, The Bollingen Series, XXXV/5, New York.

Gordon, S.
2001 ed., *Robes and Honor: The Medieval World of Investiture*, New York.

Grabar, A.
1936 *L'empereur dans l'art byzantin: recherches sur l'art officiel de l'empire d'Orient*, Faculté des Lettres: Publications de la Faculté des Lettres de l'Université de Strasbourg 75, Paris.
1951 "Les succès des arts orientaux à la cour byzantine sous les macédoniens," *Münchner Jahrbuch der bildenden Kunst* 2, pp. 32–60.
1957 *L'iconoclasme byzantin*, Paris.

Grabar, O.
1985 "Upon Reading al-Azraqi," *Muqarnas* III, pp. 1–7.
2006 *Constructing the Study of Islamic Art*, Aldershot, Hants, and Burlington, VT.

Grabar, O., and Blair, S.
1980 *Epic Images and Contemporary History: The Illustrations of the Great Mongol Shahnama*, Chicago.

Grassmann, H.
1873 *Wörterbuch zum Rig-Veda*, Leipzig, repr. Wiesbaden, 1976.

Gray, L.H.
1906 "The Jews in Pahlavi Literature," *Actes du XIV Congrès International des Orientalistes*, Paris, pp. 161–92.

Green, T.M.
1992 *The City of the Moon God: Religious Traditions of Harran*, Leiden.

Grube, E.J.
1963 "Raqqa Keramik in der Sammlung des Metropolitan Museums in New York," *Kunst des Orients* IV, Wiesbaden, pp. 48–78.
1965 "The Art of Islamic Pottery," *Bulletin of the Metropolitan Museum of Art*, February, pp. 209–28.
1967 *De Wereld van de Islam*, The Hague.
1988–9 "Notes on the Decorative Arts of the Timurid Period, II," *Islamic Art* III, pp. 175–208, pls. X–XII, figs. 1–59.
2005 "Iconography in Islamic Art," *Image and Meaning in Islamic Art*, ed. Hillenbrand, R., London, pp. 13–33.

Grube, E.J., and Johns, J.
2005 *The Painted Ceilings of the Cappella Palatina*, Genoa and New York.

Grünbaum, M.
1877 "Beiträge zur vergleichenden Mythologie aus der Hagada," *Zeitschrift der Deutschen Morgenländischen Gesellschaft* 31, pp. 183–359.

Grünwedel, A.
1912 *Altbuddhistische Kultstätten in Chinesisch-Turkistan: Bericht über archäologische Arbeiten von 1906 bis 1907 bei Kuča, Qarašahr und in der Oase Turfan*, Berlin.
1916 "Die Geschichten der vierundachtzig Zauberer (Mahāsiddhas) aus dem Tibetischen übersetzt," *Baessler-Archiv* V, no. 4/5, Leipzig, pp. 137–228.

Guguev, V.K.
1990 "Ein reiches Sarmatengrab in Rostov am Don," *Das Altertum* 36, pp. 37–42.

Gundel, W.
1936 *Neue astrologische Texte des Hermes Trismegistos: Funde und Forschungen auf dem Gebiet der antiken Astronomie und Astrologie*, Abh. der Bayerischen Akademie der Wissenschaften, phil.-hist. Abt., Munich.

Gunkel, H.
1895 *Schöpfung und Chaos in Urzeit und Endzeit - mit Beiträgen von Heinrich Zimmern*, Göttingen.

Gutas, D.
1998 *Greek Thought, Arabic Culture: the Graeco-Arabic Translation Movement in Baghdad and Early Society (2nd–4th/8th–10th Centuries)*, London.

Gyselen, R.
1995 *Sceaux magiques en Iran sassanide*, Studia Iranica, vol. 17, Paris.
2007 *Sasanian Seals and Sealings in the A. Saeedi Collection*, Acta Iranica 44, Leuven.

Hakimov, A.A.
2000 "Arts and Crafts in Transoxiania and Khurasan," *History of Civilizations of Central Asia*, vol. 4, *The Age of Achievement: A.D. 750 to the End of the Fifteenth Century, part 2, The Achievements*, Paris, pp. 411–449.

Hanaway, W.L.
1988 "Blood and Wine: Sacrifice and Celebration in Manūchihrī's Wine Poetry," *Iran* 26, pp. 69–80.

Hanson, A.
2006 "Roman Medicine," *A Companion to the Roman Empire*, ed. Potter, D.S., Oxford, pp. 492–523.

Harper, P.O.
1961–62 "The Senmurv," *Bulletin of the Metropolitan Museum of Art* 20, pp. 95–101

Haq, S.N.
1994 *Names, Natures and Things: The Alchemist Jābir ibn Ḥayyān and his Kitāb al-Aḥjār (Book of Stones)*, Dordrecht, Boston and London.

Harrak, A., and Niu Ruji
2004 "The Uighur Inscription at the Mausoleum of Mār Behnam [*sic*], Iraq," *Journal of the Canadian Society for Syriac Studies* 4, pp. 66–70.

Harrison, J.E.
1963 *Themis: A Study of the Social Origins of Greek Religion*, London, repr. 1989.

Harper, P.O.
1978 *The Royal Hunter: Art of the Sasanian Empire*, New York.

Hartmann-Schmitz, U.
1989 *Die Zahl Sieben im sunnitischen Islam: Studien anhand von Koran und Ḥadīṯ*, Europäische Hochschulschriften, Reihe 27, Asiatische und afrikanische Studien, Frankfurt a. M.

Hartmann, A.
1975 *An-Nāṣir li-dīn Allāh (1180–225): Politik, Religion, Kultur in der Späten Abbasidenzeit*, Berlin.

Hartner, W.
1938 "Pseudoplanetary Nodes of the Moon's Orbit in Hindu and Islamic Iconographies," *Ars Islamica*, vol. 5, 2, Ann Arbor, pp. 114–54.
1959 "Zur astrologischen Symbolik des »Wade Cup«," *Aus der Welt der Islamischen Kunst. Festschrift für E. Kühnel zum 75. Geburtstag*, Berlin, pp. 234–43.
1965 "Notes on Picatrix," *Isis*, vol. 56, no. 186, pp. 438–51.
1973–4 "The Vaso Vescovali in the British Museum," *Kunst des Orients*, IX, Heft 1/2, pp. 99–130.

Hartner, W., and Ettinghausen, R.
1964 "The Conquering Lion. The Life Cycle of a Symbol," *Oriens* 17, pp. 161–71; repr. *Islamic Art and Archaeology. Collected Papers [of] Richard Ettinghausen*, ed. Rosen-Ayalon, M., Berlin, 1984, pp. 693–711.

Hasluck, F.W.
1929 *Christianity and Islam under the Sultans*, ed. Hasluck, M.M., 2 vols., Oxford.

Hauptmann von Gladiss, A., and Kröger, J.
1985 *Islamische Kunst: Loseblattkatalog unpublizierter Werke aus Deutschen Museen*, vol. 2, *Metall, Stein, Stuck, Holz, Elfenbein, Stoffe*, ed. Brisch, K., Mainz.

Hauptmann von Gladiss, A.
2006 ed., *Die Dschazira: Kulturlandschaft zwischen Euphrat und Tigris*, Berlin.
2006 "Amid - Diyarbakr," *Die Dschazira: Kulturlandschaft zwischen Euphrat und Tigris*, Berlin, pp. 29–33.

Hauser, W., and Wilkinson, C.K.
1942 "The Museum's Excavations at Nīshāpūr," *Bulletin of the Metropolitan Museum of Art*, vol. 37, no. 4, The Iranian Expedition, 1938–1940 April, pp. 81 and 83–119.

Haussig, H.W.
1992 *Archäologie und Kunst der Seidenstrasse*, Darmstadt.

Hay, J.
1999 "Questions of Influence in Chinese Art History," *Res* 35, pp. 120–62.

Heidel, A.
1942 *The Babylonian Genesis: The Story of Creation*, Chicago and London, repr. 1951.

Hengstenberg, W.
1912 "Der Drachenkampf des heiligen Theodor," *Oriens christianus* 2, pp. 78–106, 241–80.

Henning, W.B.
1940 *Sogdica*, London (repr. in *W.B. Henning - Selected Papers II*, Acta Iranica 15, Tehran and Liège, pp. 1–68).
1943 "The Book of the Giants," *Bulletin of the School of Oriental and African Studies* 11, pp. 52–74 (repr. in *W.B. Henning - Selected Papers II*, Acta Iranica 15, Tehran and Liège, pp. 115–37).
1947 "Two Manichaean Magical Texts with an Excursus on the Parthian Ending *-ēndēh*," *Bulletin of the School of Oriental and African Studies* 12, pp. 39–66 (repr. in *W.B. Henning - Selected Papers II*, Tehran and Liège, pp. 273–300).

Henninger, J.
1963 "Geisterglaube bei den vorislamischen Arabern," *Festschrift Paul J. Schebesta*, Studia Instituti Anthropos, vol. 18, Vienna-Mödling, pp. 279–316.
2004 repr. as "Beliefs in Spirits Among the Pre-Islamic Arabs," *Magic and Divination in Early Islam*, ed. Savage-Smith, E., Aldershot, Hants, pp. 1–53.

Hersek, C.
2002 "General Status of Artifacts within the Region of Orkhun Monuments," *Moğolistan'daki Türk Anıtları Projesi 2000 Yılı Çalışmaları*, Ankara.

Herzfeld, E.
1920a "Der Thron des Khosrô. Quellenkritische und ikonographische Studien über Grenzgebiete des Kunstgeschichte des Morgen- und Abendlandes," *Jahrbuch der Preussischen Kunstsammlungen* 41, pp. 1–24, 103–47.
1920b *Am Tor von Asien*, Berlin.
1927 *Die Malereien von Samarra*, Berlin.
1955 *Matériaux pour un Corpus Inscriptionum Arabicum, Troisième Partie: Syrie du Nord. Inscriptions et Monuments d'Alep*, tome I, vol. 1, Institut Français d'Archéologie Orientale, Cairo.

Herzog, R.
1907 "Aus dem Asklepieion von Kos," *Archiv für Religionswissenschaft*, Leipzig.

Hill, D.R.
1976 *On the Construction of Water-Clocks, Kitāb Arshīmidas fī 'amal al-binkamāt*, Turner & Devereux Occasional Papers, 4, London.
1984 *A History of Engineering in Classical and Medieval Times*, La Salle, IL.
1990 "Alchemical Literature," *Religion, Learning and Science in the 'Abbasid Period*, ed. Young, M.J.L., Latham, J.D., and Serjeant, R.B., Cambridge and New York, pp. 328–41.
1998 *Studies in Medieval Islamic Technology: From Philo to al-Jazarī, From Alexandria to Diyār Bakr*, ed. King, D.A., Aldershot, Hants.

Hill, G.-F.
1897 *Catalogue of Greek Coins, Lycia, Pamphylia, and Pisidia*, London.

Hillenbrand, C.
1985 "The History of the Jazira, 1100–250: A Short Introduction," *The Art of Syria and the Jazira 1100–250*, ed. Raby, J., Oxford.
1999 *The Crusades: Islamic Perspectives*, Edinburgh.

Hillenbrand, R.
2006 "Mosul – Diyar Rabi'a," *Die Dschazira: Kulturlandschaft zwischen Euphrat und Tigris*, Berlin, pp. 19–22.

Hinnells, J.R.
1974 "The Iranian Background of Mithraic Iconography," *Acta Iranica*, Commémoration Cyrus, vol. 1, Hommage Universel, Tehran, Liège and Leiden, pp. 242–50.
1975 "Reflections on the Bull-slaying Scene," *Mithraic Studies*, ed. Hinnells, J.R., vol. 1, Manchester, pp. 290–312.

Hintze, A.
1995 "The Rise of the Saviour in the Avesta," *Iran and Turfan*, Beiträge Berliner Wissenschaftler, Werner Sundermann zum 60. Geburtstag gewidmet, eds. Reck, Ch., and Zieme, P., Wiesbaden, pp. 77–97.
1999 "The Saviour and the Dragon in Iranian and Jewish/Christian Eschatology," *Irano-Judaica* IV, eds. Shaked, S., and Netzer, A., Jerusalem, pp. 72–90.

Hodgson, M.G.S.
1955 *The Order of Assassins: The Struggle of the Early Nizari Isma'ilis Against the Islamic World*, The Hague.

Hoffmann, B.
2000 Waqf *im mongolischen Iran: Rašīduddīns Sorge um Nachruhm und Seelenheil*, Freiburger Islamstudien Band 20, Stuttgart.

Hoffman, E.R.F.
2001 "Pathways of Portability: Islamic and Christian Interchange from the Tenth to the Twelfth Century," *Art History*, vol. 24, no. 1, February, pp. 17–50.

Holter, K.
1937 "Die Galen-Handschrift und die Makamen des Hariri der Wiener Nationabibliothek," *Jahrbuch der kunsthistorischen Sammlungen in Wien*, N.F. 11, pp. 1–48.

Hoogasian-Villa, S.
1966 coll. and ed., *100 Armenian Tales and Their Folkloristic Relevance*, Detroit.

Hovsépian, K.
1937 "La Porte du Couvent de St.-Lazare ou des Apôtres du Daron," *Annuaire Zvarthnotz* (in Armenian).

Hübschmann, H.
1895 *Armenische Grammatik I, Armenische Etymologie*, Indogermanischer Grammatiken, vol. 6, 1.

Hüttel, H.-G.
2005 "Der Palast des Ögedei Khan – Die Ausgrabungen des Deutschen Archäologischen Instituts im Palastbezirk von Karakorum," *Dschingis Khan und seine Erben: Das Weltreich der Mongolen*, Munich, pp. 140–6.

Huys, M.
1995 *The Tale of the Hero who was Exposed at Birth in Euripidean Tragedy: A Study of Motifs*, Symbolae, Facultatis Litterarum Lovaniensis, Series A, vol. 20, Leuven.

Ibrāhīm, L.A.
1976 "Dragons on a Cairene Mosque," *Art and Archaeology Research Papers*, vol. 10 December, pp. 11–9.

Idel, M.
1988 *The Mystical Experience in Abraham Abulafia*, New York.

Ikeda, S.
1981 *Chūgoku kodai shūkyōshi kenkyū* ("Research on the History of Ancient Chinese Religion"), Tokyo.

Ilyasov, J.Y., and Rusanov, D.V.
1997–8 "A Study on the Bone Plates from Orlat," *Silk Road Art and Archaeology* 5, pp. 107–59.

İnal, G.
1970–1 "Susuz Han'daki ejderli kabartmanın Asya kültür çevresi içindeki yeri ("The Place of the Dragon Relief at Susuz Han in the Asian

Cultural Circle")," *Sanat Tarihi Yıllığı* IV, pp. 153–82 (English summary, pp. 183–4).

Ipşiroğlu, M.S.
1963 *Die Kirche von Achtamar: Bauplastik im Leben des Lichtes*, Berlin and Mainz.
1965 *Malerie der Mongolen*, Munich.

Isser, S.J.
1976 *The Dositheans: A Samaritan Sect in Late Antiquity*, Leiden.

Ittig, A.
1982 "A Talismanic Bowl," *Institut Français d'Archéologie Orientale du Caire*, vol. XVIII, pp. 79–94.

Ivanov, A.A.
1976 *Art of Kubachi*, Leningrad.
2004 tr. Rogers, J.M., "A Second "Herat Bucket" and Its Congeners," *Muqarnas* 21, Essays in Honour of J.M. Rogers, Leiden, pp. 171–9.

Jacobson, E.
1995 *The Art of the Scythians: The Interpenetration of Cultures at the Edge of the Hellenic World*, Leiden, Boston and Cologne.
1999 "Review of Bourgeois, Ignace, Massart, Claire, Mikkelsen, Jari H., and van Huele, Wim, *Ancient Nomads of the Altai Mountains*, Brussels, 2000," *Bulletin of the Asia Institute* 13, p. 173.

Jakobson, R., and Szeftel, M.
1949 "The Vseslav Epos," *Russian Epic Studies*, eds. Jakobson, R., and Simmons, E.J., Philadelphia, PA, pp. 13–87.

Jacques, R., and Wencker, R.
1967 "Die Textilien im Besitz der Schatzkammer der Kirche St. Servatius in Siegburg," *Heimatbuch der Stadt Siegburg* 2, pp. 472–527, 487–90.

Al-Janabi, T.J.
1982 *Studies in Medieval Iraqi Architecture*, Ministry of Culture and Information, State Organization of Antiquities and Heritage, Baghdad.

Janda, M.
2010 *Die Musik nach dem Chaos: Der Schöpfungsmythos der europäischen Vorzeit*, Innsbrucker Beiträge zur Kulturwissenschaft, N.F., Bd. 1, Innsbruck.

Jeffers, A.
1996 *Magic & Divination in Ancient Palestine & Syria*, Leiden.

Jeffreys, E.M.
1998 *Digenis Akritis: the Grottaferrata and Escorial Versions*, Cambridge.

Jenkins, M.
1983 ed., *Islamic Art in the Kuwait National Museum: The al-Sabah Collection*, London.

Jenkins, M., and Keene, M.
1982 *Islamic Jewelry in the Metropolitan Museum of Art*, New York.

De Jerphanion, G.
1925–42 *Les églises rupestres de Cappadoce: une nouvelle province de l'art byzantin*, Paris.

Jerusalimskaja, A.A.
2000 "Die Schule der künstlerischen Seidenweberei in Sogdiana," *Textilien Mittelasiens. Beiträge zur sasanidischen und frühislamischen Kunst Entwicklung - Ornamente - Symbolik*, vol. 1, Mittelasiatische Studien, vol. 2, ed. Schletzer, R., Berlin, pp. 81–123.

Jing, A.
2002 *The Water God's Temple of the Guangsheng Monastery: Cosmic Function of Art, Ritual and Theatre*, Leiden, Boston and Cologne, 2002.

Johnston, E.H.
1936 *Aśvaghoṣa's Buddhacarita or Acts of the Buddha*, Lahore, repr. Delhi, 2004.

Johnstone, T.M.
1976 "Knots and Curses," *Arabian Studies* 3, pp. 79–83.

Jung, C.G.
1955 "Transformation Symbolism in the Mass," *The Mysteries: Papers of the Eranos Yearbook*, vol. 2, New York, pp. 274–336.

Kadoi, Y.
2006–7 "Çintamani: Notes on the Formation of the Turco-Iranian Style," *Persica* 21, pp. 33–49.
2009 *Islamic Chinoiserie: The Art of Mongol Iran*, Edinburgh.

Kafadarian (Ġafadaryan), K.G.
1952 *Dvin kʿaġakʿę ev nra peġowmnerę: Gorod Dvin i ego raskopki*, 2 vols., Erevan.

Kahn, P.
1984 *The Secret History of the Mongols. The Origin of Chinghis Khan. An Adaptation of the Yuan Ch'ao Pi Shih. Based Primarily on the English Translation by Francis Woodman Cleaves*, San Francisco.

Kalter, J., and Schönberger, I.
2003 *Der lange Weg der Türken: 1500 Jahre türkische Kultur*, Stuttgart.

Karamağaralı, B.
1972 *Ahlat Mezartaşları*, Ankara.

Karamustafa, A.T.
2006 *God's Unruly Friends: Dervish Groups in the Islamic Middle Period 1200–1550*, Oxford.

Katz, M.H.
2002 *Body of Text: The Emergence of the Sunnī Law of Ritual Purity*, Albany, NY.

Keall, E.J.
1967 "A Sasanian Palace Stronghold in Persian Kurdistan," *Iran, Journal of the British Institute of Persian Studies*, vol. 5, pp. 99–123.

Kelhoffer, J.A.
2000 *Miracle and Mission: The Authentication of Missionaries and Their Message in the Longer Ending of Mark*, Wissenschaftliche Untersuchungen zum Neuen Testament, Reihe 2/112, Tübingen.

Kennedy, E.S.
1956 *A Survey of Islamic Astronomical Tables*, Transactions of the American Philosophical Society, n.s., vol. 46, no. 2.

Kennedy, E.S., and Pingree, D.
1971 *The Astrological History of Mashāʾallāh*, Cambridge, MA.

Kerner, J.J.
2004 *Art in the Name of Science: Illustrated Manuscripts of the* Kitāb al-diryāq, Ph.D. disserta-

tion, Institute of Fine Arts, New York University.
2007 "Art in the Name of Science: The *Kitāb al-diryāq* in Text and Image," *Arab Painting: Text and Image in Illustrated Arabic Manuscripts*, ed. Contadini, Anna, Handbook of Oriental Studies, Section 1, The Near and Middle East, Leiden and Boston, pp. 25–40.

Khal'pakh'chian (Khalpakhchian), O.K.
1971 *Grazhdanskoye zodchestvo Armenii*, Moscow.
1980 *Architectural Ensembles of Armenia: 8th century B.C. - 19th Century A.D.*, Moscow.

Khāleqī-Moṭlaq, D.
1971 *Die Frauen im Schahname: Ihre Geschichte und Stellung unter gleichzeitiger Berücksichtigung vor- und nachislamischer Quellen*, Freiburg.
1982 "Farāmarz-nāma," *Īrān nāme* 1/1, Washington, DC, pp. 22–45.

Khareghat, M.P.
1914 "The Identity of Some Heavenly Bodies Mentioned in Old Iranian Writings," *Sir Jamsetjee Jejeebhoy Madressa Jubilee Volume*, ed. Modi, J.J., Bombay, pp. 116–58.

Khoury, N.N.
1992 "The Mihrab Image: Commemorative Themes in Medieval Islamic Architecture," *Muqarnas* X, pp. 11–28.

Kilpatrick, H.
2003 *Making the Great Book of Songs: Compilation and the Author's Craft in Abû l-Faraj al-Iṣbahânî's Kitâb al-Aghânî*, London.

Kiselev, S.V.
1965 "Dvorets v Kondue," *Drevnemongol'skie goroda (Ancient Mongolian Cities)*, eds. Kiselev, S.V., Evtuchova, L.A., Kyzlasov, L.R., Merpert, N.J., Levasova, V.P., Moscow, pp. 325–69.

Kitzinger, E.
1970 "The Threshold of the Holy Shrine: Observations on Floor Mosaics at Antioch and Bethlehem," *Kyriakon. Festschrift für Johannes Quasten* II, eds., Granfield, P., and Jungmann, J.A., Münster, pp. 639–47.

Kleiss, W.
1961 "Der mongolische Bau mit den ornamentierten Türgewänden," *Takht-i Suleiman und Zendan-i-Suleiman: Vorläufiger Bericht über die Ausgrabungen im Jahre 1960*, eds. Naumann, R., Kleiss, W., and Oehler, H., Jahrbuch des Deutschen Archäologischen Instituts und Archäologischer Anzeiger 76.

Klíma, O.
1968 "Avesta. Ancient Persian Inscriptions. Middle Persian Literature," *History of Iranian Literature*, written in collaboration with Rypka, J., Kubíčková, Taurer, F., Bečka, J., Cejpek, J., Merek, J., Hrbek, I., and de Bruijn, J.T.P., tr. from the German by van Popta-Hope, P., ed. Jahn, K., Dordrecht, pp. 1–68.

Knipe, D.M.
1967 "The Heroic Theft from Ṛgveda IV and the Ancient Near East," *History of Religion* 6, 4, May, pp. 328–60.

Kolbas, J.G.
2006 *The Mongols in Iran: Chingiz Khan to Uljaytu 1220–1309*, Abingdon, Oxon.

Kopf, L.
1953 "The Book of Animals *(Kitāb al-ḥayawān)* of al-Jahiz," *Actes du VIIe Congrès international d'histoire des sciences*, ed. Bodenheimer, F.S., 4–11 août, Jerusalem, pp. 395–401.

Köprülü, M.F.
1992 *The Seljuks of Anatolia*, tr. and ed. Leiser, G., Salt Lake City.
2006 *Türk Edebiyatında ilk mutasavvıflar* ("Early Mystics in Turkish Literature"), tr. and eds. Leiser, G., and Dankoff, R., London and New York.

Kouymjian, D.
2006 "Chinese Motifs in Thirteenth-Century Armenian Art: The Mongol Connection," *Beyond the Legacy of Genghis Khan*, ed. Komaroff, L., Leiden, Boston and Cologne, pp. 303–24, pls. 23–5, figs. 58–67.

Kowalski, T.
1939–49 "Les Turcs dans le Šāh-nāme," *Rocznik Orientalistyczny* 15, Cracow, pp. 84–99.

Kramarovsky, M.G.
1991 "The Culture of the Golden Horde and the Problem of the 'Mongol Legacy.' Rulers from the Steppe. State Formation on the Eurasian Periphery," *Ethnographics Press*, The University of Southern California.
2000 "The Gold of the Chingissids: The Juchids' Treasure," *Altyn Urda khezinelere/Sokrovishcha Zolotoi Ordy/The Treasures of the Golden Horde*, exhibition catalogue organised by the State Hermitage Museum and other Institutions, St. Petersburg, pp. 202–6.
2005 "Die frühen Jöčiden: Die Entwicklungslinien einer Kultur zwischen Asien und Europa," *Dschingis Khan und seine Erben: Das Weltreich der Mongolen*, Munich, pp. 223–7.

Kraus, P.
1942 *Contribution à l'histoire des idées scientifiques dans l'Islam*, Cairo.

Kristiansen, K., and Larsson, T.B.
2005 *The Rise of Bronze Age Society: Travels, Transmissions and Transformations*, Cambridge.

Krotkoff, G.
1984 "Colour and Number in the Haft Paykar," *Logos Islamikos: Studia Islamica in Honorem Georgii Michaelis Wickens*, ed. Savory, R.M., and Dionisius, A.A., Papers in Medieval Studies 6, Toronto, pp. 97–118.

Kuehn, S.
2009 "On the Role of the Ophidian and the Quadruped Dragon within the Iconography of the Mythological Scheme of the Oxus Civilisation," *On the Track of Uncovering a Civilization. A Volume in Honor of the 80th Anniversary of Victor Sarianidi*, Transactions of the Margiana Archaeological Expedition, Vol. 3, Moscow and St. Petersburg, Aletya, November, pp. 43–67.

Kühnel, E.
1925 *Islamische Kleinkunst*, Berlin.
1950 "Drachenportale," *Zeitschrift für Kunstwissenschaft* IV, 1–2, Berlin, pp. 1–18.

Kuntzmann, R.
1983 *Le symbolisme des jumeaux au Proche-Orient*

ancien: Naissance, fonction et évolution d'un symbole, Paris.

Kunz, G.F.
1913 *The Curious Lore of Precious Stones*, Philadelphia, PA.

Kurita, I.
1988 *Gandāra bijutsu* (*Gandhāran Art*, vol. I, *The Buddha's Life Story*, vol. II), Ancient Buddhist Art Series, 2 vols., Tokyo, repr. 2003.

Kurz, O.
1983 "Cultural Relations Between Parthia and Rome," *The Cambridge History of Iran*, vol. 3, *The Seleucid, Parthian and Sasanid Periods*, eds. Fischer, W.B., Gershevitch, I., and Yarshater, E., Cambridge, pp. 559–67.

Küster, E.
1913 *Die Schlange in der griechischen Kunst und Religion*, Religionsgeschichtliche Versuche und Vorarbeiten 13, 2.

Kuzʿmina, E.E.
1987 "The Motif of the Lion-Bull Combat in the Art of Iran, Scythia, and Central Asia and its Semantics," *Orientalia Iosephi Tucci Memoriae Dicata*, eds. Gnoli, G., and Lanciotti, L., IsMEO, Serie Orientale Roma, LVI, 1–3, Rome, vol. 2, pp. 729–45.

Lane, A.
1947 *Early Islamic Pottery*, London.

Lane, A.J.
2005 *A Traditional Muʿtazilite Qurʾan Commentary: The Kashshāf of Jār Allāh Al-Zamakhsharī (d. 538/1144)*, Texts & Studies on the Qurʾan, Leiden.

Lane, E.N.
1996 ed., *Cybele, Attis and Related Cults: Essays in Memory of M.J. Vermaseren*, Leiden, New York and Cologne.

Lane Poole, S.
1877 *Catalogue of Oriental Coins in the British Museum: The Coins of the Turkumán Houses of Seljooḳ, Urtuḳ, Zengee etc. in the British Museum, Classes X–XIV*, vol. 3, ed. Stuart Poole, R., London, repr. Bologna, 1967.

Langton, E.
1949 *Essentials of Demonology: A Study of Jewish and Christian Doctrine*, London.

LaRocca, D.J.
2006 *Warriors of the Himalayas: Rediscovering the Arms and Armor of Tibet*, New Haven and London.

Laufer, B., and Walravens, H.
1987 *Sino-Tibetan Studies: Selected Papers on the Art, Folklore, History, Linguistics, and Prehistory of Sciences in China and Tibet*, repr. Delhi.

Lazard, G.
1956 "Un texte persan sur la légende de Gayomart," *Journal Asiatique*, vol. CCXLIV, no. 3, pp. 201–16.

von Le Coq, A.
1913 *Chotcho: Ergebnisse der kgl. Preussischen Turfan-Expeditionen*, Berlin.
1925 *Bilderatlas zur Kunst- und Kulturgeschichte Mittelasiens*, Berlin, repr. Graz, 1977.

von Le Coq, A., and Waldschmidt, E.
1928 *Ergebnisse der kgl. Preussischen Turfan Expeditionen: Die Buddhistische Spätantike in Mittelasien*, vol. 6, *Neue Bildwerke II, Mit einem Beitrag über die Darstellungen und den Stil der Wandgemälde aus Qyzil bei Kutscha*, Berlin, repr. Graz, 1975.

Lebedynsky, I.
1995 "Draco, Dragon Standards East and West," *The Flag Bulletin* 34, 164, pp. 90–102.

Lechler, G.
1939 "The Tree of Life in Indo-European and Islamic Cultures," *Ars Islamica*, vol. 4, pp. 369–419.

Le Goff, J.
1979 "Culture ecclésiastique et culture folklorique au Moyen Âge: Saint Marcel de Paris et le dragon," *Mélanges C. Barbagallo*, Bari, pp. 53–90, repr. in *Pour un autre Moyen Âge*, Paris, 1978, pp. 236–79; English tr., pp. 159–88.
1980 *Time, Work & Culture in the Middle Ages*, tr. Goldhammer, A., Paris.

Leisegang, H.
1924 *Die Gnosis*, Leipzig, repr. Stuttgart, 1955.
1955 "The Mystery of the Serpent," *Eranos Yearbooks* 2, repr. in *The Mysteries: Papers from the Eranos Yearbooks*, ed. Campbell, J., Princeton, NJ, 1979, pp. 194–260.

Levey, M.
1966 *Medieval Arabic Toxicology: The Book on Poisons of Ibn Waḥshiyya and Its Relation to Early Indian and Greek Texts*, Transactions of the American Philosophical Society, n.s., vol. 56, 7, Philadelphia, PA.

Levi, D.
1941 "The Evil Eye and the Lucky Hunchback," *Antioch-on-the-Orontes III: The Excavations 1937–1939*, Princeton, London and The Hague, text pp. 220–32, pls. 54–7.

Lewis, S.
1973 "The Iconography of the Coptic Horseman in Byzantine Egypt," *Journal of the American Research Center in Egypt* X, pp. 27–63, and 20 unnumbered pls. with 38 illustrations.

Lindner, R.P.
1983 *Nomads and Ottomans in Medieval Anatolia*, Research Institute for Inner Asia Studies, Bloomington, IN.

Lings, M.
1961 *A Moslem Saint of the Twentieth Century: Shaikh Aḥmad al-ʿAlawī, His Spiritual Heritage and Legacy*, London.

van Lint, T.M.
2005 "The Gift of Poetry: Khidr and John the Baptist as Patron Saints of Muslim and Armenian *Āšiks* and *Ašułs*," *Redefining Christian Identity*, eds. Ginkel, J.J., Murre-van den Berg, H.L., and van Lint, T.M., Leuven, pp. 335–78.
2009 "The Formation of Armenian Identity in the First Millenium," *Church History and Religious Culture*, 89.1–3, pp. 251–78.

Liu, M.
1958 *Die chinesischen Nachrichten zur Geschichte der Ost-Türken (T'u-küe)*, 2 vols., Wiesbaden.

L'Orange, H.P.
1953 *Studies on the Iconography of Cosmic Kingship in the Ancient World*, Instituttet for sammenlignende kulturforskning, Serie A, 23.

Loewe, M.
1987 "The Cult of the Dragon and the Invocation for Rain," *Chinese Ideas about Nature and Society*, eds. Blader, S., and Le Blanc, C., Hong Kong, pp. 195–214.

Loisy, A.
1930 *Les mystères païens et le mystère chrétien*, Paris, repr. Frankfurt, 1983.

Long, B.J.
1976 "Life Out of Death: A Structural Analysis of the Myth of the 'Churning of the Ocean of Milk,'" *Hinduism: New Essays in the History of Religion*, ed. Bardwell Smith, L., Supplement to Numen 33, Leiden, pp. 171–207.

Lowick, N.
1985 "The Religious, the Royal and the Popular in the Figural Coinage of the Jazīra," *The Art of Syria and the Jazira 1100–250*, ed. Raby, J., Oxford, pp. 159–73.

Loukonine, V., and Ivanov, A.
2003 eds., *Persian Art: Lost Treasures*, London.

MacKenzie, D.N.
1964 "Zoroastrian Astrology in the *Bundahišn*," *Bulletin of the School of Oriental and African Studies* 27, pp. 511–29.

McKinney, R.C.
2004 *The Case of Rhyme Versus Reason: Ibn al-Rūmī and His Poetics in Context*, Leiden.

Maenchen-Helfen, O.
1944–5 "The Legend of the Origin of the Huns," *Byzantion* 17, pp. 244–51.

Magistro, M.R.
2000 "Alcuni aspetti della glittica sacro-magico sasanide: il "Cavaliere nimbato,"" *Studia Iranica* 29, pp. 167–94.

Maguire, H.
1987 "Adam and the Animals: Allegory and the Literal Sense in Early Christian Art," *Dumburton Oaks Papers* 41, pp. 363–74.
1994 "Magic and Geometry in Early Christian Floor Mosaics and Textiles," *Jahrbuch der österreichischen Byzantinistik* 44, pp. 265–74.
1995 "Magic and the Christian Image," *Byzantine Magic*, ed. Maguire, H., Washington, DC, pp. 51–71.

Mahé, J.-P.
1992 "Le soleil et la lune dans la mythologie arménienne," *Caucasologie et mythologie comparée*, Actes du Colloque International du CNRS, IVe Colloque de Caucasologie (Sèvres, 27–9 juin 1988), Paris, pp. 149–75.
1994 "Un dieu guerrier à la campagne: l'example du Vahagn armenien," *Comptes rendus de l'Académie des inscriptions & belles-lettres*, July-October, pp. 779–804.
1995 "Dragons et serpents dans les traditions arménienne," *Actes du colloque "Les Lusignans et l'OutreMer," 20–4 octobre 1993*, Poitiers, pp. 181–9.

Mahdjoub, M.-D.
1988 "The Evolution of Popular Eulogy of the Imams Among the Shi'a," tr. Perry, J.R., *Authority and Political Culture in Shi'ism*, ed. Arjomand, S.A., Albany, NY, pp. 54–79.

Mango, C.
1972 *The Art of the Byzantine Empire, 312–453: Sources and Documents*, Englewood Cliffs, NJ.

Manoukian, A., and A.
1967–9 eds., *Sanahin*, Documents of Armenian Architecture, 3, Facoltà di architettura del Politecnico di Milano, Accademia delle Scienze dell'Armenia S.S.R., Missione scientifica in Armenia S.S.R.

Marazov, I.
1997 "Between Ares and Orpheus: Myth, Kingship and Art in Ancient Thrace," *Ancient Gold: The Wealth of the Thracians, Treasures from the Republic of Bulgaria*, ed. Marazov, I., New York, pp. 32–71.

Maricq, A., and Wiet, G.
1958 *Le minaret de Djam : La découverte de la capitale des Sultans Ghorides (XIIe – XIIIe siècles)*, Mémoires de la Délégation archéologique française en Afghanistan, XVI, Paris.

Markel, S.A.
1995 *Origins of the Nine Planetary Deities*, Studies in Asian Thought and Religion, vol. 16, Lewiston, NY.

Marr, N.Y., and Smirnov, V.I.
1931 *Les Vichaps*, Mémoires de l'Académie de l'histoire de la culture matérielle, Leningrad.

Marquart, J.
1914 "Über das Volkstum der Komanen," *Osttürkische Dialektstudien*, eds. Bang, W., and Marquart, J., Abh. der Königlichen Gesellschaft der Wissenschaften zu Göttingen, phil.-hist. Kl., N.F., Band XIII, Berlin, pp. 25–38.

Marshak, B.I.
1971 *Sogdijskoe serebro* ("Sogdian Silver")*: Očerki po vbostočnoj torevtike*, in Russian and English, Moscow.
1986 *Silberschätze aus dem Orient: Metallkunst des 3.–13. Jahrhunderts und ihre Kontinuität*, Leipzig.
1996 "Sogdiana, part I, Sughd and Adjacent Regions," *History of Civilizations of Central Asia*, vol. 3, *The Crossroads of Civilizations: A.D. 250 to 750*, ed. Litvinsky, B.A., Paris, repr. Delhi 1999, pp. 233–58.
2002 *Legends, Tales, and Fables in the Art of Sogdiana*, appendix by Livshits, V.A., Biennal Ehsan Yarshater Lecture Series, no. 1, New York.

Martin, F.R.
1912 *The Miniature Painting and Painters of Persia, India and Turkey, from the 8th to the 18th Century*, 2 vols., London, repr. 1968.

Martinek, M.
1996 *Wie die Schlange zum Teufel wurde: die Symbolik in der Paradiesgeschichte von der hebräischen Bibel bis zum Koran*, Studies in Oriental Religions 37, Wiesbaden.

Martinez, A.P.
1982 "Gardīzī's Two Chapters on the Turks," *Archivum Eurasiae Medii Aevi* 2, pp. 109–75.

Marzolph, U., and van Leeuwen, R., with the collaboration of Wassouf, H.
2004 *The Arabian Nights Encyclopedia*, Santa Barbara, CA.

Massé, H.
1938 *Croyances et coutumes persanes: suivies de contes et chansons populaires*, 2 vols., Paris.

Massignon, L.
1956 "Elie et son rôle transhistorique, Khadirīya, en Islam," *Élie le prophète*, Études carmélitaines, vol. 2, Au Carmel. Dans le Judaisme et l'Islam, Paris, pp. 269–90.
1950 "Inventaire de la littérature hermétique arabe," *La Révélation d'Hermès Trismégiste*, Festugière, J., vol. 1, 2, Paris, repr. 1981, pp. 384–400.

Mastrocinque, A.
2005 *From Jewish Magic to Gnosticism*, Tübingen.

Masuya, T.
1997 *The Ilkhanid Phase of Takht-i Sulaiman*, Ph.D. dissertation, New York University.
2002 "Ilkhanid Courtly Life," *The Legacy of Genghis Khan: Courtly Art and Culture in Western Asia, 1256–1353*, eds. Komaroff, L., and Carboni, S., New York, pp. 74–103.

Mathews, T.F.
1982 "The Genesis Frescoes of Ałt'amar," *Association de la Revue des Études Armenienne*, n.s., 16, Paris.

Mathews, T.F., and Sanjian, A.K.
1991 *Armenian Gospel Iconography: The Tradition of the Glajor Gospel*, Washington, DC.

Mayer, L.A.
1959 *Islamic Metalworkers and Their Works*, Geneva.

Meyerhofer, M.
1932 "Joannes Grammatikos (Philoponos) von Alexandrien und die arabische Medizin," *Mitteilungen des deutschen Instituts für ägyptische Altertumskunde in Kairo* 2, 1, Berlin, pp. 1–21.

McCown, C.C.
1922 ed., *The Testament of Solomon*, Leipzig.

McKenzie, J.
2006 *The Architecture of Alexandria and Egypt, 300 B.C. to A.D. 700*, New Haven, CN.

Meier, F.
1976 *Abu Saʿīd-i Abu 'l Ḫair (357–440/967–1049): Wirklichkeit und Legende*, Acta Iranica 11, 3, Textes et mémoires, Bibliothèque Pahlavi, Tehran, Liège and Leiden.

Meinecke, M.
1976 *Fayencedekorationen seldschukischer Sakralbauten in Kleinasien*, I and II, Istanbuler Mitteilungen, Beiheft 13, Tübingen.
1989 "Islamische Drachentüren," *Museumsjournal, Berichte aus den Museen, Schlössern und Sammlungen im Land Berlin* 3, series 4, pp. 54–8.
1996 *Patterns of Stylistic Changes in Islamic Architecture: Local Traditions Versus Migrating Artists*, New York and London.

Meisami, J.S.
1987 *Medieval Persian Court Poetry*, Princeton, NJ.
1990 "Ghaznavid Panegyrics: Some Political Implications," *Iran*, vol. 28, pp. 31–44.
1993 "The Theme of Journey in Niẓāmī's *Haft Paykar*," *Edebiyât* 4, pp. 155–72.
1999 *Persian Historiography*, Edinburgh.

Melikian-Chirvani, A.S.
1967 "Trois manuscrits de l'Iran seldjoukide," *Arts Asiatiques* 16, pp. 3–51.
1974 "The Westward Progress of Khorasanian Culture under the Seljuks," *The Art of Iran and Anatolia from the 11th to the 13th Century A.D.*, Colloquies on Asian Art and Archaeology 4, ed. Watson, W., London, pp. 110–25.
1977 "Les thèmes ésotériques et les thèmes mystiques dans l'art du bronze iranien," *Mélanges offerts à Henry Corbin (Ǧašn-nāma-i Hānrī Kurbin)*, ed. Ḥusain, N., Tehran, pp. 367–406.
1982 *Islamic Metalwork from the Islamic World, 8th-18th centuries*, Victoria and Albert Museum, London.
1984 "Le *Shāh-Nāme*, la gnose soufie et le pouvoir mongol," *Journal Asiatique* CCLXXII, 3–4, pp. 249–337.
1991 "Le livre des rois, miroir du destin II: Takht-e Soleymān et la symbolique du Shāh-Nāme" *Studia Iranica* 20, fasc. 1, pp. 33–148, pls. I–XVI.
1992 "The Wine Bull and the Magian Master," *Studia Iranica*, cahier 2, *Recurrent Patterns in Iranian Religions*, Bures-sur-Yvette, pp. 101–34, 3 pls.
1994 "The Light of the World," *The Art of the Saljūqs in Iran and Anatolia: Proceedings of a Symposium Held in Edinburgh in 1982*, ed. Hillenbrand, R., Costa Mesa, CA, pp. 146–53.
1995 "The Wine Birds of Iran from Pre-Achaemenid to Islamic Times," *Bulletin of the Asia Institute* 9, pp. 41–97, 27 figs.
1996 "The Iranian Wine Horn from Pre-Achaemenid Antiquity to the Safavid Age," *Bulletin of the Asia Institute* 10, pp. 85–139, 28 figs.
1997a "Precious and Semi-Precious Stones in Iranian Culture, Chapter I. Early Iranian Jade," *Bulletin of the Asia Institute* 11, pp. 123–73.
1997b "Conscience du passé et résistance culturelle dans l'Iran mongol," *L'Iran face à la domination mongole (Īrān dar barābar-i istīlā-yi Mughūl)*, ed. Aigle, D., Bibliothèque Iranienne 45, Tehran, pp. 135–77.
1998 "Rostam and Herakles, a Family Resemblance," *Bulletin of the Asia Institute*, n.s., Alexander's Legacy in the East: Studies in Honor of Paul Bernard, vol. 12, pp. 171–99.

Mélikoff, I.
1960 *La Geste de Melik Dāniṣmend: Étude critique du Dāniṣmendnama*, 2 vols., Paris.
1962 *Abu Muslim: Le "porte-hache" du Khorassan dans la tradition epique turco-iranienne*, Paris.
1989 *Hadji Bektach: un mythe et ses avatars. Genèse et évolution du soufisme populaire en Turquie*, Leiden, New York and Cologne.

Melville, C.
1994 "The Chinese-Uighur Animal Calendar in Persian Historiography of the Mongol Period," *Iran* 32, pp. 83–98.

Mepisaschwili, R., Zinzadze, W., and Schrade, R.
1987 *Georgien: Wehrbauten und Kirchen*, Leipzig.

Meri, J.W.
2002 *The Cult of Saints Among Muslims and Jews in Medieval Syria*, Oxford Oriental Monographs Series, Oxford and New York.
2004 tr. and intr., *A Lonely Wayfarer's Guide to Pilgrimage: ʿAlī ibn Abī Bakr al-Harawī's Kitāb al-Ishārāt ilā Maʿrifat al-Ziyārāt*, Studies in Late Antiquity and Early Islam, Princeton, NJ.

Meyvaert, P.
1980 "An Unknown Letter of Hulagu, Il-Khan of Persia, to King Louis IX of France," *Viator* 11, pp. 245–60.

Michot, Y.M.
2004 "Ibn Taymiyya on Astrology: Annotated Translations of Three Fatwas," *Magic and Divination in Early Islam*, ed. Savage-Smith, E., Aldershot, Hants, pp. 277–340.

Millet, G.
1923 "L'ascension d'Alexandre," *Syria* IV, pp. 83–133.

Minorskij (Minorsky), V.F.
1953 *Studies in Caucasian History: 1. New Light on the Shaddādids of Ganja, 2. The Shaddādids of Ani, 3. Prehistory of Saladin*, Arabic text of the chapter on the Shaddādids from Münejjim Bashi's [Munağğim Bāšī (Aḥmad b. Luṭfallāh)] Duwal al-Islām, Topkapı Sarayı Ms. 2951, London.
1942 tr. and ed., *Sharaf al-Zamān Ṭāhir Marvazī on China, the Turks and India*, Royal Asiatic Society, London.

Miroshnikov, L.I.
1992 "Appendix: A Note on the Meaning of 'Central Asia' as Used in this Book," *History of Civilizations of Central Asia*, vol. 1, *The Dawn of Civilizations: Earliest Times to 700 B.C.*, ed. Dani, A.H., and Masson, V.M., Paris, repr. Delhi, 1999, pp. 477–80.

Mnatsakanyan, A.Š.
1955 *Armyanskoe Ornamental'noe Iskusstvo/ Haykakan Zardarvest* ("Armenian Ornamental Art"), in Armenian with Russian title and summary, Erevan.

Mode, H.
2006 "Heroic Fights and Dying Heroes. The Orlat Battle Plaque and the Roots of Sogdian Art," *Ērān ud Anērān: Studies Presented to Boris Il'ič Maršak on the Occasion of His 70th Birthday*, eds. Compareti, M., Raffetta, P., and Scarcia, G., Venice, pp. 419–54.

Modi, J.J.
1894 *Charms and Amulets for Some Diseases of the Eye, and a Few Ancient Beliefs about the Eclipse*, Bombay, pp. 1–24.

Molnár, Á., with an appendix by Zieme, P.
1984 *Weather-Magic in Inner Asia*, Bloomington, IN.

Monchi-Zadeh, D.
1975 *Topographisch-historische Studien zum iranischen Nationalepos*, Wiesbaden.

Montgomery, J.E.
2006 "Spectral Armies, Snakes, and a Giant from Gog and Magog: Ibn Faḍlān as Eyewitness among the Volga Bulghārs," *The Medieval History Journal* 9, 1, pp. 63–87.

Mordtmann, A.
1864 "Studien über geschnittene Steine mit Pehlevi-Inschriften," *Zeitschrift der Deutschen Morgenländischen Gesellschaft*, vol. 18, pp. 1–53.

Morgenstern, A., and Linsider, J.A.
2006 *Hastening Redemption: Messianism and the Resettlement of the Land of Israel*, Oxford and New York.

Morgenstierne, G.
1964 "An Ancient Indo-Iranian Word for 'Dragon,'" *Dr. J.M. Unvala Memorial Volume*, Bombay, pp. 95–8 (repr. with add. in *Irano-Dardica*, Wiesbaden, 1973, pp. 24–30).
1974 *Etymological Vocabulary of the Shughni Group*, Beiträge zur Iranistik, Wiesbaden.

Moulierac, J.
1987 "Un vase d'alchimie de l'Orient médiéval islamique," *Technologia* 10, 2–4, pp. 83–90.
1996 "Les thériaques," *À l'ombre d'Avicenne: La médecine au temps des califes*, exhibition catalogue, 18 November 1996 to 2 March 1997, Institut du Monde Arabe, Paris, pp. 101–3.

Nasr, S.H.
1964a *An Introduction to Islamic Cosmological Doctrines: Conceptions of Nature and Methods Used for Its Study by the Ikhwān Al-Ṣafāʾ, Al-Bīrūnī, and Ibn Sīnā*, Cambridge, MA, repr. 1993.
1964b *Three Muslim Sages: Avicenna-Suhrawardi-Ibn Arabi*, Harvard Studies in World Religions, Cambridge, MA.

Nassar, N.
1985 "Saljuq or Byzantine: Two Related Styles of Jazīran Miniature Painting," *The Art of Syria and the Jazīra*, 1100–250, ed. Raby, J., Oxford, pp. 85–98.

Naumann, R., and E.
1976 *Takht-i Suleiman: Ausgrabungen des Deutschen Archäologischen Instituts in Iran*, exhibition catalogue, September to December 1976, Prähistorischen Staatssammlung, München, 3, Munich.

Naumann, R.
1977 *Die Ruinen von Tacht-e Suleiman und Zendan-e Suleiman und Umgebung*, Berlin.

Naveh, J., and Shaked, S.
1985 *Amulets and Magic Bowls: Aramaic Incantations of Late Antiquity*, Jerusalem, repr. 1998.

Needham, J., and Wang, L.
1954 *Science and Civilisation in China*, vol. 3, *Mathematics, The Sciences of the Heavens and of the Earth*, Cambridge.

1965 *Science and Civilisation in China*, vol. 4, *Physics and Physical Technology*, part 2, *Mechanical Engineering*, Cambridge.
1980 *Science and Civilisation in China*, vol. 5, *Chemistry and Chemical Technology*, part 4, *Spagyrical Discovery and Invention: Apparatus, Theories and Gifts*, New York.

Negmatov, N.N.
1996 "Sogdiana, part II, Ustrushan, Ferghana, Chach and Ilak," *History of Civilizations of Central Asia*, vol. 3, *The Crossroads of Civilizations: A.D. 250 to 750*, ed. Litvinsky, B.A., Paris, repr. Delhi 1999, pp. 259–80.

Der Nersessian, S.
1937 *L'illustration du roman de Barlaam and Joasaph*, Paris.
1945 *Armenia and the Byzantine Empire: A Brief Study of Armenian Art and Civilization*, Cambridge, MA.
1965 *Aght'amar, Church of the Holy Cross*, Cambridge, MA.
1969 *The Armenians*, London.
1973 *Armenian Manuscripts in the Walters Art Gallery*, Baltimore, MD.

Der Nersessian, S., and Agemian, S.
1993 with an introd. by Weyl Carr, A., *Miniature Painting in the Armenian Kingdom of Cilicia from the Twelfth to the Fourteenth Century*, Washington, DC.

Nersessian, V.
2001 *Treasures from the Ark: 1700 Years of Armenian Christian Art*, London.

Neubauer, E.
1976 *Altgeorgische Baukunst: Felsenstädte, Kirchen, Höhlenklöster*, Munich.

Nicholson, R.A.
1967 *Studies in Islamic Mysticism*, Cambridge.

Niggemeyer, J.-H.
1975 *Beschwörungsformeln aus dem "Buch der Geheimnisse" (Sefär ha-razîm): Zur Topologie der magischen Rede*, Judaistische Texte und Studien 3, ed. Maier, J., Hildesheim and New York.

Nöldeke, T.
1860 "Die Schlange nach arabischem Volksglauben," *Zeitschrift für Völkerpsychologie und Sprachwissenschaft* I, pp. 412–6.
1879 *Geschichte des Artachshîr-i-Pâpakân*, Göttingen.

Noy, D.
1971 "The Jewish Versions of the "Animal Languages" Folktale (AT670). A Typological-Structural Study," *Scripta Hierosolymitana* 22, Publications of the Hebrew University, Jerusalem, pp. 171–208.

Nyberg, H.S.
1933 "La légende de Keresāspa: Transcription des texts pehlevis, avec une traduction nouvelle et des notes philologiques," *Oriental Studies in Honour of Cursetji Erachji Pavry*, London, pp. 336–52 (repr. in *Monumentum H.S. Nyberg* IV, Acta Iranica 7, pp. 379–95).

Nylander, C.
1974 "Al-Bērunī and Persepolis," *Acta Iranica*, I, Leiden, pp. 137–50.

Oberhelman, S.M.
1994 "On the Chronology and Pneumatism of Aretaios of Cappadocia," *Aufstieg und Niedergang der römischen Welt: Geschichte und Kultur Roms im Spiegel neuerer Forschung*, part II, vol. 37.2, eds. Temporini, H., and Haase, W., Berlin and New York, pp. 941–67.

Oborin, V.A., and Tshagin, G.N.
1988 *Tschudskie drevnosti Rifeia. Permskii zverinyi stil* ("The Animal Style of Perm"), Perm.

Ocak, A.Y.
1989 *La révolte de Baba Resul ou la formation de l'Heterodoxie Musulmane en Anatolie au XIIIe siècle*, Ankara.

O'Connor, K.M.
1994 *The Alchemical Creation of Life* (Takwīn) *and Other Concepts of Genesis in Islam*, Ph.D. dissertation, University of Pennsylvania.

O'Kane, B.
2003 *Early Persian Painting: Kalila and Dimna Manuscripts of the Late Fourteenth Century*, London and New York.

Oikonomidès, N.A.
1981 "Le dédoublement de Saint Théodore et les villes d'Euchaita et d'Euchaneia," *Analecta Bollandiana* 104, pp. 327–35.

Omidsalar, M.
2001 "Rostam's Seven Trials and the Logic of the Epic Narrative in the Shāhnāma," *Asian Folklore Studies*, vol. 60, pp. 259–93.

Ölçer, N., et al.
1993 *In the Pursuit of Excellence: Works of Art from The Museum of Turkish and Islamic Arts*, Istanbul.
2002 *Türk ve İslâm Eserleri Müzesi*, Istanbul, pp. 98–9.

Oldenberg, H.
1894 *Die Religion des Veda*, Berlin, repr. Darmstadt, 1977.

Olschki, L.
1946 *Guillaume Boucher: A French Artist at the Court of the Khans*, Baltimore, 1946.

Önder, M.
1961 "Ein neugefundenes rumseldschukisches Drachenrelief," *Archäologischer Anzeiger* 76, pp. 70–4.
1987 "Neuentdeckte seldschukische Drachenfiguren," *Ars Turcica: Akten des VI. Internationalen Kongresses für Türkische Kunst, München vom 3. bis 7. September 1979*, eds. Kreiser, K., Majer, H.G., Restle, M., and Zick-Nissen, J., Munich, vol. 2, pp. 594–600, vol. 3, pl. 112.

Öney, G.
1969a "Anadolu Selçuk sanatında ejder figürleri ("Dragon Figures in Anatolian Saljuk Art")," *Belleten* XXXIII, pp. 171–92 (Turkish vers.), 193–216 (English vers. and pls.).
1969b "Anatolian Seljuq art," *Türk Tarih Kurumu, Belleten*, XXXIII, Ankara.
1969–70 "Sun and Moon Rosettes in the Shape of Human Heads in Anatolian Seljuk Architecture," *Anatolica* 3, pp. 187–203.

1978 *Anadolu Selçuklu mimarisinde süsleme ve el sanatları (Architectural Decoration and Minor Arts in Seljuk Anatolia)*, Ankara, repr. 1992.

Otavsky, K.
1998 "Zur kunsthistorischen Einordnung der Stoffe," *Entlang der Seidenstraße. Frühmittelalterliche Kunst zwischen Persien und China in der Abegg-Stiftung*, ed. Otavsky, K., Riggisberg, pp. 119–214.

Otto-Dorn, K.
1959 "Türkische Grabsteine mit Figurenreliefs aus Kleinasien," *Ars Orientalis* 3, pp. 63–76.
1961–2 "Türkisch-islamisches Bildgut in den Figurenreliefs von Achthamar," *Anatolia* 6, pp. 1–69.
1963 "Darstellungen des turco-chinesischen Tierzyklus in der islamischen Kunst," *In Memoriam Ernst Diez: Beiträge zur Kunstgeschichte Asiens*, ed. Aslapana, O., Istanbul, pp. 131–65.
1964 *Kunst des Islam*, Baden-Baden.
1978–9 "Figural Stone Reliefs on Seljuk Sacred Architecture in Anatolia," *Kunst des Orients* 12, 1–2, pp. 103–49.
1994 "The Griffin-Sphinx Ensemble," *The Art of the Saljūqs in Iran and Anatolia: Proceedings of a Symposium held in Edinburgh in 1982*, ed. Hillenbrand, R., Costa Mesa, CA, pp. 303–11.

Otto-Dorn, K., and Önder, M.
1969 "Bericht über die Grabung in Kobadabad 1966," *Archäologischer Anzeiger* 4, pp. 438–506.

Panaino, A.
2005 "Lunar and Snake Omens among the Zoroastrians," *Officina Magica: Essays on the Practice of Magic in Antiquity*, ed. Shaked, S., IJS Studies in Judaica, vol. 4, Leiden and Boston, pp. 73–89.

Pancaroğlu, O.
2000 *'A World unto Himself': The Rise of a New Human Image in the Late Seljuq Period (1150–250)*, Ph.D. dissertation, Harvard University.
2001 "Socializing Medicine: Illustrations of the *Kitāb al-Diryāq*," *Muqarnas* 18, pp. 155–72.
2003 "Sign in the Horizons: Concepts of Image and Boundary in a Medieval Persian Cosmography," *RES Anthropology and Aesthetics*, 43, Spring, vol. 43, pp. 31–41.
2004 "The Itinerant Dragon Slayer: Forging Paths of Image and Identity in Medieval Anatolia," *Gesta* 43, 2, pp. 151–64.
2007 with transcr. and tr. by Bayani, M., *Perpetual Glory: Medieval Islamic Ceramics from the Harvey B. Plotnick Collection*, New Haven and London.

Papadopoulo, A.
1979 *Islam and Muslim Art*, tr. Wolf, R.E., New York.

Parpola, S.
2001 "Mesopotamian Precursors of the Hymn of the Pearl," ed. Whiting, R.M., *Mythology and Mythologies: Methodological Approaches to Intercultural Influences*, Melammu Symposia II, Helsinki, The Neo-Assyrian Text Corpus Project, pp. 181–93.

Patterson Ševčenko, N.
1990 *Illustrated Manuscripts of the Metaphrastic Menologion*, Chicago and London.

Perdrizet, P.
1903 "Sfragis Solomònos," *Revue des études grecques*, vol. 16, pp. 42–61.
1922 *Negotium perambulans in tenebris: études de démonologie gréco-orientale*, Faculté des Lettres: Publications de la Faculté des Lettres de l'Université de Strasbourg 6, Strasbourg, Paris.

Petermann, H.
1860–1 *Reisen im Orient*, 2 vols., Leipzig.

Peters, F.E.
2004 "Hermes and Harran: The Roots of Arabic-Islamic Occultism," *Magic and Divination in Early Islam*, ed. Savage-Smith, E., Aldershot, Hants, pp. 55–85.

Peterson, E.
1926 *Eis Theos: Epigraphische, formgeschichtliche und religionsgeschichtliche Untersuchungen*, Göttingen.

Phillips, E.D.
1969 *The Mongols*, New York.

Pickett, D.
1997 *Early Persian Tilework: the Medieval Flowering of* kāshī, London.

Pielow, D.A.M.
1995 *Die Quellen der Weisheit: Die arabische Magie im Spiegel des* Uṣūl al-ḥikma *von Aḥmad Ibn ʿAlī al-Būnī*, Arabistische Texte und Studien, 8, Hildesheim.

Pinder-Wilson, R.H.
1997 "Stone Press-Moulds and Leatherworking in Khurasan," *Science, Tools and Magic*, eds. Maddison, F., and Savage-Smith, E., The Nasser D. Khalili Collection of Islamic Art, vol. 12, London, pp. 338–55.
2001 "Ghaznavid and Ghūrid Minarets," *Iran*, vol. 39, pp. 155–86.

Pingree, D.E.
1963 "Astronomy and Astrology in India and Iran," *Isis*, vol. 54, pp. 229–46.
1964–5 "Representation of the Planets in Indian Astrology," *Indo-Iranian Journal*, vol. 8, pp. 249–67.
1968 *The Thousands of Abu Ma'shar*, The Warburg Institute, London.
1990 "Astrology," *Religion, Learning and Science in the ʿAbbasid Period*, eds. Young, M.J.L., Latham, J.D., and Serjeant, R.B., Cambridge and New York, pp. 290–300.
2006 "The Byzantine Translations of Māšāʾallāh on Interrogational Astrology," *The Occult Sciences in Byzantium*, eds. Magdalino, P., and Mavroudi, M.V., Geneva, pp. 231–44.

Piotrovskiy, B.B.
1939 *Vishapy: Kamennye statui v Gorakh Armenii* ("*Vishaps*: Stone Statues in the Mountains of Armenia"), Leningrad.

Piotrovsky, M.
2000 ed., *Earthly Art – Heavenly Beauty: Art of Islam*, St. Petersburg.

Plessner, M.
1954 "The Place of the *Turba Philosophorum* in the Development of Alchemy," *Isis* XLV, pp. 331–8.

Pohl, W.
1988 *Die Awaren: ein Steppenvolk im Mitteleuropa, 567–822 n. Chr.*, Munich.

Pognon, H.
1907 *Inscriptions sémitiques de la Syrie, de la Mésopotamie et de la région de Mossoul*, vol. 1, Paris.

Porter, V.
2004 "Islamic Seals: Magical or Practical?" *Magic and Divination in Early Islam*, ed. Savage-Smith, E., Aldershot, Hants, pp. 179–200.
2006 "Talismans and Talismanic Objects," *Medieval Islamic Civilization: An Encyclopedia*, ed. Meri, J.W., New York and London, pp. 794–6.

Pope, A.U., and Ackerman, P.
1938–9 eds., *A Survey of Persian Art from Prehistoric Times to the Present*, London and New York, repr., Sopa, Ashiya, 1964–81.
1945 *Masterpieces of Persian Art*, New York.

Preisendanz, K.
1973 ed., *Papyri Graecae Magicae: Die griechischen Zauberpapyri*, vol. 1, Stuttgart (repr. of the Leipzig 1928, ed., rev. Henrichs, A.).

Preusser, C.
1911 *Nordmesopotamische Baudenkmäler altchristlicher und islamischer Zeit*, Leipzig.

Prinzing, G., and Schmidt, A.
1997 eds., *Das Lemberger Evangeliar: eine wiederentdeckte armenische Bilderhandschrift des 12. Jahrhunderts*, Wiesbaden.

Prioreschi, P.
2001 *A History of Medicine*, vol. 4, *Byzantine and Islamic Medicine*, Omaha, NE.

Pritchard, J.B.
1955 ed., *Ancient Near Eastern Texts Relating to the Old Testament with Supplement*, Princeton, NJ, repr. 1969.

Pritsak, O.
1950–5 "Qara: Studie zur türkischen Rechtssymbolik," *Zeki Velidi Togan'a Armağan: Symbolae in Honorem Z.V. Togan*, Istanbul, pp. 239–63.

Privalova, E.L.
1977 *Pavnisi*, with French summary, Tbilisi.

Propp, V.
1984a *Theory and History of Folklore*, ed. Liberman, A., tr. Ariadna, Y., and Martin, R.P., Minneapolis, MN.
1984b "Oedipus in the Light of Folklore (*Edip v svete fol'klora*, Leningrad, 1944)," *Oedipus: A Folklore Casebook*, eds. Lowell, E.E., and Dundes, A., New York and London, pp. 76–121.

Prym, E., and Socin, A.
1881 tr., *Syrische Sagen und Märchen aus dem Volksmunde gesammelt*, Göttingen.

Pugachenkova (Pugačenkova), G.A.
1956 "Dragony Mecheti Anau," *Sovietskaya Etnografiya* 2, pp. 125–9.

Pugachenkova (Pugačenkova), G.A., and Rempel', L.I.
1960 *Vydayushchiesya pamyatniki izobrazitel'nogo iskusstva Uzbekistana*, Tashkent.

P'yankov, I.V.
2006 "Scythian Genealogical Legend in "Rustamiada,"" *Ērān ud Anērān: Studies Presented to Boris Il'ič Maršak on the Occasion of His 70th Birthday*, eds. Compareti, M., Raffetta, P., and Scarcia, G., Venice, pp. 505–12.

Raby, J.
1981 "Samson and Siyah Qalam," *Islamic Art* I, pp. 160–3.

Radloff, F.W. (Radlov, V.V.)
1866–1907 ed. and tr., *Proben der Volksliteratur der türkischen Stämme Süd-Sibiriens*, St. Petersburg.
1885 ed. and tr., *Proben der Volksliteratur der nördlichen türkischen Stämme, V. Theil, Der Dialect der Kara-Kirgisen*, St. Petersburg, repr. Leipzig, 1965.

Radtke, B.
1987 "Die älteste islamische Kosmographie Muḥammad-i Ṭūsīs *'Ağā'ib ul-mahlūqāt*," *Der Islam* 64, pp. 278–88.

Rawski, E.S.
1998 *The Last Emperors: A Social History of Qing Imperial Institutions*, Berkeley, CA.

Rawson, J.
1984 *Chinese Ornament: The Lotus and the Dragon*, New York.

Redfield, J.M.
1975 *Nature and Culture in the Iliad: The Tragedy of Hector*, Chicago, repr. 1994.

Redford, S.
1990 "How Islamic Is It? The Innsbruck Plate and Its Setting," *Muqarnas* VII, pp. 119–35.
1993 "The Seljuks of Rum and the Antique," *Muqarnas* X, pp. 148–56.

Redgate, A.E.
2000 *The Armenians: The Peoples of Europe*, Malden, MA.

Regier, W.G.
2004 *Book of the Sphinx*, Lincoln, NE.

Rehatsek, E.
1873–4 "Explanations and Facsimiles of Eight Arabic Talismanic Medicine-Cups," *Journal of the Bombay Branch of the Royal Asiatic Society* 10, pp. 150–62.

Reiner, E.
1991 "First Millennium Babylonian Literature," *The Cambridge Ancient History*, vol. 3, part 2, *The Assyrian and Babylonian Empires and Other States of the Near East, from the Eighth to the Sixth Centuries B.C.*, Cambridge, repr. 2003, pp. 293–321.

Reitlinger, G.
1938 "Medieval Antiquities West of Mosul," *Iraq*, vol. 5, pp. 143–56, pls. XXI–XXVI, pp. 149–50, pls. XXII–XXIII, figs. 9–12.

Reitzenstein, R.
1904 *Poimandres: Studien zur griechisch-aegyptischen und frühchristlichen Literatur*, Leipzig.
1916 "Himmelswanderung und Drachenkampf in der alchemistischen und frühchristlichen Literatur," *Festschrift Friedrich Carl Andreas*

zur Vollendung des siebzigsten Lebensjahres am 14. April 1916 dargebracht von Freunden und Schülern, Leipzig, pp. 33–50.

1921 *Das iranische Erlösungsmysterium: religionsgeschichtliche Untersuchungen*, Bonn a. Rhein.

Remmer, U.

2006 *Frauennamen im Rigveda und im Avesta: Studien zur Onomastik des ältesten Indischen und Iranischen*, Wien.

Rempel', L.I.

1983 ed., *Khudozhestvennaya kul'tura Srednei Azii, IX–XIII veka*, Tashkent.

1987a *Tsep vremyon: Vekovye abrazy I brodyachiye syuzhrty v traditsionnom iskusstve Srednei Asii*, Tashkent.

1987b "La maquette architecturale dans le culte et la construction de l'Asie centrale préislamique," *Cultes et Monuments religieux dans l'Asie Centrale préislamique*, ed. Grenet, F., Paris, pp. 81–8, pls. XLVI–LIV.

Rhodokanakis, N., with addendum by Ehrenzweig, A.

1921 "Genesis 2–4," *Zeitschrift für die alttestamentliche Wissenschaft* 39, pp. 76–83.

Rice, D.S.

1955 *The Wade Cup in the Cleveland Museum of Art*, Paris.

1976 "The Brasses of Badr ad-Dīn Lu'Lu'," *Bulletin of the School of Oriental and African Studies* XIII, 3, pp. 627–34.

Riefstahl, R.M.

1931 *Turkish Architecture in Southwestern Anatolia*, Cambridge, MA.

Ritter, H.

1923 "Picatrix, ein arabisches Handbuch hellenistischer Magie," *Vorträge der Bibliothek Warburg 1921–2*, Leipzig.

2003 The *Ocean of the Soul: Man, the World, and God in the Stories of Farīd al-Dīn ʿAṭṭār*, tr. O'Kane, J., with ass. of Radtke, B., Handbook of Oriental Studies, Leiden.

Rhie, M.M.

1999–2002 *Early Buddhist Art of China and Central Asia: The Eastern Chin and Sixteen Kingdoms Period in China and Tumshuk, Kucha and Karashahr in Central Asia*, 2 vols., Handbook of Oriental Studies, Leiden, Boston and Cologne.

Robertson Smith, W.

1889 *Lectures on the Religion of the Semites*, Burnett Lectures 1888–9, Edinburgh, ed. and rev. Cook, S.A., London, 1927.

Rogers, M.J.

1965 "The Çifte Minare Medrese at Erzurum and the Gök Medrese at Sivas," *Anatolian Studies* 15, pp. 63–85.

1969 "Aeolipiles Again," *Forschungen zur Kunst Asiens. In Memoriam Kurt Erdmann*, ed. Aslanapa, O., and Naumann, R., Istanbul Üniversitesi/Edebiyat Fakültesi, Istanbul, pp. 147–58.

1970–1 "*Selçuklu Araştırmaları Dergisi* [Journal of Seljuk Studies] I, Selçuklu Tarihi ve Medeniyeti Enstitütüsü, Ankara, 1970, pp. 256," *Kunst des Orients* VII, 1, pp. 267–9.

1974 "The Date of the Çifte Minare Medrese at Erzurum," *Kunst des Orients* VIII 1/2, pp. 77–119.

1976 "The Mxargrdzelis between East and West," *Bedi Kartlisa* XXXIV, pp. 315–26.

1986 *The Topkapı Saray Museum: The Albums and Illustrated Manuscripts*, tr., exp. and ed. Rogers, J.M., from the original Turkish by Çağman, F., and Tandini, Z., London.

1988 "Calligraphy and Common Script: Epitaphs from Two Muslim Cemeteries, Aswan and Ahlat," *Content and Context of Visual Arts in the Islamic World. In Memoriam Richard Ettinghausen*, ed. Soucek, P., New York, pp. 105–26.

Ronca, I.

1998 "Religious Symbolism in Medieval Islamic and Christian Alchemy," *Western Esotericism and the Science of Religion*, eds., Faivre, A., Hanegraaff, W.J., Gnostica 2, Leuven, pp. 95–116.

Roscher, W.H.

1914 *Omphalos: eine philologisch-archäologisch-volkskundliche Abhandlung über die Vorstellung der Griechen und anderer Völker vom 'Nabel der Erde'*, Abh. der phil.-hist. Kl. der Sächsischen Gesellschaft der Wissenschaften, vol. XXIX, no. IX, 9 pls.

1915 *Neue Omphalosstudien: ein archäologischer Beitrag zur vergleichenden Religionswissenschaft*, Abh. der phil.-hist. Kl. der Sächsischen Gesellschaft der Wissenschaften, vol. XXXI, no. I, 7 pls.

Rosenfield, J.M.

1967 *The Dynastic Art of the Kushans*, Berkeley and Los Angeles.

Ross, M.

1962 *Catalogue of the Byzantine and Early Medieval Antiquities in the Dumbarton Oaks Collection*, I, Washington.

Rosenstiehl, J.M.

1986 "Tartarouchos-Temelouchos. Contribution à l'étude de l'Apocalypse apocryphe de Paul," *Cahiers de la Bibliothèque Copte*, Deuxième Journée d'Etudes Coptes, pp. 29–56.

Rosenthal, F.

1956 "An Ancient Commentary on the Hippocratic Oath," *Bulletin of the History of Medicine* 30, pp. 52–87.

Rossabi, M.

2002 "The Mongols and their Legacy," *The Legacy of Genghis Khan: Courtly Art and Culture in Western Asia, 1256–1353*, eds. Komaroff, L., and Carboni, S., New York, pp. 12–35.

Rostovtzeff, M.I.

1939 ed., *The Excavations at Dura Europos: Preliminary Reports VII–VIII*, New Haven, CN.

Roux, J.-P.

1972 "Le décor animé du caravansérail de Karatay en Anatolie," *Syria* XLIX, 3–4, pp. 371–97.

1978 "La prétendue représentation du calendrier des douze animaux dans l'art islamique medieval," *Journal Asiatique*, vol. 266, nos. 3–4, pp. 237–49.

1979 "Les astres chez les Turcs et les Mongols," *Revue de l'Histoire des Religions* CXCV, no. 2, April, pp. 153–92.

1980 "Mosquées anatoliennes à décor figurative sculpté," *Syria. Revue d'art oriental et d'archéologie*, vol. LVII, pp. 305–23.
1984 *La religion des Turcs et des Mongols*, Paris.
1981 "Le combat d'animaux dans l'art et la mythology irano-turcs," *Ars Asiatique* 36, pp. 5–11.

Ruska, J.
1926 *Tabula Smaragdina: ein Beitrag zur Geschichte der hermetischen Literatur*, Heidelberger Akten der von Portheim Stiftung, Heidelberg.
1931 "*Turba philosophorum*; Ein Beitrag zur Geschichte der Alchemie," *Quellen und Studien zur Geschichte der Naturwissenschaften und der Medizin* I, Berlin, pp. 1–368.

Russell, J.R.
2004 *Armenian and Iranian Studies*, Harvard Armenian Texts and Studies 9, Armenian Heritage Press, Cambridge, MA.

Russell-Smith, L.
2005 *Uygur Patronage in Dunhuang: Regional Art Centres on the Northern Silk Road in the Tenth and Eleventh Centuries*, Leiden, Boston and Cologne.

Rypka, J.
1968 "History of Persian Literature up to the Beginning of the 20th Century," *History of Iranian Literature*, written in coll. with Klíma, O., et al., tr. from the German by van Popta-Hope, P., ed. Jahn, K., Dordrecht.

Sachau, E.C., and Ethé, H.
1889 *Catalogue of the Persian, Turkish, Hindustani and Pushtu Mannuscripts in the Bodleian Library*, Oxford.

Safar, F., and Muṣṭafā, M. ʿAlī
1974 *Al-Ḥaḍar madīnat aš-šams* ("Hatra, the City of the Sun God"), Baghdad.

Sakisian, A.
1937 "Une porte en bois sculptée arménienne de 1134," *Artibus Asiae* 6, 3/4, pp. 221–9.
1939 "Thèmes et motifs d'enluminure et de décoration arméniennes et musulmanes," *Ars Islamica*, VI, I, Ann Arbor, pp. 66–87.
1940 *Pages d'art arménien*, Paris.

Salapata, G.
2006 "The Tippling Serpent in the Art of Lakonia and Beyond," *The American School of Classical Studies at Athens*, Vol. 75, 4, October to December, pp. 541–60.

Saliba, G.
1992 "The Role of the Astrologer in Medieval Islamic Society," *Bulletin d'Études Orientales* 44, pp. 45–67.

Santoro, A.
2006 "On the Two Intertwined Dragons from Pendžikent," *Ērān ud Anērān: Studies Presented to Boris Il'ič Maršak on the Occasion of His 70th Birthday*, eds. Compareti, M., Raffetta, P., and Scarcia, G., Venice, pp. 543–53.

Sarkhosh Curtis, V.
1993 *Persian Myths*, London.

Sarkhosh Curtis, V., and Stewart, S.
2005 eds., *Birth of the Persian Empire*, London and New York.

Sarre, F.
1909 *Erzeugnisse islamischer Kunst*, vol. 2, Islamische Kleinkunst, Berlin.
1910 *Denkmäler persischer Baukunst*, Berlin.
1936 *Der Kiosk von Konia*, Berlin.

Sarre, F., and Herzfeld, E.
1911/20 with a contrib. by van Berchem, M., *Arabische Inschriften Archäologische Reise im Euphrat- und Tigris-Gebiet*, 3 vols., Forschungen zur islamischen Kunst I, 1–4, Berlin.

Sarre, F., and van Berchem, M.
1907 "Das Metallbecken des Atabeks Lulu von Mosul in der Kgl. Bibliothek zu München," *Münchener Jahrbuch der bildenden Kunst*, I, pp. 18–37.

Sauvé, J.L.
1970 "The Divine Victim: Aspects of Human Sacrifice in Viking Scandinavia and Vedic India," *Myth and Law Among the Indo-Europeans*, ed. Puhvel, J., Studies in Indo-European Comparative Mythology, Berkeley, Los Angeles and London.

Savage-Smith, E.
1997 "Amulets and Related Talismanic Objects," *Science, Tools and Magic*, eds. Maddison, F., and Savage-Smith, E., The Nasser D. Khalili Collection of Islamic Art, vol. 12, London, pp. 112–9.
1997 "Sphero-Conical Vessels: A Typology of Forms and Functions," *Science, Tools and Magic*, eds. Maddison, F., and Savage-Smith, E., The Nasser D. Khalili Collection of Islamic Art, vol. 12, London, pp. 324–33.
2004 "Introduction," *Magic and Divination in Early Islam*, ed. Savage-Smith, E., Aldershot, Hants, pp. xiii-xlviii.

Saxl, F.
1912 "Beiträge zu einer Geschichte der Planetendarstellungen im Orient und Okzident," *Der Islam* 3, pp. 151–77.
1932 "The Zodiac of Quṣayr ʿAmra," *Early Muslim Architecture*, ed. Creswell, K.A.C., vol. 1, Oxford, pp. 289–95.

Scarcia, G.
1967 "Zunbil or Zanbil?" *Yádnáme-ye Jan Rypka*, Collection of Articles on Persian and Tajik Literature, Prague, pp. 41–5.
1988 "Su un rilievo di Kaxuli con l'ascensione di Alessandro e su qualche problema connesso," *Georgica II, Materiali sulla Georgia Occidentale*, *Eurasiatica* 3, Venezia, pp. 97–107.

Schafer, E.H.
1963 *The Golden Peaches of Samarkand: A Study of T'ang Exotics*, Berkeley and Los Angeles.

Scharlipp, W.E.
1992 *Die frühen Türken in Zentralasien: Eine Einführung in ihre Geschichte und Kultur*, Darmstadt.

Schefer, C.
1892 tr. and ed., *Description topographique et historique de Boukhara par Mohammed Nerchakhy, suivie de textes relatifs à la Transoxiane*, Paris.

Scheftelowitz, I.I.
1912–3 "Das Schlingen- und Netzmotif im Glauben

und Brauch der Völker," *Religionsgeschichtliche Versuche und Vorarbeiten*, vol. 12, 2, Gießen, pp. 1–64.

Scherer, A.
1953 *Gestirnnamen bei den Indogermanischen Völkern*, Heidelberg.

Schimmel, A.
1975 *Mystical Dimensions of Islam*, Chapel Hill.
1980 *The Triumphal Sun: A Study of the Works of Jalāloddin Rumi*, London, repr. 1993.
1987 "Secrecy in Sufism," *Secrecy in Religions*, ed. Bolle, Kees W., Leiden, pp. 81–103.
1994 *Deciphering the Signs of God: A Phenomenological Approach to Islam*, Albany, NY.

Schirmunski, V.
1961 *Vergleichende Epenforschung*, Berlin, vol. 1.

Schirmer, O.
1926–7 "Studien zur Astronomie der Araber," *Sitzungsbericht der Physikalisch-Medizinischen Sozietät zu Erlangen*, vol. 58, Erlangen, pp. 43–6, 63–79.

Schlumberger, G.
1878 *Numismatique de l'Orient Latin*, Paris, repr. Graz, 1954.

Schlüter, M.
1982 *"Dᵉrāqôn" und Götzendienst: Studien zur antiken jüdischen Religionsgeschichte, ausgehend von einem griechischen Lehnword in mAZ III 3*, Judentum und Umwelt, Frankfurt a. M. and Bern.

Schmidt, H.-P.
1980 "The Senmurv: Of Birds and Dogs and Bats," *Persica* 9, pp. 1–85.

Schiltz, V.
2001 ed., *L'or des Amazones: Peuples nomads entre Asie et Europe, VI siècle av. J.-C. - IV siècle apr. J.-C.*, Paris.

Schmitz, B.
1994 "A Fragmentary Mīnā'ī Bowl with Scenes from the Shāhnāmā," *The Art of the Saljūqs in Iran and Anatolia: Proceedings of a Symposium held in Edinburgh in 1982*, ed. Hillenbrand, R., Costa Mesa, CA, pp. 156–9.

Scholem, G.
1926 *Madda'ey ha-Yahadut*, vol. 2.
1957 *Die jüdische Mystik in ihren Hauptströmungen*, Frankfurt a. M., repr. 1988.

Scholz, B.E.
1982 "Die paarweise-symmetrische Darstellung des Hl. George und des Hl. Theodore Stratelates zu Pferde in der Kunst von Byzanz und Georgien vom 10.–13. Jh.," *Akten*, II, XVI. Internationaler Byzantinistenkongress, Wien, 4. bis 9. Oktober, *Jahrbuch der österreichischen Byzantinistik* 32, 5, pp. 243–53.

Schöttler, P.
1995 *Die Rumseldschuken: Gründer der Türkei. Geschichte und Kultur*, with a contrib. by Schöttler, H., *Die rumseldschukischen Handelsstraßen und ihre Karavansarays*, Freiburg im Breisgau.

Schrade, B.
2001 *Eastern Approaches to Byzantium: Papers from the Thirty-third Spring Symposium of Byzantine Studies, University of Warwick, Coventry, March 1999*, ed. Eastmond, A., Aldershot, Hants, pp. 169–98.

Schütt, H.-W.
2002 "Alchemie und Transzendenz im Spiegel zweier Symbole," *Neuzeitliches Denken: Festschrift für Hans Poser zum 65. Geburtstag*, eds. Abel, G., Engfer, H.J., and Hubig, C., Berlin and New York, pp. 101–16.

Schwartz, M.
1975 "Cautes and Cautopates," *Mithraic Studies* vol. 2, ed. Hinnells, J.R., Manchester, pp. 406–23.
1980 "Mayrhofer, M., Iranisches Personennamenbuch, Band I: Die altiranischen Namen. Faszikel 1: Die avestischen Namen," *Orientalia* vol. 49, n.s., Pontificium Institutum Biblicum, pp. 123–6.
1985 "The Old Eastern Iranian World View According to the Avesta," *The Cambridge History of Iran*, vol. 2, *The Median and Achaemenian Periods*, ed. Gershevitch, I., Cambridge, pp. 640–63.
2006 "On Haoma, and its Liturgy in the Gathas," *Proceedings of the 5th Conference of the Societas Iranologica Europaea held in Ravenna 6–11 October 2003*, Ancient & Middle Iranian Studies, vol. 1, eds. Piras, A., and Panaino, A., Milan, pp. 215–24.

Schwemer, A.M.
1994 "Elija als Araber. Die haggadischen Motive in der Legende vom Messias Menachem ben Hiskija (yBer 2,4 5a; EkhaR 1,16 § 51) im Vergleich mit den Elija und Elisch-Legenden der Vitae Prophetarum," *Die Heiden: Juden, Christen und das Problem der Fremden*, eds. Feldmeier, R., Heckel, U., and Hengel, M., Tübingen, pp. 108–57.

Schwertheim, E.
1979 "Mithras: Seine Denkmäler und sein Kult," *Antike Welt* 10, Sondernummer, Feldmeilen.

Seyrig, H.
1934 "Bas-reliefs monumentaux du temple de Bêl à Palmyre," *Syria* 15, pp. 155–86.

Sezgin, F.
1970 *Medizin-Pharmazie, Zoologie-Tierheilkunde bis ca. 430 H*, Geschichte des arabischen Schrifttums, vol. 4, Leiden.
1971 *Alchimie-Chemie-Botanik-Agrikultur bis ca. 430 H.*, Geschichte des arabischen Schrifttums, vol. 4, Leiden.

Shepherd, D.G.
1978 "A Treasure from a Thirteenth-Century Spanish Tomb," *The Bulletin of The Cleveland Museum of Art*, vol. LXV, 4 April 1978, Cleveland, OH, pp. 111–34.

Sheppard, H.J.
1962 "The Ouroboros and the Unity of Matter in Alchemy: a Study in Origins," *Ambix* 10, pp. 83–96.
1966 "Serpent Symbolism in Alchemy," *Scientia* 101, pp. 203–7.

Shahbazi, S.A.
1993 "Parthian Origins of the House of Rustam," *Bulletin of the Asia Institute* 7, pp. 155–63.

Shalem, A.
2004 *The Oliphant: Islamic Objects in Historical Context*, XVII, Islamic History and Civilization 54, Leiden.

Shani, R.
1999 "A Judeo-Persian Talismanic Textile," *Irano-Judaica* IV, eds. Shaked, S., and Netzer, A., Jerusalem, pp. 251–73.

Shatzman Steinhardt, N.
1987 "Siyah Qalem and Gong Kai: An Istanbul Album Painter and a Chinese Painter of the Mongolian Period," *Muqarnas* IV, pp. 59–71.
1988 "Towards the Definition of a Yuan Dynasty Hall," *The Journal of the Society of Architectural Historians*, vol. 47, no. 1, March, pp. 57–73.

Shokoohy, M.
1983 "The Sasanian Caravanserai of Dayr-i Gachīn, South of Ray, Iran," *Bulletin of the School of African and Oriental Studies*, vol. 43, part 3, pp. 445–61 with illustrations.

Silverstein, A.J.
2007 *Postal Systems in the Pre-Modern Islamic World*, Cambridge.

Simonenko, A.V.
1991 "Der linkshändige Sarmatenfürst von Porogi und die vornehme Dame aus dem Nogajčik-Kurgan," *Gold der Steppe: Archäologie der Ukraine*, eds. Rolle, R., Schietzel, K., and Müller-Wille, M., Schleswig, pp. 215–20.

Simpson, M.S.
1979 *The Illustration of an Epic: The Earliest Shahnama Manuscripts*, New York and London.
1985 "Narrative Allusion and Metaphor in the Decoration of Medieval Islamic Objects," *Pictorial Narrative in Antiquity and the Middle Ages*, eds. Kessler, H.L., and Simpson, M.S., Studies in the History of Art 16, Washington, DC, pp. 131–49.
2007 "Manuscripts and Mongols: Some Documented and Speculative Moments in East-West/Muslim-Christian Relations," *French Historical Studies* 30, 3, pp. 351–94.

Sims, E., with Marshak, B.I., and Grube, E.J.
2002 *Peerless Images: Persian Painting and Its Sources*, New Haven, CN.

Sinclair, T.A.
1989 *Eastern Turkey: An Architectural and Archaeological Survey*, vols. 1 and 2, London.

Sinor, D.
1982 "The Legendary Origin of the Türks," *Folklorica: Festschrift for Felix J. Oinas* (*IUUAS*, vol. 141), eds. Žygas, E.V., and Voorheis, P., Research Institute for Inner Asian Studies, Bloomington, IN, pp. 223–57.

Smirnov, J.I.
1909 *Vostočnoe serebro* ("Oriental Silver"), 2 vols., St. Petersburg.

Smith, W.R.
1889 *Lectures on the Religion of the Semites*, Burnett Lectures 1888–9, Edinburgh, ed. and rev. Cook, S.A., London, 1927.

So, J.F.
2004 "Tiny Bottles: What a Well-Dressed Qidan Lady Wears on Her Belt," *Orientations*, vol. 35, no. 7, pp. 75–9.

Soper, A.C.
1949 "Aspects of Light Symbolism in Gandhāran Sculpture," *Artibus Asiae* 12, no. 3, pp. 273–83, 314–30.
1950 "Aspects of Light Symbolism in Gandhāran Sculpture (continuation)," *Artibus Asiae* 13, no. 1/2, pp. 63–83.

Soudavar, A.
2003 *The Aura of Kings: Legitimacy and Divine Sanction in Iranian Kingship*, Costa Mesa, CA.

Soucek, P.
1997 "Byzantium and the Islamic East," *Glory of Byzantium: Arts and Culture of the Middle Byzantine Era, ad 843–1261*, ed. Evans, H., and Wixom, W., exhibition catalogue, 11 March to 6 July 1997, Metropolitan Museum of Art, New York, pp. 403–11.

Sourdel, D.
1960 "Questions de cérémonial ʿabbaside," *Revue des études islamiques* 28, pp. 121–48.

Spengler, W.F., and Sayles, W.G.
1992 *Turkoman Figural Bronze Coins and their Iconography, I: The Artuqids*, Lodi, WI.

von Spiegel, F.
1851 *Die Alexandersage bei den Orientalen. Nach den besten Quellen dargestellt*, repr. 1972, Leipzig.
1871 *Eranische Altertumskunde*, Leipzig, vol. 1.

Spier, J.
1993 "Medieval Byzantine Magical Amulets and Their Tradition," *The Journal of the Warburg and Courtauld Institutes*, vol. 56, pp. 25–62 and pls. 1–6.

Spooner, D.B.
1909–10 "Excavations at Sahribahlol," *Archaeological Survey of India*, Annual Report, Calcutta, pp. 45–62.

Spuler, B.
1939 *Die Mongolen in Iran: Politik, Verwaltung und Kultur der Ilchanzeit 1220–1350*, Berlin, repr. 1955.
1965 *Die Goldene Horde: Die Mongolen in Russland 1223–1502*, Wiesbaden.
1972 *History of the Mongols Based on Eastern and Western Accounts of the Thirteenth and Fourteenth Centuries*, tr. Drummond, H., and S., Berkeley, CA.
1976 "Iranische Einflüsse auf das abbasidische Chalifat," *Akten des VII. Kongresses für Arabistik und Islamwissenschaft, Göttingen, 15. bis 22. August 1974*, ed. Dietrich, A., Göttingen, pp. 342–7.

Stapleton, H.E., and Ḥusain, M.H.
1933 "Excursus (with relevant Appendices) on the Date, Writings, and Place in Alchemical History of ibn Umail, an Edition (with Glossary) of Early Medieval Latin Rendering of the First Half of the *Māʾ al-Waraqī*, and a Descriptive Index – Chiefly of the Alchemical Authorities Quoted by Ibn Umail," *Memoirs*

of the Asiatic Society of Bengal, 12, no. 1, pp. 117–213.

Stein, A.
1921 *Serindia: Detailed Report of Explorations in Central Asia and Westernmost China*, London and Oxford, vol. 1.

Steinbach, U.
1972 *Dât al-Himma: Kulturgeschichtliche Untersuchungen zu einem arabischen Volksroman*, Wiesbaden, Freiburger Islamstudien 4.

Strohmaier, G.
1989 Review of "Pingree, David (ed.): *Picatrix*. The Latin Version of the *Ghāyat Al-Ḥakim*. Text, Introduction, Appendices, Indices. London: The Warburg Institute. University of London, 1986 (Studies of the Warburg Institute, ed. J. B. Trapp, Bd. 39), LXXXI," *Zeitschrift für Geschichte der arabisch-islamischen Wissenschaften*, 5, pp. 265–8.

Strzygowski, J.
1918 *Die Baukunst der Armenier und Europa: Ergebnisse einer vom Kunsthistorischen Institut der Universität Wien 1913 durchgeführten Forschungsreise*, 5 vols., Vienna.

Strong, J.S.
1983 *The Legend of King Aśoka: A Study and Translation of the Aśokāvadāna*, Princeton, NJ.
1992 *Legend and Cult of Upagupta: Sanskrit Buddhism in North India and Southeast Asia*, Princeton, NJ.

Strzygowski, J.
1916 *Altai-Iran und Völkerwanderung*, Leipzig.

Sugimura, T.
1986 *The Encounter of Persia with China: Research into Cultural Contacts Based on Fifteenth Century Persian Pictorial Materials*, National Museum of Ethnology, Osaka.

Sukenik, E.L.
1932 *The Ancient Synagogue of Beth Alpha*, Jerusalem.

Sulimirski, T.
1985 "The Scyths," *The Cambridge History of Iran*, vol. 2, *The Median and Achaemenian Periods*, eds. Fischer, W.B., Gershevitch, I., and Yarshater, E., Cambridge, pp. 149–99.

Surmelian, L.Z.
1968 coll. and ed., *Apples of Immortality: Folktales of Armenia*, London.

Süslü, Ö.R.
1987 "Recherche sur une stèle," *Ars Turcica: Akten des VI. Internationalen Kongresses für Türkische Kunst, München vom 3. bis 7. September 1979*, eds. Kreiser, K., Majer, H.G., Restle, M., and Zick-Nissen, J., vol. 2, Munich, pp. 638–46, vol. 3, pls. 118 and 119.

Swietochowski, M.L., and Carboni, S.
1994 *Illustrated Poetry and Epic Images: Persian Painting in the 1330s and 1340s*, New York.

Szádeczky-Kardoss, S.
1990 "The Avars," *The Cambridge History of Early Inner Asia*, vol. 1, *From Earliest Times to the Rise of the Mongols*, ed. Sinor, D., Cambridge, pp. 206–28.

Tabbaa, Y.
1997 *Constructions of Power and Piety in Medieval Aleppo*, University Park, PA.
2002 "The Functional Aspects of Medieval Islamic Hospitals," *Poverty and Charity in Middle Eastern Context*, eds. Singer, A., and Ener, M., University of Michigan, Center for Middle Eastern and North African Studies, pp. 95–119.

Talbot-Rice, D.
1957 *The Illustrations to the "World History" of Rashīd al-Dīn*, ed. Gray, B., Edinburg.

Taylor, C.S.
1999 *The Vicinity of the Righteous: Ziyāra and the Veneration of Muslim Saints in Late Medieval Egypt*, Leiden, Boston and Cologne.

Tchukasizian, B.L.
1964 "Échos de légendes épiques iraniennes dans les "Lettres" de Grigor Magistros," *Revue des Études Armeniennes*, n.s., 1, pp. 321–9.

Tezcan, H.
2006 *Topkapı Sarayı'ndaki Şifalı Gömlekler*, Istanbul.

Texier, C.
1862 *Asie mineure, description géographique, historique et archéologique des provinces et des villes de la Chersonnèse d'Asie*, Paris.

Thierry, J.-M.
1978 *La cathédrale des Saints-Apôtres de Kars (930–43)*, Matériaux pour l'archéologie arménienne 1, Louvain and Paris.
1987 *Les arts arméniens*, documentation of principal sites by Donabédian, P., Paris.

Thierry, N.M.
1984–5 *Haut Moyen Âge en Cappadoce: Les églises de la région de Çavuşin*, vol. 2, Paris, pp. 245–54, 293–302.
1972 "Art byzantin du Haut Moyen Âge en Cappadoce: L'Église N° 3 de Mavrucan," *Journal des savants*, pp. 233–69.
1977 "Yusuf koç kilisesi, église rupestre de Cappadoce," *Peintures d'Asie Mineure et de Transcaucasie aux Xe et XIe siècles*, London.
1999 "Aux limites du sacré et du magique: un programme d'entrée d'une église de Cappadoce," *La science des cieux*, ed. Gyselen, R., Res orientales 12, pp. 233–47.
2002 *La Cappadoce de l'Antiquité au Moyen Âge*, Bibliothèque de l'Antiquité tardive 4, Turnhout.

Thompson, R.C.
1907 "The Folk-Lore of Mossul," *Proceedings of the Society of Biblical Archaeology* 29.

Thorp, R.L., and Vinograd, R.E.
2001 *Chinese Art and Culture*, New York.

Tronzo, W.
1997 *The Cultures of His Kingdom: Roger II and the Cappella Palatina in Palermo*, Princeton, NJ.
2001 "The Mantle of Roger II of Sicily," *Robes of Honor in the Medieval World of Investiture*, ed. Gordon, S., New York, pp. 241–53.

Tubach, J.
1986 *Im Schatten des Sonnengottes: der Sonnenkult in Edessa, Harrān und Hatrā am Vorabend der christlichen Mission*, Wiesbaden.

ul-Huda, Q.
2003 *Striving for Divine Union: Spiritual Exercises for Suhrawardī Ṣūfīs*, London and New York.

Ullmann, M.
1972 *Die Natur- und Geheimwissenschaften im Islam*, Handbuch der Orientalistik I, Ergänzungsband VI, 2, Leiden.
1978 *Islamic Medicine*, Edinburgh.
1992 *Das Motiv des Spiegels in der arabischen Literatur des Mittelalters*, Abh. der Akademie der Wissenschaften in Göttingen, philol.-hist. Kl., 3, Göttingen.

Uluçam, A.
1989 *Irak'taki Türk Mimari Eserleri*, Ankara.

Underwood, P.
1950 "The Fountain of Life in Manuscripts of the Gospels," *Dumbarton Oaks Papers* 5, pp. 43–138.

Al-Ush, Abu 'l-Faraj
1969 *A Concise Guide to the National Museum of Damascus*, tr. Khalifa, M., Damascus.

Vajda, G.
1953 *Index général des manuscrits arabes musulmans de la Bibliothèque nationale de Paris*, Paris.

Vámbéry, Á.
1879 *Die primitive Cultur des turko-tatarischen Volkes*, Leipzig.

Van Dalen, B.
2002 "Islamic and Chinese Astronomy under the Mongols: A Little-Known Case of Transmission," *From China to Paris*, ed. Dold-Samplonius, Y., Stuttgart, pp. 327–56.

Vajda, G.
1934 "Les Corps de Metiers en Turquie d'après deux publications de V. Gordlevskiy," *Revue des études islamiques* VIII, pp. 79–88.

Vásáry, I.
2005 *Cumans and Tatars: Oriental Military in the Pre-Ottoman Balkans, 1185-365*, Cambridge.

Vasil'kov, Y.V.
1995 "Parable of a Man, Hanging in a Tree, and Its Archaic Background," *Sthāpakaśrāddham, Professor G.A. Zograph Commemorative Volume*, eds. Gurov, N.V. and Vasil'kov, Y.V., St. Petersburg, pp. 257–69.

Vida, T.
2000 "Der Messingbeschlag aus Gic, Westungarn. Betrachtungen zu den mediterranen Beziehungen der spätawarischen Kunst im Karpatenbecken," *Die Awaren am Rand der byzantinischen Welt: Studien zu Diplomatie, Handel und Technologietransfer im Frühmittelalter*, ed. Daim, F., Vienna, pp. 305–26.

Viennot, O.
1954 "Typologie du makara et essai du chronologie," *Arts Asiatiques* 1, pp. 189–208.

Vierck, H.
1978 "La "Chemise de Sainte-Bathilde" à Chelles et l'influence byzantine sur l'art de cour mérovingien au VIIe siècle," *Centenaire de l'Abbé Cochet, 1975: Actes du Colloque International d'Archéologie*, Rouen 3-4-5 juillet 1975, ed. Chirol, É., Rouen, pp. 521–64.

Vogel, J.P.
1926 *Indian Serpent-lore: Or, The Nāgas in Hindu Legend and Art*, London.
1929–30 "Le makara dans la sculpture de l'Inde," *Revue des Arts Asiatiques* 6 (3), pp. 133–47.

Wakeman, M.K.
1973 *God's Battle with the Monster: A Study in Biblical Imagery*, Leiden.

Waldschmidt, E.
1970 "Buddha Frees the Disc of the Moon (*Candrasūtra*)," *Bulletin of the School of Oriental and African Studies* XXXIII, pp. 179–83.

Wallace, H.N.
1985 *The Eden Narrative*, Harvard Semitic Monographs, 32, Atlanta, GA.

Walter, C.
1989a "The Thracian Horseman: Ancestor of the Warrior Saints?" *Byzantine Thrace, Image and Character. Symposium for Thracian Studies*, Komotini, 1987, ed. Bakirtzis, C., Byzantinische Forschungen, vol. 14, pp. 659–73.
1989b "The Cycle of Saint George in the Monastery of Dečani," *Dečani i vizantijska umetnost sredinom XIV veka: međunarodni naučni skup povodom 650 godina manastira Dečani, septembar 1985 (Dečani et l'art byzantin au milieu du XIVe siècle)*, ed. Đurić, V.J., Belgrade, pp. 347–58.
1995 "The Origins of the Cult of St. George," *Revue des études byzantines* LIII, pp. 295–326.
1999 "Theodore, Archetype of the Warrior Saint," *Revue des études byzantines* LVII, pp. 163–210.
2003 *The Warrior Saints in Byzantine Art and Tradition*, Aldershot, Hants.

Wang, E.Y.
2005 *Shaping the Lotus Sutra: Buddhist Visual Culture in Medieval China*, Seattle.

Ward, R.
1985 "Evidence for a School of Painting at the Artuqid Court," *The Art of Syria and the Jazīra, 1100–250*, ed. Raby, J., Oxford, pp. 69–84.
1993 *Islamic Metalwork*, London.

Wardwell, A.E.
1988–9 "*Panni Tartarici*: Eastern Islamic Silks Woven with Gold and Silver (Thirteenth and Fourteenth Centuries)," *Islamic Art* 3, pp. 95–173, figs. 1–79, pls. VIII, IX.

Watkins, C.
1995 *How to Kill a Dragon: Aspects of Indo-European Poetics*, Oxford and New York.

Watson, O.
1985 *Persian Lustre Ware*, London.

Watson, W.
1971 *Cultural Frontiers in Ancient East Asia*, The Rhind Lectures 1965–6, Edinburgh.

Watt, J.C.Y., and Wardwell, A.E., with an essay by Rossabi, M.
1997 *When Silk Was Gold: Central Asian and Chinese Textiles*, New York.

Wellhausen, J.
1897 *Reste arabischen Heidentums*, Berlin, repr. Saarbrücken, 2007.

Wensinck, A.J.
1916 *The Ideas of the Western Semites Concerning the Navel of the Earth*, Verhandelingen der Koninklijke Akademie van Wetenschappen te Amsterdam, Afdeeling Letterkunde, Nieuwe Reeks, Deel XVII, no. 1, Amsterdam, repr. in *Studies of A.J. Wensinck*, Amsterdam, New York, 1978.
1918 *The Ocean in the Literature of the Western Semites*, Verhandelingen der Koninklijke Akademie van Wetenschappen te Amsterdam, Afdeeling Letterkunde, Nieuwe Reeks, Deel XIX, no. 2, Amsterdam, repr., Vaduz Liechtenstein, 1968, and repr. in *Studies of A.J. Wensinck*, Amsterdam, New York, 1978.
1921 *Tree and Bird as Cosmological Symbols in Western Asia*, Verhandelingen der Koninklijke Akademie van Wetenschappen te Amsterdam, Afdeeling Letterkunde, Amsterdam, repr. in *Studies of A.J. Wensinck*, Amsterdam, New York, 1978.
1923 "The Semitic New Year and the Origin of Eschatology," *Acta Orientalia*, Leiden, vol. 1, pp. 158–99.

Wenzel, M.
2005 "Fire-Making, and its Influence on the Background to some Mysterious Iconography in Medieval Islamic Art," *Image and Meaning in Islamic Art*, ed. Hillenbrand, R., London, pp. 140–58.

Wesselofsky, A.
1876–7 "Die Sage vom Babylonischen Reich," *Archiv für slavische Philologie*, 2 vols., pp. 129–43, 308–32.

West, M.L.
1962 "Three Presocratic Cosmologies," *The Classical Quarterly* 12, pp. 154–76.

Wheeler, B.M.
2002 *Prophets in the Quran: An Introduction to the Quran and Muslim Exegesis*, London and New York.

Whelan, E.J.
1980 "A Contribution to Dānishmendid History: the Figured Copper Coins," *American Numismatic Society Museum Notes*, vol. 25, pp. 133–66, pls. 16–7.

White, J.M., and Bunker, E.C., with contrib. by Peifen, C.
1994 *Adornment for Eternity: Status and Rank in Chinese Ornament*, Denver.

White, D.G.
1991 *Myths of the Dog-Man*, Chicago.
1996 *The Alchemical Body: Siddha Traditions in Medieval India*, Chicago and London.

Whitfield, R., Whitfield, S., and Agnew, N.
2000 *Cave Temples of Dunhuang*, London.

Widengren, G.
1955 *Muhammad, the Apostle of God, and His Ascension: King and Saviour*, 5, Uppsala Universitets Arsskrift, no. 1, Wiesbaden.
1960 *Iranisch-semitische Kulturbegegnung in parthischer Zeit*, Cologne.
1965 *Die Religionen Irans*, Stuttgart.
1966 "The Mithraic Mysteries in the Greco-Roman World with Special Regard to Their Iranian Background," *La Persia e il Mondo Greco-Romano*, Accademia Nazionale dei Lincei, Anno 363, Quad. 76, pp. 433–55.
1969 *Der Feudalismus im alten Iran*, Cologne and Opladen.

Wiedemann, E., and Hauser, F.
1921 "Über eine Palasttür und Schlösser nach al-Ǧazarī," *Der Islam* 11, pp. 214–31, figs. 1–16.

Wiedemann, E.
1970 *Aufsätze zur islamischen Wissenschaftsgeschichte*, 2 vols., repr. Hildesheim.

Wiet, G.M.
1930 *Album du Musée Arabe du Caire*, Cairo.

Wikander, S.
1938 *Der arische Männerbund*, Lund.

von Wilckens, L.
1991 *Die textilen Künste: Von der Spätantike bis um 1500*, Munich.
1992 *Mittelalterliche Seidenstoffe: Bestandskatalog XVIII des Kunstgewerbemuseums*, Berlin.
1997 "Fatimidisches Gewebe mit gewirktem Dekor im Vergleich mit spanischen und sizilischen," *Riggisberger Berichte*, Islamische Textilkunst des Mittelalters, Aktuelle Probleme 5, pp. 157–71.

Wilkinson, C.K.
1973 *Nishapur, Pottery of the Early Islamic Period*, New York.

Williams, J.G.
1982 *The Art of Gupta India: Empire and Province*, Princeton, NJ.

Williams, J.
1994 *The Illustrated Beatus: A Corpus of the Illustrations of the Commentary on the Apocalypse*, vol. 1, *Introduction*, vol. 2, *The Ninth and Tenth Centuries*, vol. 3, *The Tenth and Eleventh Centuries*, London.

Williams, M.A.
1996 *Rethinking "Gnosticism": An Argument for Dismantling a Dubious Category*, Princeton, NJ.

Wilson, L.S.
2001 *The Serpent Symbol in the Ancient Near East. Nahash and Ashera: Death, Life and Healing*, Lanham, New York and Oxford.

Winfield, D.
1968 "Some Early Medieval Figure Sculpture from North-East Turkey," *Journal of the Warburg and Courtauld Institutes*, vol. 31, pp. 33–72.

Winkelmann, S.
2004 *Katalog der parthischen Waffen und Waffenträger aus Hatra*, Materialien des SFB "Differenz in Integration," vol. 4, Halle.

Winkler, H.A.
1930 *Siegel und Charaktere in der muhammedanischen Zauberei*, Berlin and Leipzig.
1931 *Salomo und die Karina*, Stuttgart.

Wittek, P.
1936 "Deux chapitres de l'histoire des Turcs de Roum," *Byzantion* XI, pp. 285–302.

Wittfogel, K.A., and Fêng, C.-S.
1949 *History of Chinese Society: Liao (907–1125)*, Philadelphia.

Wolper, E.S.
1995 "The Politics of Patronage: Political Change and the Construction of Dervish Lodges in Sivas," *Muqarnas* 12, pp. 39–47.
2000 "Khiḍr, Elwan Çelebi and the Conversion of Sacred Sanctuaries in Anatolia," *The Muslim World*, vol. 90, 3–4, pp. 309–22.

Wood, P.C.
1916 "The Religion of Canaan from the Earliest Times to the Hebrew Conquest," *Journal of Biblical Literature* 35, pp. 1–133, 163–279.

Wu Hung
1986 "Buddhist Elements in Early Chinese Art (2nd and 3rd Centuries AD)," *Artibus Asiae*, vol. 47, no. 3/4, pp. 264–303.

Wünsche, A.
1905 *Die Sagen vom Lebensbaum und Lebenswasser*, Ex Oriente Lux I, Leipzig.

Yaldiz, M.
1987 *Archäologie und Kunstgeschichte Chinesisch-Zentralasiens (Xinjiang)*, Leiden.

Yamamoto, K.
2003 *The Oral Background of Persian Epics: Storytelling and Poetry*, Leiden and Boston.

Yarshater, E.
1983a "Iranian Historical Tradition," *The Cambridge History of Iran*, vol. 3, *The Seleucid, Parthian and Sasanid Periods*, eds. Fischer, W.B., Gershevitch, Ilya, and Yarshater, E., Cambridge, pp. 343–80.
1983b "Mazdakism," *The Cambridge History of Iran*, vol. 3, *The Seleucid, Parthian and Sasanid Periods*, eds. Fischer, W.B., Gershevitch, I., and Yarshater, E., Cambridge, pp. 991–1026.

Zaehner, R.C.
1955 *Zurvan: a Zoroastrian Dilemma*, Oxford, repr. New York, 1972.
1961 *The Dawn and Twilight of Zoroastrianism*, London.

Zbinden, E.
1953 *Die Djinn des Islam und der altorientalische Geisterglaube*, Bern.

Zieme, P.
2000 "Verse des *Candrasūtra* nach chinesisch-uighurischen Bilinguen," *Türk Dilleri Araştırmaları* 10, pp. 65–80.

Zürcher, E.
1959 *The Buddhist Conquest of China: The Spread and Adaptation of Buddhism in Early Medieval China*, vol. 1, Leiden.

LIST OF ILLUSTRATIONS

Kuwait, al-Sabāh Collection, Dar al-Athar al-Islamiyyah, Kuwait National Museum, inv. no. LNS 617 T. Photograph by courtesy of the al-Sabāh Collection, Kuwait.

69. a (plate 16) and b (plate 62). **Double-headed eagles with outspread dragon-headed wings.** Detail of a textile fragment, probably Anatolia. *c.* 1250. Silk. Length 58 cm, width 37 cm. Preserved as relic cover from the shrine of Saint Apollinaris, church of Saint Servatius, Siegburg. Photograph by courtesy of the church of Saint Servatius, Siegburg.

70. a and b. **Double-headed eagles with outspread dragon-headed wings** (plate 63). Relief carving from the western portal, a. left side, b. right side, Ulu Cami of Divriği. 1228.

71. **Confronted dragon-headed birds with interlaced necks** (plate 16). Missal, Armenia. Ninth or tenth century. Ejmiatsin, State Library, Ms. 958, fol. 10. After Sakisian, 1939, p. 84, fig. 31.

72. **A dragon-tailed *regardant* bird** (plate 63). Marginal ornament in the canon tables, L'viv Gospel, monasteries of Mlich and Skevra. 1193–1198/99. Transcribed and illustrated by the priest Grigor. Tempera and gold on vellum. Height 31 cm, width 24 cm. Gniezno, Archiwum Archidiecezjalne, MS 667, fol. 9v (detail). After Prinzing and Schmidt, eds., 1997, pl. VIII.

73. **A pair of confronted dragon-tailed *regardant* birds flanking a cross** (plate 64). L'viv Gospel, monasteries of Mlich and Skevra. 1193–1198/99. Transcribed and illustrated by the priest Grigor. Tempera and gold on vellum. Height 31 cm, width 24 cm. Gniezno, Archiwum Archidiecezjalne, MS 667, fol. 207r (detail). After Prinzing and Schmidt, eds., 1997, pl. XV.

74. **A pair of confronted dragon-tailed *regardant* birds** (plate 16). Relief carving above the southern outer door, monastery of Mār Behnām/Deir al-Khiḍr, southeast of Mosul. Thirteenth century. Photograph by courtesy of Yasser Tabbaa.

75. **A pair of addorsed dragon-tailed lions *couchant*** (plate 64). Matrix from a set of 77 matrices for belt/strap fittings. Putative origin: Minaret of Jam, Ghūr. Late eleventh century. Copper alloy. Length 4.62 cm, width 1.93 cm. Kuwait, al-Sabāh Collection, Dar al-Athar al-Islamiyyah, Kuwait National Museum, inv. no. LNS 2558 J a-x2 'x2.'

76. **A single dragon-tailed lion *couchant*** (plate 64). Matrix from a set of 77 matrices for belt/strap fittings. Putative origin: Minaret of Jam, Ghūr. Length 2.69 cm, width 1.53 cm. Late eleventh century. Copper alloy. Kuwait, al-Sabāh Collection, Dar al-Athar al-Islamiyyah, Kuwait National Museum, inv. no. LNS 2558 J a-x2 's2.'

77. **A seated dragon-tailed lion (one of a pair)** (plate 17). Relief carving above the southern outer door, monastery of Mār Behnām/Deir al-Khiḍr, southeast of Mosul. Thirteenth century. After Fiey, 1959, fig. 12.

78. **A seated dragon-tailed lion (one of a pair)** (plate 17). Relief carving on the main portal of the Jacobite church, Cizre (Jazīrat ibn ʿUmar). Thirteenth century. Height 45 cm, width 56 cm. After Preusser, 1911, p. 25, pl. 34.2.

79. **Initial surmounted by confronted seated dragon-tailed lions** (plate 64). Painting in a Gospel, Siunikʿ province. 1315. Painted by Bartholemew (Bardagh). Yerevan, Matenadaran Manuscript Museum, Ms. 9721. Photograph by courtesy of the Matenadaran Manuscript Museum, Yerevan.

80. **A dragon-tailed lion with bird** (plate 17). Relief carving to the right side of the portal of Kesikköprü Han, south of Kırşehir, Kesikköprü village. 667/1268–69. Height 50 cm, length 70 cm. Photograph by courtesy of Joachim Gierlichs.

81. **Pairs of addorsed dragon-tailed lions in rampant posture inscribed with the name of *sulṭān* Kay Qubādh** (plate 65). Section of a chasuble, probably Anatolia. First half of the thirteenth century. Silk. Length 102 cm, width 74.5 cm. Lyon, Musée Historique des Tissus, inv. no. 23.475. Photograph by courtesy of the Musée Historique des Tissus, Lyon.

82. **Double doors of the Ulu Cami at Cizre with the dragon knockers *in situ*** (plate 18). First half of the thirteenth century. Wood, copper alloy. Istanbul, Türk ve İslam Eserleri Müzesi, inv. no. 4282.

83. **A pair of confronted dragons with entwined bird-headed tails flanking a lion-headed knob** (plate 18). Door knocker, Cizre (Jazīrat ibn ʿUmar). First half of the thirteenth century. Copper alloy. Height 27 cm, width 24 cm, depth 3 cm. Istanbul, Türk ve İslam Eserleri Müzesi, inv. no. 3749 (complete knocker).

84. **"Elephant clock"** (plate 66). Illustration from al-Jazarī, *Kitāb fī maʿrifat al-ḥiyāl al-handasiyya*, Anatolia. Early thirteenth century. Transcribed by Muḥammad ibn Yūsuf ibn ʿUthmān al-Ḥaṣkafī. Opaque pigment and ink on paper. Height 35.8 cm, width 22.5 cm. Istanbul, Topkapı Sarayı Müzesi, Ms. Ahmet III 3472, fol. 46a. Photograph by courtesy of the Topkapı Sarayı Müzesi, Istanbul.

85. a (plate 19) and b (plate 66). **Elephants and winged quadruped dragons with benedictory inscription naming the owner, Qāʾid Abu 'l-Manṣūr Bākh-tigīn.** Textile fragment, Khurasan. Before 349/960–61. Silk samite. Large fragment: length 52 cm,

width 94 cm; small fragment: length 24.5 cm, width 62 cm. Preserved as shroud of Saint Josse, Saint-Josse-sur-Mer. Paris, Musée du Louvre, département des arts de l'Islam, inv. no. OA 7502. Photograph by courtesy of the Musée du Louvre, Paris.

86. a and b. **Investiture of Ardashīr I** (plate 20). Rock relief, Naqsh-i Rustam. Third century.

87. **A horseman fighting a seven-headed dragon** (plate 21).
Seal, Iranian world. Sasanian period. Brown-red jasper mottled with black. Height 1.9 cm, bezel 2.5 cm × 2 cm. Formerly in the collection of the counts Shuvalov. St. Petersburg, State Hermitage Museum, inv. no. Gl. 883. Photograph by courtesy of the State Hermitage Museum, St. Petersburg.

88. **Rustam fighting a dragon** (plate 67).
Wall painting in a private house, northern wall of room 41/VI, Panjikent. *c.* 740. St. Petersburg, State Hermitage Museum, inv. no. SA 15902. Photograph by courtesy of the State Hermitage Museum, St. Petersburg.

89. **Rustam departing after killing the dragon** (plate 67).
Wall painting in a private house, northern wall of room 41/VI, Panjikent. *c.* 740. St. Petersburg, State Hermitage Museum, inv. no. SA 15902. Photograph by courtesy of the State Hermitage Museum, St. Petersburg.

90. **A horseman fighting a dragon** (plate 68).
Detail from the Bobrinski bucket, possibly Herat. Muḥarram 559/December 1163. Made by Muḥammad ibn ʿAbd al-Wāḥid and Masʿūd ibn Aḥmad. Copper alloy, inlay in silver, copper and niello. Height to rim 18.5 cm, diameter 22 cm. St. Petersburg, State Hermitage Museum, inv. no. JR-2268 (detail). Photograph by courtesy of the State Hermitage Museum, St. Petersburg.

91. **A horseman fighting a dragon** (plate 68).
Detail from the Fould bucket, possibly Anatolia. Late twelfth or early thirteenth century. Made by Muḥammad ibn Nāṣir ibn Muḥammad al-Harawī. Copper alloy, gilded, inlay in silver and copper. Height to rim 18.8 cm, diameter 21.5 cm. St. Petersburg, State Hermitage Museum, inv. no. IR-1668 (detail). Photograph by courtesy of the State Hermitage Museum, St. Petersburg.

92. **A horseman fighting a dragon** (plate 21).
Detail on faceted shoulder of a ewer, possibly Herat. Late twelfth or early thirteenth century. Copper alloy, silver inlay. Private Collection.

93. **A pair of confronted horsemen fighting an upright double-headed dragon and a lion** (plate 21).
Base of a penbox, Iran. 680/1281–2. Signed by Maḥmūd ibn Sunqur. Height 3.2 cm, length 19.7 cm, width 4.3 cm. London, British Museum, inv. no. ME OA 1891.6–23.5 After *Furūsiyya*, 1996, p. 173 (drawing).

94. **A horseman fighting a dragon** (plate 69).
Roundel, Western Central Asia. Twelfth or thirteenth century. Copper alloy, gilded. Kuwait, al-Sabāh Collection, Dar al-Athar al-Islamiyyah, Kuwait National Museum, inv. no. LNS 28 M. Photograph by courtesy of the al-Sabāh Collection, Kuwait.

95. **A horseman fighting a dragon** (plate 69).
Twelve-pointed star tile, Iran. Late twelfth or early thirteenth century. Fritware, overglaze painted *(mīnāʾī)*. Height 18.5 cm, width 1.7 cm. Washington, DC, Smithsonian Institution, Freer Gallery of Art, Gift of Charles Lang Freer, F1911.319. Photograph by courtesy of the Freer Gallery of Art, Washington, DC.

96. **A horseman fighting a dragon** (plate 22).
Bowl, Iran. Early thirteenth century. Fritware, overglaze painted *(mīnāʾī)*. Zurich, Vollmoeller Collection. After Shepherd, 1978, p. 122, fig. 16 (upper left photograph).

97. **A warrior on foot fighting a dragon** (plate 22).
Detail from the base of the so-called "Freer Plate." Late twelfth or early thirteenth century. Fritware, overglaze painted *(mīnāʾī)*. Height 11.1 cm, width 47.8 cm, depth 47.8 cm. Washington, DC, Smithsonian Institution, Freer Gallery of Art, Gift of Charles Lang Freer, F1943.3 (detail). Photograph by courtesy of the Freer Gallery of Art, Washington, DC.

98. **A pair of confronted horsemen fighting a winged dragon and a lion** (plate 23).
Relief frieze from the pavilion of Qılıch Arslan II (Alaeddin Köşkü), Konya. Second half of the twelfth century (probably 551/1156–588/1192). Height 29 cm, width 58 cm. Istanbul, Türk ve İslam Eserleri Müzesi, inv. no. 2831. After Sarre, 1909, vol. 2, pl. III.

99. **A horseman fighting a dragon** (plate 23).
Detail from a candlestick base, the Jazīra. Probably *c.* 637/1230. Copper alloy, silver inlay. Height 34 cm, diameter at base 31 cm. Formerly Harari Collection, Cairo. Cairo, Museum of Islamic Art, inv. no. 15121. After *L'orient de Saladin*, 2002, p. 148, cat. no. 124.

100. a and b. **A pair of warriors on foot fighting confronted dragon-tailed winged dragons with forelegs** (plate 24).
a. Relief carving on the gateway of al-Khān/Khān al-Harārāt, between Mosul and Sinjār. Second quarter of the thirteenth century (631/1233–4–656–7/1257–8). Photograph by courtesy of Joachim Gierlichs. b. Drawing of the relief carving on the gateway, right side. After Sarre, 1936, p. 15, fig. 10 (after a drawing by Ernst Herzfeld dated 19 December 1907, Museum für Islamische Kunst, Staatliche Museen zu Berlin).

101. **A pair of warriors on foot fighting addorsed winged dragons with forelegs and entwined bodies** (plate 25).
Relief carving on the portal of the Mosul gate,

Peshawar Museum. Photograph by courtesy of Isao Kurita.

165. **A pair of entwined quadruped dragons** (plate 84).
Relief carving on the inscribed memorial stele of Köl Tigin. Eastern Turkish empire. *c.* 732. Height 333 cm, width 132 cm, thickness 46 cm. Mongolia, Archangajin Province, Chöshöö Cajdam.

166. **One of a pair of entwined quadruped dragons** (plate 84).
Fragment of a relief carved monumental stele, Qarabalghasun. Uighur empire, 744–840, probably after 761.

167. **A pair of upright confronted quadruped dragons with a quadripartite knot** (plate 40).
Wall painting, Shorchuk. Sixth to eighth century. After Stein, 1921, vol. 1, Pl. CXXVI, Mi. xviii, 0014).

168. **A pair of addorsed quadruped dragons with a quadripartite knot** (plate 40).
Wall painting, Bezeklik. Probably tenth century. After Grünwedel, 1912, fig. 590.

169. **A pair of confronted double-headed dragons with a quadripartite knot** (plate 85).
Matrix. Putative origin: Minaret of Jam, Ghūr. Late eleventh century. Matrix from a set of 77 copper alloy matrices for belt/strap fittings. Length 10.62 cm, width 5.98 cm, thickness 1.74 cm. Kuwait, al-Sabāh Collection, Dar al-Athar al-Islamiyyah, Kuwait National Museum, inv. no. 2559 J.

170. **A pair of confronted dragons with forelegs with a Herakles knot** (plate 40).
Fragment of a relief frieze, *iwan*, Temple II, Panjikent. Possibly late seventh or early eighth century. Clay. Height 27 cm, diameter 18 cm. Excavated in 1952. Tajikistan, Panjikent Museum. After Belenizkii, 1980, fig. 92.

171. **A pair of confronted dragons with a quadripartite knot** (plate 85).
Sphero-conical vessel, Golden Horde (Juchi Ulus). Probably late twelfth or early thirteenth century. Unglazed earthenware. Moscow, State Historical Museum.

172. **Pairs of confronted dragons with quadripartite knots** (plate 41).
Jug with filter, northern Syria. Twelfth or thirteenth century. Unglazed earthenware. Height 13.5 cm. Damascus, National Museum, inv. no. 1462 A. After *À l'ombre d'Avicenne*, 1996, p. 204, cat. no. 128.

173. **A pair of addorsed dragons with a quadripartite knot** (plate 41).
Bowl, Raqqa. Late twelfth or thirteenth century. Earthenware, underglaze painted in blue and black. Diameter 12.7 cm. New York, Metropolitan Museum of Art, acc. no. 20.52.3. Photograph by courtesy of the Metropolitan Museum of Art, New York.

174. **A pair of confronted dragons with a quadripartite knot** (plate 41).
Detail from a talismanic bowl. Twelfth to fourteenth century. Copper alloy. Height 3.4 cm, diameter 10.5 cm. Toronto, Royal Ontario Museum, inv. no. 976.34. After Ittig, 1982, pls. II–VII.

175. **A pair of confronted dragons with a quadripartite knot** (plate 41).
Relief carving on the hospital *(darüşşifa)*, Çankırı. 633/1235. Height 25 cm, width 100 cm. Line drawing by courtesy of the Turkish Historical Society.

176. **A personification of the Moon enclosed within interlaced dragons** (plate 85).
Detail of the right half of the double-page frontispiece painting in the *Kitāb al-diryāq*, Mosul (?), the Jazīra. Rabīʿ al-awwal of the year 595/31 December 1198–29 January 1199. Opaque pigment and ink on paper. Paris, Bibliothèque Nationale, Ms. Arabe 2964; current pagination 36–37. Photograph by courtesy of the Bibliothèque Nationale, Paris.

177. **A musician with a dragon-headed stringed instrument** (plate 86).
Detail of an enthronement scene of a Mongol ruler, Tabriz (?). First quarter of the fourteenth century. Opaque pigment on paper. Height 38.8 cm, width 29.2 cm. Berlin, Staatsbibliothek zu Berlin – Preußischer Kulturbesitz, Orientabteilung, Ms. Diez A fol. 70, p. 21 (detail). Photograph by courtesy of the Staatsbibliothek zu Berlin – Preußischer Kulturbesitz, Orientabteilung.

178. a and b. **A musician with a dragon-headed stringed instrument** (plate 87).
Wall painting, Panjikent. Eight century. Dushanbe National Museum.

179. **Two pairs of interlaced confronted dragons** (plate 87).
Relief carving around the wall arch above the altar in the funerary chapel of Surb Grigor, monastic complex of Noravankʿ, Vayots Dzor. 1275.

180. **"The Perils of Life"** (plate 42).
Illustration from the *Kalīla wa Dimna*, Baghdad (?). 663/1265–679/1280. Opaque pigment on paper. Fol.: height 29.9 cm, width 26.9 cm; painting: height 19.7 cm, width 12.7 cm. Rabat, Bibliothèque Royale, Ms. 3655, fol. 17 B. After O'Kane, 2003, fig. 8.

181. **The angel Abi 'l-Ḥanaf as crowned lion rider holding a dragon-sceptre** (plate 42).
Painting in a copy of Nāṣir al-Dīn Muḥammad ibn Ibrāhīm ibn ʿAbdallāh al-Rummal al-Muʿaẓẓam al-Saʿatī al-Haykalī, *Daqāʾiq al-Ḥaqāʾiq*, Aksaray. Mid- to late thirteenth century (variously dated 10 Ramaḍān 670/10 April 1272 and mid-Shawwāl 671/early May 1273); illustrations of various dates. Paris,

GENERAL INDEX

In the arrangement adopted here, the Arabic definite article *(al-)* at the beginning of an entry, the transliteration symbols for the Arabic letters *hamza (ʾ)* and *ʿayn (ʿ)*, and distinctions between different letters transliterated by the same Latin character (e.g. *d* and *ḍ*) are ignored for purposes of alphabetisation. Numbers in **bold** type refer to figures; numbers in *italics* refer to *sūras* and *sūra* verses.

1. **A pair of winged confronted dragons with forelegs.** Relief carving on the West Gate of the city wall, Diyārbakr.

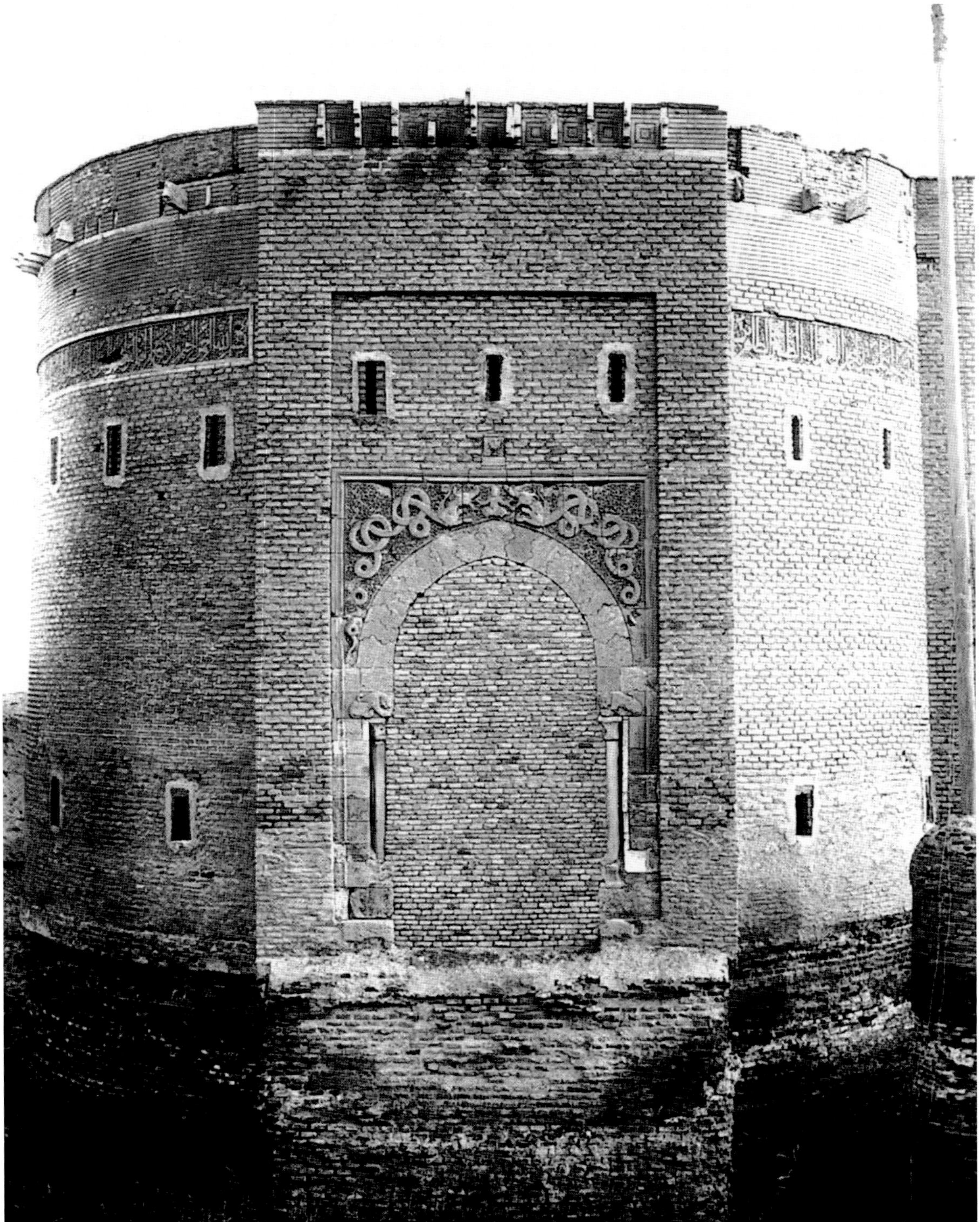

2. **A seated human figure between a pair of winged confronted dragons with forelegs.** Relief carving on the archivolt of the so-called Talisman Gate (Bāb al-Ṭilasm), Baghdad.

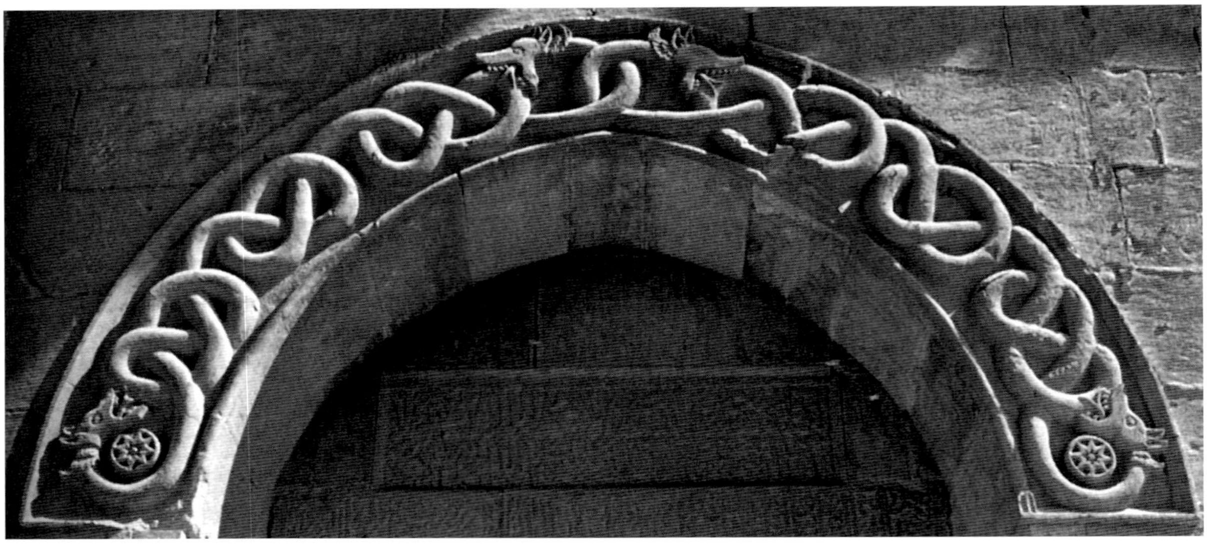

3a and b. A pair of intertwined winged double-headed dragons. Relief carving on the so-called Gate of the Serpents (Bāb al-Ḥayyāt), citadel of Aleppo, Aleppo.

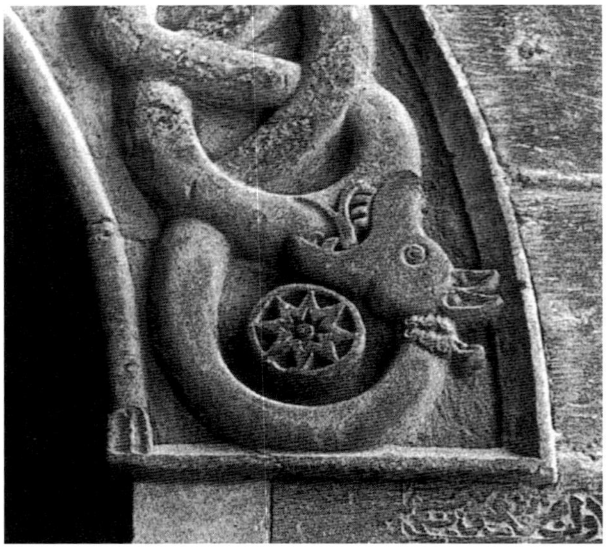

3b

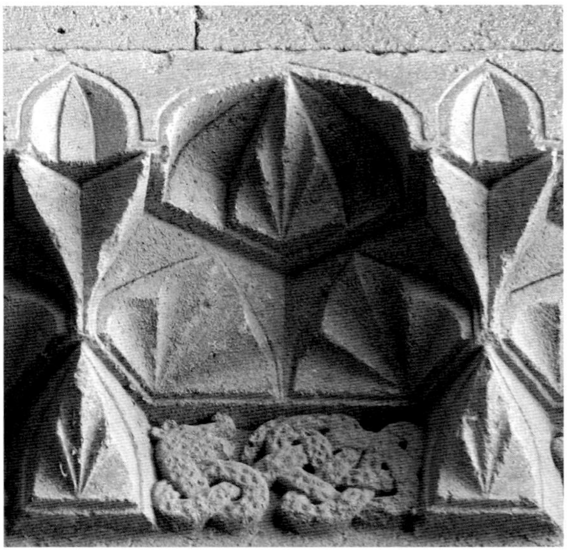

5. A single *regardant* dragon with elaborately knotted tail. *Muqarnas* frieze at the portal arch (to the left) above the entrance to a tomb, Karatay Han, east of Kayseri.

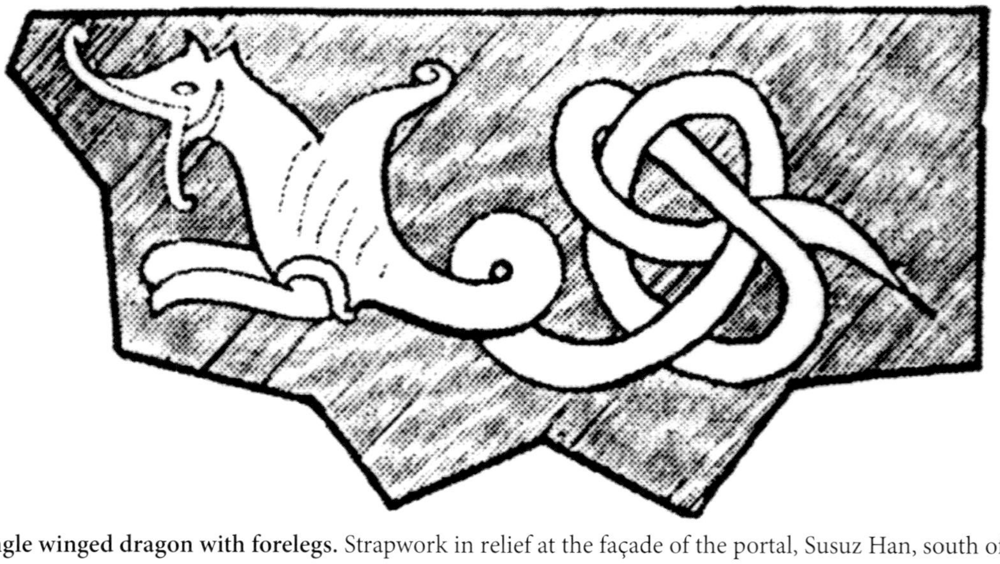

6. A single winged dragon with forelegs. Strapwork in relief at the façade of the portal, Susuz Han, south of Bucak.

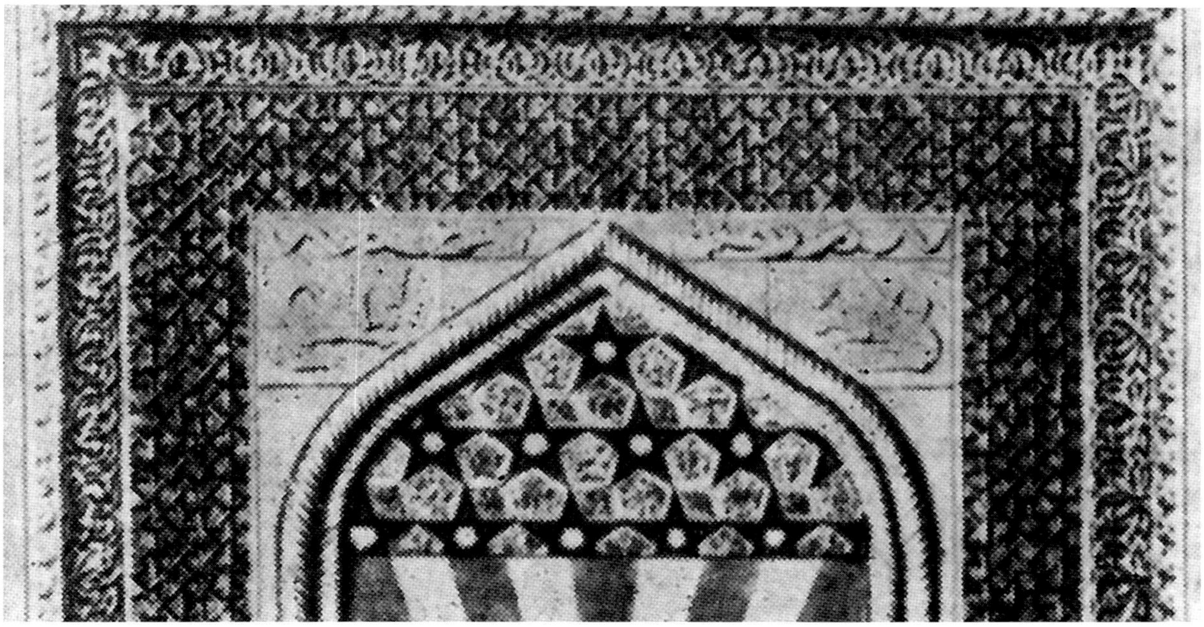

8. **A pair of confronted dragons.** Relief carving on the spandrels of the portal arch, entrance façade of the southern caravanserai, Ani.

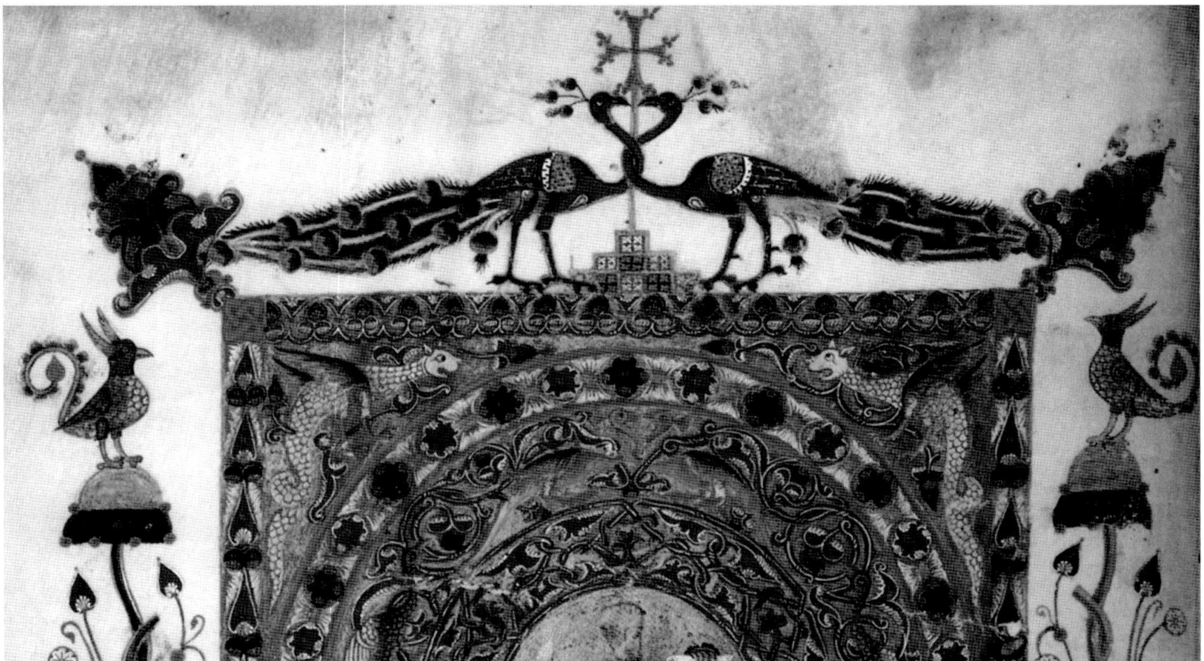

9. **A pair of confronted winged dragons with forelegs.** Top register of an opening page of canon tables, L'viv Gospel, monasteries of Mlich and Skevra.

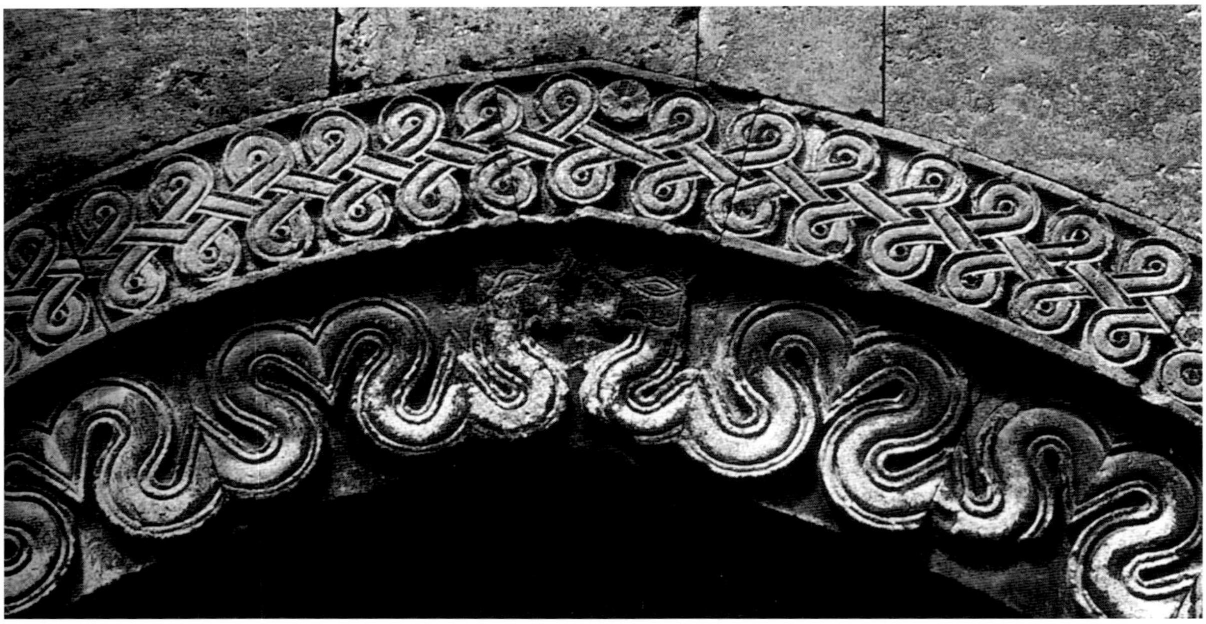

12. **Apex of a dragon festoon with a pair of confronted dragons.** Relief carving on the south-facing arch, mosque of Sultan Han, northeast of Kayseri.

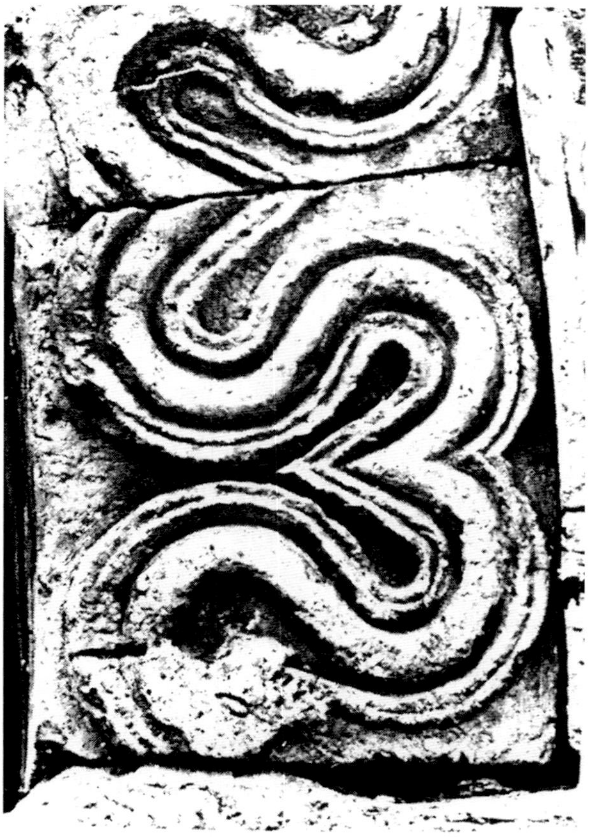

13. **A dragon festoon ending in small inverted dragon heads, the open jaws holding the tip of the outer edge of the festoon-band.** Relief carving on the south-facing arch (detail of the lower left end), mosque of Sultan Han, northeast of Kayseri.

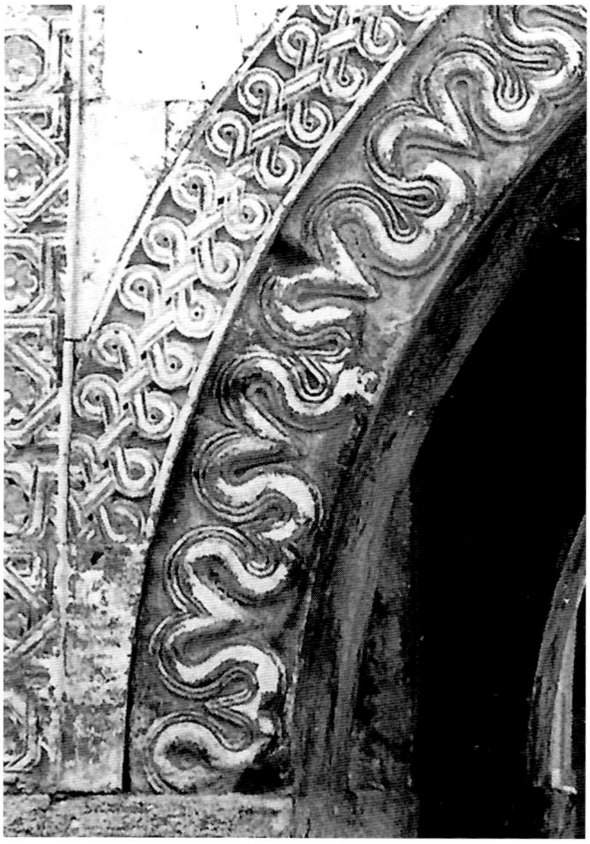

14. **A dragon festoon with a small dragon head growing out of one of the bends.** Relief carving on the east-facing arch (detail of the lower left end), mosque of Sultan Han, northeast of Kayseri.

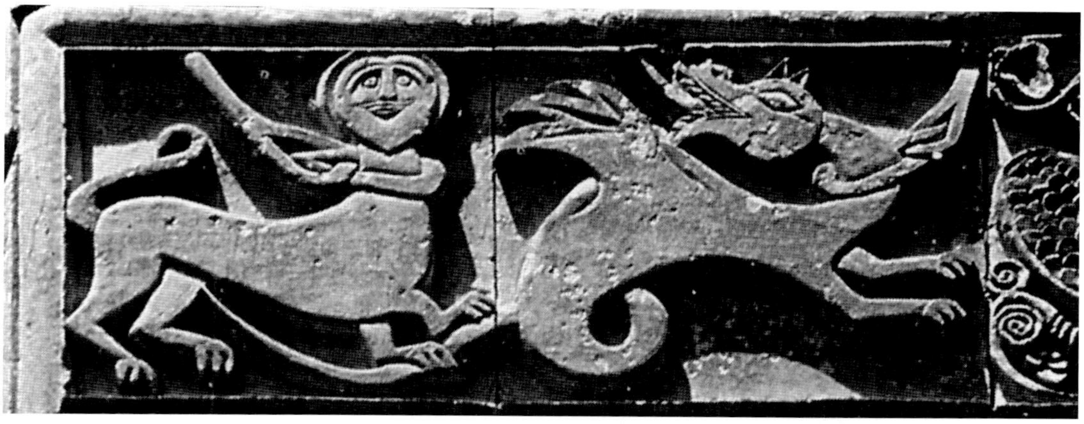

15. **A winged *regardant* dragon with forelegs flanked by a centaur-like creature.** Relief carving on the eastern façade of the church of the Virgin, Mart'vili.

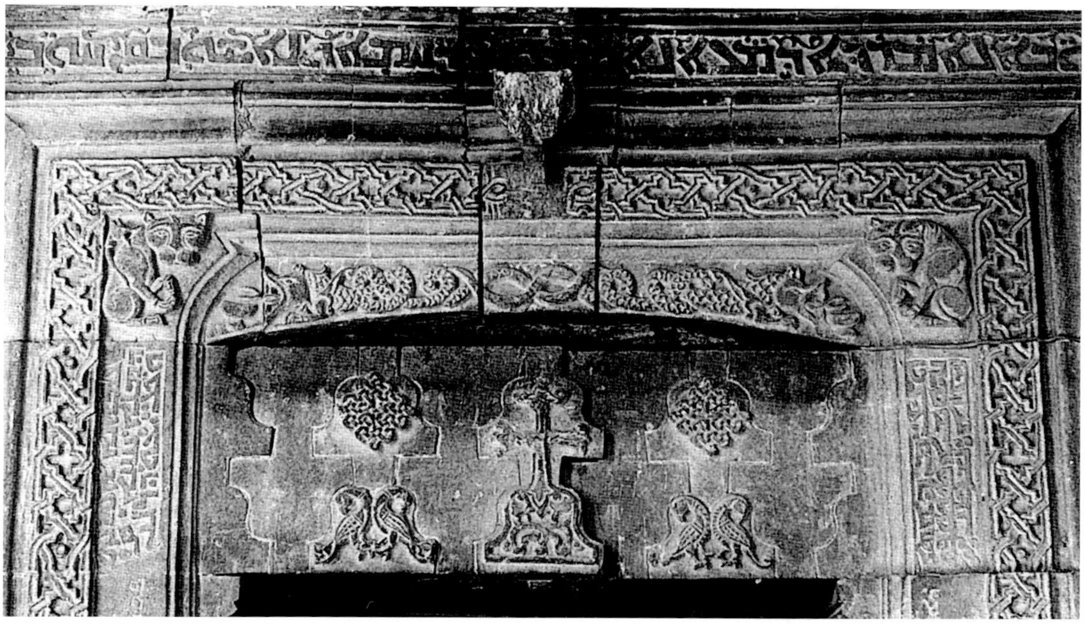

17a and b. A pair of addorsed interlaced drinking dragons with wings and forelegs surmounting a dragon-cross with dragon-winged birds and flanked by seated dragon-tailed lions. Relief carving above the southern outer portal, monastery of Mār Behnām/Deir al-Khiḍr, southeast of Mosul.

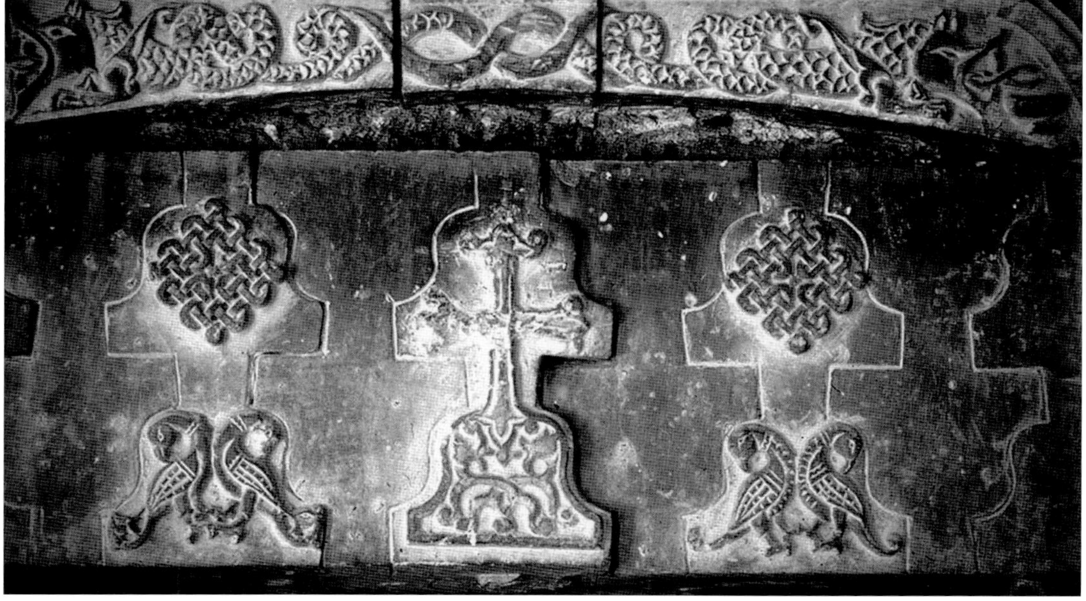

17b

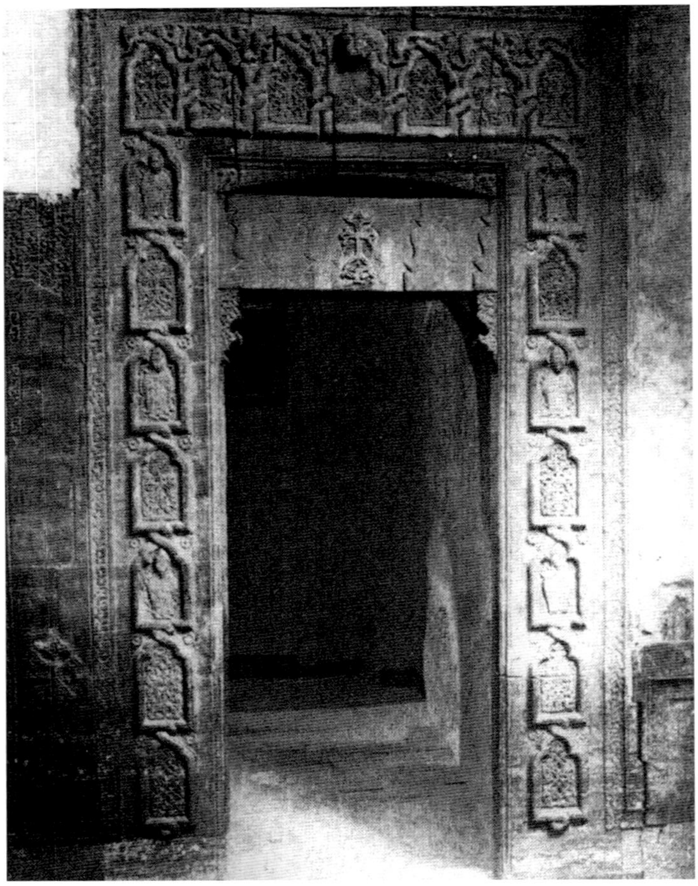

18. A knotted interlace composed of six paired dragons enclosing a total of twenty-one niches. Relief carving on the second southern portal leading to the chapel of the baptistery, monastery of Mār Behnām/Deir al-Khiḍr, southeast of Mosul.

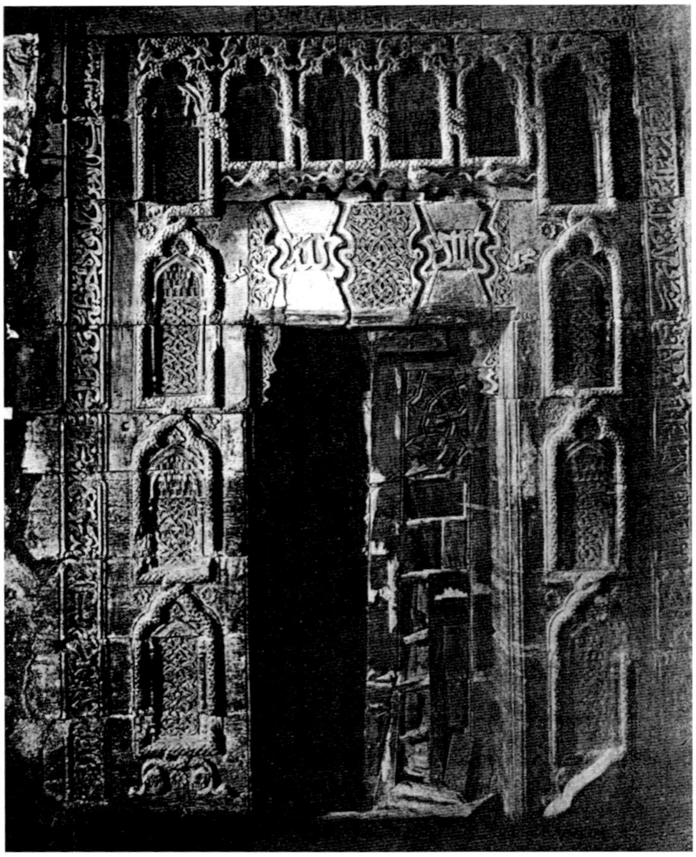

19. A knotted interlace composed of six paired dragons enclosing a total of twelve niches. Relief carving on the portal leading to the vestibule, mausoleum of Imām Bahir, Mosul.

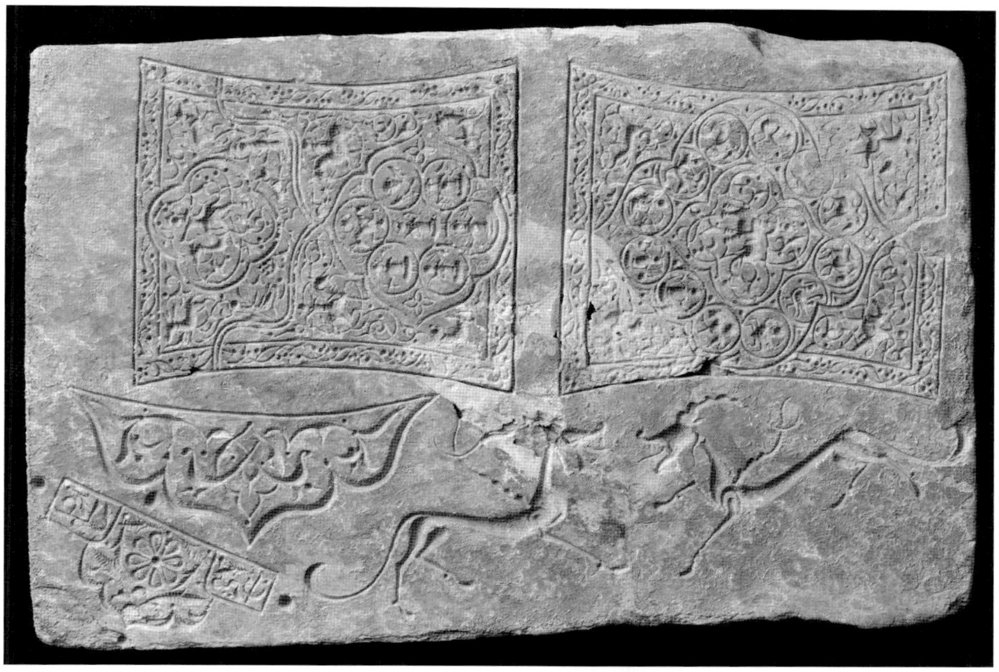

29a and b. **A pair of confronted winged quadruped dragons.** Mould for tooling leather, Herat.

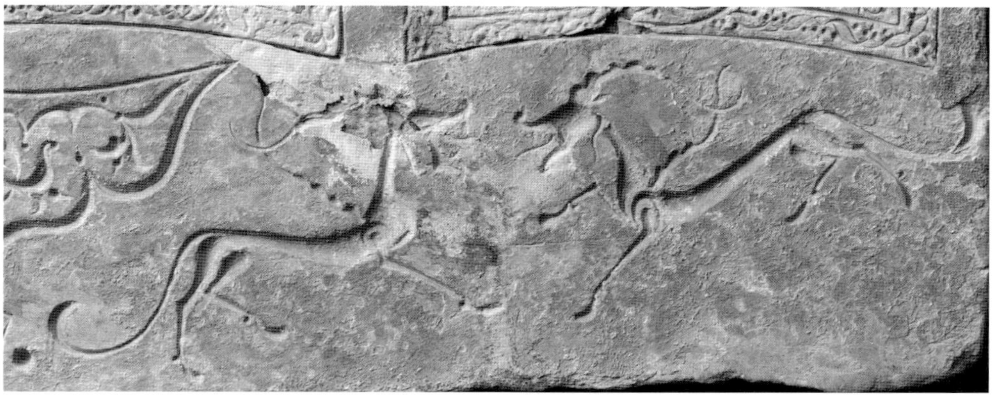

29b

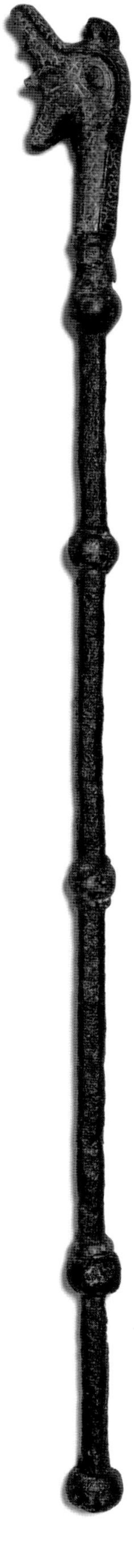

20. **A staff terminating in a dragon head.** Afghanistan.

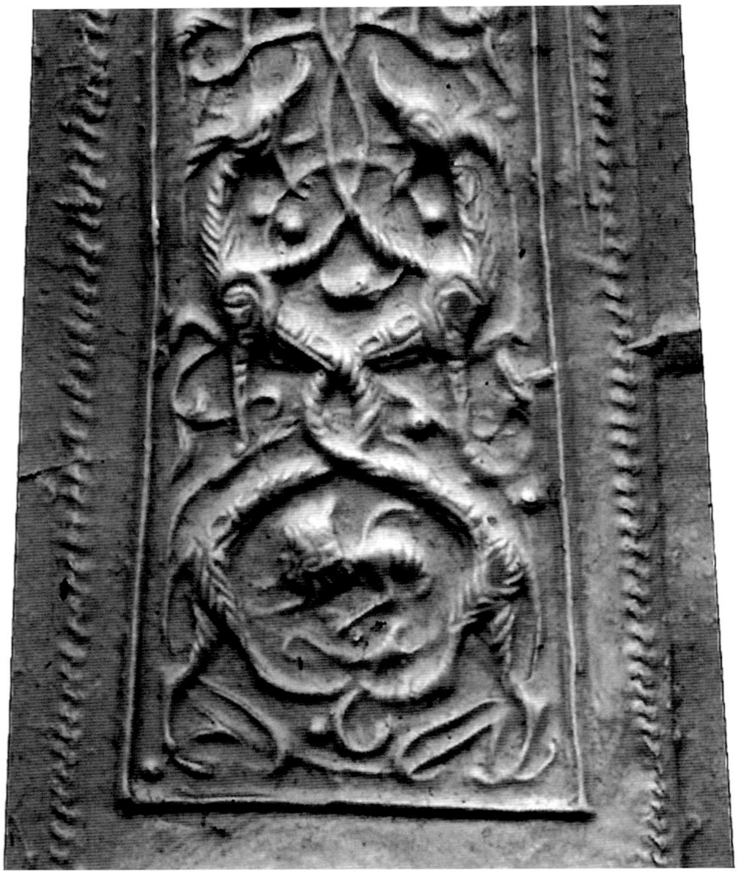

31a and b. A pair of upright addorsed quadruped dragons *regardant* with forelegs, wings and entwined bodies. Press-mould, Balkh.

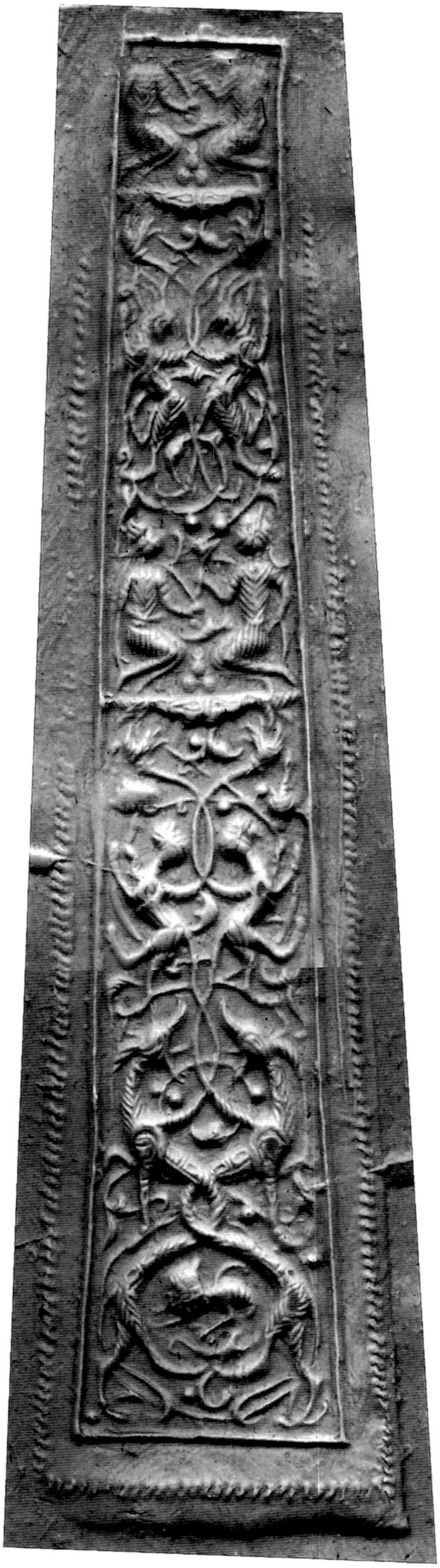

31b

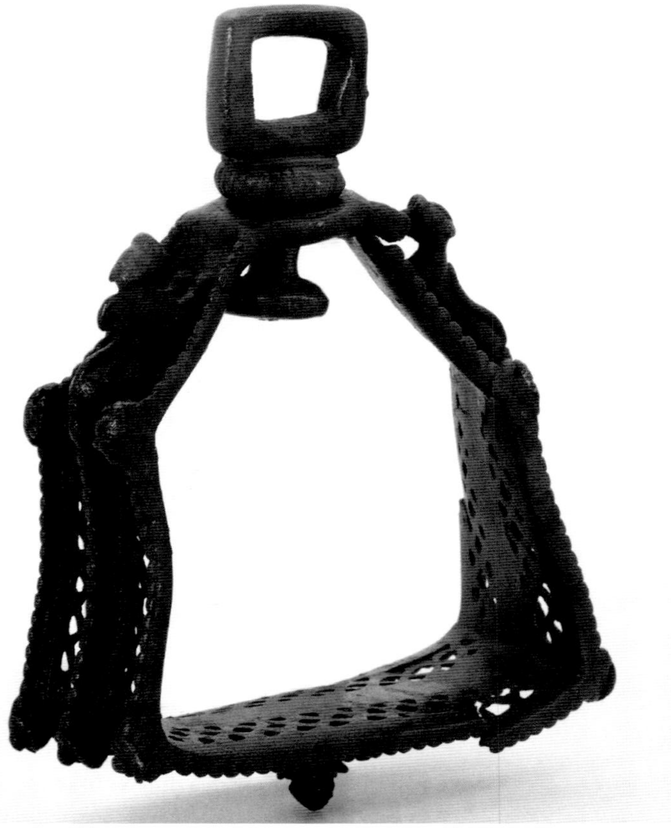

28. A pair of confronted winged quadruped dragons on the shoulders of a horse stirrup. Afghanistan.

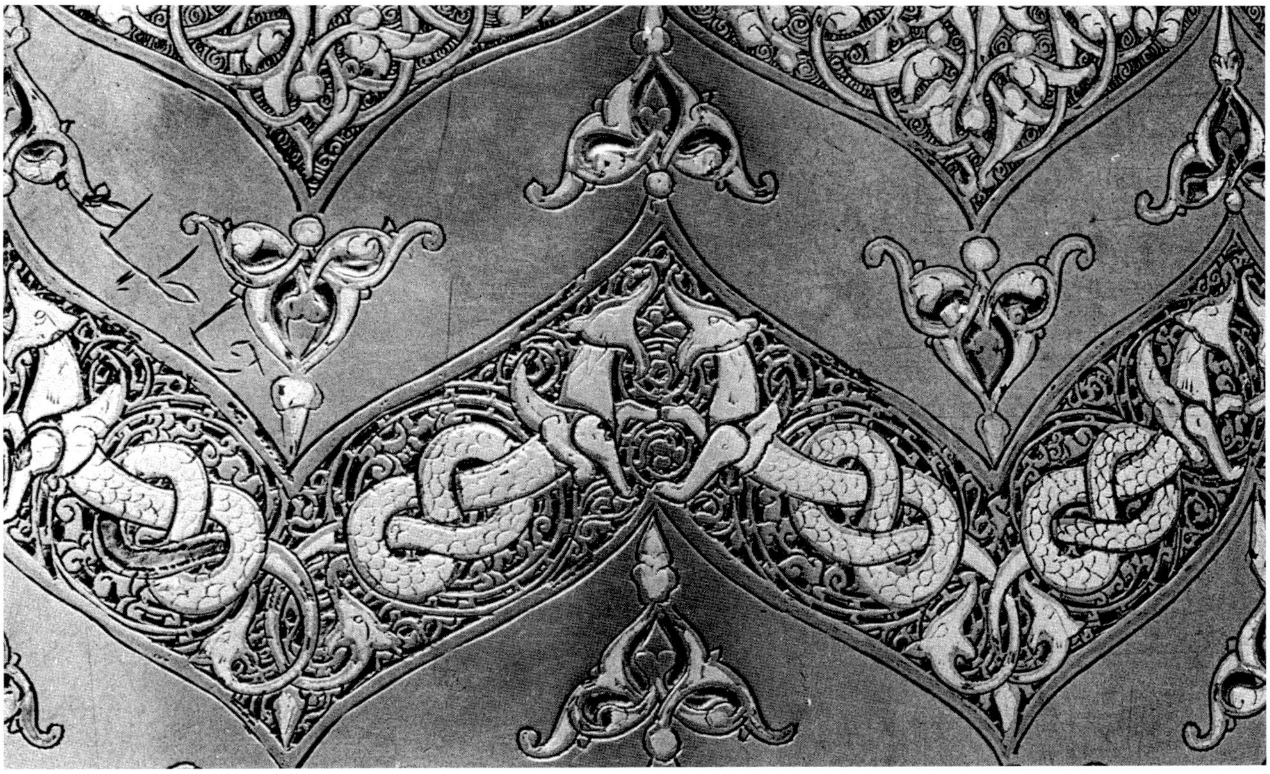

36. Confronted pairs of winged dragon-tailed dragons with forelegs. Detail from a candlestick base, the Jazīra.

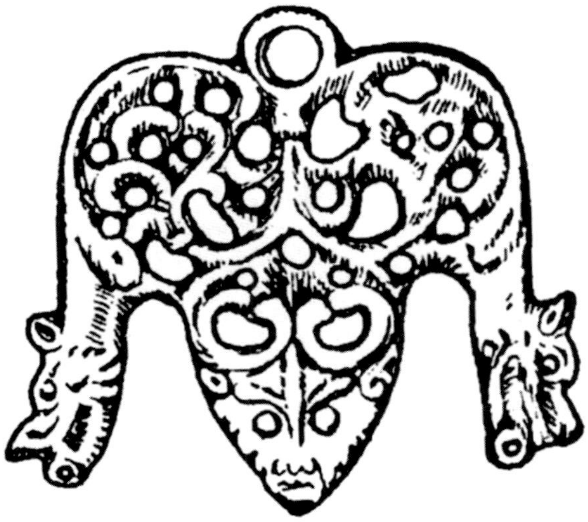

38. A pair of addorsed dragon protomes emerging from a vegetal composition that springs from a mask-like head. Fork-shaped harness pendant ornament, Kebinai, southern Siberia.

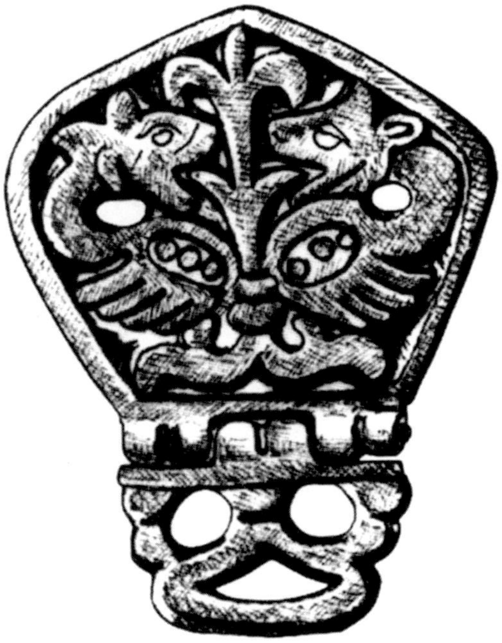

39. A pair of confronted winged dragon protomes springing from a vegetal composition. Belt fitting, Novocherkassk, Lower Don region.

Plate 10

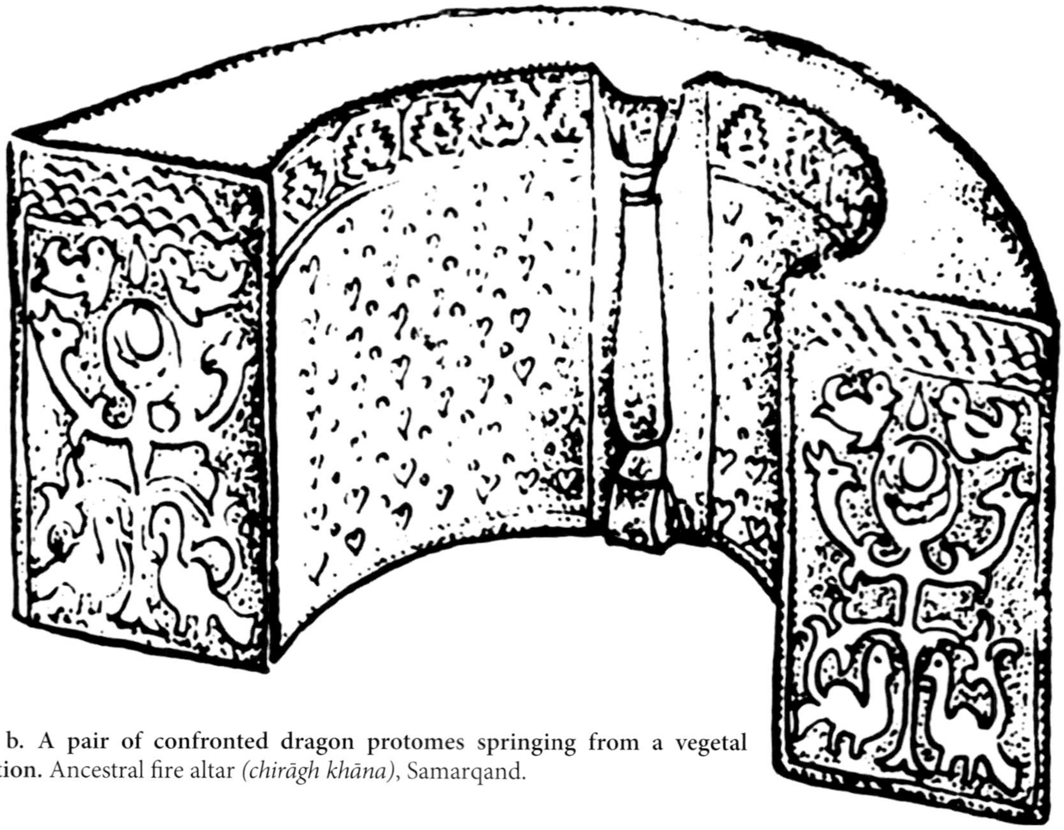

40a and b. A pair of confronted dragon protomes springing from a vegetal composition. Ancestral fire altar *(chirāgh khāna)*, Samarqand.

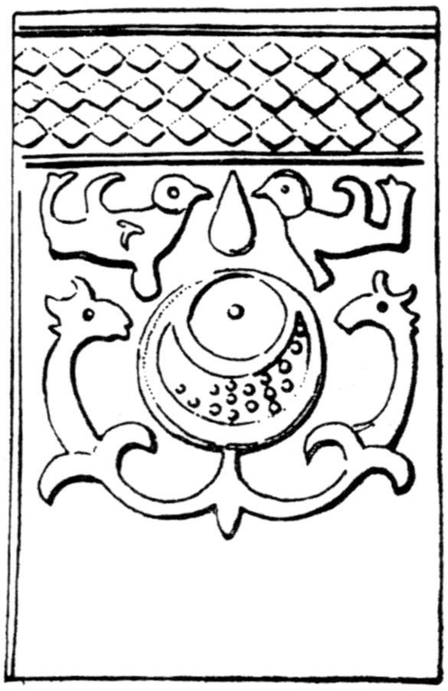

40b

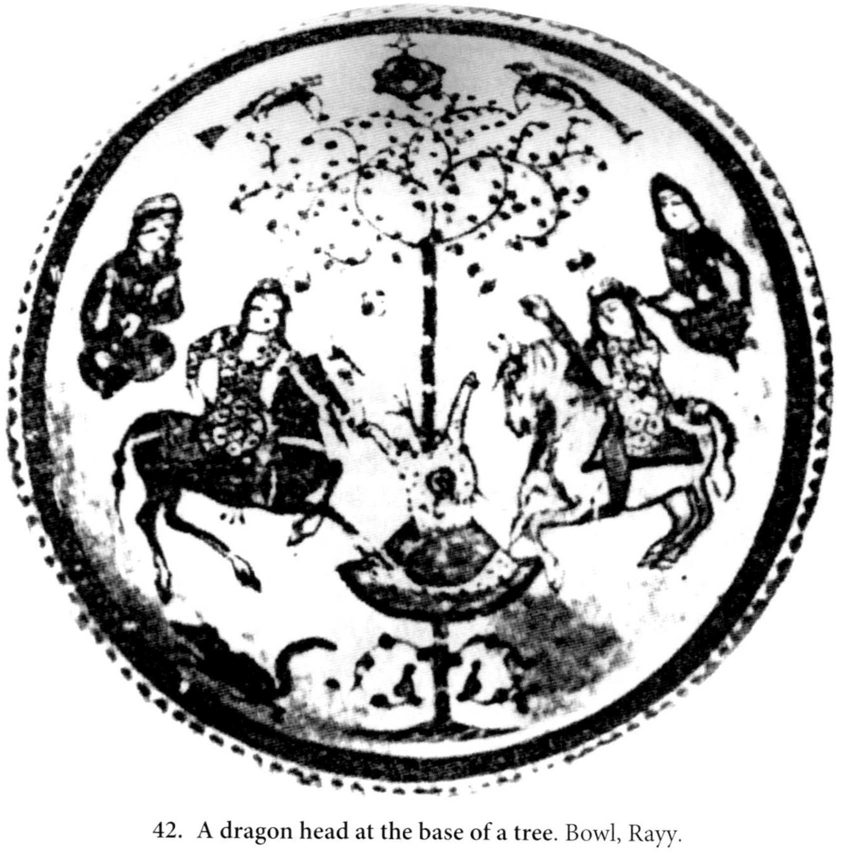

42. A dragon head at the base of a tree. Bowl, Rayy.

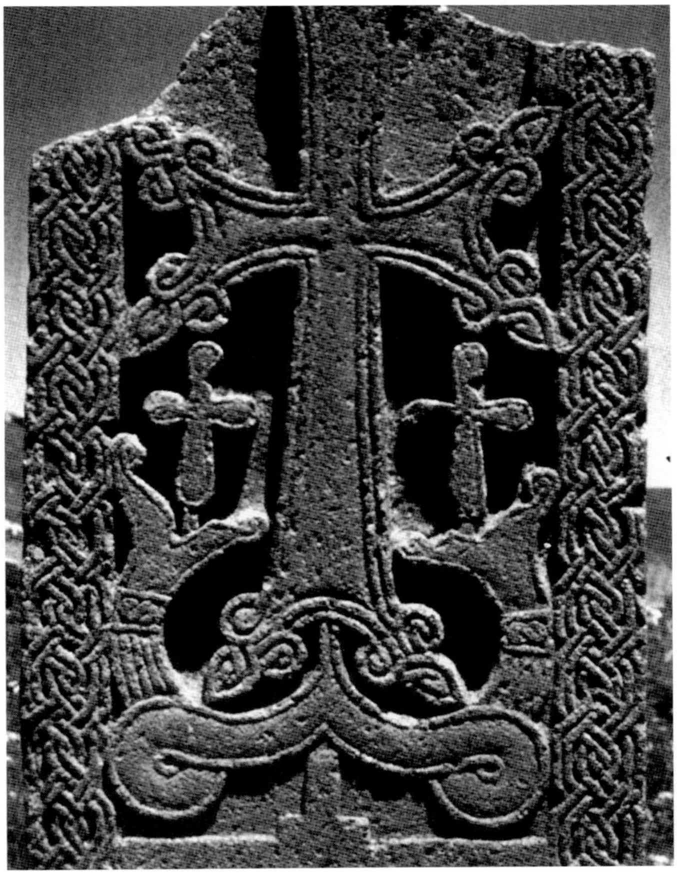

46. A pair of stylised dragon protomes springing from the base of a cross, their open mouths issuing small crosses. *Vishap*-type *khatchk'ar*, Makravank'.

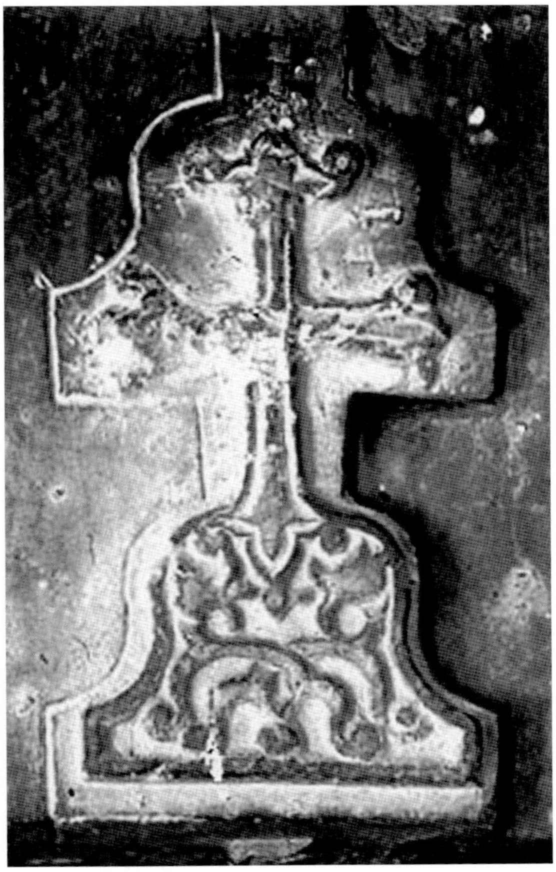

50. A cross with an arched cartouche at its base enclosing a pair of stylised *regardant* quadruped dragons with crossed bodies. Relief carving above the southern outer portal, monastery of Mār Behnām/Deir al-Khiḍr, southeast of Mosul.

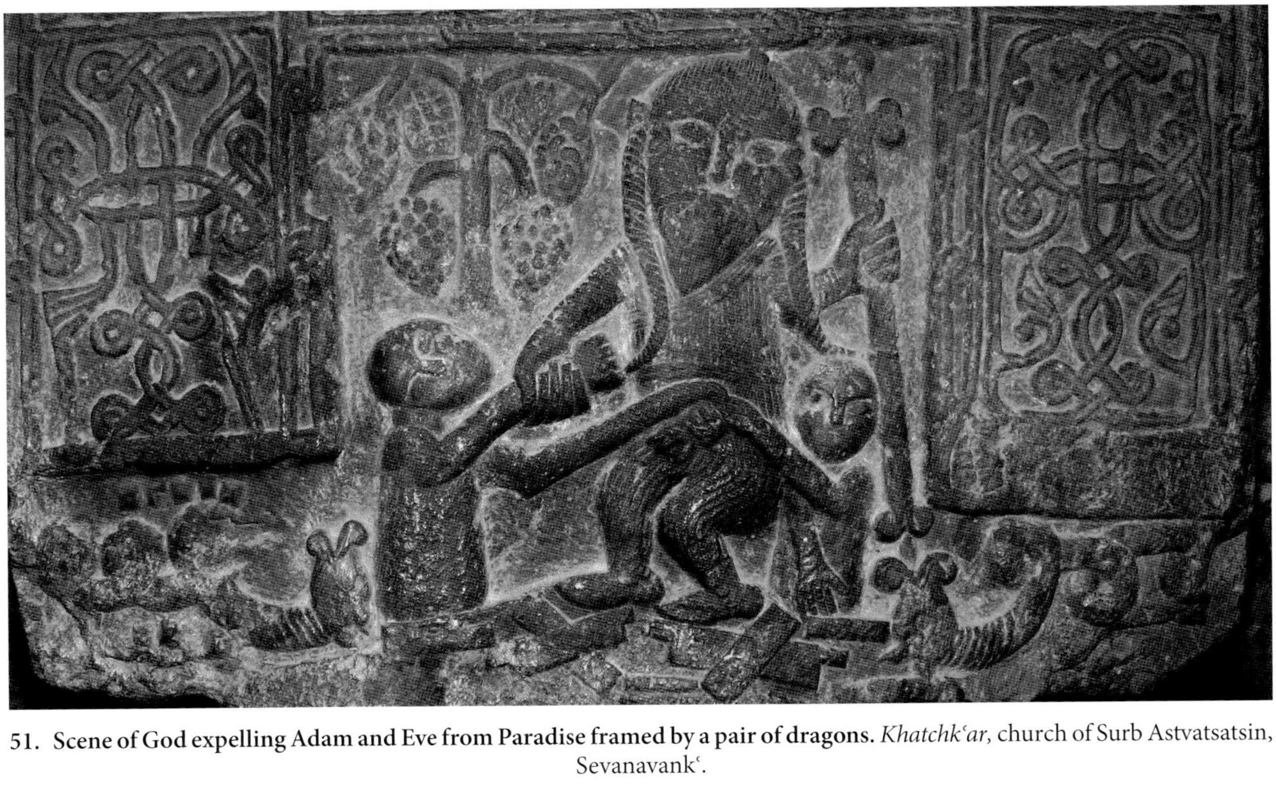

51. Scene of God expelling Adam and Eve from Paradise framed by a pair of dragons. *Khatchk'ar*, church of Surb Astvatsatsin, Sevanavank'.

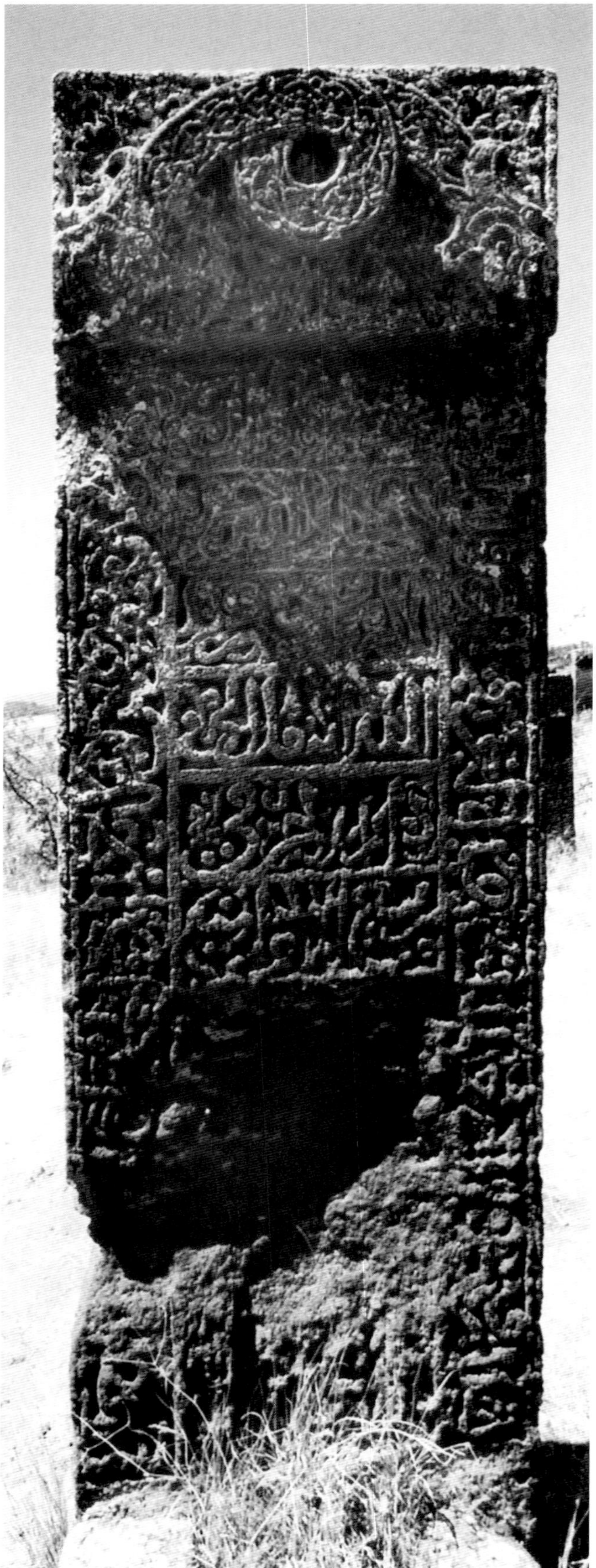

48. A double-headed dragon. Relief carving on a funerary stele, Akhlāṭ cemetery.

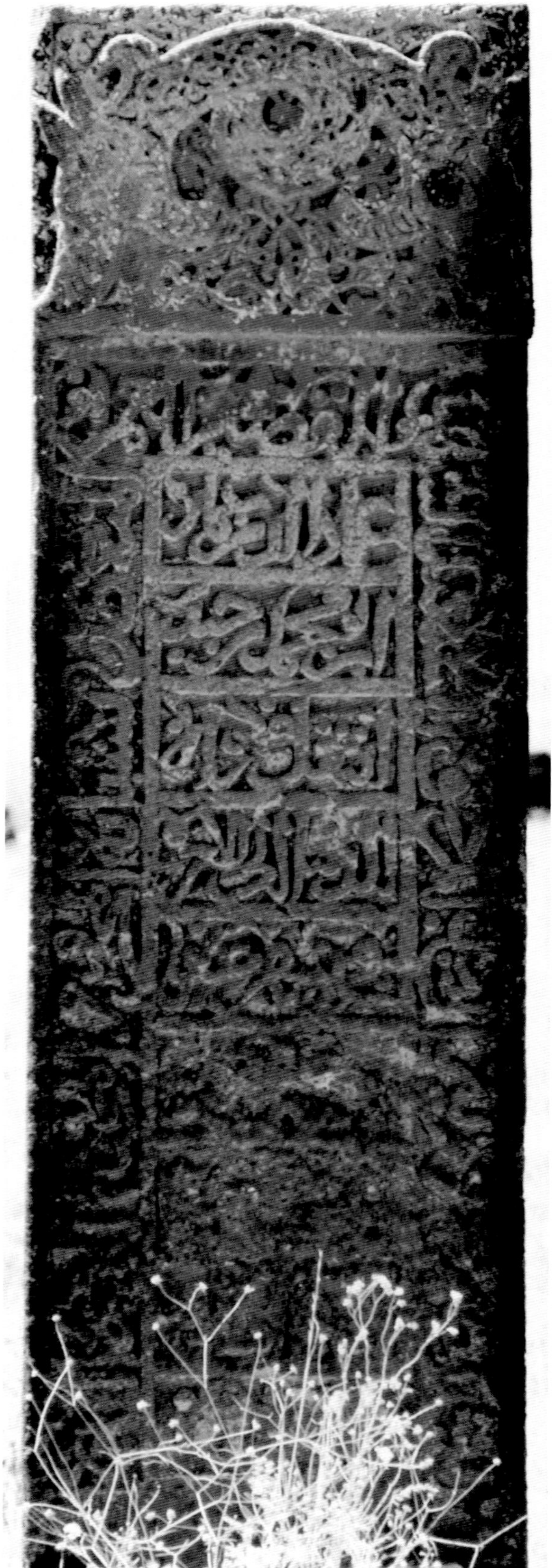

49. A double-headed dragon. Relief carving on a funerary stele, Akhlāṭ cemetery.

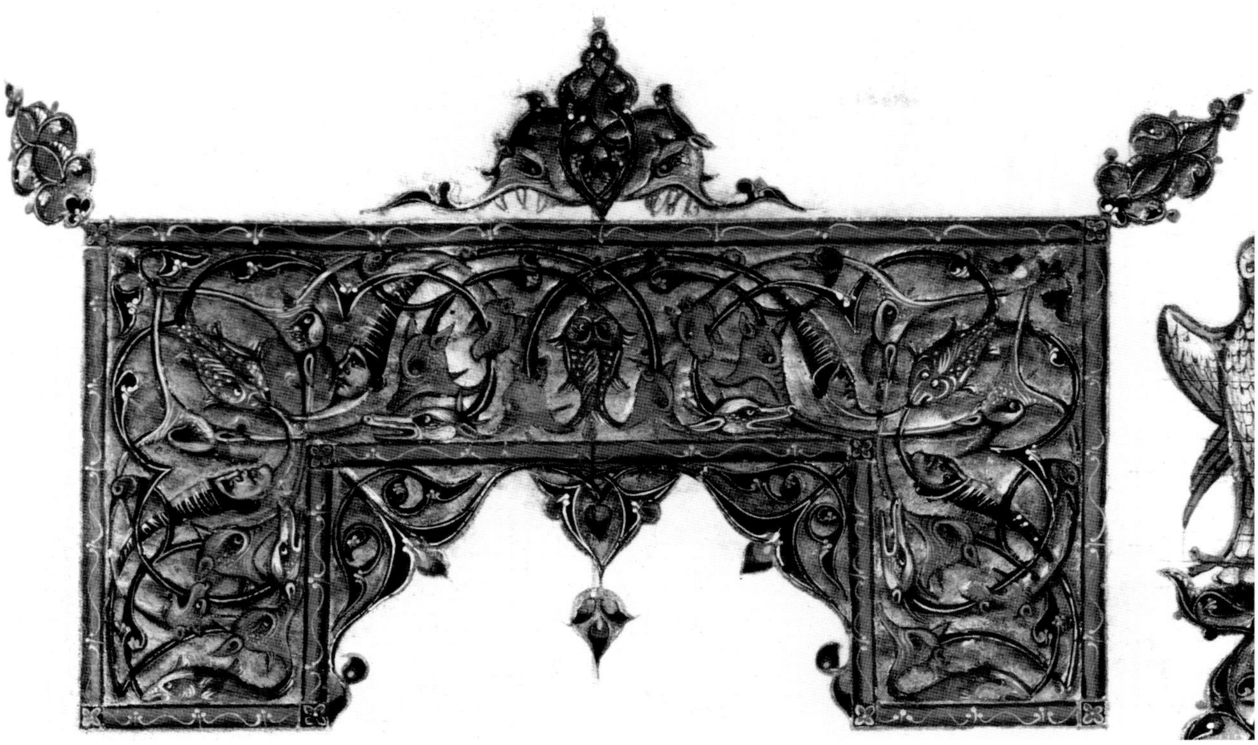

54. **A headpiece filled with an all-over foliate interlace bearing animal, in particular dragon, and human heads.** Gospel of Luke, Sis.

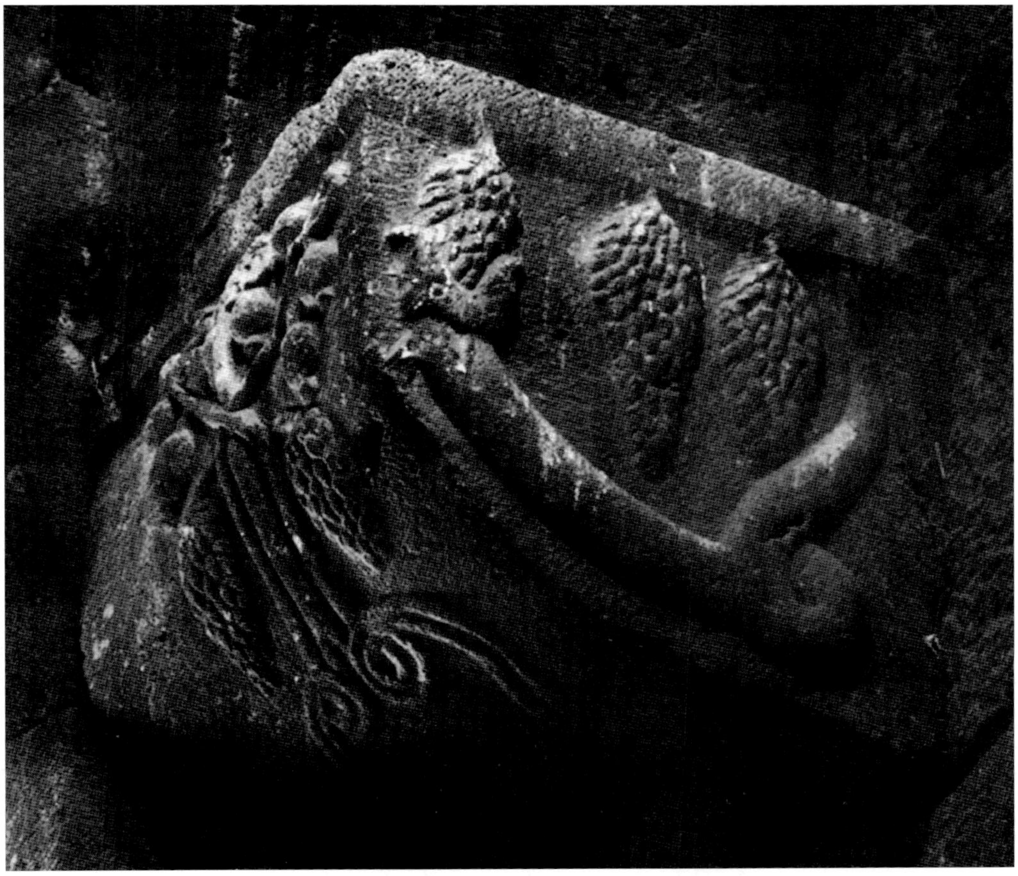

58. **A recumbent serpent reaching towards a bunch of grapes suspended above its mouth.** Relief carving on the northern capital, Çengelli kilise, southwest of Kars.

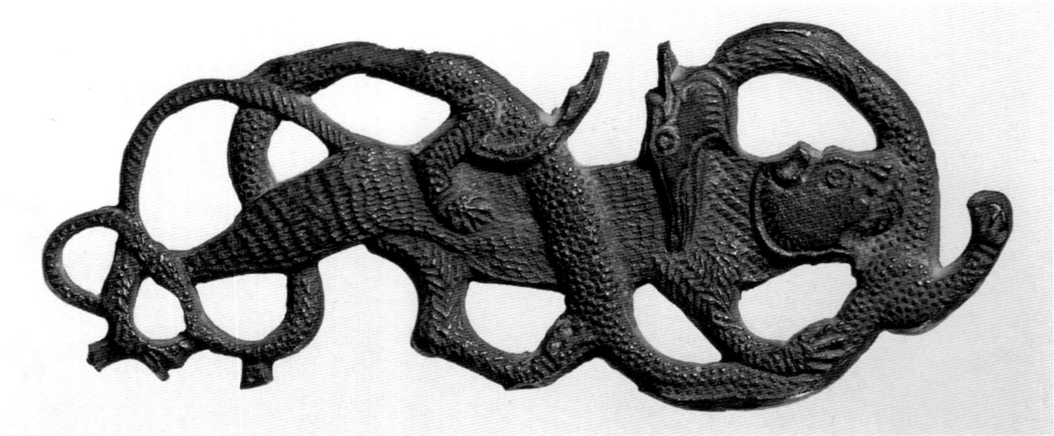

59. **A winged quadruped dragon and a feline in combat.** Openwork decoration from a brazier (?), Iran or Anatolia.

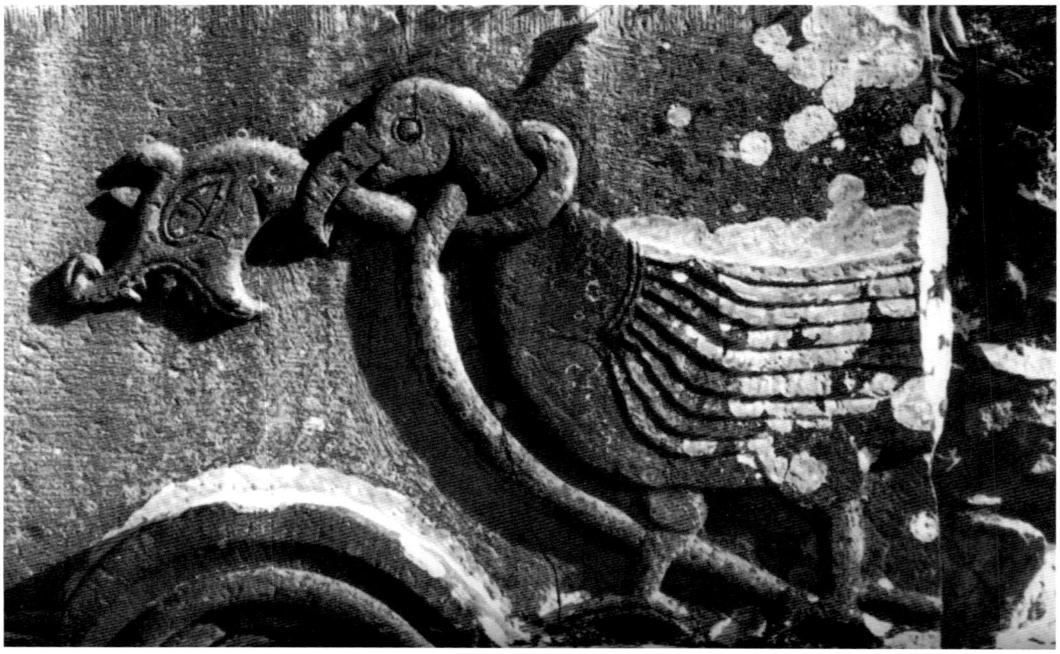

62. **A bird in combat with a dragon.** Relief carving over a window edge on the southern façade, small chapel behind the main church of Surp Astvatsatsin, Makaravankʿ monastic complex, Tavush province.

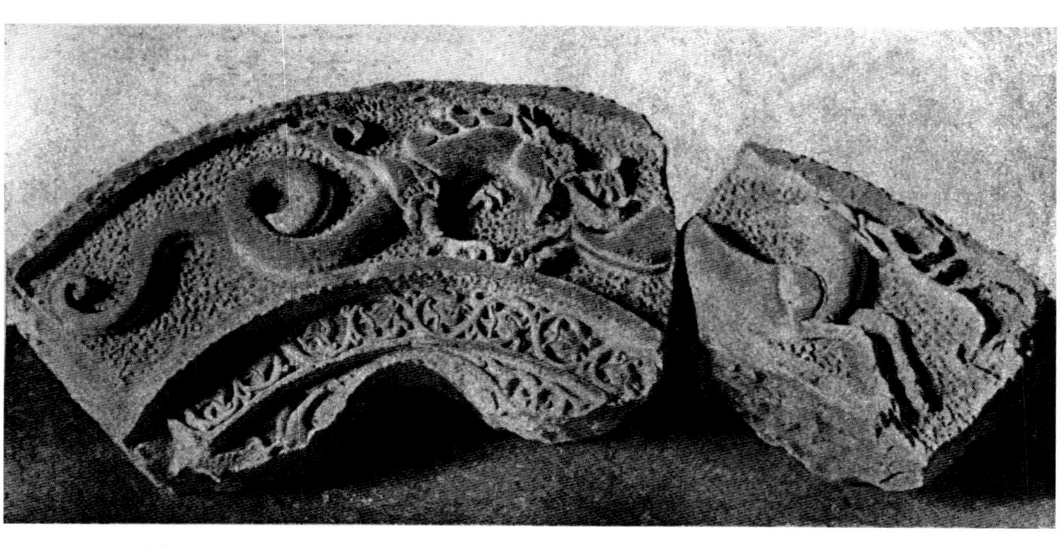

63. **A winged dragon with forelegs in combat with a cervid.** Relief carving on an archivolt fragment, Daghistan.

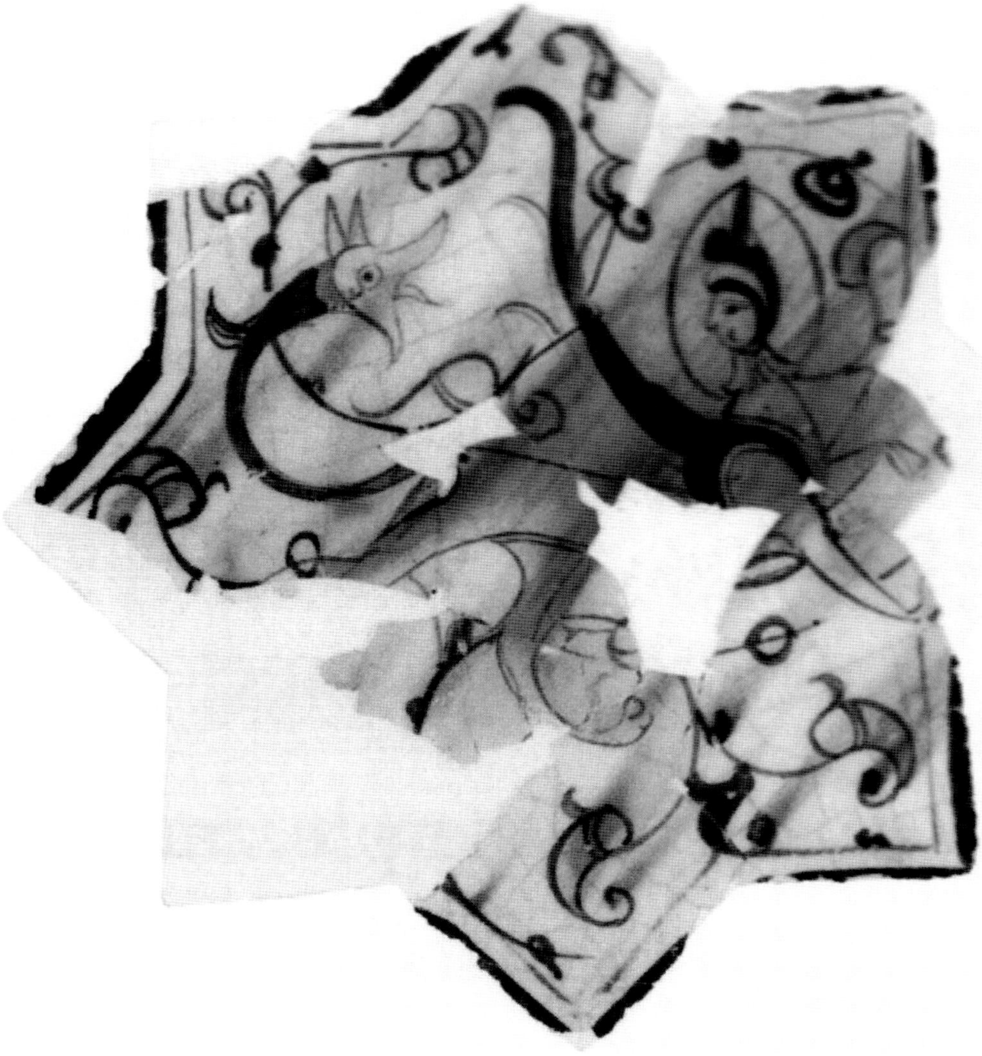

65. **A dragon-tailed *regardant* sphinx**. Star tile fragment, small palace in Kubadabad.

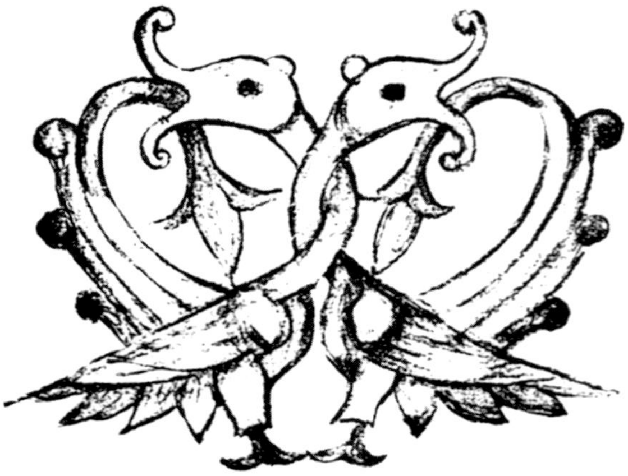

71. Confronted dragon-headed birds with interlaced necks. Missal, Armenia.

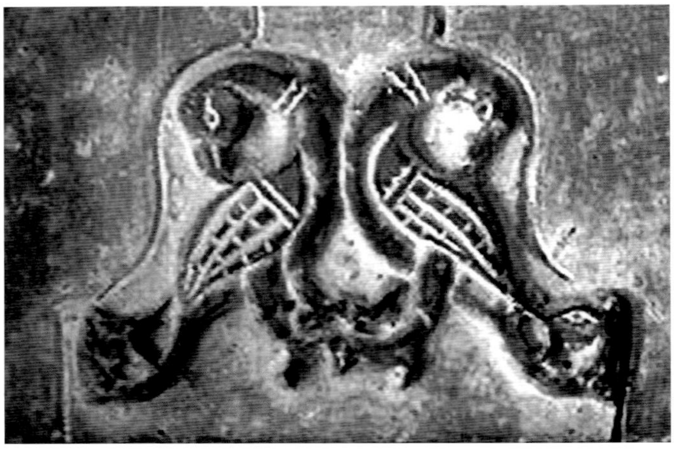

74. A pair of confronted dragon-tailed *regardant* birds. Relief carving above the southern outer portal, monastery of Mār Behnām/Deir al-Khiḍr, southeast of Mosul.

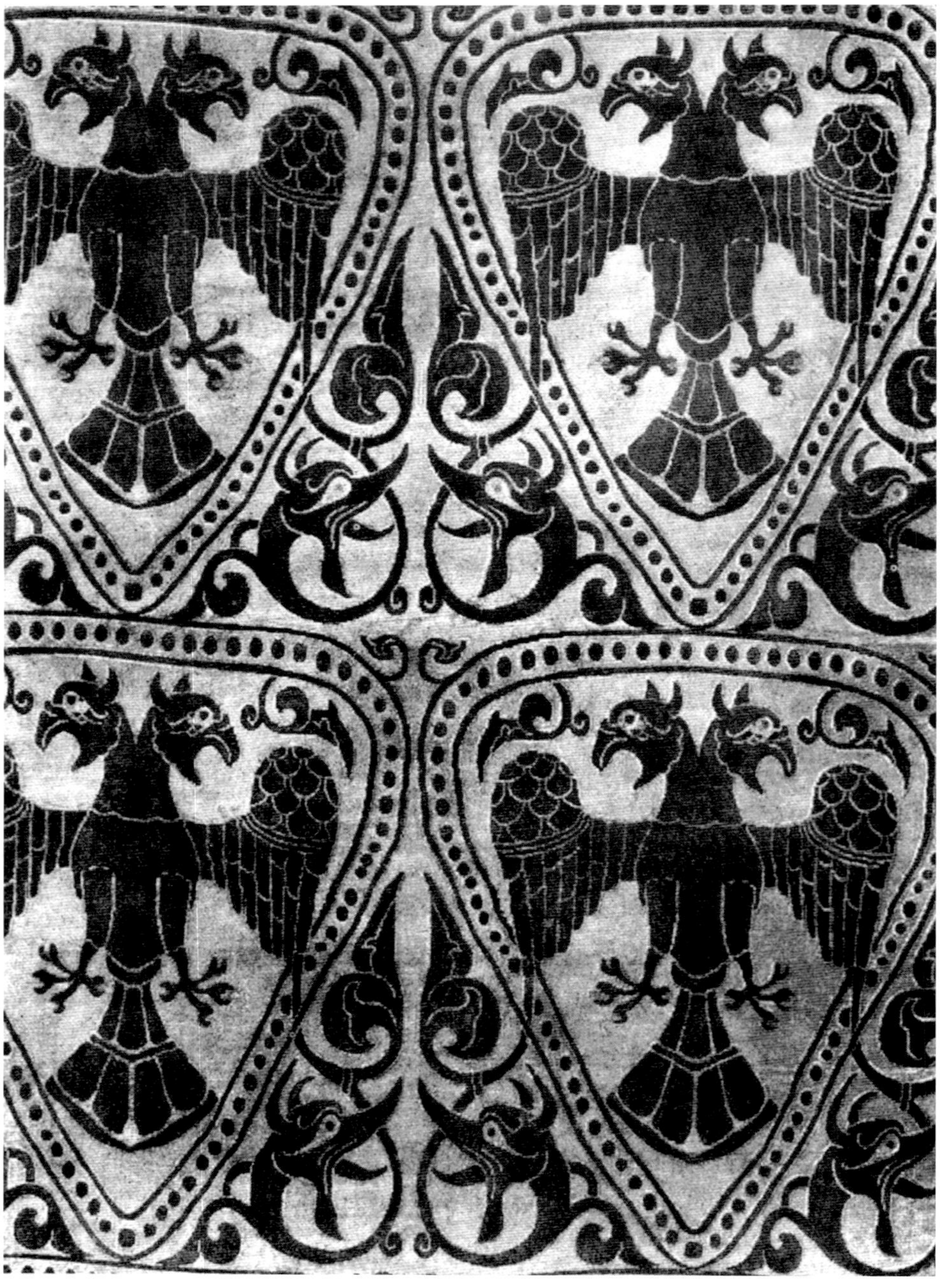

69a. Double-headed eagles with outspread dragon-headed wings. Detail of a textile fragment, probably Anatolia.

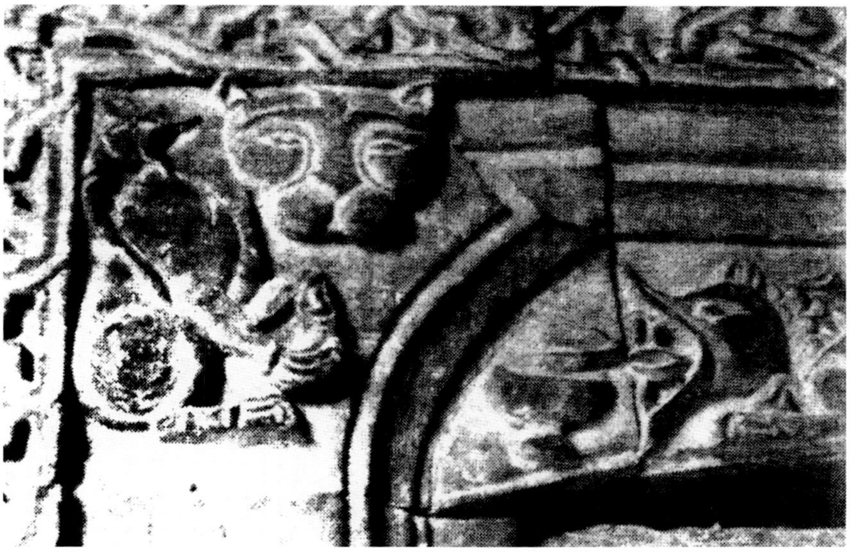

77. A seated dragon-tailed lion (one of a pair). Relief carving above the southern outer portal, monastery of Mār Behnām/Deir al-Khiḍr, southeast of Mosul.

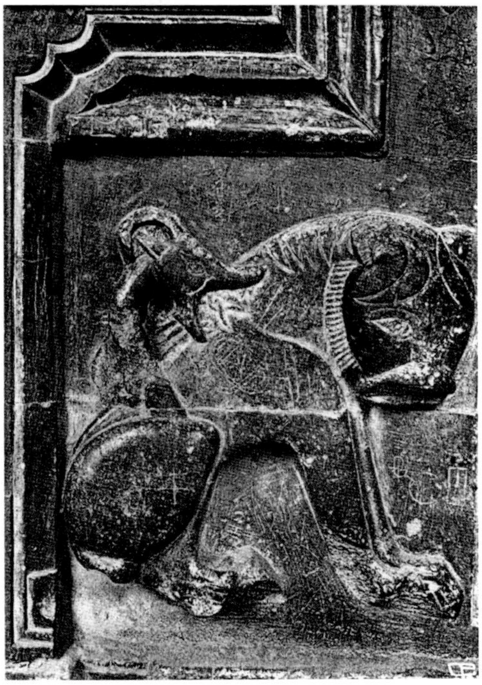

78. A seated dragon-tailed lion (one of a pair). Relief carving on the main portal of the Jacobite church, Cizre.

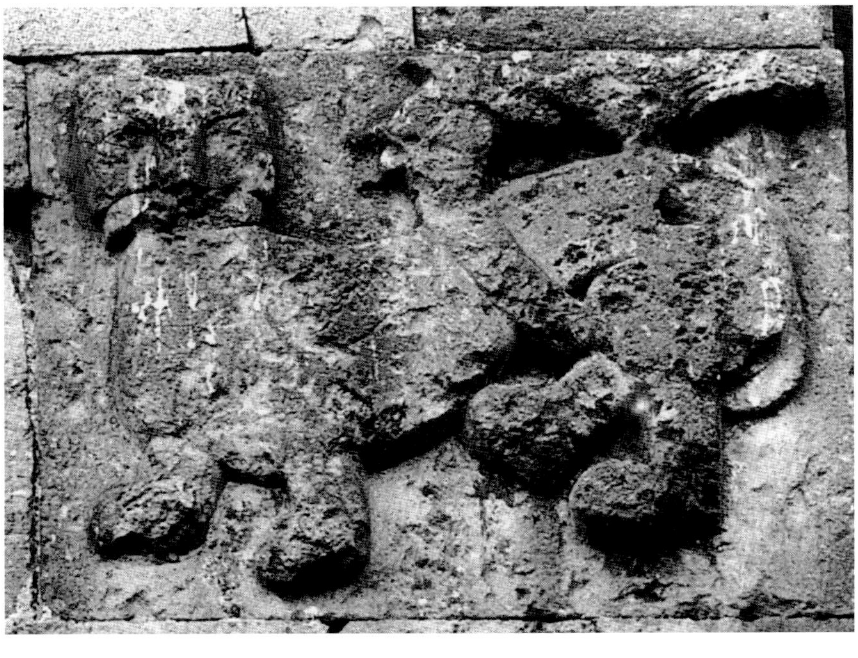

80. A dragon-tailed lion with bird. Relief carving to the right side of the portal of Kesikköprü Han, south of Kırşehir.

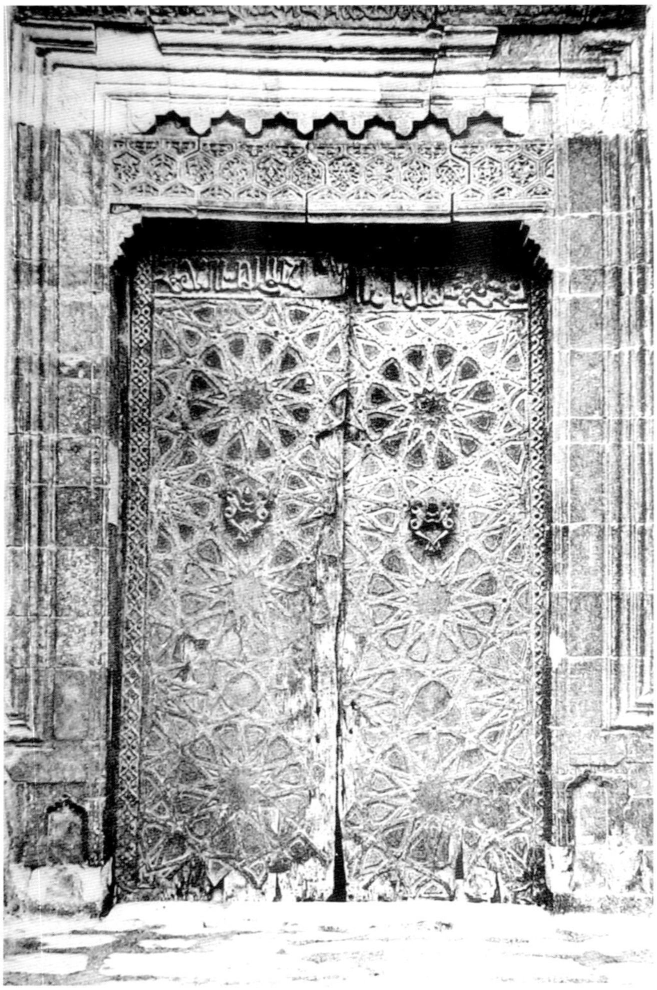

82. Double doors of the Ulu Cami of Cizre with the dragon knockers *in situ*.

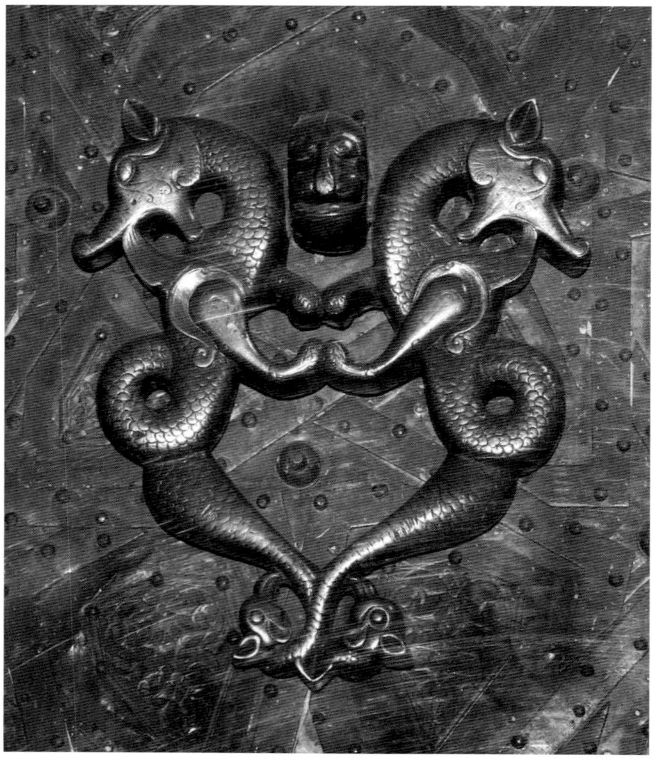

83. A pair of confronted dragons with entwined bird-headed tails flanking a lion-headed knob. Door knocker, Cizre.

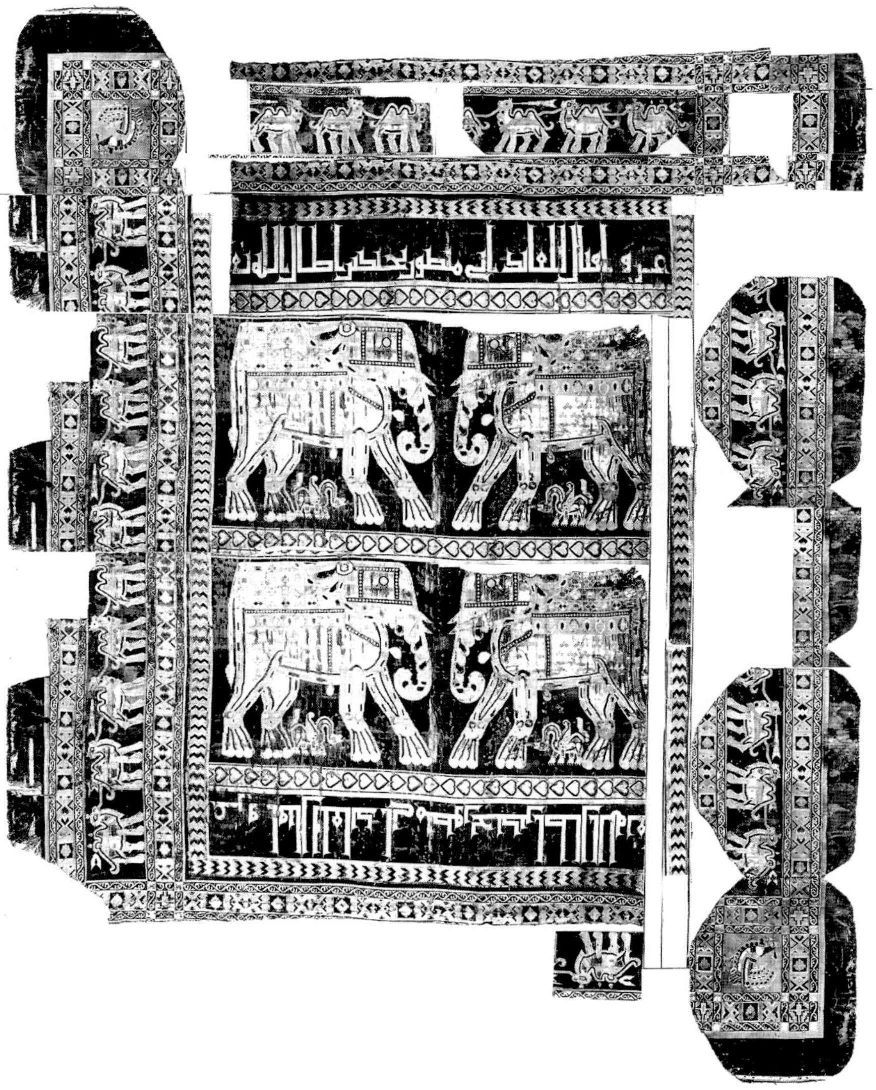

85a. Elephants and winged quadruped dragons with benedictory inscription naming the owner, Qā'id Abu 'l-Manṣūr Bākh-tigīn. Textile fragment, Khurasan.

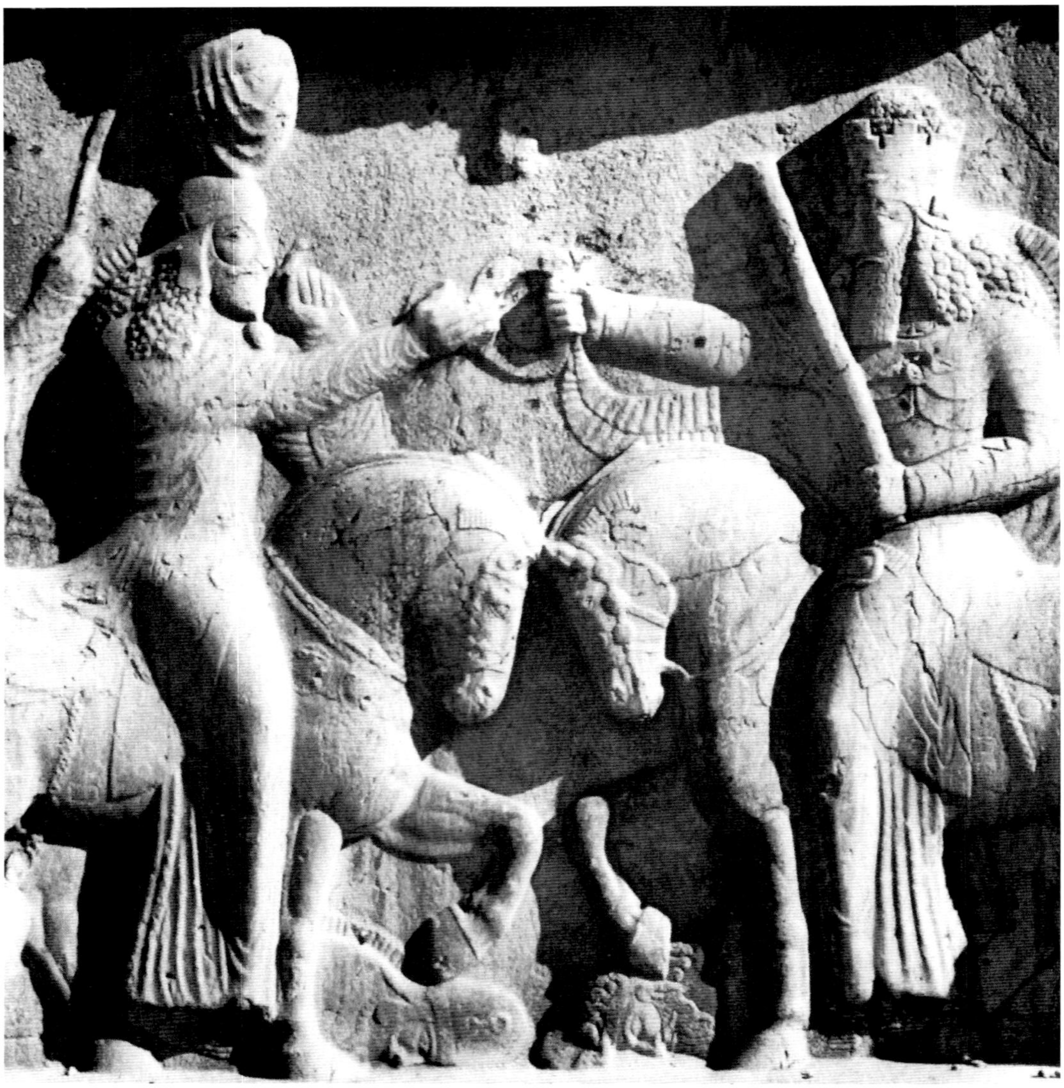

86a and b. Investiture of Ardashīr I. Rock relief, Naqsh-i Rustam.

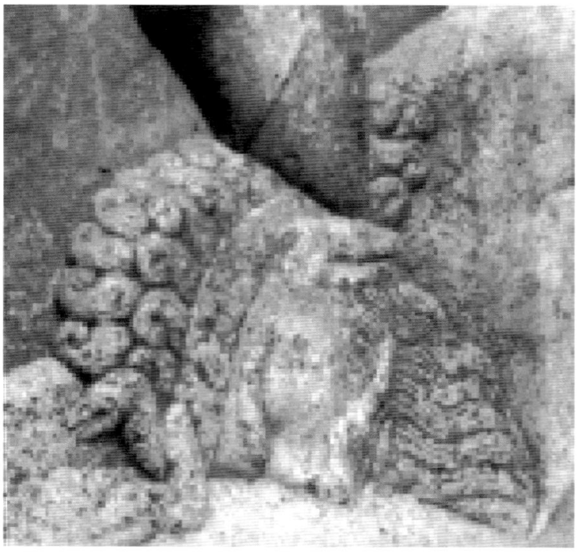

86b

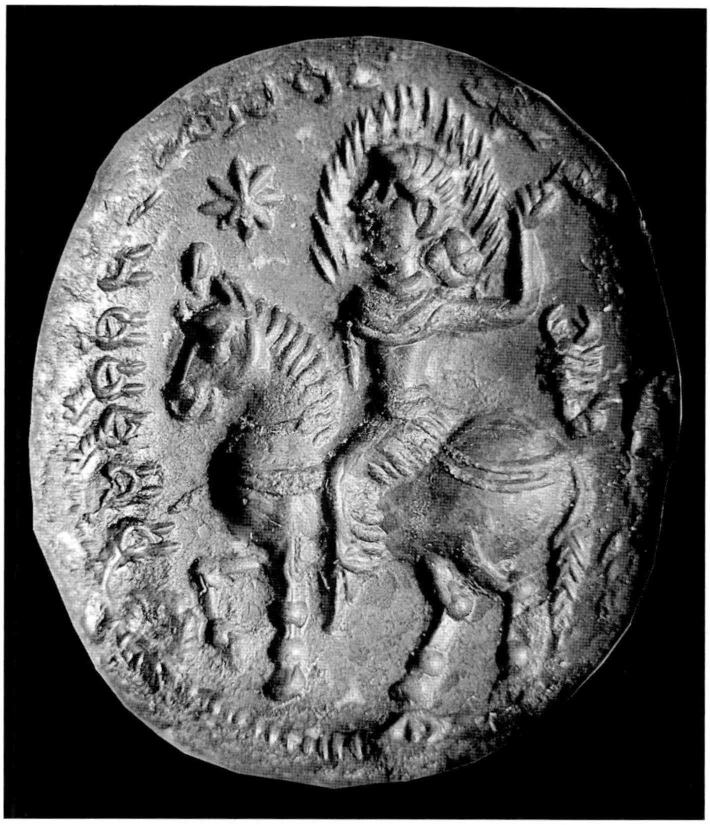

87. **A horseman fighting a seven-headed dragon.** Seal, Iranian world.

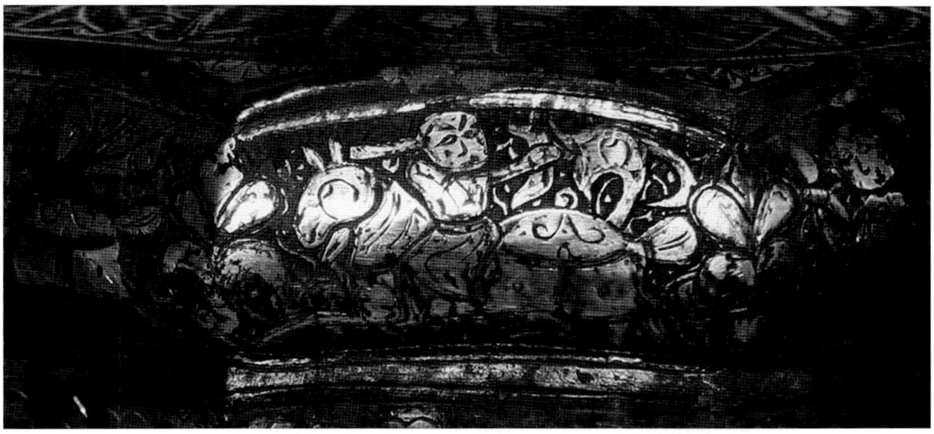

92. **A horseman fighting a dragon.** Detail on faceted shoulder of a ewer, Herat.

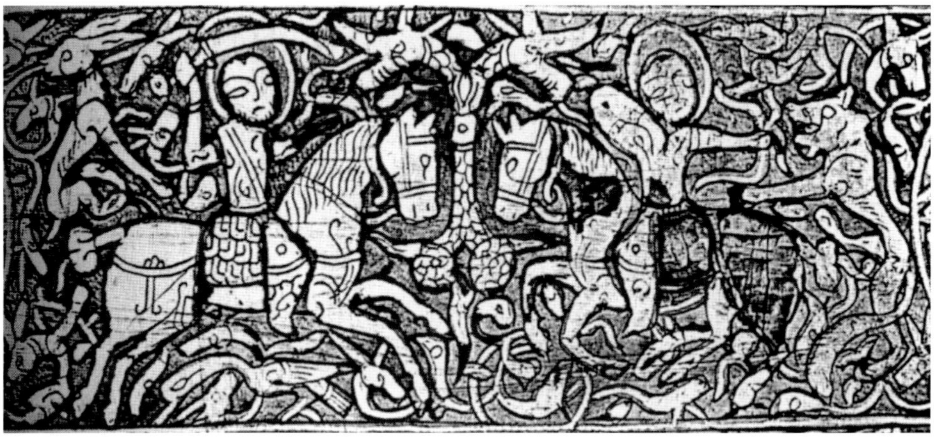

93. **A pair of confronted horsemen fighting an upright double-headed dragon and a lion.** Base of a penbox, Iran.

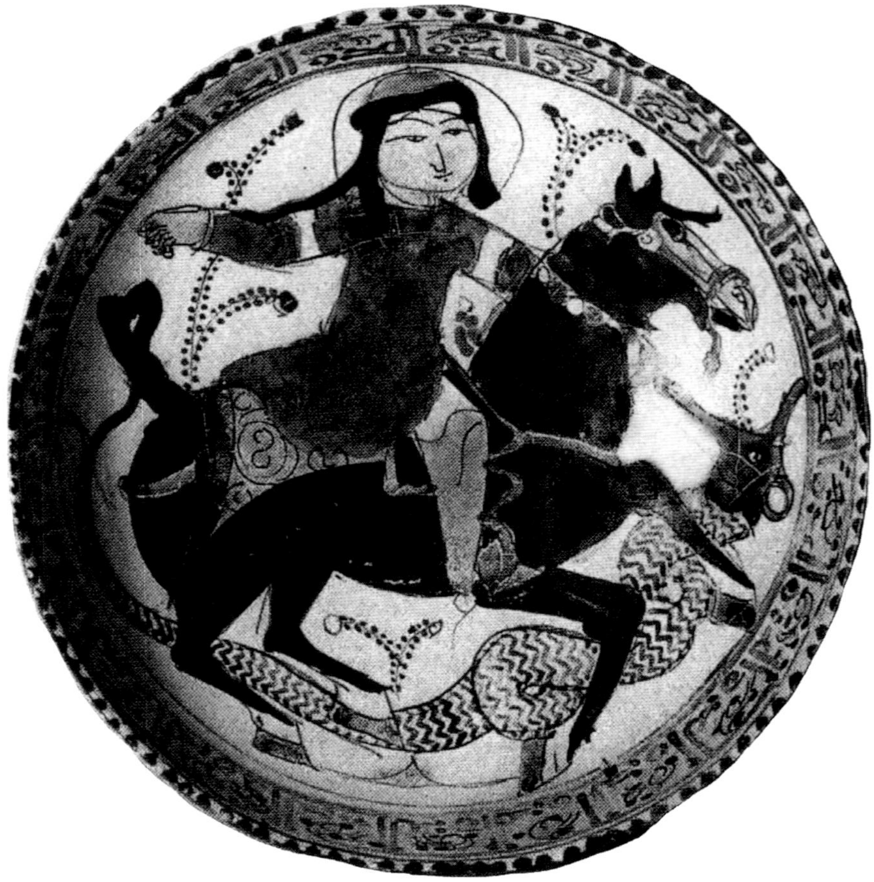

96. **A horseman fighting a dragon.** Bowl, Iran.

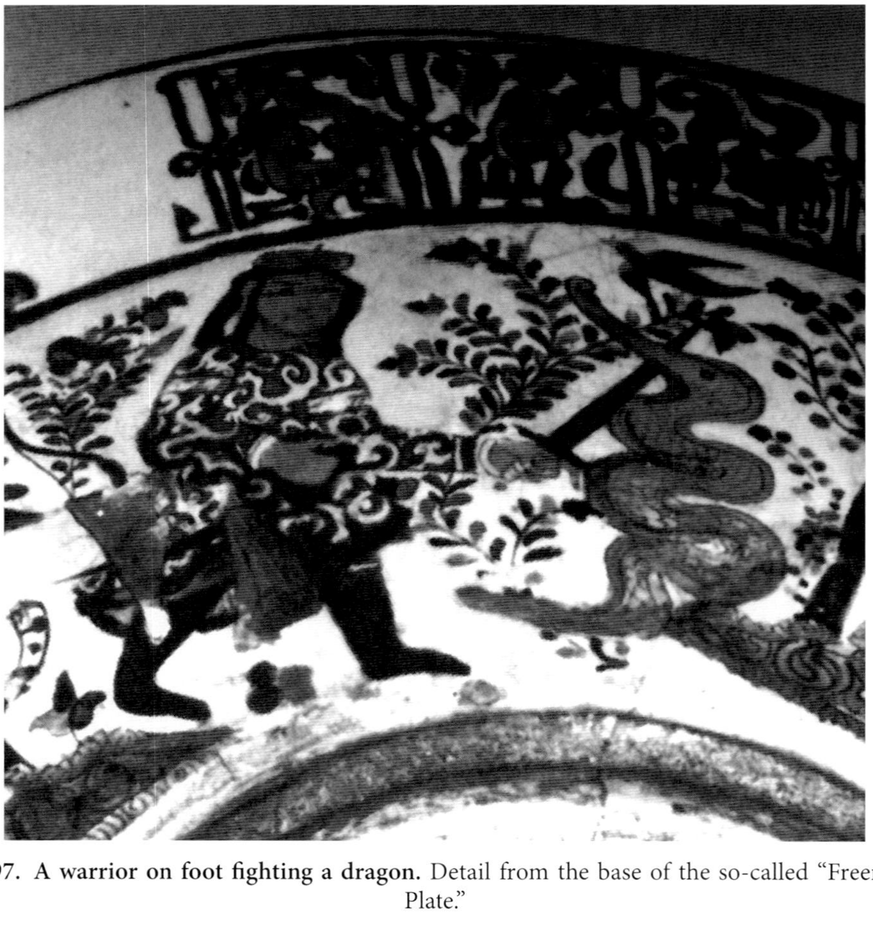

97. **A warrior on foot fighting a dragon.** Detail from the base of the so-called "Freer Plate."

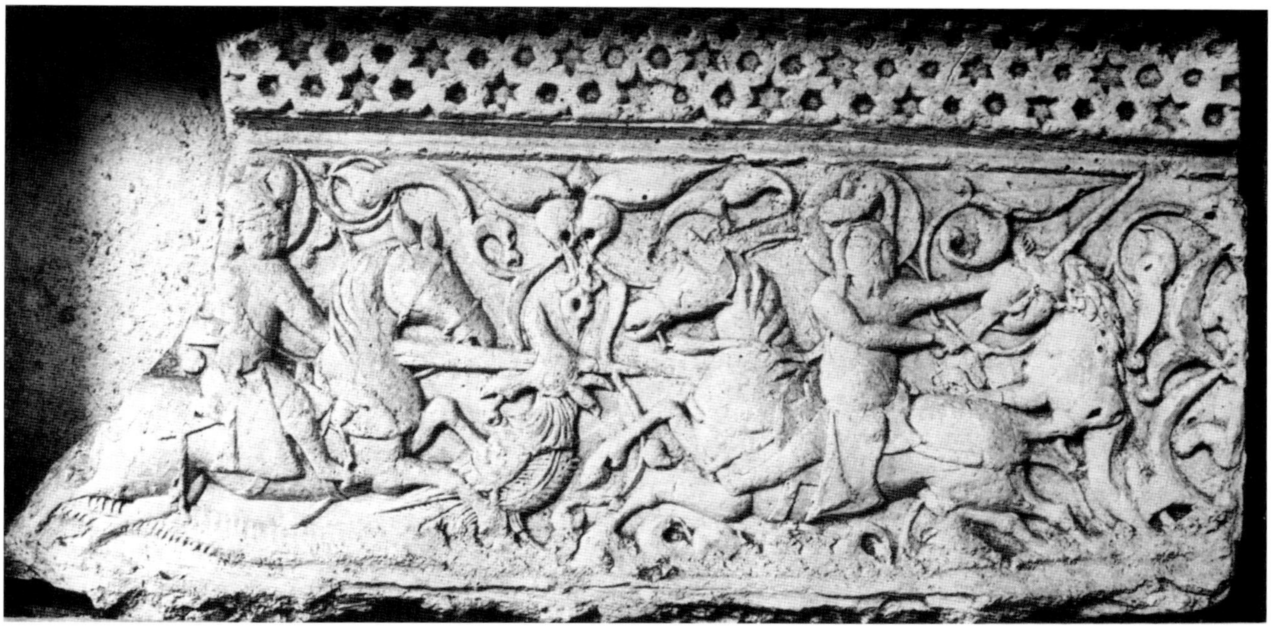

98. A pair of confronted horsemen fighting a winged dragon and a lion. Relief frieze from the pavilion of Qılıch Arslan II (Alaeddin Köşkü), Konya.

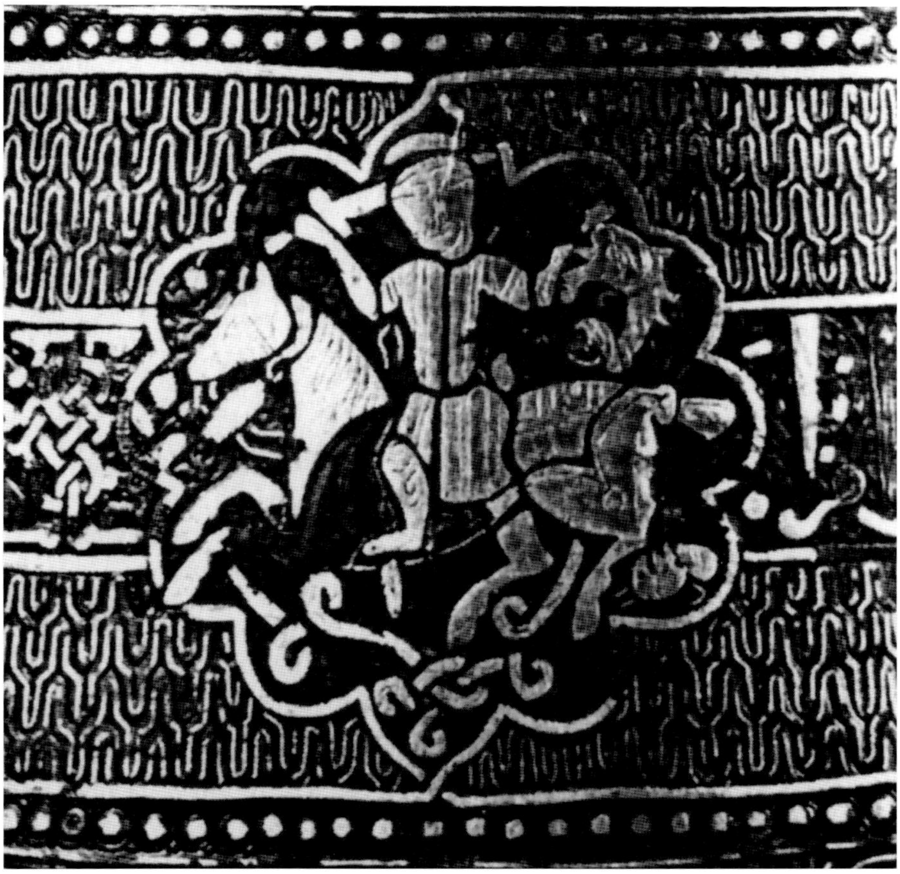

99. A horseman fighting a dragon. Detail from a candlestick base, the Jazīra.

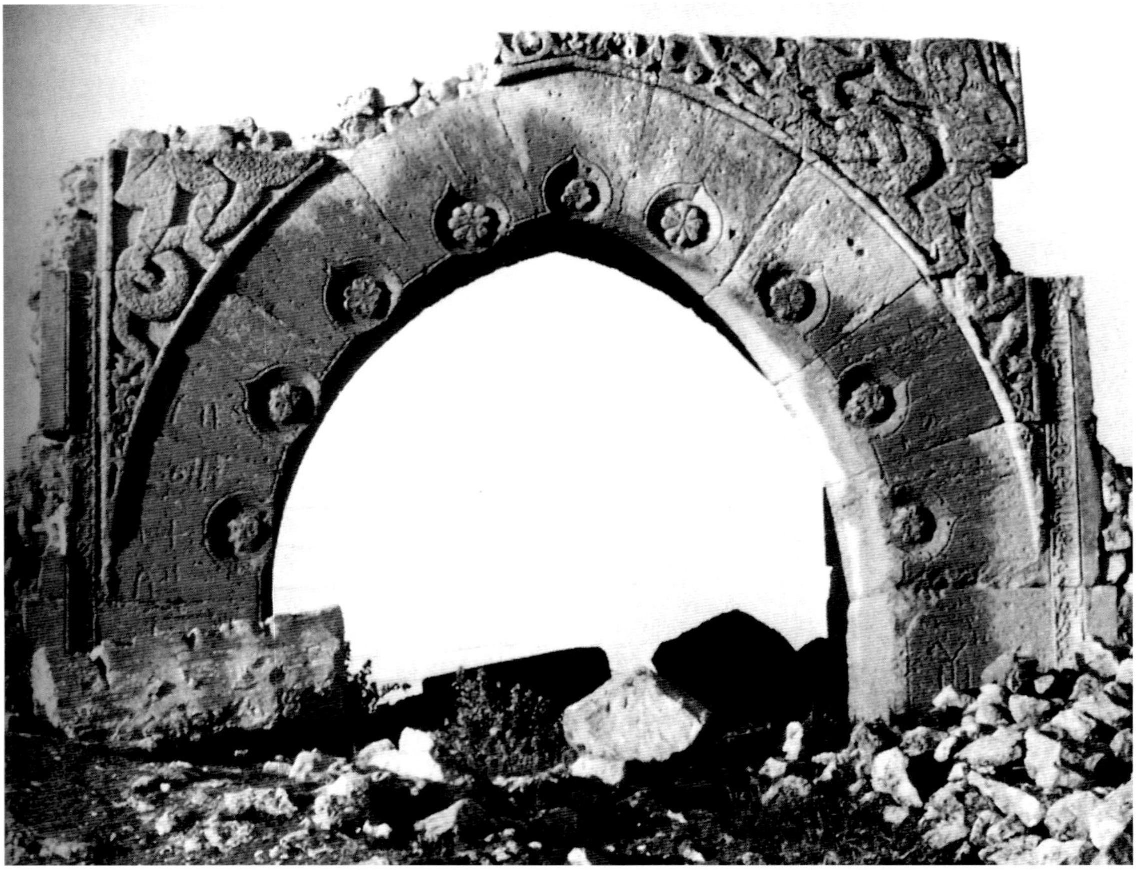

100a and b. A pair of warriors on foot fighting confronted dragon-tailed winged dragons with forelegs. Relief carving on the gateway of al-Khān, between Mosul and Sinjār.

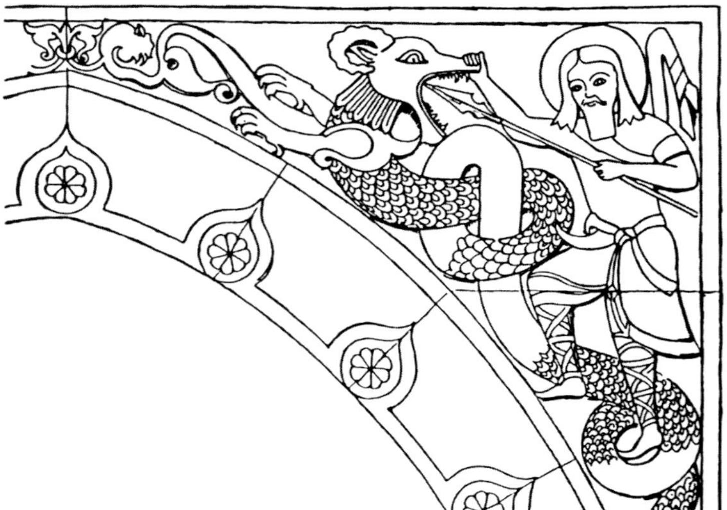

100b

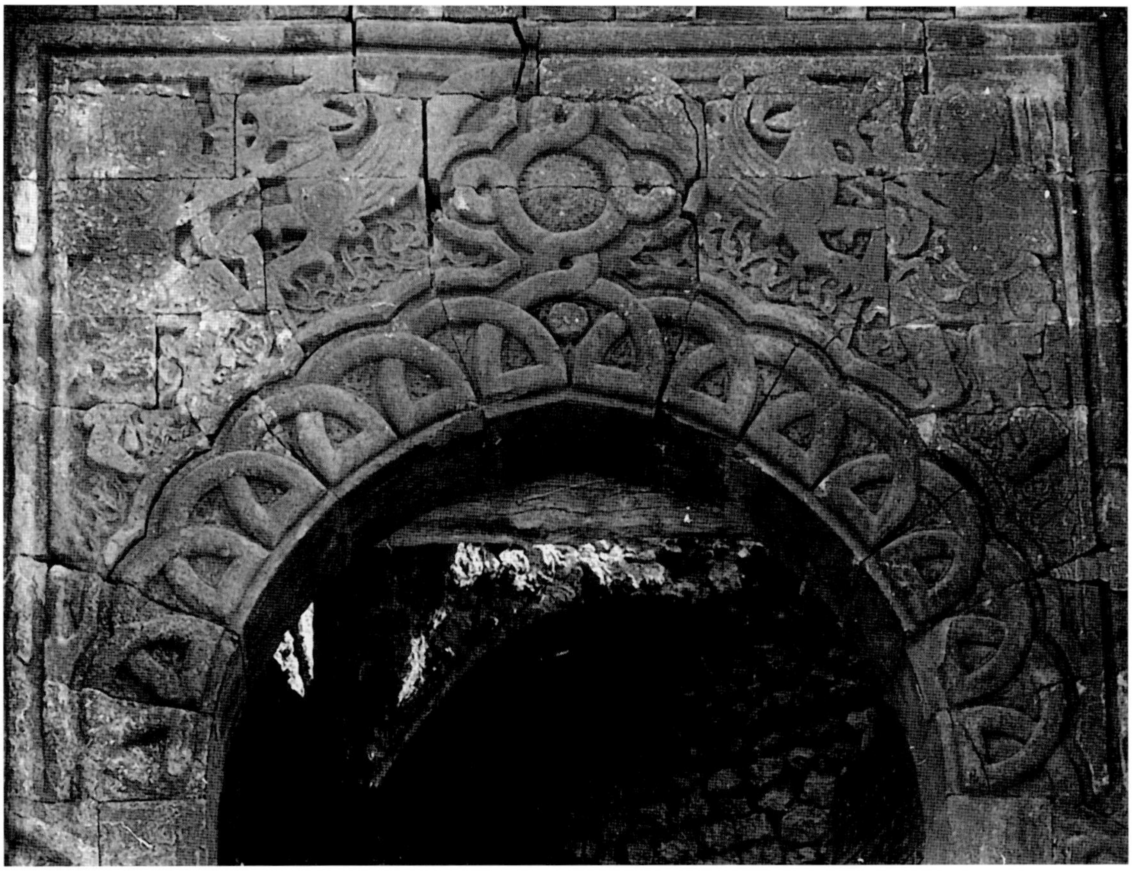

101. A pair of warriors on foot fighting addorsed winged dragons with forelegs and entwined bodies. Relief carving on the portal of the Mosul gate, ʿAmādiya, northeast of Mosul.

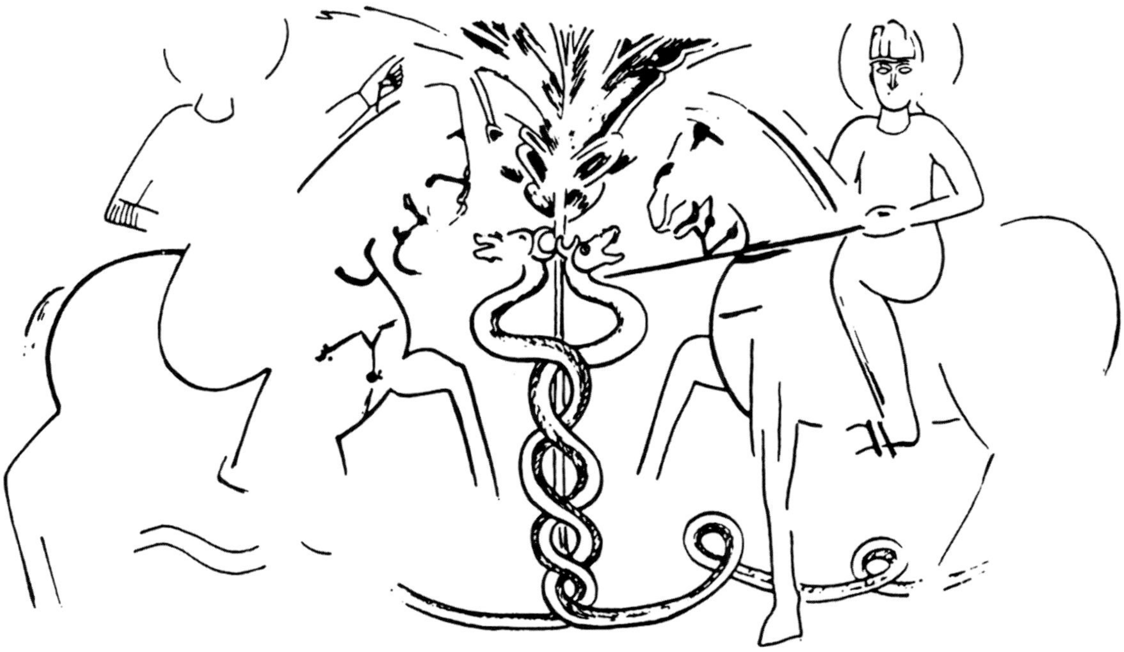

104. A pair of confronted equestrian saints fighting dragons coiled around a tree trunk. Wall painting in the Mistikan kilise, village of Güzelöz, region of Çavuşin.

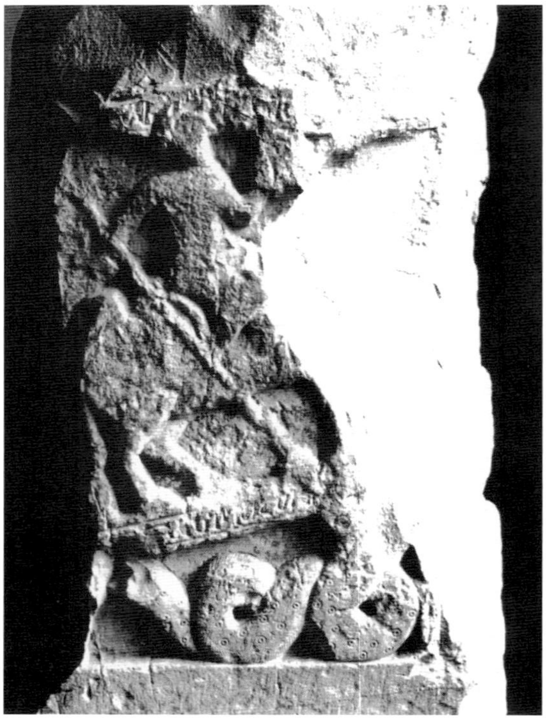

103. A horseman fighting a dragon. Relief carving on Ekikilise, Kartli region.

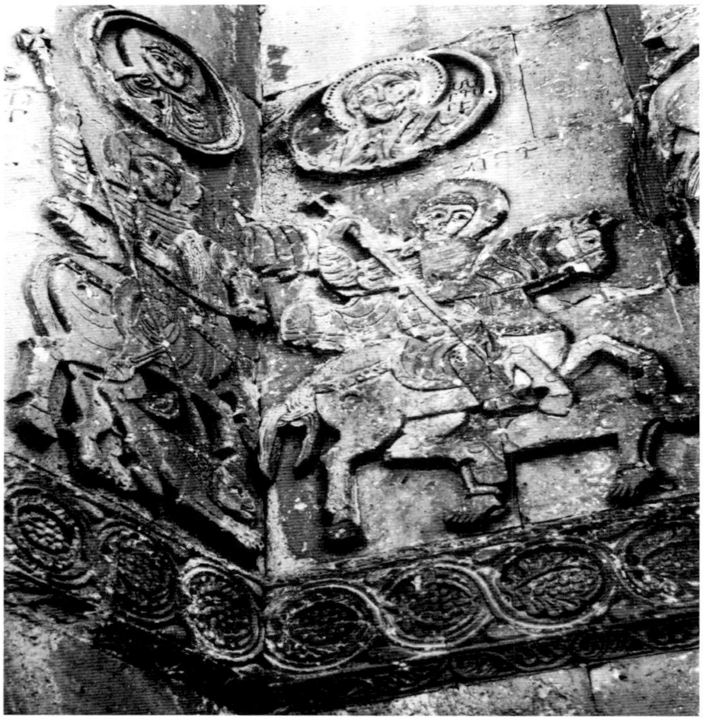

108. The saints Sergios and George killing a feline and a supine human figure. Relief carving on the northwestern façade of the church of the Holy Cross, Akht'amar island.

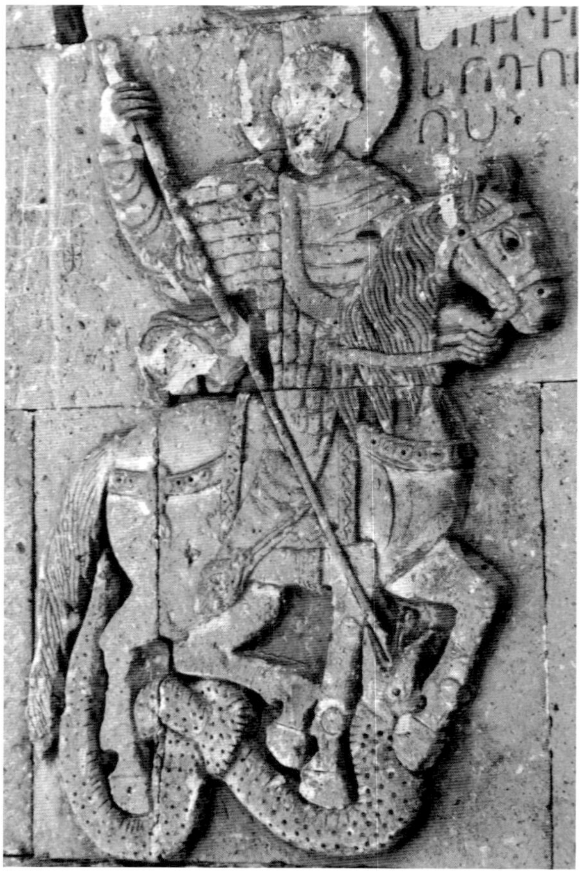

109. Saint Theodore killing a dragon. Relief carving on the northwestern façade of the church of the Holy Cross, Akht'amar island.

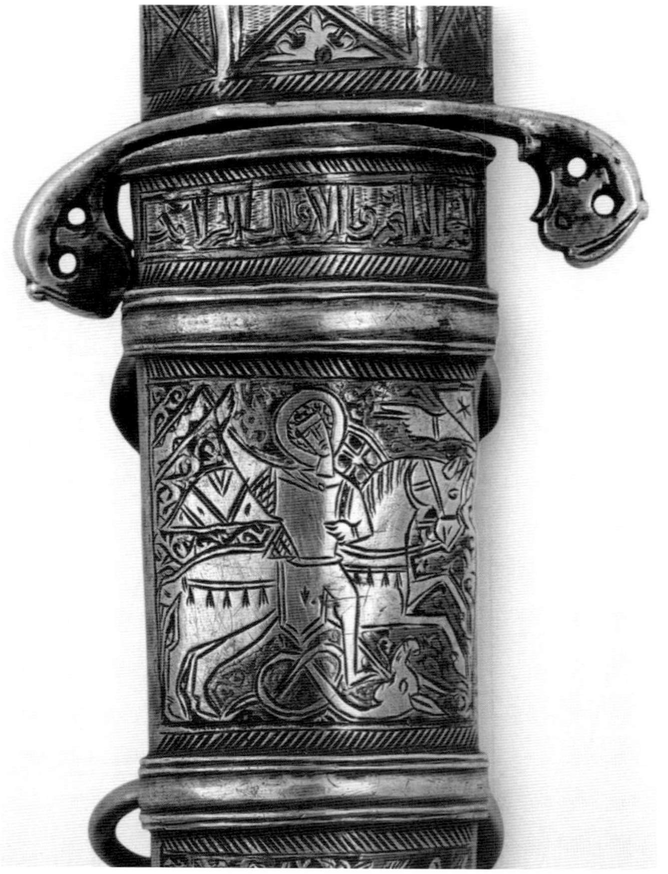

111. An equestrian saint killing a dragon; the sloping quillons terminating in dragon heads. Detail from a dagger with scabbard, Syria or Palestine.

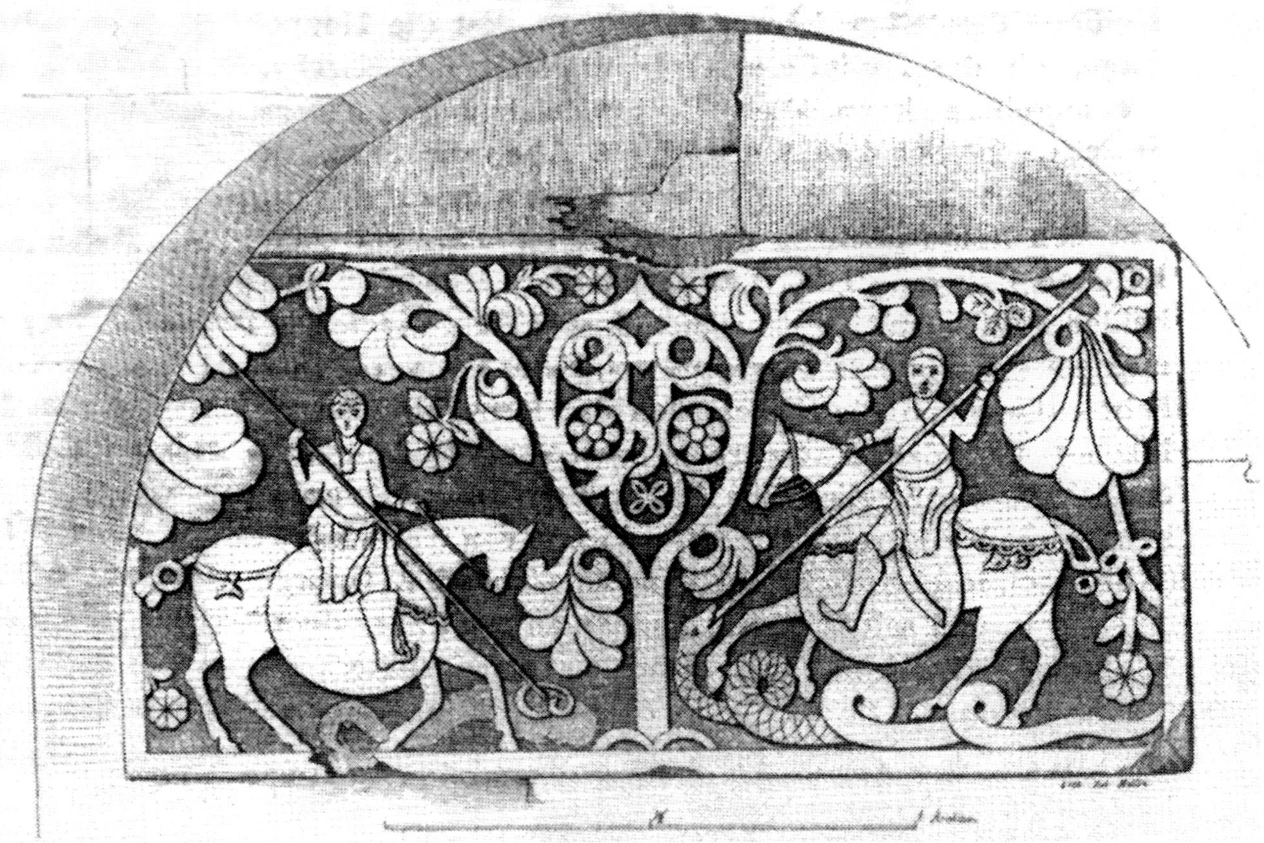

105. **A pair of confronted horsemen separated by a tree fighting dragons.** Drawing of a relief carving, Ani.

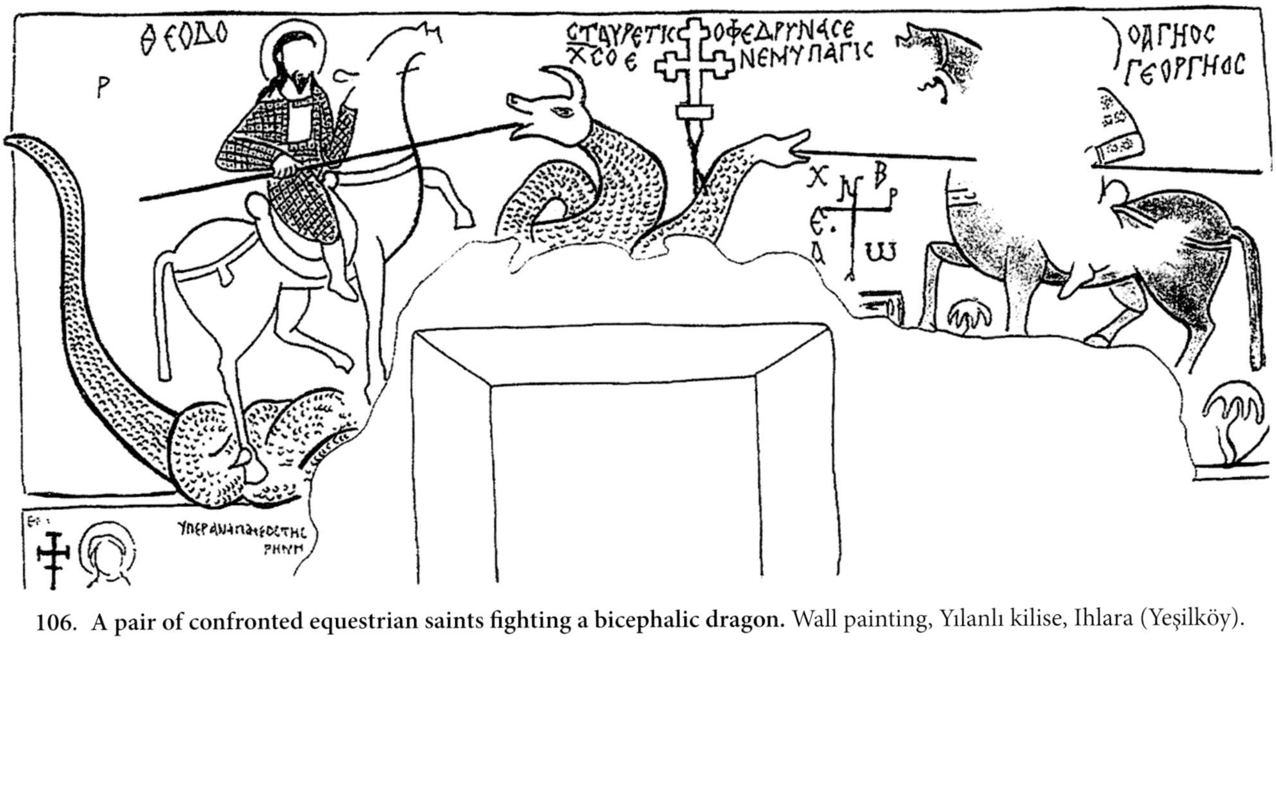

106. **A pair of confronted equestrian saints fighting a bicephalic dragon.** Wall painting, Yılanlı kilise, Ihlara (Yeşilköy).

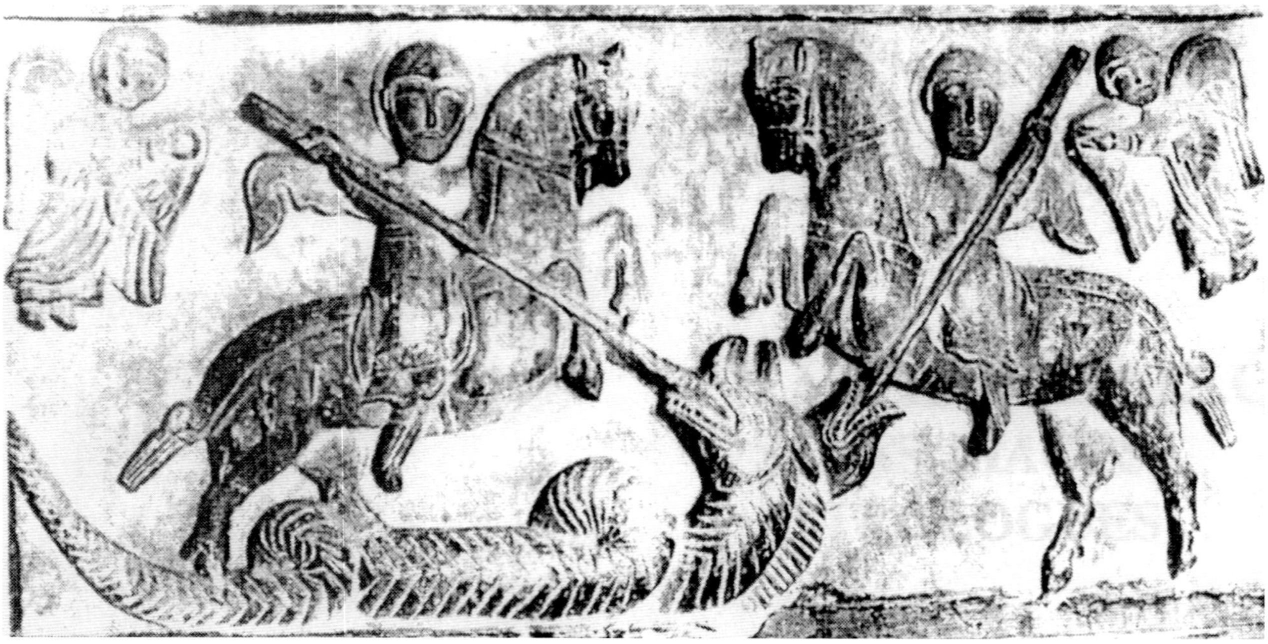

107. A pair of confronted equestrian saints fighting a bicephalic dragon. Relief carving above the western entrance, church of the Virgin, Mart'vili.

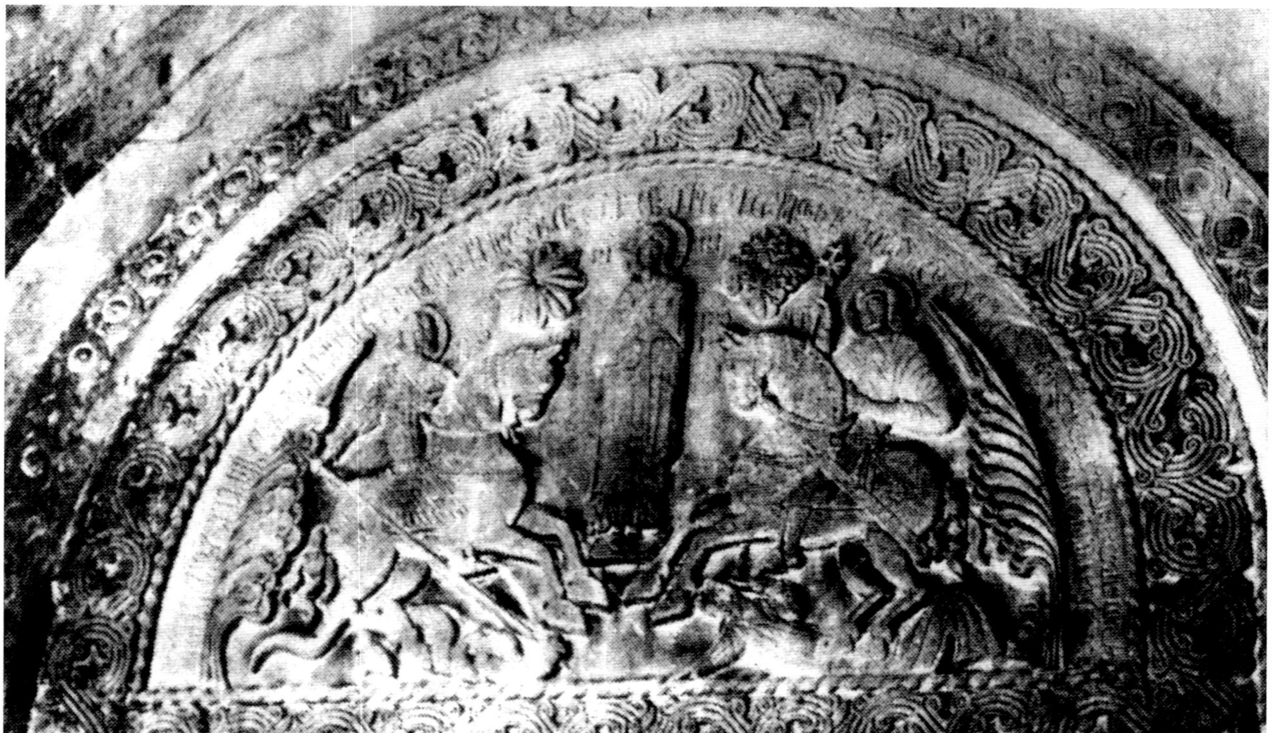

110. A pair of confronted equestrian saints, identified as George and Theodore, killing a supine human figure and a dragon. Relief carving on the eastern façade of the church of Nik'orc'minda, Racha.

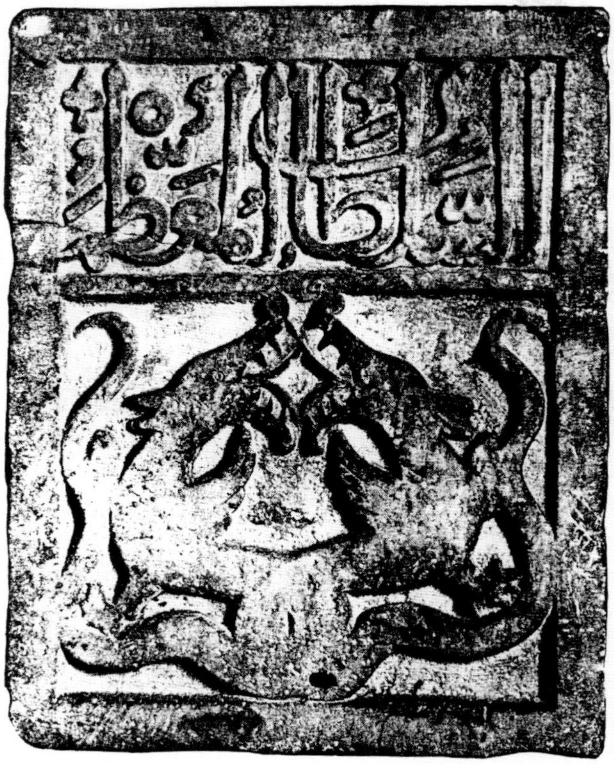

112. **A pair of addorsed winged *regardant* dragons with interlaced tails surmounted by an epigraphic frieze, reading *al-sulṭān al-muʿaẓẓam*.** Relief carving, Mesopotamia.

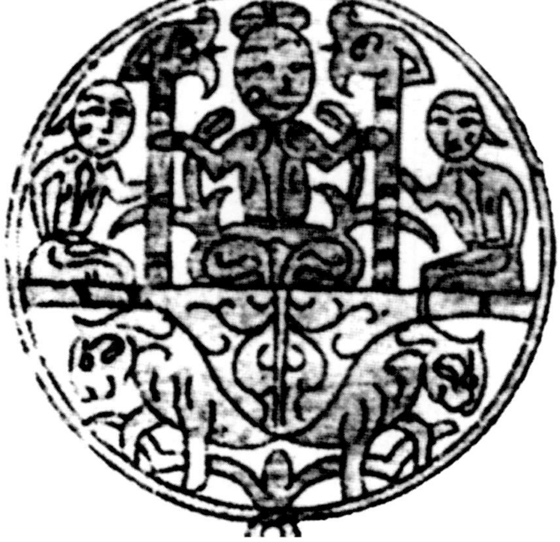

113. **The planet *jawzahar*.** Detail from the "Vaso Vescovali," lidded bowl, possibly Herat.

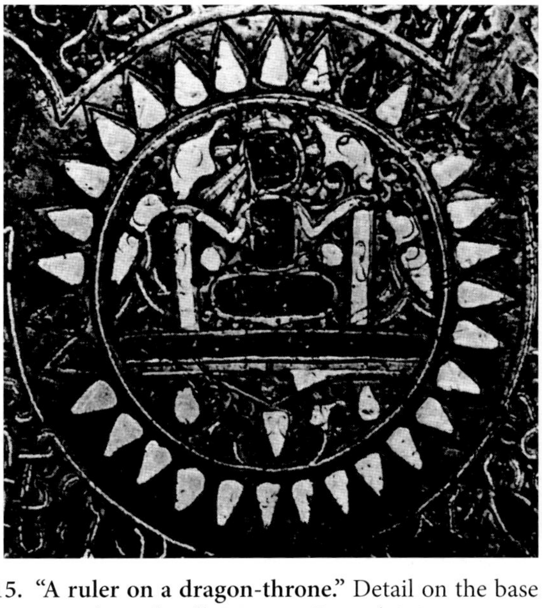

115. **"A ruler on a dragon-throne."** Detail on the base of an inkwell, Western Central Asia.

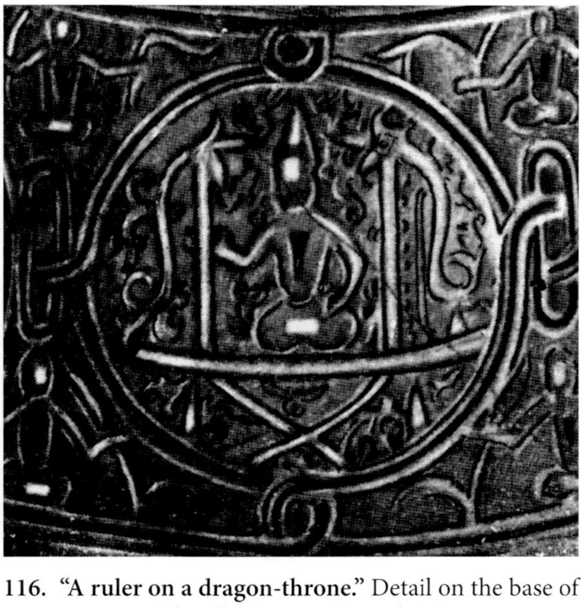

116. **"A ruler on a dragon-throne."** Detail on the base of an inkwell, Western Central Asia.

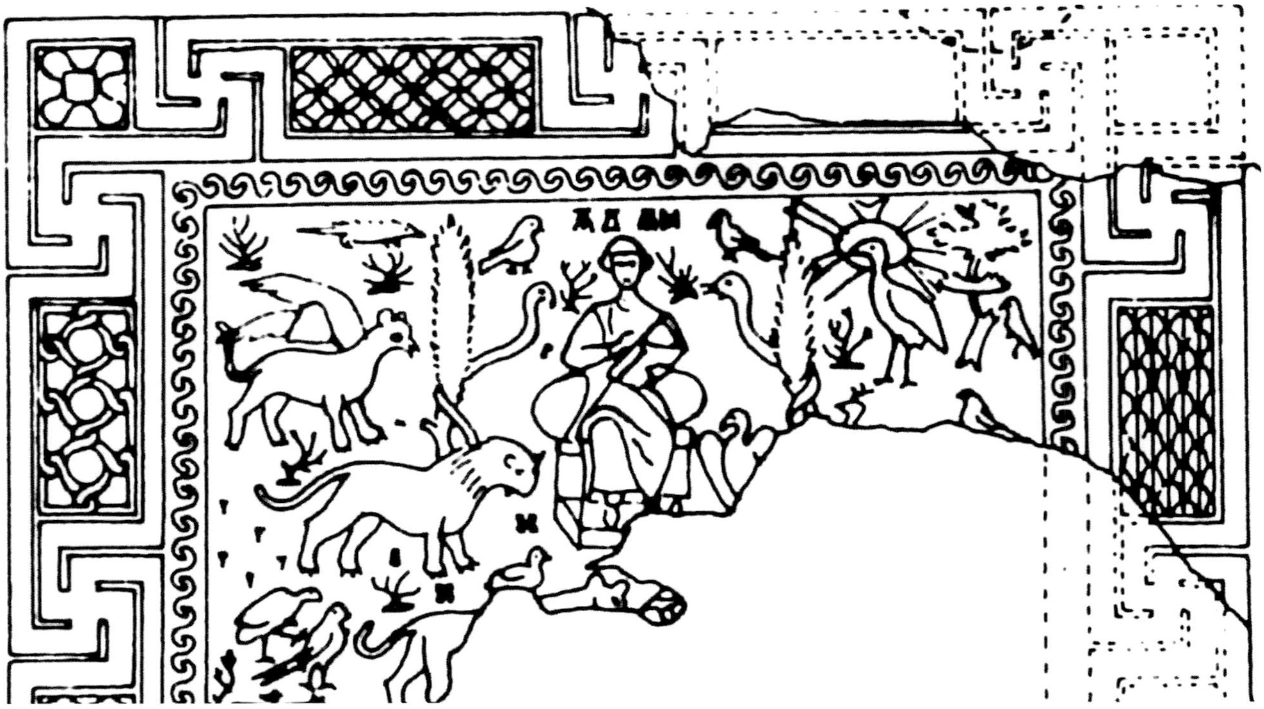

117. **Adam naming the animals framed by serpent-twined trees.** Floor mosaic of apse and nave of the north church, Huarte.

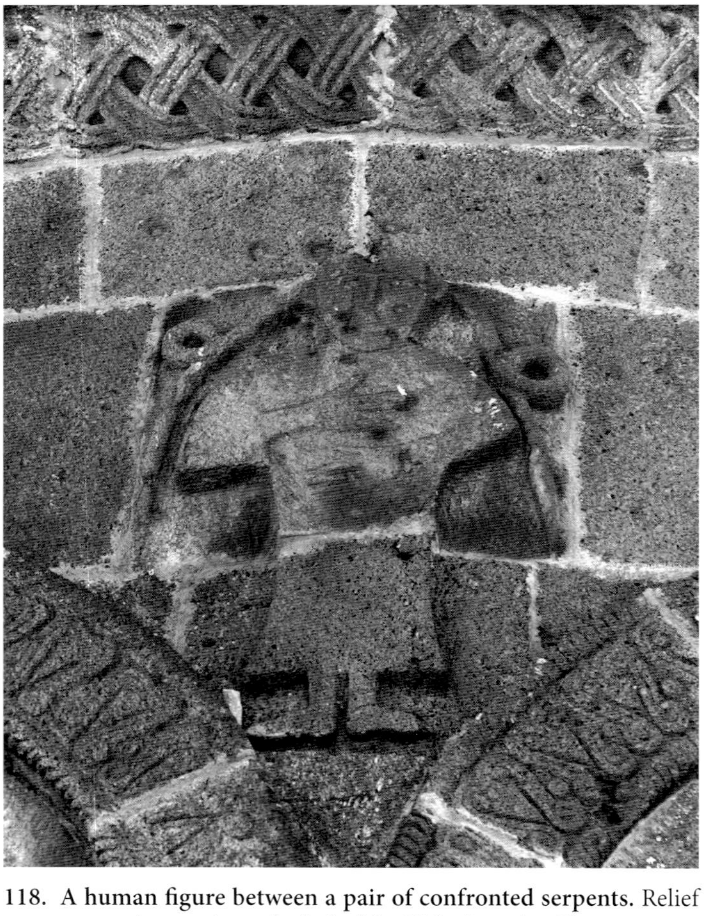

118. **A human figure between a pair of confronted serpents.** Relief carving on the cathedral of the Holy Apostles, Kars.

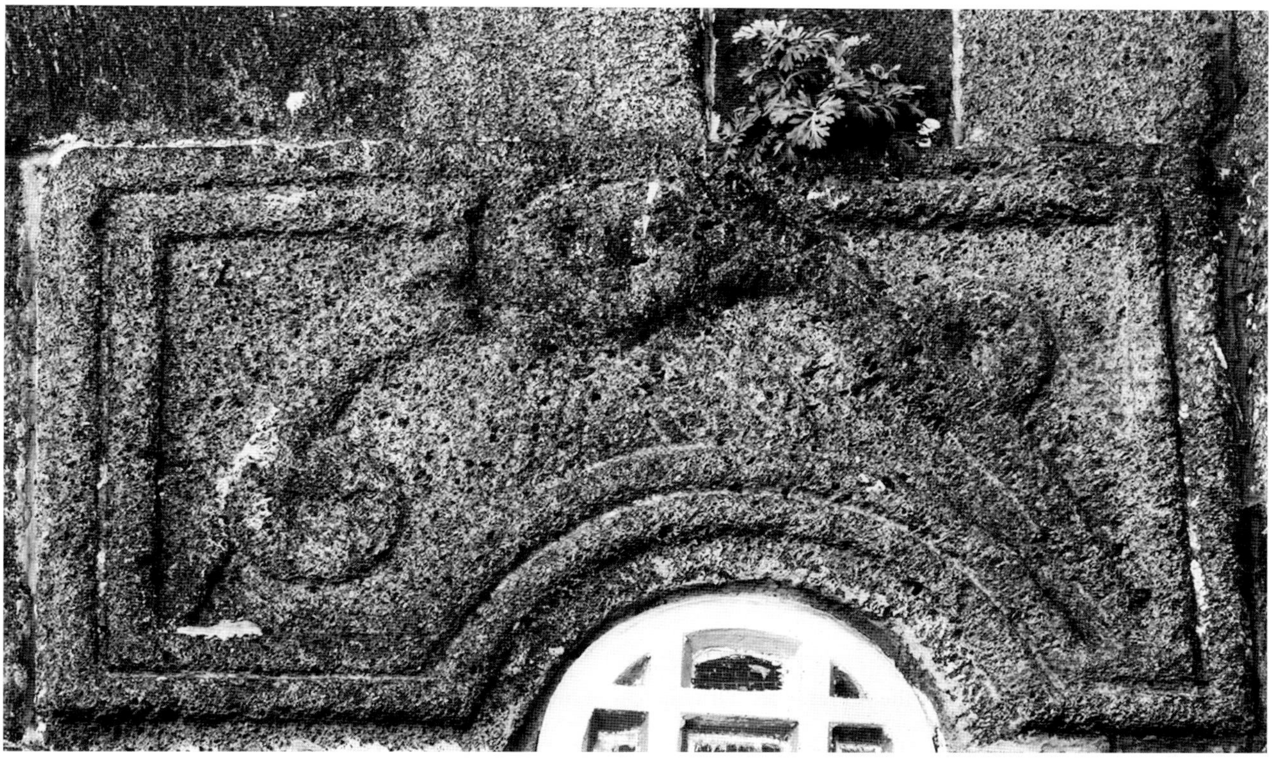

119. A human bust between a pair of confronted serpents. Relief carving on the cathedral of the Holy Apostles, Kars.

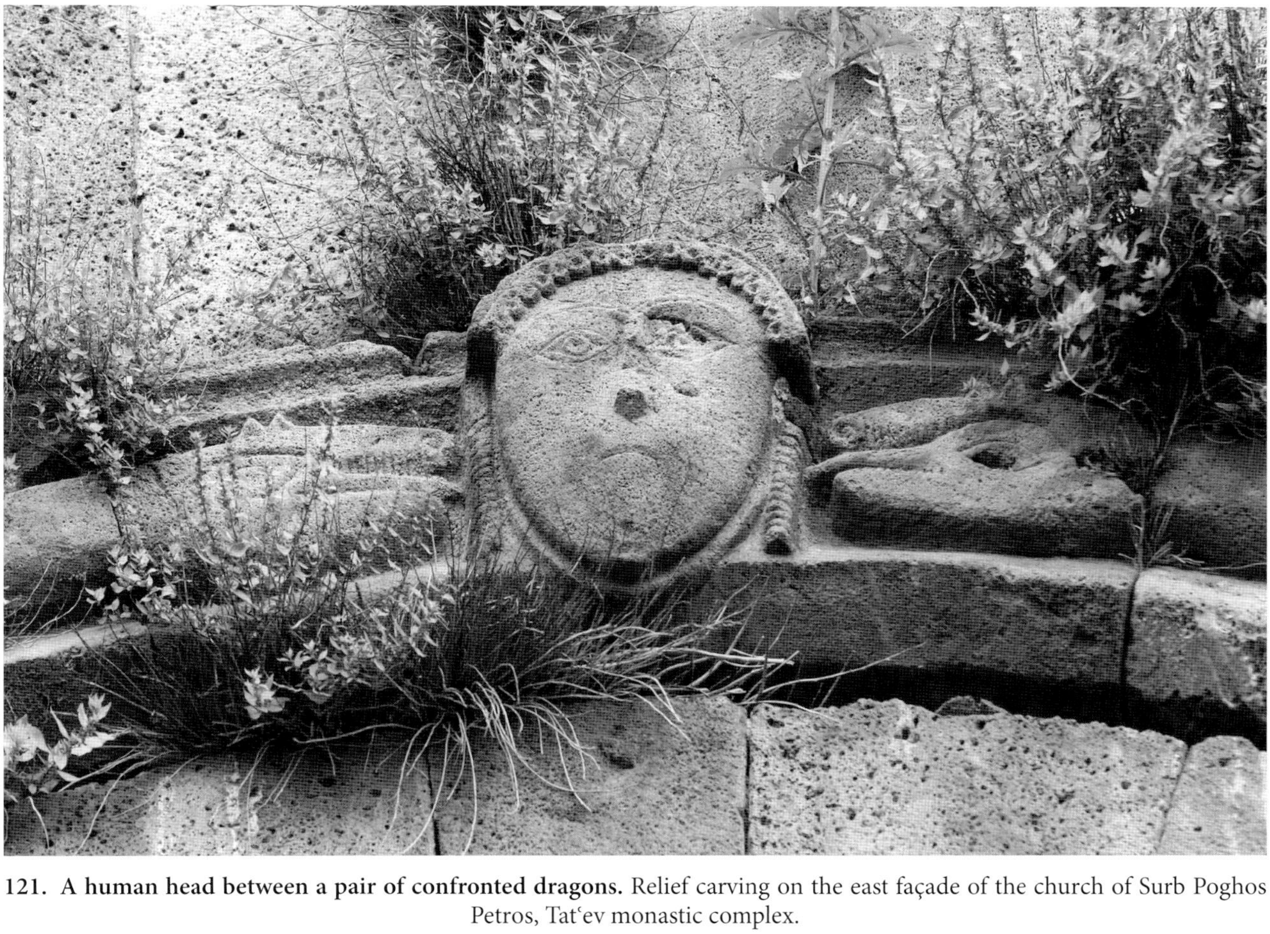

121. A human head between a pair of confronted dragons. Relief carving on the east façade of the church of Surb Poghos Petros, Tat'ev monastic complex.

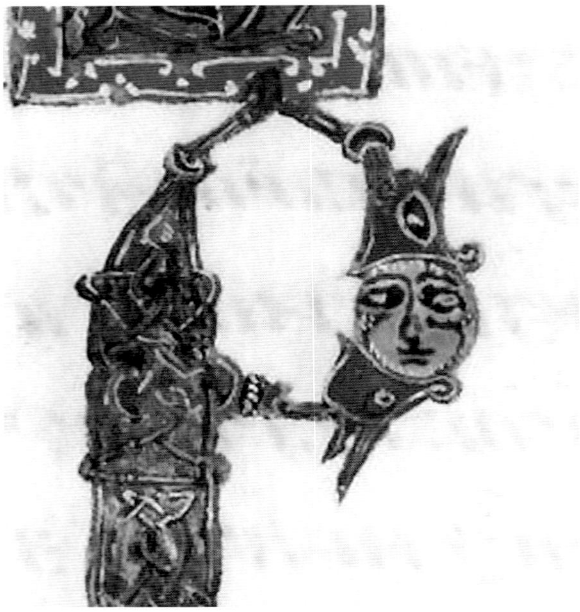

123. **A human head between a pair of confronted dragon heads inserted in the loop of the initial letter.** Ornament on the first page of the Gospel of Luke, monastery of Paughoskan, region of Mlich.

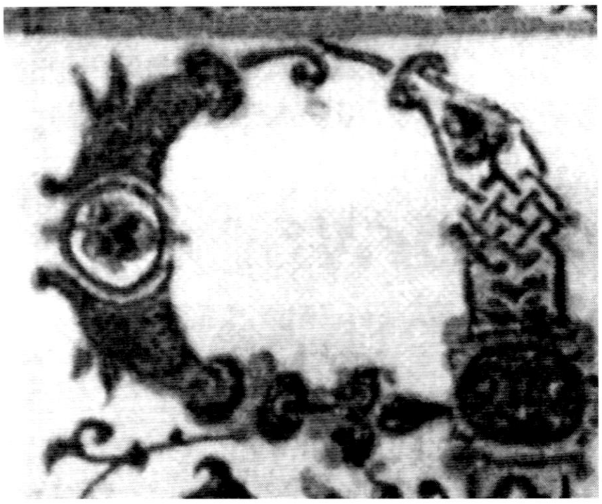

125. **A palmette between a pair of confronted dragon heads inserted in the loop of the initial letter.** Ornament on the first page of the Gospel of Matthew, Armenia.

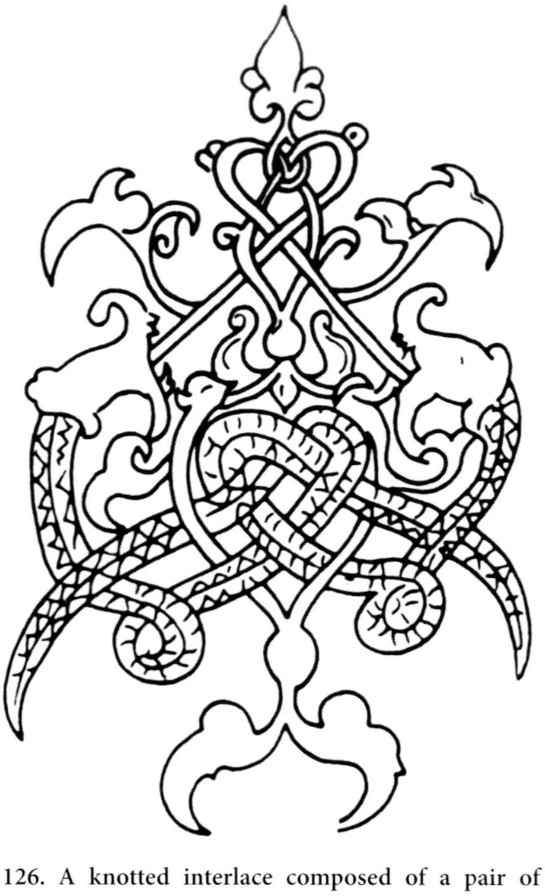

126. **A knotted interlace composed of a pair of confronted dragons issuing vegetation.** Marginal ornament in the Mush Homiliary, monastery of Avagvank‘, Erznga(n).

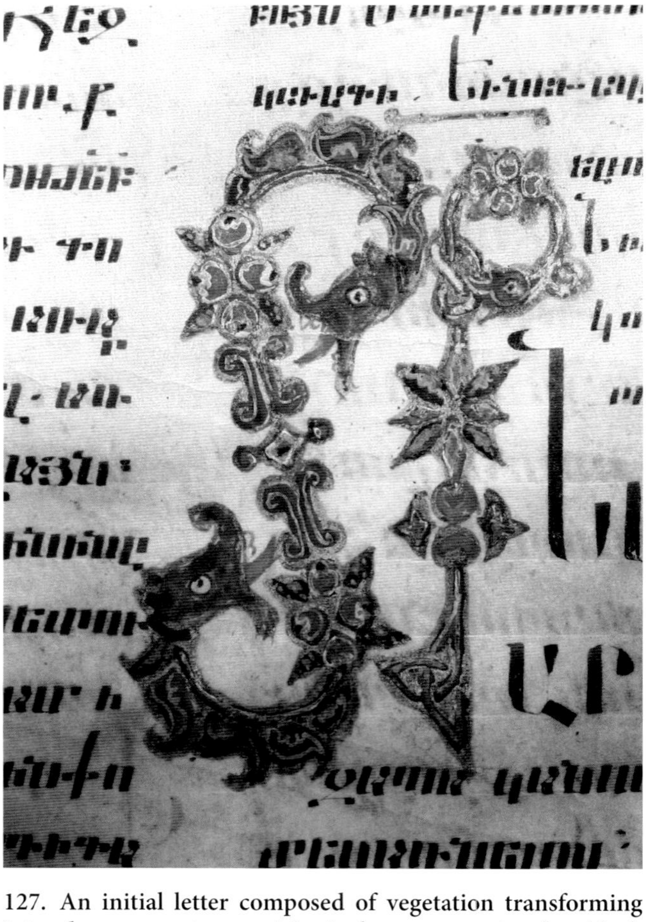

127. **An initial letter composed of vegetation transforming into dragon protomes.** Marginal ornament in the Mush Homiliary, monastery of Avagvank‘, Erznga(n).

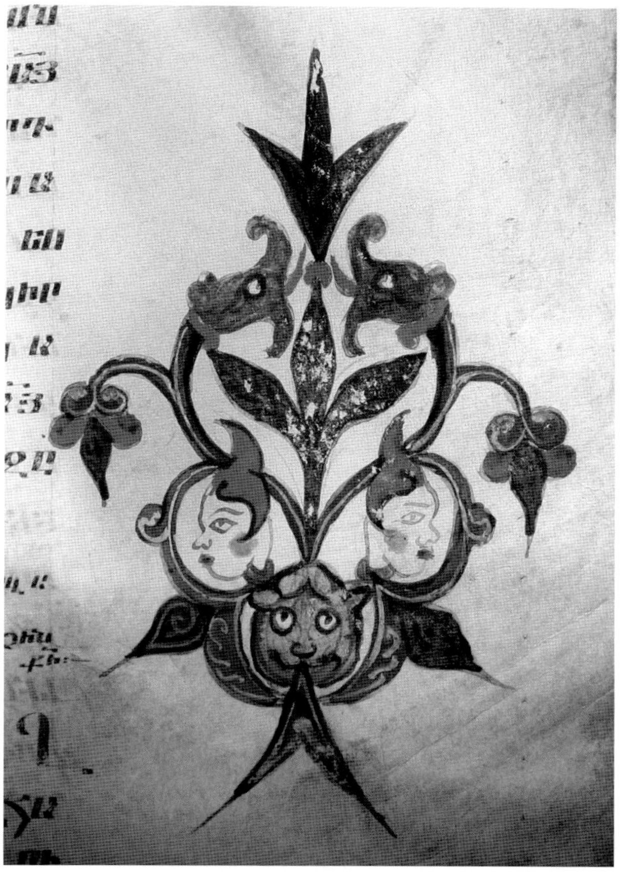

132. A lion head with a pair of addorsed human heads and a pair of confronted dragon heads linked by means of a vegetal interlace. Marginal ornament in the Mush Homiliary, monastery of Avagvank', Erznga(n).

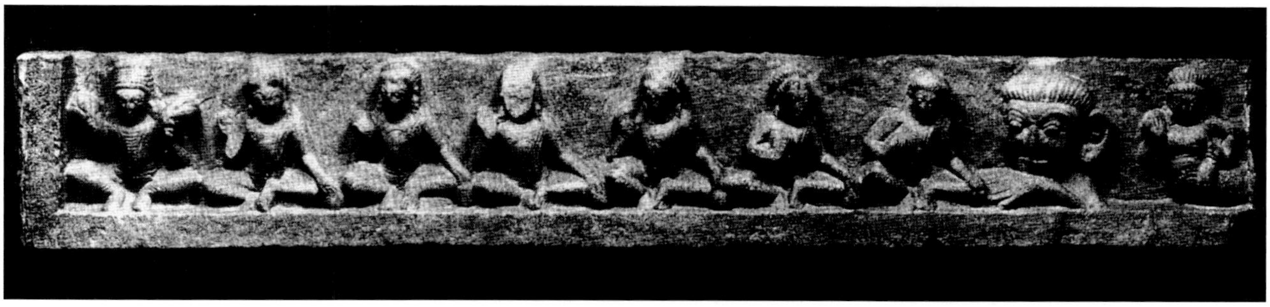

140. Nine planetary deities including Rāhu and Ketu. Relief carving, Uttar Pradesh.

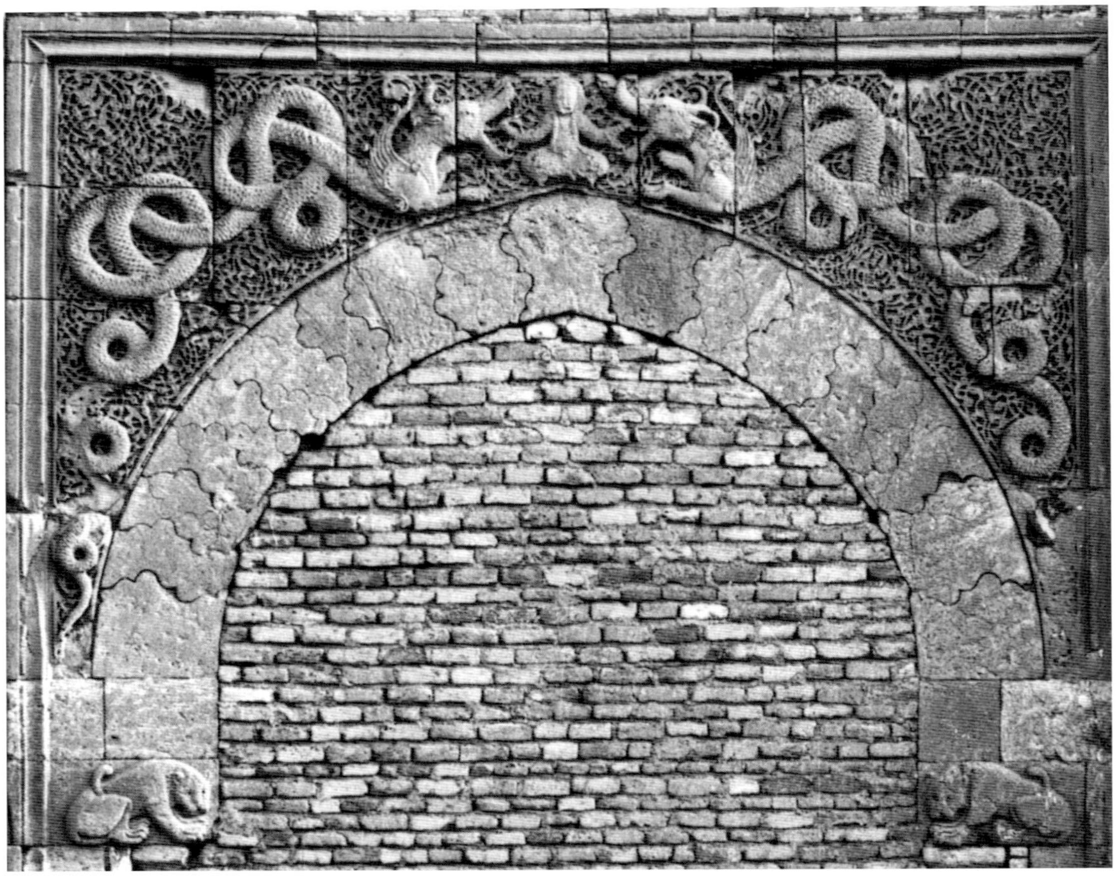

139a and b. A seated human figure between a pair of winged confronted dragons with forelegs. Relief carving on the archivolt of the so-called Talisman Gate (Bāb al-Ṭilasm), Baghdad.

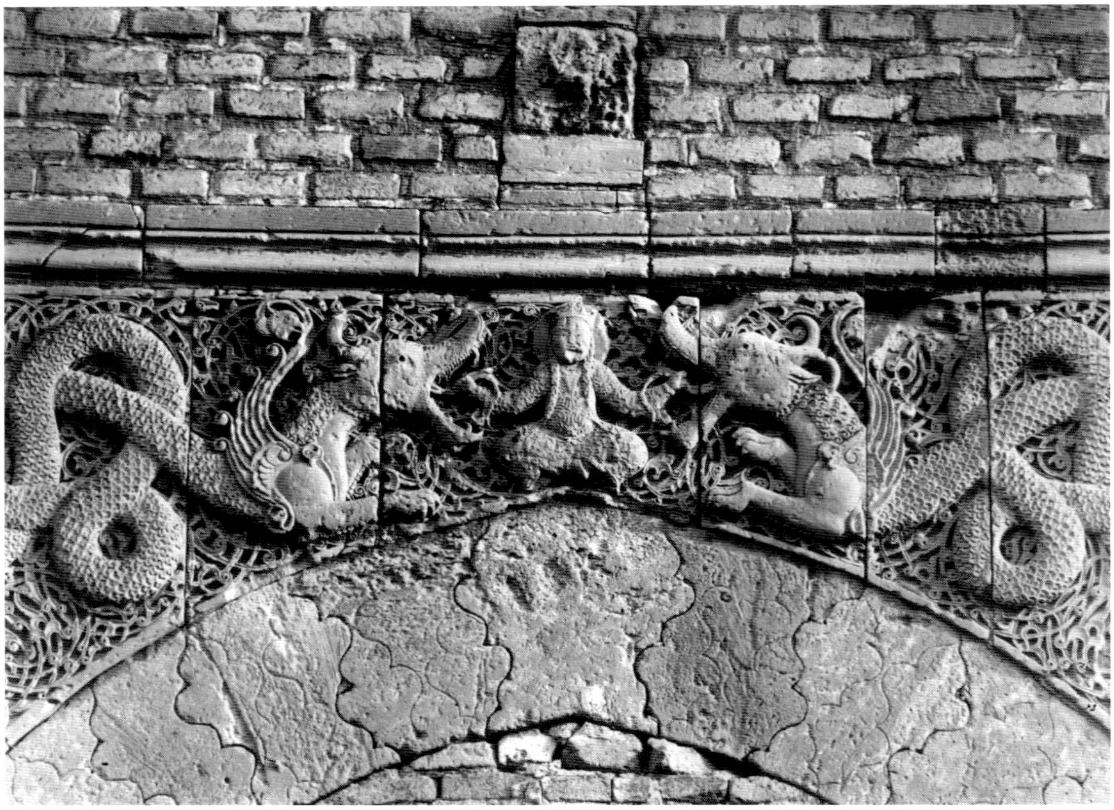

139b

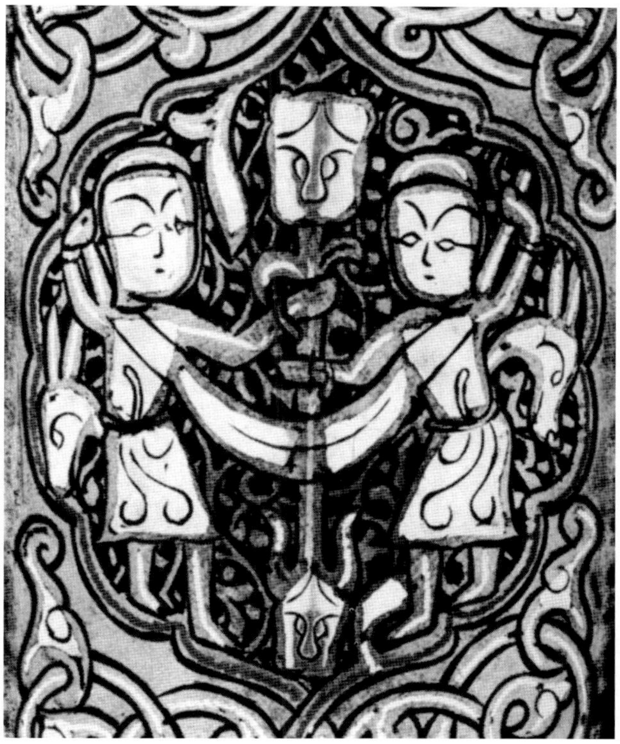

141. **Sign of the zodiac featuring the eclipse pseudo-planet *(al-jawzahar)* at the points of exaltation of its head or tail in Gemini.** Detail from the body of a ewer, possibly Herat.

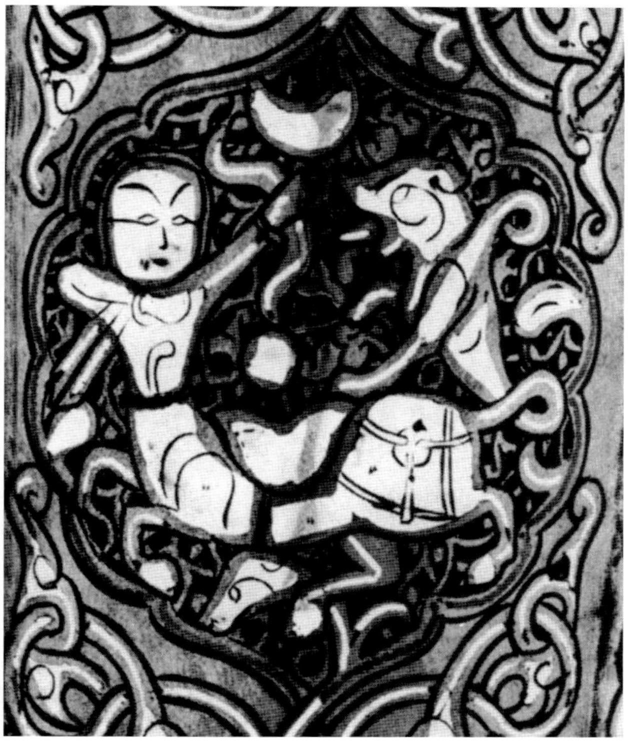

142. **Sign of the zodiac featuring the planetary eclipse in Sagittarius shown as dragon-tailed centaur.** Detail from the body of a ewer, possibly Herat.

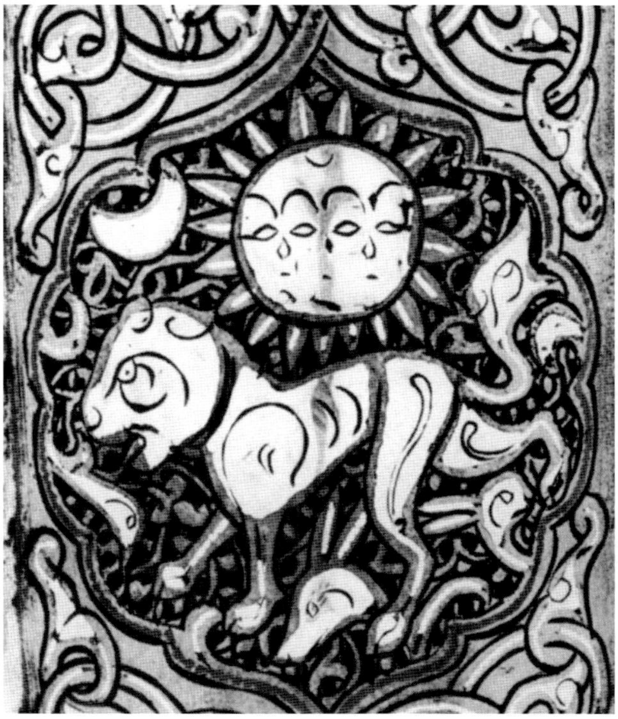

143. **Sign of the zodiac featuring the planetary eclipse *(al-jawzahar)* threatening the Sun in Leo.** Detail from the body of a ewer, possibly Herat.

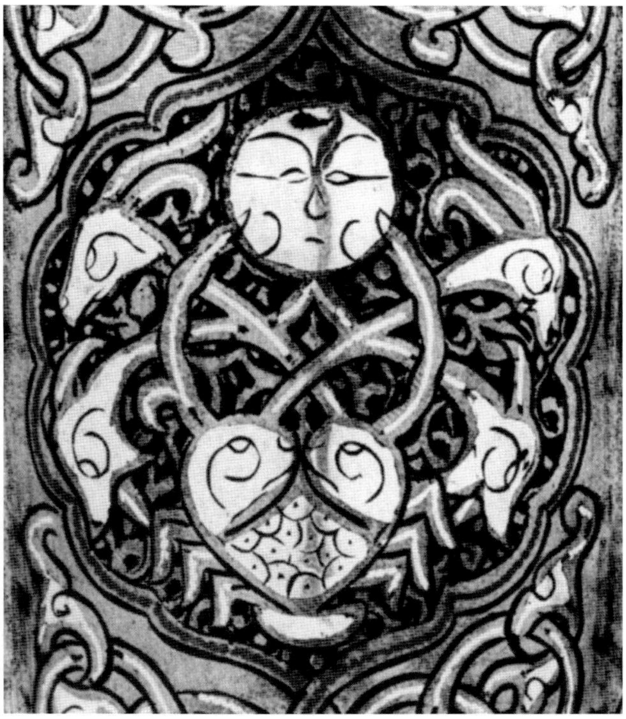

144. **Sign of the zodiac featuring the planetary eclipse *(al-jawzahar)* threatening the Moon in Cancer.** Detail from the body of a ewer, possibly Herat.

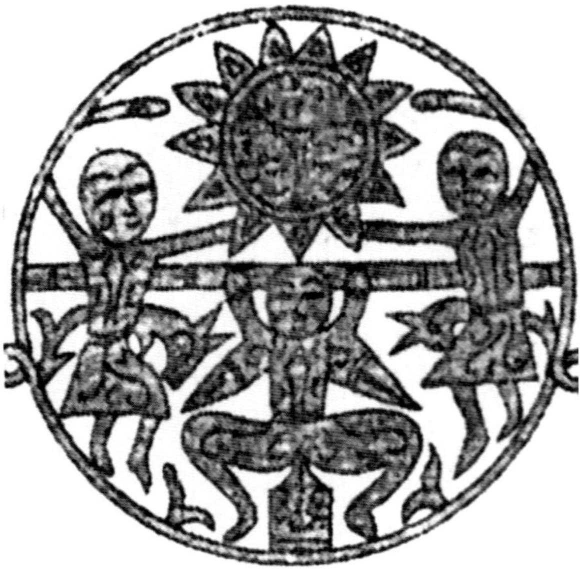

145. Sign of the zodiac featuring the Sun. Detail from the "Vaso Vescovali," lidded bowl, possibly Herat.

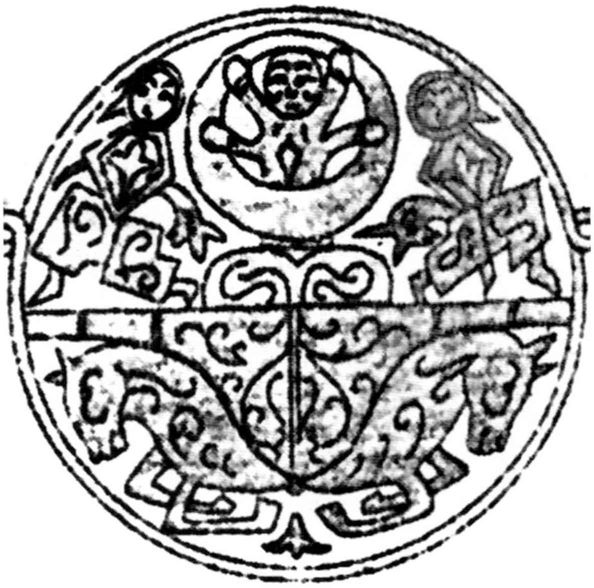

146. Sign of the zodiac featuring the Moon. Detail from the "Vaso Vescovali," lidded bowl, possibly Herat.

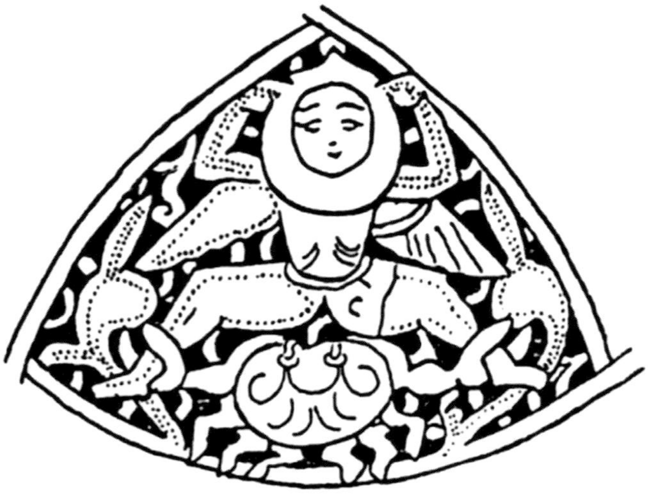

147. Sign of the zodiac featuring the Moon in Cancer. Detail from the so-called Wade Cup, northwest Iran.

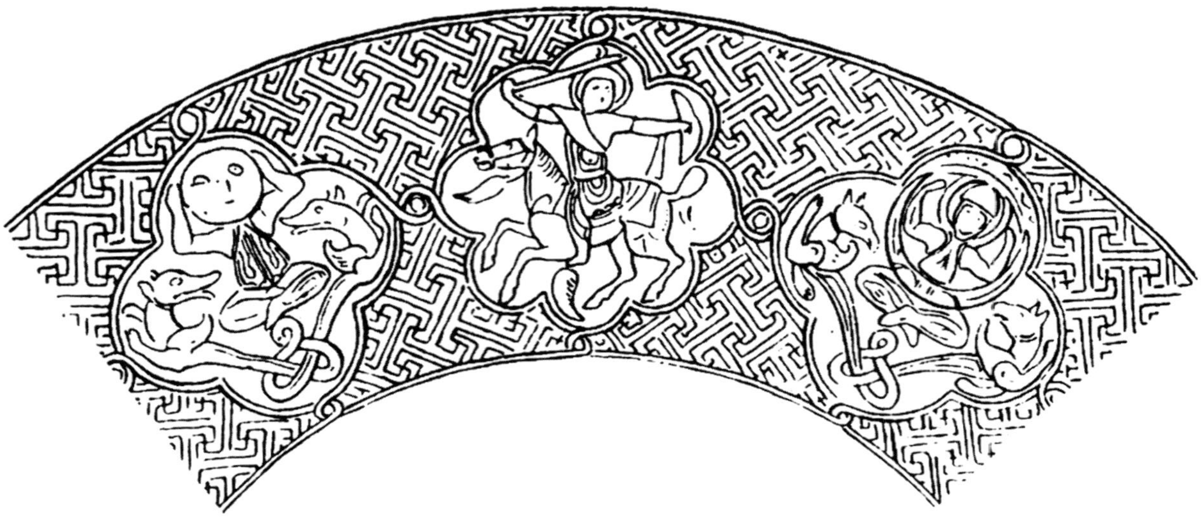

148. Sol and Luna above a pair of addorsed winged *regardant* dragons. Detail from a basin of the *atābeg* Badr al-Dīn Lu'lu', Mosul.

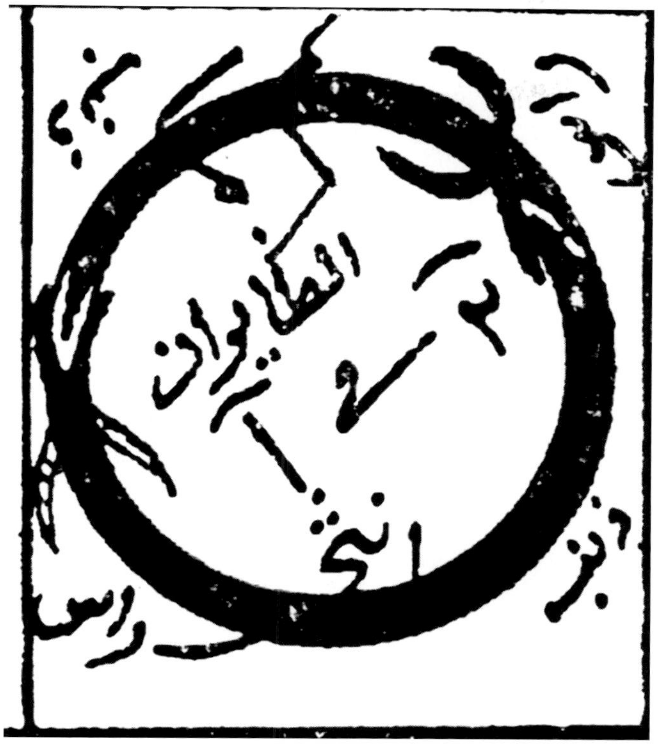

149. A pair of fabulous creatures in circular arrangement biting each other's tails. Painting in a copy of Muḥammad ibn Umayl's *Kitāb al-Māʾ al-Waraqī wa ʾl-Arḍ al-Najmīya*.

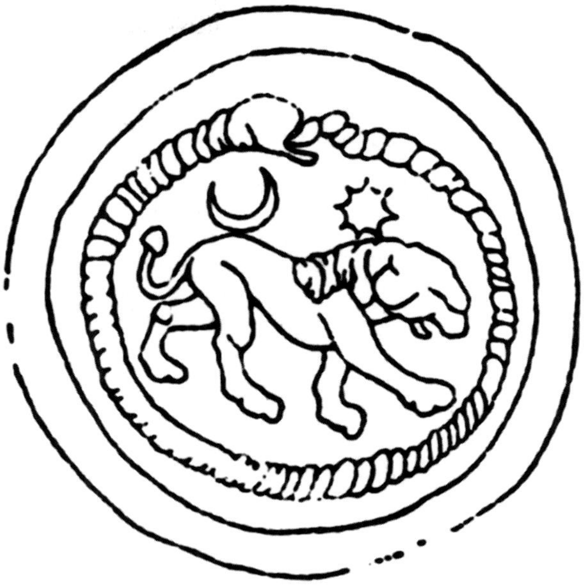

150. A crescent and stars above a lion, encircled by an *ouroboros* serpent. Seal, Iranian world.

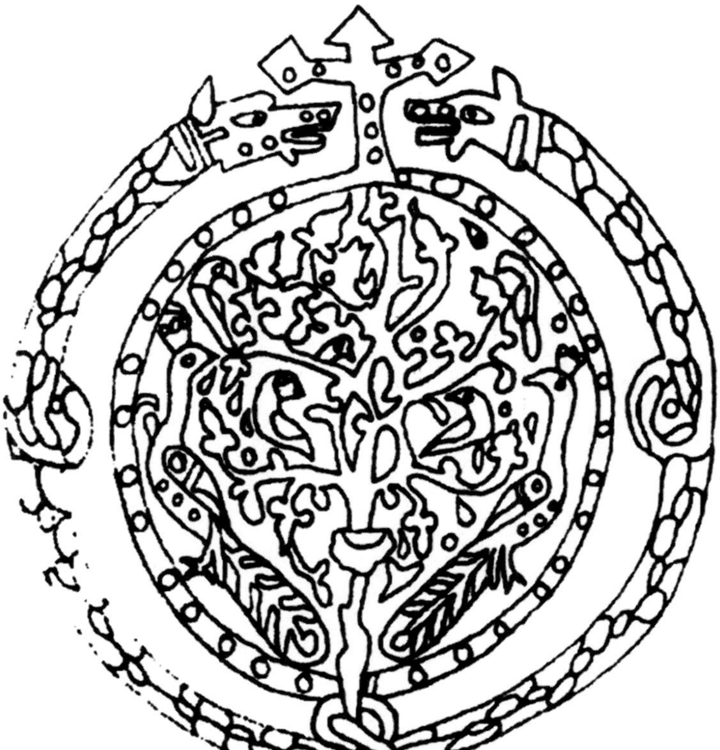

151. The world as seen by Alexander. Medallion from the Pala d'Oro, Constantinople.

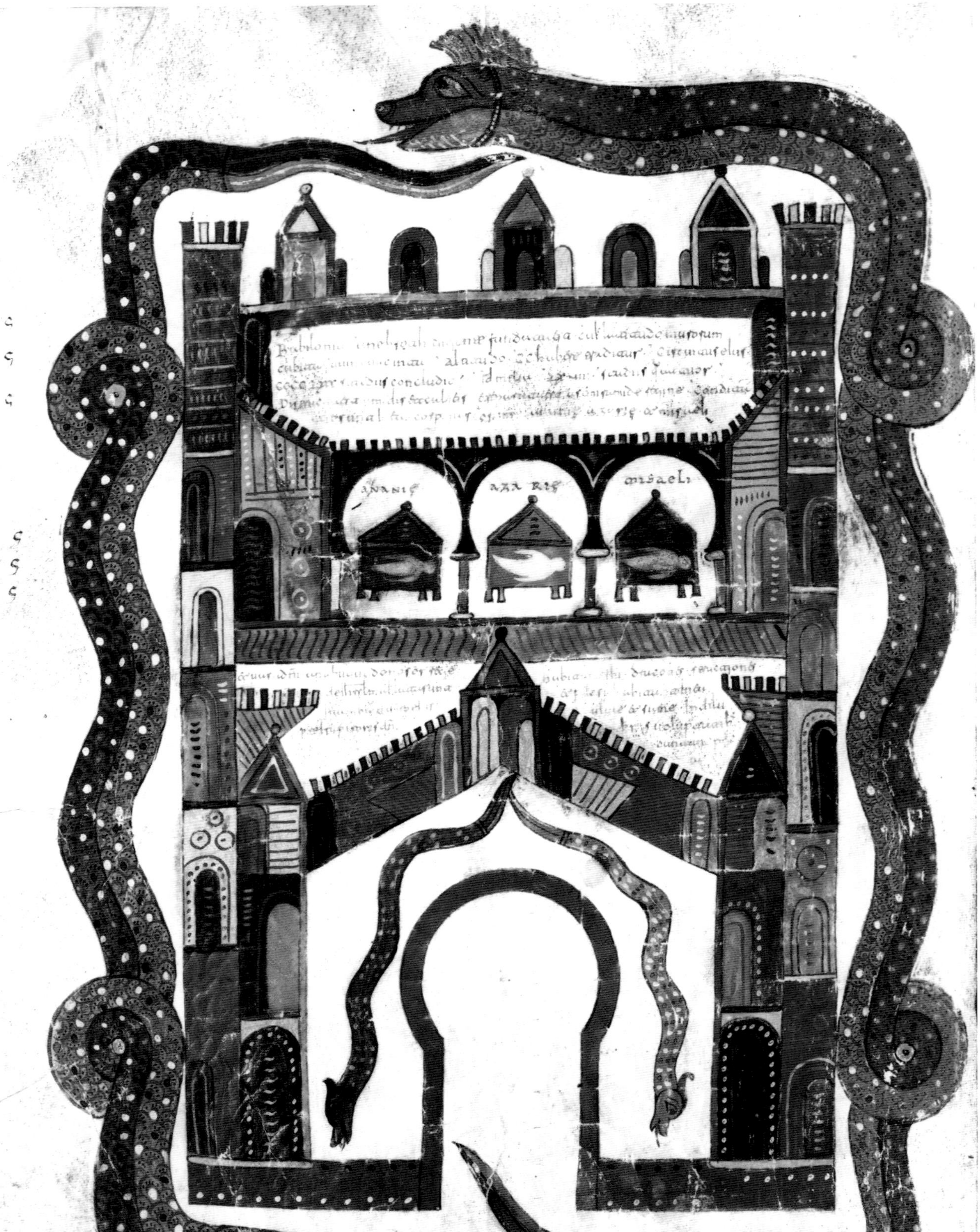

152. The city of Babylon enclosed by a pair of dragons. Illustration from the Morgan Beatus, kingdom of Léon.

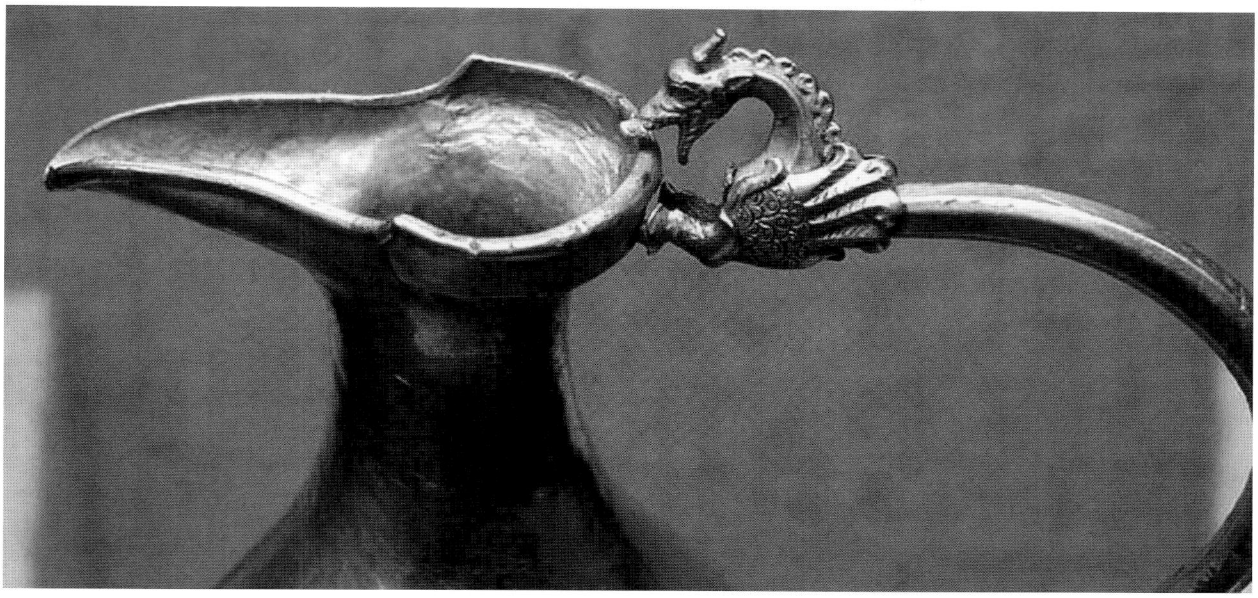

162. **A winged dragon protome.** The top of a jug handle. Provenance unknown.

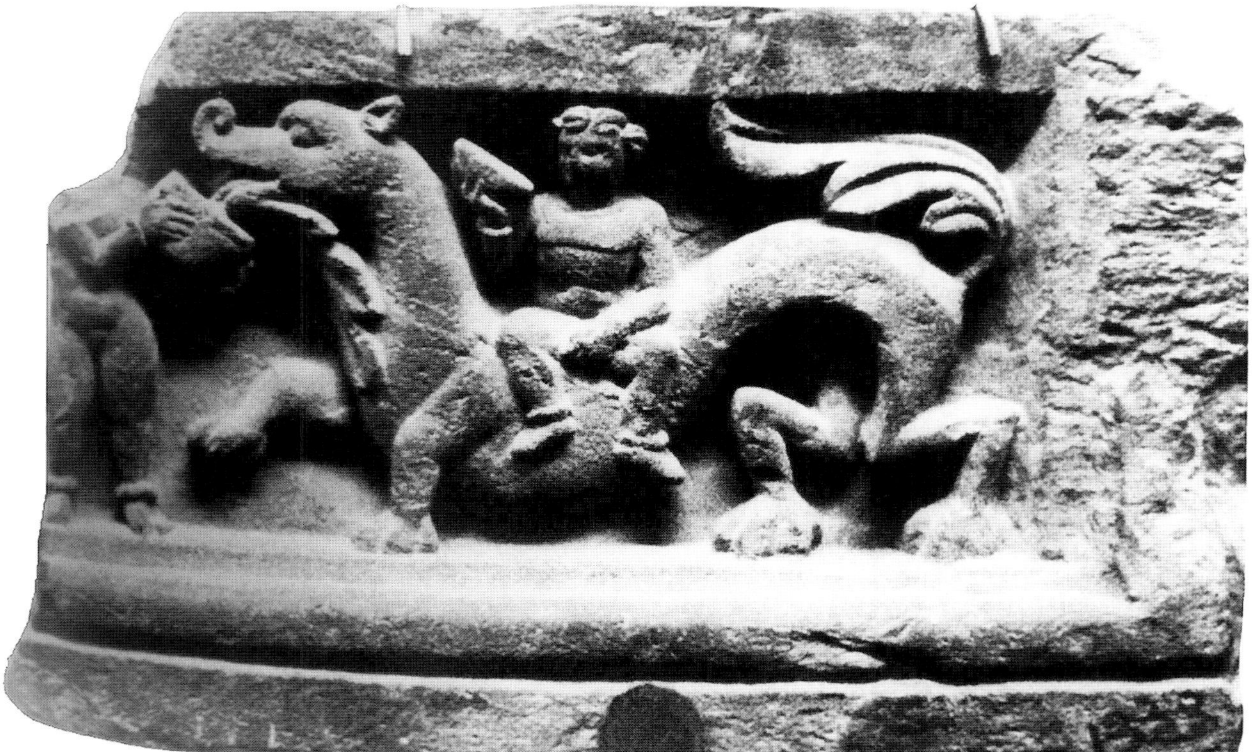

164. **A quadruped dragon drinking from a cup.** Relief carving, Gandhāra region.

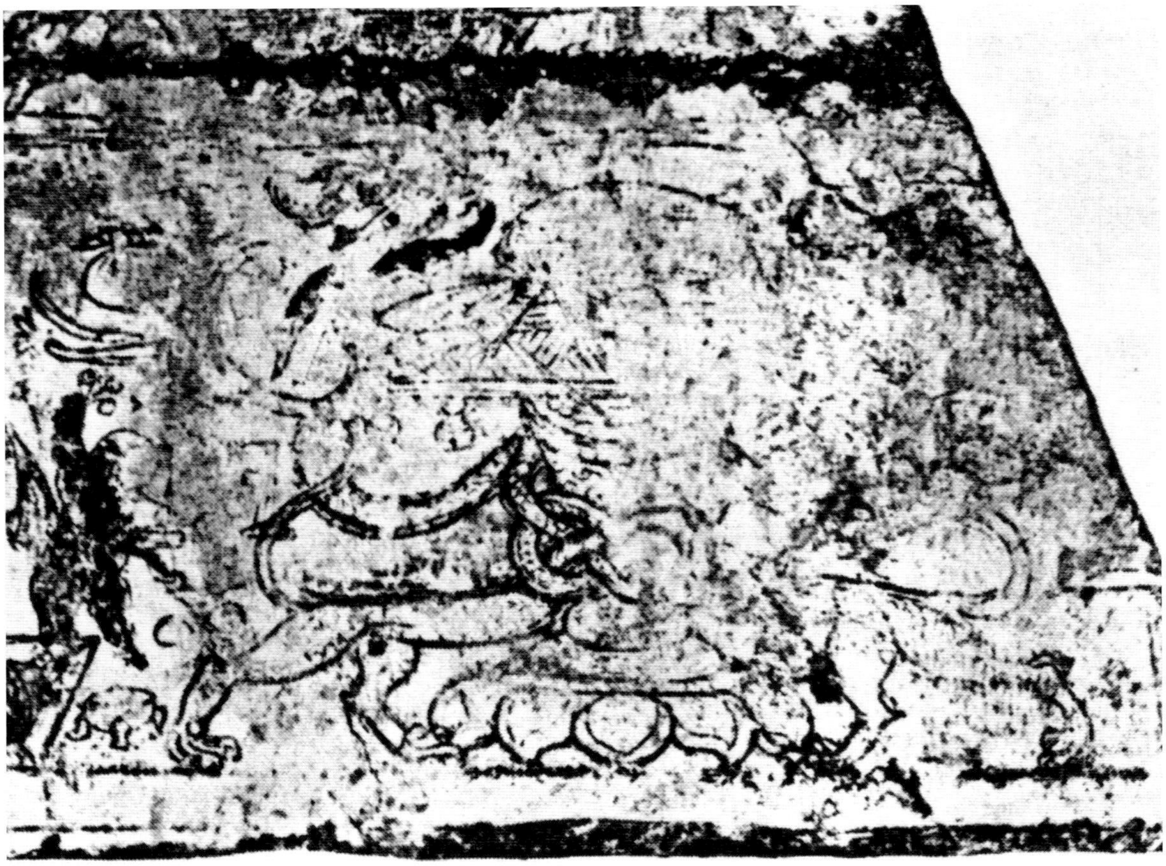

167. A pair of upright confronted quadruped dragons with a quadripartite knot. Wall painting, Shorchuk.

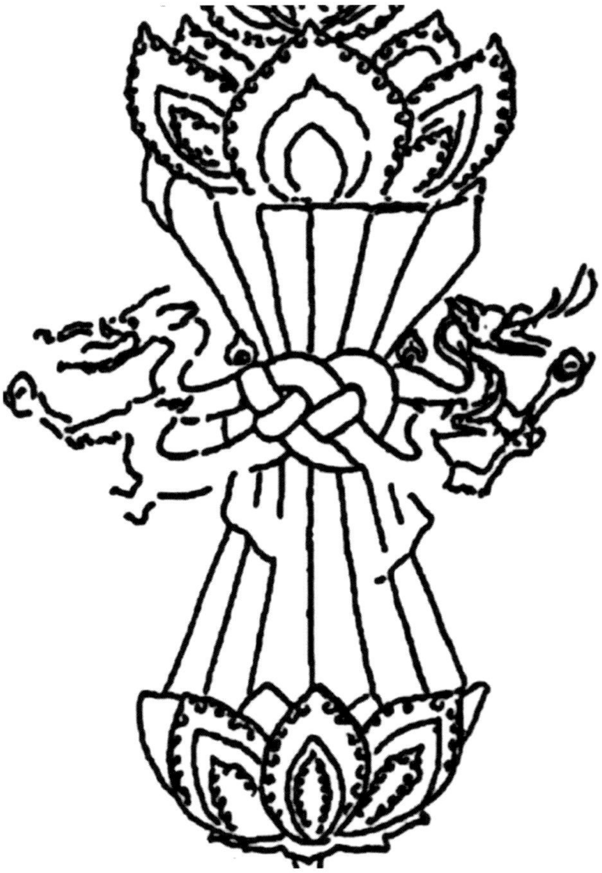

168. A pair of addorsed quadruped dragons with a quadripartite knot. Wall painting, Bezeklik.

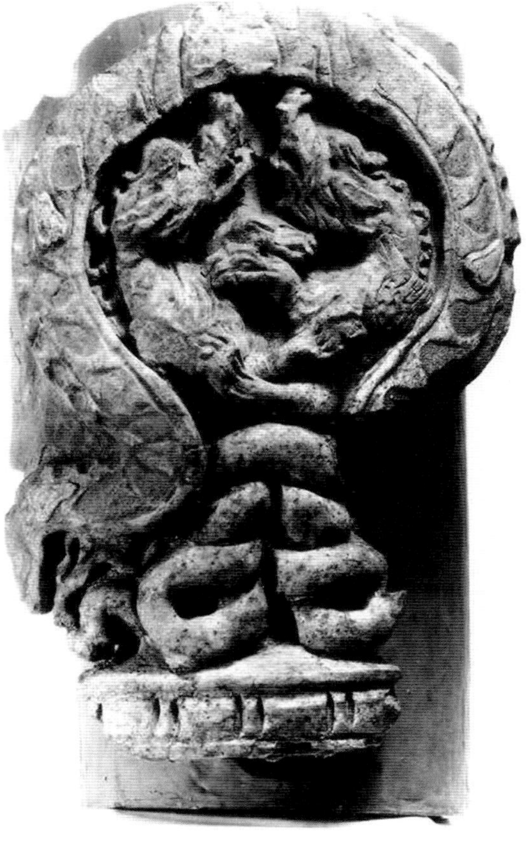

170. A pair of confronted dragons with forelegs with a Herakles knot. Fragment of a relief frieze, Panjikent.

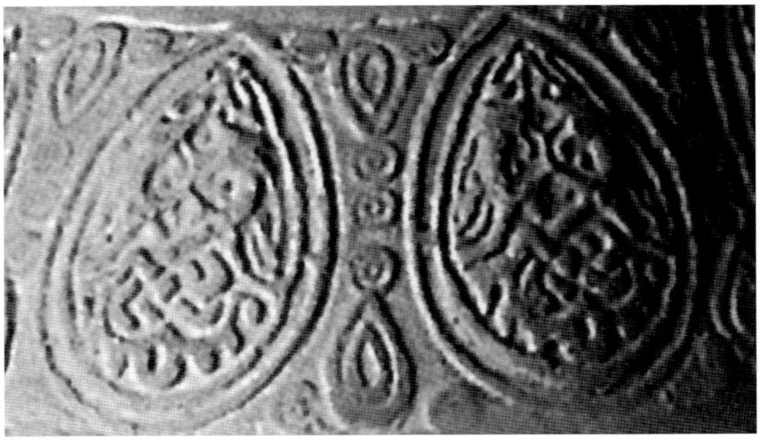

172. **Pairs of confronted dragons with quadripartite knots.** Jug with filter, northern Syria.

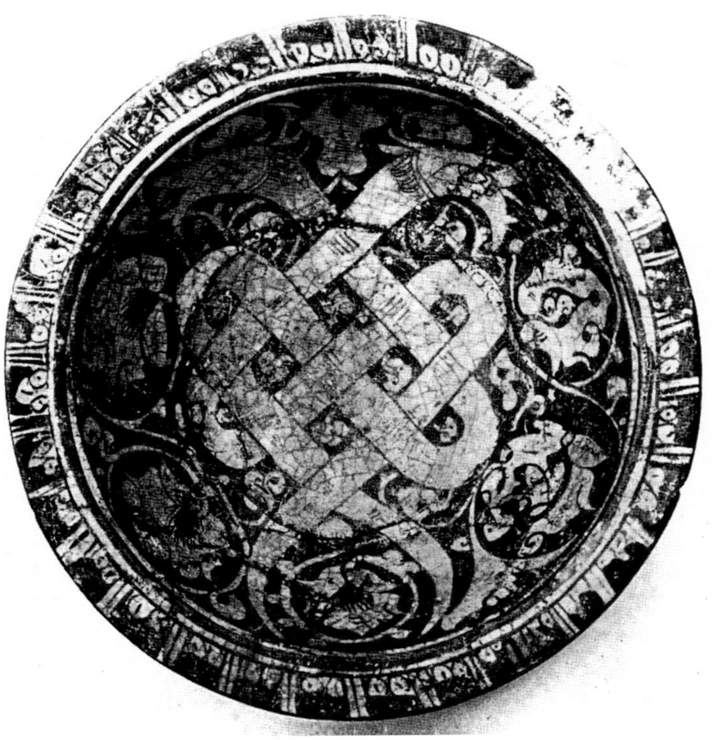

173. **A pair of addorsed dragons with a quadripartite knot.** Bowl, Raqqa.

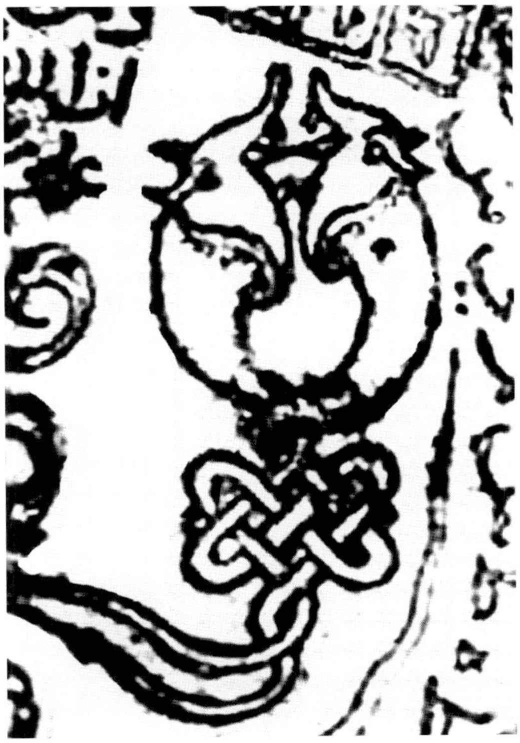

174. **A pair of confronted dragons with a quadripartite knot.** Detail from a talismanic bowl.

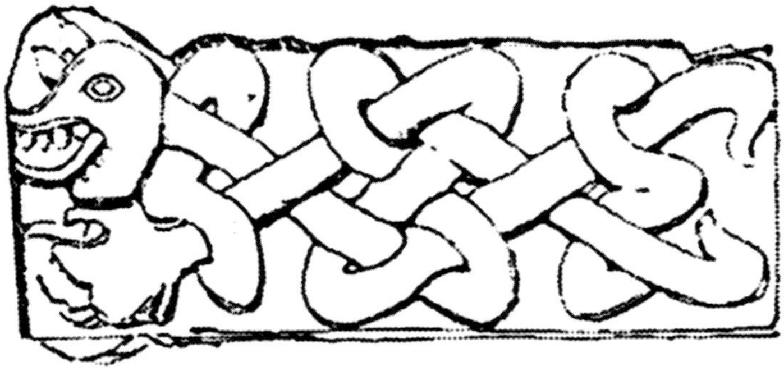

175. **A pair of confronted dragons with a quadripartite knot.** Relief carving on the hospital *(darüşşifa)*, Çankırı.

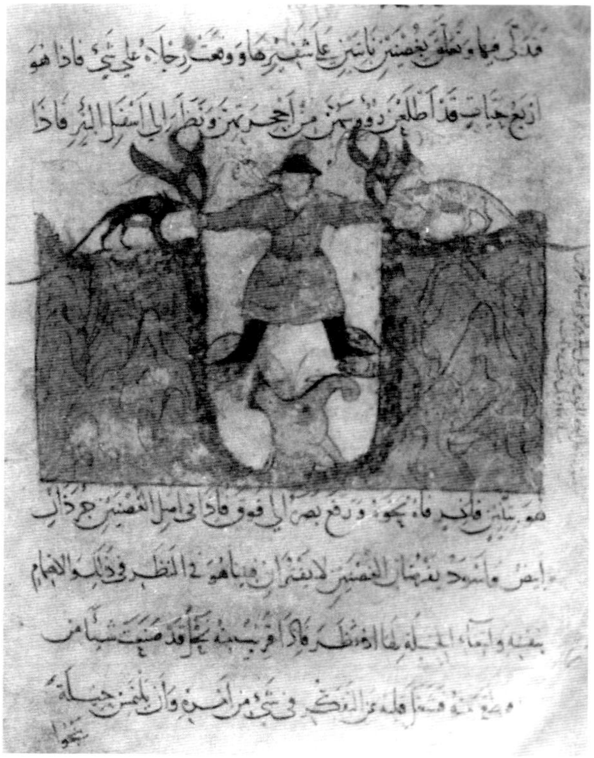

180. **"The Perils of Life."** Illustration from the *Kalīla wa Dimna*, Baghdad (?).

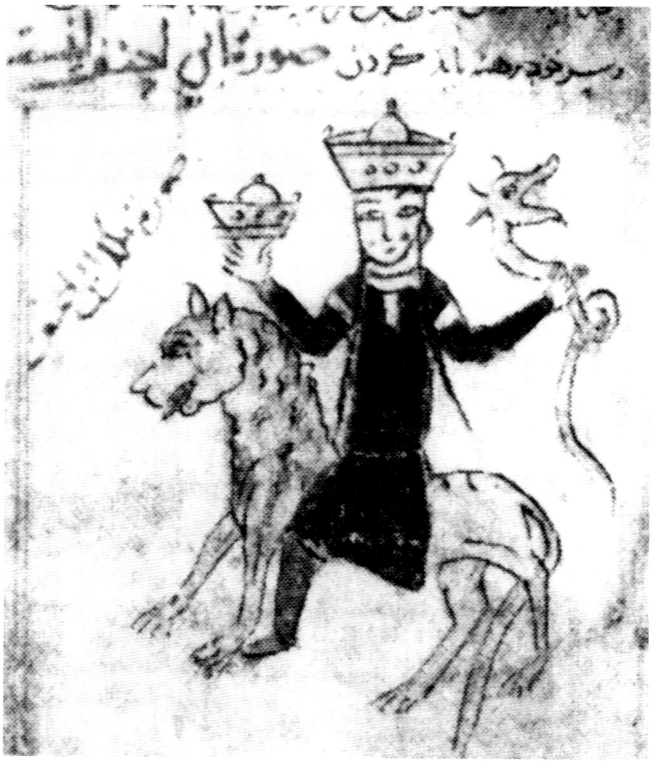

181. **The angel Abi 'l-Ḥanaf as crowned lion rider holding a dragon-sceptre.** Painting in a copy of the *Daqā'iq al-Ḥaqā'iq*, Aksaray.

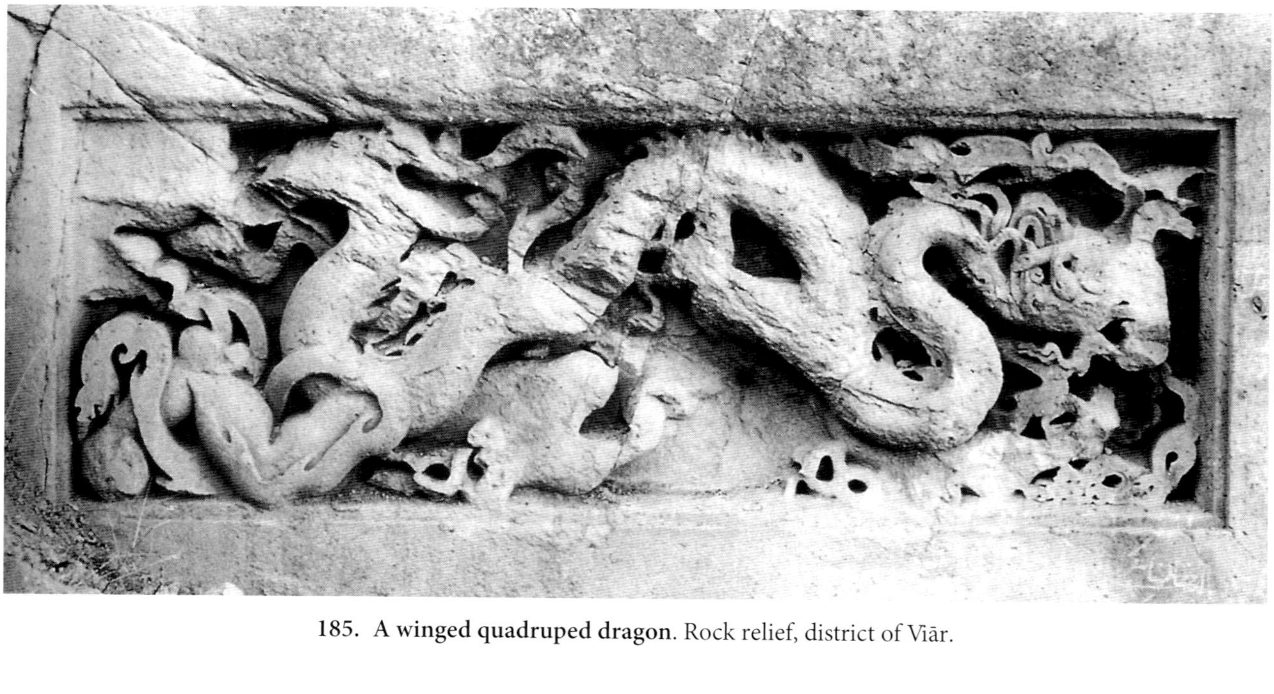

185. **A winged quadruped dragon**. Rock relief, district of Viār.

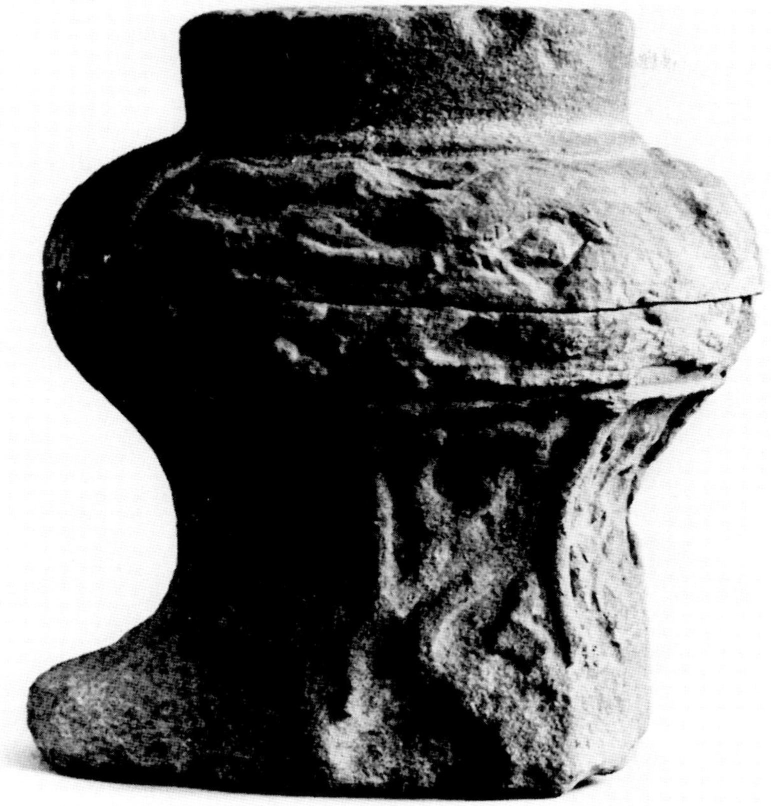

187a and b. A winged quadruped dragon. Relief carving around the torus of the round capitals, Takht-i Sulaimān.

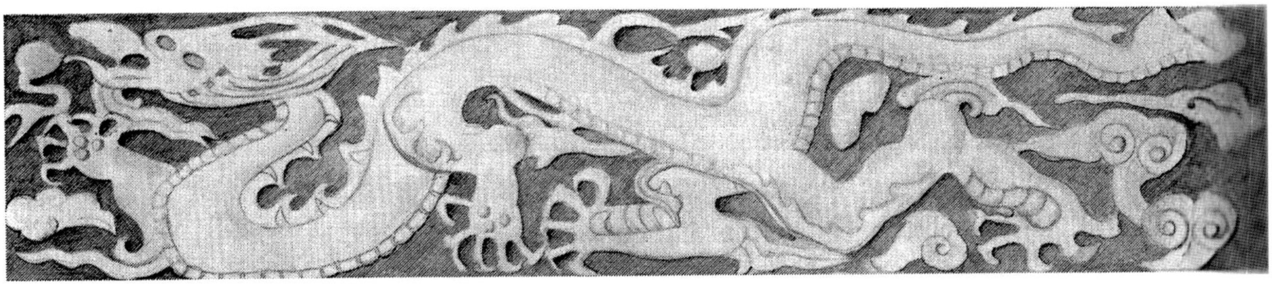

187b

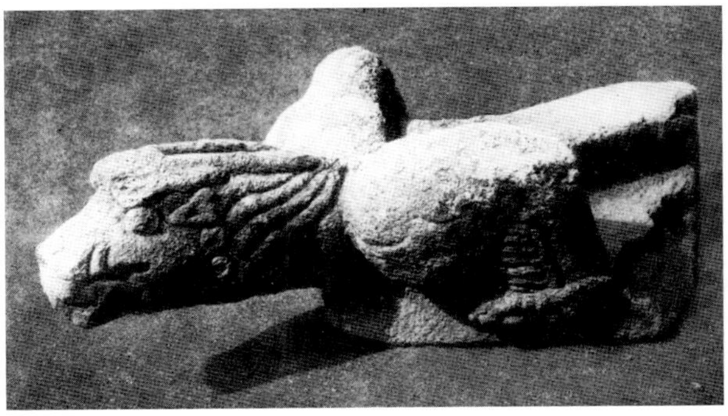

188. A dragon protome. Relief carving, Kondui palace, Transbaikal region.

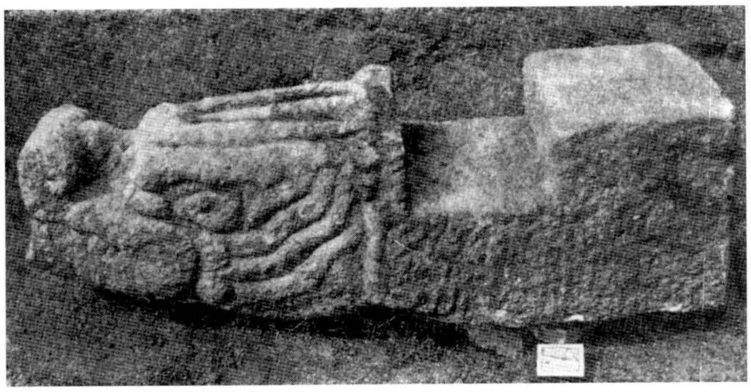

189. A dragon protome. Relief carving, Kondui palace, Transbaikal region.

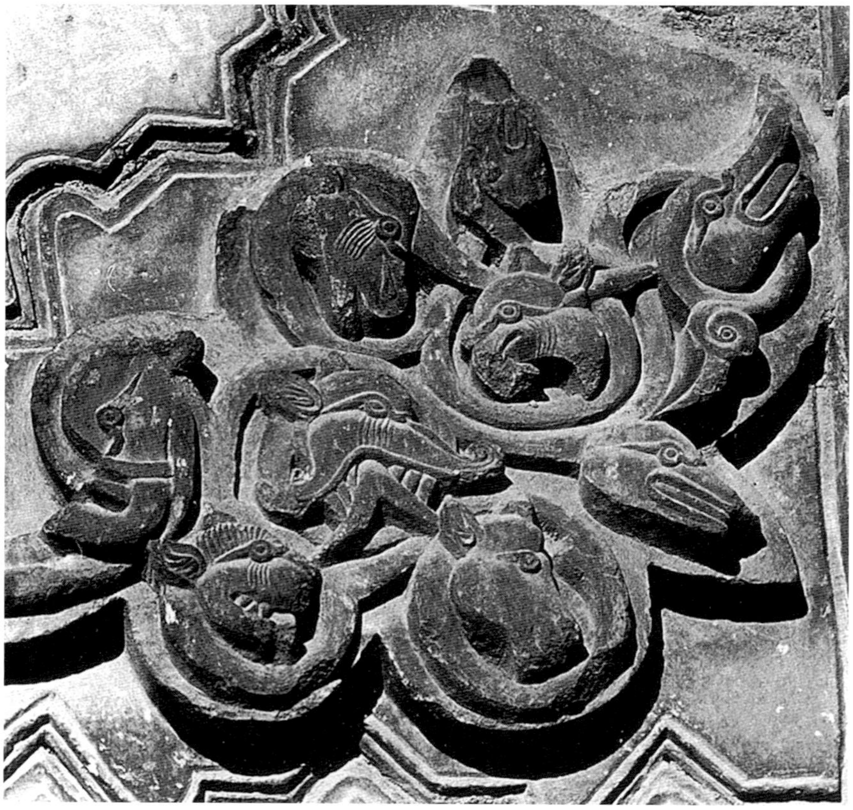

190. A dragon head projecting from amidst a cluster of animal heads. Relief sculpture at the portal façade of the Gök *madrasa*, Sivas.

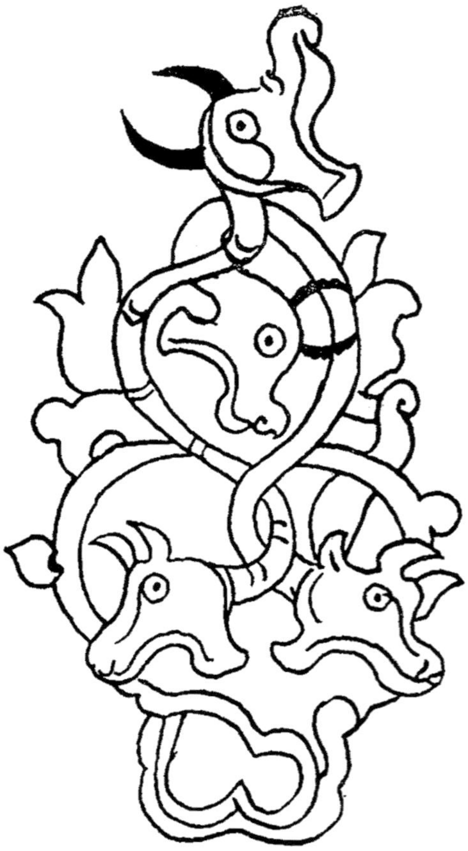

191. Four dragon heads issuing from a vegetal interlace. Marginal ornament from a collection of sermons, monastery of Surb Karapet, Baghesh.

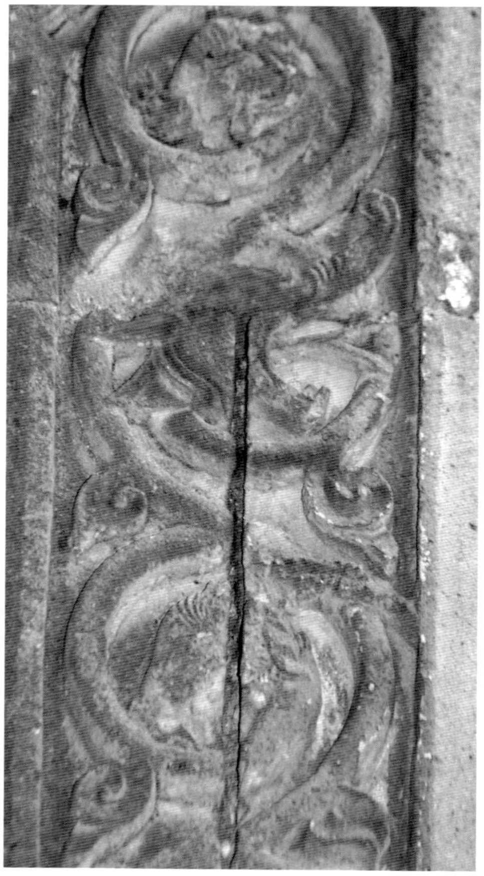

192. A dragon head in a *rinceau* of animal heads. Side panel flanking the portal of the Sunqur Beg Mosque, Niğde.

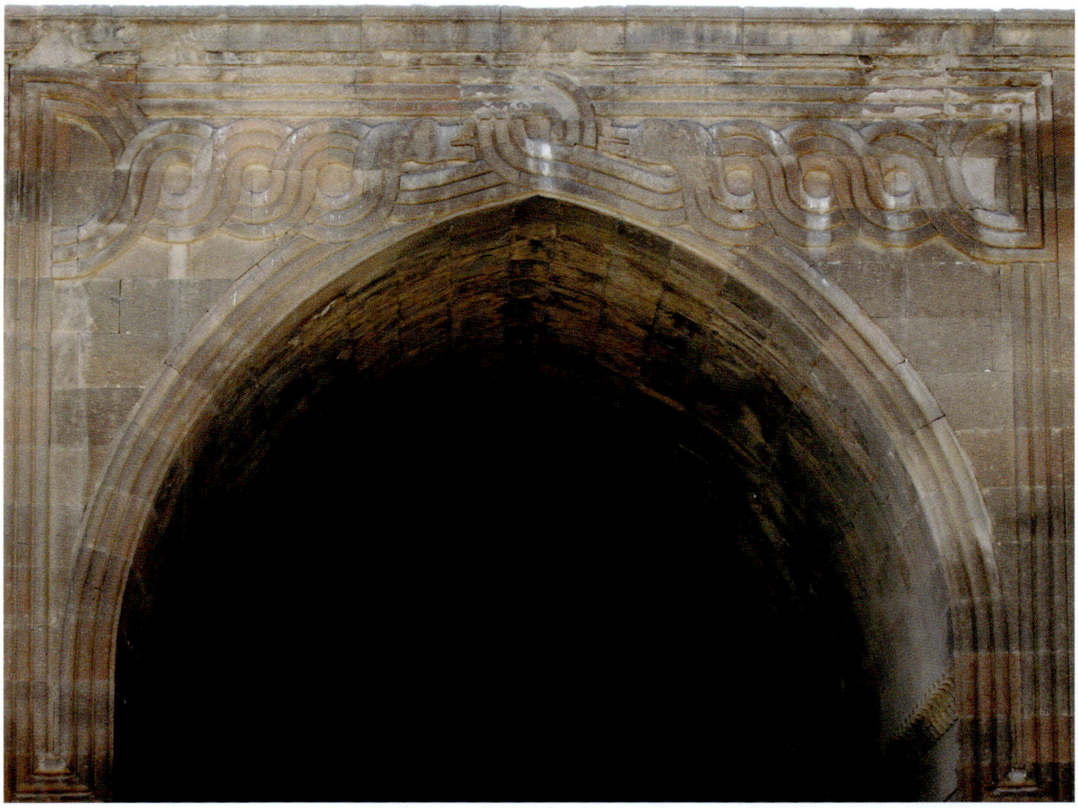

4a and b. A pair of monumental confronted dragons with entwined bodies. Relief carving at the back of the entrance-*īwān*, Karatay Han, east of Kayseri.

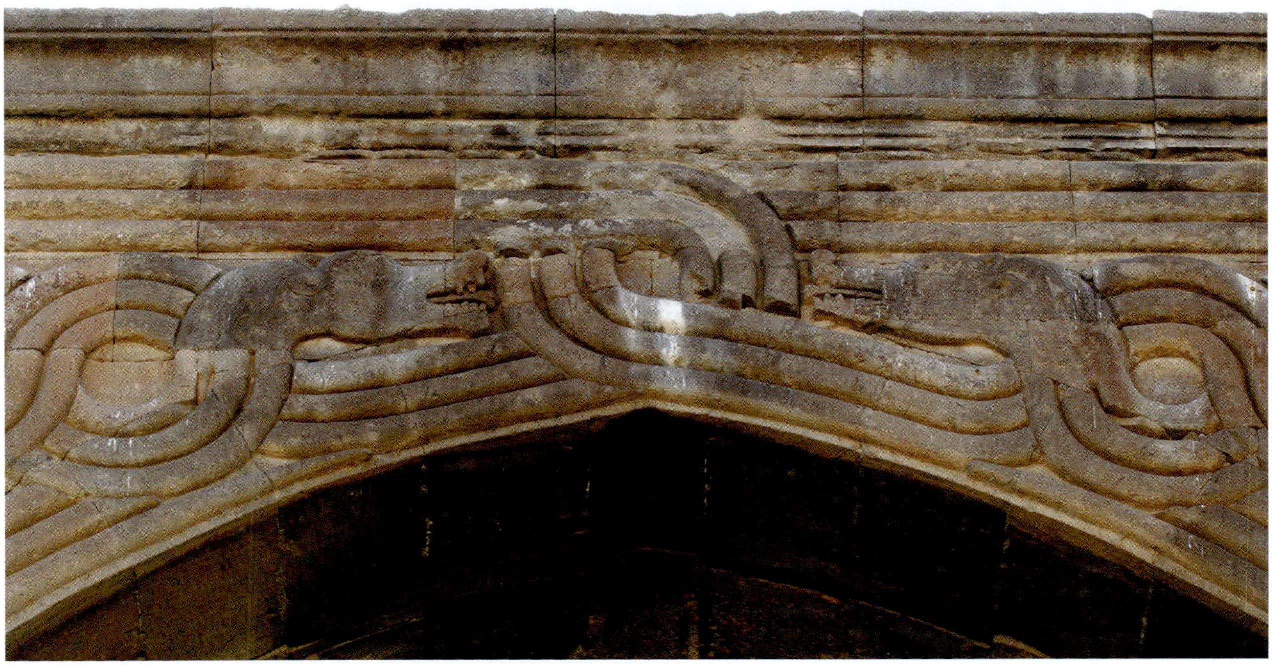

4b

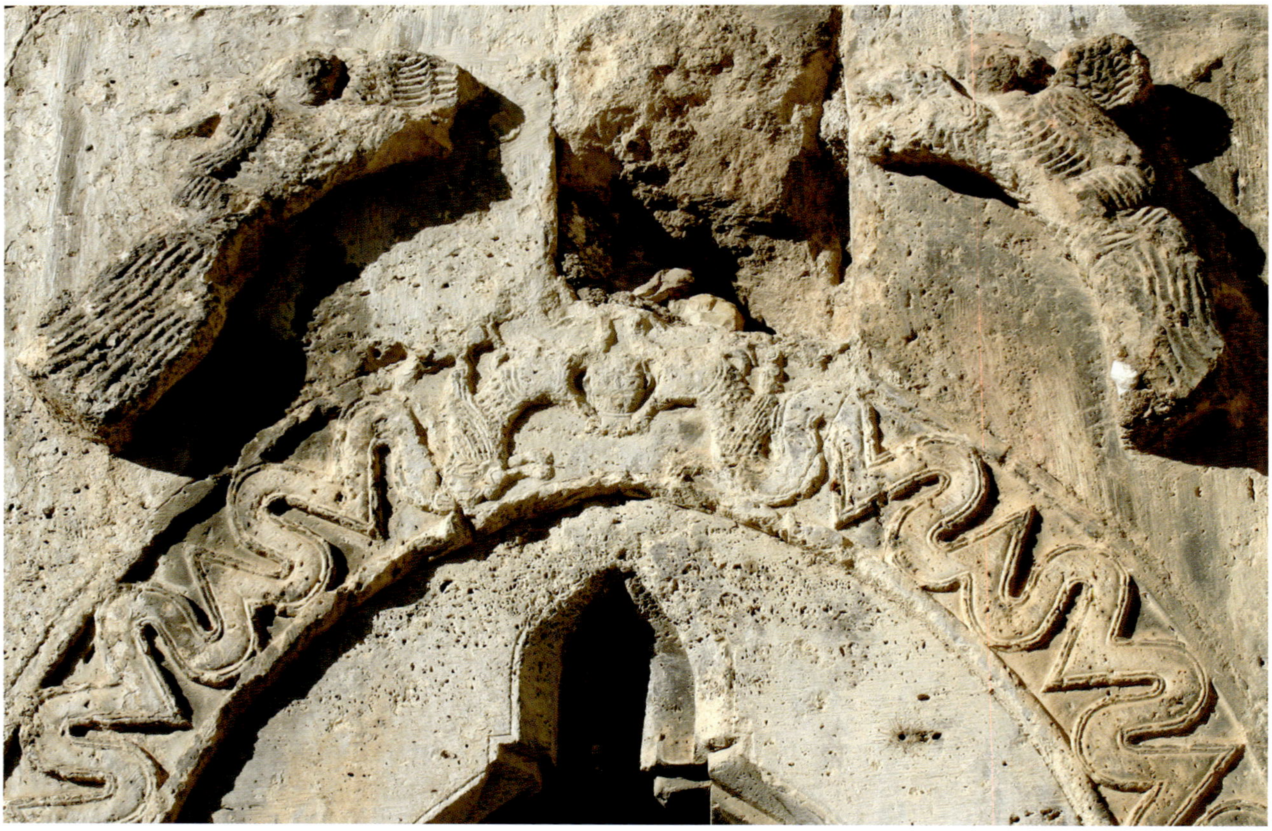

7. **A human head between a pair of winged confronted dragons with forelegs surmounted by winged figures.** Relief carving above the two niches that flank the main portal, Susuz Han, south of Bucak.

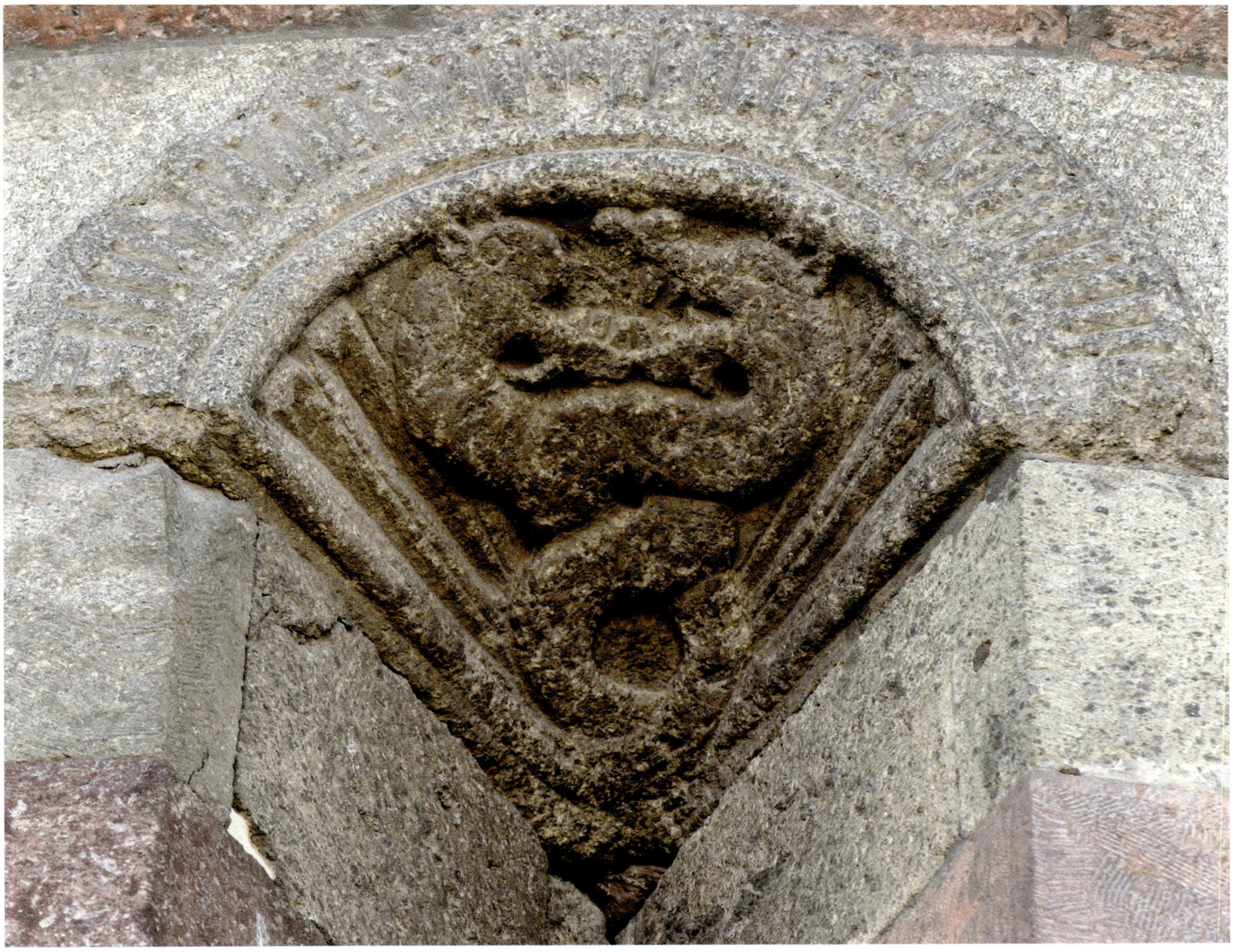

10. **A pair of upright confronted dragons with entwined bodies.** Relief carving on the *türbe* of Emir Saltuq, Erzurum.

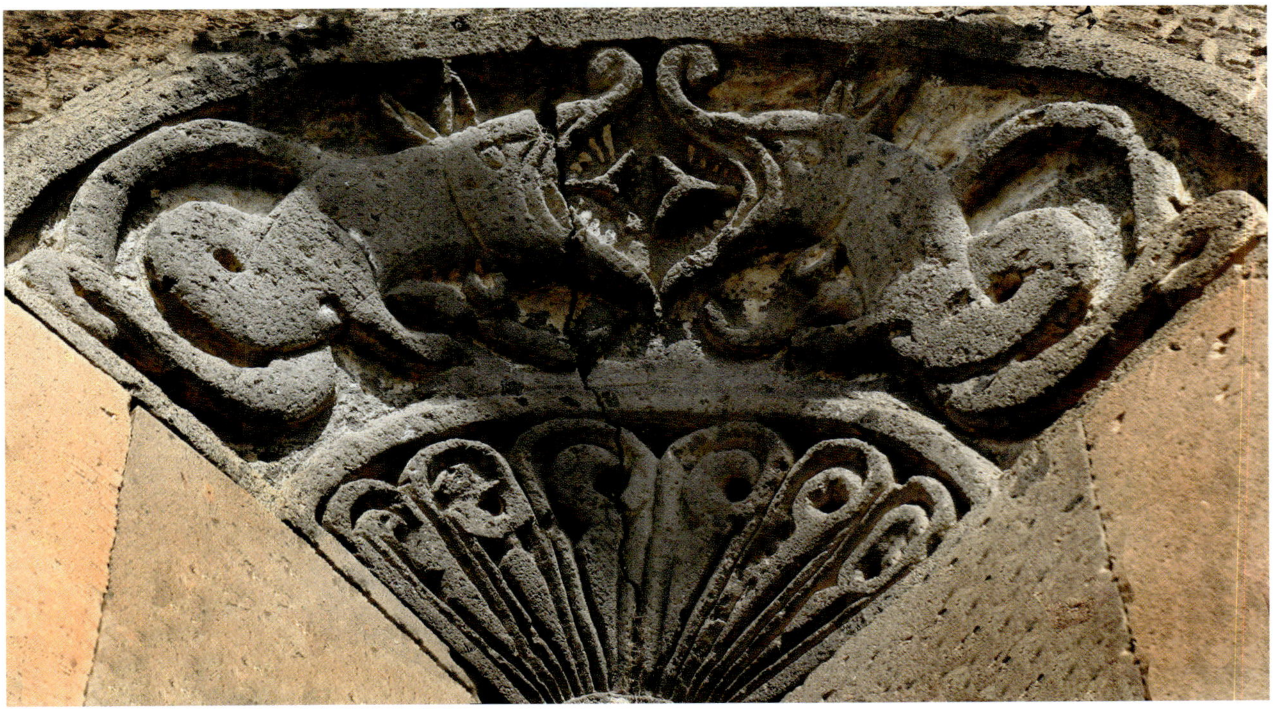

11. **A pair of confronted dragons with forelegs.** Relief carving on the church of Saint Gregory, Ani.

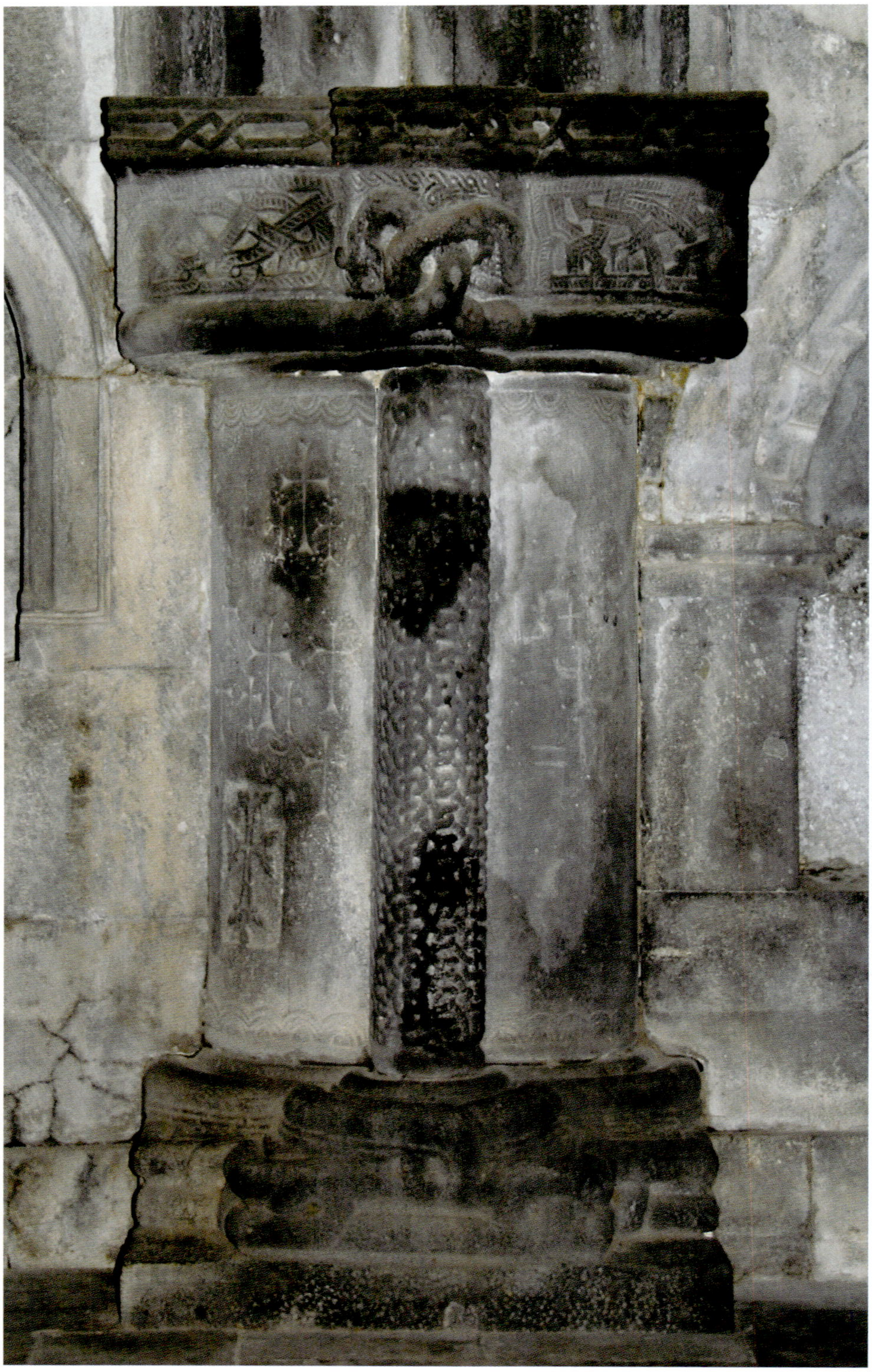

16. A pair of interlaced dragons. Column capital in the library, monastery of Sanahin, Alaverdi.

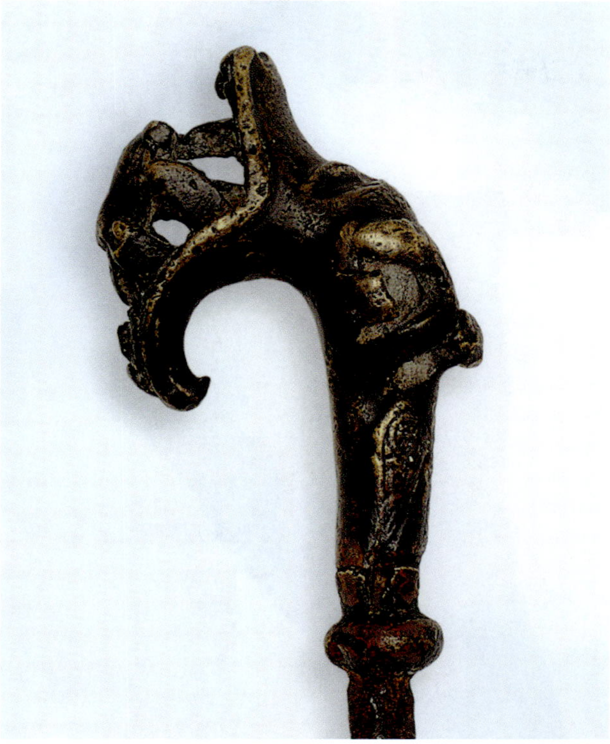

21. **A dragon head holding a quadruped, probably a feline, in its maw.** Mace head, Anatolia.

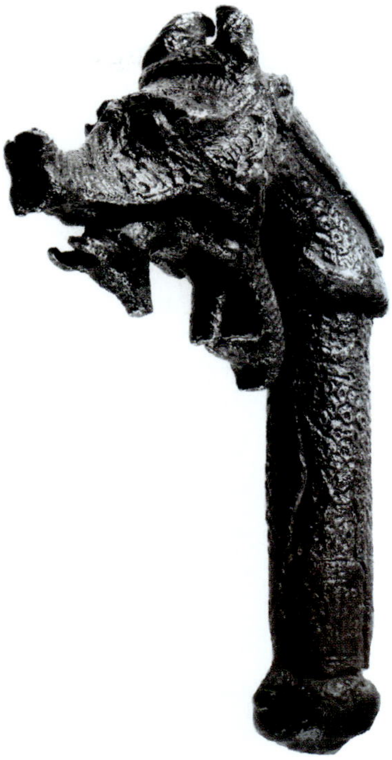

23. **A dragon head holding a bovid in its maw.** Finial, Iran or Afghanistan, perhaps Anatolia.

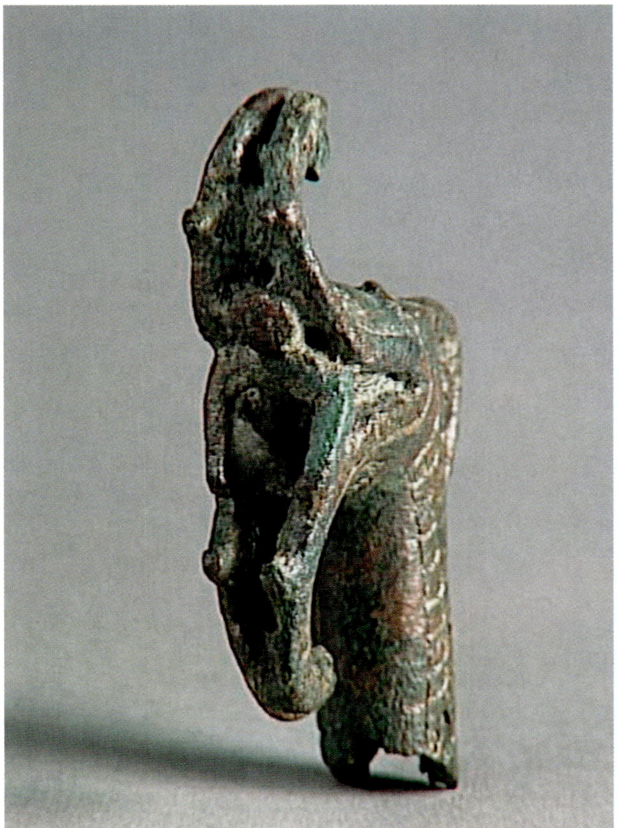

22a and b. A dragon head holding a human figure in its maw. Finial, Iran or the Jazīra.

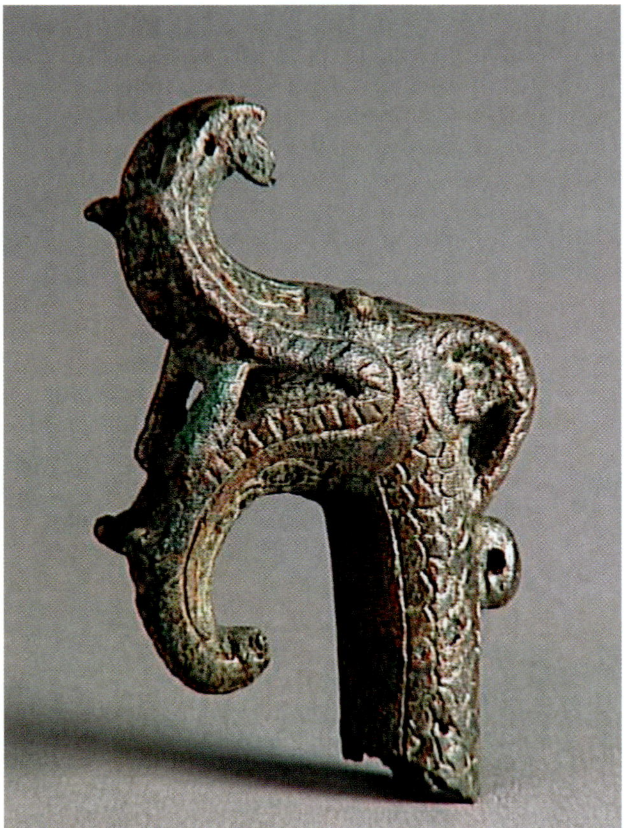

22b

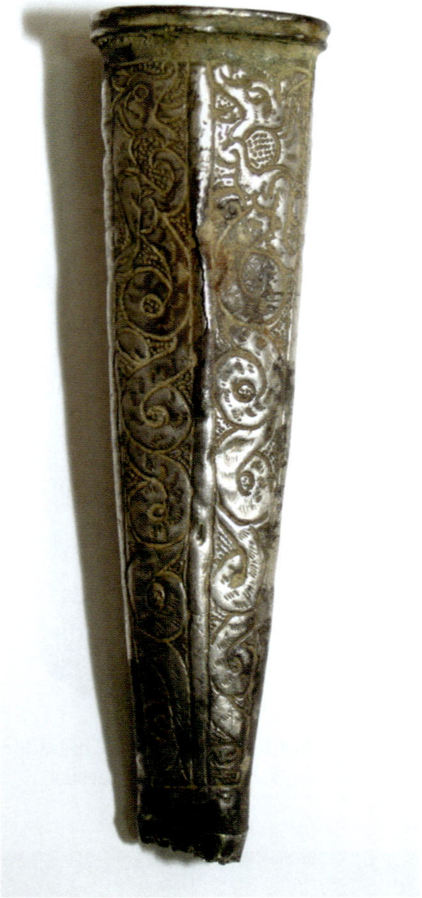

24. A pair of upright addorsed winged *regardant* dragons with forelegs. Chape, Herat.

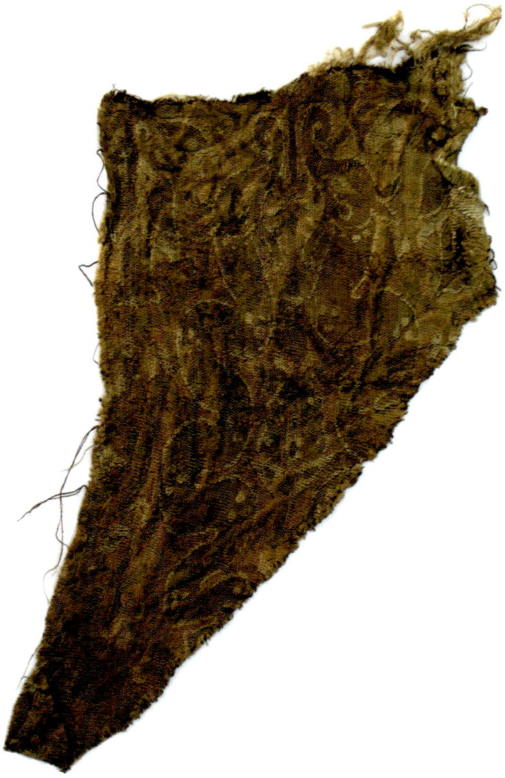

25. A pair of upright confronted dragons. Textile fragment, Dar-i Suf, Samangan province.

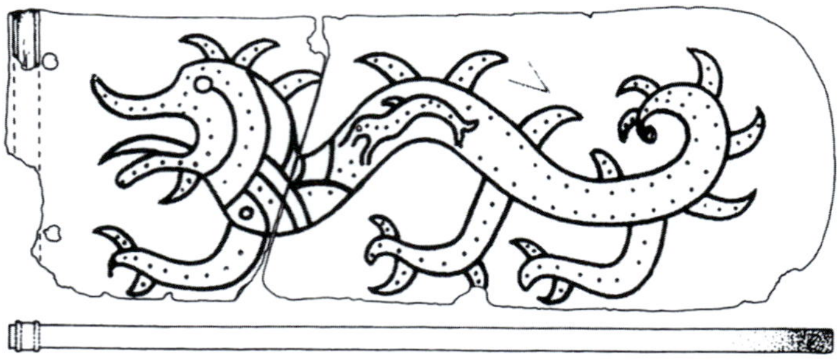

26. A single winged quadruped dragon. Tongue-strap fitting, Avar necropolis in Abony.

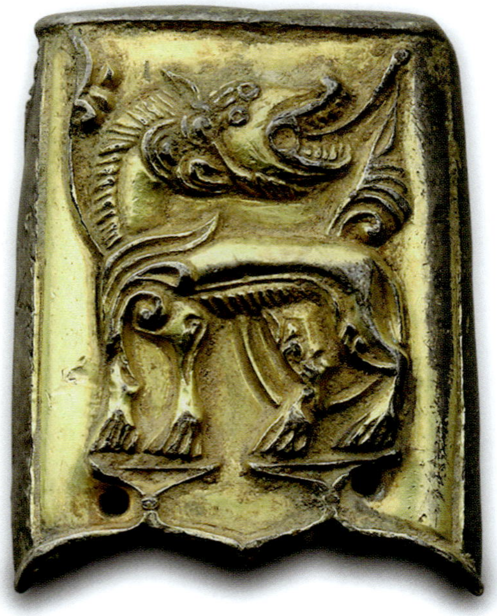

27. A winged *regardant* quadruped dragon. Fitting, greater Khurasan region.

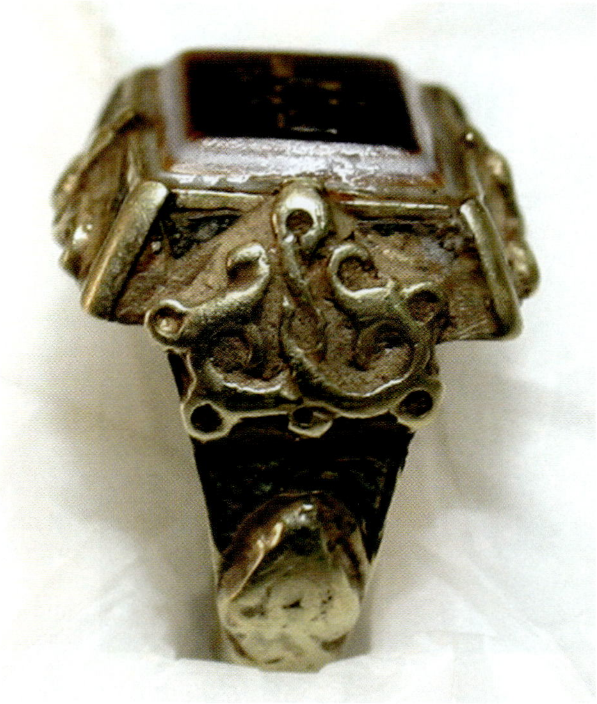

30. A pair of intertwined confronted dragon protomes. Appliqués at the shoulders of a finger ring, greater Khurasan region.

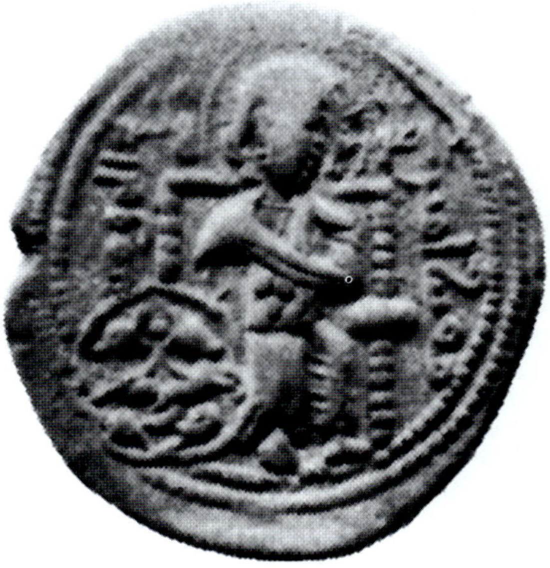

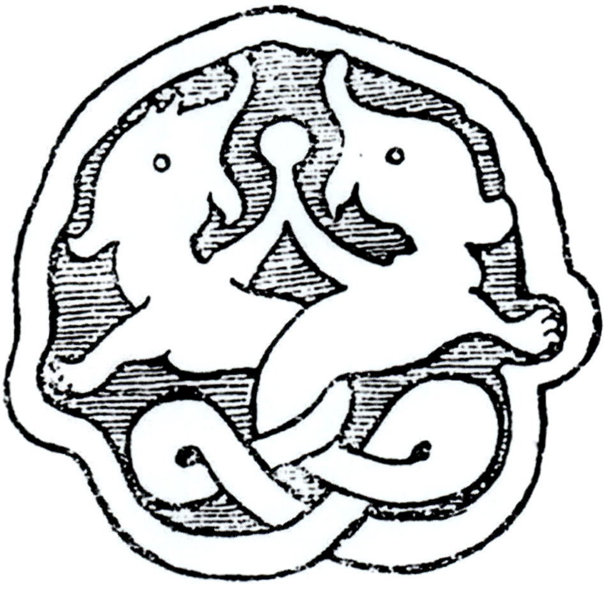

32a and b. An emblem with a pair of interlaced addorsed *regardant* dragons with wings and forelegs on a late Byzantine image of an enthroned Christ. Coin (reverse) of Qara Arslan (539/1144–562/1167), the Artuqid ruler of Ḥiṣn Kayfā and Khartpert.

32b

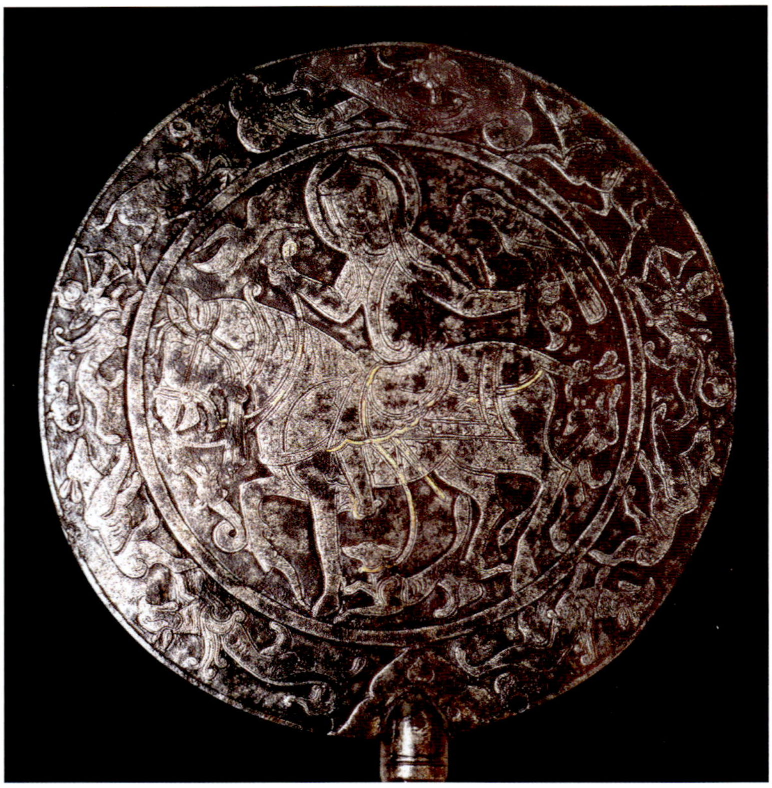

33. A mirror with three representations of dragons: a pair of winged dragons with forelegs and with crossed bodies at the apex, a dragon trampled by a horse and a dragon-tailed centaur. Anatolia or the Jazīra.

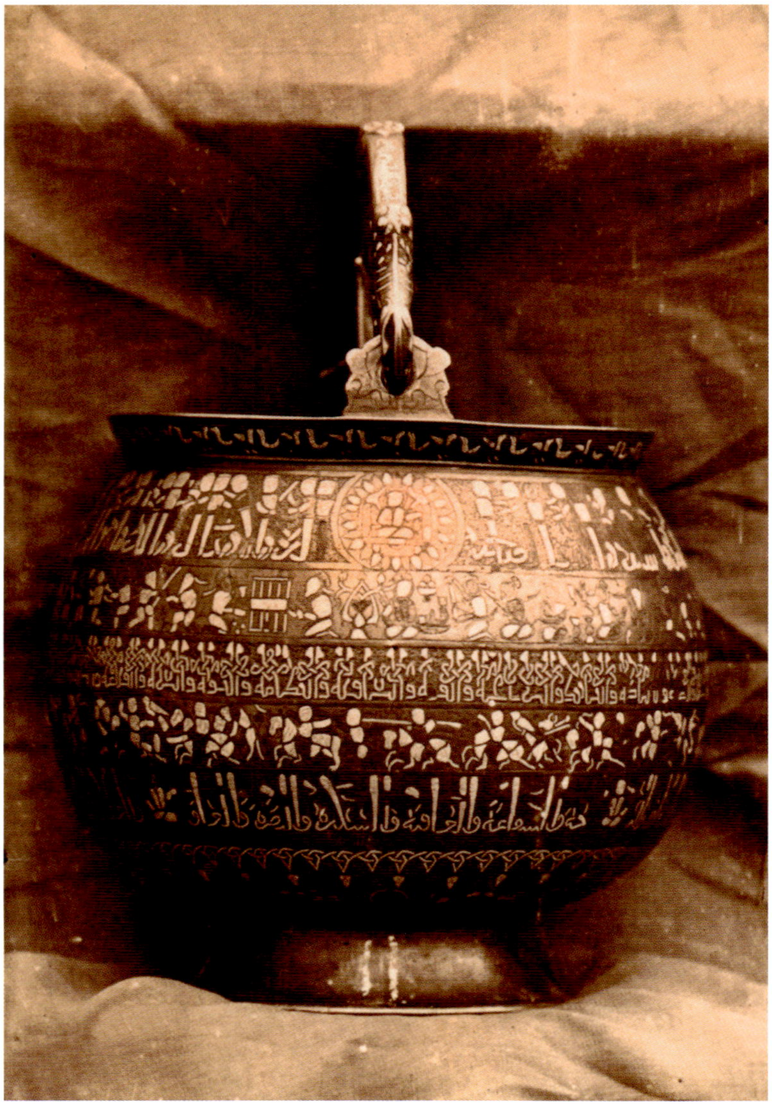

34. The so-called Bobrinski bucket. Possibly Herat.

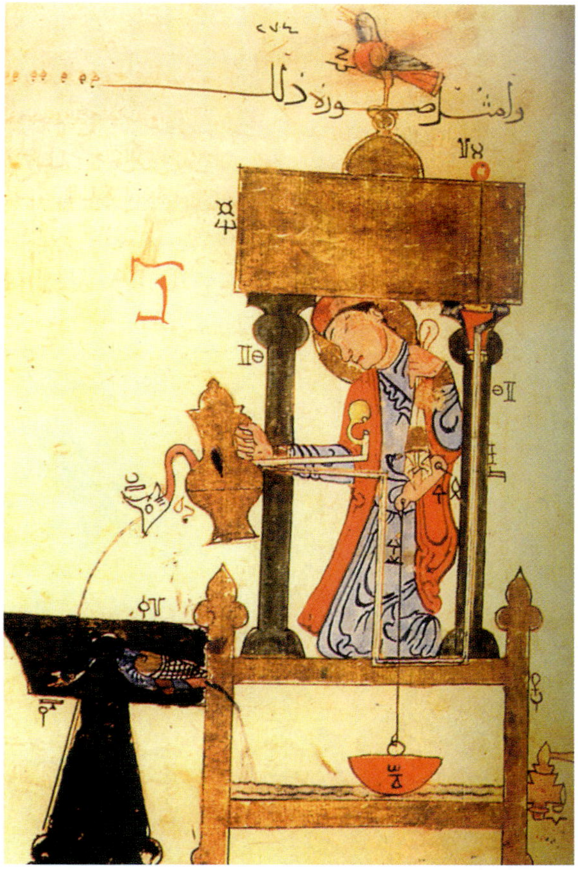

35. **"Hand-washing machine."** Illustration from al-Jazarī, *Kitāb fī maʿrifat al-ḥiyāl al-handasiyya*, Anatolia.

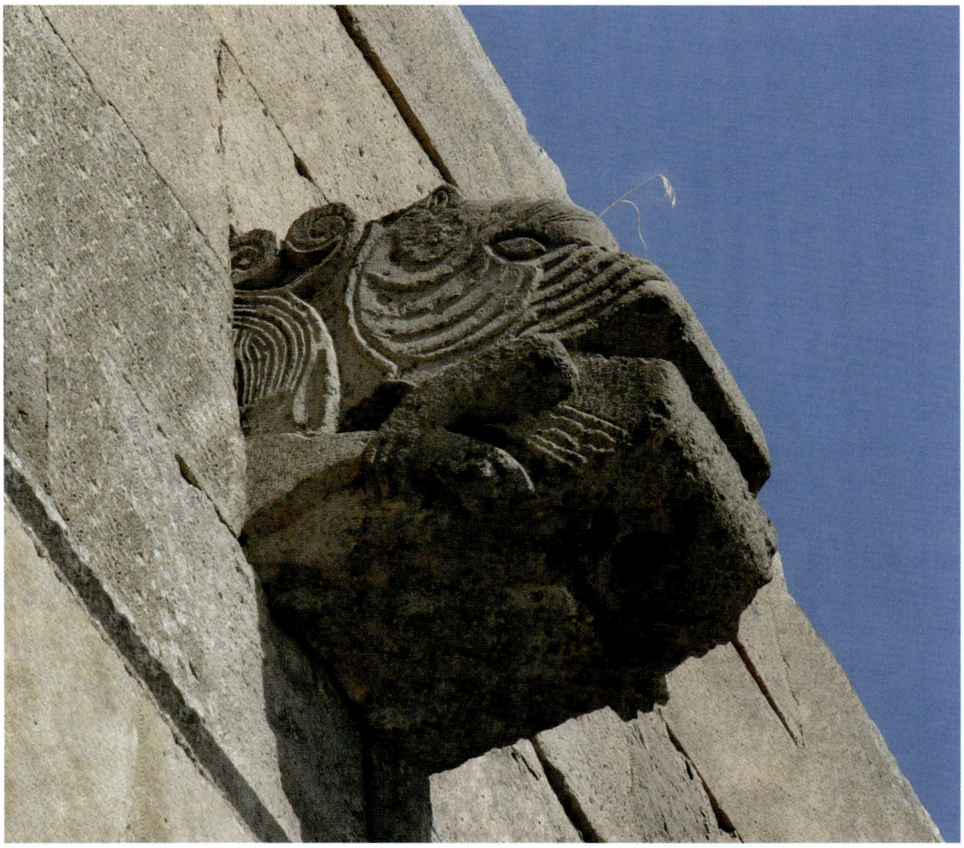

37. **A protome of a winged dragon holding in its jaws a stylised human being whose hands grip the dragon's forelegs.** Waterspout on the façade to the right of the main gate, Karatay Han, east of Kayseri.

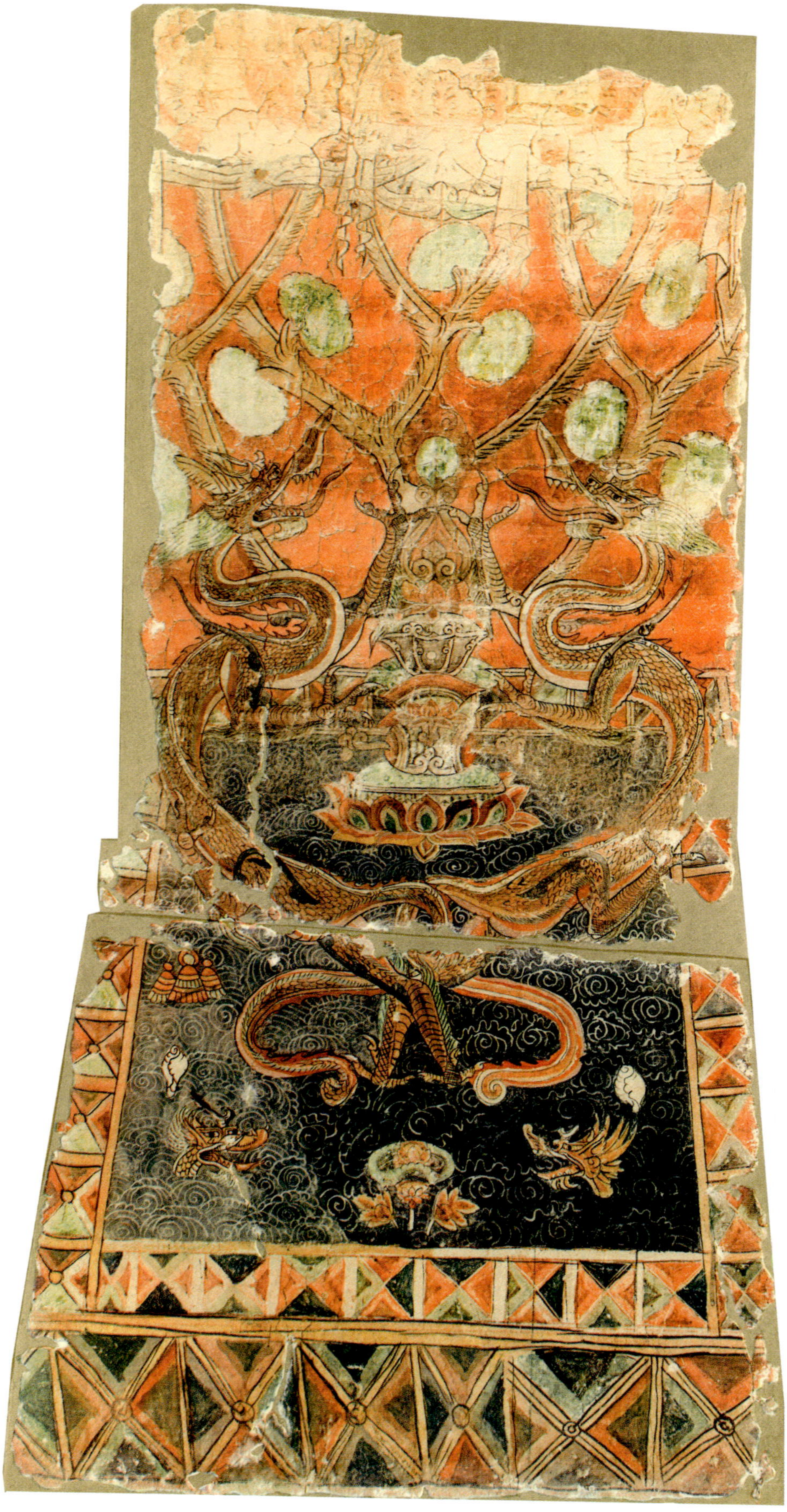

41. **A pair of upright confronted quadruped dragons with interlaced tails guarding a treasure.** Wall painting in Temple 19, Bezeklik.

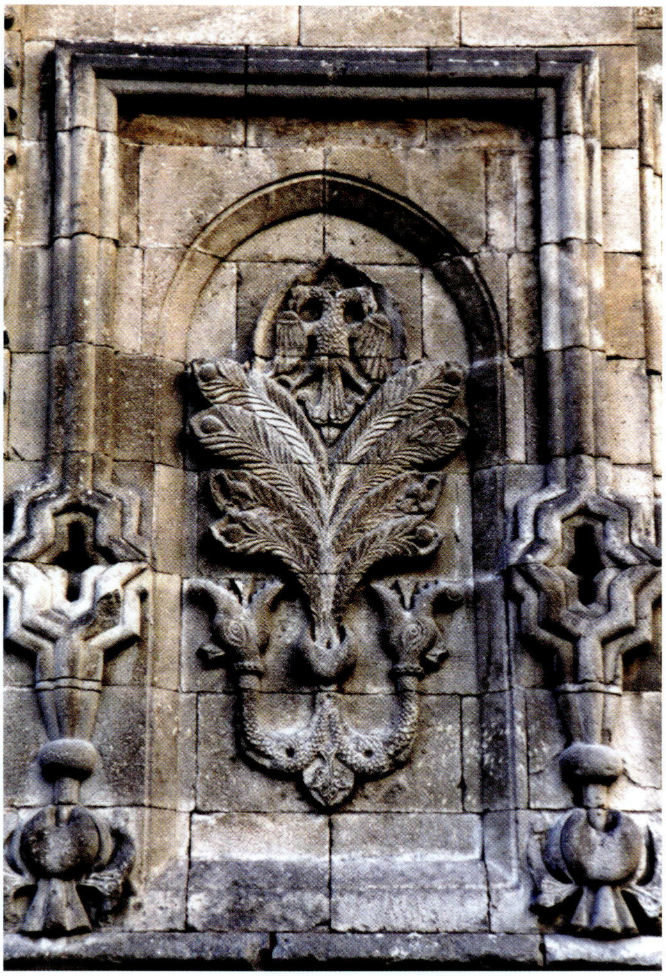

43. A pair of dragon protomes springing from the base of a vegetal composition topped by a double-headed eagle. Relief carving on the façade of the Çifte Minare *madrasa*, Erzurum.

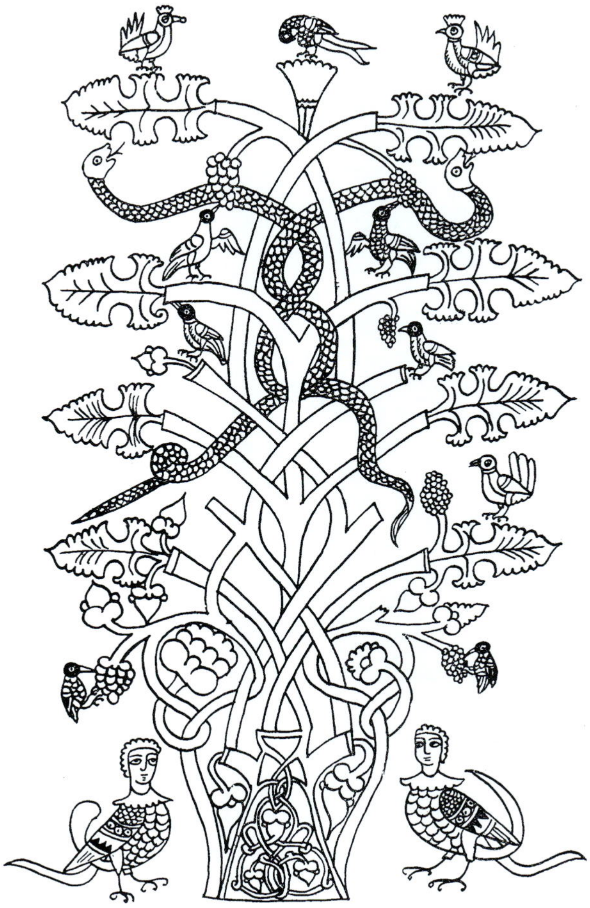

44. A pair of large serpents coiled around a tree trunk. Marginal ornament in a *Yachakhapatum*, monastery of Skevra.

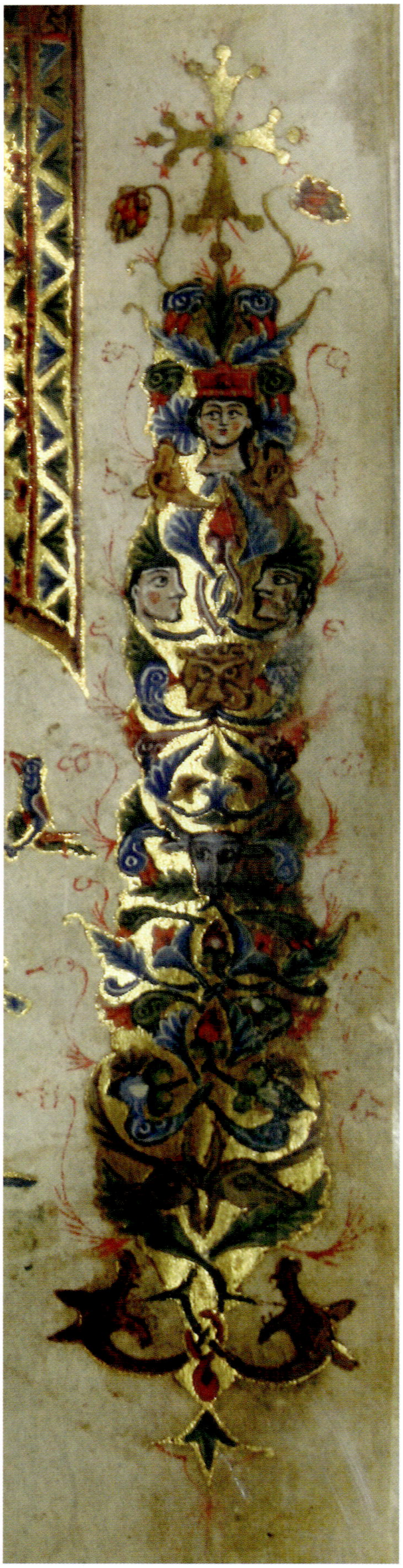

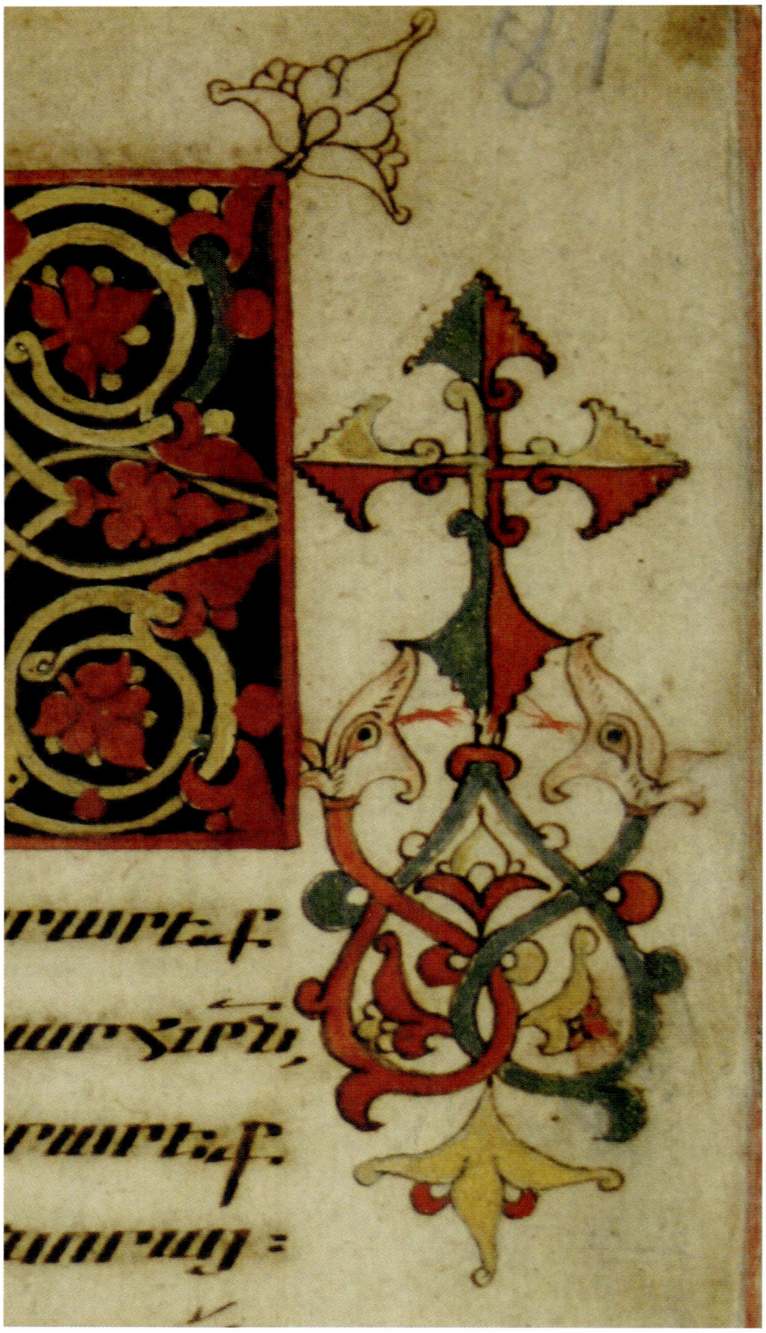

47. **A cross springing from a vegetal interlace transforming in a pair of confronted dragon heads.** Marginal ornament in a copy of the Gospel of Mark, Edessa.

45. **A pair of confronted dragon heads at the base of a vegetal composition bearing the heads of the four Evangelists topped by a cross.** Marginal ornament in a copy of the Gospel of Luke, monastery of Gladzor.

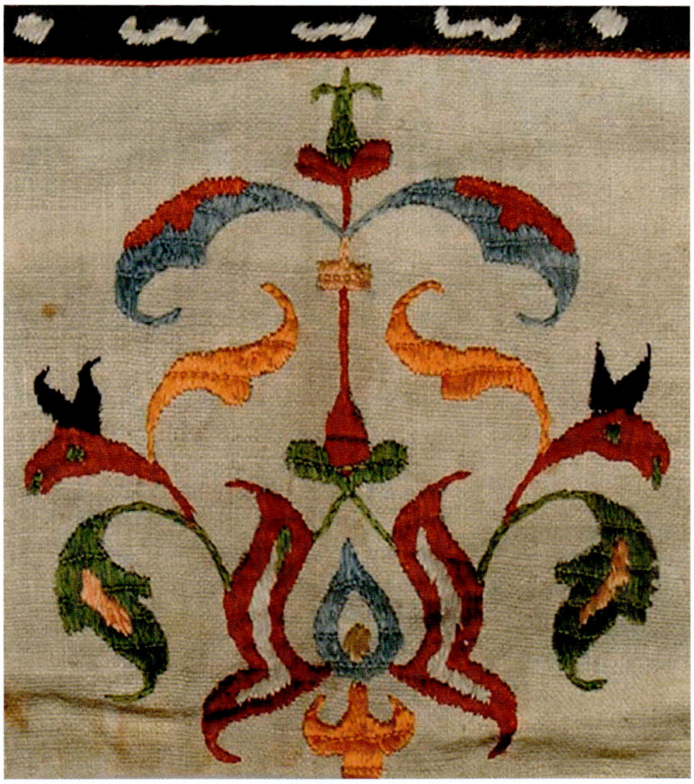

52. A pair of addorsed dragon heads springing from a vegetal composition. Textile fragment, greater Khurasan.

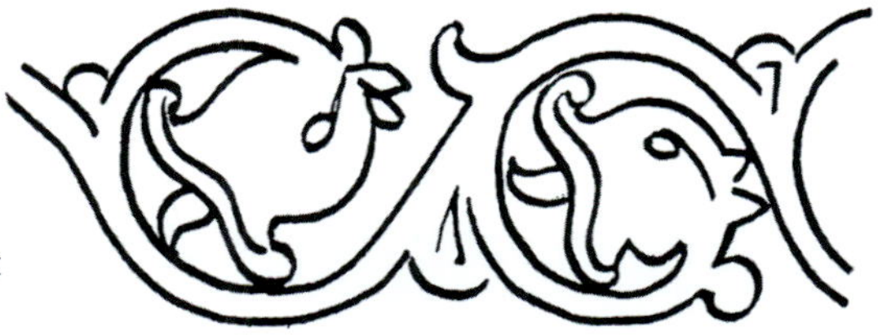

53. A dragon head *rinceau*. Relief carving on an archivolt fragment, Daghistan.

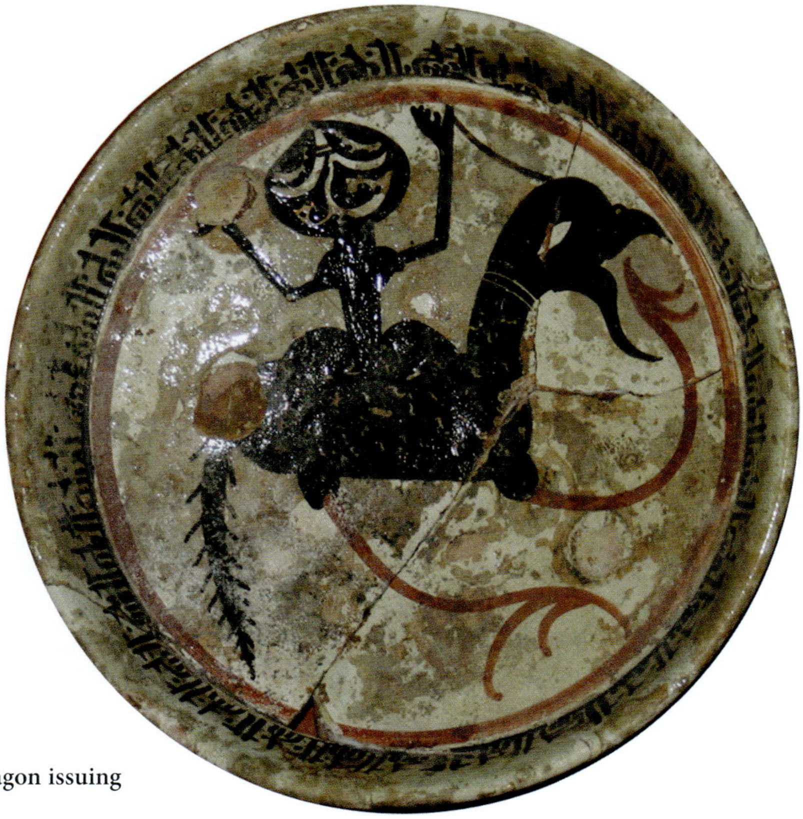

55. A rider on a recumbent quadruped dragon issuing vegetation. Bowl, Tashkent.

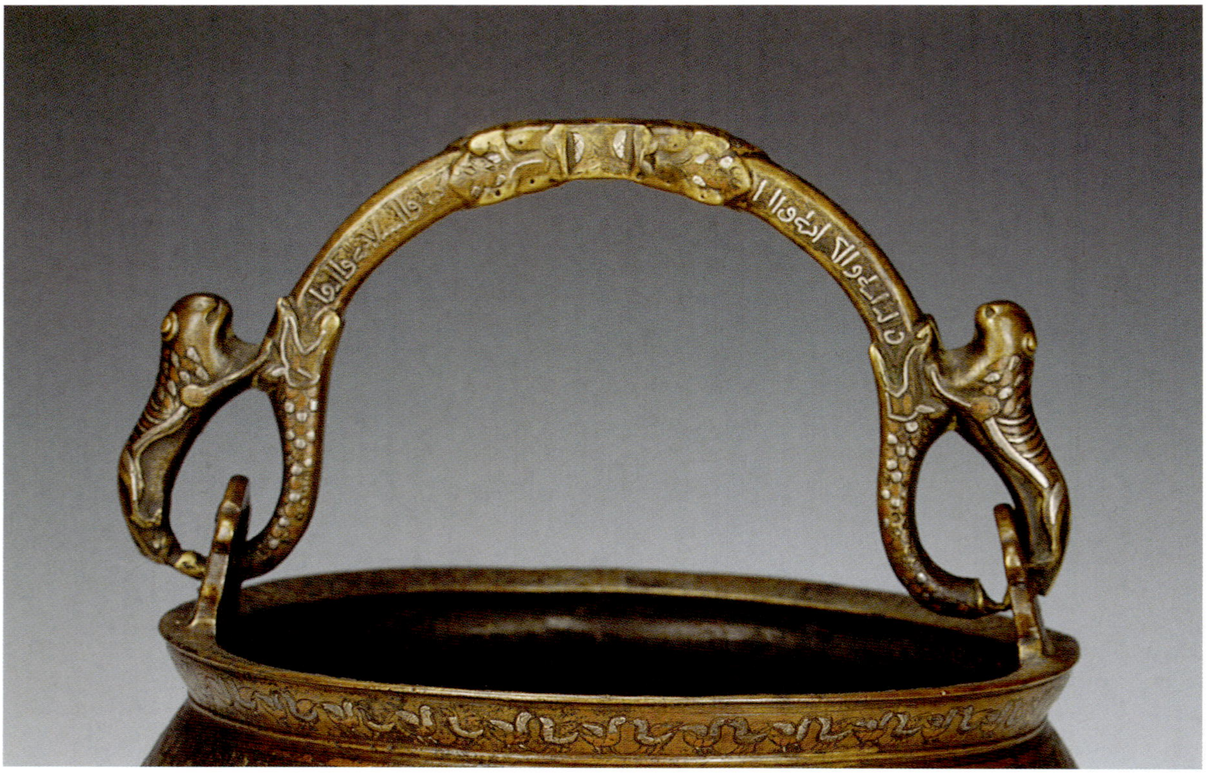

56. **Leaping lions and dragon protomes, the gaping mouths issuing benedictory inscriptions.** Arched faceted handle of the so-called Bobrinski bucket, possibly Herat.

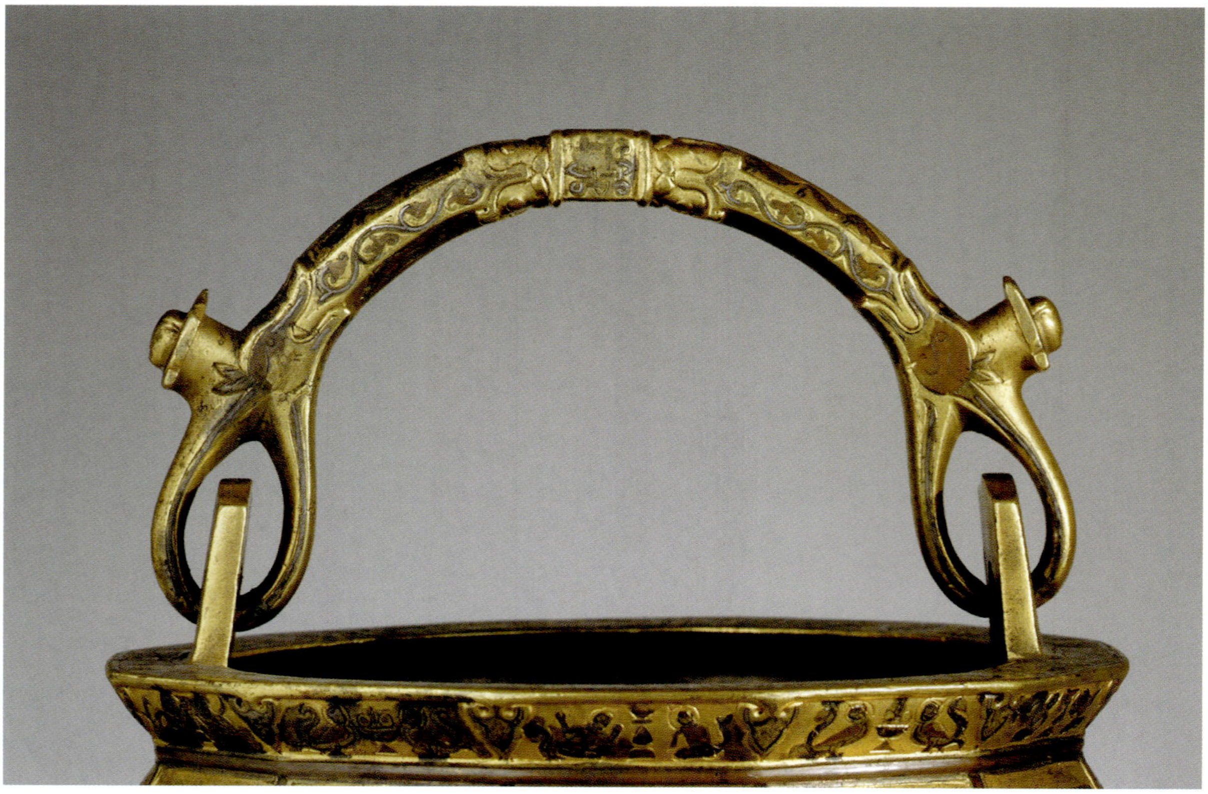

57. **Lion heads and dragons, the gaping mouths issuing vegetal scrolls.** Arched faceted handle of the so-called Fould bucket, possibly Anatolia.

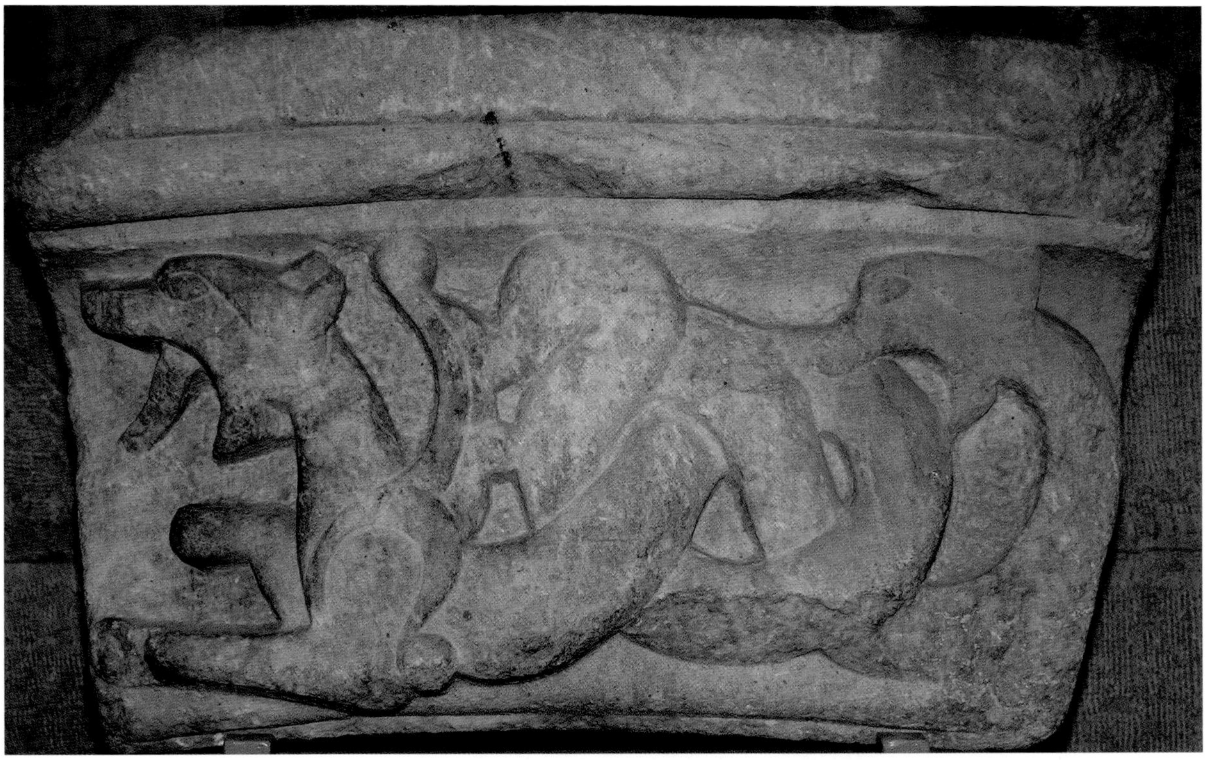

60. **A winged dragon with forelegs and with a dragon-tail snapping at its own coils.** Relief carving, Konya.

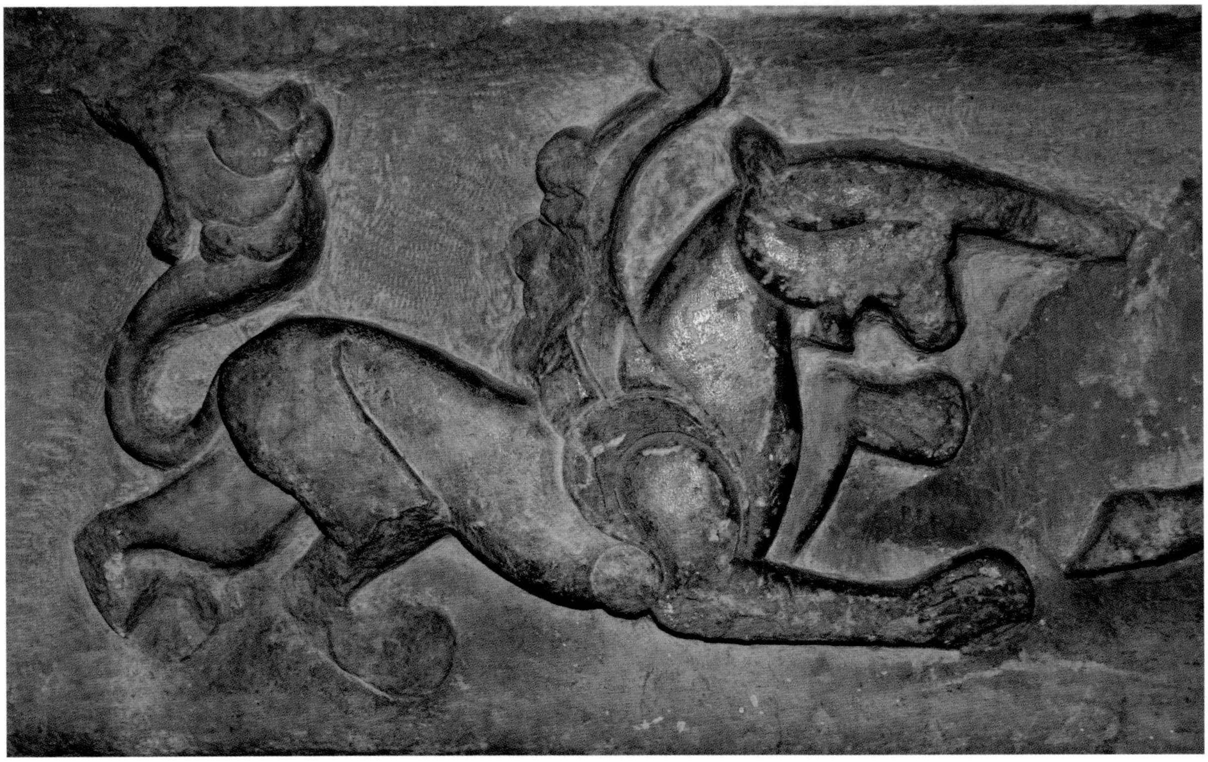

64. **A dragon-tailed unicorn.** Relief carving, Konya.

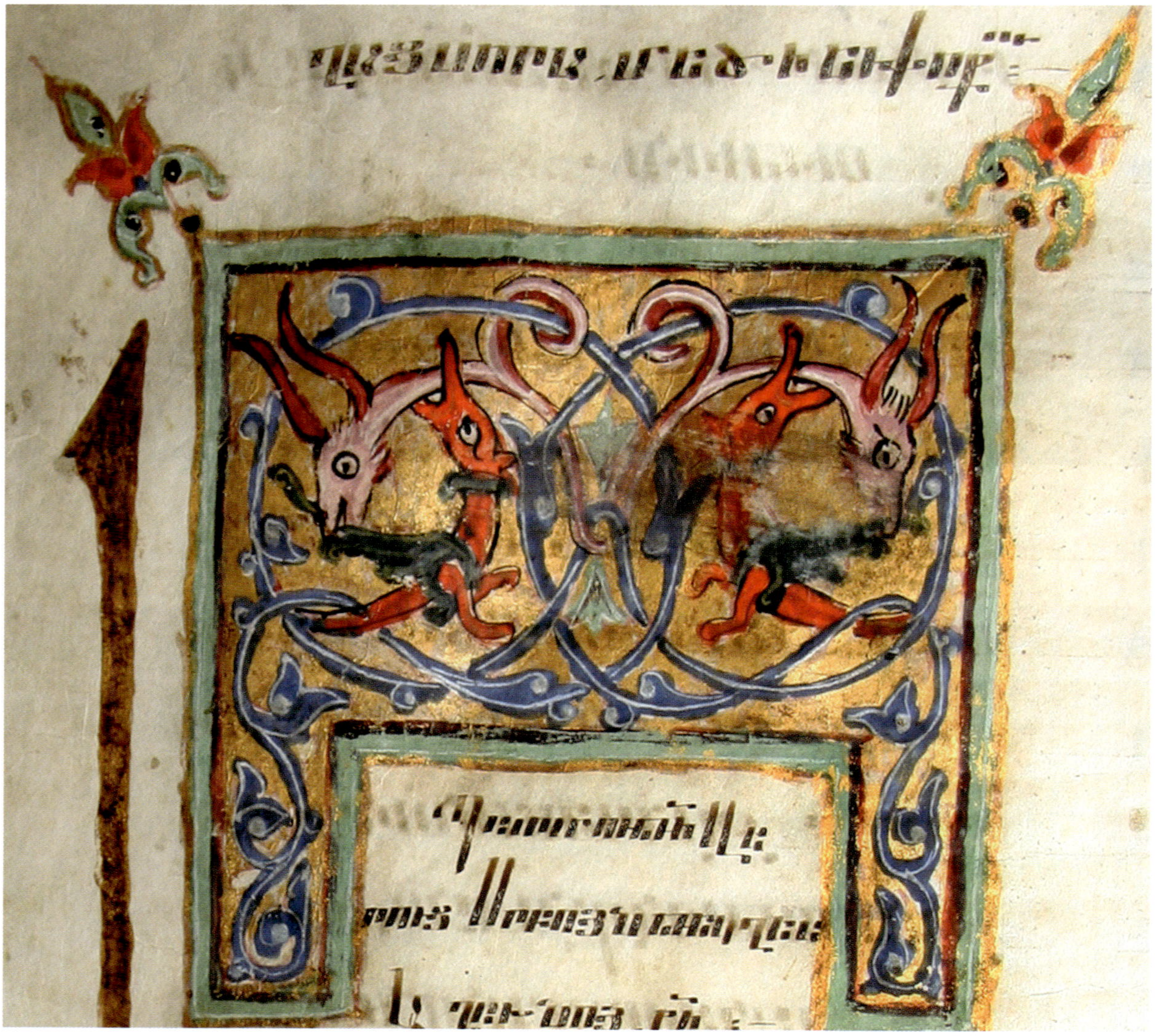

61. Headpiece with foliate interlace issuing pairs of winged dragon protomes with forelegs and goat heads that are locked in combat with each other. Painting in the Mush Homiliary, monastery of Avagvankʿ, Erznga(n).

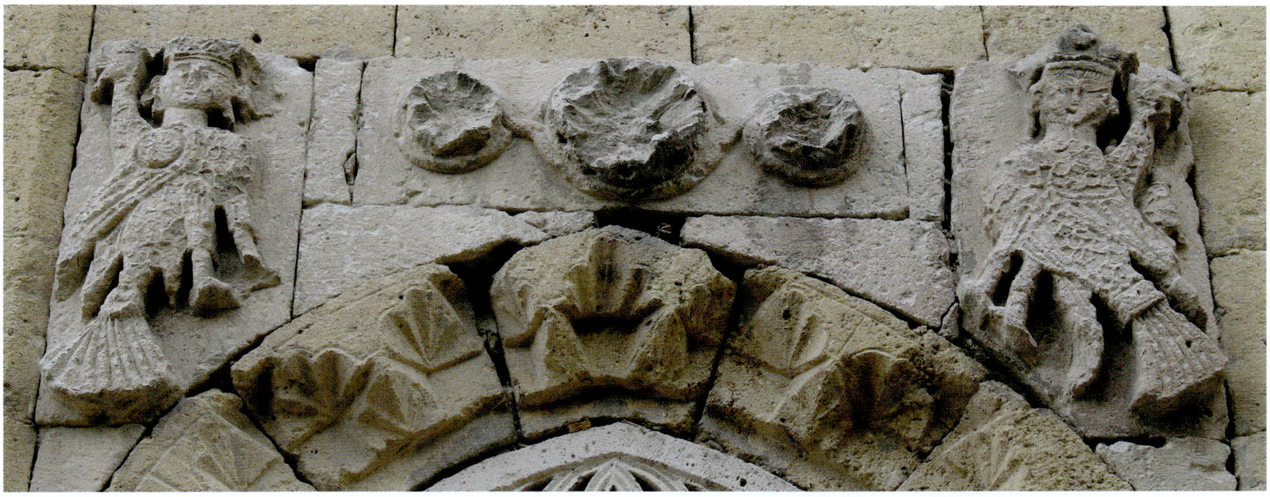

66. **A pair of confronted harpies with dragon-headed wing tips.** Relief carving on the *türbe* of Hüdavend Hatun, Niğde.

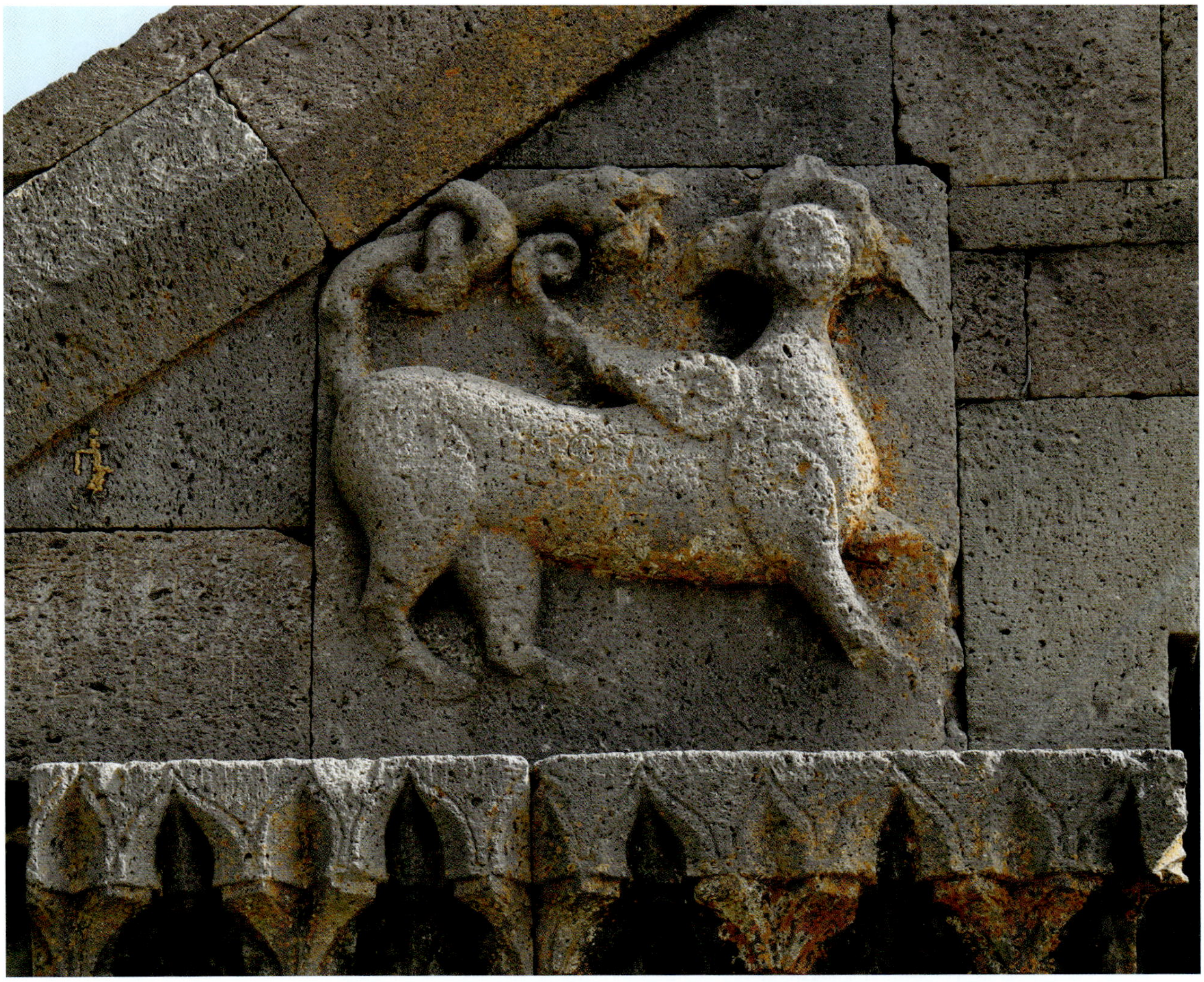

67. **A dragon-tailed sphinx.** Relief carving on the left side of the portal of Selim caravanserai, Vayots Dzor province.

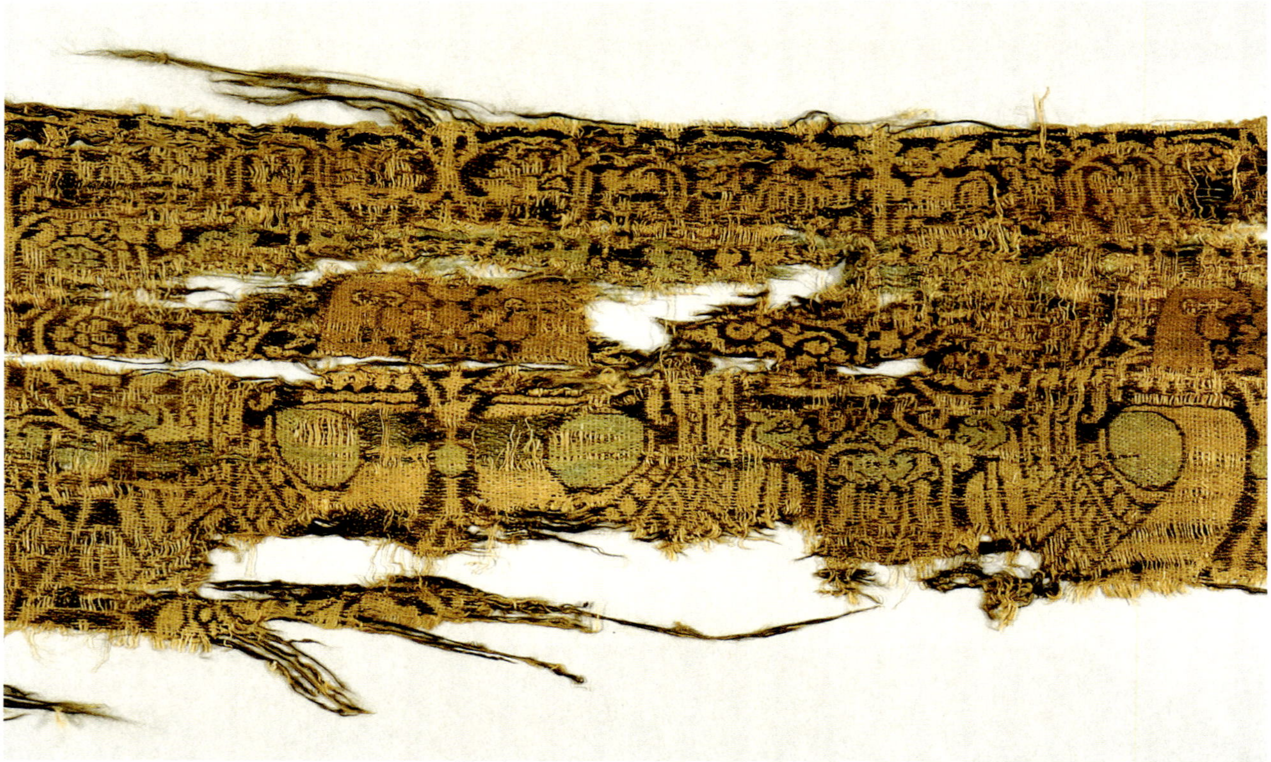

68. Pairs of confronted roosters with dragon-headed tails. Detail of a textile fragment, Samangan province.

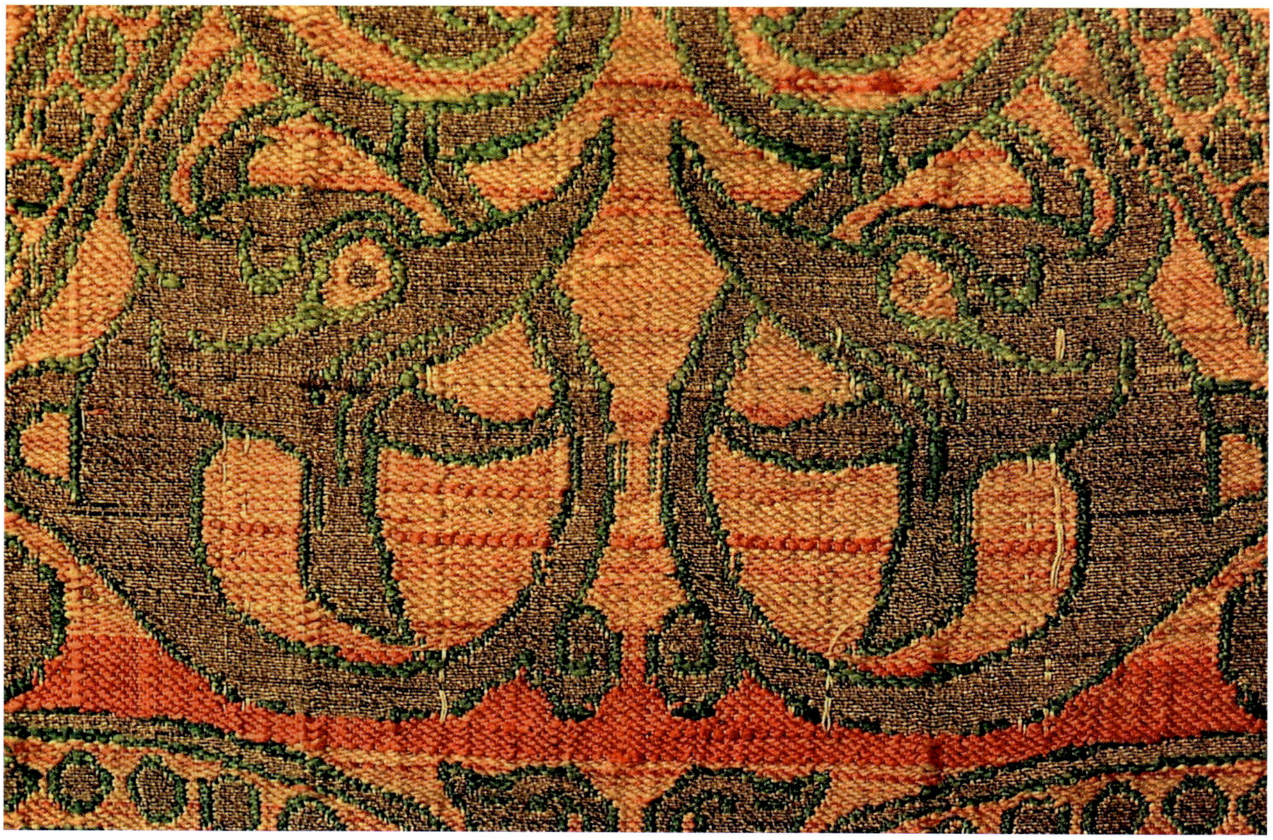

69b. Double-headed eagles with outspread dragon-headed wings. Detail of a textile fragment, probably Anatolia.

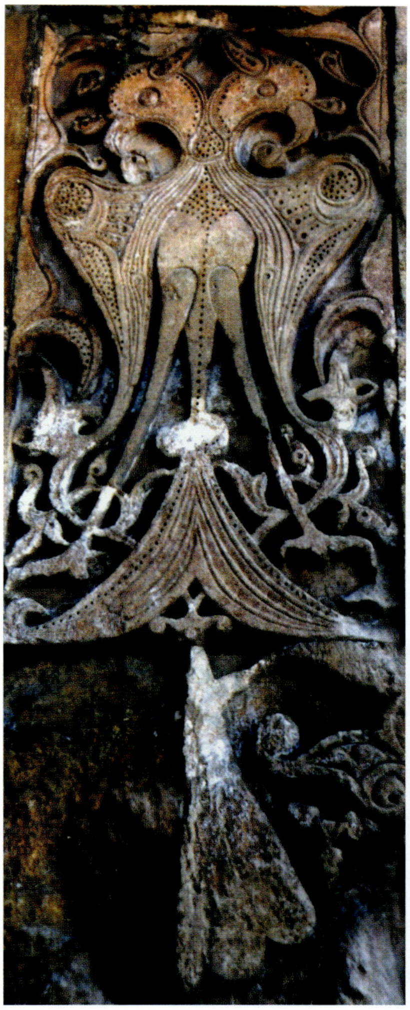

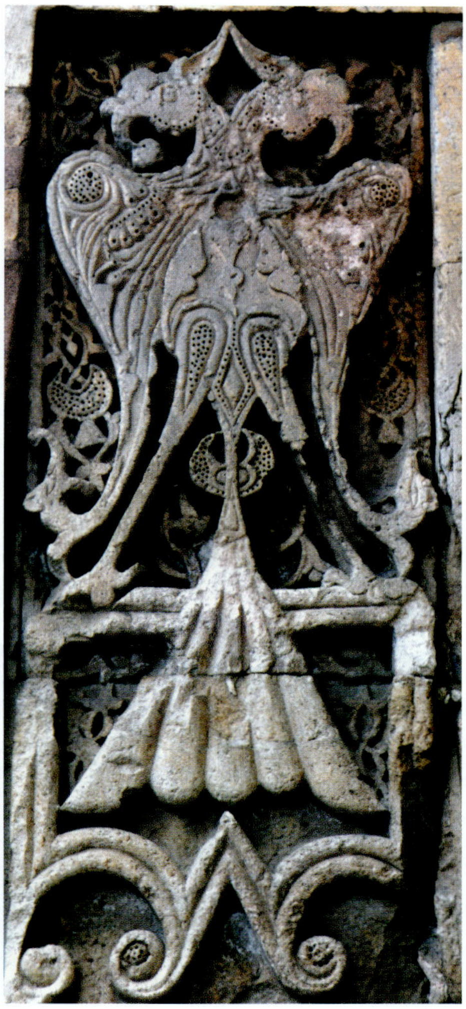

70a and b. Double-headed eagles with outspread dragon-headed wings. Relief carving from the western portal, a. left side, b. right side, Great Mosque of Divriği.

70b

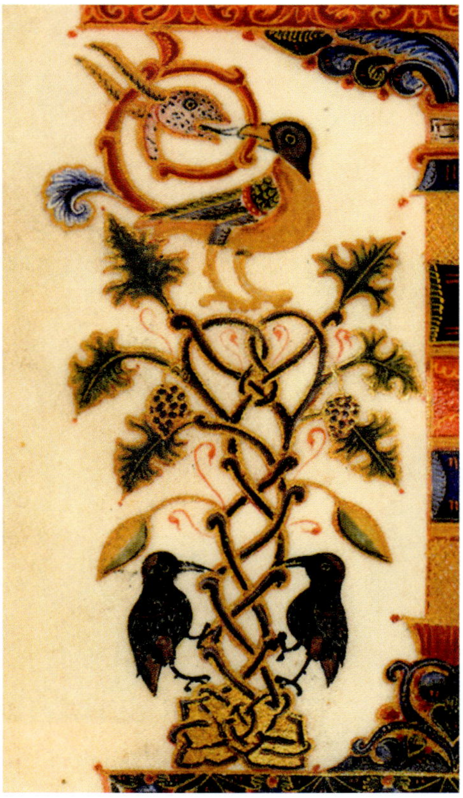

72. A dragon-tailed *regardant* bird. Marginal ornament in the canon tables, L'viv Gospel, monasteries of Mlich and Skevra.

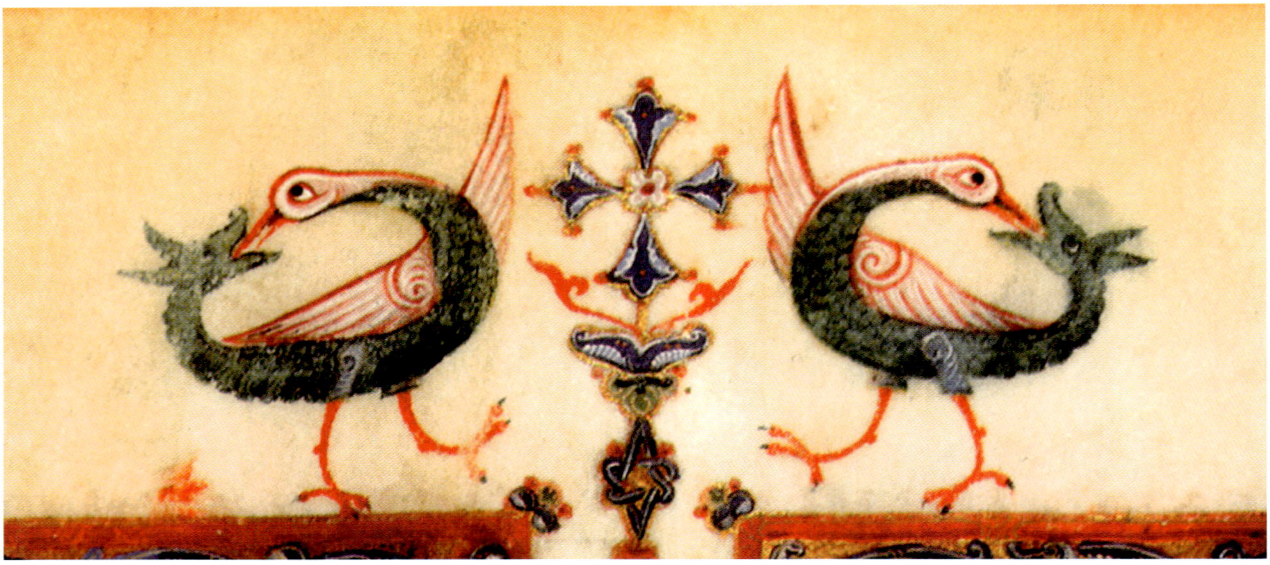

73. A pair of confronted dragon-tailed *regardant* birds flanking a cross. L'viv Gospel, monasteries of Mlich and Skevra.

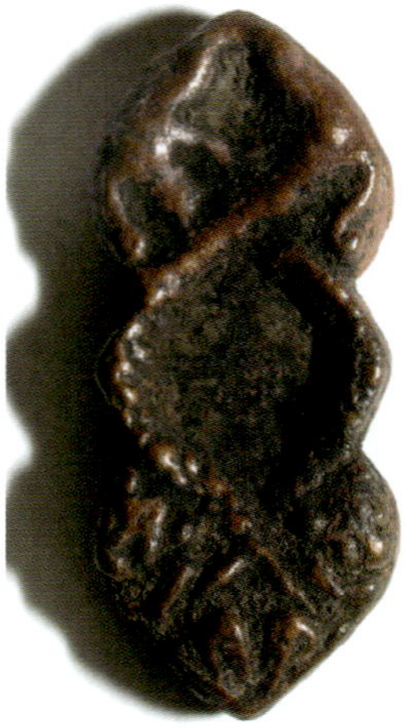

75. A pair of addorsed dragon-tailed lions *couchant*. Matrix, Ghūr.

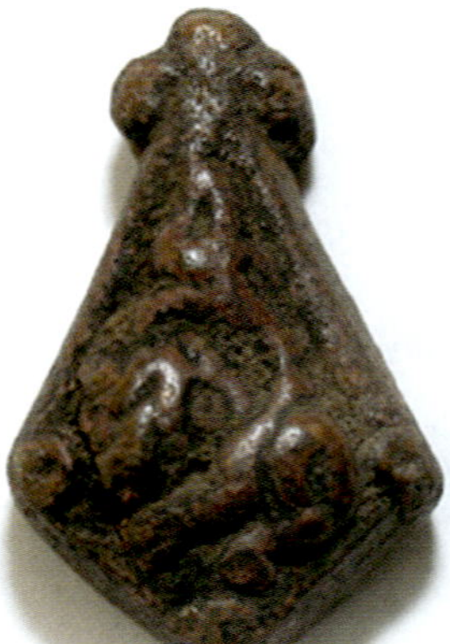

76. A single dragon-tailed lion *couchant*. Matrix, Ghūr.

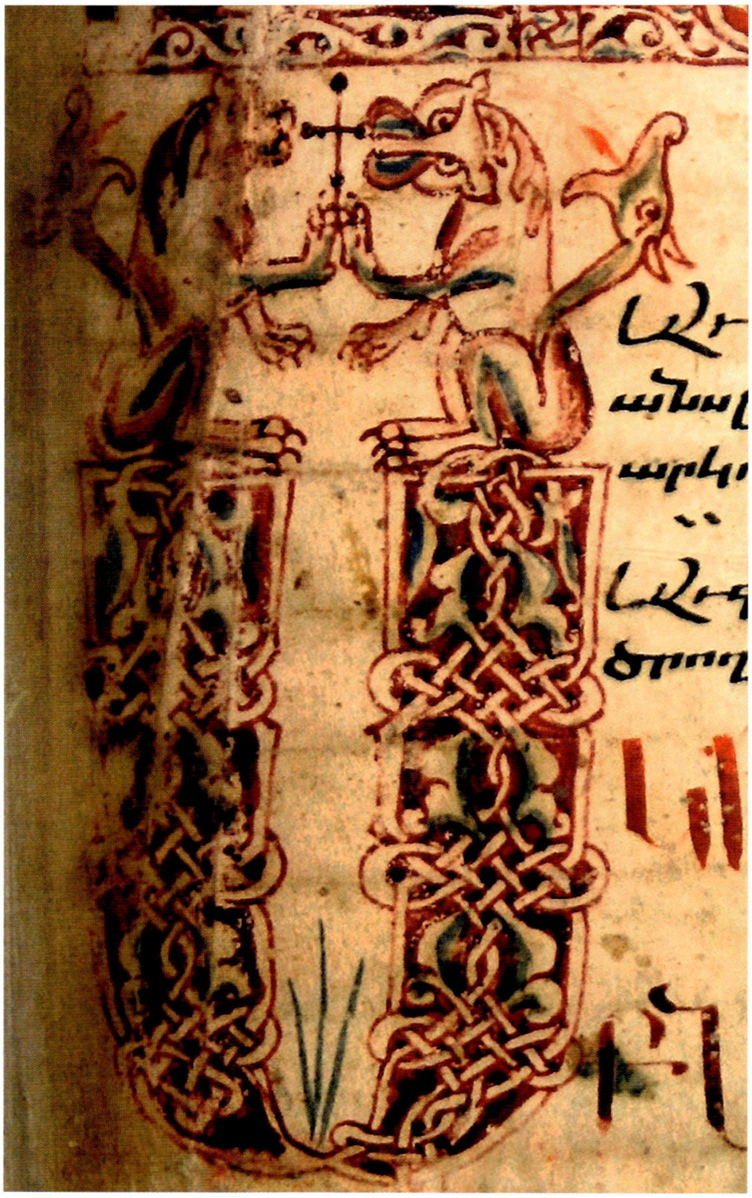

79. Initial surmounted by confronted seated dragon-tailed lions. Painting in a Gospel, Siunikʿ province.

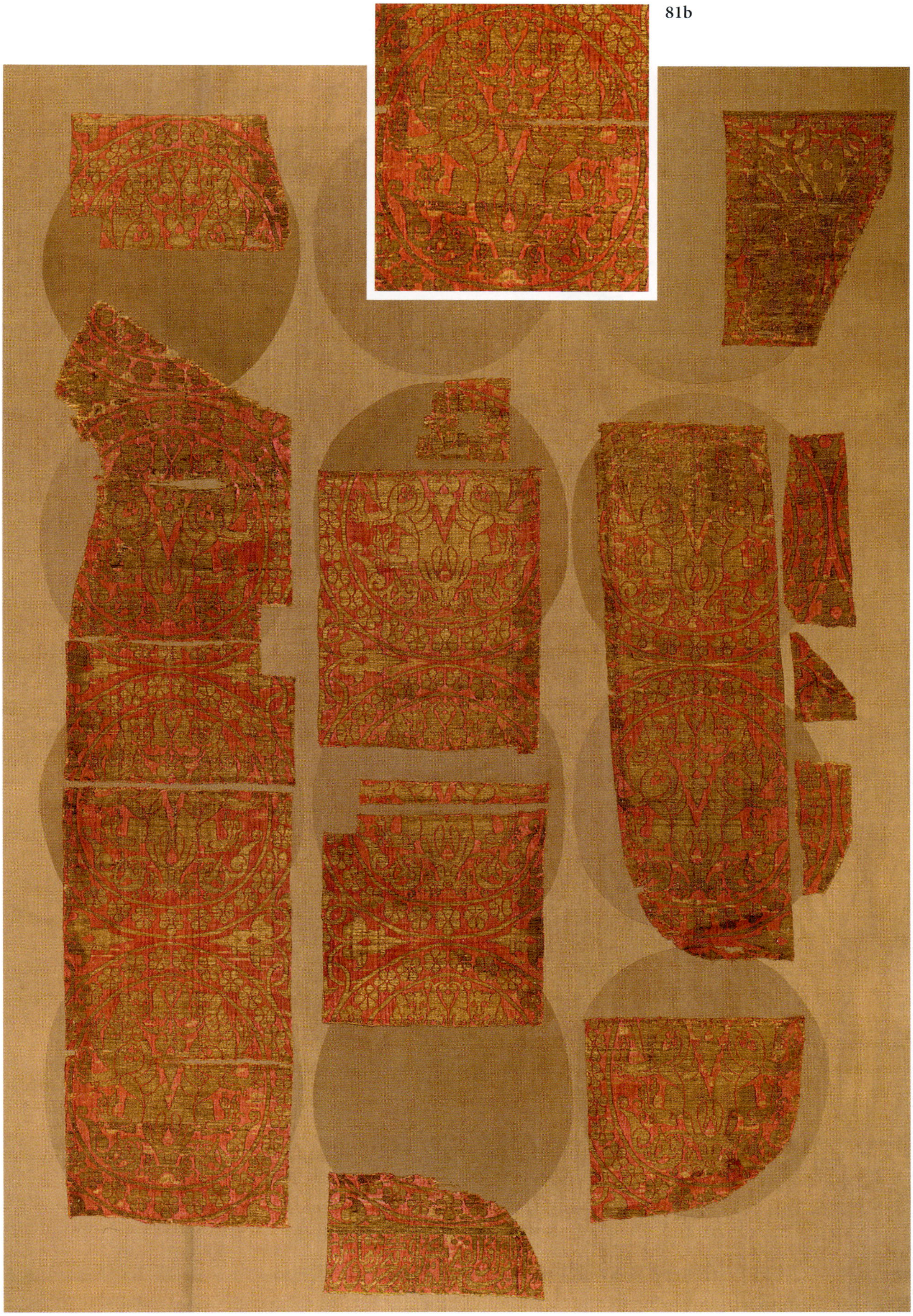

81b

81a and b. Pairs of addorsed dragon-tailed lions in rampant posture inscribed with the name of *sulṭān* Kay Qubādh. Section of a chasuble, probably Anatolia.

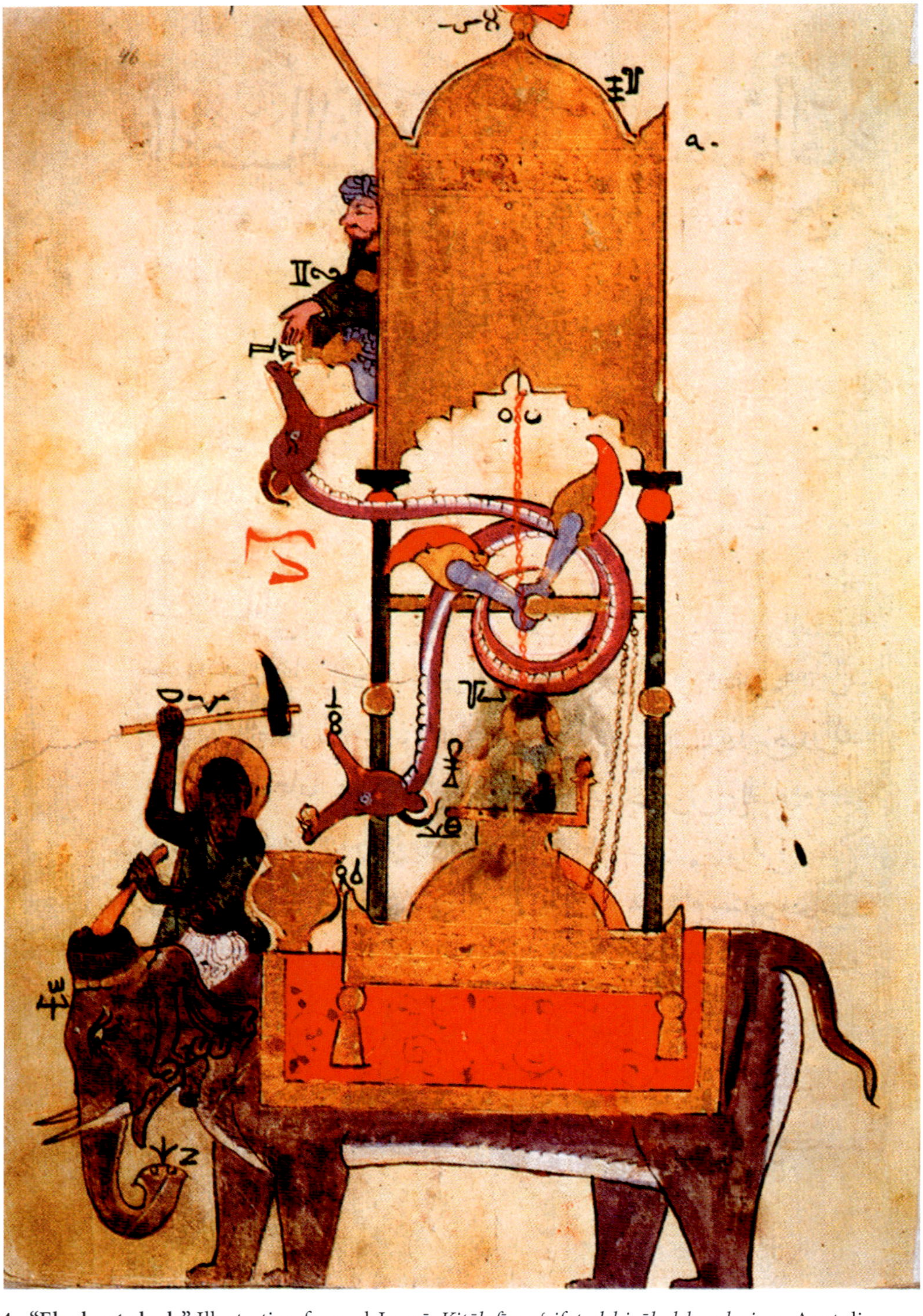

84. **"Elephant clock."** Illustration from al-Jazarī, *Kitāb fī maʿrifat al-ḥiyāl al-handasiyya*, Anatolia.

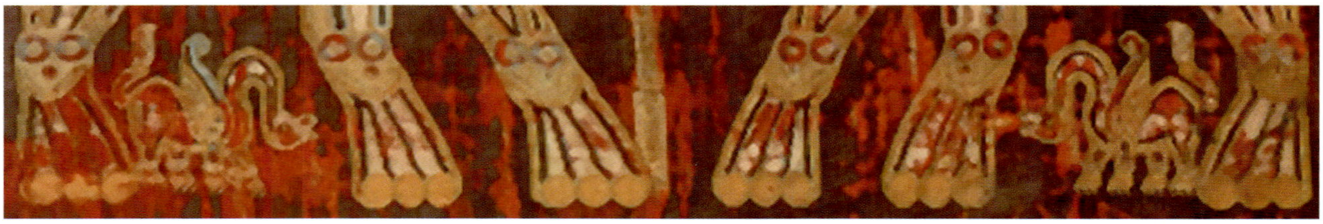

85b. Elephants and winged quadruped dragons with benedictory inscription naming the owner, Qāʾid Abu ʾl-Manṣūr Bākh-tigīn. Textile fragment, Khurasan.

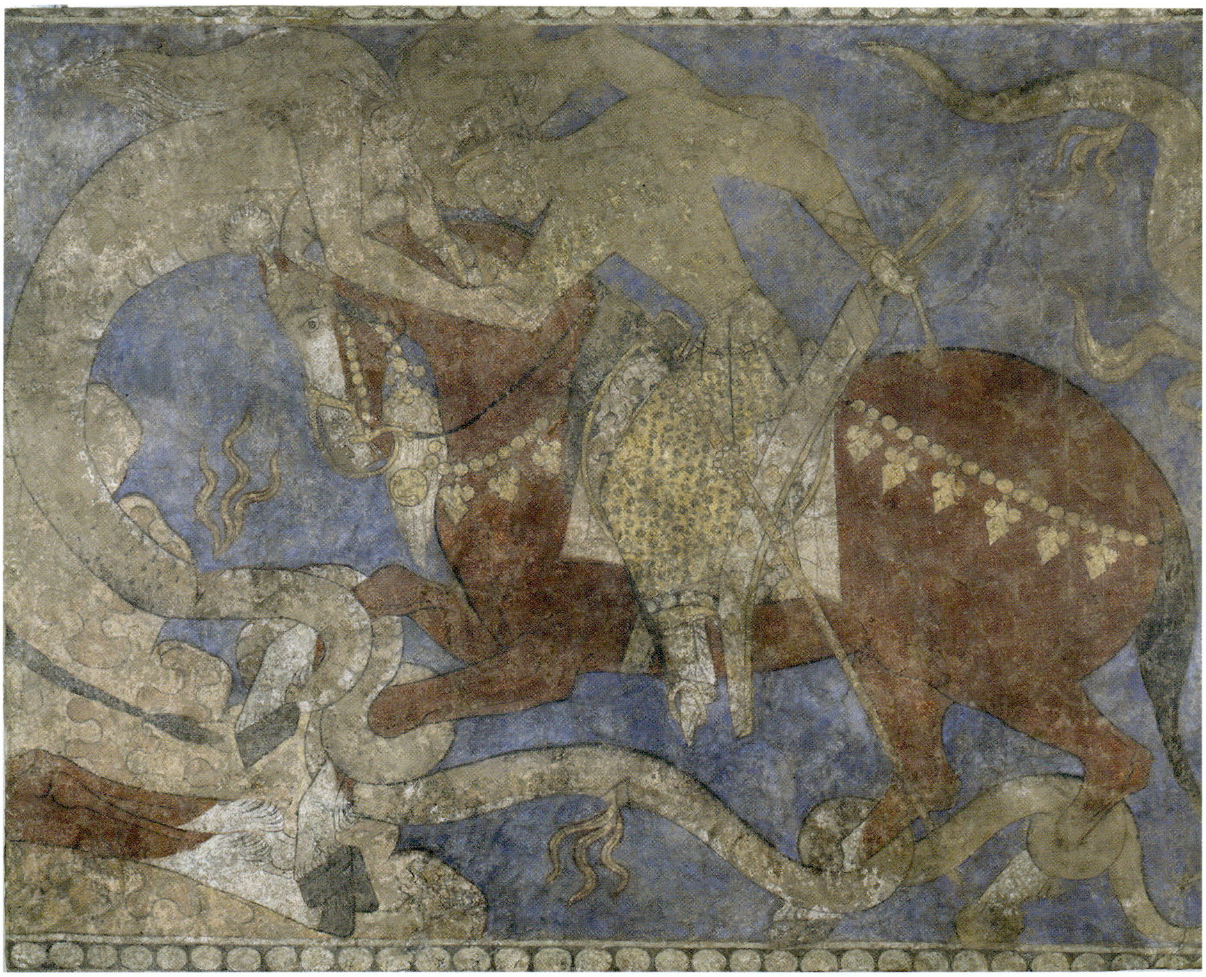

88. Rustam fighting a dragon. Wall painting, Panjikent.

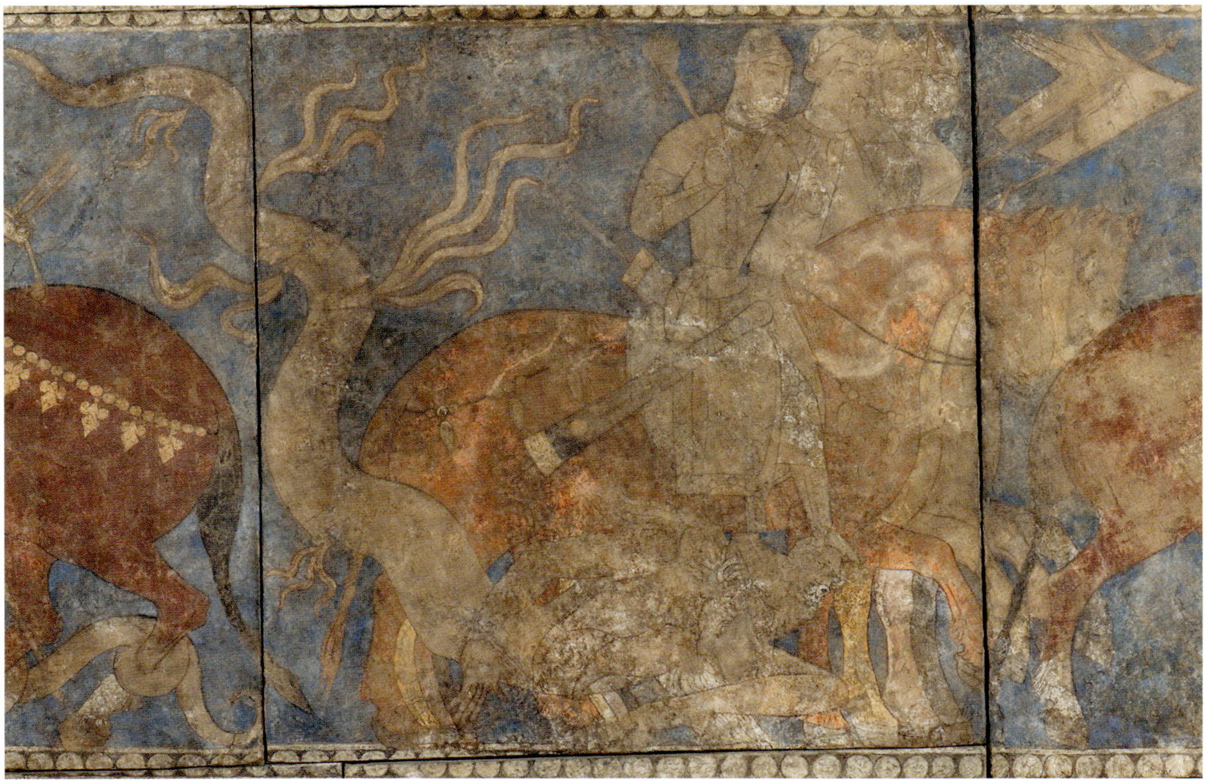

89. Rustam departing after killing the dragon. Wall painting, Panjikent.

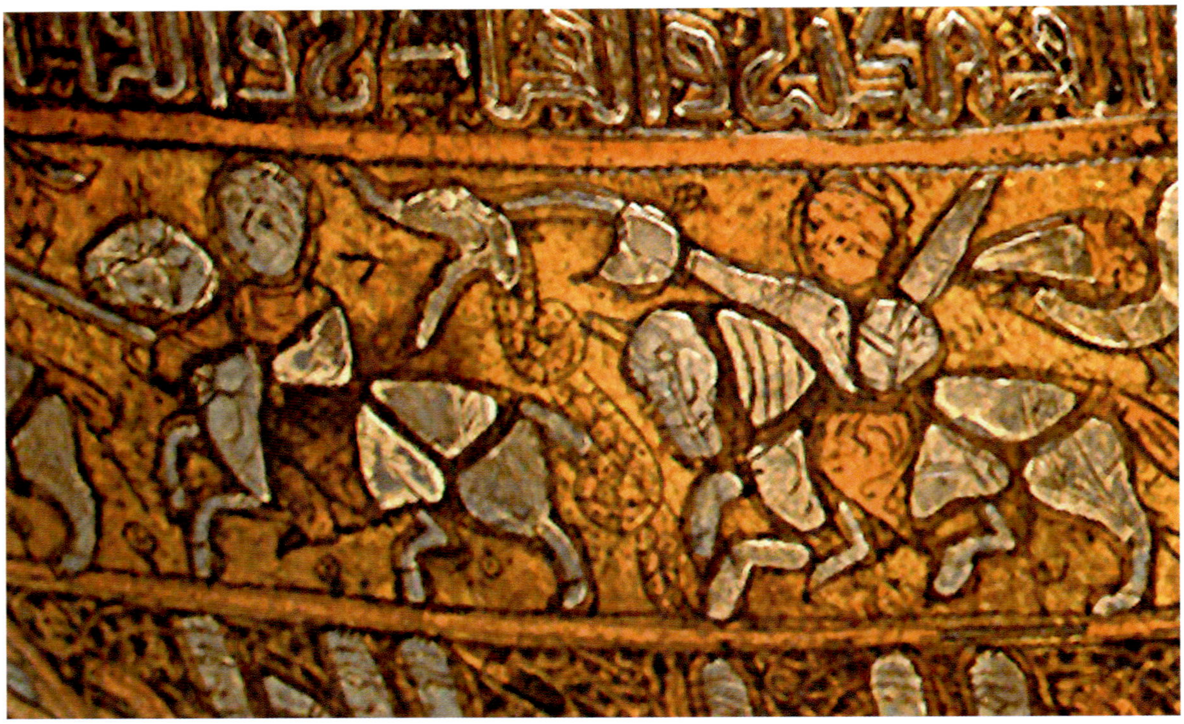

90. A horseman fighting a dragon. Detail from the Bobrinski bucket, possibly Herat.

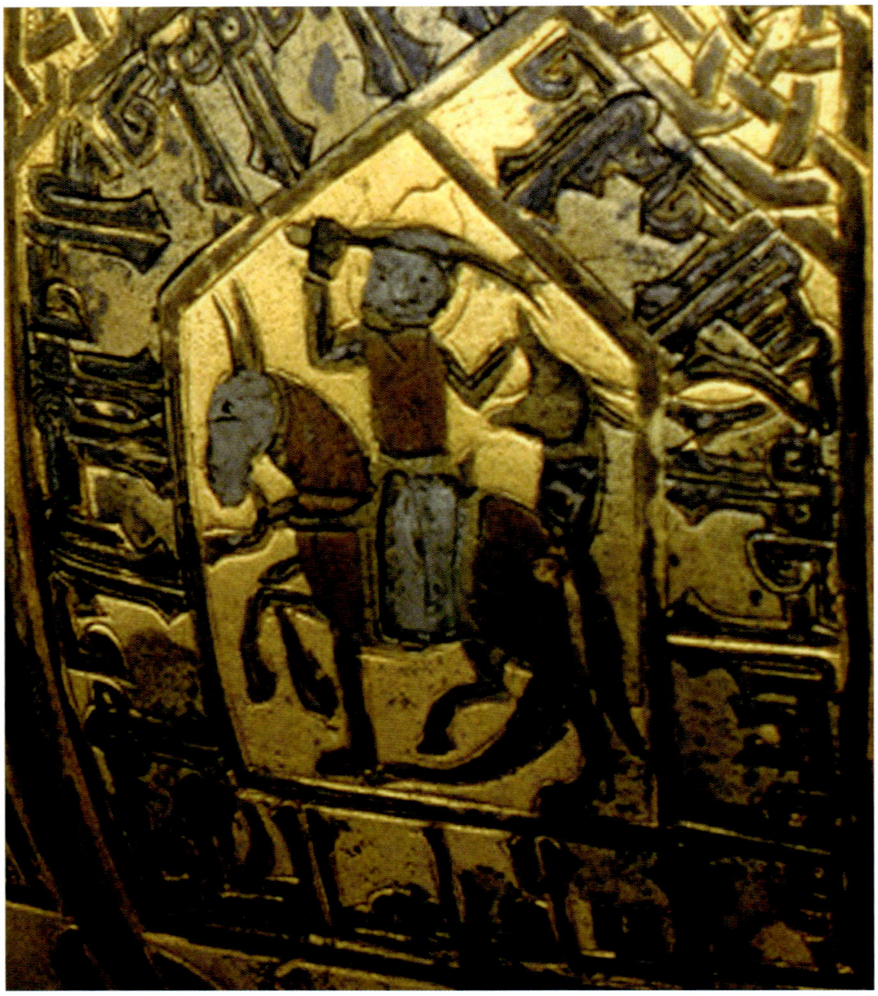

91. A horseman fighting a dragon. Detail from the Fould bucket, possibly Anatolia.

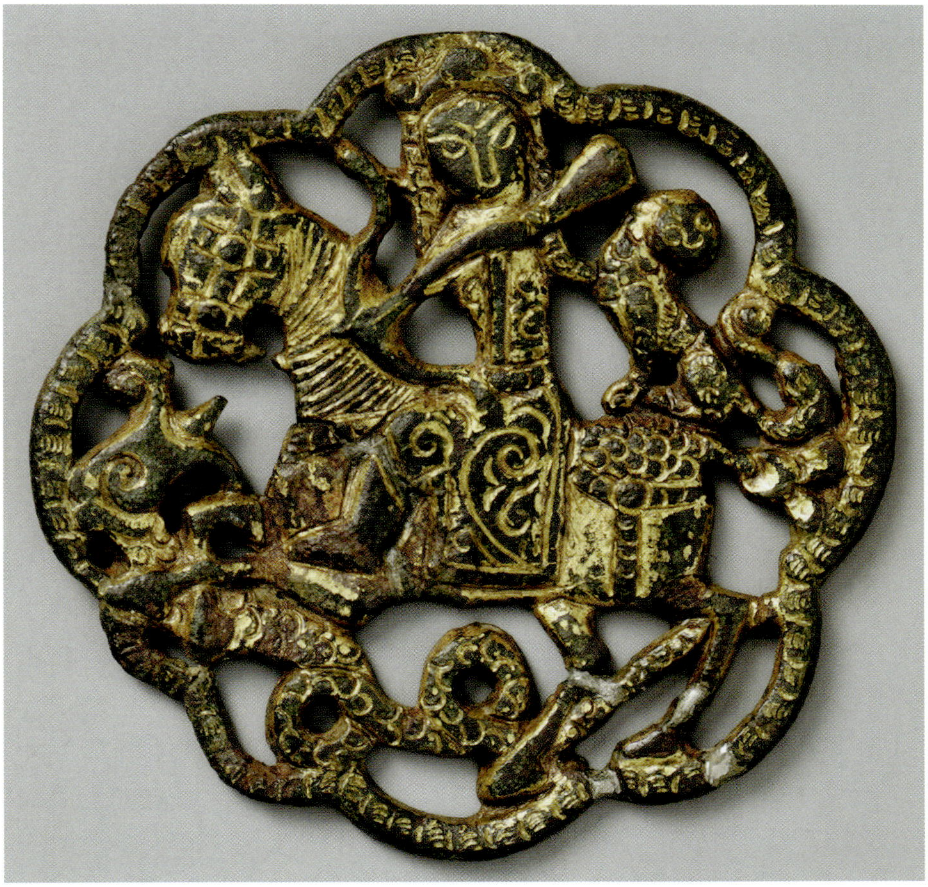

94. A horseman fighting a dragon. Roundel, Western Central Asia.

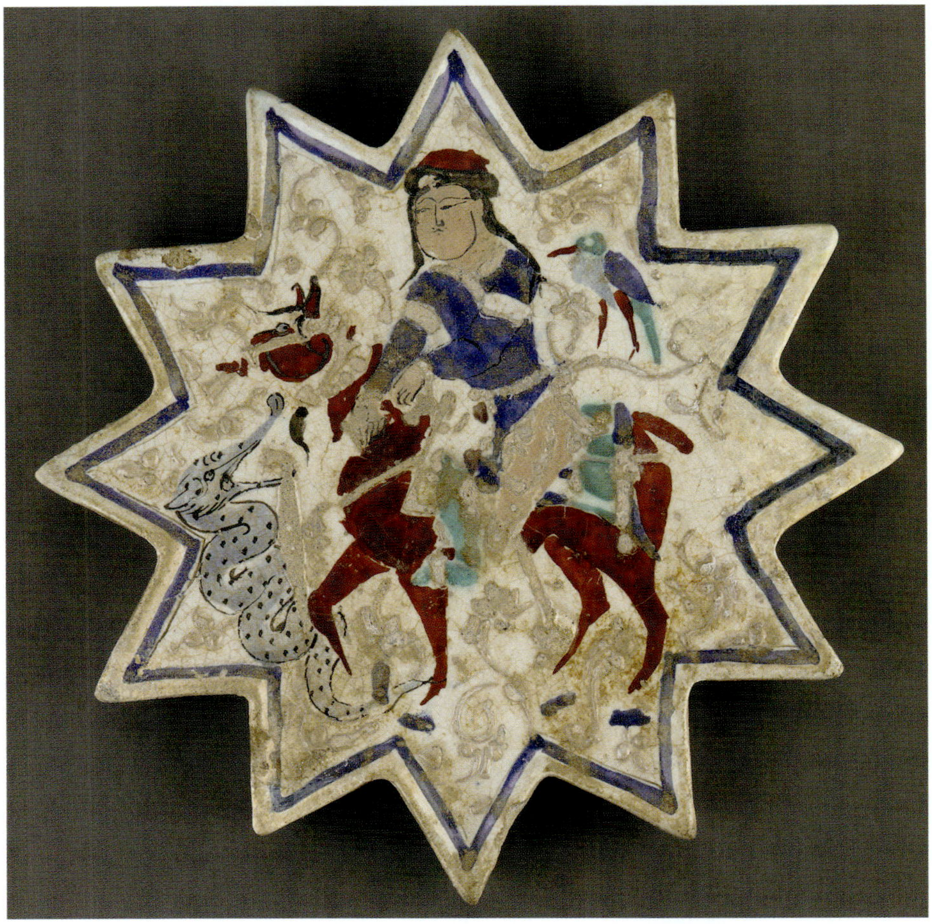

95. A horseman fighting a dragon. Twelve-pointed star tile, Iran.

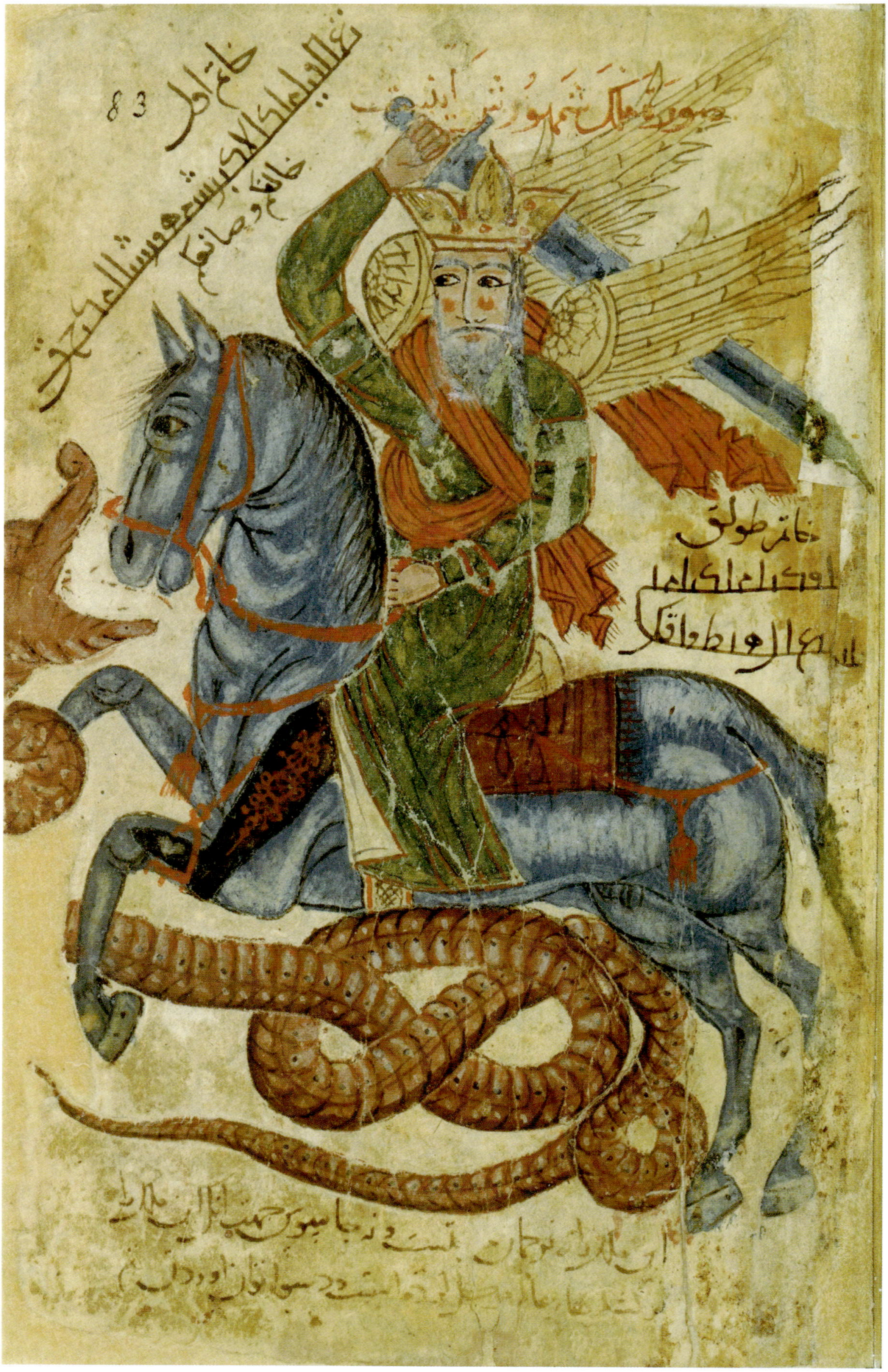

102. The angel Shamhūrash as mounted dragon-fighter. Painting in a copy of the *Daqā'iq al-Ḥaqā'iq*, Aksaray.

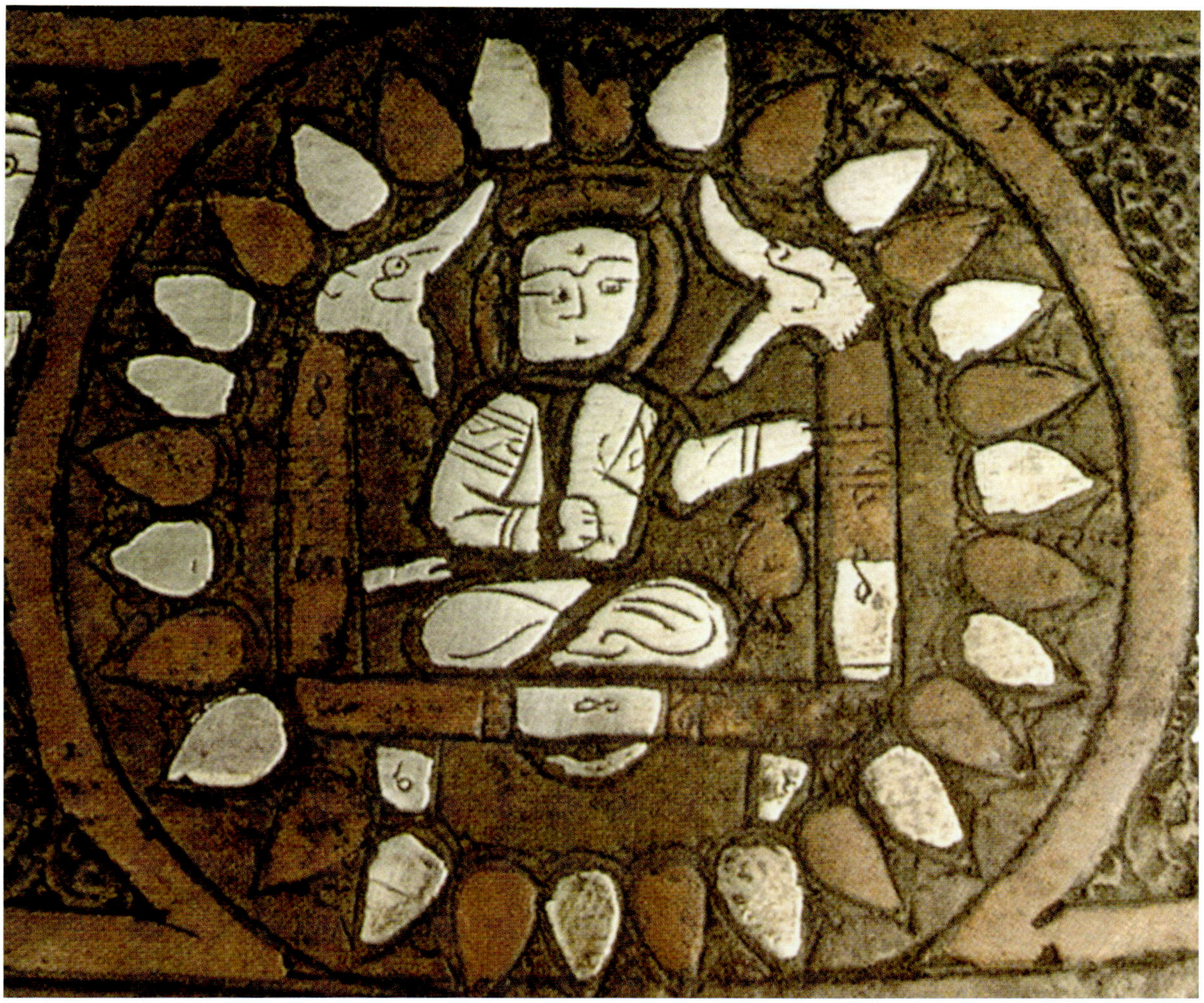

114. "A ruler on a dragon-throne." Detail from the Bobrinski bucket, possibly Herat.

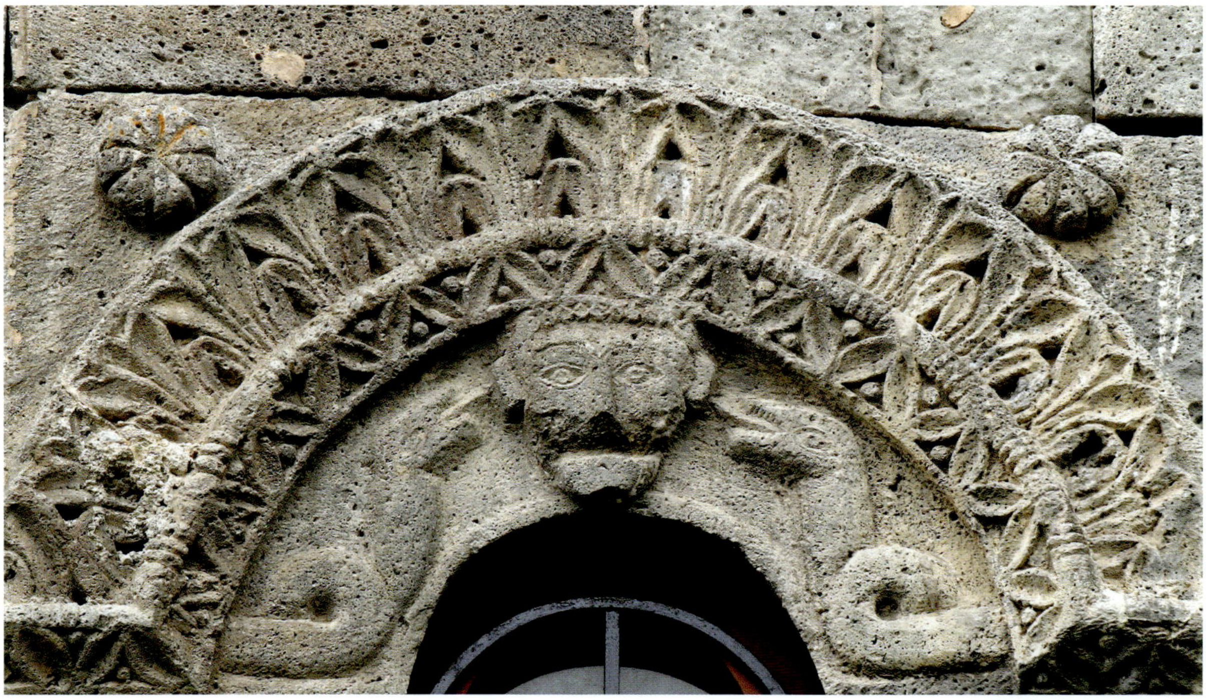

120. A human head between a pair of confronted dragons. Relief carving on the north façade of the church of Surb Poghos Petros, Tat'ev monastic complex.

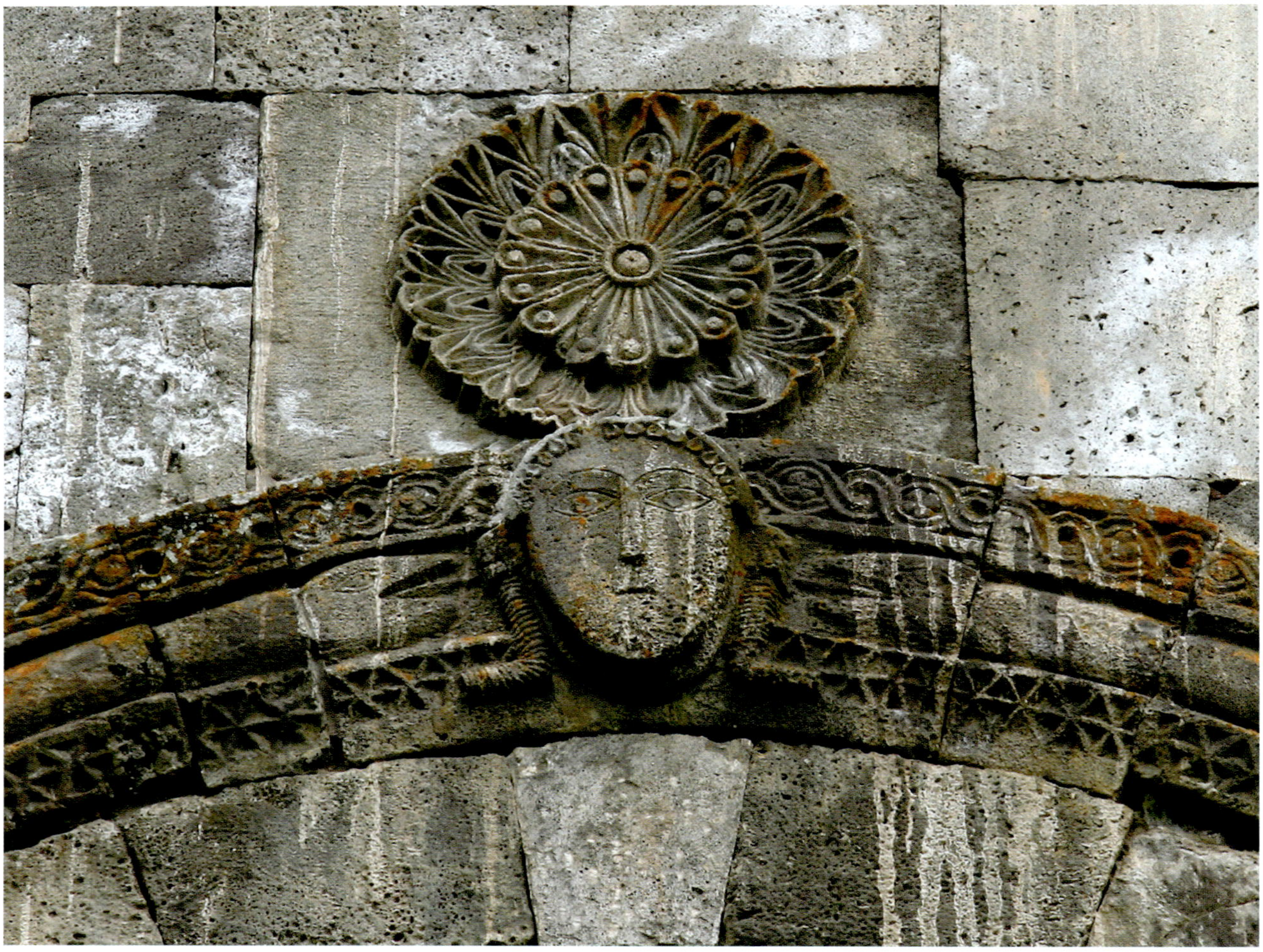

122. A human head between a pair of confronted dragons. Relief carving on the east façade of the church of Surb Poghos Petros, Tatʿev monastic complex.

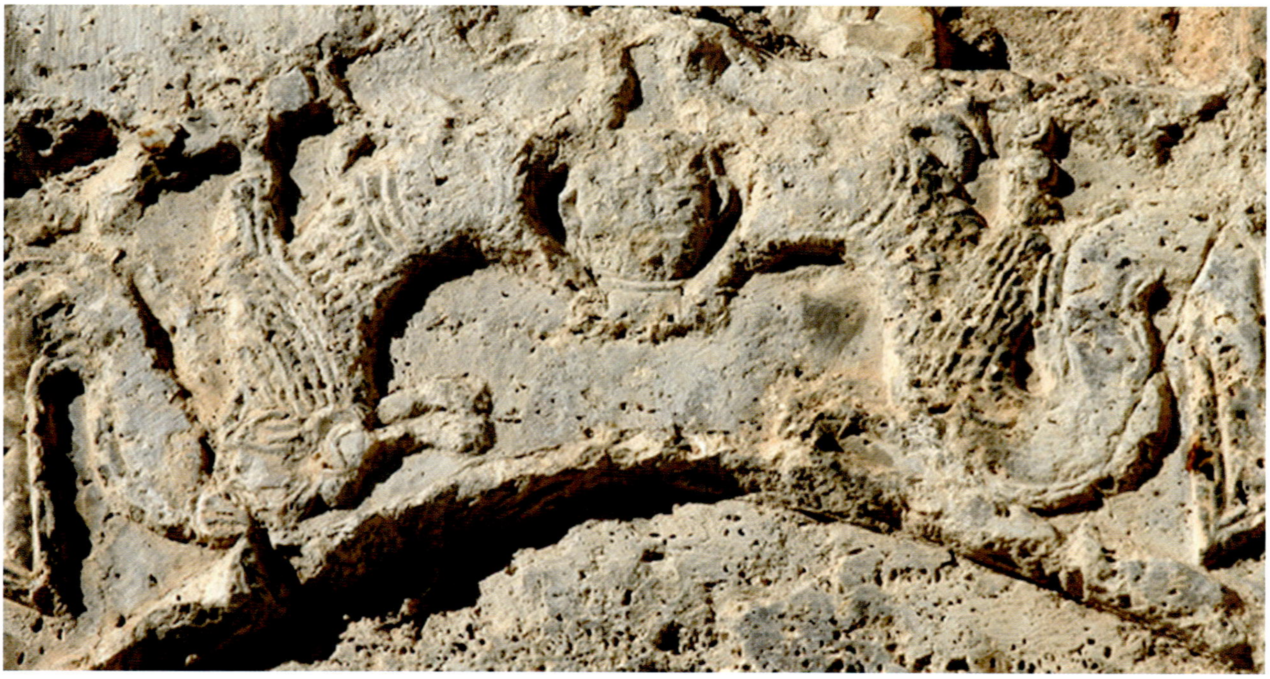

124. A human head between a pair of confronted winged dragons with forelegs. Relief carving above the two niches that flank the main portal, Susuz Han, south of Bucak.

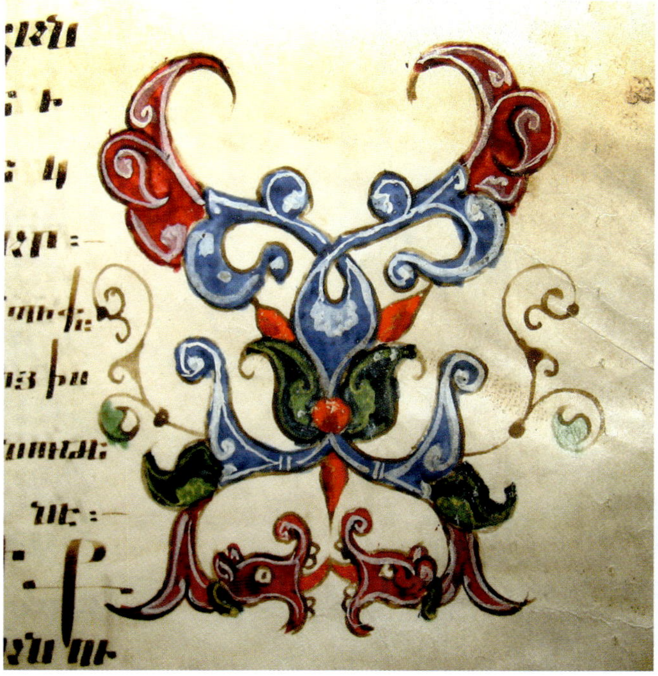

128. A pair of confronted dragon heads springing from interlaced vegetation. Marginal ornament in the Mush Homiliary, monastery of Avagvankʿ, Erznga(n).

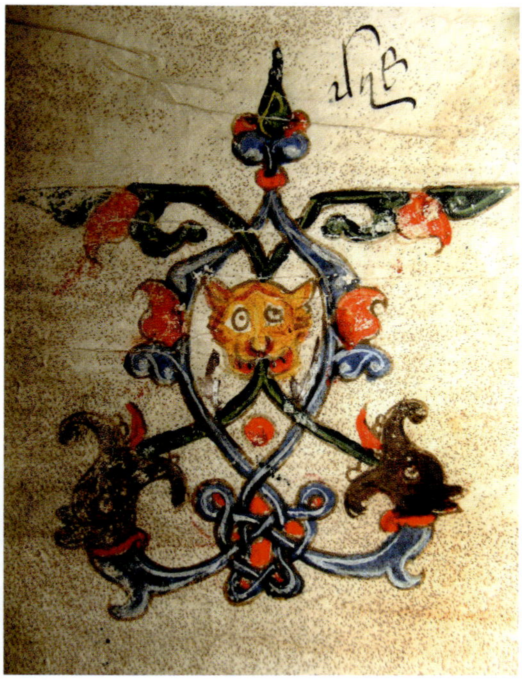

131. A lion head above a pair of confronted dragons issuing a vegetal interlace. Marginal ornament in the Mush Homiliary, monastery of Avagvankʿ, Erznga(n).

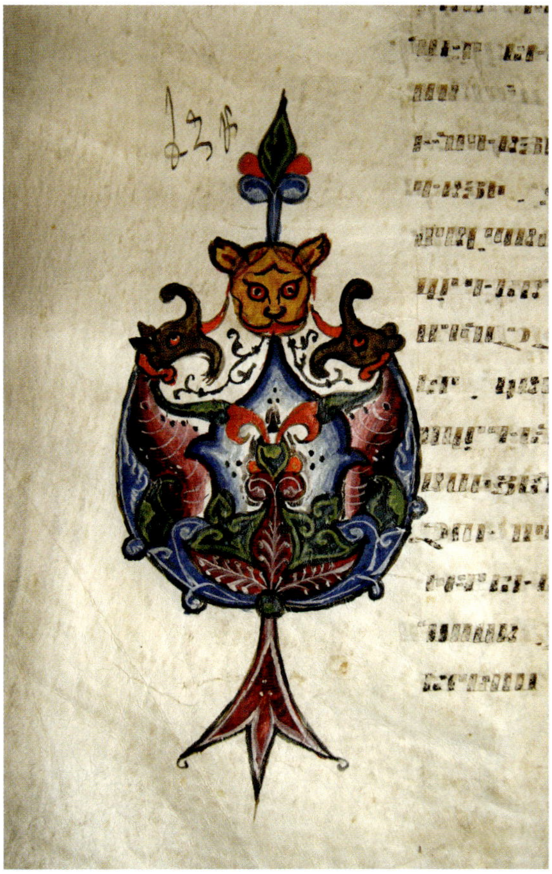

133. A pomegranate enclosing a lion head between a pair of confronted dragons. Marginal ornament in the Mush Homiliary, monastery of Avagvankʿ, Erznga(n).

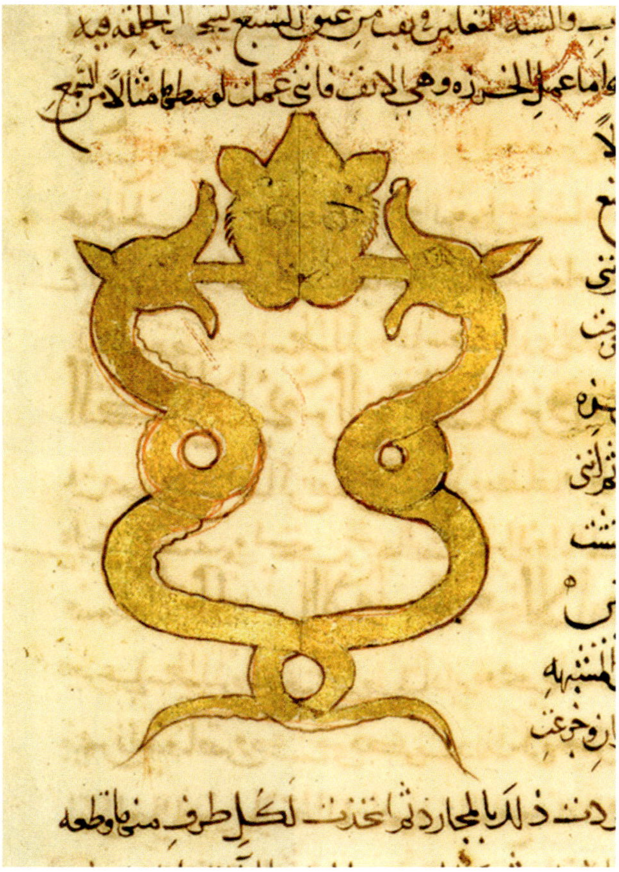

134. A knocker in the form of a pair of confronted dragons framing a lion-headed knob. Drawing of the doors of the Diyārbakr palace, illustration in a copy of al-Jazarī, *Kitāb fī maʿrifat al-ḥiyāl al-handasiyya*, Anatolia.

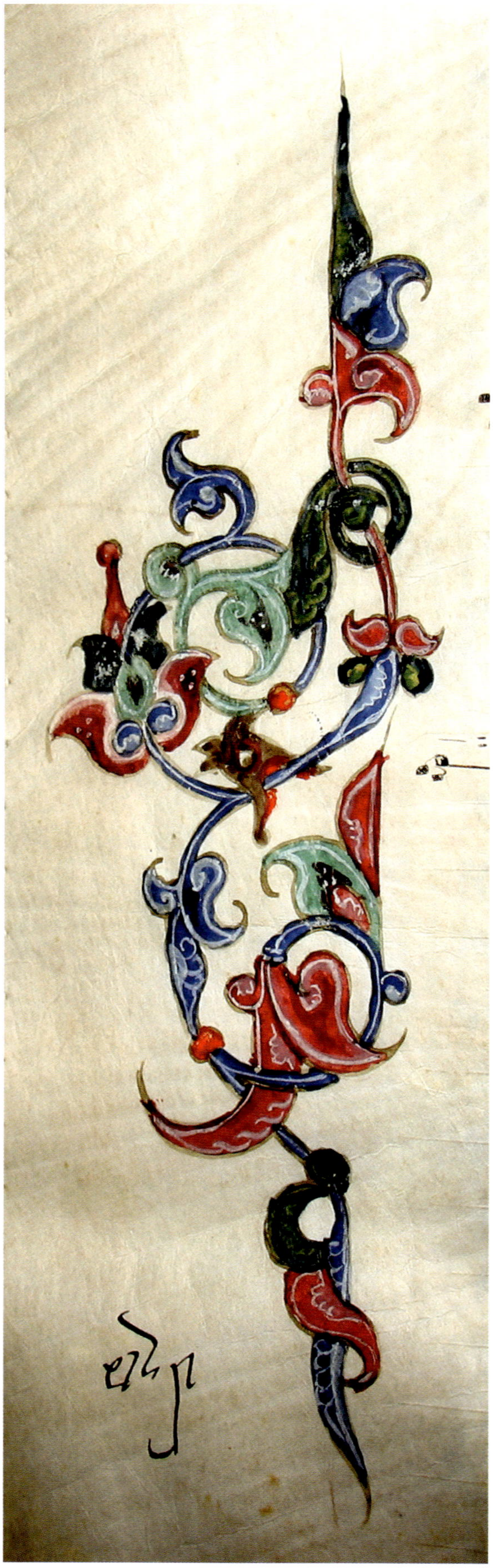

129. A vegetal stalk issuing a single dragon head. Marginal ornament in the Mush Homiliary, monastery of Avagvank‘, Erznga(n).

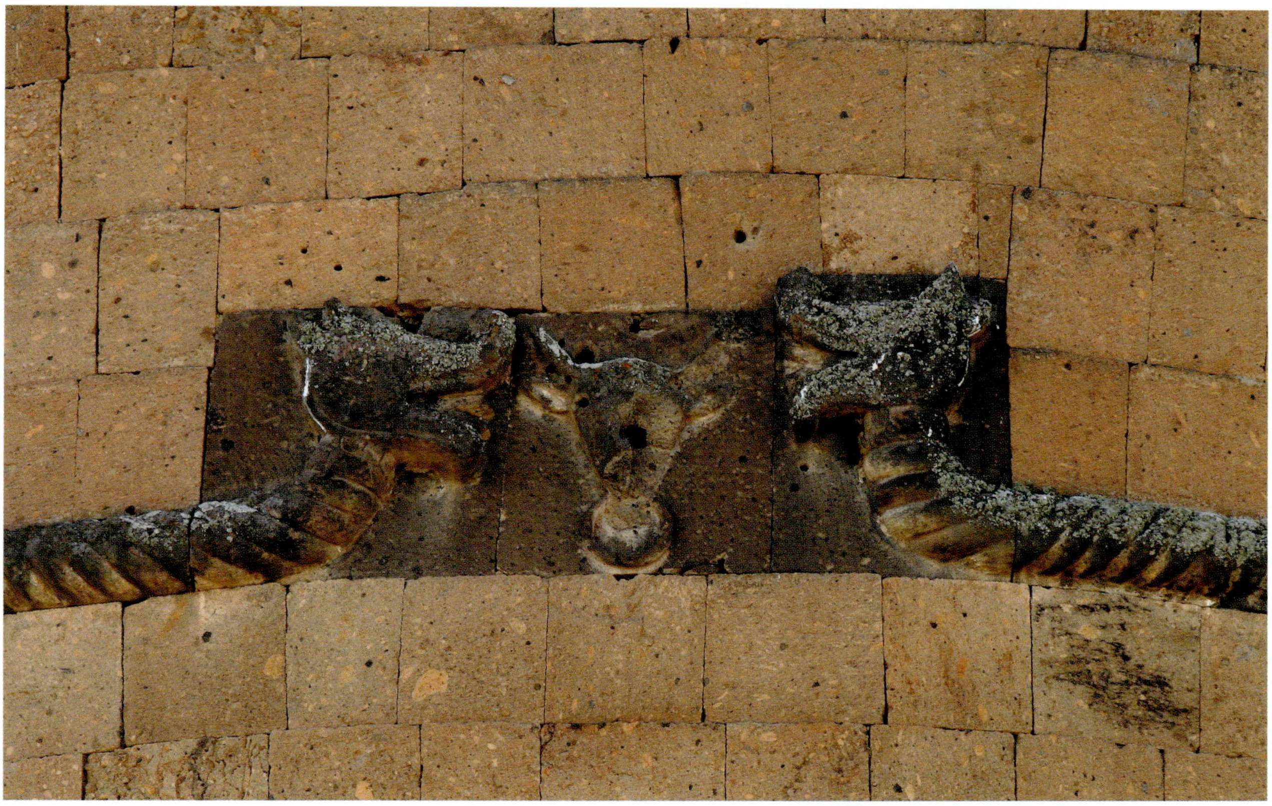

130. A bovine head holding a ring between a pair of confronted dragons. Relief carving on a round tower of the northern city wall, Ani.

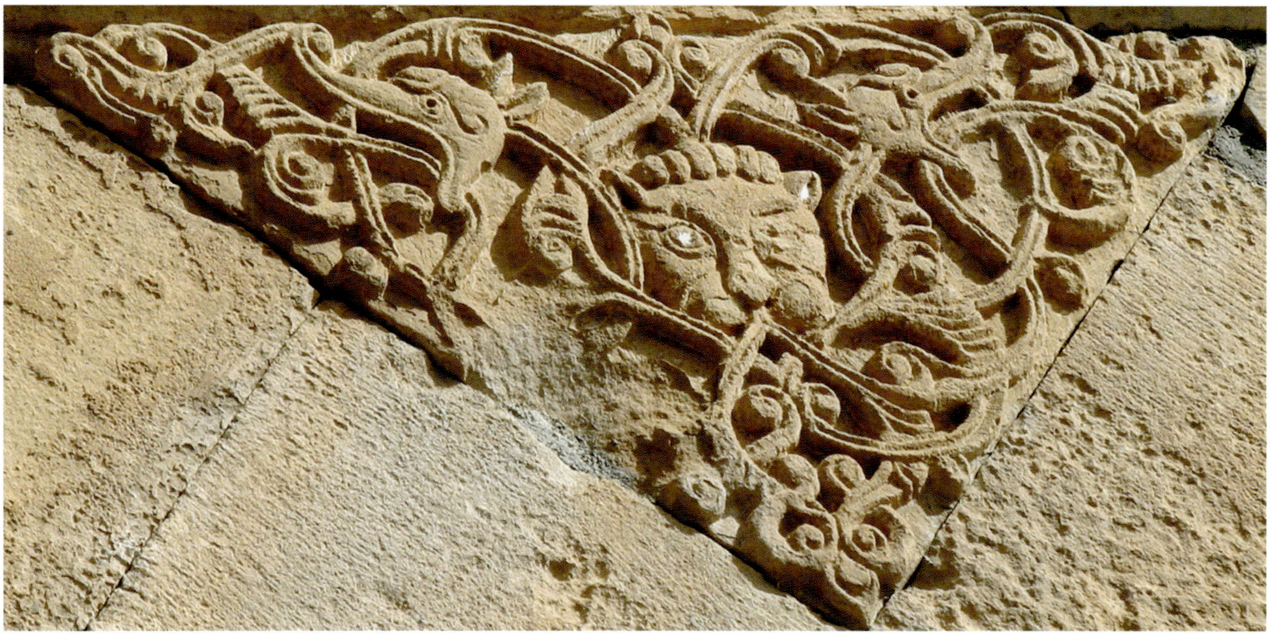

135. A lion head issuing spiralling tendrils that transform into a pair of addorsed dragon heads. Relief carving at the upper corners just below the roof of the church of Surb Karapet, monastic complex of Noravankʿ.

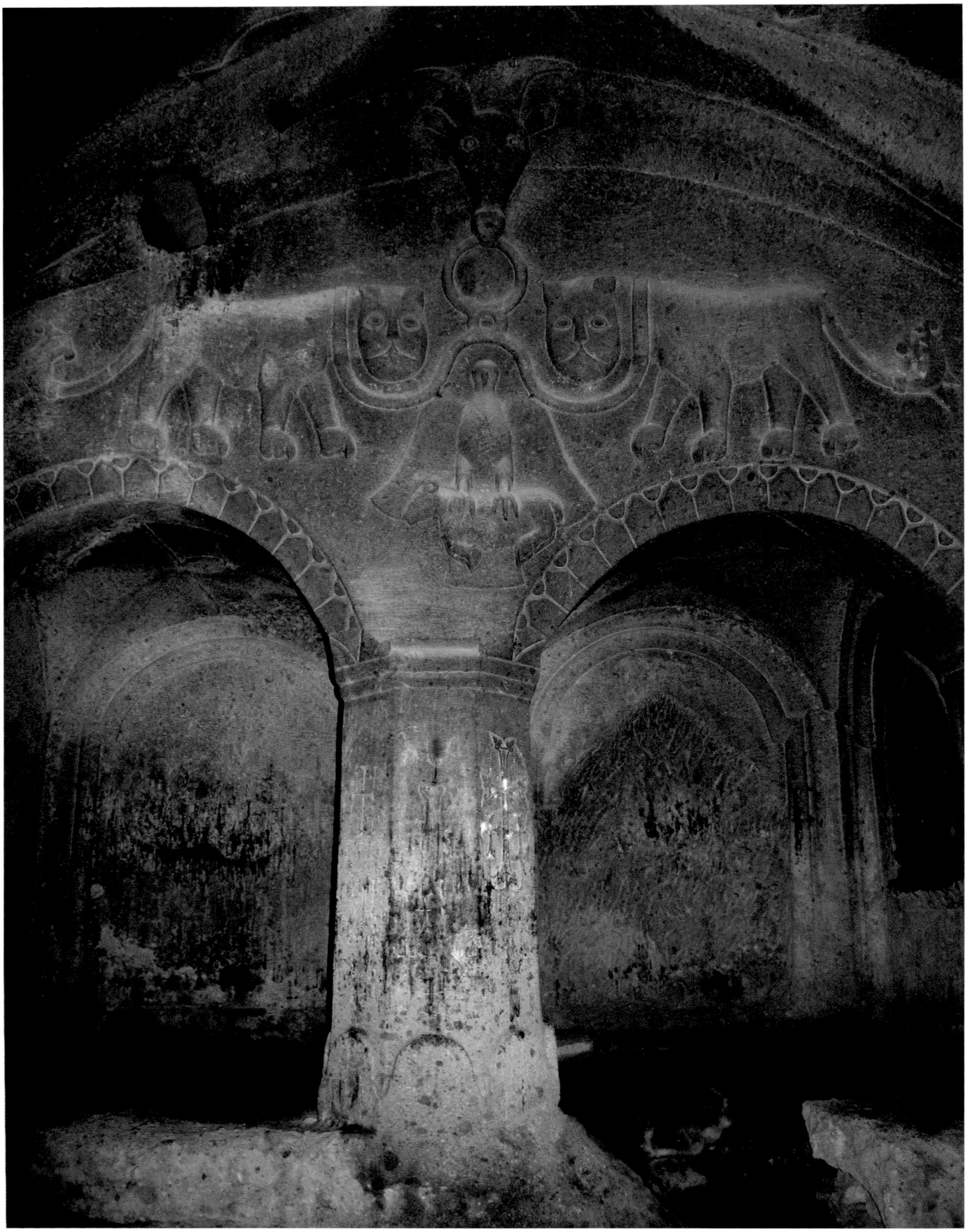

136. A bovine head holding a ring fastened to chains that are attached to a pair of confronted dragon-tailed lions surmounting an eagle grasping an ungulate. Rock relief on the northern wall of the Prosh family mausoleum, monastic complex of Geghard, Kotaykʿ.

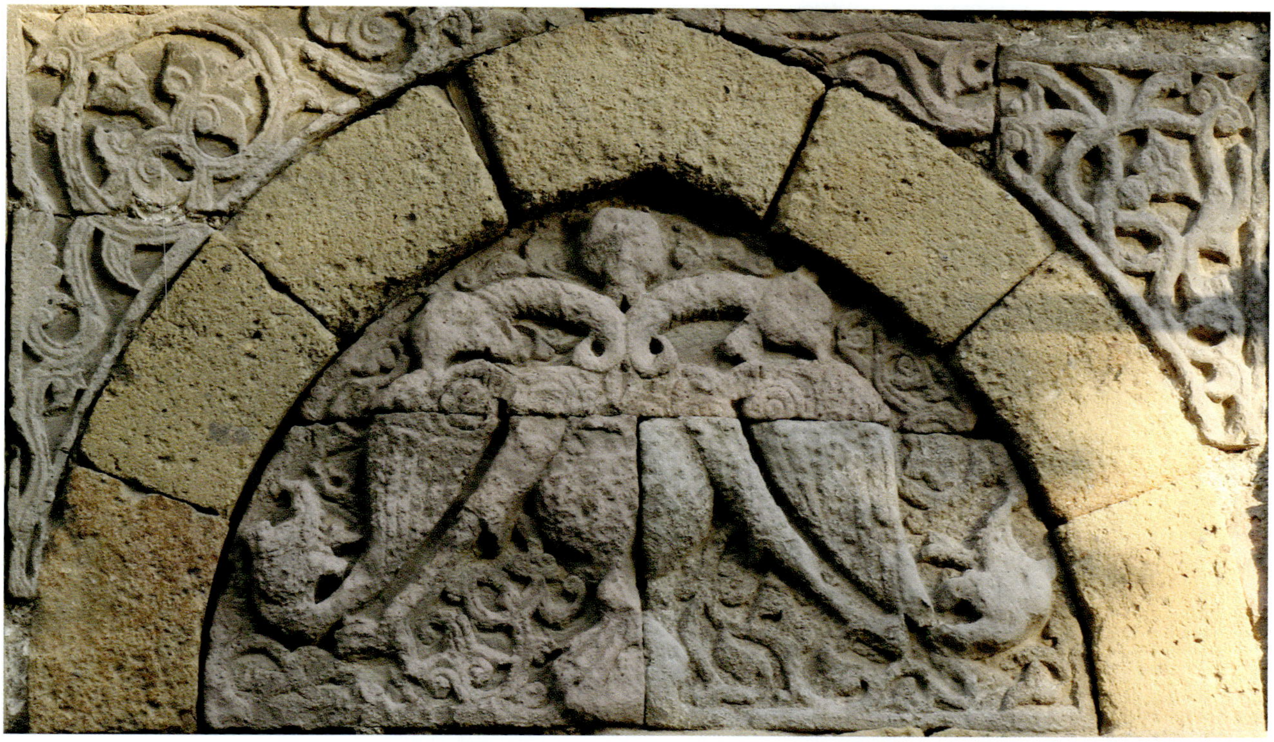

137. A human face surmounting a double-headed eagle with dragon-headed wing tips. Relief carving on the *türbe* of Hüdavend Hatun, Niğde.

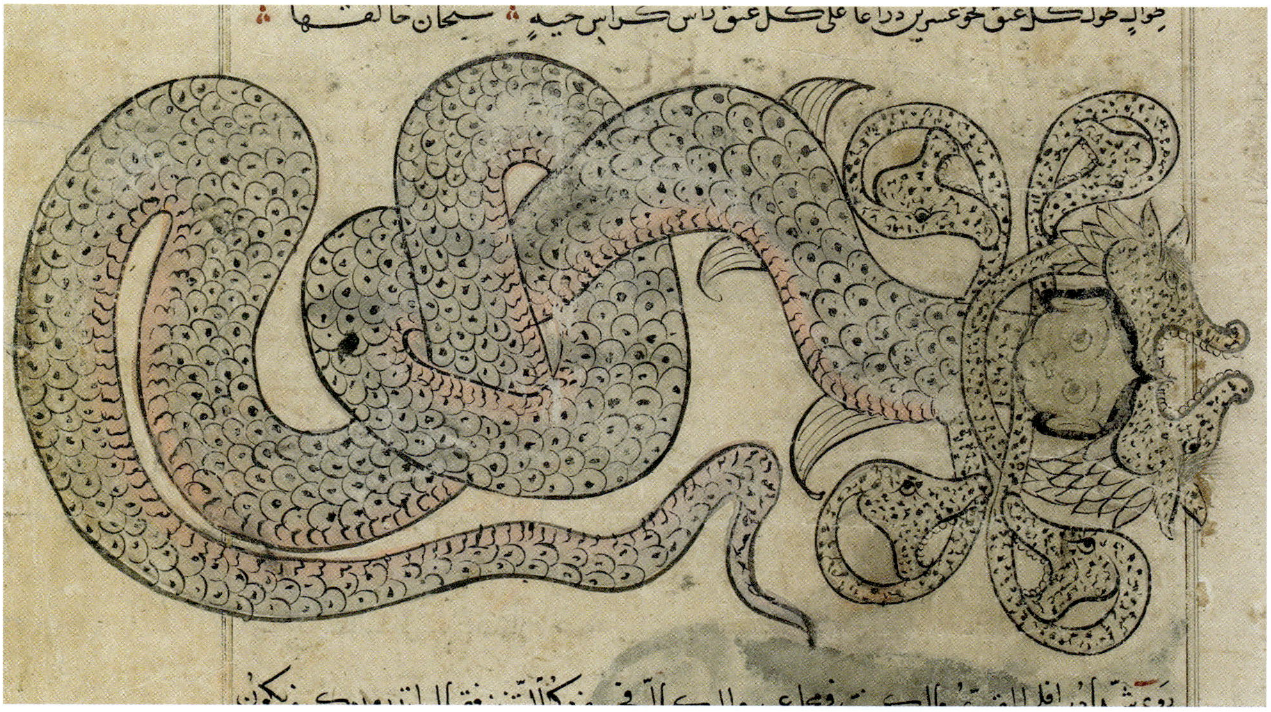

138. "The Dragon." Illustration from the Sarre Qazwīnī, attributed to southern Anatolia, perhaps Diyārbakr.

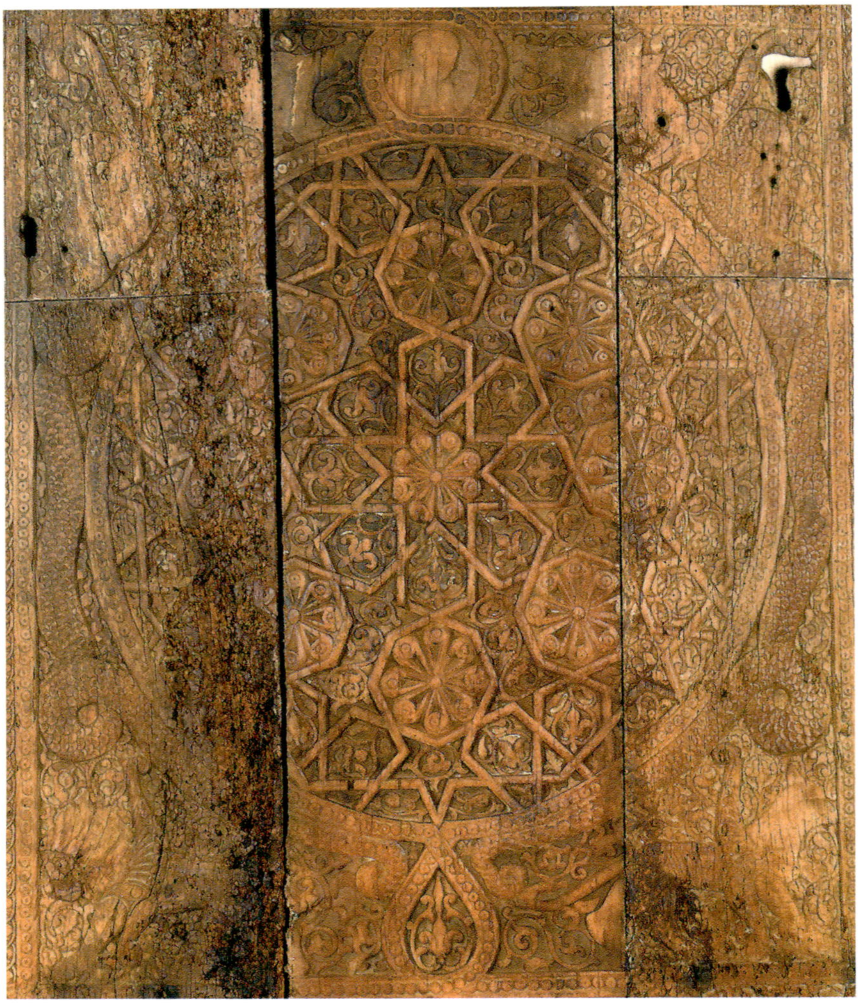

153. A pair of confronted winged dragons with forelegs flanking a human bust (?) and enclosing a large medallion containing a star pattern. Relief carving of a door, the Jazīra.

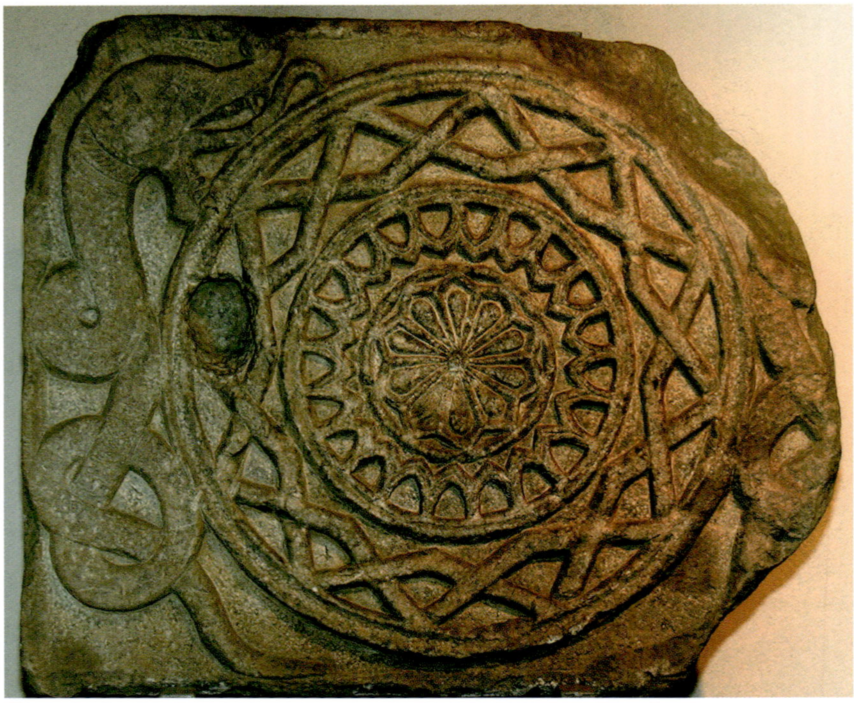

154. A pair of dragons enclosing a large medallion containing a star pattern. Relief carving, Anatolia.

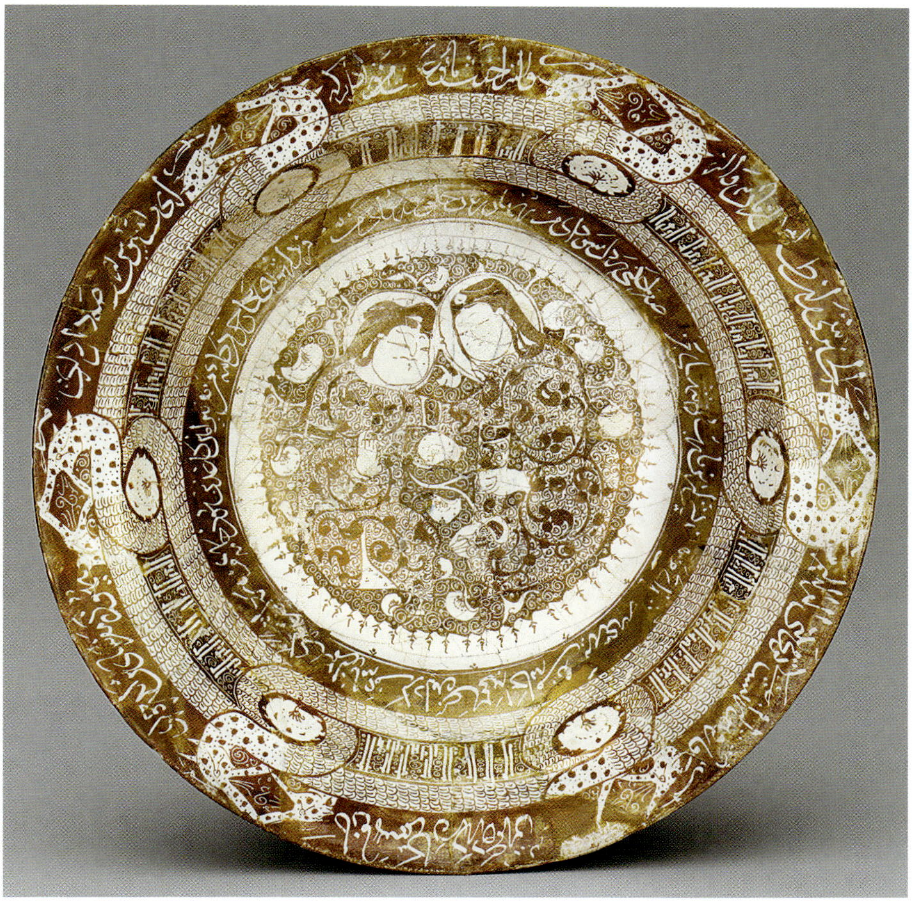

155. **Intertwined dragons and epigraphic bands framing a seated couple.** Bowl, Iran.

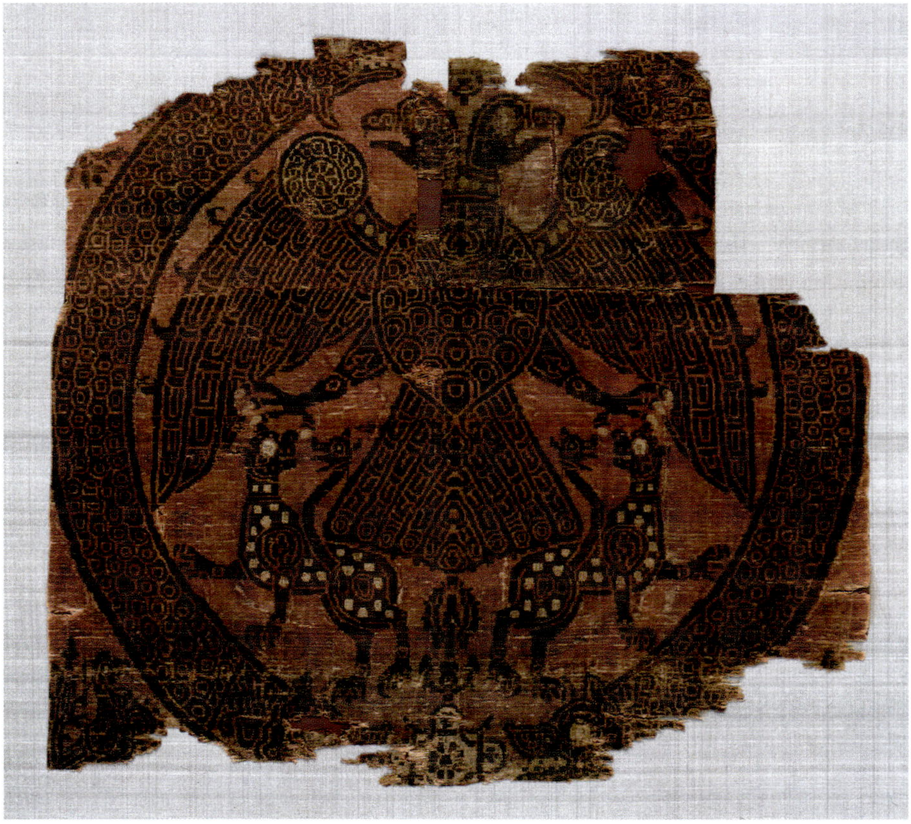

156. **A pair of double-headed confronted dragons enclosing a double-headed eagle and two dragon-tailed lions.** Textile fragment, preserved as relic cover of Saint Amandus, Western Central Asia.

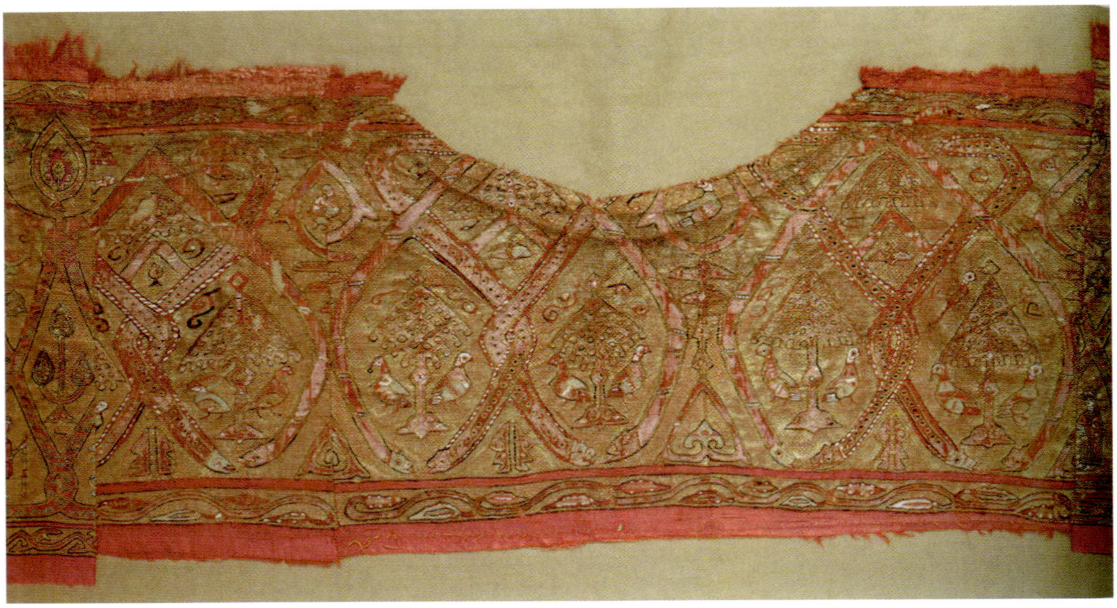

157a and b. **The "Bird Cloth."** Lining fabric of the coronation mantle of king Roger II of Sicily and southern Italy.

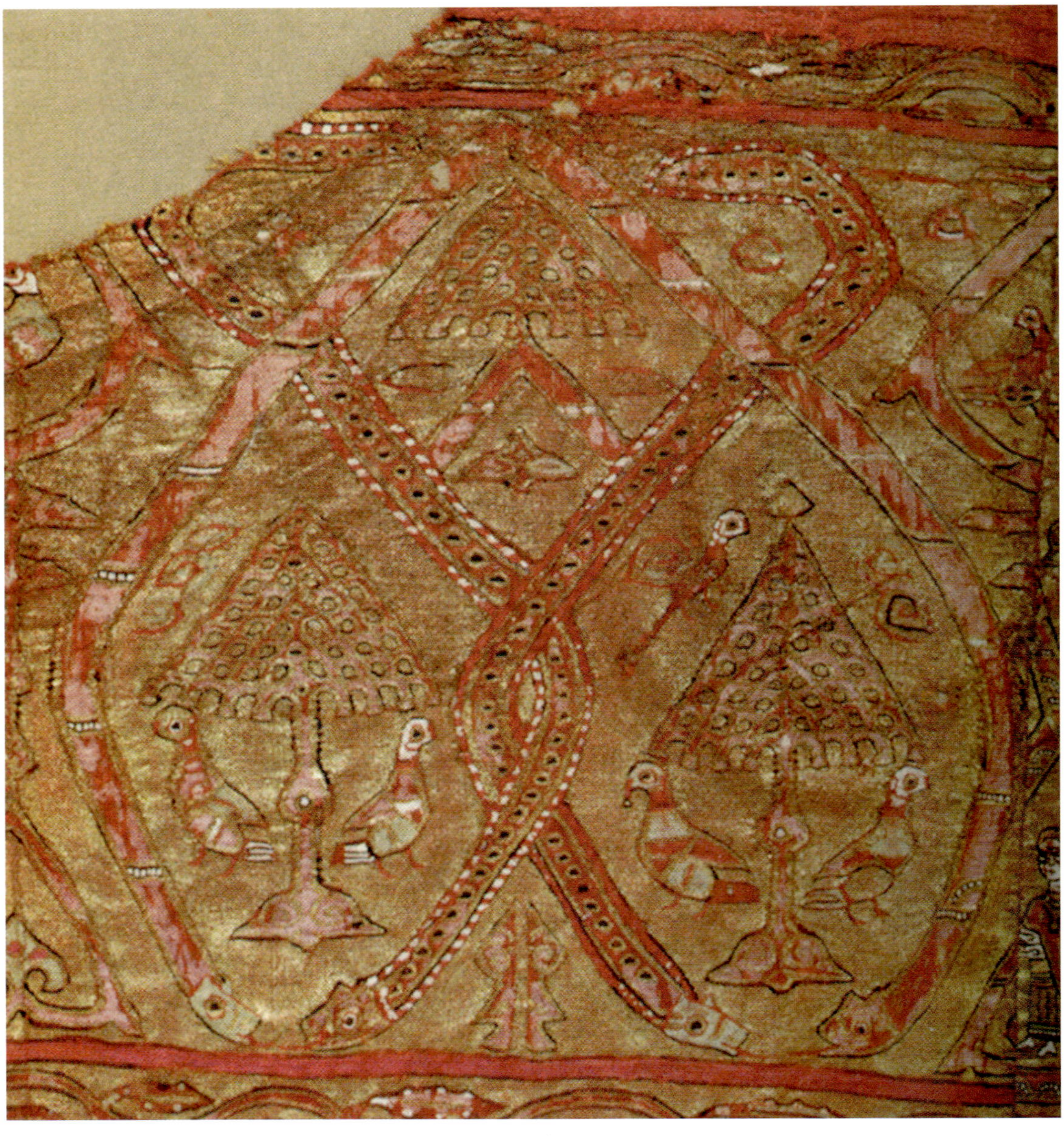

157b

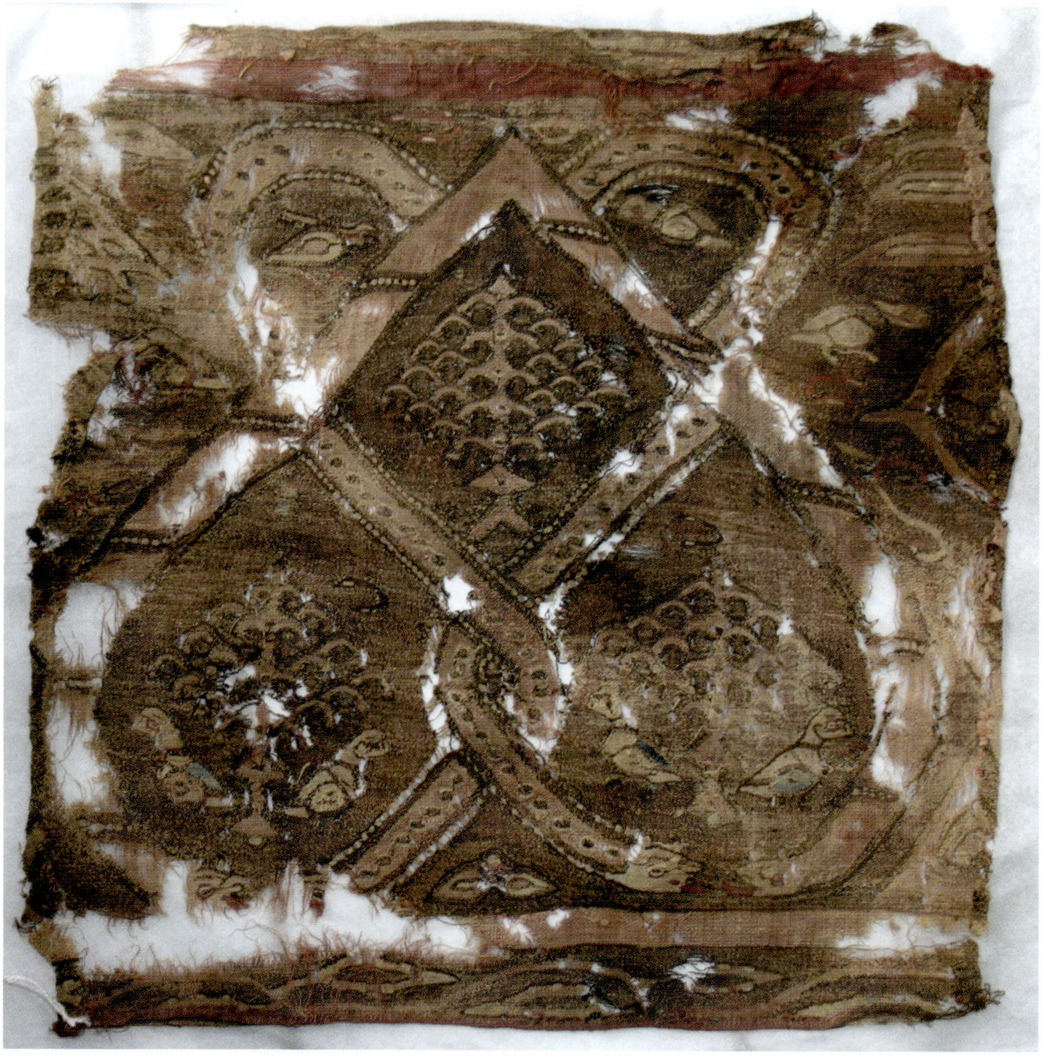

158a and b. A lattice formed by two pairs of confronted dragons enclosing trees flanked by addorsed birds. Textile fragment, Dar-i Suf, Samangan province.

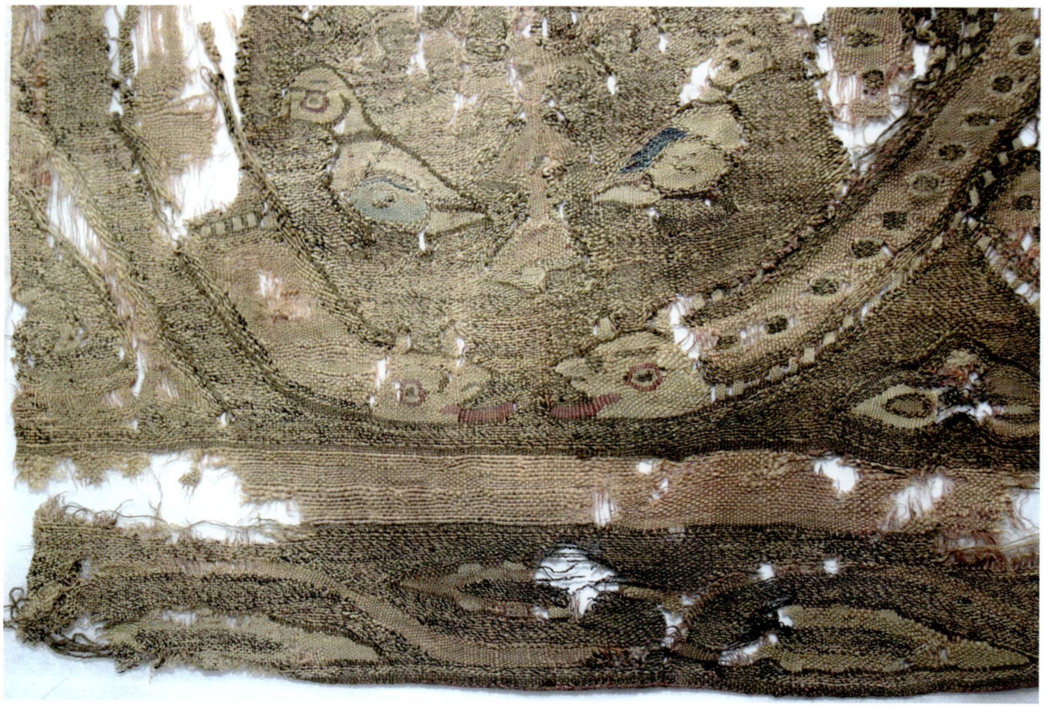

158b

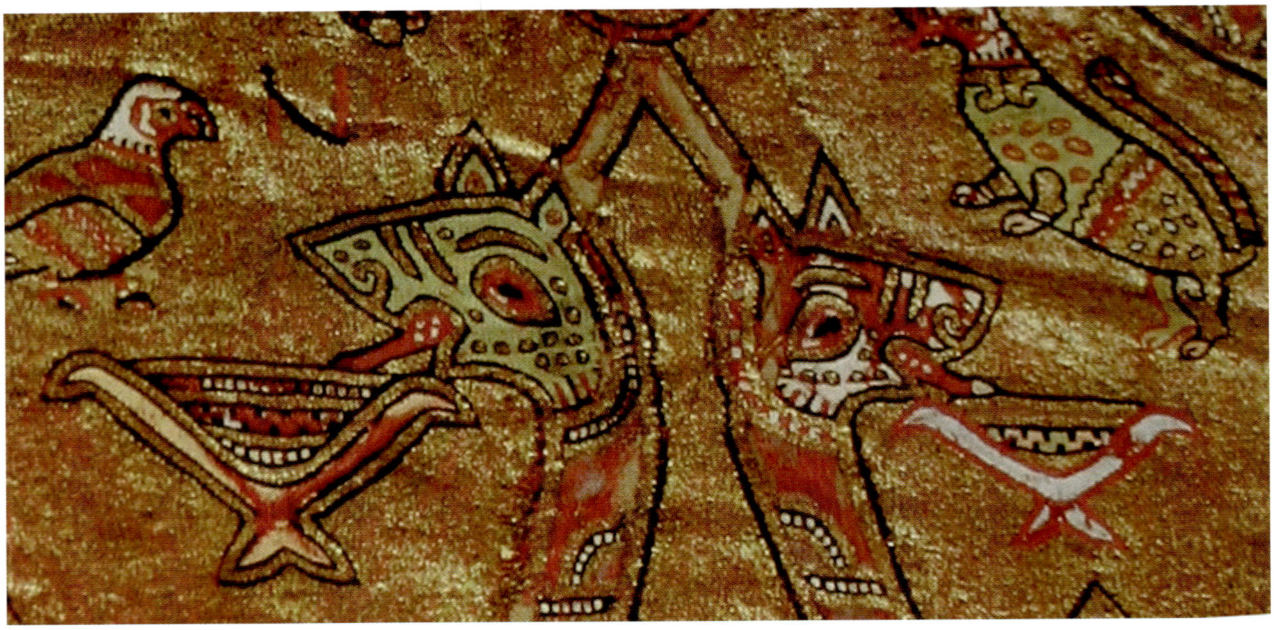

159. Dragons drinking from stemmed cups. Detail of the "Dragon Cloth," lining fabric of the coronation mantle of king Roger II of Sicily and southern Italy.

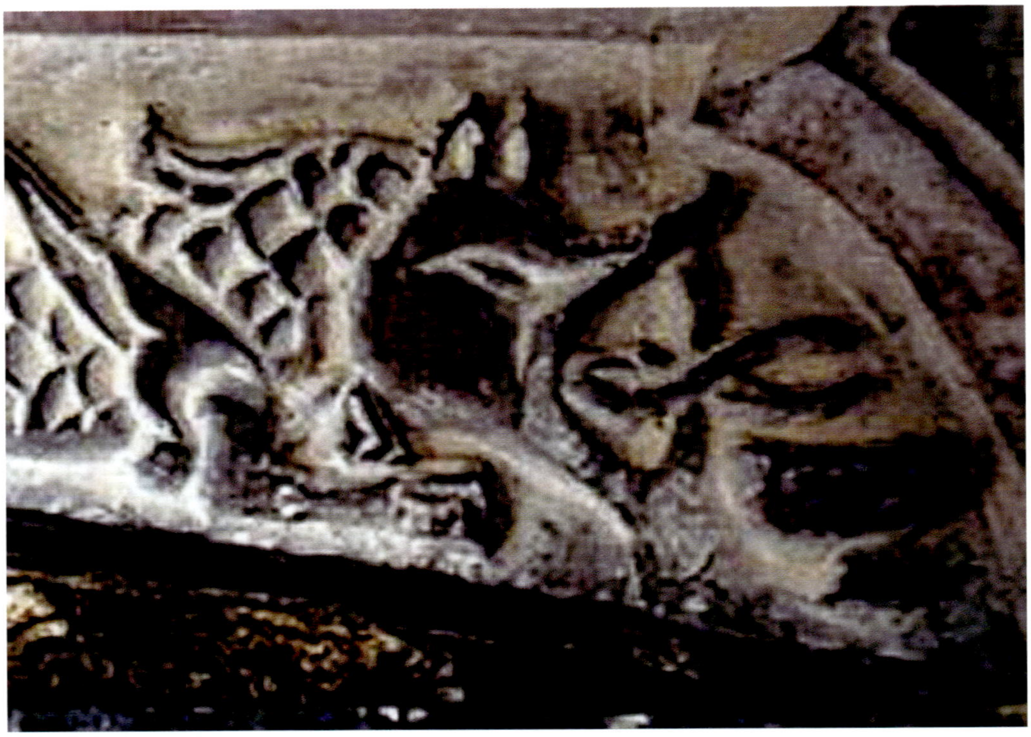

160. A pair of dragons drinking from stemmed cups. Detail of the relief carving above the southern outer portal, monastery of Mār Behnām/Deir al-Khiḍr, southeast of Mosul.

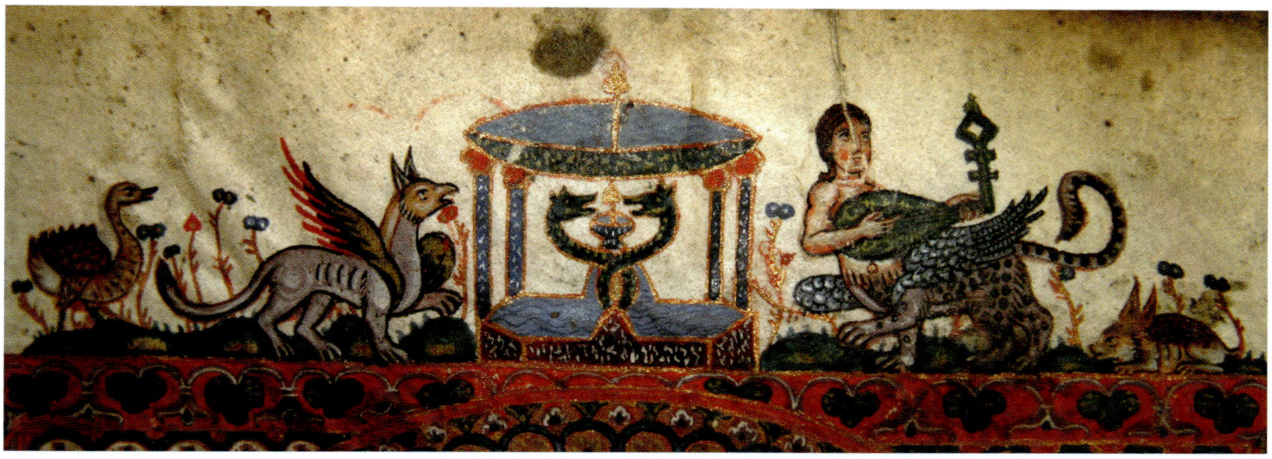

161. **A pair of confronted serpents drinking from a chalice.** Canon table in the Vani Gospels, Constantinople.

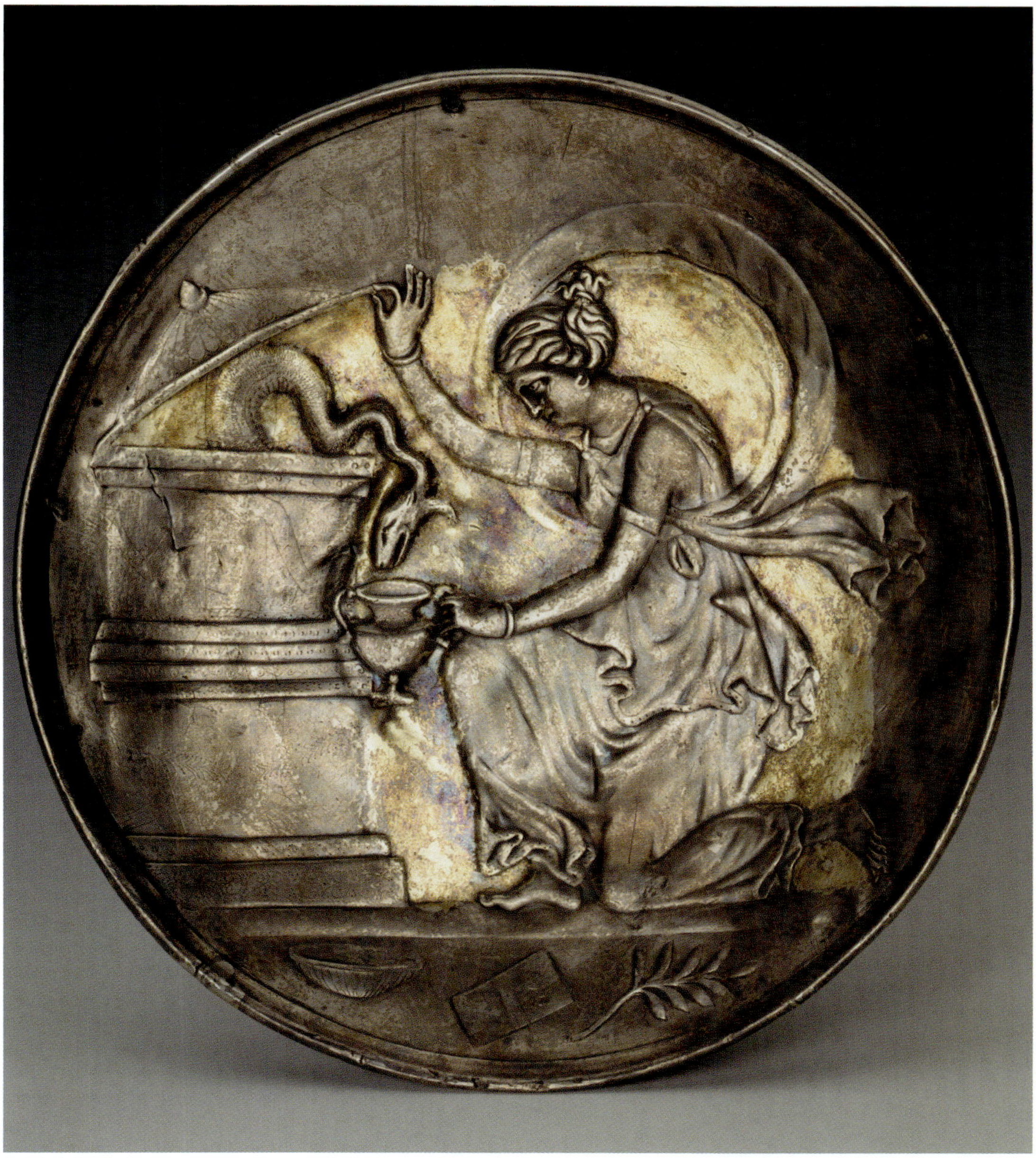

163. **A maenad feeding a serpent from a calyx-like vessel.** Dish, Byzantium.

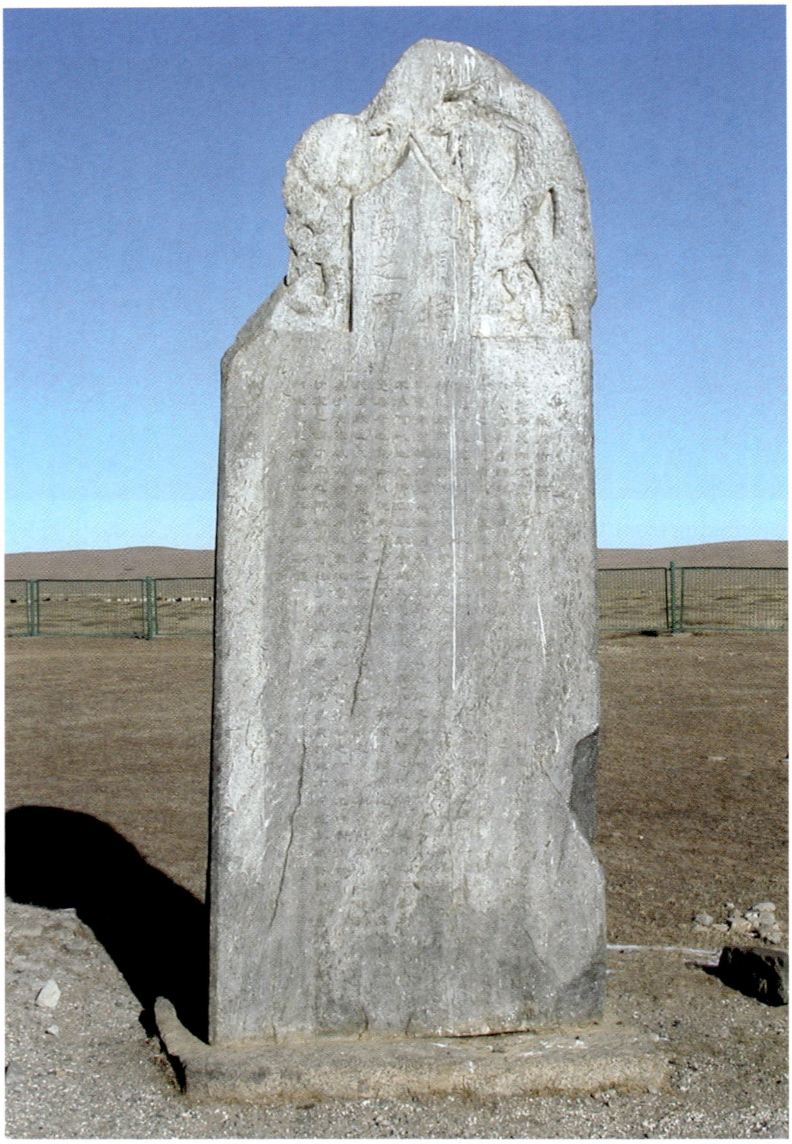

165. A pair of entwined quadruped dragons. Relief carving on the inscribed memorial stele of Köl Tigin.

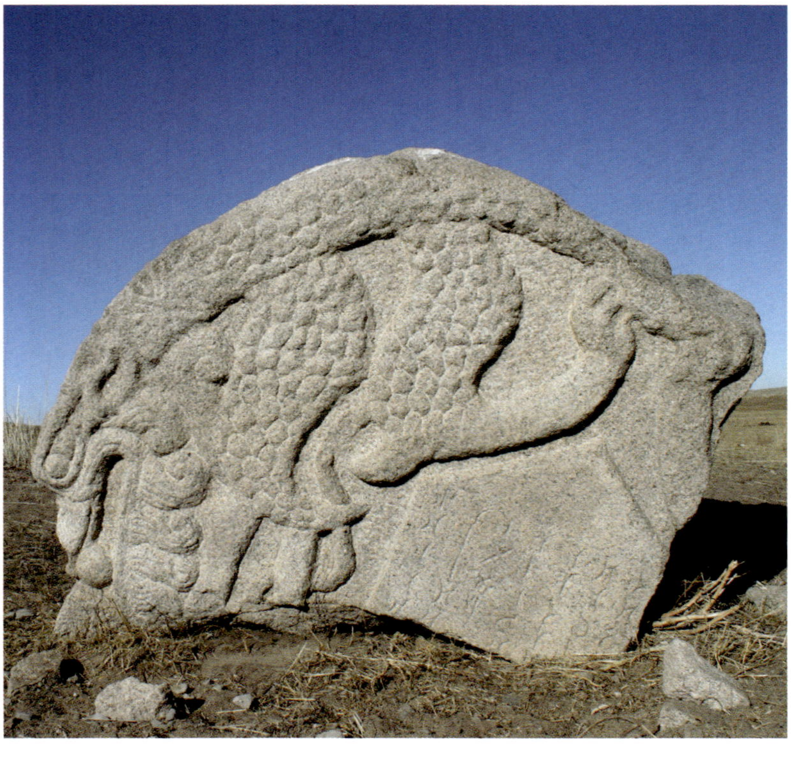

166. One of a pair of entwined quadruped dragons. Fragment of a relief carved monumental stele, Qarabalghasun.

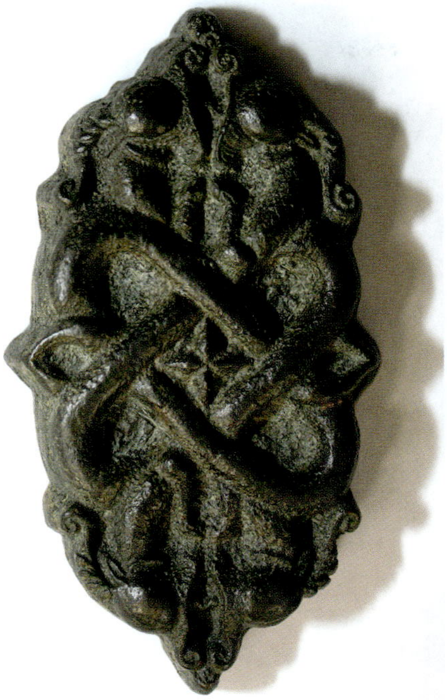

169. A pair of confronted double-headed dragons with a quadripartite knot. Matrix, Ghūr.

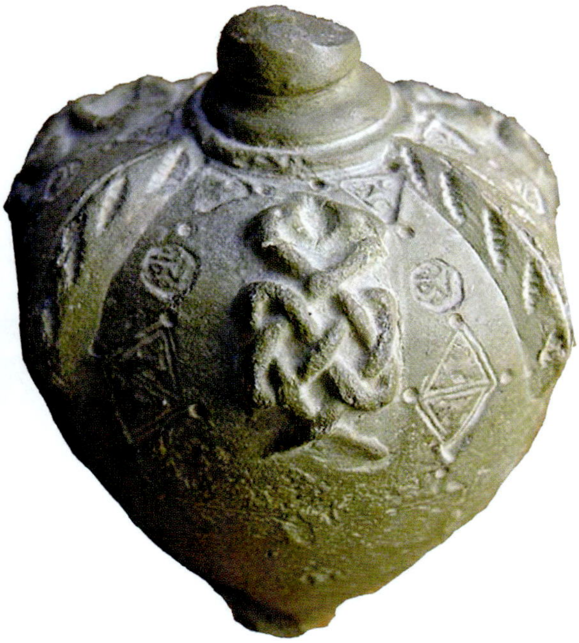

171. A pair of confronted dragons with a quadripartite knot. Sphero-conical vessel, Golden Horde (Juchi Ulus).

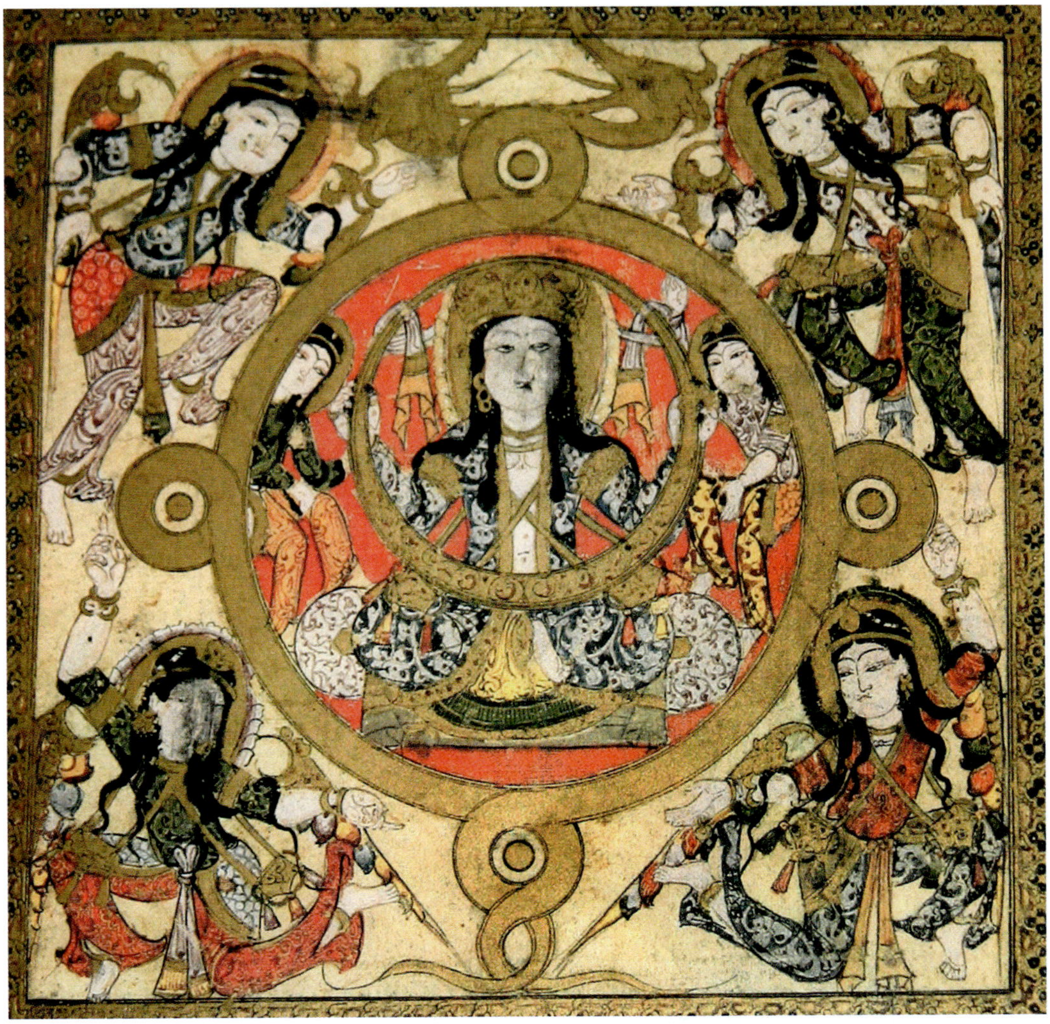

176. A personification of the Moon enclosed within interlaced dragons. Detail of the right half of the double-page frontispiece painting in the *Kitāb al-diryāq*, Mosul (?).

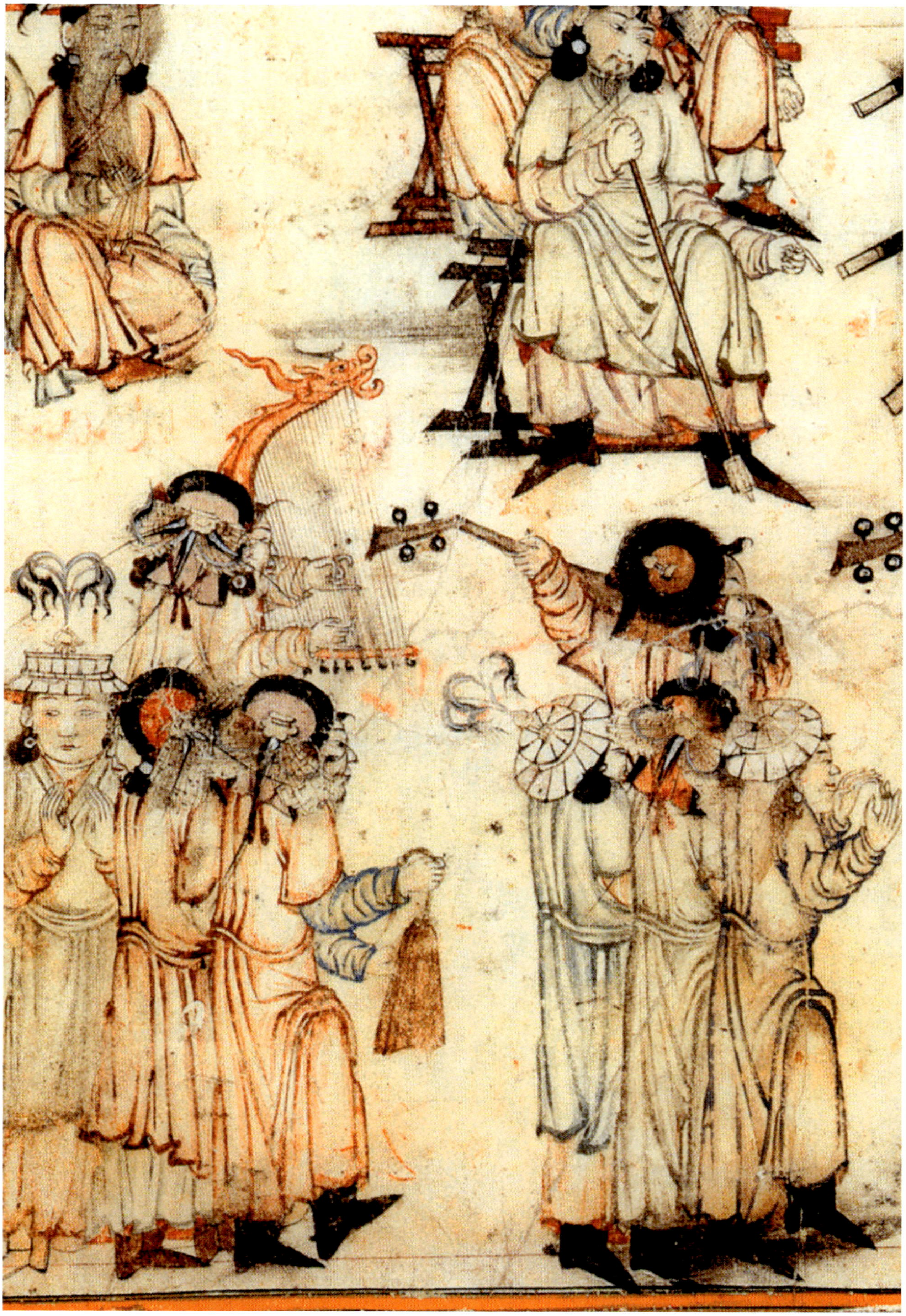

177. **A musician with a dragon-headed stringed instrument.** Detail of an enthronement scene of a Mongol ruler, Tabriz (?).

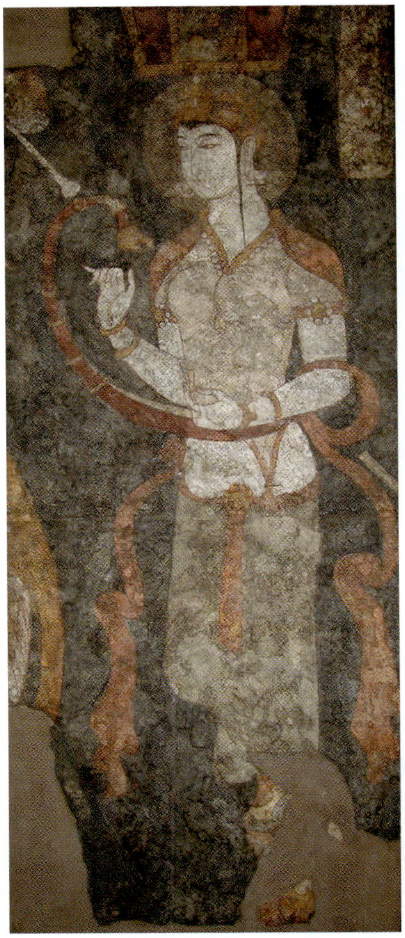

178a and b. A musician with a dragon-headed stringed instrument. Wall painting, Panjikent.

178b

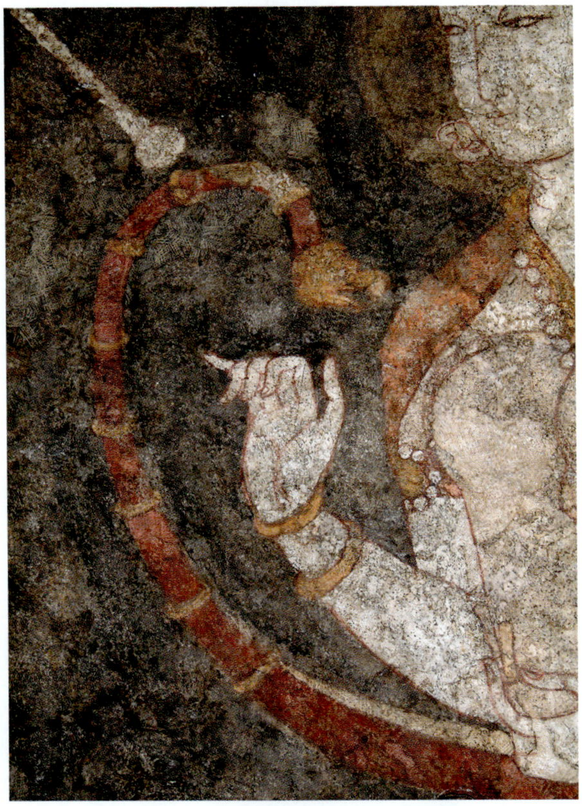

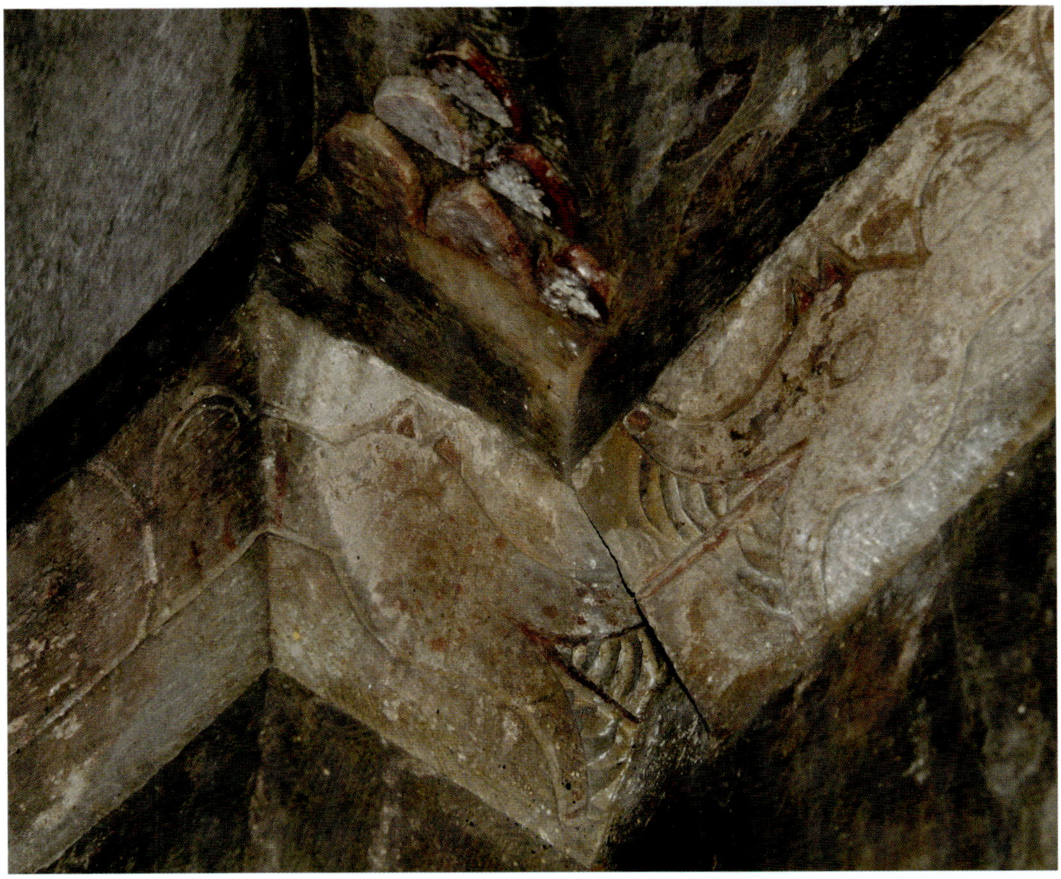

179. Two pairs of interlaced confronted dragons. Relief carving around the wall arch above the altar in the funerary chapel of Surb Grigor, monastic complex of Noravank‘.

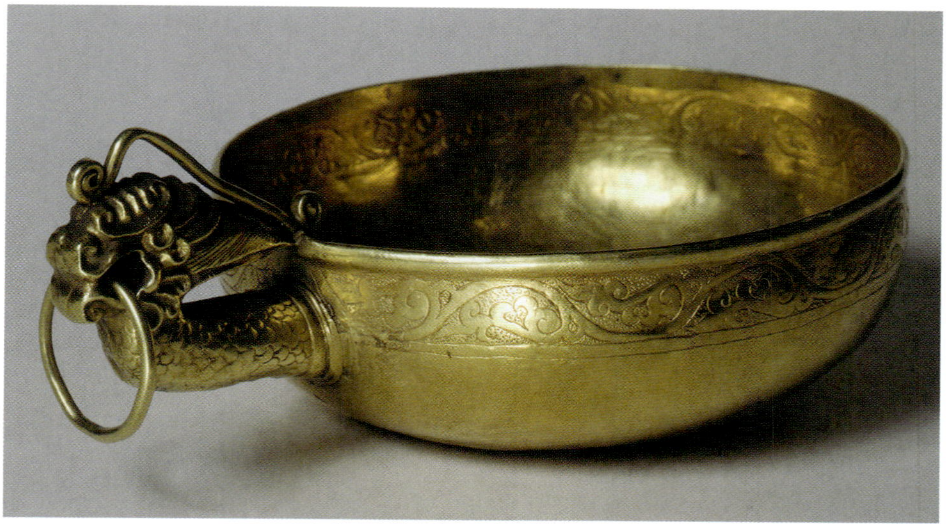

182. A dragon-handled cup. Siberian Collection of Peter the Great.

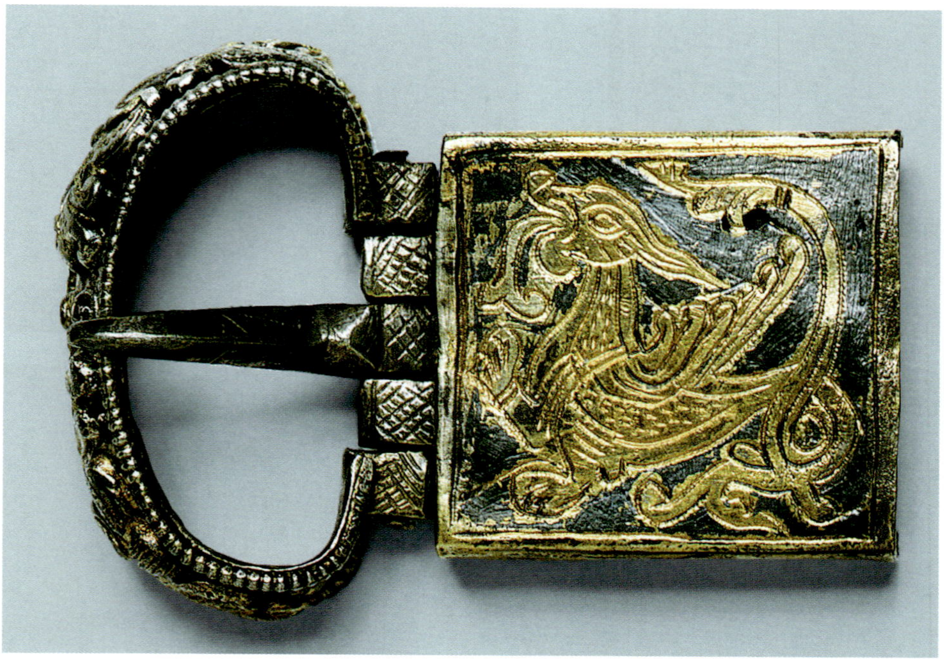

183. A winged dragon with forelegs. Buckle of a belt, Mongol empire (Ulus Juchids), Astrakhan region.

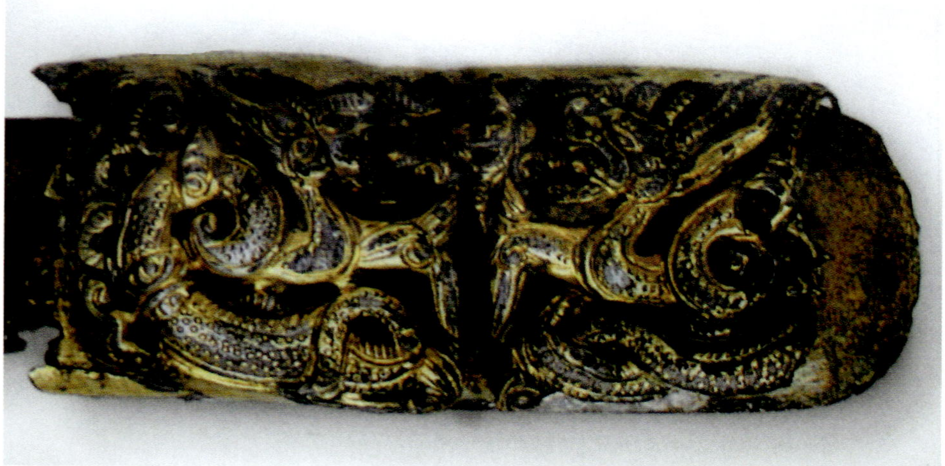

184. A "Master of Dragons." Strap-end fitting of a belt, Mongol empire (Ulus Juchids), Astrakhan region.

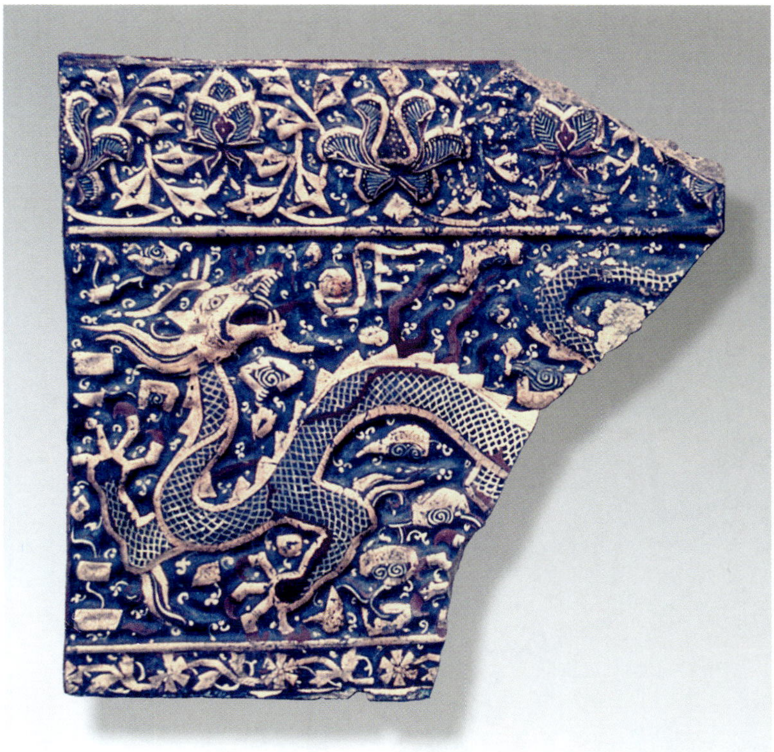

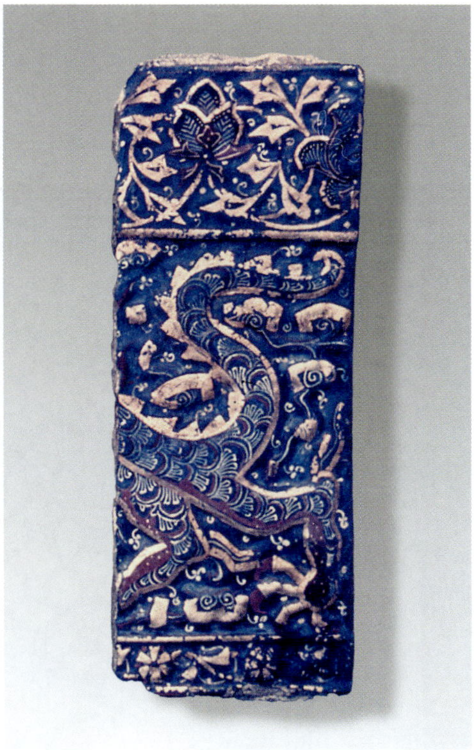

186a and b. A *regardant* quadruped dragon. Two tile fragments, Takht-i Sulaimān.

186b

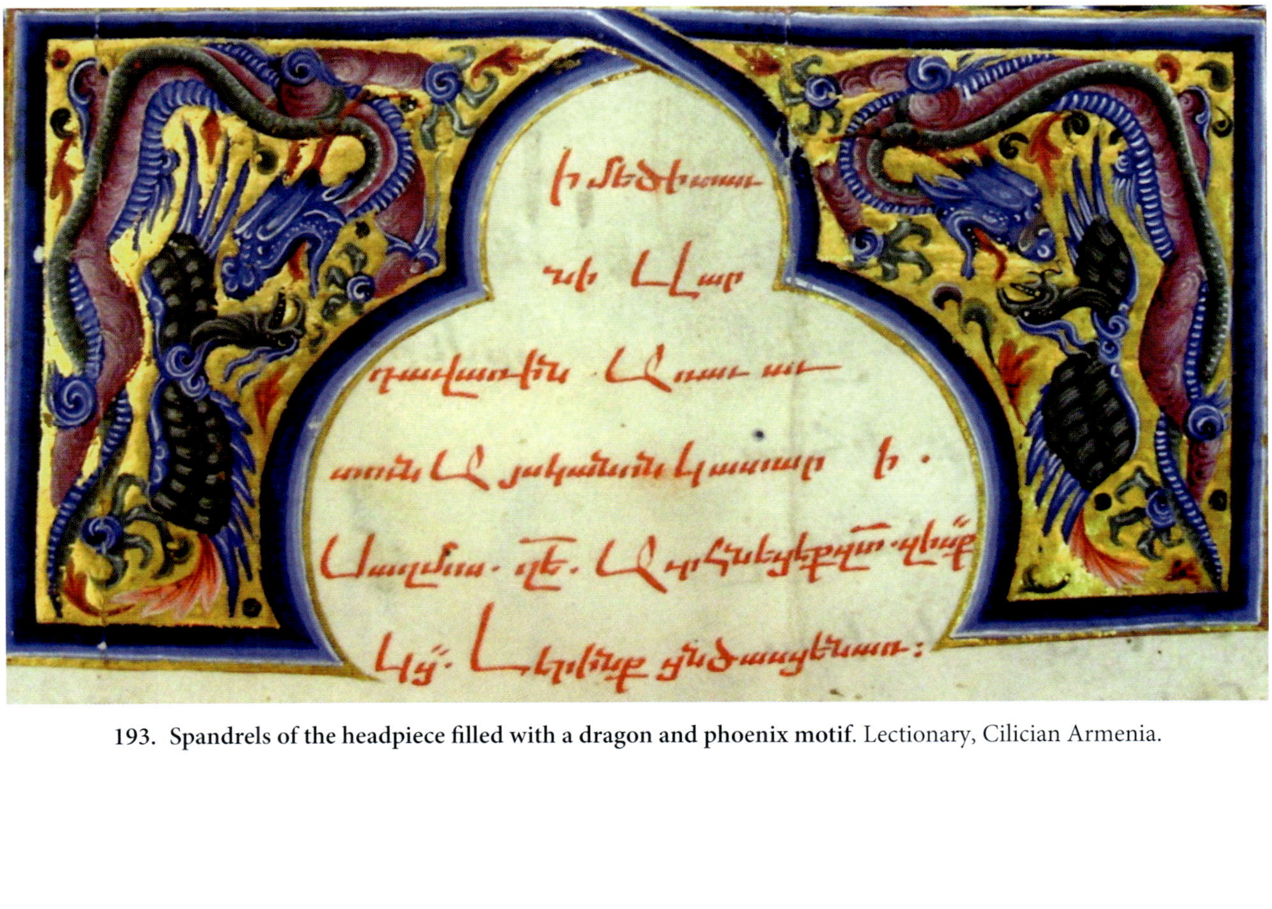

193. Spandrels of the headpiece filled with a dragon and phoenix motif. Lectionary, Cilician Armenia.

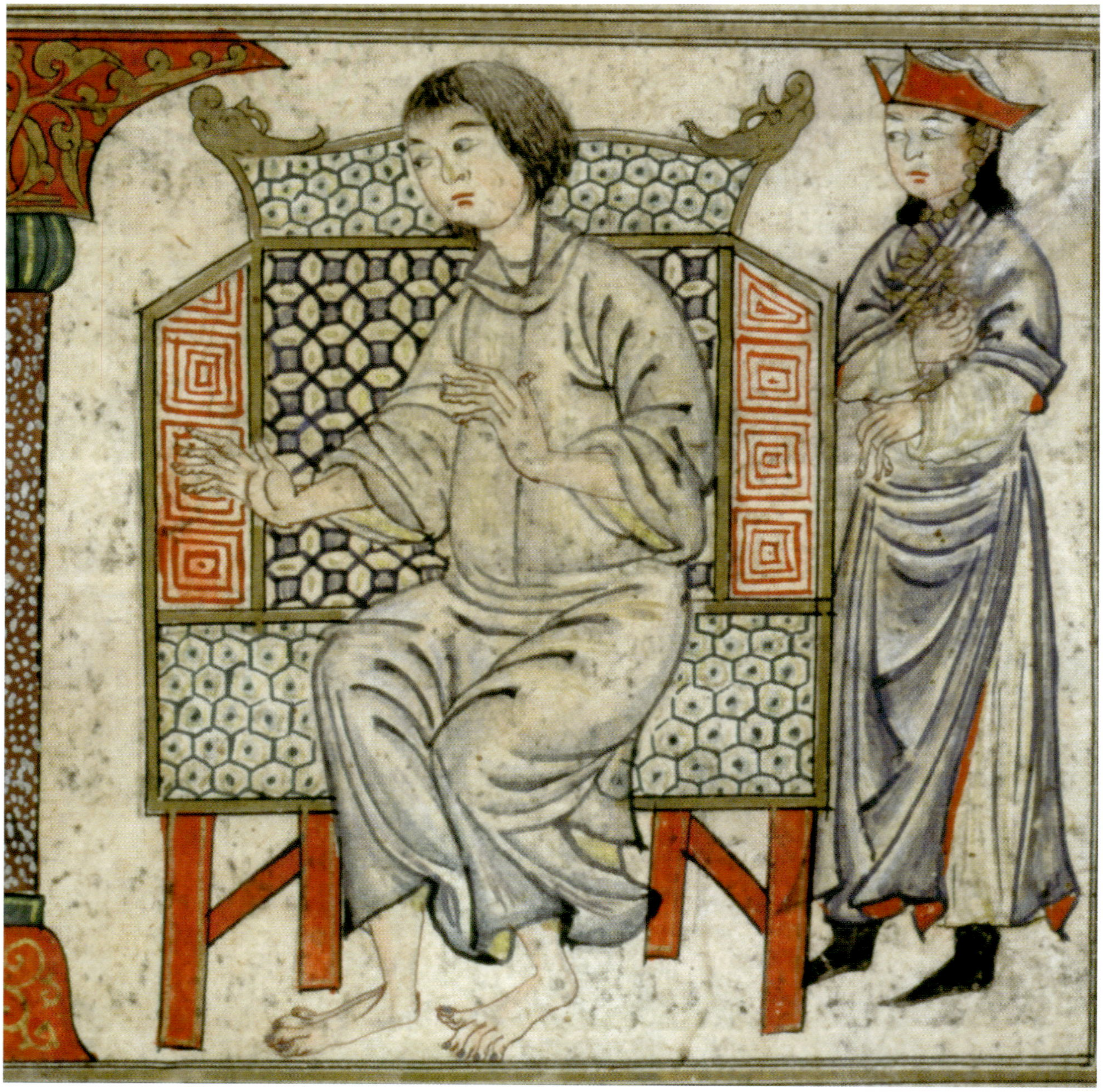

194. A *faqīr* on a dragon-throne. Painting in the reconstructed manuscript of the section of the *Jāmiʿ al-tawārīkh*, Tabriz.

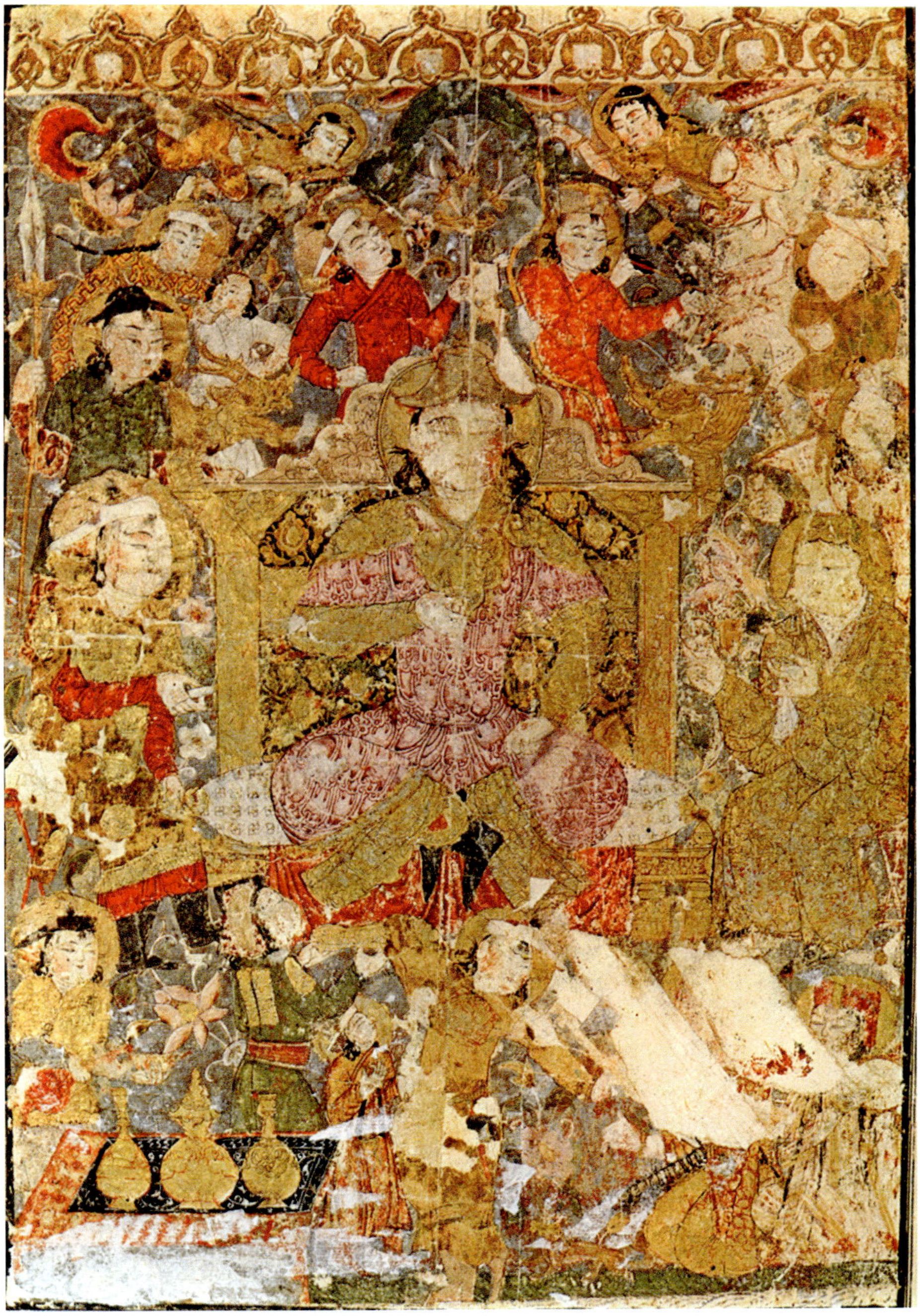

195. A ruler on a dragon-throne. Painting from a dispersed manuscript known as the "Saray album paintings."

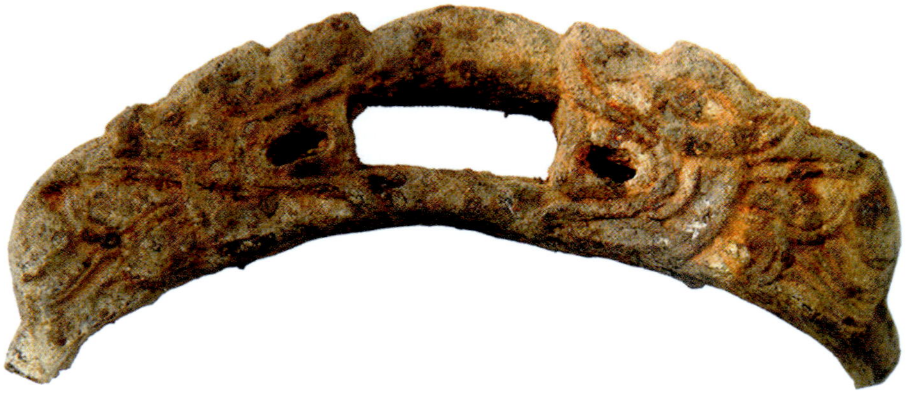

196. Inward-facing dragon heads. Stirrup crossbar fragment, Qaraqorum.

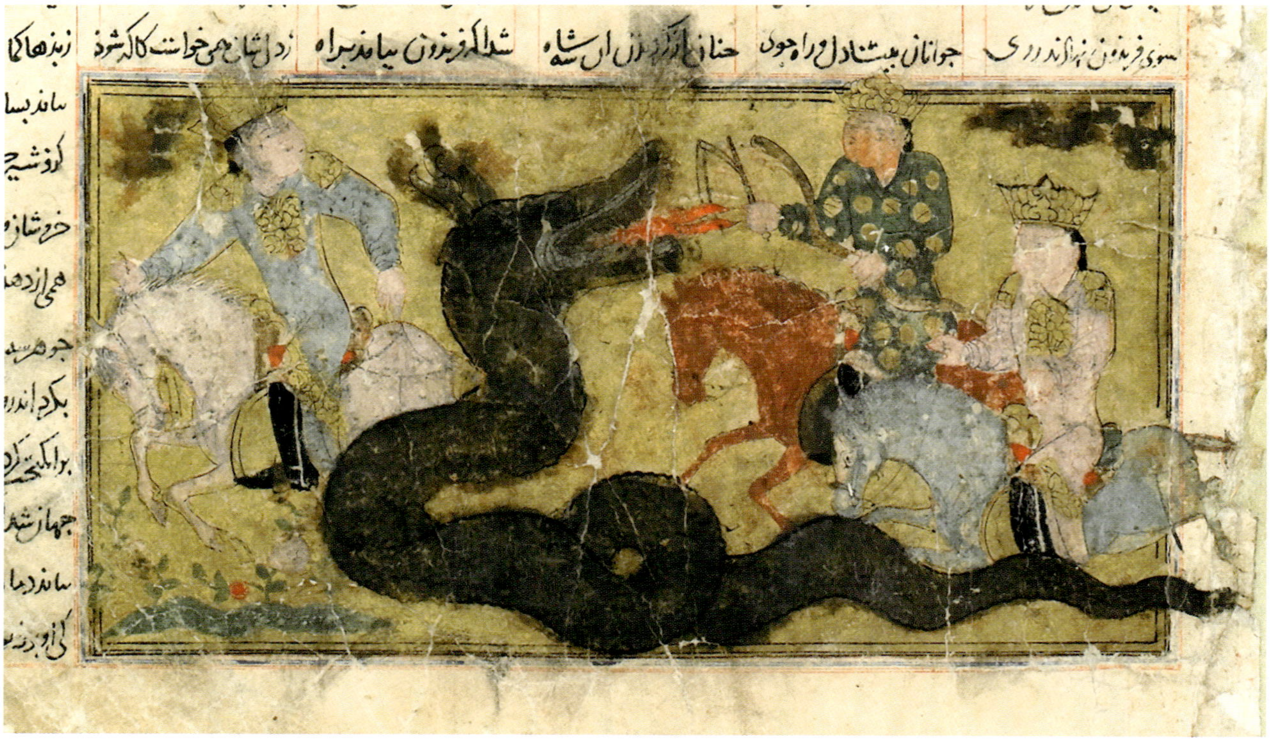

197. Farīdūn in the guise of a dragon testing his three sons. Painting in a copy of the so-called "Small *Shāh-nāma*" group of manuscripts.

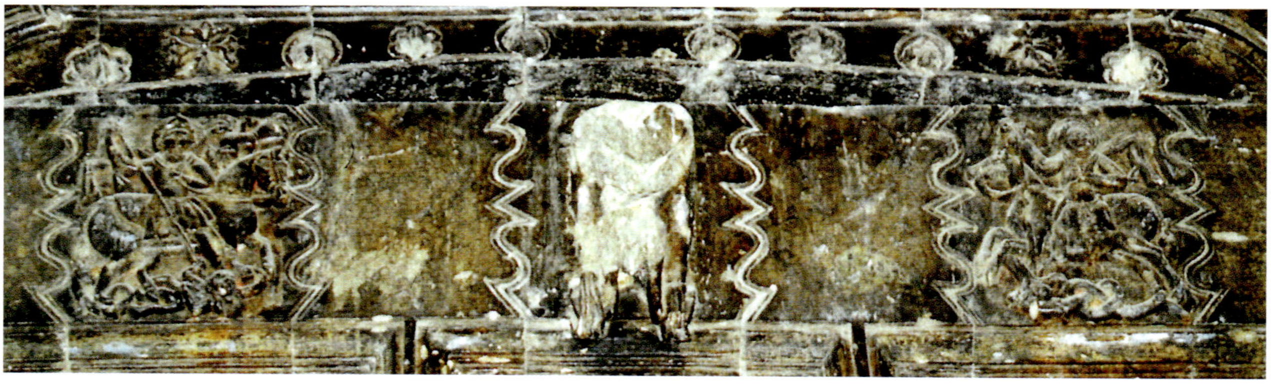

198. A pair of confronted horsemen killing a dragon and an anthropomorphic figure representing Satan. Relief carving on the lintel above the royal portal leading to the burial chamber of Saint Behnām, monastery of Mār Behnām/Deir al-Khiḍr, southeast of Mosul.